Federal Regulatory Directory

Federal Regulatory Directory

Eleventh Edition

CQ PRESS

A DIVISION OF CONGRESSIONAL QUARTERLY
WASHINGTON, D.C.

Federal Regulatory Directory, Eleventh Edition
Researched by Jankowski Associates, Inc.,
Frederick, Maryland

CQ Press
1255 22nd Street, N.W., Suite 400
Washington, D.C. 20037

Phone, 202-729-1900
Toll-free, 1-866-4CQ-PRESS (1-866-427-7737)

www.cqpress.com

Contributors: Rebecca Adams, Mary Agnes Carey, Susan
Ferrechio, Brian Hansen, Liriel Higa, Grace Hill, Scott
Kuzner, January Layman-Wood, Daphne Levitas, Mary
Marshall, David Masci, and Jon Preimesberger.
Cover: Naylor Design, Inc.
Subject index: Julia Petrakis, Facts OnLine

♾ The paper used in this publication exceeds the
requirements of the American National Standard for
Information Sciences—Permanence of Paper for Printed
Library Materials, ANSI Z39.48-1992.

**The library of Congress cataloged the first edition of this
title as follows:**
Federal regulatory directory. 1979/80—
Washington. Congressional Quarterly Inc.
KF5406.A15F4   0195–749X   79–644368

ISBN 1-56802-812-1
ISSN 0195-749X

Printed and bound in the United States of America
07   06   05   04   03   5   4   3   2   1

Contents

Preface

The world of federal regulation goes on regardless of who is in control at either end of Pennsylvania Avenue, and federal agencies and the independent regulatory commissions remain actively engaged in the economic and social life of the nation. They deal with complex issues in society that often remain stubbornly present for years, as well as brand-new or newly highlighted issues that face the nation.

For example, the terrorist attacks of September 11, 2001, prompted the most far-reaching reorganization of the federal government since World War II: the consolidation of twenty-two federal agencies into the newly created Homeland Security Department, which is expected to become the third-largest cabinet-level department in the federal government and the employer of almost 170,000 people. This reorganization, announced by the administration of George W. Bush in 2002, merged agencies and offices in four primary areas: border and transportation security; emergency preparedness and response; science and technology; and information analysis and infrastructure protection. The Homeland Security Department assumed the enforcement activities and personnel from the Border Patrol, the Coast Guard, the Customs Service, and the Immigration and Naturalization Service, as well as the Federal Emergency Management Agency, the Secret Service, and the new Transportation Security Administration.

In addition, accounting scandals within several of the nation's largest publicly traded companies, as well as consolidation in the telecommunications industry, prompted changes in other regulatory agencies. The Federal Energy Regulatory Commission began a formal investigation into natural gas pricing when energy trading companies like Enron and Dynegy admitted to falsifying price data, and the Securities and Exchange Commission launched investigations and filed fraud charges against those and several other companies. Such corporate malfeasance prompted reform and led to the Sarbanes-Oxley Act, which put in motion one of the most extensive overhauls of U.S. business practices since Franklin Roosevelt's New Deal policies. The Federal Communications Commission also faced issues arising from the expansion of the telecommunications sector, including the repeal of a prohibition on large mergers in the cell phone industry.

PURPOSE OF THE BOOK

Such challenges and structural changes within regulatory agencies can make the regulatory process particularly difficult to understand. It can take more than a Web site or a few phone calls to understand issues and find needed resources or personnel.

The *Federal Regulatory Directory,* eleventh edition, provides easy access to in-depth and essential information on regulation and regulatory agencies. This volume not only clarifies who the agencies are and what they do but also helps to navigate the organizational transformations, new legislation, and judicial decisions that regulatory agencies commonly encounter.

PLAN OF THE BOOK

The book opens with a comprehensive essay that gives readers a close look at federal regulation, detailing the origins and social impact of regulation; the legislative process; the political predominance of various presidents, congressional representatives, and other influential policymakers; and the judicial decisions that have affected the regulatory process.

The next section covers the twelve largest regulatory agencies in depth. Each agency profile includes

- an introduction to the history and current developments in the agency;
- contact information, including biographies of key personnel;
- organizational charts that reflect recent agency restructuring;
- updated summaries of regulatory legislation and congressional committee information; and
- information sources, both internal and external.

The sections that follow provide detailed information on other independent regulatory agencies, including the Federal Election Commission and the Social Security Administration; cabinet department agencies that have regulatory responsibilities, like the Agriculture and Treasury Departments; and offices responsible for oversight and coordination in the Executive Office of the President. Each entry includes

- an overview of the regulatory body and its mission;
- contact information;
- updated summaries of regulatory legislation and congressional committee information; and
- information sources, both internal and external.

The appendix offers several useful resources, including a ready reference list of Web sites included in the book for quick access to online information, directions on how to order government publications, a guide on how to use the *Federal Register* and the *Code of Federal Regulations,* and the text of executive orders and congressional acts covering federal regulation. Comprehensive subject and name indexes conclude the book.

Federal Regulatory Directory

Federal Regulation: An Introduction

For much of American history, regulation was a modest and relatively obscure government function. Conflict over regulation, when it occurred, generally was muted and played out in court. Over time, as the role of regulation in American society grew, so too did the controversy that attended each manifestation of its considerable power. Because regulation continues to be a pervasive presence in American economic and social affairs, controversy over it provides much of the fuel for the U.S. political system.

Conflict is inevitably a part of virtually every significant element of regulation. Statutes creating or amending regulatory programs are hotly contested when under consideration by Congress. Affected parties frequently challenge regulations mandated or authorized by legislation during the agency rulemaking process or in court after the rules are completed. The implementation and enforcement of regulations generate thousands of hearings and lawsuits. Students and practitioners of regulation debate virtually all aspects of regulatory programs, from their origins in American political culture to their actual impact on society. They even disagree on an issue as basic as the definition of *regulation.*

Anyone asked to provide a defensible definition of regulation is well advised to err on the side of generality. Many experts, including members of the Senate Committee on Governmental Affairs and the staff of the Office of Management and Budget (OMB), have attempted to be specific. But they have found regulation is difficult to capture because of its many variations and nuances. Even efforts to develop comprehensive lists of regulatory programs or regulated activities usually are frustrated by the remarkable diversity of forms and functions. One scholar on regulation, Kenneth Meier, offers a definition that may be sufficiently general: regulation is "any attempt by the government to control the behavior of citizens, corporations, or subgovernments." This definition encompasses programs and activities in which regulation is either the primary goal or secondary effect. After all, many programs in which the primary mission is to deliver benefits or services in fact develop eligibility criteria, reimbursement policies, and other requirements that in effect serve to regulate program participants.

Regulation is also a process, complex and continuous. It occurs in identifiable stages—legislation, rulemaking, implementation, enforcement, and dispute resolution. But the sequence of these stages is neither neat nor predictable. For example, any stage can lead directly to dispute resolution. Rulemaking by an agency can stimulate interest groups to demand new legislation. While the institutional focus shifts from stage to stage, regulation engages the time and resources of all the major institutions and actors in the U.S. political system: Congress, the president, agencies, departments and commissions of all sorts, the ubiquitous interest groups, the press, business, and individuals.

In a real sense, regulation is always being redefined. Once it was confined largely to economic concerns, such as entry to markets by individual companies, the rates they charged, and the products or services provided in defined industries. This form of regulation has declined in importance, overshadowed today by programs that seek broader social objectives—equity, health, safety, protection, aesthetics—and cut across all economic sectors and activities. Regulation is today the dominant form of domestic policy, and the regulatory process is the chosen method of policy making.

REASONS FOR REGULATION

Proponents of regulation justify the implicit limitations on freedom by arguing that the free market and private decisions either create inequitable and inefficient conditions or fail to achieve optimal social benefits. Opponents frequently scoff at such justifications, arguing that regulation usually substitutes one type of inequity or inefficiency for another and that purported benefits rarely are achieved because regulatory programs are either fundamentally misguided or mismanaged. The debate reached a crescendo in the late 1970s and early 1980s, when some of the most thoughtful critiques and defenses of regulation were offered by scholars and professionals.

After an ebb, the 1994 elections that brought the first Republican Congress to power since the Eisenhower administration reinvigorated the regulatory debate. As long as the Republicans controlled Congress and a Democrat occupied the White House, the legislative branch's efforts to bring about major regulatory change was doomed to yield more heat than light. But with the election of George W. Bush in 2000, the landscape changed. One of Bush's first actions on Inauguration Day in 2001 was to slap a sixty-day freeze on new rules and regulations, during which time the new White House vowed to review hundreds of measures proposed in the final months of Bill Clinton's administration. Emboldened, the Republican Congress immediately moved to begin its review of the Clinton regulatory legacy.

While a number of the late Clinton administration regulations, such as the rules on arsenic levels in drinking water, ultimately took effect, many were rolled back permanently. The new administration also changed the paradigm for justifying new regulations—focusing more on cost-benefit analysis, especially on those regulations that affected businesses. But the changes under Bush were just the latest salvo in a long war between those who favor a more thorough regulatory scheme as a means to soften the sharper edges of the market economy and those who view such a scheme as an obstacle to wealth creation and prosperity.

This section reviews some of the classic arguments for and against regulation.

Economic Regulation

Competition is the cornerstone of the American economy, and a major purpose of economic regulation is to ensure the proper continuation of a competitive atmosphere. The justification for regulation is that it corrects market failures that occur when competition either does not exist in an industry or does not allocate resources efficiently.

NATURAL MONOPOLY

One such failure is the existence of a "natural monopoly," or exclusive control of a commodity or service in a specified area. Unregulated monopolies can restrict output and elevate prices compared with those in a competitive market structure. The regulation of public utilities is the classic example of government controls on natural monopolies. A public utility commission determines what the single supplier (the monopolist) may charge for output, the minimum quality of the service, and what profit the monopolist is entitled to earn. The ongoing debate in Congress over the proposed deregulation of the electricity industry highlights the limits and lengths lawmakers and regulators have already gone to end such "natural monopolies." The electricity industry stands as the last major regulated monopoly in the country. But the deregulatory fiasco in California that led to rolling blackouts and nearly bankrupt utilities in the winter of 2000–2001 may doom efforts to further deregulate the industry.

In fact, what once seemed a natural monopoly often ceases to be one with changes in the market or the advent of new technology. The railroads, for example, were considered natural monopolies in the nineteenth century; as such, the rates they could charge, as well as other aspects of their business, were regulated. But with the development of other viable methods of transportation in the twentieth century, this natural-monopoly rationale for government regulation ceased to exist. The same held true for providers of local telephone service, which were regulated as monopolies until the Telecommunications Act of 1996 allowed the phase-in of competition for local service.

Monopolies may also occur when a company or a group of companies takes deliberate action to set prices or control supply and thus drive other competitors out of business. Since it was enacted in 1890, the Sherman Antitrust Act has made such combinations in restraint of trade illegal. Critics of this justification for regulation scrutinize any activity for which natural-monopoly status is proposed. The Department of Justice in 1998 moved against two powerful corporations consolidating power in the computer age, Microsoft and Intel. Both were accused of unfair trade practices that had left them with near-total control over the software and microprocessor markets. Intel quietly settled its antitrust case with the government, but in 1999, U.S. District Court Judge Thomas Penfield Jackson ordered a defiant Microsoft to be broken up into two companies; he set into motion the most momentous antitrust action since AT&T was broken up in the 1980s.

Although Jackson's order to break up Microsoft was overturned by a federal appeals court in 2001, his contention that the company was an illegal monopoly was affirmed. Still, the reversal gave impetus to the Bush Justice Department—which was much less enthusiastic about breaking up the software maker than was the department under Clinton—to cut a deal with the company later that year. Under the agreement, Microsoft would remain whole in exchange for altering certain business practices that had allowed it to use the monopoly it enjoyed with its Windows operating system to shut competitors out of certain parts of the software market.

Overall, antitrust activity has subsided substantially in President Bush's first two-and-a-half years in office. Ironically, European regulators have been more aggressive in their pursuit of possible U.S. monopolists. For instance, General Electric's bid to buy Honeywell was approved by U.S. regulators only to be nixed by their European counterparts, who worried that the two firms would unfairly dominate the world market for jetliner components.

DESTRUCTIVE COMPETITION

Overly vigorous competition within an industry can lead to a deterioration in product quality, bankruptcy, and monopoly. The railroad price wars that raged in the 1870s and 1880s demonstrated the harm imposed by destructive competition—prices and services fluctuated wildly, consumer demands went unsatisfied, and industry planning became increasingly difficult. Both the railroads and the public suffered from this instability. The Interstate Commerce Commission (ICC) was created in 1887 in part to end the destructive competition.

Advocates of free markets note that such industry-threatening conditions are sometimes caused by those seeking monopoly or oligopoly through predatory pricing. For example, they argue that the savings and loan problems in the 1980s arose as much because of conflict of interest, fraud, and mismanagement as because of destructive competition. Cases of unadulterated destructive competition are rare; anticompetitive and illegal practices are usually lurking in the background.

EXTERNALITIES

Another form of market imperfection involves what economists call "externalities," or spillovers, which develop when the production or use of a product has an effect on third parties. Positive externalities are benefits enjoyed by third parties; negative externalities are costs borne by third parties.

Air pollution, which harms the health of the public in general, is a negative externality. Resources such as clean air and water are scarce and exhaustible, but manufacturers treat them as a "free" input in the production process; consequently production costs do not include the expenses of the pollution. From a social point of view, therefore, the company's goods will not reflect the true costs of production. Those costs are shared by the public, and the price can include illness and expensive health care.

No one seriously questions the existence of externalities or the inefficiencies and inequities they create. However, many take issue with the regulatory mechanisms that deal with them. The use of "command and control" regulation, with its uniform rules and enforcement through monitoring and sanctioning, frequently is criticized as inappropriate, ineffective, and inefficient. Critics much prefer regulations that set standards (but leave to regulated parties decisions as to how to comply). This type of system, critics argue, avoids a cumbersome bureaucracy and draws on the ingenuity of American business and proven market forces to achieve important social goals such as pollution reduction. Programs launched by the Environmental Protection Agency (EPA), the Department of Agriculture,

and the Occupational Safety and Health Administration (OSHA) during the Clinton administration sought to do just that, setting goals in areas as diverse as workplace safety, pollution control, and food safety, then letting industry find the way to reach those goals. Proponents of the existing mode of regulation question the ability and willingness of the private sector to find these solutions.

But, if anything, such cooperative programs are expanding. Under the Bush administration, agencies such as the EPA and OSHA have worked to increase their outreach efforts to the businesses they regulate and, in some cases, have pushed for forms of voluntary or self-regulation. An example of this is Bush's Clear Skies Initiative, a 2002 proposal that aimed to lower smog and acid-rain causing emissions by allowing utilities to buy and sell pollution credits.

SPECIAL GOODS AND SERVICES

Some goods and services have characteristics that prevent the free market from handling them in an efficient manner. Many socially beneficial goods or services would not be produced without government intervention, such as highways, air traffic control, national defense, and clean air. Other goods and services might be exploited, depleted, or foreclosed for other beneficial purposes if use was unregulated. The use of resources such as groundwater, common grazing areas, and free-flowing rivers are typically regulated by the government.

Again, critics find fault with the typical regulatory response. Some support more user charges for the goods and services government provides to ensure that those who enjoy the benefits pay the costs. Some would provide access to resources that could be threatened by unlimited use through an auction, with use going to the highest bidder. Others prefer to entrust such decisions to regulatory agencies, which are charged with the responsibility to define and defend an always elusive "public interest."

Social Aspects of Economic Regulation

Many, if not most, types of economic regulation are social in nature. The nation seeks to control damage from pollution, illness, or injuries to workers and consumers, preserve multiple uses of rivers, and protect endangered species for more than economic reasons. Issues of social equity have driven a number of other regulatory programs, notably in employment. Arguments over equal employment opportunity regulation have raged since 1964 and show no signs of abating. Charges of quotas and reverse discrimination arising from these programs are all too familiar and still unresolved.

The rationing of energy supplies or controls on their prices also can be seen as social regulation, and these practices often are attacked on efficiency grounds. "Supplement incomes," say the critics, "and let the market determine prices." Ultimately, they claim, the market eliminates shortages by encouraging production or generating substitutes.

There is another form of social regulation the mere mention of which triggers fierce reactions. The content of art and entertainment can offend the moral code or aesthetic sensibilities of some viewers or listeners. What might otherwise be protected by basic constitutional rights of free expression becomes a potential object of regulation when public monies or licenses are involved. The Federal Communications Commission (FCC) took similar action to prevent its radio and television licenses from exposing children to "indecent" programming. The Telecommunications Act of 1996 ordered that new televisions contain circuitry capable of blocking programs rated for violence or adult content. The law broke new and controversial ground by barring the transmission or display of indecent material on an interactive computer service such as the Internet. Indecency in this case extended not just to sexually explicit material but to information about drugs and devices for producing abortions. The reaction to such initiatives has been predictable. What is most significant about these cases is that they illustrate how deeply regulation affects fundamental constitutional freedoms and personal values.

However sophisticated and esoteric they become, the arguments for and against the regulatory system always return to fundamental questions of effectiveness, efficiency, and equity. That regulatory programs fall short of achieving the goals set for them is indisputable, but this fact ignores the extraordinary tasks set before them. The Occupational Safety and Health Act, for example, called upon OSHA to "set . . . standard(s) which most adequately assures to the extent feasible, on the basis of the best available evidence, that no employee will suffer material impairment of health or functional capacity even if such employee has regular exposure to the hazard dealt with by such standard for the period of his working life."

The 1972 Clean Water Act required the EPA to issue regulations governing all point sources of water pollution within one year and to bring all regulated parties into compliance with strict standards within ten years. Realistic criteria for an "effective" program are elusive when regulatory statutes promise so much to so many. If taken literally, these laws doom their regulatory progeny to failure and the public to disappointment.

EARLY HISTORY AND GROWTH OF REGULATION

Article I, Section 8, of the U.S. Constitution empowers Congress to "regulate Commerce with foreign Nations, and among the several States." One of the earliest cases in American administrative law involved delegation of a regulatory power—the imposition and suspension of tariffs—to the president of the United States. The federal government in its first 100 years established numerous offices that performed regulatory functions. Designed largely to promote and develop the young nation and its industries, these agencies included the Army Corps of Engineers (1824), the Patent and Trademark Office (1836), the Comptroller of the Currency (1863), the Copyright Office of the Library of Congress (1870), and the Bureau of Fisheries (1871). Two other agencies, the Internal Revenue Service (1862) and the Civil Service Commission (1883), were established to facilitate administration of the government.

In 1887, in response to widespread dissatisfaction with the state of the railroads, Congress created the ICC to regulate that industry. The ICC can be seen as the start of the modern era of regulation for a number of reasons. It represented a shift of regulatory power from the states to the federal government, a trend that continues today, though a strong current of "federalism" is seeking to reshift the balance toward the states. The "independent commission," multimember and politically balanced, became a model used in regulation of other industries and economic activities. The original statute, the Interstate Commerce Act, was amended several times to correct perceived defects in its design or alleged abuses and limitations in the responsible agency. Early on, the judiciary emerged as a major force in railroad regulation, as the ICC's decisions were routinely and successfully challenged by regulated parties. These aspects in the development of the ICC have been repeated to some degree in all the other regulatory agencies. The ICC's later history is less typical, though it may also provide a prototype for the critics of government regulation: deregulation in the 1980s led to the ICC's elimination in 1995, with its remaining regulatory functions being transferred to the new Surface Transportation Board in the Transportation Department.

Between 1915 and the beginning of the New Deal, Congress created seven more agencies and commissions to regulate parts of the nation's commercial and financial systems. These were the Coast Guard (1915), the Tariff Commission (1916), the Commodities Exchange Authority (1922), the Customs Service (1927), the Federal Radio Commission (1927), the Federal Power Commission (1930)—to replace the Water Power Commission, which was established in 1920—and the Food and Drug Administration (1931). Some of these agencies were later absorbed into larger departments.

The New Deal marks the next major landmark in the history of regulation. A network of entities designed to regulate the economy out of the Great Depression, President Franklin D. Roosevelt's program was an unprecedented incursion by government into the private sector. The regulatory legacy of the New Deal is threefold. The first legacy is economic regulation. Some of the agencies and legislation dealing with economic regulation and created during the New Deal are:

- The Federal Home Loan Bank Board (FHLBB), established in 1932 to regulate federally chartered savings and loan associations.
- The Federal Deposit Insurance Corporation (FDIC), created in 1933 to be the primary regulator and insurer of state-chartered banks that were not members of the Federal Reserve System.
- The Securities and Exchange Commission (SEC), started in 1934 to protect the public against fraud and deception in the securities and financial markets.
- The National Labor Relations Board (NLRB), established by the Wagner Act of 1935 to prevent "unfair labor practices" and to protect the right of employees to bargain collectively.
- The Motor Carrier Act of 1935, which gave the ICC authority over the burgeoning trucking industry.
- The U.S. Maritime Administration, created in 1936 to oversee shipbuilding and ship operations during World War II. Eventually these functions, among others, were transferred to the Transportation Department and the independent Federal Maritime Commission (FMC).

At Roosevelt's urging, Congress in 1934 established the independent FCC to consolidate federal regulation of all common carriers in interstate communications, which then were radio, telephone, and telegraph. During this period, the growing competition among airlines necessitated coordination of airline routes and regulation of flight operations. Because the ICC was already heavily burdened with increased responsibility for surface transportation, Congress in 1938 created the Civil Aeronautics Authority (CAA) to promote and regulate the industry, and then replaced it in 1940 with the Civil Aeronautics Board (CAB), an independent commission.

The second legacy of the New Deal is the establishment of a federal responsibility for social welfare through Social Security and related programs. In this way the New Deal set the stage for the massive expansion of benefit programs in the 1960s and regulatory programs concerned with social problems in the 1970s. The third legacy is the revolution in administrative procedure that still influences the operation of regulatory programs. Perceived abuses by New Deal agencies in the way they made and implemented regulatory decisions led directly, if slowly, to the Administrative Procedure Act of 1946 (APA). Both social regulation and regulatory procedures will be discussed subsequently.

From the end of World War II until the mid-1960s relatively few new programs of federal regulation appeared. The Atomic Energy Commission and the expansion of aviation regulation were the major additions.

THE DEVELOPMENT OF SOCIAL REGULATION

The origins of much contemporary social regulation can be traced back to the 1960s. This new form of regulation is characterized by broad social objectives, greatly diversified government activities, and a vastly expanded reach into the private sector. Some mark the beginning with passage of the Civil Rights Act of 1964; others fix the date later, with the National Environmental Policy Act of 1969. Whichever date is chosen as the start, the 1970s were unquestionably the most significant years in the history of regulation. More than 100 regulatory statutes were enacted during this decade alone, and many new regulatory institutions were created.

Consumer Protection

The consumer movement reached its zenith in the early 1970s and made a deep imprint on American life and the marketplace. Before his foray into electoral politics—and his role as Green Party spoiler in the 2000 election, Ralph Nader was, above all, a regulatory crusader. In the 1970s consumers, led by Nader, organized to demand safer, higher-quality products, goods that lived up to advertised claims, and lower prices for food, medical care, fuel, and other products. Nader's activities influenced passage of auto safety legislation in 1966. The new law established federal motor vehicle and tire safety standards and brought the automobile industry under permanent regulation for the first time. In 1970 the National Highway Traffic Safety Administration (NHTSA) was created within the Transportation Department with authority to set auto safety and fuel efficiency standards as well as standards for state highway safety programs. Other agencies created to protect consumers of transportation included the Federal Highway Administration (FHWA) in 1966, which establishes highway safety standards, and the Federal Railroad Administration (FRA) also in 1966, which sets rail safety standards.

Financial and banking matters also came under new regulations. Between 1968 and 1977 Congress enacted the Truth in Lending Act, the Fair Credit Billing Act, the Equal Credit Opportunity Act, the Home Mortgage Disclosure Act, the Consumer Leasing Act, and the Fair Debt Collection Practices Act. Congress in 1975 also passed legislation strengthening regulation of consumer warranties. The National Credit Union Administration (NCUA) was created in 1970 to regulate member credit unions.

Consumers also won passage of the Consumer Product Safety Act in 1972. That law established the Consumer Product Safety Commission (CPSC) as an independent regulatory commission to protect the public against unreasonable risk of injury from hazardous products.

Environmental Quality

Paralleling consumer activism was an equally enthusiastic public voice calling for a cleaner environment. Disasters, such as the 1969 oil spill off the coast of Santa Barbara, California, strengthened the environmentalists' case.

One result of the environmental movement was the consolidation of the federal government's widespread environmental protection efforts into a single agency. The EPA, created in 1970 by President Richard Nixon's executive order, soon became one of the most controversial agencies in government. It remains so today. In the course of a single decade, Congress delegated vast authority to the EPA, through the Clean Air Act (1970, amendments in 1977), the Clean Water Act (1972, amendments in 1972), the Safe Drinking Water Act (1974, amendments in 1996), the Toxic Substances Control Act (1976), and the Resource Conservation and Recovery Act (1976).

Other regulatory agencies were established to protect certain elements of the environment, such as the Office of Surface Mining Reclamation and Enforcement (now the Office of Surface Mining) created in 1977 to regulate the strip-mining industry.

Workplace Safety

Safety in the workplace was the focus of another new regulatory agency that had an immense impact on U.S. business. OSHA was created in 1970 as an agency within the Labor Department to promulgate and enforce worker safety and health standards. The agency was authorized to conduct workplace inspections, require employers to keep detailed records on worker injuries and illness, and conduct research. Within one month of its creation, the agency adopted some 4,400 standards from existing federal regulations, industry codes, and the National Standards Institute. The agency also was authorized to issue standards for health hazards such as inhalation of cotton dust and exposure to toxic chemicals.

Congress in 1973 established the Mining Enforcement and Safety Administration within the Interior Department to promulgate and enforce mine safety and health standards. In 1977 the agency was reorganized as the Mine Safety and Health Administration (MSHA) and placed in the Labor Department.

Energy Regulation

Another major area of expanded federal regulation in the 1970s was the energy sector, in which the United States was repeatedly confronted with the twin problems of dwindling energy supply and soaring costs. In 1973 Congress set up the Federal Energy Administration (FEA) to manage short-term fuel shortages. In 1974 Congress abolished the Atomic Energy Commission (AEC), creating in its place the Energy Research and Development Administration (ERDA), which was authorized to develop nuclear power and new energy sources while maintaining the nation's nuclear arsenal through a complex web of nuclear weapons plants and laboratories. That year, Congress also created an independent Nuclear Regulatory Commission (NRC), which assumed the AEC's nuclear safety and regulatory responsibilities.

In 1977 President Jimmy Carter created the cabinet-level Department of Energy (DOE) to consolidate the vast array of evolving energy powers, programs, and agencies throughout the government. The DOE assumed the powers and functions of the Federal Power Commission (FPC), the FEA, and ERDA, all of which were abolished. Authority to set prices for natural gas, oil, and electricity was given to the Federal Energy Regulatory Commission (FERC), an independent commission set up within, but separate from, the DOE.

The Reagan and First Bush Administrations

If the 1970s demonstrated extraordinary faith in regulation as an instrument for achieving social objectives, the 1980s were a decade of doubt, criticism, and reconsideration. Elected in 1980 on a platform highly critical of government roles in society in general and the economy in particular, President Ronald Reagan acted quickly, broadly, and decisively to alter the federal regulatory process.

In 1981 President Reagan issued Executive Order 12291 (*for text of order, see p. 778*), which gave the OMB extensive powers over the regulatory apparatus—perhaps the single most important reform of the rulemaking process since the APA in 1946. The order empowered the OMB to identify duplication, overlap, and conflict in rules, which federal agencies then were required to rectify; and to review existing and new rules for consistency with administration policies. The order required the use of cost-benefit analysis and established a "net benefit" criterion for rulemaking. The order also called for the serious consideration of alternatives, including nonregulatory options, when attempting to solve problems, and selecting the approach that creates the least burden for affected parties.

In the 1980s both the process and substance of regulation changed. The deregulation movement, which actually had begun in the late 1970s, accelerated and engulfed airlines, telecommunications, securities, trucking, railroads, buses, cable television, oil, natural gas, financial institutions, and even public utilities. In some areas the changes were profound. For example, the ICC, the institution that started it all in 1887, was left a shadow of its former self by deregulation legislation of the early 1980s. (The ICC was finally abolished in 1995.) Almost all the areas affected by deregulation were economic: rates, entry to markets, or business practices that critics believed were better left to the free market.

The Reagan administration attacked social regulation with different, more subtle means. Administration officials imposed a temporary moratorium on new rules, altered procedures, cut budgets, and questioned policy decisions. New regulations faced a more arduous path from initiation to publication in the *Federal Register*.

It must also be said that an examination of the 1980s also finds new regulatory statutes. But these statutes usually were amendments to legislation enacted earlier. Examples include the Government Securities Act (1986); the Hazardous and Solid Waste Amendments of 1984, which amended the Resource Conservation and Recovery Act; the Safe Drinking Water Act Amendments (1986); and the Electric Consumers Protection Act (1986), which amended the Federal Power Act. There were some new initiatives as well, such as the Commercial Space Launch Act of 1984 and Superfund hazardous waste regulations of 1980.

During the administration of George Bush, the president was often described, perhaps unfairly, as lacking interest in domestic policy. He attempted to respond to these criticisms with numerous assertions of intent, including his widely quoted aspiration to be known as the "environmental president." Whatever his actual interests and hopes, it was certainly true that regulatory activity during the first years of his presidency continued a revival that had actually begun in Reagan's second term.

Alarmed by apparent backsliding on the regulation issue, Bush's conservative supporters mounted an organized and concerted effort to drag their president back to the path of reduction and reform. He imposed and then extended a moratorium on new rules and tightened cost-benefit analysis requirements for those that were issued. He began instituting programs to set standards, then allowing businesses to develop the means to meet them. The EPA's 33/50, developed under the Bush administration, was one example. The program allowed more than 1,300 companies to cut back voluntarily toxic emissions 33 percent by 1993 and 50 percent by 1995. In exchange, EPA regulators would ease up on oversight and compliance rules. But Bush's most dramatic response was the creation of the Council on Competitiveness, chaired by Vice President Dan Quayle. The council was given authority to roam the full range of regulation in search of relief for American business, and it soon became an aggressive advocate for relaxed requirements. A major source of controversy concerned the way the council conducted its business. It attempted to maintain strict secrecy in its deliberations and repeatedly refused to disclose those people in the private sector it communicated with or consulted. Those critics who were upset earlier with the possibilities of "backdoor rulemaking" were livid when they learned about the council's operations. It never altered its procedures; the election of 1992 did.

The Clinton Administration

President Clinton's arrival in Washington was greeted with relief by liberal groups that felt the Reagan and Bush administrations had eased up too much on protection for the environment, workplace safety, and public health. Clinton's actions, however, elicited both applause and concern from those groups. Ironically, business groups also gave Clinton mixed reviews, approving of many industry-friendly initiatives but decrying a few tough new regulations. Clinton geared his reforms toward easing the regulatory burden on industry, the interest group that offered him the least political support. But his advocacy of "keeping the regulatory cop on the beat" quieted the criticism of liberal interest groups, as did the more public process his agencies instituted for rulemaking. A remarkable slew of "midnight" regulations—issued in the waning days of the Clinton White House—solidified his reputation as a regulatory activist. Forty-six finalized regulations—from sweeping rules governing repetitive motion injuries in the workplace to antidiscrimination protections for homosexuals—were published between Nov. 2, 2000, and the day Clinton left office.

From 1994 to the end of his term, Clinton's attitudes toward regulation could not be seen in isolation from those of Congress. The 1994 elections brought to power a group of Republicans whose contempt for regulation was unprecedented. Although they failed to enact their most ambitious legislative items, the self-described Republican revolutionaries forced the Democratic administration to institute regulatory changes that preempted and defused some antiregulatory zeal. The Republican Congress succeeded in invigorating Clinton's reform efforts. At times, they even pushed agencies further to the right than they would have gone otherwise. On the other hand, a hostile Congress emboldened Clinton to use his regulatory powers where his legislative powers failed him. From homosexual rights to patient protections against managed care insurers, Clinton was able to use the power of the presidency to circumvent Congress.

The Clinton approach to regulation and the regulatory process was outlined in two different documents. His Executive Order 12866, "Regulatory Planning and Review" (*for text of order, see p. 784*), established the principles guiding the development of regulations in federal agencies and the review of those regulations in the White House. The National Performance Review (NPR), written under the direction of Vice President Al Gore, contained a number of proposals to "reinvent" regulation. While Clinton was generally viewed as more sympathetic to regulatory programs than his Republican predecessor, Clinton's program for improving regulation contained much that is familiar from previous administrations.

The executive order, under the section titled "The Principles of Regulation," established twelve policies that the president expected agencies to observe in their regulatory work. These included:

- Identification of problems to be addressed by regulation and their magnitude.
- Review of existing regulations for possible elimination or modification.
- Assessment of nonregulatory alternatives to solving problems.
- Use of risk assessment to establish regulatory priorities.
- Establishing steps to ensure that the benefits of regulation justify the costs and that regulations adopted are cost-effective.
- Use of the best available information when developing regulations.
- Use of performance objectives whenever possible. Wide consultation with state, local, and tribal governments. Avoidance of inconsistent, incompatible, or duplicative regulations.
- Tailoring of regulations to produce the least burden possible on society.
- Writing regulations that are simple and easy to understand.

The NPR, in a brief chapter titled "Eliminating Regulatory Overkill," provided a number of more specific objectives that the Clinton administration sought to achieve. These were mostly related in some way to the principles set forth in Executive Order 12866. Among these objectives were very ambitious plans to reduce existing rules—50 percent—within three years and set up better interagency coordination to reduce "red tape."

Interagency coordination would be heightened through the creation of a high-level Regulatory Working Group. An NPR report noted the need for such coordination with the example of chocolate manufacturers who faced conflicting regulations from separate agencies. OSHA demanded porous insulation to reduce noise from machinery, while the Food and Drug Administration (FDA) insisted such insulation could not be kept clean enough to meet food-safety standards. The group also assumed the task of identifying priority rules for OMB review. By easing the review burden on OMB, the coordinating group allowed rule reviewers to consider new rules in new ways, such as using more detailed cost-benefit analyses and examining the various segments of society and the economy the rule was impacting. The group also quieted criticism of "backdoor" rulemaking by taking away from OMB some of the responsibility Reagan and Bush had given it.

The administration also let it be known, both in the NPR and at the press conference announcing Executive Order 12866, that it strongly supported the expanded use of regulatory negotiation. The administration subsequently named the EPA, OSHA, and FDA as the vanguard agencies for its reform efforts, stressing cooperation and consultation over punishment and oversight.

To complement the Bush administration's 33/50 program, the EPA under President Clinton created Project XL and the Common Sense Initiative. Project XL allows large companies with good environmental track records to demonstrate their own paths toward emissions reduction outside those prescribed by EPA rule-writers. The Common Sense Initiative identified six industry sectors—automobiles, electronics, iron and steel, metal finishing, petroleum refining, and printing—and then formed teams of business, environmental, and community representatives to come up with industry-specific ways to cut red tape, reduce emissions, and end the one-size-fits-all approach to environmental regulations. Through the program, the EPA reached an agreement with the metal finishing industry, granting it regulatory relief in exchange for efforts that went beyond mere compliance with environmental law. Some 11,000 metal finishing shops would be brought under the agreement, which envisions slashing emissions by up to 75 percent of 1992 levels.

Starting in 1993, OSHA's Maine 200 Program identified companies with high injury rates, then gave those firms the choice between partnering with OSHA to develop new worker-safety programs or facing stepped-up enforcement. In December 1997 OSHA transformed the Maine pilot program into a national effort involving 12,250 employers, dubbed the Cooperative Compliance Program (CCP). But cooperation could only go so far. About 10,000 out of 12,000 employers invited to join the CCP had signed up by February 1998. But that month, the program was thrown out by a federal appeals court, responding to a major lawsuit by the U.S. Chamber of Commerce, the National Association of Manufacturers, the American Trucking Associations, and the Food Marketing Institute. The court found that the program amounted to an unfair club in the hands of the regulators. OSHA could promise fewer inspections, but to participate, businesses would have to institute some workplace safety programs that had not gone through a formal rulemaking procedure. That, the court ruled, was an end run around the regulatory process.

In 1996 the FDA announced a series of new cooperative programs. One pilot effort allowed medical device manufacturers to select an FDA-recognized third-party reviewer to assess the safety of low and moderate risk products, thus speeding the regulatory process. A series of meetings between the FDA and medical device manufacturers produced changes to FDA inspection procedures to permit advance notification of inspections and an opportunity for firms to note on inspection records that a violation had been immediately corrected.

In July 1996 the Department of Agriculture's (USDA) Food Safety and Inspection Service announced the first overhaul of its meat and poultry inspection system in ninety years, and again, cooperation was a key component. Slaughterhouses and processing plants, with the help of USDA inspectors, were required to develop hazard analysis plans and sanitation standards. Regulators had to approve those plans and standards, and their implementation was to be monitored. But administration officials stressed that the new system allowed plants to develop strategies best suited to their situations rather than follow a system devised in Washington.

But just as it emphasized cooperation with industry, the Clinton administration also moved to protect its regulatory powers, in some cases flouting the notion of regulatory relief. By executive order, EPA was given new authority to force polluters to clean up toxic waste sites. The USDA's new meat inspection rules may have involved cooperation, but they also tightened safety controls. The rules mandated, for instance, that slaughter plants regularly test carcasses for the generic E. coli bacteria to verify the effectiveness of plant procedures designed to prevent fecal contamination. The rules also created the first regulatory performance standard for salmonella contamination rates.

Bridling under such regulations, a coalition of industry groups in 1997 mounted perhaps the most significant challenge to the government's regulatory authority since the modern regulatory era began in 1970. The group's lawsuit was triggered by tough new smog- and soot-reduction standards adopted in 1997 by the EPA under the authority of the Clean Air Act. Industry lawyers contended that Congress had ceded too much of its lawmaking power to regulators when it approved the Clean Air Act, and that the EPA should be obligated to balance compliance costs against health benefits when setting standards. But in a unanimous decision (*Whitman v. American Trucking Associations*) that could become a landmark in regulatory affairs, the Supreme Court ruled in February 2001 that the EPA—and by extension, all regulatory agencies—had the right to issue rules under the authority vested by Congress. Specifically, the justices ruled, the Clean Air Act bars the EPA from weighing compliance costs against health benefits.

The ruling was a victory for Clinton, whose second term was marked by an increasing interest in new regulatory efforts. The Department of Agriculture approved new rules to regulate food labeled "organic." In

1997 the White House signed the international agreement reached in Kyoto, Japan, to stem global warming through strict new limits on emissions of greenhouse gases such as carbon dioxide. Although there was not enough support in Congress to ratify the Kyoto accords immediately, the Clinton administration continued to work on emissions piecemeal. In 1999 the White House completed new emissions standards for the rapidly growing numbers of minivans and sport-utility vehicles, so-called "light trucks." These vehicles escaped automotive regulatory standards through a loophole originally intended for trucks used for business purposes, such as hauling and construction.

A Congress once marked by antiregulatory zeal was also joining the act. Its Congressional Review Act, passed in March 1996 to give lawmakers the authority to overturn any regulation by a simple majority vote, lay dormant for the remainder of the Clinton years. That same year, the Telecommunications Act created a new discount "e-rate" that firms must provide schools, libraries, and nonprofit groups for access to the Internet. In 1998 Congress again waded into the telecommunications market and drafted legislation banning the practice of "slamming," where companies unilaterally change an unsuspecting customer's long-distance service provider.

Any credit the Clinton administration may have gotten for regulatory innovation was swamped by the ill will of business garnered in the final years of the Clinton White House. In an August 1996 report, Thomas D. Hopkins of the Center for the Study of American Business (CSAB) at Washington University calculated that the total costs of regulation during the Clinton administration jumped from $642 billion in 1992 and 1993 to $677 billion in 1996, using constant 1995 dollars. Those costs were to climb steadily to $721 billion by 2000.

The growth in funding and staffing for both economic and social regulation was considerable from 1970 to 1980. The rate of growth slowed in the 1980s, but by the end of the decade it was increasing once again. Staffing levels during the early years of the Clinton administration declined, because of cuts mandated by the NPR and others necessitated by congressional and administration budget cuts. OSHA employment declined from 2,409 in 1992 to 2,208 in 1997, bouncing back to 2,370 in 2001. The Equal Employment Opportunity Commission (EEOC) payroll fell from 2,791 full-time employees in 1992 to 2,544 in 1998 but was back up to 2,852 in 2000. EPA employment declined to 16,790 in 2000 from 18,398 in 1992. Still, by 2001, total staffing at fifty-four regulatory agencies was expected to rebound

to a record 131,983, according to CSAB. The administrative costs of running those agencies were forecast to reach $19.8 billion, a 4.8 percent increase over 2000. Funding levels in 2000 also marked an 8.2 percent increase over 1999.

Another barometer of regulatory activity, the number of pages printed annually in the *Federal Register*, shows a similar trend. In 1970 the *Federal Register* had 20,032 pages; in 1980, it had 87,012. The number had declined to 47,418 by 1986, but stood at 68,530 pages in 1997. Then the numbers soared. In 2000, the final full year of the Clinton administration, 83,178 pages were published. Clinton's final three months alone saw 25,605 pages printed in the *Federal Register*. On Jan. 22, 2001, three days after Clinton officially left office, last-minute rules, regulations, and other measures still in the pipeline filled 944 register pages.

The Arrival of George W. Bush

From the day of his inauguration, George W. Bush signaled his regulatory approach would be more similar to Reagan's than Clinton's—or even Bush's father's. As Reagan had done, Bush immediately froze all new rules and regulations, pending a sixty-day review by the new administration. He also quickly put a conservative ideological stamp on his executive decision making. In his first month in office, Bush ordered that all companies contracting with the federal government notify unionized employees that they have the right to withhold the portion of their union dues slated to be used for political purposes. Republicans had been trying for years to enact this so-called "paycheck protection" measure as a way to curb funding for union political activities that were heavily biased toward the Democratic Party. Bush also rescinded Clinton-era orders favoring unionized contractors that bid on federally funded construction projects.

President Bush also tapped John Graham, a vocal critic of business regulation, to head his Office of Information and Regulatory Affairs (OIRA), the regulatory gatekeeper within the OMB. OIRA was created during the last days of the Carter administration but was first staffed and shaped during Reagan's tenure in the White House. The office aims to watch over and guide regulators. In this role, it reviews regulations—roughly 600 per year—and guards against bureaucratic overreach.

As the director of the industry-backed Harvard Center for Risk Analysis, Graham has been a strong advocate of cost-benefit analyses. For instance, he had questioned the EPA's efforts to regulate second-hand cigarette smoke, opposed efforts to ban the use of cell phones by drivers, and raised concerns about the safety of mandatory air bags in cars.

After winning a bruising confirmation battle in the Senate, 61–37, Graham lost no time in applying his tough standards to regulations under review. During his first six months in office, the new OIRA head sent twenty rules back to their agencies of origin for redrafting. During the previous seven years under Clinton, the office had sent back just seven regulations.

But Graham was not entirely predictable. For instance, early in his tenure he argued against an administration decision not to regulate carbon dioxide as a pollutant. The decision was a reversal of a pledge Bush had made during the 2000 campaign. Such regulation would have been a powerful tool to combat global climate change, but the administration argued that the cost to industry—especially to energy producers—would have been too high. In March 2001 the president further angered environmentalists when the EPA announced it would revoke a Clinton administration rule that would have sharply reduced the acceptable level of arsenic in drinking water. That same month the White House announced that the United States was withdrawing completely from the Kyoto accords.

Like Graham though, Bush also defied predictability, making decisions that surprised opponents and supporters alike. For example, during his first few months in office he earned the praise of environmentalists by declining to reverse Clinton's decision to set aside millions of acres of land as national monuments. He also backed away from his earlier decision to rescind the arsenic rules.

Meanwhile, with the White House canceling or at least reviewing many Clinton-era regulations, the Republican-controlled Congress dusted off the 1996 Congressional Review Act in March 2001 and put it to use for the first time to overturn the Clinton administration's tough new regulations guarding against repetitive motion disorders, such as carpal tunnel syndrome and tendonitis. The review act had passed with little fanfare as a means to diffuse stronger regulatory "reform" measures. But it granted Congress extraordinary new powers to combat regulatory efforts. The act sets aside traditional legislative procedures, such as hearings, bars filibusters, disallows amendments to so-called "resolutions of disapproval," and forbids an agency from reissuing a regulation that is "substantially the same" without explicit congressional approval. The highly controversial ergonomics rule—developed by the Department of Labor over the course of a decade—would have covered 6 million workplaces and 100 million workers.

Annual compliance cost estimates ranged wildly, from $4.5 billion to more than $100 billion.

But seven months before the rule was to go into force, Congress scuttled it with remarkable speed. Bush's signature sent a clear signal that the regulatory activism of the Clinton era was over. "There needs to be a balance between and an understanding of the costs and benefits associated with federal regulations," Bush said in a statement the day the rule was officially revoked.

But the Republicans would soon have to put their congressional efforts to scale back regulations on hold. In June 2001 Sen. James Jeffords of Vermont announced that he was leaving the Republican Party to become an Independent. Even though Jeffords officially belonged to neither major party, he began to caucus with the Democrats, giving them fifty-one votes and majority status in the closely divided Senate.

Still, efforts to change the regulatory environment continued apace within the executive branch. In 2001, for instance, the administration tried to formalize the process of OIRA review by actively soliciting groups—business associations, nonprofit organizations, think tanks, and universities as well as government agencies—to suggest regulations for review and possible change. The nominated regulations, seventy-one in all, were handed over to Graham and his staff at OIRA, where they were subjected to strict cost-benefit analysis. Of these, twenty-three were categorized as "high priority" and many were eliminated or changed. For example, a Clinton-era regulation mandating greater energy efficiency on new air conditioners was scaled back. Another rule banning the use of snowmobiles in national parks was largely rescinded.

But despite the work of OIRA, regulatory activity did not ground to a halt under Bush. During the new president's first year in office, the federal government issued 4,132 regulations, while 4,313 were issued in 2000, the last year of the Clinton presidency. The numbers are a testament to the fact that though regulatory philosophy may change one way or another with the comings and goings of presidents, the work of regulating goes on. After all, most regulation is the fruit of legislation, often enacted long before a president arrives at the White House.

The shock of the terrorist attacks on Sept. 11, 2001, changed the political and social dynamic of the nation, literally, in a matter of hours. By the time President Bush returned to Washington late on the afternoon of the day of the attacks, he had a completely new mission—to protect the homeland. Bush and his team acted swiftly, asking Congress for $40 billion in new funds to help a devastated New York City and to begin waging the new war on terrorism, both at home and abroad. Legislation appropriating the funds cleared Congress a mere three days after the attack.

The administration also asked for new law enforcement powers. Attorney General John Ashcroft sought new wiretapping and search authority as well as broader power to detain and deport immigrants. Legislation granting almost everything Ashcroft had asked for, called the USA Patriot Act, cleared Congress on Oct. 25. The new law granted expanded regulatory authority to a large number of agencies, including the Immigration and Naturalization Service (INS), the Customs Service, and the FBI.

In November Congress created the Transportation Security Administration (TSA) within the Department of Transportation, charged with administering security at airports. Under the legislation creating the new agency, the federal government had until the end of 2002 to replace all 28,000 privately employed airport baggage screeners with federal workers. The same deadline was set for airports to have the capacity to screen all luggage. It was the first major agency created since 1977, the year the Department of Energy came into existence. It would not be the last.

One criticism that came out of the 2001 attacks was that federal agencies did not adequately coordinate their counterterrorism activities. The charge stuck especially to intelligence and law enforcement agencies—notably the FBI and CIA. Bush sought to overcome this handicap by creating an Office of Homeland Security, to coordinate the government's domestic response to terrorism. The president appointed popular Pennsylvania governor Thomas Ridge to fill the post.

Many in Congress called for legislation that would define the powers of the new office and subject the president's choice to confirmation. They argued that formalizing Ridge's role and appropriating a budget for the new office would give him the clout he needed to work within the federal bureaucracy. But the administration opposed the idea, arguing that Ridge had "the president's ear," which was all the clout he needed to do his job. By the end of May 2002 impatient members of Congress were beginning to float other proposals. Then, surprising many on Capitol Hill, the White House released a new plan for homeland security, one that was much broader and more far-reaching than most of the congressional proposals it had earlier rejected.

The Bush plan called for reorganizing the entire federal government to create a whole new department, the Department of Homeland Security. After initial congressional enthusiasm for the new department, the issue became bogged down over labor issues. The administration wanted to be able to design a new personnel system, setting pay and performance rules free of the strictures of the civil service rules. The president also wanted to be able to rearrange parts of the agencies and their budgets without congressional approval. Finally, on Nov. 22 Congress cleared a bill that virtually mirrored Bush's initial proposal and that largely gave the president his way on personnel issues.

The new Department of Homeland Security was created out of twenty-two different agencies with just under 170,000 employees and a budget approaching $40 billion. After the Department of Defense, it was the largest cabinet department (in terms of personnel) in the federal government. The new department merged agencies in four basic areas: border and transportation security; emergency preparedness; countermeasures against weapons of mass destruction; and information analysis and infrastructure protection. It included the Coast Guard, the Customs Service, the INS, the Federal Emergency Management Agency, the Secret Service, and the new TSA. The new department also absorbed smaller functions of other agencies, such as the Department of Health and Human Service's National Pharmaceutical Stockpile, the Department of Agriculture's Animal and Plant Health Inspection Service, and the Department of Energy's Nuclear Energy Search Team.

REGULATORY TOOLS

The wide variety of issues and conditions dealt with by regulation requires similarly diversified mechanisms and procedures. Nevertheless, there are common elements that, taken together, form the outlines of contemporary regulation.

Legislation

Contrary to views held by some, regulation does not grow mushroom-like in the dark recesses of Washington bureaucracy. All regulation starts with an act of Congress. Statutes define the goals of regulatory programs, identify the agency responsible for achieving them, and contain substantive and procedural guidance as to how the agency is to conduct its work. The first and most important tool of regulation is the law that establishes the authority and basic architecture of the program.

In the matter of guidance, regulatory statutes vary tremendously. A perennial criticism of regulatory statutes is that they are vague, giving far too much substantive and procedural discretion to bureaucrats in the programs they administer. There is no question that the provisions of some statutes are quite general. The Federal Power Act, for example, directs FERC to license those hydroelectric power projects that "are best adapted to a comprehensive plan for development of the waterway." The comprehensive plan and what constitutes a project that is "best adapted" is left to FERC's discretion. Similarly the statutory language that created OSHA gave that agency a very broad mandate.

On the other hand, statutes can be quite specific when establishing the substantive jurisdiction of agencies. The Safe Drinking Water Act amendments of 1996 upheld regulations the EPA had been drafting on the by-products of disinfectants, such as chlorine. The Delaney Amendment to the Food, Drug and Cosmetic Act gave the FDA strict guidelines for dealing with suspected carcinogens. The "zero-tolerance" standard of Delaney was replaced in 1996 by a new pesticide law establishing a uniform safety standard to ensure that the chemicals on both raw and processed foods pose a "reasonable certainty" of no harm. Such a standard is commonly interpreted to mean a lifetime cancer risk of no more than one in a million. In some instances, the subject matter of the regulatory statute is so narrow, like the Surface Transportation Assistance Act's provisions relating to tandem truck trailers, that substantive discretion is negligible.

The trend since 1965 is toward more narrowly defined statutes and limiting amendments, which are the result of accumulated experience with programs. For example, the first Clean Air Act in 1970 was much less specific about hazardous air pollutants.

Procedural guidance in statutes varies as well. But, as with substantive provisions, the trend is for Congress to provide more direction to agencies on how to make decisions and what factors to take into account when doing so. The 1996 safe drinking water law rescinded a requirement that the EPA set standards for twenty-five new drinking water contaminants every three years. Instead, the agency must publish every five years a list of unregulated contaminants found in drinking water. The EPA would then use that list to propose the regulation of new contaminants, taking the costs and benefits of any new regulation into account. Some statutes require agencies to balance conflicting interests or to conduct specified analyses during the process of making regulatory decisions. Amendments to the Federal Power Act tell FERC to balance power and nonpower interests in hydropower licensing, and they make it plain that environmental and recreational concerns are the nonpower interests most important to Congress. In addition to balancing multiple interests, Congress expects regulatory agencies to study different facets of proposed regulations.

Rules and Rulemaking

Rulemaking is usually the most important function performed by regulatory agencies. It transforms the provisions of statutes into specific mandates which, in turn, structure the behaviors of implementing officials and affected parties in the private sector. Since the earliest Congresses, which required the president to write rules related to trade with Native Americans and uses of public lands, rulemaking has been the source of law people turn to in order to learn exactly what they can expect from government and what government can expect from them.

The process by which rules are made can be quite complex. Congress first established uniform methods for rulemaking in the APA in 1946 (*for text of act, see p. 739*). The rulemaking provisions of that statute stressed three principles that remain central today: information, participation, and accountability. The act required a notice in the *Federal Register* that described the rule the issuing agency was proposing, opportunity for the public to comment in writing on the proposal, and a notice of the final rule and its effective date. The act promoted accountability by authorizing the courts to review any rule that was challenged as illegal. Still, the provisions were quite flexible, balancing a modest degree of public scrutiny and involvement with considerable discretion for rulemaking agencies.

Since 1946 the number of legal requirements for creating new rules have grown enormously, although most requirements apply selectively to individual rulemakings. Virtually all of these additional requirements enhance in some way one or more of the principles established in the APA. There are general statutes such as the Regulatory Flexibility Act, Paperwork Reduction Act, National Environmental Policy Act, and Unfunded Mandates Act of 1995, which require additional studies and forms of public participation when rules affect the interests that these laws seek to protect. Agency- and program-specific authorizing and appropriations bills establish similar procedures. Presidential executive orders also impose additional requirements, ranging from cost-benefit analysis to special consideration of private property, the family, and state and local governments. Individual judicial decisions can require agencies to conduct special studies or consult extensively with interest groups. Overall, the weight of these requirements is to transform the APA model of rulemaking into a process that may be so encumbered that Thomas

McGarrity of the University of Texas has used the term "ossification" to describe it. The pendulum has clearly swung away from agency flexibility in favor of public participation, especially by interest groups, broadly defined.

Any governmental function that is so important, frequent, and complex is bound to attract controversy and criticism, and rulemaking is certainly no exception. The complaints are numerous and, at times, contradictory. Some charge there is simply too much rulemaking and that it is choking the private sector. Others will argue for more rulemaking, either because they favor more extensive regulation or they believe government too often makes law or policy without observing the proper procedures. Critics also fault the time it takes to issue rules; in some agencies the average is measured in years. Finally, there are persistent concerns in both the private and public sectors about the quality of the rules that the process ultimately produces. The private sector has questioned the quality of information and analysis on which rules are based and has found them difficult to understand and comply with and, most disturbing, biased in favor of large, established firms and organizations. Some in the public sector undoubtedly share some or all of these views, but they focus more on the difficulties created by unrealistic deadlines set by Congress and the courts, rules that are written in Washington without regard for resources available to implement them in the field, and ambiguous or otherwise faulty language in rules that impede their enforcement. The recent battle between the Department of Energy and Congress over the establishment of a permanent nuclear waste repository at Yucca Mountain, Nevada, is a case in point. Members of Congress, echoing the anger of the nuclear power industry, complained bitterly when the federal government failed to meet its statutory obligation in accepting commercial nuclear waste by January 1998. But Energy Department officials snapped back that Congress created that deadline in 1982 without a realistic assessment of the difficulty in creating a repository that must remain safe and stable for 10,000 years.

It should not be surprising that rulemaking is a function that requires a substantial amount of proactive management. It is now common to find priority setting, budgeting, and scheduling systems in agencies that issue a substantial number of rules. Most use some form of cross-agency work group to write rules to ensure that all relevant legal, technical, and political issues are considered. Rulemaking also attracts the attention of Congress, which conducts oversight by a variety of means; of the White House, which reviews both pro-posed and final rules; and of the courts when litigation over rules occurs.

However troubled and difficult, rulemaking is and will continue to be an elemental regulatory function that structures much of what follows.

Licenses and Permits

Granting licenses and issuing permits are common regulatory activities. States license doctors, lawyers, and a variety of other professionals and service providers to protect the public from the unqualified or unscrupulous. At the federal level the focus is different. Here it is more common to find programs that license activities, usually those with implications for health, safety, or the environment. For example, licenses are required to build and operate nuclear power plants and hydroelectric facilities. The National Pollution Discharge Elimination System (NPDES) issues permits to discharge all sources of pollution into America's waterways. The handling of pesticides and hazardous wastes must be cleared through the EPA.

Control of licenses and permits serves several interrelated purposes. In some instances those seeking the government's permission to engage in certain activities, such as operating a nuclear power plant, are expected to demonstrate that they are competent to perform them or that the activity poses no risk to health, safety, or the environment. Permits and licenses also are used to impose conditions on the activity for which the permission is being granted. A pesticide registration may be accompanied by the limitations on its use or the precautions those administering it are required to take.

Because a considerable amount of environmental, health, safety, and natural resource regulation involves licenses and permits, the procedures used to issue them are painstaking. Most require an applicant to submit extensive background information. The government then evaluates the applicant's qualifications, the threats the proposed activity might pose to health, safety, or environmental quality, and the steps the applicant will take to eliminate or mitigate the potential for harm.

For environmental, safety, and natural resource licenses, the agency's rules usually require that applicants consult in advance with other agencies or groups and report the comments they receive from these third parties in the application. In its procedures for licensing hydroelectric power plants, FERC requires preapplication consultation with federal and state agencies responsible for fisheries, wildlife, recreation, aesthetics, water quality, geology and soils, historic preservation, and Native American lands.

It is also common for the licensing agency to circulate the completed applications it receives to other agencies for formal comment. Notices to the public about the proposed action are published in the *Federal Register* and other outlets. Negotiations between the applicant and agencies or groups often result in agreements written into the license or permit.

At some point, the agency decides whether to issue a license or permit and what, if any, conditions to impose. Again, the hydropower licensing process is instructive. It is not uncommon for FERC to issue such a license containing dozens of conditions, or "articles," designed to protect natural resources and historic sites and to preserve other values and uses of the waterway on which the project will be built. Most agencies also have procedures to reconsider the content of licenses or permits at the request of the applicant or a third party, and, like rules, licenses and permits can be challenged in court.

Because licenses and permits have policy implications that affect multiple interests and are in effect for long periods of time, the procedures employed to issue them have come to resemble those associated with rulemaking.

IMPLEMENTATION TECHNIQUES

Once the rules or licenses are written, their provisions must be implemented. At this stage the behavior of regulated parties becomes important, and regulatory agencies engage in a variety of activities to ensure compliance.

Informing the Public

The *Federal Register* is the official means of communicating regulatory policies and decisions to the public. Yet few in the regulated community learn about their obligations through it. Many have on-staff specialists to track new and changing requirements and to fashion approaches to compliance. Others rely on trade associations and professional newsletters to supply information; some hire expert consultants. The Internet has become a new resource for public participation. The Clinton administration pushed agencies to establish Web sites and to publish new regulatory policies electronically. Still, some people only learn about regulatory obligations by being cited for violating one or more of them.

To keep the public better informed, regulatory agencies provide information beyond what is found in the *Federal Register*. At times, agencies may communicate directly with regulated parties, especially in emergency situations, such as when defects are discovered in aircraft. Agencies also provide technical supplements to rules to assist regulated parties. The NRC provides this type of guidance with each new rule that requires significant changes in equipment or operations. The supplement tells what the NRC considers acceptable, effective means of complying with new requirements and standards. OSHA has taken this approach a step further by performing "regulatory audits" for businesses. Under this program OSHA officials conduct a no-fault survey of the company's compliance record and make recommendations for change. In this way the company obtains authoritative information about how to avoid noncompliance without the threat of an enforcement action. The audit program has been explored by other agencies as well; it is perhaps the most ambitious method of keeping regulated parties aware of their obligations.

Monitoring

However they communicate requirements to the regulated parties, agencies do not rely solely on the provision of information to ensure that obligations are met. Agencies use a variety of means to monitor restricted activities and behaviors. Some programs require regulated parties to monitor their activities and to submit periodic reports. The reports might consist of raw data or summaries that follow a standard format. In some instances data and reports may not be required routinely but must be made available to the agency on request when an inspector visits.

Inspection is the customary way to monitor for workplace safety, protection of natural resources, and compliance in some environmental programs. For some programs, such as OSHA's, the number of regulated premises far outnumber the available staff. OSHA's 1,123 inspectors cannot possibly visit all 6 million workplaces that fall under their jurisdiction. Such programs rely on complaints from the public when establishing their inspection priorities. An inspection program can become so intensive that it resembles supervision of the regulated activity. The USDA's 7,400 food safety inspectors are a constant presence at the nation's 6,200 slaughterhouses and processing plants. There tends to be a direct relationship between the potential danger to the public posed by the regulated activity and the amount of agency monitoring.

Intervention and Enforcement

When an agency discovers that a violation has occurred, it must intervene to bring the offending party into compliance. Some inspectors, notably those associated with occupational safety, have been criticized for issuing citations for minor offenses and, in the process, trivializing the program and infuriating the affected businesses. But many cases have been reported of inspectors overlooking minor, often inadvertent violations to get quick agreements from regulated parties to correct more serious problems. Citations may or may not be issued in such instances. And, there are the rare but disturbing reports of corruption in programs—inspectors overlooking violations in return for personal rewards.

Sanctions

The approach an agency takes to intervention depends to some extent on the nature and severity of sanctions it can impose on parties who fail to comply. Generally, regulatory statutes establish a range of sanctions that agencies can impose. Agencies match the type of sanction to the type of noncompliance through rules and management directives to their inspection staff.

Sanctions come in the form of warnings, fines, more frequent inspections, product recalls, temporary or permanent cessation of activities, suspension or termination of licenses or permits, and criminal penalties. Sanctions also have serious indirect consequences. An airline, such as ValuJet in 1996, that has its airworthiness certification suspended by the FAA can suffer a loss of consumer confidence. ValuJet shut down and reopened under the name AirTran. A manufacturing plant cited for polluting a waterway can suffer serious public relations problems. Both may expect to lose business.

The mechanisms by which sanctions are imposed also vary across programs. Some regulatory statutes grant significant authority to agencies to impose sanctions; others require the responsible agency to seek court orders. The EEOC had to file a federal lawsuit against Mitsubishi in April 1996 to take action on one of the biggest sexual harassment cases in history. When criminal penalties may be involved, the agency usually refers the matter to the Department of Justice for prosecution. The FDA in June 1996 asked Justice Department prosecutors to investigate whether the Upjohn Co. hid safety concerns about its controversial sleeping pill Halcion. In 1998 the Justice Department's regulators in the agency's antitrust division began pursuing a major lawsuit against Microsoft. The following year, using a racketeering statute created to pursue organized crime, the department sued the tobacco industry for health-care costs incurred by taxpayers. Then, in 2000, the Department of Housing and Urban Development, with the Justice Department's help, threatened to sue

gun manufacturers if they did not cooperate with state and local governments pursuing their own lawsuits to restrict the sale and marketing of firearms.

Recently, financial services and accounting firms have come under increased state and federal scrutiny as a result of a series of scandals ranging from shady accounting practices to the defrauding of investors. As a result, an increasing number of fines have been levied against these companies. For instance, in March 2003 Merrill Lynch, one of the nation's top brokerage houses, paid an $80 million fine to the SEC in exchange for the agency's dropping charges against the firm. Merrill had been accused of aiding bankrupt energy giant Enron in its efforts to hide losses and inflate earnings. In May the SEC fined telecommunications giant WorldCom $500 million for its uncovered accounting fraud. Similar fines were likely to be leveled against other firms that lied about their financial health.

DISPUTE RESOLUTION

Conflict is common between an agency enforcing regulations and the regulated parties. Disputes arise regarding alleged violations and the sanctions imposed for noncompliance. Congress has established a two-tiered system for resolving these disputes. The first tier is based in the agencies; the second is in the federal court system.

Adjudication of disputes in agencies is governed by provisions in the APA and the procedural regulations of individual agencies that apply to the conduct of hearings. Adjudication usually involves fewer parties and is more judicial in nature than other forms of regulatory procedure. Formal adjudication involves a court trial in which the agency charges a named individual or company with violating a law or regulation. The APA outlines a strict format of notice, hearings, procedures, evidence, oral argument, and formal judicial decision that adjudication proceedings must follow. Consequently, adjudication is often a time-consuming and cumbersome process.

Participation

Companies and industries affected by federal regulations always have been well represented at agency proceedings. But intervention by citizens and consumer groups involves the question of standing—whether petitioners have a legitimate right to be heard before an agency because their interests and well-being are affected. While the right to appeal an agency decision before the courts is subject to limits imposed by the Constitution and court decisions, agencies enjoy broad discretion in setting and enforcing rules for participation in their proceedings.

The ability of groups other than the regulated industries to participate has been influenced by the regulatory system itself. Delay in the procedure is costly, and many small businesses and interest groups have found that they cannot afford to participate in a lengthy series of hearings and appeals. Although notice is required to be given in the *Federal Register,* unless a group has been following a particular issue closely, it may not be aware of a proposed ruling. Moreover, there might not always be adequate notice of a pending case, necessitating a hasty response by interested parties. In general, the regulated industries are better equipped to keep themselves abreast of forthcoming rules that fall within their interests.

The expense of participation has raised the question of whether there is a need to facilitate representation by consumer and citizen groups. It has been argued that their greater representation would provide the agencies with new or different information and lead to better informed judgments. Others have contended that because regulation exists to protect consumers and workers as well as industry interests, such views should be heard. Congress, however, has been unwilling to create an agency to represent consumer interests before other regulatory agencies. Programs to reimburse citizens who take part in agency proceedings also have met with mixed success and spotty government support. The Clinton administration broadened federal outreach to "stakeholder" groups, including activists and citizens, but with mixed results. Business groups complained that the citizens participating in hearings and roundtable discussions were really the representatives of special interests, such as environmental groups. The citizens complained that their opinions carried no weight in the final decision.

Adjudicatory Process

Many disputes are resolved by consent order, which is a regulatory "plea bargain." Using this device a regulated party agrees to cease violation of regulations. A proposed order is drafted, published in the *Federal Register* for comment, and then recommended by the agency. Comments are considered part of the record of the case and, based on them, the agency may issue a consent order in final form. This substantial role for the public is another manifestation of the importance of participation in regulatory procedure. If a case is not dropped or settled through a consent order, the agency may initiate adjudicatory proceedings by issuing a formal complaint against the alleged violators.

Formal adjudication is conducted in a manner very similar to a court proceeding. After the agency's complaint has been served, the charged party (the respondent) must provide a written response within a stipulated time. The case is assigned to an administrative law judge (ALJ) who presides over the trial. The litigating parties usually meet in an informal pretrial conference, at which oral arguments are presented and documents exchanged.

After the case has been narrowed to the substantive issues involved, the formal trial begins. The APA requires the agency to notify the affected parties of the hearing's time and place, the statute involved, and the factual dispute to be decided. The parties may submit oral or written evidence, present a defense and rebuttal, and cross-examine witnesses. The ALJ is prohibited from consulting any party on an issue of fact unless all parties have a chance to participate. Generally, regulatory agencies are more lenient than law courts on the evidence that may be admitted; this leniency is based on the assumption that regulatory officials are experts and thus highly qualified to evaluate evidence. But agencies must be careful that the evidence they admit will stand in a court of law should the decision in the case be appealed.

The record is closed when the hearing ends. Each party then submits a memorandum to the ALJ and responds to the other side's presentation. After reviewing the record, the ALJ issues a decision with respect to the facts of the case and the applicable law. A proposed order to remedy any found violations of law is then served on the involved parties.

Appeals

After an agency order has been served, the parties may appeal the ALJ's decision to the full commission or the agency administrator. After completion of its review, which may range from cursory to thorough, the agency can adopt the ALJ's decision, reject it, or return it for further consideration. At this point the agency's determination of the facts of the case is considered final.

The volume of cases handled under the adjudicatory systems of regulatory agencies has been substantial. In fiscal year 2002, for example, OSHA alone docketed 2,026 new cases arising from disputed OSHA citations.

This review of regulatory tools, while brief, underscores the complexities of the regulatory process, which is properly seen as a process by which a fundamental decision to regulate passes through successively finer procedural filters until the obligations of individual parties are established in specific terms. The procedures vary at each stage and become more formal when they shift from essentially legislative decisions and executive actions to judicial determinations. Perhaps the most compelling characteristic of regulatory procedure is the interdependence of the procedural steps and its appearance of perpetual motion. Decisions made at each point are being continually reexamined, altered, or supplemented at the next. At each stage of the regulatory process, analysis of some kind is being conducted.

ANALYSIS IN THE REGULATORY PROCESS

Analysis plays a role at each stage of every significant decision made during the regulatory process. Congressional staffers perform analyses when regulatory legislation is considered; the clerks of federal judges prepare analyses of conflicting testimony when a policy or decision is challenged in a lawsuit. But in terms of cumulative effect, the analyses performed in agencies by bureaucrats and their surrogates during the rulemaking process are the most important and wide-ranging in regulatory program operations.

Legal Analysis

Every rulemaking begins with an assessment of the provisions in legislation or judicial decisions that will govern the development of the regulation. What the statute mandates or allows the agency to do must be determined. Legislation may impose deadlines, require certain types of studies, or call for specific forms of public participation beyond the written comment mandated by the APA. Usually, this legal analysis is straightforward because the legislative provisions are easy to understand. At times, the staff responsible for writing the rule may have to consult the agency's office of general counsel to determine what is expected under the statute. Legal analysis of this sort is an essential prerequisite to other rulemaking activities.

Policy Analysis

As noted earlier, President Reagan at the outset of his first term announced a set of "regulatory principles" that he expected agencies of the executive branch to follow when they developed rules or made other regulatory decisions. Other presidents have done the same. In addition to the president's general policies, rule writers must be aware of the priorities and preferences of the political leadership of their agency. During the Clinton administration, EPA rule writers showed a keen awareness of EPA Administrator Carol M. Browner's background as an environmental agency chief for the state of Florida

when they crafted their state "performance partnership grants," which give state governments more flexibility with federal environmental funds. While many of Clinton's agency heads have been relatively low-key, FDA Commissioner David A. Kessler (1990–1997) was notably aggressive in his regulatory role. FDA rule writers took their cue, especially with their tough tobacco regulations. In contrast, a succession of free-market FERC chairs kept that regulatory agency's hands off the increasingly deregulated wholesale electricity market. When California began facing severe electricity shortages and soaring power costs during the winter of 2000 and 2001, state officials implored FERC to step in to cap wholesale electricity prices, at least temporarily. First, FERC's Clinton-appointed chair, James Hoecker, then FERC's Bush-appointed chair, Curt Hebert Jr., declined. Indeed, throughout the crisis that lasted into 2002, the White House argued that such controls would only discourage the building of new power generating facilities and prolong the shortage.

Failure to incorporate policy preferences into rules can lead to problems when the rules are reviewed at higher levels. Therefore, at the outset of a rulemaking, agencies analyze the policy issues associated with the regulation to determine whether a particular substantive approach or set of procedures should be adopted.

Scientific and Technical Analysis

Every rule has a purpose that its substantive content is expected to achieve. In many cases the content deals with comparatively minor matters, and staff draws on readily available information. Analysis is minimal. For example, when it first came into being, OSHA simply adopted as rules more than 4,000 standards that a panoply of testing and professional societies had developed to protect worker safety. Other rules respond to individual problems as they arise. An airline disaster caused by a technical malfunction usually brings a wave of new rules as aviation experts in the FAA analyze the problem and take steps to prevent its recurrence.

In still other cases, rules change to incorporate state-of-the-art practices and innovations. In fact, the NRC has been criticized for engaging in the serial "ratcheting up" of engineering requirements that draw on newly developed equipment or practices that promise increases in safety. Similarly, the EPA is required to locate and mandate the "best available technology" to limit pollution or its discharge into the water and air. This requirement also involves analysis of available means and how they perform. As science develops techniques capable of detecting the presence of even the most minute trace of a pollutant, industries and even the scientists themselves fear regulators will become more and more strict with allowable exposures.

On the other hand, technical analyses to support new rules are most difficult to perform when Congress mandates regulatory solutions for problems about which little is known. Environmental and worker health programs frequently are pushed beyond available knowledge. For example, the disputes over regulation of benzene in the workplace, asbestos in schools, and radon in houses hinge, at least in part, on studies of long-term health effects that cannot be conducted quickly or cheaply. Congress has thus far prevented OSHA from developing regulations on repetitive stress injuries in the workplace, fearing that effective solutions could be difficult to find and expensive to implement.

Agencies are organized to perform these analyses in a variety of ways. Many have offices of research and development to conduct studies. In a distinctive arrangement, all worker health regulations written by OSHA originate with research conducted by the National Institute of Occupational Safety and Health (NIOSH), a separate agency. More common is the use of contractors to supplement agency staff in conducting the basic data collection and analysis. Bottlenecks develop in studies when the necessary data is in the hands of the very industries to be regulated. Claiming proprietary rights, these sources often are loath to release information to help the agency write a rule that will end up costing them money.

Delays in completing rules, and successful legal challenges to completed ones, often result from the unavailability of information or its poor quality. But technical analysis is about more than time or potential litigation. The accuracy of technical analysis determines the success of a regulatory program. If problems are inadequately assessed or their solutions improperly devised, regulations will fail to achieve their goals.

Risk Analysis

Environmental, health, and safety regulatory programs are premised on conceptions of risk to human life or to valuable animal and plant life. Determining the nature and degree of risk posed by a given substance or activity is essential to any regulatory effort aimed at its elimination, reduction, or mitigation. This is the goal of a scientific technique known as risk analysis or risk assessment. A number of statutes require agencies to conduct studies of risk and use the results as the basis for regulation.

A number of high-profile regulatory disputes, such as occupational exposure to benzene and dioxin contamination in the food chain, have hinged on the quality of risk assessments. In those cases determining acceptable levels of exposure or ingestion has been stalled by protracted disagreements among scientists regarding the conduct of the risk analyses. Overall research designs, the ability to measure minute amounts of substances thought to be highly toxic, methods of data collection, statistical techniques used to analyze available data, conclusions drawn from statistical analyses, and proposed levels of pollution control based on the results of analyses have all been disputed in these and other cases. Further, Congress has not adopted uniform standards to guide risk assessment. Even in a single agency the criteria can vary across programs. EPA administers at least three statutes—the Safe Drinking Water Act, the Federal Insecticide, Fungicide and Rodenticide Act, and the Toxic Substances Control Act—that seek different levels of risk reduction. Clinton's Executive Order 12881 established the National Science and Technology Council within the White House. The council's risk-assessment subcommittee has been reviewing federal risk assessment research to help improve its quality and implementation.

The Republican 104th Congress dramatically raised the issue's profile when it made risk assessment and cost-benefit analysis cornerstones of its regulatory efforts. The 1996 safe drinking water law mandated that EPA publish a nonbinding analysis of the costs, benefits, and risks of new drinking water regulation. In response, some regulators have complained that Congress should not call for increased risk assessment while simultaneously cutting agency budgets.

While the overuse of risk analysis can stop or slow the regulatory process, high-quality risk analysis and assessment remains a powerful tool in efforts to build regulatory programs that work. As a scientific technique it is developing rapidly. But these methodological advances do not transfer automatically to the regulatory process, and the day that risk analyses are no longer disputed is well in the future.

Cost-Benefit Analysis

If there was a dominant theme in the Reagan administration's assault on the regulatory process, it was the simple, appealing notion that a regulatory action should generate more benefit than cost. That theme reemerged in 1995 with the swearing in of the Republican-led 104th Congress. The vehicle offered by the Republicans to ensure "net benefit" was cost-benefit analysis. This technique had been in use long before the Reagan administration. President Gerald R. Ford in 1974 directed agencies to prepare "inflation impact statements" to accompany their rules. At the end of 1976 the program was extended and its title changed to the economic impact statement program. Although the cost estimates were reasonably accurate, the assessment of benefits usually was weak, as was the study of alternatives. Agencies found that the program was useful in formulating their regulations and that the paperwork and time involved were not excessive.

President Carter also supported this approach. Shortly after taking office in 1977 he asked that full consideration be given to the "economic cost of major government regulations, through a more effective analysis of their economic impact." In March 1978 Carter issued Executive Order 12044, which set criteria for agencies to follow in performing regulatory impact analyses (*for text of order, see p. 776*). The analysis had to include a description of the major alternative ways of dealing with the problem that were considered by the agency; an analysis of the economic circumstances of each of these alternatives; and a detailed explanation of the reasons for choosing one alternative over the others. The order did not extend to independent commissions. Nor did it require a strict cost-benefit analysis.

Carter also created the Regulatory Analysis Review Group (RARG), chaired by a member of the Council of Economic Advisers, to improve such analysis. The Carter administration "always took pains to stress that its requirements for regulatory analysis should not be interpreted as subjecting rules to a [strict] cost-benefit test," said former RARG chair George C. Eads.

In contrast, in February 1981 Reagan issued Executive Order 12291, which replaced Carter's Executive Order 12044, and required a cost-benefit analysis from agencies. It required executive agencies to prepare a regulatory impact analysis for all new and existing major regulations. Major rules were defined as those likely to have an annual effect on the economy of $100 million or more, lead to a major increase in costs or prices, or have "significant adverse effects" on business.

Regulatory analyses had to be submitted to OMB for review 60 days prior to publication in the *Federal Register*. However, OMB was empowered to waive the regulatory impact analysis for any rule. Agencies had to apply cost-benefit analyses to all rulemaking and adopt the least costly alternative.

The rise of cost-benefit analysis as a decision-making tool in the development of specific regulations remains controversial. As an analytical technique, cost-benefit analysis is limited, sometimes severely, by the lack of data or skepticism about the data's sources and accuracy. Even more fundamental are problems in measuring benefits and costs that may occur over a long period of time or involve intangibles that are difficult

to value. It has been widely reported, for example, that different agencies use different estimates for the value of a human life that might be saved by a given regulatory intervention. Many people are appalled by the very notion of placing dollar values on life, health, or safety. The fact that studies are conducted before regulations are actually implemented means agencies should be estimating compliance rates, another complicating factor.

The first Bush administration retained Executive Order 12291's approach to cost-benefit analysis. The Clinton administration embraced the technique, as well, often using it as a means to justify many of its regulatory initiatives. For instance, in 1997 the Clinton administration estimated the cost of a new nutritional labeling campaign for food at $4 million per year, with a benefit ranging from $275 million to $360 million a year. The FDA's proposed regulations of tobacco were estimated to cost $180 million a year at a benefit of up to $10.4 billion.

But it was the Republican 104th Congress that pushed hardest for its broad implementation, and with some success. The unfunded mandates law of 1995 requires the Congressional Budget Office (CBO) to estimate the impacts of all new mandates that would cost state or local governments $50 million or more a year. The CBO also must estimate the impacts of any mandate that would cost private companies $100 million or more a year. Before issuing rules that would cost businesses more than $100 million yearly, regulatory agencies now must prepare a cost-benefit analysis. A rider attached to a 1996 law raising the federal debt ceiling instructs the EPA and OSHA to collect advice and recommendations from small businesses to improve their analyses of a proposed regulation's impact.

Such mandates are not necessarily cheap. A 1998 study by CBO found that eighty-five randomly selected "regulatory impact analyses" finished in 1997 cost federal agencies anywhere from $14,000 to $6 million to implement. OSHA spent as much as $5 million performing risk assessments and regulatory analyses on the single rule it issued in 1997. The EPA spends about $120 million a year on regulatory analyses.

Not surprisingly, compliance with these mandates has been spotty at best. In a 2000 report, the Center for the Study of American Business concluded that OMB has largely failed to supply independent cost-benefit analyses, relying instead on the regulatory agencies' efforts—efforts that have been suspect. For instance, in 1997 EPA reported—and OMB dutifully repeated—that the annual benefits of environmental regulation were worth $3.2 trillion. At EPA's request, the number was revised radically downward, to $1.45 trillion, in 2000 to respond to charges of gross exaggeration.

Meanwhile the cost to businesses of all regulation has remained high. According to a recent study issued by the Weidenbaum Center at Washington University in St. Louis, regulations cost the private sector $1.13 trillion in 2002.

Other Analyses Required by Statutes

As noted above, several types of analysis may be required by legislation. For example, the Regulatory Flexibility Act (RFA) requires agencies to determine and consider the effects of rules on small business. The National Environmental Policy Act (NEPA) may require an environmental impact statement (EIS) if the rule is likely to have major ecological effects.

An EIS is a significant analytical task and is governed by guidelines issued by the Council on Environmental Quality (CEQ). In addition to covering a wide range of potential impact, the EIS must be made available in draft form for review and comment by the public. Hence, the process side of NEPA is substantial, as well.

Since its passage in 1980, one piece of analytical legislation has created tremendous controversy and difficulty for the regulatory process. The Paperwork Reduction Act (PRA) was intended to force discipline in the government's information collection efforts (*for text of act, see p. 760*). The act established the Office of Information and Regulatory Affairs as a principal unit of OMB. Its main task is to oversee the actions of regulatory agencies to determine if the paperwork required in any regulatory effort is the least burdensome, not duplicative, and "of practical utility." The goal of obtaining good quality, useful information was as important as the more widely known objective of reducing the burden of paperwork on the public. Clearly the PRA requires agencies to think carefully about their information requests. But OMB's role in this process has been the object of intense controversy in Congress. (See Accountability and Oversight, below.)

REGULATORY PERSONNEL

Much of the debate on reforming the federal regulatory process centers on two important areas—the people chosen to direct the agencies and the procedures they use to regulate. The president appoints and the Senate confirms the heads of most regulatory agencies, but there are few guidelines for the selection process. Many critics believe that federal regulators are not as well qualified for their jobs as they should be.

Numerous experts, task forces, and study commissions have examined the twin problems of the quality of administrators and regulatory procedures, and they have made hundreds of recommendations for improvements. But few of these recommendations have been implemented in any formal way, and the debate on how to solve these problems is likely to continue.

Selection of Officials

Most regulatory agency heads and commissioners are selected in accordance with Article II, Section 2, of the Constitution, which states that the president "shall nominate, and by and with the Advice and Consent of the Senate, shall appoint Ambassadors, other public Ministers and Consuls, Judges of the Supreme Court, and all other Officers of the United States." Dividing the power of appointment between the president and the Senate was one of the checks the framers of the Constitution felt was necessary to ensure that one branch of government did not dominate the others.

The president may remove for any or no reason heads of regulatory agencies that are within the executive branch. Once the Senate has confirmed a nominee and he or she has been sworn in, the Senate may not reconsider the nomination. Independent regulatory commission members generally may be removed only for cause, such as inefficiency, neglect of duty, or misconduct.

The Constitution does not specify any qualifications to be a regulator. Congress, however, has required that appointees to particular agencies sit for fixed terms and meet certain criteria. For example, the act establishing the Federal Reserve Board stipulates that members be chosen with "due regard to a fair representation of the financial, agricultural, industrial, and commercial interests and geographical divisions of the country." The requirements can be even more precise. For example, the FAA administrator is to "be a civilian and shall have experience in a field directly related to aviation."

To ensure a degree of bipartisanship in regulatory decisions, Congress has required that most independent regulatory commissions have no more than a simple majority of commissioners from the same political party. The president is authorized to designate the chairs of most independent regulatory commissions, and most presidents choose someone of their political party.

NOMINATIONS

There is no established formal process for the selection of presidential appointees, although recent administrations have followed roughly the same procedures.

Generally the president has an appointments adviser who oversees the process of searching out, screening, and recommending potential nominees. Members of Congress and special interest groups are often consulted in an effort to obtain informal clearance for the candidate. But few people will be nominated who are not politically acceptable to the White House, and in some cases politics and patronage may be the chief determinant in a person's selection.

The president, along with advisers, will consider several other points in deciding whom to nominate to a regulatory agency. These factors can include the potential nominee's educational background and employment record, familiarity with the matter to be regulated, age, health, and the region of the country he or she comes from.

Another connection that has been useful to dozens of regulatory agency appointees is congressional sponsorship. In its study of thirty-eight regulatory appointments to four agencies over a fifteen-year period, the Senate Governmental Affairs Committee found that congressional sponsorship was often an important, if not the predominant, factor in the selection process.

President Clinton explicitly introduced diversity as a criterion in presidential appointments. In order to form a government that "looks like America," his White House personnel office sought qualified women, African Americans, Hispanics, and other minorities to fill vacancies in regulatory and other agencies. President George W. Bush has carried on the practice, appointing minorities to top slots, including secretaries of State, Transportation, and Education and heads of the National Security Council and the White House Counsel's Office.

CONFIRMATIONS

The purpose of congressional confirmation proceedings is to determine the character and competence of the nominee. The committee with oversight for the agency holds hearings at which the nominee and others may testify. Once the committee has approved a nominee, the name is submitted to the full Senate. The Senate may approve, reject, or recommit a nomination to the committee that considered it. Controversial nominations sometimes are debated at length, but few are brought to the floor if there is any chance the nominee will be rejected. A nominee having that much opposition usually withdraws before the appointment is considered by the full Senate.

The Senate's advice-and-consent role gives Congress an important mechanism for monitoring the quality of regulatory agency appointments. Critics have charged, however, that the Senate does not take full advantage of this power. In general, the Senate does not closely examine presidential choices for regulatory positions in the executive branch on the theory that presidents should be allowed to choose their staffs. A check of the candidate's basic qualifications, rather than a full-scale examination of his or her views, generally suffices.

Appointments to the independent regulatory commissions are a somewhat different matter. Until the early 1970s presidential nominations to the independent agencies also were routinely confirmed. But after the Watergate scandal heightened sensitivity to potential abuses of government office, the Senate began to scrutinize nominations more carefully, looking at a nominee's economic views and political philosophy, as well as potential conflicts of interest.

QUESTION OF QUALITY

The quality of regulatory commissioners has been an issue for many decades. James M. Landis, President John F. Kennedy's regulatory adviser, wrote in 1960 that poor administrators can "wreak havoc with good law." Landis attributed many of the agencies' shortcomings to "a deterioration in the quality of our administrative personnel" since World War II, "both at the top level and throughout the staff."

Studying the problem seventeen years later, the Senate Governmental Affairs Committee did not find the situation much improved. "[T]here is something lacking in overall quality," the committee wrote. "It is not a matter of venality or corruption or even stupidity; rather, it is a problem of mediocrity."

There is little agreement on the reasons for the lack of quality and even less agreement on what should be done about it. Some have argued that the multimember structure of the independent commissions, not the personnel, is responsible for mediocrity. "Even if the best qualified person filled each position, the collegial structure would impede effective performance," the Ash Council, a task force set up by President Nixon, wrote in 1971.

The selection process is also blamed for the lack of qualified regulators in government service. Critics say it is haphazard and too often governed by factors other than a candidate's professional qualifications. Finding a candidate who is politically acceptable is oftentimes more important than finding one who is technically qualified.

The Regulatory Civil Service

The quality of political leadership in regulatory institutions is unquestionably important. These individuals have the power to influence the policies implemented by their agencies and are constantly involved in important decisions. But concern for top officials should not obscure the crucial importance of career staff in the performance of regulatory agencies. It is the civil servant whose work determines if and how well higher-level policies are carried out and priorities met. They draft the rules, carry out the inspections, and resolve most disputes. The problems associated with these regulatory personnel are different from, but every bit as serious as, those that affect the political leadership of any agency.

The education, skills, and experiences that are represented in the professional staff of regulatory agencies constitute a microcosm of American society. For every regulated activity there must be appropriate expertise. A large number of professions are represented in the regulatory civil service. The FCC requires the services of a substantial number of attorneys as well as engineers, economists, accountants, and electrical technicians. A review of the professional backgrounds of employees of the EPA would find attorneys, economists, engineers, chemists, biologists, statisticians, and persons with advanced degrees in public administration and policy analysis.

Additionally, those working in each of these agencies, whatever their academic training, must have, or acquire on the job, intimate working knowledge of the private industry or activity they are engaged in regulating. It goes without saying that persons with these combinations of education, skills, and experience are often sought after by the private or nonprofit sectors. So attracting highly qualified persons to government service is only part of the challenge; keeping them there when government salaries, benefits, working conditions, and promotional opportunities lag behind the private sector has become difficult. Qualified persons must be recruited for public service, and once in place they must be retained.

The report of the National Commission on the Public Service, Leadership for America: Rebuilding the Public Service, points to a gradual erosion in the caliber of government personnel due mainly to the difficulty with attracting and keeping qualified workers. Those familiar with regulatory requirements, procedures, and compliance techniques are much in demand in affected industries, businesses, and organizations where salaries, benefits, and opportunities are greater. This dilemma has no easy solution. The investment the nation needs to make to attract experienced and talented professionals to leave the private sector for careers in regulatory agencies is substantial indeed.

ACCOUNTABILITY AND OVERSIGHT

There is intense conflict over the accountability of those who make regulatory decisions. A few observers find nothing less than a total perversion of the constitutional system, with unelected bureaucrats wielding vast regulatory powers essentially unchecked by direct popular will. Others find the governmental agencies greatly hindered by external checks. There is no question that bureaucrats in regulatory agencies make important decisions, but in doing so they are constrained. They are accountable to the popular will, but indirectly, through the actions of elected representatives—Congress and the president—and those of the unelected branch of government—the judiciary.

Presidential Influence

Presidents sought to exert control over regulation almost as soon as the first agency came into being. In 1908 President Theodore Roosevelt urged that all independent commissions be placed in the executive branch under the immediate supervision of a cabinet secretary. A task force appointed in 1937 by Franklin Roosevelt amplified that view. It found that "important powers of policy and administration" were routinely parceled out "to a dozen or more irresponsible agencies."

In 1949 the Hoover Commission recommended that the "purely executive functions of quasi-legislative and quasi-judicial agencies" be brought within the regular executive departments. In 1971 the Ash Council proposed that rulemaking functions of the independent commissions be placed directly under the president. Although Congress ignored these proposals, the powers of the president remained formidable.

The appointment process (discussed in a previous section) obviously is an important mechanism to ensure accountability of regulatory officials to the president. The use of the budget and executive orders are other controls available.

BUDGET CONTROL

The budget is one of the most important controls presidents have over the regulatory agencies. Presidents, not the agencies, decide how much money to request from Congress and for what purposes. In this way presidents can cut back regulatory efforts they disapprove of and give a boost to those they favor. Although the budget is one of its main oversight tools, Congress in the past has generally made only insignificant changes to the presidential budget request for the regulatory agencies.

That changed dramatically in 1995. The Republican-led Congress used the appropriations process to try to curb regulations through attrition. House appropriators tried to slash the EPA's budget by a third. OSHA's budget was slated for a 16 percent cut. Budgetary attacks on regulatory agencies, coupled with riders on appropriations bills to curb the agencies' enforcement powers specifically, helped lead to the government shutdowns of 1995 and 1996. Most of the funds were eventually restored. The EPA, for instance, wound up with a 9.8 percent cut. But fiscal uncertainties during the budget battles had the temporary effect of curbing much regulatory action.

In the latter years of the Clinton administration, many regulatory agencies made remarkable budgetary recoveries. But with his March 2001 budget blueprint, President George W. Bush signaled a return to austerity for some agencies, while other, more politically favored offices would thrive. EPA and the Labor Department were scheduled for budget cuts, while the EEOC would remain flush, a sign of the new president's continuing outreach to minorities. These trends continued in the president's next two budget requests.

Since 1921, when the Budget and Accounting Act was passed, presidents have had the authority to review and revise budget estimates for all executive branch agencies before they were submitted to Congress. In 1939 that authority was extended to the independent regulatory commissions.

Congress did not object to this executive control over the independent commissions' budgets until President Nixon created the OMB in 1970. Built around the nucleus of the old Budget Bureau, OMB was given new authority to coordinate the executive branch budget requests and legislative proposals. Unlike its predecessor, which had retained an image of neutrality, OMB was quickly identified as the president's agency, a tool for pushing the presidential budget and legislative proposals through Congress.

President Reagan, for example, used the budget to promote his antiregulation policies. The biggest cuts in regulatory spending, 37 percent from 1981 to 1985, occurred in agencies that regulate specific industries such as airlines, trucking, railroads, and intercity bus lines. On the other hand, the budgets of agencies concerned with banking and finance and general business matters, such as the FDIC, the SEC, and the Patent and Trademark Office, increased substantially during Reagan's first term.

Staffing reductions occurred across the board, but safety, health, and energy and environmental programs took the biggest cuts. The CPSC lost 225 employees between 1981 and 1985. OSHA had lost 654 full-time staffers by the end of Reagan's first term, and the EEOC, 285. Most of the cuts occurred during the first year Reagan had full control over agency budgets and personnel.

After 1985 the cuts slowed down and in some cases were reversed. The change in direction was attributed to several factors. Observers of the regulatory scene noted that the analytical requirements called for by Executive Order 12291 would be expensive for the agencies to implement. In addition, Democratic congresses appeared to be less willing to acquiesce in regulatory budget cutting after the EPA was convulsed by scandal in 1983. Stung by charges of being antienvironment, the Republican 104th Congress began showing similar reluctance to cut in 1996.

EXECUTIVE ORDERS

In addition to the appointments and budget powers, presidents also are free to issue directives and statements to the agencies in the form of executive orders. In February 1981 President Reagan issued Executive Order 12291, which imposed strict new rules on cabinet and agency regulators, gave OMB extensive powers, and required the use of cost-benefit analysis. In January 1985 Reagan issued Executive Order 12498, which required agencies to clear their regulations with OMB while they were in the early stages of development (*for text of order, see p. 782*). The order called for each agency to submit to OMB in January of each year lists of significant regulatory actions it expected to propose in the coming year. According to OMB, this procedure would give the agency the opportunity to clear regulations while they were under development instead of when they were about to be proposed to the public. The executive order also called for the annual publication of the rules each agency planned to propose.

The changes wrought by these executive orders were among the most significant alterations in the regulatory process since passage of the APA. Their significance was underscored by the firestorm of criticism, litigation, and political conflict they generated. OMB critics charged that the agency improperly altered proposed regulations and was a secret conduit for industry lobbyists who wished to weaken regulatory proposals. Lawsuits challenged the constitutionality of OMB's intervention. Although the use of OMB by the president to manage the regulatory process emerged largely intact from this litigation, the controversy did not go away.

Soon after taking office, President Clinton issued Executive Order 12866, which repealed the Reagan executive orders and outlined the Clinton approach to presidential oversight of rulemaking. In addition to articulating a number of principles to guide rulemakers, he limited the use of OMB review and cost-benefit analysis to "significant" rules, as determined by a number of criteria set out in the order. The president required that OMB's Office of Information and Regulatory Affairs disclose all manner of communication with agencies and outside parties during the course of its review and imposed strict time periods for completion of the review process. The order also established a "Regulatory Working Group," consisting of the vice president, the director of OIRA, and the heads of all government agencies involved in domestic regulation, that is charged with developing "innovative regulatory techniques." In all, Clinton issued 364 executive orders during his eight years in office, fewer than Reagan's 381 but still a respectable total. In his first two years in office, President George W. Bush issued eighty-one executive orders—an annual pace that put him slightly behind Clinton and Reagan.

Congressional Oversight

Although any president can exert a strong influence on the regulatory process through the powers of appointment, budget, and executive order, congressional powers are also substantial. In its 1977 study of regulation, the Senate Governmental Affairs Committee listed six primary goals of congressional oversight. They were: (1) ensuring compliance with legislative intent; (2) determining the effectiveness of regulatory policies; (3) preventing waste and dishonesty; (4) preventing abuse in the administrative process; (5) representing the public interest; and (6) preventing agency usurpation of legislative authority.

"[O]versight is not simply hindsight," the report noted. "Oversight involves a wide range of congressional efforts to review and control policy implementation by regulatory agencies. Congressional oversight thus includes both participation before agency action and review after the fact."

The fundamental congressional control over independent and executive branch regulatory agencies is statutory—the passage of legislation establishing new agencies and commissions, and spelling out their powers and limitations. Once the agencies are created, Congress exercises its control by assigning new responsibilities to them. Members of Congress also may influence the selection of nominees to head the commissions and agencies, and even more important is the Senate's authority to confirm them.

After the agencies are established and their members confirmed, Congress uses several tools to ensure that the agencies remain politically accountable to the legislative branch. One tool is investigation: Congress can examine agency practices in light of possible abuses, costs and benefits of regulation, potential reforms, and agency responsiveness to the elusive "public interest." But the two principal tools are appropriations and authorization statutes.

The appropriations process enables the House and Senate appropriations committees to scrutinize proposed agency budgets. Oversight through appropriations has been strengthened through the annual review of most agency budgets. In approving them, Congress may specify the purposes for which funds are to be used—a direct and unambiguous method of control.

At times, Congress has been unable to ensure that appropriated funds actually are spent. Nevertheless, Congress has used the appropriations process to order the agencies to take specific regulatory actions or to refrain from them. For example, Congress repeatedly used a rider to an appropriations bill to prevent the Agriculture Department from abolishing certain marketing orders targeted for elimination by Reagan's OMB staff in the early 1980s. In 1995 House members tried to use a rider to bar OSHA from developing standards or issuing regulations on repetitive motion injuries, like carpal tunnel syndrome. After Republicans battled for months with the Clinton administration, a compromise was reached to allow the standards to be developed but to block new regulations. After the GOP came to power in 1995, a little-noticed provision in the energy and water development appropriations bill has prevented federal regulators from tightening corporate average fuel efficiency (CAFE) standards for automakers. The congressional prohibition has recently taken on more urgency with the booming popularity of "light trucks"—sport utility vehicles and minivans—because such vehicles are exempt from the tougher CAFE standards for cars. In 1998 House Republicans inserted a provision into the spending plan for the departments of Veterans Affairs and Housing and Urban Development blocking the Consumer Products Safety Commission from developing a new standard for upholstery flammability.

Traditionally, the appropriations review has not focused on the agencies' policies and goals. If it has occurred at all, such scrutiny has come during the authorization process when Congress determines whether to continue the agency. Again, the 104th Congress broke from this tradition, although it ultimately failed to get its plans enacted. Riders on its fiscal 1996 appropriations bill would have severely curtailed OSHA's enforcement power while increasing funds for counseling and technical assistance, essentially changing it from an enforcement agency to one focused on safety awareness and technical support. The House's original 1996 budget for the EPA contained seventeen legislative provisions aimed at limiting EPA's ability to enforce regulations on sewer systems, wetlands, refineries, oil and gas manufacturing, radon in water, pesticides in processed foods, lead paint, and water pollution. The budget wars of 1995 and 1996 chased Congress back to the position that substantive changes to agency policies should be the purview of authorizing committees. A number of agencies have been given permanent authorization status, among them the FCC and the EPA. Aware that permanent authorizations decrease its ability to oversee regulatory actions, Congress in recent years has required periodic authorization for some of the more controversial agencies, including the CPSC and the Federal Trade Commission (FTC).

More often than not, Congress gives up some of its control by couching agency authorizing statutes in vague generalities, giving the regulators considerable leeway in the performance of their functions. Occasionally, agencies have taken actions that ran counter to congressional intent. In a few such cases, Congress then has felt obliged to narrow the agency's mandate.

Besides these "formal" oversight powers, Congress has other ways to regulate the regulators, among them hearings, informal contacts, and directives contained in committee reports, sunset provisions, and individual casework. These nonstatutory controls may be the most common form of congressional oversight. A number of statutes require regulatory agencies to submit detailed reports to committees. Committee investigations not only provide information but also publicize the performance of agencies.

Casework is intervention by a member of Congress on behalf of a constituent who is involved in a proceeding before an agency. There are no reliable figures on the number of times members attempt to assist constituents with regulatory problems. Anecdotes suggest that a significant percentage of "congressional mail" received by some regulatory agencies involves this type of inquiry. It may be too strong to characterize this political ombudsman role as oversight, but it clearly puts affected agencies on notice that Congress is watching their decisions as they affect individuals, as well as overall programs and general policies.

The legislative veto, once a popular device, allowed Congress to manage the regulatory process through rejection of individual rules. In 1983 the Supreme Court ruled its use unconstitutional in *Immigration and Naturalization Service v. Chadha.*

Limits on Oversight

The Senate Governmental Affairs Committee in 1977 detailed a number of major roadblocks to effective oversight, which remain in place today. These include

- Committee Structure. Because several committees usually share jurisdiction over an agency, oversight is fragmented, and coordination and cooperation among legislative panels is difficult to achieve, particularly among House and Senate committees.

- Information Lag. Committees sometimes have experienced difficulties and delays in obtaining requested information. Agencies may refuse to supply information, or they simply may not have it available. Moreover, filtering most regulatory agency budget and legislative requests through OMB reduces the ability of Congress to obtain independent information.

- Inadequate Staff. According to the committee report, the professional staff members on legislative committees having oversight responsibility for the regulatory agencies numbered only several hundred, reflecting the great disparity in size between congressional staffs and the agencies they oversee. Perhaps more important is the problem of developing the necessary staff expertise for effective oversight, the committee said.

- Other intangible factors can hinder congressional oversight, among them the demand on members' time and the belief that members gain more politically from sponsoring new legislation than from policing what has already been enacted. Bonds that develop between congressional committees and agencies also may impede a full and critical review of regulatory performance.

Judicial Review

As with the other branches, the courts have always been significantly involved in regulatory decision making. The Supreme Court's decisions invalidating New Deal regulatory programs set the stage for the APA. More recently, the courts have played a profoundly important role in setting the limits of congressional, presidential, and even judicial influence over regulatory policy making in the agencies. Their rulings have altered whole regulatory programs and countless individual decisions. Although critics of judicial activism deplore such decisions, judicial review is not without substantial constraints.

The judiciary is the most passive branch, awaiting the filing of lawsuits before it can take action. The courts are empowered to hear a variety of challenges to regulatory decisions, ranging from the delegation of authority to agencies by Congress to the legality and fairness of agency dealings with individual regulated parties.

There are, however, criteria that must be satisfied before the courts can hear a case brought by a complaining party.

Litigants must establish standing to sue; the court must agree that the timing of the lawsuit is correct; and all other possible remedies must be exhausted. To establish standing, potential litigants must demonstrate that they have a personal stake in the outcome of the lawsuit and that the damage suffered is related to the regulatory action in dispute. Courts will not entertain a lawsuit until an agency has completed its work on the matter in question. The principles of "finality" and "ripeness for review" are well-settled tenets of administrative law; they prevent premature review of issues that may be resolved by agency deliberations. "Exhaustion of remedies" is a similar concept that forecloses court review if there are opportunities remaining in the administrative process to redress the grievances. Lawsuits also must be brought to the proper level of court. Most regulatory statutes contain provisions that determine which federal courts have the authority to hear cases arising from different types of regulatory actions.

If a litigant satisfies these criteria and presents the lawsuit in the proper court, a decision of some sort will be rendered on the merits of the case. A critical question is the extent to which courts will question the judgment of regulators when they are sued. This is the "scope of review" issue, and on this matter the judiciary has sent decidedly mixed signals. In 1983 the Supreme Court announced in the case of *Motor Vehicle Manufacturers v. State Farm* that the courts would take a "hard look" when regulators made decisions to ensure that they were doing what Congress had intended in a careful and well-reasoned manner. One year later, however, the Court appeared to back off from this aggressive approach in its decision in *Chevron USA v. NRDC*, which stated that the judicial inquiry should end as soon as the judges satisfied themselves that the agency had interpreted the statute in question in a manner that is "permissible."

Courts continue to shape regulatory issues. A 1996 Supreme Court ruling in *Seminole Tribe v. Florida* could affect the enforcement of federal statutes and regulations against states deemed in violation. The ruling did not directly involve regulation. Instead, it was prompted by a dispute over Native American gaming. But if the decision is broadly interpreted, regulators may be unable to sue states in federal court. States could find themselves protected against federal regulations by the 11th Amendment, which states in part, "The judicial power of the United States shall not be construed to extend to any suit in law or equity, commenced or prosecuted against one of the United States." Protections for state governments against federal regulation were bolstered again in 2001, when a divided Supreme Court ruled 5–4 that a woman employed by the state of Alabama could not sue the state under the Americans with Disabilities Act.

A wide variety of decisions are possible when a court reviews actions of regulatory agencies. Courts can uphold the agency decision, invalidate the agency decision, or specify corrective procedures for the agency or litigant. Courts may even decide whether an agency has jurisdiction at all, as in 1997, when a federal court in Greensboro, N.C., ruled that the FDA could regulate tobacco and its contents as a drug but did not have the power to regulate tobacco advertising. Both the Clinton administration and the tobacco industry appealed the ruling, and understandably so. Different courts facing different circumstances at different times will reach different results. In 1998 a three-judge panel from the 4th Circuit U.S. Court of Appeals in Richmond overturned the ruling. Finally, in 1999 the Supreme Court ruled that the FDA had no jurisdiction over tobacco.

But just as the judiciary can restrict regulatory activity, it can affirm the power of regulators to do their jobs. The Supreme Court's February 2001 *Whitman v. American Trucking Associations* decision may prove to be a landmark. The ruling unambiguously found that the EPA was not taking too much lawmaking power away from Congress by filling in the blanks left by vague congressional requests in the Clean Air Act. Such fill-in-the-blank exercises have become part of the daily routine for all federal regulatory agencies.

Whatever the prevailing general philosophy of judicial review, there is no question that judges and their decisions influence the regulatory process. In some instances, courts have been quite aggressive in substituting their judgment for those of agency experts. In July 1998 U.S. District Court Judge William Osteen of North Carolina undercut all regulation of indoor smoking by striking down a landmark 1993 EPA finding that secondhand tobacco smoke increases the risk of cancer. Some courts have ordered a redistribution of agency resources, a reduction in agency discretion, and redistributions of power among the various types of professionals in regulatory agencies.

Overall, then, the view that holds that regulatory agencies are subject to an elaborate network of controls is most certainly true. The issue is not whether agencies are accountable; rather, the issue is how agencies sort out the multiple and often conflicting messages they get from the president, Congress, the courts, and interest groups.

REFORM AND THE FUTURE

Frequently, reform triggers reaction. Consider the calls in 1990 for reregulation in many areas deregulated since 1975. To varying degrees, reform restored unfettered market forces in civil aviation, trucking, telecommunications, energy, and banking. These returns to the free market have indeed paid dividends. The Center for the Study of American Business at Washington University estimated the consumer benefits of airline deregulation amount to $10 billion annually while accident rates have fallen. Deregulation of railroads has led to savings of between $3.5 and $5 billion a year for shippers. Trucking deregulation more than doubled the number of carriers, increased jobs by 30 percent, and saved the economy $7.8 billion per year. But experience with some of the side effects of deregulation—concerns for safety in air travel, poor quality service in cable television, the monumental mismanagement and fraud in the savings and loan industry, and the distributional consequences of market-based prices generally—have convinced many that only a return to regulation will restore satisfaction with and confidence in these industries.

Consider also the reaction to presidents' attempts to better manage the regulatory process, particularly rulemaking. President Reagan's uses of OMB review of new rules, cost-benefit analysis, the Paperwork Reduction Act, and regulatory planning were attacked by powerful, vocal critics who saw them as thinly veiled efforts to usurp congressional powers, delay essential regulations, and provide a convenient back channel by which special interests could influence the content of regulatory policy. Bitter exchanges between Congress and the White House over continued authorization and funding for some of these OMB functions became a hallmark of the late 1980s and early 1990s. Legislation proposed in the 104th Congress would have shifted responsibility for rulemaking from the regulatory agencies back to the Capitol, a reaction to growing presidential power but a recipe for legislative gridlock, critics contend.

Regulatory negotiation, an innovation in rulemaking, may offer a way to alleviate conflict. But even ideas that have wide appeal may take a long time to put into practice. This idea, developed in the early 1980s, calls for the development of rules through a form of collective bargaining. Regulatory negotiation brings together parties interested in the content of a new rule with the responsible agency in an effort to draft the rule in a collective and consensual process. The advantages to this approach are many. It eliminates the distant and often adversarial relations between the regulators and the regulated that characterize much important rulemaking. Information flows freely, and the resulting rule is based on an informed consensus, which eases the task of implementation, compliance, and enforcement.

Regulatory negotiation is not appropriate for all rules. There are limits on the types of issues and numbers of affected parties that this form of rulemaking can accommodate. Nevertheless, in 1990 Congress enacted legislation that required agencies to consider this method of rulemaking for new regulations. Several agencies, including the EPA, OSHA, and the FAA, have used the device. The OSHA Compliance Act of 1998, signed by President Clinton that summer, directed OSHA by statute to establish and fund consultation programs that allow employers to identify violations and correct them without penalty. But this innovation has not caught on in the regulatory agencies to the extent justified by its many apparent advantages.

Although the regulatory negotiations attempted to date have not been uniformly successful, at the very worst they should be characterized as encouraging. Why, then, with the thousands of regulations written and planned since the concept first emerged have only a few dozen such negotiations taken place? There is no definitive answer, but in all likelihood a complex mix of economic, political, and bureaucratic factors have retarded its growth. Up-front costs of participating in regulatory negotiation for an interest group may be higher than those of participating in conventional rulemaking. For groups working with limited budgets and concerned with a large number of issues, cost may be an obstacle. Moreover, some groups may prefer the distance and tension of conventional rulemaking to the collaboration and tacit acceptance of regulation that involvement in negotiation implies. Corporate attorneys fear that a regulatory compliance plan negotiated with an agency may not protect their clients from third-party lawsuits. If the EPA allows a company to operate outside its rigid regulatory framework to reduce emissions, who is to say an environmental group will not file suit to force the firm back into that framework? Clinton administration officials found just such wariness.

Agencies may resist change because of bureaucratic inertia or because regulatory negotiation involves the sacrifice of the obscurity and relative autonomy of normal rulemaking. Analysts working on Vice President Gore's NPR team in the 1990s conceded they had been asking regulatory agencies to change an entrenched, confrontational culture, a process that has been far slower than they had anticipated. Whatever the reasons, the acceptance of regulatory negotiation is widespread in theory but so far limited in practice.

While eschewing the harsh rhetoric of Reagan and George Bush and seemingly dedicated to a better, more open process, Clinton set in motion a number of initiatives that created great stress in the regulatory process. Compounded by congressional attacks, his proposals in the NPR to cut 252,000 federal jobs, reduce the number of existing regulations by 50 percent, and eliminate the deficit meant leaner, more difficult times for regulators. Agencies complained that the ongoing reviews of existing rules took huge amounts of their time, leaving precious little left for traditional enforcement or nontraditional negotiations. Because rule writers tend to be the more powerful, senior members of staff, budget cuts may be taking a disproportionate toll on enforcement staff.

Clinton's success in implementing his ambitious agenda was also spotty. On the NPR's fifth anniversary in April 1998, Vice President Al Gore appeared to have plenty to boast about: the elimination of more than 200 federal programs, the cutting of more than 16,000 pages of regulations, and the saving, by Gore's estimate, of more than $137 billion. But the surge in new regulations during the administration's final days showed the limits of Clinton's efforts.

As it turns out, many of these last-minute regulations were overturned by the incoming administration of George W. Bush. As already noted, the new workplace ergonomic standards and 175 new environmental regulations were nullified. Bush justified the action by arguing that he should not be bound by decisions made by his predecessor at the last minute.

The process of rolling back previous regulations has gathered stream in the Bush administration. On Dec. 18, 2002, the administration announced that for its second referendum on current regulations to review, the OIRA would look at 267 rules. The number greatly exceeded the seventy-one regulations chosen in 2001. Most of the regulations nominated for review came from just a few agencies: the Departments of Health and Human Services, Labor, and Transportation as well as EPA and the FCC. Among the regulations that would be subject to future review were rules to strengthen standards for salmonella, requiring crash recorders on trucks, and minimum staffing standards for nursing homes.

In other areas, regulatory activity has increased dramatically, largely as a result of the 2001 terrorist attacks, and mostly from agencies now under the Homeland Security Department's umbrella. Indeed, new rules have touched all areas of domestic security. For in-

stance, the new TSA has promulgated a large number of new regulations—from tougher baggage screening requirements to the rules on the storage of guns in airliner cockpits—all aimed at improving air travel security.

A host of other new regulatory schemes have arisen since the enactment of the 2001 Patriot Act. The Customs Service, for example, implemented new safety guidelines for freight shippers and movers in an effort to improve security without slowing down the speed of shipping. The INS also promulgated new regulations requiring men visiting the United States, from twenty-five mostly Muslim countries, to register with the agency. The men also are fingerprinted and questioned by INS agents. The Department of Homeland Security took this a step further in May 2003 when it announced that it would, beginning in 2004, fingerprint and photograph all foreign visitors arriving with visas in the United States. The department hoped this would allow it to screen for possible terrorists and to keep track of visitors during their U.S. stay.

Even in realms other than domestic security, the administration has moved the regulatory ball forward. The EPA, for instance, has been working on tough new standards to reduce pollution from diesel fuel as well as regulations requiring higher fuel efficiency for light trucks. Meanwhile the FDA has announced that it would renew efforts to regulate ephedra, a popular diet drug that has been called harmful by some. Under the 1994 Dietary Supplement and Health Education Act, the agency must prove a health supplement, such as a diet aid or vitamin pill, is harmful before taking it off the market. The reverse is true with prescription drugs; pharmaceutical companies must prove their safety before winning FDA approval to market it to the public.

Indeed, one of the biggest outcomes of the terrorist attacks and subsequent war on terrorism, many analysts said, was a change in the administration's philosophy that was previously focused on limiting the role of government in people's lives. A sign of this trend was the increase in federal discretionary spending—4 percent in the fiscal 2004 budget proposed by Bush in early February 2003.

Still, the impetus to rein in regulation did not disappear after September 2001. In addition to the work of OIRA, many agencies have sought alternatives to regulation on their own. For instance, when the Department of Homeland Security announced that it was going to create a huge database to catalog and track all of the nation's vital infrastructure in sectors such as transportation and energy, it indicated it wanted to avoid drafting new regulations to do so. Deputy Secretary Gordon England told business leaders at a recent U.S. Chamber of Commerce meeting that the department would instead create incentives for businesses to cooperate. Clinton-era officials would have been more likely to set down disclosure and reporting requirements for businesses.

The coming years will likely see new challenges for the regulatory community. Recently enacted laws such as the Telecommunications Act, the pesticide and safe drinking water amendments, and the Patriot Act will require new approaches to regulation. Some of these laws, such as the safe drinking water amendments, call for increased flexibility, more cost-benefit analysis, and the novel "right to know" concept. Others, such as the Patriot Act, allow for the more direct imposition of requirements on the private sector, in the name of domestic security. Indeed, the Justice Department and new Homeland Security Department were likely to grapple with new regulations, on issues ranging from immigration requirements to search and seizure rules in terrorism-related cases, for years to come.

By mid-2003 a number of important regulatory statutes, such as superfund, were long past due for reauthorization, and these promised new initiatives. Congressional efforts to amend such regulatory standards as the Endangered Species Act and the Food and Drug Act were ongoing, as were broad bills to overhaul the entire regulatory apparatus. Congress was also considering legislation that would significantly overhaul the Medicare program, adding, among other things, a new prescription drug benefit for seniors.

In spite of the Bush administration's ongoing efforts to scale back some rules and rulemaking, regulation will remain a primary vehicle for domestic public policy in America. Its varied processes will continue to attract the interest and efforts of powerful political forces. Americans will rely on it to formulate and implement solutions to some of the most serious, intractable, and contentious problems that face society. Regulation will command ever-increasing shares of the attention and resources of public and private institutions. The results it achieves will have a profound effect on the quality of American life.

Major Regulatory Agencies

Consumer Product Safety Commission

4330 East-West Hwy., Bethesda, MD 20814
Internet: http://www.cpsc.gov

▣ INTRODUCTION

The Consumer Product Safety Commission (CPSC) is an independent regulatory agency that was established by the 1972 Consumer Product Safety Act. The commission began operations on May 14, 1973. It is composed of five commissioners, not more than three of whom may be members of the same political party. The commissioners are appointed to seven-year terms by the president and confirmed by the Senate. The president designates one of the commissioners to serve as chair. In 1986 Congress restricted funds for two commissioners and their staffs. Since then the CPSC has functioned as a three-member commission.

Responsibilities

The commission's statutory purposes are to (1) protect the public against unreasonable risks of injury associated with consumer products; (2) assist consumers in evaluating the comparative safety of consumer products; (3) develop uniform safety standards for consumer products and minimize conflicting state and local regulations; and (4) promote research and investigation into the causes and prevention of product-related deaths, illnesses, and injuries.

The CPSC:

- Works with industry to develop voluntary product standards.
- Establishes mandatory safety standards governing the performance and labeling of more than 15,000 consumer products when voluntary efforts prove inadequate.
- Develops rules and regulations to enforce standards.
- Bans the sale of products that present unreasonable risk of injury.

- Researches and develops test methods for consumer product standards.
- Develops broad consumer and industry education programs.
- Establishes flammability standards for fabrics.
- Prohibits introduction into interstate commerce of misbranded or banned substances and products.
- Establishes packaging requirements for poisonous substances.
- Enforces standards through litigation and administrative actions.
- Collects data on hazardous consumer products and accidents involving consumer products through the National Injury Information Clearinghouse.
- Requires manufacturers, distributors, and retailers to notify consumers and/or recall, repair, or replace consumer products that present a substantial hazard.
- Requires manufacturers of products subject to a consumer product safety standard to certify that the products conform to all applicable safety standards.
- Works with U.S. Customs Service to identify and prevent the entry of hazardous consumer products into the United States.

Powers and Authority

In addition to the authority assigned to the commission when it was created by the Consumer Product Safety Act, major consumer programs were transferred to the new agency from the Food and Drug Administration, the Health, Education and Welfare Department, and the Commerce Department. Included were the Federal Hazardous Substances Act of 1960, as amended by the Toy Safety Acts of 1969 and 1984 and the Child Protection Amendments of 1966, the Poison Prevention Packaging Act of 1970, the Flammable Fabrics Act of 1953, and the Refrigerator Safety Act of 1956.

The 1984 Toy Safety amendments to the Federal Hazardous Substances Act give the CPSC authority to recall dangerous toys from the market quickly when warranted. When the CPSC was created, it was given authority under the Consumer Product Safety Act to begin the process of ordering a recall immediately when a substantial hazard is discovered. But the recall of toys was left under different procedures in the Federal Hazardous Substances Act.

The CPSC's power to regulate products containing substances such as asbestos and formaldehyde, which present risks of cancer, birth defects, or gene mutations, is tempered by a requirement that the agency form a chronic hazard advisory panel (CHAP) to review the available scientific data. The commission must consider the CHAP report before issuing an advance notice of proposed rulemaking involving the substance.

In 1988 the Labeling of Hazardous Art Materials Act was passed giving the CPSC power to regulate art products that pose a chronic health hazard. In 1992 the agency issued guidelines for evaluating these products.

OTHER AGENCIES

Certain consumer products, including foods, drugs, and automobiles, continue to be regulated by other agencies and do not fall under the commission's broad domain. However, responsibility for administration of several existing consumer programs was transferred from other agencies when the CPSC was created.

Any differing state or local law cannot preempt standards set by the CPSC. However, states and localities may obtain permission to set different product safety standards if the resulting standard produces a greater degree of protection than that offered by the CPSC and if there would be no undue burden on interstate commerce. The Consumer Product Safety Act also gives the commission flexibility in choosing which of the five laws it administers to use in regulating a particular product. It can choose the Consumer Product Safety Act over the others if it publishes a formal explanation of the decision in the *Federal Register*. The CPSC may not regulate firearms, tobacco products, aviation and boating equipment, motor vehicles, food and drugs, cosmetics, insecticides, fungicides, and rodenticides.

SECTION 15

The heart of the Consumer Product Safety Act is the requirement under Section 15(b) that any importer, distributor, or manufacturer who knows of a product defect that poses a substantial product hazard must report that product to the CPSC in a timely manner or face severe civil penalties. The Office of Compliance *(see p. 45)* is responsible for identifying product defects that present substantial product hazards but are not subject to safety standards or banning regulations. The office also identifies products that violate existing standards and guidelines. In addition, it is responsible for developing and enforcing adequate corrective action plans designed to remove such products from the marketplace. A substantial product hazard is defined in the act as a product defect that, because of the pattern of defect, the number of products distributed in commerce, or the severity of the risk, creates a substantial risk of injury to the public.

In most cases companies work cooperatively with the CPSC to develop and implement voluntary corrective action plans to recall or otherwise correct products that may present possible substantial hazards.

The Consumer Product Safety Improvement Act, signed by President George Bush in 1990, gave a major boost to the commission's power. This legislation increased industry's obligation to report substantial product hazards to the CPSC. The act made reporting requirements tougher by requiring companies to report not only products that create "an unreasonable risk of serious injury or death" but also products that fail to comply with applicable voluntary standards upon which the commission has relied under Section 9 of the Consumer Product Safety Act.

The Improvement Act also created a new Section 37, an automatic lawsuit reporting requirement. Under this provision, manufacturers and importers must report to the CPSC if a "particular model" of a product is the subject of three or more civil actions—alleging death or grievous bodily injury and resulting in a final settlement or in a judgment in favor of the plaintiff—filed in federal or state courts in a prescribed two-year period.

This latest fine-tuning of the Section 15 reporting requirements followed a 1984 policy statement clarifying industry's obligation and the 1989 *Recall Handbook,* which spelled out in detail the substantial hazard reporting requirements. The handbook listed the various types of product hazards the commission considers serious enough to report. Since publication of the handbook and the issuance of stricter reporting requirements, the number of Section 15 reports and product recalls has steadily increased.

STANDARDS DEVELOPMENT

Since its establishment, the CPSC has assisted industry in developing more than 300 voluntary standards. Voluntary standards often are arrived at by revising existing industry standards, by repealing existing mandatory standards, or after notifying an industry of an emerging hazard.

Since 1973 the CPSC opted for voluntary negotiated guidelines over mandatory standards and bans. When industry has adopted a voluntary rule dealing with a risk of injury, the commission must find that compliance with the voluntary standard is not likely to result in adequate reduction of the risk or that it is unlikely that there will be substantial compliance before it can issue mandatory safety rules. The benefits of such a mandatory rule also must bear a reasonable relationship to the costs of compliance and impose the least burdensome requirement in preventing or adequately reducing the risk of injury.

The commission also is responsible for monitoring enforcement of existing mandatory standards, bans, or labeling requirements (among them toys and children's articles), restrictions on the sale of clothing treated with the chemical Tris (a flame retardant identified as a carcinogen), and compliance with provisions of the Poison Prevention Packaging Act that require child-resistant tops on oral prescription drugs.

The Consumer Product Safety Act allows the commission to issue a rule that prohibits manufacturers from stockpiling products that may be banned or that will fail to comply with a standard that has been issued but has not yet gone into effect.

Information from surveillance activities that uncovers violations of standards or regulations under the Consumer Product Safety Act, the Federal Hazardous Substances Act, and the Poison Prevention Packaging Act is transmitted to commission headquarters where, if voluntary action is not forthcoming, federal court action may result. Violations of standards issued under the Flammable Fabrics Act may be turned over to an administrative law judge who will preside over an administrative hearing and make an initial decision on the case. A judge's decision may be appealed to the full commission.

The commission also has the authority to impose civil fines for violations of its standards and for failure to observe cease-and-desist orders. In some cases the commission negotiates consent agreements whereby a company agrees to stop engaging in activities that violate commission rules but does not admit any wrongdoing.

Background

The CPSC was created at the zenith of the consumer movement. In 1968 President Lyndon Johnson, heeding the demand for safer products, established the National Commission on Product Safety. In June 1970 this fact-finding commission recommended establishment of a permanent agency. Just two years later, Congress created the CPSC, the first independent agency since the New Deal.

The national commission based its recommendation on the finding that an estimated 20 million Americans were injured annually by consumer products. Of those injured, the commission stated, approximately 110,000 were permanently disabled and 30,000 killed. The commission's chair, Arnold Elkind, told Congress that an effective agency could prevent as many as four million injuries and 6,000 deaths each year.

President Richard Nixon, who took office while Congress was debating the need for a product safety agency, supported the establishment of such a function in the executive branch but opposed establishment of an independent commission. Nevertheless, Congress passed the Consumer Product Safety Act, which granted the new agency unusual independence from the executive branch. Its chair was to serve a fixed term. (This practice was changed in 1976.) Other innovative provisions required the agency to open its proceedings to the public and to ensure public participation.

These provisions, some of which inhibited the commission's progress, were intended to answer the often-heard criticism of regulatory agencies—that they become captives of the industries they regulate. The congressional intent was to keep business and industry at arm's length and to substitute consumers as the primary participants in the agency's decision-making processes.

In another attempt to give the CPSC independence, the legislation required the agency to deliver its budget requests to Congress at the same time they were forwarded to the Office of Management and Budget (OMB). Nixon had created OMB just two years earlier to screen agency requests for funds or changes in the law before they were sent to Congress.

The law establishing the CPSC incorporated elaborate mechanisms for assuring maximum public participation in agency proceedings. Money was authorized to underwrite some of the costs of public participation. Through a procedure called the "offeror" process, any interested and competent outside group was invited to offer, or propose, mandatory consumer product safety standards for eventual adoption by the agency. Until 1978 the CPSC was permitted to develop its own mandatory safety standards only when no acceptable outside group had offered to do so.

The innovative procedures prescribed by Congress absorbed a good deal of the commission's attention during its formative years. Some procedures, such as the offeror process, were repealed; but the agency's original rules regarding open proceedings stand, having been amended just once to open the originally closed commission meetings.

Another forerunner of change in all regulatory agencies was the requirement that CPSC regulations take economic considerations into account. The requirement to perform cost-benefit analysis eventually became part of most substantive federal regulatory activities.

The greatest change in the agency during its first decade was in its relationship to the industries it regulates. Amendments to the law gradually shifted the commission's functions from handing down mandatory design standards and bans to promoting and nurturing the voluntary industry standard-setting process. Fostered by the shift from mandated consumer protection to deregulation and helped by a consumer activist constituency that has, in some part, developed its ability to work with business and industry, successive commissions have abandoned their hostility toward manufacturers of consumer products.

EARLY HISTORY

Lacking the wholehearted support of President Nixon (who delayed appointing a commission for five months after Congress authorized its creation), the CPSC's first chair, Richard Simpson, spent much of his three-year term asserting the independence of the agency. The White House and OMB followed traditional patterns, recommending party-loyal candidates for top staff positions and expecting to agree informally on a budget without congressional advice. Simpson found neither procedure consistent with the CPSC's congressional mandate.

Congress supported Simpson, passing an amendment exempting agency employees from political clearance at the White House. Simpson was not reappointed to the commission when his term expired.

President Gerald R. Ford chose S. John Byington, a native of Ford's hometown, Grand Rapids, Mich., to succeed Simpson in 1976. Byington was a known opponent of consumer legislation pending before Congress. In addition to the enmity of consumerists—both those in Congress and those who sought to influence the developing CPSC—Byington soon faced a barrage of critical government evaluations of the agency, including studies by the General Accounting Office, the Civil Service Commission, and the House Commerce Oversight and Investigations Subcommittee.

Matters came to a head in early 1978 when Sen. Wendell H. Ford, D-Ky., chair of the Senate Consumer Subcommittee, asked Byington to resign. Ford's request followed release of a Civil Service Commission report alleging thirty cases of CPSC abuse of government personnel rules. The violations occurred, the report stated, "against a backdrop of management unconcern for and, in some instances, outright contempt for principles of merit." Byington resigned to "depoliticize" congressional hearings on extending the agency's authorization.

REAUTHORIZATION AND REFORM

By 1978 President Jimmy Carter had appointed a number of consumer advocates to top administration positions. Congress, while it was beginning to talk about deregulation, was still giving regulatory agencies substantial funds and support. Susan King, Carter's appointee to head the CPSC, was the first commission chair to enjoy good relations simultaneously with the White House, Congress, and consumer activists.

Midway through Carter's term, some of the president's advisers recommended that the agency be abolished and that its functions be transferred to other agencies to streamline federal health and safety regulatory activities. However, after vigorous lobbying by the commissioners and consumer advocates, the president announced in April 1978 that he would support a three-year reauthorization.

Congress concurred, extending the agency through Sept. 30, 1981. It also agreed to some changes requested by Carter. These included:

▪ Authorizing the commission to participate directly in the development of mandatory safety standards in certain circumstances.

▪ Authorizing the commission to make existing voluntary standards mandatory and to delay imposition of a mandatory standard to permit an industry to develop a voluntary standard.

- Requiring manufacturers to notify the commission if they planned to export products that the commission had banned or that were not in conformity with applicable mandatory standards. The commission, in turn, would notify the government of the country that would be receiving the goods.

The 1978 reauthorization also required that the commission make a study of its goals, accomplishments, effectiveness, and impact of its regulatory activities on industry and the economy. As a result, the agency initiated a program to review existing standards to determine if any of them were conflicting, overlapping, obsolete, or ineffective. Regulations were reviewed for clarity and the burden they imposed on industry. The commission's approach to its regulatory mission was to target the most significant product hazards in a manner that least impinged on product utility, consumer demand, manufacturers' costs, and marketplace competition.

CPSC IN THE 1980S

After the 1980 election of Ronald Reagan, the fortunes of the CPSC took a decidedly downward turn. When the agency came up for review in 1981, its detractors, bolstered by the antiregulatory mood of the country, again attempted to abolish it. In May OMB director David Stockman announced that the Reagan administration wanted to dismantle the CPSC because it had "adventured too far in some areas of regulation." Others wanted to reorganize it into an executive branch agency or put it into the Commerce Department where it would be accountable to the president.

Consumer groups won the battle to keep the commission independent, but the Product Safety Amendments of 1981 cut the agency's budget authorization and circumscribed its powers in several respects, most notably by directing the commission not to set a mandatory safety standard without exhausting every possible means of arriving at a voluntary one.

These amendments reinforced the commission's duty to make economic analyses before regulatory decisions. They abolished the process through which outside organizations drafted standards for the commission to approve, they restricted the release of information business considered confidential, and they allowed one chamber of Congress to veto CPSC regulations if the other chamber did not object. This type of congressional veto provision, however, was found unconstitutional by the Supreme Court in *Immigration and Naturalization Service v. Chadha* (1983).

It fell to Nancy Harvey Steorts, Reagan's first appointment to the CPSC chair, to change direction under the

1981 amendments and accompanying budget slashing. The amendments also:

- Eliminated CPSC authority to issue safety standards containing product design requirements and required the agency to express standards in terms of performance requirements, warnings, and instructions.

- Directed the CPSC to amend its controversial mandatory safety standard for lawn mowers, which required mowers to stop when the user was not touching the handle and to restart automatically. The commission was required to provide an alternative that would allow the engine to be started manually.

- Abolished three of the four statutory advisory committees: the Product Safety Advisory Council, the National Advisory Committee for the Flammable Fabrics Act, and the Technical Advisory Committee on Poison Prevention Packaging. The Toxicological Advisory Board continued in existence.

Steorts is credited with creating an atmosphere of cooperation with industry. She began by reevaluating mandatory standards established by earlier commissions. Among these was the unvented gas heater standard, which was revoked in favor of a voluntary industry standard. This regulatory philosophy also was applied to enforcement, substituting voluntary corrective action plans, whenever possible, for outright bans of products found defective by the agency. Still, Steorts was not reappointed to a second term—perhaps because she never completely embraced the Reagan deregulatory philosophy, and she appealed to OMB to restore agency funds that had been cut.

The reductions in the CPSC's 1982 budget were dramatic. In fiscal 1980 the CPSC had a budget of $41 million and 871 full-time positions. In fiscal 1982 Congress agreed to Reagan's request of $32 million and a ceiling of 631 full-time employees—30 percent lower than Carter's budget recommendation for fiscal 1982, and a 27 percent cut in its staff, the largest reduction for any federal health and safety agency.

In an attempt to set priorities and to increase efficiency, the commission established in 1981 a priority list of twelve hazard projects. Criteria for selecting priorities focused on the severity of the risk involved, size and characteristics of the population exposed, and the circumstances of the exposure. A number of the agency's former critics applauded this more focused approach. They noted that in the early years of the CPSC the agency had listed more than 180 priorities.

By fiscal 1986 the list of priorities was down to five: electrocution hazards, fire toxicity, gas heating systems, portable electric heaters, and riding mowers. In its request for funds for fiscal 1986 the CPSC explained that by selecting priority projects that present the most serious consumer safety problems the commission was able "to focus its very limited resources on these important projects." In practice, however, priority projects sometimes were postponed, having been superseded by a more serious hazard.

Terrence Scanlon, appointed to a four-year term as chair in 1984, favored increasing cooperation with state and local government through contracts under which local inspectors would spend a portion of their time working for the CPSC. In fiscal 1986 nearly one-fourth of the agency's budget was allocated to field activity with the continuing aim of reducing the ratio of administrators to investigators.

Scanlon also attempted to foster the development of voluntary standards. By 1990 the commission staff had participated in the development of nearly 300 voluntary standards. Some notable accomplishments included revision of the National Electrical Code to require ground fault circuit interrupters in household wiring to help prevent electrocutions (the changes in the code were made at the request of CPSC staff); modification of swimming pool standards to help prevent child drownings; changes in the kerosene heater voluntary standard to require nitrogen dioxide sensors; changes in the voluntary standard for hair dryers to include protection from water immersion electrocution; and limiting the amount of methylene chloride in consumer products such as paint strippers, paint thinners, spray paints, and adhesive removers.

CPSC IN TROUBLE

For the last half of the 1980s the CPSC faced three major problems—dwindling resources, a bitter internal power struggle among the commissioners, and a protracted battle with the all-terrain vehicle (ATV) industry.

From 1985 to 1990 the CPSC's budget was between $33 million and $36 million. Each year the commission's operating plan was trimmed to accommodate the figures set by OMB and Congress, and contract money for major research projects was eliminated. Priority setting became narrower and more focused. By 1990 the CPSC had resources sufficient to select only two priority projects for fiscal year 1992—smoke detectors and carbon monoxide/fuel gas detection.

Although some observers and agency officials said that budget and staff reductions had resulted in increased efficiency, streamlined procedures, and improved management techniques, others argued that the cuts were designed more to hamper the CPSC's ability to function than to effect real savings.

The internal power struggle began in 1986 with the resignation of two commissioners—leaving the agency with only three sitting commissioners. The House and Senate Appropriations committees restricted funds for the salaries for the two vacancies. In effect the CPSC had, by an act of Congress, been changed from a five-member to a three-member commission. When Scanlon attempted a staff re-

organization without consulting the other two commissioners, months of public squabbling resulted. The ill will remained until Scanlon resigned in January 1989.

The commission's involvement with ATVs began in 1985 with the publication of an *Advance Notice of Proposed Rulemaking*, which was based on reports of 161 deaths and 89,000 injuries, primarily to young children. Public hearings were held around the nation, and by October 1986 the CPSC was recommending a ban of ATVs for children under twelve and an extensive consumer notification program. In December the CPSC asked the Justice Department to represent it in a lawsuit against the ATV manufacturers; the suit sought a refund program for all three-wheel ATVs, development of a voluntary standard, consumer notification, and driver training for new purchasers. After a year of negotiations, the commission entered into a consent agreement with the industry. The agreement included everything except the refund program for current owners of ATVs.

Critics called the agreement a sellout and a victory for the industry. By June 1990 the industry stopped work on developing a voluntary standard, saying it could not produce one that would be satisfactory to the commission. In 1992 the CPSC officially terminated rulemaking proceedings for ATVs. A coalition of consumer groups brought a suit against the commission saying that its decision was "arbitrary and capricious." The U.S. District Court for the District of Columbia upheld the commission's decision, however.

During the last half of the 1980s, the commission was able to accomplish little else in the way of mandatory standards or bans. One notable success was the ban of steel-tipped lawn darts, which had caused the death of a seven-year-old girl.

CPSC IN THE 1990S

The commission was without its third member—and thus without a quorum—for ten months until President Bush appointed Jacqueline Jones-Smith as the new chair in November 1989. One of the major accomplishments of Jones-Smith was the relocation of the CPSC headquarters staff from several Washington, D.C., offices to one building in Bethesda, Md. The major regulatory achievement of her four years as chair proved to be the development of a mandatory standard for child-resistant cigarette lighters. The standard was the result of a cooperative effort between the commission and lighter manufacturers, who favored the idea of a safety standard as a defense against product liability lawsuits. The standard was built on research started in 1988 and was issued in 1992.

Two significant developments that occurred during Jones-Smith's term came about not through commission initiative, but rather because of the intervention of

Congress. First was the passage of the Consumer Product Safety Improvement Act, which created tighter reporting requirements under Section 15. Second was the passage of the Child Safety Protection Act, which mandated placing labels that warned of choking hazards on certain toys and the reporting of choking incidents to the commission.

In March 1994 President Bill Clinton replaced Jones-Smith as chair with consumer advocate Ann Brown. Brown came to the commission with a reputation as an activist with a flair for gaining media attention. She was widely known for her annual Christmas toy hazard list, which she announced at a preholiday press conference highlighted by dangerous toys being dumped into a trash can. During the first four months of her term more rulemaking proceedings were initiated by the commission than in the entire four years of the previous term. Proposed rules were published to address such hazards as fireworks that could kill and strings on children's garments that could strangle.

During her first year Brown held news conferences that received nationwide news coverage. A news conference announcing the recall of crayons that contained lead garnered one of the largest consumer responses in the commission's history in terms of calls to the agency's hotline. Brown also made frequent radio and television appearances promoting CPSC activities, and she often called in industry and consumer representatives to discuss safety problems and regulatory approaches. For example in 1995 the CPSC launched a new educational program, called "baby safety showers," aimed at informing new parents of infants of safe products and potential hazards. Brown also instituted an annual public relations push to review the previous year's recalls and actions.

Confronting the budget-cutting proposals of the Republican Congress back in 1995, Brown declared that "regulation is a last resort" and offered the CPSC, with its perennially small appropriations and staff, as a model for government regulatory agencies in the new era of federal downsizing. Brown's proactive stance helped the CPSC survive essentially intact against a hostile Congress from 1995 through 2000. Budget requests at the agency reflected the need to keep up with inflation but not the addition of new programs.

Under Brown, voluntary recalls that gained attention included those for plastic lawn chairs that were prone to collapse, net minihammocks without spreader bars, and tubular metal bunk beds. In the area of indoor air pollution, CPSC laboratory tests confirmed in 1996 that some imported vinyl miniblinds contained lead. Manufacturers of the blinds agreed to change the formula for the plastic in the blinds, and some retailers voluntarily pulled the products from their shelves. Later, the agency worked with industry to prevent the accidental strangulation deaths of children caught in window blind and drapery pull cords.

In another area of child safety, the CPSC in June 1996 issued recommendations on safer new protective equipment for children's baseball, citing the statistic that the sport caused 162,000 injuries to children in 1995. In the highly controversial report, the commission urged baseball leagues to use softer baseballs. The CPSC study found eighty-eight deaths between 1973 and 1995—sixty-eight of them caused by balls hitting children in the head or chest and thirteen caused by bat impact. However, few leagues adopted the recommendations while most clung to the traditional ball.

Another study released by the CPSC in June 1996 found that child-resistant packaging had reduced the death rate for children who accidentally swallow medicine by 45 percent since 1974. The CPSC in 1995 had ordered a redesign of child-resistant packaging of medicine, to take effect by January 1998; the new design was tested both by children and by adults aged fifty to seventy and received strong industry support.

In 1997 the commission targeted for voluntary recall the popular halogen torchiere lamps that have been linked to 100 fires and ten deaths since 1992. After negotiations, Underwriters Laboratories (UL), the nation's leading independent product testing service, agreed to distribute for free in-home repair kits for the 40 million lamps sold as well as update the store packages with wire guards.

In 1998 the commission settled a lawsuit with Central Sprinkler Co. by recalling 8.4 million Omega fire sprinklers. The commission found that the popular fire sprinklers—a dozen of which were installed in the East and West Wings of the White House—contained a basic defect that could cause them to fail during a fire. The incident increased scrutiny of the safety of fire sprinklers and of UL, which had vouched for the sprinkler's efficacy. In June 2000, in part because of the controversy that was generated by concern about the testing performed on the sprinklers, UL announced that it would improve its safety standards and allow more public oversight over the testing process.

In 1998 the commission also continued its focus on children's products and toys. It issued a voluntary recall of old-style rolling baby walkers and urged parents instead to buy newer, wider walkers that do not fit through doorways and cannot fall down stairs. In conjunction with the National Highway Traffic Safety Administration, the CPSC in March 1998 issued a massive recall of 800,000 Evenflo On My Way infant car seat/carriers. The agency said that while the seats/carriers met rigorous crash standards when used inside the car, they caused numerous injuries, including skull fractures, concussions, and bruises, when the seat was used improperly outside the car.

In 1999 there were more than 300 federal recalls of faulty products. However, most of these recalls were voluntary rather than mandatory.

CPSC IN THE 2000S

The agency enjoyed slight budget increases throughout the final years of Clinton's administration. By fiscal 2001 the agency was funded at $52.5 million and had approximately 480 full-time workers. However, the size of the workforce was about half of its strength in its prime at the end of the Carter administration in 1980.

The commission continued to take a particular issue in regulating products for children. In early 2001 voluntary recalls included the removal of about 171,000 baby bungee jumpers that allow babies to bounce while supported by a seat that is suspended from a doorway. Additionally, about 125,000 fleece pants were recalled voluntarily because a cord had a tendency to break off. The commission also blocked Burger King Corp. from giving out about 400,000 riverboat toys with children's meals and another 234,000 toy bugs that had been distributed through McDonald's Happy Meals program. Both toys posed a choking hazard, the commission said.

By 2000 the commission finished consolidating its information systems into one comprehensive system to make them more available to business officials and consumers than they had been in past years. The new computer system integrated information received from various sources, including industry, consumer groups, and the National Electronic Injury Surveillance System. In addition to an expanded hotline service, the commission's Web site was improved so that consumers could get quick information about recalls and safety alerts.

The commission received unwanted attention in 2001 when President George W. Bush's nominee to head the agency, Mary Sheila Gall, was widely rejected on Capitol Hill. Gall, who had been a CSPC commissioner since 1991, had upset consumer groups by voting against recalls and safety standards. Democrats charged that during her tenure Gall had not looked out for consumers. Many cited her vote in 1994 against beginning a safety review for a type of baby walker. She said the review was unnecessary because the injuries related to that style of walker could have been prevented by better supervision of the child. After the Senate Commerce Committee rejected her nomination in August 2001 on a party-line vote, Gall asked Bush to withdraw her name from consideration.

In July 2002 the Senate confirmed Bush's second nominee, Harold D. Stratton Jr. As state attorney general for New Mexico, Stratton had brought a number of fraud cases on issues such as high-pressure sales tactics and telemarketers and art fraud. But some consumer groups felt that Stratton's antiregulatory stance would undercut the commission's mission. Stratton had helped found an organization called the Rio Grande Foundation, which promoted "limited government, economic freedom and individual responsibility." Stratton also had served on the board of the Defenders of Property Rights, a group that aimed to, as described on their Web site, "counterbalance the governmental threat to private property as a result of a broad range of regulations."

In his defense, Stratton told lawmakers what while he was philosophically opposed to regulation, the government must play a role on consumer safety issues. Noting that he was the father of two young daughters, Stratton said "we all believe in the safety of our consumer products when it comes to kids."

Stratton's confirmation put the CSPC back in business again. For months the panel had been without a quorum, which meant that it could not issue subpoenas or refer investigations to the Justice Department for further action. Without a quorum present, only voluntary recalls had been possible.

Current Issues

The CSPC has continued its focus on working with manufacturers to recall a product voluntarily when a defect is discovered. Each month, the agency's Web site features a lengthy list of recalls that include a vast array of products. Hazards to children are the focus of many listings, such as a recall of 360,000 children's boardbook sets that were sold in cardboard boxes with plastic snaps. The snaps could detach, posing a choking hazard to young children.

The number of products the agency has recalled has been increasing, in part because some federal agencies have been more aggressive in forcing companies to comply with product safety laws. But CPSC officials have said the commission has also increased its enforcement of consumer laws and collection of fines from companies who violate those laws.

In 2002 the agency completed thirteen civil penalty cases that resulted in more than $4 million in fines for failure to report a hazardous defect or violation of federal safety laws. The agency also secured eight criminal convictions. For example, the commission announced a $1 million settlement with General Electric for charges that the company failed to report defects involving more than three million dishwashers made in the 1980s. In a separate case, the commission tied the deaths of twelve children to chests made by Lane, a Tupelo, Miss., company.

Despite those high-profile cases, the agency has its critics, including former CPSC head Brown. Brown has charged that a loophole in federal law was leading to deaths from products even after they were recalled. Because companies did not have to keep records of consumers who buy their products, consumer could not be notified about recalls. Brown and consumer groups said that consumers have to rely instead on advertising campaigns and news reports, and that the commission should take steps to remedy the problem. Stratton, who was slated to serve as chair of the commission until October 2006, and fellow commissioner Gall opposed a request from consumer groups to mandate that a product-registration card be included with children's products. In a statement, Stratton said he turned down the petition because of its "broad and indefinite scope" and its cost.

A February 2003 report to Congress charted an ambitious agenda for the agency. The CPSC's strategic goals included reducing the death rate from fires by 10 percent, reducing the number of deaths from electrocutions by 20 percent, and reducing the head injury rate for children by 10 percent. The agency also aimed to increase the number of onsite investigations and launch a study on improving the safety of residential panelboards, also known as circuit breakers, to reduce home electrical fires originating in the breaker panel.

■ AGENCY ORGANIZATION

Biographies

HAROLD D. (HAL) STRATTON JR., CHAIRMAN

Appointment: Nominated by President George W. Bush as commissioner, confirmed by the Senate July 25, 2002; term expires Oct. 2006.

Born: Dec. 6, 1950; Muskogee, OK.

Education: University of Oklahoma, B.A., 1973; University of Oklahoma School of Law, J.D., 1976.

Profession: Lawyer.

Political Affiliation: Republican.

Previous Career: After law school, Mr. Stratton served in the U.S. Army and then moved to Albuquerque. He served in the New Mexico House of Representatives from 1979–1986 and as New Mexico attorney general from 1987–1990. Mr. Stratton also served on the Western Conference of the Council of State Governments, the National Conference of State Legislatures, the National Conference of Commissioners on Uniform State Laws, the New Mexico Judicial Council, and the BLM Citizens Advisory Committee (Albuquerque district).

MARY SHEILA GALL, COMMISSIONER

Appointment: Nominated by President George Bush to a seven-year term as commissioner, confirmed by the Senate Dec. 9, 1991; term expired Oct. 1998. Renominated and confirmed by the U.S. Senate to a seven-year term.

Born: July 19, 1949; Buffalo, NY.

Education: Rosary Hill College, B.A., 1971.

Profession: Government official.

Political Affiliation: Republican.

Previous Career: Gall served from 1971 to 1979 in various legislative positions on the staffs of several members of the U.S. Congress (Sen. James Buckley, R-N.Y.; Rep. Jack Kemp, R-N.Y.; Rep. Tom Coleman, R-Mo.). From 1980 to 1981, she worked as a senior legislative analyst and consultant to the Reagan-Bush Presidential Campaign and Transition Team. From 1981 to 1986 she served at the White House as deputy policy advisor to Vice President Bush. Gall served as counselor to the director at the OPM from 1986 to 1989, and in 1989 she was appointed assistant secretary at the Health and Human Services Department, serving in that position until her appointment to the CPSC.

THOMAS HILL MOORE, COMMISSIONER

Appointment: Nominated by President Clinton to an unexpired term, confirmed by the Senate April 1995; term expired Oct. 26, 1996. Renominated by President Clinton for a full term, confirmed by the Senate Aug. 2, 1996; term expires Oct. 26, 2003.

Born: Feb. 2, 1937, Washington, GA.

Education: Jacksonville University, B.S., 1971; University of Florida, J.D., 1974.

Profession: Lawyer.

Political Affiliation: Democrat.

Previous Career: Moore served as assistant dean at the University of Florida College of Law from 1974 to 1977, directing programs for minority students. From 1977 to 1980 he was a legislative assistant to Sen. Richard Stone, D-Fla. Moore also has held positions as a government relations consultant, as legislative affairs director for a private law firm, as a staff attorney at the National Consumer Law Center, and as executive vice president at the National Medical Association. Moore served as legislative counsel to Sen. John Breaux, D-La., from 1988 to 1995, until being appointed to the CPSC.

Headquarters and Divisions

OFFICE OF THE COMMISSIONERS

The chair is the principal executive officer of the commission and has authority over all executive and administrative functions. The commission annually elects a vice chair to act in the absence of the chair. The commissioners have general authority over all functions of the CPSC (see Responsibilities, p. 35). These responsibilities are generally delegated to various offices within the CPSC; the commissioners retain the final approval over their recommendations.

The 1981 Consumer Product Safety Amendments provided for formation of ad hoc chronic hazard advisory panels to advise the commission concerning the risk

CONSUMER PRODUCT SAFETY COMMISSION

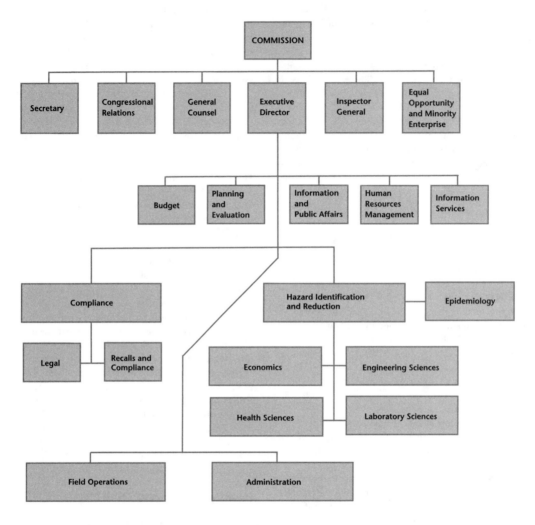

of cancer, birth defects, or gene mutations associated with consumer products. A panel would be formed when the commission decided there was a need for one and would consist of seven members appointed by the commission from a list of scientists nominated by the president of the National Academy of Sciences.

Chair

Hal Stratton .... (301) 504-7900
Fax..................................... (301) 504-0057

Commissioners

Mary Sheila Gall .... (301) 504-7901
Fax..................................... (301) 504-0768

Thomas H. Moore .... (301) 504-7902
Fax..................................... (301) 504-0813

OFFICE OF THE EXECUTIVE DIRECTOR

The executive director acts as the agency's chief operating manager under the broad direction of the chair; assists with development of the agency's budget and operating plan, and, after commission approval, manages execution of those plans. The office oversees the offices of the Budget, Compliance, Hazard Identification and Reduction, Human Resources Management, Information Services, Planning and Evaluation, and Information and Public Affairs.

The commission's directorates report to the executive director, as do the regional offices.

Executive Director

Patsy Semple .... (301) 504-7899

Fax .... (301) 504-0121

Deputy Executive Director

Thomas W. Murr Jr. .... (301) 504-7881

Fax .... (301) 504-0354

DIRECTORATE FOR ADMINISTRATION

Responsible for administrative functions supporting the commission in the areas of finance, management and organizational analysis, procurement, security, and property management. It also operates the reference library.

Associate Executive Director

Robert Frost .... (301) 504-7116

Administrative Services Branch, Building Services

Marcia Fulham .... (301) 504-7091

Administrative Services Branch, Support Services

Iris Parks .... (301) 504-7078

Financial Services Branch

Deborah Hodge .... (301) 504-7130

DIRECTORATE FOR FIELD OPERATIONS

Responsible for all commission field operations. Field staff are located in 37 cities across the country and support the full range of commission programs. The directorate also negotiates and monitors recalls of hazardous products and provides advice and guidance to industry. (For a list of regional offices, see p. 47.)

Director

Carol Cave .... (301) 504-7677

Fax .... (301) 504-0354

State and Local Programs

Denise Beatty .... (301) 504-7676

OFFICE OF THE BUDGET

Carries out budget development and analysis, and prepares the commission's operating plan in consultation with other offices and directorates. Also manages execution of the commission's budget and recommends to the executive director actions to enhance the effectiveness of the commission's programs and activities.

Director

Edward E. Quist .... (301) 504-7655

Fax .... (301) 504-0121

OFFICE OF COMPLIANCE

Identifies and takes action to have manufacturers correct or recall any defective consumer product already in distribution; establishes industry compliance with existing safety standards through development of surveillance and enforcement programs as well as the conduct of enforcement litigation; and provides legal advice and case guidance to field offices.

Assistant Executive Director

Alan H. Schoem .... (301) 504–7519

Fax .... (301) 504–0008

Litigation

Eric Stone .... (301) 504–7585

Recalls and Compliance

Marc Schoem .... (301) 504–7520

OFFICE OF CONGRESSIONAL RELATIONS

Provides information and assistance to Congress on matters of commission policy; coordinates written and oral testimony by commissioners and agency personnel before Congress.

Director

Jack Horner .... (301) 504–7660

Fax .... (301) 504–0016

OFFICE OF EQUAL EMPLOYMENT AND MINORITY ENTERPRISE

Oversees CPSC compliance with laws, regulations, and internal policies relating to equal employment opportunity and ensures compliance with relevant provisions of the Small Business Act.

Director

Kathy Buttrey .... (301) 504–7771

Fax .... (301) 504–0107

OFFICE OF THE GENERAL COUNSEL

The general counsel prepares the commission's legislative program and reviews legislative proposals originated elsewhere, conducts or supervises the conduct of litigation to which the commission is a party, and reviews and approves the litigation aspects of enforcement matters. Staff also provides final legal review of and makes recommendations to the commission on proposed product safety standards, rules, laws, regulations, petition actions, and substantial consumer hazard actions; provides legal review of certain procurement, personnel, and administrative actions; and drafts documents for publication in the *Federal Register*.

General Counsel

Bill DuRoss .... (301) 504–7626

Fax .... (301) 504–0403

Enforcement and Information

Alan Shakin .... (301) 504–7632

Regulatory Affairs

Stephen Lemberg .... (301) 504-7630

OFFICE OF HAZARD IDENTIFICATION AND REDUCTION

Manages hazard-related programs delineated in the commission's operating plan or assigned by the executive director; analyzes petitions requesting development of standards submitted to the commission; provides direction and support to all projects including mandatory and voluntary standards and petitions, data collection and analysis, and emerging hazards, especially where responsibility involves more than one directorate. Staff ensures that technical, environmental, economic, and social impacts of projects are coordinated when presented to the commission for decision; exercises program review and is active in setting commission priorities; oversees CPSC involvement with voluntary standard-setting groups; and coordinates international liaison activities on consumer product safety.

Assistant Executive Director

Jacqueline Elder..........................(301) 504–7645

Fax ....(301) 504–0354

Directorate for Economic Analysis

Conducts studies to determine the impact of CPSC regulations on consumers, the economy, industry, and production. Also studies potential environmental effects of commission actions. Most of the directorate's resources are located in the hazard programs, where they provide the economic information necessary to make decisions concerning the best options to reduce unreasonable risks of injury associated with consumer products.

Associate Executive Director

Warren Prunella .... (301) 504–7703

Fax ....(301) 504–0124

Regulatory Analysis

Dale Ray................................(301) 504–7704

Research and Data Analysis

Gregory Rodgers........................(301) 504–7702

Directorate for Engineering Sciences

Provides scientific and technical expertise to the commission to support agency regulatory activity. Develops and evaluates product performance criteria, design specifications, and quality control standards; conducts engineering tests, evaluates test methods; provides advice on proposed safety standards; performs and monitors research in the engineering sciences; and supervises the CPSC engineering laboratory and other test facilities.

Associate Executive Director

Hugh McLaurin .... (301) 504–7531

Fax ....(301) 504–0533

Electrical Engineering

Elinda Edwards........................ (301) 504–7535

Human Factors

Robert B. Ochsman.....................(301) 504–7686

Mechanical Engineering

Mark Kommagai........................(301) 504–7532

Directorate for Laboratory Sciences

Associate Executive Director

Andrew Stadnik.........................(301) 424–6421

Fax ....(301) 413–7107

Chemistry

Warren K. Porter Jr. .... (301) 424–6421

Directorate for Epidemiology and Health Sciences

Collects data on consumer product related hazards and potential hazards; determines the frequency, severity, and distribution of the various types of injuries and investigates their causes; and assesses the effects of product safety standards and programs on consumer injuries. Staff also conducts epidemiological studies and research in the fields of consumer-related injuries.

This directorate also is responsible for management of the commission's chemical hazards program; development and evaluation of the scientific content of product safety standards and test methods; and the conduct and evaluation of specific product testing to support general agency regulatory activity. It conducts and evaluates scientific tests and test methods, collects scientific and technical data, performs risk assessments, and monitors research. The directorate is the commission's primary source of expertise for implementation of the Poison Prevention Packaging Act, and the directorate provides technical liaison with the National Toxicological Program, the National Cancer Institute, the Environmental Protection Agency, and other federal programs related to chemical hazards. It also manages activities of the chronic hazard advisory panels.

Associate Executive Director

Mary Ann Danello.....................(301) 504–7237

Fax ....(301) 504–0079

Hazard Analysis

Susan Ahmed .... (301) 504–7416

Hazard and Injury Data Systems

Arthur MacDonald ....(301) 504–7422

Health Sciences

Marilyn L. Wind.......................(301) 504–7246

OFFICE OF HUMAN RESOURCES MANAGEMENT

Provides management support to the commission in the areas of recruitment and placement, training and executive development, employee and labor relations, benefits and retirement assistance, disciplinary actions, and grievances and appeals.

Director

Randall Redmond .... (301) 504–7222

Fax .... (301) 504-0025

OFFICE OF PUBLIC AFFAIRS AND MEDIA RELATIONS

See Information Sources.

OFFICE OF INFORMATION SERVICES

See Information Sources.

OFFICE OF THE INSPECTOR GENERAL

Reviews, analyzes, and reports on commission programs and organization to assess compliance with appropriate laws, regulations, and procedures. Recommends ways to promote economy, efficiency, and effectiveness within the commission's programs and operations. Receives complaints and investigates possible violations of law, rules, and regulations; mismanagement; abuse of authority; and waste of funds.

Inspector General

Vacant .... (301) 504–7905

Fax .... (301) 504-0124

OFFICE OF PLANNING AND EVALUATION

Develops the CPSC's goals, and program and resource plans in coordination with other offices; develops and uses analytical methods, standards, and techniques in the measurement of program accomplishments; and recommends changes to increase CPSC effectiveness.

Director

N.J. Scheers .... (301) 504–7670

Fax .... (301) 504-0025

OFFICE OF THE SECRETARY

The major point of contact for consumer information. Prepares the commission's agenda; prepares, distributes, and stores official records; and schedules and coordinates commission business at official meetings. The secretary also exercises joint responsibility with the Office of the General Counsel for interpretation and implementation of the Privacy Act, the Freedom of Information Act, and the Government in the Sunshine Act. Staff prepares and coordinates reports required by law under these acts, issues *Federal Register* documents, supervises and administers the dockets of adjudicative proceedings before the commissioners, administers the public reading room, maintains a master calendar of commission meetings, and publishes the *Public Calendar*.

Director

Todd Stevenson .... (301) 504–6836

Fax .... (301) 504–0127

Regional Offices

Eastern Regional Center

(CT, DC, DE, FL, MA, MD, ME, NC, NH, NJ, NY, PA, PR, RI, SC, VA, VT, WV, VI)
201 Varick St., #903
New York, NY 10014
(212) 620-6180
Gerry Naylis, director

Central Regional Center

(AL, GA, IA, IL, IN, KS, KY, MI, MN, MO, ND, NE, OH, SD, TN, WI)
230 S. Dearborn St., #2944
Chicago, IL 60604-1601
(312) 353-8260
Eric Ault, director

Western Regional Center

(AK, AR, AS, AZ, CA, CO, GU, HI, ID, LA, MT, NM, NV, OK, OR, TX, UT, WA, WY)
1301 Clay St., #610-N
Oakland, CA 94612
(415) 643–4053
Frank Nava, director

▪ CONGRESSIONAL ACTION

Congressional Liaison

Jolin Homer .... (301) 504–7660

Committees and Subcommittees

HOUSE APPROPRIATIONS COMMITTEE

Subcommittee on VA, HUD, and Independent Agencies
H143 CAP, Washington, DC 20515
(202) 225-3241

HOUSE COMMERCE COMMITTEE

Subcommittee on Finance and Hazardous Materials
2125 RHOB, Washington, DC 20515
(202) 225-2927

HOUSE GOVERNMENT REFORM AND OVERSIGHT COMMITTEE

Subcommittee on National Economic Growth, Natural Resources, and Regulatory Affairs
B377 RHOB, Washington, DC 20515
(202) 225-4407

SENATE APPROPRIATIONS COMMITTEE
Subcommittee on VA, HUD, and Independent Agencies
SD-130, Washington, DC 20510
(202) 224-7211

SENATE COMMERCE, SCIENCE, AND
TRANSPORTATION COMMITTEE
Subcommittee on Consumer Affairs, Foreign Commerce,
and Tourism
SH-425, Washington, DC 20510
(202) 224-5183

Legislation

The CPSC was established under authority of the **Consumer Product Safety Act,** signed by the president Oct. 27, 1972. The act was later amended by the **Consumer Product Safety Commission Improvements Act of 1976** (90 Stat. 503, 15 U.S.C. 2051 note), the **Emergency Interim Consumer Product Safety Standard Act of 1978** (92 Stat. 386), the **Consumer Product Safety Amendments of 1981** (Title 12, subtitle A, 95 Stat. 703), and the **Consumer Product Safety Improvement Act of 1990** (104 Stat. 3110, 15 U.S.C. 2051 note).

Major legislation administered by the CPSC includes:

Flammable Fabrics Act (67 Stat. 111, 15 U.S.C. 1191). Signed by the president June 30, 1953. Prohibited the introduction or movement in interstate commerce of highly flammable clothing or material.

Refrigerator Safety Act (70 Stat. 953, 15 U.S.C. 1211). Signed by the president Aug. 2, 1956. Required that all refrigerators sold in interstate commerce be equipped with a safety device enabling them to be easily opened from the inside.

Federal Hazardous Substances Act (74 Stat. 372, 15 U.S.C. 1261). Signed by the president July 12, 1960. Required precautionary labels and regulated distribution and sale of hazardous substances suitable for household use.

Poison Prevention Packaging Act of 1970 (84 Stat. 1670, 15 U.S.C. 1471). Signed by the president Dec. 30, 1970. Required special packaging to protect children from serious injury or illness from handling or swallowing household substances.

Consumer Product Safety Act (86 Stat. 1207, 15 U.S.C. 2051). Signed by the president Oct. 27, 1972. Established the CPSC to protect consumers against unreasonable risk of injury from hazardous products.

Lead Contamination Control Act of 1988 (102 Stat. 2884, 42 U.S.C. 201 note). Signed by the president Oct. 31, 1988. Amended the Safe Drinking Water Act to allow the CPSC to recall drinking-water coolers with lead-lined tanks.

Regulations Regarding Lawn Darts (102 Stat. 3183, 16 C.F.R. 1500.86(a)(3)). Signed by the president Nov. 5, 1988. Banned the sale of lawn darts and similar sharp-pointed toys.

Labeling of Hazardous Art Materials (102 Stat. 4568, 15 U.S.C. 1277). Signed by the president Nov. 18, 1988. Amended the Federal Hazardous Substances Act by adding Sec. 23, which sets forth requirements for labeling art materials that the commission deems potentially hazardous to the health of children and adults.

Consumer Product Safety Improvement Act of 1990 (104 Stat. 3110, 15 U.S.C. 2051 note). Signed by the president on Nov. 16, 1990. Title I amended the Consumer Product Safety Act, the Federal Hazardous Substances Act, and the Flammable Fabrics Act to require the commission to devise procedures to monitor compliance with certain voluntary standards; and to terminate a proposed consumer product safety rule only if a voluntary standard has been approved. Title II required the commission to issue a standard for automatic garage door openers to protect against entrapment.

Child Safety Protection Act (108 Stat. 722, 15 U.S.C. 1261 note). Signed by the president on June 16, 1994. Title I required legible and conspicuous choking hazard warning labels on packages of balloons, marbles, small balls, and toys with small parts intended for children over three. Title II, the Children's Bicycle Helmet Safety Act of 1994, authorized funding for helmets and helmet safety programs through the National Highway Traffic Safety Administration and specified that helmets must meet CPSC standards.

Amendment to Consumer Product Safety Act (116 Stat. 2776, 15 U.S.C. 2085). Signed by the president on Dec. 4, 2002. Amended the Consumer Product Safety Act to provide that low-speed electric bicycles are consumer products and shall be subject to CPSC regulations. The law changed the regulation of low-speed electric bicycles, treating them as normal bicycles and not as motorcycles.

■ INFORMATION SOURCES

Internet

Agency Web Site: http://www.cpsc.gov
E-mail: info@cpsc.gov

For information, call (800) 638–2772. News releases about recalls and product hazards along with the CPSC's news releases are available online. Information on how consumers can report hazardous products to the agency also is available.

Telephone Contacts

Consumer Hotline.........................(800) 638–2772
  Hotline TTY .... (800) 638–8270
Employee Locator .... (301) 504–7218

Information and Publications

KEY OFFICES

CPSC Public Affairs and Media Relations

4330 East-West Hwy.
Bethesda, MD 20814-4408
(301) 504–7908
Fax (301) 504–0862
Bruce Richardson, director

Distributes health and safety information to the news media and issues press releases. Coordinates media coverage of commission events and information activities within the commission's regional offices. Distributes commission publications.

CPSC Information Services

4330 East-West Hwy.
Bethesda, MD 20814-4408
(800) 638–2772
Fax (301) 504–0025
Pat Weddle, assistant executive director

Manages the commission's data processing resources and networks, toll-free hotlines, and Internet and fax-on-demand services; operates the National Injury Information Clearinghouse (see Data and Statistics, p. 49). Works to improve agency operations through information technology. The Hotline provides information on recalls and handles consumer complaints about unsafe products or product-related injuries; it operates at all times, with staff available weekdays from 8:30 a.m. to 5:00 p.m.

Freedom of Information

4330 East-West Hwy.
Bethesda, MD 20814-4408
(301) 504–6821
Fax (301) 504–0127
Sandy Bradshaw, FOI officer

Requests should specify product or manufacturer's name, exact titles, dates, file designation, or other information to identify the records requested. Fees for search and reproduction costs vary.

PUBLICATIONS

Contact CPSC Information and Public Affairs, the Office of the Secretary, or the Consumer Hotline to order or to request the *Publications Listing*. Publications cover all aspects of consumer product safety, including Christmas decorations, playground equipment and toys, power tools, and kitchen products. To request a publication by title and item number, write:

Publication Request

CPSC Public Affairs and Media Relations
Washington, DC 20207

Publications also may be obtained from the CPSC's regional offices, which also have staff members who specialize in consumer affairs. Single copies are available free from the CPSC; multiple copies are for sale from the U.S. Government Printing Office (GPO): see appendix, Ordering Government Publications. Titles available include:

Annual Report. Summarizes commission activities; lists policies, advisory opinions, regulations, and proposals.

Recall Handbook. A guide for manufacturers, importers, distributors, and retailers to help in understanding obligations and responsibilities under the Consumer Product Safety Act.

Hotline Flyer and *Hotline Brochure.* Fact sheets outlining the functions and purpose of the hotline, as well as how the hotline operates.

Safety for Older Consumers: Home Safety Checklist.

Who We Are, What We Do. General brochure on CPSC organization and activities.

DATA AND STATISTICS

The CPSC *Annual Report* lists data on deaths, injuries, and costs of injuries from consumer products; it also provides an index of products regulated by the commission. More information is available from:

CPSC National Injury Information Clearinghouse

4330 East-West Hwy.
Bethesda, MD 20814-4408
(301) 504–7921
Fax (301) 504–0025
Ann DeTemple, director

Maintains databases on product-related deaths and injuries. Obtains data and statistics from state agencies, such as police departments and coroners' offices, and through the National Electronic Surveillance System. Most data requests are answered free of charge. However, when costs exceed $50, the requestor will be notified of the amount due, with payment required in advance. Information on the following databases is available from the clearinghouse or through the agency's Internet services:

Accident Investigations. Information on accident sequence, product brand name, involvement of product, environmental circumstances, behavior of people involved, photographs, or diagrams. Police, fire, or coroners' reports may be included as supplemental data. Investigation reports are filed by calendar year, area office or contractor, type of injury, type of consumer product, age, sex, etc.

DCRT—Death Certificate System. Information on victim's residence, age, sex, race, date and place of accident, accident mechanism, manner of death, whether or not the accident was work related, nature of injuries, external causes, consumer products involved, general location of the accident, and up to four lines of narrative detail.

NEISS—National Electronic Injury Surveillance System. Data on product-related injuries collected from statistically representative hospital emergency rooms nationwide. Data include victim's age, sex, diagnosis, body part affected, disposition of the case, product involved, any indication of a second product involved, and the general location of the accident.

Reported Incidents. Narrative reports of actual or potential product hazards taken from consumers' letters to the CPSC, hotline calls, newspaper articles, and notices from coroners and medical examiners.

MEETINGS

The commissioners generally meet Wednesday and Thursday. These meetings usually are open to the public but participation is limited to observation. Notices of meetings, with a tentative agenda, are published in the "Sunshine Act Meetings" section of the *Federal Register,* and are also available on a recorded message: (301) 504–6836.

The CPSC Office of the Secretary maintains the master calendar of the agency, which it distributes through a mailing list. The secretary's office also can usually provide minutes of executive session meetings. Call (301) 504-6836.

Reference Resources

LIBRARY

CPSC Library
4330 East-West Hwy.
Bethesda, MD 20814-4408
(301) 504–7622
Hours: 1:00 p.m. to 5:00 p.m.

Maintains a collection of publications and periodicals with an emphasis on product safety, product liability, engineering, economics, biomedical sciences, and consumer affairs. Open to the public; research assistance provided. Interlibrary loan service is available.

DOCKETS

CPSC Office of the Secretary
4330 East-West Hwy.
Bethesda, MD 20814-4408
(301) 504–6833
Rocky Hammond, docket control specialist
Hours: 8:30 a.m. to 5:00 p.m.

Maintains a reading room containing CPSC documents and other records that are available for public inspection.

RULES AND REGULATIONS

CPSC rules and regulations are published in the *Code of Federal Regulations,* Title 16, Part 1000 to end. Proposed rules, new final rules, and updates to the *Code of Federal Regulations* are published in the *Federal Register.* (See appendix for information on how to obtain and use these publications.)

Other Information Sources

RELATED AGENCY

Consumer Information Center
General Services Administration
(See appendix, Ordering Government Publications.)

NONGOVERNMENTAL ORGANIZATIONS

The following are some key organizations that monitor the CPSC and consumer product safety issues.

Consumer Alert
1001 Connecticut Ave. N.W., #1128
Washington, DC 20036
(202) 467-5809
Fax (202) 467-5814
Internet: http://www.consumeralert.org/index.htm

Consumer Federation of America
1424 16th St. N.W., #604
Washington, DC 20036
(202) 387-6121
Fax (202) 265-7989

Consumers Union of the United States
101 Truman Ave.
Yonkers, NY 10703
(914) 378-2000
Fax (914) 378-2905
  Washington office
  1666 Connecticut Ave. N.W., #310
  Washington, DC 20009
  (202) 462-6262
  Fax (202) 265-9548
Publishes *Consumer Reports magazine.*
Internet: http://www.consumersunion.org

Council of Better Business Bureaus
4200 Wilson Blvd., #800
Arlington, VA 22203
(703) 276-0100
Fax (703) 525-8277
Internet: http://www.bbb.org

National Consumers League
1701 K St. N.W., #1200
Washington, DC 20006
(202) 835-3323
Fax (202) 835-0747
Internet: http://www.aoa.dhhs.gov/aoa/dir/148.html

Public Citizen
1600 20th St. N.W.
Washington, DC 20009
(202) 588-1000
Fax (202) 588-7798
Internet: http://www.citizen.org

United States Public Interest Research Group (USPIRG)
218 D St. S.E.
Washington, DC 20003
(202) 546-9707
Fax (202) 546-2461
Internet: http://www.igc.apc.org/pirg/uspirg/index.htm

Bureau of National Affairs (BNA), Inc.
1231 25th St. N.W.
Washington, DC 20037
(202) 452-4200
Fax (800) 253-0332
Internet: http://www.bna.com

Commerce Clearing House (CCH), Inc.
2700 Lake Cook Rd.
Riverwoods, IL 60015
(847) 267-7000
Fax (847) 267-7878
Internet: http://www.cch.com

Gale Group
27500 Drake Rd.
Farmington Hills, MI 48331-3535
(800) 877-4253
Internet: http://www.gale.com

Matthew Bender & Co., Inc.
11 Penn Plaza
New York, NY 10001-2006
(800) 223-1940
Internet: http://www.bender.com

Pergamon Press
P.O. Box 945
New York, NY 10159-0945
(212) 633-3730
(888) 437-4636
Fax (212) 633-3680
Internet: http://www.elsevier.nl

Pierian Press
P.O. Box 1808
Ann Arbor, MI 48106
(800) 678-2435
Fax (734) 434-6409

PUBLISHERS

The following companies and organizations publish on the CPSC and related issues through books, periodicals, or electronic media.

Environmental Protection Agency

401 M St. S.W., Washington, DC 20460
Internet: http://www.epa.gov

▪ INTRODUCTION

Established in 1970, the Environmental Protection Agency (EPA) is an independent agency in the executive branch. It is headed by an administrator who is assisted by a deputy and nine assistant administrators, all nominated by the president and confirmed by the Senate.

Responsibilities

In the area of air quality, the EPA:

- Establishes U.S. air quality standards.
- Sets limits on the level of air pollutants emitted from stationary sources such as power plants, municipal incinerators, factories, and chemical plants.
- Establishes emission standards for new motor vehicles.
- Sets allowable levels for toxic substances like lead, benzene, and toluene in gasoline.
- Establishes emission standards for hazardous air pollutants such as beryllium, mercury, and asbestos.
- Supervises states in their development of state implementation plans (SIPs).

In the area of water quality and protection, the EPA:

- Issues permits for the discharge of any pollutant into navigable waters.
- With the Coast Guard, coordinates cleanup of oil and chemical spills into U.S. waterways.
- Develops "effluent guidelines" to control discharge of specific water pollutants, including radiation.
- Develops criteria that enable states to set water quality standards.
- Administers grants program to states to subsidize the cost of building sewage treatment plants.
- Regulates disposal of waste material, including sludge and low-level radioactive discards, into the oceans.

- Cooperates with the Army Corps of Engineers to issue permits for the dredging and filling of wetlands.
- Sets national drinking water standards to ensure that drinking water is safe.
- Regulates underground injection of wastes to protect purity of ground water.

To control the disposal of hazardous waste, the EPA:

- Maintains inventory of existing hazardous waste dump sites.
- Tracks more than 500 hazardous compounds from point of origin to final disposal site.
- Sets standards for generators and transporters of hazardous wastes.
- Issues permits for treatment, storage, and disposal facilities for hazardous wastes.
- Assists states in developing hazardous waste control programs.
- Maintains a multibillion-dollar fund, the "superfund," from industry fees and general tax revenues to provide for emergency cleanup of hazardous dumps when no responsible party can immediately be found.
- Pursues identification of parties responsible for waste sites and eventual reimbursement of the federal government for superfund money spent cleaning up these sites.

To regulate chemicals, including pesticides, and radioactive waste, the EPA:

- Maintains inventory of chemical substances now in commercial use.
- Regulates existing chemicals considered serious hazards to people and the environment, including fluorocarbons, asbestos, and PCBs.
- Issues procedures for the proper safety testing of chemicals and orders them tested when necessary.
- Requires the registration of insecticides, herbicides, or fungicides intended for sale in the United States.
- Requires pesticide manufacturers to provide scientific evidence that their products will not injure humans, livestock, crops, or wildlife when used as directed.
- Classifies pesticides for either general public use or restricted use by certified applicators.
- Sets standards for certification of applicators of restricted-use pesticides. (Individual states may certify applicators through their programs based on the federal standards.)
- Cancels or suspends the registration of a product on the basis of actual or potential unreasonable risk to humans, animals, or the environment.
- Issues a "stop sale, use, and removal" order when a pesticide already in circulation is found to be in violation of the law.
- Requires registration of pesticide-producing establishments.

GLOSSARY

Chlorofluorocarbons (CFCs)—chemical compounds, such as refrigerants, suspected of causing the depletion of the ozone layer in the atmosphere.

Greenhouse effect—the trapping of carbon dioxide and other gases within the atmosphere, leading to global warming and health hazards.

Radon—an odorless and colorless gas produced from the decay of radium 226 in soil and rocks. High levels of radon trapped indoors can pose health hazards.

State implementation plans (SIPs)—Plans created by the states in place of national EPA directives. The EPA oversees the development of such plans, which must be at least as stringent as EPA plans.

Superfund—A multibillion-dollar fund set up in 1980 to provide for emergency cleanup of hazardous sites when no responsible party can be found.

Wetlands—marshes, swamps, or bogs. Many environmentalists see wetlands as providing wildlife habitat and other valuable ecological functions.

- Issues regulations concerning the labeling, storage, and disposal of pesticide containers.
- Issues permits for pesticide research.
- Monitors pesticide levels in the environment.
- Monitors and regulates the levels of radiation in drinking water, oceans, and air.
- Conducts research on toxic substances, pesticides, air and water quality, hazardous wastes, radiation, and the causes and effects of acid rain.
- Provides overall guidance to other federal agencies on radiation protection matters that affect public health.

Powers and Authority

The EPA encourages voluntary compliance by government agencies, private industries, and communities and, as mandated by federal environmental laws, encourages state and local governments to perform direct enforcement activities needed to meet local environmental standards. If state and local agencies fail to produce effective plans for pollution abatement, or if they do not enforce the programs they develop, the EPA is authorized to do so under provisions of major environmental laws.

National enforcement functions are carried out by the EPA where delegation to the states is not practical. For example, the EPA inspects and tests automobiles to ensure compliance with air pollution control standards. The agency also can recall vehicles that fail to meet those standards. The agency maintains a staff of inspectors who spot-check compliance with unleaded gasoline regulations, monitor air and water quality, check radiation levels in the environment, and collect other data to use in enforcing environmental laws.

The Office of Enforcement and Compliance Assurance is responsible for overseeing all of the EPA's enforcement activities. The office gathers and prepares evidence and conducts enforcement proceedings for water quality, stationary and mobile sources of air pollution, radiation, pesticides, solid wastes, toxic substances, hazardous wastes, and noise pollution (see p. 65).

EPA's ten regional counsels review administrative enforcement actions and develop judicial enforcement cases for headquarters' review. In addition they provide regional administrators and regional program managers with legal advice and assistance for all program areas in an attorney-client relationship.

Under the terms of most statutes administered by the agency, the alleged polluter is notified of a violation of EPA standards and ordered to stop. If the violation is not corrected, informal negotiations begin. If the informal meeting fails, the agency has authority to start civil court proceedings to force compliance.

Penalties for violations of environmental laws can be severe. For example, the court can order civil penalties for violations of the Clean Air Act Amendments of up to $25,000 per day for as long as each violation continues and impose a one-year jail sentence.

Without going into federal court the EPA may revoke or suspend licenses and permits for activities regulated by the agency. Under the Toxic Substances Control Act, for example, the EPA may order the seizure of any substances found to be toxic. It also may order the manufacturer of the toxic substances to publicize the violation and issue a notice of possible risk of injury.

The Resource Conservation and Recovery Act mandated a record-keeping system to keep track of the handling and disposal of hazardous wastes. The system was designed specifically to thwart "midnight dumpers," who dump toxic wastes in sewers, woods, fields, or streams under cover of darkness.

The Enforcement Office also has a criminal investigation unit to prosecute persons who willfully discharge wastes into waterways, engage in midnight dumping of toxic substances, and deliberately destroy or falsify vital environmental reports. Willful violators may be subject to imprisonment and be personally liable for fines.

Among the major laws administered by the EPA are those dealing with clean air and water, safe drinking water, pesticides, waste treatment and disposal, control of toxic substances, and the superfund program to deal with release of hazardous substances in spills and abandoned disposal sites.

The statutes take two basic approaches in their civil enforcement provisions: administrative and judicial. Administrative enforcement encompasses a wide range of responses, including informational orders, notices of noncompliance, notices of violation, administrative orders, and administrative penalty complaints. An administrative penalty complaint is a notice sent to a violator informing the recipient that he or she is in violation and that he or she is entitled to an administrative hearing. An administrative law judge presides over the hearing and renders a final decision that may in turn be appealed to the EPA administrator. The administrator's decision may be further appealed to the federal court system and ultimately to the Supreme Court. However, the vast majority of these administrative cases never reach the courts.

The second basic approach to enforcement is judicial action. Here the violator again receives notice that he or she is in violation. If the problem cannot be resolved at this level, the EPA refers the case to the Justice Department for prosecution. The Justice Department reviews the case and then sends it to a U.S. attorney who initiates the case at the federal district court level.

The authority to take enforcement action varies under each statute. The following summarizes the statutory powers granted to the EPA under the major environmental laws and its enforcement powers under those laws.

Background

Since its establishment, the EPA has evolved into one of the largest, as well as most criticized, federal regulatory agencies. Controversy over the agency stemmed partly from its wide-ranging responsibilities, involving the administration of a multitude of complex and costly laws. In most cases of EPA action or inaction to implement those statutes, environmentalists and industry representatives squared off to fight for or against a deadline, a delay, or a new standard. And at times the agency was the target of complaints from both supporters and opponents of the environmental movement. Nonetheless, over time it has succeeded in forcing significant reductions in the levels of pollutants in the environment.

EARLY HISTORY

When the EPA came into being in 1970, it took over the air pollution, water pollution, solid waste, pesticide, and radiation programs scattered around the federal government. Between the EPA's establishment and the early 1980s those programs were broadened and improved, and Congress heaped major new responsibilities on the agency. "Many of EPA's difficulties over the years can be traced to the fact that Congress loaded the agency with far more statutory responsibilities within a brief period of time than perhaps any agency could effectively perform," commented Russell Train in 1982. Train served as EPA administrator from 1973 to 1977.

The EPA was established at a time when the nation was becoming increasingly concerned about declining air and water quality and a general deterioration of the environment. The dramatic blowout of an oil well in the channel off the coast of Santa Barbara, Calif., in January 1969 focused public attention on the seriousness of environmental problems. Miles of beaches were covered with oil, and thousands of fish and wildfowl were killed.

Some months after the Santa Barbara incident, on June 3, President Richard Nixon established by executive order the Cabinet-level Environmental Quality Council (EQC). Congress was not satisfied and in December 1969 it passed the National Environmental Policy Act (NEPA), which made environmental protection a matter of national policy. The act required all federal agencies to submit environmental impact statements for all proposed actions and created the three-member Council on Environmental Quality (CEQ) within the executive office of the president to replace the EQC. Many industry groups denounced NEPA, but conservation organizations such as the Sierra Club hailed it as "an environmental Magna Carta."

During the early days of his administration, Nixon was widely criticized for lacking a strong commitment to environmental protection. As the pressure for corrective action mounted, the president in 1970 submitted to Congress a plan to consolidate the federal government's widespread environmental protection efforts into a single agency. Against little congressional opposition, the EPA was created by executive order. Most existing environmental programs were transferred to the EPA from other government departments. The EPA's first administrator was William D. Ruckelshaus, a vigorous enforcer of water and air quality standards; he infused the EPA with an enthusiasm and sense of mission not unlike that associated with the Peace Corps.

The CEQ continued to exist as an advisory and policy-making body. While the EPA was charged with setting and enforcing pollution control standards, the CEQ focused on broad environmental policies and coordination of the federal government's environmental activities.

Enthusiasm for environmental legislation continued throughout the early 1970s. Congress passed several laws designed to limit or halt the entry of pollutants into the environment, including the Water Quality Improvement Act and the Clean Air Act Amendments, both of 1970, and the Federal Environmental Pesticide Control Act, the Noise Control Act, the Marine Protection, Research and Sanctuaries Act, and the Water Pollution Control Act Amendments, all of 1972. Responsibility for enforcing these laws was given to the EPA.

The energy shortage created by the 1973 Arab oil embargo slowed the rush of environmental programs as legislators sought to balance the benefits of a sometimes costly antipollution program against the need for a stable and productive economy. Opponents of stricter environmental standards argued that the costs of complying with EPA regulations slowed industrial expansion. In some cases companies reportedly closed their doors rather than attempt to meet EPA-imposed standards. Moreover, the environmental movement, which was the impetus behind many of the environmental laws passed by Congress, had lost much of its momentum by the mid-1970s.

Nonetheless, the EPA's responsibilities expanded in certain areas. The Safe Drinking Water Act of 1974 set standards for chemical and bacteriological pollutants in water systems. The Toxic Substances Control Act of 1976 gave the EPA responsibility for studying the risks attached to toxic substances and protecting the public from them. The Resource Conservation and Recovery Act (RCRA) of 1976 was intended to ensure that hazardous and nonhazardous wastes were disposed of in environmentally sound ways. During 1977 clean water standards were redefined and deadlines extended.

Carter's EPA head, Douglas M. Costle, who had served on an advisory council that recommended establishing the agency, focused on dealing with the concerns of industry while continuing to protect the environment. The EPA undertook a review of existing regulations and attempted to streamline its regulatory process and to be more cost conscious in its enforcement procedures.

During Costle's tenure in office, the innovative "bubble" and "offset" methods of getting private industry to comply with air emission standards were introduced. Instead of determining emission standards for every process within a factory, in the first approach, the EPA puts an imaginary bubble over the plant and sets allowable standards for the entire operation. This procedure gives factory managers greater incentive to make changes in basic plant operations rather than just adding pollution control devices.

The second approach is to grant "offsets" in areas where pollution standards are not being met. If a new factory wants to move into an over-polluted area, it must induce existing factories to reduce their pollution levels by more than the amount the new factory will produce. Another variation allows a company having more than one factory in the same area to offset higher-than-standard emissions at one factory by lower-than-standard emissions at another.

SUPERFUND

More responsibilities in the hazardous waste area were given to the EPA with the passage of the controversial

Superfund legislation in the waning days of the 96th Congress. In December 1980 President Jimmy Carter signed the Comprehensive Environmental Response, Compensation and Liability Act of 1980, which established a $1.6 billion emergency fund to clean up toxic contaminants spilled or dumped into the environment. The major part of the Hazardous Substance Response Trust Fund (Superfund)—86 percent—was scheduled to come from the chemical and oil industries; appropriations of general revenue in fiscal years 1981–1985 would provide the remaining 14 percent. The EPA was given responsibility for administering the fund.

Under the Superfund authority, the EPA first notifies responsible parties of their potential liability. If the responsible parties are unwilling to perform appropriate abatement measures, the EPA will either issue an order requiring cleanup (the violation of which subjects the respondent to punitive damages); bring suit to obtain a judicial order requiring cleanup; or tap superfund monies to finance the necessary removal or remedial activities. If the EPA performs the cleanup, the agency will later bring an action against the responsible parties to recover the costs.

Complaints about the way the EPA carried out the Superfund law prompted congressional investigations through the years. Congressional probers found that the EPA was slow in spending money in the fund, preferred to negotiate rather than litigate against dumpers to collect costs, and settled for inadequate cleanups at some sites. The agency also has been criticized for spending more on lawyers than on site cleanup.

THE EPA IN THE 1980S

President Ronald Reagan's first term produced little in the way of new legislation. The RCRA, which had governed "cradle-to-grave" handling of hazardous wastes since its enactment in 1976, was reauthorized at the end of 1984 with stronger controls. But the legislative mandates for other major environmental laws, such as the Clean Water Act, the Clean Air Act, the Safe Drinking Water Act, the Ocean Dumping Act, and laws governing the use of pesticides, expired and were funded only on a year-to-year basis. In general, neither industry-sponsored measures for relaxation of controls nor environmentalists' proposals for tighter regulations made much headway.

Rather than environmental issues, personalities, scandal, and internal problems dominated the agency in the early 1980s. Critics of Reagan's first administrator, Anne M. (Gorsuch) Burford, complained that she circumvented the legislative process by using regulatory decisions and budget cuts to undermine the agency's effectiveness.

In response Burford claimed that she was carrying out her mandate from the president to make the agency more efficient, cost conscious, and a part of the "new federalism"

program. She tried to reduce the agency's budget and to cut funding for many of its programs. But Congress consistently appropriated more money for the EPA than the administration requested.

Of particular concern to environmentalists and their supporters in Congress was the reduction Burford made in the Office of Enforcement and the number of enforcement cases earmarked for court action. She defended the moves, saying violations should be dealt with at the lowest appropriate level wherever possible. And she claimed her enforcement methods, which stressed voluntary compliance, were yielding better results than those of the Carter administration.

The House Energy and Commerce Subcommittee on Oversight and Investigations disagreed. In an October 1982 report the panel criticized the EPA's enforcement program and noted a 69 percent decline between calendar years 1980 and 1981 in the number of civil case referrals from the agency to the Justice Department under the major acts the EPA administered.

In December 1982 the House cited Burford for contempt for refusing—on Reagan's orders—to turn over documents sought by a subcommittee regarding the agency's management of the superfund program. She was the highest executive branch official ever cited for contempt by Congress. But the constitutional issue of executive privilege, Reagan's justification for withholding the documents, was never resolved. In the end, administration and congressional representatives struck a compromise that allowed the committees to examine nearly all the documents they sought. In August 1983 the House dropped the contempt citation.

The political damage to the agency was enormous. The controversy drew widespread publicity to charges that some EPA officials had been lax in enforcing toxic waste laws, made "sweetheart deals" with polluters, stood to profit from conflicts of interest, manipulated toxic cleanup grants to influence elections, shredded papers subpoenaed by Congress, and used political "hit lists" to terminate the appointments of science advisers and career employees who disagreed with the administration's environmental policies. Although none of the charges was prosecuted by the Justice Department, the White House began distancing itself from Burford. She resigned in March 1983.

More than a dozen top EPA aides resigned or were fired during the turmoil of this period. Among them was Rita M. Lavelle, head of the superfund program and the only EPA official to face criminal charges in the scandal. Lavelle was convicted of perjury and obstructing a congressional investigation. In January 1984 she was sentenced to six months in prison and fined $10,000.

With the EPA in disarray, Reagan tapped the EPA's first administrator, William Ruckelshaus, to restore public and congressional confidence in the beleaguered agency.

Ruckelshaus convinced the administration to reverse several years of decline in its operating budget. He also made several significant regulatory decisions.

Under the new administrator's direction, a 91 percent reduction in the lead content of gasoline was initiated. Despite requirements in effect since 1975 that all new cars sold in the United States use unleaded gasoline, leaded fuel accounted for nearly 40 percent of total gasoline sales in 1984. The EPA found that to be disproportionately high given the number of late-model vehicles in operation. It estimated that 16 percent of all cars that should be using lead-free gasoline were using leaded gasoline.

The agency's revised rules on lead were issued March 4, 1985. They required gasoline lead content to be cut from 1.1 grams per gallon to 0.5 grams by July and to 0.1 gram by Jan. 1, 1986.

Another major Ruckelshaus action was the EPA's move against the pesticide ethylene dibromide (EDB), widely used as a fumigant of grains and food products. The agency declared an emergency ban on EDB as a grain fumigant Feb. 4, 1984, and placed interim limits on its content in food still in the pipeline. Later it limited its use on citrus fruits before banning it altogether on Sept. 1, 1984.

But Ruckelshaus was frustrated in his effort to get the administration to take action on acid rain. With studies linking sulfur dioxide emissions from coal-burning power plants in the Midwest to acid rain problems in the northeastern United States and Canada, the issue divided lawmakers along regional lines and became an irritant in U.S.-Canadian relations. Debate over acid rain stalled renewal of the Clean Air Act.

Central to the dispute was the cost of cutting emissions and who would pay. The administration took the coal and utility industry position that not enough scientific evidence had been gathered to justify costly controls and proposed doubling acid rain research funding. The move was announced by President Reagan in his 1984 State of the Union address.

Ruckelshaus left the EPA soon after and was replaced by Lee Thomas, former head of the EPA's toxic waste programs. Under Thomas, the EPA established a major enforcement precedent in May 1985 when it reached an agreement with Westinghouse Corp. that required the company to spend up to $100 million, the largest such settlement to date, to clean up toxic waste sites it used at six locations in Indiana.

But in February 1988 the EPA imposed an even larger fine for environmental damage. Shell Oil Co. and the U.S. Army pledged to spend up to $1 billion to clean up toxic contamination from production of chemical weapons at the Rocky Mountain Arsenal in Denver. The settlement required the parties to clean up the dump site for the debris from two decades of chemical weapons development. The EPA was to supervise the project, with the costs shared between Shell and the army.

In 1986 Congress enacted a major expansion of the superfund program. The bill set strict standards for cleaning up sites and required the EPA to begin work at 375 sites within five years. It stressed the use of permanent cleanup methods, calling for detoxifying wastes whenever possible, instead of burying them in landfills. The measure also required industries to provide local communities with information on what chemicals they handled or dumped, and it gave victims of toxic dumping a longer opportunity to sue those responsible.

After the low environmental focus of the Reagan administration, environmental issues again moved to the front burner of national concerns when George Bush moved into the White House. Bush promised during his campaign that he would be "the environmental president," and he pleased many environmentalists by appointing William Reilly as administrator of the EPA. Reilly was the first professional environmentalist to hold the post; he had been head of an important mainstream environmental group, the U.S. branch of the Swiss-based World Wildlife Fund. Reilly had gained attention by promoting the use of economic incentives as a way to break the logjam between industry and environmental activists over the cost of pollution controls. Instead of mandating what each utility should do to curb pollution, Reilly advocated the trading of "pollution credits" between polluters who cleaned up and those who could not or who needed to expand plants that might add pollution.

This formula might allow Utility A, which spent $5 million to install new smoke-cleaning equipment, to gain a credit that could be swapped with Utility B 100 miles away, which needed a credit to avoid penalties imposed by the EPA. This market-based approach, he argued, would help finance cleanup efforts and provide incentives lacking in the usual environmental government-by-directive regulations.

In 1989 the EPA released a report claiming that indoor pollution, especially exposure to radon gas, posed one of the greatest environmental risks to Americans. Indoor pollutants were thought to cause more than 14,000 deaths annually.

Also in 1989, Reilly's activist approach gained impetus from an environmental disaster that alarmed the nation. The *Exxon Valdez*, running aground at Valdez, Alaska, spilled more than 11 million gallons of crude oil, spreading a slick over hundreds of miles of pristine coastline. This oil spill, the worst in the nation's history, set the tone for debate in Congress over major environmental legislation, much like the earlier Santa Barbara Channel incident.

Although the captain of the *Valdez* was convicted for the negligent discharge of oil, it was Exxon, target of lawsuits totaling billions of dollars in damages, that was put on trial by the public. Despite spending some $2 billion and enlisting thousands of Alaskans in an effort to clean up the mess, Exxon was portrayed as an environmental villain. A poll taken in the wake of the *Exxon Valdez* spill found renewed interest in environmental issues. More than 70 percent of Americans considered themselves environmentalists.

In October 1991 Exxon agreed, as part of an out-of-court settlement, to pay the government more than $1 billion in fines and damages. The bulk of the money—$900 million—was set aside over a ten-year period to pay civil claims brought as a result of the damage. Additionally, on Sept. 16, 1994, a federal court ordered Exxon to pay a record $5 billion in punitive damages to 34,000 Alaskan residents affected by the spill. Exxon has appealed the damage award.

THE EPA IN THE 1990S

The Alaska disaster set the stage for the Bush administration to rewrite the nation's major pollution law, the Clean Air Act, which had last been revised in 1977. Signed on Nov. 15, 1990, the overhaul of the act was designed to markedly improve air quality by the end of the century and became the most significant environmental achievement of the Bush administration.

The act imposed new standards for smog-producing emissions: reducing nitrogen oxides by 60 percent and hydrocarbons by 40 percent by 1994. Further reductions in these emissions would be required in 2003 unless the EPA determined that they were not technologically possible. In addition, cars had to be built to meet the new emissions standards for ten years or 100,000 miles by 1996.

In provisions to reduce sulfur dioxide and nitrogen oxide emissions from utilities that cause acid rain, the act established five classes of nonattainment for smog problems in each metropolitan area ranging from marginal to extreme. The timetable for cleanup—which would involve refitting many industries with pollution control devices—depended on the severity of the problem. Areas with marginal smog problems had only three years to achieve attainment, while extreme areas would be granted twenty years to reduce smog to acceptable levels. All but marginal areas would be required to reduce nonautomotive smog by 15 percent annually for the first six years and 3 percent for each year after that.

The act also sought by 2000 to phase out U.S. production of chlorofluorocarbons and methyl chloroform, two chemicals widely used as refrigerants and in electronics. These chemicals are blamed for the depletion of the ozone shield in the upper atmosphere, which allows more dangerous ultraviolet rays from the sun to penetrate, raising the risk of cancers.

The global focus on the environment reached its apex in May 1992, when representatives of more than 150 countries met in Rio de Janeiro, Brazil, to discuss environmental issues. The conference hit a snag when the Bush administration balked at international caps on the emission of carbon dioxide and other gases causing the greenhouse effect, which in turn is believed by many scientists to lead to global warming and health hazards. The European Community and Japan had already agreed to limit greenhouse gases to their 1990 level by the year 2000.

American negotiators argued that the United States was already doing its part to combat global warming. They pointed out that the country had already banned some greenhouse gases, namely chlorofluorocarbons, and had initiated a program to plant one billion trees. In the end, a treaty limiting greenhouse gas emissions to 1990 levels was passed. But at U.S. insistence, no timetables were set.

The conference passed a second treaty requiring a full inventory of all of the world's plants and animals and the development of a strategy for preserving biodiversity.

But the United States refused to sign the so-called Biodiversity Treaty, arguing that it would ultimately impose limitations on the pharmaceutical and biotechnology industries. But the U.S. position on the treaty changed with administrations and President Bill Clinton signed the pact in 1993.

Clinton chose Carol M. Browner to be EPA administrator in 1993. Browner served as Al Gore's Senate legislative director from 1990 to 1991. She became secretary of the Florida Department of Environmental Regulation, where she built a reputation as a tough environmentalist with a commensurate understanding of business concerns.

Browner's first major challenge as administrator was to help negotiate and sell an environmental side agreement for the North American Free Trade Agreement (NAFTA) among the United States, Canada, and Mexico.

NAFTA negotiations were completed in the last year of the Bush administration. The treaty largely eliminated tariffs and other trade barriers among the three countries. During the 1992 campaign, Clinton had been in favor of NAFTA but had conditioned his support on the negotiation of additional side agreements aimed at strengthening treaty provisions on the environment, labor laws, and other areas.

Environmental groups had worried that NAFTA would allow Mexico to successfully challenge tough U.S. state and local environmental laws as trade barriers. They also feared that provisions of the treaty requiring the three countries to work toward common environmental standards would lead to weakening of laws, since Mexico's standards were much lower than those of its northern neighbors. The final agreement did not require harmonization of laws. Instead, the countries were encouraged to adopt the highest standard.

The agreement also established a Commission for Environmental Cooperation, responsible for monitoring environmental laws. Initially, the administration had proposed allowing the commission to impose trade sanctions against any country that failed to enforce its own environmental laws. But this was dropped in favor of fines or other sanctions that could be levied only after a long and drawn-out process. In addition, the commission had no authority to compel any government to pay a fine.

Browner also put her philosophy to work in programs that favored broad goals, not prescriptive solutions. Browner's marquee program was Project XL, which required companies to meet standards but gave them flexibility to do so. In June 1996 Browner announced administrative changes to the Superfund program to free some small businesses and municipalities from the program's costly web of litigation by no longer making them responsible for cleanup costs. The Clinton administration ostensibly reflected an approach to environmental protection that favored consensus over confrontation.

But despite Browner's background and new regulatory approaches, the Clinton administration still found itself early on the target of a backlash toward what many perceived as overly restrictive rules and regulations. During the Democratically controlled 103rd Congress, Republicans and some conservative Democrats lambasted the EPA for offering programs they considered only a token response to the call for more leeway in environmental laws.

A bill to elevate the EPA to cabinet-level status died after being caught up in a larger movement to curb regulations by requiring EPA and other agencies to weigh the costs and benefits of new rules. Clinton continued to allow Browner to sit in on Cabinet meetings, underlining the importance of the agency and its administrator.

Ironically, it was the Republican-controlled 104th Congress that resurrected the environment as a vibrant issue and trained President Clinton's attention on it. The ground began to shift in the spring and summer of 1995 when the GOP attempted to push through a rewrite of the Clean Water Act and endorsed environment-related legislative provisions in appropriation bills. Both moves were roundly criticized as regulatory rollbacks, and Republicans faced harsh criticism. Clinton seized the opening, exploiting the Republican's credibility gap to paint the Republican Congress as "extremists" and positioning himself as the chief protector of the environment.

By August 1996 the political ground had shifted sharply as Congress, hoping to shore up its environmental image, sent Clinton a sweeping bipartisan rewrite of the federal drinking water law. The drinking water act gave more flexibility to regulators in revising health standards, created a grant and loan fund to pay for water system improvements, and required that drinking water suppliers inform customers of contaminants. The contamination of drinking water in the United States was more widespread than

was commonly believed. According to the EPA, there were more than 700 harmful contaminants in drinking water. Long-term exposure to some of these chemicals can lead to problems such as birth defects. The 1996 act was seen as an important step in improving the nation's drinking water quality.

President Clinton also signed in 1996 an overhaul of pesticide regulations. The Food Quality Protection Act sought to protect people from dangerous levels of cancer-causing pesticides in food. At the same time, the act allowed some chemical residues in food, enabling farmers to continue to use certain pesticides. In addition, provisions sought to safeguard the health of infants and children, restrict the ability of states to pass laws stricter than federal regulations, and educate the public about the risks and benefits of agricultural chemicals.

At the end of 1996, the EPA proposed stringent new clear air standards. The regulations, the most significant rewrite of the Clean Air Act since the 1970s, tightened an existing rule for ozone, the main component of smog. In addition, the act created a new standard for airborne particles of soot produced by sources such as diesel engines and power plants fueled by coal.

The proposed regulations produced a firestorm of criticism, especially from the business community. Industries, including utilities and automobile manufacturers, argued that the new rules would cost millions of dollars to implement and produce no appreciable environmental benefit. These and other critics lobbied the Clinton administration to eliminate or at least significantly soften the EPA's clean air plan. But in July 1997, environmentalists scored a huge victory, when the president announced that he would support the agency's new rules.

The announcement outraged many Republicans and some Democrats on Capitol Hill. But an effort to reverse the regulations legislatively stalled after supporters of the bill realized that they could not muster the two-thirds majority needed in both houses to override a promised presidential veto.

The administration also angered many on Capitol Hill near the end of 1997 with its performance at a conference held in Kyoto, Japan, that addressed the issue of global warming. After being accused by environmentalists and others of inflexibility and foot-dragging, the administration agreed to deep cuts in greenhouse gases, produced largely through the burning of oil and coal. Under what became known as the Kyoto protocol, the United States agreed to cut national greenhouse emissions to 7 percent below 1990 levels during the following fifteen years.

Many Republicans and some Democrats in Congress, joined by business groups, criticized the need for the Kyoto agreement, especially one so far-reaching. They argued that global warming was a theory that had yet to be proven. In addition, they said, the treaty would cost businesses billions and leave millions of U.S. workers jobless.

While President Clinton signed the treaty in November 1998, intense opposition to it in Congress forced him to delay sending it to the Senate for ratification. Soon after, the administration realized that any attempt at ratification would have to wait until after the 2000 elections, producing more charges of foot-dragging from the Europeans and others.

Meanwhile, efforts to come up with compromises on how to implement various parts of the accord deadlocked at a United Nations conference in November 2000. The United States, backed by Japan, Canada, and Australia, proposed a system by which it could offset a failure to meet reduced air pollution targets by "buying" emission credits from countries that were polluting less than their quota allowed. But delegates from the European Union accused the United States—which produces a quarter of the world's carbon emissions—of trying to buy its way out of its obligations, instead of changing its wasteful ways.

In 1998 EPA began its review of potentially dangerous pesticides, as required by the 1996 Food Quality Protection Act. The action set off a battle between chemical producers and farmers on one hand and environmentalists and public health advocates on the other. Still, by 1999 the agency had begun to take action, banning most applications of methal parathion and increasing restrictions on azinphos methyl. Both substances are popular organophosphates, which kill insects by disrupting their nervous systems. They have also been shown to cause illness in farm workers and others. The EPA was particularly concerned that the two pesticides might cause neurological disorders in small children. The following year, the agency banned chlorpyrifos (used in insecticides and flee collars) and reached a voluntary agreement with the chemical company Syngenta to phase out home and garden use of diazinon, a very common organophosphate used to control roaches and other pests.

THE EPA IN THE 2000S

In the last few years, the agency also has come under fire for its role in encouraging the use of methyl tertiary butyl ether (MTBE), a gasoline additive that makes fuel burn cleaner by reducing the amount of carcinogens cars emit. The EPA touted MTBE as a way for states with high levels of air pollution to meet tougher air quality standards under the Clean Air Act Amendments of 1990. But while the substance did help improve air quality, it also leaked from underground storage tanks, contaminating water supplies everywhere.

In March 2000 the EPA called for a prohibition on the use of MTBE and urged oil companies to use the more expensive ethanol instead. Ethanol, derived from corn, is another petroleum additive that some believe makes gasoline burn cleaner. The agency was criticized, however, for its decision regarding ethanol. Some environmentalists charged that the substance was not an appropriate substitute because it actually boosted emissions of some smog-forming chemicals.

As it grappled with the fuel additive issue, the agency also proposed new regulations aimed at reducing emissions from trucks and buses that burn diesel fuel, which causes a disproportionate amount of air pollution. The new regulations, which were proposed in May 2000, called for removing 97 percent of the sulfur found in diesel fuel. Along with other steps, EPA aimed to reduce pollution caused by diesel emissions by 90 percent over the next decade.

The agency's efforts to clean up the nation's air received a boost from the Supreme Court in the winter of 2001. In late February, the Court ruled that, when setting new clean air standards, the EPA did not have to consider their potential economic impact on industry. Although U.S. businesses had claimed that new regulations on ozone and soot would cost untold billions of dollars in unnecessary expense, the Court ruled that the agency only had to weigh public health considerations when deciding on acceptable levels of pollution.

The 2000 presidential election created a dramatically new situation for the EPA. The traditionally more environment-friendly Democrats were no longer in charge of the executive branch. In addition, the agency lost its biggest champion with the defeat of presidential candidate Gore, a longtime environmentalist. In his place were a new president and vice president who had spent part of their professional lives in the oil industry. Moreover, during the campaign, the Republican presidential nominee, Gov. George W. Bush of Texas, had alarmed environmentalists by advocating oil drilling in Alaska's Arctic National Wildlife Refuge.

On the other hand, most EPA boosters were satisfied with Bush's pick to run the agency—Gov. Christine Todd Whitman of New Jersey. Whitman, a moderate Republican, did not have her predecessor's direct experience in environmental policy. Still she had a reputation as a good manager and a familiarity with some environmental concerns—such as superfund cleanup and coastal management issues—from her six-year tenure as the governor of a highly industrial state.

At her confirmation hearing in January 2001, Whitman signaled a new direction for the agency by promising to emphasize market-based solutions to problems. Moreover she indicated that in the future, the EPA would more thoroughly consider the economic impact of a policy before proposing new regulations. These remarks worried environmentalists, who wondered whether the EPA would "cooperate" with polluters more than other interests. But Whitman tried to assuage their concerns by promising that the EPA would become more open to cooperating with all sides in the environmental debate, including business, environmental advocacy groups, and state governments. In addition, she said, the agency would be more "flexible" in trying to come up with solutions.

But if Whitman had hoped for a honeymoon period with environmentalists while she settled in, the administration's early moves on the environment guaranteed that the new secretary would have to start her term fighting. The battle began on the day Bush took office, when he put a hold on 175 new environmental regulations promulgated by Clinton in the waning days of his administration. Among these were new rules lowering the allowable levels of arsenic in drinking water. Putting the new arsenic regulations on hold set off a furor among Democrats and earned the new president some of his first bad press.

In the months immediately following, Bush further enraged environmentalists by announcing that he would not submit the Kyoto protocol to the Senate for consideration. The protocol negotiated by the Clinton administration was unlikely to win Senate approval anyway, because of the enormous cost to business and others associated with reducing carbon emissions. Indeed, after signing Kyoto Clinton did little to push for its ratification. But Bush's action incensed environmentalists around the globe, who said that such a stark repudiation by the world's top economy and largest producer of greenhouse gases would seriously dilute the efforts of other countries that had signed the treaty.

Bush countered that Kyoto would cost the American economy a total of $400 billion and 4.9 million jobs—too high a price to pay for a treaty that would only slow the rate of increase of greenhouse gas emissions. Instead, the president promised to come up with a new plan to limit greenhouse gases that would not damage the economy.

After these first rocky months, the administration made more of an effort to shore up its green credentials, beginning by reinstating the arsenic rules. It also unveiled a number of large and small policy proposals in key environmental areas.

The most significant of these new proposals, the Clear Skies Initiative, was announced on Feb. 13, 2002. Clear Skies would amend the Clean Air act to cut power plant emissions of sulfur dioxide, nitrogen oxide, and mercury—pollutants that contribute to smog and acid rain—by 70 percent. This would be accomplished through a market-based system that would allow utilities to buy and sell pollution credits. In other words, those firms with emissions below proscribed levels would be able to sell the difference to utilities with power plants that were exceeding the limits.

Clear Skies also called for Green House emissions to be reduced by 18 percent over the next ten years through the development of new, cleaner-burning technologies. Bush hoped that these cleaner technologies—zero-emission fuel cells for cars and power plants—would be able to bring carbon dioxide levels down without damaging the American economy. "In the next decade alone, Clear Skies will eliminate 35 million more tons of pollution than the current Clean Air Act, bringing cleaner air to millions of Americans," Bush said on July 29, the day the initiative was presented in legislative form to Congress.

But environmentalists argued that Clear Skies would allow polluters to avoid cleaning up dirty plants by using bookkeeping tricks. Only mandated pollution reductions, such as those already in the Clean Air Act, would improve air quality, they said.

Meanwhile, the EPA was taking action in another major environmental sphere: water. In July 2001 the agency announced that it was delaying the implementation of major new clean water rules that would have required states to come up with plans to protect and clean up some 21,000 streams, rivers, and lakes that had already been declared "impaired" by the EPA. A year later, the agency gave the first indications of how it was going to change the rules, saying that states would be given more flexibility in how they clean up waterways. Efforts would be made to encourage voluntary compliance. The agency also said it was considering a market-based system that would allow polluters to buy and sell credits, similar to the one proposed in the president's Clear Skies Initiative.

The rules, originally drafted during the Clinton administration, had come under heavy fire from states, farm groups, and many members of Congress, who worried that they would impose high costs on local governments and the agricultural industry. Environmental groups countered that the administration was using the strong objections from these groups as an opportunity to weaken the rules so as to make them ineffective.

Environmentalists also were angered by a delay of other Clinton-era clean water rules—requiring small construction sites to develop plans for storm water runoff. In March 2002 the EPA announced that the rules, which were just coming into force, would not apply to oil and gas companies for at least another two years. Energy companies had argued that the new regulations should not apply to them because, unlike other kinds of construction, oil and gas drilling was usually set up quickly. The EPA said that it would study the issue during the two-year exemption and then decide what to do. But environmentalists and their allies argued that the exemption was a payoff to the Bush administration's many allies in the oil and gas industry.

On the other hand, the EPA surprised environmentalists in August 2001 when it ordered General Electric to pay $500 million to clean up toxic materials it had dumped into the Hudson River. The agency order came even as the company and business groups lobbied the administration, saying that the dredging required to clean the river floor would do more harm than good.

Environmentalists also lauded Whitman's statement that the nation's water infrastructure—including pipes and water treatment facilities—was aging and that $535 billion above the current spending levels would be needed over the next twenty years to ensure that drinking water was safe and rivers and lakes were not further soiled.

Current Issues

Congress will likely take up the president's Clear Skies Initiative in 2003. Republicans in both houses have conceded that they will probably have to compromise with Democrats and environmental groups to push the proposal through Congress. Still, Bush was encouraged by the creation early in 2003 of a voluntary carbon emissions trading program in Chicago involving many of America's largest companies. The firms have pledged to reduce emissions by 4 percent over the next four years by allowing those businesses that exceed that goal to sell their excess reductions to those companies that have lagged behind.

Meanwhile some environmentalists have been heartened by a number of actions by the Bush administration in 2003, including a proposal to increase the fuel efficiency standards for Sports Utility Vehicles, pick-ups, and minivans by 1.5 miles over three years. Light trucks, which now make up more than half of all U.S. car sales, have long been derided as gas-guzzlers. While some environmental groups have criticized the proposal as a token gesture, others have seen it as a step in the right direction. The move was closely followed by an announcement, in Bush's 2003 State of the Union Address, that the federal government would spend $1.2 billion in coming years to help the American auto industry develop clean-burning fuel cells.

The agency also pleased environmentalists with its announcement that it would thoroughly review cleanup efforts, past, present, and future, at many of the nation's 1,500 superfund sites because of recent research showing that one contaminant, trichloroethylene, is more toxic than previously thought. The substance, used as a solvent to clean electronic parts, may be between five and sixty-five times more toxic for pregnant women than originally estimated.

Many observers said that the recent proposals and actions were evidence that the administration wanted to burnish its environmental credentials ahead of the 2004 election. Indeed, polling showed that among crucial suburban swing voters, especially women, the environment was an important issue. In spite of recent efforts, environmentalists still gave the EPA poor marks and expressed their intention to fight "Clear Skies" in Congress.

In May 2003 EPA chief Whitman announced she would leave her post in June to spend more time with her family. Some EPA watchers had been hinting of such a departure for a while, suggesting that Whitman—a GOP moderate—was unhappy over the administration's antienvironment positions. Arguing to the contrary, Whitman had long said that administration and EPA proposals have not been antienvironment, but more open to new solutions. The proof, she said, will be whether they are effective, whether the nation's air and water become cleaner in coming years.

The White House did not indicate an immediate replacement for Whitman. Word shortly leaked out, however, of a few of those under consideration by President Bush, including former Michigan governor John Engler; David B. Struhs, secretary of the Florida Department of Environmental Protection; and Josephine Cooper, chief operating officer of the Alliance of Automobile Manufacturers, a trade association of car and light truck manufacturers. One thing is certain: the nominee can expect a close scrutiny by environmental groups.

■ AGENCY ORGANIZATION

Headquarters and Divisions

OFFICE OF THE ADMINISTRATOR

The administrator is responsible to the president for overall supervision of the agency.

Administrator
Vacant................................... (202) 564–4700
Fax...................................... (202) 501–1450
Deputy Administrator
Linda J. Fisher .... (202) 564–4711
Fax...................................... (202) 501–1450
Chief of Staff
Eileen McGinnis....................... (202) 564–6999
Fax...................................... (202) 501–1450

Office of Administrative Law Judges

The administrative law judges conduct formal administrative hearings.

Chief Administrative Law Judge
Susan L. Biro........................... (202) 564–6255
Fax...................................... (202) 565–0044

Office of Civil Rights

Implements and monitors the agency's equal employment opportunity program and processes discrimination complaints. Monitors general contractors who have received EPA grants for compliance with various sections of the civil rights acts.

Director
Ann E. Goode .... (202) 564–7272
Fax...................................... (202) 501–1836

ENVIRONMENTAL PROTECTION AGENCY

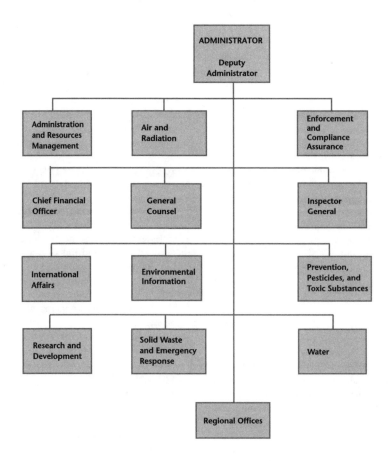

Office of Small and Disadvantaged Business Utilization

Assists small, minority-owned and women-owned businesses in applying for EPA grants and contracts.

Director

Jeanette L. Brown .... (202) 564–4100

Fax .... (202) 501–0756

Science Advisory Board

Advises the administrator on scientific and technical issues pertaining to the environment.

Director

Donald G. Barnes .... (202) 564–4533

Fax .... (202) 501–0323

Office of Cooperative Environmental Management

Provides the administrator with technical assistance and focused information dissemination on issues concerning technology transfer.

Director

Gordon Schisler (acting) .... (202) 233–0090

Fax .... (202) 501–0661

Office of Executive Support

Provides the administrator and deputy administrator, their staffs, and other agency offices with administrative, financial management, automatic data processing, and budget support.

Director

    Diane N. Bazzle .... (202) 564–0444

    Fax .... (202) 564–2744

Executive Secretariat

Manages executive correspondence for the Office of the Administrator. Also handles the EPA's freedom of information activities. (See Information Sources.)

Director

    William H. Meagher III .... (202) 564–7311

    Fax .... (202) 501–1818

Environmental Appeals Board

The final EPA body responsible for appeals under all major EPA administrative statutes. Duties include adjudicating appeals in the implementation and enforcement of environmental regulations. The three-member board's caseload consists primarily of permit and civil penalty decisions and Superfund cases.

Environmental Appeals Judges

    Fax .... (202) 501–7580

    Kathie A. Stein .... (202) 233–0122

    Scott C. Fulton .... (202) 233–0122

    Ronald L. McCallum .... (202) 233–0122

    Edward E. Reich .... (202) 233–0122

Office of Children's Health Protection

In May 1997 the Office of Children's Health Protection was established to address environmental threats to children's health. This action was in response to Executive Order 12606 to Protect Children from Environmental Health and Safety Risks.

Director

    E. Ramona Trovato .... (202) 564–6665

    Fax .... (202) 564–2733

Coordinator, Regulatory Affairs Team

    Vacant .... (202) 564–2188

    Fax .... (202) 564–2733

Office of Regional Operations

Serves as the primary communications link between the EPA administrator and the regional administrators.

Director

    Judy Kertcher (acting) .... (202) 564–3103

    Fax .... (202) 501–0062

ASSOCIATE ADMINISTRATOR FOR PUBLIC AFFAIRS

Implements the Environmental Education Program. Provides policy direction for the agency in the areas of public information and press services. Provides information to the media and the public and publishes the *EPA Journal.*

Associate Administrator

    Joseph Martyak .... (202) 564–9828

    Fax .... (202) 501–1474

Communications

    Vacant .... (202) 564–4455

    Fax .... (202) 501–1747

Environmental Education

    C. Michael Baker (acting) .... (202) 564–0443

    Fax .... (202) 564–2754

Media Relations

    Lisa Harrison .... (202) 564–1490

    Fax .... (202) 501–1789

ASSOCIATE ADMINISTRATOR FOR CONGRESSIONAL AND INTERGOVERNMENTAL RELATIONS

The principal adviser to the administrator for communications and public affairs with respect to congressional activities and the main point of congressional contact with the agency. Develops and drafts legislative initiatives for the EPA. Prepares EPA testimony before congressional committees; prepares reports and recommendations on pending and enacted legislation; and represents the agency in legislative dealings with Congress, other departments and agencies.

Associate Administrator

    Edward D. Krenik .... (202) 564–5200

    Fax .... (202) 501–1519

Congressional Affairs

    John E. Reeder .... (202) 564–3699

    Fax .... (202) 501–1545

State and Local Relations

Senior Policy Advisor

    Michelle Hiller .... (202) 564–3702

    Fax .... (202) 501–1545

Information and Management Division

Coordinates responses to congressional mail, maintains the EPA's legislative library, notifies members of Congress of EPA grants and awards, and edits congressional transcripts.

Director

    Julie Tate (acting) .... (202) 564–2022

    Fax .... (202) 501–1519

ASSOCIATE ADMINISTRATOR FOR POLICY, ECONOMICS, AND INNOVATION

The principal adviser to the administrator for environmental policy and innovation, environmental economics, and business and community innovation.

Associate Administrator

    Jessica Furey .... (202) 564–4715

    Fax .... (202) 501–1688

National Center for Environmental Economics

Albert M. McGarland................. (202) 566–3354

Business and Community Innovation

Alexander Cristofaro................... (202) 564–7253

Environmental Policy and Innovation

Elizabeth Shaw .... (202) 566–0495

ASSISTANT ADMINISTRATOR FOR ADMINISTRATION AND RESOURCES MANAGEMENT

Has primary responsibility for policy and procedures governing resources management, environmental health and safety, administration, organization and management analyses and systems development, facilities management, information management, automated data processing systems, procurement through contracts and grants, and human resource management. Also serves as liaison to the Office of Management and Budget and other federal agencies involved in the conduct of budget and administrative activities.

Assistant Administrator

Vacant................................. (202) 564–4600

Fax..................................... (202) 564–0233

Policy and Resources Management

David E. Osterman (acting) .... (202) 564–6778

Director (Cincinnati, OH)

William Henderson .... (513) 569–7910

Fax..................................... (513) 569–7903

Director (Research Triangle Park, NC)

William Laxton........................ (513) 569–7910

Fax..................................... (919) 541–3552

Office of Administration

Responsible for personnel programs and procedures. Oversees property and space management, personal and property security, and occupational health and safety programs. Also develops procurement procedures, such as grants, contracts, and interagency agreements. North Carolina office also handles certain agencywide services for automated data processing.

Director

Rich Lemley .... (202) 564–8400

Fax..................................... (202) 564–8408

Facilities Management and Services

Renee Page (acting) .... (202) 564–2030

Safety, Health, and Environmental Management

Dennis Bushta........................ (202) 564–1640

Office of Acquisition Management

Responsible for the policies, procedures, operations, and support of the EPA's procurement and contracts management program, from contract planning through closeout.

Director

Vacant................................. (202) 564–4310

Fax..................................... (202) 565–2473

Office of Grants and Debarment

Responsible for EPA's grants and other forms of assistance programs, including cooperative agreements.

Director

Howard Corcoran..................... (202) 564–1903

Fax..................................... (202) 565–2469

Office of Human Resources and Organizational Services

Oversees human resources, information management and systems, labor and employee relations, organization and management consulting services, planning and budgeting, and strategic planning and policy systems.

Director

Daiva A. Balkus....................... (202) 233–0066

Fax..................................... (202) 564–4613

ASSISTANT ADMINISTRATOR FOR ENFORCEMENT AND COMPLIANCE ASSURANCE

Serves as the EPA's national program manager and principal adviser to the administrator for matters concerning national crime enforcement, forensics, and training program. OCEA also manages the agency's regulatory, site remediation, and federal facilities enforcement and compliance assurance programs, as well as the agency's environmental justice program responsibilities.

Assistant Administrator

Vacant................................. (202) 564–2440

Fax..................................... (202) 501–3842

Administration and Resource Management

Teresa Gauger (acting) .... (202) 564–0204

Compliance

Michael M. Stahl (acting)............. (202) 564–2280

Criminal Enforcement, Forensics, and Training

Letterio (Leo) D'Amico............... (202) 564–2480

Enforcement Capacity and Outreach

Peter D. Rosenberg (acting) .... (202) 564–2611

Environmental Justice

Barry Hill .... (202) 564–2515

Federal Activities

Anne N. Miller (acting)............... (202) 564–7127

Federal Facilities Enforcement

Craig E. Hooks .... (202) 566–6372

Planning and Policy Analysis

Mary K. Lynch (acting) .... (202) 564–2574

Regulatory Enforcement

Eric V. Schaeffer...................... (202) 564–2220

Site Remediation Enforcement

Barry N. Breen .... (202) 566–0200

OFFICE OF THE GENERAL COUNSEL

Provides legal support for all programs and activities of the agency, including legal opinions, counsel, and litigation support; and assists as legal adviser in the formulation and administration of the agency's policies and programs.

General Counsel
Robert Fabricant .... (202) 564–8040
Fax .... (202) 564–1788
Air and Radiation
Lisa Friedman .... (202) 564–5501
Civil Rights Law Office
Vacant .... (202) 564–4606
Cross-Cutting Issues
James C. Nelson .... (202) 564–5532
Finance and Operations
Marla E. Diamond .... (202) 564–5323
International Environmental Law
Vacant .... (202) 564–1810
Pesticides and Toxic Substances
Patricia A. Roberts .... (202) 564–5375
Solid Waste and Emergency Response
Earl Salo (acting) .... (202) 564–5504
Water
Susan G. Lepow .... (202) 564–5472

ASSISTANT ADMINISTRATOR FOR ENVIRONMENTAL INFORMATION

OEI advances the creation, management, and use of data as a strategic resource to enhance public health and environmental protection, inform decision making, and improve public access to information about environmental conditions.

Assistant Administrator
Kim T. Nelson .... (202) 564–6665
Fax .... (202) 501–1622
Planning, Resources, and Outreach
Margaret Mitchell .... (202) 566–0959
Quality Staff
Nancy Wentworth .... (202) 564–6830

Office of Information Analysis and Access

Oversees environmental analysis, information access, and the Toxic Release Inventory Program.

Director
Elaine G. Stanley .... (202) 566–0600
Fax .... (202) 401–2727
Environmental Analysis
Steven E. Young .... (202) 566–0608
Fax .... (202) 401–0906
Information Access
Emma J. McNamara .... (202) 566–0707
Fax .... (202) 401–1617

Toxic Release Inventory Program
Maria J. Doa .... (202) 566–0718
Fax .... (202) 401–0237

Office of Information Collection

Plans and coordinates collection services and strategies.

Director
Mark A. Luttner .... (202) 566–1630
Fax .... (202) 401–4544
Collection Services
Joseph D. Retzer .... (202) 566–1685
Collection Strategies
Oscar Morales .... (202) 566–1641

Office of Technology Operations and Planning

Oversees technology operations and planning.

Director
Mark E. Day .... (202) 566–0300
Fax .... (202) 401–4542
Headquarters and Desktop Services
Myra J. Galbreath .... (202) 566–1010
National Technology Services
Richard A. Martin .... (919) 541–2838

ASSISTANT ADMINISTRATOR FOR INTERNATIONAL ACTIVITIES

Coordinates the EPA's international activities and assists the administrator in determining policies and programs conducted by the EPA overseas.

Assistant Administrator
Judith Ayres .... (202) 564–6600
Fax .... (202) 565–2407
International Environmental Policy
Paul F. Cough .... (202) 564–6459
Technology Cooperation and Assistance
Martin Dieu (acting) .... (202) 564–6442
Management Operations
Kathy Petruccelli .... (202) 564–4672
Western Hemisphere and Bilateral Affairs
Joan Fidler .... (202) 564–6611

OFFICE OF THE INSPECTOR GENERAL

Conducts and supervises audits and investigations of EPA programs and operations. Reviews existing and proposed legislation and regulations to promote effectiveness and prevent fraud or abuse in agency programs. Reports semiannually to the EPA administrator and Congress.

Inspector General
Nikki L. Tinsley .... (202) 566–0847
Fax .... (202) 260–0711
Audit
Melissa Heist .... (202) 260–4942

Counsel

Mark Bialek............................. (202) 566–0861

Human Capital

Gary L. Johnson (acting) .... (202) 566–0848

Investigations

Emmett D. Dashiell (acting)........... (202) 564–2480

Mission Systems

John C. Jones.......................... (202) 260–3137

Planning, Analysis, and Results

Elissa Karpf............................ (202) 260–3486

Program Evaluation

Kwai-Cheung Chan .... (202) 566–0827

ASSISTANT ADMINISTRATOR FOR RESEARCH AND DEVELOPMENT

Performs research and development to identify, understand, and solve current and future environmental problems. Provides responsive technical support to EPA's mission. Provides leadership in addressing emerging environmental issues and in advancing the science and technology of risk assessment and risk management

Assistant Administrator

Paul Gilman .... (202) 564–6620

Fax.................................... (202) 565–2430

National Center for Environmental Assessment

Serves as a resource center for the overall process of risk assessment. Operates branches in Cincinnati, OH; Research Triangle Park, NC; and Washington, DC.

Director

William H. Farland..................... (202) 564–6620

Fax.................................... (202) 565–0090

National Center for Environmental Research

Promotes the highest possible quality scientific research by the EPA. Operates the Science to Achieve Results (STAR) program, which seeks to focus the work of leading research scientists from universities and nonprofit centers to meet specific science needs of the agency. Offers grants and graduate fellowships.

Director

Peter W. Preuss........................ (202) 564–6825

Fax.................................... (202) 565–2444

National Exposure Research Laboratory

Conducts human and ecosystem exposure assessments. Headquartered in Research Triangle Park, NC; divisions listed below.

Director

Gary J. Foley........................... (919) 541–2106

Fax.................................... (919) 541–0445

Human Exposure and Atmospheric Sciences

Larry T. Cupitt......................... (919) 541–0349

Atmospheric Modeling

Frank A. Schiermeier................... (919) 541–4542

Environmental Sciences (Las Vegas, NV)

John G. Lyon........................... (702) 798–2525

Ecological Exposure (Cincinnati, OH)

M. Kate Smith......................... (513) 569–7577

Ecosystems Research (Athens, GA)

Rosemarie C. Russo.................... (706) 355–8001

Microbiological and Chemical Exposure Assessment Research (Cincinnati, OH)

Alfred P. DuFour .... (513) 569–7303

National Health and Environmental Effects Research Laboratory

Performs laboratory and field research on health and ecological effects of exposures to man-made stressors, particularly under conditions of environmental exposure. Located in Research Triangle Park, NC.

Director

Lawrence W. Reiter..................... (919) 541–2281

Fax.................................... (919) 541–4324

National Risk Management Research Laboratory

Provides the scientific basis for risk management involving pollutants. Conducts research to reduce the uncertainty associated with making and implementing risk management decisions. Headquartered in Cincinnati, OH.

Director

E. Timothy Oppelt .... (513) 569–7904

Fax.................................... (513) 569–7680

Office of Resources Management and Administration

Provides support services, including human resources, budgeting, training, and information systems and technology, to laboratories and centers in the Office for Research and Development.

Director

Deborah Y. Dietrich.................... (202) 564–8600

Fax.................................... (202) 564–8222

Office of Science Policy

Administers the programs of two standing interoffice committees: the Science Policy Council and the Risk Assessment Forum.

Director

Deborah Y. Dietrich.................... (202) 564–8600

Fax.................................... (202) 564–8222

OFFICE OF THE CHIEF FINANCIAL OFFICER

Responsible for the agency's budget, resources management, financial management, program analysis and planning, funding allotments and allocations, and accounting and payroll systems.

Chief Financial Officer

Linda Combs .... (202) 564–1151

Fax .... (202) 501–0771

Comptroller

Joseph L. Dillon .... (202) 564–9673

Fax .... (202) 501–1606

ASSISTANT ADMINISTRATOR FOR AIR AND RADIATION (OAR)

Advises the administrator and oversees the air activities of the agency. Air activities include development of national programs, technical policies, and regulations for air pollution control.

Assistant Administrator

Robert (Bob) Brenner .... (202) 564–7409

Fax .... (202) 501–0394

Office of Air Quality Planning and Standards

Develops national air quality standards, including emission standards for new stationary sources of pollution and for hazardous pollutants. Assesses national air pollution control programs and provides assistance to states, industry, and other groups through personnel training and technical information. Maintains the national air programs data system, which includes information on air quality, emissions, and other technological data. Also devises ways to apply technological advances to pollution control procedures. Located in Research Triangle Park, NC.

Director

John S. Seitz .... (919) 541–5616

Fax .... (919) 541–2464

Air Quality Strategies and Standards

Lydia N. Wegman .... (919) 541–5505

Emission Standards

Sally L. Shaver .... (919) 541–5572

Emissions, Monitoring, and Analysis

David J. Mobley .... (919) 541–4676

Information Transfer and Program Integration

William (Bill) T. Harnett .... (919) 541–4979

Office of Atmospheric Programs

Develops technical policy, procedures, and regulations for programs to control acid deposition. Also develops policy and regulations regarding the impact of ozone-depleting chemicals on the stratospheric ozone layer and implements voluntary pollution prevention programs to control global warning.

Director

Paul M. Stolpman .... (202) 564–9140

Clean Air Markets

Brian J. McLean .... (202) 564–9140

Climate Protection Partnerships

Kathleen B. Hogan .... (202) 564–9190

Global Programs

Drusilla J.C. Hufford .... (202) 564–9101

Toll-free .... (800) 296–1996

Office of Transportation and Air Quality

Identifies characteristics of mobile source emissions (vehicles and engines) and fuels. Assesses technology to control such emissions. Develops emission standards for mobile sources and works to ensure compliance.

Director

Margo Oge .... (202) 564–1682

Fax .... (202) 564–1686

(The following divisions are in Ann Arbor, MI.)

Advanced Technology

Charles L. Gray Jr. .... (734) 214–4404

Assessment and Standards

Chester (Chet) J. France .... (734) 214–4338

Certification and Compliance

Greg Green .... (734) 214–4488

Laboratory Operations

Michael A. Sabourin .... (734) 214–4316

Transportation and Regional Programs

Robert Larsen (acting) .... (734) 214–4277

Office of Radiation and Indoor Air Programs

Develops radiation and indoor air pollution protection criteria, standards, and policies. Works with other EPA programs and other agencies to control radiation and indoor air pollution exposure and provides technical assistance to states through EPA's regional offices. Also directs an environmental radiation monitoring program, responds to radiological emergencies, and evaluates the overall risk and impact of radiation and indoor air pollution. Serves as EPA's lead office for intra- and interagency activities coordinated through the Committee for Indoor Air Quality. Responsibilities also include establishing standards for disposal of radioactive wastes and guidelines relating to control of radiation exposure under the Atomic Energy Act, the Clean Air Act, and other applicable legislation.

Director

Steven D. Page .... (202) 564–9320

Fax .... (202) 565–2043

Indoor Environments

Mary T. Smith .... (202) 566–1000

National Air and Radiation Environmental Laboratory (Montgomery, AL)

Edwin L. Sensintaffar .... (334) 270–3401

Radiation and Indoor Environments National Laboratory (Las Vegas, NV)
    Jed Harrison . . . . (702) 798–2476
Radiation Protection
    Frank Marcinowski III (acting) . . . . (202) 564–9290

ASSISTANT ADMINISTRATOR FOR PREVENTION, PESTICIDES, AND TOXIC SUBSTANCES

Develops strategies for toxic substance control; establishes criteria for assessing chemical substances, including new chemicals. Develops and enforces procedures for industry reporting and regulations for controlling hazardous substances. Promotes reduced use of pesticides; establishes tolerance levels for pesticides in food; investigates pesticide accidents.

Assistant Administrator
    Steve Johnson . . . . (202) 564–2902
    Fax . . . . (202) 260–1847
Program Management and Operations
    Marylouise N. Uhlig . . . . (202) 564–0545

Office of Pesticide Programs

Responsible for control of pesticide pollution and the review of research and monitoring programs. Establishes tolerance levels for pesticide residues in or on food, and requires registration of pesticides and monitors pesticide residues in food, people, and certain fish and wildlife and their environment. Also imposes restrictions on the sale and use of pesticides and investigates accidents and incidents involving pesticides. Establishes guidelines for inspection of products; prepares model legislation to be used by the states to improve pesticide control; provides assistance to technical and personnel training programs related to pesticides; and reviews environmental impact statements that relate to pesticide use.

Director
    Marcia E. Mulkey . . . . (703) 305–7090
    Fax . . . . (703) 308–4776
Antimicrobials
    Frank T. Sanders . . . . (703) 308–6411
Biological and Economic Analysis
    Denise Keehner . . . . (202) 566–1566
Biopesticides and Pollution Prevention
    Janet L. Andersen . . . . (703) 308–8712
Environmental Fate and Effects
    Elizabeth M. Leovey (acting) . . . . (703) 305–7328
Field and External Affairs
    Anne E. Lindsay . . . . (703) 305–5265
Health Effects
    Margaret J. Stasikowski . . . . (703) 305–7351
Information Resources and Services
    Richard D. Schmitt (acting) . . . . (703) 305–5484

Registration
    James J. Jones . . . . (703) 305–7090
Special Review and Reregistration
    Lois A. Rossi . . . . (703) 308–8000

Office of Pollution Prevention and Toxics

Responsible for administration of the Toxic Substances Control Act. Develops policies for programs designed to control toxic substances; determines research priorities; and develops scientific, technical, economic, and social databases for the health evaluation of toxic substances. Also responsible for communicating with the industrial community on implementation of the regulations.

Director
    William H. Sanders III . . . . (202) 564–0554
    Fax . . . . (202) 260–0575
Chemical Control
    Charles M. Auer . . . . (202) 564–3810
National Program Chemical Division
    Linda Moos (acting) . . . . (202) 564–1866
Economics, Exposure and Technology
    Mary Ellen Weber . . . . (202) 564–8770
Environmental Assistance
    Barbara A. Cunningham (acting) . . . . . (202) 564–8198
Information Management
    Allan Abramson . . . . (202) 564–8800
Pollution Prevention
    John F. Cross (acting) . . . . (202) 564–8844
Risk Assessment
    Oscar Hernandez . . . . (202) 564–7641

Office of Science Coordination and Policy

Oversees exposure assessment coordination and policy and hazard assessment coordination and policy.

Director
    Steven K. Galson . . . . (202) 260–6900
    Fax . . . . (202) 401–0849

ASSISTANT ADMINISTRATOR FOR WATER

Responsible for the agency's water quality activities, which represent a coordinated effort to restore the nation's waters. In addition, this office furnishes technical direction, support, and evaluation of regional water activities. The office oversees the provision of training in the fields of water quality, economic and long-term environmental analysis, and marine and estuarine protection.

Assistant Administrator
    Vacant . . . . (202) 260–5700
    Fax . . . . (202) 260–5711
American Indian Environmental Office
    Carol Jorgensen . . . . (202) 564–0303

Office of Ground Water and Drinking Water

Develops standards for drinking water quality and promulgates regulations to preserve underground sources of drinking water. Monitors and evaluates compliance. Develops and coordinates the agency's ground water policy; distributes grants to states for the development of ground water strategies. Also maintains an information program and develops plans to handle water emergencies.

Director
Cynthia C. Dougherty .... (202) 564–3750
Fax .... (202) 260–4383
Drinking Water Protection
William R. Diamond .... (202) 564–3751
Standards and Risk Management
Ephraim S. King .... (202) 564–3752

Office of Science and Technology

Coordinates national water-related activities and sets effluent and water quality guidelines. Maintains data systems on water quality, discharge, and programs.

Director
Geoffrey H. Grubbs .... (202) 566–0430
Fax .... (202) 260–5394
Engineering and Analysis
Sheila E. Frace .... (202) 564–0749
Standards and Health Protection
Elizabeth Southerland .... (703) 603–8960

Office of Wastewater Management

Develops and oversees programs to protect the nation's watersheds and conserve water resources in cooperation with EPA regional offices, states, municipalities, and the public. Administers permit programs for sewage treatment plants and industrial waste, regulates sewage sludge disposal and storm water collection systems, and manages revolving funds for municipalities to finance publicly owned treatment works.

Director
James A. Hanlon .... (202) 564–0748
Fax .... (202) 501–2338
Municipal Support
Sheila E. Frace .... (202) 564–0749
Water Permits
Linda Boornazian .... (202) 564–0221

Office of Wetlands, Oceans, and Watersheds

Oversees EPA programs that manage and protect the aquatic sewage systems of inland and coastal watersheds. Promotes wetlands protection through both regulatory and cooperative programs, develops criteria to evaluate ocean dumping proposals and issuing permits for the dumping of all wastes, oversees the marine san-

itation device program, manages grants programs for abating nonpoint source pollution, and oversees surface water quality monitoring and water quality assessment activities.

Director
Diane Regas .... (202) 566–1146
Fax .... (202) 566–1147
Assessment and Watershed Protection
Charles Sutfin .... (202) 566–1155
Oceans and Coastal Protection
Suzanne E. Schwartz .... (202) 566–1200
Policy, Communications, and Resource Management
Arnold Layne (acting) .... (202) 566–1300
Wetlands
John W. Meagher .... (202) 566–1348

ASSISTANT ADMINISTRATOR FOR SOLID WASTE AND EMERGENCY RESPONSE

Provides agency-wide policy, guidance, and direction for solid waste and emergency response programs. Responsibilities include: program policy development and evaluation, development of appropriate hazardous waste standards and regulations, program policy guidance and overview, technical support and evaluation of regional solid waste and emergency response activities, and development of programs for technical and programmatic assistance to state and local government.

Assistant Administrator
Marianne Lamont Horinko .... (202) 566–0200
Federal Facilities Restoration and Reuse
James E. Woolford .... (703) 603–9089

Chemical Emergency Preparedness and Prevention Office

Responsible for emergency program implementation and coordination.

Director
Debbie Dietrich .... (202) 564–8600
Fax .... (703) 260–9927

Office of Emergency and Remedial Response (Superfund/Oil Programs)

Coordinates with regional offices on remedial responses to cleanup sites, including oil pollution cleanup. This includes screening, evaluating, ranking, and planning. The planning process consists of the Remedial Action Master Plan, including determination of the states' role, remedial investigation, solution selection, and remedial design/construction.

Director
Mike Cook .... (703) 603–8960
Fax .... (703) 603–9146

Office of Solid Waste

Establishes program policy for the regulation of solid and hazardous waste management throughout the country.

Director

Robert Springer (acting)............... (202) 564–9205

Fax.................................... (703) 308–0513

Office of Technology Innovation

Oversees technology users support program and technology and markets programs.

Director

Walter W. Kovalick Jr................... (703) 603–9910

Fax.................................... (703) 603–9135

Office of Underground Storage Tanks

Controls releases of petroleum products and other regulated substances from underground storage tanks.

Director

Cliff Rothenstein .... (703) 603–9900

Fax.................................... (703) 603–9163

Office of Program Management

Oversees information management and data quality, organizational management and integrity, policy analysis and regulatory management, and acquisition and resource management.

Director

Devereaux Barnes .... (202) 566–1884

Regional Offices

REGION 1

(CT, MA, ME, NH, RI, VT)
One Congress St., #1100
Boston, MA 02114-2023
(617) 918-1111
(888) 372-7341
Ira Leighton (acting), regional administrator

REGION 2

(NJ, NY, PR, VI)
290 Broadway
New York, NY 10007-1866
(212) 637-3000
Fax (212) 637–3526
William Muszynski (acting), regional administrator

REGION 3

(DC, DE, MD, PA, VA, WV)
1650 Arch St.
Philadelphia, PA 19103-2029
(215) 814–5000
(800) 438–2474
Fax (215) 814–5103
Thomas Voltaggio (acting), regional administrator

REGION 4

(AL, FL, GA, KY, MS, NC, SC, TN)
61 Forsythe St., SW
Atlanta, GA 30303-3104
(404) 562–9900
(800) 241–1754
Fax (404) 562–8174
Stan Meiberg (acting), regional administrator

REGION 5

(IL, IN, MI, MN, OH, WI)
77 W. Jackson Blvd.
Chicago, IL 60604-3507
(312) 353–2000
(800) 621–8431
David A. Ullrich, regional administrator

REGION 6

(AR, LA, NM, OK, TX)
1445 Ross Ave., #1200
Dallas, TX 75202-2733
(214) 665–2200
(800) 887–6063
Gregg A. Cooke, regional administrator

REGION 7

(IA, KS, MO, NE)
901 N. Fifth St.
Kansas City, KS 66101
(913) 551–7003
(800) 223–0425
William W. Rice (acting), regional administrator

REGION 8

(CO, MT, ND, SD, UT, WY)
999 18th St., #500
Denver, CO 80202-2466
(303) 312–6312
(800) 227–8917
Jack McGraw (acting), regional administrator

REGION 9
(AS, AZ, CA, GU, HI, NV)
75 Hawthorne St.
San Francisco, CA 94105
(415) 947–8000
Laura Yoshii (acting), regional administrator

REGION 10
(AK, ID, OR, WA)
1200 Sixth Ave.
Seattle, WA 98101
(206) 553–1200
(800) 424–4372
Fax (206) 553-0149
Charles E. Findley (acting), regional administrator

■ CONGRESSIONAL ACTION

Congressional Liaison
Edward D. Krenik .... (202) 260–5200

Committees and Subcommittees

HOUSE APPROPRIATIONS COMMITTEE
Subcommittee on VA, HUD, and Independent Agencies
H-143 CAP, Washington, DC 20515
(202) 225–3241

HOUSE ENERGY AND COMMERCE COMMITTEE
Subcommittee on Environment and Hazardous
 Materials
2125 RHOB, Washington, DC 20515
(202) 225–2927
Subcommittee on Energy and Air Quality
2125 RHOB, Washington, DC 20515
(202) 225–2927

HOUSE GOVERNMENT REFORM COMMITTEE
Subcommittee on Energy Policy, Natural Resources, and
 Regulatory Affairs
2157 RHOB, Washington, DC 20515
(202) 225–5074

HOUSE SCIENCE COMMITTEE
Subcommittee on Environment, Technology, and
 Standards
2320 RHOB, Washington, DC 20515
(202) 225–9662

SENATE APPROPRIATIONS COMMITTEE
Subcommittee on VA, HUD, and Independent Agencies
S-128 CAP, Washington, DC 20510
(202) 224–3471

**SENATE ENVIRONMENT AND PUBLIC WORKS
COMMITTEE**
SD-410, Washington, DC 20510
(202) 224–6176

**SUBCOMMITTEE ON CLEAN AIR, WETLANDS,
PRIVATE PROPERTY, AND NUCLEAR SAFETY**
SD-410, Washington, DC 20510
(202) 224–6176

**SUBCOMMITTEE ON, FISHERIES, WILDLIFE, AND
WATER**
SD-410, Washington, DC 20510
(202) 224–6176

**SUBCOMMITTEE ON TRANSPORTATION AND
INFRASTRUCTURE**
SD-410, Washington, DC 20510
(202) 224–6176

SENATE ENERGY AND NATURAL RESOURCES
SD-364, Washington, DC 20510
(202) 224–4971

Legislation
The EPA was established by Reorganization Plan No. 3, an executive order submitted to Congress July 9, 1970, by President Nixon. The House of Representatives defeated a resolution to block approval of the plan creating the new agency; there was no formal opposition to the reorganization in the Senate.

The EPA administers most of the environmental statutes in force. (The Agriculture Department has responsibility for parts of some laws governing pesticide use and the Interior Department has responsibility for some conservation measures related to environmental law.) The following laws are administered by the EPA:

National Environmental Policy Act of 1969 (83 Stat. 852, 42 U.S.C. 4321). Signed by the president Jan. 1, 1970. Established the Council on Environmental Quality (CEQ) and required the development of a national policy on the environment.

Water Quality Improvement Act of 1970 (84 Stat. 94, 33 U.S.C. 1251). Signed by the president April 3, 1970. Made oil companies partially liable (up to $14 million) for oil spills and outlawed flushing of raw sewage from boats. Increased restrictions on thermal pollution from nuclear power plants. Created the Office of Environmental Quality to serve as staff for the CEQ.

Clean Air Act Amendments of 1970 (84 Stat. 1676, 42 U.S.C. 1857b). Signed by the president Dec. 31, 1970. Set initial deadlines for auto emission standards and gave the EPA administrator power to establish the standards. Gave citizens and public interest groups the right to bring suit against alleged polluters, including federal agencies.

Federal Environmental Pesticide Control Act of 1972 (86 Stat. 975, 7 U.S.C. 135). Signed by the president Oct. 1, 1972. Required the registration of pesticides and gave the EPA authority to ban the use of hazardous pesticides.

Federal Water Pollution Control Act Amendments of 1972 (Clean Water Act) (86 Stat. 816, 33 U.S.C. 1254). Vetoed by the president Oct. 17, 1972; veto overridden Oct. 18, 1972. Set up a program of grants to the states for construction of sewage treatment plants. Established industrial and municipal pollutant discharge permit programs.

Marine Protection, Research, and Sanctuaries Act of 1972 (86 Stat. 1052, 33 U.S.C. 1401). Signed by the president Oct. 23, 1972. Outlawed dumping of waste in oceans without an EPA permit and required the EPA to designate sites to be used by permit holders.

Noise Control Act of 1972 (86 Stat. 1234, 42 U.S.C. 4901). Signed by the president Oct. 27, 1972. Gave the EPA the authority to set national noise standards for commercial products. Required the EPA to assist the Federal Aviation Administration in developing noise regulations for airports and aircraft.

Safe Drinking Water Act (88 Stat. 1661, 42 U.S.C. 300f). Signed by the president Dec. 16, 1974. Set standards for allowable levels of certain chemicals and bacteriological pollutants in public drinking water systems.

Toxic Substances Control Act (90 Stat. 2005, 15 U.S.C. 2601). Signed by the president Oct. 11, 1976. Banned use of polychlorinated biphenyls (PCBs) and gave the EPA power to require testing of chemical substances that present a risk of injury to health and the environment.

Resource Conservation and Recovery Act of 1976 (RCRA) (90 Stat. 95, 42 U.S.C. 6901). Signed by the president Oct. 21, 1976. Set safety standard regulations for handling and storage of hazardous wastes and required permits for the operation of hazardous waste treatment, storage, and disposal facilities.

Clean Air Act Amendments of 1977 (91 Stat. 685, 42 U.S.C. 7401). Signed by the president Aug. 7, 1977. Delayed auto emission deadlines for an additional two years and tightened emission standards for 1980 and 1981 model year automobiles. Set new standards to protect areas with clean air from deterioration of air quality. Extended air quality standards for most cities and industries.

Clean Water Act of 1977 (91 Stat. 1566, 33 U.S.C. 1251). Signed by the president Dec. 27, 1977. Created "best conventional technology" standard for water quality by 1984, continued grants to states, and raised liability limit on oil spill cleanup costs.

Comprehensive Environmental Response, Compensation and Liability Act of 1980 (CERCLA) (94 Stat. 2767, 42 U.S.C. 9601 note). Signed by the president Dec. 11, 1980. Created a $1.6 billion Hazardous Substance Response Trust Fund (Superfund) to clean up toxic contaminants spilled or dumped into the environment. Imposed liability for government cleanup costs and natural resource damages of up to $50 million on anyone releasing hazardous substances into the environment.

Hazardous and Solid Waste Amendments of 1984 (98 Stat. 3221, 42 U.S.C. 6901 note). Signed by the president Nov. 8, 1984. Revised and strengthened EPA procedures for regulating hazardous waste facilities. Prohibited land disposal of certain hazardous liquid wastes. Authorized EPA to regulate underground storage tanks containing petroleum products and hazardous materials.

Safe Drinking Water Act Amendments of 1986 (100 Stat. 642, 42 U.S.C. 201 note). Signed by the president June 19, 1986. Revised EPA safe drinking water programs, including grants to states for drinking water standards enforcement and ground water protection programs.

Comprehensive Environmental Response, Compensation and Liability Act Amendments of 1986 (CERCLA) (100 Stat. 1613, 42 U.S.C. 9601 note). Signed by the president Oct. 17, 1986. Provided $8.5 billion for the Hazardous Substance Response Trust Fund (Superfund) for fiscal years 1987 through 1991. Required the EPA to start work on 375 sites within the five-year funding period.

Water Quality Act of 1987 (101 Stat. 7, 33 U.S.C. 1251 note). Signed by the president Feb. 4, 1987. Amended the Clean Water Act of 1972 and expanded EPA enforcement authority. Revised EPA water pollution control programs, including grants to states for construction of wastewater treatment facilities and implementation of mandated nonpoint-source pollution management plans. Established a national estuary program.

Federal Insecticide, Fungicide, and Rodenticide Act Amendments of 1988 (FIFRA) (102 Stat. 2654, 7 U.S.C. 9601 note). Signed by the president Oct. 25, 1988. Required chemical companies to determine, over a nine-year period, whether their pesticide products had adverse health effects.

Toxic Substances Control Act Amendments of 1988 (102 Stat. 2755, 15 U.S.C. 2601). Signed by the president Oct. 28, 1988. Authorized federal aid to help states develop programs to mitigate the effects of radon gas in homes, schools, and other buildings.

Ocean Pollution Dumping Act of 1988 (102 Stat. 3213, 16 U.S.C. 1438). Signed by the president Nov. 7, 1988. Amended the Marine Protection, Research, and Sanctuaries Act of 1972 to end all ocean disposal of sewage sludge and industrial waste by Dec. 31, 1991. Established dumping fees, permit requirements, and civil penalties for violations of ocean dumping laws.

Pollution Prevention Act of 1990 (104 Stat. 1388, 42 U.S.C. 13101 note). Signed by the president Nov. 5, 1990. Established the Office of Pollution Prevention in the EPA to coordinate agency efforts at source reduction. Mandated that businesses submit a source reduction and recycling report to accompany annual toxic release inventory.

Clean Air Act Amendments of 1990 (104 Stat. 2399, 42 U.S.C. 7407 note). Signed by the president Nov. 15, 1990. Set new requirements and deadlines for major urban areas to meet federal clean air standards. Imposed new emissions standards for motor vehicles and mandated cleaner fuels. Required reduction in emissions of sulfur dioxide and nitrogen oxides by power plants to limit acid deposition. Prohibited the use of chlorofluorocarbons (CFCs) by the year 2000 and established phaseout schedules for other ozone-depleting chemicals.

Reclamation Projects Authorization and Adjustment Act of 1992 (106 Stat. 4600, 43 U.S.C. 371 note). Signed by the president Oct. 30, 1992. Authorized completion of major water projects. Mandated extensive wildlife and environmental protection, mitigation, and restoration programs.

Waste Isolation Pilot Plant Act (106 Stat. 4777). Signed by the president Oct. 30, 1992. Authorized the storage of certain defense-related nuclear waste at the Energy Department's underground storage facility near Carlsbad, NM.

Small Business Regulatory Enforcement Fairness Act of 1996 (110 Stat. 847, 5 U.S.C. 601 note). Signed by the president March 29, 1996. Required SBA to assist small businesses with regulatory compliance through community information clearinghouses and resource centers; to establish a Small Business and Agriculture Regulatory Enforcement Ombudsman, and to establish a Small Business Regulatory Fairness Board in each SBA regional office.

Food Quality Protection Act of 1996 (110 Stat. 1489, 7 U.S.C. 136 note). Signed by the president on Aug. 3, 1996. Amended the Federal Insecticide, Fungicide, and Rodenticide Act of 1947 and the Federal Food, Drug and Cosmetic Act of 1958 (FFDCA) to allow the EPA to issue an emergency order to suspend pesticides that pose a risk to public health before a pesticide goes through the cancellation process.

Safe Drinking Water Amendments of 1996 (42 U.S.C. 201 note). Signed by the president Aug. 6, 1996. Changed the process by which new contaminants become regulated. Required the EPA to publish a cost-benefit analysis of all proposed regulation.

Chemical Safety Information, Site Security and Fuels Regulatory Relief Act (113 Stat. 207, 42 U.S.C. 7401 note). Signed by the president on Aug. 5, 1999. Amended the Clean Air Act to exempt propane and similar flammable fuels from EPA emergency management requirements.

Beaches Environmental Assessment and Coastal Health Act of 2000 (114 Stat. 870, 33 U.S.C. 1251 note). Signed by the president on Oct. 10, 2000. Amended the Federal Water Pollution Control Act to require states to establish water quality standards and monitoring programs for coastal recreational areas.

Small Business Liability Relief and Brownfields Revitalization Act (115 Stat. 2356, 42 U.S.C. 9601 note). Signed by the president on Jan. 11, 2002. Title I, the Small Business Liability Protection Act, amended the Comprehensive Environmental Response, Compensation and Liability Act of 1980 (CERCLA) to provide small businesses certain relief from liability under CERCLA. Title II, the Brownfields Revitalization and Environmental Restoration Act of 2001, amended CERCLA to provide grants to states for the cleanup and reuse of contaminated industrial sites, or brownfields.

Public Health Security and Bioterrorism Preparedness and Response Act of 2002 (116 Stat. 594, 42 U.S.C. 201 note). Signed by the president on June 12, 2002. Amended the Safe Drinking Water Act to require communities with more than 3,330 residents to evaluate the vulnerability of their water system to a terrorist attack or other act intended to affect the safety and reliability of the water supply. Required the establishment of an emergency response plan based upon the evaluation.

▣ INFORMATION SOURCES

Internet

Agency Web Site: http://www.epa.gov. Provides links to many EPA offices, programs, and publications.

(See also Reference Resources and Other Information Sources, below.)

Telephone Contacts

The EPA maintains many hotline and clearinghouse numbers, which are directed to state and local agencies, the private sector, environmental and health groups, and the public. For fax-on-demand services, see Publications.

Administrator's Hotline .... (202) 260–1000
Air Quality Planning and
    Standards .... (919) 541–5615

Environmental Financing
Information .... (202) 564–4994
Hazardous Waste Ombudsman .... (800) 262–7937
Indoor Air Quality Information
Clearinghouse .... (800) 438–4318
Inspector General Hotline .... (888) 546–8740
National Lead Information Center .... (800) 532–3394
National Radon Hotline .... (800) 767–7236
Resource Conservation/Superfund
Hotline .... (800) 424–9346
TDD .... (800) 553–7672
DC area .... (703) 412–9810
Safe Drinking Water Hotline .... (800) 426–4791
Small Business Ombudsman .... (800) 368–5888
Stratospheric Ozone Information
Hotline .... (800) 296–1996
Wetlands Information Hotline .... (800) 832–7828

Information and Publications

KEY OFFICES

EPA Information Resources Center
401 M St. S.W., #2904
Washington, DC 20460
(202) 260–5922
publicaccess@epa.gov
Hours: 8:00 a.m. to 5:00 p.m.

Distributes information to the public, including selected publications. Handles general correspondence and inquiries.

EPA Communications, Education, and Media Relations
401 M St. S.W.
Washington, DC 20460
(202) 564–9828
Fax (202) 501–1474
Joseph Martyak, associate administrator

Provides information to the media and the public, including information on environmental education programs. Publishes the *EPA Journal* and maintains a clipping service.

EPA Press Relations
401 M St. S.W.
Washington, DC 20460
(202) 564–4355
Fax (202) 501–1761
Cornelia (Ronnie) M. Piper (acting), director

Provides information to the media. Issues news releases and radio announcements and coordinates news conferences. News releases are also available online.

Freedom of Information
1200 Pennsylvania Ave., N.W.
Washington, DC 20460
(202) 566–1667
Fax (202) 566–2147
Betty Lopez, FOIA officer

GRANTS
Contact the nearest regional office for information. For specific guides, see Publications, below.

PUBLICATIONS
General information. Contact the EPA Public Information Center for the booklet *ACCESS Express*, which provides an overview of EPA information resources, and for other nontechnical information. The more comprehensive guide, *ACCESS EPA*, may be purchased from either the Government Printing Office (GPO) or the National Technical Information Service (NTIS): see appendix, Ordering Government Information. The text of *ACCESS EPA* is also available online, via the EPA's Online Library Service (OLS).

Technical material. Available through the EPA Library and NTIS. The NTIS publishes the *EPA Publications Bibliography: Quarterly Abstract Bulletin*, which contains abstracts of EPA research reports and is indexed by individual author, corporate author, EPA sponsoring office, subject, title, and NTIS reference number. The fourth quarter index covers the entire year.

Grants. EPA grants are described in the *EPA Assistance Administration Manual*, available from the NTIS. Information on EPA grants and copies of grant application forms also are available from the nearest regional office or the EPA Grant Operations Branch; (202) 260-5252. Related listings appear in the *Catalog of Federal Domestic Assistance*, available for purchase from the GPO or from its Web site.

Fax-on-demand. The following services will fax EPA documents automatically upon request:

Automated Imports Helpline. Provides information on importing cars, trucks, motorcycles, and their parts. Call (202) 233–9660.

Green Light Program. Provides information on how companies and individuals can conserve energy by upgrading to more energy-efficient lighting systems. Call (202) 233–9659.

DATA AND STATISTICS
EPA data and statistics are available on a wide range of topics. There is no central office that provides all EPA

information; good places to start include the EPA Headquarters Library, the agency's Internet sites, and the publication *ACCESS EPA*.

Reference Resources

LIBRARIES

EPA regional offices and many EPA laboratories also maintain libraries.

EPA Headquarters Library

401 M St. S.W., # 2904
Washington, DC 20460
(202) 260–5922
Fax (202) 260–6257
Hours: 8:00 a.m. to 5:00 p.m.

A large collection of material on the environment and pollution, including specialized reports, with an emphasis on environmental policy and management. Receives a wide range of periodicals dealing with environmental problems. Limited reference services are available to the general public; non-EPA users may borrow materials only through interlibrary loans.

EPA Legislative Reference Library

401 M St. S.W.
Washington, DC 20460
(202) 564–2782
Fax (202) 501–1519
Pamela Abraham, head librarian
Hours: 9:00 a.m. to 12:30 p.m.; 1:30 p.m. to 4:00 p.m.

Receives all congressional documents for the agency. Also tracks the status of current environmental legislation and provides limited reference services to the general public. (Operated by EPA Congressional and Legislative Affairs.)

DOCKETS

Dockets are maintained by individual offices within the EPA. The booklet *Access Express* provides a list of locations where major EPA dockets may be inspected. The Headquarters Library also can refer inquiries to the appropriate office.

ONLINE

EPA Online Library System (OLS). Consists of several databases with bibliographic information on topics including hazardous waste, environmental project financing, and chemicals. Data cover both EPA documents and library holdings of the agency. OLS can be accessed via Telnet using the host address, epaibm.rtpnc.epa.gov; to log in

via modem, call (919) 549–0720 or (800) 445–2795. There is no fee for access, apart from applicable telecommunications charges. The EPA publishes a *User Guide* for public access to the OLS; technical assistance also is available by calling the EPA's National Computer Center; (800) 334–2405 or, outside the U.S., (919) 541–7862.

Environmental Financing Information Network (EFIN). A database of abstracts from publications and other documents that deal with environmental financing. The database can be accessed via Telnet using the host address, epaibm.rtpnc.epa.gov, or it may be accessed via a modem by dialing (919) 549–0720. Instructions on accessing the database can be obtained via the Internet at: http://www. epa.gov/efinpage/efindata.htm.

National Drinking Water Clearinghouse (NDWC). Maintains a database and bulletin board system (BBS) with information about small communities' drinking water. The database may be downloaded or obtained on disk for a small fee. To access the BBS, call (800) 624–8301. It also can be accessed via the Internet at: http://www.estd.wvu.edu.

National Small Flows Clearinghouse (NSFC). Maintains databases and a bulletin board system (BBS) with information on wastewater treatment. To access the BBS, visit the web site, http://www.estd.wvu.edu. Dial the hotline for both NDWC and NSFC at (800) 624–8301 or (304) 293–4191; they can provide BBS technical assistance. Write both clearinghouses at P.O. Box 6064, Morgantown, WV 26506.

Subsurface Remediation Information Center (SRIC). Maintains a database of this EPA center's research. Accessible via OLS or by contacting SRIC, 919 Kerr Research Dr., DAALI, Ada, OK 74820; (580) 436–8651.

Other online services and databases that are sponsored by or maintained jointly with EPA offices are listed in the publication, *ACCESS EPA* (the text of which is also available electronically, via OLS).

See Other Information Sources, below, for related online services that are not maintained by the EPA.

RULES AND REGULATIONS

EPA rules and regulations are published in the *Code of Federal Regulations*, Title 40, parts 1–792. Proposed rules, new final rules, and updates to the *Code of Federal Regulations* are published in the daily *Federal Register*. (See appendix for information on how to obtain and use these publications.)

Other Information Sources

ONLINE

The following services are available outside the EPA:

Clean-Up Information (CLU-IN). A bulletin board system (BBS) of files on hazardous waste remediation technologies. Available from CLU-IN, Environmental Management Support, Inc., 8601 Georgia Ave., #500, Silver Spring, MD 20910; (301) 589–8368 (operator), (301) 589–8366 (system access).

Environment Information Clearinghouse (EIC). A clearinghouse for energy and environmental information supported by the United States Agency for International Development. Products include computer microfiche systems, abstracts, journals, indexes, handbooks, and directories as well as Environline and Energyline databases. Databases are available from the following online services: BRS (800) 468–0908; DIALOG (800) 3-DIALOG; or ORBIT (800) 45-ORBIT.

National Environmental Data Referral Service (NEDRES). A computerized system that provides information on environmental data files offered by federal, state, and local governments, universities, research institutes, and private industry in the United States and elsewhere. Available from the National Oceanic and Atmospheric Administration. *(Call (202) 606–4548 for more information.)*

National Technical Information Service (NTIS) Database. Supported by the Commerce Department. It lists U.S. government-sponsored research, development, and engineering reports from the EPA and other agencies. Available from NTIS; (703) 605–6000.

Pollution Abstracts. International technical literature is abstracted and indexed. It is available in a bimonthly journal, an online database, on CD-ROM, or through magnetic tape lease. Available from Cambridge Scientific Abstract Co., 7200 Wisconsin Ave., Bethesda, MD 20814; (301) 961–6700.

Watershed Information Resource System (WIRS). A database of information on water issues, including articles and periodicals. The database can be accessed via the Internet at: http://www.terrene.org. Available from the Terrene Institute, 4 Herbert St., Alexandria, VA 22305; (703) 548–5473; hotline: (800) 726–5253.

NONGOVERNMENTAL ORGANIZATIONS

The following are some key organizations that monitor the EPA and environmental protection issues:

American Rivers
1025 Vermont Ave. N.W., #720
Washington, DC 20005
(202) 347–7550
Internet: http://www.amrivers.org

Center for Marine Conservation
1725 DeSales St. N.W., #600
Washington, DC 20036
(202) 429–5609
Internet: http://ww.cmc-ocean.org/

Environmental Defense Fund
257 Park Ave. South
New York, NY 10010
(212) 505–2100
Washington office
1875 Connecticut Ave. N.W.
Washington, DC 20009
(202) 387–3500
Internet: http://www.edf.org

Environmental Working Group
1436 U St., N.W., #100
Washington, DC 20009
(202) 667–6982
Internet: http://www.ewg.org

Greenpeace USA
702 H St. N.W., #300
Washington, DC 20001
(800) 326–0959
Internet: http://www.greenpeaceusa.org

The Keystone Center
1628 Saints John Rd.
Keystone, CO 80435
(970) 513–5800
Fax (970) 262–0152
Washington office
1020 16th St., N.W., 2nd Floor
Washington, DC 20036
(202) 452–1590
Internet: http://www.keystone.org

League of Conservation Voters
1920 L St. N.W., #800
Washington, DC 20036
(202) 785–8683
Internet: http://www.lcv.org

National Wildlife Federation
11100 Wildlife Center Dr.
Reston, VA 20190
(703) 438–6000

Washington Office
1400 16th St. N.W.
Washington, DC 20036
(202) 797-6800
Internet: http://www.nwf.org

Natural Resources Defense Council
40 W. 20th St.
New York, NY 10011
(212) 727–2700
Fax (212) 727–1773
  Washington office
  1200 New York Ave. N.W., #400
  Washington, DC 20005
  (202) 289–6868
Internet: http://www.nrdc.org

Political Economy Research Center
502 S. 19th Ave.
Bozeman, MT 59718
(406) 587–9591
Internet: http://www.perc.org

Resources for the Future
1616 P St. N.W.
Washington, DC 20036
(202) 328–5000
Fax (202) 939–3460
Internet: http://www.rff.org

Sierra Club
85 2nd St., 2nd Floor
San Francisco, CA 94105-3441
(415) 977–5500
Fax (415) 977–5799
  Washington office
  408 C St. N.E.
  Washington, DC 20002-5818
  (202) 547–1141
  Fax (202) 547–6009
Internet: http://www.sierraclub.org

The Wilderness Society
1615 M St. N.W.
Washington, DC 20036
(800) THE-WILD
Internet: http://www.wilderness.org

World Wildlife Fund
1250 24th St. N.W.
Washington, DC 20037
(202) 293–4800
Fax (202) 293–9211
Internet: http://www.worldwildlife.org

PUBLISHERS

The following companies and organizations publish on the EPA and related issues through books, periodicals, or electronic media.

American Law Institute-American Bar Association
Committee on Continuing Professional Education
4025 Chestnut St.
Philadelphia, PA 19104
(800) CLENEWS
Internet: http://www.ali-aba.org

Bureau of National Affairs (BNA), Inc.
1231 25th St. N.W.
Washington, DC 20037
(800) 372–1033
Internet: http://www.bna.com

Business Publishers, Inc.
8737 Colesville Rd., #110
Silver Spring, MD 20910-3928
(800) 274–6737
(301) 589–5103
Internet: http://www.bpinews.com

Cambridge Scientific Abstracts
7200 Wisconsin Ave., #601
Bethesda, MD 20814
(301) 961–6700
(800) 843–7751
Internet: http://www.csa.com/siteV3/newhome.html

Government Institutes, Inc.
4 Research Place
Rockville, MD 20850
(301) 921–2300
Internet: http://www.govinst.com

Matthew Bender & Co., Inc./Lexis-Nexis
2 Park Ave.
New York, NY 10016
(212) 448–2000
(800) 833–9844
Internet: http://www.bender.com

Equal Employment Opportunity Commission

1801 L St. N.W., Washington, DC 20507
Internet: http://www.eeoc.gov

■ INTRODUCTION

The Equal Employment Opportunity Commission (EEOC) is an independent agency that was established in 1965. It is composed of five commissioners, not more than three of whom may be members of the same political party. The commissioners are appointed by the president and confirmed by the Senate for five-year terms. The president designates one member to serve as chair and another to serve as vice chair. In addition, the general counsel is nominated by the president and confirmed by the Senate for a four-year term.

Responsibilities

The EEOC is charged with enforcing laws that:
- Prohibit employment discrimination on the basis of race, color, national origin, religion, or sex.
- Prohibit employment discrimination based on pregnancy, childbirth, or related medical conditions.
- Protect men and women against pay discrimination based on sex.
- Protect workers of ages forty or older from arbitrary age discrimination in hiring, discharge, pay, promotions, and other aspects of employment.
- Prohibit discrimination against individuals with disabilities within the federal government.

Also, the commission:
- Coordinates all federal equal employment efforts.
- Oversees affirmative action plans to eliminate discriminatory practices.
- Has jurisdiction over federal employees' complaints concerning equal employment discrimination.

GLOSSARY

Alternative dispute resolution (ADR)—A less formal and less adversarial method of resolving employment practice disputes, such as mediation.

Charging party—A person or group making a charge of employment discrimination.

Deferral—The process whereby the EEOC turns over a discrimination charge it has received to a state or local fair employment practices agency (706 agency) for action.

FEP agencies—State and local government agencies, known as FEPAs, that enforce fair employment practice (FEP) laws.

No cause—A finding by the commission that a charge of discrimination does not have merit under the law.

Respondent—The firm, union, employment agency, or individual against whom a charge of employment discrimination is filed.

706 agencies—State and local agencies described in section 706(c) of Title VII of the Civil Rights Act. They are FEP agencies that meet certain criteria. The 706 agencies enforce state and local laws prohibiting job discrimination as well as Title VII on a contract basis with the EEOC.

Systemic discrimination—Employment "systems" that show a pattern or practice of employment discrimination throughout an industry or large company, as opposed to individual acts of discrimination.

Title VII—The section of the Civil Rights Act of 1964 that created the EEOC.

Powers and Authority

The EEOC has the authority to investigate, conciliate, and litigate charges of discrimination in employment. It also has the authority to issue guidelines, rules, and regulations and to require employers, unions, and others covered by Title VII of the Civil Rights Act of 1964 to report regularly on the race, ethnic origin, and sex of their employees and members. In cases where a charge of discrimination cannot be conciliated, the EEOC has the authority to file a lawsuit in federal district court to force compliance with Title VII.

Under Title VII, as amended, the EEOC has broad authority. The commission is charged with prohibiting employers from discriminating in hiring on the basis of race, color, religion, sex, or national origin. The law applies to all private concerns that ship or receive goods across state lines and employ fifteen workers. EEOC enforces the Equal Pay Act of 1963, which requires equal pay for equal work, and the Age Discrimination in Employment Act of 1967,

as amended. This legislation formerly came under the jurisdiction of the Labor Department.

The EEOC is responsible for the administration of Executive Order 11478, which protects people with disabilities and aged workers from discrimination in federal government employment. It also administers the employment sections of the 1990 Americans with Disabilities Act, which outlawed discrimination against the estimated 54 million Americans with disabilities in employment, public services, and public accommodations. It took effect July 26, 1992, for employers with twenty-five or more employees. Beginning on July 26, 1994, the law applied to employers with fifteen or more employees.

The EEOC administers Executive Order 12067, which requires oversight and coordination of all federal equal employment opportunity regulations, practices, and policies. The commission enforces the Pregnancy Discrimination Act, which was written into Title VII and forbids discrimination on the basis of pregnancy, childbirth, or related medical conditions; and Section 501 of the Rehabilitation Act of 1973, which pertains to employment discrimination against individuals with disabilities in the federal government.

The EEOC now uses a system of "negotiated rulemaking," meaning it tries to bring all potentially affected parties into a working group during the drafting of a proposed rule, rather than relying on traditional procedures of receiving public comment after a rule has been devised and proposed. Under this system, the agency creates a committee made up of labor, industry, and other representatives to work out the details of a proposed rule. While admitting this does not solve all differences, the agency says it reduces legal challenges to new rules.

Employees of the U.S. Congress are protected by the EEOC under the Congressional Accountability Act.

SYSTEMIC DISCRIMINATION

The commission has the authority to investigate and prosecute cases of systemic discrimination—a pattern or practice of employment discrimination throughout an entire company or industry.

Systemic Investigations and Review Programs, under the Office of the General Counsel, monitors equal employment opportunity reports from private employers to identify possible cases of systemic discrimination. Regional offices take the worst-first approach by targeting companies whose profiles show the greatest underrepresentation of minorities and women. An investigation is carried out if a pattern or practice of discrimination is discovered. Based on the evidence developed, one of the commissioners then decides whether to lodge a charge. After a charge has been filed, the office requests additional information from the company about its employment practices. During the investigation, the EEOC tries to make a predetermination settlement. If the matter is not settled and discrimination is found to exist, the regional office issues an administrative decision and tries to settle the matter through conciliation. If this fails, the regional office seeks the commission's authority to litigate the matter in federal district court.

Class action suits, like systemic cases, deal with patterns or practices of discrimination within an industry or group. Class action cases are initiated by individuals rather than by a commissioner.

Any member of the public or any organization or agency may request that the commission investigate a case of systemic discrimination, but the EEOC is not required to undertake investigations based on outside requests.

AFFIRMATIVE ACTION

Congress enacted Title VII to overcome the effects of past and present employment practices that perpetuated discrimination. In addition to prohibiting specific acts of employment discrimination, Title VII encouraged voluntary affirmative action by employers to eliminate barriers to equal employment opportunity. Since the enactment of Title VII, therefore, many employers, labor organizations, and others have developed programs to improve employment opportunities for groups that previously suffered from discrimination. These programs include efforts to recruit women and minorities and to offer them special training to improve their chances of promotion. Some of these actions and programs have been challenged under Title VII. These so-called "reverse discrimination" cases charge that affirmative action programs are in conflict with requirements that employment decisions not be based on race, color, religion, sex, or national origin.

The EEOC has published affirmative action guidelines to help employers develop programs that would encourage increased employment opportunities for minorities and women while at the same time meeting the requirements of Title VII.

PROCEDURES

The commission decided in 1983 that the EEOC should no longer rely on its rapid charge processing system, which had been instituted in the 1970s, and instead should consider in each and every case whether the charge deserved investigation and perhaps litigation. The processing takes place at the nearest field office or at a 706 agency, with assistance from headquarters. The person making the charge (the charging party) first meets with an EEOC investigator (the intake officer) to determine whether the charge falls under the commission's jurisdiction (that is, discrimination in employment). If it does, a formal complaint

is drawn up. Then the field office makes a decision as to whether the charge deserves rapid processing aimed at settlement or extended processing aimed at litigation and assigns it to the appropriate unit. The business, group, or individual against whom the charge is filed (the respondent) is then notified of the charge and asked to provide information. If the respondent fails to provide the information, the commission may issue a subpoena. After the EEOC field office gets the information, it may hold a fact-finding conference attended by both parties. The charging party and the respondent may reach a settlement during this process. If no settlement is reached, or if the charge is in extended processing, a formal investigation then commences.

The formal investigation uses the administrative powers of the commission. Witnesses are interviewed, field visits are made, and relevant documents are examined. The investigator then confers with an EEOC attorney to make a determination of "reasonable cause"—a decision as to whether the charge has merit under the law.

An effort of conciliation (a Title VII term signaling a settlement only after issuance of a decision) among the parties is made. However, according to a 1985 policy statement, the EEOC is committed to seeking "full remedial, corrective, and preventive relief" in every case where reasonable cause was found to believe that there had been illegal discrimination. Yet the statement also said that "reasonable compromise" could be considered during conciliation efforts.

If conciliation does not occur, the investigator and attorney then make a recommendation to the district director. If the director agrees, the case is recommended to the general counsel who, in turn, recommends it to the commission. The commission, at its weekly meeting, makes the final decision on filing a suit in the public interest. If the commission decides to sue, the case is sent back to the office where it originated and charges are filed against the respondent in federal district court. If the commission decides against litigation, the claimant is informed and issued a right-to-sue notice. Claimants who have been issued right-to-sue notices may file suit on their own, if they wish, but the EEOC will not provide any further assistance.

Age, Pay, and Disability Discrimination

Procedures for filing age, pay, and disability discrimination complaints and charges are similar to those used for Title VII charges. Anyone alleging age, pay, or disability discrimination can file either a complaint or a charge at the nearest EEOC district or area office.

For charges filed under the Equal Pay Act and the Age Discrimination Act, the complaint protects the identity of the individual making the filing, and the respondent is not notified of an investigation until the commission makes a determination of reasonable cause. When a charge is filed, the respondent is notified within ten days and the identity of the person making the charge is not protected.

Charges filed under the Americans with Disabilities Act and Title VII do not carry the same confidentiality provision for employees but, as in all cases, charges are kept confidential from the public.

Concurrent charges that allege discrimination under Title VII in addition to pay or age bias also may be filed.

Federal Employment Discrimination

Federal employment discrimination complaints are first made informally to the accused agency's equal employment opportunity counselor, who makes an inquiry and seeks a solution. If the matter cannot be resolved, a formal complaint may be filed with the agency's director of equal employment opportunity or other appropriate official, who investigates the complaint and proposes a disposition. The complainant may request a hearing, in which case the agency asks the EEOC to assign an administrative judge to conduct a hearing. After the hearing, the administrative judge makes a recommendation to the agency head (or designee), who makes a final decision. The complainant has the right to appeal the decision to the EEOC's Office of Federal Operations or to file a civil suit in federal district court. If dissatisfied with the appellate decision, the complainant still may file a civil suit.

If the complaint is of age discrimination, the complainant may avoid this administrative process by filing a Notice of Intent to Sue and giving the EEOC thirty days' notice of intent to file suit. Complaints of violations of the Equal Pay Act (EPA) must be filed directly with the EEOC at any of its district or area offices. In addition, an EPA suit may be brought in federal court before filing an administrative complaint.

In October 1992 new regulations about the federal agency complaint process went into effect. Under the so-called Part 1614 regulations, EEOC's administrative judges must close new requests for hearings within 180 days.

Part 1614 provided that an employee or applicant generally must contact a counselor within forty-five days of the discriminatory event but also allowed the time to be extended when warranted. It limited the time spent in counseling to thirty days, with the possibility of extending an additional sixty days if agreed to by both parties.

It also required the agency to complete its investigation and issue a notice of final action on a complaint within 180 days of its filing.

The EEOC reported that this procedure increased average hearings productivity for each administrative judge by 11 percent during fiscal 1993, its first year of implementation.

In May 1998, to the disdain of conservatives in and out of government, President Bill Clinton expanded the list of categories that are protected from federal hiring and contracting discrimination. Along with such classifications as age and gender, Clinton by executive order said sexual orientation could not be the basis of discrimination.

REPORTING REQUIREMENTS

The commission enforces several reporting requirements that apply to employers, unions, and employment agencies. Generally only aggregate and nonconfidential information from these reports is available to the public *(see Other Information Sources, p. 97)*.

Private employers of 100 or more individuals must annually file reports (EEO-1 reports) on the composition of their workforce by occupational category, broken down by race, sex, and national origin. All government contractors and subcontractors with fifty or more employees and contracts in excess of $50,000 also must file this report.

Others required to file EEOC reports include:

• Local unions with 100 or more members (EEO-3 reports, biannual).

• State and local governments with fifteen or more employees (EEO-4 reports, biannual).

• Elementary and secondary school districts that employ 100 or more individuals (EEO-5 reports, biannual).

• Private and public colleges and universities that employ fifteen or more individuals (EEO-6 reports, biannual).

• Employers are required to post in a conspicuous place a notice that gives a summary of fair employment laws and information on the procedures for filing a charge of employment discrimination.

Background

The EEOC was established by Title VII of the Civil Rights Act of 1964 and began operations July 2, 1965. The creation of the EEOC was the culmination of more than two decades of effort by civil rights activists to establish a federal fair employment agency. In 1941 President Franklin D. Roosevelt set up a Fair Employment Practices Committee (FEPC). Largely advisory, the committee sought to end discrimination in hiring by the federal government and its defense contractors. Four years later, after a bitter debate over appropriations, Congress directed that the agency end its activities in 1946.

President Harry S. Truman in 1948 submitted a civil rights program to Congress calling for a new fair employment agency, but bills to establish such an agency were kept from the floor of both chambers until 1950. During that year the House of Representatives passed a fair employment bill, but a Republican-sponsored amendment, supported by southern Democrats, deleted the agency's enforcement powers. Efforts to pass a stronger measure in the Senate also failed that year.

In 1961 President John F. Kennedy, by executive order, established the Equal Employment Opportunity Committee, headed by Vice President Lyndon B. Johnson. Kennedy told the committee to use its powers "to remove permanently from government employment and work performed for the government every trace of discrimination."

A government-wide racial employment census was undertaken for the first time, and all government departments and agencies were directed to report to the committee their plans and recommendations for eliminating employment discrimination. The committee sought to persuade corporations doing business with the government to adopt "Plans for Progress" designed to provide for the training and employment of African Americans. Such agreements were voluntary, however, and the reach of the committee's authority was uncertain.

EARLY HISTORY

In 1963, when the drive for civil rights began to dominate national headlines, legislation again was introduced in Congress to create a fair employment agency. It came in the form of an amendment to a civil rights package submitted by Kennedy. With the strong backing of President Johnson, the Civil Rights Act, including a section creating the EEOC, was enacted by Congress in 1964.

As originally structured, the EEOC had authority to encourage compliance with the equal employment provisions of Title VII by using conciliation proceedings. If conciliation failed, the commission could recommend that the U.S. attorney general file suit in federal district court to force compliance. If the attorney general declined to prosecute, the aggrieved individual (the charging party) could file a suit on his or her own behalf. The commission lacked the power to compel an employer to obey the law.

The enactment of the Equal Employment Opportunity Act of 1972 amended Title VII and gave the commission authority to file lawsuits against private employers, employment agencies, and unions when conciliation efforts failed. It also allowed the commission to file suit in cases of alleged systemic discrimination. Authority to file suit against alleged discriminatory practices in state and local governments, however, was not given to the EEOC; that power remained in the Justice Department.

During the commission's first decade of operation, it gained the reputation of being among the worst managed government agencies. By 1976 it had gone through six chairs and several acting chairs, as well as a like number of executive directors. It also was burdened with a backlog that by some estimates exceeded 120,000 cases.

Criticism of the commission came from all sides. Minorities and women asserted that it took so long to process

charges that the victims often lost patience and dropped their complaints. Employers and unions, on the other hand, argued that the commission provoked confrontation and was biased in favor of employees. The EEOC also was accused of encouraging preferential hiring and using discriminatory quota systems.

Eleanor Holmes Norton, who was appointed chair by President Jimmy Carter in 1977, instituted several revisions. She reorganized the commission's internal structure and field offices and established a new system for handling complaints. Norton's system, called rapid charge processing, reduced the commission's case backlog, which had been significantly increased by the transfer of age and equal pay regulation from the Labor Department in 1979. By 1981 the commission's backlog had been reduced to fewer than 33,000 cases. The average case required less than three months to process and resolve, as compared with two years under the former procedures.

EEOC IN THE 1980S

During the course of the presidency of Ronald Reagan, the EEOC underwent a complete change in leadership and direction. With the appointment of Clarence Thomas, the assistant secretary for civil rights in the Education Department as chair in 1982, the EEOC scrapped the use of goals and timetables to promote the hiring of minorities and women.

In fact, Thomas was so vehemently opposed to goals and timetables that during his term of office EEOC attorneys inserted new clauses in some of the consent decrees obtained during the Carter administration. The clauses announced that the EEOC would not enforce any sections of the decrees calling for the use of goals and timetables to increase the hiring of minorities and women.

In 1985 the commission adopted a statement of policy to seek "full remedial, corrective, and preventive relief" in every case where reasonable cause was found to suspect illegal discrimination. That policy statement was widely seen as heralding a shift in EEOC emphasis—away from systemic discrimination cases against large companies or entire industries and toward cases involving discrimination against specific individuals.

Criticism of the agency continued, in large part because of the backlog of cases—due, as some critics charged, to Thomas's belief in litigating as many valid cases as possible. The backlog affected both the private-sector enforcement activities of the commission and its role in enforcing laws against discrimination in federal employment.

Congress continually was frustrated with the federal equal employment opportunity (EEO) complaint process and had pressed Thomas and the commission for more than three years to come up with a better system. Each agency was responsible for investigating and resolving its own complaints. But with no pressure to resolve cases quickly, the investigations dragged on.

Federal workers and civil rights organizations condemned the system as containing built-in conflicts of interest. In 1989 Congress introduced a bill to give the EEOC full responsibility for handling discrimination complaints in the federal government, just as it had in the private sector. But Thomas resisted the measure, saying that the agency did not have the money or the staff to handle federal workers' complaints on top of its existing workload.

In September 1987 the Senate Special Committee on Aging made inquiries into the way the EEOC handled claims of discrimination filed under the Age Discrimination in Employment Act (ADEA), focusing on the EEOC's failure to file class action suits that would have a broad impact on discrimination against older workers. At the same time, Senate investigators discovered that the statute of limitations had expired on approximately 7,500 cases and the EEOC had failed to notify the complainants of that fact in many of the cases.

To preserve the rights of older workers to sue under the ADEA, in 1988 the House and Senate passed, and President Reagan signed, the Age Discrimination Claims Assistance Act, giving older workers an additional eighteen months to file a lawsuit once the statute of limitations expired.

In response to criticism about the agency's lack of work on discrimination on the basis of national origin, the EEOC set up "expanded presence" offices—temporary facilities located in churches or other community gathering places in areas removed from the EEOC district offices.

Thomas also attempted to mend EEOC relations with the small business community by starting the Voluntary Assistance Program, in which district offices held seminars for business owners to educate them about antidiscrimination laws.

One final set of events significant to the future course of the EEOC were the six 1989 Supreme Court rulings that narrowed the scope of antibias laws and put the responsibility for proving discrimination on employees rather than the employer. The best known of these decisions was *Wards Cove Packing Co. v. Antonio*, which required the worker to identify a particular employment practice that resulted in an underrepresentation of minorities in the workplace, and gave the worker the job of proving the practice was not required in the course of running a business.

CIVIL RIGHTS LEGISLATION

Two major pieces of legislation redefined the work of the EEOC in the 1990s: the Civil Rights Act of 1991 and the Americans with Disabilities Act of 1990. These laws greatly increased the workload and the complexity of cases under the jurisdiction of the EEOC.

Congress first addressed civil rights discrimination issues when it sought to counter the effects of the six 1989 Supreme Court decisions that made it harder for workers to sue their employers for discrimination. Sen. Edward M. Kennedy, D-Mass., and Rep. Augustus F. Hawkins, D-Calif., introduced legislation to give women and religious and ethnic minorities the right to seek monetary damages in job discrimination cases. Previously, African Americans and other racial minorities were the only groups allowed to sue for monetary damages, as opposed to back pay. The administration of George Bush opposed the bill, maintaining that the introduction of monetary damages and a jury trial would turn the EEOC mediation process into an adversarial one. However, on Nov. 7, 1991, Congress passed a compromise civil rights bill that Bush signed. The Civil Rights Act of 1991 allowed limited money damages for harassment victims and those discriminated against on the basis of sex, religion, or disability, permitting women for the first time the right to seek limited money damages for sex discrimination.

It required the EEOC to establish a Technical Assistance Training Institute to provide training and technical assistance on the laws and regulations enforced by the commission. It also required the EEOC to carry out educational and outreach activities, including targeting those who historically had been targets of discrimination and distributing information in other languages besides English.

The second major piece of legislation, the Americans with Disabilities Act (ADA), was signed into law July 26, 1990. It outlawed discrimination against the estimated 43 million Americans with disabilities in employment, public services, and public accommodations. The EEOC was responsible for enforcing the sections of the ADA dealing with employment. Although changes that would involve "undue hardship" were excluded, employers were required to make "reasonable accommodations" for workers who have disabilities. The law did not spell out what these accommodations might be.

The ADA created a special challenge for the EEOC because the commission had to develop manuals and pamphlets for use by people with disabilities. This requirement meant publishing materials in Braille or on tape for the blind and expanding the use of telecommunication devices for the deaf. Moreover, the ADA required the EEOC to determine whether certain specific conditions should be regarded as disabilities. For example, persons with acquired immune deficiency syndrome (AIDS) were covered under the law "implicitly," under an interpretation of the Rehabilitation Act of 1973, issued by the Justice Department, which described AIDS patients as disabled. In July 1998 the Supreme Court ruled that those people with the human immune deficiency virus (HIV), which causes AIDS, were covered by the act. By a 5–4 vote, the Court said it did not matter whether a person had developed symptoms of the disease.

The agency itself made clear the scope of the law in 1997, issuing guidelines stating that mental illness is a disability and that employers must accommodate those suffering from it. The guideline raised the ire of many who worried about unstable workers being protected. For the EEOC, the law meant a broad expansion of its jurisdiction and workload. In subsequent years the EEOC requested increasing amounts of appropriations from Congress in order to keep up with its increased workload under the ADA.

In October 1990 Congress also passed the Older Workers Benefit Protection Act, legislation to reverse a 1989 Supreme Court ruling that allowed age-based discrimination in employee benefits. Regulations dating from 1969 prohibited age-based differentials in benefits unless they were justified by "significant cost considerations." Those so-called "equal cost or equal benefit" regulations were invalidated by a 1989 Supreme Court decision. The 1990 act codified the "equal cost or equal benefit" regulations. As the act was originally opposed by many business groups, members incorporated a compromise that gave employers exemptions for two widely used early retirement incentive plans.

EEOC IN THE 1990S

In addition to having major legislative additions to its responsibility, the EEOC also remained under public scrutiny with ongoing criticism and investigations. In 1990, when EEOC chair Clarence Thomas won confirmation to the U.S. Court of Appeals for the District of Columbia Circuit, some Senate Judiciary Committee members expressed concern about the commission's handling of age-discrimination cases and halting of efforts to meet minority hiring goals and timetables in job discrimination cases under Thomas's stewardship.

Thomas brought the EEOC back into the spotlight a year later, during his Supreme Court nomination hearings. During the initial hearings, Thomas again was criticized on age discrimination; some groups also complained that he failed to challenge gender-based wage discrimination. University of Oklahoma law school professor Anita Hill then came forward to testify in a second set of hearings that Thomas had sexually harassed her while both worked at the EEOC. Thomas denied the charges and later won confirmation to the Supreme Court, although not without sparking national dialogue about sexual harassment in the workplace.

The EEOC's guidelines on sexual harassment, ironically, had come to be the accepted workplace standard: "Unwelcome sexual advances, requests for sexual favors, and other verbal or physical conduct of a sexual nature constitute sexual harassment when (1) submission to such conduct is made either explicitly or implicitly a term or condition of an individual's employment, (2) submission to or rejection of such conduct by an individual is used as the basis for employment decisions affecting such individual, or (3) such conduct has the purpose or effect of unreasonably interfering with an individual's work performance or creating an intimidating, hostile, or offensive working environment."

A series of hearings and reports in the early 1990s marked a trail of ongoing criticism of the agency. A General Accounting Office (GAO) report in July 1993 detailed concerns about the EEOC's operations, including the increasing time it took the EEOC to investigate and process charges, the inventory of charges awaiting investigation, and the adequacy of investigations. The GAO also expressed concerns about the high proportion of findings that the discrimination charges were not warranted and the limited number of litigation actions and systemic investigations initiated by the EEOC.

Another concern had been the hiring and promotion of women and minorities in the federal workforce. In October 1991 the GAO testified before the Senate Governmental Affairs Committee that representation of women and minorities in the federal workforce had improved overall between 1982 and 1990; but the GAO noted that white women and minorities still had fewer numbers in upper-level positions. The GAO recommended that the EEOC require agencies to analyze hiring, promotion, and other personnel action data to identify equal employment barriers better. In March 1993 the GAO still found white women and minorities underrepresented in key higher-level government jobs.

Revisions to the EEOC's structure and procedures continued to be a topic of discussion. In a report to the Senate Special Committee on Aging in February 1994, the GAO warned that the EEOC's workload would continue to increase unless the agency changed its policies and practices. Among the options mentioned in the report were using alternative dispute resolution (ADR) approaches such as mediation to achieve agreement through less formal and less adversarial procedures. The report also suggested that the EEOC could increase its systemic actions by working with constituency groups and making greater use of testers—people who apply for jobs with the sole purpose of uncovering discriminatory hiring practices.

The beginning of the Clinton administration did not seem to herald a new era of effectiveness for the EEOC. President Clinton took fifteen months to nominate Gilbert Casellas as chair, and for much of Clinton's first year and a half the agency made do with three commissioners rather than five. Meanwhile, the backlog of complaints continued to swell, nearing the 100,000 mark by late 1994.

Under Casellas, however, the EEOC made some attempt to answer its critics, through both greater efficiency and increased activism. After taking office in October 1994, Casellas declared that "we must reevaluate how we do business." Coming from a career in corporate law rather than in civil rights organizations, Casellas set up a task force to increase the use of alternative methods of dispute resolution in cases handled by the EEOC.

A second task force, headed by EEOC commissioner Paul Igasaki, recommended that the agency divide complaints into three categories and stop fully examining complaints that were deemed to have little merit. Field offices were given authority to dismiss some complaints and were relieved of the burden of writing letters to explain each dismissal. By April 1995 the EEOC had enacted these recommendations.

The EEOC under Casellas did increase both its activism and its pragmatism, resulting in a somewhat mixed and ambiguous record. A case in point was the agency's handling of the ADA, which many critics faulted for a dramatic increase in the number of discrimination cases filed with the EEOC. In April 1995 the EEOC expanded its interpretation of the ADA to include employment discrimination based on a worker's genetic predisposition toward particular diseases or disorders, thereby staking out new authority over a type of case that was anticipated but not yet common. In October 1995, on the other hand, the EEOC refined its guidelines on the ADA to relax the rules on questions about "reasonable accommodations" that employers can ask job applicants: this came in response to businesses' confusion under the initial guidelines.

The EEOC's handling of its most high-profile cases also brought mixed results. In 1996 the EEOC took up a class-type lawsuit against Mitsubishi Motors, alleging sexual harassment of some 500 women at a plant in Normal, Ill. In April the company staged a worker rally against the EEOC; but on July 11, 1998, the agency announced it had secured the largest sexual harassment litigation payment in history. The $34 million settlement, along with the company's apology to more than 300 female workers, gave the agency a well-publicized victory.

Ida L. Castro, the first Hispanic to head the agency, took over as chair of the commission in October of 1998 and quickly made clear she would be an aggressive advocate of workers and would be willing to go places that the agency had not previously gone. In controversial moves, the agency issued new rules in 1999 making clear that a company does not have to know about a particular case of worker harassment to be held liable, and ruled in late 2000 that an employer who does not offer contraception as part of an insurance drug benefit is guilty of sexual discrimination.

In other policy guidelines, the agency tackled the salary differentials of male and female coaches at the high school and college level and the rights of temporary employees. In a highly publicized announcement, the agency said pay variances among male and female coaches are acceptable, as long as they can be justified. The guideline addressed the common practice of paying male coaches more than their female counterparts and took into account the fact that men's sports often bring in more revenue than female athletics.

In March 1999 the agency worked out a $2.1 million settlement against a Missouri nursing home that discriminated against Filipino registered nurses. The agency was not involved in a 1999 settlement between black workers and Coca-Cola Co. The $492.5 million settlement was the largest racial discrimination settlement in history.

Some of the biggest acts affecting the agency in recent years, however, have come from the U.S. Supreme Court and not from the agency itself. A series of rulings have limited the scope of the ADA, such as two in 1999 that exempted from the law those workers whose conditions can be corrected by medication or other treatments, such as glasses. The cases involved nearsighted pilots and a mechanic who suffered from hypertension. While treatable, the agency argued that many such conditions negatively impact the ability of individuals to gain employment. The Court also ruled that state government workers cannot sue their employer in federal court under the act.

In a major victory for the agency, however, the Court in 1999 overturned an appellate court ruling that said the agency did not have the power to impose compensatory damages. The lower court ruling, if left intact, would have stripped the agency of much of its power, backers said.

The agency in the latter part of the decade focused its attention on those workers who report allegations of discrimination. With a nearly double increase in retaliation complaints since 1991, the EEOC issued guidelines in 1997 making it clear it is illegal to retaliate against workers, or former workers, that file discrimination complaints.

EEOC IN THE 2000S

Until her tenure ended in August 2001, Castro had stressed the need to educate employers, especially small businesses, about the ways to avoid ending up on the receiving end of a complaint. Under her leadership the agency has urged workers and employers to mediate, rather than litigate, cases. The rate of voluntary mediations has risen dramatically in recent years.

In fiscal 2000 the EEOC won $245.7 million in settlements. In one case the EEOC successfully filed suit on behalf of a man who was fired by a Ryder Systems subsidiary because he suffered from epilepsy. The man, a former trucker, received $5.5 million. The agency ruled that temporary employment agencies and contracting companies are responsible for making sure workers with disabilities are treated fairly. In June 2000 the agency secured a $1 million settlement of a class action lawsuit on behalf of twenty-two Hispanic women against Grace Culinary Systems and Townsend Culinary. The agency had alleged wide-ranging sexual harassment against the women at the Laurel, Md., food processing plant.

Castro, a former labor lawyer, took additional steps to protect immigrant and migrant workers, pointing to statistics that show harassment allegations against workers based on their nationality have grown in recent years. The agency issued guidelines in 2000 stating that undocumented workers "are entitled to the same remedies as any other workers: back pay, reinstatement if the employee was unlawfully terminated, hiring . . . except in the very narrow situations where an award would directly conflict with the immigration laws."

In early 2001 the agency convinced Burlington Northern Santa Fe Railroad to stop testing its workers for genetic defects. The case, supporters said, was an important step toward protecting the medical privacy of workers and complemented a Clinton administration executive order blocking the federal government from basing hiring decisions on such information.

The agency's authority was strengthened in some cases through a 2002 U.S. Supreme Court decision, *EEOC v. Waffle House Inc.*, which affirmed that the EEOC could sue employers who discriminate against workers, even if the workers had signed an arbitration agreement that sought to bar employees from suing their employers for discrimination.

The appointment of Cari M. Dominguez by President George W. Bush in August 2001 as the new chair of the commission marked a shift in direction for the agency. Dominguez, who was the first person without a law degree to head the commission, relied on her private-sector business experience and previous work at the Labor Department as she embarked on efforts to streamline the agency.

In early 2002 Dominguez introduced a five-point plan encouraging the agency to use more cost-efficient techniques. The five elements of Dominguez's plan were (1) proactive prevention of discrimination through educational outreach; (2) cost-effective and timely resolution of charges; (3) strategic enforcement that targets the most egregious cases; (4) expansion of mediation and arbitration techniques; and (5) strict antidiscrimination safeguards at the EEOC for its workers.

With her business background, Dominguez used the plan to emphasize her interest in getting the "biggest bang for the buck." She hoped to use the media and the agency's Web site as low-cost ways to educate the public about discrimination and how to prevent it. Her second stated goal—to streamline and expedite the resolution of cases—was intended to save both time and money. The purpose of Dominguez's third point was to litigate cases that would "provide the greatest benefit to the greatest number of people," such as situations involving widespread, systemic discrimination. An expanded emphasis on mediation and arbitration, which had been used extensively in the Clinton administration as well, was another way that Dominguez believed the agency could reduce the funding and time involved in resolving cases. The fifth point of her plan simply involved making the EEOC a "model workplace" and improving coordination among its offices.

The EEOC addressed an increased number of cases in 2002—the highest level since 1995. Complaints rose to 84,442 during the 2002 budget year, up from 80,840 the previous year. (In 1995 the number had reached 87,529.) The poor economy, an aging and multinational workforce, and backlash from the 2001 terrorist attacks were all cited as reasons by Dominguez. Complaints based on religion spiked by a 21 percent jump, while complaints of age discrimination rose by 14.5 percent and national origin complaints rose by 13 percent. The commission resolved 95,222 cases that year, which marked a 5 percent increase from 2001.

Dominguez credited part of the reason for the improved timeliness of resolution to her increased use of alternative dispute resolution approaches, which grew out of the Clinton administration's program. A report commissioned by Dominguez showed that, from October 1996 through September 2001, about 91 percent of federal employment discrimination lawsuits by the EEOC were successfully resolved through consent decrees, settlement agreements, and favorable court orders, according to an extensive five-year litigation study released by the EEOC.

Current Issues

EEOC chief Dominguez planned to continue to rely on mediation and arbitration as tools to keep the annual number of case resolutions high. She initiated pilot projects in 2003 to expand the use of mediation in disputes between private-sector employers and workers. Serving with Dominguez in 2003 were Paul Steven Miller, a Clinton appointee whose nearly ten years at the commission made him one of the longest serving commissioners in the 40-year history of the EEOC; Leslie E. Silverman, a lawyer and former Republican congressional aide who was sworn in during March 2002; and Naomi Churchill Earp, who was given a recess appointment by President George W. Bush in April 2003.

Dominguez also hoped to continue to build on her five broad goals through a complete reorganization of the agency's complaint process, which she sought to make faster and cheaper. She planned to unveil an overhaul plan in 2003, with implementation of the proposal to occur during fiscal 2004.

In formating her overhaul plan, Dominguez sought suggestions in 2003 from a number of advocacy groups. The National Academy of Public Administration (NAPA) also released a report in February suggesting that the agency should consolidate its administrative support staff and consider relocating some workers away from Washington, D.C., where rental and salary costs may be lower. The NAPA study noted that the agency's rental expenses were increasing more than $1 million each year. The study proposed that the commission experiment with technology to improve efficiency. It recommended experiments with telecommuting and suggested that the agency invest in software that could help manage its caseload. Dominguez charged a task force with examining the recommendations and creating plans to incorporate ideas that could save money.

Part of the impetus behind Dominguez's long-range goals came from the demands of a budget crisis at the agency. President Bush did not push for increased funding to attain gender pay equity at the agency, as Clinton did at the end of his term. EEOC officials had also made it clear by the end of 2000 that the agency's resources were stretched thin. The strains on the agency continued to grow, leading to a projected shortfall of resources in 2003. Soaring lease costs, an increase in cases, and payroll increases all contributed to the deficit.

◼ AGENCY ORGANIZATION

Biographies

CARI M. DOMINGUEZ, CHAIR

Appointment: Nominated by President George W. Bush on May 10, 2001, to serve as Chair.

Born: March 8, 1949, Havana, Cuba.

Education: American University, B.A., 1971; M.A., 1977.

Profession: Consultant.

Political Affiliation: Republican.

Previous Career: Dominguez has held positions in government and business and currently runs her own consulting firm, Dominguez and Associates, specializing in senior management recruitment, diversity evaluations, expert witness testimony on employment-related cases, and workforce preparedness assessments. She has served as assistant secretary of labor for employment standards.

NAOMI CHURCHILL EARP, VICE CHAIR

Appointment: Nominated by President George W. Bush on April 22, 2003; five-year term expires July 1, 2005.

Born: February 15, 1950.

Education: Norfolk State University, B.A., 1972; Indiana University, M.A., 1977; Catholic University of America's Columbus School of Law, J.D., 1982.

Profession: Consultant, attorney advisor.

Political Affiliation: Republican.

Previous Career: Earp's work experience in promoting diversity in the EEO field includes a series of progressively responsible leadership positions with various federal agencies, including the National Institute of Science and Technology, the National Institutes of Health, the Federal Deposit Insurance Corporation, and the U.S. Department of Agriculture. At NIH, Earp spearheaded the development of a world-class diversity initiative and a nationally-recognized Alternative Dispute Resolution Program. At the Department of Agriculture she headed the Equal Opportunity Program, which included minority small businesses and minority farmers. Earp also served as an Attorney Advisor at the EEOC during the mid-1980s. In addition, to being an attorney advisor, Earp has worked as an independent consultant providing services to private employers and public agencies on a variety of employment-related issues and programs.

PAUL STEVEN MILLER, COMMISSIONER

Appointment: Nominated by President Clinton to fill an unexpired term, confirmed by the Senate Sept. 29, 1994; confirmed for a second term in July 1999; term expires July 2004.

Born: May 4, 1961, New York, NY.

Education: University of Pennsylvania, B.A. 1983; Harvard University, J.D. 1986.

Profession: Lawyer.

Political Affiliation: Democrat.

Previous Career: Prior to his appointment to the EEOC, Miller was deputy director of the U.S. Office of Consumer Affairs and the White House liaison to the disability community. Prior to that, he was director of litigation for the Western Law Center for Disability Rights. Miller has taught law courses at Loyola Law School in Los Angeles and at the University of California at Los Angeles.

LESLIE E. SILVERMAN, COMMISSIONER

Appointment: Nominated by President Bush on Feb. 11, 2002 to fill an unexpired term; confirmed by the Senate March 1, 2002; term expires July 2003.

Born: 1965, Boston, MA.

Education: University of Vermont, B.A.; American University, Washington College of Law, J.D.; Georgetown University Law Center, M.A.

Profession: Lawyer.

Political Affiliation: Democrat.

Previous Career: Silverman served five years as labor counsel to the Senate Health, Education, Labor, and

EQUAL EMPLOYMENT OPPORTUNITY COMMISSION

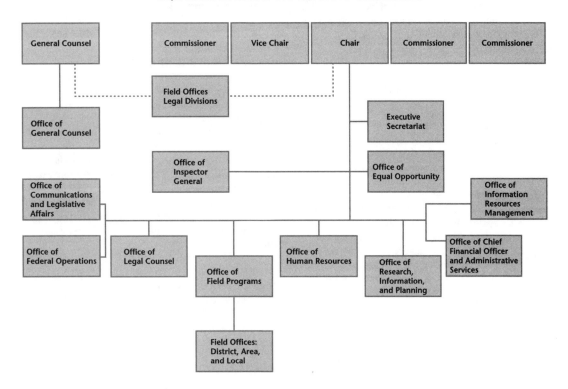

Pensions Committee. From 1990 to 1997, she was an associate specializing in employment law and litigation with Keller and Heckman, a Washington, D.C.-based law firm. Silverman has also worked as a law clerk for the U.S. Attorney's Office for the District of Columbia and for the Antitrust Division of the U.S. Department of Justice.

Headquarters and Divisions

COMMISSION

The commission is responsible for receiving and investigating charges of employment discrimination. Individual commissioners may initiate charges if they receive information that indicates the law has been violated. The commission approves the filing of lawsuits under Title VII of the Civil Rights Act of 1964, as amended, the Equal Pay Act of 1963, the Age Discrimination in Employment Act of 1967, and the Americans with Disabilities Act of 1990. It conducts public and closed hearings on employment discrimination in various industries and on proposed employment guidelines. It also rules on the designation of state and local 706 agencies and makes final judgments on appeals of denials of Freedom of Information Act requests.

The commission reviews selected decisions of the Merit Systems Protection Board in which federal employment discrimination is an issue.

The chair, as executive officer, is responsible for the successful implementation of commission policy and the supervision of the commission staff. The chair recommends policies, procedures, and programs for consideration by the commission.

Chair
    Cari M. Dominguez.................... (202) 663–4001
    TTY.................................... (202) 663–4141
Vice Chair
    Paul M. Igasaki .... (202) 663–4027
    TTY.................................... (202) 663–7129
Commissioners
    Paul Steven Miller...................... (202) 663–4036
    TTY.................................... (202) 663–7172
    Leslie E. Silverman .... (202) 663–4026
    TTY.................................... (202) 663–4062
    Naomi Churchill Earp .... (202) 663–4081

OFFICE OF THE EXECUTIVE SECRETARIAT

Serves as the focal point for the receipt, documentation, review, coordination, and monitoring of all policy-related activities and all the decisions flowing to and from the chair, commissioners, and program offices. Responsible for the coordination of the commission meetings and the administration of responsibilities under the Government in the Sunshine Act.

Director

Frances Hart	(202) 663–4070
TTY	(202) 663–4077

OFFICE OF COMMUNICATIONS AND LEGISLATIVE AFFAIRS

The Legislative Affairs Division responds to congressional communications and tracks, researches, and analyzes legislation and issues. Communications Division staff inform employees, employers, the general public, and all other stakeholders about EEOC policies and programs, participate in seminars and exhibits, produce publications and annual reports, and serve as a liaison to the media. The Public Information Unit answers general public inquiries. Agency public information publications are available free of charge through a toll-free number.

Director

Joan Ehrlich (acting)	(202) 663–4900
TTY	(202) 663–4494

Communications

Vacant	(202) 663–4900

Legislative Affairs

Sylvia Anderson	(202) 663–4900

Public Information Unit

All areas	(202) 663–4900

Publications Distribution Center

All areas	(800) 669-3362
TTY	(800) 669-3302

OFFICE OF EQUAL OPPORTUNITY

Counsels, investigates, and recommends disposition of complaints of commission employees and applicants for employment who believe they have experienced discrimination in the workplace, or in the application process. Provides alternative dispute resolution opportunities (principally mediation) at all steps of the foregoing processes. Coordinates with other EEOC components to promote affirmative employment and diversity, and establishes and monitors special employment programs for disabled and veteran employees. Develops and promotes special emphasis programs to celebrate historic months and causes such as Women's History Month, Black History Month, the disabled, diverse sexual orientation, and ethnic groups (Hispanics, Asian American and Pacific Islanders, and Native Americans).

Director

Veronica Venture	(202) 663–7081
TTY	(202) 663–7002
Fax	(202) 663–7003

OFFICE OF FEDERAL OPERATIONS

Provides leadership and guidance to federal agencies regarding the federal government's equal employment opportunity program; develops proposed policies; and implements programs to ensure hiring, placement, and advancement of women, minorities, and individuals with disabilities.

Also receives appeals of discrimination decisions handed down by the Merit Systems Protection Board (MSPB) and from final action taken on discrimination complaints made by the heads of federal agencies. Drafts proposed decisions for the commissioners, who then adopt a recommendation for a ruling.

Director

Carlton M. Hadden	(202) 663–4599
TTY	(202) 663–4593

Appellate Review Programs

Hilda D. Rodriguez	(202) 663–4601

Compliance and Control

Robert Barnhart	(202) 663–4599

Federal Sector Programs

R. Edison Elkins	(202) 663–4519

Special Services

Donald E. Names	(202) 663–4599

OFFICE OF THE GENERAL COUNSEL

Responsible for litigation authorized by the commission, represents the commission in litigation, and provides legal advice to the commission and its officers. Also concurs in the appointment of regional attorneys and advises them on litigation. Oversees, with the Office of Field Programs, enforcement litigation programs in the headquarters and field offices. The division of Systemic Investigations and Review Programs advises the Office of Field Programs during the investigation of systemic and individual charges to ensure EEOC standards are met before cases are litigated. Develops programs designed to encourage compliance with EEO laws and reports to the commission on legal issues raised in enforcement litigation that may affect commission policy.

General Counsel

Vacant	(202) 663–4702
TTY	(202) 663–7181

Deputy General Counsel

Nicholas M. Inzeo (acting)	(202) 663–4702

Associate General Counsel

Gwendolyn Young Reams	(202) 663–4702

Appellate Services

Philip B. Sklover........................ (202) 663–4736

Litigation Management Services

Jerome Scanlon........................ (202) 663–4719

Research and Analytic Services

Joseph Donovan........................ (202) 663–4749

Systemic Investigations and Review Programs

James Finney .... (202) 663–4863

OFFICE OF THE INSPECTOR GENERAL

Principal responsibilities under the Inspector General Act of 1978, as amended, include providing policy direction, and conducting, supervising, and coordinating independent internal and external audits, investigations, and evaluation of all EEOC programs and operations. Works to promote economy and efficiency in the administration of, and to prevent and detect fraud, waste, and abuse in, EEOC programs and operations. OIG keeps the Chair and Congress fully and currently informed about commission problems and deficiencies, and the need for corrective action. OIG focuses its resources on issues that represent the greatest risk and maximum opportunity to add value to the agency.

Hotline................................. (800) 849-4239

Inspector General

Aletha Brown........................... (202) 663–4379

Deputy Inspector General

Milton A. Mayo Jr. .... (202) 663–4379

Counsel to Inspector General

Joyce T. Willoughby................... (202) 663–4379

OFFICE OF THE LEGAL COUNSEL

Serves as principal adviser to the commission in all nonenforcement legal matters. Provides legal advice to the public and, upon request, to federal agencies, state and local governments, fair employment practice agencies, and members of Congress. Develops and recommends commission decisions on cases for which there is no commission precedent. Drafts regulations, enforcement guidances, and compliance manual sections for commission approval; responds to requests under the Freedom of Information Act; manages the administration of Executive Order 12067, which calls for governmentwide coordination of equal employment opportunity statutes, regulations, and policies, and provides advice on the EEOC's ethics program.

Legal Counsel

David L. Franks........................ (202) 663–4637

TTY..................................... (202) 663–7026

Deputy Legal Counsel

Legal Services Programs

Richard Roscio (acting)................ (202) 663–4640

Associate Legal Counsel

Coordination and Guidance Programs

Peggy Mastroiazzi...................... (202) 663–4638

FINANCIAL AND RESOURCES MANAGEMENT

Establishes, monitors, and maintains control over federal funds appropriated for commission operations. Responsible for accounting for such funds. Administers the commission's contracts and procurement programs.

Director

Jeffrey A. Smith........................ (202) 663–4046

Financial Management Division

Jeffrey A. Smith........................ (202) 663–4200

Resource Management Division

George R. Betters...................... (202) 663–4263

OFFICE OF HUMAN RESOURCES

Provides leadership in the recruitment, development, and retention of a high quality and diverse workforce. Encourages line managers to take responsibility and accountability for human resources management by simplifying human resources systems and investing in employee development.

Director

Angelica E. Uberguen.................. (202) 663–4306

TTY.................................... (202) 663–4399

Fax.................................... (202) 663–4324

OFFICE OF INFORMATION RESOURCE MANAGEMENT

Plans, develops, and implements all aspects of the agency's IRM/IT program including policies and procedures concerning the automated information systems, deployed technology, and related resources and services. Provides a variety of computer services to all EEOC offices, and manages technology infrastructure, primary information systems, and telecommunications systems on an agencywide basis.

Director/Chief Information Officer

Sallie Hsieh .... (202) 663–4447

Fax.................................... (202) 663–4451

Charge Data System Division

Pierrette J. Hickey..................... (202) 663–4429

Systems Support and Services Division

Everett J. Barnes....................... (202) 663–4440

Technology Planning and Design Division

    Robert E. Fuller......................... (202) 663–4496

Telecommunications and Networking Division

    Lori Renner............................ (202) 663–4411

OFFICE OF RESEARCH, INFORMATION, AND PLANNING

Researches, collects, and analyzes enforcement data; reviews and analyzes organizational activities; makes recommendations to improve operations; manages agency Web site and library services; and provides resource, technical, and research support to the commission and the public.

Director

    Deidre Flippen .... (202) 663–4853

Research and Technical Information

    Patrick R. Edwards..................... (202) 663–4959

Program Research and Surveys

    Joachim Neckere .... (202) 663–4958

Program Planning and Analysis

    James Goldweber....................... (202) 663–4850

Strategic Planning and Management Controls

    Jay Friedman .... (202) 663-4094

Library and Information Services

    Susan Taylor........................... (202) 663-4630

Web Site Contact Manager

    Susan Farris........................... (202) 663-4160

OFFICE OF FIELD PROGRAMS

Manages EEOC's 50 field offices. Advises and assists field offices in meeting the challenges of managing large and complex workloads. Coordinates field office enforcement and litigation, as well as hearings and Federal Affirmative Action functions. Gathers and assembles data from field offices to present to Congress and oversight agencies. Designs and develops national training programs for field office staff, coordinates outreach programs aimed at EEOC's stakeholders, including fee-based training under the EEOC revolving fund, and oversees the national mediation program. Manages and supports the resolution of charges by state and local agencies under worksharing agreements and contracts, and contracts with Tribal Employment Rights Offices to protect Title VII and special preference rights of Indians. Also works with the commission's management offices to administer budgetary, financial, and training services to the field offices.

Director

    Reuben Daniels (acting) .... (202) 663–4801

    TTY.................................... (202) 663–7063

State/Local Programs

    Michael Dougherty .... (202) 663–4944

Field Management Programs

    James Lee (acting)..................... (202) 663–4814

Field Coordination Programs

    Paula J. Choate .... (202) 663–4831

Regional Offices

The EEOC has 24 district offices, 1 field office, 17 area offices, and 8 local offices. Offices are responsible for the receipt, mediation, investigation, conciliation, and litigation of charges of employment discrimination. Offices also provide education outreach and technical assistance to employers and others on the laws EEOC enforces. Certain offices also have hearings and federal affirmative action functions.

Section 706 of Title VII provides that the EEOC may contract with designated state and local fair employment practice agencies; the 706 agencies play a major role in processing discrimination charges within their jurisdictions.

Below is a list of EEOC district offices. For information about area, local, and 706 agency offices, contact the closest district office or call (800) 669–4000 (voice) or (800) 669-6820 (TTY).

ALBUQUERQUE

505 Marquette N.W., #900
Albuquerque, NM 87102
(505) 248–5201
TTY (505) 248–5240
Georgia Marchbanks (acting), director

ATLANTA

100 Alabama St., #4R30
Atlanta, GA 30303
(404) 562–6800
TTY (404) 562–6801
Bernice Williams-Kimbrough, director

BALTIMORE

City Cresent Bldg.
10 S. Howard St., 3rd Floor
Baltimore, MD 21201
(410) 962–3932
TTY (410) 962–6065
Gerald Kiel (acting), director

BIRMINGHAM

Ridge Park Pl., #2000
1130 22nd St. SE
Birmingham, AL 32205
(205) 731–0082
TTY (205) 731–0095
Cynthia G. Pierre, director

CHARLOTTE

129 W. Trade St., #400
Charlotte, NC 28202
(704) 344–6682
TTY (704) 344–6684
Michael A. Whitlow (acting), director

CHICAGO

500 W. Madison St., #2800
Chicago, IL 60661
(312) 353–2713
TTY (312) 353–2421
John P. Rowe, director

CLEVELAND

1660 W. Second St., #850
Cleveland, OH 44113–1454
(216) 522–2001
TTY (216) 522–8441
Michael C. Fetzer, director

DALLAS

207 S. Houston St., 3rd Floor
Dallas, TX 75202–4726
(214) 655–3355
TTY (214) 655–3363
Chester Bailey (acting), director

DENVER

303 E. 17th Ave., #510
Denver, CO 80203
(303) 866–1300
TTY (303) 866–1950
Francisco J. Flores, director

DETROIT

477 Michigan Ave., #865
Detroit, MI 48226–9704
(313) 226–7636
TTY (313) 226–7599
James R. Neely Jr., director

HOUSTON

1919 Smith St., 7th Floor
Houston, TX 77002
(713) 209–3320
TTY (713) 209–3367
Jim Sacher (acting), director

INDIANAPOLIS

101 W. Ohio St., #1900
Indianapolis, IN 46204–4203
(317) 226–7212
TTY (317) 226–5162
Danny G. Harter, director

LOS ANGELES

255 E. Temple St., 4th Floor
Los Angeles, CA 90012
(213) 894–1000
TTY (213) 894–1121
Olophius Perry (acting), director

MEMPHIS

1407 Union Ave., #521
Memphis, TN 38104
(901) 544–0115
TTY (901) 544–0112
Doris Woods (acting), director

MIAMI

1 Biscayne Tower
2 S. Biscayne Blvd., #2700
Miami, FL 33131
(305) 536–4491
TTY (305) 536–5721
Federico Costales, director

MILWAUKEE

310 W. Wisconsin Ave., #800
Milwaukee, WI 53203–2292
(414) 297–1111
TTY (414) 297–1115
Chester V. Bailey, director

NEW ORLEANS

701 Loyola Ave., #600
New Orleans, LA 70113–9936
(504) 589–2329
TTY (504) 589–2958
Patricia T. Bivins, director

NEW YORK

33 Whitehall St.
New York, NY 10004
(212) 336–3620
TTY (212) 336–3622
Spencer H. Lewis Jr., director

PHILADELPHIA
21 S. Fifth St., 4th Floor
Philadelphia, PA 19106–2151
(215) 440-2600
TTY (215) 440-2610
Marie M. Tomasso, director

PHOENIX
3300 N. Central Ave., #690
Phoenix, AZ 85012–1848
(602) 640–5000
TTY (602) 640–5072
Charles Burtner, director

SAN ANTONIO
5410 Fredericksburg Rd., #200
San Antonio, TX 78229–3555
(210) 281-7600
TTY (210) 281-7610
Pedro Esquivel, director

SAN FRANCISCO
901 Market St., #500
San Francisco, CA 94103
(415) 356–5100
TTY (415) 356–5098
Susan L. McDuffie, director

SEATTLE
Federal Office Bldg.
909 First Ave., #400
Seattle, WA 98104–1061
(206) 220–6883
TTY (206) 220–6882
Jeanette M. Leino, director

ST. LOUIS
Robert A. Young Bldg.
122 Spruce St., #8.100
St. Louis, MO 63103
(314) 539–7800
TTY (314) 539–7803
Lynn Bruner, director

■ CONGRESSIONAL ACTION

Congressional Liaison
Vacant......................................(202) 663–4900

Committees and Subcommittees

HOUSE APPROPRIATIONS COMMITTEE
Subcommittee on Commerce, Justice, State, and
 Judiciary
H309 CAP, Washington, DC 20515
(202) 225–3351

HOUSE EDUCATION AND THE WORKFORCE COMMITTEE
2181 RHOB, Washington, DC 20515
(202) 225–4527
Subcommittee on Employer-Employee Relations
B346A RHOB, Washington, DC 20515
(202) 225–7101

HOUSE GOVERNMENT REFORM AND OVERSIGHT COMMITTEE
2157 RHOB, Washington, DC 20515
(202) 225–5074
Subcommittee on Civil Service
B371C RHOB, Washington, DC 20515
(202) 225–6427
Subcommittee on Human Resources
B372 RHOB, Washington, DC 20515
(202) 225–2548

SENATE APPROPRIATIONS COMMITTEE
Subcommittee on Commerce, Justice, State, and
 Judiciary
S146A CAP, Washington, DC 20510
(202) 224–7277

SENATE COMMITTEE ON HEALTH, EDUCATION, LABOR, AND PENSIONS
SD-428, Washington, DC 20510
(202) 224–5875

Legislation
The EEOC was created by **Title VII of the Civil Rights Act of 1964** (78 Stat. 241, 42 U.S.C. 2000e), signed by the president July 2, 1964. Title VII contained the provisions of the law to be enforced by the EEOC. It outlawed discrimination in employment on the basis of race, color, religion, national origin, and sex (pregnancy-related discrimination was specifically prohibited by the **Pregnancy Discrimination Act of 1978,** 92 Stat. 2076, 42 U.S.C. 2000e). It also applies to employers of 15 or more employees, state and local government, employment agencies, and labor unions.

The provisions of Title VII did not apply to elected officials, their personal assistants, and appointed policy-making officials. Title VII also provided that employers could make distinctions on the basis of sex, religion, or national origin if sex, religion, or national origin was a *bona fide* occupational qualification for the job.

Enforcement powers contained in the 1964 law gave the EEOC authority only to investigate, find cause, and attempt conciliation. However, passage of the **Equal Employment Opportunity Act** (86 Stat. 103, 42 U.S.C. 2000e), signed by the president March 24, 1972, gave EEOC authority to prosecute cases of employment discrimination against private employers. It also brought all federal employees under the protection of Title VII, with enforcement initially assigned to the Civil Service Commission.

A 1978 presidential reorganization plan gave EEOC authority to enforce the EEO laws prohibiting discrimination by the federal government.

The same reorganization also transferred responsibility for equal pay and age discrimination statutes from the Labor Department to the EEOC. In 1990, EEOC was given responsibility for the enforcement of the Americans with Disabilities Act.

In addition to Title VII, EEOC currently enforces the following laws:

Equal Pay Act of 1963 (77 Stat. 56, 29 U.S.C. 206). Signed by the president June 10, 1963. Forbade discrimination in wages and fringe benefits based on sex.

Age Discrimination in Employment Act of 1967 (81 Stat. 602, 29 U.S.C. 621). Signed by the president Dec. 15, 1967. Outlaws discrimination against workers or applicants over the age of 40. It applies to private employers of 20 or more workers; federal, state, and local governments and employment agencies; and labor unions with 25 or more members or that operate a hiring hall or office that recruits or attempts to recruit employees for a covered employer.

Rehabilitation Act of 1973, Section 501 (86 Stat. 355, 29 U.S.C. 791). Signed by the president Sept. 26, 1973. Prohibits disability-based discrimination against federal employees and requires federal agencies to undertake affirmative action in connection with the employment of persons with disabilities.

Title I of the **Americans with Disabilities Act** (104 Stat. 327, 42 U.S.C. 1201 note). Signed by the president July 26, 1990. Prohibits employment discrimination against qualified individuals with disabilities. Applies to employers with 15 or more employees, unions, employment agencies, and state and local government.

Civil Rights Act of 1991 (105 Stat. 1071, 42 U.S.C. 1981 note). Signed by the president Nov. 21, 1991. Amended the Civil Rights Act of 1964 by strengthening the scope and effectiveness of civil rights protections. Provided compensatory and punitive damages for intentional discrimination under Title VII of the Civil Rights Act and under the Americans with Disabilities Act.

■ INFORMATION SOURCES

Internet

The EEOC can be reached via the Internet using the host address: Internet: http://www.eeoc.gov. The site contains contact information, an introduction about the commission, and links to other relevant sites.

Telephone Contacts

Publications Orders .... (800) 669–3362
Information Line .... (800) 669–4000
TTY .... (800) 669–6820

Information and Publications

KEY OFFICES

EEOC Communications and Legislative Affairs
1801 L St. N.W., Room 9027
Washington, DC 20507
(202) 663–4900
TTY 663–4494
Vacant, director

Answers general questions from the press and the public. Also issues news releases and publications and maintains a mailing list.

Freedom of Information
Office of the Legal Counsel
1801 L St. N.W., Room 6206
Washington, DC 20507
(202) 663–4669
TTY 663–7026
Stephanie Garner, contact

EEOC Office of Field Programs
1801 L St. N.W., Room 8002A
Washington, DC 20507
(202) 663–4801
TTY 663–7063
James Lee (acting), director

Provides information on complaints and charges. Complaints alleging employment discrimination must be made at the EEOC field office nearest the dispute or at a 706 agency. If conciliation fails to settle the matter, the commissioners vote on whether to litigate on behalf of the party alleging discrimination.

Charges must be filed within 180 days of the alleged law violation (up to 300 days if a state or local fair employment practices agency was first contacted).

To file a charge, a claimant must use Form EEOC-5, which is available from any EEOC office. The initial charge may be made without this form, but it must be in writing. This initial charge need contain only the claimant's name, address, place of employment, and a statement indicating that he or she has been discriminated against by an employer.

This information constitutes a charge, although the claimant should be willing to give further information at later stages of the investigation.

Charges are kept confidential. A charge may be filed by one party on behalf of another party.

PUBLICATIONS

Contact the EEOC Publications Distribution Center, (800) 669–3362, for the following titles, which are available free:

Annual Report. Commission decisions and compliance activities; includes list of complaints acted on by the commission.

The ADA: Your Rights as an Individual with a Disability. Explains rights under the Americans with Disabilities Act. Also in Spanish.

EEOC Poster. Gives a summary of federal fair employment laws and information on how to file a charge of employment discrimination. Must be displayed in a conspicuous place by all employers subject to EEOC supervision. Also in Spanish and Mandarin Chinese.

Information for the Federal Sector. Contains detailed explanation of complaint process for charges involving federal employees or applicants, of appeal process of federal EEOC decisions, and of the rights of federal employees.

Information for the Private Sector. Contains detailed explanation of the laws the EEOC enforces and the charge filing process. Also in Spanish.

National Origin Discrimination. Includes overview and background of revised guidelines on discrimination because of national origin.

Pregnancy Discrimination. Includes overview of guidelines for compliance with the Pregnancy Discrimination Act of 1978.

Religious Discrimination. Provides brief overview and background of revised guidelines on discrimination because of religion.

Sexual Harassment. Gives brief overview of sexual harassment as a form of discrimination. Also in Spanish.

DATA AND STATISTICS

Program Research and Survey Division

Office of Research, Information, and Planning
(202) 663–4958
Joachim Neckere, director

Provides information on reports required by the EEOC, which supply data on the composition of the nation's working population. (Most information has been "sanitized" to protect the confidentiality of employers and employees alike.) The following reports are kept on microfilm:

Elementary and Secondary Staff Information (EEO-5). Data provided biennially by public school districts with 100 or more full-time employees. Full-time employees are categorized by race/ethnic and sex groups and by 18 job assignment classes. Part-time and new hire data also are collected. Aggregate data available to the public.

Employer Information Report (EEO-1). Annual data provided by all private employers with 100 or more employees and all government contractors with 50 or more employees and a contract of $50,000 or more. Collected by race/ethnic and sex groups, by nine occupational categories, and by Standard Industrial Classification codes; currently reported for any payroll period in July through September. Data available to the public.

Local Union Report (EEO-3). Data provided biennially by all local referral unions with 100 or more members; data include total and minority group membership, job referrals, applicants for membership and referrals, sex of members, trades, and geographic location. Aggregate data available to the public.

State and Local Government Information (EEO-4). Employment data on state and local governments with 100 or more full-time employees are collected biennially by race/ethnic and sex categories, by eight job categories, and by eight salary intervals for full-time employment. Data also collected for part-time employment and new hires. Aggregate listings available to the public.

Charge Data System Division

Information Resources Management Services
(202) 663–4429
Pierrette J. Hickey, director

Maintains the Charge Data System (CDS). CDS contains data on individuals who filed charges of employment discrimination, organizations against which charges were filed, receipt and violation dates of charges, issues involved, geographic locations, and processing and disposition information. Includes charges filed with 706 referral agencies as well as the EEOC. Selected tabular material is available in the EEOC annual report. Information on respondents and charging parties is confidential.

MEETINGS

The commission members meet formally as needed. Notices of upcoming meetings are posted in the lobby of the EEOC headquarters outside the offices of the executive secretariat, the chair, and the legal counsel. Notices are published in the *Federal Register* and available from a 24-hour telephone recording: (202) 663–7100.

At open sessions, the commission considers EEOC policy, proposed guidelines, proposals to fund various agencies and programs, and the general operations of the EEOC. Closed EEOC sessions typically involve complaints filed and/or internal personnel matters.

Reference Resources

LIBRARY

EEOC Library
1801 L St. N.W., Room 6502
Washington, DC 20507
(202) 663–4630
TTY 663-4641
Susan Taylor, chief
Hours: 8:30 a.m. to 5:00 p.m.

Open to the public. An appointment is recommended but not required.

INTERPRETATIONS AND OPINIONS

Office of the Legal Counsel
1801 L St. N.W., Room 6002
Washington, DC 20507
(202) 663–4637
TTY (202) 663–7026
David L. Frank, legal counsel

Anyone may request that the commission issue an interpretation of or an opinion on an employment discrimination question, but formal opinions are made available at the discretion of the commission. Requests must be written and should include the name of the person making the request, a statement of known facts, and the reason why the interpretation or opinion should be issued.

DECISIONS

When the commission makes a significant decision—one that affects an area on which the commission had not

previously ruled or one that expands a previous EEOC decision—it makes the text of the decision available to trade publishers for inclusion in their coverage of EEOC laws and regulations. The publishers are the Bureau of National Affairs and Commerce Clearing House. (*see Publishers, p. 98*)

RULES AND REGULATIONS

EEOC rules and regulations are published in the *Code of Federal Regulations,* Title 29, parts 1600–1612. Proposed rules, new final rules, and updates to the *Code of Federal Regulations* are published in the *Federal Register.* (See appendix for information on how to obtain and use these publications.) All EEOC rules, regulations, and policies are available on its Web site.

Other Information Sources

RELATED AGENCY

Office of Personnel Management
Workforce Information
1900 E St. N.W.
Washington, DC 20415
(202) 606–2704

Compiles and distributes statistical data on federal affirmative employment, covering race and national origin, sex, disability and veteran status, years of service, and age. Publications include *Demographic Profile of the Federal Workforce.*

COMPLIANCE MANUAL

The EEOC also prepares a compliance manual detailing requirements of Title VII. The manual is not distributed or sold by the government, but it is available from private publishers who have been given the right to reprint it. The compliance manual also is available for use at all EEOC district offices and at the EEOC Library.

NONGOVERNMENTAL ORGANIZATIONS

The following are some key organizations that monitor the EEOC and equal employment opportunity issues.

Center for Equal Opportunity
815 15th St. N.W., #928
Washington, DC 20005
(202) 639–0803
Fax (202) 639–0827
Internet: http://www.ceousa.org

Commission on Professionals in Science and Technology
1200 New York Ave. N.W., #390
Washington, DC 20005
(202) 326–7080
Fax (202) 842–1603
Internet: http://www.aaas.org/cpst

Equal Employment Advisory Council
1015 15th St. N.W., #1200
Washington, DC 20005
(202) 789–8650
Fax (202) 789–2291
TTY (202) 789–8645
Internet: http://www.eeac.org

Human Rights Campaign
1101 14th St. N.W., #200
Washington, DC 20005
(202) 628–4160
Fax (202) 347–5323
Internet: http://www.hrcusa.org

Leadership Conference on Civil Rights
1629 K St. N.W., #1010
Washington, DC 20006
(202) 466–3311
Fax (202) 466–3435
TTY (202) 785–3859

NAACP Legal Defense and Educational Fund
99 Hudson St., 16th Floor
New York, NY 10013
(212) 219–1900
Fax (212) 226–7592
  Washington office
  1275 K St. N.W., #301
  Washington, DC 20005
  (202) 682–1300
  Fax (202) 682–1312

National Organization for Women (NOW)
1000 16th St. N.W., #700
Washington, DC 20036
(202) 331–0066
Fax (202) 785–8576
TTY (202) 331–9002
Internet: http://www.now.org

National Organization on Disability
910 16th St. N.W., #600
Washington, DC 20006–2988
(202) 293–5960
Fax (202) 293–7999
TTY (202) 293–5968
Internet: http://www.nod.org

9 to 5, National Association of Working Women
238 W. Wisconsin Ave., #700
Milwaukee, WI 53203
(414) 274–0925
Fax (414) 272–2870
Job problems hotline: (800) 522–0925

PUBLISHERS
The following companies and organizations publish on the EEOC and related issues through books, periodicals, or electronic media.

Bureau of National Affairs (BNA), Inc.
1231 25th St. N.W.
Washington, DC 20037
(202) 452–4200
Fax (800) 253–0332
Internet: http://www.bna.com

Commerce Clearing House (CCH), Inc.
2700 Lake Cook Rd.
Riverwoods, IL 60015
(847) 267–7000
Fax (800) 835–5224
Internet: http://www.cch.com

Equal Rights Advocates
1663 Mission St., #550
San Francisco, CA 94103
(415) 621–0672
Fax (415) 621–6744
Internet: http://www.equalrights.org

Garrett Park Press
P.O. Box 190
Garrett Park, MD 20896
(301) 946–2553
Fax (301) 949–3955

ILR Press
Cornell University Press
P.O. Box 6525
750 Cascadilla St.
Ithaca, NY 14851–6525
(607) 277–2211
Fax (800) 688–2877
Internet: http://www.ilr.cornell.edu/depts/ILRpress

Warren, Gorham & Lamont, Inc.
31 St. James Ave.
Boston, MA 02116
(800) 999–9336
Fax (617) 695–9699
Internet: http://www.wgl.com

West Publishing Co.
P.O. Box 64526
St. Paul, MN 55164
(800) 328–9352
Internet: http://www.westpub.com

Federal Communications Commission

445 12th St. S.W., Washington, DC 20554
Internet: http://www.fcc.gov

INTRODUCTION

The Federal Communications Commission (FCC) is an independent regulatory agency that was established by the Communications Act of 1934. It is composed of five commissioners, not more than three of whom may be members of the same political party. The commissioners are nominated by the president and confirmed by the Senate. The president designates one of the members to serve as chair. Terms are for five years with staggered expiration dates, arranged so that no two terms expire in the same year. Originally there were seven commissioners with longer terms, but legislation enacted by Congress in 1982 reduced both. The change became effective June 30, 1983.

Responsibilities

The FCC oversees all interstate and foreign communication by means of radio, television, wire, cable, and satellite. It controls licenses for about three million companies and individuals that rely on the airwaves for communications, ranging from amateur radio operators to regional Bell telephone companies and cable television systems.

Specifically, the FCC:

• Allocates portions of the radio spectrum to nongovernmental communications services and assigns specific frequencies within those spectrum bands to individual users. It also governs the use of the spectrum for other purposes, such as remote-control devices.

• Licenses and regulates all commercial audio, video, and communications services that use the radio spectrum.

• Regulates common carriers in interstate and foreign communications by telegraph, telephone, and satellite. It also sets national standards for competition in local telephone service.

GLOSSARY

Broadcasting—The multidirectional transmission of sound, images, data, or other electronically encoded information over the air by means of electromagnetic radiation in the radio spectrum, such as in radio or television.

Cable—Transmission of sound, images, data, and other electronically encoded information by means of wires, usually a combination of fiber-optic and coaxial cables capable of carrying sixty or more video channels simultaneously.

Cellular telephone—Transmission of telephone calls via radio to mobile receivers. Metropolitan areas are divided into "cells," each with an antenna to relay signals to and from the mobile phones. The call is handed off from one cell to the next as the receiving phone moves, allowing the first cell to use the same frequency for a new call.

Common carrier—A regulatory category that includes any company offering telecommunications services to the general public, such as telephone and telegraph companies. Common carriers must offer their transmission services at nondiscriminatory rates to any interested customer, and for regulatory purposes are treated much like electric or gas utilities.

Direct broadcast satellite (DBS)—The transmission of video images and sound directly from a programming source to viewers' homes via satellite. The service typically is offered via subscriptions, like cable, and the satellite dishes are roughly eighteen inches in diameter.

Low power television—Television stations with ranges of only a few miles. The FCC licenses low-power stations to increase the number of channels serving a community without electronically interfering with transmissions in nearby communities.

Multipoint microwave distribution services (MMDS), or wireless cable—Television broadcasting systems that transmit over the microwave portion of the radio spectrum. Microwave broadcasts can carry multiple channels but have a limited range because their signals do not pass through objects.

Personal communications service (PCS)—A digital version of cellular telephone service that the FCC started licensing in 1994. Typically, PCS phones are capable of more functions than other mobile units. For example, they can simultaneously act as phones, pagers, and answering machines.

Radio spectrum—The range of radiation frequencies available for use by the broadcasting and mobile communications services. These frequencies are divided into discrete channels and allocated to the various users by the FCC.

Telecommunications—Transmission of information chosen by a customer to points selected by the customer, without changing the form or content of the information.

- Regulates cable television and video services provided over telephone lines.
- Promotes safety through the use of radio on land, water, and in the air.

The commission also participates in an advisory capacity in U.S. delegations to international communications forums of the International Telecommunication Union (ITU). The ITU coordinates international spectrum allocations by treaty.

The FCC does not control every aspect of communications or broadcasting, largely because of the limits imposed by the First Amendment to the U.S. Constitution. It has little say over the broadcast networks or programming practices of individual stations or cable franchises. It does not control the content of broadcasts, although it has rules governing obscenity, slander, and political programs. And it does not regulate the advertising practices of broadcasters or claims made by advertisers on radio or television, other than limiting the amount of advertising during children's television programs. Instead, those matters are handled by the Federal Trade Commission (FTC).

The FCC has no authority over any form of government communication. Nor does it have jurisdiction over communications media other than broadcasters, cable, and telecommunications companies. For example, it does not regulate the motion picture industry, newspapers, or book publishers.

Finally, the FCC has only a limited role in local telephone or telecommunications services, which are regulated primarily by state utility commissions. In 1996 Congress gave the FCC authority to promote competition in local phone service and encourage the availability of low-cost telecommunications services in all areas, a policy known as "universal service." The FCC was given the power to preempt any state or local rule that was inconsistent with its regulations in those areas.

Powers and Authority

The five FCC commissioners adopt regulations to implement the telecommunications laws enacted by Congress. The regulations are developed and carried out by the six FCC bureaus: Common Carrier, Wireless

Telecommunications, Mass Media, Cable Services, International, and Compliance and Information. All of the bureaus are assisted when necessary by the Office of the General Counsel and the Office of Engineering and Technology.

The commission's power to regulate is strictly limited by Congress, but its power to deregulate is broad and discretionary. In the Telecommunications Act of 1996, Congress instructed the FCC to stop enforcing any regulation that was no longer needed to protect consumers or the public interest. That provision effectively gave the FCC the power to deregulate any segment of the industry that had become competitive, such as long-distance phone service.

Some of the specific areas the FCC controls are broadcast licenses, radio and television technical matters, interstate telephone and telegraph rates and charges, international communications by satellite and undersea cable, amateur (ham) radio equipment and practices, maritime communications, police and fire department communications, cable and pay television rates and program distribution, data transmission services, educational broadcasting, antitrust cases involving broadcast and telephone companies, consumer electronics standards (that is, specifications for radio and television receivers), industrial radio use such as radio dispatch of motor vehicle fleets, and aviation radio communication. The commission also is responsible for the equal employment opportunity practices of the industries it regulates.

COMMON CARRIER

Communications common carriers provide telephone, telegraph, facsimile, data, telephoto, audio and video broadcast program transmission, satellite transmission, and other electronic communications services for hire. The Communications Act requires common carriers to charge reasonable and nondiscriminatory prices, and most of the responsibility for enforcing that requirement falls to the Common Carrier Bureau. Technically, the commission has jurisdiction only over interstate and related telephone and telegraph services. Its reach extends to local phone companies, however, because those companies' networks are financed in part by interstate calls carried by long-distance companies.

Through the Common Carrier Bureau, the commission sets caps on the prices that phone companies charge for interstate and related services, writes accounting and depreciation rules, and determines whether companies may build new telephone facilities or discontinue or reduce services. It also requires regular financial and operating reports, reviews proposed phone company mergers and acquisitions, and promotes competition in the telephone markets.

Other duties include evaluating new technologies and utilization of facilities; conducting economic studies and investigations in industry structure and practice; overseeing telephone numbering, network reliability, and equipment registration; and regulating the rates and conditions for cable companies' use of utility poles.

The commission attempts to clear the way for new services through proceedings such as the Computers 2 and 3 inquiries, which determined the computer services that were properly subject to FCC regulation, and the Open Network Architecture proposal, designed to provide the building blocks for enhanced services. All three proceedings were completed by the FCC in the 1980s.

In the late 1990s the commission ended the requirement that phone companies file tariffs for domestic long-distance service because of the extensive competition in that market. The move all but deregulated prices in the interstate telephone business, although the FCC still retained the power to investigate complaints about excessive rates.

WIRELESS TELECOMMUNICATIONS

Cellular telephone, paging, public-safety dispatching, private radio, aviation radio, and other mobile communications services must obtain licenses from the FCC in order to use frequencies in the radio spectrum. The job of assigning those frequencies and issuing licenses falls to the Wireless Telecommunications Bureau, which the FCC established in 1994 to replace the Private Radio Services Bureau.

In the case of commercial services, the FCC has been given temporary power to conduct auctions and assign licenses to the highest qualified bidders. The bureau also promotes competition in wireless services and regulates the frequencies used, transmitting power, call signals, permissible communications, and related matters.

Unlike the wireline local phone companies, wireless operators face at least one competitor in every market. For that reason, they are subject to less regulation by the FCC and state authorities than their wireline counterparts. For example, the FCC does not require mobile communications companies to file tariffs, and Congress in 1993 barred state and local governments from regulating those companies' rates.

MASS MEDIA

Radio and television stations also must obtain licenses from the FCC before going on the air. The commission assigns the task of issuing licenses and developing broadcast regulations to the Mass Media Bureau. The bureau also sets technical standards and power limits for transmissions, assigns call letters, sets operating hours, and licenses the technicians who operate broadcast equipment.

In the interest of promoting competition and diversity of media ownership, the commission exerts a limited degree of control over television and radio networks. For example, the FCC reviews the restrictions that networks place on their affiliates' programs and advertising, and it limits the number of stations under common ownership locally and (in the case of television stations) nationally.

The FCC's principal leverage over broadcasters is its control over license renewals. When a station seeks to renew its license, the Mass Media Bureau reviews its performance to determine whether it has met the requirement to serve the public interest. For new licenses, the bureau conducts lotteries to determine which of the competing applicants will be authorized.

The commission only has limited power over the content of programs because, in addition to their First Amendment rights, broadcasters are not common carriers—they are not compelled to provide airtime to all would-be programmers or advertisers. The commission can and does restrict obscene and indecent programming, require television broadcasters to carry a certain amount of educational programming, and limit advertising during children's programs.

The commission's political broadcasting rules require stations that sell air time to one candidate to provide equal time to other major candidates for that office and to keep strict records of candidate requests for air time. The FCC also acts as arbiter in disputes concerning political broadcasts. The commission no longer requires stations to present contrasting views on nonpolitical programs, having concluded in 1987 that its Fairness Doctrine was unconstitutional. The decision remains a sore point with Congress, where efforts to restore the policy are ongoing.

In addition to the typical television and radio stations, the Mass Media Bureau licenses and regulates noncommercial educational stations, low-power television stations, and instructional television fixed service (ITFS) for in-school reception. ITFS uses higher frequencies than broadcast television and is not considered a broadcast service. It also licenses microwave-based "wireless cable" systems, a competitor to conventional cable television systems that the commission has tried to promote.

CABLE SERVICES

As in phone service, the regulation of cable television operators is split between the FCC and state and local agencies. Generally, local agencies are allowed to regulate franchising, basic subscriber rates, and leased access services. The FCC reviews rates for certain cable services, sets standards for customer service and picture quality, and enforces the federal requirements on cable programming. The latter includes the mandates that cable systems carry local broadcast stations, pay for the broadcast programs they retransmit, and make channels available to public, educational, and governmental programmers.

The commission also regulates other forms of video service and program distribution; ensures compatibility of programming with home electronic equipment; restricts indecent cable programs; and monitors competition in video services and oversees certain technical aspects of cable operation.

The Cable Services Bureau was split off from the Mass Media Bureau in 1993 to heighten the oversight of the rapidly expanding cable industry. Congress ordered the increased regulation in 1992, giving the FCC and local authorities the power to set "reasonable" rates for basic and expanded basic services, equipment rentals, and installation in areas where there was no effective competition.

In 1996 Congress reduced the FCC's power over cable rates and system ownership, particularly in relation to small cable systems. The same law also set out new regulatory requirements for telephone companies' video systems, and the Cable Services Bureau developed rules for such "open video systems" later that year.

INTERNATIONAL

In addition to communications within the United States, the FCC also has domestic authority over satellite communications systems, telephone services that link the United States with foreign countries, and international broadcasting stations. The commission established the International Bureau in 1994 to consolidate the commission's international policies and activities. It licenses satellite communications systems, regulates international telecommunications and broadcasting services, and represents the FCC at international telecommunications organizations.

The FCC's international mission includes enhancing U.S. competitiveness overseas and promoting an interconnected, global telecommunications network. Through the International Bureau, it researches the development of international telecommunications regulations and facilities, promotes the international coordination of spectrum use and orbital assignments, advises the U.S. Trade Representative on international telecommunications negotiations and standard-setting, monitors compliance with licenses, and conducts training programs for foreign telecommunications officials.

COMPLIANCE AND INFORMATION

The job of enforcing federal radio law and FCC rules generally falls to the Compliance and Information Bureau, formerly known as the Field Operations Bureau. It operates sixteen field offices and thirteen automated monitoring facilities across the United States, serving as the commission's window onto the communications world it regulates. In addition to acting as the commission's police, it also educates the public and the communications industries about FCC rules and policies.

Through the bureau, the FCC monitors the use of the spectrum to identify violations of the law or license terms. Its staff inspects radio stations and investigates complaints of interference, unauthorized transmission, or unlawful interception of calls. The bureau also is a leading authority on direction finding and other methods to identify the source of transmissions.

In 1996 the bureau began operating a national call center to field complaints about communications companies and other matters within its jurisdiction. In addition to providing information to the public, the bureau also advises the commission on the impact of regulations, the level of compliance, problems in the communications industries, and the merits of discontinuing old rules.

ENGINEERING AND TECHNOLOGY

To guard against conflicts in the radio spectrum, the FCC regulates most equipment that makes or interferes with radio transmissions—including computers, garage-door openers, cordless telephones, radio and television transmitters, and microwave ovens. New equipment in that category must meet FCC specifications and be authorized by the commission before it can be marketed.

The commission's Office of Engineering and Technology tests and authorizes equipment to ensure compliance. The office also works on technical standards, monitors and experiments with new technology, coordinates use of the frequencies shared by U.S. companies and international users or federal agencies, and provides the bureaus with scientific and technical advice.

Background

Federal regulation of interstate electrical communication began with the Post Roads Act in 1866, which authorized the postmaster general to fix rates annually for government telegrams. In 1887 Congress gave the Interstate Commerce Commission (ICC) authority to require telegraph companies to interconnect their lines for more extended service to the public.

Government regulation of the accounting practices of wire communication carriers began with the Mann-Elkins Act of 1910. That act authorized the ICC to establish uniform systems of accounts for telegraph and telephone carriers and to require certain reports of them. The Mann-Elkins Act also gave the ICC certain powers over radiotelegraph (wireless) carriers. This statute, in effect, extended provisions of the Interstate Commerce Act of 1887 to cover wireless telegraph.

As the number of radio users increased, it became necessary to organize the way the radio spectrum was used. A series of international radio conferences, starting in 1903, led to the development of regulations specifying uniform practices for radiotelegraph services. The enforcement of the regulations in the United States was delegated to the secretary of commerce and labor.

In 1912 Congress passed the Radio Act, the first law for the domestic regulation of radio communications in general. The Radio Act governed the character of emissions and transmissions of distress calls. It also set aside certain frequencies for government use and placed licensing of wireless stations and operators under the secretary of commerce and labor. The first stations were licensed that year.

After World War I commercial radio broadcasting began to grow. Because the Radio Act of 1912 had not anticipated commercial broadcasting, no federal safeguards had been adopted to prevent stations from interfering with or overpowering one another's signals. These problems were dealt with on an ad hoc basis by four National Radio Conferences held during the early 1920s.

In 1926 President Calvin Coolidge urged Congress to rewrite the 1912 law. The result was the Dill-White Radio Act of 1927. It created a five-member Federal Radio Commission with regulatory powers over radio, including the issuance of station licenses, the allocation of frequency bands to various services, the assignment of specified frequencies to individual stations, and the control of station power. The secretary of commerce was delegated the authority to inspect radio stations, examine and license radio operators, and assign radio call signals.

While the creation of the Federal Radio Commission solved many problems, the responsibility for electronic communications remained divided. The ICC still retained major responsibilities, and some aspects of telegraph service were under the jurisdiction of the Post Office Department and the State Department.

EARLY HISTORY

In 1933 President Franklin D. Roosevelt urged the creation of a new agency to regulate all interstate and foreign communication by wire and radio, including telephone, telegraph, and broadcasting. In response Congress enacted the Communications Act of 1934, which consolidated in the new Federal Communications Commission the regulatory authority previously exercised by the Federal Radio Commission (which was abolished), the secretary of commerce, and the ICC.

The 1934 act would stand for sixty-two years as the foundation for federal telecommunications policy. It provided the basis for strict federal regulation of the communications media, a level of control intended to protect consumers and the public interest in the face of powerful monopolies. The most significant changes during the next six decades were the Communications Satellite Act of 1962, which created the Communications Satellite Corporation (Comsat) and gave the FCC authority to regulate the corporation and its activities; the 1984 and 1992 cable acts, which deregulated and reregulated the cable industry; and the Omnibus Budget Reconciliation Act of 1993, which required the FCC to auction off portions of the radio spectrum instead of awarding those frequencies by lottery.

Congress tried repeatedly and unsuccessfully in the 1970s, 1980s, and early 1990s to overhaul the 1934 act. With competing interest groups facing off over the complex legislation, lawmakers demurred rather than appearing to take sides.

FROM TELEPHONE MONOPOLY TO COMPETITION

For many years, the FCC and state officials agreed with AT&T that the phone system was a natural monopoly; indeed, one effect of state and federal regulation was to sustain that monopoly against would-be competitors. In the local phone arena, the country was divided into regional monopolies dominated by AT&T's twenty-two Bell affiliates. In long-distance service, AT&T was effectively the sole provider. In addition, AT&T purchased all its equipment from its Western Electric subsidiary, and all Bell customers were required to use that equipment.

To give consumers some degree of protection, the FCC and state utility commissions regulated telephone rates and limited the profits earned by AT&T and the local phone companies. The FCC also imposed surcharges to shift costs from local to long-distance services; this shift was designed to hold down the cost of local phone lines. The main principles observed by the FCC were promoting the availability of low-cost phone service and insuring nondiscriminatory pricing.

The commission's approach to telephone service began to change in the 1960s, when it made two major moves toward competition: it allowed MCI and other upstart long-distance companies to offer specialized services in markets already served by AT&T, and it ended the requirement that consumers use the telephone sets and office switchboards provided by AT&T. In the early 1970s, the commission's Common Carrier Bureau allowed the competing long-distance companies to expand their offerings to the public, extending the battle with AT&T into more types of service.

AT&T responded by underpricing the competition, a move that the FCC tried repeatedly to block. Meanwhile, the Justice Department filed another antitrust lawsuit against AT&T—its third—seeking to split the Bells from the long-distance operations of AT&T and Western Electric. The Justice Department argued that AT&T was using the Bells' regulated monopoly power in local phone service to gain an illegal advantage in the newly competitive field of long-distance service.

That lawsuit led in 1982 to the consent decree that split the Bells from AT&T. The decree also released AT&T from the restrictions imposed under a previous settlement with the Justice Department, which had confined AT&T to markets regulated by the government. Those restrictions had kept AT&T out of the data-processing business and other computer- and information-related markets. At the same time, the Bells were barred from carrying long-distance calls, providing information services, and manufacturing telecommunications equipment until the federal courts ruled that there would be no threat of anticompetitive behavior.

The consent decree took effect Jan. 1, 1984, requiring a major new undertaking by the FCC: ensuring that all long-distance companies had equal access to the local phone companies' customers. It also came up with a new mechanism for shifting costs from local to long-distance services, establishing "access charges" that the local companies applied to each long-distance call.

DEREGULATION AT THE FCC

During the period of the breakup of AT&T, the FCC was transforming its interpretation of the law, moving toward a less strict regulatory regime. The move was prompted partly by political philosophy and partly by the rapid advance of technology, which strained the restrictions imposed by the FCC.

Deregulation first began in the common carrier area under Richard Wiley, a Republican chair appointed by President Richard Nixon. A series of court cases started to chip away AT&T's monopoly over long-distance telephone service. Using the court decisions as precedent, the FCC made several decisions that had the effect of promoting competition in long-distance services.

When Charles Ferris, a Democrat appointed by President Jimmy Carter, became chair, deregulation spread to the other communications services regulated by the FCC. By the time Mark Fowler, President Ronald Reagan's chair, was sworn in, the nature of the FCC's role in regulating telecommunications had undergone a fundamental change. Rather than restrict the development of new technologies and tightly regulate each component of the nation's communications network, the commission began to allow a free and open marketplace in telecommunications products and services.

Lotteries were introduced in the 1980s to grant low-power television, multichannel and multipoint distribution, cellular mobile telephone, electronic paging, and private radio services. Minority ownership rules were suspended. The Fairness Doctrine and other content-oriented broadcast regulations were dropped. Marketplace regulations based on pricing replaced traditional rate-of-return rules for common carriers. Tariff proceedings were expedited to speed delivery of new long-distance services to businesses and consumers. Station antitrafficking rules were eliminated. The multiple station ownership rules were eased. And regulation after regulation was dismantled for AT&T.

In the process, the commission reduced the paperwork burden imposed on many of its licensees and the backlog of some license applications, but it also alienated the more regulatory-minded majority in Congress. The result was several confrontations in the late 1980s and early 1990s as lawmakers tried to reassert their leadership on communications issues.

FCC IN THE 1990S

Congress reacted to the efforts of Fowler and Dennis Patrick, the succeeding FCC chair, by seeking to influence, obstruct, or overturn FCC decisions. With tensions growing, President George Bush appointed a Republican moderate, Alfred Sikes, who was well liked in Congress, to be his commission chair. Although the appointment of Sikes was designed to be a calming influence, it did not stop Congress from approving sweeping legislation in 1992 to reregulate the cable industry, even overriding Bush's veto.

President Bill Clinton's choice for FCC chair, Reed Hundt, drew mixed reviews from the industry and Congress. The broadcasters, for example, accused him of heavy-handedness in pushing to mandate three hours of educational television programming per week, and the cable companies decried his implementation of the 1992 cable act. Their complaints found a sympathetic ear among Republicans on Capitol Hill. Some leading congressional Democrats, on the other hand, praised Hundt for trying to protect consumers while also looking for ways to lighten the industry's regulatory load.

Hundt remained at the FCC until November 1997, leaving after the commission completed its major telephone reform in local exchange interconnection, universal service, and lower access charges. William Kennard, the commission's general counsel during Hundt's tenure, took over as chair at the same time as three new commissioners took their seats, marking 1997 as a hectic year in leadership changeover at the FCC.

When Republicans took control of Congress in 1995, GOP conservatives targeted the FCC for cuts or even elimination. The most deregulatory proposals were opposed by many segments of the industry, however, for fear that the Bells would run roughshod over their competition. Instead, a consensus gradually emerged in favor of a regulated transition to competition overseen by the FCC.

By the end of the year, lawmakers had fashioned a rewrite of the 1934 act that satisfied most segments of the industry, their allies in Congress, and the Clinton administration. The Telecommunications Act of 1996, which was signed into law in February, attempted to expand competition in the telephone and cable industries while paring the amount of regulation on all telecommunications companies and broadcasters. The new law represented a 180-degree shift in policy from the 1934 act as Congress sought to have competition and market forces take the place of strict federal and state controls.

As competition flourished in the long-distance market, the FCC gradually had eased its regulation of AT&T's long-distance services. In 1995 the FCC declared that AT&T was no longer a "dominant" carrier in the domestic long-distance market, lifting the added regulatory burden that AT&T had been forced to meet.

State regulators also were warming to the idea of competition in the local phone markets, but many technical and regulatory barriers stood in the way. The 1996 act eliminated the legal obstacles to competition in those markets, and it instructed the FCC to help remove the technical barriers on two main fronts: interconnection and universal service.

"Interconnection"—hooking into the incumbent local phone company's network—enables customers on competing phone networks to make calls to one another. Otherwise, a competitor would have to install new lines and phones into every home and business. The 1996 act required the incumbent phone companies to allow their competitors to interconnect with their networks at reasonable and nondiscriminatory rates. It also required them to give competitors a wholesale discount if the competitors chose to resell the incumbent's services rather than installing their own networks.

The FCC was left to translate the act's general instructions into specific rules within six months. In August 1996 the commission adopted a set of minimum interconnection standards that left many of the details to be negotiated by competitors or ironed out by state regulators. For example, the FCC established a method for determining what prices incumbents could charge their competitors, as well as default ceilings for those prices, but left the states to set the actual prices. Similarly, the FCC established rules to help the states calculate an appropriate wholesale discount, as well as setting a default discount of 17 to 25 percent below the retail price.

New FCC rules dealing with universal service were also not well received. State and federal universal service policies had posed a threat to competition because they distorted prices, with businesses and toll callers paying higher rates to keep the prices for residential lines low and affordable. The 1996 act required the FCC to create a new, competitively neutral system of explicit subsidies that would ensure the wide availability of low-cost phone service. Under the FCC's rules released in May 1997, companies had to use forward-looking formulas to determine how much a typical telephone line in an area would cost to replace five years in the future. The FCC then stipulated that the federal Universal Service Fund would cover 25 percent of those costs incurred over a national benchmark price. The other 75 percent would be left to the states to pay.

These May 1997 rules drew sharp criticism and litigation from the states and the Bells. As the 1990s drew to a close, the federal court system, including the U.S. Supreme Court, began sorting out these rules and lawsuits. Although the act and FCC rules left the states in primary control of the move to local-phone competition, the FCC was given the power to intervene if a state strayed from the mandates of the new law or failed to resolve disputes among competitors.

The act also gave the FCC, not the courts, control over the Bells' expansion into long-distance service and telecommunications equipment manufacturing. Before applying to the FCC, a Bell was required to face competition in at least a portion of its local phone market, meet a fourteen-point test that its network and operational support systems could handle interconnection, and be in the public interest. But by summer 1998, more than two years after the act was passed, no Bell companies had been admitted into the long-distance market, although several had applied. Southwestern Bell Communications prevailed in a Texas district court with its claims that Section 271 of the Telecommunications Act, which bars the Bell companies from this line of business until the FCC gives its okay, constituted a bill of attainder—an obscure section of the U.S. Constitution that prohibits Congress from singling out an individual for punishment without due process. The case was appealed in 1998 to the 5th U.S. Circuit Court of Appeals in New Orleans and the initial ruling was stayed pending that appeal.

CABLE REVERSALS

For cable companies, the 1996 act represented the third major shift in regulatory policy in twelve years. The 1984 Cable Communications Policy Act had deregulated the cable industry and relieved the commission and local municipalities of their rate and other regulatory authority. To give the fledgling cable companies a buffer against competition, the act barred the local phone companies from offering video programming services over the phone lines—a major restriction that the Bells would eventually challenge in court.

The deregulation was followed by the explosion of the cable industry into a $20 billion giant and complaints of poor service and discriminatory business practices. After a three-year fight, Congress reversed itself in 1992, giving the commission the power to set certain rates and requiring that cable program producers, such as MTV and ESPN, offer their programs to cable competitors at fair prices and terms.

The FCC was left to implement the 1992 act, and its interpretation won plaudits from consumer advocates but brickbats from industry. Using its authority, the commission ordered rates reduced up to 10 percent in 1993 and an additional 7 percent in 1994, cuts that saved consumers an estimated $4 billion. Hundt called the cuts "one of the greatest cost savings in the face of monopoly pricing in the history of American business regulation."

The 1996 act lifted the federal price controls on "cable programming services"—channels in the expanded basic tier, such as Cable News Network and ESPN—after March 31, 1999. The act also made it much harder for the FCC to review a proposed rate increase before the price controls were lifted and allowed cable operators to escape price controls earlier in the face of threatened competition. Finally, the act eliminated price controls on "cable programming services" for many small cable systems.

Some GOP congressional leaders wanted to go further in limiting the FCC's authority over cable. Consumers did not need regulators to protect them, these Republicans argued, because cable was hardly the only source of video entertainment. But opposition from the White House—Vice President Al Gore had helped to write the 1992 act as a Democratic senator from Tennessee—forced Republicans to agree to leave some price controls in place for three years.

The 1996 act also gave the FCC jurisdiction over the telephone companies' video efforts, although the companies were allowed to choose how extensively they would be regulated. One new option, called "open video systems," required the operator to make two-thirds of its channels available to unaffiliated programmers. It also exempted the operator, however, from many of the regulations on cable systems.

The FCC adopted its rules for open video systems in June 1996, prohibiting operators from discriminating among programmers, favoring their own programs, or charging unaffiliated programmers excessively to use the system. The rules, like the regulations adopted in 1993 for cable systems, also required operators to carry the signals of local television stations and obtain permission before retransmitting a station's broadcasts.

MASS MEDIA

The FCC loosened the reins significantly on broadcasters in the 1980s and 1990s, opening the door to more players and new services. One of the early deregulatory moves came in April 1981, when the commission eliminated many of its radio record-keeping requirements, all of its requirements governing minimum amounts of news and public affairs programming, and its rules requiring station executives to poll their communities regularly to ascertain their listeners' concerns and programming preferences.

In June 1984 the FCC extended those changes to television broadcasters when it eliminated guidelines concerning minimum amounts of news and public affairs programs and maximum amounts of commercial time. The commission also abolished program logs and requirements that stations meet certain program needs of the communities in which they operate.

More recently, the commission granted a major new freedom to television networks in 1995 when it repealed its twenty-five-year-old financial interest and syndication rules. Those rules had deterred CBS, NBC, and ABC from owning television programming. It also repealed the twenty-five-year-old prime time access rule that had prohibited those networks and their affiliates in large cities from filling their prime-time schedules with network-originated programs.

In addition to giving broadcasters more control over their schedules and programs, the rule changes eased the path to license renewal. In the 1996 act, Congress extended the terms of licenses to eight years—up from seven for radio and five for television stations—and ordered the FCC to renew a license automatically if a station had served the public interest, made no serious violations of FCC rules or federal communications law, and committed no pattern of abuse of FCC rules or federal law. In deciding whether to renew a license, the FCC could not consider whether the public interest would be served better by another applicant for that license.

The FCC and Congress also steadily increased the number of stations that a network or ownership group could control. For radio, the limit rose from twelve AM and twelve FM stations in late 1984 to twenty AM and twenty FM in 1994 and to an unlimited number in the 1996 act. For television, the limit rose from twelve stations reaching no more than 25 percent of the national viewing audience in late 1984 to an unlimited number of stations reaching no more than 35 percent of the national audience in the 1996 act.

Congress also eased the limits on local ownership of radio stations, allowing a single company or group to control as many as eight stations in large markets. It left intact the ban on networks owning more than one television station in a single market, although the FCC was ordered to reconsider that restriction and other ownership limits every two years. The law also ordered the FCC to let broadcast networks own cable systems. The FCC would have to ensure, however, that cable systems controlled by a network did not discriminate against broadcasters not affiliated with that network.

The 1996 changes in ownership limits sparked a flurry of mergers and buyouts. Two of the biggest deals, announced while the legislation was still moving through Congress, came in the area of television and cable: Walt Disney's purchase of Capital Cities/ABC and Westinghouse's purchase of CBS. In 1997 Time Warner acquired Turner Broadcasting Company to form another notable media titan. The merger wave quickly swept up radio stations and the baby Bells—by 1998 deals were pending that would combine the original seven Bells into four telephone giants.

The FCC and Congress generally justified the diminished control over broadcasters by citing the numerous and expanding sources of audio and video programming. Indeed, the FCC authorized almost 700 new FM stations in the mid-1980s and authorized a new, satellite-based digital audio broadcasting service in the 1990s. It also oversaw the emergence of direct broadcast satellites and attempted to speed the deployment of multipoint microwave distribution services (also known as wireless cable).

One significant potential source of video programming that emerged in the mid-1990s was digital television. In 1993 a group of manufacturers formed the Grand Alliance to develop a standard format for digital broadcasts. They eventually proposed a flexible format that would allow stations to transmit multiple channels on a single frequency or to broadcast one "high definition" signal with enhanced sound and picture quality. In May 1996 the FCC proposed to make the Grand Alliance format mandatory for all digital broadcasts. Broadcasters strongly backed the proposal, but the computer industry protested and urged that the marketplace, not government, should set the standard. In April 1997 the FCC set a timetable for build-out of the digital television system that would have all broadcasters converted to digital television and relinquishing their analog frequencies by 2006. Those frequencies will be reauctioned at that time.

One area where the FCC and Congress resisted the deregulatory tide was in television programming for children. In 1974 the commission issued the Children's Television Report and Policy Statement, which established guidelines for broadcasters. Sixteen years later, Congress enacted the Children's Television Act in a bid to improve the quality of commercial programming for children. The law ordered the FCC to determine whether a television station had served the educational needs of children before renewing its license.

After adopting an initial set of rules for children's programming in 1991, the FCC struggled for almost five years to clarify the requirements for broadcasters. Democrats sought to mandate a specific amount of educational programming that stations had to broadcast and Republicans resisted any quantitative standard. The logjam broke in August 1996, when the commission ordered stations to carry at least three hours of educational programming per week for viewers under the age of seventeen. The order represented a compromise among the commissioners, the White House, and broadcasters.

In 1997 the FCC approved a set of TV ratings developed by the broadcasting industry. The system, which displays a series of letters at the start of the program warning parents of sexual situations, violence, language, or dialogue, work with the "V-chip"—a device that can block the display of programs with certain ratings.

LICENSE FEES AND AUCTIONS

The FCC grew rapidly from the Nixon administration on, its budget multiplying from $25 million in fiscal 1970 to $278 million in fiscal 2003. Its approximately 1,900 employees are located primarily in Washington, D.C.

For many years the FCC has offset its expenses by charging fees on the telecommunications industry, but by the early 1990s the revenue had fallen far behind the commission's costs. In 1993 Congress approved an FCC plan for doubling new user fees ranging from $200 to $900 for radio stations and from $4,000 to $18,000 for television stations.

Congress also authorized the FCC to auction portions of the radio spectrum for commercial use. Long advocated by the FCC, the auctions represented a radical change in the way the spectrum was parceled out to users. They also reflected the growing role played by wireless technologies in telecommunications.

The bulk of the usable spectrum has been reserved for the Defense Department and other federal agencies. The next largest users are radio and television broadcasters; the FCC awards those licenses for free after holding hearings to decide which applicant would best serve the public interest.

The FCC used similar "comparative hearings" to award licenses for the early mobile communications systems, which were akin to two-way radios. As technology advanced and competition for licenses increased, the commission switched to a lottery system that awarded licenses on the basis of luck, not public interest.

The FCC started using lotteries to award cellular-phone licenses in 1983, and it followed the same route for paging systems. An unintended byproduct, however, was a new industry of license speculators who would apply for licenses only for the sake of selling whatever they won to the highest bidder.

By auctioning licenses, the FCC effectively transferred the speculators' bounty to the U.S. Treasury. The first licenses offered at auction were for a new, digital form of mobile phone and paging called "personal communications services." Those auctions raised an estimated $10 billion.

The enormous amount of money raised by the auctions led numerous lawmakers to call for more of the government-reserved spectrum to be converted to pri-

vate use through auctions. The interest in spectrum led the FCC to make more frequencies available in relatively small blocks, both for licensed and unlicensed services. By summer 1998, the commission had raised $23 billion through these auctions, with the Broadband C-block auction pulling in nearly $10 billion.

But all was not rosy with the auctions. Several of the C-block license winners defaulted on their loans and the FCC was left to straighten out the mess. Congress, as part of its Balanced Budget Act of 1997, also required the commission to set minimum prices for each license after the April 1997 Wireless Communications Services auction ended with several winning bids of less than $5 for major metropolitan licenses.

MERGERS AND CONSOLIDATIONS

The 1996 Telecommunications Act spurred more than $500 billion in mergers, as telephone companies, broadcast and cable system owners, and content providers retrenched in the deregulated environment. Major deals included America Online's purchase of Time-Warner—which combined the nation's largest Internet service provider with the second-largest cable-system owner; Bell Atlantic's purchase of GTE; AT&T's acquisition of cable giants MediaOne and Tele-Communications; and WorldCom's purchase of MCI. The FCC under Kennard was responsible for assessing whether these combinations ultimately benefited consumers. Because some merged entities began "bundling" services—simultaneously selling voice, cable, and high-speed Internet, all transmitted over high-capacity fiber-optic lines—the agency also was thrust into the role of regulating some new digital services that had previously fallen outside of its purview.

The FCC came under particular scrutiny for its role in promoting competition in local telephone service. Competitors tried to break the local monopolies of the Bells, which were strengthened by mergers and which sought to enter new markets. One area the Bells coveted was the transmission of computer data over long distances. Several Bells submitted to lengthy FCC reviews of whether they had opened their local phone markets to competition—for instance, by allowing smaller vendors to install equipment in the Bells' central switching offices—hoping in exchange to win approval to begin to offer long-distance service. Verizon Communications, formed by the merger of Bell Atlantic and GTE Corp., won approval for long-distance service in New York early in 2000, and SBC Communications later that year similarly received approval in Texas, Oklahoma, and Kansas. However, congressional Republicans and some Democrats traditionally sympathetic to the Bells complained the FCC was dragging its feet and not opening local markets quickly enough. Conversely, consumer groups bitterly criticized the agency for not doing enough to prevent a "re-monopolization" of the telecommunications market.

The act also gave the FCC control over the Bells' expansion into long-distance service. Before FCC approval, however, a Bell was required to face competition in at least a portion of its local phone market. But by summer 1998, no Bell companies had been admitted into the long-distance market, although several had applied. Southwestern Bell Communications prevailed in a Texas district court with its claims that Section 271 of the Telecommunications Act, which bars the Bell companies from long-distance service until the FCC gives its okay, constituted a bill of attainder—an obscure section of the U.S. Constitution that prohibits Congress from singling out an individual for punishment without due process. The lower court ruling was stayed pending the FCC's appeal. In 1998 the Supreme Court upheld all but one of the FCC rules that were challenged. The Court struck down only the rule that assured new telephone companies access to most of the "elements" of the local phone system. The Court ruled that the FCC had exceeded its authority in drafting so broad a rule.

FCC IN THE 2000S

Kennard's efforts to offset media consolidation also were evident in a January 2000 initiative to license approximately 1,000 new low-power FM radio stations. The permits for 100-watt, noncommercial stations were seen as a way of giving schools, churches, and community groups an opportunity to create niche programming at low cost. Central to the plan was allowing the tiny stations to be located closer to existing stations on the FM dial than had been previously permitted. But the proposal triggered an intense lobbying effort by opponents including the National Association of Broadcasters and National Public Radio, who charged spacing the signals closer would result in signal interference. Upset at what some viewed as an independent, activist agenda, Congress late in 2000 included a provision in a year-end spending bill disallowing the closer spacing. The move had the effect of gutting the program by eliminating 70 to 80 percent of qualified applicants. Only applicants in outlying areas where signal interference was not likely were allowed to proceed.

The FCC in 2000 also had difficulty planning a much-anticipated auction of broadcast spectrum prompted by the gradual changeover to digital television. Television stations were supposed to give up the space by the end of 2006 or when the national penetration for digital TV reaches 85 percent, whichever came later. The auction of analog spectrum held by broadcasters occupying channels 60 to 69, and a follow-up auction of airwave channels 52 to 59 was anticipated to raise more than $11 billion, with wireless phone companies eager to offer advanced telecommunications services expected to do most of the bidding. However, the slower-than-anticipated transition to digital TV,

because of slow consumer acceptance of the new medium, added to the uncertainty and forced the FCC to delay the auction several times. The administration of George W. Bush gave the FCC some breathing room by giving the agency until Sept. 30, 2004, to deposit proceeds from the auction, effectively allowing the agency to delay the anticipated 2001 auction.

In January 2001 President Bush elevated then commissioner Michael K. Powell to FCC chair. Powell, the son of the Secretary of State Colin Powell, had been serving on the commission since 1997. Before that, Powell had worked at the antitrust division of the Justice Department. Powell began his new job with the support of powerful Republican lawmakers, especially Sen. John McCain of Arizona who headed up the Senate Commerce Committee (which oversaw telecommunications) and Rep. Billy Tauzin of Louisiana who chaired the counterpart House committee. Many had high hopes that Powell would usher in a period of more collegial relations between Congress and the FCC.

Early in his tenure, the new FCC chair vowed to adopt a less activist agenda and argued for a scaled-back role for telecommunications regulators in the marketplace. Indeed, he proposed deregulating many parts of the industry, especially local telephone companies and large media firms. Powell also promised to take the notoriously slow FCC and make it faster and more decisive, especially when it came to ruling on proposed mergers, something that had often taken a year or more in the past.

During his first year in office Powell initiated a number of reforms with the aim of making the agency more nimble. In an effort to combat institutional parochialism and myopia, he shifted 500 of the FCC's 2,000 employees to different divisions with the idea of forcing them to learn about different industries that the agency regulated. He also created an "FCC University" to keep employees up to date on the newest trends and technologies in the industries under the agency's regulatory umbrella.

Powell arrived at the FCC at just the moment when the telecommunications industry was tipping into crisis. Companies had overbuilt capacity (especially fiber-optic cable) and had taken on enormous debt to do so. As a result, a number of large firms, including giants such as Worldcom and rising stars such as Global Crossing and PSINet, slipped into bankruptcy. In the first eighteen months of the new commissioner's tenure, the industry as a whole lost $2 trillion in market valuation and shed 500,000 jobs. At the same time, broadcasters and cable operators were reeling from a slowdown in the advertising market, cutting deeply into their revenues and profits. "There's never been a downturn like this," said Reed Hundt, former chair of the FCC.

Industry contraction led to less competition in some areas. For instance, during the first six months of 2001, the cost of broadband Internet service provided by the Baby Bells rose 25 percent, reflecting a dearth of other providers. Instead of calling for new regulations, Powell proposed doubling fines the agency levies against those Baby Bells that did not adequately open their local networks to competitors, as mandated by the 1996 Telecommunications Act.

At the same time, Powell faced intense pressure from these same Bell companies to undo a number of restrictions imposed on them as a result of the 1996 act. In particular, the phone companies wanted to be freed from having to lease out their local phone lines to outside competitors at discount rates. The act required the discounts—ultimately determined by state regulators with guidelines provided by the FCC—in an effort to create an environment by which other phone companies could crack the Bells' traditional local phone monopoly. But Verizon, SBC, and other former Bells argued that the discounts allowed their competitors an unfair advantage in the fight for local phone customers.

Competitors such as AT&T and MCI complained that the Bells were stalling by mounting legal challenges to the efforts of many state regulators to establish a discount fee for new local providers. In addition, these companies said that the Baby Bells often took days or even weeks to hand over the records of those customers who were switching to a new provider.

The discounts also were supposed to ensure the viability of a class of small vendors known as competitive local exchange carriers (CLECs). However, regional Bells complained that some CLECs had struck exclusive agreements with Internet service providers and were only routing one-way calls to the provider, ensuring that they only receive payments for connecting the calls.

In an effort to split the difference, Powell proposed a two-year phaseout of the FCC guidelines, which raised the ire of the new big competitors and CLECS, who argued that eliminating the discounts too soon would slow their progress, just as they were beginning to take market share away from the Bells and create a competitive environment. The debate continued through 2002 with the federal courts weighing in on both sides. First, on May 14 the Supreme Court affirmed the part of the 1996 law that required the discounts. But on May 25, the D.C. Circuit Court of Appeals struck down a part of those rules, when it decided that the discounts from the Bells did not apply to phone lines the CLECs were using to provide customers with Internet access.

The resulting confusion was a powerful argument for Powell's proposed phaseout of the discounts, and many analysts predicted that the rules would not remain in effect for much longer. On Feb. 20, 2003, the FCC voted on Powell's proposal. Given the fact that the commission had three Republicans (all appointed by Bush) and only two

Democrats, industry watchers expected the chair to win the day. But the vote to phase out local discounted rates was defeated 3–2.

The vote was a huge blow to Powell. The local discount rate had clearly been the most important issue before the commission since he had assumed the chair, and it had not gone his way. Even worse, the dissenting Republican, Kevin J. Martin, was now deemed to be a swing vote, which gave him enormous leverage. Martin emerged as a powerful force on the commission and a rival to Powell. The ruling was also a blow to the Bells. Not only were the discounts not eliminated or phased out, but the state role in determining rates remained, leaving in place a chaotic fifty-state patchwork of rules and proposed rules, subject to court challenges, lobbying, and years of delay.

Powell was more successful in his efforts to repeal a prohibition on large mergers in the cell phone industry. There were six national carriers, including Verizon Wireless, Cingular, and Sprint PCS, and the commission previously had effectively banned consolidation among these providers by restricting the amount of wireless spectrum one company could own in each market. The restriction was intended to prevent one or two firms from dominating a market, but studies showed the ban was hurting the industry. The big six all had national networks and all could compete in every market, which would make competition especially fierce and prices very low, benefiting consumers. So, on Nov. 1, 2001, the agency voted to phase out the cap on spectrum ownership by 2003.

Current Issues

By early 2003 none of the wireless giants have taken advantage of the easing of restrictions on mergers. One reason has been that the companies each use one of three incompatible cell phone technologies. For instance, while Verizon used a technology called CDMA, Cingular and AT&T wireless used another called GSM. Because these technologies were incompatible, only those companies that used the same standard could conceivably combine their operations. This severely limited the number of merger choices.

Meanwhile by the end of 2002, the agency had returned almost $3.3 billion to Verizon and a number of other wireless firms that had deposited the money with the FCC as part of a $16 billion purchase of spectrum that was auctioned off in 2001. Legal delays—the spectrum had been originally sold to and then reclaimed from now bankrupt Nextwave Telecom—stopped the agency being able to outright give the space to its new buyers. The companies complained the agency was holding their licenses too long, causing too much uncertainty. But other analysts said that buying $16 billion in new spectrum was a luxury the strapped telecommunications industry could no longer afford, and the FCC's decision saved them from overextending themselves financially.

Additional good news for wireless carriers came in the form of an agency report that showed that in the near future, new technologies would allow companies to squeeze more traffic into existing spectrum. The development could allow companies to offer new services, such as wireless Internet, without having to buy more spectrum space.

Recently the FCC voted 3–2 to scale back significantly media cross-ownership rules that prohibited one company from owning a large number of media outlets—such as television and radio stations and newspapers—in one market. The old rules also prevented a business from owning television stations that reach more than 35 percent of all households nationwide. Under the new FCC-approved guidelines, one company can own up to three television stations, eight radio outlets; one daily newspaper, and one cable operator in one large market. Companies can also own television stations reaching up to 45 percent of all households in the country.

Powell defended the decision, arguing that the old rules were anachronistic in the fast-paced information age, where the Internet and cable have caused a proliferation of new sources of information. Moreover, he said, the FTC and the Justice Department's Antitrust Division would still have the authority to review media mergers and stop those deals that would hurt consumers. But consumer advocates, entertainers, and others decried the change, arguing that eliminating the rules further threatens the independence of the press as well as that of independently owned radio and television stations, which tend to provide communities with more local programming than network-owned stations.

In Congress there was an immediate push to reverse the decision. A bill restoring most of the old guidelines won the approval of the Senate Commerce Committee in June 2003 and was likely to pass the full Senate. Its ultimate fate was unknown though, as the bill enjoyed less support in the House of Representatives and was opposed by President Bush.

■ AGENCY ORGANIZATION

Biographies

MICHAEL K. POWELL, CHAIRMAN

Appointment: Designated chairman by President Bush Jan. 22, 2001. Nominated by President Clinton and confirmed by the Senate Oct. 28, 1997; renominated by President George W. Bush for a second term and confirmed by the Senate May 25, 2001; term expires June 30, 2007.

Born: March 23, 1963, Birmingham, AL.

Education: College of William and Mary, B.A. in government, 1985; Georgetown University Law School, J.D., 1990.

Profession: Lawyer.

Political Affiliation: Republican.

Previous Career: Powell served as chief of staff of the Antitrust Division of the Justice Department. He also practiced law with the firm of O'Melveny & Myers, LLP. He has held positions as a judicial clerk for a U.S. Court of Appeals judge and as a policy advisor to the Secretary of Defense.

KATHLEEN Q. ABERNATHY, COMMISSIONER

Appointment: Nominated by President Bush and confirmed by the Senate on May 25, 2001; term expires June 30, 2004.

Education: Marquette University, B.S.; The Catholic University of America, Columbus School of Law, J.D.

Profession: Lawyer.

Political Affiliation: Republican

Previous Career: Abernathy was director for government affairs at BroadBand Office Communications, Inc.; a partner in the Washington, D.C., law firm of Wilkinson Barker Knauer, LLP; vice president for regulatory affairs at U.S. West; and vice president for federal regulatory affairs at AirTouch Communications.

MICHAEL J. COPPS, COMMISSIONER

Appointment: Nominated by President Bush and confirmed by the Senate on May 25, 2001; term expires June 30, 2005.

Education: Wofford College, B.A.; University of North Carolina at Chapel Hill, Ph.D.

Profession: Professor, government official.

Political Affiliation: Democrat

Previous Career: Copps served as assistant secretary of commerce for Trade Development at the U.S. Department of Commerce, where he was previously deputy assistant secretary of commerce for Basic Industries. Copps served for over 12 years as chief of staff for Sen. Ernest Hollings (D-SC).

KEVIN MARTIN, COMMISSIONER

Appointment: Nominated by President Bush on April 30, 2001, and confirmed by the Senate May 25, 2001, for a five-year term expiring June 30, 2006.

Education: University of North Carolina at Chapel Hill, B.A.; Duke University, M.A., Harvard University, J.D.

Profession: Attorney.

Political Affiliation: Republican.

Previous Career: Martin was Special Assistant to the President for Economic Policy and was Deputy General Counsel for Bush for President. Martin served at the FCC as Legal Advisor to Commissioner Furchtgott-Roth from 1997 to 1999.

JONATHAN S. ADELSTEIN, COMMISSIONER

Appointment: Nominated by President George W. Bush on July 10, 2002, and confirmed by the Senate November 14, 2002, for a term expiring June 30, 2003.

Born: Dec. 20, 1953, San Juan, PR.

Education: Stanford University, B.A., 1985; M.A., 1986.

Profession: Commissioner.

Political Affiliation: Democrat.

Previous Career: Before joining the FCC, Adelstein served for 15 years as a staff member in the U.S. Senate. He was a senior legislative aide to U.S. Senate Minority Leader Tom Daschle (D-SD) for seven years. Previously, he served as professional staff member to Senate Special Committee on Aging chairman David Pryor (D-AR), including an assignment as a special liaison to Senator Harry Reid (D-NV) and as a legislative assistant to Senator Donald W. Riegle Jr. (D-MI).

Headquarters and Divisions

COMMISSION

The commissioners hold final authority (subject to review by federal courts) in all matters under the jurisdiction of the FCC. The commissioners also coordinate FCC activities with other federal agencies and with state regulatory bodies.

The chair presides at all commission meetings, coordinates and organizes commission work, and represents the FCC in legislative matters and in relations with other departments and agencies.

Chair

Michael K. Powell .... (202) 418–1000
Fax .... (202) 418–2801

Commissioners

Kathleen Abernathy .... (202) 418–2400
Fax .... (202) 418–2820
Jonathan Adelstein .... (202) 418–2300
Fax .... (202) 418–2377
Michael Copps .... (202) 418–2000
Fax .... (202) 418–2802
Kevin Martin .... (202) 418–2100
Fax .... (202) 418–0982

OFFICE OF THE ADMINISTRATIVE LAW JUDGES

The administrative law judges are responsible for presiding at and conducting proceedings assigned by the commission in cases requiring adjudicatory hearings. The assigned judge prepares initial decisions and forwards them to the commissioners for final decision.

Administrative Law Judge

Richard L. Sippel .... (202) 418–2280
Arthur I. Steinberg .... (202) 418–2255

OFFICE OF COMMUNICATIONS BUSINESS OPPORTUNITIES

The main contact for small business owners and investors in communications services. Provides research materials on small businesses and on minority and female ownership and employment in the communications industry. Advises the commission on policy and rules that affect small businesses.

Director

Carolyn Fleming Williams .... (202) 418–0990
Fax .... (202) 418–0235

OFFICE OF ENGINEERING AND TECHNOLOGY

Advises the commission on characteristics of the radio frequency spectrum, its uses, and the types of equipment using the spectrum. Responsible for the examination and approval of equipment, domestic and international frequency allocation, and research into spectrum propagation and innovation in the field. Identifies and reviews new developments in telecommunications and related technologies. The chief engineer also advises the commission on the development of U.S. telecommunications policy.

Chief Engineer

Edmond Thomas .... (202) 418–2470
Fax .... (202) 418–1944

Electromagnetic Compatibility

Robert M. Bromery .... (202) 418–2475

Laboratory (Columbia, MD)

Rashmi Doshi .... (301) 362–3000

Network Technology

Jefferey Goldthorp .... (202) 418–1096

Policy and Rules

Alan Scrime .... (202) 418–2472

OFFICE OF THE GENERAL COUNSEL

Handles legal matters for the commission including litigation, recommendations on legislation, interpretation of statutes and treaties, and review of rules for consistency and legality. Works with the chief engineer on frequency allocation proceedings and advises on rulemaking proceedings involving more than one bureau. Also advises the commission on the preparation and revision of rules and the implementation and administration of the Freedom of Information, Privacy, and Sunshine acts.

General Counsel

John Rogovin .... (202) 418–1700
Fax .... (202) 418–2822

FEDERAL COMMUNICATIONS COMMISSION

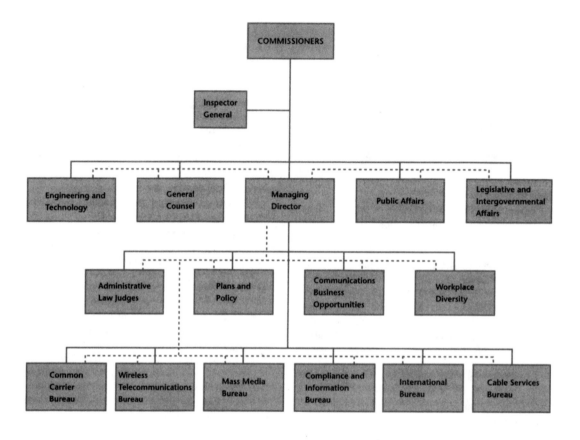

— Lines of policy and judicial authority
···· Lines of management and administrative authority

Administrative Law
 Susan H. Steiman .... (202) 418–1720
Ethics
 Patrick Larney........................... (202) 418–1720
Litigation
 Daniel M. Armstrong.................. (202) 418–1740

OFFICE OF THE INSPECTOR GENERAL
 Conducts independent internal audits and investigations of the commission's operations, and reports directly to Congress and the chair of the FCC.
Inspector General
 H. Walker Feaster III................... (202) 418–0470
 Fax..................................... (202) 418–2811

 Hotline................................. (202) 418–0473
 (Outside of D.C.)....................... (800) 863–2244

OFFICE OF LEGISLATIVE AFFAIRS
 Advises the commission on legislative proposals and responds to congressional inquiries.
Director
 Martha Johnson........................ (202) 418–1900
 Fax.................................... (202) 418–2806

OFFICE OF THE MANAGING DIRECTOR
 Responsible for internal administrative matters, including personnel, budget planning, labor relations, information processing, records, security, data automation,

health and safety, and implementation of the Public Information Act of 1966.

Also serves as principal adviser to and spokesperson for the commission on matters of administration and management, and has management and administrative responsibilities over the agency's bureau and staff offices.

Managing Director

Andrew Fishel .... (202) 418–1919
Fax .... (202) 418–2808

Administrative Operations

Jeffrey Ryan .... (202) 418–1950

Human Resources Management

Michele Sutton .... (202) 418–0137

Information Technology Center

Ron Stone .... (202) 418–2022

Financial Operations

Mark A. Reger .... (202) 418–1925

Performance Evaluation and Records Management

Kathy Fagan .... (202) 418–0448

Secretary

Marlene Dortch .... (202) 418–0300

OFFICE OF STRATEGIC PLANNING AND POLICY ANALYSIS

Responsible for working with the Chairman, Commissioners, Bureaus, and Offices to develop a strategic plan identifying short- and long-term policy objectives for the agency; to help prepare the agency's annual budget ensuring that budget proposals mesh with agency policy objectives and plans; and to work with the office of the chairman and the managing director in developing a workforce strategy consistent with agency policy-related requirements.

OSP continues the tradition of sophisticated and timely policy analysis and development set by the former Office of Plans and Policy. OSP is responsible for monitoring the state of the communications industry to identify trends, issues, and overall industry health, and produces staff working papers and acts as expert consultants to the commission in areas of economic, business, and market analysis and other subjects that cut across traditional lines, such as the Internet. OSP also reviews legal trends and developments not necessarily related to current FCC proceedings, such as intellectual property law, Internet and e-commerce issues.

Director

Jane Mago .... (202) 418–2030
Fax .... (202) 418–2807

Chief, Policy Planning

Robert Pepper .... (202) 418–2030

OFFICE OF MEDIA RELATIONS

Responsible for the commission's media information and Internet programs. Also issues daily news releases and other FCC publications.

Director

David Fiske .... (202) 418–0500
Fax .... (202) 418–7286

OFFICE OF WORKPLACE DIVERSITY

Director

Barbara Douglas .... (202) 418–1799
Fax .... (202) 418–0379

WIRELINE COMPETITION BUREAU

The Wireline Competition Bureau develops and recommends policy goals, programs, and plans for the commission on matters concerning wireline telecommunications. The wireline competition bureau's overall objectives include: 1) ensuring choice, opportunity, and fairness in the development of wireline telecommunications services and markets; 2) developing deregulatory initiatives; 3) promoting economically efficient investment in wireline telecommunications infrastructure; 4) promoting the development and widespread availability of wireline telecommunications services; and 5) fostering economic growth. The wireline competition bureau is organized into four divisions and an administrative and management office.

Bureau Chief

William Maher .... (202) 418–1500
Fax .... (202) 418–2825

Competition Policy Division

Michelle Carey .... (202) 418–1580

Pricing Policy Division

Tamara Preiss .... (202) 418–1520

Telecommunications Access Policy Division

Eric Einhorn .... (202) 418–7400

Industry Analysis Technology Division

Alan Feldman (acting) .... (202) 418–0940

CONSUMER AND GOVERNMENTAL AFFAIRS BUREAU

Handles public inquiries and informal consumer complaints. Also responsible for promoting partnerships with other FCC bureaus and offices, consumer groups, industry groups, and state and local municipalities to enhance consumer awareness, solicit feedback, and encourage more public participation in the work of the commission.

Chief

K. Dane Snowden .... (202) 418–1400

Chief-of-Staff

P. June Taylor .... (202) 418–1400

Deputy Chief (Policy)
Margaret Egler.......................... (202) 418–1400
Deputy Chief (Inquiries and Complaints)
Thomas Wyatt......................... (202) 418–1400
Deputy Chief (Consumer Outreach and Intergovernmental Affairs)
Kris Monteith.......................... (202) 418–1400
Reference Information Center
Bill Cline............................... (202) 418–0267
Consumer Centers
Toll-free................................ (800) 225–5322

ENFORCEMENT BUREAU

Primary FCC organization responsible for enforcement of the Communications Act, as well as Commission rules, orders, and authorizations.
Chief
David H. Solomon..................... (202) 418–7450
Investigations and Hearings
Maureen Del Duca.................... (202) 418–1420
Market Disputes Resolution
Alex Starr.............................. (202) 418–7330
Technical and Public Safety
Joseph Casey.......................... (202) 418–1160
Telecommunications Consumers
Colleen Heitkamp..................... (202) 418–7320

INTERNATIONAL BUREAU

Administers the FCC's international telecommunications policies and obligations; promotes a high-quality, reliable, globally interconnected, and interoperable international infrastructure; and promotes U.S. interests in international communications and the competitiveness of U.S. industry domestically and abroad.
Chief
Donald Abelson....................... (202) 418–0437
Fax..................................... (202) 418–2818
Satellite Division
Thomas Tycz........................... (202) 418–0719
Policy Division
James Ball.............................. (202) 418–1460
Strategic Analysis and Negotiations Division
Kathryn O'Brien .... (202) 418–2150

MEDIA BUREAU

The media bureau develops, recommends, and administers the policy and licensing programs relating to electronic media, including cable television, broadcast television, and radio in the United States and its territories. The media bureau also handles post-licensing matters regarding direct broadcast satellite service.

Chief
W. Kenneth Ferree .... (202) 418–7200
Fax...................................... (202) 418–1195
Office of Broadcast License Policy
Roy Stewart............................ (202) 418–2600
Audio Division
Peter Doyle .... (202) 418–2780
Video Division
Barbara Kreisman..................... (202) 418–1600
Policy Division
Mary Beth Murphy.................... (202) 418–2120
Industry Analysis Division
Royce Sherlock .... (202) 418–7200
Engineering Division
John Wong.............................. (202) 418–7200
Office of Communications and Industry Information
Michael Perko .... (202) 418–7200
Management and Resources
Janet Amaya .... (202) 418–7200

WIRELESS TELECOMMUNICATIONS BUREAU

Handles all FCC domestic wireless telecommunications programs and policies, except those involving satellite communications or broadcasting. Conducts licensing and regulatory functions for cellular telephones, pagers, and other personal communications services, as well as two-way radio used by police, fire, and public safety officials; state and local government; marine and aviation operators; land transportation companies (railroads, buses, trucks, taxis, automobile emergency services); amateur (ham) operators; and private citizens. Also responsible for spectrum auctions, as authorized by the 1993 Omnibus Budget Reconciliation Act. Some divisions are based in Gettysburg, Pa.
Chief
John Muleta .... (202) 418–0600
Fax...................................... (202) 418–0787
Auctions and Industry Analysis
Margaret Weiner .... (202) 418–0638
Commercial Wireless
William Kunze.......................... (202) 418–7887
Data Management (Gettysburg, Pa.)
John Chudovan......................... (717) 338–2510
Policy
Blaise Scino (acting) .... (202) 418–1310
Public Safety and Private Wireless
D'wana Terry........................... (202) 418–0680

Regional Offices

People interested in contacting the regional or district offices must dial (888) 225–5322 to reach the FCC's Consumer Centers for referral to the desired region or district.

NORTHEAST REGION
(CT, DC, DE, IL, IN, KY, MA, MD, ME, MI, MN, NH, NJ, NY, PA, OH, RI, VT, WI)
Park Ridge Center
1550 Northwest Hwy., #306
Park Ridge, IL 60068–1460
Russell D. Monie, regional director

Boston District
1 Batterymarch Park
Quincy, MA 02169–7495
Vincent F. Kajunski, district director

Chicago District
Park Ridge Center
1550 Northwest Hwy., #306
Park Ridge, IL 60068–1460
George M. Moffitt, district director

Columbia District
9200 Farm House Ln.
Columbia, MD 21046
Charles Magin, district director

Detroit District
24897 Hathaway St.
Farmington Hills, MI 48335–1552
James A. Bridgewater, district director

New York District
201 Varick St., #1151
New York, NY 10014–4870
Alexander J. Zimny, district director

Philadelphia District
One Oxford Valley Bldg., #404
2300 E. Lincoln Hwy.
Langhorne, PA 19047–1859
John Rahtes, district director

SOUTH CENTRAL REGION
(AL, AR, CO, FL, GA, IA, KS, LA, MO, MS, NC, ND, NE, NM, OK, PR, SC, SD, TN, TX, VA, VI)
520 N.E. Colburn Rd.
Lee's Summit, MO 64086
Dennis P. Carlton, regional director

Atlanta District
3575 Koger Blvd., #320
Duluth, GA 30096–4958
Fred L. Broce, district director

Dallas District
9330 LBJ Freeway, #1170
Dallas, TX 75243–3429
James D. Wells, district director

Denver District
215 S. Wadsworth Blvd., #303
Lakewood, CO 80226-1544
Leo Cirbo, district director

Kansas City District
520 N.E. Colburn Rd.
Lee's Summit, MO 64086
Robert McKinney, district director

New Orleans District
2424 Edenborn Ave., #460
Metairie, LA 70001
James C. Hawkins, district director

Tampa District
2203 N. Lois Ave., #1215
Tampa, FL 33607–2356
Ralph M. Barlow, district director

WESTERN REGION
(AK, AZ, CA, HI, ID, MT, NV, OR, UT, WA, WY)
5653 Stoneridge Dr., #105
Pleasanton, CA 94588-8543
Charles (Wayne) Craig, regional director

Los Angeles District
Cerritos Corporate Tower
18000 Studebaker Rd., #660
Cerritos, CA 90701–3684
James R. Zoulek, district director

San Diego District
Interstate Office Park
4542 Ruffner St., #370
San Diego, CA 92111–2216
William Zears, district director

San Francisco District
5653 Stoneridge Dr., #105
Pleasanton, CA 94588-8543
Tom van Stavern, district director

Seattle District
11410 N.E. 122nd Way, #312
Kirkland, WA 98034–6927
Dennis Anderson, district director

■ CONGRESSIONAL ACTION

Congressional Correspondence

Vacant...................................... (202) 418–1910

Committees and Subcommittees

HOUSE APPROPRIATIONS COMMITTEE
Subcommittee on Commerce, Justice, State,
 and Judiciary
H309 CAP, Washington, DC 20515
(202) 225–3351

HOUSE COMMERCE COMMITTEE
Subcommittee on Telecommunications, Trade
 and Consumer Protection
2125 RHOB, Washington, DC 20515
(202) 225–2927

SENATE APPROPRIATIONS COMMITTEE
Subcommittee on Commerce, Justice, State,
 and Judiciary
S146A CAP, Washington, DC 20510
(202) 224–7277

**SENATE COMMERCE, SCIENCE, AND
TRANSPORTATION COMMITTEE**
Subcommittee on Communications
SH-227, Washington, DC 20510
(202) 224–5184

Legislation

The FCC exercises authority under the following major pieces of legislation:

Communications Act of 1934 (48 Stat. 1064; 15 U.S.C. 21; 47 U.S.C. 35, 151–609). Signed by the president June 19, 1934. Created the FCC and gave it basic authority to regulate interstate and international communications by wire and radio. Numerous amendments over the years have expanded the commission's power.

A copy of the Communications Act of 1934 and its amendments, the Administrative Procedure Act, the Judicial Review Act, and selected sections of the criminal code pertaining to broadcasting is available from the GPO: see appendix, Ordering Government Publications.

Communications Satellite Act of 1962 (76 Stat. 419; 47 U.S.C. 701–744). Signed by the president Aug. 31, 1962. Created the Communications Satellite Corp. and gave the FCC authority to regulate the corporation.

Cable Communications Policy Act of 1984 (98 Stat. 2779; 47 U.S.C. 521). Signed by the president Oct. 30, 1984. Maintained the dual roles of the FCC and local government in regulating cable, and eliminated the regulation of cable rates by local governments in markets where there is effective competition after 1987. Designated the FCC to define effective competition and oversee equal employment opportunity in cable operations.

Children's Television Act of 1990 (104 Stat. 996-1000, 47 U.S.C. 303a, 303b, and 394). Signed by the president on Oct. 17, 1990. Required each TV station in the U.S. to serve the educational and information needs of children through its overall programming.

National High-Performance Computer Technology Act (105 Stat. 1594, 15 U.S.C. 5501). Signed by the president Dec. 9, 1991. Provided for a coordinated federal research program to ensure continued U.S. leadership in high-performance computing. Created a high-capacity national research and education network to link up supercomputers and databases in the United States.

Automated Telephone Consumer Protection Act of 1991 (105 Stat. 2394, 47 U.S.C. 227 note). Signed by the president Dec. 20, 1991. Prohibited sending an unsolicited ad by fax; using automated telephone equipment to call emergency telephone lines, pagers, or cellular telephones; or initiating unsolicited, auto-dialed telephone calls to residences, except as regulated by the FCC.

Cable Television Consumer Protection and Competition Act of 1992 (106 Stat. 1460, 47 U.S.C. 521 note). Signed by the president Oct. 5, 1992. Amended the Communications Act of 1934 to provide increased consumer protection and to promote increased competition in the cable television and related markets.

Telephone Disclosure and Dispute Resolution Act (106 Stat. 4181, 15 U.S.C. 5701). Signed by the president Oct. 28, 1992. Provided regulation and oversight of the applications and growth of the pay-per-call industry to protect public interest.

Telecommunications Act of 1996 (47 U.S.C. 609 note). Signed by the president Feb. 8, 1996. Revised provisions of the Communications Act of 1934 to reduce regulation and increase competition in communications markets, and to speed deployment of new telecommunications technologies. Also included provisions regarding obscenity in broadcast and Internet transmissions. Charged the FCC with more than 80 rulemakings required to implement the new provisions.

Satellite Home Viewer Improvement Act of 1999 (SHVIA) (113 Stat. 1501). Signed by the president on Nov. 29, 1999. Incorporated into the fiscal 2000 omnibus spending bill, the SHVIA amended the Communications Act of 1934 to permit satellite carriers to air local television broadcasts. Required the FCC to establish rules for satellite companies with regard to mandatory carriage of broadcast signals, retransmission consent, and program exclusivity.

Open-market Reorganization for the Betterment of International Telecommunications Act (ORBIT) (114 Stat. 48, 47 U.S.C. 701/761 note). Signed by the president on March 17, 2000. Amended the Communications Satellite Act of 1962 to add a new chapter concerning competition and privatization in satellite communications. Required the privatization of Intelsat, the International Telecommunications Satellite Organization, and Inmarsat, the International Maritime Satellite Organization.

FCC Regulations Regarding Use of Citizens Band Radio Equipment (P.L. 106-521). Signed by the president on Nov. 22, 2000. Amended the Communications Act of 1934 to authorize state and local governments to enforce FCC regulations that limit the signal strength of citizens band (CB) radio amplifiers. Under previous law, state and local governments were unable to stop such broadcasts because the FCC had total regulatory authority over the use of CB radios.

Auction Reform Act of 2002 (116 Stat. 715, 47 U.S.C. 609 note). Signed by the president on June 19, 2002. Amended the Communications Act of 1934 to require the FCC to determine the deadlines for competitive bidding and auctioning of electromagnetic spectrum used by analog television broadcasters. Required the FCC to postpone indefinitely auctions of portions of the 700 megahertz band of spectrum. Directed the FCC to submit a report to Congress within a year describing the agency's progress in promoting the transition to digital television (DTV) and developing a comprehensive spectrum allocation plan for advanced wireless communications services.

■ INFORMATION SOURCES

Internet
Agency Web Site: http://www.fcc.gov. Provides links to many FCC offices, programs, and publications. Includes consumer information and details on the Telecommunications Act of 1996.

Telephone Contacts
Inspector General Hotline .... (202) 418–0473
National Call Center .... (888) 225–5322
TTY .... (888) 835–5322

Information and Publications

KEY OFFICES

FCC Media Relations
445 12th St. S.W.
Washington, DC 20554
(202) 418–0500
Fax (202) 418–7286
David Fiske, director

Provides general information; issues news releases daily. Also issues the *Daily Digest,* an index and summary of each day's releases. Does not maintain a mailing list. Staff also provides a list of commercial messenger and press services that will pick up and forward releases upon request.

Freedom of Information
445 12th St. S.W.
Washington, DC 20554
(202) 418–0440
Fax: (202) 418–2826
e-mail: foia@fcc.gov
Shoko Hair, FOI officer

FCC Consumer Centers
445 12th St. S.W.
Washington, DC 20554
(202) 418–0232
TTY (888) 835–5322

COMPLAINTS
If a direct complaint to a broadcast station, a telephone or telegraph company, or a cable television system does not resolve the problem, contact the FCC's Consumer

Centers, the nearest regional office, or the agency headquarters. Staff can assist in filing a complaint. Written complaints should be specific, including when and where the problem occurred and other pertinent details. Include copies of all correspondence with the station or company when you contact the FCC. Regional offices handle complaints involving private radio.

PUBLICATIONS

Contact the FCC Consumer and Governmental Affairs Bureau.

FCC Record. Biweekly; a comprehensive listing of FCC actions, including texts released to the public daily. Contains proposed rulemaking and some other public notices.

MEETINGS

The commission usually meets once a month at the FCC, 445 12th St. S.W., Washington, DC 20554. Meetings are generally open to the public. Agendas for meetings are published one week in advance in the "Sunshine Act Meetings" section of the *Federal Register.* They also are available on the FCC Web site: www.fcc.gov. For more details and information on last-minute changes in schedule and agenda, contact the Office of Media Relations (202) 418–0500.

Reference Resources

LIBRARIES

FCC Library

445 12th St. S.W., #TW-B505
Washington, DC 20554
(202) 418–0450
Gloria Jean Thomas, librarian
Hours: 1:00 p.m. to 4:00 p.m.

Open to the public. Maintains a collection of books and periodicals on broadcasting and telecommunications and a complete collection of FCC opinions.

FCC Reference Information Center

445 12th St. S.W.
Washington, DC 20554
(202) 418–0270
William Cline, chief
Hours: Mon.–Thurs. 8:00 a.m.–4:30 p.m.,
Fri. 8:00 a.m.–11:00 a.m.

The Reference Information Center (RIC) contains all publicly available files, including International and Broadcast Station files, Cable and Wireless files and microfilm, and active Docket and Rulemaking files. The RIC research area has a seating capacity for 100 visitors and is equipped with 20 public computer workstations. The RIC provides electronic access to the commission's public information databases, allowing the capability to query data for immediate status, research, verification, and printing by the FCC copy contractor.

RULES AND REGULATIONS

FCC rules and regulations are published in the *Code of Federal Regulations,* Title 47, Chapter I. Chapter I is divided into four volumes: (1) General, parts 1–19; (2) Common Carrier Services, parts 20–69; (3) Broadcast Radio Services, parts 70–79; and (4) Safety and Special Radio Services, parts 80–end. Proposed rules, new final rules, and updates to the *Code of Federal Regulations* are published in the daily *Federal Register.* (See appendix for information on how to obtain and use these publications.)

Other Information Sources

NONGOVERNMENTAL ORGANIZATIONS

The following are some key organizations that monitor the FCC, telecommunications issues, and emerging technologies.

Alliance for Telecommunications Industry Solutions (ATIS)

1200 G St. N.W., #500
Washington, DC 20005
(202) 434–8850
Fax (202) 393–5453
Internet: http://www.atis.org

American Mobile Telecommunications Association

1150 18th St. N.W., #250
Washington, DC 20036
(202) 331-7773
Fax (202) 331-9062

Association of Communication Enterprises

1401 K St. N.W., #600
Washington, DC 20005
(202) 835-9898
Fax (202) 835-9893
Internet: http://www.ascent.org

Association of America's Public Television Stations

1350 Connecticut Ave. N.W., #200
Washington, DC 20036
(202) 887-1700
Fax (202) 293-2422
Internet: http://www.apts.org

**Association of Telemessaging
Services International**
1200 19th St. N.W.
Washington, DC 20036
(202) 429-5151
Fax (202) 223-4579
Internet: http://www.atsi.org

Broadcast Education Association
1771 N St. N.W.
Washington, DC 20036–2891
(202) 429–5354
Fax (202) 429–5343
Internet: http://www.beaweb.org

**Cellular Telecommunications Industry
Association (CTIA)**
1250 Connecticut Ave. N.W., #200
Washington, DC 20036
(202) 785–0081
Fax (202) 467–6990
Internet: http://www.wow-com.com

Center for Democracy and Technology
1634 Eye St. N.W., #1100
Washington, DC 20006
(202) 637–9800
Fax (202) 637–0968
Internet: http://www.cdt.org

Center for Media Education
1511 K St. N.W., #518
Washington, DC 20002
(202) 628–2620
Fax (202) 628–2554
Internet: http://www.cme.org

Communications Workers of America
501 3rd St. N.W.
Washington, DC 20001
(202) 434-1100
Fax (202) 434-1279
Internet: http://www.cwa-union.org

Competitive Telecommunications Association
1900 M St. N.W., #800
Washington, DC 20036
(202) 298–6650
Fax (202) 296–7585
Internet: http://www.comptel.org

Electronic Frontier Foundation
1550 Bryant, #725
San Francisco, CA 94103
(415) 436–9333
Fax (415) 436–9993
Internet: http://www.eff.org

Federal Communications Bar Association
1722 Eye St. N.W., #300
Washington, DC 20006
(202) 736–8640
Fax (202) 736-8740

**Independent Telephone and
Telecommunications Alliance**
1300 Connecticut Ave. N.W., #600
Washington, DC 20036
(202) 775–8116
Fax (202) 223–0358

Industrial Telecommunications Association
1110 N. Glebe Rd., #500
Arlington, VA 22201-5720
(703) 528-5115
Fax (703) 524-1074
Internet: http://www.ita-relay.com

**Information Technology Association
of America**
1616 N. Fort Myer Dr., #1300
Arlington, VA 22209
(703) 284–5300
Fax (703) 525–2279
Internet: http://www.itaa.org

**International Communications
Industries Association**
11242 Waples Mill Rd., #200
Fairfax, VA 22030
(703) 273–7200
(800) 659–7469
Fax (703) 278–8082
Internet: http://www.infocomm.org

The Internet Society
12020 Sunrise Valley Dr., #210
Reston, VA 22091–3429
(703) 648–9888
(800) 468–9507
Fax (703) 648–9887
Internet: http://www.isoc.org

The Media Institute
1000 Potomac St. N.W., #301
Washington, DC 20007
(202) 298-7512
Fax (202) 337-7092
Internet: http://www.mediainst.org/

National Association of Broadcasters
1771 N St. N.W.
Washington, DC 20036
(202) 429-5300
Fax (202) 429-5343
Internet: http://www.nab.org

National Cable Television Association
1724 Massachusetts Ave. N.W.
Washington, DC 20036
(202) 775–3669
Fax (202) 775-3692
Internet: http://www.ncta.com

National Coalition on Television Violence
5132 Newport Ave.
Bethesda, MD 20816
(301) 986–0362
Fax (301) 656–7031
Internet: http://www.nctvv.org

National Telephone Cooperative Association
2626 Pennsylvania Ave. N.W.
Washington, DC 20037
(202) 298–2391
Fax (202) 298–2320
Internet: http://www.ntca.org

Organization for the Promotion and Advancement of Small Telecommunications Companies
21 Dupont Circle N.W., #700
Washington, DC 20036
(202) 659–5990
Fax (202) 659–4619
Internet: http://www.opastco.org

Personal Communications Industry Association
500 Montgomery St., #700
Alexandria, VA 22314
(703) 739-0300
Fax (703) 836-1608
Internet: http://www.pcia.com

The Progress & Freedom Foundation
1301 K St. N.W., #550E
Washington, DC 20005
(202) 289–8928
Fax (202) 289–6079
Internet: http://www.pff.org

Telecommunications Industry Association
2500 Wilson Blvd., #300
Arlington, VA 22201
(703) 907–7721
Fax (703) 907–7727
Internet: http://www.tiaonline.org

U.S. Telephone Association
1401 H St. N.W., #600
Washington, DC 20005
(202) 326–7300
Fax (202) 326–7333
Fax-on-Demand (888) 682–4636
Internet: http://www.usta.org

Viewers for Quality Television
P.O. Box 195
Fairfax Station, VA 22039
(703) 425-0075
Fax (703) 425-8143
Internet: http://www.vqt.org

PUBLISHERS

The following companies and organizations publish on the FCC and related issues through books, periodicals, or electronic media.

Artech House Publishers
685 Canton St.
Norwood, MA 02062
(781) 769–9750
(800) 225–9977
Fax (781) 769–6334
Internet: http://www.artech-house.com

Broadcasting and Cable Magazine
1705 DeSales St. N.W.
Washington, DC 20036
(202) 659–2340
Fax (202) 429–0651
Internet: http://www.broadcastingcable.com

Broadcasting and the Law
1 S.E. 3rd Ave., #1450
Miami, FL 33131
(305) 530–8322
Fax (305) 530–9417

BRP Publications, Inc.
1333 H St. N.W., #1100 West Tower
Washington, DC 20005
(202) 842–0520
(800) 822–6338
Internet: http://www.brp.com
Newsletters include *Telecommunications Reports.*

Bureau of National Affairs (BNA), Inc.
1231 25th St. N.W.
Washington, DC 20037
(202) 452–4200
Fax (800) 253–0332
Internet: http://www.bna.com

Communications Week
600 Community Dr.
Manhasset, NY 11030
(516) 562–7611
Fax (516) 562–7013
Internet: http://www.techweb.cmp.com

Crain Communications Inc.
814 National Press Bldg.
Washington, DC 20045
(202) 662–7200
Fax (202) 638–3155
Publications include *RCR Radio Communications Report.*

Electronic Media
814 National Press Bldg.
Washington, DC 20045
(202) 662–7208
Fax (202) 638–3155
Internet: http://www.emonline.com

Foundation Press, Inc.
615 Merrick Ave.
Westbury, NY 11590–6607
(516) 832–6950
Fax (516) 832–6957
Internet: http://www.fdpress.com

IMAS Publishing
P.O. Box 1214
Falls Church, VA 22041
(703) 998-7600
Fax (703) 820-3245
Internet: http://www.imaspub.com
Publishes *Radio World* biweekly.

Inside Washington Publishers
P.O. Box 7167, Ben Franklin Station
Washington, DC 20044
(703) 416–8500
Fax (703) 416–8543
Publications include *Washington Telecom Week.*

Intertec Publishing
P.O. Box 12901
Overland Park, KS 66828-2901
(800) 441–0294
Fax (913) 967–1899
Internet: http://intertec.com

Law Journal Seminars-Press
345 Park Ave. South
New York, NY 10010
(212) 545–6111
(800) 888–8300
Fax (212) 696–1517
Internet: http://www.legalseminars.com
Publishes *All About Cable,* a loose-leaf service.

Matthew Bender & Co., Inc.
11 Penn Plaza
New York, NY 10001–2006
(800) 223–9844
Fax (518) 487–3507
Internet: http://www.bender.com

Paul Kagan Associates
126 Clock Tower Place
Carmel, CA 93923
(408) 624–1536
Fax (408) 624–5974
Publishes the *Pay TV Newsletter.*

Phillips Business Information
1201 Seven Locks Rd., #300
Potomac, MD 20854
(301) 340–7788
Fax (301) 424–2390
Internet: http://www.phillips.com
Publications include *Telecommunications Today.*

Pike and Fischer, Inc.
4600 East-West Hwy., #200
Bethesda, MD 20814
(800) 255–8131
Fax (301) 654–6297
Publishes *Pike and Fischer Radio Regulation.*

Primedia Intertec
98 Metcalf
Overland Park, KS 66212
(913) 341–1300
Fax (913) 967–1899
Internet: http://www.intertec.com

Reed Reference Publishing
121 Chanlon Rd.
New Providence, NJ 07974
(800) 521–8110
Internet: http://www.reedref.com

RTNDA Communicator
1000 Connecticut Ave. N.W., #615
Washington, DC 20036
(202) 659-6510
Fax (202) 223-4007
Internet: http://www.rtnda.org

Scarecrow Press, Inc.
4720 Boston Way
Lanham, MD 20706
(301) 459–3366
Fax (301) 459–2118
Internet: http://www.scarecrowpress.com

Warren Publishing, Inc.
2115 Ward Ct. N.W.
Washington, DC 20037
(202) 872–9200
Fax (202) 293–3435
Internet: http://www.telecommunications.com
Newsletters include *FCC Report.*

Federal Deposit Insurance Corporation

550 17th St. N.W., Washington, DC 20429
Internet: http://www.fdic.gov

■ INTRODUCTION

The Federal Deposit Insurance Corporation (FDIC) is an independent agency of the federal government; that is, no taxpayer money supports it. It is managed by a five-member board of directors. One of the directors is the comptroller of the currency; another is the director of the Office of Thrift Supervision (OTS). The three others are appointed by the president and confirmed by the Senate. One of the appointed members is designated chair, and all three serve six-year terms. No more than three of the board members may be of the same political party.

Responsibilities

The FDIC insures funds at the nation's 9,354 banks and savings associations up to a $100,000 limit. The agency also acts as the primary federal regulator of 5,352 insured commercial banks, including small savings banks and banks that hold state charters and are not members of the Federal Reserve System (state nonmember insured banks).

The FDIC:

• Operates two insurance funds—the Bank Insurance Fund (BIF) for commercial banks and the Savings Association Insurance Fund (SAIF) for thrifts.

• Assesses premiums on all insured deposit accounts of commercial banks and thrifts.

• Requires periodic reports of condition and income and other financial data about regulated banks.

• Examines banks annually to determine their condition.

• Approves proposals to relocate main offices and relocate or establish branch offices.

• Approves reduction or retirement of capital.

• Approves bank mergers when the resulting institution will be a bank subject to FDIC regulation.

GLOSSARY

National bank—A bank that is chartered and regulated by the comptroller of the currency. National banks are required to have FDIC insurance.

State member bank—A bank that is chartered by a state and is a member of the Federal Reserve System. State member banks are required to have FDIC insurance.

State nonmember bank—A bank that is chartered by a state and has FDIC insurance, but is not a member of the Federal Reserve System. The FDIC monitors the performance of all banks it insures, but it is the principal federal regulator of state nonmember banks and mutual savings banks (a form of a thrift owned and operated by its depositors).

• Issues cease-and-desist orders to, or obtains agreements from, banks and bank officers to stop engaging in unsound, unsafe, dishonest, or illegal practices.

• Acts as receiver for failed insured national banks and, when appointed by state authorities, for failed state-chartered banks.

• Enforces fair credit, consumer, community reinvestment, and truth-in-lending legislation affecting banks.

• Administers the regulations and reporting provisions of the Securities Exchange Act with respect to banks whose securities are publicly traded.

• Requires reports of changes in ownership of outstanding voting stock of a bank that results in a change in control of the bank.

• Approves the acquisition of controlling interest of a bank by an individual or group.

• Requires banks to maintain an adequate security system to discourage burglaries and robberies.

• Has authority to terminate insurance coverage of a bank that continues, after notice and hearing, to engage in unsafe and unsound practices in violation of laws and regulations.

• Publishes quarterly reports on the condition of the commercial banking industry.

Powers and Authority

Unlike most other government agencies, the FDIC receives no annual appropriation from Congress. The corporation received its initial funding from assessments levied against the members of the Federal Reserve System and a $150 million loan from the U.S. Treasury, which was paid back in full by 1948. Since then it has been funded by assessments on deposits held by insured banks and from interest on the required investment of its surplus funds in government securities.

Most states require state-chartered banks that are not members of the Federal Reserve System to apply to the FDIC for federal insurance coverage. After receiving the application, the corporation undertakes a thorough investigation of the bank. The factors reviewed include the bank's financial history and current condition, the adequacy of its capital structure, its prospects for future earnings, the general character of the bank's management, and the needs of the community in which the bank is located.

National banks and state banks that are members of the Federal Reserve System receive FDIC insurance with their charters and do not require investigation by the corporation before becoming members. In 1990 165 new charters were granted. The number dropped to forty-six in 1993 and has been on the upturn since then as the nation experienced a stronger economy and troubles in the industry faded. The number continued rising to 232 in 1999 but then, as the economy stumbled, began declining again. In 2000 there were 192; in 2001, 129; and in 2002, the number dropped to 94 new bank charters.

REPORTING REQUIREMENTS

All federally insured banks are required to file reports on condition and income with the FDIC. Reports on condition must be filed quarterly; reports on income are required twice a year for most banks and quarterly for banks with assets in excess of $300 million. The data is used to keep track of economic conditions and trends in the banking industry. The data also is fed into the Integrated Monitoring System (IMS), a computerized analysis system for monitoring bank performance between examinations. Summaries of the reports are available from the Office of Public Affairs (*p. 142*).

BANK EXAMINATIONS

The FDIC Improvement Act of 1991 requires an annual examination of all banks to determine their financial health. Before that, regulators had set the priorities, focusing mainly on troubled banks. The corporation makes four types of examinations—safety and soundness, compliance with consumer protection and civil rights laws and regulations, performance of fiduciary responsibilities in trust departments, and adequacy of internal controls in electronic data processing operations.

A full-scale examination includes evaluation of assets, capital structure, income and changes in capital, loan policies, concentrations of credit, loans to bank officers and stockholders, investment policies, borrowing practices, management, internal controls, compliance with laws and regulations, and review of the bank's premises and other real estate. A less rigorous checkup, called a modified examination, emphasizes management policies and the bank's financial performance.

The number of banks examined for safety and soundness peaked in 1990 at 6,234. More than 11,000 examinations were carried out that year when other types of exams are included. In each of the next three years, the FDIC completed more than 5,300 safety and soundness exams. By 1998 that number was down to 2,399, though the number increased slightly to 2,540 in 1999. The number of exams hovered around 2,500 in the three years since then: There were 2,486 in 2000; 2,566 in 2001; and 2,534 in 2002.

The FDIC also relies on the states to share the burden of periodic bank examinations. Because state-chartered banks are examined regularly by both federal and state regulators, the FDIC follows a program of divided responsibility, under which the states and the corporation alternate their examinations.

ENFORCEMENT ACTIVITIES

If the FDIC examiners determine that a bank is faltering, in poor condition, or engaged in illegal activities, the corporation can respond in several ways. Usually the FDIC attempts to work with the bank management informally by obtaining its approval of a corrective agreement or privately issuing a proposed notice of charges and a proposed cease-and-desist order. If, after a meeting with the bank and the appropriate state supervisory authority, the bank does not consent to comply with the proposed order, the FDIC will initiate formal proceedings by publicly issuing the notice of charges and holding a hearing before an administrative law judge.

Banking practices that might result in an informal cease-and-desist action or hearing include: inadequate capital in relation to the kind and quality of assets; inadequate provisions for liquidity; failure of the bank to diversify its portfolio resulting in a risk to capital; extension of credit to officers and affiliates of the bank who are not creditworthy; poor management practices; hazardous lending practices involving extension of credit with inadequate documentation or for the purpose of speculation in real estate; an excessive portfolio of poor-quality loans in relation to capital; and failure to comply with consumer protection laws and regulations.

The FDIC also has the authority to terminate a bank's insurance if it finds that the bank has been conducting its affairs in an unsound and unsafe manner. The bank is notified when termination-of-insurance proceedings are started and has 120 days to correct the problems cited by the FDIC. If the deficiencies are not corrected, an administrative hearing is held. If the hearing results in a decision to terminate, depositors are given notice that the insured

FDIC COVERAGE

Per Depositor 1934–2003

Amount	Effective Date
$ 2,500	1/1/34
5,000	6/1/34
10,000	9/21/50
15,000	10/16/66
20,000	12/23/69
40,000	11/27/74
100,000*	3/31/80

*Time and savings deposits of government units (except state and local government deposits held in out-of-state banks) had been covered at this level since 1974.

status of the bank has been revoked and that two years from the date of termination their funds no longer will be insured.

The FDIC also has the authority to remove an officer, director, or other manager if it determines that the person has engaged in illegal or unsafe activities that have caused substantial financial damage to the insured bank. To protect the bank, the corporation also has the power to suspend such persons until the removal proceedings can be completed.

If all of the preventive activities of the FDIC fail and a bank becomes insolvent, the corporation acts as the receiver for the bank; it assumes the bank's liabilities and assets and pays out funds to the depositors up to the $100,000 limit. In most cases, the FDIC arranges for a takeover of a failed bank by a healthy one and does not make direct deposits to the failed bank. From 1934 through 1994, a total of 2,069 banks failed, of which 2,050 required disbursements by the FDIC to pay off insured depositors. More than two-thirds of the failures took place in the ten years from 1983 to 1992. The deposits in all failed banks for the period 1934–1994 totaled nearly $212 billion.

In 1996 five banks and one thrift failed. For a fifteen-month period from mid-1996 until the end of 1997 there was not a single bank failure. This was the longest period in U.S. history without the failure of an FDIC-insured bank. But there were three failures in 1998, eight in 1999, seven in 2000, four in 2001 and eleven in 2002.

Background

The FDIC was created by the Banking Act of 1933 to help stem the rash of bank failures that swept the country after the stock market crash of October 1929. A root cause of the failures was the involvement of many banks in investment companies that had speculated extensively in securities and real estate, often with their depositors' funds. At the time of the crash and during the Great Depression that followed, both the investment companies and their parent banks suffered tremendous losses: 9,106 banks were forced to close their doors between 1930 and 1933. Depositors in failed banks could not always recover their money, and those banks that did survive were badly damaged when their customers, fearful of the spreading failures, withdrew their funds.

To restore public confidence in the banking system, the FDIC offered federally guaranteed insurance for an individual's deposit up to $2,500. This insurance limit was soon raised to $5,000, and Congress periodically has increased the maximum coverage. The most recent increase, in March 1980, raised the maximum to $100,000.

EARLY HISTORY

The FDIC was the third agency created to regulate the U.S. banking industry. Federal regulation began with the National Currency Act of 1863, which established the Office of the Comptroller of the Currency (p. 692). The comptroller's office was given the power to charter and supervise national banks as a way to provide and promote a stable national currency. The comptroller of the currency remains the primary regulator of all nationally chartered banks. State regulation of banking had begun earlier in the nineteenth century when state legislatures passed chartering laws for local banks.

The Federal Reserve Act that created the Federal Reserve System was passed by Congress in 1913. Under that law, national banks were required to become members of the Federal Reserve; state-chartered banks were given the option of joining, but membership was not mandatory. The Federal Reserve System assumed responsibility as primary regulator of those state banks that chose to join the system (state member banks).

When the FDIC was first set up, its insurance coverage was made mandatory for all members of the Federal Reserve that could meet the corporation's requirements for admission, including adequate capitalization, reserve strength, and financial stability. Originally, only members of the Federal Reserve System could obtain FDIC insurance. In 1939 that requirement was dropped, and the availability of FDIC coverage was extended to state-chartered banks that were not members of the Federal Reserve System.

Under the 1933 Banking Act, a group of amendments to the 1913 Federal Reserve Act, the FDIC was to institute a program of bank examinations to detect potential problem areas in bank management and funding. It was authorized to promulgate regulations to promote safe and sound banking practices and thereby protect both banks and their depositors. The original legislation also forced banks to divest themselves of ownership or control of investment companies. FDIC examiners were authorized to review the operations of banks under FDIC jurisdiction, including loans, status of investments, assets, and liabilities. The legislation further established the FDIC as receiver for all failed national banks and declared that the FDIC could be appointed receiver of failed state banks if requested by a state banking authority.

Two years later, the Banking Act of 1935 gave the FDIC power to cancel insurance for banks engaging in unsafe banking practices and banks in violation of laws or regulations. It also authorized the FDIC to approve the reduction or retirement of capital and the establishment of branch offices for banks under its jurisdiction, to require reports of a bank's condition, to regulate payment of interest on deposits, and to issue regulations necessary to carry out its functions. The 1935 law also authorized the FDIC to make loans or purchase assets to facilitate the absorption of a faltering bank by an insured bank in sound financial condition.

GROWING AUTHORITY

In 1951 authority for the FDIC was withdrawn from the Federal Reserve Act and made part of a separate law called the Federal Deposit Insurance Act. This new legislation gave the FDIC two additional powers. It permitted the corporation to provide funds through loans or deposits to a bank experiencing difficulty, if the FDIC determined that continued operation of the bank was crucial for the local community. It also extended FDIC examination authority to national and state-chartered banks that are members of the Federal Reserve System, a power seldom exercised.

The Bank Mergers Act of 1960 gave the FDIC power to approve mergers between insured and noninsured banks when the resulting institution would be a state-insured bank that would not be a member of the Federal Reserve System.

In 1966 the supervisory powers of the corporation again were increased when Congress authorized the FDIC to issue cease-and-desist orders to institutions persisting in unsafe banking practices and to remove bank officers engaging in dishonest or illegal dealings.

During the 1960s and 1970s the corporation also was given enforcement responsibility for various consumer laws that apply to banks regulated by the FDIC. These include the Truth in Lending Act, the Fair Credit Reporting Act, the Real Estate Settlement Procedures Act, the Equal Credit Opportunity Act, the Open Housing Act, the Home

Mortgage Disclosure Act, and the Community Reinvestment Act.

REFORMS IN THE 1970S

Except for the disasters of the Depression era, until the mid-1970s only a handful of banks had failed. Since the mid-1970s, however, the number of bank closings has increased steadily. A number of well-publicized failures called into question the adequacy of the existing regulatory system. A 1977 study by the FDIC showed that 60 percent of bank failures between 1960 and 1975 were because of "insider loans," which are preferential or excessive loans provided to bank officers and stockholders.

In 1978 Congress passed the Financial Institutions Regulatory and Interest Rate Control Act, which limited loans that could be made to a bank's officers and major stockholders to no more than 10 percent of the capital accounts of the bank. Banks were required to report loans to their officers, and preferential loans to insiders and overdrafts by bank officers were prohibited.

The act also restricted most forms of interlocking directorates (overlapping memberships on the board of directors) among financial institutions. Enforcement powers were increased, allowing the FDIC to impose civil penalties, issue cease-and-desist orders to individual officers, order the removal of executives and directors who threatened the safety and soundness of financial institutions, and require depository holding companies to divest themselves of holdings that endangered the soundness of banking subsidiaries.

The measure required individuals wishing to acquire a bank or savings institution to give sixty days' notice to the appropriate regulatory agency. The agencies were given the authority to reject such acquisitions.

The 1978 legislation also created the Federal Financial Institutions Examination Council (FFIEC) to coordinate the regulatory activities of the agencies responsible for supervising financial institutions. The purpose of the council is to promote uniform supervision of financial institutions.

In addition, consumer safeguards were increased by the 1978 law. Most important was a provision limiting to $50 the liability of a customer for unauthorized fund transfers involving automated bank tellers and other forms of electronic banking.

The FDIC's involvement in international banking also increased significantly under the 1978 regulatory act as well as under the International Banking Act of 1978. The regulatory act required state nonmember insured banks to obtain the prior written consent of the FDIC before establishing or operating a foreign branch and before obtaining any interest in a foreign bank or financial institution.

The International Banking Act of 1978 gave the FDIC primary examining authority over U.S. branches of foreign banks that are chartered by a state and carry FDIC insurance but are not members of the Federal Reserve System. FDIC insurance of commercial deposits in branches of foreign banks is available but is not mandatory. However, FDIC insurance is mandatory if the branch accepts retail domestic deposits, which are defined as deposits of less than $100,000.

Also in 1978 Congress approved legislation authorizing the General Accounting Office to audit the performance of the FDIC, the Federal Reserve System, and the Office of the Comptroller of the Currency.

DEREGULATION IN THE 1980S

In March 1980 Congress passed the Depository Institutions Deregulation and Monetary Control Act, which made far-reaching changes in the federal regulation of the nation's banking industry and opened the door to the eventual deregulation of depository institutions. Among its provisions, the landmark banking reform legislation more than doubled FDIC insurance protection from $40,000 to $100,000 per depositor. Although the 1980 law did not provide for any significant increase in FDIC funding, it stipulated a revised formula by which the corporation computes deposit insurance assessment credits. Banks were required to pay the cost of FDIC insurance through assessments based on their volume of deposits.

The Monetary Control Act was intended to allow for increased competition between commercial banks and traditional thrift institutions. The bill also phased out interest rate ceilings on time and savings accounts.

In October 1982 President Ronald Reagan signed into law the Depository Institutions Act, a bill intended to help banks cope with the highly competitive financial environment that had developed in the early 1980s during the rapid growth of money market mutual funds. The money markets' higher yields had drained banks of a large proportion of the funds that consumers previously had deposited in checking accounts and low-interest savings accounts. The 1982 law allowed banks to develop new products to compete with these money market funds, including checking accounts that paid interest—NOW accounts—and their own money market accounts, which paid higher interest. But banks had to pay more for the funds they needed to operate, straining profit margins and weakening the industry's financial health.

The 1982 legislation gave the FDIC greater flexibility and additional powers to deal with troubled and failed banks through financial aid and merger assistance. It permitted financial institutions with plunging net worths to obtain emergency infusions of capital from the FDIC to help prevent them from going under. The FDIC was authorized to provide new forms of assistance, including assumptions of liabilities, deposits and contributions, and the purchase of securities.

For the first time, the agency was authorized to arrange for interstate and interindustry acquisitions of failing or failed institutions under certain limited circumstances. To help equalize competition between banks and savings and loan associations, the legislation provided for the elimination of all federal interest rate ceilings by Jan. 1, 1984. The ceilings originally were established to ensure savings and loan associations a slight competitive edge over commercial banks in attracting savings deposits, thus indirectly encouraging the home mortgage marketplace.

The Competitive Equality Banking Act of 1987 gave the FDIC power to establish a bridge bank when an insured bank is closed, no immediate buyer is available, it would be less expensive to continue operating the bank than to liquidate it and pay off depositors, and the continued operation of the bank is in the best interest of depositors and the public. A bridge bank is a full-service national bank that can be operated for up to three years by a board of directors appointed by the FDIC. The FDIC used its bridge bank authority for the first time Oct. 30, 1987, when it closed the Capital Bank & Trust Co. in Baton Rouge, La.

At the time of the 1987 legislation, farmers were being hurt by declining land values, depressed crop prices, and soft export markets. The legislation permitted agricultural banks to amortize losses on agricultural loans and losses resulting from reappraisal of other related assets over a seven-year period.

Both the industry and its federal regulators were unprepared for the upheaval in the financial services industry unleashed by congressional actions of the early 1980s. These moves resulted in the rapid expansion by securities brokers, insurance companies, and even retailers such as Sears, Roebuck and Company and the Kroger Company into the markets formerly reserved for banks. In the newly competitive financial marketplace, consumers began to turn more and more toward these alternative purveyors of financial services, causing the banks to founder.

To meet the challenge of these new less-regulated rivals, many states enacted laws that allowed banks to engage in nontraditional banking activities such as securities brokerage, real estate investment, and insurance operations. The FDIC accommodated these changes by allowing these operations through separate subsidiaries.

To help commercial banks avoid losing corporate customers, the banking regulators pressed Congress to allow commercial banks to engage in more investment banking activities, including underwriting and dealing in corporate securities, commercial paper, and municipal bonds. Many banks also faced new competition from other commercial banks as interstate banking restrictions began to crumble with the development of regional banking pacts. These agreements allowed banks to set up operations in states within the pact. By the late 1980s only a few states were not part of regional banking pacts. Ironically, the regulatory changes designed to prop up the banking industry ended up laying the foundation for the demise of many institutions. By the late 1980s the banking industry had suffered the largest number of failures since the Depression. Banks concentrating in energy and agriculture loans were particularly vulnerable because of falling oil and farm prices. Problems also spread to commercial real estate loans.

The number of banks on the FDIC's problem bank list jumped from 848 in 1984 to a peak of 1,575 at the end of 1987, and hovered around the 1,100 mark until 1992. In 1988 the insurance fund suffered the first operating loss in its fifty-five-year history. It did not see a profit until four years later. In 1989 the number of bank failures peaked at 206. The trend reversed after that but each of the next four years saw more than one hundred banks close because of financial difficulties. The growing number of banks in trouble, especially in the oil and farm belts, prompted federal regulators to tighten capital standards. The FDIC and other regulators adopted capital standards stipulating that banks with the riskiest investment portfolio would have to build larger capital cushions against potential losses.

Although the number of bank failures was making post-Depression records, it was the more widespread and much larger failures of savings and loan institutions insured by the FDIC's sister agency, the Federal Savings and Loan Insurance Corporation (FSLIC), that forced attention on the future of the federal deposit insurance system. In 1989 President George Bush signed into law the historic Financial Institutions Reform, Recovery, and Enforcement Act (FIRREA).

That legislation established a financing corporation to raise the money needed to close failed savings and loan associations and pay off insured depositors. The process was projected to cost U.S. taxpayers more than $500 billion over forty years.

The FSLIC fund, although broke, was placed under the FDIC, and the name was changed to the Savings Association Insurance Fund (SAIF). The FDIC board was assigned to manage the Resolution Trust Corporation (RTC), a temporary agency created to take control of failed savings and loan associations and sell their assets. (The bill also expanded the FDIC board to five members.)

To strengthen the FDIC fund, the bill raised the insurance premium on bank deposits. The bill added enforcement powers of both thrift and banking regulators and significantly increased civil penalties for unsafe and abusive activities by bank directors and officers. It also made it easier for regulators to take control of banks operating with insufficient capital.

FDIC IN THE 1990S

The early 1990s were a time of rebuilding for the FDIC and the banking industry, as regulators and banks alike faced a dire need for new capital, while the late 1990s saw financial institutions basking in a wave of unprecedented prosperity. The new century came, however, with concerns about the health of the industry.

Before the prosperity could be enjoyed, the BIF had to be restored to health to avert the need for Treasury support and the threat of a taxpayer bailout. The insurance fund dropped to 7 cents for every $100 of insured bank deposits by the end of 1989—well below the historic level of $1.25 for every $100 in deposits.

To build the fund back up, the Omnibus Budget Reconciliation Act of 1990 waived caps on the FDIC's insurance premiums and allowed the agency to make midyear premium adjustments, rather than only annual changes. The premium later shifted from a flat rate to a risk-related system on Jan. 1, 1993; the premium banks pay is determined by a formula based on an institution's capital level and its management strength.

During the administration of Bill Clinton, the FDIC saw restored prosperity both in the BIF and in the banking industry. In 1995 the FDIC lowered deposit-insurance premiums twice for most banks: first from 23 cents to 4 cents per $100 of deposits, then to the statutory minimum requirement of $2,000 a year per insured institution. The latter move, which took effect in January 1996, came after the insurance fund passed the $25 billion mark, at the time a record in FDIC history. By late 1995 the insurance fund had exceeded the requirement of 1.25 percent of insured deposits, where it remained in 2001.

In 1991, when the insurance fund was still severely undercapitalized, the FDIC Improvement Act put a time frame on getting the fund back to the 1.25 percent level, requiring the FDIC to meet this goal within fifteen years. To ensure that the agency could continue to protect deposits in failed banks without having to tap taxpayer funds, the act also increased a direct line of credit from the Treasury from $5 billion to $30 billion.

Meanwhile, to avoid having the FDIC dip into bank insurance funds for savings and loan cleanups, the SAIF was given its own appropriations authority. The SAIF, too, was experiencing unprecedented financial success by the latter part of the 1990s, reaching its own record balance of $9.5 billion in the first quarter of 1998.

In September 1996 Congress passed legislation to merge the BIF and SAIF in 1999, provided an additional law was passed to eliminate the SAIF charter. However, by the beginning of the 108th Congress in 2003, Congress had yet to act. Because the insurance fund for thrifts continued to lag behind the fund for banks, the 1996 law more immediately levied a one-time assessment on thrifts, of 68 cents per $100, to bring the SAIF to its required 1.25 percent level.

The 1991 FDIC Improvement Act also changed the way the agency approached its regulatory role. First, the act required the FDIC to examine every bank every year, a departure from the historical method of giving troubled banks priority over healthy banks. Second, the 1991 law changed the way the FDIC handled failed banks. Previously, regulators used a "least-costly resolution," which gave them latitude to consider how a community might be affected by a failed bank, allowing them more time to find a prospective buyer or otherwise dispose of assets. Now they must use a "least cost resolution," making their decisions dollar-driven only, with no regard for the economic condition of the area.

The FDIC Improvement Act also phased out the "too big to fail" doctrine that led regulators to prop up such behemoths as the Bank of New England because of the potentially damaging ripple effect its failure would have had on the people of Boston. The 1991 law also prohibited state charter banks from engaging in activities not allowed for national banks, which took many more bankers out of the real estate business once and for all.

After the banking crisis of the late 1980s and the resulting tightening of lending restrictions, it did not take long for bank owners to claim those restrictions hurt business. Such pressure led Congress in 1992 to pass a number of tax laws to ease the regulatory burden. For example, the value of property requiring a certified appraisal for a loan was raised from $100,000 to $250,000, which translated into less red tape for the majority of home loans.

Barriers to interstate banking also fell in the 1990s. Since 1933, branching across state lines had been prohibited. Large banking empires had to charter new banks in each state, hiring separate bank presidents and boards of directors. Bank industry lobbyists claimed this restriction cost the industry billions of dollars each year. The Interstate Banking Efficiency Act, passed in 1994, removed these restrictions, allowing banks to operate in more than one state under the same corporate structure.

President Clinton appointed Ricki Helfer in 1994 as the FDIC's first female chair. Helfer described her mission as an "effort to shift the FDIC from an agency that resolves bank failures to an agency working to keep banks open and operating safely and soundly." She instituted an extensive reorganization of the agency, whereby most divisions report to three deputies rather than directly to the chair. Reorganization continued as the 1993 RTC Completion Act required the RTC to consolidate its staff and functions with the FDIC by the end of 1995.

Helfer created a task force to study how derivatives and other new financial instruments affect deposit insurance funds; a so-called "early warning system," to help prevent bank failures; and increased consumer education. The FDIC sought to help member banks clarify to customers the differences between federally insured investments, such as certificates of deposit (CDs), and uninsured investments, including mutual funds—especially when these two types of investments are marketed by the same financial institution.

In addition to the proposed BIF-SAIF merger, banking provisions attached to appropriations legislation at the end of 1996 included "regulatory relief"—some forty changes in banking laws to ease regulation—and decreased the liability borne by banks for environmental problems on properties they obtain through foreclosure.

Helfer resigned in mid-1997. Almost a year later, the Senate confirmed her successor, Hawaiian corporate lawyer Donna Tanoue. Under Tanoue, the FDIC continued efforts to streamline regulations, expedite application procedures for well-capitalized, well-managed banks, and simplify deposit insurance rules. Additionally, FDIC worked with other financial regulators to coordinate the handling of merger requests.

The FDIC downsized in the late 1990s, as the number of bank failures diminished and the workload decreased. It closed regional offices, offered employee buyouts, and relied on traditional attrition. By 2001 the agency was down to about 6,700 workers, a decrease of about 5,000 employees in four years.

In the midst of the economic boom of the 1990s, regulators became increasingly concerned that lending standards were slipping dangerously. Although the thriving economy had brought tremendous benefits for banks, it also had led to increased competition for loans. That meant lower profit margins and increased lending to those with tarnished credit histories. Fears that a downturn in the economy would have seriously negative consequences for many banks led the FDIC in May 1997 to issue a letter warning banks about risky subprime lending. Later that year, the agency said one out of every five auto loans was considered subprime. In October 2000 the agency said "risky underwriting practices" had increased after a brief decline. Though the rate of such loans was down from historic highs of 1998, the agency said 26 percent of construction lenders were making "speculative" loans that warranted notice and that there were concerns in the real estate and home equity lending sectors, among others.

As the twentieth century came to a close the agency's image was tarnished by missteps. Under pressure in 1999, it dumped a highly criticized plan calling for banks to track the actions of their customers. The agency also agreed to a $14 million race discrimination settlement of a lawsuit filed by former African American workers. In 1999 the agency announced a "diversity strategic plan," which called for increased recruiting of minority job applicants.

FDIC IN THE 2000S

In November 1999 President Clinton signed into law a major banking overhaul bill, known as Gramm-Leach-Bliley for its sponsors, that broke down many of the Depression-era barriers that had separated banks, brokerages, and insurance firms. The FDIC spent the subsequent time period crafting rules dealing with various provisions in the new law and preparing for a potential increase in its oversight responsibilities.

The FDIC in 2000 also adopted new "sunshine" guidelines called for by Gramm-Leach-Bliley, setting disclosure requirements for agreements that banks and private groups reach to abide by the Community Reinvestment Act. The agency also adopted guidelines requiring new safeguards to protect consumer information and records. Also related to the legislation, the agency in May 2000 approved a consumer privacy regulation that required financial institutions to describe their privacy policies clearly and allow customers to "opt out of disclosures to nonaffiliated third parties." The agency gave banks until July 2001 to comply with the regulation, a delay that irritated many consumer rights advocates.

As her tenure drew to a close, Tanoue moved ahead with a plan to reform the deposit insurance program. Many of the tenets of the plan have been discussed for years. One priority in the reform was merging the BIF and the SAIF as first proposed in 1996. Backers of this plan said it would help further diversify the overall fund and make one safer fund than the two separate funds. But this goal required action from Congress. Although many lawmakers supported that goal, members were unable to reach agreement on other related issues while Tanoue was in office under the Clinton administration and the first months of the administration of George W. Bush.

Becoming FDIC chair on Aug. 29, 2001, Texas banker Donald E. Powell said he wanted to raise the profile of the agency. Powell also promised to continue efforts to overhaul deposit insurance. His stated priorities for the overhaul included merging the two insurance funds, indexing insurance coverage limits to inflation, and increasing the insurance limit for retirement accounts.

The FDIC in early 2001 issued guidelines making clear it would more closely scrutinize "subprime lending programs," those aimed at borrowers with sketchy credit histories and a willingness to pay higher interest rates. The agency put a new emphasis on following the effects of mergers within the industry, creating a task force in 1998 to study what would happen if one of the new, large banks failed. In 1999 there were 341 mergers, down from 390 in 1998 and 419 in 1997. The number rose again in

2000 to 456 mergers but declined to 360 in 2001 and 294 in 2002.

Current Issues

The 108th Congress, which began in January 2003, was expected to take up the thorny issue of increasing the $100,000 federal deposit insurance limit. The increase would be the first since the current limit was established in 1980. While many banking groups support this proposal, key members of Congress have opposed it.

Some members of Congress also wanted to change the way banks were charged for deposit insurance, tying it to the level of risk in a bank's portfolio but allowing all banks to pay some fee. Currently, only those institutions with weak ratings are charged fees, which means more than nine out of ten institutions pay no fee. The agency has also called for a plan to issue rebates to institutions when the insurance funds grows higher than necessary.

The House twice passed legislation, in 2002 and 2003, that would have increased the federal deposit insurance ceiling from $100,000 to $130,000 for each account at banks, thrift institutions, and credit unions. The bill, which passed 411–11 in 2003, also would have provided for future increases pegged to inflation beginning in 2005, set a $260,000 coverage limit for retirement accounts, and given the FDIC more leeway in setting premiums and reserve levels. As the FDIC requested, the bill also would have merged the BIF and SAIF.

Among supporters of the boost in individual deposit insurance limit have been small banks, which depend more on deposits as a source of lending capital than do large banks. However, the Bush administration and Federal Reserve have contended that increasing the insurance limit would boost the government's risk without benefiting consumers. In the Senate, Richard C. Shelby, head of the Banking, Housing and Urban Affairs Committee, also voiced opposition to the increase. Shelby was working on a proposal of his own that varied from the House's bill.

On the regulatory front, Powell sought to operate the agency more like a private company and less as a bureaucracy. The FDIC chair streamlined the agency, significantly reducing the number of management positions. In another move that stripped some senior officials of power, Powell delegated more authority to lower-ranking officials, hoping to move decision making closer to the ground level. He said his goal was to make the agency more responsive to the banking community that it regulates.

The agency also created new internal procedures to shift agency resources to the institutions that policymakers believed could pose the greatest risk to the stability of the insurance funds. One new program was established to provide greater oversight over the eight largest insured banking institutions.

In the wake of the recent corporate accounting scandals, the FDIC also said it was boosting its oversight of troubled financial institutions even as Powell tried to incorporate an industry-friendly attitude in daily relations with banks. Agency officials said that the FDIC was reviewing auditor independence requirements, ethics policies, and practices of FDIC-supervised institutions.

▪ AGENCY ORGANIZATION

Biographies

DONALD E. POWELL, CHAIRMAN

Appointment: Nominated by President Bush to be a Member of the Board of Directors of the Federal Deposit Insurance Corporation for a term of six years and Chairperson for a term of five years.

Education: West Texas State University, B.S., 1963, Southwestern Graduate School of Banking at Southern Methodist University, M.S.

Profession: Banker.

Political Affiliation: Republican.

Previous Career: Prior to his appointment, Powell was the President and CEO of First National Bank in Amarillo, Texas, and was formerly with the Boatman's First National Bank of Amarillo. Mr. Powell was appointed to the Board of Regents by Governor George W. Bush in 1995. He was elected Chairman of the Board in 1997 and re-elected to a two-year term in 1999.

JOHN REICH, VICE-CHAIRMAN

Appointment: Nominated by President Clinton; confirmed by the Senate Dec. 15, 2000; term expires Dec. 15, 2006. Became Vice-Chairman on Nov. 15, 2002, had served as a board member since Jan 16, 2001.

Born:. Oct. 7, 1939, Matoon, Il.

Education: Southern Illinois University, B.S. in accounting; University of Southern Florida, MBA

Profession: Lawyer.

Political Affiliation: Republican.

Previous Career: Prior to his appointment, Reich was for ten years Chief of Staff to now-retired U.S. Senator Connie Mack. He also was President and CEO of First Commercial Bank in Fort Myers, FL.

JOHN D. HAWKE JR., COMPTROLLER OF THE CURRENCY

Appointment: Nominated by President Clinton; confirmed by the Senate Oct. 13, 1999; term expires Oct. 13, 2004.

Born:. June 26, 1933, New York, N.Y.

Education: Yale University, B.A. in English; Columbia University, J.D.

Profession: Lawyer.

Political Affiliation: Democrat.

Previous Career: Prior to his appointment, Hawke served for three and a half years as Under Secretary of the Treasury for Domestic Finance. He also served as Chairman of the Advanced Counterfeit Deterrence Steering Committee and as a member of the Securities Investor Protection Corporation.

JAMES E. GILLERAN, DIRECTOR, OFFICE OF THRIFT SUPERVISION

Appointment: Nominated by President George W. Bush; sworn to office on Dec. 7, 2001.

Education: Pace University, 1955; Northwestern California University, J.D., 1996.

Profession: Banker, CPA, Lawyer.

Previous Career: Prior to his appointment, Gilleran served in the U.S. Army from 1955–1957. He also served as Chairman of the Conference of State Banking Supervisors from 1993–1994, and was a member of CSBS's Bankers Advisory Council until 2000. Gilleran was Chairman and CEO of the Bank of San Francisco from October 1994 until December 2000.

Headquarters and Divisions

BOARD OF DIRECTORS

The board is responsible for formulating and executing policy and administering the affairs of the corporation. It bears final responsibility for FDIC activities involving protection of bank depositors and is accountable to the president and Congress. The board adopts rules and regulations, supervises state nonmember insured banks, determines the course of action to take when an insured bank has difficulties, and decides how to deal with potential and actual bank failures. The board makes final decisions on conversions, mergers, and consolidations of banks; proposals to reduce or retire capital; requests to establish or move branch offices; issuance of cease-and-desist orders; and applications for insurance by noninsured banks.

Chair

Donald E. Powell . . . . (202) 898–6974

Fax . . . . (202) 898–3500

Vice-Chair

John Reich . . . . (202) 898–3888

Fax . . . . (202) 898–3778

Directors

John D. Hawke Jr., Comptroller
of the Currency . . . . (202) 874–4900

James E. Gilleran, Director of the
Office of Thrift Supervision . . . . (202) 906–6280

(The Comptroller of the Currency and the Director of the Office of Thrift Supervision are required by law to be members of the FDIC Board of Directors.)

Deputy to the Chair for Finance/Chief Financial Officer

Steven O. App . . . . (202) 898-8732

Deputy to the Chair/Chief Operating Officer

John F. Bovenzi . . . . (202) 898–6949

Deputy to the Vice Chairman

Robert W. Russell . . . . (202) 898–8952

Deputy to the Appointive Director

Vacant . . . . (202) 898–3855

Special Advisor to the Chairman

C. K. Lee . . . . (202) 898–3673

Deputy to the Director, Comptroller of the Currency

Thomas Zemke . . . . (202) 898–6960

Deputy to the Director, Office of Thrift Supervision

Walter B. Mason . . . . (202) 898–6965

OFFICE OF PUBLIC AFFAIRS

See Information Sources.

OFFICE OF DIVERSITY AND ECONOMIC OPPORTUNITY

Directs affirmative action programs for FDIC employees and employment applicants.

Director

D. Michael Collins . . . . (202) 416–2172

Fax . . . . (202) 416–2466

OFFICE OF THE EXECUTIVE SECRETARY

Responsible for the maintenance and custody of official records of the board of directors and any standing or special committees. Certifies and seals documents, issues certificates of insurance to insured banks, and issues public notices of all meetings of the board and any standing or special committees. Publishes proposed and final rules in the *Federal Register*.

Executive Secretary

Robert E. Feldman . . . . (202) 898–3811

Fax . . . . (202) 898–3838

Operations

Valerie Best . . . . (202) 898–3812

OFFICE OF THE INSPECTOR GENERAL

Audits and evaluates the FDIC's fiscal and accounting activities, systems of internal controls, bank liquidations, data processing operations, and any other activities and operations as specified by the board of directors.

FEDERAL DEPOSIT INSURANCE CORPORATION

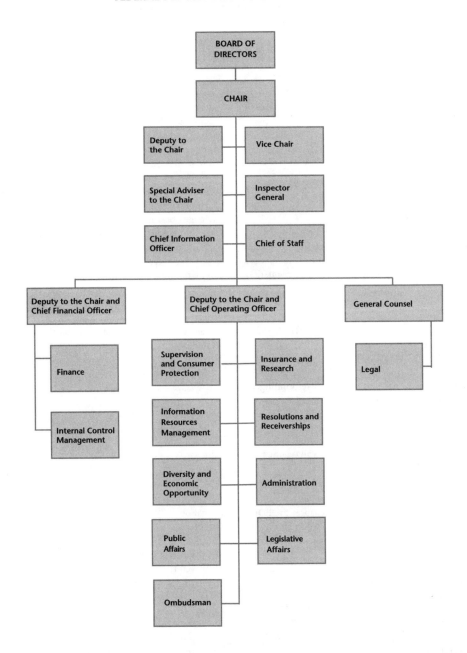

BOARD OF DIRECTORS

CHAIR

Deputy to the Chair

Vice Chair

Special Adviser to the Chair

Inspector General

Chief Information Officer

Chief of Staff

Deputy to the Chair and Chief Financial Officer

Deputy to the Chair and Chief Operating Officer

General Counsel

Finance

Internal Control Management

Supervision and Consumer Protection

Insurance and Research

Information Resources Management

Resolutions and Receiverships

Diversity and Economic Opportunity

Administration

Public Affairs

Legislative Affairs

Ombudsman

Legal

Inspector General

Gaston L. Gianni Jr. .... (202) 416–2026

Fax .... (202) 416–2906

Deputy Inspector General

Patricia Black .... (202) 416–2474

Audits

Russel A. Rau .... (202) 416–2543

Field Audits

Sharon Smith .... (202) 416–2430

Supervision and Resolution Audits

Herbert Davis .... (202) 416–2421

Information Systems Audits

Scott Miller .... (202) 416–2485

Investigations

Samuel M. Holland .... (202) 416–2912

OFFICE OF OMBUDSMAN

Is an independent, neutral, and confidential source of assistance for the public. Provides answers to the public in the areas of depositor concerns, loan questions, asset information, bank closing issues, and any FDIC regulation or policy.

Director

Cottrell L. Webster .... (202) 942–3715

Fax .... (202) 942–3041

OFFICE OF LEGISLATIVE AFFAIRS

Advises the FDIC on legislative policy, which includes developing congressional testimony, and responding to congressional inquiries regarding pending legislation and to congressional constituent complaints and inquiries.

Director

Alice C. Goodman .... (202) 898–8730

Fax .... (202) 898–3745

OFFICE OF INTERNAL CONTROL MANAGEMENT

Serves as the corporate oversight manager for internal controls and risk management and ensures the FDIC operates within an environment conducive to strong internal controls that are essential to the agency's ongoing operations and management.

Director

Michael MacDermott (acting,

rotational basis)   (202) 736–0075

Fax .... (202) 736–3115

Assistant to the Director

Wilma H. Lekan .... (202) 736–3129

Training and Outreach

Kenneth T. Jones .... (202) 736–0409

Internal Control Operations

Corinne Watts .... (202) 736–0076

Audit Follow-up and Resolutions

Howard D. Furner .... (202) 736–0304

DIVISION OF ADMINISTRATION

Branches and sections handle a variety of support services within the FDIC.

Director

Arleas Upton Kea .... (202) 942–3859

Fax .... (202) 942–3555

Acquisition & Corporate Services

Michael Rubino .... (202) 942–3215

Human Resources Branch

Miguel A. Jorrado .... (202) 942–3311

DIVISION OF RESOLUTIONS AND RECEIVERSHIPS

Supervises the liquidation of failed insured banks and savings associations, verifies claims of depositors, and pays out insurance up to the $100,000 limit. Administers a portfolio of assets of failed insured banks and savings associations and keeps a complete record of the details of each liquidation case. Also coordinates the FDIC's response to failed and failing banks and savings associations, including the development, negotiation, and monitoring of all aspects of the resolution process; manages and disposes of equity positions acquired in resolutions; and develops related policies and financing strategies.

Director

Mitchell Glassman .... (202) 898–6525

Fax .... (202) 898–6857

DIVISION OF FINANCE

Manages the FDIC's corporate and receivership funds; provides necessary financial statements and reports; administers responsibilities under the Chief Financial Officers Act, and conducts audits of and collects premiums from insured financial institutions; and provides other services, including accounting, budgeting, travel, and relocation.

Director

Fred Selby .... (202) 416–6960

Deputy Director, Resource Management

Steven P. Anderson .... (202) 416–6975

Deputy Director, Treasury

Steve W. Black .... (202) 416–4440

Deputy Director, Accounting and Reporting

Karen J. Hughes .... (202) 416–7201

DIVISION OF SUPERVISION AND CONSUMER PROTECTION

Promotes stability and public confidence in the nation's financial system by examining and supervising insured financial institutions to ensure they operate in a safe and sound manner, that consumers' rights are protected, and that FDIC-supervised institutions invest in their communities. DSCP also provides timely and accurate deposit insurance information to financial institutions and the public.

Director

Michael J. Zamorski .... (202) 898–8946

Deputy Director, Strategic Planning, Budget, and Reporting

Sandra L. Thompson .... (202) 898–3696

Deputy Director, Risk Management

John M. Lane .... (202) 898–6771

Deputy Director, Policy and Examination Oversight

George French .... (202) 898–3929

Deputy Director, Compliance and Consumer Protection

Donna J. Gambrell .... (202) 898–6549

DIVISION OF INSURANCE AND RESEARCH

Researches, analyzes, and develops policy on banking and deposit insurance; identifies existing and emerging risks to the deposit insurance funds; manages and evaluates the risk-related premium system; and provides comprehensive and statistical information on banking.

Director

Arthur J. Murton .... (202) 898–3938

Fax .... (202) 898–8636

Deputy Director, Financial Risk Management and Research

Fred S. Carns .... (202) 898–3930

Deputy Director, Risk Analysis and Banking Statistics

Maureen E. Sweeney .... (202) 898–8746

DIVISION OF INFORMATION RESOURCES MANAGEMENT

Coordinates the FDIC's computer operations and data analysis used by agency officials involved in regulation and insurance activities; and fosters the sharing and integration of information.

Director

Vijay Deshpande (acting) .... (703) 516–1076

Fax .... (703) 516–5119

LEGAL DIVISION

Handles all legal matters affecting the FDIC, including litigation; legal correspondence; interpretation of federal and state laws; and preparation of rules, regulations, opinions, and legal documents.

General Counsel

William F. Kroener III .... (202) 898–3680

Fax .... (202) 898–7394

Deputy General Counsel for Corporate Operations

Erica Cooper .... (202) 898–8530

Deputy General Counsel of Litigation Branch

Jack D. Smith .... (202) 898–3706

Deputy General Counsel of Supervision and Legislation

Douglas H. Jones .... (202) 898–3700

Regional Offices

Division of Supervision Consumer Protection

ATLANTA

(AL, FL, GA, NC, SC, VA, WV)
1 Atlantic Center
1201 W. Peachtree St. N.E., #1600
Atlanta, GA 30309
(404) 817–1300
Fax (404) 817–2810
Mark S. Schmidt, regional director

BOSTON

(CT, MA, ME, NH, RI, VT)
15 Braintree Hill Office Park
Braintree, MA 02184
(781) 794–5501
Fax (781) 794–5533
Patrick J. Rohan, regional director

CHICAGO

(IL, IN, MI, OH, WI)
500 W. Monroe St., #3200
Chicago, IL 60661
(312) 382–7552
Fax (312) 382–6901
Scott M. Polakoff, regional director

DALLAS

(CO, NM, OK, TX)
1910 Pacific Ave., #1900
Dallas, TX 75201
(972) 761–2092
John F. Carter, regional director

KANSAS CITY

(IA, KS, MN, MO, ND, NE, SD)
2345 Grand Ave., #1500
Kansas City, MO 64108
(816) 234–8137
Fax (816) 234–8182
Lawrence Morgan, regional director

MEMPHIS
(AR, KY, LA, MS, TN)
5100 Poplar Ave., #1900
Memphis, TN 38137
(901) 821–5201
Fax (901) 821–5308
Cottrell L. Webster, regional director

NEW YORK
(DC, DE, MD, NJ, NY, PA, PR, VI)
452 Fifth Ave., 19th Floor
New York, NY 10018
(212) 320–2570
Fax (212) 704–1495
Daryl P. Stum, regional director

SAN FRANCISCO
(AK, AZ, CA, GU, HI, ID, MT, NV, OR, UT, WA, WY)
25 Ecker St., #2300
San Francisco, CA 94105
(415) 808–8044
Fax (415) 543–2624
George J. Masa, regional director

Compliance and Consumer Affairs Division

ATLANTA
(AL, FL, GA, NC, SC, VA, WV)
One Atlantic Center
1201 W. Peachtree St. N.E., #1600
Atlanta, GA 30309
(404) 817–1300
Fax (404) 817–8806
Jimmy Loyless, regional director

BOSTON
(CT, MA, ME, NH, RI, VT)
15 Braintree Hill Office Park
Braintree, MA 02184
(781) 794–5500
Fax (781) 794–5633
Carl W. Schnapp, regional director

CHICAGO
(IL, IN, MI, OH, WI)
500 W. Monroe St., #3200
Chicago, IL 60661
(312) 382–7500
Fax (312) 382–6945
David K. Mangian, regional director

DALLAS
(CO, NM, OK, TX)
1910 Pacific Ave., #1900
Dallas, TX 75201
(214) 754–0098
Fax (214) 761–2362
Thomas P. Anderson, regional director

KANSAS CITY
(IA, KS, MN, MO, ND, NE, SD)
2345 Grand Ave., #1500
Kansas City, MO 64108
(816) 234–8000
Fax (816) 234–8088
John P. Misiewicz, regional director

MEMPHIS
(AR, KY, LA, MS, TN)
5100 Poplar Ave., #1900
Memphis, TN 38137
(901) 685–1603
Fax (901) 821–5272
Sylvia Plunkett, regional director

NEW YORK
(DC, DE, MD, NJ, NY, PA, PR, VI)
452 Fifth Ave., 19th Floor
New York, NY 10018
(212) 704–1200
Fax (212) 827–4529
Richard Pazereckas, regional director

SAN FRANCISCO
(AK, AZ, CA, GU, HI, ID, MT, NV, OR, UT, WA, WY)
25 Ecker St., #2300
San Francisco, CA 94105
(415) 546–0160
Fax (415) 543–2624
James Densmore, regional director

■ CONGRESSIONAL ACTION

Congressional Liaison
Alice Goodman........................ (202) 898–8730

Committees and Subcommittees

HOUSE APPROPRIATIONS COMMITTEE
Subcommittee on VA, HUD, and Independent Agencies
H143 CAP, Washington, DC 20515
(202) 225–3241

HOUSE BANKING AND FINANCIAL SERVICES COMMITTEE
Subcommittee on Financial Institutions and Consumer Credit
2129 RHOB, Washington, DC 20515
(202) 225–2258

HOUSE GOVERNMENT REFORM AND OVERSIGHT COMMITTEE
Subcommittee on National Economic Growth, Natural Resources, and Regulatory Affairs
B377 RHOB, Washington, DC 20515
(202) 225–4407

SENATE APPROPRIATIONS COMMITTEE
Subcommittee on VA, HUD, and Independent Agencies
SD-130, Washington, DC 20510
(202) 224–7211

SENATE BANKING, HOUSING AND URBAN AFFAIRS COMMITTEE
SD-534, Washington, DC 20510
(202) 224–7391

Legislation

The FDIC was organized under the **Banking Act of 1933** (48 Stat. 162, 12 U.S.C. 227), signed by the president June 16, 1933, which added a new section (12B) to the **Federal Reserve Act** (38 Stat. 251, 12 U.S.C. 226), signed by the president Dec. 23, 1913. The **Banking Act of 1935** (49 Stat. 684, 12 U.S.C. 228), signed by the president Aug. 23, 1935, extended and expanded the power of the FDIC. In 1951 Section 12B of the **Federal Reserve Act** was withdrawn from that act and enacted as a separate law known as the **Federal Deposit Insurance Act** (64 Stat. 873, 12 U.S.C. 1811–1831), signed by the president Sept. 21, 1951. This law embodies the basic authority for the operations of the FDIC.

The FDIC also is responsible for the administration of several other laws, many of them having to do with fair consumer practices. In almost all cases where the FDIC holds authority under a law, that authority extends only to insured state nonmember banks regulated by the agency.

Major legislation administered in part by the FDIC includes:

Securities Exchange Act of 1934 (48 Stat. 881, 15 U.S.C. 78b). Signed by the president June 6, 1934. Required the registration of securities by U.S. banking institutions.

Bank Holding Company Act of 1956 (70 Stat. 133, 12 U.S.C. 1841). Signed by the president May 9, 1956. Regulated the creation and expansion of bank holding companies.

Bank Mergers and Consolidation Act of 1960 (74 Stat. 129, 12 U.S.C. 1828). Signed by the president May 13, 1960. Required bank mergers to receive prior approval from the federal regulatory agency having jurisdiction over the surviving bank.

Bank Service Corporation Act (76 Stat. 1132, 12 U.S.C. 1861). Signed by the president Oct. 23, 1962. Permitted certain federally supervised banks to form service corporations to perform clerical, bookkeeping, and data processing services.

Truth in Lending Act (82 Stat. 146, 15 U.S.C. 1601). Signed by the president May 29, 1968. Required lenders and merchants to inform consumers of the total cost of loans and installment purchase plans and to clearly state annual percentage rate. Also prohibited unsolicited distribution of credit cards and limited the owner's liability for unauthorized use of a lost or stolen card.

Bank Protection Act of 1968 (82 Stat. 294, 12 U.S.C. 1881). Signed by the president July 7, 1968. Required establishment of minimum security system standards for banking institutions.

Fair Credit Reporting Act (84 Stat. 1128, 15 U.S.C. 1681). Signed by the president Oct. 26, 1970. Regulated credit information collection and use.

NOW Accounts Act (87 Stat. 342, 12 U.S.C. 1832). Signed by the president Aug. 16, 1973. Regulated interest-bearing checking accounts.

Equal Credit Opportunity Act (88 Stat. 1521, 15 U.S.C. 1691). Signed by the president Oct. 28, 1974. Prohibited credit discrimination against women. Amended by the **Equal Credit Opportunity Act Amendments of 1976** (90 Stat. 251, 15 U.S.C. 1691 note). Signed by the president March 23, 1976. Barred credit discrimination based on age, race, religion, or national origin.

Real Estate Settlement Procedures Act of 1974 (88 Stat. 1724, 12 U.S.C. 2601–2616). Signed by the president Dec. 22, 1974. Minimized settlement charges for home buyers; confirmed the authority of the Department of Housing and Urban Development to set standards for settlement charges on homes financed through federally backed mortgages.

Home Mortgage Disclosure Act (89 Stat. 1125, 12 U.S.C. 2801). Signed by the president Dec. 31, 1975. Required lending institutions within standard metropolitan statistical areas (SMSAs) to disclose the number and amount of mortgage loans made yearly to determine if banks are discriminating against certain city neighborhoods by refusing to make mortgage loans regardless of the creditworthiness of the potential borrower (practice known as "redlining").

Fair Debt Collection Practices Act (91 Stat. 874, 15 U.S.C. 1692). Signed by the president Sept. 20, 1977. Regulated methods used by debt collecting agencies.

Community Reinvestment Act of 1977 (91 Stat. 1147, 12 U.S.C. 2901–2905). Signed by the president Oct. 12, 1977. Required federal bank regulators to encourage institutions they regulate to help meet the credit needs of their communities, including low- and moderate-income neighborhoods, consistent with safe and sound operations.

International Banking Act of 1978 (92 Stat. 607, 12 U.S.C. 3101–3108). Signed by the president Sept. 17, 1978. Provided for the federal regulation of foreign banks in domestic financial markets.

Electronic Fund Transfer Act of 1978 (92 Stat. 3728, 15 U.S.C. 1601 note). Signed by the president Nov. 10, 1978. Established rules relating to consumer liability for unauthorized use of an electronic fund transfer card and unsolicited issuance of cards by financial institutions. Prohibited creditors from making automatic repayment of loans a condition of extending credit; overdraft credit plans were exempted.

Financial Institutions Regulatory and Interest Rate Control Act of 1978 (92 Stat. 3641, 12 U.S.C. 226 note). Signed by the president Nov. 10, 1978. Regulated the activities of individual bank officers; provided for tighter controls on insider lending and interlocking directorates among financial institutions and expanded the authority of bank regulators.

Depository Institutions Deregulation and Monetary Control Act of 1980 (94 Stat. 132, 12 U.S.C. 226 note). Signed by the president March 31, 1980. Extended reserve requirements to all financial institutions, phased out interest rate ceilings over a six-year period, and allowed thrift institutions to offer a wider range of financial services. Established the Depository Institutions Deregulation Committee. Increased FDIC insurance coverage to $100,000 per depositor.

Garn-St. Germain Depository Institutions Act of 1982 (96 Stat. 1469, 12 U.S.C. 226 note). Signed by the president Oct. 15, 1982. Expanded the FDIC's powers to assist troubled banks by allowing either direct or merger-related assistance (1) to prevent the closing of or to reopen any insured bank or (2) when severe financial conditions threaten the stability of a significant number of banks or banks with substantial financial resources. Increased the powers of federally chartered savings and loan associations and savings banks (thrift institutions) to conduct a wider range of commercial operations and thus be able to compete with recently established investment institutions.

Federal Deposit Insurance Act, Amendment (97 Stat. 189, 96 U.S.C. 1492). Signed by the president May 16, 1983. Provided that the issuance of net worth certificates did not constitute default under existing debt obligations. This amendment took effect retroactively on Oct. 15, 1982, the date of enactment of the Garn-St. Germain Depository Institutions Act of 1982.

Supplemental Appropriations Act, 1984; Domestic Housing and International Recovery and Financial Stability Act, Titles VII and IX (97 Stat. 1153, 12 U.S.C. 1701a note). Signed by the president Nov. 30, 1983. Title VII amended the Federal Deposit Insurance Act by permitting any sitting member of the FDIC board of directors to remain in office until a successor is confirmed by the Senate. Title IX, the **International Lending Supervision Act of 1983**, increased FDIC supervisory and regulatory powers over banking institutions engaged in international borrowing and lending.

Bankruptcy Amendments and Federal Judgeship Act of 1984 (98 Stat. 333, 28 U.S.C. 151 note). Signed by the president July 10, 1984. Permitted the FDIC to act as a member of an unsecured creditor's committee when acting as a receiver or liquidator of banks failing after Oct. 9, 1984.

Continuing Appropriations, 1985—Comprehensive Crime Control Act of 1984 (98 Stat. 1837, 43 U.S.C. 1715). Signed by the president Oct. 12, 1984. Prohibited the receipt of stolen property from a bank and the bribing of bank personnel.

The Competitive Equality Banking Act of 1987 (101 Stat. 552, 12 U.S.C. 226 note). Signed by the president Aug. 10, 1987. Granted the Federal Savings and Loan Insurance Corporation (FSLIC) new borrowing authority in order to reimburse depositors as it shut down bankrupt thrifts. Suspended the expansion of banks into insurance, securities underwriting, and real estate and prohibited the expansion of limited service banks. Eased regulatory requirements for savings and loans in economically depressed areas and required faster clearing of depositors' checks.

Technical and Miscellaneous Revenue Act of 1988 (102 Stat. 3342, 26 U.S.C. 1 note). Signed by the president Nov. 10, 1988. Extended until Dec. 31, 1989, special tax treatment to troubled banks assisted by the FDIC.

Financial Institutions Reform, Recovery and Enforcement Act of 1989 (FIRREA) (103 Stat. 183, 12 U.S.C. 1811 note). Signed by the president Aug. 9, 1989. Approved the use of $50 billion to finance the closing of insolvent savings and loans. Created the Resolution Trust Corporation (RTC) to manage the disposal of the assets of bankrupt thrifts. Dissolved the Federal Home Loan Bank Board, assigning its regulatory responsibilities to the Treasury Department and assigning its role in insuring depositors through the Federal Savings and Loan Insurance Corporation (FSLIC) to the FDIC. Savings and loans were required to maintain a minimum amount of tangible capital equal to 1.5 percent of total assets.

Federal Deposit Insurance Corporation Improvement Act of 1991 (105 Stat. 2236, 12 U.S.C. 1811 note). Signed by the president Dec. 19, 1991. Required banks to increase capital and pay higher deposit insurance premiums. Provided Treasury funding to the BIF.

Depository Institutions Disaster Relief Act of 1992 (106 Stat. 2771, 12 U.S.C. 1811 note). Signed by the president Oct. 23, 1992. Facilitated recovery from disasters by providing greater flexibility for depository institutions and their regulators.

Housing and Community Development Act of 1992 (106 Stat. 3672, 42 U.S.C. 5301 note). Signed by the president Oct. 28, 1992. Established regulatory structure for government-sponsored enterprises (GSEs), combated money laundering, and provided regulatory relief to financial institutions.

Resolution Trust Corporation Completion Act (107 Stat. 2369, 12 U.S.C. 1421 note). Signed by the president Dec. 17, 1993. Amended the Inspector General Act of 1978; it made the position of the inspector general a presidential appointment. Set forth structural changes for the FDIC as well as the Resolution Trust Corporation (RTC). Prescribed the termination of the RTC on Oct. 1, 1995 and delegated all remaining authorities, duties, responsibilities, and activities to the FDIC thereafter. Directed the FDIC Board of Directors to prescribe regulations regarding conflicts of interest, ethical responsibilities, and the use of confidential information; establish minimum standards of competence, experience, and integrity for its contractors; and prohibit the sale of a failed institution's assets to any person engaged in unethical conduct with respect to such institution.

Interstate Banking Efficiency Act of 1994 (108 Stat. 2338, 12 U.S.C. 1811 note). Signed by the president Sept. 29, 1994. Permitted banks to operate networks of branch offices across state lines without having to set up separately capitalized subsidiary banks.

Gramm-Leach-Bliley Act. (113 Stat. 1338, 12 U.S.C. 1811 note). Signed by the president on Nov. 12, 1999. Title I repealed provisions of the Banking Act of 1933 and the Bank Holding Act of 1956 to allow affiliations between banks and any financial company, including brokerage and insurance firms. Required the FDIC to enforce privacy and fair credit reporting standards.

American Homeownership and Economic Opportunity Act of 2000. (114 Stat. 2944, 12 U.S.C. 1701). Signed by the president on Dec. 27, 2000. Title I, the Housing Affordability Barrier Removal Act of 2000, amended the Housing and Community Development Act of 1992 to authorize $15 million for the next five years for states, local government, and consortiums to create regulatory relief strategies. Title XII, the Financial Regulatory Relief and Economic Efficiency Act of 2000, provided regulatory relief to banks, including a provision permitting banks to own some of their stock.

Uniting and Strengthening America by Providing Appropriate Tools Required to Intercept and Obstruct Terrorism Act of 2002 (USA Patriot Act). (115 Stat. 272, 18 U.S.C. 1 note). Signed by the president on Oct. 26, 2001. Title III, the International Money Laundering Abatement and Anti-Terrorist Financing Act of 2001, amended various federal banking laws, including the Bank Holding Company Act of 1956, the Fair Credit Reporting Act, the Federal Reserve Act, and the Federal Deposit Insurance Act. Directed certain government agencies, principally the Treasury Department in consultation with the Federal Reserve (Fed), to investigate and curtail money laundering and other activities that might be undertaken to finance terrorist actions or disrupt legitimate banking operations. Required securities brokers and dealers to submit reports regarding suspected money-laundering transactions. Required the Fed to consider an institution's ability to combat money laundering when evaluating proposed bank shares or mergers. Provided protection for Fed facilities and staff, including law enforcement officers authorized to carry firearms and make warrantless arrests. Allowed written employment references to contain suspicions of involvement in illegal activity.

Investor and Capital Markets Fee Relief Act. (115 Stat. 2390, 15 U.S.C. 78a note). Signed by the president on Jan. 16, 2002. Amended the Securities Exchange Act of 1934 to reduce fees on the purchase and sale of securities, on trades of single stock futures, on merger and tender offers, and on fees companies pay to register securities. Eliminated fees on Trust Indenture applications. Required the SEC to adjust its fees annually after fiscal 2002 to account for changing market conditions. Increased SEC staff salaries by authorizing the SEC to establish an employee compensation system outside of the existing federal civil service system.

■ INFORMATION SOURCES

Internet
Agency Web Site: http://www.fdic.gov. Provides general information and links to specific FDIC offices and programs.

Telephone Contacts
Consumer Hotline . . . . (800) 934–3342
    TDD . . . . (800) 925–4618
    Washington, DC, area . . . . (202) 898–3773
Member Banks Help Line . . . . (800) 934–3342
Public Information Center . . . . (877) 275–3342

Information and Publications

KEY OFFICES

FDIC Office of Public Affairs
550 17th St. N.W.
Washington, DC 20429
(202) 898–6993
Fax (202) 898–3543
James Phillip Battey, director

Issues news releases; topics include notices of failed banks, policy statements, addresses by FDIC officials, and personnel changes. Distributes most FDIC publications.

Freedom of Information
FDIC Executive Secretary
550 17th St. N.W.
Washington, DC 20429
(202) 898–3819
Fax (202) 898–8778
Robert Feldman

PUBLICATIONS
For a list or to order a specific title, contact FDIC Corporate Communications or:

FDIC Public Information Center
801 17th St. N.W., Room 100
Washington, DC 20429
(202) 416–6940
Fax (202) 416–2076
Hours: 9 a.m. to 5 p.m.

Provides the following FDIC publications free of charge unless otherwise indicated; requests may be made in person, by telephone, or by mail.

Annual Report. Contains FDIC operations, enforcement actions, legislation and regulations, and statistics on closed banks and deposit insurance.

Consumer Information. This and other consumer pamphlets, including *Truth in Lending, Fair Credit Billing, Fair Credit Reporting Act, Equal Credit Opportunity and Age,* and *Equal Credit Opportunity and Women,* are available from Compliance and Consumer Affairs, many also in Spanish. Bulk quantities may be ordered free of charge.

Data Book. Annual summary of accounts and deposits in all commercial and mutual savings banks and domestic branches of foreign banks. All operating banks and branches are listed.

Merger Decisions. Reports merger decisions by the corporation (approvals and denials of bank absorptions).

Statistics on Banking. Contains several categories of year-end statistical data formerly provided by the *Annual Report,* including information on assets, income, and liabilities of insured banks.

Symbol of Confidence. Describes the history, rules, and regulations of the FDIC, including how the corporation protects depositors' accounts and promotes sound banking practices. Single copies available at no charge.

Trust Assets of Banks and Trust Companies. Data from all insured commercial banks by type of account, asset distribution, and size of the trust department; lists trust assets for trust departments of all insured commercial and mutual savings banks.

Your Insured Deposit. Provides examples of insurance coverage under the FDIC's rules on certain types of accounts commonly held by depositors in insured banks.

In addition, the Office of the Executive Secretary issues a loose-leaf service on the laws, regulations, and related acts that affect the operation of insured banks. This three-volume reporting service is updated every two months and is available by subscription. For details, call (202) 898–6757.

Finally, some FDIC publications, including *Quarterly Banking Profile, Real Estate Survey,* and *Banking Review,* can be subscribed through listserv. If interested, visit: http://www.fdic.gov/publish/publctns.html and follow the instructions.

DATA AND STATISTICS

FDIC Division of Insurance and Research
550 17th St. N.W.
Washington, DC 20429
(202) 898–3946
Fax (202) 898–7499
Arthur J. Murton, director

Compiles statistics on bank deposit insurance and banking in general. Prepares special reports, surveys, and studies, and analyzes policy issues, proposed legislation, economic trends, and other developments affecting financial institutions and markets. The following titles are available via listserv (see Publications for more information) or in printed form via the FDIC Public Information Center:

FDIC Banking Review. Journal presenting research on banking and deposit insurance issues and information on federal and state legislation and regulatory actions.

Historical Statistics on Banking. Contains annual data on FDIC-insured institutions from 1934. Includes state-level tables and annual lists of failed commercial banks and savings institutions.

Quarterly Banking Profile. Published within seventy-five days after the end of each quarter; provides the earliest comprehensive summary of financial results from all insured institutions.

Report on Underwriting Practices. Biannual; monitors trends and practices in new loan underwriting at FDIC-supervised banks.

Statistics on Banking. Quarterly; provides aggregate financial information on FDIC-insured institutions, with summary totals by state and charter type.

The Survey of Real Estate Trends. Quarterly; provides aggregate national and regional developments in local real estate markets.

FDIC Division of Supervision Disclosure Group
550 17th St. N.W.
Washington, DC 20429
(202) 898–7112

Data on banks and savings associations and their financial condition are available from the FDIC for a nominal service charge. Contact this office for details on specific prices. All information and reports must be requested in writing by name of bank, city, and state. Information available includes:

Bank Branch Master File. Quarterly publication of all banks and branches, listed by name of bank and address only. Available on magnetic tape.

Reports of Condition and Income. Retained for ten years; reports of condition available quarterly.

Summary of Deposits. All banking offices within a given city, county, standard metropolitan statistical area (SMSA), or state (on a computer printout).

Trust Asset File. Annual; a trust asset form file of all banks with trust assets, giving bank name and address. Available on magnetic computer tape; paper copy is available from FDIC Corporate Communications.

Trust Asset List. Annual report containing all banks with trust assets listed in descending order. Paper copy is available from FDIC Corporate Communications.

MEETINGS
The directors of the FDIC hold monthly meetings. Notices are posted in the lobby of the FDIC headquarters and are published in the *Federal Register*. The Office of the Executive Secretary can provide further details; (202) 898–3811.

Reference Resources

LIBRARY

FDIC Library
550 17th St. N.W., Room 4060
Washington, DC 20429
(202) 898–3623
Fax (202) 898–3984
Dianna Smith, head librarian

Specializes in banking law and maintains separate banking, legal, and economic sections. Open to the public Tuesday, Wednesday, and Thursday by appointment only.

RULES AND REGULATIONS
FDIC rules and regulations are published in the *Code of Federal Regulations*, Title 12, vol. 2, sections 301–351. Proposed rules, new final rules, and updates to the *Code of Federal Regulations* are published in the daily *Federal Register*. (See appendix for information on how to obtain and use these publications.)

Other Information Sources

NONGOVERNMENTAL ORGANIZATIONS
The following are some key organizations that monitor the FDIC and banking issues.

American Bankers Association
1120 Connecticut Ave. N.W.
Washington, DC 20036
(202) 663–5000
Fax (202) 828–4532
Internet: http://www.aba.com

America's Community Bankers
900 19th St. N.W., #400
Washington, DC 20006
(202) 857–3100
Fax (202) 296–8716
Internet: http://www.acbankers.org

American Financial Services Association
919 18th St. N.W., #300
Washington, DC 20006
(202) 296–5544
Fax (202) 223–0321

Bank Administration Institute
1 N. Franklin St.
Chicago, IL 60606
(800) 323–8552
Publications (800) 224–9889
Fax (800) 375–5543
Internet: http://www.bai.org

The Bankers' Roundtable
805 15th St. N.W., #600
Washington, DC 20005
(202) 289–4322
Fax (202) 289–1903
Internet: http://www.bankersround.org

Conference of State Bank Supervisors
1015 18th St. N.W., #1100
Washington, DC 20036–5275
(202) 296–2840
(800) 866–2727
Fax (202) 296–1928
Internet: http://www.csbsdal.org

Consumer Bankers Association
1000 Wilson Blvd., #3012
Arlington, VA 22209–3908
(703) 276–1750
Fax (703) 528–1290
Internet: http://www.cbanet.org

Independent Bankers Association of America
1 Thomas Circle N.W., #400
Washington, DC 20005
(202) 659–8111
(800) 422–8439
Fax (202) 659–9216
Internet: http://www.ibaa.org

PUBLISHERS
The following companies and organizations publish on the FDIC and related issues through books, periodicals, or electronic media.

American Banker
1 State St. Plaza
New York, NY 10004
(800) 221–1809
Fax (800) 803–8200
Internet: http://www.americanbanker.com

Bureau of National Affairs (BNA), Inc.
1231 25th St. N.W.
Washington, DC 20037
(202) 452–4200
Fax (800) 253–0332
Internet: http://www.bna.com

Commerce Clearing House (CCH), Inc.
2700 Lake Cook Rd.
Riverwoods, IL 60015
(847) 267–7000
Fax (847) 267–7878
Internet: http://www.cch.com

Journal of Money, Credit and Banking
Ohio State University Press, Journals Dept.
1070 Carmack Rd.
Columbus, OH 43210–1002
(614) 292–1407
(800) 437–4439
Fax (614) 292–2065
Internet: http://www.sbs.ohio-state.edu/osu-press/
jmcbmain.htm (to contact OSU Press)
http://www.jstor.org/journals/00222879.html (to browse
the journal's archives)

Moody's Investors Service, Inc.
99 Church St.
Attn: FIS 1st Floor Sales Dept.
New York, NY 10007
(800) 342–5647
Fax (212) 553–4700
Internet: http://www.moodys.com

Phillips Business Information
1201 Seven Locks Rd., #300
Potomac, MD 20854
(301) 340–7788
Internet: http://www.phillips.com

Warren, Gorham & Lamont, Inc.
31 St. James Ave.
Boston, MA 02116
(800) 999–9336
Fax (617) 695–9699
Internet: http://www.wgl.com

Federal Energy Regulatory Commission

888 1st St. N.E., Washington, DC 20426
Internet: http://www.ferc.fed.gov

▌ INTRODUCTION

Established as an independent regulatory agency, the Federal Energy Regulatory Commission (FERC) is within, but separate from, the Department of Energy (DOE). It was created by the Department of Energy Organization Act of 1977 to replace the Federal Power Commission (FPC).

The commission has five members appointed by the president and confirmed by the Senate. Before 1990, members served four-year terms. But in April 1990, President George Bush signed a law providing for five-year terms of office for members. The president appoints one commissioner to serve as chair.

Responsibilities

The commission:

• Regulates the transmission of natural gas in interstate commerce.

• Regulates the construction, operation, and abandonment of interstate pipeline facilities.

• Reviews curtailment plans proposed by gas companies to reduce service to certain areas.

• Oversees construction and operation of facilities needed by pipelines at the point of entry to import or export natural gas.

• Reviews rates set by the federal power marketing administrations and certifies small power production and cogeneration facilities.

• Regulates the rates and practices of oil pipeline companies engaged in interstate transportation.

• Regulates the transmission and sale (wholesale) of electricity in interstate commerce.

• Authorizes the conditions, rates, and charges for interconnections among electric utilities.

GLOSSARY

Abandonment—The cessation of service certificated under the Natural Gas Act from a gas well or facilities dedicated to the interstate market.

Blanket Certificate—Allows pipelines to conduct certain transactions and services on a self-implementing basis.

Curtailment—A cutback in acceptance of delivery by pipelines from gas producers during periods of oversupply; a cutback in the availability of "interruptible" transportation service during periods of high demand.

Electronic Bulletin Board—The use of computerized information systems to exchange information about pipeline capacity, rates, and deliveries. FERC, in Order 889, required electric utilities to obtain information about their transmission using the Open Access Same-time Information System (OASIS), sharing information about available transmission capacity with competitors.

ISO—Independent system operator.

Interconnection—A joining of the transmission networks of two or more electric utilities. Interconnection allows utilities to share facilities and power reserves and provides service to larger areas.

LDC—Local distribution company.

NOPR—Notice of proposed rulemaking.

Open-Access Transportation Program—A program that allows pipelines to apply for "blanket" transportation certificates that require transportation to be carried out on a nondiscriminatory basis. Transportation requests are fulfilled on a first-come, first-served basis.

Pooling—The voluntary agreement among utilities to sell power to one another. Pooling offers a sales outlet for power produced in excess of immediate system requirements, and a supply source when demand exceeds immediate system generating capacity. Pools may or may not be operated by independent system operators.

Stranded Costs—Costs that a utility has incurred to serve wholesale requirements or retail franchise customers that are stranded when a customer stops buying power from the utility and simply pays for transmission services to reach a different supplier.

Take-or-Pay—Requires pipelines either to buy and take the agreed-upon volumes from the producer or to pay a fee to the producer if it fails to take the gas.

Unbundling—The separation of services into discrete components with separate charges for each service.

Wheeling—An arrangement in which one electric company allows another company to use its lines to transmit power to customers in its service area. Retail wheeling allows any customer to buy from any supplier.

- Issues licenses, conducts safety inspections, and reviews environmental compliance for nonfederal hydroelectric projects.
- Regulates security (stock) issues and mergers of electric utilities; approves interlocking directorships among electric utilities.
- Reviews appeals from DOE remedial orders and denials of adjustments.

Powers and Authority

NATURAL GAS REGULATION

The natural gas industry consists of three major segments: producers; pipeline companies, which transport gas from producing areas to consuming markets; and local distribution companies (LDCs), which sell gas to ultimate consumers.

The commission sets the rates that interstate pipeline companies may charge for the transmission of natural gas. Local distribution companies, which buy gas from pipelines and sell it to homes and industries, generally are regulated by state public utility commissions. The commission no longer regulates the rates for wellhead sales of natural gas and is phasing out regulation of rates charged by the gathering systems owned by interstate pipelines.

FERC approves construction of interstate pipeline facilities In acting on a proposal to build a major pipeline facility, the commission must take into account a number of factors, including the market for the gas, environmental impact, and financial viability. FERC also reviews proposals by interstate pipeline companies to provide service to new customers or to modify existing service, to abandon pipeline facilities, and to transport gas directly to industrial and other endusers.

The commission can exercise authority in several areas where little regulation has been required since the return of normal market conditions in the 1980s: authority over the siting, construction, and operation of liquefied natural gas (LNG) terminals to receive and regasify imported LNG; and the approval of curtailment plans, which are used by pipelines to allocate available supplies among customers during periods when gas supplies are inadequate to satisfy demand.

WHOLESALE ELECTRIC RATE REGULATION

The commission regulates the rate and service standards for wholesale electricity. These sales of electricity for resale—between utilities or by a utility to a municipality—make up more than a quarter of total U.S. electricity sales. Retail sales of electricity to consumers, such as homeowners and businesses, are regulated by state public utility commissions. The traditional split between state and federal jurisdiction has been complicated by the commission's assertion in Order 888 of jurisdiction over the rates for unbundled retail transmission in interstate commerce.

The commission ensures that rates for wholesale transactions in interstate commerce are just and reasonable and not unduly discriminatory. The commission reviews agreements for the interconnection of utility systems and the transfer of power among utilities, with the aim of achieving reliable service at just and reasonable rates.

In addition to the review of rates and service standards, the commission has authority over the mergers of regulated utilities, certain issuances of utility stock, and the existence of certain interlocking relationships between top officials in utilities and major firms doing business with utilities. It also approves the rates of the five power marketing agencies, which are federally owned utilities operated by the DOE. Finally, FERC determines whether the operations of independent power producers and cogeneration facilities qualify for purposes of selling electricity to utilities at preferential rates under the Public Utility Regulatory Policy Act of 1978 (PURPA).

HYDROELECTRIC POWER PROJECT LICENSING

FERC issues licenses to construct and operate hydroelectric power projects, except those owned by other federal agencies. Hydroelectric power generation represents 98 percent of the country's current renewable energy resources; hydropower projects under FERC's jurisdiction are approximately 50 percent of the national total. The commission seeks to preserve environmental quality at hydroelectric sites by including protective measures in its licensing orders. FERC is responsible for licensing and regulating about 1,670 nonfederal hydroelectric projects. Licenses issued by the commission contain conditions for protection of fish and wildlife, water quality, historical and archeological sites, scenic and cultural values, as well as providing for recreational opportunities, flood control, and the efficient, safe operation of project dams.

OIL PIPELINE REGULATION

The commission regulates the rates and practices of the approximately 150 pipeline companies transporting oil in interstate commerce. The overall objective of FERC is to establish just and reasonable rates that will encourage the optimal use, maintenance, and construction of oil pipeline systems—a relatively inexpensive mode of oil transportation—while protecting consumers against unjustified costs. The commission also has the authority to prohibit certain anticompetitive oil pipeline company practices.

RELATIONSHIP TO DOE

The commission functions as an independent regulatory body within the DOE. The energy secretary exercises no control over the decisions of the commission, although the secretary may recommend issues for its consideration. Commission decisions are final for the DOE; they may be appealed to the U.S. Court of Appeals.

FERC also reviews certain rules proposed by the DOE. If a proposed rule could significantly affect its functions, FERC may consider the rule, receive comments from the public, and make recommendations to the secretary of energy on whether and how it should be implemented. The secretary must incorporate all changes proposed by the commission before a rule becomes final.

FORMAL PROCEEDINGS

The commission may initiate formal rulemakings, major rate cases, applications for curtailments, and other issues it considers of sufficient merit. Proposals for rulemaking may originate from within the commission or from the general public. FERC staff proposals are placed on the agenda of an open commission meeting and published in the *Federal Register*; important public proposals likewise are placed on the agenda and published. At the commission meeting the commissioners may accept the proposed rule, reject it, or send it back to the staff for further study. If approved, it is published in the *Federal Register* as a Notice of Proposed Rulemaking (NOPR) and public comment is solicited.

An administrative law judge (ALJ) presides over hearings on cases in which the commission wants an evidentiary record. A hearing is conducted like a courtroom hearing; participants may examine and cross-examine witnesses, file briefs, and submit evidence and exhibits. After the hearing, the ALJ issues an "initial decision" or recommendation for the consideration of the commission. The commission may adopt the ALJ's recommendation, modify, reject, or remand it for further proceedings in an opinion that is published in the *Federal Register*. These opinions, along with other orders of the commission, are posted on the FERC's Web site. Parties to the decision may request a rehearing, which is held at the commission's discretion. FERC decisions may be appealed to the U.S. Court of Appeals.

Company requests for rate increases, adjustments, and curtailments follow a similar procedure. After the commission receives a request for action and the FERC staff reviews it, a Notice of Application is issued and published in the

Federal Register to solicit public comment. Following further staff analysis, the case is placed on the commission meeting agenda. After considering the staff's recommendation, the commission may approve, modify, reject, or set certain issues for an evidentiary hearing before an ALJ.

ENFORCEMENT

FERC has the authority to enforce compliance with its statutes, rules, orders, and regulations. Most enforcement is by administrative or judicial action. Compliance orders may be appealed to the commission. Failure to comply may result in proceedings in a U.S. district court. Preliminary enforcement proceedings also can take the form of special investigations and examinations.

CERTIFICATES AND LICENSES

The commission requires several different types of licenses and certificates of regulated industries. Actions that require FERC approval include:

- Construction of nonfederal hydroelectric projects (license). Similar to the certificates required for gas.
- Maintenance of facilities at international borders for the transmission of electric energy or natural gas between the United States and another country (permit).
- Construction of gas pipelines and facilities (certificate). This certificate is the most common authorized by FERC. It ensures that the builder's financial resources are in order and that the pipeline or facility will be able to meet anticipated demand. Relaxations under the blanket certificate program have enabled pipelines to start construction on certain projects without prior FERC authorization.

REPORTING REQUIREMENTS

FERC maintains a uniform system of accounts that almost all large electric utilities and pipelines use. FERC collects detailed financial information on the revenues, costs, and balance sheets of the larger industry participants. In recent years, authority to collect some types of data, such as gas storage operations, has been reassigned to the DOE's Energy Information Administration. Most of the detailed financial reports are available for public inspection.

Background

Although FERC technically is one of the newer federal agencies, its history stretches back more than three-quarters of a century. FERC was created by the Department of Energy Organization Act and began operations Oct. 1, 1977. Its primary responsibilities, however, are those previously administered by the FPC, which was established in 1920. In addition to taking over the FPC's functions, FERC assumed the oil pipeline valuation and rate regulation functions of the Interstate Commerce Commission.

EARLY HISTORY

The FPC, FERC's predecessor, was created by the Federal Water Power Act of 1920 in response to demands for the government to encourage and coordinate the construction of hydroelectric projects on federal lands and waterways. Before the FPC's creation, a special act of Congress was required before a private hydroelectric project could be built on federal lands or waterways. The FPC originally consisted of the secretaries of the departments of war, interior, and agriculture. However, as the demand for electric power expanded, this arrangement proved too unwieldy, and in 1930 the commission was reorganized into a five-member bipartisan group.

In the FPC's early days, the commission's sole responsibility was the approval or disapproval of hydroelectric projects, but during the 1930s the body's regulatory powers were increased. In 1935 the Federal Water Power Act of 1920 was made part of a new Federal Power Act. In addition to its existing functions, the FPC assumed responsibility for regulating electric utilities' wholesale rates and transactions. The bill also authorized the commission to prescribe a uniform system of accounts and to inspect the records of licensees and public utilities.

The Natural Gas Act of 1938 extended FPC jurisdiction to the wholesale sales and transportation of natural gas in interstate commerce by pipeline companies. In 1942 the Natural Gas Act was amended to make the FPC responsible for certifying, as well as regulating, facilities for the transportation and wholesale sale of natural gas in interstate commerce.

The FPC's interest in natural gas grew as demand for the fuel increased after World War II. In 1954 the Supreme Court ruled that independent local producers selling natural gas for resale in interstate commerce were subject to FPC regulation. Consequently, the rates for gas produced and sold within the same state were left to the discretion of state governments, but the FPC maintained responsibility for setting rates for natural gas sold by producers in interstate commerce.

During the 1950s and 1960s, when natural gas was relatively plentiful, these two different approaches to rate setting did not cause serious problems. However, as the difference in the average prices of interstate and intrastate gas began to widen, producers increasingly made the decision to sell their gas in the higher-priced intrastate market, which was free of federal regulation. By the mid-1970s only 19 percent of newly discovered natural gas was being sold on the interstate market.

Severe shortages, culminating in a natural gas crisis in the winter of 1976–1977, developed in the consuming states that were dependent on federally regulated gas, while gas surpluses grew in the producing states where prices usually were unregulated. The need for reform of natural gas

FEDERAL ENERGY REGULATORY COMMISSION ORDERS

Order 436: Issued October 1985. Established the principle of open-access transportation by encouraging pipelines to apply for "blanket certificates" under which they provide carriage in a nondiscriminatory fashion. Transportation requests are fulfilled on a first-come, first-served basis. (D.C. Circuit Court of Appeals remanded to FERC in June 1987 so the commission could "more convincingly" address the take-or-pay issue.)

Order 451: Issued June 1986. Permitted first sellers of "old" natural gas—which may be contractually priced below current market levels—to initiate "good faith negotiations" (GFNs) to settle on a new price. If the seller and purchaser engaging in GFN are unable to agree on a price, each is entitled to abandon the sale or purchase. (Vacated by the 5th U.S. Circuit Court of Appeals in September 1989. Court ruled that FERC exceeded its statutory authority in establishing new pricing structure for old gas that collapsed the previous vintage, or classification, system into a single, higher ceiling price. It also criticized the abandonment provision. The Supreme Court upheld the order in 1991.)

Order 497: Issued June 1988. Set a number of requirements for natural gas pipelines and their marketing affiliates, including the separation of operating personnel "to the maximum extent practicable" and reports of affiliate transactions.

Order 500: Issued August 1987 to meet the D.C. Circuit Court of Appeals' concerns with Order 436. Established mechanisms to prevent the accumulation of take-or-pay when a pipeline transports; spread take-or-pay liabilities among all parties—producers, pipelines, and customers. (The D.C. Circuit Court of Appeals ruled October 1989 that Order 500 failed to provide the reasoned take-or-pay explanation it had sought in the Order 436 case. The court remanded the case to FERC.)

Order 500-H: Issued December 1989 to comply with D.C. Circuit Court's remand.

Order 636: Issued April 1992. Mandated the complete separation of pipeline services, or unbundling. Required pipelines to provide open-access firm and interruptible transportation services for all gas suppliers. Allowed pipelines to sell gas at unregulated prices.

Order 888: Issued April 1996. Required electric utilities and transmission companies to file tariffs that offered competitors open-access to transmission grids. Provided for the recovery of stranded costs. Asserted FERC jurisdiction over retail wheeling as a last resort where state regulatory commissions lacked jurisdiction to order recovery of stranded costs.

Order 2000: Issued December 1999. Called for the creation of regional transmission organizations (RTOs) to increase the operating efficiency of electric transmission systems while eliminating opportunities for discriminatory transmission practices.

---

pricing was evident. The Natural Gas Policy Act (NGPA) of 1978 extended federal price controls to the intrastate market to end the distortions caused by the dual system. The act also established a schedule for phased deregulation of new gas beginning in 1985. Gas drilled before April 20, 1977, was to remain under control.

NATURAL GAS REGULATION IN THE 1980S

The NGPA also established categories of natural gas that could be priced at different levels. The tiered pricing system was intended to encourage the discovery of new gas supplies. But proponents of ending federal price controls said the system only encouraged producers to drill for the most expensive gas.

By the winter of 1981–1982 natural gas prices began to surge. The highly regulated market did not conform to traditional supply-demand price and cost models. Long-term contracts signed during the 1970s when supplies were tight were blamed for some of the price increases. Because federal regulators allowed pipelines to earn a fixed rate of return on their costs, they had little incentive to keep gas

costs down. Meanwhile, incremental demand was increasingly being met from the several tiers of deregulated gas permitted by the NGPA. And each new increment of supply was commanding prices unheard of before or since. Rising costs were simply averaged into the total supply mix, most of it purchased by pipelines at controlled prices, and passed on to consumers.

In many cases pipelines—which not only transported gas but also sold, stored, and processed some of it—had agreed to pay the highest price allowed by the NGPA. Many producer-pipeline contracts contained "take-or-pay" provisions requiring pipelines to pay for almost all of the gas they contracted for, even if they did not take delivery of it. Some pipelines were farsighted enough to protect themselves with "market out" clauses that dropped the take-or-pay obligation if demand for gas fell, but most were not. These pipelines were stuck with huge and growing liabilities once gas demand started to fall.

During the last months of 1984, FERC had begun a broad inquiry on gas transportation issues. In October 1985 FERC issued Order 436, which embodied comprehensive changes in its regulations governing the transportation of natural gas by pipelines. Among other things, Order 436 broadened access for shippers and consumers to transportation services offered by pipelines. The rules required pipelines that accepted federal authorization to carry gas for others to do so on a nondiscriminatory basis.

In April 1986 the DOE unveiled a bill designed to correct the flaws in Order 436 while also providing for decontrol of old-gas prices. Under the open-access transportation program, pipelines holding open-access blanket certificates had to transport gas on a nondiscriminatory, first-come, first-served basis.

Despite opposition from some producer-states, the DOE convinced FERC to develop a rule that would eliminate old-gas price "vintaging." (Gas was classified by vintage for pricing ceiling purposes, according to the date the gas well was drilled, the method used for drilling, and the degree of difficulty in drilling.) Order 451, which took effect in July 1986, obligated pipelines in certain situations to transport gas, and the order required renegotiation of high gas prices if they were contained in multivintage contracts.

Congress repealed the incremental pricing provisions of the NGPA as well as the gas-use restrictions contained in the Power Plant and Industrial Fuel Use Act in January 1987. President Ronald Reagan signed the bill in May 1987, spurring talk in the industry of new markets for natural gas.

Meanwhile, the take-or-pay problem was growing. Estimating that take-or-pay costs could go as high as $14 billion by the end of 1986, pipelines urged FERC to develop a mechanism allowing them to bill customers directly for expenses related to buying out expensive take-or-pay contracts. The commission responded in March 1987 with a plan allowing pipelines and their customers to split the costs on a 50-50 basis.

But FERC's solution was not satisfactory to the D.C. Circuit Court of Appeals. In June 1987, the court remanded Order 436 to FERC so the commission could "more convincingly address" the take-or-pay issue. Although the appeals court decision (*Associated Gas Distributors v. FERC*) generally upheld Order 436, the appeals court told FERC to give "reasoned consideration" to claims that the open-access transportation program would aggravate pipelines' take-or-pay obligations.

In August 1987 the commission issued an interim rule, Order 500, designed to meet the court's concerns. The commission established a crediting mechanism to prevent the accumulation of take-or-pay when an open-access pipeline transported gas. The rule also set out an equitable sharing mechanism to spread take-or-pay liability among all parties—producers, pipelines, and customers.

The commission at this time began to explore more fully a fee that would allow pipelines to recover future take-or-pay costs. FERC's open-access policies had prodded pipelines to "unbundle" or charge separately for services, rather than charge one fee for all services. The innovative "gas inventory charge" provided a mechanism for pipelines to recover costs of maintaining gas supplies to satisfy the demand of their remaining sales customers, whether or not the customers actually purchased the gas.

In the fall of 1989 the commission issued its "final" version of Order 500, which made few changes to the previous interim rule and concluded that pipelines had resolved the bulk of their take-or-pay problems. But the D.C. Circuit Court remanded the record to FERC, holding that the order failed to provide the reasoned explanation it had sought about whether the open-access transportation program would aggravate pipeline take-or-pay obligations. The Supreme Court resolved the issue. On Jan. 8, 1991, the Court unanimously upheld the validity of FERC's Order 451. The decision was lauded by consumer groups, who said that the ruling would ensure consumers got the most competitive price possible for gas.

NATURAL GAS RESTRUCTURING IN THE 1990S

During 1990 and 1991 the movement in Washington toward creating a more competitive natural gas industry intensified. In May 1991 a public conference was held to air views of new, overall pipeline regulations aimed at revising pipeline service obligations, rate structure, and comparability of service. The conference concluded with industry-wide agreement that any new regulations should reflect the natural gas industry's need for flexible guidelines for making a pipeline's merchant function comparable to its transportation function.

In August 1991 FERC proposed a new rule, officially known as Docket No. RM91-11. Industry observers dubbed it the "Mega-NOPR" because of its far-reaching implications for the natural gas industry. The rule had several key provisions:

▪ Pipelines could continue to market gas to customers. But because marketing was a separate area of business than shipping, pipelines had to set up discrete marketing affiliates.

▪ Pipelines would have to unbundle their services. In the past, pipelines had worked package deals—where they might purchase and resell the gas, store it, and transport it. Under Mega-NOPR, pipelines would not be allowed to force a customer to buy more than one of these services at a time.

▪ Pipelines would have to set separate prices for each of the services that they offered. This would allow customers to choose from a menu of services. It granted blanket certification for services that pipelines unbundled.

▪ Pipelines would retain the right to abandon service without first getting FERC approval in cases where they provided interruptible and short-term firm transportation service.

- Pipelines would have to use the straight-fixed variable method of rate design (placing all fixed costs in the demand component and all variable costs in the commodity component) and to provide customers access to certain information through the use of electronic bulletin board systems.

The commission billed the new rule as a major step toward enhancing consumer benefits. Initially, there was some negative reaction to Mega-NOPR from pipelines as well as LDCs. Because the rule would force contract renegotiation, many were concerned that there would be increased litigation in the courts.

Pipeline companies also said the rule would affect their ability to secure short-term, no-notice supplies of gas—reliability had always been a key reason behind the industry's extensive regulation. Before Mega-NOPR, pipelines could offer access to stored gas on a no-notice basis under bundled rates. But LDCs and pipeline operators expressed concern that once access was stripped away under an unbundled system, they would lose control of the gas availability. Pipeline operators and gas utilities also argued that the new rule would impair their ability to secure supplies and could raise prices.

The sweeping changes were the subject of extensive debate. One analyst said the rule would reverse the "historic one-stop shopping monopoly" the pipelines always had been afforded. Among the strongest supporters of Mega-NOPR was the Natural Gas Supply Association, whose members would be able to take over the gas sales function once it was unbundled from the pipelines. In comments to the commission, the association urged it to stand firm on the rule: "The ultimate payoff for the commission, the gas industry and the consumer will be an efficient, competitive, free market for natural gas that encourages long-term contracting and supply diversification."

In March 1992 the commission outlined the rule officially. It retained many features of the initial guidelines and included a provision aimed at providing pipelines with greater operational control of their facilities. It also responded to LDC concerns about supply with a provision that required pipelines to provide no-notice, unbundled firm transportation service. On April 8, 1992, the commission issued Order 636, the long-awaited 250-page final version of Mega-NOPR.

In August FERC issued orders on rehearing, called 636-A, which kept largely intact the previous thrust of the regulations. Additional adjustments were made in December 1992, officially known at 636-B. On Jan. 8, 1993, the commission denied all requests for rehearings and set to work revising its regulations for all seventy-nine interstate pipelines.

Congress passed and signed into law the Energy Policy Act in fall 1992. Among other things, the law loosened existing restrictions on Canadian natural gas, blocked the need for special import approvals, and specified that neither federal nor state regulators could treat Canadian gas differently than domestic natural gas once it was in the country.

The law also directed FERC to simplify its method for setting "just and reasonable" rates for interstate oil pipelines. However, the statute allowed rates that were approved at least one year before enactment and that were not subject to challenge to remain in effect. It also directed the commission to streamline consideration of rate changes.

After the issuance of Order 636, restructuring in the natural gas industry continued. FERC decisions focused on some of the so-called "leftover 636 issues." One of these centered around requirements in the order that interstate pipelines post information about their capacity release guidelines on electronic bulletin boards.

One of the primary reasons for the inclusion of electronic notification in Order 636 was to ensure that pipelines were able to use their storage and transportation space most efficiently. The electronic notification system was designed so that customers who contracted for firm capacity could resell that capacity if demand dropped—as during the summer months—by posting an electronic notice of freed-up capacity. FERC's aim was to standardize the computer systems and information so that businesses could download information and manipulate it according to their needs. The result was the Gas Pipeline Data bulletin board, available to anyone with a computer modem to download pipeline tariffs and similar information.

The commission has moved to further standardize access and information by requiring by June 1, 1999, that pipelines provide all information and conduct all business using the public Internet and common protocols. This will make it easier for shippers to move gas across multiple pipelines.

A second "leftover 636" issue was reform of gas gathering systems—the methods by which interstate pipelines collect and retrieve the natural gas from suppliers. Interstate pipelines are not necessarily located near gas wells or gas fields. Gathering systems collect the gas from the wells or fields, take it to a processing plant, separate out the natural gas from the other petroleum liquids, and transport the gas to an appropriate pipeline.

During the time when natural gas was regulated, the gathering business had largely been done by independent companies. Only about a third of natural gas was gathered by pipelines. The gathering systems run by pipelines were regulated by FERC, but those run by independent companies were unregulated. As a result, pipeline operators were anxious to set up unregulated affiliates to take over their gathering requirements.

Following the introduction and enactment of Order 636, gathering regulation became increasingly divisive. Pipelines argued that their affiliated gathering systems could not compete against unregulated independents. The operators supported deregulation of gathering systems.

But producers maintained sufficient competition did not exist in all cases and that protecting nonaffiliated gatherers could prove difficult in a deregulated environment. The challenge was to put protections in place for gathering systems that were already operating.

In a series of eight decisions on gathering, FERC announced policy changes that had the effect of phasing out federal regulation. Gathering systems run by pipelines were still regulated, but pipelines were permitted to sell gathering systems to unregulated affiliates or third parties so long as (1) the new arrangement did not operate to frustrate the commission's regulation over the interstate gas pipeline grid, and (2) the gathering system's customers agreed to new contracts or were offered a default contract at favorable rates.

The final deregulation issue concerned capacity release. Order 636 allows those who control a portion of a pipeline's capacity to release it either temporarily or permanently if they no longer need to use it. Usually, this means renting it out for short periods to a broker or large shipper that happens to need additional capacity. Many of these transactions are arranged over electronic bulletin boards.

The commission in March 1995 issued Order 577 to change the former rule that prearranged capacity releases had to be for less than thirty days. The revision permitted transactions for a full calendar month without meeting the commission's advanced notice and bidding requirements.

The benefits of natural gas restructuring became evident in the late 1990s. By 1996 the commission estimated that about $3 billion in transition costs and $10 billion in take-or-pay costs had been recovered by industry participants. By 1998, six years after Order 636, markets had become dynamic and were being driven by short-term and even intraday transactions. However, providing adequate protection to captive customers—those who have no options in choosing their natural gas supplier—remained a concern for FERC. For this reason, the commission issued an NOPR in July 1998 that proposed expanding options for captive customers and examining ways to keep long-term contracts attractive.

The proposed rule would end price caps for transactions of less than one year while continuing cost-based regulation in the long-term market. FERC's intention was to create a more open and efficient short-term market, while eliminating any regulation-based bias against long-term transactions. Pipelines also would be given greater flexibility in negotiating terms and conditions of service with individual customers.

NATURAL GAS RESTRUCTURING IN THE 2000S

Natural gas prices swung wildly at certain times during the first years of the decade, as charges of deception and malfeasance were lodged against energy trading companies. In California FERC eventually found evidence that some companies, including the giant El Paso Corporation, withheld gas pipeline capacity, creating an artificial shortage that led to higher prices. Prices did not come down significantly, until FERC imposed general price restraints in the western states in June of 2001.

In the summer of 2002 FERC began a formal investigation into natural gas pricing. In addition to examining allegations of withholding pipeline capacity, the commission began looking into charges that natural gas traders fed inaccurate price data to trade journals in an effort to boost prices for the commodity. The price indexes, published by the trade journals, are used to calculate the value of contracts between natural gas providers and their customers. During this time, some large traders, including Enron, Dynegy, and Williams Transcontinental Gas Pipe Corp., admitted that some of their employees had reported false data in an effort to drive up prices.

These revelations especially had a great impact in California. In November 2002 the state government filed a massive lawsuit (asking for an undisclosed sum) against dozens of natural gas companies and two trade journals alleging that the false data had driven up prices and contributed to the state's energy crisis during 2000–2001.

Other kinds of market-altering violations also occurred. For instance, in March 2003 the commission imposed the largest fine in its history, forcing Williams to pay $20 million over the following four years. Williams had been found to have given price discounts to its gas marketing unit, which violated a federal law requiring pipeline owners to give equal treatment to all competitors.

In the spring and summer of 2002 natural gas prices began rising again, increasing from $3.65 per million btu's to $6 in under a year. This time though, legitimate market forces rather than manipulation were blamed. Demand for gas has been increasing, in large part because, unlike coal or oil, gas is a clean-burning fuel and hence not environmentally controversial. As a result, nearly all the power plants built since 1998 are fired by natural gas.

By spring 2003 new gas drilling had increased by 25 percent. But supply was still running short, in part because much of the new drilling work had been done in gas fields that had already been heavily exploited, producing much lower returns. The amount of stored natural gas was the lowest it has been in more than twenty-five years and 30 percent lower than the average during the past five years.

In June 2003 Alan Greenspan, head of the Federal Reserve, warned that continued shortages could erode economic growth. Energy experts said that one way to ramp up supplies would be to explore new domestic fields, but many of these areas, most notably the Alaskan National Wildlife Reserve, were protected. Another option would be to import more liquefied natural gas. But increasing exports would require a huge new infrastructure investment, because additional port terminals would be needed to offload the gas.

ELECTRICITY RESTRUCTURING IN THE 1990S

While natural gas regulation dominated the commission's work during the 1980s and early 1990s, the restructuring of the interstate electricity market became the commission's main focus by the mid-1990s. This change was caused by the need to address serious financial problems faced by many large electricity generators and a desire to provide a competitive market for power generation. The problems the industry faced were similar to those that the commission had successfully addressed when restructuring interstate natural gas shipments.

Traditional electric utilities got into trouble because of changes in the underlying economics of electricity generation. During the 1970s the industry built too many large and sometimes ruinously expensive central generating facilities, which usually lacked the heat recovery facilities to be optimally efficient. This prompted larger industrial customers to either cogenerate their own electricity from the process heat left over from manufacturing, or to buy electricity at cheaper rates from new, small independent power generators. The independent producers used highly efficient new technology, such as natural gas turbines, and could sell electricity at rates well below those charged by the traditional utilities. This reversed the long-term trend where unit production costs could only be lowered by taking advantage of the economies of scale inherent in ever larger generating plants. The new generating facilities could produce electricity at lower unit cost, even though they were many times smaller in scale. The only problem was whether they could get access to the transmission lines owned by the traditional utilities in order to deliver their power to their new customers.

The process of restructuring wholesale electricity sales got under way in early 1988 when the commission considered four NOPRs addressing revisions to regulation of the electricity industry. These proposals were never formalized but they were an important first step in restructuring.

The next step was taken by Congress in the Energy Policy Act of 1992. In the section of the law that amended the 1935 Public Utility Holding Company Act (PUHCA), FERC was authorized to order a utility to transmit the power from wholesale electricity generators whenever the

transaction was in the public interest. Under the new law, wholesale producers who requested such a transmission would have to pay for it, and those charges had to cover the utility's transmission costs plus a reasonable return on investment. Mandatory transmission orders would not be allowed when they jeopardized the reliability of established electric systems.

The law banned FERC from issuing a transmission order that would result in a wholesale power producer selling directly to consumers or in "sham transactions" whereby a third party buys electricity wholesale and resells it to disguise what is basically a retail transaction.

Before 1992, it was not possible for an electric utility wholesale customer to purchase electricity from any other provider than the one that served the grid in their area. After the 1992 energy bill, wholesale customers—primarily rural electric cooperatives and municipalities—were able to shop around for electricity sources and could apply to FERC to ask the utilities to transmit the power.

The bill also created a category of wholesale power producers exempted from PUHCA. The change was added to allow utilities to operate independent wholesale plants outside their service territories and encourage independent producers to operate generating plants. Power producers had to apply to FERC for the designation on a case-by-case basis. The exemption applied only to producers that generated and sold electricity wholesale.

FERC spent the next several years implementing the new law's section 211 provisions, but the commission saw the need for a broader rule (as opposed to a case-by-case approach). Meanwhile, nearly a dozen states announced plans to proceed with some version of restructuring on their own, and the financial problems of the traditional generating industry continued to grow. Often the financial problem was not actual losses, so much as concern over what would happen to the industry's balance sheet if the large, expensive, but inefficient generating facilities had to be written off as more and more traditional customers were lost to competition. For some utilities, the threat was not just to less efficient assets. All assets could be at risk if enough large industrial customers pursued other alternatives. Various attempts were made to measure the amount of "stranded costs." Moody's, a well-known financial rating agency, put the figure at $135 billion and warned that it could go as high as $300 billion.

Finally, FERC took action. The commission issued a proposed rule on April 7, 1995, that called for open access to utility electricity transmission facilities, and recovery of stranded costs by public utilities. Among the many controversial questions was the environmental impact of the proposed rule. This issue touched off a cross-agency dispute with EPA that was resolved by the issuance of an environmental impact statement that adopted FERC's view that the impact of a restructured electric utility industry would be minimal.

The many issues raised by the proposed rules were debated for a nearly a year, until the commission took final action in the form of Orders 888 and 889, issued in April 1996. Order 888 specified how the electricity generation industry would be restructured, while Order 889 detailed the electronic information systems that would be used by utilities to make known how much transmission capacity was available at any given time.

Under Order 888, all public utilities that owned, controlled, or operated interstate transmission facilities were required to file new tariffs that specified the rates for nondiscriminatory access to their transmission facilities. Public utilities were required to file a single open access tariff that offered both network, load-based service, and point-to-point contract-based service. Related ancillary services incident to normal electricity generation had to be provided. These services were scheduling, system control, and dispatch; reactive supply and voltage control from generation sources service; regulation and frequency response service; energy imbalance service; operating reserve—spinning reserve service; and operating reserve—supplemental reserve service. The power company pools that handled bulk power transactions between utilities were required to revise their pooling agreements and joint pool-wide transmission tariffs to remove provisions that discriminated against outsiders.

FERC asserted authority for the first time over the rates and terms for unbundled retail transmission of electricity in interstate commerce. The commission announced seven indicators for deciding where its jurisdiction ended and state regulatory authority began.

With regard to the recovery of "stranded costs" related to wholesale requirements contracts executed on or before July 11, 1994, FERC permitted a public utility to seek recovery from departing customers. Recovery of stranded costs related to wholesale requirements contracts executed after July 11, 1994, was permitted only if the contract provided for such recovery.

FERC ordered that utilities seeking to recover stranded costs from retail wheeling should first look to the state regulatory commissions, but that it would review cases when state commissions lacked authority at the time retail wheeling was required to order stranded cost recovery. Parties to requirements contracts entered into before July 11, 1994, could seek to have them modified on a case-by-case basis. Utilities seeking market rates for sales from new capacity did not need to show lack of generation dominance in new capacity.

The initial implementation phase went smoothly. FERC announced in July 1996 that it had received either the newly ordered tariffs or waiver requests from all of the

166 interstate utilities that had been expected to respond. Nearly 200 parties challenged the orders, however, and it took another four years to settle the dispute.

In June 2000 the U.S. Court of Appeals for the District of Columbia Circuit upheld FERC's Orders 888 and 889. The court ruled that FERC could use its powers under the Federal Power Act and the Energy Policy Act of 1992 to create regional wholesale power markets and to check anticompetitive behavior. The court turned away arguments from utilities that the orders represented an unconstitutional "taking" under the Fifth Amendment as well as claims from environmental groups and the U.S. Environmental Protection Agency that the orders could lead to increased pollution from coal-fired power plants. The court sent two issues to the commission for review—one involving the treatment of energy costs under FERC's market option for stranded cost recovery, the other dealing with FERC's failure to provide a "reasonable" cap on contract extensions for transmission customers who wanted to renew contracts for transmission capacity.

ELECTRICITY RESTRUCTURING IN THE 2000S

In December 1999 FERC issued Order 2000, calling for the creation of regional transmission organizations (RTOs) throughout the country. The order required utilities that owned, operated, or controlled interstate electric transmission facilities—but had not already chosen to participate as an independent system operator (ISO) or other regional transmission entity—to file a proposal for joining an RTO by October 2000. Utilities that chose not to file this proposal could file an alternate plan.

Order 2000 also outlined any characteristics that proposed RTOs were required to meet and allowed utilities some flexibility in their proposals to meet FERC requirements. FERC hoped that Order 2000 would significantly increase the operating efficiency of electric transmission systems while eliminating opportunities for discriminatory transmission practices and improving the estimates of available transmission capacity, system reliability, and pricing.

California became the first state to introduce a statewide competitive electric industry, opening its market to competition in March 1998. By late 2000, however, the lower prices had not materialized and the state found itself in a power crisis, caused by a lack of new electric generation and increased demand for electricity.

With two of the state's largest electric utilities on the brink of bankruptcy and the system near collapse, President Bill Clinton in December 2000 directed FERC to authorize California officials to reimpose rate controls on most electricity generated in the state. President George W. Bush extended the rate caps for two weeks shortly after his January 2001 inauguration, but then he allowed them to expire. The head of FERC, Curt Hebert Jr., also was opposed to price caps, saying they would not bring in new supplies of electricity. By April 2001 one large electricity supplier had filed for bankruptcy. Customers of another large utility, San Diego Gas & Electric Co., received higher costs because the utility had recovered its "stranded costs" through the sale of its generation facilities, a move that allowed it to fully deregulate prices.

With its utilities on the ropes, the state government was forced to step in and spend $9.5 billion to buy power on their behalf. In spite of these steps, state residents were subjected to rolling blackouts during the winter months late in 2000 and early in 2001. In April 2001 FERC issued an order requiring price restraints in California during times of emergency, defined as whenever the state's power reserves dropped to below 7.5 percent. But by the late spring the agency was under intense pressure from Congress to do more to alleviate California's energy crisis. Members of both parties had been threatening to push through legislation that would have forced FERC to institute price caps or wholesale rates based on cost.

In June the commission unanimously voted to make semipermanent the existing price restraints on electricity sales. In addition, FERC expanded the restraints to eleven western states to ensure that utilities in California would not be tempted to send power to neighboring states to sell it at a higher price. The restrictions were to remain in effect for fifteen months. FERC chair Hebert called the order "a market-based decision" that was preferable to strict price caps, which critics say destroy incentives for power companies to add capacity.

But California Governor Gray Davis said that the action was "too little, too late" and called on the federal government to force electricity generators to refund the billions of dollars the governor said they overcharged California. Davis charged that the state had been overcharged close to $9 billion. Within days, FERC responded to this charge, saying that if the state and utilities were unable to come to an agreement in two weeks, it would ask one of its administrative judges to propose a solution.

The judge, Curtis Wagner Jr., tried to broker a deal between the state and its energy suppliers, which included Reliant Energy, Duke Energy, Enron, and Dynegy. After weeks of unsuccessful negotiations, Wagner issued his proposal, arguing that California's $9 billion claim was unsupportable and that the state was owed no more than $1 billion in refunds. The state did however receive some good news. The new price restraints coupled with a milder summer and energy conservation measures led to lower energy prices during the months of July and August 2001, giving the state and consumers some much needed relief.

California received a second boost with the announcement that FERC chair Hebert would resign by the end of August and be replaced by Pat Wood III, former chief energy regulator of Texas. Wood was much more sympathetic to the state's arguments that it had been grossly overcharged by energy providers.

The trouble in California alerted federal policymakers to the potential for energy shortages around the country and prompted FERC to take a number of actions aimed at preventing another power supply meltdown. The first of these occurred in July 2001, when the agency announced that it would ask most utilities to hand over control of their power lines to four new regional authorities that would be established in 2002. These four groups would have the power to build new lines to connect up power grids and ensure the free flow of electricity around the country.

The idea was to create the equivalent of an interstate highway system for electricity that would prevent price gouging by creating a free flow of power around the country and prevent large energy suppliers from enacting monopolistic pricing policies. With a larger, more integrated grid, a local utility that needed power would have a much greater number of suppliers to choose from, hence ensuring a more competitive pricing environment.

In September Wood put some teeth in the new proposal by announcing that any electric utility that did not join one of the four regional authorities would lose the right to set market-based prices for power. FERC took the proposal even further in November, announcing that it would impose price controls on utilities that were in a position to raise prices because of their dominance in a local market.

The new regional authorities and the price controls were opposed by many utilities and free-market thinkers, who argued that the actions amounted to unnecessary overregulation that would stifle competition and lead to disincentives for power suppliers to build new plants. But Wood countered that the big utilities had to be brought to heel to level the playing field for new competitors to enter the market.

Early in 2002, California was back in the news, as it once again accused power suppliers, most notably fallen energy-giant Enron, of overcharging in some of the long-term contracts they had signed with the state. Davis asked FERC to rescind $40 billion in long-term contracts he had signed during the crisis a year before, in an effort to guarantee the state sufficient power in the coming decade. By the late spring, evidence was emerging showing that Enron and other companies had indeed used power shortages in California to manipulate the market. In August FERC launched an investigation into the matter.

But the commission also came in for severe criticism over the price gouging issue. In November the Senate Energy Committee released a report accusing the agency of ignoring signs that power companies were taking advantage of California during the energy crisis. Wood, who was not FERC chair during that period, agreed that the commission could have done more. As FERC continued to investigate Enron and others into 2003, a number of companies were fined and ordered to pay $3.3 billion in refunds to California. Moreover, some energy companies were forced to renegotiate some of the long-term contracts they had signed with California.

Current Issues

It is clear that with its plan to establish superregional authorities, FERC hopes to use its authority to promote the transition to a more competitive national electric market in which prices are roughly equal around the country. The move comes in large part as an effort to ensure that the electric grid problems and price spikes in wholesale electricity spot markets that characterized the recent energy crisis in California are avoided in the future.

But opposition to the plan is strong, especially from big utilities in the South and West. These companies and others have been pushing Congress to eliminate or at least limit FERC's plan. In April 2003 they succeeded in convincing members of the House Energy and Commerce Committee to insert provisions into the omnibus energy bill limiting the commission's authority to go ahead with its plan. A similar provision has yet to be included in the Senate version of the bill, but the issue is expected to be brought when an energy bill goes to conference.

The fact that Congress is possibly moving to rein in FERC's regulatory authority surprises many industry watchers, who expected Bush appointees on the commission, such as Chairman Wood, to favor less government regulation. But the energy crisis in California as well as the bankruptcy of energy giants, such as Enron and Dynegy, exposed the dangers of at least some types of deregulation, making FERC's subsequent actions more understandable. Wood also has argued that the new superregional authorities are a promarket step, because they aim to increase competition and deny large regional suppliers monopolistic power.

In spite of the failed experiment in California, the bankruptcies, and the arguments over regulation and competition, there is an issue that ultimately unites most parties in the energy field: The need for growth. Recently, Vice President Richard B. Cheney, who headed up an energy task force for the Bush administration, predicted that the country would need to build one relatively large-sized power plant a week for the next twenty years if the nation was to meet its future energy needs.

With a weak economy dampening demand, the United States can afford to dither on a plan for the future of the country's power supply. But if economic activity picks up, as is predicted for the second half of 2003 and 2004, those parts of the country without a healthy and growing power

generation sector could find themselves in the same place that California was less than two years ago. Rolling blackouts and high prices could drive businesses out of certain regions and deprive these same areas of much needed new investment.

■ AGENCY ORGANIZATION

Biographies

PATRICK HENRY WOOD, III, CHAIRMAN

Appointment: Nominated by President Bush on April 30, 2001, and confirmed by the Senate on May 25, 2001, for the remainder of a five-year term expiring June 30, 2005. Named Chairman by President George W. Bush in Sept., 2001.

Education: Texas A&M University, B.S; Harvard Law School, J.D.

Profession: Attorney.

Political Affiliation: Republican.

Previous Career: Wood was Chairman of the Public Utility Commission of Texas. He served as staff member of the Federal Energy Regulatory Commission from 1991 to 1993 and as legal counsel to the Chairman of the Texas Railroad Commission.

NORA MEAD BROWNWELL, COMMISSIONER

Appointment: Nominated by President Bush on April 30, 2001, and confirmed by the Senate May 25, 2001, to serve for an additional five-year term expiring June 30, 2006.

Education: Syracuse University.

Profession: Banker.

Political Affiliation: Republican.

Previous Career: Brownell was appointed by Governor Tom Ridge to the Public Utilities Commission of Pennsylvania. Until 1997, she acted as the Executive Director of the Performing Arts Center in Philadelphia.

WILLIAM L. MASSEY, COMMISSIONER

Appointment: Nominated by President Clinton on April 29, 1993, to an unexpired term, confirmed by the Senate on May 20, 1993; term expired June 30, 1998. Confirmed for a second term on June 26, 1998; term expires June 30, 2003.

Born: Oct. 19, 1948, Little Rock, AR.

Education: Ouachita University, B.A., 1970; University of Arkansas, J.D., 1973; Georgetown University, Master of Laws, 1985.

Profession: Lawyer.

Political Affiliation: Democrat.

FEDERAL ENERGY REGULATORY COMMISSION

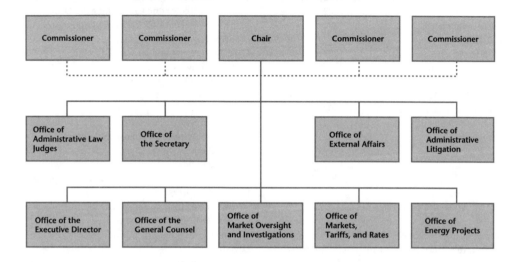

Previous Career: From 1989 to 1992, Massey worked on the Presidential Transition Team for the Energy Department and was a partner in the Washington, DC, firm of Mitchell, Williams, Selig, Gates, and Woodyard.

Headquarters and Divisions

COMMISSION

The commissioners make all final decisions on matters regulated by FERC. These include: setting limits on rates and charges for the interstate transportation and sale of natural gas; issuing certificates for the construction and operation of facilities for the transportation of gas by pipeline and approving abandonment of such facilities and service; setting rates, terms, and conditions for interstate transmission and wholesale sales of electric energy; issuing licenses and permits for hydroelectric plants; acting on proposed mergers involving electric utilities and dispositions of facilities; acting on certain issuances of securities and assumptions of liabilities by electric utilities; acting on certain interlocking directorates involving electric utilities; setting limits on oil pipeline rates, charges, and valuations; and requiring regulated electric and natural gas companies to follow a uniform system of accounts.

The chairman is responsible for the executive and administrative operation of the commission, including appointment of administrative law judges, the selection of personnel (including the executive director), and the supervision of FERC personnel.

Chairman
Pat Wood, III.............................(202) 502–8000
Fax......................................(202) 208–0064
Commissioners
William L. Massey.......................(202) 502–8366
Fax......................................(202) 208–0608
Nora Mead Brownwell..................(202) 502–8383
Fax......................................(202) 219–2917

OFFICE OF ADMINISTRATIVE LAW JUDGES

Presides over hearings for the resolution of issues concerning the Federal Power Act and the Natural Gas Act. Conducts hearings and issues initial decisions on actions taken under the authority of the secretary of energy on which a departmental level hearing and on-the-record determination have been made. Also conducts hearings delegated to FERC under the Interstate Commerce Act, the Natural Gas Policy Act, and the Public Utility Regulatory Policies Act. The Administrative Law Judges play a judicial role and are, in effect, the trial judiciary of the agency. On all cases set for hearing by the Commission, the Administrative Law Judges preside over the hearing and issue an initial decision at its conclusion.

Chief Administrative Law Judge
Curtis Wagner Jr.......................(202) 502–8500
Fax......................................(202) 219–3289
Legal and Special Assistant to the Chief Judge
Martha E. Altamar ....(202) 502–8654

Administrative Law Judges

Isaac D. Benkin	(202) 502–8507
Bruce Birchman	(202) 502–8544
Lawrence Brenner	(202) 502–8539
Carmen Cintron	(202) 502–8545
Judith Dowd	(202) 502–8557
Herbert Grossman	(202) 502–8524
David Harfeld	(202) 502–8514
Karen V. Johnson	(202) 502–6412
Jeffie J. Massey	(202) 502–8523
Bobbie McCartney	(202) 502–8534
Joseph Nacy	(202) 502–8508
Edward Silverstein	(202) 502–8556
H. Peter Young	(202) 502–8550
Raymond Zimmet	(202) 502–8549

OFFICE OF ADMINISTRATIVE LITIGATION

The Office of Administrative Litigation litigates or otherwise resolves cases set for hearing. The lawyers and technical staff in this office represent the public interest and seek to litigate or settle cases in a timely, efficient, and equitable manner while ensuring the outcomes are consistent with Commission policy.

Director

William J. Froehlich	(202) 502–6100
Fax	(202) 219–0285

OFFICE OF THE EXECUTIVE DIRECTOR

The Office of the Executive Director supports the Federal Energy Regulatory Commission in the accomplishment of its mission. Provides efficient and effective equal employment opportunity, administrative support, information technology, human resources, organizational management, logistics, procurement, financial services, financial policy, budgets, internal control and evaluations, and management, administrative and payroll system (MAPS) strategic plan. Advises the Chairman of potential issues and concerns in the areas of management studies and related financial reviews, productivity, and performance audits.

Under the Federal Power Act, the Natural Gas Act, and the Interstate Commerce Act, the Federal Energy Regulatory Commission requires that organizations subject to its jurisdiction keep financial and related records in accordance with rules and regulations contained in the applicable Uniformed Systems of Accounts established under each of the respective acts. The Chief Accountant (CA) administers the Uniform Systems Accounts through programs such as onsite performance and regulatory audits, granting authority to record certain accounting entries, and interpreting the accounting systems rules and regulations providing regulatory accounting policy. In addition, the CA and staff provide accounting counsel to the commission in connection with orders, ratemaking issues, rulemakings, hearing, and administrative actions.

Executive Director and Chief Financial Officer

Thomas R. Herlihy	(202) 502–8300
Fax	(202) 208–1259

Chief Accountant and Deputy Director

John Delaware	(202) 502–8600

Deputy Chief Information Officer

Fernenda Young	(202) 502–1055

Budget

Stacie Davis	(202) 502–8427

Equal Employment Opportunity Adviser

Madelaine Lewis	(202) 502–8120

Financial Policy

Matt Sweet	(202) 502–8926

Financial Services

Anton Parker	(202) 502–8728

Human Resources

James Feeney	(202) 502–8705

Logistics

Tamrah Semega	(202) 502–6030

Management, Administration, and Payroll Support

Craig Chapman	(202) 502–6162

Organizational Management

Antonio Javonillo	(202) 502–8966

Procurement

Andrew Sakallaris	(202) 502–8122

Regulatory Audits

Michael Oliva	(202) 502–6597

Regulatory Accounting Policy

James Guest	(202) 502–6614

OFFICE OF EXTERNAL AFFAIRS

See Information Sources.

OFFICE OF THE GENERAL COUNSEL

Provides legal services to the commission. OGC represents the commission before the courts and Congress and is responsible for the legal phases of the commission's activities.

General Counsel

Cynthia A. Marlette	(202) 502–6000
Fax	(202) 208–2115

Deputy General Counsel

Marsha L. Gransee	(202) 502–8448

Administration

Merle O. Bess	(202) 502–8628

Markets, Tarriffs, and Rates

Michael A. Bardee	(202) 502–8068

Energy Projects

Robert F. Christin	(202) 502–6022

Solicitor

   Dennis Lane .... (202) 502–8954

General and Administration Law

   Susan Court .... (202) 502–8182

OFFICE OF THE SECRETARY

Acts as the liaison between the commission and those doing business with it. Receives and distributes all material filed with the commission; sets the agenda and records minutes and votes at commission meetings; and issues approved orders. The secretary also performs regulatory support services; records and distributes all regulatory filings; records and processes filing fees; issues commission orders, notices, and other formal documents; maintains files of agency publications and arranges publication of FERC documents in the *Federal Register;* and maintains service lists for all proceedings. Serves as the official focal point through which all filings are made for proceedings before the commission.

Secretary

   Magalie R. Salais .... (202) 502–8400

   Fax.................................... (202) 208–2268

Deputy Secretary

   Vacant..................................

Agenda and Minutes/Document Control

   Linda Mitry............................ (202) 502–8125

Agenda and Minutes

   Philis Posey .... (202) 502–6208

Dockets

   Brooks Carter.......................... (202) 502–8195

Registry and Service

   Tiquana Taylor .... (202) 502–8551

DISPUTE RESOLUTION SERVICE

The Dispute Resolution Service fosters the use of alternative dispute resolution processes (ADR) in oil, gas, electric, and hydroelectric proceedings, and for disputes within the commission. It is neutral and independent, and provides ADR services, such as convening sessions, facilitation, and mediation. It is available to assist parties in screening disputes for ADR application, and also helps develop programs for ADR education and training.

Director

   Richard Miles.......................... (877) 337–2237

OFFICE OF ENERGY PROJECTS

The mission of the office is to foster economic and environmental benefits for the nation through the approval and oversight of hydroelectric and natural gas pipeline energy projects that are in the public interest.

Director

   Mark Robinson........................ (202) 502–8700

   Fax.................................... (202) 219–0205

Deputy Director for Policy

   Robert J. Capian....................... (202) 502–8700

Senior Legal/Policy Adviser

   Mark Schaffer.......................... (202) 502–6807

Management and Operations

   Bernie Mosley .... (202) 502–8625

Pipeline Certificates

   Vacant..................................

Environmental and Engineering Review

   Rich Hoffman .... (202) 502–8066

Hydropower Administration and Compliance

   Joeseph Morge.......................... (202) 502–6377

Dam Safety and Inspections

   Gus Tjoumas .... (202) 502–6734

OFFICE OF MARKETS, TARIFFS, AND RATES

The Office of Market, Tariffs, and Rates (OMTR) was created to integrate the commission's economic regulation of the electric, natural gas, and oil industries. OMTR deals with matters involving markets, tariffs, and rates relating to electric, natural gas, and oil pipeline facilities and services. The office plays a lead role in monitoring, promoting, and maintaining competitive markets and refining compliance auditing. As a result of the commission's FERC First undertaking, the commission will be looking at how it can ensure lighter-handed regulation for energy transactions in competitive markets, while standardizing terms and conditions for those transactions that will continue to be regulated on a cost basis. This office reflects the convergence of electric and natural gas concerns already taking place in the energy industry.

Director

   Daniel Larcamp .... (202) 502–8088

   Fax.................................... (202) 208–0193

Deputy Director

   Shelton Cannon .... (202) 502–8213

OFFICE OF MARKET OVERSIGHT AND INVESTIGATIONS

The Office of Market Oversight and Investigations (OMOI) will help the commission improve its understanding of energy market operations and ensure vigilant and fair oversight of those areas under commission jurisdiction.

OMOI oversees and assesses the operations of the nation's gas, oil pipeline, and electricity markets. Its functions include understanding energy markets and risk management, measuring market performance, investigating compliance violations, and analyzing market data. The office is made up of a multidisciplinary team of economists, engineers, attorneys, auditors, data management specialists, financial analysts, regulatory policy analysts, energy analysts, and support staff.

Director

    William Hederman.................... (202) 502–8100

    Fax..................................... (202) 502–6449

Deputy Director Market Oversight and Assessment

    Stephen Harvey (202) 502–6372

Deputy Director Investigations

    Dennis O'Keefe........................ (202) 502–8032

ENFORCEMENT HOTLINE

    (Toll-free).............................. (877) 337–2264

Regional Offices
FERC/Hydropower Licensing

ATLANTA

3125 Presidential Pkwy., #300

Atlanta, GA 30340

(770) 452–3777

Jerold W. Gotzmer, regional director

CHICAGO

230 S. Dearborn St., #3130

Chicago, IL 60604

(312) 353–7478

Peggy Harding, regional director

NEW YORK

19 West 34th St., #400

New York, NY 10001

(212) 273–5900

Anton Sidoti, regional director

PORTLAND

101 S.W. Main St., #905

Portland, OR 97204

(503) 944–6710

Harry T. Hall, regional director

SAN FRANCISCO

901 Market St., #305

San Francisco, CA 94103–1778

(415) 369–3390

Takeshi Yamashita, regional director

■ CONGRESSIONAL ACTION

Congressional Liaison

Don Chamblee .... (202) 502–8870

Committees and Subcommittees

HOUSE APPROPRIATIONS COMMITTEE

Subcommittee on Energy and Water Development

2362 RHOB, Washington, DC 20515

(202) 225–3421

HOUSE COMMERCE COMMITTEE

2125 RHOB, Washington, DC 20515

(202) 225–2927

Subcommittee on Energy and Power

2125 RHOB, Washington, DC 20515

(202) 225–2927

SENATE APPROPRIATIONS COMMITTEE

Subcommittee on Energy and Water Development

SD-127, Washington, DC 20510

(202) 224–7260

SENATE ENERGY AND NATURAL RESOURCES COMMITTEE

SD-304, Washington, DC 20510

(202) 224–4971

Subcommittee on Energy Research, Development, Production, and Regulation

SD-308, Washington, DC 20510

(202) 224–6567

Legislation

FERC was created by the **Department of Energy Organization Act** (91 Stat. 565, 42 U.S.C. 7101 note). Section 401(a) of that act assigned to FERC all of the responsibilities that had been carried out by the Federal Power Commission under the Federal Power Act, the Natural Gas Act, the Emergency Petroleum Allocation Act, and the Energy Policy and Conservation Act. The oil pipeline valuation and rate regulation functions of the Interstate Commerce Commission also were transferred to FERC. Signed by the president Aug. 4, 1977, the Energy Organization Act brought together in one central Cabinet-level agency all the federal government's energy responsibilities. FERC began operations on Oct. 1, 1977.

The Energy Organization Act also gave FERC powers over oil pricing and some administrative procedures in the

Energy Department. Although oil pricing has been deregulated, FERC still has jurisdiction over appeals of Economic Regulatory Administration decisions concerning oil pricing violations that occurred from 1973 to 1980.

FERC administers the following acts in full or in part:

Federal Water Power Act of 1920 (41 Stat. 1063, 16 U.S.C. 791). Signed by the president June 10, 1920. Established the Federal Power Commission (FPC), which then consisted of the secretaries of war, interior, and agriculture. The FPC was empowered to grant preliminary licenses, to study potential sites, and to issue licenses for the development of hydroelectric power plants on the nation's waterways. The act became part I of the Federal Power Act in 1935.

Federal Power Act of 1935 (41 Stat. 1063, 16 U.S.C. 791–828c). Signed by the president Aug. 26, 1935. Incorporated the Federal Water Power Act and added two new parts. Part II gave the commission responsibility for regulating the interstate transmission and wholesale sale of electric energy and empowered the Federal Power Commission to encourage voluntary interconnection and coordination of facilities for the generation, transmission, and sale of electric energy. Part III gave the commission authority to prescribe a uniform system of accounts and to inspect the books and records of licensees and public utilities.

Natural Gas Act of 1938 (52 Stat. 821, 15 U.S.C. 717). Signed by the president June 21, 1938. Gave the Federal Power Commission jurisdiction over the interstate transportation of natural gas, the wholesale price of natural gas in interstate commerce, and the accounting systems used by natural gas companies.

Natural Gas Policy Act of 1978 (92 Stat. 3350, 15 U.S.C. 3301 note, 42 U.S.C. 7255). Signed by the president Nov. 9, 1978. One of five parts of the National Energy Act, the act deregulated the price of natural gas over a five-year period, established a program of incentive prices for newly discovered gas, and required the development of an incremental pricing plan to transfer the burden of higher gas prices to the largest users of natural gas.

Public Utility Regulatory Policies Act of 1978 (92 Stat. 3117, 16 U.S.C. 2601). Signed by the president Nov. 9, 1978. One of five parts of the National Energy Act, the act required state utility commissions and other regulatory agencies to consider energy-saving methods, such as pricing electricity at lower levels in off-peak hours. It also gave FERC greater control over electric ratemaking.

Electric Consumers Protection Act of 1986 (100 Stat. 1243, 16 U.S.C. 791a note). Signed by the president Oct. 16, 1986. Amended the Federal Power Act to enhance competition among applicants in hydroelectric power relicensing cases and to provide that equal consideration be given to developmental and environmental concerns in the licensing of hydroelectric power projects.

Natural Gas Wellhead Decontrol Act of 1989 (103 Stat. 157, 15 U.S.C. 3301 note). Signed by the president July 26, 1989. Provided for the phased elimination of all remaining wellhead price and nonprice controls on the first sale of natural gas by Jan. 1, 1993.

Federal Energy Regulatory Commission Member Term Act of 1990 (104 Stat. 135, 42 U.S.C. 7101 note). Signed by the president April 11, 1990. Amended the Department of Energy Organization Act to provide for five-year, staggered terms for members of the commission. The new terms apply only to those appointed or reappointed as members of the commission after the date of enactment.

Energy Policy Act of 1992 (106 Stat. 2775, 42 U.S.C. 13201 note). Signed by the president on Oct. 24, 1992. Promoted energy conservation and efficiency and increased domestic energy production to ensure economic growth and to protect national security.

Energy Act of 2000 (114 Stat. 2029, 42 U.S.C. 6201 note). Signed by the president Nov. 9, 2000. Reauthorized a program under the Energy Policy and Conservation Act that provided for continued operation of U.S. strategic petroleum reserves. Amended the Federal Power Act to direct FERC to discontinue its licensing and regulatory authority over certain small hydroelectric power projects in Alaska. Directed FERC to review federal hydroelectric licensing procedures.

■ INFORMATION SOURCES

Internet

Agency Web Site: http://www.ferc.gov. Provides access to documents filed with, and issued by, the commission through its e-Library system (FERRIS), which also provides access to Docket Sheets listings.

Information on commission meetings is also posted on the Web site, along with FERC regulations and enabling legislation. FERC Online will provide a range of e-Services. Available services include e-Filing, and e-Subscription.

For assistance . . . . (202) 502–6652

Telephone Contacts

Recorded information . . . . (202) 502–8627
Commission agenda . . . . (202) 208–0200

Information and Publications

KEY OFFICES

FERC External Affairs
888 1st St. N.E.
Washington, DC 20426
(202) 502–8004
Fax (202) 208–2106
Kevin Cadden, director

The Office of External Affairs is the commission's primary contact point with the Congress, the general public, international, federal, state, and local government offices, interest groups, and the news media. It is responsible for developing public relations and other outreach strategies for the commission. Congressional and executive correspondence is analyzed and processed through a computerized correspondence tracking system. Divisions include:

Congressional, Intergovernmental, and Public Affairs Division
888 1st St. N.E.
Washington, DC 20426
(202) 502–8870
Fax (202) 208–2106
Don Chamblee, director/senate liaison
Carol Connors, deputy director/house liaison

Provides information on litigation and public participation; answers consumer questions; and disseminates energy information among federal, state, and local governments.

Press Services Division
888 1st St. N.E.
Washington, DC 20426
(202) 502–8680
Hedley M. Burrell, press secretary

Responds to questions from the press, prepares news releases, and organizes news conferences and coverage of public hearings and proceedings.

Public Inquiries
888 1st St. N.E.
Washington, DC 20426
(Toll-free) (866) 208–3372

Responds to questions from the public and other government agencies. It assists in identifying sources for FERC-related information, processes Freedom of Information requests, prepares informational and educational materials, and assists in organizing public proceedings.

Public Reference Room
888 1st St. N.E., Room 2A
Washington, DC 20426
(202) 502–8371

Issues a *Guide to Public Information,* which details all reports, forms, orders, and similar materials that are available from FERC and indicates the office responsible for issuing them. Also operates the Public Reference Room *(see Dockets, below).*

Freedom of Information
The director of FERC External Affairs serves as FOI officer. Requests can be made through Public Inquiries, above.

PUBLICATIONS
Contact Public Inquiries or the Public Reference Room. FERC publications are listed in the *Federal Energy Regulatory Commission Publications Catalog.* Subjects include FERC programs and products, electric power, natural gas, and oil pipelines. Among titles available through the Public Reference Room, the following are free:

The Federal Energy Regulatory Commission—Its Organization and Operations. Provides a detailed description of functions and commission authority including office contacts.

Guide to Public Information at the Federal Energy Regulatory Commission. Describes information and services available in the commission's Public Reference Room and types of data contained in report forms and publications.

How to Intervene. Describes procedures to intervene in a proceeding before the commission.

Water Power—Use of a Renewable Resource. Discusses hydroelectric power generation and FERC's licensing role.

DATA AND STATISTICS
FERC requires regulated industries to file various reports on production, income, expenditures, and other items. These reports generally adhere to a format designed by FERC and are assigned a form number and title. Reports

are available through the Public Reference Room, and the FERC Web site. *(See Internet, p. 161.)*

MEETINGS

Commission meetings usually are scheduled every other Wednesday and held in Room 2C of FERC headquarters, 888 1st St. N.E., Washington, DC 20426.

Meetings are open to the general public, as are most hearings, conferences, and other regulatory proceedings. Transcripts of special meetings usually are available the morning following the hearing in the Public Reference Room.

The Office of the Secretary can supply details on meeting schedules and agenda; (202) 502–8400.

Reference Resources

LIBRARY

FERC Library
888 1st St. N.E., Room 95-01
Washington, DC 20426
(202) 502–8179
TTY (202) 502–8345
Robert Kimberlin, chief
Hours: 8:30 a.m. to 5:00 p.m.

Open to the public and has a wide range of holdings on the topic of energy. References available include:

FERC Statutes and Regulations. Set of six loose-leaf volumes devoted to the federal laws that give the commission its authority and responsibilities and to the regulations the commission issues pursuant to those laws.

FERC Reports. Contains documents issued by the commission that are decisional or precedent setting, but do not amend the regulations in Title 18 of the *Code of Federal Regulations* (CFR). Loose-leaf pages are transferred to a numbered semipermanent binder at the end of each calendar quarter.

Federal Power Commission Reports. Hardcover volumes containing opinions, decisions, and orders of the Federal Power Commission, FERC's predecessor. The reports are useful for determining commission interpretation of regulations; however, they lag several years behind in publication. Material not yet published in bound volumes is available in the Public Reference Room.

DOCKETS

FERC Public Reference Room
888 1st St. N.E., Room 2A
Washington, DC 20426
(202) 502–8371
Hours: 8:30 a.m. to 5:00 p.m.

The files for rulemaking proceedings and other formal activities of the commission are under the jurisdiction of the Office of the Secretary. However, dockets may be examined and copied at the Public Reference Room.

Docket numbers are included in all press releases and in *Federal Register* notices; they also can be obtained from FERC reference staff.

Copying services may be arranged for those unable to visit. Transcripts from public hearings also are available for inspection and copying.

RULES AND REGULATIONS

FERC rules and regulations are published in the CFR, Title 18. Proposed rules, new final rules, and updates to the *Code of Federal Regulations* are published in the *Federal Register. (See appendix for information on how to obtain and use these publications.)*

Other Information Sources

RELATED AGENCIES

National Energy Information Center
DOE Energy Information Administration
1000 Independence Ave. S.W.
Washington, DC 20585
(202) 586–8800
Fax (202) 586–0727
Internet: http://www.eia.doe.gov

Provides statistical data on energy; publishes twenty analytical reports and approximately sixty periodicals annually. Topics covered include supply and demand data, pricing, imports and exports, and projections regarding electricity, nuclear energy, and fossil fuels. The *Energy Information Administration Publications Directory* is available free.

DOE Office of Scientific and Technical Information
P.O. Box 62
Oak Ridge, TN 37831
(423) 576–1272 or 576–1175
Fax (423) 576–3609

Handles inquiries about the *Energy Data Base,* which stores and analyzes international energy information.

NONGOVERNMENTAL ORGANIZATIONS

The following are some key organizations that monitor FERC and related energy issues.

American Petroleum Institute

1220 L St. N.W.
Washington, DC 20005
(202) 682–8000
Fax (202) 682–8029
Internet: http://www.api.org

American Public Power Association

2301 M St. N.W.
Washington, DC 20037
(202) 467–2900
Fax (202) 467–2910
Internet: http://www.appanet.org

Association of Oil Pipelines

1101 Vermont Ave. N.W., #604
Washington, DC 20005
(202) 408–7970
Fax (202) 408–7983

Edison Electric Institute

701 Pennsylvania Ave. N.W.
Washington, DC 20004
(202) 508–5000
Fax (202) 508–5759
Internet: http://www.eei.org

Federal Energy Bar Association

2175 K St., N.W., #600
Washington, DC 20037
(202) 833–5625
Fax (202) 833–5596
Internet: www.eba-net.org

National Association of Regulatory Utility Commissioners

1101 Vermont Ave., N.W., #200
Washington, DC 20005
(202) 898–2200
Fax (202) 898–2213
Internet: www.naruc.org

National Rural Electric Cooperative Association

4301 Wilson Blvd.
Arlington, VA 22203
(703) 907–5500
Fax (703) 907–5515
Internet: www.nreca.org

U.S. Chamber of Commerce

Environment, Energy, and Food Policy
1615 H St. N.W.
Washington, DC 20062–2000
(202) 659–6000
Internet: http://www.uschamber.org

U.S. Energy Association

1300 Pennsylvania Ave., N.W., #550
Mailbox 142
Washington, DC 20004-3022
(202) 312–1230
Fax (202) 682–1682
Internet: www.usea.org

PUBLISHERS

The following companies and organizations publish on FERC and related issues through books, periodicals, or electronic media.

Advanstar Communications

545 Boylston St.
Boston, MA 02116
(617) 267–6500
Fax (617) 267–6900
Internet: www.advanstar.com

Barrows Company

116 E. 66th St.
New York, NY 10021
(212) 772–1199
(Toll-free) (800) 227–7697
Fax (212) 288-7242
Internet: http://www.barrowscompany.com

Commerce Clearing House (CCH), Inc.

2700 Lake Cook Rd.
Riverwoods, IL 60015
(847) 267–7000
Fax (847) 267–7878
Internet: http://www.cch.com

The Dialog Corporation

11000 Regency Parkway, #10
Cary, NC 27511
(919) 462–8600
(Toll-free) (800) 3DIALOG
Fax (919) 468–9890
Internet: http://www.dialog.com
Provides access to the *Energyline* database.

Hart Publications, Inc.
(a Phillips Publishing, Inc. company)
1201 Seven Lakes Road, #300
Potomac, MD 20854
(301) 354–2045
Fax (301) 424–7260
Internet: www.hartenergynetwork.com

The Energy Daily
King Communications Group, Inc.
1325 G St., N.W., #1003
Washington, DC 20005
(202) 638–4260
(800) 926–5464
Fax (202) 662–9719
Internet: www.kingpublishing.com

McGraw-Hill Companies
1221 Avenue of the Americas
New York, NY 10020
(800) 722–4726
Internet: http://www.mcgraw-hill.com

> **Platt's Division**
> (800) 752–8878
> Fax (212) 904–3070
> Internet: http://www.platts.com
> **Utility Data Institute**
> 1200 G St. N.W., #250
> Washington, DC 20005–3802
> (202) 942–8788
> Fax (202) 942–8789
> Internet: http://www.platts.com/udidata

PennWell Publishing Co.
1421 S. Sheridan Rd.
Box 21288
Tulsa, OK 74121
(800) 331–4463
Fax (918) 835–3161
Internet: http://www.pennwell.com

The WEFA Group
800 Baldwin Tower
Eddystone, PA 19022
(610) 490–4000
Energy department (617) 221–0340
Internet: http://www.wefa.com
Provides access to the *Energy* database.

Federal Reserve System

20th and C Sts. N.W., Washington, DC 20551
Internet: http://www.federalreserve.gov

■ INTRODUCTION

The Federal Reserve System (the Fed) is an independent regulatory and monetary policy-making agency, established by the Federal Reserve Act in 1913.

The Fed is administered by a board composed of seven governors, nominated by the president and confirmed by the Senate. The president also designates two of the members to serve as chair and vice chair for four years. Both the chair and vice chair may be redesignated. A governor's term is fourteen years, but few serve that long, and often an individual is appointed to fill the remaining portion of a term. Members who have served a full term may not be reappointed.

Responsibilities

The Fed's major responsibility is to conduct the federal government's monetary policy. Through the buying and selling of government securities, the Fed directly influences the supply of credit and the level of key short-term interest rates, which in turn strongly affect the pace of economic activity, unemployment, and prices.

In addition, the Fed regulates certain credit activities, collects economic data, oversees the activities of bank holding companies, and acts as the primary federal government supervisor of state-chartered banks that have joined the Federal Reserve System. These banks are referred to as state member banks. State-chartered banks that are not members of the Fed are supervised by the Federal Deposit Insurance Corporation (p. 125); federally chartered banks are regulated by the Office of the Comptroller of the Currency (p. 133).

GLOSSARY

Bank holding company (BHC)—A company that owns or controls one or more banks. The Federal Reserve System regulates and supervises BHCs and approves bank mergers and acquisitions. The Fed maintains authority over a BHC even if the banks it owns are under the supervision of the Federal Deposit Insurance Corporation or Office of the Comptroller of the Currency.

Discount rate—The interest rate district Federal Reserve banks charge on loans to depository institutions (banks, savings banks, thrifts, and credit unions).

Discount window—An expression used to describe the mechanism by which the Fed makes loans to depository institutions.

Fed—A widely used nickname for the Federal Reserve System.

Federal funds rate—The rate commercial banks pay to borrow money from each other on a short-term basis, generally overnight, and typically to meet reserve requirements.

Interlocking directorates—Boards of directors having some members in common, so that the corporations concerned are to some extent under the same control.

National bank—A bank that is chartered and regulated by the Office of the Comptroller of the Currency. National banks are required to be members of the Federal Reserve System.

NOW Accounts (Negotiable-order-of-withdrawal accounts.)—These are interest-bearing accounts on which checks may be drawn.

Reserves—Money that financial institutions must keep as cash in their vaults.

State member bank—A bank that is chartered by a state and is a member of the Federal Reserve System, which supervises these banks.

State nonmember bank—A bank that is chartered by a state but is not a member of the Federal Reserve System. These banks are supervised by the Federal Deposit Insurance Corporation.

In executing its monetary policy-making functions, the Fed:

- Determines the level of reserves that must be kept on deposit with the twelve Federal Reserve district banks by all financial institutions.

- Lends money through its "discount window" to banks that encounter unexpected deposit fluctuations and need to enlarge their reserves or pay depositors. Serves as the "lender of last resort" when financial markets are in disarray. Reviews and confirms the "discount rate" charged on such loans by the Federal Reserve district banks.

- Buys and sells government securities in the open market, thereby directly increasing or reducing the amount of bank cash reserves and short-term market interest rates ("open market operations").

- Collects and analyzes extensive data on the money supply, credit, industrial production, and other economic activity.

- Supervises and examines the activities of the twelve Federal Reserve district banks.

- Supervises the issuance and distribution of Federal Reserve notes and monitors the amount of currency in circulation.

- Regulates various types of credit, such as for purchasing stocks and other equity securities.

- Serves as fiscal agent for the U.S. government, selling, servicing, and redeeming U.S. Treasury securities.

- Buys and sells foreign currencies, in cooperation with the Treasury Department or on behalf of foreign central banks, to counteract disorderly conditions in foreign exchange markets.

- Supervises the government securities broker and dealer activities of state member banks, foreign banks and their uninsured U.S. branches, and foreign branches and affiliates of U.S. banks.

As one of the five major federal regulatory agencies for financial institutions, the Fed:

- Registers, regulates, and supervises bank holding companies; reviews acquisition and expansion plans of bank holding companies to ensure they do not foster anticompetitive and monopolistic behavior.

- Approves establishment of foreign branches of member banks and regulates their activities; regulates and supervises the foreign activities of U.S. banks.

- Charters and regulates international banking subsidiaries (known as Edge corporations) of member banks.

- Approves acquisitions of banks, thrifts, and commercial lending offices in the United States by foreign-owned banks; approves opening of branch offices by foreign banks; has authority to close state-chartered branches and affiliate offices of foreign banks that are not subject to comprehensive regulation in their home countries (and recommend such action to the Office of the Comptroller of the Currency for federally chartered branches of foreign banks); supervises certain nonbank offices of state-chartered, foreign-owned banks; enforces consumer protection laws as they apply to foreign-owned U.S. banks; monitors capital standards for foreign banks in the United States.

- Provides check clearing, settlement, wire transfer, automated clearinghouse, and other services to the banking system.

- Issues regulations requiring meaningful disclosure of credit terms offered by state member banks.

- Issues rules prohibiting discrimination by banks in granting credit.
- Participates in the deliberations of the Federal Financial Institutions Examination Council, which was established in 1978 to develop uniform examination and supervision practices for all depository institutions' regulatory agencies. Other members of the council include the Office of the Comptroller of the Currency (OCC), the Federal Deposit Insurance Corporation (FDIC), the Office of Thrift Supervision (OTS) *(p. 704)*, and the National Credit Union Administration (NCUA) *(p. 343)*.

As the primary regulator of state-chartered banks that have joined the Federal Reserve System (state member banks), the Fed:

- Regulates and supervises the activities of state member banks, including their lending practices and financial condition.
- Approves establishment of new facilities and branches by state member banks.
- Authorizes the issuance of orders requiring state member banks and bank holding companies to cease and desist from violations of law and unsafe business practices.
- Authorizes the removal from office of bank officers and directors who violate the law, engage in unsafe and unsound practices, or engage in insider loans and arrangements.
- Regulates issuance of credit cards by state member banks.
- Establishes minimum standards for installing and maintaining security systems.
- Enforces statutory restrictions that greatly limit interlocking directorates and overlap of officers among banking companies.
- Regulates mergers, consolidations, and acquisitions when the resulting institution would be a state member bank.

Powers and Authority

The Federal Reserve System is the nation's central bank and is charged with making and administering policy for the nation's credit and monetary affairs. It also has supervisory and regulatory power over bank holding companies, state-chartered banks that are members of the system, overseas activities of U.S. banks, and U.S.-based operations of foreign-owned banks.

STRUCTURE

The Federal Reserve System consists of five major parts: (1) the board of governors, (2) the Federal Open Market Committee (FOMC), (3) the twelve Federal Reserve banks, (4) the three advisory councils, and (5) the member banks of the system.

The Board of Governors

The board is responsible for administering and supervising the Federal Reserve System. It consists of seven members who are appointed by the president and confirmed by the Senate. Board members are appointed for fourteen-year terms, and no two members may come from the same Federal Reserve district. The chair and vice chair of the board are named by the president to four-year terms and may be renamed as long as their terms have not expired.

Although the Fed is designed to be independent of political influences, the chair often meets with administration officials to discuss economic policy and since 1978 is required by law to appear biannually before the House and Senate Banking committees to give lawmakers an economic update. In practice, members of the board testify much more often than that on a wide variety of economic issues.

The board supervises the twelve Federal Reserve District banks and appoints some members of each bank's board of directors. Each bank's board appoints its president and vice presidents, but the Federal Reserve Board confirms those appointments. In addition, the Fed board coordinates the Reserve System's economic research and data collection and reviews all publications. It must vote to approve acquisitions by bank holding companies, some bank mergers, and certain other commercial bank actions.

The board's primary function, however, is the formulation of monetary policy. In addition to approving proposed changes in the discount rate, it has authority to change reserve requirements within specified limits and to set margin requirements for the financing of securities traded on national securities exchanges.

Federal Open Market Committee

The FOMC, with twelve voting members, is the system's most important monetary policy-making body. The committee meets eight times a year in Washington, D.C., and consults by telephone when a change of policy is called for between meeting dates. It is composed of the board of governors plus the president of the New York Reserve Bank. Four other voting positions rotate among the eleven remaining Reserve bank presidents, though all twelve Reserve bank presidents typically attend each session of the FOMC and participate in discussions.

The committee's main responsibility is to establish open market operations and thereby the general course of monetary policy. The FOMC decides the extent to which the system buys and sells government and other securities. Purchases and sales of securities in the open market are undertaken to supply the credit and money needed for long-term economic growth, to offset cyclical economic swings, and to accommodate seasonal demands of businesses and consumers for money and credit. The committee also issues regulations regarding administration of the discount window.

In addition, the committee oversees the system's operations in foreign exchange markets. Foreign currency transactions are undertaken in conjunction with the Treasury to safeguard the value of the dollar in international exchange markets and to facilitate growth in international liquidity in accordance with the needs of an expanding world economy.

The New York Reserve Bank serves as the committee's agent in making actual purchases and sales. Government securities bought outright are then prorated among the twelve Reserve banks according to a formula based upon their reserve ratios. The foreign department of the New York bank acts as the agent for foreign exchange transactions.

The Federal Reserve Banks

The operations of the Federal Reserve System are conducted through a nationwide network of twelve Federal Reserve banks located in Atlanta, Boston, Chicago, Cleveland, Dallas, Kansas City, Minneapolis, New York, Philadelphia, Richmond, San Francisco, and St. Louis. Branches of Reserve banks have been established in twenty-five additional cities *(p. 184)*.

Each Reserve bank is an incorporated institution with its own board of directors, consisting of nine members. The Federal Reserve Act requires that directors be divided into three classes. Class A directors, who represent member banks, and Class B directors, who are engaged in pursuits other than banking, are elected by the member banks in each Federal Reserve district. The board of governors appoints the three Class C directors and designates one of them as chair and another as deputy chair of the bank's board. No Class B or Class C director may be an officer, director, or employee of a bank; in addition, Class C directors are prohibited from being stockholders of any bank.

The directors of each Reserve bank oversee the operations of their bank under the overall supervision of the board of governors. They establish, subject to approval by the board, the interest rates the bank may charge on short-term collateral loans to member banks and on any loans that may be extended to nonmember institutions. The directors appoint the bank's president and first vice president subject to approval of the Fed board of governors.

Advisory Councils

To aid the Fed in its work, three advisory councils monitor various issues and offer suggestions to the board and the FOMC.

The Federal Advisory Council consists of one member from each of the Federal Reserve districts. The board of directors of each bank annually selects one council member, usually a banker from the district. The council is required to meet in Washington, D.C., at least four times a year. It confers with the board of governors on economic and banking matters and makes recommendations regarding the affairs of the system.

The Consumer Advisory Council meets three times a year to discuss consumer issues relating to Fed responsibilities. The thirty-member body is made up of bankers, consumer group representatives, academics, and legal experts.

The twelve-member Thrift Institutions Advisory Council provides the Fed with information and views on the needs and problems of thrifts. The council is composed of representatives from savings banks, savings and loan associations, and credit unions.

Agency Budget

The Fed receives no appropriation from Congress, and its budget is largely free from congressional scrutiny. Interest paid on government securities purchased by the Fed accounts for about 90 percent of the Fed's earnings. In addition, the Fed earns money from the fees it charges for its services, from interest on discount window loans, and from its foreign currency operations.

Technically, the Federal Reserve System is owned by its member banks. To be admitted to membership, a bank must subscribe a certain percentage of its capital stock and surplus to the Reserve bank in its district. Member banks receive a dividend of 6 percent annually on the value of their paid-in stock. The dividend is exempt from federal, state, and local tax.

The Fed's earnings go first to pay expenses and to pay the 6 percent dividend to member banks on their paid-in stock. Earnings also are used to make any additions to each Reserve bank's surplus to keep it equal to the bank's paid-in stock. Remaining earnings then are paid to the U.S. Treasury. About 90 percent of the Fed's annual income has been paid to the Treasury since the system was established.

Although Congress has no say in the budgets of the Federal Reserve board of governors or the twelve district banks, since 1978 the General Accounting Office (GAO) has been authorized to audit certain records of the Fed. The GAO is barred from examining: international monetary and financial transactions; monetary policy matters, including discount window operations, member bank reserves, securities credit, interest on deposits, and open market operations; FOMC activities; and all communications among Fed personnel relating to exempted activities. The comptroller general is required to report to Congress on the results of the GAO audits.

MONETARY POLICY

The Fed closely monitors and takes regular steps to affect the supply of credit and its price, or interest rates, which in turn influence the level of spending and production in the economy. Long-term monetary policy is set by the Fed's board of governors through the discount rate and bank reserve requirements. But short-term policy, which is more central to the economy and market observers, is set in meetings of the FOMC.

The Fed requires all depository institutions to maintain reserves—in the form of cash in their vaults or held in noninterest-bearing accounts at Federal Reserve banks—equal to a certain percentage of their deposits. When the central bank buys Treasury securities from banks, it pays for them by crediting the banks' reserve accounts, giving banks additional money to lend to individuals and corporations. Conversely, when the Fed sells Treasury securities, it prompts banks to draw down their reserves. To maintain the required level of reserves, banks are forced to pull money out of the system by slowing down their rate of lending or perhaps even calling in some loans.

Most banks meet their reserve requirements by borrowing, usually on an overnight basis, from other institutions that have a temporary surplus. The market-based interest rate for such short-term borrowing, dubbed the federal funds rate, is closely controlled by Fed open market operations, and it is closely watched by financial markets as a sign of changes in available credit. When the Fed seeks to move interest rates up or down, it buys or sells Treasury securities and thereby expands or contracts bank reserves, altering the supply of money to meet reserve requirements. A tighter supply of lendable reserves results in a higher price to borrow, or a higher federal funds rate; a looser supply results in a lower rate. Fed open market operations are carefully geared to keep the federal funds rate fairly steady and to move it generally in increments of a quarter of a percentage point.

The Fed often engages in open market transactions simply to iron out temporary fluctuations in the demand for money and credit in the economy. These shifts in demand can result from a variety of factors, such as seasonal variations in economic activity and the weather, among others. But open market transactions also influence longer-term trends in credit conditions.

Since the mid-1950s the Fed has used monetary policy to moderate the degree of inflation or recession in the economy. To counteract inflation, the central bank has followed a restrictive policy, making it more difficult for consumers, businesses, and governments to borrow money. Tighter credit tends to reduce the demand for goods, in turn decreasing inflationary pressures on prices; but it also risks increasing unemployment. At other times, to fight recession, the central bank has eased credit conditions, bringing down interest rates and encouraging borrowing. That tends to increase the demand for goods, raising production and employment; but it also creates the danger of inflationary wage and price scales.

The challenge to monetary policymakers has always been to find an appropriate guide for their activities. The effects of a change in policy on growth or inflation may not show up in the economy until many months after the change has occurred. As a result, the FOMC must predict the effects of its actions using imperfect indicators.

During World War II and immediately after, the FOMC was guided by the need to prevent interest rates on the government debt from rising. The government had borrowed heavily to finance the war, and increasing rates would add greatly to the federal budget. If the rates the Treasury had to pay to borrow money started to rise, the Fed would follow an easier policy, creating more reserves and encouraging interest rates to fall. Such a policy, however, was powerless to prevent inflation. As the rate of inflation began to rise during the Korean War, the Fed formally ended its support of Treasury financing.

The Fed continued to pay attention to interest rates, however, as well as to various measures of the money supply and other indicators of economic activity. It was not until October 1979 that the Fed decided to ignore interest rates and set a policy designed to slow the growth of the money supply in a vigorous attempt to curtail double-digit inflation.

The close focus on money supply measures came to an end in 1982. The FOMC claimed that the principal measure of the money supply—known as M1—had become distorted. M1 was supposed to include currency in circulation plus checking accounts, but not savings accounts. But the rise of NOW accounts and money market accounts made the line between checking and savings accounts increasingly vague. As a result, Fed officials claimed, M1 had become an unreliable guide to policy. Perhaps more important than those technical arguments, however, was the fact that the money supply was rising rapidly in late 1982, and the Fed knew that any attempt to rein it in would exacerbate an already deep recession and a looming international debt crisis. An increasingly global economy and a resulting increase in "Eurodollars"—U.S. dollars held and traded in Europe—added to the Fed's difficulty in controlling the money supply.

Since 1982 the FOMC has followed a varied set of policy guides. Because meetings are held in private, it is difficult to say precisely what determines committee decisions. A statement of policy directives adopted by the FOMC and minutes of the meetings are released five to eight weeks after they occur—typically a few days after the following meeting.

Not only is it difficult to know what guides Fed policy decisions; sometimes the decisions themselves are obscure. In fact, it has long been the Fed's practice to allow the financial markets, businesses, governments, and other observers to guess at its intentions. Its silence has led to severe criticism. In response to such objections, the Fed on several occasions in 1994 released public statements that the FOMC had decided to boost the federal funds rate.

Despite the apparent policy reversal, the FOMC's policy actions remain somewhat ambiguous, particularly the rationale for policy decisions. It is, however, apparent from a careful reading of FOMC policy statements and minutes that in making monetary policy the committee keeps a close eye not only on the behavior of money supply measures but also on other indicators, such as economic growth rates, including gross measures of the economy and narrow statistics of regional and sectoral activity, inflation, the value of the dollar on foreign exchange markets, lending activity, and the health of the financial system.

Moreover, it is plain that the Fed chair, being the most visible member of the Fed board and also serving as chair of the FOMC, wields enormous influence. To the extent that the chair's thinking reflects a general view of the board of governors and the FOMC, it is sometimes possible to discern what influences the committee. The Fed chair testifies twice yearly to the House and Senate Banking committees, explaining Fed monetary policy, and makes frequent other appearances before congressional committees to discuss economic concerns. Financial markets follow closely every statement the Fed chair makes, looking for clues to the direction of Fed monetary policy.

BANK SUPERVISION AND REGULATION

The Bank Holding Company Act of 1956 granted to the Federal Reserve regulatory authority over bank holding companies (BHCs). A BHC was defined as any company controlling at least 25 percent of a bank's voting stock or the election of a majority of its governing body.

The purpose of the act was to control BHC expansion, prevent the formation of monopolies, and discourage restraint-of-trade in banking. The act required a company to obtain prior approval from the Fed before becoming a BHC. It also required prior approval for a BHC to do any of the following: acquire more than 5 percent of a bank's voting stock, acquire a bank's assets or merge with another BHC, or acquire a bank's assets in another state unless state law specifically authorizes out-of-state acquisition. (The prohibition on out-of-state acquisitions was repealed in 1994.) It prohibited expansion into nonbanking areas except those deemed by the Fed to be permissible bank-related activities or "so closely related to the business of banking or of managing or controlling banks as to be a proper incident thereto."

A 1970 amendment to the Bank Holding Company Act closed a major loophole by giving the Fed regulatory authority over bank holding companies that only own a single bank—companies that previously had been exempted.

The Bank Mergers Act of 1966 granted the board of governors partial authority to administer bank mergers. The Fed approves mergers between *state member* banks and national or state nonmember banks if the resulting institution is to be a state member bank.

Throughout the 1980s and 1990s the Fed several times expanded its interpretation of closely related activities to allow some banking companies to engage in securities activities. Those decisions required a relaxed interpretation of the Glass-Steagall Act of 1933, the Depression-era barriers that barred banks from engaging in most securities sales and underwriting activities and from affiliating with companies "principally engaged" in those securities activities.

In November 1999 a historic overhaul of the Glass-Steagall Act, known as Gramm-Leach-Bliley, was signed by President Bill Clinton. The long-awaited modernization of the financial services industry allows banks, securities firms, and insurance companies to enter into each other's markets to a certain degree. Under the new system, banks can form holding companies that engage in traditional banking activities as well as insurance and securities underwriting, merchant banking, and real estate development. Each endeavor operates as a separate business under the umbrella of the new financial services conglomerates—still closely regulated by the Fed. Other federal agencies, such as the Securities and Exchange Commission and the Office of the Comptroller of the Currency, continue to regulate activities within their jurisdiction, regardless of whether they were carried out by a bank.

International Banking

The Fed issues licenses for foreign branches of Federal Reserve member banks and regulates the scope of their activity. It also charters and regulates international banking subsidiaries, called Edge corporations after Sen. Walter Edge, R-N.J. (1919–1929), who introduced the legislation in 1919, and it authorizes overseas investments of commercial banks, Edge corporations, and bank holding companies.

The International Banking Act of 1978 gave the Fed the primary authority for regulating U.S. branches of foreign banks and overseas branches of U.S. banks. Two years later the Monetary Control Act required U.S. branches of foreign banks and Edge corporations to meet the Fed's reserve requirements. The Foreign Bank Supervision Enhancement Act of 1991 greatly expanded the Fed's jurisdiction over U.S. activities of foreign banks, including by requiring advance approval of the Fed for the acquisition or establishment of a branch, agency, representative office, or commercial lending company.

In addition to these regulatory responsibilities, the Fed advises and consults with agencies of the federal government in discussions with international organizations and maintains contacts with the central banks of other countries.

Consumer Credit Protection

The board shares with other banking regulators enforcement responsibility for several consumer-protection laws. These include the Truth in Lending Act, the Truth in Savings Act, the Fair Credit Billing Act, the Fair Debt Collection Practices Act, the Home Mortgage Disclosure Act, the Equal Credit Opportunity Act, the Community Reinvestment Act, and certain provisions of the Real Estate Settlement Procedures Act and the Federal Trade Commission Act that apply to banks.

Bank Examinations

The Fed has the authority to conduct examinations of all member banks, including national as well as state-chartered banks. However, the comptroller of the currency has primary responsibility for the supervision and regulation of nationally chartered member banks and furnishes the Fed with reports on their operations. The FDIC examines and regulates state nonmember insured banks.

Because its primary role is formulating monetary policy, the board of governors has delegated the responsibility for field examination of member banks to the twelve Federal Reserve banks around the country. The mechanics and standards of examinations, as well as enforcement activities, are similar to those carried out by the FDIC (p. 125).

Field examiners have the authority to examine a bank's financial condition, enforce regulations and statutory provisions, such as restrictions on asset holdings, and require that unsatisfactory operating conditions of member banks be corrected. Under a major banking law enacted in 1991, bank regulators, including the Fed, were required to take direct action to prevent financial institutions from becoming undercapitalized and to take control of or close institutions whose capital fell below a designated "critical" level.

Most state member banks must be examined by Federal Reserve bank officials every year. Only smaller banks that received the highest of five regulatory ratings are examined every eighteen months.

SUPPORT SERVICES

The Monetary Control Act of 1980 required the board to charge for Federal Reserve bank services, which include currency and coin services of a nongovernmental nature; check clearing and collection; wire transfers; automated clearinghouse; settlement; securities safekeeping; Federal Reserve float (the Fed gives one institution credit for a check before it has collected funds from the institution where the check was written); and payment services for electronic funds transfer.

Issuing Currency

Reserve banks provide a convenient and accessible source of currency and coin for banks. If a bank needs cash, it replenishes its supply by obtaining shipments from a Reserve bank. If a bank accumulates more currency and coin than it needs, it is allowed to return this money to a Reserve bank and receive credits to its reserve accounts.

Federal Reserve banks also replace worn or damaged currency or coin with new money obtained from the U.S. Mint or the Bureau of Engraving and Printing.

The Federal Reserve collects substantial quantities of bank checks and noncash items such as drafts, promissory notes, and bond coupons for the public.

When a check remains in the community near the bank on which it is drawn, presentation for payment usually is made by an exchange of checks through a local clearing arrangement. For checks leaving the local community, however, the Federal Reserve assists the timely presentation of that check by accepting millions of checks daily and then sorting and directing them to the banks on which they are drawn.

Banks receive credit for checks deposited with a Federal Reserve bank based on a published availability schedule, with credit being passed to the depositor the same day payment is scheduled to be received from the bank on which the check is written.

Securities Credit

Through regulations T, U, and X, the board of governors sets the amount of credit that may be used to buy equity securities. These regulations are known as "margin" requirements.

Wire Transfer of Funds

A member bank may transfer funds from its reserve account to another member bank anywhere in the country within a matter of minutes. Such transactions formerly were processed on a private communications system known as the Federal Reserve Communications System (FRCS). In 1994 the twelve Federal Reserve district banks and member banks began using a new completely interconnected Fednet system.

Automated Clearinghouses

Reserve banks and their branches operate automated clearinghouses (ACHs) that provide for the exchange of payments on magnetic tape. The ACH receives a tape of transaction information from a commercial bank and electronically directs each item to the appropriate receiving bank where customer accounts are posted. Examples of ACH transactions are the direct deposit of a payroll by an employer and payment of a customer's recurring bills such as mortgages. In 2002 the Fed processed nearly five billion of these transactions, totaling more than $13.1 trillion.

Background

The Federal Reserve System was created by Congress in December 1913. It was the nation's third attempt to establish a central bank. The first Bank of the United States was chartered by Congress in 1791. When its twenty-year charter expired, Congress, fearing the central bank vested too much control over the economy in the hands of the federal government, refused to extend it.

In 1816 Congress established the second Bank of the United States. But again, members of Congress grew distrustful of their creation and allowed its charter to expire in 1836. Both national banks also were criticized for benefiting the moneyed aristocracy over the general population.

For the next twenty-five years, the banking system consisted of a network of unregulated state-chartered banks and was plagued by insufficient capital, a high level of risky loans, fluctuating currency values, and insufficient reserves to back bank notes and deposits. The situation continued to deteriorate until 1863, when Congress passed the National Bank Act, which established federally chartered banks and created the Office of the Comptroller of the Currency to regulate them. A primary purpose was to establish a uniform national currency that would be issued through national banks, with the intent of stabilizing money in the Union and devaluing that in the Confederacy during the Civil War.

The economy continued to suffer from periodic banking and currency crises, however, leading Congress to pass the Federal Reserve Act in 1913.

EARLY HISTORY

The architects of the Federal Reserve System were concerned principally with the need for an efficient payments system that would allow money to be transferred among financial institutions across the nation. They also believed the new Federal Reserve banks could smooth out fluctuations in the nation's money supply and help avoid financial panics by making loans to banks through the discount window. Authors of the Federal Reserve Act said that the bill's purpose was "to provide for the establishment of Federal Reserve banks, to furnish an elastic currency, to afford a means of rediscounting commercial paper [and] to establish a more effective supervision of banking in the United States."

During the 1920s, however, the Fed learned that the sale and purchase of U.S. Treasury securities provided an even more powerful tool for influencing money creation than the discount window. When the Fed bought securities from a bank, it increased the bank's reserves and enabled it to make more loans; as a result, interest rates on loans tended to fall. When the Fed sold securities, on the other hand, bank reserves fell and credit shrank; as a result, interest rates tended to rise.

At first, sales and purchases of Treasury securities by the Federal Reserve district banks were uncoordinated, sometimes contributing to disarray in financial markets. But in 1922 the Fed established the Open Market Investment Committee to coordinate dealings in securities.

In the spring of 1933, in the midst of the Great Depression, the Fed failed to avert panic by providing sufficient cash to banks experiencing depositor runs. President Franklin D. Roosevelt was forced to declare a "bank holiday," closing all the banks in the nation on March 6, two days after he was sworn into office. Several thousand banks never reopened their doors. This severe crisis prompted passage of landmark banking laws in 1933 and 1935 that established the FDIC to insure bank deposits and stabilize banks.

The FDIC also was charged with supervising state-chartered banks that were not members of the Fed and, therefore, previously had not been subject to federal regulation. The Fed continued to supervise state-chartered banks that were members, and the comptroller regulated national banks.

The banking acts of the 1930s also increased the power and the autonomy of the Fed by removing the secretary of the Treasury and the comptroller from its board of governors. The acts also stripped the regional Fed banks of their power to buy and sell securities and concentrated that power in the hands of the Federal Open Market Committee—successor to the Open Market Investment Committee—which operated through the Federal Reserve Bank of New York.

From the outset, all national banks were required to be members of the Fed, and state-chartered banks could choose to be members if they wished. Member banks were required to keep interest-free reserves at the Fed, and in return they received certain Fed services. The rise of interest rates in the 1970s, however, caused dramatic growth in the cost to banks of keeping interest-free reserves at the Fed. As a result, many state banks withdrew from Fed membership, and some national banks converted to state charters so they also could withdraw.

Fearing that a loss of Fed members would hamper the central bank's ability to manage the money supply, Congress passed the Monetary Control Act in 1980. That law required all depository institutions to keep reserves at the Fed, regardless of whether they were members. The Fed also was required to charge fees for its check clearing and other services, and to offer them to nonmember banks.

THE FED IN THE 1980S

In the 1980s, confronted with major upheavals in the economy and the performance of financial markets, the Fed attracted severe criticism for its monetary policy. With inflation topping 10 percent in 1979, Fed chair Paul A. Volcker began a "war on inflation," convincing the FOMC to stop trying to control interest rates and focus on restraining the growth of the money supply. Prices had been brought under control by 1982, when inflation settled in at about 4 percent, as measured by the Consumer Price Index. But price stability came at the cost of soaring interest rates—prime rates charged by commercial banks exceeded 20 percent in 1981—and a pair of back-to-back recessions that stretched from January 1980 to November 1982.

The war on inflation was ultimately considered a success. Though Volcker was branded as a pariah in the early 1980s, by the time he left the Fed in 1987, the economy was in its fifth consecutive year of economic growth, and the chair was hailed for the prosperity.

But notwithstanding its success in reining in prices, the Fed was left struggling with interest rates that remained high, particularly as the economy grew with gusto in the mid-1980s. The prime rate fell in 1987 to just above 8 percent before it began climbing, and the central bank came under renewed pressure from policymakers—in Congress and the White House—who thought that rates were too high.

Alan Greenspan, who took the helm in the summer of 1987, continued the vigorous approach of his predecessor, but whereas Volcker had battled inflation to get the economy back on track, Greenspan has tried to prevent inflationary pressures from gaining a foothold to keep economic growth at a stable and sustained pace.

The Fed did not hesitate to intervene when the stock and futures markets were in disarray. After Oct. 19, 1987, when stock markets around the world crashed and the Dow Jones Industrial Average dropped 508 points, the central bank took steps to assure brokers that credit would be extended if needed. The move calmed investors' biggest fears—that credit would not be available to cover margin requirements and their stocks would have to be sold in a deeply depressed market.

Likewise, in October 1989, after the Dow dropped 190 points on a Friday, Fed officials spent the weekend assuring investors that money would be available to meet credit needs. When trading began the following Monday, the markets rebounded.

THE FED IN THE 1990S

Greenspan's emphasis on price stability often came at the expense of economic growth. The economy stalled again in July 1990 and recovered slowly from a recession that lasted until March 1991, in technical terms, and continued for a year or more after that in practical effect. The result, however, was a further decline in inflation and interest rates.

The Fed had taken a deliberate route of pulling rates down during the 1990 recession and after: in just twelve months from late 1990 to late 1991, the Fed cut the discount rate in half, from 7 percent to 3.5 percent. Six months later, in mid-1992, the discount rate fell to 3 percent, a level where it had not been since 1962. "Real" short-term rates—or rates after the effects of inflation were discounted—were near zero, providing what the Fed later said was needed accommodation to the economy's recovery.

In July 1991, expressing confidence in his inflation-fighting skills, President George Bush nominated Greenspan for a second four-year term as chair and a full fourteen-year term on the board of governors.

The Fed board took one other monetary policy step in the aftermath of the 1990 recession to ease what it viewed as a credit crunch threatening the economy. In April 1992 the board reduced from 12 percent to 10 percent the number of bank deposits above a threshold amount ($51.9 million in 1994) that must be set aside as reserves in vault cash or on deposit with the Fed. Deposits less than the threshold were subject to a statutory 3 percent reserve requirement.

The Fed also actively—and successfully—sought changes in international banking laws in 1991 following the scandal involving the Bank of Credit and Commerce International (BCCI) and its secret ownership of several large U.S. banks. The Fed eventually fined a top BCCI official $37 million. Nonetheless, the Fed's regulation of foreign banks suffered a blow in 1995: When it closed the U.S. operations of Japan's Daiwa Bank for fraud in bond trading, critics faulted both the Fed and the Federal Reserve Bank of New York for overlooking a problem that dated back more than a decade.

In February 1994, somewhat to the consternation of financial markets and policymakers, the FOMC began edging rates higher, as a stronger economy posed the threat of resurgent inflation. Six more hikes followed over twelve months. By late 1995 the rates began to lower, and from January through November 1996 the short-term interest rates held steady at 5.25 percent. Through all these fluctuations the Fed's objectives continued to be low inflation and an unemployment rate no lower than 6 percent. In return, the Fed received some credit for a recovery that, though never robust, had been fairly steady.

In 1994, when the administration of Democratic President Bill Clinton proposed consolidating the federal government's banking regulators into a single agency—stripping the Fed of much of its bank regulatory authority—the Fed led the charge that blocked the proposed change. However, Greenspan suffered little lasting enmity from the administration or from Congress: he was renominated to his third term as chair by Clinton in 1996 and was confirmed with strong bipartisan support. Greenspan's consistent emphasis on "slow growth" had helped lower the unemployment rate to 5.1 percent and kept the annual inflation rate to 2.6 percent, a thirty-year low.

But the Fed under Greenspan has not just focused on inflation. It has also worked aggressively to transform the U.S. financial services industry. In particular, the Fed pushed hard for repeal of the Glass-Steagall Act of 1933, which had prohibited banks from dealing in and underwriting securities other than those issued by the government and backed by tax receipts. The Glass-Steagall Act also had prevented banks from affiliating with companies "principally engaged" in prohibited securities activities.

Despite Greenspan's strong backing for financial services overhaul and the efforts of federal regulators, including the Fed, to allow banks to dabble in securities and insurance products, Congress failed several times during the 1980s and 1990s to overturn Glass-Steagall, largely because compromise among the three main industry groups affected—banks, securities firms, and insurance companies—remained elusive.

In 1998 Congress took another run at overhauling the law, and Greenspan shed some of his natural reserve to stump for the cause. Greenspan also argued publicly with opponents of the bill, namely his close partner in overseeing the nation's economy, Treasury Secretary Robert E. Rubin. The disagreement between Greenspan and Rubin centered on how new financial conglomerates in a post–Glass-Steagall world would organize their banking, brokerage, and insurance arms, and on who would regulate the new conglomerates. Greenspan favored a system in which banks could form holding companies that engaged in traditional banking activities as well as insurance and securities underwriting, merchant banking, and real estate development. Under Greenspan's plan, each endeavor would be under the umbrella of the holding company but would function as a separate business with its own bottom line. The new financial services conglomerates would be regulated by the Fed. Rubin argued that such a structure would disadvantage smaller institutions that could not afford to set up an elaborate system. Rubin favored allowing the organization of operating subsidiaries without a holding company, which would essentially leave the brokerage and insurance operations as a part of the parent bank.

Greenspan's plan received a boost early in 1999, when Rubin's retirement as Treasury secretary removed a major opponent to the chair's proposal. At the same time, various finance-related industries put aside their differences and began aggressively pushing legislation that resembled Greenspan's proposal. Such a bill cleared Congress and was signed into law by Clinton in November of that year.

Meanwhile, the economy had continued to improve, culminating in record-breaking stock market highs during the late 1990s and into 2000. Despite the financial peaks, the Fed remained on guard for inflationary trends that could sidetrack the country's growth. A brief dip in the stock market during the summer of 1998 had prompted the Fed to make three quarter-point rate cuts, bringing the federal funds rate down to 4.75 percent. The tactic worked, and the market rose to new highs.

But by the middle of 1999 the Fed had once again become concerned about the threat of inflation. These fears were reinforced when the unemployment rate reached a twenty-nine-year low of just above 4 percent, driving up demand for skilled workers. The Fed chair and others worried that the high demand for workers would drive up wages, which would in turn increase the cost of products, fueling inflation.

Moreover, economic growth continued at what Greenspan believed was an unsustainable pace, with growth rates averaging 4.6 percent between 1997 and 1999. Even the serious fiscal crisis in Asia in 1997 did not slow down the American economy. In the first half of 2000 the economy was well into its ninth year of growth—humming along at 5 percent rate of growth.

In June 1999—just a year after the slight decrease in rates—the bank had made the first of six interest rate increases, in an effort to slow down the economy and prevent inflation. Over the next year, the federal funds rate was increased from 4.75 percent to 6.5 percent. The goal of the increases was to engineer what financial analysts called a "soft landing," an economy with slower but steady growth, coupled with low inflation.

THE FED IN THE 2000S

At first the Fed's strategy to slow the economy seemed to be working. In the second half of 2000, economic growth began to slow down. However, by early 2001 the "soft landing," according to some indicators, appeared to be turning into a "hard landing" or even a recession. Growth in the first months of the year almost sputtered to a halt, slowing to 1 percent. The formerly high-flying stock market dropped precipitously. In particular, the tech-heavy NASDAQ lost more than half its value in the last quarter of 2000 and first quarter of 2001.

Greenspan, renominated to a fourth term in 2000, took a drubbing. Some members of the financial community questioned why the Fed chair, who had coined the term "irrational exuberance" to describe investors' feverish purchase of overvalued stock back in 1996, had not done more to prick the bubble in its early stages.

Still, Greenspan continued to be generally regarded as a good steward of the economy. The new president, George W. Bush, helped to reinforce this image by meeting with the Fed chief before his inauguration to express total confidence in his abilities. Greenspan returned the favor in January 2001 by endorsing tax cuts—the cornerstone of Bush's economic agenda—as a way of giving the economy a much-needed boost.

The Fed took its own steps to respond to the slowdown with a number of deep interest rate cuts. The first came in early January 2001 and took investors by surprise. The half-point reduction gave the markets a short-term boost but did little to dispel the general gloom hanging over the economy. When the Fed cut rates for a third time in March—once again by a half point, leaving short-term rates at 5 percent—the markets actually dropped precipitously. By August the Fed had slashed rates to 3.75 percent, down from 6.5 percent at the beginning of the year.

The terrorist attacks in September dealt a major blow to the economy. When the stock market reopened six days after the attacks, understandably skittish investors reacted by selling: equity markets tumbled—7 percent on the first day and an additional 5 percent later that week. The Fed sought to reassure with two cuts of 0.5 percent each within three weeks of the attacks. By December the Fed had cut rates a record eleven times that year, leaving rates at a forty-year low of 1.75 percent.

Despite the uncertainties created by the terrorist attacks, Greenspan gave a guardedly encouraging assessment of the economy in testimony to Congress early in 2002. It was at that time, however, that news of the Enron scandal broke, and the country learned that the energy company had been using stock options bestowed on its executives to inflate its stock prices artificially. Corporate accountability leapt onto the congressional agenda. Although President Bush denounced the financial shenanigans, he was put on the defense when the GAO decided to sue the administration to obtain the list of participants in Vice President Dick Cheney's energy task force sessions the previous year.

Greenspan and Bush had their first significant public disagreement over how to reform the expensing of stock options. As news broke that other major companies—WorldCom, Tyco, and Xerox—also used stock options to inflate earnings, Greenspan advocated for corporations being required to state stock options as expenses, warning of the "infectious greed" of executives. Meanwhile, Bush supported maintaining the status quo of requiring companies to include unexercised options in their calculations of the number of outstanding shares.

Current Issues

With Republicans regaining control of both chambers of Congress following the 2002 elections, President Bush seemed poised to enact further tax cuts in 2003, touting them as a necessary stimulant to the still skittish economy. However, Greenspan sent mixed signals regarding Bush's proposed tax cut. While stating that the elimination of dividend taxation was sound economic policy, the Fed chair noted that the effects would be negligible in the short term. Furthermore, he said that any cuts should be offset by cuts in spending to prevent further ballooning of the federal deficit.

In the months leading up to the war in Iraq, energy prices spiked, with prices peaking in late February. Analysts were unsettled by unexpected news that the country had lost 308,000 jobs in February, with nationwide unemployment rising to 5.8 percent. When the Fed met for their March meeting, war seemed imminent and uncertainty about which way the economy was headed abounded. The Fed declined to cut interest rates below the current 1.25 percent but signaled that it would keep a close watch on war developments and act quickly if necessary.

As the United States made steady progress in toppling the Iraqi regime in March and April, energy prices dropped and the stock market rallied. Greenspan continued to be cautiously optimistic about the future of the economy, citing its ability in dealing with shocks of the past few years, including the terrorist attacks, the accounting scandals, and the decline in stock prices. Some economists dissented, saying that the problems were deeper than the war and high energy prices.

At its May 2003 meeting the Fed again left interest rates unchanged at the historically low levels. Greenspan even hinted at further cuts in the near future. Greenspan's new concern was the "unwelcome substantial fall in inflation"—or deflation. Deflationary spirals are a dire threat to the economy: consumers and businesses reduce spending while unemployment rises. Whether fighting inflation or deflation, the Fed chair retained the confidence of the administration, and Bush announced in April that Greenspan had done a "good enough job" to be reappointed when his term was up in 2004.

■ AGENCY ORGANIZATION

Biographies

ALAN GREENSPAN, CHAIR

Appointment: Nominated by President Reagan, confirmed by the Senate Aug. 3, 1987; term expired Jan. 31, 1992. Renominated by President Bush, confirmed by the Senate Feb. 27, 1992; term expires Jan 31, 2006.

Born: March 6, 1926, New York, NY.

Education: New York University, B.S. in economics, 1948, M.A. in economics, 1950, Ph.D. in economics, 1977.

Profession: Economist.

Political Affiliation: Republican.

Previous Career: Greenspan was chair and president of Townsend-Greenspan & Co. from 1954 to 1974 and from 1977 to 1987. He served on the board of economists for *Time magazine* from 1971 to 1974 and from 1977 to 1987. He was an adjunct professor at New York University's Graduate School of Business Administration from 1977 to 1987. From 1974 to 1977 and from 1981 to 1987, Greenspan served as chair of the President's Council of Economic Advisers. From 1981 to 1983 he was chair of the National Commission on Social Security Reform and the President's Foreign Intelligence Advisory Board. As chair of the Federal Reserve Board, Greenspan also is chair of the Federal Open Market Committee.

ROGER W. FERGUSON JR., VICE CHAIR

Appointment: Nominated by President Clinton to an unexpired term, confirmed by the Senate Nov. 5, 1997; confirmed by President Bush July 26, 2001; term expires Jan. 31, 2004.

Born: Oct. 28, 1951, Washington, DC.

Education: Harvard University, B.A. in economics, 1973; Harvard University, J.D. in law, 1979; Harvard University, Ph.D. in economics, 1981.

Profession: Investment firm executive/researcher.

Political Affiliation: Democrat.

Previous Career: Ferguson was a partner at McKinsey and Company, an international management consulting firm where he managed studies for various financial institutions from 1984 to 1997. From 1981 to 1984, Ferguson was an attorney with the New York City office of Davis Polk and Wardwell.

EDWARD M. GRAMLICH, GOVERNOR

Appointment: Nominated by President Clinton to an unexpired term, confirmed by the Senate Nov. 5, 1997; term expires Jan. 31, 2008.

Born: June 18, 1939, Rochester, NY.

Education: Williams College, B.A., 1961; Yale University, M.A. in economics, 1962; Yale University, Ph.D. in economics, 1965.

Profession: Government official and educator.

Political Affiliation: None.

Previous Career: Prior to his appointment, Gramlich served as the Dean of the School of Public Policy at the University of Michigan. He also was a professor of economics and public policy at the University of Michigan from 1976 to 1997. He also served as the chair of the Quadrennial Advisory Council on Social Security and as deputy and acting director of the Congressional Budget Office in 1986 to 1987. He also served as the director of the Policy Research Division at the Office of Economic Opportunity (1971 to 1973) and was a senior fellow at the Brookings Institution (1973 to 1976).

DONALD L. KOHN, GOVERNOR

Appointment: Took office on Aug. 5, 2002, for a full term; term expires Jan. 31, 2016.

Born: Nov. 7, 1942, Philadelphia, PA.

Education: College of Wooster, B.A. in economics, 1964; University of Michigan, Ph.D. in economics, 1971.

Profession: Economist.

Previous Career: Dr. Kohn is a veteran of the Federal Reserve System. Before becoming a member of the Board, he served on its staff as Advisor to the Board for Monetary Policy (2001–2002), Secretary of the Federal Open Market Committee (1987–2002), Director of the Division of Monetary Affairs (1987–2001), and Deputy Staff Director for Monetary and Financial Policy (1983–1987). He also held several positions in the Board's Division of Research and Statistics; Associate Director (1981–1983), Chief of Capital Markets (1978–1981), and Economist (1975–1978).

SUSAN SCHMIDT BIES, GOVERNOR

Appointment: Confirmed by the Senate Dec. 7, 2001; term expires Jan. 31, 2012.

Born: May 5, 1947, Buffalo, NY.

Education: State College of N.Y., B.S. in education, 1967; Northwestern University, M.A. in economics, 1968; Northwestern University, Ph.D. in economics, 1972.

Profession: Professor, Economist.

Previous Career: Before becoming a member of the Board, Dr. Bies was Executive Vice President for Risk Management and Auditor at First Tennessee National Corporation, Memphis, Tennessee (1995–2001). From 1979–1995, she served in various other positions at First Tennessee, including Executive Vice President and Chief Financial Officer, Senior Vice President and Treasurer, Vice President for Corporate Development, Tactical Planning Manager, and Economist. Dr. Bies was also an Associate Professor of Economics, Rhodes College (1977–1979), Assistant Professor of Economics, Wayne State (1972–1977), and Chief Regional and Banking Structure Economist at the Federal Reserve Bank of St. Louis (1970–1972).

MARK W. OLSON, GOVERNOR

Appointment: Took office on Dec. 7, 2001, to fill an expired term; term expires Jan. 31, 2010.

Born: March 17, 1943, Fergus Falls, MN.

Education: St. Olaf College, B.A. in economics, 1965.

Profession: Government official and businessman.

Previous Career: Before becoming a member of the Board, Mr. Olson served as Staff Director of the Securities Subcommittee of the Banking, Housing, and Urban Affairs Committee, U.S. Senate (2000–2001). From 1988–1999, Mr. Olson served as a partner with Ernst & Young LLP and its predecessor, Arthur Young & Company. From 1991–1992 Mr. Olson was selected to join a Treasury Department effort to assist Eastern European bankers in adapting to a free-market economy.

BEN S. BERNANKE, GOVERNOR

Appointment: Took office on Aug. 5, 2002, to fill an expired term; term expires Jan. 31, 2004.

Born: Dec. 13, 1953, Augusta, GA.

Education: Harvard University, B.A. in economics, 1975; Massachusetts Institute of Technology, Ph.D. in economics, 1979.

Profession: Professor.

Previous Career: Before becoming a member of the Board, Dr. Bernanke was the Howard Harrison and Gabrielle Snyder Beck Professor of Economics and Public Affairs and Chair of the Economics Department at Princeton University (1996–2002). Dr. Bernanke had served as a Professor of Economics and Public Affairs at Princeton since 1985. At the time of his appointment, he had already served the Federal Reserve System in several roles. He had been a visiting scholar at the Federal Reserve Banks of Philadelphia (1987–1989), Boston (1989–1990), and New York (1990–1991, 1994–1996), and he had served on the Academic Advisory Panel at the Federal Reserve Bank of New York (1990–2002).

Headquarters and Divisions

BOARD OF GOVERNORS

Establishes and implements the government's monetary policy. Has broad supervisory and regulatory responsibilities over state-chartered banks that are members of the Federal Reserve System, bank holding companies, and operations of foreign banks in the United States.

Establishes reserve requirements for all depository institutions that offer transaction accounts or nonpersonal time accounts, reviews and acts on discount rate recommendations of the boards of directors of Federal Reserve banks, and issues regulations governing the administration of the discount window at those banks.

Exercises supervisory and regulatory responsibilities over the laws that regulate foreign operations of member banks and administers the laws that regulate the actions of foreign bank operations in the United States. Directed by Congress to write rules for and to implement a number of major consumer credit protection laws, including the

Truth in Lending Act and the Equal Credit Opportunity Act.

Submits an annual report to Congress and makes available detailed statistics and other information relating to the system's activities and the nation's money supply through a variety of publications, including the monthly *Federal Reserve Bulletin*.

Submits a biannual written report to Congress on the state of the economy and monetary policy.

Chair

Alan Greenspan .... (202) 452–3201
Fax .... (202) 452–3819

Vice Chair

Roger W. Ferguson Jr. .... (202) 452–3735
Fax .... (202) 452–3819

Governors

Edward M. Gramlich................... (202) 452–3213
Susan Schmidt Bies
Mark W. Olson
Ben S. Bernanke
Donald L. Kohn

FEDERAL OPEN MARKET COMMITTEE

The principal instrument used by the Federal Reserve to implement national monetary policy. Responsible for determining what transactions the Federal Reserve will conduct in the open financial marketplace. Through frequent buying and selling of U.S. government securities or the securities of federal agencies, the manager of the System Open Market Account increases or decreases bank reserves in keeping with the instructions and directives issued by the committee. When purchases are made on behalf of the Open Market Account, reserves are increased and more money is injected into the financial system. When sales are made by the account manager, the buyers must take money out of circulation to pay for the securities acquired, thus reducing the money supply. In addition to operations in the domestic securities market, the FOMC authorizes and directs operations in foreign exchange markets. The Federal Reserve Bank of New York executes all such transactions and makes allocations among the Reserve banks according to a formula approved by the board of governors.

The FOMC is composed of the seven members of the board of governors and five Reserve bank presidents, one of whom is the president of the Federal Reserve Bank of New York, who serves on a continuous basis. The other bank presidents serve one-year terms, Jan. 1 to Dec. 31, on a rotating basis. One member is elected from each of the following groups of Reserve banks: (1) Boston, Philadelphia, Richmond; (2) Cleveland, Chicago; (3) Atlanta, St. Louis, Dallas; and (4) Minneapolis, Kansas City, San Francisco. By statute the committee determines its own organization,

FEDERAL RESERVE SYSTEM

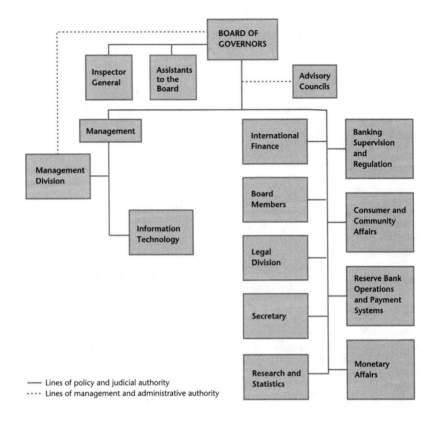

— Lines of policy and judicial authority
···· Lines of management and administrative authority

and by tradition it elects the chair of the board of governors to serve as its chair and the president of the Federal Reserve Bank of New York as its vice chair. The committee meets in the board's offices in Washington, DC, eight times yearly.

Chair
Alan Greenspan

Vice Chair
William J. McDonough (New York)

Other Members:
Board of Governors
Bank Presidents (for 2001)
1. Cathy E. Minehan (Boston)
2. William J. McDonough (New York)
3. William Poole (St. Louis)
4. Thomas M. Hoenig (Kansas City)
5. Michael H. Moscow (Chicago)

Bank Presidents (for 2002)
1. Anthony M. Santomero (Philadelphia)
2. William J. McDonough (New York)
3. Robert D. McTeer Jr. (Dallas)
4. Gary H. Stern (Minneapolis)
5. Jerry L. Jordan (Cleveland)

Bank Presidents (for 2003)
1. J. Alfred Broaddus Jr. (Richmond)
2. Michael H. Moscow (Chicago)
3. Jack Guynn (Atlanta)
4. Robert T. Parry (San Francisco)
5. William J. McDonough (New York)

Economists
David J. Stockton .... (202) 452–3301
Karen H. Johnson .... (202) 452–2345

General Counsel
J. Virgil Mattingly Jr. .... (202) 452–3430

Manager for Foreign Operations,
System Open Market Account

    Peter Fisher .... (212) 720–6180

Secretary and Economist

    Donald Kohn .... (202) 452–3761

ADVISORY COUNCILS

Consumer Advisory Council

Composed of thirty members representing the interests of the financial industry and consumers. Advises the board on the exercise of the Federal Reserve System's responsibilities under the Consumer Credit Protection Act. Meets approximately three times a year.

Chair

    Lauren Anderson

Vice Chair

    Dorothy Broodman

Contact

    Sandra Braunstein...................... (202) 452–3378

Federal Advisory Council

Composed of a representative from each Federal Reserve district. Members are selected annually by the board of directors of each Federal Reserve bank and may be reappointed. Meets four times a year. Confers with the board of governors on banking, business conditions, credit, and monetary policies, and makes recommendations regarding the affairs of the Federal Reserve System.

President

    Douglas A. Warner III

Vice President

    Lawrence K. Fish

Contact

    Sandra Putman-Hunter................ (202) 452–3379

Thrift Institutions Advisory Council

Composed of representatives from savings and loan associations, savings banks, and credit unions. Provides information and advice concerning the special needs and problems of thrift institutions.

President

    Charles R. Rinehart

Vice President

    William A. Fitzgerald

Contact

    Sandra Putman-Hunter................ (202) 452–3379

Academic Consultants

This ad hoc committee provides a forum for the exchange of views between the board and the academic community in economics and banking. Meetings are held in

Washington, DC, three to four times a year. For information, contact the Office of the Secretary *(p. 179)*.

DIVISION OF BANKING SUPERVISION AND REGULATION

Informs the board about current developments in bank supervision and banking structure. Coordinates the system's bank supervision and examining activities and processes applications for permission to form or expand bank holding companies or make other changes in bank structure, such as adding branches. Administers the examiner training program.

Director

    Richard Spillenkothen .... (202) 452–2773

      Fax..................................... (202) 452–2770

Deputy Director

    Stephen Schemering .... (202) 452–2433

Application and Enforcement

    Herbert Biern.......................... (202) 452–2620

Accounting Policy and Regulatory Reporting

    Gerald A. Edwards Jr. .... (202) 452–2741

Global and Foreign Organizations

    Stephen M. Hoffman Jr. .... (202) 452–5271

Financial Analysis, Surveillance, and Risk Assessment

    James Houpt........................... (202) 452–3358

Capital Markets and Specialized Activities

    Michael G. Martinson .... (202) 452–3640

Staff Development and Program Review

    Sidney Sussan.......................... (202) 452–2638

Domestic Organizations

    Molly Wassom......................... (202) 452–2305

OFFICE OF BOARD MEMBERS

Provides direct staff support to the seven members of the board, provides secretarial help, implements actions taken by the board, assists divisions in implementing policy actions, assists board members in speech preparation, conducts special surveys and research assignments for board members, and answers selected correspondence. Responsible for public affairs and congressional liaison functions.

Congressional Liaison

    Donald J. Winn......................... (202) 452–3456

      Fax..................................... (202) 452–2611

Deputy Congressional Liaison

    Winthrop P. Hambley.................. (202) 452–3456

Public Affairs

    Lynn Fox............................... (202) 452–3204

DIVISION OF CONSUMER AND COMMUNITY AFFAIRS

Drafts, interprets, and administers regulations governing consumer protection laws, community reinvestment, and fair lending. Coordinates the system's supervision and examining activities to make sure state member banks comply with consumer protection regulations, and investigates consumer complaints against banks. Oversees a community affairs program that encourages banks to engage in community development projects. The Consumer Advisory Council, established in 1976 and composed of thirty members from across the country, meets quarterly to represent consumer and creditor interests before the board.

Director
Dolores S. Smith .... (202) 452–2631
Fax...................................... (202) 872–4995
Compliance, Fair Lending, and Enforcement
Shawn McNulty .... (202) 452–3946
Consumer Complaints
Maureen English .... (202) 452–3401
Regulations
Adrienne Hurt.......................... (202) 452–2412
Community Affairs and Consumer Advisory Council
Sandra Braunstein..................... (202) 452–3378

DIVISION OF RESERVE BANK OPERATIONS AND PAYMENT SYSTEMS

Ensures the accuracy of the Reserve bank balance sheets and the safekeeping of the bank's assets. Exercises control over Reserve bank expenditures and financial planning as well as coordinating currency and coin requirements for Reserve banks. Oversees the production and distribution of the Federal Reserve System's financial reports. Makes recommendations to the board on plans for new Reserve bank buildings and renovations to existing facilities; and reviews Reserve bank automation systems, including check, data processing, communications, and research systems. Also makes recommendations to the board on the payment system, and provides liaison with the Treasury Department in matters concerning government payment programs.

Director
Louise L. Roseman .... (202) 452–2789
Fax (202) 452–6474
Associate Director
Paul W. Bettge......................... (202) 452–3174
Assistant Director
Kenneth D. Buckley.................... (202) 452–3646
Assistant Director
Tillena G. Clark .... (202) 452–5810
Assistant Director
Joseph H. Hayes Jr..................... (202) 452–3660
Assistant Director
Jeffrey C. Margquardt................. (202) 452–2360
Assistant Director
Edgar A. Martindale .... (202) 452–3341

Assistant Director
Marsha Reidhill....................... (202) 452–2767
Assistant Director
Jeff J. Stehm.......................... (202) 452–2217
Assistant to Director
Lisa Hoskins .... (202) 452–3437

OFFICE OF THE INSPECTOR GENERAL

Investigates suspected cases of impropriety, wrongdoing, fraud, or waste and abuse in programs and operations administered or financed by the board.

Inspector General
Barry Snyder.......................... (202) 973–5003
Fax...................................... (202) 973–5044
Deputy Inspector General
Donald Robinson .... (202) 973–5020

DIVISION OF INTERNATIONAL FINANCE

Provides the board, the Federal Open Market Committee, and other Federal Reserve officials with assessments of current international economic and financial developments, principally those relating to the effects on the U.S. economy and world activity, and the effects of the world economy on U.S. economic and financial conditions. Provides economic data and analyses for public release.

Director
Karen H. Johnson .... (202) 452–2345
Fax...................................... (202) 452–6424
Deputy Director
David H. Howard .... (202) 452–3796
Deputy Director
Vincent R. Reinhart................... (202) 452–2007
Associate Director
Thomas A. Connors................... (202) 452–3639
Associate Director
Dale W. Henderson .... (202) 452–2343
Assistant Director
Richard T. Freeman .... (202) 452–2344
Assistant Director
William L. Helkie..................... (202) 452–3836
Assistant Director
Steven B. Kamin...................... (202) 452–3339
Assistant Director
Ralph W. Tryon....................... (202) 452–2368
Assistant to the Director
Michael D. Gilbert .... (202) 452–2308

LEGAL DIVISION

Provides legal advice in support of board statutory and regulatory responsibilities. Prepares legal analyses and drafts proposals for use by the board in implementing statutory provisions. Represents the board in civil litigation and in administrative proceedings. Aids other divisions in the following areas: contracting; fiscal agency activities; Federal Reserve Bank matters; environment and labor law; personnel and supervisory enforcement matters; preparing draft legislation or comments on proposed legislation; and assisting in the preparation of board member testimony. Also prepares, interprets, and distributes information about board decisions, regulations, rules, and instructions. Advises the board of governors and acts as general counsel to the FOMC.

General Counsel
> J. Virgil Mattingly Jr. .... (202) 452–3294
> Fax .... (202) 452–3101

International Banking
> Kathleen O'Day .... (202) 452–3786

Litigation and Enforcement
> Richard Ashton .... (202) 452–3750

Monetary and Reserve Bank Affairs
> Oliver Ireland .... (202) 452–3625

Bank Holding Company
> Scott Alvarez .... (202) 452–3583

OFFICE OF STAFF DIRECTOR FOR MANAGEMENT

Responsible for planning and coordinating the board's operations and activities, including building administration, budget preparation, accounting, and personnel management. Coordinates contingency planning operations and equal employment opportunity programs. The staff director is a designated official of the board's occupational safety and health program.

Staff Director
> Stephen R. Malphrus .... (202) 452–3764
> Fax .... (202) 728–5832

MANAGEMENT DIVISION

Maintains the board's account books and directs its internal financial management program, draws up the annual budget, and supervises the receipt and disbursement of funds. Reviews and analyzes the board's use of resources and makes recommendations on developing new programs and improving existing ones.

Financial Function
> Stephen J. Clark .... (202) 452–3551
> Fax .... (202) 452–6490

Human Resources Function
> Darrell R. Pauley .... (202) 452–3486

Equal Employment Opportunity
> Sheila Clark .... (202) 452–2883

DIVISION OF SUPPORT SERVICES

Provides building management and maintenance; security; publications printing and distribution; and purchasing, contracting, and supply services.

Director
> Robert E. Frazier .... (202) 452–3816

DIVISION OF INFORMATION RESOURCES MANAGEMENT

Provides telecommunication services for the board of governors, including maintenance and storage of data files and an extensive distribution processing network facility.

Director
> Richard Stevens .... (202) 452–2664
> Fax .... (202) 872–7566

Deputy Director
> Marianne Emerson .... (202) 452–2045

Associate Director
> Ray Massey .... (202) 452–2042

Associate Director
> Maureen Hannan .... (202) 452–3618

C & CA & FFIEC Systems
> Wayne Edmondson .... (202) 728–5814

Financial Systems
> Ray Massey (acting) .... (202) 452–2042

Security, Systems, and Data Center
> Day Radebaugh Jr. .... (202) 452–2052

SECY & Regulatory Systems
> Geary Cunningham. .... (202) 452–3886

Statistical Services
> Po Kim .... (202) 452–3842

Supervisory Systems
> Sharon Mowry .... (202) 452–2554

Telecommunications
> Sue Marycz .... (202) 728–5839

DIVISION OF MONETARY AFFAIRS

Plans and coordinates the development of monetary policy, which includes market discount policy and reserve requirement policy. Directs the activities of the FOMC staff and conducts research on domestic and international finance and securities credit regulation. Also involved in interagency activities to coordinate the planning and development of economic policy. Acts as liaison with the trading desk at the Federal Reserve Bank of New York in connection with open market operations. Also acts as a liaison with the Treasury Department and other agencies in the domestic financial area. On foreign exchange market operations, coordinates with the system account manager and the Treasury Department.

Director

Donald Kohn .... (202) 452–3761

Fax .... (202) 452–2301

Deputy Director

David Lindsey .... (202) 452–2601

Monetary and Financial Market Analysis

Brian Madigan.......................... (202) 452–3828

Banking Analysis

Brian Madigan.......................... (202) 452–3828

Monetary Studies

Richard Porter.......................... (202) 452–2661

Monetary and Reserve Analysis

Bill Whitesell .... (202) 452–2967

DIVISION OF RESEARCH AND STATISTICS

Prepares and develops economic and financial information needed by Fed officials to formulate credit and monetary policies and to maintain current operations of the board and the Federal Reserve System. Also supplies economic data and analyses for public release. Most of the data is available in various publications *(see Publications, p. 191)*.

Director

David Stockton.......................... (202) 452–3301

Fax .... (202) 452–5296

Automation and Research Computing

Michael Cringoli .... (202) 728–5806

Capital Markets

Nellie Lang.............................. (202) 452–2918

Macroeconomic Analysis

William Wascher .... (202) 452–3702

Economic Information Management

Sandra Connor.......................... (202) 452–3710

Economic Editing

Ellen Dykes .... (202) 452–3952

Financial Reports

Mary West .... (202) 452–3829

Financial Structure

Robin Proger .... (202) 452–3906

Fiscal Analysis

Wolfhard Ramm........................ (202) 452–2381

Flow of Funds and Savings

Eric Engen .... (202) 452–2980

Industrial Output

Carol Corrado.......................... (202) 452–3521

Macroeconomic and Quantitative Studies

David Reisheimer .... (202) 452–2941

Microstatistics

Daryl Parke .... (202) 452–2470

Monetary and Financial Studies

Diana Hancock.......................... (202) 452–3019

Research Library

Susan Vincent.......................... (202) 452–3398

Trading Risk Analysis

Michael Gibson........................ (202) 452–2495

OFFICE OF THE SECRETARY

Coordinates and handles items requiring board action including the following: preparing agendas for board meetings; implementing actions taken at board meetings; preparing, indexing, and circulating minutes of board meetings; and participating in the drafting of Federal Reserve regulations, rules, and procedures. Also performs the same functions for the Federal Advisory Council and coordinates communication between the board and the conference of presidents and the conference of first vice presidents of Federal Reserve banks. Makes arrangements for individuals and groups visiting the board and maintains custody of and provides reference service for official records of the board. Produces the *Federal Reserve Regulatory Service* and handles correspondence and freedom of information requests.

Secretary

Jennifer Johnson .... (202) 452–3257

Fax .... (202) 452–3819

Associate Secretaries

Robert deV. Frierson................... (202) 452–3711

Barbara R. Lowrey .... (202) 452–3742

Clearing and Correspondence

Marilyn Barron......................... (202) 452–2506

Freedom of Information

Jeanne McLaughlin..................... (202) 452–2407

Protocol

Barbara F. Driggins..................... (202) 452–3126

Records

Anita Pintado........................... (202) 452–1927

Regulatory Improvement

Barbara R. Lowrey .... (202) 452–3742

FEDERAL RESERVE BANKS

The twelve Federal Reserve districts were created on the basis of trade areas and related economic considerations and do not always follow state lines. There is a Federal Reserve bank in each district, and ten of the banks have branch offices. The Reserve banks are the principal medium through which the policies and supervisory powers of the Federal Reserve System are implemented. Responsibilities of the banks include providing local and nationwide facilities for the processing of checks and other money instruments, meeting the currency needs of the country, holding the reserve accounts required of financial institutions, extending credit to depository institutions, supervising and collecting data on the banking system, acting as a fiscal agent for the government, maintaining government accounts, selling and redeeming government securities, and administering regionally the policies of the board of governors and the FOMC. The chief executive officer of each bank is its president. The president and first vice president are appointed by the board of directors, with approval of the Fed's board of governors, for a term of five years.

Directors of Federal Reserve District Banks

Each of the twelve Federal Reserve district banks has nine directors, elected or appointed for staggered three-year terms. They are divided into three classes of three directors each; the term of one director in each class expires every year.

The classes represent member banks (Class A) and the public (Classes B and C). Class A and B directors are elected by the member banks in the district. Class C directors are appointed by the board of governors.

Member banks are divided into categories according to capitalization: Group 1 (large banks), Group 2 (medium banks), and Group 3 (small banks). Each group elects one Class A and one Class B director.

Class A directors are almost always member bank officers or directors. Class B directors are selected with consideration to agricultural, commercial, industrial service, labor, and consumer interests. Class B and C directors may not be officers, directors, or employees of any bank. Class A and B directors may be reelected.

One of the Class C directors is appointed by the board to act as chair, and another is appointed as deputy chair. In the absence of the chair and deputy chair, the third Class C director acts as chair. Class C directors are not reappointed if they have served two full terms of three years each.

The directors help formulate monetary policy through biweekly recommendations to the board of governors on the discount rate their banks charge on collateralized loans to depository institutions. They prescribe the bylaws under which the bank's general business is conducted, and oversee management of the bank. The directors appoint all officers and recommend their salaries, decide on promotion or change in office personnel, supervise internal auditing, and approve the annual budget for their bank.

Directors of Federal Reserve Branch Banks

Branches have either five or seven directors. A majority of these are appointed by the board of directors of the parent Reserve bank; the others are appointed by the Fed's board of governors. The chair of a branch bank board is chosen from among the directors appointed by the board of governors. Branch bank directors must be individuals whose business and financial interests are primarily within and representative of the branch territory. Directors serve for three years when the branch board consists of seven people, or for two years when the branch board consists of five people.

Branches perform for their territories most of the functions performed at the district level.

Federal Reserve District Banks

DISTRICT 1
(northern CT, MA, ME, NH, RI, VT)

Federal Reserve Bank of Boston
600 Atlantic Ave.
Boston, MA 02106
(617) 973–3000
Cathy E. Minehan, president

DISTRICT 2
(southern CT, northern NJ, NY, PR, VI)

Federal Reserve Bank of New York
33 Liberty St.
New York, NY 10045
(212) 720–5000
William J. McDonough, president

Buffalo Branch
160 Delaware Ave.
P.O. Box 961
Buffalo, NY 14240–0961
(716) 849–5000
Carl Turnipseed, vice president

DISTRICT 3
(DE, southern NJ, eastern and central PA)

Federal Reserve Bank of Philadelphia
10 Independence Mall
Philadelphia, PA 19106
(215) 574–6000
Edward G. Boehne, president

DISTRICT 4
(eastern KY, OH, western PA, northern WV)

Federal Reserve Bank of Cleveland
1455 E. 6th St.
P.O. Box 6387
Cleveland, OH 44101
(216) 579–2000
Jerry L. Jordan, president

Cincinnati Branch

150 E. 4th St.
P.O. Box 999
Cincinnati, OH 45201–0999
(513) 721–4787
Charles Cerino, vice president

Pittsburgh Branch

717 Grant St.
P.O. Box 299
Pittsburgh, PA 15230
(412) 261–7800
Robert B. Schaub, vice president

DISTRICT 5

(DC, MD, NC, SC, VA, eastern and southern WV)

Federal Reserve Bank of Richmond

701 E. Byrd St.
P.O. Box 27622
Richmond, VA 23261
(804) 697–8000
J. Alfred Broaddus Jr., president

Baltimore Branch

502 S. Sharp St.
P.O. Box 1378
Baltimore, MD 21203
(410) 576–3300
William Tignanelli, vice president

Charlotte Branch

530 E. Trade St.
P.O. Box 30248
Charlotte, NC 28230
(704) 358–2100
Dan M. Bechter, vice president

DISTRICT 6

(AL, FL, GA, southern LA, southern MS, central and eastern TN)

Federal Reserve Bank of Atlanta

104 Marietta St. N.W.
Atlanta, GA 30303
(404) 521–8500
Jack Guynn, president

Birmingham Branch

1801 5th Ave. North
P.O. Box 830447
Birmingham, AL 35283–0447
(205) 731–8500
Fred Herr, vice president

Jacksonville Branch

800 Water St.
P.O. Box 929
Jacksonville, FL 32231–0044
(904) 632–1000
James Hawkins, vice president

Miami Branch

9100 N.W. 36th St.
P.O. Box 520847
Miami, FL 33152–0847
(305) 591–2065
James Curry III, vice president

Nashville Branch

301 8th Ave. North
Nashville, TN 37203
(615) 251–7100
Mel Purcell, vice president

New Orleans Branch

525 St. Charles Ave.
P.O. Box 61630
New Orleans, LA 70130–1630
(504) 593–3200
Robert Musso, vice president

DISTRICT 7

(IA, northern IL, central and northern IN, southern MI, southern WI)

Federal Reserve Bank of Chicago

230 S. La Salle St.
P.O. Box 834
Chicago, IL 60690–0834
(312) 322–5322
Michael H. Moskow, president

Detroit Branch

160 W. Fort St.
P.O. Box 1059
Detroit, MI 48231
(313) 961–6880
David Allardice, vice president

DISTRICT 8

(AR, southern IL, southern IN, western KY, northern MS, eastern MO, western TN)

Federal Reserve Bank of St. Louis

411 Locust St.
P.O. Box 442
St. Louis, MO 63166
(314) 444–8444
William Poole, president

Little Rock Branch

325 W. Capitol Ave.
P.O. Box 1261
Little Rock, AR 72203–1261
(501) 324–8300
Robert Hopkins, vice president

Louisville Branch

410 S. 5th St.
P.O. Box 32710
Louisville, KY 40232–2710
(502) 568–9200
Thomas Boone, vice president

Memphis Branch

200 N. Main St.
P.O. Box 407
Memphis, TN 38101–0407
(901) 523–7171
Martha Perine Beard, vice president

DISTRICT 9

(northern MI, MN, MT, ND, SD, northwestern WI)

Federal Reserve Bank of Minneapolis

90 Hennepin Ave.
P.O. Box 291
Minneapolis, MN 55480–0291
(612) 204–5000
Gary H. Stern, president

Helena Branch

100 Neill Ave.
Helena, MT 59601
(406) 447–3800
John Johnson, vice president

DISTRICT 10

(CO, KS, western MO, NE, northern NM, OK, WY)

Federal Reserve Bank of Kansas City

925 Grand Blvd.
P.O. Box 2076
Kansas City, MO 64188–0001
(816) 881–2000
Thomas M. Hoenig, president

Denver Branch

1020 16th St.
P.O. Box 5228, Terminal Annex
Denver, CO 80217
(303) 572–2300
Carl M. Gambs, vice president

Oklahoma City Branch

226 Dean A. McGee Ave.
P.O. Box 25129
Oklahoma City, OK 73125
(405) 270–8400
Mark L. Mullinix, vice president

Omaha Branch

2201 Farnam St.
P.O. Box 3958
Omaha, NE 68103
(402) 221–5500
Bradley C. Cloverdyke, vice president

DISTRICT 11

(northern LA, southern NM, TX)

Federal Reserve Bank of Dallas

2200 N. Pearl St.
Dallas, TX 75222
(214) 922–6000
Robert D. McTeer Jr., president

El Paso Branch
301 E. Main St.
P.O. Box 100
El Paso, TX 79999
(915) 544–4730
Sammie Clay, vice president

Houston Branch
1701 San Jacinto St.
P.O. Box 2578
Houston, TX 77252
(713) 659–4433
Robert Smith III, vice president

San Antonio Branch
126 E. Nueva St.
P.O. Box 1471
San Antonio, TX 78295
(210) 224–2141
James Stull, vice president

DISTRICT 12
(AK, AZ, CA, HI, ID, NV, OR, UT, WA)

Federal Reserve Bank of San Francisco
101 Market St.
P.O. Box 7702
San Francisco, CA 94120
(415) 974–2000
Robert T. Parry, president

Los Angeles Branch
950 S. Grand Ave.
P.O. Box 2077, Terminal Annex
Los Angeles, CA 90051
(213) 683–2300
Mark Mullinix, vice president

Portland Branch
915 S.W. Stark St.
P.O. Box 3436
Portland, OR 97208
(503) 221–5900
Ray Lawrence, vice president

Salt Lake City Branch
120 S. State St.
P.O. Box 30780
Salt Lake City, UT 84125
(801) 322–7900
Andrea Wolcott, vice president

Seattle Branch
1015 2nd Ave.
P.O. Box 3567
Seattle, WA 98124
(206) 343–3600
Gordon Werkema, vice president

■ CONGRESSIONAL ACTION

Congressional Liaison
Donald Winn............................ (202) 452–3456

Committees and Subcommittees

HOUSE BANKING AND FINANCIAL SERVICES COMMITTEE
Subcommittee on Domestic and International Monetary Policy
B303 RHOB Washington, DC 20515
(202) 226–0473

HOUSE GOVERNMENT REFORM AND OVERSIGHT COMMITTEE
Subcommittee on National Economic Growth, Natural Resources, and Regulatory Affairs
B377 RHOB, Washington, DC 20515
(202) 225–4407

SENATE BANKING, HOUSING AND URBAN AFFAIRS COMMITTEE
SD-534, Washington, DC 20510
(202) 224–7391

Legislation
The Federal Reserve System was established under authority of the **Federal Reserve Act,** approved Dec. 23, 1913 (38 Stat. 251, 12 U.S.C. 221). The act was substantially amended by the **Banking Act of 1933,** also known as the **Glass-Steagall Act** (48 Stat. 162, 12 U.S.C. 227) and the **Banking Act of 1935** (49 Stat. 684, 12 U.S.C. 228). This legislation, as amended, embodies the basic authorization for the activities of the Federal Reserve System.

The Fed also has responsibility for the administration of other legislation. Although it has supervisory powers over all member banks, its regulatory powers for the legislation listed below extend only to state-chartered banks that have voluntarily become members of the system. The following is a list of the major legislation administered in part by the

Federal Reserve. The regulation letter in brackets after each statute refers to the Federal Reserve regulation that covers that law.

Federal Trade Commission Act of 1914 (38 Stat. 719, 15 U.S.C. 41). Signed by the president Sept. 26, 1914. Prohibited unfair or deceptive banking practices. [Regulation AA]

Securities Act of 1933 (48 Stat. 74, 15 U.S.C. 77a). Signed by the president May 27, 1933. Originally administered by the Federal Trade Commission, the act exempted banks from registering securities.

Securities Exchange Act of 1934 (48 Stat. 881, 15 U.S.C. 78b). Signed by the president June 6, 1934. Required registration of securities (applicable to state member banks with more than $1 million in assets and more than 500 stockholders). [Regulations T, U, G, and X]

Defense Production Act of 1950 and **Executive Order 10480** (64 Stat. 798, 50 U.S.C. app. 2091). Signed by the president Sept. 8, 1950. Guaranteed the financing of contractors, subcontractors, and others involved in national defense work. [Regulation V]

Bank Holding Company Act of 1956 (70 Stat. 133, 12 U.S.C. 1841). Signed by the president May 9, 1956. Regulated the creation and expansion of bank holding companies. [Regulation Y]

Bank Mergers and Consolidation Act of 1960 (74 Stat. 129, 12 U.S.C. 1828). Signed by the president May 13, 1960. Required that all proposed bank mergers receive prior approval from the federal regulatory agency that will have jurisdiction over the surviving bank.

Bank Service Corporation Act (76 Stat. 1132, 12 U.S.C. 1861). Signed by the president Oct. 23, 1962. Permitted certain federally supervised banks to form service corporations to perform clerical, bookkeeping, and data processing functions.

Bank Mergers Act of 1966 (80 Stat. 7, 12 U.S.C. 1828). Signed by the president Feb. 21, 1966. Established a procedure for review of proposed bank mergers so as to eliminate the necessity for dissolution of merged banks.

Truth in Lending Act (82 Stat. 146, 15 U.S.C. 1601). Signed by the president May 29, 1968. Required lenders and merchants to inform customers of the total cost of loans and installment purchase plans in terms of annual rates to be charged; permitted customers to make valid cost comparisons between lending rates or installment plans of different stores or lending institutions. Also prohibited unsolicited distribution of credit cards and limited the owner's liability for unauthorized use of lost or stolen cards. [Regulation Z]

Bank Protection Act of 1968 (82 Stat. 294, 12 U.S.C. 1881). Signed by the president July 7, 1968. Required establishment of security system standards for banking institutions. [Regulation P]

Credit Control Act of 1969 (83 Stat. 376, 12 U.S.C. 1901). Signed by the president Dec. 23, 1969. Authorized the board of governors, at the direction of the president, to impose controls on all forms of consumer credit.

Currency and Foreign Transactions Reporting Act (84 Stat. 1118, 31 U.S.C. 1051). Signed by the president Oct. 26, 1970. Required banks, citizens, and businesses to maintain adequate records of foreign currency transactions. [Regulations M, N]

Fair Credit Reporting Act (84 Stat. 1128, 15 U.S.C. 1681). Signed by the president Oct. 26, 1970. Regulated credit information and use. [Regulation Z]

NOW Accounts Act (87 Stat. 342, 12 U.S.C. 1832). Signed by the president Aug. 16, 1973. Regulated interest-bearing checking accounts. [Regulation J]

Equal Credit Opportunity Act (88 Stat. 1521, 15 U.S.C. 1691). Signed by the president Oct. 28, 1974. Prohibited credit discrimination against women; amended in 1975 to include discrimination based on age, race, color, religion, or national origin. [Regulation B]

Home Mortgage Disclosure Act of 1975 (89 Stat. 1125, 12 U.S.C. 2801). Signed by the president Dec. 31, 1975. Required lending institutions within standard metropolitan statistical areas (SMSAs) to disclose the number and amount of mortgage loans made annually to determine if banks are discriminating against certain city neighborhoods by refusing to make mortgage loans regardless of the creditworthiness of the potential borrower (practice known as "redlining"). [Regulation C]

Consumer Leasing Act of 1976 (90 Stat. 257, 15 U.S.C. 1601). Signed by the president March 23, 1976. Required full disclosure of terms of leases of personal property, including vehicles, appliances, and furniture. [Regulation Z]

Community Reinvestment Act of 1977 (91 Stat. 1147, 12 U.S.C. 2901–2905). Signed by the president Oct. 12, 1977. Required federal regulators of banks and savings and loan associations to encourage institutions they regulate to help meet the credit needs of their communities, particularly low- and moderate-income neighborhoods. [Regulation BB]

International Banking Act of 1978 (92 Stat. 607, 12 U.S.C. 3101–3108). Signed by the president Sept. 17, 1978. Provided for the federal regulation of foreign banks in domestic financial markets.

Electronic Fund Transfer Act of 1978 (92 Stat. 3728, 15 U.S.C. 1601 note). Signed by the president Nov. 10, 1978. Established rules relating to consumer liability for unauthorized use of an electronic fund transfer card and unsolicited issuance of cards by financial institutions. Prohibited creditors from making automatic repayment of loans a condition of extending credit; overdraft credit plans were exempted. [Regulation E]

Financial Institutions Regulatory and Interest Rate Control Act of 1978 (92 Stat. 3641, 12 U.S.C. 226 note). Signed by the president Nov. 10, 1978. Regulated the activities of individual bank officers. Provided for tighter controls on insider lending and interlocking directorates among financial institutions and expanded the authority of bank regulators.

Depository Institutions Deregulation and Monetary Control Act of 1980 (94 Stat. 132, 12 U.S.C. 226 note). Signed by the president March 31, 1980. Extended reserve requirements to all financial institutions, phased out interest rate ceilings over a six-year period, and allowed thrift institutions to offer a wider range of financial services.

Garn-St. Germain Depository Institutions Act of 1982 (96 Stat. 1469, 12 U.S.C. 226 note). Signed by the president Oct. 15, 1982. Expanded the Federal Deposit Insurance Corporation's (FDIC) powers to assist troubled banks by allowing either direct or merger-related assistance (1) to prevent the closing of or to reopen any insured bank, or (2) when severe financial conditions threaten the stability of a significant number of banks or banks with significant financial resources. Provided FDIC assistance to holding companies, Federal Savings and Loan Insurance Corporation (FSLIC) insured institutions, or other persons relating to a merger with, or an acquisition of, an insured bank. Allowed commercial banks and mutual savings banks with assets of $500 million or more that are closed or, in the case of mutual savings banks, are in danger of closing, to be acquired on an interstate and/or cross-industry basis. Authorized the FSLIC and the FDIC to use their respective insurance funds to administer a three-year program in which qualified federally insured institutions may exchange their own capital instruments for promissory notes issued by federal insurance agencies. The program was designed for insured institutions having a net worth equal to or less than 3 percent of assets. Provided increased powers for federally chartered savings and loan associations and savings banks (thrift institutions), including: more liberal chartering options; the ability to offer stock; the authority to accept demand deposits from commercial, corporate, and agricultural customers who have established a loan relationship with the thrift institution; expanded real estate investment authority; and the ability to invest in a broad range of government securities (up to 10 percent of capital accounts for any one governmental unit). Authorized thrift institutions to originate or participate in commercial, corporate, and agricultural loans up to 5 percent of assets beginning Oct. 15, 1982 (7.5 percent for federal savings banks), and 10 percent after Jan. 1, 1984.

International Lending Supervision Act of 1983 (97 Stat. 1278, 12 U.S.C. 3901). Signed by the president Nov. 30, 1983. Increased the oversight responsibilities of the Federal Reserve in terms of the international lending procedures of U.S. banks. Required federal banking agencies to establish minimum capital levels for banking institutions, accounting fee regulations on international loans, and regulations for collection and disclosure of international lending data regarding the status of banks' outstanding loans to particular countries. Also required banks to maintain special reserves against loans that were unlikely to be paid off by a foreign borrower.

Competitive Equality Banking Act of 1987 (101 Stat. 581, 12 U.S.C. 1841 note). Signed by the president Aug. 10, 1987. Redefined "banks" as institutions that take deposits or write commercial loans. Prohibited limited service banks from engaging in banking activities without regulation.

Expedited Funds Availability Act (101 Stat. 635, 12 U.S.C. 4001). Signed by the president Aug. 10, 1987. Mandated timetables for check clearing and availability of funds. Required the Federal Reserve to reduce the amount of time for checks to clear.

Federal Deposit Insurance Corporation Improvement Act of 1991 (105 Stat. 2236, 12 U.S.C. 1811). Signed by the president Dec. 19, 1991. Required the most cost-effective method of resolving banks in danger of failing and improved supervisory and examination procedures. It also made additional resources available to the Bank Insurance Fund. Gave the Federal Reserve Board jurisdiction over all foreign banks in the United States.

Depository Institutions Disaster Relief Act of 1992 (106 Stat. 2771, 12 U.S.C. 1811 note). Signed by the president Oct. 23, 1992. Facilitated recovery from recent disasters by providing greater flexibility for depository institutions and their regulators.

Futures Trading Practices Act of 1992 (106 Stat. 3628, 7 U.S.C. 1 note). Signed by the president Oct. 28, 1992. Title 5 directed any contract market in stock index futures or options on stock index futures to submit to the board of governors any rule establishing or changing levels of either initial or maintenance margin on such contracts. Also permitted the board to delegate to the Commodity Futures Trading Commission its authority over margin levels for stock index contracts.

Housing and Community Development Act of 1992 (106 Stat. 3672, 42 U.S.C. 5301 note). Signed by the president Oct. 28, 1992. Established regulatory structure for government-sponsored enterprises (GSEs), combated money laundering, and provided regulatory relief to financial institutions.

Depository Institutions Disaster Relief Act of 1993 (107 Stat. 752, 12 U.S.C. 4008 note). Signed by the president Aug. 12, 1993. Authorized the board to make exceptions to the Truth in Lending and Expedited Funds Availability acts within major disaster areas.

Government Securities Act Amendments of 1993 (107 Stat. 2344, 15 U.S.C. 78a note). Signed by the president Dec. 17, 1993. Extended and revised rulemaking authority with respect to government securities under the federal securities laws.

Home Ownership and Equity Protection Act of 1994 (108 Stat. 2160, 12 U.S.C. 4701 note). Signed by the president Sept. 23, 1994. Part of a larger bill. Under title I, subtitle B, section 157, Fed's board of governors was directed to: (1) study and report to Congress on the adequacy of federal consumer protections in connection with an open-ended credit transaction secured by the consumer's principal dwelling; (2) report to Congress on whether, for purposes of such transactions, a more appropriate interest rate index exists than the yield on Treasury securities; and (3) conduct periodic public hearings on the home equity loan market and the adequacy of existing consumer protection laws to protect low-income consumers.

Interstate Banking Efficiency Act of 1994 (108 Stat. 2338, 12 U.S.C. 1811 note). Signed by the president Sept. 29, 1994. Permitted banks to operate networks of branch offices across state lines without having to set up separately capitalized subsidiary banks.

Farm Credit System Reform Act of 1996 (110 Stat. 162, 12 U.S.C. 20001 note). Signed by the president Feb. 10, 1996. Required federal reserve banks to act as depositaries, fiscal agents, or custodians of the Federal Agricultural Mortgage Corporation (FAMC). Required the book-entry system of the Fed to be made available to FAMC.

Economic Growth and Regulatory Paperwork Reduction Act of 1996 (110 Stat. 3009-32, 5 U.S.C. 3109). Signed by the president Sept. 30, 1996. Authorized the board of governors to exempt those transactions from the Truth in Lending Act (TILA) disclosure requirements when the board determined: (1) they are not necessary to effectuate its purposes; or (2) they do not provide a measurable benefit in the form of useful information or consumer protection. Required the board to publish its rationale for exemption at the time a proposed exemption is published for comment.

To Amend the Federal Reserve Act to Broaden the Range of Discount Window Loans. (113 Stat. 1638). Signed by the president on Dec. 6, 1999. Amended the Federal Reserve Act to allow the Federal Reserve to print more money for its "discount window," which extended credit to banks and served as a buffer against unexpected fluctuations in bank reserves. Permitted banks to offer additional types of collateral to receive credit at the discount window, including receipts of deposits and collections and agricultural securities.

Gramm-Leach-Bliley Act. (113 Stat. 1338, 12 U.S.C. 1811 note). Signed by the president on Nov. 12, 1999. Title I repealed provisions of the Banking Act of 1933 and the Bank Holding Act of 1956 to allow affiliations between banks and any financial company, including brokerage and insurance firms. Gave Federal Reserve supervisory oversight authority and responsibility for bank holding companies.

Uniting and Strengthening America by Providing Appropriate Tools Required to Intercept and Obstruct Terrorism Act of 2002 (USA Patriot Act) (115 Stat. 272, 18 U.S.C. 1 note). Signed by the president on Oct. 26, 2001. Title III, the International Money Laundering Abatement and Anti-Terrorist Financing Act of 2001, amended various federal banking laws, including the Bank Holding Company Act of 1956, the Fair Credit Reporting Act, the Federal Deposit Insurance Act, and the Federal Reserve Act. Directed certain government agencies, principally the Treasury Department in consultation with the Fed, to investigate and curtail money laundering and other activities that might be undertaken to finance terrorist actions or disrupt legitimate banking operations. Required securities brokers and dealers to submit reports regarding suspected money-laundering transactions. Required the Fed to consider an institution's ability to combat money laundering when evaluating proposed bank shares or mergers. Provided protection for Fed facilities and staff, including law enforcement officers authorized to carry firearms and make warrantless arrests. Allowed written employment references to contain suspicions of involvement in illegal activity.

▨ INFORMATION SOURCES

Internet

Board of Governors Web Site: http://www.federalreserve.gov. Includes information on Federal Reserve Banks nationwide and provides links to their Internet sites.

Telephone Contacts

Federal Reserve News Recording.......... (202) 452–3206

Information and Publications

KEY OFFICES

Board of Governors Public Affairs
20th and C Sts. N.W., Room B-2120
Washington, DC 20551
(202) 452–3204
Fax (202) 452–3819
Lynn S. Fox, assistant to the board

Acts as the spokesman for the board of governors and prepares all press releases. Also operates a daily telephone recording of Fed activities and releases; (202) 452–3206. Pamphlets and audio-visual materials are available from Publications Services, which also maintains all mailing lists for publications.

Board of Governors Consumer and Community Affairs

20th and C Sts. N.W.
Washington, DC 20551
(202) 452–2631
Dolores S. Smith, director

Administers the board's consumer protection responsibilities. Writes rules to implement consumer-related laws, for which the board has administrative responsibility, supervises enforcement with regard to state member banks, and operates a program to monitor and respond to consumer complaints. Oversees a program that encourages banks to engage in community economic development. Administers a program to educate financial institutions and assists the board's Public Affairs Office in developing consumer education materials. Also produces consumer education pamphlets, available from Publications Services.

Freedom of Information

Board of Governors Office of the Secretary
20th and C Sts. N.W., Room MP-500
Washington, DC 20551
(202) 452–2407
Jeanne McLaughlin, FOI officer

Federal Reserve Publications Services

20th and C Sts. N.W., Room MP-510
Mail Stop 138
Washington, DC 20551
(202) 452–3244
Linda Kyles, chief
Provides publications and price lists.

PUBLICATIONS

Contact Federal Reserve Publications Services for specific titles or a price list; the catalog, *Federal Reserve Board Publications*, is also available from any Federal Reserve district bank. Titles include:

Annual Report. Reviews monetary policy and the state of the economy for the previous year and reports on system operations. Also contains statistical charts and tables. Free.

Annual Statistical Digest. Provides economic and financial data for a broad range of users. Provides historical perspective and detailed series of statistics for years covered. No text accompanying tables; all explanations contained in notes to the tables.

Federal Reserve Bulletin. Monthly; includes articles on selected topics in economics, domestic and international business activity, and recent developments in banking. Separate tables include substantial statistics related to activity of various sectors of the economy.

Federal Reserve Regulatory Service. Monthly; loose-leaf service that includes all board statutes, rulings, regulations, staff opinions, and related interpretations and documents. Consists of three publications, with subject and citation indexes. The service includes the *Securities Credit Transactions Handbook* (Regulations G, T, U, and X and a list of over-the-counter margin stocks); *Monetary Policy and Reserve Requirements Handbook* (Regulations A, D, Q, and rules of the Depository Institutions Deregulation Committee); and the *Consumer and Community Affairs Handbook* (Regulations B, C, E, M, Z, AA, and BB). Handbooks also available individually.

The Federal Reserve System: Purposes and Functions. A detailed explanation of the work of the system, especially in developing monetary policy. Free.

Regulations of the Board of Governors of the Federal Reserve System. Full texts of regulations A through EE; each regulation is issued as an individual booklet, updated. Free.

Welcome to the Federal Reserve. Illustrated pamphlet outlining the system's background, structure, and functions. Includes description of the historical and architectural features of the board building.

Consumer Education Pamphlets. Issued by the board of governors and suited for classroom use. Single and multiple copies available at no charge. Titles include:

Consumer Handbook on Adjustable Rate Mortgages
Consumer Handbook to Credit Protection Laws
A Consumer's Guide to Mortgage Lock-Ins
A Consumer's Guide to Mortgage Refinancing
A Consumer's Guide to Mortgage Settlement Costs
A Guide to Business Credit for Women, Minorities, and Small Businesses
How to File a Consumer Credit Complaint
Making Deposits: When Will Your Money Be Available?
Series on the Structure of the Federal Reserve System:
- *The Board of Governors of the Federal Reserve System*
- *The Federal Open Market Committee*
- *Federal Reserve Bank Board of Directors*
- *Federal Reserve Banks*
- *Organization and Advisory Committees*

When Your Home Is on the Line: What You Should Know About Home Equity Lines of Credit

DATA AND STATISTICS

See Publications, above, for titles that include statistical information.

MEETINGS

The board of governors meets twice a week, usually on Monday and Wednesday, to consider matters relating to its supervisory, regulatory, and monetary responsibilities. Notices of open meetings are published in the *Federal Register* and are usually available in advance from the Freedom of Information and Public Affairs offices and the Treasury Department press rooms. Information about agenda items may be obtained from the Web site, www.federalreserve.gov/general, or from Public Affairs; (202) 452–3206. A daily news recording also gives details on meetings and press releases; (202) 452–3206.

Notices of meetings closed to the public are published in the *Federal Register,* identifying the official designated to provide information about the meeting. After the meeting has been held, a cassette recording and agenda are available. Special facilities are provided in the Freedom of Information Office, Room MP-500, for listening to recordings; cassettes may also be purchased.

Reference Resources

LIBRARIES

Federal Reserve Law Library
20th and C Sts. N.W., Room B-1066
Washington, DC 20551
(202) 452–3284
Rick McKinney, law librarian
Hours: 9:00 a.m. to 5:00 p.m.

Open to the public by appointment. Holds more than 26,000 volumes on banking legislation and regulation. Interlibrary loan service available within the Washington, DC, area.

Federal Reserve Research Library
20th and C Sts. N.W., Room B-C-241
Washington, DC 20551
(202) 452–3332
Susan Vincent, chief librarian
Hours: 9:00 a.m. to 5:00 p.m., Thursday only

Open to the public for research in fields of banking, finance, monetary and fiscal policy, economics, and the history and operation of the Federal Reserve System. Makes limited interlibrary loans within the Washington, DC, area.

Rules and Regulations
Federal Reserve System rules and regulations are published in the *Code of Federal Regulations,* Title 12. Proposed regulations, new final regulations, and updates to the *Code of Federal Regulations* are published in the daily *Federal Register.* (See appendix for information on how to obtain and use these publications.)

The pamphlet, *A Guide to Federal Reserve Regulations,* gives a brief summary of the regulations. Individual copies of each regulation also are available. They include the full text of each regulation, text of relevant statutes, and, in some cases, a section on interpretations. Both the *Guide* and the individual regulations may be obtained from Federal Reserve Publication Services.

Other Information Sources

NONGOVERNMENTAL ORGANIZATIONS
The following are some key organizations that monitor the Federal Reserve and related economic issues.

American Bankers Association
1120 Connecticut Ave. N.W.
Washington, DC 20036
(202) 663–5000
Fax (202) 828–4532
Internet: http://www.aba.com

American Business Conference
1730 K St. N.W., #1200
Washington, DC 20006
(202) 822–9300
Fax (202) 467–4070

American Enterprise Institute for Public Policy Research
Economic Policy Studies
1150 17th St. N.W.
Washington, DC 20036
(202) 862–5846
Fax (202) 862–7177
Internet: http://www.aei.org

Bank Administration Institute
1 N. Franklin St.
Chicago, IL 60606
(800) 323–8552
Publications (800) 224–9889
Fax (800) 375–5543
Internet: http://www.bai.org

The Brookings Institution
Economic Studies Program
1775 Massachusetts Ave. N.W.
Washington, DC 20036–2188
(202) 797–6121
Fax (202) 797–6181
Internet: http://www.brookings.org

The Business Council
888 17th St. N.W.
Washington, DC 20006
(202) 298–7650
Fax (202) 785–0296

The Business Roundtable
1615 L St. N.W., #1100
Washington, DC 20036
(202) 872–1260
Fax (202) 466–3509
Internet: http://www.brtable.org

Economic Policy Institute
1660 L St. N.W., #1200
Washington, DC 20036
(202) 775–8810
Fax (202) 775–0819
Internet: http://epinet.org

The Heritage Foundation
214 Massachusetts Ave. N.E.
Washington, DC 20002
(202) 546–4400
Fax (202) 544–6979
Internet: http://www.heritage.org

U.S. Chamber of Commerce
Economic Policy
1615 H St. N.W.
Washington, DC 20062–2000
(202) 463–5620
(800) 649–9719
Fax (202) 463–3174
Internet: http://www.uschamber.com

PUBLISHERS

The following companies and organizations publish on the Federal Reserve and related issues through books, periodicals, or electronic media.

American Banker
1 State St. Plaza
New York, NY 10004
(800) 221–1809
Fax (800) 235–5552
Internet: http://www.americanbanker.com

Bureau of National Affairs (BNA), Inc.
1231 25th St. N.W.
Washington, DC 20037
(202) 452–4200
Fax (800) 253–0332
Internet: http://www.bna.com

Commerce Clearing House (CCH), Inc.
2700 Lake Cook Rd.
Riverwoods, IL 60015
(847) 267–7000
Fax (847) 267–7878
Internet: http://www.cch.com

Journal of Money, Credit and Banking
Ohio State University Press, Journals Dept.
1070 Carmack Rd.
Columbus, OH 43210–1002
(614) 292–1407
(800) 437–4439
Fax (614) 292–2065
Ohio State University Press homepage:
http://www.sbs.ohio-state.edu/osu-press/jmcbmain.htm
To browse the *Journal* online:
http://www.jstor.org/journals/00222879.html

Lexis Law Publishing
P.O. Box 7587
Charlottesville, VA 22906
(800) 562–1197
Fax (800) 643–1280
Internet: http://www.michie.com

Moody'S Investors Service, Inc.
99 Church St.
Attn: FIS 1st Floor Sales Dept.
New York, NY 10007
(800) 342–5647
Fax (212) 553–4700
Internet: http://www.moodys.com

Warren, Gorham & Lamont, Inc.
31 St. James Ave.
Boston, MA 02116
(800) 999–9336
Fax (617) 695–9699
Internet: http://www.wgl.com

Federal Trade Commission

6th St. and Pennsylvania Ave. N.W., Washington, DC 20580
Internet: http://www.ftc.gov

◼ INTRODUCTION

Created in 1914, the Federal Trade Commission (FTC) is an independent agency headed by five commissioners who are nominated by the president and confirmed by the Senate for seven-year terms. One commissioner is designated chair by the president. No more than three of the commissioners may be members of the same political party.

As a quasi-judicial and quasi-legislative administrative authority, the FTC deals with trade practices by identifying and seeking to end unfair competition and deceptive practices. Although it has no authority to punish, the commission uses its powers to prevent unfair practices or issue cease-and-desist orders.

The agency also is charged with consumer protection. It works to ensure truth in advertising, marketing, and product labeling. Additionally, it seeks to prevent creditors from unlawful practices, when issuing credit, operating collection services, and collecting debts.

Responsibilities

The FTC:

▪ Promotes free and fair competition in interstate commerce through the prevention of trade restraints such as price-fixing, boycotts, illegal combinations of competitors, and similar unfair practices.

▪ Protects the public from false and deceptive advertising.

▪ Prevents practices that tend to lessen competition.

▪ Receives prior notice of large mergers and acquisitions. Such transactions cannot occur before the expiration of a waiting period during which the FTC may challenge them on antitrust grounds.

▪ Prohibits interlocking directorates that restrain competition.

- Prevents unlawful price discrimination.
- Prevents fraudulent telemarketing schemes and deceptive sales tactics.
- Regulates the packaging and labeling of consumer products to prevent deception.
- Requires accurate labels on fur, wool, and textile products.
- Informs consumers and industry of major FTC decisions, programs, statutes, and rules, defining the legality of certain business practices.
- Prohibits credit discrimination on the basis of sex, race, marital status, national origin, age, or receipt of public assistance.
- Requires nondepository creditors including retailers and finance companies to give borrowers accurate and complete information about the true cost of credit.
- Prohibits debt-collection agencies from harassing consumers.
- Requires sellers to give consumers notice of their three-day cancellation rights for sales, such as door-to-door and telephone sales, made away from the seller's place of business.
- Prohibits the sending of unordered merchandise to consumers and then charging for it.
- Requires that consumers ordering merchandise through the mail, by telephone, or fax be informed if shipment cannot be made by the promised date (or within thirty days). Customers must then be given the opportunity to agree to a new shipping date or to cancel the order and receive a full refund.
- Requires funeral directors to disclose prices and other information about funeral goods and services.
- Requires operators of (900) number telephone services to disclose fees and to avoid sales to minors without parental consent.
- Requires packaging and labeling of energy-consuming appliances, other devices, and vehicles to assist consumers in selecting those that are most energy efficient.

Powers and Authority

The FTC derives its authority under the Federal Trade Commission Act and the Clayton Act, both passed in 1914. The FTC Act prohibits the use of "unfair methods of competition" and "unfair or deceptive acts or practices." The Clayton Act makes illegal certain practices that may lead to monopolies. Since 1914, Congress also passed numerous other statutes expanding the duties of the commission (*See Background, p. 197*).

The FTC is authorized to investigate cases involving alleged unfair competition or deceptive practices. Once it determines that a company may have engaged in illegal activities, it may either negotiate an agreement in which the company voluntarily agrees to stop the practice and,

GLOSSARY

Advisory opinion—Advice given by the commission in response to a request from an individual or company as to the legality of a specific course of action.

Consent orders—Orders issued by the commission in which a company neither admits nor denies violating the law, but it agrees to discontinue certain practices.

Trade regulation rules (TRRs)—Rules that set standards and define which industry practices the commission holds to be unfair and deceptive. TRRs have the force of law.

in appropriate cases, pays civil penalties and consumer redress, or it may initiate adjudicative proceedings. Investigations, consent agreements, and adjudication related to anticompetitive behavior are handled by the Bureau of Competition. Matters related to consumers and consumer problems are handled by the Bureau of Consumer Protection. Both bureaus have personnel assigned to monitor and enforce specific provisions of FTC statutes. The regional offices have staff assigned to both consumer protection and business competition.

ADMINISTRATIVE PROCEEDINGS

The FTC initially attempts to ensure compliance by voluntary means, usually through nonbiding staff advice. The commission also can issue advisory opinions, guides, and policy statements clarifying legal practices. However, enforcement largely depends on several administrative procedures used to inform the business community and consumers of the legality of certain acts or practices.

Advisory Opinions

The advisory opinion procedure was established to enable business executives to learn, before implementing a practice, whether the practice might violate the laws the FTC administers. Because they clarify and interpret the law regarding a specific proposed action, advisory opinions do not usually involve consumers.

Advisory opinions are promulgated by the commission at the request of a business or an individual and apply specifically to a practice that the business or the individual is considering. The opinions define the limits of the law as they relate to that particular business practice. The commission at any time may overturn advisory opinions. If they are overturned, however, the commission must give the individual or business originally affected by the opinion a reasonable amount of time to alter practices to conform to the new ruling. Any individual or any business may apply to the commission for an advisory opinion; the commission will issue an advisory opinion if it involves a substantial or novel question. The FTC staff may issue advice when a case does not warrant an advisory opinion.

Adjudicative Proceedings

Adjudicative proceedings are instituted to resolve a complaint that alleges a company is engaging in anticompetitive, unfair, or deceptive acts or practices. Complaints can arise from several sources: the public, Congress, the White House, other government agencies, consumer or business groups, or the commission itself. The adjudicative proceeding begins after the commission has conducted an investigation and issued a formal complaint alleging some form of illegal behavior. The party charged (respondent) is notified and given thirty days to respond to the complaint. If the respondent decides not to dispute the charge, the illegal practice must be stopped and, in some cases, restitution must be made to the consumers adversely affected by the behavior of the respondent. If the respondent wishes to dispute the charge, an administrative law judge is named and a hearing is scheduled.

At the hearing, both sides present their arguments to the administrative law judge. Witnesses are examined and cross-examined and exhibits can be placed in the record. After considering the case, the administrative law judge issues an initial decision. This decision automatically becomes the order of the commission within thirty days if neither party files a notice of intention to appeal to the commission within ten days of being served the decision and if the commission unilaterally declines to review the decision. If a matter is appealed to the commission, an opinion is rendered. Respondents retain the right to appeal that decision to any U.S. Court of Appeals. If, after adjudication, it is determined that the violative conduct also is dishonest or fraudulent, the commission may begin a district court proceeding to seek redress for injured consumers.

Consent Orders

The commission often is able to stop lengthy adjudicative proceedings by negotiating a consent order with the respondent. Typically, the respondent neither admits nor denies any wrongdoing, but it agrees to discontinue the practice and, as appropriate, to take some type of affirmative action to rectify past actions. In such cases the commission issues a proposed consent order, spelling out any corrective action that must be taken.

This proposed order is placed on the public record, including publication in the *Federal Register*, and is open for public comment for sixty days. The comments become a part of the record and are considered by the commission in deciding whether to issue the order in final form. The comments may result in a commission decision, or if the respondent does not agree to the change, the matter may be adjudicated.

Trade Regulation Rules

The FTC's farthest-reaching power is the authority to issue trade regulation rules (TRRs). The commission was authorized to issue TRRs by the Magnuson-Moss Warranty-Federal Trade Commission Improvement Act of 1974. TRRs have the force of law and can apply to an entire industry or only to industries in a specific geographical region.

Generally, when the FTC staff finds an unfair or deceptive practice to be prevalent in an entire industry, it recommends that the commissioners begin rulemaking proceedings. Alternatively, the public may petition the commission to make a rule. However, before beginning the rulemaking process, the commission first publishes an advance notice of the proposed rule and solicits public comment.

If the FTC then decides to begin rulemaking, a presiding officer is appointed and a notice again is published in the *Federal Register* outlining the proposed rule and what the commissioners believe are the central issues to be discussed. At that time, individuals can comment, testify on the rule, or suggest additional issues to be discussed.

The presiding officer conducts public hearings that include cross-examination of witnesses on certain issues. When the hearings are completed, the FTC staff submits a report and the presiding officer recommends a decision on the issues. At that time the public can comment on the entire rulemaking record.

The matter then goes before the commission for deliberation on the record, which includes the presiding officer's decisions, the FTC staff report, and comments from the general public. The commission makes the final decision whether to issue the trade regulation rule. The commission can decide instead to make changes in the provisions of the rule and issue a Revised Version. The commission's rule may be challenged in an U.S. Court of Appeals. When a rule becomes final, it has the force of law.

ENFORCEMENT

If a respondent fails to comply with an FTC final cease-and-desist order or a TRR, the commission can request the attorney general to seek a district court order imposing a civil penalty of up to $11,000 for alleged violations of the rule or order. In the case of continuing violations, civil penalties of up to $11,000 per day may be requested. In the event of a court judgment for civil penalties and equitable relief, further failure to comply will result in contempt of court charges. The order becomes final sixty days after service, unless the respondent petitions a U.S. Court of Appeals to review the order and petitions the commission to stay the order pending review. The appeals court can affirm, modify, or overturn the order. Depending on the action, the respondent can then petition the Supreme Court for redress.

The FTC Act empowers the commission to seek a preliminary injunction to aid in obtaining effective relief pending the outcome of subsequent administrative proceedings with respect to any law enforced by the commission. This provision often is used to obtain preliminary injunctions blocking mergers and acquisitions if there are commission administrative complaints challenging such transactions as anticompetitive. In one such 1989 case involving an acquisition (*FTC v. Elders Grain*) the 7th Circuit held that the parties' consummated acquisition could be rescinded.

In appropriate cases, often involving fraud, the commission may seek permanent injunctions in court. No administrative proceeding is required.

OTHER POWERS

The agency also devotes its efforts to consumer protection to fulfill its obligations under a variety of statutes: the Wheeler-Lea Act, the Clayton Act, the Consumer Protection Act, the Robinson-Patman Protection Act, the Magnuson-Moss Warranty-Federal Trade Commission Improvements Act of 1980, the Smokeless Tobacco Health Education Act of 1986, the Telephone Disclosure and Dispute Resolution Act, the FTC Improvement Act of 1994, the International Antitrust Enforcement Assistance Act of 1994, and the Telemarketing and Consumer Fraud and Abuse Prevention Act and FTC Act Amendments of 1994.

It focuses much of its consumer protection efforts on advertising and marketing, including health and nutrition claims, environmental advertising and labeling, telemarketing, and franchise investments. It works to ensure truthful, not misleading, advertising and to curtail fraudulent or deceptive marketing practices. Under the Consumer Protection Act, it seeks to prohibit creditors from illegal practices when issuing credit, maintaining credit information, collecting debts, and operating credit systems.

Under the Wool Products Labeling Act, the Fur Products Labeling Act, and the Textile Fiber Products Identification Act, the commission requires the registration of certain types of products, including labeling for content, country of origin, and identity of manufacturer. These statutes also give the FTC power to issue rules and regulations related to these products, to test and inspect products, to institute condemnation proceedings, and to issue cease-and-desist orders.

The commission's outreach program apprises the business community of laws and regulations. The FTC believes that most businesses will comply voluntarily, and it can then concentrate its enforcement on those who do not. The FTC also publishes guidelines, pamphlets, and other materials for consumers to warn them of fraudulent practices they may encounter and to inform them of their rights under the law. Publications often are prepared in cooperation with businesses or business associations.

REPORTING REQUIREMENTS

Section 6(a) of the FTC Act gives the commission extensive power to request information from any business in the country. This power is backed up by the commission's authority to compel a business to submit the materials it wants to inspect. If the business does not comply, the FTC may seek a court order to enforce the process. The court then decides if enforcement is appropriate.

The FTC is prohibited from publishing trade secrets or privileged financial information and is required to ensure the confidentiality of data collected in its statistical reporting program.

Despite its power to seek information, the FTC does not maintain a single, across-the-board reporting program for the business community. It does, however, operate several separate reporting programs *(see Data and Statistics, p. 211)*.

Background

The formation in the late nineteenth century of several large and extremely powerful industrial trusts led Congress in 1898 to create the Industrial Commission to study the monopolistic behavior of corporations. The commission recommended that Congress establish a federal bureau to collect information on corporations. This recommendation led to the creation in 1903 of the Bureau of Corporations, in what was then the Department of Commerce and Labor. The bureau had no enforcement powers, and its main activity was gathering data from businesses, often at the instigation of Congress, which at the time had few investigative staff.

The Federal Trade Commission Act of 1914 created the FTC, which was designed to act as the federal government's chief trust-buster. The Bureau of Corporations was merged into the FTC in 1915 and made up most of the original staff of the commission. The reliance on voluntary compliance was continued at the new commission, but the FTC was given additional power to investigate business practices and to order them stopped. The wording of the legislation was intentionally flexible; Section 5 of the act gave the FTC broad powers to define business practices that constituted "unfair methods of competition." Congress also passed the Clayton Act (frequently referred to as the Clayton Antitrust Act) in 1914. This statute prohibited specific business activities that tended to lessen competition or to create monopolies.

EARLY HISTORY

During its infancy the FTC issued broad orders designed to promote competition. However, Congress, after initial enthusiasm, ignored the commission. Court decisions limited the agency's power to take action against practices that injured consumers but not competition. The commission fell into a period of inactivity.

The FTC's authority was increased in 1938 with the passage of the Wheeler-Lea Amendment to the original FTC Act. Designed to provide some degree of consumer protection to those who previously had been at the mercy of business interests, the amendment authorized the commission to prohibit "unfair or deceptive" business acts and practices. In this way the FTC could move against a business on behalf of consumers without first proving the existence of anticompetitive behavior.

In the 1940s the commission again began the active pursuit of cases. The courts were especially willing to uphold commission orders related to false advertising, which, as a result, became one of the agency's main areas of investigation and enforcement. The commission also moved into specialized regulation with the passage of the Wool Products Labeling Act. Success in that area led to the passage of the Fur Products Labeling Act, the Textile Fiber Products Identification Act, and the Flammable Fabrics Act (implementation of which was shifted subsequently to the Consumer Product Safety Commission).

In the 1950s and 1960s the FTC made few waves, except for a 1964 rule that would have required cigarette packages and all cigarette advertising to carry a health-hazard warning. However, the tobacco industry lobbied successfully to weaken the rule. The result was passage of the 1965 Federal Cigarette Labeling and Advertising Act, which required warnings on packages only. Subsequent legislation strengthened this law. The Public Health Cigarette Smoking Act of 1969 prohibited radio and television cigarette advertising, required printed ads to include a health warning, and strengthened the wording of the messages. In 1973 the law was amended to include small cigars, and in 1984 the Comprehensive Smoking Education Act strengthened the warning again and required four different messages to appear on a quarterly, rotating basis. A 1986 amendment, the Smokeless Tobacco Act, added chewing tobacco and snuff to the list of tobacco products banned from advertisements on television and radio and required that their packages also carry health warnings.

REVITALIZATION OF THE AGENCY

In 1969 a group of students working for consumer activist Ralph Nader issued a study of the FTC, charging that the commission was mired in trivial matters, that its reliance on case-by-case enforcement slowed progress, and that voluntary compliance was not stopping illegal or unfair business practices. In reaction to the Nader report, President Richard Nixon requested that the American Bar Association (ABA) appoint a committee to study the FTC. The ABA committee report also was critical of the commission.

The Nader and ABA reports made it politically advantageous for Nixon to begin upgrading the agency. He appointed Caspar Weinberger, who had developed a reputation as a first-rate manager, to the chair's post in 1969, replacing him seven months later with Miles Kirkpatrick, who had coordinated the ABA report on the FTC.

Under Weinberger and Kirkpatrick the FTC hired a number of young, activist lawyers. Greater emphasis was placed on consumer affairs and public participation. As a result, the commission gained a favorable reputation among consumer groups, while some business people charged that the commission was ignoring its responsibilities toward industry.

The push for improvements at the FTC resulted in the passage, in 1974, of the Magnuson-Moss Warranty-Federal Trade Commission Improvement Act, which gave the FTC authority to use industry-wide rulemaking—having the force and effect of law—as an alternative to challenging unfair or deceptive advertising and trade practices of an entire industry. The legislation also granted funds to public participants in rulemaking procedures. This provision designed to encourage greater public participation in the rulemaking process was later repealed in 1994.

The warranties provisions authorized the FTC for the first time to spell out standards to be met by written warranties given by manufacturers or sellers of products priced at $10 or more.

Passage of the Magnuson-Moss bill, which possibly marked the last big legislative success of the consumer movement, was just one of several indications in the early 1970s that the public and its representatives on Capitol Hill still favored a vigorous FTC.

The agency's activism was strongly supported by President Jimmy Carter, who appointed consumer proponent Michael Pertschuk to chair the FTC. Under Pertschuk, the FTC continued to push for consumer protection rules and regulations and took on some of the giants in the business and professional communities. The FTC reached its peak size of about 1,800 employees during the Carter administration.

CONGRESS CURBS THE FTC

A decade after it helped rouse the FTC from its somnolence, Congress began showing irritation with the agency. The FTC, using its broad mandate to ferret out "unfair or deceptive acts or practices," had antagonized a number of powerful industries and professional associations, as well as various individual retailers.

In 1977 the House of Representatives attempted to stall industry-wide rulemaking by attaching to the FTC's authorization bill a requirement that trade regulation rules be submitted to Congress for approval before taking effect. Both the Senate and President Carter objected to this legislative veto, calling it unconstitutional because it encroached on the authority of the executive branch. Because of this disagreement the agency was funded for the next three years by continuing resolutions, bypassing the normal authorization process. The stalemate continued until 1980, when certain House members announced they would not continue to fund the commission until an agreement was reached on the veto issue.

Compromise legislation that authorized FTC funds through fiscal 1982 provided for a two-house veto of the commission's rules and cut back other agency powers. Carter indicated that he would accept the legislative veto only if no major FTC proceedings would be terminated. Therefore, proposed rules to regulate children's advertising, funeral homes, and agricultural cooperatives survived when the compromise authorization bill was signed May 28, 1980.

The 1980 authorization bill also restricted FTC rulemaking authority governing commercial advertising to deceptive—not to unfair—practices. It prohibited the agency from providing citizens or consumer groups the funds necessary to enable them to participate in agency proceedings, and it prohibited the FTC from further study of the insurance industry. Congress also demanded that the FTC consider whether the children's advertising it sought to regulate was deceptive, not merely unfair. This forced the FTC to drop the children's advertising proceeding in 1981.

THE FTC IN THE 1980S

Groups that had chafed for years under FTC restrictions saw an opportunity when the Republican Party took over the White House and Senate in 1981. While President Ronald Reagan chose board members who were philosophically aligned with the administration's goal of reducing the regulatory burden on U.S. businesses, opposition groups also pressed Congress to rein in the FTC still further.

Associations of doctors, lawyers, and other professionals, the U.S. Chamber of Commerce, dairy groups, advertising groups, and the National Association of Manufacturers were among leaders of the movement to curb the FTC. The pressure group campaign fit in neatly with the new administration's plans to cut the budget of the regulatory agency and thus limit its activity.

When the FTC authorization expired at the end of 1982, Congress took another two years to reauthorize the agency. Each time Congress tried and failed to reauthorize the FTC new restrictions appeared in the bills that did not pass.

Other restrictions in other unpassed bills, such as one requiring the FTC to notify Congress before it gave testimony or made comments before any other federal or state body, were similarly honored by the agency. Some of the numerous restrictions were included in the FTC authorization bill finally passed in 1994.

During this time the FTC issued rules in two controversial areas—used cars and funeral homes. These rules prompted Congress to use, for the first time, the veto power it had given itself in 1980. The veto was challenged by consumer groups, and in July 1983 the Supreme Court ruled the veto unconstitutional. The used-car rule, after a further challenge on its merits, was repromulgated by the FTC in 1985 without a controversial provision that would have required used-car dealers to inform consumers of any major known defect in a used car.

Reagan's two terms brought eight consecutive years of budget and personnel cuts for the commission. The FTC workforce was cut in half, from 1,800 people when Pertschuk was chair, to fewer than 900. The budget shrank along with the size of the agency.

Although Reagan's first FTC chair, James Miller III, urged Congress to limit the FTC's authority to correct unfair and deceptive business practices to abuses that caused consumers "substantial injury," he fought off Congress's and American Medical Association proposals to curb the FTC's antitrust authority over state-licensed professional groups. Begun under Miller, the agency's campaign against professionally imposed boycotts, restrictions on locations of clinics and doctors' offices, collusion to fix prices, and bans on advertising continued into the 1990s and was an acknowledged success. The FTC was aided by the Supreme Court which, in a unanimous 1986 decision, upheld a lower court in *FTC v. Indiana Federation of Dentists*. Subsequently, the agency challenged the practices of a range of associations including pharmacists, veterinarians, real estate professionals, and college football teams.

After Miller became director of the Office of Management and Budget in 1985, Reagan appointed Daniel Oliver to chair the FTC. Oliver, who was considered very conservative by many and who acted as an outspoken proponent of Reagan's views on matters far removed from the business of the FTC, managed to alienate Congress, state officials, his fellow commissioners, and the FTC staff.

FTC IN THE 1990S

Janet Steiger, appointed FTC chair by President George Bush in 1989, gave new life to a demoralized agency. Steiger, the first woman to chair the commission, undertook to improve the FTC's image. Consumer groups, supported by former chair Pertschuk, had been critical of the commission's failure to act on what they saw as flagrantly deceptive advertising and ever more prevalent mergers, most of which went unchallenged by the agency. Steiger set up working groups with the agency's critics, most notably the National Association of Attorneys General (NAAG). She set three goals:

- To eliminate the perception that the FTC had ceased to be a vigorous law enforcement agency.
- To eliminate the appearance of a confrontational attitude toward Congress, the states, the legal community, and other public interest constituencies.
- To attempt to halt the decline in resources at the FTC.

Congress gave the agency its first budget boost in a decade soon after Steiger's appointment, and it continued to heed her requests for additional funds in subsequent years.

To counter criticism of the commission's poor record of regulating mergers during the 1980s, Steiger embarked on an internal study of the agency's merger activities and, together with the state attorneys general and the Justice Department's Antitrust Division, formed an executive working group on antitrust. Not only did the agency challenge more mergers in the ensuing years; it also produced the first *Joint Horizontal Merger Guidelines* with Justice's Antitrust Division in 1992. In 1993 the same two entities cooperated to produce Statements of Antitrust Enforcement Policy in the health care area to help reduce business uncertainty about mergers and other conduct that might give rise to antitrust actions during a time of rapid change in the health care industry. These guidelines were supported by Congress and the legal profession.

Under Steiger, the agency's efforts on advertising brought mixed results. In 1994 the FTC announced that it would harmonize its food advertising enforcement policies with the Food and Drug Administration's food labeling regulations that strictly limit health and other dietary claims. Also in 1994, however, the commission voted not to act on allegations that the "Joe Camel" cigarette ads were aimed at young people. The vote was a setback to Steiger, who had identified action on tobacco advertising as a priority early in her tenure.

However, the telemarketing law passed in late 1994 gave the FTC a clear mandate to make rules for the telemarketing industry. Rules implemented in 1995 barred telemarketers from repeatedly disturbing individual consumers with unsolicited telephone calls, limited the hours during which telephone sales could be solicited, and required telemarketers to "promptly and clearly disclose" the sales nature of any telephone call. The rules allowed nationwide injunctions against telemarketing companies, not merely refunds for individual consumers. Working with the NAAG, the FTC also set up the Telemarketing Fraud Data Base, which allowed law enforcement agencies to review consumer complaints and information about investigations and enforcement. By 1996 the FTC was targeting telemarketing fraud by so-called "scholarship search services."

When Congress enacted a bill authorizing continued operation for the FTC in August 1994, it was seen as an indication of the FTC's improved relationship with lawmakers. The legislation reinstated the agency's power to make rules governing unfair conduct, although it first required the FTC to prove that any practice it deemed unfair was a prevalent practice. FTC attorneys suspected that the definition of unfair in the new law might limit them to bringing cases in which consumers have suffered economic injury and exclude those which charge that an act or practice is harmful to health.

Another measure of the FTC's rejuvenation in the 1990s was the agency's ability to attract top-notch law school graduates: this sign of a healthy, well-run agency had not been seen since the 1970s. In April 1995 Democrat Bill Clinton appointed Robert Pitofsky chair of the FTC—but the election of a Republican Congress in the meantime decreased the likelihood that Pitofsky's approach to the agency would diverge markedly from Steiger's. Although he headed the FTC's Consumer Protection Bureau in the early 1970s and served as a commissioner of the agency under President Carter, Pitofsky nonetheless declared himself a centrist politically, noting that "It's just that the center has moved to the right during the past twenty years."

Under Pitofsky the FTC sought to update itself through both regulatory reform and a fuller understanding of regulatory implications of new technology. Vowing to repeal 25 percent of its trade regulatory rules, the FTC in 1996 eliminated some 10,000 directives that were more than twenty years old and not frequently implemented. By September 1998 the agency had vacated 35 percent of its guides and rules, effectively "cleaning out the regulatory closet," Pitofsky said. However, the agency has remained active on battling cases in court, winning more cases than previous administrations and losing only one case in three years.

Pitofsky approached the regulation of corporate mergers with a new emphasis. He gave more weight to increased efficiencies, such as lower unit and production costs, that pass on savings to consumers—whereas antitrust enforcement traditionally assumes that decreasing competition will raise prices. Pitofsky also directed FTC staff to examine how proposed mergers might affect market share and product development and innovation, especially in light of increased international competition.

At first glance, Pitofsky's appointment increased the antitrust activism of the FTC. In fiscal 1995 the agency challenged thirty-five corporate mergers—the highest since 1980—and observers remarked that the FTC was becoming more effective at enforcement than the Antitrust Division of the Justice Department. However, with the largest mergers in the media and defense industries, Pitofsky's FTC proved to be quite accommodating. In April 1996 the agency also approved Lockheed Martin's $9.1 billion acquisition of Loral Corp. (Lockheed Martin itself being the offspring of an FTC-approved merger in January 1995.) A year later, the commission approved a $15 billion merger between Boeing and McDonnell Douglas Corp. In mid-1998, running counter to the FTC, the Justice Department objected to a proposed merger of the last of the major defense contractors: Lockheed Martin Corp.'s proposed $12 billion purchase of Northrop Grumman Corp. In 1996 the FTC also approved the merger of Time Warner and Turner Broadcasting without any divestiture of assets.

The FTC was not reluctant to take on giants, particularly in the area of retail superstores. In July 1997 the commission blocked the proposed $4 billion merger of office suppliers Staples and Office Depot. The FTC contended that the proposed merger would essentially reduce competition to two major players, the new Staples-Office Depot entity and Office-Max. Countering the companies argument that additional competition would still exist with small stationery shops and large discount stores, such as Wal-Mart, the commission said their unusual variety of products constituted their own market.

In 1998 the FTC charged the largest manufacturer of computer microprocessors, Intel Corporation, that it used its monopoly power to dominate the entire market. The FTC alleged that Intel illegally used its market power against its three competitors who had sought to enforce patents in microprocessor technology. Similarly, the FTC alleged that Toys "R" Us forced all the leading toy manufacturers, including Hasbro and Mattel, into withholding best-selling merchandise from warehouse stores such as Sam's and Price Club, leading to higher prices for consumers. The company, which controls nearly 20 percent of the American toy market, also compelled manufacturers to sell those products only in combinations that made it difficult for consumers to compare prices, the agency argued.

In health care, the FTC in early 1996 rejected a merger of the Rite Aid and Revco drugstore chains as well as launched an investigation into whether pharmaceutical companies conspired to overcharge independent pharmacies for drugs. Then again in 1998, the courts upheld the FTC's request to stop two mergers of wholesale drug manufacturers: McKesson Corp. from buying AmeriSource Health Corp., and Cardinal Health Inc. from acquiring Bergen Brunswig Corp. The FTC contended that the mergers would have left only two companies in control of nearly 80 percent of the drug wholesale market. With new business arrangements cropping up frequently, the dynamic health care industry may face more scrutiny in the future.

The FTC also overhauled its tar and nicotine ratings for cigarettes, a system that had been widely regarded as inaccurate for much of its history. The agency also continued its litigation against "Joe Camel," or "unfair" advertising aimed at children in spite of a 1998 federal appeals court ruling that the Food and Drug Administration lacked jurisdiction in its fight against tobacco.

The FTC also voiced concern that the Telecommunications Act of 1996 might infringe on privacy, as it allowed companies to share customer data in the name of increased competition. In an action hailed by privacy advocates, the agency in August 1998 targeted for the first time a popular Web site on the Internet to enforce laws against deception and the misuse of personal information. The agency forced GeoCities to stop releasing personal information about its users to advertisers without notification. Pitofsky predicted that unless the telecommunications industry improved its self-regulation, the FTC would become more active and even seek new statutes from Congress. However, he recognized the pitfalls of seeking regulatory or legislative remedies first, saying "we are more open to self-regulations. The economy is too big and we are too small."

While the business growth of the Internet provided new challenges for the agency, the Internet also made the FTC more accessible to the public. In 1997 the agency established the Consumer Response Center to receive consumer complaints and inquiries by mail, telephone, and the Internet. Toll-free numbers established in 1999 and 2000 also made the agency more accessible. In fiscal 2000 the FTC received more than 833,000 complaints and inquiries from the public—more than one-third above its target number of 600,000 for that year and producing an estimated $265 million in savings to consumers.

In handling complaints, the FTC worked with partners such as the National Fraud Information Center of the National Consumers League, local chapters of the Better Business Bureau, and PhoneBusters, the Canadian fraud database. Fraud complaints are collected, analyzed to identify trends and patterns, new scams, and companies that engage in fraudulent, deceptive, or unfair business practices; the complaints are also shared with law enforcement agencies in the United States, Canada, and Australia via Consumer Sentinel, a secure Web site. The analysis allows the agency to stop unlawful or deceptive practices that included online auction fraud, pyramid schemes, scams for travel and health care, and unauthorized billing for unwanted services, known as "cramming."

The 1990s came to an end with corporate mergers continuing at an accelerated pace, rising in 1991 to 4,642 in 1999. The dollar value of the mergers increased even more dramatically, from $169 billion to approximately $3 trillion. The FTC saw the rise in mergers, and a corresponding increase in their complexity, as requiring greater antitrust review to prevent mergers that could diminish healthy competition. To meet the challenge in this area, the agency worked with industry and antitrust lawyers to find ways of making the merger investigation process more efficient. It also continued to undertake internal reforms to speed merger investigations and provide more complete information on the issues that require an investigation.

FTC IN THE 2000S

The merger wave continued into the early 2000s. The FTC required divestitures before a $27 billion merger between BP Amoco/Atlantic Richfield Company (ARCO) was allowed to proceed in April 2000. Specifically, the FTC required the company to divest all of ARCO's assets relating to oil production on Alaska's North Slope to Phillips Petroleum Company (Phillips) or another commission-approved purchaser.

The FTC also sanctioned the merger of America Online and Time Warner after requiring AOL Time Warner to fulfill several requirements. Among them, it had to open its cable system to competitor Internet service providers (ISPs). The FTC prohibited the company from interfering with content passed along the bandwidth contracted for by nonaffiliated ISPs and from interfering with the ability of nonaffiliated providers of interactive TV services to interact with interactive signals, triggers, or content that AOL Time Warner has agreed to carry. The FTC also set up regulations preventing the company from discriminating on the basis of affiliation in the transmission of content, or from entering into exclusive arrangements with other cable companies with respect to ISP services or interactive TV services.

In the area of nonmerger enforcement, the FTC focused on competition in the pharmaceutical industry. For example, the FTC in 2000 settled a monopolization case against Mylan Laboratories, resulting in a record $100 million settlement. Mylan was charged with conspiring to eliminate its competition for generic versions of two drugs used to treat anxiety, making unavailable the key active ingredients for those drugs. In settling the case, Mylan agreed to pay $100 million into a fund to compensate affected consumers and state agencies.

When in 2001 the number of mergers began declining, the FTC reinvigorated its nonmerger enforcement program. Particularly notable in the nonmerger area were the FTC's actions to stop branded pharmaceutical company practices that delay generic drug entry. In July 2002 the FTC also released a comprehensive study of generic drug entry prior to patent expiration. In this report, the FTC recommended legislative changes to the Hatch-Waxman Amendments to ensure that provisions of this law do not delay generic drug entry into the market.

In the spring of 2003 the FTC announced "Operation Bidder Beware"—a program to combat Internet auction fraud. Most auction fraud—the top complaint of consumers about the Internet—dealt with consumers paying for an auction item and then never receiving it. Under the program the FTC was to work with state and local law enforcement agencies to police Internet auction sites while the agency launched a campaign to educate consumers about Internet auction fraud.

Current Issues

The FTC plans to continue bringing law enforcement actions that address issues of importance to consumers, including identity theft, telemarketing fraud, Internet fraud, deceptive lending practices, and false and unsubstantiated claims for health and weight-loss products. The FTC also plans on focusing on deceptive advertising cases, in particular cases that involve health or safety issues or significant economic injury.

Health care remains a significant concern of the FTC. In addition to the pharmaceutical cases, the FTC has charged several groups of physicians with engaging in collusive practices that drove up consumer costs. These practices included physicians agreeing among themselves to fix fees and to refuse to deal with health plans, except on collectively agreed-upon terms. The FTC also has been conducting a retrospective study of hospital mergers to determine whether particular mergers have led to higher prices.

Another continuing priority of the FTC is the protection of consumer privacy. The FTC recently launched its most far-reaching privacy initiative to date, the National Do-Not-Call Registry, a centralized database of telephone numbers of consumers who have indicated they do not want to receive telemarketing calls. The registry will be legally binding and will allow consumers to stop most telemarketing calls simply by clicking on a Web site or making a toll-free call. The agency also has undertaken other privacy initiatives, including targeted law enforcement actions, consumer and business education, and research on emerging issues to reduce the serious consequences to consumers that can result from the misuse of personal information.

In addition to focusing on the increasing use of business practices designed to give companies market power or otherwise restrict competition in industries that are important to consumers, merger enforcement continues to be a staple of the FTC's enforcement agenda. Stopping mergers that substantially may lessen competition ensures that consumers pay lower prices and have greater choice in their selections of goods and services.

Finally, the FTC continues to expand its public profile through an information campaign promoting its toll-free numbers and Web site. The agency also has established a program that allows military personnel to enter complaints online and has expanded domestic and international participation in the Consumer Sentinel Web site, a database of consumer fraud complaints used by the FTC and its law enforcement partners.

◼ AGENCY ORGANIZATION

Biographies

TIMOTHY J. MURIS, CHAIRMAN

Appointment: Nominated by President Bush on April 23, 2001, and confirmed by the Senate May 25, 2001, to a term of seven years beginning September 26, 2001.

Born: Nov. 18, 1949.

Education: San Diego State University, B.A., 1971; University of California at Los Angeles, J.D., 1974.

Profession: Attorney.

Political Affiliation: Republican.

Previous Career: Muris has served at the FTC during previous administrations, holding down three different posts. He separately headed up FTC's Bureau of Competition and its Bureau of Consumer Protection under the Reagan Administration. He also served as assistant to the director of the Office of Policy, Planning, & Evaluation. During the 2000 presidential campaign, he was an economic adviser to George W. Bush. Muris has taught at George Mason University's Arlington law school since he left the Reagan administration in 1988.

SHEILA F. ANTHONY, COMMISSIONER

Appointment: Nominated by President Clinton, confirmed by the Senate Sept. 24, 1997; term expired. Remains in position.

Born: Nov. 8, 1940, Hope, AR.

Education: University of Arkansas, B.A., 1962; American University Washington College of Law, J.D., 1985.

Profession: Lawyer.

Political Affiliation: Democrat.

Previous Career: Before her appointment as FTC commissioner, Anthony served as assistant attorney general for legislative affairs at the Justice Department. Previously, she was an attorney with the Washington, DC, law firm of Dow, Lohnes and Albertson.

ORSON SWINDLE, COMMISSIONER

Appointment: Nominated by President Clinton, confirmed by the Senate March 19, 1998. Term expires Sept. 2004.

Born: March 8, 1937, Camilla, GA.

Education: Georgia Institute of Technology, B.S. in industrial management; Florida State University, M.B.A., 1973.

Military Service: U.S. Marine Corps, 1959–1979; POW in Hanoi for six years.

Profession: Businessman, government official, political organizer.

Political Affiliation: Republican.

Previous Career: During the Reagan administration, Swindle was assistant secretary of commerce for development. He also served as state director of the Farmers Home Administration of the Agriculture Department. Candidate for U.S. Congress, first district in Hawaii, in 1994 and 1996.

MOZELLE W. THOMPSON, COMMISSIONER

Appointment: Appointed by President Clinton during Senate recess Dec. 17, 1997. Term expires in 2003.

Born: Dec. 11, 1954, Pittsburgh, PA.

Education: Columbia University, A.B., 1976; Princeton University, M.P.A., 1980; Columbia School of Law, J.D., 1981.

Profession: Government official, lawyer.

Political Affiliation: Democrat.

Previous Career: Prior to joining the FTC, Thompson worked as principal deputy assistant secretary of the Treasury. Before his career at the Treasury Department, he held the position of senior vice president and general counsel to the New York State Finance Agency. He also taught courses as an adjunct professor at the Fordham University School of Law. He practiced law with Skadden, Arps, Slate, Meagher and Flom. Thompson began his legal career as a law clerk to U.S. District Court Judge William F. Hoeveler in Miami, FL.

THOMAS B. LEARY, COMMISSIONER

Appointment: Nominated by President Clinton and sworn in on November 17, 1999. His term on the Commission expires in 2005.

Education: Princeton University, B.A., economics; Harvard Law School, J.D.

Profession: Attorney.

Political Affiliation: Republican.

Previous Career: Mr. Leary was a partner at Hogan & Hartson, in Washington, D.C., as of 1983. His practice was principally in the area of antitrust and trade regulation. Before becoming a partner at Hogan & Hartson, Mr. Leary was the Assistant General Counsel of General Motors.

Headquarters and Divisions

COMMISSION

The commissioners make final decisions on trade regulation rules (TRRs), advisory opinions, investigatory subpoenas, consent orders, and appeals of administrative law

FEDERAL TRADE COMMISSION

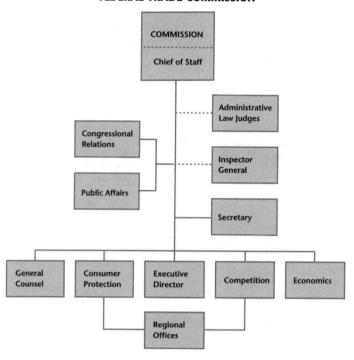

judges' decisions. They vote on ordering companies and individuals to file reports and answer questions in FTC investigations, and on issuing complaints alleging unfair competition and deceptive business practices. The commissioners grant extensions of deadlines, supervise the rulemaking process, and approve the appointment of top FTC employees. The chairman, as chief officer of the FTC, has final responsibility for the operations of the agency. The whole commission, however, votes on matters related to the FTC's policymaking, regulatory, and law enforcement activities.

Chair
Timothy J. Muris .... (202) 326–2100
    Fax .... (202) 326–2396
Commissioners
Sheila F. Anthony .... (202) 326–2171
    Fax .... (202) 326–3441
Orson Swindle .... (202) 326–2150
    Fax .... (202) 326–3436
Mozelle W. Thompson .... (202) 326–3400
    Fax .... (202) 326–3442
Thomas B. Leary .... (202) 326–2145
    Fax .... (202) 326–3446

Chief of Staff
MaryAnne Kane .... (202) 326–2450
Attorney Advisers to the Chairman
Daryn Bowie .... (202) 326–2018
Jeanne Balbach .... (202) 326–2568
Maame Gyamfi .... (202) 326–2886
Bilal Sayyed .... (202) 326–3658
Staff Assistant to Commissioner Anthony
LarVerne H. Harris .... (202) 326–2170
Attorney Advisers to Commissioner Anthony
Katherine E. Armstrong .... (202) 326–3250
Sean D. Hughto .... (202) 326–2199
Tara Isa Koslov .... (202) 326–2877
Staff Assistant to Commissioner Swindle
Barbara A. Cook .... (202) 326–2150
Special Assistant to Commissioner Swindle
Daniel W. Caprio Jr. .... (202) 326–2414
Attorney Advisers to Commissioner Swindle
Laura DeMartino .... (202) 326–3030
Robin Moore .... (202) 326–3133
Lynda M. Rozell .... (202) 326–2977
John H. Seesel .... (202) 326–2702

Staff Assistant to Commissioner Thompson
June Young.............................. (202) 326–2105
Attorney Advisers to Commissioner Thompson
Erica Lee .... (202) 326–3400
Kellie Cosgrove .... (202) 326–3400
Paden Magee........................... (202) 326–3400
Casey Triggs .... (202) 326–3400
Staff Assistant to Commissioner Leary
Deborah M. Blunt...................... (202) 326–2145
Attorney Advisers to Commissioner Leary
Tom Klotz.............................. (202) 326–2139
Lisa Kopchik........................... (202) 326–3139
Holly Vedova .... (202) 326–2896

OFFICE OF ADMINISTRATIVE LAW JUDGES

Performs the initial fact finding in adjudicative cases, conducts hearings, examines evidence, and issues decisions. Initial decisions become final unless reviewed by the full commission or appealed. The judges also act as presiding officers assigned to conduct rulemaking proceedings, with the chief judge serving as chief presiding officer.

Chief Judge
Stephen J. McGuire..................... (202) 326–3626
Fax..................................... (202) 326–2427
Administrative Law Judge
D. Michael Chappell .... (202) 326–3632
Administrative Officer
Patricia A. Harriger .... (202) 326–3626

OFFICE OF CONGRESSIONAL RELATIONS

Provides information for congressional members and staff who have questions concerning proposed legislation, commission activities, and constituent requests. Also advises the commission on congressional policies, procedures, interests, and pending legislative initiatives.

Director
Anna Davis .... (202) 326–2195
Fax..................................... (202) 326–3585

OFFICE OF THE EXECUTIVE DIRECTOR

The executive director has executive and administrative supervisory authority over all FTC offices, bureaus, and employees. Staff is responsible for publication of all commission documents and notices in the *Federal Register* and for other publications.

Executive Director
Rosemarie A. Straight................. (202) 326–2207
Fax..................................... (202) 326–3599
Equal Employment Opportunity
Barbara B. Wiggs...................... (202) 326–2196

DEPUTY EXECUTIVE DIRECTORS

Responsible for administration and management of FTC operations.

Administrative Services
Sherron G. Greulich.................... (202) 326–2271
Fax..................................... (202) 326–2731
Financial Management
Henry Hoffman .... (202) 326–2664
Fax..................................... (202) 326–2329
Human Resources Management
Janet Silva............................. (202) 326–2344
Fax..................................... (202) 326–2328

OFFICE OF INFORMATION TECHNOLOGY MANAGEMENT

Responsible for the development, implementation, and maintenance of information solutions. Major responsibilities include: litigation support, program support, end-user support, software development, technology infrastructure, and administration of the FTC library.

Director and Chief Information Officer
Stephen Warren .... (202) 326–2898
Fax..................................... (202) 326–2360
Associate Chief Information Officer
Keith Golden .... (202) 326–2410

OFFICE OF THE GENERAL COUNSEL

The general counsel acts as the commission's chief law officer and adviser and provides legal services to the commission, the operating bureaus, and other offices.

The assistant general counsel for legal counsel advises the commission on questions of law and policy, as well as legislative matters. The legal counsel also ensures FTC compliance with the Freedom of Information and Privacy acts and related statutes.

The assistant general counsel for litigation represents the commission in all federal court proceedings, except certain matters such as compliance with outstanding cease-and-desist orders. The Litigation Office handles appeals of final orders and represents the commission in orders to file special reports, subpoenas, injunctions, and reviews of FTC decisions under the Freedom of Information Act. For general inquiries, call (202) 326–2424.

General Counsel
William E. Kovacic .... (202) 326–3661
Fax..................................... (202) 326–2477
Deputy General Counsel
John D. Graubert....................... (202) 326–2186
Legal Counsel
Christian S. White..................... (202) 326–2476
Litigation
John F. Daly............................ (202) 326–2244

OFFICE OF THE INSPECTOR GENERAL

Conducts and supervises audits and investigations of FTC programs and operations. Reviews existing and proposed legislation and regulations to promote effectiveness and to prevent fraud and abuse.

Inspector General

Frederick J. Zirkel .... (202) 326–2800

Fax .... (202) 326–2034

POLICY PLANNING

Researches, develops, and drafts policy recommendations to the commission on a wide variety of issues, as guidance during commission deliberations or as proposals for future enforcement policy. Through its advocacy program, advises other governmental and self-regulatory organizations about the potential effects on consumers of proposed legislation, rules, or industry guides or codes.

Director

Jenny Ellig (Acting) .... (202) 326–3528

Fax .... (202) 326–3275

OFFICE OF PUBLIC AFFAIRS (PRESS OFFICE)

See Information Sources.

OFFICE OF THE SECRETARY

Responsible for the minutes of commission meetings and acts as the custodian of the FTC's seal, papers, and records including all legal and public records gathered by the commission. Receives all incoming congressional correspondence and coordinates the agency's response. The secretary signs all commission orders and official correspondence and coordinates all liaison activities with the executive and administrative departments and agencies. The secretary also issues and serves all official agency documents and maintains the commission's rules of procedure.

Secretary

Donald S. Clark .... (202) 326–2514

Fax .... (202) 326–2496

Commission Services

C. Landis Plummer .... (202) 326–2520

Congressional Correspondence

Elizabeth M. Foster.................... (202) 326–2187

BUREAU OF COMPETITION

Enforces antitrust laws that are under the administration of the FTC (Clayton Antitrust Act and Federal Trade Commission Act). Investigates and litigates cases of alleged anticompetitive or monopolistic behavior, including anti-merger enforcement, that are in violation of those acts, and advises the commission on rules and procedures. Also enforces the Export Trade Act, which allows the formation, monitoring, and regulation of certain export trade associ-

ations. Requires prior notice of certain mergers (typically in which a company worth $100 million or more plans to acquire or merge with a company worth $10 million or more) and reviews these cases to determine whether the action will reduce competition. For general inquiries, call (202) 326–3300.

Director

Joseph J. Simons........................ (202) 326–3667

Fax .... (202) 326–2884

Accounting and Financial Analysis

Gabriel Dagen .... (202) 326–2573

Compliance

Daniel P. Ducore .... (202) 326–2526

Fax .... (202) 326–2655

General Litigation

Health Care

Jeffrey Brennon .... (202) 326–3688

Fax .... (202) 326–3384

Merger 1

Ann B. Malester....................... (202) 326–2820

Fax .... (202) 326–2655

Merger 2

Vacant .... (202) 326–2821

Fax .... (202) 326–3383

Merger 3

Phillip L. Broyles...................... (202) 326–2805

Fax .... (202) 326–3383

Anticompetition Practices

Richard G. Dagen..................... (202) 326–2628

International Antitrust

Randolph W. Tritell................... (202) 326–3051

Fax .... (202) 326–2884

Policy and Evaluation

Aldea Abbott.......................... (202) 326–2881

Fax .... (202) 326–2884

Premerger Notification

Marian R. Bruno...................... (202) 326–5100

Fax .... (202) 326–2624

Regions/States/Federal Relations

D. Bruce Hoffman .... (202) 326–2924

BUREAU OF CONSUMER PROTECTION

Investigates, attempts to foster compliance, and litigates instances of alleged unfair or deceptive business practices that harm the consuming public. Advises the commission on rules and proceedings and recommends cases for litigation. Seeks to educate both consumers and the business community about the laws it enforces, and informs Congress of the impact proposed actions could have on consumers. Administers product registration numbers for wool, fur, and textile fiber products through its Enforcement division.

Director

J. Howard Beales III. .... (202) 326–3665

Fax .... (202) 326–3799

Advertising Practices

Mary K. Eagle .... (202) 326–3161

Fax .... (202) 326–3259

Consumer and Business Education

Carolyn Shanoff .... (202) 326–3268

Fax .... (202) 326–3574

Financial Practices

Joel C. Winston .... (202) 326–3153

Fax .... (202) 326–2558

Enforcement

Elaine D. Kolish .... (202) 326–3042

Fax .... (202) 326–2558

Marketing Practices

Eileen Harrington .... (202) 326–3127

Fax .... (202) 326–3395

Planning and Information

Lois Greisman .... (202) 326–3404

International Consumer Protection

Hugh Stevenson .... (202) 326–3511

BUREAU OF ECONOMICS

Advises the commission on the economic aspects and effects of FTC actions. Prepares economic surveys and reports for use by the commission and by other FTC bureaus. Areas of analysis include industry and trade practices and behavior, consumer protection, antitrust, and government and self-regulatory entities. For general inquiries, call (202) 326–3419.

Director

David T. Scheffman .... (202) 326–3687

Fax .... (202) 326–2380

Antitrust

Mary Coleman .... (202) 326–2291

Fax .... (202) 326–2625

Consumer Protection

Paul A. Pautler .... (202) 326–3357

Economic Policy Analysis

Denis A. Breen .... (202) 326–3447

Special Projects

Pauline M. Ippolito .... (202) 326–3477

Regional Offices

EAST CENTRAL REGION

(DC, DE, MD, MI, OH, PA, VA, WV)
Federal Trade Commission
1111 Superior Ave., #200
Cleveland, OH 44114–2507
216–263–3410
John M. Mendenhall, director

NORTHEAST REGION

(CT, ME, MA, NH, NJ, NY, PR, RI, VT, VI)
Federal Trade Commission
1 Bowling Green, #318
New York, NY 10004
212–607–2829
Barbara Anthony, director

NORTHWEST REGION

(AK, ID, MT, OR, WA, WY)
Federal Trade Commission
2896 Federal Bldg., 915 2nd Ave.
Seattle, WA 98174
206–220–6350
Charles A. Harwood, director

SOUTHEAST REGION

(AL, FL, GA, MS, NC, SC, TN)
Federal Trade Commission
60 Forsyth St., SW, #5M35
Atlanta, GA 30303-2322
404–656–1390
Andrea Foster, Director

SOUTHWEST REGION

(AR, LA, NM, OK, TX)
Federal Trade Commission
1999 Bryan St., #2150
Dallas, TX 75201-6808
214–979–9350
Bradley Elbein, regional director

WESTERN REGION

(AZ, CA, CO, HI, NV, UT)
Federal Trade Commission
901 Market St., #570
San Francisco, CA 94103
415–848–5100
Jeffrey A. Klurfeld, director

Federal Trade Commission
10877 Wilshire Blvd., #700
Los Angeles, California 90024
310–824–4343
Jeffrey A. Klurfeld, director

CONGRESSIONAL ACTION

Congressional Liaison
Anna Davis .... (202) 326–2195

Committees and Subcommittees

HOUSE APPROPRIATIONS COMMITTEE
Subcommittee on Commerce, Justice, State,
  and Judiciary
H309 CAP, Washington, DC 20515
(202) 225–3351

HOUSE COMMERCE COMMITTEE
Subcommittee on Health and Environment
2125 RHOB, Washington, DC 20515
(202) 225–2927

HOUSE JUDICIARY COMMITTEE
Subcommittee on Commercial and Administrative Law
B353 RHOB, Washington, DC 20515
(202) 225–2825

SENATE APPROPRIATIONS COMMITTEE
Subcommittee on Commerce, Justice, State, and Judiciary
S146A CAP, Washington, DC 20510
(202) 224–7277

SENATE COMMERCE, SCIENCE AND TRANSPORTATION COMMITTEE
Subcommittee on Consumer Affairs, Foreign Commerce, and Tourism
SH-425, Washington, DC 20510
(202) 224–5183

SENATE JUDICIARY COMMITTEE
Subcommittee on Antitrust, Business Rights, and Competition
SD-161, Washington, DC 20510
(202) 224–9494

Legislation

The FTC was created by the **Federal Trade Commission Act of 1914** (38 Stat. 717, 15 U.S.C. 41). Signed by the president Sept. 26, 1914. The commission's primary function is to define and outlaw unfair methods of competition. The FTC Act was amended in 1938 by the passage of the **Wheeler-Lea Act** (52 Stat. 114, 15 U.S.C. 52). The 1938 amendment extended protection to consumers by forbidding unfair or deceptive acts or practices in commerce. The FTC Act was amended again with passage of the

Federal Trade Commission Improvements Act of 1980 (94 Stat. 374, 15 U.S.C. 58 note). Signed by the president May 28, 1980. Permitted Congress to veto FTC regulations or actions without presidential approval.

The commission also administers several other laws, all of which either prohibit anticompetitive practices or promote consumer protection. They include, as amended:

Sherman Antitrust Act (26 Stat. 209, 15 U.S.C. 1). Signed by the president July 2, 1890. Prohibited restraint of trade and the monopolization of any part of trade or commerce.

Clayton Act (38 Stat. 730, 15 U.S.C. 12). Signed by the president Oct. 15, 1914. Outlawed mergers or acquisitions that could substantially lessen competition or help to create monopolies.

Export Trade Act (40 Stat. 516, 15 U.S.C. 61). Signed by the president April 10, 1918. Promoted export trade by permitting certain types of cooperative business activities.

Robinson-Patman Protection Act (49 Stat. 1526, 15 U.S.C. 13). Signed by the president June 19, 1936. Prohibited specified practices, such as unlawful price discrimination and related acts.

Wool Products Labeling Act of 1939 (54 Stat. 1128, 15 U.S.C. 68). Signed by the president Oct. 14, 1940. Required manufacturers to disclose composition of spun, woven, knitted, felted, and other types of manufactured wool products.

Lanham Trademark Act of 1946 (60 Stat. 427, 15 U.S.C. 1051). Signed by the president July 5, 1946. Required registration and protection of trademarks used in commerce.

Fur Products Labeling Act (65 Stat. 175, 15 U.S.C. 69). Signed by the president Aug. 8, 1951. Prohibited false advertising, false invoicing and false branding of furs and fur products.

Textile Fiber Products Identification Act (72 Stat. 1717, 15 U.S.C. 70). Signed by the president Sept. 2, 1958. Prohibited use of false brands or false advertising of the fiber content of textile fiber products.

Federal Cigarette Labeling and Advertising Act (79 Stat. 282, 15 U.S.C. 1331 note). Signed by the president July 27, 1965. Required health warnings on cigarette packages. This act was amended by the **Public Health Cigarette Smoking Act of 1969** (84 Stat. 87, 15 U.S.C. 1331 et seq.). Signed by the president April 1, 1970. Prohibited radio and television cigarette advertising, required printed ads to include a health warning, and strengthened the wording of the messages. The **Federal Cigarette Labeling and Advertising Act** was again amended by the **Little Cigar Act of 1973** (87 Stat. 352, 15 U.S.C. 1331), which was signed by the president Sept. 21, 1973 and brought little cigars under its jurisdiction. The final amendment to the 1965 act was the **Comprehensive Smoking Education Act of 1984**

(98 Stat. 2200, 15 U.S.C. 1331 note). Signed by the president Oct. 12, 1984. This act strengthened the warning again and required four different messages to appear on a quarterly, rotating basis.

Fair Packaging and Labeling Act (80 Stat. 1296, 15 U.S.C. 1451). Signed by the president Nov. 3, 1966. Prohibited unfair or deceptive packaging and labeling of certain consumer products.

Truth in Lending Act (82 Stat. 146, 15 U.S.C. 1601). Signed by the president May 29, 1968. Required full disclosure of credit terms before a consumer credit account is opened or a credit transaction completed. Also established limits on a consumer's liability for unauthorized use of a credit card.

Fair Credit Reporting Act (84 Stat. 1128, 15 U.S.C. 1681). Signed by the president Oct. 26, 1970. Required that credit reports be accurate and allowed consumers to correct faulty information in their reports. Also required that credit reports be kept confidential and that only properly authorized parties be allowed access to the reports.

Equal Credit Opportunity Act (88 Stat. 1521, 15 U.S.C. 1691). Signed by the president Oct. 28, 1974. Prohibited the denial of credit on the basis of sex, marital status, age, race, religion, or national origin.

Fair Credit Billing Act (88 Stat. 1511, 15 U.S.C. 1666). Signed by the president Oct. 28, 1974. Amended the Truth in Lending Act by setting up a mechanism that consumers can use to dispute billing errors and requiring creditors to take steps to correct billing errors.

Magnuson-Moss Warranty–Federal Trade Commission Improvement Act (88 Stat. 2183, 15 U.S.C. 2301–12, 15 U.S.C. 45–58). Signed by the president Jan. 4, 1975. Authorized the FTC to establish standards for written warranties on products that cost more than $10; gave the FTC authority to promulgate trade regulation rules that carry the force of law to deal with unfair or deceptive practices throughout an industry rather than on a case-by-case basis; allowed the commission to represent itself in court and to request redress and civil penalties for violations of the Federal Trade Commission Act; and expanded the FTC's jurisdiction to cover activities "affecting commerce" as well as "in commerce."

Hart-Scott-Rodino Antitrust Improvement Act of 1976 (90 Stat. 1383, 15 U.S.C. 1311 note). Signed by the president Sept. 30, 1976. Required companies to notify the FTC and the Justice Department of an intention to merge if one of the companies involved is worth in excess of $100 million and the other company is worth in excess of $10 million and if the transaction would affect in excess of $50 million in stocks or assets, or 15 percent of the voting securities of the acquired company.

Fair Debt Collection Practices Act of 1977 (91 Stat. 874, 15 U.S.C. 1601 note). Signed by the president Sept. 20, 1977. Established a national system of controls on the activities of debt collection agencies.

Electronic Fund Transfer Act (92 Stat 3728, 15 U.S.C. 1693). Signed by the president Nov. 11, 1978. Enacted as Title IX of the Consumer Credit Protection Act to provide a framework for consumer rights regarding electronic fund transfer systems. The FTC was given authority for the administrative enforcement of this statute, excepting oversight of financial institutions, air carriers, and securities brokers and dealers.

Comprehensive Smokeless Tobacco Health Education Act (100 Stat. 30, 15 U.S.C. 4401 note). Signed by the president Feb. 27, 1986. Required manufacturers of "smokeless tobacco" products such as chewing tobacco and snuff to print warning labels on their packages. Prohibited radio and television advertising of such products.

Telephone Disclosure and Dispute Resolution Act of 1992 (106 Stat. 4181, 15 U.S.C. 5701). Signed by the president Oct. 28, 1992. Title II amended the Communications Act of 1934 by adding section 228 (42 U.S.C. 228). Authorized the FTC to regulate pay-per-call telephone services to protect consumers. Also authorized regulation of unfair and deceptive advertising regarding pay-per-call.

Telemarketing and Consumer Fraud and Abuse Prevention Act (108 Stat. 1545, 15 U.S.C. 6101). Signed by the president Aug. 16, 1994. Prohibited unfair or deceptive telemarketing practices. Required a limit on the hours during which telephone sales can be solicited; required telemarketers to "promptly and clearly disclose" the purpose of the call; barred telemarketers from repeatedly disturbing consumers with unsolicited calls.

Federal Trade Commission Act Amendments of 1994 (108 Stat. 1691, 15 U.S.C. 58 note). Signed by the president Aug. 26, 1994. Amended the Federal Trade Commission Act to deny authority to the FTC to study, investigate, or prosecute agricultural cooperatives for any action not in violation of antitrust acts, or to study or investigate agricultural marketing orders. Prohibited the FTC from instituting a civil action, in cases involving consent orders, to obtain civil penalties for unfair or deceptive acts or practices. Prohibited the FTC from using authorized funds for submitting statements to, appearing before, or intervening in the proceeds of, any federal or state agency or legislative body concerning proposed rules or legislation that the agency or legislative body is considering, without notifying relevant congressional committees in a timely manner.

Consumer Credit Reporting Reform Act of 1996 (110 Stat. 3009-426, 15 U.S.C. 1601 note). Required the FTC to take action to achieve consumer standardization and comprehensibility. Authorized the FTC to commence a civil action to recover a civil penalty in a federal district court in the event of a knowing violation constituting a pattern or practice of the Fair Credit Reporting Act (FCRA) violations. Limited such penalty to $2,500. Precluded the FTC from promulgating trade regulation rules with respect to the FCRA.

Credit Repair Organizations Act (110 Stat. 3009-455, 15 U.S.C. 1601 note). Signed by the president Sept. 30, 1996. Delegated to the FTC the responsibility of enforcing the following provisions: (1) prohibited any credit repair organizations (CRO) from advising consumers to make an untrue or misleading statement or to alter a consumer's credit record; (2) prohibited any fraud or deceptive actions by a CRO; and (3) prohibited a CRO from charging or receiving valuable consideration for any service before such service is fully rendered. Established a five-year statute of limitations for actions to enforce liability under this title.

Do-Not-Call Implementation Act (117 Stat. 557, 15 U.S.C. 6101 note). Signed by the president on March 11, 2003. Authorized the FTC to collect fees for use in establishing a national "do-not-call" registry for telemarketers. Directed the FTC and the Federal Communications Commission (FCC) to align their telemarketing regulations for the purposes of consistency.

INFORMATION SOURCES

Internet
Agency Web Site: http://www.ftc.gov. Provides information on FTC offices and programs, news releases, and extensive consumer information.

Telephone Contacts
News Developments (recording).......... (202) 326–2710
Calendar (recording)...................... (202) 326–2711

Information and Publications

KEY OFFICES

FTC Public Affairs (Press Office)
600 Pennsylvania Ave. N.W.
Washington, DC 20580
(202) 326–2718
Fax (202) 326–3366
Cathy MacFarlane, director
(202) 326–2181
Claudia Bourne Farrell and Mitchell Katz, senior press officers

Issues news releases on actions of the commission, including investigations, consent orders, settlements, court cases, trade regulation rules, staff reports, and hearings. Also issues a detailed *Weekly Calendar and Notice of "Sunshine" Meetings* and the *FTC News Notes,* a weekly summary

of releases; maintains a mailing list for each. Much of this information is also available online and via recorded messages *(see Telephone Contacts).* For general inquiries, call (202) 326–2180.

FTC Consumer Response Center
600 Pennsylvania Ave. N.W.
Washington, DC 20580
Toll-free (877) 382–4357
Fax (202) 326–2012

Responds to inquiries from the public, the business community, and government. Distributes copies of FTC reports, speeches, regulations, and press releases. Receives complaints involving antitrust matters and unfair or deceptive trade practices. Maintains complaint databases that are shared with other federal agencies, state attorneys general, and international partners. Operates a walk-in public reference room, a general information telephone line, and a consumer hotline. Consumers may also contact the FTC regional office in their area.

FTC Consumer and Business Education
Bureau of Consumer Protection
601 New Jersey Ave. N.W.
Washington, DC 20580
(202) 326–3268
Fax (202) 326–3574
Carolyn S. Shanoff, chief

Provides information about FTC consumer programs to consumers, attorneys, and business executives.

Freedom of Information
Freedom of Information Act Request
Planning and Information Division
600 Pennsylvania Ave. N.W.
Washington, DC 20580
(202) 326–2430
Joan Fina, manager

PUBLICATIONS
Contact the FTC Consumer Response Center; most of the following general titles are available free:

Consumers Guides and *Buyers Guides.* A series of short pamphlets telling consumers about their rights and warning against unfair practices.

Federal Trade Commission—"Best Sellers, for Consumers." Contains a partial list of FTC publications and ordering information.

Federal Trade Commission: Organization, Procedures, Rules of Practice and Standards of Conduct. Contains complete information on procedures of the commission, updated as needed.

A Guide to the Federal Trade Commission.

Trade Regulation Rules (copies of individual rules).

What's Going On at the FTC? Brochure describing consumer protection programs.

For the *Annual Report,* contact U.S. Government Printing Office (GPO): see appendix, Ordering Government Publications. Recent volumes of the following reference works are also available from the GPO. Complete sets may be consulted at the FTC.

Federal Trade Commission Decisions. Hardcover volumes covering all FTC decisions, from 1915. Each generally covers a six-month period.

Trade Regulation Rules (complete set). Contained in *Code of Federal Regulations,* Title 16—Commercial Practices.

DATA AND STATISTICS

All FTC documents, studies, reports, summaries, dockets, files, and investigations that are open to the public are available for inspection and copying in the Public Reference Room. The *Annual Report* provides an overview of agency data; also available:

FTC Report to Congress Pursuant to the Federal Cigarette Labeling and Advertising Act. Issued twice yearly by the Bureau of Consumer Protection; lists the "tar" and nicotine content of domestic cigarettes. Available free from the FTC Public Reference Branch.

MEETINGS

The commissioners usually meet in Room 432 of the FTC headquarters. Schedules and agendas for meetings are published in the *FTC Weekly Calendar and Notice of "Sunshine" Meetings.* This information also is available in the FTC Public Reference Room, in the "Sunshine Meetings" section of the *Federal Register,* and on a recorded message maintained by FTC Public Affairs: (202) 326–2711.

Any member of the public whose interest could be directly affected if a certain part of a meeting is open may request that the commission consider closing that portion of the meeting. Requests for a closed meeting should be directed to the Office of the General Counsel.

Reference Resources

LIBRARIES

FTC Library
6th St. and Pennsylvania Ave. N.W., Room 630
Washington, DC 20580
(202) 326–2395
Fax (202) 326–2732
Elaine Sullivan, director

Open to the public. Holds materials on law, related antitrust matters, and consumer and economic affairs. Subscribes to the following search services: LRS, LEXIS-NEXIS, DIALOG, Information America, Westlaw, ELSS, and Dow Jones. Interlibrary loan service is available.

FTC Consumer Response Center
600 Pennsylvania Ave. N.W., Room 130
Washington, DC 20580
Toll-free (877) 382–4357
Fax (202) 326–2050
Hours: 9:00 a.m. to 5:00 p.m.

Provides public dockets for all FTC proceedings for inspection and copying. Other information available to the public includes an index of opinions, orders, statements of policy, and interpretations; administrative staff manuals; a record of the final votes of commissioners in agency proceedings; records of adjudicative proceedings and hearings; petitions filed with the secretary regarding rules and regulations; transcripts of hearings and written statements filed in connection with rulemaking proceedings; published FTC reports on economic surveys and investigations; registration statements and annual reports filed by export trade associations; requests for advice on proposed mergers, divestitures, and acquisitions; reports of compliance; administrative interpretations; notices of rulemaking, including proposals; news releases; reprints of the FTC's principal laws; FTC annual reports; and *Federal Trade Commission Decisions.*

DOCKETS

Contact the FTC Consumer Response Center.

RULES AND REGULATIONS

FTC rules and regulations are published in the *Code of Federal Regulations,* Title 16, parts 0–999. Proposed rules, new final rules, and updates to the *Code of Federal Regulations* are published in the daily *Federal Register.* (See appendix for information on how to obtain and use these publications.)

Other Information Sources

RELATED AGENCIES

Antitrust Division
Justice Department
See p. 547.

Consumer Information Center
General Services Administration
See appendix, Ordering Government Publications.

NONGOVERNMENTAL ORGANIZATIONS

The following are some key organizations that monitor the FTC and related trade and consumer protection issues.

Action on Smoking and Health

2013 H St. N.W.
Washington, DC 20006
(202) 659–4310
(800) 427–4228
Internet: http://www.ash.org

The American Advertising Federation

1101 Vermont Ave. N.W., #500
Washington, DC 20005
(202) 898–0089
Fax (202) 898–0159
Internet: http://www.aaf.org

The Business Roundtable

1615 L St. N.W., #1100
Washington, DC 20036
(202) 872–1260
Fax (202) 466–3509
Internet: http://www.brtable.org

Consumer Federation of America

1424 16th St. N.W., #604
Washington, DC 20036
(202) 387–6121
Fax (202) 265–7989

Consumers Union of the United States

101 Truman Ave.
Yonkers, NY 10703
(914) 378–2000
Fax (914) 378–2905
Internet: http://www.consunion.org
  Washington office
  1666 Connecticut Ave. N.W., #310
  Washington, DC 20009
  (202) 462–6262
  Fax (202) 265–9548
  Publishes *Consumer Reports.*

National Association of Attorneys General

750 1st St. N.W., #1100
Washington, DC 20002
(202) 326–6000
Fax (202) 408–7014
Internet: http://www.naag.org

National Consumers League

1701 K St. N.W., #1200
Washington, DC 20006
(202) 835–3323
Fax (202) 835–0747
Internet: http://www.natlconsumersleague.org

Public Citizen

1600 20th St. N.W.
Washington, DC 20009
(202) 588–1000
Fax (202) 588–7798
Internet: http://www.citizen.org

U.S. Chamber of Commerce

1615 H St. N.W.
Washington, DC 20062-2000
(202) 463–5500
(800) 649–9719
Fax (202) 887–3445
Internet: http://www.uschamber.com

PUBLISHERS

The following companies and organizations publish on the FTC and related issues through books, periodicals, or electronic media.

American Council on Consumer Interests

240 Stanley Hall
University of Missouri
Columbia, MO 65211
(573) 882–3817
Fax (573) 884–6571
Internet: http://acci.ps.missouri.edu
Publishes the *Journal of Consumer Affairs.*

Anderson Publishing Co.
2035 Reading Rd.
Cincinnati, OH 45202
(800) 582–7295
Fax (513) 562–8116
Internet: http://www.legalpubs.com

Bureau of National Affairs (BNA), Inc.
1231 25th St. N.W.
Washington, DC 20037
(202) 452–4200
Fax (800) 253–0332
Internet: http://www.bna.com

Commerce Clearing House (CCH), Inc.
2700 Lake Cook Rd.
Riverwoods, IL 60015
(847) 267–7000
Fax (847) 267–7878
Internet: http://www.cch.com

Gale Research Co.
2700 Drake Rd.
Farmington Hills, MI 48331
(800) 877–4253
Internet: http://www.gale.com

Journal of Consumer Research
University of Chicago Press, Journals
5720 S. Woodlawn Ave.
Chicago, IL 60637
(312) 753–3347
Fax (312) 753–0811
Internet: http://www.journals.uchicago.edu

West Group
P.O. Box 64526
St. Paul, MN 55164
(800) 344–5008
Fax (612) 687–7302
Internet: http://www.westgroup.com

Food and Drug Administration

5600 Fishers Lane, Rockville, MD 20857
Internet: http://www.fda.gov

INTRODUCTION

The Food and Drug Administration (FDA) is an agency within the Health and Human Services Department (HHS). The president appoints and the Senate confirms the FDA commissioner.

The Food and Drug Act of 1906 called for the protection of the public from the potential health hazards presented by adulterated and mislabeled foods, drugs, cosmetics, and medical devices. That law was joined by the Food, Drug and Cosmetic (FDC) Act of 1938 and various amendments to it (including the FDA Modernization Act of 1997), the Public Health Service Act (PHS) of 1944, the 1968 Radiation Control for Health and Safety Act amending the PHS Act, the Fair Packaging and Labeling Act of 1966, and the Drug Price Competition and Patent Term Restoration Act of 1984. By force of these major laws, as well as others, the FDA regulates those foods, drugs, cosmetics, and medical devices found in interstate commerce. Meat and poultry are regulated by the Agriculture Department, and products such as child-proof medicine bottle caps and tobacco are regulated elsewhere in the federal government.

Responsibilities

The FDA:

- Regulates the composition, quality, safety, and labeling of food, food additives, food colors, and cosmetics and carries out some research in these areas.

- Monitors and enforces regulations through the inspection of food and cosmetics producers' facilities, surveillance of advertising and media reports, and follow-up of consumer complaints.

- Regulates the composition, quality, safety, efficacy, and labeling of all drugs for human use and establishes, in part through research, scientific standards for this purpose.

GLOSSARY

Adulterated—Products or materials that are defective and unsafe because they are contaminated or were produced under unsanitary conditions.

ANDA (Abbreviated new drug application)—An application that must be filed and approved before a manufacturer can market a copy of an already approved drug. ANDAs require information showing that the copy is bioequivalent to the original product but do not require original test results proving safety and efficacy.

Bioequivalent—A drug product is considered a bioequivalent if it demonstrates the same therapeutic effect as the drug it copies.

Biologics—Medical products, such as vaccines and serums, derived from living organisms.

Carcinogen—A substance that is shown to cause cancer.

Delaney Amendment—A 1958 amendment to the Food, Drug and Cosmetic Act that requires the FDA to ban any food or color additive that has been shown to cause cancer in laboratory test animals. Named after the chief sponsor, Rep. James J. Delaney, D-N.Y. (1945–1947, 1949–1978).

Generic drug—A copy of an already approved drug product whose patent protection has expired. To gain approval of a generic drug product, the manufacturer must submit an ANDA including laboratory tests demonstrating that the copy is bioequivalent to the original product.

Listed drug—A product with an approved NDA.

Misbranded—Products or materials with labels that mislead or lack necessary information.

NCE (New chemical entity)—A new chemical that has not been adequately characterized in the literature with regard to its physical and chemical properties.

NDA (New drug application)—An application that a pharmaceutical company must submit before the FDA will allow it to market a new drug. NDAs require supporting evidence that the new drug is both safe and effective.

OTC (Over-the-counter)—A drug product that can be sold directly to the consumer without a doctor's prescription.

- Requires premarket testing of new drugs and evaluates new drug applications and requests to approve drugs for experimental use.
- Develops standards for the safety and effectiveness of over-the-counter drugs.
- Develops guidelines on good drug manufacturing practices and makes periodic inspections of drug manufacturing facilities in the United States and overseas.

- Monitors the quality of marketed drugs through product testing, surveillance, and compliance and adverse reaction reporting programs.
- Conducts recalls or seizure actions of products found to violate federal laws and pose hazards to human health.
- Conducts research and establishes scientific standards for the development, manufacture, testing, and use of biological products.
- Inspects and licenses manufacturers of biological products.
- Requires premarket testing of new biological products and evaluates the claims for new drugs that are biologics.
- Tests biological products, often on a lot-by-lot basis.
- Collects data on medical device experience and sets standards for medical devices.
- Regulates the safety, efficacy, and labeling of medical devices and requires premarket testing of medical devices categorized as potentially hazardous.
- Establishes standards and makes regulations for good manufacturing practices for medical devices and inspects manufacturers' facilities.
- Conducts research on the biological effects of radiation exposure and develops programs to reduce human exposure to radiation.
- Determines standards for the quality of radiation-emitting products, such as television sets and X-ray machines, inspects radiological product manufacturing facilities, and provides certification for products meeting FDA standards.
- Develops programs and standards dealing with veterinary drugs, particularly in the areas of good manufacturing practices and the handling of livestock destined for human consumption.
- Occasionally conducts or solicits research on potentially toxic substances and distributes information on toxic substances under agency jurisdiction.

Powers and Authority

The FDA commissioner is assisted by seven associate commissioners who are responsible for legislation and public information; planning and evaluation; management and operations; and regulatory, health, and consumer affairs. The FDA's investigations, analysis, research, and compliance monitoring take place through the National Center for Devices and Radiological Health, the Center for Biologics Evaluation and Research, the Center for Drug Evaluation and Research, and the Centers for Food Safety and Applied Nutrition and for Veterinary Medicine.

ENFORCEMENT ACTIVITIES

In fulfilling its statutory duties, the FDA engages in three broad categories of activity: analysis, surveillance, and correction. Most, although not all, analytical work is preventive, occurring in the process of clearing new products for the market. Rather than conducting research on new drugs, food additives, veterinary drugs, biological drugs, and some medical devices from scratch, each section of the agency reviews scientific literature and test results and consults with advisory boards on the products under its jurisdiction. To the degree that the agency oversees and makes standards for bioresearch carried out by product sponsors (for example, drug manufacturers and processed food manufacturers), it has a hand in the analytical process itself. Insulin and a few other products must be tested batch by batch before going on the market; in September 1982 antibiotics were exempted from this process. In the FDA's field offices, chemists analyze samples from products already on the market to ensure that they meet FDA standards.

The FDA's surveillance duties are performed by field office inspectors authorized to inspect factories and other establishments that produce food, drugs, cosmetics, medical devices, and radiation-emitting products. Inspectors have access to every link in the commercial chain, overseeing research and development, production, distribution, and storage for the products regulated by the FDA. In addition, the FDA keeps track of developments in relevant markets by means of programs such as its "adverse reaction reporting system" and by attention to consumer complaints. The FDA licenses blood banks and manufacturers of biologic drugs.

Finally, when the FDA encounters violations of its rules—such as adulterated or misbranded products—it has several enforcement options:

Regulatory Letter. The FDA can send an enforcement document to the top management of a firm, stating that legal action will be taken unless the apparent violative product conditions are corrected.

Recall. After the FDA, or a manufacturer, finds that a product is defective, a recall may be initiated to remove the product from the marketplace. Recalls may be made voluntarily by the manufacturer or conducted at the request of the FDA. In some cases recalls may involve correction rather than removal of the product. The administration monitors the progress of recalls to ensure that all affected inventory is corrected or removed from sale.

Injunction. The FDA also may initiate civil court proceedings against the individual or company involved. Such actions usually seek to stop the continued manufacture or distribution of products that are in violation of the law.

Citation. In the event of a possible law violation, the FDA may send to a firm or to an individual notification that criminal action is contemplated and an invitation to provide information indicating that no violation has occurred.

Seizure. The FDA can initiate a seizure by filing a complaint with the U.S. District Court where the goods to be seized are located. A U.S. marshal is directed by the court to take possession of the goods until the matter is resolved.

Prosecution. On recommendation of the FDA, the U.S. attorney general may file a criminal action against an individual or a company that is charged with violating the laws administered by the agency.

Civil Money Penalty. On recommendation by the FDA that violations related to radiation-emitting electronic devices have occurred, monetary fines may be imposed by a court.

REGULATIONS AND STANDARDS

The FDA commissioner has initial authority to issue regulations and standards for the industries under the agency's jurisdiction. All regulations are subject to review by the HHS secretary. Major regulations administered by the FDA include:

- FDA Food Standards, which establish specifications for foods and food products.
- Current Good-Manufacturing Practice Guidelines, which establish quality controls, including requirements for sanitation, inspection of materials, and finished products.
- New Drug Regulations, which establish requirements for new drug approvals and for a drug's continued safety and efficacy.
- Regulations may be formulated or amended by a process of hearings and other administrative proceedings.

Once a proposed regulation is published in the *Federal Register,* any party may submit comments to the commissioner on the proposal. After taking these public comments into account, the commissioner issues a final rule. The decisions of the commissioner may be appealed to a U.S. circuit court of appeals.

The FDA also issues guidelines and advisory opinions. The guidelines state procedures or standards that are not legally binding, but they are recommended by the FDA. Guidelines are announced in the *Federal Register* and placed on file with the dockets management office. Advisory opinions are formulated, when feasible, upon receiving a request from any member of the public.

To assist the commissioner with decisions, the FDA has established advisory committees whose members review and recommend policy and technical decisions to the commissioner. There are currently more than fifty standing advisory committees. An advisory committee may be established to examine any area regulated by the FDA. The committees are composed of experts in particular areas, and they also may include representatives of consumer groups.

The advisory committees play a particularly crucial role in the drug approval process, holding lengthy detailed hearings on experimental therapies to determine whether there is sufficient scientific evidence to find the drugs safe and effective in their intended use. Although such hearings are not required under federal drug law, the FDA typically calls on the committees to screen any pending drug, especially one for which approval might engender controversy, to bolster the decision-making process. The committees' views are not binding on the FDA, but they typically carry great weight with agency decision makers.

ADMINISTRATIVE PROCEEDINGS

The FDA has several types of administrative proceedings for rulemaking. Some are mandated by statute; others may be requested by interested persons or initiated by the commissioner. The rulemaking process is complex, with various opportunities for hearings depending on factors such as whether the rulemaking is considered formal or informal by the agency. Detailed information is contained in Title 21 of the *Code of Federal Regulations*.

The commissioner has several administrative proceedings by which to consider a petition from a member of the public; to issue, amend, or revoke a rule; or to otherwise review and discuss regulations. In several cases, the FDA commissioner has the authority to issue regulations without going through the process of administrative hearings.

A hearing, required in certain rulemaking procedures, may be initiated in a number of ways, most frequently by objections to proposed FDA regulations or upon the initiative of the commissioner.

REPORTING AND REGISTRATION

The FDA has several reporting programs for its regulated industries. The major programs are:

Drug Listing and Establishment Registration. Owners and operators of establishments that manufacture or process pharmaceuticals in the United States are required to register and list all their products with the FDA.

Products that must be listed include all drugs for human use, biologics, blood and blood derivatives, veterinary drugs, medicated pre-mixes for animal feed, and in vitro diagnostic products (those that are drugs). Establishments that are required to register include all facilities that manufacture or process drugs and those that repackage or otherwise change the container, wrapper, or labels. Foreign drug manufacturers must list drugs as well, although they do not have to register.

Low-Acid Canned Foods Registration. All commercial processors of low-acid canned food must register their facilities and products with the FDA. Processors also are required to file processing information for each food product they handle.

Medical Device Registration. As with drug manufacturers, owners and operators of establishments that manufacture medical devices must register and list all their products with the FDA.

Radiation Registration. Manufacturers of certain electronic products that emit radiation (such as microwave ovens, X-ray machines, and color television sets) must furnish the FDA with initial product reports prior to marketing as well as reports of model changes.

Cosmetics Registration. The FDA has a voluntary reporting program for the registration of cosmetics manufacturers and their products.

Background

The origins of the FDA can be traced to one individual, Harvey W. Wiley, chief chemist of the Agriculture Department's Bureau of Chemistry. Soon after joining the bureau in 1883, Wiley began experimenting with food and drug adulteration. His most famous experiments took the form of feeding small doses of poisons to a group of human volunteers. The substances fed to the volunteers were similar or identical to those found in food preservatives common at the time.

Dubbed the "Poison Squad," the volunteers generated publicity for Wiley's experiments and created a public awareness of the dangers of eating adulterated foods. This publicity led Congress to enact the Food and Drug Act of 1906.

Wiley's Bureau of Chemistry began administering the act in 1907. Twenty years later, responsibility for administering the legislation was transferred to the Agriculture Department's newly created Food, Drug and Insecticide Administration. In 1931 the name was changed to the Food and Drug Administration.

The FDA's powers were expanded in 1938 with the passage of the Food, Drug and Cosmetic Act. The most significant part of the legislation required that a manufacturer prove the safety of a new drug before the FDA would allow it to be placed on the market. Congress was spurred into action by the death in 1937 of more than one hundred people who had taken a dose of a seemingly harmless cure-all, elixir of sulfanilamide.

In 1940 the administration was transferred from the Agriculture Department to the Federal Security Agency, a new agency established to protect the public health. The Federal Security Agency was incorporated into the Department of Health, Education and Welfare (HEW) when that department was created in 1953.

Today the FDA maintains a wide influence over U.S. products—it regulates products that account for 25 cents of every dollar spent and oversees almost one-third of the products in the U.S. market.

EXPANDED POWERS

The regulatory authority of the administration was broadened in 1958 with the passage of an amendment to the Food, Drug, and Cosmetic Act. Known as the Delaney Amendment, after its sponsor, New York representative James Delaney, it required manufacturers to prove the safety of food additives and required the FDA to prohibit the use of any food additive that induced cancer in humans or animals.

In 1962 it was discovered that pregnant women who had taken the drug thalidomide ran a very high risk of giving birth to deformed children. Thalidomide had been widely marketed in Europe, but the drug had been kept off the U.S. market largely through the efforts of an FDA chemist who was not convinced of its safety. Again, public awareness of the problem roused Congress to enact stronger FDA legislation.

The Food and Drug Act Amendments of 1962 required drug manufacturers to prove the effectiveness as well as the safety of their products before they could be marketed. The FDA also was authorized to order the immediate withdrawal of dangerous drugs from the market. It was given additional powers in 1976 when Congress passed legislation requiring regulation of complex medical devices and diagnostic products.

In 1979 Congress passed legislation removing education functions from HEW to a new Education Department. What remained, including the Food and Drug Administration, was renamed the Health and Human Services Department.

FDA IN THE 1980S

In 1983 President Ronald Reagan signed into law a bill providing financial incentives to the developers of new therapies for diseases that were rare or otherwise had such small markets as to make them unprofitable. The FDA, two years earlier, had instituted a program to encourage the development of so-called orphan drugs, which the government defined as drugs intended for the treatment of diseases with 200,000 or fewer U.S. victims. But the 1983 law and its 1985 amendments formalized the FDA program and offered eligible orphan drug developers seven years' marketing exclusivity, tax credits, research grants, and other federal incentives and subsidies.

The Drug Price Competition and Patent Term Restoration Act, which became law in 1984, was intended by its drafters to make the drug industry more competitive by speeding the entry into the marketplace of generic drugs, which are copies of brand-name products whose patent protection has expired. The law allowed manufacturers of generic drugs simply to demonstrate that their product was "bioequivalent," or therapeutically identical, to the brand-name product they were copying. They accomplished this by filing an Abbreviated New Drug Application (ANDA), a much shorter procedure than the New Drug Application (NDA) required for a new drug. At the same time the measure offered enhanced patent protection for brand-name drug products, to offset the growing period of time required for FDA review of new drug marketing applications.

The 1984 law had made immediately eligible for generic competition more than one quarter of the two hundred largest-selling prescription drugs, as well as many less popular products. Once the new law was in place, drug companies swamped the FDA with applications to market new generic drugs. In the first six months of the law's life, the FDA approved 206 ANDAs but was slow to complete formal regulations to flesh out the details of the process to approve new generic drugs.

The law also enabled the holder of a patent for a drug, medical device, or food additive to extend it for a maximum of five years, depending on the time required by the FDA to complete its review of the product and provided the post-approval patent life did not exceed fourteen years. The longer patent life responded to the brand-name industry's complaints that lengthy FDA review times had decreased the effective life of a patent from sixteen years in 1961 to ten years by 1984.

A scandal uncovered in the FDA's Generic Drugs Division during 1989 devastated congressional and administration confidence in the FDA. The lack of regulations and controls had made it easier for unscrupulous FDA drug reviewers to act unfairly or arbitrarily by, for example, moving one company's applications through the bureaucracy at a faster pace than a competitor's or repeatedly "losing" another company's paperwork. By April 1992 Congress had passed legislation that provided stricter HHS oversight of the FDA and tightened the generic drug approval process.

FDA IN THE 1990S

In 1990 President George Bush appointed David A. Kessler, medical director of the Albert Einstein College of Medicine in New York, commissioner of the agency. Kessler, who had both medical and law degrees, waged an aggressive effort to improve the FDA's image, enforce regulations, and streamline its product-testing efforts. Kessler played a high-profile role, becoming one of the most recognized figures in the federal bureaucracy.

An attempt in the early 1990s to increase and standardize the FDA's enforcement powers had powerful House supporters, but never went to the floor for a vote. Advocates of the legislation argued that FDA authority had never been seriously reviewed since 1938, and its powers had been delegated piecemeal over decades. But opposition from food producers and the makers of drugs and medical devices helped kill the legislation.

The FDA in 1990 completed a review of the safety and effectiveness of the active ingredients of all over-the-counter drugs, a project it had begun in 1972 under orders from Congress. In 1990 the FDA banned 111 unproven ingredients used in nonprescription diet aids and appetite suppressants, and another 223 ingredients in nineteen other classes of over-the-counter drugs used to treat a wide variety of medical conditions. In August 1992 the FDA released a list of 415 ingredients that the agency said were not shown to be effective.

In the early 1990s the FDA approved important new drugs to treat cystic fibrosis and to combat Alzheimer's disease. It also approved Taxol, a drug used to treat advanced ovarian cancer, and Depo-Provera, a birth control drug for women that prevents pregnancy with four injections per year. The FDA also approved over-the-counter use of the painkiller naproxen sodium and the hair-growth drug Rogaine.

A furor over the safety of silicone breast implants prompted the FDA in April 1992 to ban almost all of their cosmetic uses, limiting them to breast cancer patients and others with valid medical needs. The agency said they would be banned until scientific proof of their safety was established. With roughly 80 percent of implant surgery done for cosmetic purposes, the decision substantially curbed the practice. In 1994 the FDA opened an inquiry into the safety of saline breast implants, which were still widely available.

President Bill Clinton reappointed Kessler in 1993. The FDA under the Clinton administration followed a program of cutting bureaucratic delays and red tape, speeding agency actions, and eliminating unnecessary regulation. With health concerns rising, the FDA continually found itself in the middle of several national debates, ranging from the health risks of dietary supplements and cigarettes to tighter regulation of medical devices.

The FDA in February 1994 ended a ten-year-long debate over a genetically engineered drug that boosts milk production in cows when it approved recombinant bovine somatotropin (rBST), a bovine growth hormone. Consumer groups had fought the approval, voicing concerns about genetic engineering. Numerous studies, however, found that milk from hormone-treated cows posed no risk to human health. The FDA also approved in 1994 the genetically engineered Flavr-Savr tomato, opening the door to more genetically modified foods in the future.

In May 1994 the agency promulgated new requirements for uniform and understandable food labels, culminating in a four-year process to give consumers more information about the food they bought. Manufacturers were barred from making certain nutritional claims about their products on the label—such as promoting a product as "high fiber"—when other important information such as cholesterol level was not mentioned.

In a similar effort, the FDA in August 1995 unveiled an education program aimed at giving patients better written information on prescription drugs, such as a product's approved uses and serious adverse reactions. The program established quality standards for health professionals in distributing written leaflets with prescriptions. These standards focused on seven areas—scientific accuracy, consistency in a standard format, nonpromotional tone and content, specificity, comprehensiveness, understandable language, and legibility.

In 1995 the FDA turned its attention to claims by makers of dietary supplements. For two decades the agency had sought tighter regulations on the growing billion-dollar industry. New FDA rules forced makers of vitamins, minerals, and herbal remedies to back up the health claims made on their labels with evidence supported by "significant scientific agreement." Supporters of the labeling requirements contended that dietary supplement producers had misled consumers with exaggerated or unsubstantiated health claims. "Consumers should have access to dietary supplements that are truthfully labeled and marketed," said Kessler.

The FDA in January 1996 approved the fat substitute olestra, developed over twenty-five years by Procter & Gamble at a cost of $300 million. The food additive, which adds no fat or calories, was marketed under the trademark Olean in certain snacks. Because the substance may inhibit the body's absorption of some vitamins and nutrients, the company was required to add the vitamins A, D, E, and K to products containing olestra. All products containing olestra also had to carry an explicit warning about the fat substitute's possible side effects. In June 1998 an FDA advisory panel recommended that the agency consider changes to the warning labels following industry-sponsored studies that reportedly showed no increased side effects among olestra users.

The FDA approved in July 1996 the first nicotine patch to be sold over the counter to adults who wish to stop smoking. The skin patches, which have been available by prescription since 1992, were designed to help adults overcome their craving for a cigarette by releasing nicotine through the skin. Although the FDA has not been bound by the recommendations of its advisory committees, the action came after the Nonprescription Drugs Advisory Committee recommended the move in April. In a related move, the FDA approved in February 1996 an over-the-counter chewing gum called Nicorette that contains nicotine.

Although there was evidence that a few drug companies were making lavish profits from drugs brought to market under the 1983 orphan drug program, Congress and President Clinton extended tax credit for manufacturers of orphan drugs in August 1996. The FDA counseled against altering the terms of the program, for fear changes might discourage the development of life-saving remedies for obscure maladies.

President Clinton also signed into law in August 1996 bipartisan legislation that broke a decades-old logjam on pesticide regulations. The new law created a unified health standard for both raw and processed foods with guidelines to protect children from pesticides. The compromise wording imposed a safety standard to ensure that pesticide residues on foods pose no reasonable risk of harm, meaning that there likely would be no more than one in a million cases of cancer related to the residue in question.

THE AIDS EPIDEMIC

From the initial discovery of the first cases of Acquired Immune Deficiency Syndrome (AIDS), AIDS has remained the biggest challenge for the FDA as well as the entire health-related federal bureaucracy. As the numbers of people infected with HIV, the virus that causes AIDS, dramatically increased from the early 1980s through the 1990s, AIDS activists pressured the FDA to reform its conservative approach to more aggressive testing of new drugs.

In May 1990, after months of study, HHS formally proposed what it labeled a "parallel track" mechanism for the evaluation of drugs for AIDS and related conditions. Under the parallel track plan, unproven drugs would be widely distributed to patients under minimal medical supervision at the same time FDA testing was taking place. FDA implemented the policy in April 1992, allowing certain drugs that show promise of combating the AIDS virus to be made available to people unable to take standard therapy.

In June 1994 the FDA approved four drugs to treat AIDS and the HIV infection—Ziduvudine (AZT), didanosine (ddI), Zalcitabine (ddc), and Stavudine (D4T). None of these drugs is a cure for AIDS, but they may delay the onset of symptoms for some patients.

In December 1995 the FDA approved Invirase (saquinavir), the first protease inhibitor, a new class of drugs that inhibit the production of an enzyme key to HIV reproduction. The drug was approved in just three months, prompting the agency to tout its ability to review and get promising new drugs to dying patients quickly. In July 1996 the agency approved yet another drug, neviripine, for treating HIV. Neviripine.

With the medical community struggling for a cure, the FDA and other federal agencies also focused on prevention. In the mid-1990s the Clinton administration launched an aggressive public awareness campaign to promote the use of condoms. The FDA also approved the first home blood test kit for detecting the HIV virus in 1996 and an at-home urine HIV test in 1998.

The first broad-based international trial of a vaccine to protect against HIV was approved by the FDA in 1998, a year after President Clinton issued a call for such a vaccine by 2007. A San Francisco-based company, VaxGen, began testing a vaccine composed of a genetically engineered molecule that resembles part of HIV. The vaccine trial, which lasted three years, had mixed results.

MOVEMENT TOWARD TOBACCO REGULATION

In February 1994 Kessler announced a major FDA policy change, asserting that the agency had the authority to regulate the sale of cigarettes. Kessler said that evidence indicated that nicotine levels in cigarettes were being manipulated, which made cigarettes a drug and thus placed it under FDA jurisdiction. "A strict application of these provisions could mean, ultimately, removal from the market of tobacco products containing nicotine at levels that cause or satisfy addiction," he said.

Kessler's decision was followed by a number of allegations that Philip Morris Co., the nation's largest tobacco company, had suppressed a 1983 study concluding that nicotine was addictive. When Republicans gained control of Congress in 1995, congressional action on the issue was effectively halted. In the summer of 1996, however, the Clinton administration took the initiative by essentially recasting smoking as a "pediatric disease."

In August 1996 President Clinton announced that he would allow the FDA to regulate nicotine as an addictive drug and impose strict limits on tobacco advertising in an effort to prevent children and teenagers from smoking cigarettes or using smokeless tobacco. The president's decision was significant because for the first time the FDA was given oversight authority over tobacco advertising—a jurisdiction that had previously fallen to the Federal Trade Commission.

Coinciding with the White House announcement, the FDA issued its rule to reduce the access and appeal of tobacco products by making it harder for young people under eighteen to buy cigarettes and smokeless tobacco. The rule required anyone who looked younger than twenty-six to show proof of age to buy cigarettes and that tobacco products be placed behind sales counters to deter youngsters from shoplifting. Cigarette vending machines were prohibited in many public places, and cigarette billboards were banned within 1,000 feet of schools and playgrounds. Tobacco ads in magazines with a high ratio of underage readers were restricted to black-and-white text.

Hours after the FDA's announced rule, tobacco and advertising industries filed a complaint in federal district court alleging that only Congress could give the FDA regulatory authority over tobacco. Moreover, they said the new regulatory action would affect adults because it restricted tobacco companies' ability to use billboards, sponsor major sporting events, and use in-store tobacco displays. In addition, critics of the government's action said the move to declare nicotine in tobacco as an addictive drug could eventually lead to a ban on cigarette sales to adults. HHS secretary Donna Shalala denied, however, that the Clinton administration planned to pursue an outright ban on tobacco sales.

In April 1997 U.S. District Judge William Osteen let stand FDA's regulation of tobacco sales to minors and of vending machine sales but halted parts of the 1996 rule that restricted advertising and promotional activities. Both sides hastily appealed the ruling.

In an about-face, the five major tobacco companies on June 20, 1997, agreed to many of the same or more stringent restrictions in a legal settlement with forty state attorneys general. Beginning in Mississippi in May 1994, state officials had filed lawsuits in state and federal courts seeking recoupment of Medicaid funds used to treat state smokers. In the June 1997 settlement, the five companies agreed to pay $368.5 billion over the first twenty-five years of the lawsuit and comply with a number of restrictions on its marketing if they were granted legal protections, such as the settling of punitive damage claims based on past actions and the resolution of lawsuits brought by the state attorneys general. The settlement also would have capped the amount of money that the tobacco companies would have paid out for other lawsuits such as individual actions in any given year.

The enactment of the settlement proved to be more difficult than state officials or the industry had envisioned. Congress demanded a strong role in crafting a national tobacco policy. In April 1998, after months of deliberations, a national version of the settlement was approved by the Senate Commerce, Science and Transportation Committee on a 19–1 vote. However, Republicans criticized the bill—which had been introduced by Sen. John McCain, the Republican chair of the committee—as overly regulatory. By the time the bill reached the Senate floor, requirements on the industry had increased, with payments over twenty-five years rising to $516 billion, while legal protections had been stripped down essentially to an annual cap on payouts.

The industry protested by removing its support and launching a $40 million national ad campaign against the legislation. The full Senate conducted a freewheeling debate on the bill before the measure died on a pair of procedural votes in June 1998.

In another courtroom victory for the tobacco industry, a three-judge circuit court panel ruled in a 2–1 vote in August 1998 that the FDA had no authority to impose any restrictions on the tobacco industry without congressional approval. The ruling reversed the April 1997 decision that allowed FDA regulation of tobacco sales to teenagers. The

Justice Department quickly appealed the ruling to the full circuit court, the last stop on the way to the Supreme Court.

In March 2000 the Supreme Court voted 5–4 to strike down the FDA's authority to regulate tobacco, saying that only Congress could confer such authority on the agency. Several lawmakers tried in 2000 to give FDA the power to regulate tobacco, although the Republican leadership appeared firmly opposed to such moves. The proposals—which never became law—would have taken a far narrower approach to government regulation than the McCain bill.

For example, McCain joined forces with Sen. Bill Frist, a heart and lung transplant surgeon, on legislation that would have revived some provisions in McCain's 1998 bill. Similar to that proposal, the measure would have allowed the FDA to regulate tobacco because of the health risks associated with smoking. Frist, who has performed thousands of heart and lung transplants on longtime smokers with cancers and circulatory diseases, thought it was critical to stop teenagers from taking up smoking. So his bill would have required regulators who wanted to bar an advertising campaign to prove that such a ban would limit children's access to tobacco products.

The Frist bill also would have encouraged the development of so-called reduced risk cigarettes, which tobacco companies claim reduce harmful byproducts in smoke by heating tobacco instead of burning it. Public health officials, however, balked at the idea of the government declaring that a "safer" cigarette existed.

Separately Sen. Edward M. Kennedy of Massachusetts pushed a bill that would have revived many elements of McCain's 1998 measure, which would have raised the price of cigarettes, capped tobacco companies' legal liability, and restricted tobacco advertising. Kennedy's action put McCain and Frist in the awkward position of opposing legislation they had championed just two years earlier. By the start of the 108th Congress in 2003, however, neither the Frist nor Kennedy bill had advanced.

FDA OVERHAUL

In 1997 the FDA underwent a major overhaul under the Food and Drug Administration Modernization Act. The impetus behind the legislation was to combat complaints that the FDA was dragging its feet in approving new drugs and medical devices. Congressional Republicans and some Democrats criticized the agency's extensive testing practices by saying they prevented needed, life-improving drugs from reaching the public.

Consumer advocates and other Democrats, concerned that a speedy approval process might unnecessarily endanger the lives and safety of Americans, opposed the bill. Opponents argued that the agency had already made great strides in reducing the review time of new drugs and medical devices. After months of negotiations, vocal opponents such as Senator Kennedy supported the final version of the bill. The overhaul affected almost every major responsibility of the FDA. The legislation laid out specific timelines for the FDA to act upon various applications.

Among the requirements was a mandated faster review of clinical trials for new drugs. Prior to the law's enactment, the preapproval process took an average of about seven years as the drug companies evaluated the safety of the proposed drug on a pool of generally fewer than one hundred volunteers. After that stage, the companies were required to conduct another trial on a larger pool of patients to double-check the drug's effects because previous law mandated "substantial evidence of effectiveness." The 1997 law clarified that only one clinical trial could offer enough study for a new drug approval. The FDA was not required to accept more than one trial before approving a drug, but it was given the option if the trial was "well-controlled."

In exchange for shortening the time frame for drug approval, drug companies were required to pay an increase of about 21 percent in user fees. The fees for new drug applications were scheduled to rise from $233,000 in fiscal 1997 to $258,451 in fiscal 2002.

The law also expanded the parallel track process for approving new drugs, including vaccines and biological products that are intended to fight life-threatening or serious diseases. Producers may request that their application be given the faster parallel track review. If the HHS secretary approves the product for parallel track consideration under certain criteria, the FDA would be able to review further studies and any proposed promotional materials at least thirty days before the product was released to the public. The FDA would still have the authority to withdraw its backing of a product if further tests raised concerns.

Further evidence of a desire to change the culture of FDA was evident in a new rule to require advisory panels of expert consultants to review drugs within sixty days of its submission and to require the FDA to report the panel's recommendation within ninety days of receiving it. Medical devices, from pacemakers to hearing aids to bandages, also were affected by the legislation. Simple devices such as bandages, toothbrushes, and tongue depressors were exempted from approval procedures unless they posed a danger to society or were of "substantial importance." Priority for review was given to rare devices that are considered breakthrough technologies that are significantly different from products already on the market.

Most devices had been reviewed through a procedure, known as the 510(k) process, reserved for devices similar to others already on the market. The new legislation offered a more collaborative manner for the review of such applications by encouraging FDA officials to suggest minor improvements to manufacturers in the clinical review

phase. Manufacturers would not have to submit an additional application for approval to implement suggested changes to the device or to clinical testing procedures.

HHS officials also were required to meet with manufacturers to determine what type of scientific evidence would be needed for the FDA to evaluate the efficacy of a device that the manufacturer planned to later submit for approval. Within thirty days of a meeting, officials would have to describe the necessary scientific evidence in writing to the manufacturer.

Evaluation of devices by outside third-party consultants was encouraged in the legislation. The measure expanded a demonstration project that allowed the HHS secretary to accredit reviewers. Manufacturers were to pay the reviewers to consult with them under the oversight of the secretary. Certain complicated devices were exempted.

Health and nutrient claims that food producers want to use in labeling were expected to be reviewed more quickly as a result of the law. Under the legislation, a proposed claim would be considered denied if officials did not approve it within one hundred days unless an extension was granted.

Another provision allows drug and device manufacturers to distribute information from a medical journal or textbook about a product's other, unapproved uses if the FDA approves it through a secondary "off-label" use application. The FDA could force the manufacturer to disclose conflicting reports of the secondary use or ban the manufacturer from distributing the information if the use was not legal. In October 1996 the FDA began allowing some limited uses of such information.

One of the first applications of the FDA's new speedy parallel track process was the quick approval of the first approved oral pill to treat impotence dysfunction. The drug Viagra, or sildenafil citrate, was approved less than six months after submission. Viagra caused a stir among the public, with 2.7 million prescriptions dispersed between March and June 1998. Some concerns arose about the safety of the activity for elderly patients. During that time, at least seventy-seven patients reportedly died after being prescribed the drug, with twenty-four reported to have suffered from cardiac problems.

Some lawmakers remain concerned that the new procedures initiated by the 1997 overhaul could jeopardize consumer safety. The July 1998 approval by the FDA of the drug thalidomide for leprosy raised eyebrows. The agency had banned the drug in 1962 because of safety concerns. Later, it was established that the drug caused severe birth defects. The FDA said that its approval in 1998 was based on a limited use of the drug. Officials argued that the large amount of publicity that the drug had received lowered the likelihood that it would be misused.

However, some lawmakers pointed to this approval as evidence that public safety was taking second priority to the need to push through approval of drugs. The September 2000 report to Congress found that many of the required changes mandated in the FDA overhaul bill were occurring at the agency. The report found that new drugs and biologics were being approved in just six months and that in 1999 the agency had approved new drugs to treat several diseases, including osteoarthritis, influenza, obesity, HIV, and diabetes.

The report also found that nearly two-thirds of 4,000 manufacturers of drugs, biological agents, and medical devices said that the FDA's guidance on submission requirements made the approval process faster and easier than it was in 1997. The agency also had improved the safety of seafood by installing a quality control system in all domestic seafood plants, worked with other federal agencies to establish a nationwide food safety surveillance network, and launched a nationwide public information campaign to help reduce injuries and other adverse events caused by improper use of medicines, vaccines, medical devices, and foods.

The 1997 overhaul also required the FDA to compile a new publicly available database of clinical trials used to treat serious conditions, a goal the agency met during 1999. In November 2000 the agency launched an improved Web site to allow the public access to information about FDA activities, such as safety alerts and product approvals.

FDA IN THE 2000s

The year 2000 brought a variety of new challenges for the agency that reflected the changing nature—and complexity—of the many issues under FDA regulations. That year, for example, the FDA came under scrutiny for its monitoring of gene therapy trials after an eighteen-year-old volunteer, Jesse Gelsinger, died. Gene therapy is a process in which faulty genes linked to certain diseases are replaced by healthy ones. During congressional hearings lawmakers questioned whether both FDA and the National Institutes of Health (NIH), which share oversight of biomedical trials, had adequately monitored potentially serious side effects that may arise from gene therapy. Gelsinger's father told lawmakers that researchers did not disclose that laboratory monkeys died following a procedure similar to the one done on his son, or that several earlier human subjects sustained serious liver damage.

Legislators have debated whether tighter federal oversight would discourage researchers from exploring the field. Congress has also considered—but has yet to reach consensus—on giving NIH a greater share of jurisdiction in part because NIH in the past had been quicker than the FDA in publicly disclosing adverse reactions in clinical trials.

FDA clashed with Congress again in September 2000 when it approved the marketing of RU-486, the so-called abortion pill. Conservatives were outraged. "The FDA's mission is to promote health, not facilitate the taking of life," said former representative Tom Coburn, R-Okla. Liberals such as Rep. Nita M. Lowey, D-N.Y., said the approval was "an important day for American women. . . . the FDA put science first and left politics out." HHS Secretary Tommy G. Thompson has expressed concerns about the safety of RU-486, but as of early 2003 he had taken no action to ban use of the pill.

While the FDA claims it has jurisdiction over human cloning, some lawmakers, backed by President George W. Bush, tried in both the 2002 and 2003 to pass legislation that would ban the use of the procedure to create human embryos. Proponents of a ban said that there was no way that FDA could stop the practice, even if it did have the regulatory power to do so. Agency officials claim that the act of taking an adult cell and implanting it into a woman's egg stripped of its DNA is subject to provision in the Public Health Service Act of 1944 and the Food, Drug and Cosmetic Act of 1938.

In December 2002 Congress reauthorized the drug user fee program and expanded it to include medical devices. The medical device industry had shied away from paying user fees to underwrite additional FDA staff, although the user fee program for the drug industry has been hailed for speeding up approvals for new drugs. The 2002 bill allowed private contractors to assume some of the FDA's duties to inspect manufacturing facilities of medical devices. Democrats won inclusion of funding to expand FDA studies of the safety of new products after they reach the market. The bill also established new regulations for the sterilization and reuse of catheters and other products currently approved only for single use.

In AIDS research, the FDA in 2002 approved a test that could detect within as little as twenty minutes if someone was infected with HIV. Experts said that advance might encourage thousands of Americans to get tested, which in turn might slow the spread of the disease.

In March 2003 the agency approved the use of the drug Fuzeon to treat advanced HIV infection in adults and children ages six and older. According to the FDA, the drug was the first product in a new class of medications called fusion inhibitors to receive marketing approval. Drugs in that class interfere with the entry of HIV into cells by inhibiting the fusion of viral and cellular membranes. That inhibition blocks the virus's ability to infect certain components of the immune system. While AIDS advocates were pleased with the drug's approval, they feared that its price—$20,000 a year for patients—would make the drug out of reach for many of the patients who could benefit by it.

FDA was thrust into the spotlight in the 107th Congress when Democrats and some Republicans pushed proposals that would make it easier to import prescription drugs approved by the agency from nations that cap prices. Proponents of such measures say the practice, known as drug reimportation, would allow consumers to pay less—perhaps as much as 50 percent less in some cases—for the same drugs they now purchase at higher prices in the United States. Drug manufacturers said that drug importation should not be allowed because it would jeopardize patient safety by increasing the flow of counterfeit drugs into the country and that it would be virtually impossible for the FDA to police how drugs are produced, shipped, or stored overseas. When the issue was debated in Congress in 2002, FDA officials, as well as HHS Secretary Thompson said that the agency could not guarantee the safety of "reimported" drugs, but proponents of such bills said that FDA had the power to make sure the drugs were safe.

With prescription drug prices increasing—and much of the rise being attributed to ads that target some of the newest and most expensive drugs on the market—the FDA will likely have rigorous oversight of so-called "direct to consumer advertising," the proliferation of television and magazine advertising that drug companies have done since 1997 when the FDA loosened its rules on such ads. According to the General Accounting Office (GAO), prescription drug spending increased at an annual rate of about 18 percent from 1997 through 2001. During that same period, spending on direct-to-consumer advertising surged 145 percent to $2.7 billion from $1.1 billion, the GAO found.

Pharmaceutical companies have said the advertising gives patients important information about drugs and may convince them to seek treatment for many medical conditions that often go undiagnosed, such as depression or hypertension. But critics say ads create undo pressure to prescribe a particular medication whether or not it is needed. Mark B. McClellan, a Texas-born physician and economist named by President Bush in late 2001 to head the agency, has pledged to take tougher and quicker action against misleading drug ads and dietary supplement labels. "Advertising must be truthful and not misleading," McClellan told reporters shortly after his confirmation. "We will not be afraid to go to court when necessary." Should the FDA move to regulate such ads, lawmaker sympathetic to the drug industry may try to block the agency's efforts.

McClellan, who also served in the Clinton administration from 1998 to 1999 as a deputy assistant Treasury secretary for economic policy, has said he wanted to streamline the agency's drug-approval process, shortening the time and reducing the cost of getting new drugs to market. The agency's key mission, McClellan has said, is protecting public health.

Current Issues

McClellan's focus on making the FDA more accountable on public health issues has brought a renewed consumer focus to the agency. The FDA chief's interest in direct-to-consumer advertising is a clear example of his zest to reinvigorate FDA, which had not had a commissioner since Jane E. Henney, the first woman ever to head the agency, left in early 2001 after President Bush took office.

McClellan's tenure will likely be marked in ways his predecessors' terms were not. The threat of bioterrorism, for example, will bring new emphasis to the agency's regulatory powers, including its ability to protect the nation's food supply from contamination. The agency will be heavily involved in protecting the nation from health threats, such as a smallpox epidemic, which public health experts have not confronted for decades.

Early in the 108th Congress, lawmakers and President Bush were moving to expand funding for the research, production, and availability of vaccines that would be used to protect citizens against biological and chemical terrorist attacks. Under the legislation, the FDA would be given the authority to expedite the approval process for vaccines and treatments.

The vast array of medical devices, from the recently FDA-approved cardiac defibrillator designed for the home to contacts that are designed solely to change the color of the eye—a product the FDA has warned consumers not to use—present an array of challenges for the agency, because consumers expect FDA to protect them from products that could cause harm.

One of the more pressing consumer issues that immediately demanded McClellan's attention was how to deal with the increasing number of consumers who use the Internet to purchase medication—sometimes from foreign countries at lesser cost—rather than using the traditional method of filling a physician's prescription at the local pharmacy.

The agency has issued a series of "import alerts" to let FDA and U.S. Customs personnel and consumers know about possible dangers with some imported drugs. A December 2002 alert, for example, included accutane, which is used in the treatment of acne, and actiq, which is used to treat severe cancer pain. Consumers using versions of those and other listed drugs not approved by FDA could cause harm to themselves, McClellan said.

Another high-profile consumer issue for FDA will be its regulation of hormone replacement therapy for postmenopausal women. Early in 2003 the agency approved new labels for estrogen and estrogen with progestin

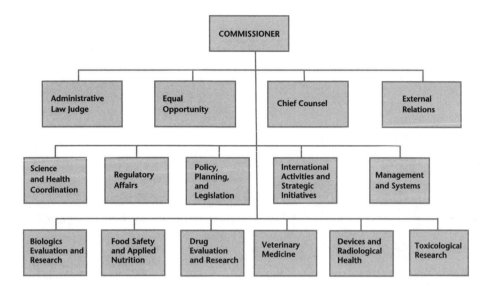

AGENCY ORGANIZATION

Headquarters and Divisions

(Listings for the FDA's research centers begin on p. 226.)

OFFICE OF THE COMMISSIONER

The commissioner is the chief administrative officer of the FDA, an agency within the Department of Health and Human Services (HHS). The commissioner is responsible for making final decisions on actions against food and drug manufacturers and distributors. Any decision of the FDA commissioner is subject to review and revision by the secretary of health and human services. The Office of Management and Budget may review proposed regulations with significant economic impact. The commissioner oversees all FDA operations and develops policy. The deputy commissioner/senior advisor assists the commissioner with the administration of the FDA centers and offices.

Commissioner

Mark McClellan . . . . (301) 827–2410

Fax . . . . (301) 443–3100

Deputy Commissioner

Lester Crawford . . . . (301) 827–3310

Chief Mediator and Ombudsman

Suzanna O'Shea . . . . (301) 827–3390

Executive Assistant to the Commissioner

Carol Crim . . . . (301) 827–2410

therapies to help women and their physicians evaluate the risks and benefits of such treatment. FDA's labeling changes included a new boxed warning, the highest level of warning information in labeling, that highlights the increased risk for heart disease, heart attacks, strokes, and breast cancer. The warnings follow an analysis of data from the Women's Health Initiative Study, a study sponsored by the NIH, that raised concern about the risks of using hormone replacement products.

McClellan has also focused on using the FDA's powers to help eliminate the number of medical errors that hurt and even kill thousands of Americans each year. Early in 2003 the FDA announced it would require bar codes on all medications used by hospitals to help reduce medical medication errors. McClellan estimated that the bar code requirement would prevent 400,000 bad drug reactions over the next two decades. Medication errors have been blamed on a variety of factors, including overworked nursing staff, poor physicians' handwriting, and computer-entry errors.

Lawmakers and the FDA have been focused on the idea of reducing medical errors since 1999 when the National Institute of Medicine estimated that medical errors killed as many as 98,000 people a year in the United States, more than car crashes. When FDA announced its bar coding proposal, McClellan said it would be "part of a comprehensive strategy to build a medical patient protection system for the twenty-first century."

Principal Associate Commissioner
  Murray M. Lumpkin.................. (301) 827–5709
Associate Commissioner for Science
  Norris Alderson .... (301) 827–3340

OFFICE OF EQUAL EMPLOYMENT AND CIVIL RIGHTS

Develops, implements, and monitors the FDA's affirmative action plans.

Director
  Rosamelia T. Lecea .... (301) 827–4830
  Fax..................................... (301) 827–0053

OFFICE OF THE ASSOCIATE COMMISSIONER FOR EXTERNAL RELATIONS

Advises the commissioner and other key agency officials on agency-level activities and issues that affect agency-wide programs, projects, strategies, and initiatives. Coordinates activities involving emergency or crisis situations and resolves complex problems and issues related to agency programs that are sensitive and controversial and affect agency relations with other federal agencies and foreign governments.

Senior Associate Commissioner
  Peter J. Pitts............................ (301) 827–3330
  Fax..................................... (301) 827–3052

CHIEF MEDIATOR AND OMBUDSMAN

Chief Mediator and Ombudsman
  Vacant.................................. (301) 827–3390
  Fax..................................... (301) 827–8039

OFFICE OF THE EXECUTIVE SECRETARIAT

The executive secretariat coordinates communication on program formulation and priorities, assigns and reviews agency correspondence, and serves as a liaison between the FDA and the Department of Health and Human Services.

Executive Secretariat
  LaJuana D. Caldwell.................... (301) 827–4450
  Fax..................................... (301) 827–1412

OFFICE OF INTERNAL AFFAIRS

Conducts investigations into allegations of wrongdoing by FDA employees.

Special Agent-in-Charge
  Donald Briggs .... (301) 827–0243
  Fax..................................... (301) 827–0273

OFFICE OF EXECUTIVE OPERATIONS

Director
  Linda Brna.............................. (301) 827–3440
  Fax..................................... (301) 594–0113

ORPHAN PRODUCTS DEVELOPMENT

Reviews and approves requests for orphan product designation (designation reserved for products to treat rare diseases that affect fewer than 200,000 people in the United States).

Director
  Marlene Haffner, M.D., M.P.H. .... (301) 827–3666
  Fax..................................... (301) 443–4915

OFFICE OF PUBLIC AFFAIRS

Serves as the agency's primary liaison with the news media and develops much of the material FDA uses to communicate its public health and consumer protection mission.

Associate Commissioner
  Lawrence Bachorik..................... (301) 827–6250
  Fax..................................... (301) 827–1219

Print Media Staff

Handles FDA press relations and news releases, distributes publications, and answers questions about programs and policies. Rockville office handles press inquiries on human and animal drugs, vaccines and other biological products, medical devices, or health fraud. Washington office handles press inquiries on food and cosmetics.

Senior Director, Media Affairs
  Bradford Stone .... (301) 827–6250
  Fax..................................... (301) 827–1681
Deputy Director, Washington
  Ruth Welch .... (202) 205–4144
  Fax..................................... (202) 205–5169

Broadcast Media Staff

Serves as primary contact for national electronic media for all of FDA. Handles requests for radio and on-camera interviews and background information on agency position and policies.

Director, Rockville
  Sharan Jayne........................... (301) 827–3434
  Fax..................................... (301) 443–8512
Deputy Director, Washington
  Monica Revelle .... (202) 205–4144
  Fax..................................... (202) 205–5169

Operations Staff

Coordinates and schedules requests for FDA speakers; coordinates agency exhibits for national meetings and conferences; works with associate commissioner in the allocation and management of financial and human resources; and assists the Associate Commissioner in establishing and maintaining efficient and productive management systems.

Director

Theresa Hoog Stone.................... (301) 827–6250

Fax...................................... (301) 827–1681

Website Management Staff

Oversees the content, design, and management of FDA's Web site (www.fda.gov), develops, and promotes creative uses of the Internet to help fulfill all aspects of the agency's mission.

Director

William Rados.......................... (301) 827–7140

Fax...................................... (301) 827–1682

Communications Staff

Produces most FDA publications, including consumer brochures and audiovisual materials about the agency and the products it regulates.

Director

Michael Herndon (acting)............. (301) 827–7130

Fax...................................... (301) 827–5308

OFFICE OF THE CHIEF COUNSEL

The office of the chief counsel provides legal services involving FDA's regulatory activities. The office's attorneys support the agency's public health and consumer protection missions by handling litigation matters and providing counseling advice. They represent FDA in judicial and administrative hearings by actively participating in case development and prosecution. They also prepare legal opinions, participate in rulemaking proceedings, legislative matters, policy deliberations, and international negotiations. The office works closely with other federal agencies.

Chief Counsel

Dan Troy................................ (301) 827–1137

Fax...................................... (301) 827–3054

OFFICE OF INTERNATIONAL PROGRAMS

Responsible for overseeing agency constituency efforts and supporting FDA centers and field offices. Has four component offices.

Deputy Commissioner

Melinda Plaisier .... (301) 827–3450

Fax...................................... (301) 827–1335

Office of Special Health Issues (OSHI)

The Office of Special Health Issues (OSHI) works with patients and their advocates to encourage and support their active participation in the formulation of FDA regulatory policy. The staff is familiar with the concerns confronting patients and families dealing with a life-threatening illness. OSHI serves the public by answering their questions about the FDA activities related to HIV/AIDS, cancer, and other special health issues, and provides information about the FDA drug approval process and clinical trials.

Director

Theresa A. Toiga....................... (301) 827–4460

Fax...................................... (301) 443–4555

Office of International Programs

Responsible for overall leadership, policy, and coordination of FDA international activities. Serves as focal point and liaison with foreign countries and international organizations. Coordinates FDA participation in a variety of international standard-setting and harmonization organizations and activities. Focal point for international agreements, including Memoranda of Understanding and mutual recognition activities. Also processes approvals for export of international drugs, manages requests for international, technical assistance, develops strategies for international partnering activities, and develops international strategic plans.

Director

Walter Batts............................(301) 827–4480

Fax...................................... (301) 827–0003

International Relations Staff

Walter Batts............................(301) 827–4480

International Agreements Staff

Linda Horton..........................(301) 827–3344

International Planning and Resource Management Staff

Beverly Corey..........................(301) 827–0855

International Scientific Activities and Standards Staff

Janet Jenkins Showalter...............(301) 827–0865

Office of Legislative Affairs

Acts as liaison between the FDA and Congress, monitors hearings and legislation relevant to the agency, and prepares FDA reports, testimony, and position papers on proposed legislation. Drafts legislative proposals, provides explanations of the laws and regulations administered by the FDA, and provides technical assistance to members of Congress and their staffs on matters related to the FDA. (*See also Congressional Action.*)

Associate Commissioner

Amit Sachdev..........................(301) 443–3150

Office of Women'S Health

Serves as a focal point for women's health issues. Responsibilities include coordinating efforts to correct gender disparities in drug, device, and biologics testing, and regulation, policy, and monitoring FDA clinical trial guidelines to ensure that women are represented and that gender analyses are included in product applications.

Director

Susan F. Wood.......................... (301) 827–0350

Fax..................................... (301) 443–0926

OFFICE OF MANAGEMENT AND SYSTEMS

Oversees agency management activities, including budget and finance, human resources, ethics, grants and contracts, procurement information systems and management, and record keeping. Also processes public responses to proposed FDA rulemaking.

Senior Associate Commissioner

Jeffrey M. Weber........................ (301) 827–3443

Fax..................................... (301) 594–6774

Deputy Associate Commissioner

Vacant.................................. (301) 827–3443

Office of Information Resources Management

Develops and implements agency policy and procedure related to information technology. Plans and coordinates information technology development to support agency programs. Manages Freedom of Information and Paperwork Reduction activities.

Chief Information Officer

William M. Bristow II.................. (301) 827–4280

Fax..................................... (301) 443–3470

Deputy Chief Information Officer

E. Glenn Rogers........................ (301) 827–4280

Software Engineering Services

Ray Russo.............................. (301) 827–6496

Planning, Resources and Information Systems Management

Roderick Bond.......................... (301) 827–6459

Operations and Technology Services

Mike Buster............................ (301) 827–4640

Information Services and Policy

Laura Rodin............................ (301) 827–4282

Freedom of Information

Betty Dorsey........................... (301) 827–6547

Facilities Telecommunications and Planning Support

John Robbins........................... (301) 827–7143

Office of Financial Management

Responsible for the formulation and execution of agency budget; development and maintenance of agency financial systems; oversight of the agency's financial audit activities; and management of all financial activities for FDA.

Director

Helen Horn............................. (301) 827–5001

Fax..................................... (301) 443–9987

Accounting

Dave Petak............................. (301) 827–5004

Budget Execution

Bob MacLeod........................... (301) 827–3923

Budget Formulation

Lisa Siegel............................ (301) 827–5022

Financial Systems

Mike Fullen............................ (301) 827–2788

Office of Human Resources and Management Services

Responsible for personnel, labor relations, and training policies. Manages agency ethics program and public responses to proposed rulemaking.

Director

Mary Babcok........................... (301) 827–4120

Fax..................................... (301) 443–6684

Deputy Director

Pat Foley.............................. (301) 827–4120

Classification Services Staff

George Calvert......................... (301) 827–4040

Information Resources Staff

Tony Wilson............................ (301) 827–4118

Commissioner Personnel Operations

Connie Roos............................ (301) 827–4039

Employee & Labor Management Relations

Gail Pierpoint (acting)................ (301) 827–4150

Compensation, Benefits and Training

Gail Pierpoint......................... (301) 827–4150

Recruitment & Staffing

Dolores Beebe.......................... (301) 827–4070

Management Programs

Gail Kohlhorst......................... (301) 827–4810

Office of Facilities, Acquisitions and Central Services

Responsible for grants and contracts, procurement, facilities planning, facilities management, safety, and security in the FDA.

Director

James Tidmore.......................... (301) 827–6890

Fax   (301) 827–7029

Deputy Director (Acquisitions)

Wayne Slaughter........................ (301) 827–6890

Associate Director for Acquisitions

Cynthia Hawley......................... (301) 827–7041

Contracts and Procurement Management

    Olia Hopkins .... (301) 827–7184

Grants Management

    Peggy Jones .... (301) 827–7160

OFFICE OF POLICY, PLANNING AND LEGISLATION

Advises the Commissioner and other key agency officials on matters relating to agency policy, regulations development, legislative issues, and planning and evaluation activities.

Senior Associate Commissioner

    William Hubbard...................... (301) 827–3370

    Fax.................................... (301) 594–6777

Management Adviser

    Fay Fink................................ (301) 827–3360

Office of Policy

Directs and coordinates the FDA's rulemaking activities and regulations development system. Also responsible for initiating more efficient regulatory procedures and overseeing agency regulatory reform efforts. Develops and maintains policies and communications regarding international regulation harmonization, including international standard setting and bilateral agreements on inspections.

Associate Commissioner

    Margaret Dotzel .... (301) 827–3360

    Fax.................................... (301) 443–6607

International Policy Staff

Develops and coordinates FDA's international policies, including harmonization, trade negotiations, and international standard setting, and advises the commissioner and other senior agency staff on international regulatory policy. Represents the agency on international policy matters with other federal agencies and at international meetings.

Director

    Linda Horton........................... (301) 827–3344

Policy Development and Coordination Staff

Advises the deputy commissioner on current and proposed FDA policies and establishes and monitors procedures for policy formulation throughout the agency. Negotiates the resolution of policy issues involving more than one component of the agency and coordinates the review and analysis of policy. Also serves as the agency liaison for intergovernmental policy development.

Director

    Catherine Lorraine .... (301) 827–3360

    Fax.................................... (301) 594–6777

Policy Research Staff

Proposes and researches policy alternatives and identifies the impact of FDA policies on national health issues and technological advances. Also researches the impact of external factors on policy formulation.

Director

    Karen Hulebak .... (301) 827–3380

Regulations Policy and Management Team

The administrative center for FDA regulatory and rulemaking activities. Reviews proposed and final regulations and other agency documents before publication in the *Federal Register* to ensure that regulations are necessary; consistent with agency policy; clearly written; enforceable; coordinated with other agency components and federal, state, and local governments; responsive to public participation requirements and applicable executive orders; and responsive to requirements for assessment of economic and environmental effects.

Also ensures that all regulations mandated by statute are promulgated and identifies regulations that require revision to correspond with current standards or those that should be revoked due to obsolescence. During the preparation of *Federal Register* documents the office arbitrates policy disagreements among agency components and provides all document development support functions.

Director

    Edwin Dutra........................... (301) 443–3480

    Fax.................................... (301) 443–2946

Deputy Director

    Ken Smith.............................. (301) 443–3480

Regulations Editorial Section

    Vacant................................. (301) 827–7010

Office of Planning

Coordinates FDA planning, program evaluation, and economic analysis. Conducts economic studies of regulatory policies, forecasts trends and problems that might affect the FDA, and measures agency performance and productivity.

Associate Commissioner

    Theresa Mullin (acting)............... (301) 827–5292

    Fax.................................... (301) 594–6777

Evaluation Staff

    Vacant................................. (301) 827–5292

Economics Staff

    Lawrence Braslow .... (301) 827–5331

Planning Staff

    Morris Bosin........................... (301) 827–5210

Management Initiatives Staff

    Vacant................................. (301) 827–3445

Management Specialist

Diane Fink............................. (301) 827–5293

Office of Legislation

Acts as liaison between the FDA and Congress, monitors hearings and legislation relevant to the agency, and prepares FDA reports, testimony, and position papers on proposed legislation. Drafts legislative proposals, provides explanations of the laws and regulations administered by the FDA, and provides technical assistance to members of Congress and their staffs on matters related to the FDA.

Associate Commissioner

Amit Sachdev........................... (301) 827–3793
Fax...................................... (301) 827–1960

Congressional Affairs Staff I

Michael Eck............................. (301) 827–3793

Congressional Affairs Staff II

Jarilyn Dupont .... (301) 827–3793

Congressional Affairs Support Staff

Lisa Granger............................ (301) 827–3793

Management Specialist

Donald L. Banks........................ (301) 827–3793

OFFICE OF REGULATORY AFFAIRS

Responsible for agency-wide programs to ensure compliance with FDA rules.

Associate Commissioner

John Taylor .... (301) 827–3101
Fax...................................... (301) 443–6591

Regional Operations

Deborah D. Ralston.................... (301) 443–6230

Enforcement

John M. Taylor .... (301) 827–0429

Criminal Investigations

Terrell Vermillion .... (301) 294–4030

CENTER FOR BIOLOGICS EVALUATION AND RESEARCH

CBER is responsible for ensuring the safety and efficacy of biological products from premarket review and clinical investigations to manufacturing and inspections to postmarketing requirements and enforcement actions. The center conducts mission-related regulatory research that focuses on safety, provides supporting information to the review process, and establishes national standards. Postmarketing activities include adverse event monitoring, both active and passive, inspections, lot release, surveillance and enforcement. CBER is responsible for the safety of the nation's blood supply and the products derived from blood, vaccines, allergenic extracts, antitoxins, therapeutics, related drugs and devices, and a wide variety of the products of new technologies such as DNA-derived biotechnology products, somatic cell therapy, gene transfer products, conventional banked human tissues, and xenotransplantation.

Director

Jesse Goodman .... (301) 827–0372
Fax...................................... (301) 827–0440

Deputy Director for Operations

Mark A. Elengold...................... (301) 827–0372

Deputy Director for Medicine

Vacant................................... (301) 827–0372

Biostatics and Epidemiology

Susan S. Ellenberg..................... (301) 827–3034

Blood Research and Review

Jay S. Epstein .... (301) 827–3518

Communication, Training and Manufacturers Assistance

Mary T. Meyer.......................... (301) 827–2000

Compliance and Biologics Quality

Steven A. Masiello..................... (301) 827–6190

Management

Joseph A. Biviano (acting)............. (301) 827–1320

Policy

Diane Maloney.......................... (301) 827–0372

Quality Assurance

Sherry Lard............................. (301) 827–0379

Review Management

Robert A. Yetter .... (301) 827–0372

Therapeutics Research and Review

Jay P. Siegel .... (301) 827–5098

Vaccine Research and Review

Karen Midthun......................... (301) 827–0655

CENTER FOR DEVICES AND RADIOLOGICAL HEALTH

Helps ensure that medical devices are safe and effective, and helps reduce unnecessary exposure to radiation from medical, occupational, and consumer products. Medical devices under the center's jurisdiction range widely in complexity and potential risk, and include such products as contact lenses, heart valves, artificial joints, and condoms. Radiation-emitting products include microwave ovens, television sets, sunlamps, and lasers. In regulating medical devices, the center has several functions: evaluating the safety and effectiveness of new devices before they can be marketed; conducting a postmarket surveillance program to identify and correct problems that occur with devices already on the market; working with the FDA field force in the inspection of medical device firms; educating health professionals and consumers about how to use devices safely; and conducting laboratory research to help make regulatory decisions and to identify safety problems that cross product lines. In regulating radiation-emitting products, the center promulgates and enforces performance standards with which manufacturers must comply.

Director
David W. Feigal Jr. .... (301) 443–4690
Fax .... (301) 594–1320

Associate Director for Systems and Management
Donald J. Sauer .... (301) 443–8120

Deputy Director for Science
Lillian J. Gill .... (301) 443–4690

Compliance
Larry D. Spears (acting) .... (301) 594–4692

Device Evaluation
Bernard E. Statland .... (301) 594–2022

Education and Communications
Mark Barnett .... (301) 443–6220

Health and Industry Programs
Lireka P. Joseph .... (301) 428–2845

Science and Technology
Donald E. Marlowe .... (301) 827–4777

Surveillance and Biometrics
Larry G. Kessler .... (301) 594–2812

CENTER FOR DRUG EVALUATION AND RESEARCH

Regulates the testing, manufacture, and labeling of drugs; reviews and evaluates new drug and investigational drug applications; monitors the quality and safety of drug products; regulates the advertising and promotion of prescription drugs; provides ongoing surveillance for adverse events and use problems; and promotes informational and educational programs that address both medical and consumer interests. Additional information can be found at www.fda.gov/cder. For general drug information, contact the center's Division of Drug Information by mail at CDER Division of Drug Information, (HFD-210), 5600 Fishers Ln., Rockville, MD 20857, by telephone at (301) 827-4573, or by email at dibcder.fda.gov. For registering a complaint, contact the Ombudsman by mail at CDER Ombudsman (HFD-001), 5600 Fishers Ln., Rockville, MD 20857, by telephone at (301) 594-5443, or by email at morrisonjcder.fda.gov. To report an adverse event associated with the use of an FDA regulated drug, biologic, device, or dietary supplement, call (301) 443-1246 or submit a report at www.fda.gov/medwatch.

Director
Janet Woodcock .... (301) 594–5400
Fax .... (301) 594–6197

Deputy Director
Steven Galson .... (301) 594–5400

Compliance
David Horowitz .... (301) 594–0054

Electronic Review
Randy Levin (acting) .... (301) 594–5400

Executive Operations
Deborah Henderson .... (301) 594–6779

Information Technology
Ralph Lillie .... (301) 827–6240

International Affairs
Justina Molzon .... (301) 594–5400

Management
Russell Abbott .... (301) 594–6741

Medical Policy
Robert Temple .... (301) 594–6758

Pharmaceutical Science
Helen Winkle .... (301) 594–2847

Policy
Jane Axelrod .... (301) 594–5400

Review Management
Sandy Kweder (acting) .... (301) 594–5400

Review Standards
Lisa Rarick .... (301) 594–5400

Training & Communications
Nancy Smith .... (301) 827–1651

CENTER FOR FOOD SAFETY AND APPLIED NUTRITION

(200 C St. S.W., Washington, DC 20204)

Responsible for developing FDA policy, standards, and regulations on foods (with the exception of red meats and poultry, which are under the jurisdiction of the Agriculture Department), food additives, artificial colorings, and cosmetics. Develops programs to monitor the implementation of quality assurance programs, provides information on the levels of compliance achieved by the food and cosmetic industries, and plans and manages seminars and workshops on topics related to food and cosmetics, including the protection of consumers from economic fraud.

Also conducts research on composition and safety of foods; methods to detect and identify microorganisms in foods that may cause human illness; health hazards associated with cosmetics and color additives; food hygiene and sanitation; processing, packaging, and handling procedures for food and cosmetics; chemical composition of cosmetics and color additives; the nutritional composition of food; and methods to detect pesticides and chemical contaminants.

Develops rules and guidelines for safety and sanitation of foods and inspecting facilities where food products and additives are manufactured. Also determines the accuracy of nutritional labeling statements and collects and studies data on food consumption patterns and food composition.

Director

    Joseph A. Levitt......................... (202) 205–4850

    Fax....................................... (202) 205–5025

Deputy Director

    Janice F. Oliver.......................... (202) 205–4307

Constituent Operations

    Catherine W. Carnevale............... (202) 205–5032

Cosmetics and Colors

    Adele Dennis (acting)................. (202) 205–4530

Dean, CFSAN Staff College

    George Jackson   (202) 205–4051

Equal Employment Opportunity

    Joan K. Jappa .... (202) 205–4284

Field Programs

    Joseph Baca.............................. (202) 205–4187

Food Safety Initiatives

    Louis J. Carson .... (202) 260-3470

Management Systems

    Juanita Wills............................. (202) 205–4637

Nutritional Products, Labeling and Dietary Supplements

    Christine J. Lewis....................... (202) 205–4561

Plant & Dairy Foods and Beverages

    Terry C. Troxcell........................ (202) 205–4064

Premarket Approval

    Alan Rulis............................... (202) 418–3100

Regulation and Policy

    L. Robert Lake.......................... (202) 205-4160

Science

    Robert L. Buchanan.................... (202) 205–4499

Scientific Analysis and Support

    Kenneth Falci............................ (202) 205–5817

Seafood

    Philip C. Spiller........................ (202) 418–3133

CENTER FOR VETERINARY MEDICINE

Develops FDA policy, standards, and regulations on the safety and efficacy of animal drugs, feed additives, and veterinary devices (instruments and implements intended for use in the diagnosis, cure, treatment, and prevention of disease). Works with federal and state agencies to ensure animal health and the safety of food derived from animals. Evaluates applications to market new animal drugs, food additives, feed ingredients, and devices; coordinates the veterinary medicine aspects of inspection and investigation programs; assesses the environmental impact of product approvals; and plans, directs, and evaluates the agency's surveillance and compliance programs for all animal drugs, feed additives, and devices.

Director

    Stephen F. Sundlof..................... (301) 827-2950

    Fax....................................... (301) 827-4401

Deputy Director

    Linda A. Tollefson...................... (301) 827–2953

Animal Health Policy and Operations

    Andrew J. Beaulieu..................... (301) 827–2954

Management and Communications

    Robert Sauer............................. (301) 827–4410

New Animal Drug Evaluation

    Claire M. Lathers....................... (301) 594–1620

Policy and Regulations

    G. A. Mitchell........................... (301) 827–2957

Research

    Norris E. Alderson .... (301) 827–8010

Surveillance and Compliance

    Daniel G. McChesney.................. (301) 827–6648

NATIONAL CENTER FOR TOXICOLOGICAL RESEARCH

(3900 NCTR Rd., Jefferson, AR 72079, www.fda.gov/nctr)

Conducts peer-reviewed fundamental research that is targeted to: (1) develop new strategies, standards, and systems to predict toxicity and anticipate new product technology to support FDA's commitment to bring this technology to market more rapidly; and (2) understand the mechanisms of toxicity and design better risk assessment/detection techniques for use in review and surveillance of FDA-regulated products. Key performance goals include the integration of new genetic systems and computer-assisted toxicology into the review process and the integration of gene chip, gene array, and proteomic technologies as standards for FDA review/risk management. NCTR actively involves its stakeholders in planning and evaluating its research agenda, and partners with other agencies, academia, and industry to address critical research issues such as individual susceptibility to drugs, toxicity due to drug interactions, standard markers for foodborne pathogens, and phototoxicity of cosmetics and foods.

Director

    Daniel A. Casciano..................... (870) 543–7517

    Fax....................................... (870) 543–7576

Deputy Director/Management

    Victor Atwood.......................... (870) 543–7130

Deputy Director/Washington Operations

    James T. MacGregor.................... (301) 827–6696

Management Services

    Vicky L. Ross-Barsh.................... (870) 543–7569

Planning, Finance and Information Technology

    Jeanne F. Anson .... (870) 543–7359

Research

    Daniel A. Casciano (acting) .... (870) 543–7516

Regional Offices

NORTHEAST REGION
(CT, MA, ME, NH, NY, RI, VT)
158-15 Liberty Ave.
Jamaica, NY 11433-1034
(718) 662–5416
Diana Kolaitis, regional director

CENTRAL REGION
(DC, DE, IN, IL, KY, MD, MI, MN, ND, NJ, OH, PA, SD, VA, WV, WI)
Philadelphia Office
U.S. Custom House, #900
Second and Chestnut Sts.
Philadelphia, PA 19106
(215) 597–8058
Susan M. Setterberg, regional director

Chicago Office
20 N. Michigan Ave., #550
Chicago, IL 60606
(312) 353–9400

SOUTHEAST REGION
(AL, FL, GA, LA, MS, NC, PR, SC, TN)
60 Eighth St. N.E.
Atlanta, GA 30309
(404) 347–4266
Gary J. Dykstra, regional director

SOUTHWEST REGION
(AR, CO, IA, KS, MO, NE, NM, OK, TX, UT, WY)
7920 Elmerbrook Rd., #102
Dallas, TX 75247-4982
(214) 655–8100
Gary Pierce, regional director

PACIFIC REGION
(AK, AZ, CA, HI, ID, MT, NV, OR, WA)
1301 Clay St., #1180–N
Oakland, CA 94612-5217
(510) 637–3960
Brenda Holman, regional director

■ CONGRESSIONAL ACTION

Congressional Liaison
Melinda Plaisier .... (301) 443–3793

Committees and Subcommittees

HOUSE AGRICULTURE COMMITTEE
1301 LHOB, Washington, DC 20515
(202) 225–2171

ENERGY AND COMMERCE COMMITTEE
2125 RHOB, Washington, DC 20515
(202) 225–2927

Subcommittee on Health
2125 RHOB, Washington, DC 20515
(202) 225–2927

Subcommittee on Oversight and Investigations
2125 RHOB, Washington, DC 20515
(202) 225–2927

HOUSE GOVERNMENT REFORM COMMITTEE
2157 RHOB, Washington, DC 20515
(202) 225–2577

Subcommittee on Criminal Justice, Drug Policy & Human Resources
B373 RHOB, Washington, DC 20515
(202) 225–2577

HOUSE APPROPRIATIONS COMMITTEE
Subcommittee on Agriculture, Rural Development, FDA, and Related Agencies
2362 RHOB, Washington, DC 20515
(202) 225–2638

SENATE AGRICULTURE, NUTRITION, AND FORESTRY COMMITTEE
SR-328A Russell Senate Office Bldg., Washington, DC 20510
(202) 224–2035

SENATE HEALTH, EDUCATION, LABOR &
PENSIONS COMMITTEE
SD-428 Dirksen Senate Office Bldg., Washington,
  DC 20510
(202) 224–5375

SENATE GOVERNMENTAL AFFAIRS PERMANENT
SUBCOMMITTEE ON INVESTIGATIONS
SR-100 Russell Senate Office Bldg., Washington,
  DC 20510
(202) 224–3721

SENATE APPROPRIATIONS COMMITTEE
Subcommittee on Agriculture, Rural Development, and
  Related Agencies
SD-136 Dirksen Senate Office Bldg., Washington,
  DC 20510
(202) 224–5270

Legislation

The original legislation giving the federal government regulatory control over foods and drugs was the **Food and Drug Act of 1906** (34 Stat. 768, 21 U.S.C.). Signed by the president June 30, 1906. The act prohibited interstate commerce in misbranded and adulterated foods, drinks, and drugs. The power to administer the law was placed in the Agriculture Department's Bureau of Chemistry.

A major overhaul of the basic food and drug legislation occurred in 1938 with the passage of the **Federal Food, Drug and Cosmetic (FFDCA) Act of 1938** (52 Stat. 1040, 21 U.S.C. 301-395). Signed by the president June 25, 1938. This act broadened the original legislation by extending FDA regulatory power to cover cosmetics and medical devices; requiring predistribution approval of new drugs; requiring that tolerance levels be set for unavoidable poisonous substances; authorizing standards of identity, quality, and fill levels for containers for foods; authorizing inspections of factories where regulated products are manufactured; and adding court injunctions to FDA enforcement powers.

Humphrey Amendment (65 Stat. 648, 21 U.S.C. 333, note). Signed by the president Oct. 26, 1951. Required that drugs that cannot be safely used without medical supervision must be labeled for sale and dispensed only by prescription of a licensed practitioner.

Food Additives Amendment or **Delaney Amendment** (72 Stat. 1784, 21 U.S.C. 321, 331, 342, 346, 348). Signed by the president Sept. 6, 1958. Prohibited the use of new food additives until the manufacturer had proven they were safe for public consumption. The act further provided that any food containing a substance found to be carcinogenic had to be removed from the market.

Color Additive Amendments of 1960 (74 Stat. 397, 21 U.S.C. 321, 331, 333, 342, 343, 346, 351, 361, 362, 371, 376). Signed by the president July 12, 1960. Gave the FDA authority to establish standards for safe use of color additives.

Drug Amendments of 1962 (76 Stat. 780, 21 U.S.C. 321, 331, 332, 348, 351-353, 355, 357-360, 372, 374, 376, 381). Signed by the president Oct. 10, 1962. Authorized the administration to require that all drugs be proven effective as well as safe before they could be marketed. The Drug Amendments also gave the FDA responsibility to regulate prescription drug advertising.

Drug Abuse Control Amendments (79 Stat. 226, 18 U.S.C. 1114, 21 U.S.C. 321, 331, 333, 334, 360, 360a, 372). Signed by the president July 15, 1965. Established controls to prevent illicit traffic of groups of abused drugs—depressants, stimulants, and hallucinogens.

Vitamins and Minerals Amendments (90 Stat. 410, 21 U.S.C. 321, 333, 334, 343, 350, 378). Signed by the president April 22, 1976. Amended the FFDC Act to prevent the FDA from establishing standards limiting the potency of vitamins and minerals in food supplements or regulating such products as drugs.

Medical Device Amendments of 1976 (90 Stat. 539, 21 U.S.C. 321, 331, 334, 351, 352, 358, 360, 360c-360k, 374, 376, 379, 379a, 381). Signed by the president May 28, 1976. Empowered the FDA to regulate medical devices. The amendments allowed the FDA to ban risky medical devices, to establish categories for medical devices, to set performance standards for less hazardous devices, and to require that the safety of the most complex medical devices be demonstrated prior to their being marketed.

Other legislation administered by the FDA includes:

Public Health Service Act (58 Stat. 682, 42 U.S.C. 201, et seq.). Signed by the president July 1, 1944. Gave the FDA authority to ensure safety, purity, and potency of vaccines, blood, serum, and other biological products. Also empowered the FDA to ensure safety of pasteurized milk and shellfish, as well as the sanitation of food services and sanitary facilities for travelers on buses, trains, and planes.

Federal Hazardous Substances Act (74 Stat. 372, 15 U.S.C. 1261-1277). Signed by the president July 12, 1960. Gave the FDA power to declare as a hazardous substance any material containing a residue of an insecticide, pesticide, fungicide, or similar chemical.

Fair Packaging and Labeling Act (80 Stat. 1296, 15 U.S.C. 1451-1461). Signed by the president Nov. 3, 1966. Gave the FDA authority to require that labels on packages of food, drugs, cosmetics, and medical devices be uniform and accurate.

Radiation Control for Health and Safety Act (82 Stat. 1173, 21 U.S.C. 360hh-360ss). Signed by the president Oct. 18, 1968. Authorized the FDA to set performance standards for television sets, microwave ovens, X-ray machines, and other products that emit radiation.

Drug Listing Act of 1972 (86 Stat. 559, 21 U.S.C. 331, 355, 360). Signed by the president Aug. 16, 1972. Required registration with the FDA of producers of drugs or medical devices and the filing of lists of drugs and devices produced by registrants.

Infant Formula Act of 1980 (94 Stat. 1190, 21 U.S.C. 301 note, 321, 331, 350a, 374, 830, 841-843, 873). Signed by the president Sept. 26, 1980. Set standards for content and processing of infant formulas.

Orphan Drug Act of 1983 (96 Stat. 2049, 21 U.S.C. 301 note, 360aa-360dd, 904). Signed by the president Jan. 4, 1983. Authorized financial incentives for companies to develop drugs for the treatment of rare illnesses.

Federal Anti-Tampering Act (97 Stat. 831, 18 U.S.C. 1365). Signed by the president Oct. 13, 1983. Made it a felony to tamper with packaged consumer products such as foods, drugs, and cosmetics. Gave investigatory authority to the FDA where products within its jurisdiction are involved.

Drug Price Competition and Patent Term Restoration Act (98 Stat. 1585, 21 U.S.C. 301 note, 355, 360cc). Signed by the president Sept. 24, 1984. Designed to expedite the approval of generic versions of "pioneer" drugs and to extend patent protection to compensate sponsors for time required by the FDA to consider new drug approvals.

Orphan Drug Amendments of 1985 (99 Stat. 387, 21 U.S.C. 301 note, 360aa, 360aa note, 360bb, 360cc, 360ee). Signed by the president Aug. 15, 1985. Extended the authorizations for research grants, expanded the marketing protection to sponsors of approved orphan drugs, and established a National Commission on Orphan Diseases to evaluate government research activities on rare diseases.

Orphan Drug Amendments of 1988 (102 Stat. 90, 21 U.S.C. 301 note, 360aa note, 360bb, 360ee). Signed by the president April 18, 1988. Extended authorizations for grant money and required manufacturers of designated orphan drugs who intended to halt production to notify the FDA one year in advance so the agency could try to find a new production source. Required a study to be completed by 1990 to determine the necessity of incentives to encourage companies to develop medical devices and foods for rare diseases and conditions.

Prescription Drug Marketing Act of 1987 (102 Stat. 95, 21 U.S.C. 301 note, 331, 333, 353, 353 notes, 381). Signed by the president April 22, 1988. Banned the reimportation of drugs produced in the United States, placed restrictions on the distribution of drug samples, banned certain resales of drugs by hospitals and charitable institutions, and required federal standards for the licensure of drug wholesalers.

Health Omnibus Programs Extension of 1988 (102 Stat. 3048, 21 U.S.C. 301 note, 393, 393 notes). Signed by the president Nov. 5, 1988. The **Food and Drug Administration Act**, Title V of this act, established in statute the FDA within the Health and Human Services Department and required that the FDA commissioner be appointed by the president and confirmed by the Senate. Title II of this act, the **AIDS Amendments of 1988** (102 Stat. 3062, 42 U.S.C. 201 note, 242c, 247d, 286, 289f, 300cc-300aaa), required development of research and education programs, counseling, testing, and health care for AIDS patients. It also required the FDA to develop a registry of experimental AIDS drugs.

Nutrition Labeling and Education Act (104 Stat. 2353, 21 U.S.C. 301 note, 321, 331-334, 335b, 341-343, 346a, 352, 355, 358, 360b-360i, 360cc, 360hh-360ss). Signed by the president Nov. 8, 1990. Mandated uniform nutrition labeling on packaged food items, including most processed food products and some raw agricultural products, fish, and shellfish. Required manufacturers' labels to provide detailed information on caloric levels and amounts of fat and cholesterol in food items. Directed the FDA to test products for such claims as "natural" and "low-fat" before those terms could be used on food labels.

FDA Revitalization Act (104 Stat. 4583, 21 U.S.C. 301 note, 379b, 379c, 379d, 394). Signed by the president Nov. 28, 1990. Consolidated FDA headquarters offices and provided for the automation of the FDA approval application process. Authorized the commissioner to appoint technical and scientific review panels and to pay appointees not employed by the federal government.

Safe Medical Devices Act of 1990 (104 Stat. 4511, 21 U.S.C. 301 note, 321, 333, 333 note, 351, 353, 360, 360c, 360d-360j, 360l, 360gg-360ss, 383). Signed by the president Nov. 28, 1990. Strengthened FDA procedures for approving new medical devices and recalling defective products already on the market. Required medical facilities to report faulty or dangerous devices to manufacturers and, in the case of a death, to the FDA. Imposed monetary fines for violations.

Generic Drug Enforcement Act of 1992 (106 Stat. 149, 21 U.S.C. 301 note, 321, 335a, 335a notes, 335b, 335c, 336, 337, 355). Signed by the president May 13, 1992. Expanded the authority of the FDA to oversee the generic drug industry. Prescribed civil penalties for fraud and abuse of the approval process for generic copies of brand-name prescription drugs, including monetary fines, debarment from future dealings with the FDA, withdrawal of FDA approval, and suspension of distribution.

Mammography Quality Standards Act of 1992 (106 Stat. 3547, 42 U.S.C. 201, 263b, 263b note). Signed by the president Oct. 27, 1992. Required all U.S. mammography facilities to be accredited and fully certified. Mandated collection of fees from facilities to cover cost of annual inspections.

Prescription Drug User Fee Act of 1992 (106 Stat. 4491, 21 U.S.C. 321, 331, 342, 343, 346a, 351, 352, 360j, 361, 362, 372a, 376, 379c-379h, 453, 601, 1033); **Dietary Supplement Act of 1992** (106 Stat. 4500, 21 U.S.C. 301 note, 343 notes, 343-1 note, 393 note). Signed by the president Oct. 29, 1992. Required prescription drug manufacturers to pay "user fees" to help underwrite the cost of federal safety and efficiency reviews. Established rates for annual "facilities" fees and an "application fee," to be paid when a drug is submitted for approval. Imposed a moratorium on enforcing new fees on vitamins and dietary supplements until Dec. 15, 1993.

Dietary Supplement Health and Education Act of 1994 (108 Stat. 4325 21 U.S.C. 321, 331, 342, 343, 343-2, 350, 350b; 42 U.S.C. 281, 287c-11). Signed by the president Oct. 25, 1994. Established a regulatory framework and specific labeling requirements for dietary supplement manufacturers.

FDA Export Reform and Enhancement Act of 1996 (110 Stat. 1321-313, 21 U.S.C. 301 note, 331, 381, 382; 42 U.S.C. 262). Signed by the president April 26, 1996. Part of a larger bill. The act amended the Food, Drug, and Cosmetic Act (FFDCA) to revise requirements regarding the importing and exporting of any component of a drug, biological product (including a partially processed biological product), device, food or color additive, or dietary supplement.

Food Quality Protection Act of 1996 (110 Stat. 1489, 7 U.S.C. 136 note). Signed by the president on Aug. 3, 1996. Amended the Federal Insecticide, Fungicide, and Rodenticide Act of 1947 and the Food, Drug and Cosmetic Act of 1958 (FFDCA) to allow the EPA to issue an emergency order to suspend pesticides that pose a risk to public health before the pesticide goes through the cancellation process. Replaced the FFDCA's Delaney Amendment with a single health standard requiring the EPA to ensure that pesticide residue in both raw and processed food posed a "reasonable certainty of no harm." Required the EPA to establish programs to screen for estrogen-like substances and provide increased information to the public on the amounts of pesticides found in foods.

The FDA Modernization Act of 1997 (111 Stat. 2296, 21 U.S.C. 301 note et seq.). Signed by the president on Nov. 21, 1997. The act amended certain provisions in the FFDCA and the Prescription Drug User Fee Act of 1992 (PDUFA). Reauthorized the PDUFA for five more years. Streamlined the regulation and approval of a product by codifying FDA's regulations and practice to increase patient access to experimental drugs and medical devices and to accelerate review of important new medications. An expanded database on clinical trials was to be made available for patients. Enabled the FDA to contract outside experts to conduct the initial review of all class I and low-to-intermediate risk class II devices. Eliminated the requirement of FDA's premarket approval for most packaging and other substances that come in contact with food and may migrate into it.

Best Pharmaceuticals for Children Act (115 Stat. 1408, 21 U.S.C. 301 note). Signed by the president on Jan. 4, 2002. Amended the Federal Food, Drug and Cosmetic Act and the Public Health Service Act to improve the safety and efficacy of pharmaceuticals for children. Required drug manufacturers to revise labeling of drugs based on findings of a five-year $200 million pediatric study. Established an Office of Pediatric Therapeutics within the FDA to oversee activities that deal with pediatric health and pharmacy issues.

Public Health Security and Bioterrorism Preparedness and Response Act of 2002 (116 Stat. 594, 42 U.S.C. 201 note). Signed by the president on June 12, 2002. Authorized funding for the FDA and the Agriculture Department (USDA) to hire new border inspectors and develop new methods for detecting crop and food contaminations. Mandated the annual registration of foreign manufacturers who import drug and device products into the United States Authorized the FDA to detain suspicious foods and required prior notice of all food imports. Required the FDA to inform states if it received information of a possible shipment of tainted food. Reauthorized the Prescription Drug User Fee Act for another five years.

Health Care Safety Net Amendments of 2002 (116 Stat. 1621, 42 U.S.C. 201 note). Signed by the president on Oct. 26, 2002. Amended the Public Health Service Act to reauthorize and improve its Consolidated Health Center Program and the National Health Service Corps (NHSC).

Established a grant program to improve the quality of health care by rural and other small health care providers. Created a Healthy Communities Access Program, which provides grants to communities and groups of health care providers to develop or strengthen integrated health care delivery.

Medical Device User Fee and Modernization Act (MDUFMA) of 2002 (116 Stat. 1588, 21 U.S.C. 301 note). Signed by the president on Oct. 26, 2002. Amended the Federal Food, Drug and Cosmetic Act to establish a new program that imposed fees on medical device manufacturers to help pay for faster FDA approval of their products. Allowed manufacturers to hire independent contractors to conduct safety inspections of their factories. Established new regulations governing the sterilization and reuse of catheters and other products originally approved for use one-time only.

INFORMATION SOURCES

Internet

Agency Web Site: http://www.fda.gov. Provides a range of information about the agency's regulatory operations, including the activities of all FDA centers. Press releases, reports, and newsletters also are available.

Telephone Contacts

FDA General Inquiries	(888) 463–6332
FDA's 24-hour Emergency Line	(301) 443–1240
Locator	(301) 827–4160
Consumer Affairs and Inquiries	(888) 463–6332
Consumer Products Complaint Line	(800) 638–2041

The FDA maintains the following hotline and clearinghouse numbers:

Advisory Committee Information Hotline	(800) 741–8138
AIDS Clinical Trials Information Service	(800) 874–2572
Center for Biologics Evaluation and Research Voice Information Service	(800) 835–4709
Center for Drug Evaluation and Research Fax-on-Demand	(301) 827–4573
Center for Food Safety and Applied Nutrition (Documents)	(800) 332–4010
DC area	(202) 205–4314
Center for Food Safety and Applied Nutrition Outreach and Information	(888) 723–3366
Adverse Event Reporting System/Medwatch	(800) 332–1088
Center for Veterinary Medicine Adverse Drug Reporting System	(888) 332–8387
Vaccine Adverse Event Reporting System	(800) 822–7967

Information and Publications

KEY OFFICES

FDA Public Affairs
Print Media Staff, Rockville
5600 Fishers Lane
Rockville, MD 20857
(301) 827–6242
Fax (301) 827–1680
Bradford Stone, director

Print Media Staff, Washington
200 C St. S.W.
Washington, DC 20204
(202) 205–4144
Fax (301) 305–5169
Ruth Welch, deputy director

Handles FDA press relations and news releases, distributes publications, and answers questions about programs and policies. Rockville office handles press inquiries on human and animal drugs, vaccines, medical devices, or health fraud. Washington office handles press inquiries on food or cosmetics.

Communications Division
5600 Fishers Lane
Rockville, MD 20857
(301) 827–7130
Fax (301) 827–5308
Michael Herndon (acting), director

Produces most FDA publications, including consumer brochures and audiovisual materials about the agency and the products it regulates.

Freedom of Information
Office of Management & Systems
5600 Fishers Lane, Room 12A-30
Rockville, MD 20857
(301) 827–6547
Fax (301) 443–2896
Betty Dorsey, director

Public reading room open 9:00 a.m. to 4:00 p.m., Monday through Friday.

GRANTS

Office of Facilities, Acquisitions and Central Services
Office of Management & Systems
5600 Fishers Lane
Rockville, MD 20857
(301) 827–6890
Fax (301) 827–7029
Vacant, director

The FDA makes grants to assist public, nonprofit, and other institutions with the establishment, expansion, and improvement of research concerned with poison control, drug and cosmetic hazards, human and veterinary drugs, medical devices and diagnostic products, biologics, and radiation-emitting devices and materials. All qualified institutions, firms, and individuals are eligible for contracts that are awarded competitively. (Some contracts may be awarded noncompetitively.)

There are no application forms for contracts; proposals should be made in response to requests from the agency published in *Commerce Business Daily*. Subscriptions are available from the U.S. Government Printing Office (GPO): see appendix, Ordering Government Publications.

PUBLICATIONS

Each FDA center provides information on scientific papers and publications currently available. Many publications and documents also are available from the FDA's Web site, and from the field offices.

Two agency periodicals are available from the GPO *(see appendix, Ordering Government Publications)*:

FDA Consumer. Official magazine of the FDA, published six times a year and written for the general public.

FDA Veterinarian. Bimonthly publication covering animal drugs, food additives, and devices.

Many FDA documents, including audiovisual materials and lists of substances that the agency has determined are generally recognized as safe (GRAS) for each year, are available from the National Technical Information Service (NTIS): see appendix, Ordering Government Publications. (A GRAS list also is published in Title 21 of the *Code of Federal Regulations*.)

NTIS provides the public with titles and price information. Microfiche copies of all FDA materials handled by the NTIS are available for inspection in this office.

The FDA operates the following liaison office with the NTIS:

FDA Office of Information Resources Management
Information Collection and Dissemination Branch
5600 Fishers Lane
Rockville, MD 20857
(301) 827–1686
Fax (301) 443–3470
Charity Smith, chief

DATA AND STATISTICS

FDA Center for Drug Evaluation and Research
1901 Chapman Ave.
Rockville, MD 20852
(301) 827–4583
Carolann Hooton, chief, FOI branch

Provides information on use of several computerized FDA databases related to drugs.

(Databases for other products under FDA jurisdiction are maintained by the various centers; see listings beginning on p. 226.)

MEETINGS

FDA Public Affairs issues a *Public Calendar* that lists upcoming meetings open to the public; meetings held by key FDA officials, with the names of other participants; and meetings held the previous week. For copies, contact the Communications Division; (301) 443–3220.

Advisory committee meetings open to the public are also announced in the *Federal Register*.

Reference Resources

LIBRARIES

Center for Devices and Radiological Health Library
9200 Corporate Blvd., #30
Rockville, MD 20850
(301) 827–6901
Hours: 8:00 a.m. to 4:30 p.m.
Internet: www.cdhr.fda.gov/library/homepage.htm
Harriet Albersheim, chief

Collection focuses on medical devices and radiology.

Center for Food Safety and Applied Nutrition Library
200 C St. S.W., Room 3321
Washington, DC 20204
(202) 205–4235
Hours: 8:00 a.m. to 4:30 p.m.
Anna Therese McGowan, director

Contains technical literature related to the chemistry of food and cosmetic research. Open to the public; photocopying machines not available.

FDA Medical Library

Center for Drug Evaluation and Research
5600 Fishers Lane, Room 11 B-40
Rockville, MD 20857
(301) 827–5703
Hours: 7:30 a.m. to 4:30 p.m.
Carol Assouad, director

Collection scope is biomedical with emphasis on pharmaceutical science and regulatory science. Open to the public by appointment.

National Center for Toxicological Research Library

Bldg. 10, Library & Conference Center
Jefferson, AR 72079
(870) 543–7323
Susan Laney-Sheehan, head librarian

A collection of toxicology literature.

DOCKETS

FDA Office of Management and Systems

Dockets Management Branch
5600 Fishers Lane, Mail Stop HFA–305
Rockville, MD 20852
(301) 827–6860
Fax (301) 827-6870
Jennie Butler, branch chief

Serves as the official FDA repository for documents submitted to administrative proceedings and rulemaking and *Federal Register* documents. Types of documents include comments, transcripts, motions, briefs, and petitions to establish, amend, or revoke an FDA action. Also available are minutes, transcripts, slides, briefing materials for advisory committee meetings, panel reports, public comments on rulemakings, and Freedom of Information Summaries for animal drugs. Dockets are now accessible via the FDA Web site. The most frequently requested FDA documents are available for viewing or may be downloaded at the site. A search engine is available. Comments may be submitted electronically through the Dockets Web site at http://www.fda.gov or via e-mail at fdadocketsoc.fda.gov. The Dockets Public Reading Room is open 9:00 a.m. to 4:00 p.m., Monday through Friday.

RULES AND REGULATIONS

FDA rules and regulations are published in the *Code of Federal Regulations*, Title 21. Proposed rules, new final rules, rulings by the commissioner, and updates to the *Code of Federal Regulations* are published in the daily *Federal Register*. (See appendix for information on how to obtain and use these publications.)

Two sources of information detailing the laws and regulations administered by the FDA, *Requirements of Laws and Regulations Enforced by the U.S. FDA* and *Food and Drug Administration Acts*, are available on the FDA Web site, http://www.fda.gov.

Other Information Sources

Related Agency

National Library of Medicine (NLM)

8600 Rockville Pike
Bethesda, MD 20894
(301) 594–5983
(888) 346–3656
Health professional inquiries (800) 272–4787
Internet: http://www.nlm.nih.gov

Part of the National Institutes of Health. Maintains MEDLINE, a Web-based database of eleven million references and abstracts to medical journal articles. PubMed is the access system for MEDLINE. Other databases cover toxicology, chemical substances, and environmental health. MEDLINE Plus is an information service available on the Web containing health information for the public. Links are available at the NLM Web site to access these and other services. Additional help, including reference assistance, is available at custservnlm.nih.gov. Many NLM fact sheets and reports are available via the agency Web site; other publications may be purchased from the GPO and NTIS (see appendix, Ordering Government Publications.)

NONGOVERNMENTAL ORGANIZATIONS

The following are some key organizations that monitor the FDA and related food and drug issues.

American Council on Science and Health

1995 Broadway, 2nd Floor
New York, NY 10023
(212) 362–7044
Fax (212) 362–4919
Internet: http://www.acsh.org

American Public Health Association

800 I St. N.W.
Washington, DC 20001
(202) 777–2742
Fax (202) 777–2534
Internet: http://www.apha.org

Center for Science in the Public Interest

1875 Connecticut Ave. N.W., #300
Washington, DC 20009
(202) 332–9110
Fax (202) 265–4954
Internet: http://www.cspinet.org

Consumer Federation of America

1424 16th St. N.W., #604
Washington, DC 20036
(202) 287-6121
Internet: http://www.consumerfed.org

Food and Drug Law Institute

1000 Vermont Ave. N.W., #200
Washington, DC 20005
(202) 371–1420
Fax (202) 371–0649
Internet: http://www.fdli.org
Publishes the *Food and Drug Law Journal.*

Food Research and Action Center

1875 Connecticut Ave. N.W., #540
Washington, DC 20009
(202) 986–2200
Fax (202) 986–2525
Internet: http://www.frac.org

National Consumers League

1701 K St. N.W., #1201
Washington, DC 20006
(202) 835-3323
Fax (202) 835-0747
Internet: http://www.nclnet.org

National Pharmaceutical Council

1894 Preston White Dr.
Reston, VA 22091
(703) 620–6390
Fax (703) 476–0904
Internet: http://www.npcnow.org

U.S. Pharmacopeia

12601 Twinbrook Pkwy.
Rockville, MD 20852
(800) 822–8772
Fax (301) 816–8299
Internet: http://www.usp.org

PUBLISHERS

The following companies and organizations publish on the FDA and related issues through books, periodicals, or electronic media.

Commerce Clearing House (CCH), Inc.

2700 Lake Cook Rd.
Riverwoods, IL 60015
(847) 267–7000
Fax (847) 267-7878
Internet: http://www.cch.com

The Dialog Corporation

2440 W. El Camino Real
Mountain View, CA 94040
(650) 254–7000
Fax (650) 254–8058
Provides access to the Pharmaceutical News Index (PNI) database.

ECRI

5200 Butler Pike
Plymouth Meeting, PA 19462
(610) 825–6000
Fax (610) 834–1275
Internet: http://www.ecri.org

Food Chemical News

1725 K St. NW
Washington, DC 20006
(202) 887–6320
Fax (202) 887–6337
Internet: http://www.crcpress.com

Foundation Press, Inc.

11 Penn Plaza, 10th Floor
New York, NY 10001
(212) 760–8700
Fax (212) 760–8705
Internet: http://www.fdpress.com

National Academy Press

2101 Constitution Ave. N.W. Box 285
Washington, DC 20055
(202) 334–3313
(800) 624–6242
Fax (202) 334–2451
Internet: http://www.nap.edu

National Labor Relations Board

1099 14th St. N.W., Washington, DC 20570
Internet: http://www.nlrb.gov

▓ INTRODUCTION

The National Labor Relations Board (NLRB) is an independent agency established by the National Labor Relations Act (Wagner Act) of 1935. The board is composed of a general counsel and five members who are nominated by the president and confirmed by the Senate. The president designates one of the members to serve as chair. Board members serve five-year terms, and the general counsel serves a four-year term; incumbents may be reappointed.

Responsibilities

The NLRB:

▪ Conducts elections to determine if workers in a plant, factory, or business wish to be represented by a union.

▪ Conducts elections to determine which of two or more unions attempting to organize a workplace the workers prefer.

▪ Conducts elections to determine if workers wish to remove their union.

▪ Certifies results of elections.

▪ Acts to prevent employers and unions from engaging in unfair labor practices.

Powers and Authority

The NLRB does not initiate cases; it has the power to act only when cases are brought before it and only in cases in which the employer's operation or the labor dispute affects commerce. In practice, this restriction means that the agency has authority to act in all but purely local cases. However, the board may decline to exercise jurisdiction over a category of employers when the labor dispute does not have a substantial impact on commerce.

The agency will not consider cases involving race tracks; owners, breeders, or trainers of horses; and real estate

GLOSSARY

Charge—Form used for filing an allegation of unfair labor practices.

Closed shop—An establishment in which the employer by agreement hires only union members in good standing.

Complaint—Formal allegation issued by an NLRB regional office after investigation indicates merit to a charge.

Jurisdictional standards—Board's criteria for acting on a case, based on an enterprise's annual amount of business or annual sales or purchases.

Petition—Form used to request a representation election.

Right-to-work laws—State laws that prohibit labor-management agreements requiring union membership to obtain or keep a job.

Union shop—An agreement that requires an employee to join a union to obtain or keep a job.

---

brokers. The following employees also are exempt from coverage under the act: agricultural laborers; domestic servants; individuals employed by a parent or spouse; independent contractors; managers or supervisors; individuals subject to the Railway Labor Act; federal, state, or local government employees; employees of Federal Reserve banks; and employees of church-affiliated schools.

Most NLRB activity takes place in the field offices, with less than 5 percent of unfair labor practice cases making it all the way to the board for review. In addition to the broad discretion that regional directors have because of this arrangement, they have the authority to define bargaining units.

PETITIONS

The NLRB may perform its duties only after the filing of a petition or charge. A petition, which requests the NLRB to hold a representation election, may be filed by an employee, a group of employees, any individual or labor organization acting on their behalf, or an employer. A petition filed by or on behalf of employees must show that at least 30 percent of the employees desire an election and that their employer refuses to acknowledge their representative.

A petition filed by an employer must allege that one or more individuals or organizations have made a claim for recognition as the exclusive representative of the same group of employees. Petitions must be sworn to or affirmed under oath, and filed with the NLRB regional office where the employee unit is located (*addresses, p. 252*).

ELECTIONS

Once a petition has been filed, the NLRB regional director must investigate it. The purpose of the investigation is to determine: whether the agency has jurisdiction to conduct the election; if there is a sufficient showing of employee interest to justify an election; if a question of representation actually exists; whether the representative named in the petition is qualified; if there are any barriers to an election such as an existing contract or previous election; and what is the scope and composition of the appropriate bargaining unit.

An election may be held by agreement between the employer and individual or labor group claiming to represent the employees. In such a case, the parties determine who is eligible to vote and authorize the NLRB regional director to conduct the election. Employees are given a choice of one or more bargaining representatives, or they may choose not to have any representative at all. To be certified as the bargaining representative, an individual or labor organization must receive a majority of the votes cast.

If the parties are unable to reach an agreement, the NLRB must hold a hearing to resolve disputed issues and decide whether to direct a secret ballot election. Election details are left to the discretion of the regional director and are decided in accordance with established board rules and precedents. Elections generally are held thirty days after they are ordered.

Any party that believes a board election standard was not met may file an objection with the regional director who supervised the election. The director will then issue a ruling on the objection, which usually may be appealed to the NLRB for a decision.

An election will be set aside if the board determines that one of the parties acted in such a way as to interfere with the employees' free expression of choice.

UNFAIR LABOR PRACTICES

To file an unfair labor practice complaint with the NLRB, a charge must be registered with the regional director for the district in which the practice occurred. Charges may be filed by employee representatives against an employer or vice versa. The regional director then investigates the charge to determine its validity. If the regional director agrees that an unfair labor practice was or is occurring, a complaint will be issued notifying the offending party that a hearing is to be held concerning the charges.

Every effort is made to resolve the dispute before the hearing date. If the decision reached between the participating parties is fair and acceptable to both parties and to the NLRB, the board may defer to that decision. If the arbitration procedure does not result in an acceptable agreement, the board resumes jurisdiction. Only one-third of the cases filed are found to have merit; another third are settled before the hearing stage.

Unsettled unfair labor practice cases are conducted before an NLRB administrative law judge in accordance with procedures that apply in U.S. District Court. The administrative law judge makes findings and recommendations to the board based upon testimony taken at the hearing. Any party involved may appeal the administrative law judge's decision to the board. If the NLRB agrees that an unfair labor practice was or is occurring, it is authorized to issue a cease-and-desist order requiring the offending party to take appropriate affirmative action.

Any party to proceedings in an unfair labor practices case may appeal a board decision to the appropriate U.S. Court of Appeals. At this point, the general counsel represents the board and may not appeal its ruling. The court of appeals may enforce the order, remand it to the board for reconsideration, change it, or set it aside entirely.

Board cases provide more litigation in these courts than any other federal agency. The circuit courts are obligated to accept NLRB cases. Either party in an NLRB case may appeal proceedings to the Supreme Court.

If an employer or a union fails to comply with a board order, the board is empowered to petition the U.S. Court of Appeals for a court decree enforcing the order. Further failure to comply with the order can result in a fine or imprisonment for contempt of court.

Background

Until the 1930s federal and state laws favored management; union activity was discouraged by employers, who sometimes used force to prevent unions from coming into their plants or businesses. In spite of antiunion activity, the movement to organize employees into labor unions for self-protection gradually began to make progress.

During World War I, a National War Labor Board was created to establish policies covering labor relations. The board—operating from April 1918 until August 1919—served to protect the right of employees to bargain collectively and barred management from interfering in the process. Employers also were barred from discriminating against employees engaging in legitimate union activity.

The Railway Labor Act of 1926 required the railroads and their employees to exert every reasonable effort to make employment agreements through representatives chosen by each side, free from interference by the other. A board for mediation of disputes was established, and the act later was extended to cover airline employees. Employees covered by this act were exempted from the National Labor Relations Act.

The Norris-LaGuardia Act of 1932 restricted the federal courts' power to issue injunctions against unions engaged in peaceful strikes. It declared that workers had a right to organize and engage in collective bargaining. In addition, the act prohibited federal courts from enforcing "yellow dog" contracts in which employees promised not to join a union or to quit one if already a member.

LABOR AND THE NEW DEAL

The National Industrial Recovery Act (NIRA), symbolized by a blue eagle, took effect on June 16, 1933. The act sought to preserve the employee's right to collective bargaining and to ensure that no employee would be required to join a union or refrain from joining a union as a condition of employment. Critics complained that employers were not complying with the codes and were refusing to recognize or meet with committees of employees to discuss grievances. The need for an agency to administer NIRA became apparent.

That administrative body, the National Labor Board (NLB), was created by President Franklin D. Roosevelt on Aug. 5, 1933, with Sen. Robert Wagner, D-N.Y. (1927–1949) as its first chair. In addition to the chair, the board consisted of three industry members and three labor members. To handle the volume of disputes brought before the NLB, twenty regional boards composed of industry and labor representatives were created to hold hearings wherever controversies arose. This procedure expedited cases as the parties involved were no longer required to travel to Washington to plead their cases.

However, flagrant defiance of the board, especially by large employers, soon became a serious obstacle to its effectiveness. Theoretically, the NLB could report violations to the U.S. attorney general for possible prosecution, but in reality the only sanction the board could apply was to take away from the offender the symbol of compliance, the agency's blue eagle. This lack of enforcement authority, coupled with a lack of explicit legislative authority, ultimately led to the board's demise.

NATIONAL LABOR RELATIONS ACT

The NLRB as it currently exists dates from the passage in 1935 of the National Labor Relations Act, commonly known as the Wagner Act, after its sponsor. The newly created board supplanted the earlier NLB that Wagner had chaired; the NLB had been declared unconstitutional by the Supreme Court. The Wagner Act went further in protecting the rights of workers than the Railway Labor Act and the Norris-LaGuardia Act. It gave the board more enforcement tools, such as the power to issue subpoenas, cease-and-desist orders, and remedies. In addition to establishing the NLRB, the Wagner Act barred employers from engaging in five kinds of illegal labor practices. Prohibited were:

- Interference with employees who exercise their right to organize (by threatening or even questioning employees about their union activities).
- Establishing or contributing to the support of a union (a so-called company, or sweetheart, union).
- Discrimination against actual or potential employees on the basis of union membership (by firing or refusing to hire union or nonunion members). This provision did not prohibit the closed shop agreement, under which an employer agrees to hire only union members, or the union shop agreement, in which employers agree to require all employees, once hired, to join a union.
- Discrimination against employees who testify or file charges under the act.
- Refusal to bargain collectively with employees' chosen union.

Thus protected from the sometimes violent antiunion practices of employers that characterized organizing activity before the Wagner Act became law, unions rapidly increased their membership, growing from 3.6 million in 1935 to more than 10 million by 1941. But the hard-won protection that unions had gained under the Wagner Act was not destined to remain unchallenged for very long.

TAFT-HARTLEY ACT

The constitutionality of the Wagner Act was upheld by the Supreme Court in five challenges brought by employer groups. But the act was altered substantially by the Taft-Hartley amendments of 1947 and the Landrum-Griffin amendments of 1959. The 1947 Taft-Hartley Act was passed by Congress over President Harry S. Truman's veto and was bitterly opposed by organized labor groups. For the first time, a means to protect employers as well as employees was established. A detailed list of unfair labor activities that unions were forbidden to practice was added to the original legislation, along with a "free speech" amendment allowing employers to propagandize against unions prior to an NLRB election, if no threats or promises were made. After passage of Taft-Hartley, union election rates started dropping.

The Taft-Hartley Act still protected the employees' right to bargain collectively, join a union, strike, and petition the NLRB to hold a certification election to determine union representation, but it added their right to refrain from such activities and allowed a union to be sued for contract violations and held liable for damages resulting from illegal actions. Closed shops were forbidden but union shops remained legal. Union officials had to file financial reports and swear they were not communists. Strikes against the government were outlawed. Federal courts were empowered to issue injunctions against national emergency strikes, providing for an eighty-day cooling-off period.

Under other provisions of the act, the NLRB was reorganized to its present five-member form and the Federal Mediation and Conciliation Service and Joint Committee on Labor-Management Relations were established. The act also created an independent general counsel to remove the appearance of conflict between the board's dual roles as prosecutor and judge.

LANDRUM-GRIFFIN ACT

After a series of hearings on union corruption, Congress in 1959 passed a tough labor anticorruption bill entitled the Labor-Management Reporting and Disclosure (Landrum-Griffin) Act. The act required all unions to adopt constitutions and bylaws and to register them with the secretary of labor. In addition, unions were required to submit annual reports detailing assets, liabilities, revenue and sources, payments to union members exceeding $10,000, loans to union members and businesses, and other financial disbursements.

NLRB IN THE 1970S

In 1970 Congress passed the Postal Reorganization Act, which put the U.S. Postal Service under NLRB jurisdiction. The National Labor Relations Act was further amended in 1974 to extend protection under the act to employees of all private health care institutions, whether or not they were profit-making enterprises.

Efforts on the part of organized labor to halt the gradual erosion by Congress and the courts of the protections granted to organized labor by the Wagner Act generally have failed. Many union leaders were optimistic that the tide would change under the administration of President Jimmy Carter. Carter, a Democrat, was much more in tune with union interests than his Republican predecessors had been, but labor's agenda in Congress still fared poorly.

A big disappointment to labor was the 1977 defeat of a bill to legalize common-site picketing in the construction industry. A twenty-five-year battle had been waged by the construction trade unions to permit a form of secondary boycott by allowing unions with a grievance against one contractor to picket an entire construction site.

The following year, labor geared up to push a labor law reform bill that would have, among other things, simplified and sped up union certification elections. But a filibuster led by conservative senators defeated the measure, and the leadership sent the bill back to the Senate Labor and Human Resources Committee, where it died at the end of the Congress. The bill was viewed suspiciously as an attempt to revive unions' lagging organizing successes. Nonetheless, critics in industry charged that Carter was attempting to bring about the reforms that Congress had refused to enact by appointing members to the board who were sympathetic toward labor's position.

Over the years several important Supreme Court cases have modified coverage for workers and employers under the National Labor Relations Act, as well as the scope of the NLRB's authority. In March 1979, the Supreme Court ruled that the NLRB did not have jurisdiction over teachers in church-affiliated schools; and in February 1980, the Court overturned a board decision that maintained faculty members at a private university had the right to bargain collectively under federal labor law. The Court held that if faculty members had authority over academic matters and institutional policies, they were, in effect, managers, and not entitled to the protections of the act if they organized a union.

NLRB IN THE 1980S

President Ronald Reagan came into office promising to rein in the government and reduce regulation. Nowhere did he have a better opportunity than at the NLRB. Attrition allowed him to appoint new board members who shared his conservative philosophy. Virtually all of his nominations to the NLRB were opposed by labor and supported by management.

During the Reagan administration, the NLRB handed down a number of decisions that reversed previous rulings. The board affirmed the right of employers to demand loyalty from supervisors, relaxed rules on management neutrality when rival unions compete to represent workers, and indicated it would refrain from involvement in minor workplace disputes.

In a ruling that was decried by labor groups, the board in January 1984, and again on remand in 1987, upheld the firing of a truck driver who refused to drive an unsafe truck. The NLRB said that while it was "outraged" by the action of Meyer Industries of Tennessee, the driver was not protected by the National Labor Relations Act because he did not act in concert with other employees. The ruling reversed the finding of an administrative law judge and also reversed a policy set in a 1975 case involving the Alleluia Cushion Co. In the earlier case, the board had said that an employee who acted to protect his own safety for good cause was engaged in "concerted activity" because safety involved all employees.

Also in 1984 the NLRB ruled that an employer could relocate work to another, nonunion plant to avoid the higher union labor costs, as long as relocation was not barred in the union contract. But three years later, the Supreme Court ruled in *Fall River Dyeing and Finishing Corp. v. NLRB* that in the case of a new owner, bargaining obligations carry over if they represent substantially the same operation and jobs.

According to an AFL-CIO study released in 1985 the NLRB had ruled in favor of employers in 60 percent of the cases it decided in 1984, more than double the promanagement decisions made by two previous boards examined by the study. The Reagan board's goal of keeping government out of the collective bargaining process had some success, as disgruntled labor officials sought other avenues, such as arbitration, to resolve disputes.

Some of the controversy surrounding the NLRB in the mid-1980s focused on a huge case backlog, a problem that has historically plagued the agency. A report issued by the Employment and Housing Subcommittee of the House Government Operations Committee following a series of hearings throughout the 1980s found the NLRB to be "in a crisis" because of slowness in decision making.

Unlike most federal regulatory agencies, the board has rarely initiated substantive rulemaking, which it considers a measure of last resort. Pressed by an ever-increasing number of cases in the health care field, the board in 1987 proposed to recognize eight appropriate bargaining units in acute care hospitals, replacing the old system of defining units on a case-by-case basis. In effect, the rule made it easier for hospital staff to organize unions. The hospital industry immediately challenged NLRB's authority to issue the rules, which were to have gone into effect in May 1989. A federal appeals court upheld the NLRB's authority in 1990, and, in a major victory for labor forces, a unanimous Supreme Court upheld the new NLRB rules in 1991.

In 1988 the Supreme Court in *Edward J. De Bartolo Corp. v. Florida Gulf Coast Building & Construction Trades Council* overturned a board decision that a union's peaceful distribution of handbills urging consumers to boycott secondary employers—not the employer with whom the union had a dispute—violated the act's secondary boycotting provision. The Court reasoned that unlike picketing, passing out handbills was not coercive and, therefore, not illegal. In 1992 however, the Supreme Court ruled in *Lechmere, Inc. v. National Labor Relations Board* that a store owner who had prevented union representatives who were not employees from giving out handbills in the parking lot in order to organize the labor force at his shop was acting within the scope of the National Labor Relations Act. The Court rejected the board's rule allowing the distribution of the handbills because the union had not proven that there was no other reasonable means of communicating with the employees.

In 1989 the board was rebuffed when it tried to force an employer to hire a union organizer. A federal appeals court ruled in *H. B. Zachry Co. v. NLRB* that the board "chose form over substance" in its attempt to prevent worker discrimination based on union sympathy. But workers won a major battle when the Supreme Court ruled in the 1994 case, *ABF Freight Systems, Inc. v. National Labor Relations Board*, that the NLRB was acting within its authority when it reinstated a fired worker, even though the worker had lied during the administrative proceedings in the case.

One controversial decision of the NLRB occurred in 1989 when the NLRB general counsel ruled that drug testing was a subject for collective bargaining and could not be unilaterally imposed. The board later overruled part of that order, saying that it applied only to current employees, leaving employers free to test job applicants.

NLRB IN THE 1990S

In 1990 President George Bush appointed James M. Stephens, former counsel of the Senate Labor and Human Resources Committee, to head the NLRB. Under Stephens's leadership, the board was credited by both labor and management with bringing a more balanced, impartial approach to board decisions. Board members were still considered somewhat conservative, but earnest about an even-handed application of the law.

By the 1990s there was a slight upturn in union victories in representational elections. In 1980 they won 3,498 elections, less than half of the 7,296 conducted by the NLRB, but by 1995 unions had won 1,468 of the 2,911 representation elections held, or a full 50 percent. Unions also did slightly better in the decertification elections. Whereas unions won only 24 percent of these elections in the early 1980s, between 1990 and 1995 they won 1,000 of the 3,278 elections or roughly 31 percent.

Bill Clinton's election as president did not immediately produce positive results for labor. Despite having a Democrat in the White House, unions and labor leaders suffered several major defeats in Congress and the courts. Notwithstanding vocal and intense labor opposition to the North American Free Trade Agreement (NAFTA), Congress approved the measure in 1993. The same battle was fought and lost against the General Agreement on Tariffs and Trade (GATT), which passed in 1994.

In 1992 the NLRB announced it would initiate rules to comply with the 1988 Supreme Court decision in *Beck v. Communications Workers of America*. The Court ruled that nonunion workers who had to pay fees to a union were entitled to withhold the portion of the fee that went to activities other than negotiating with the employer or administering the labor union. The nonunion workers did not have to pay the portion of the dues that went to lobbying, organizing new workers, supporting strikes elsewhere, or running community service activities. Though the NLRB had promulgated these rules since 1992, it was not until two 1995 cases, *California Saw and Knife Works* and *Weyerhaeuser*, that the board cited the *Beck* case in rendering decisions against organized labor.

In 1994 the Supreme Court struck down the NLRB's test to determine whether nurses should be considered supervisors. (Supervisors are not protected under the National Labor Relations Act.) In *National Labor Relations Board v. Health Care & Retirement Corporation of America,* the Court held that the NLRB's test—which relied on whether the nurse was acting for the benefit of the employer or the patient—was inconsistent with the National Labor Relations Act.

The outlook for organized labor took a decided turn for the better with the appointment of William B. Gould IV as NLRB chair, the first African American named to that position. Gould, who took office in March 1994 after an acrimonious nine-month Senate confirmation fight, made no secret of his belief that the board tilted too far toward management during the Reagan and Bush administrations and that he was determined to correct that perceived bias.

Many Republicans and business executives believe during his tenure he went too far in the opposite direction. Daniel Yager, the general counsel of the Labor Policy Association, which represents 230 large firms, said of Gould: "Under his leadership, the board has been the most politicized in recent memory." When the Supreme Court sided with the NLRB in 1995 *(NLRB v. Town & Country Electric, Inc.),* ruling that union activists who take jobs in nonunion companies to try to organize from within cannot be fired for their prounion activities, Gould called the decision "a big victory," saying that this ruling is likely to increase such organizing efforts, which are called "salting" campaigns.

Gould also was openly opposed to the so-called TEAM bill (the Teamwork for Employees and Management Act), which would have modified the 1935 National Labor Relations Act to make clear that U.S. businesses are permitted to form worker-management groups to address issues such as quality control, productivity, and safety. Organized labor strongly opposed the measure, fearing that it would lead to sham or "company" unions, whereas business argued such groups would provide for more flexibility and cooperation in the workplace. President Clinton vetoed the legislation on July 30, 1996.

Gould was not invariably prounion, however. In January 1995 he cast the deciding vote in two rulings that union members had improperly picketed employers of other, nonunion workers. Gould cited a 1992 Supreme Court decision that employers are within their rights to bar nonemployee union members who attempt to organize workers on private property.

In 1995 the board issued a record number of injunctions ordering companies to reverse antiunion actions. This increase in injunctions signals a major change in operations for the NLRB, which had previously depended far more on standard litigation to resolve cases.

Injunctions are part of a trend in labor relations that has de-emphasized the strike in favor of legal action, thus increasing the importance of the NLRB in everyday collective bargaining. At the root of this trend is workers' fear of being permanently replaced if they go on strike. In 1994 labor failed to secure passage in Congress of a bill to prohibit the hiring of permanent replacements for some striking workers. The practice had been sanctioned by the Supreme Court in its 1938 decision *NLRB v. Mackay Radio and Telegraph Co.,* but it had not been widely practiced until the 1980s, when management seized on it as a method of breaking unions who were striking for better pay.

Because this practice is illegal if the strike is called because of unfair labor practices, it has become part of unions' defense against the threat of permanent replacement workers to file complaints of unfair labor practices with the NLRB. For example, the United Auto Workers lodged more than 180 complaints of unfair labor practices during their seventeen-month-long strike against Caterpillar Inc. Caterpillar ultimately won the strike, however, by using managers, office workers, and skilled temporaries rather than permanent replacements to maintain production.

The board's increasingly active role in labor disputes did not go unnoticed on Capitol Hill, where the pro-labor Democratic majority was replaced in 1995 by the more probusiness Republican Party. GOP members accused Gould of being shamelessly prounion and claimed that he was unable to intervene fairly in labor disputes.

Gould, for his part, argued that the GOP and probusiness groups were angered by his willingness to actually apply laws designed to protect workers rights. "I wasn't aware of the deeply held tenacity of those who really do not accept the idea of the National Labor Relations Act," he said in an August 1998 interview in the *New York Times.* He also accused Republicans of directly interfering in specific NLRB cases, something members of Congress had never done before, he said.

The rhetoric heated up almost immediately after Republicans took charge of both houses of Congress in early 1995. That year Congress rescinded a recently proposed NLRB rule that would have allowed a company's employees at one workplace site to unionize, even if workers at its other nearby sites did not. In other words, even if workers did not vote to unionize company-wide, employees at one site could still form a union.

Implementation of the rule was blocked in the fiscal 1996 spending bill funding the agency. This recision was renewed by Congress in the next two annual spending bills covering the NLRB. These bills also cut the agency's budget by 2 percent in fiscal 1996 and froze it the following two years.

Gould accused Congress of micromanaging and second-guessing the board. But on Feb. 18, 1998, over his objections, the entire board voted to withdraw the proposed regulation. Shortly afterwards, Gould announced that he would not seek another four-year term when his first stint as chair ended on Aug. 27. Although the sixty-two-year-old Stanford University law professor did not always make prounion rulings, his actions and statements generally reflected a greater concern and empathy for workers.

In his place, President Clinton nominated John C. Truesdale, a labor lawyer who joined the NLRB in 1948 and served in a variety of capacities, including five different times as a board member. Not as controversial as Gould, Truesdale promised to focus on reducing the agency's backlog of unresolved cases. He won unanimous Senate confirmation.

In spite of Gould's absence, the board continued to issue what many in the business community regarded as controversial, prounion decisions. One of the most highly publicized of these rulings came in August 1998 and involved a 1995 strike by workers at Detroit's two daily newspapers, the *News* and the *Free Press.* Claiming that the newspapers had not bargained in good faith, the NLRB ruled that both had to reinstate strikers, even if it meant laying off permanent replacements who had long ago been brought on to work at the papers. It also ordered the newspapers to pay strikers back wages, estimated at $80 million.

The agency also weighed in on the contentious issue of whether doctors should be able to unionize. Health maintenance organizations and private hospitals have long opposed collective bargaining for doctors, arguing that they are private contractors. While only about 5 percent of the nation's physicians belong to a union, their numbers grew dramatically during the 1990s. The NLRB gave a boost to these efforts in November 1999 by ruling that interns and residents at privately owned hospitals had the right to unionize.

NLRB IN THE 2000S

The agency raised its profile at the start of the new millennium with a potentially far-reaching decision, granting some temporary workers the right to organize and form unions. Under the ruling, handed down in September 2000, temporary employees were allowed to form a union if they were supervised by the company they were assigned to work for, and if they did the same work as the firm's full-time employees. The decision had long-term implications, as more and more businesses relied on temporary workers to do jobs formerly held by permanent employees.

Two months later, the board weighed in on a similar issue, in this case involving graduate teaching assistants (TAs) at private universities. Two decades earlier the NLRB had ruled that TAs did not have the right to form a union. But a new case, brought by graduate students from New York University, prompted the board to reverse itself and allow unionization. The decision had a broad impact, fueling new labor organizing drives at scores of public and private universities around the country, including Columbia University, the University of Michigan, and the University of Illinois.

Meanwhile, important personnel issues were coming to the fore. By the end of 2000, retirements left the board with only three members. Of those remaining, one member, NRLB chief Truesdale, was slated to retire in the fall of 2001. At the end of the year, President Clinton brought board membership up to four by making a recess appointment that allowed the new member, Democrat Dennis Walsh, to serve only a year.

During his first year in office, Clinton's successor, Republican George W. Bush did not make any appointments. But Truesdale's retirement and the end of Walsh's temporary appointment at the end of the 2001 left the board with only two members, one shy of a quorum needed to issue rulings. In January 2002 Bush made two recess appointments, both Republicans, to fill in some of the gaps. He also reappointed Democrat Wilma Liebman in August. Finally, at the end of 2002, Bush appointed three Republicans to full terms on the board, including new chair Robert J. Battista. The president also brought back Democrat Walsh to round out the board, giving it the traditional three-to-two split in favor of the administration's party.

Battista, a well-respected labor lawyer from Detroit, spent most of his career in private practice representing management clients. At his Senate confirmation hearing, he said he wanted to reduce rancor and partisanship on the board.

Battista and the other new Republican board members were easily confirmed, even though President Bush's had begun his term at odds with organized labor. A little over a month after taking office, the president upset unions when he signed an executive order requiring federal contractors to post notices at the workplace informing their unionized employees of a 1988 Supreme Court decision giving them the right to withhold that portion of their dues that goes to political activities. At the same time, the new president signed another executive order reversing a policy that requires some federal contractors to be union shops.

During his first two years, Bush continued to rankle labor groups. Unions accused the president of stepping into a number of labor disputes on the side of management. For instance, after labor talks between machinists and Northwest Airlines collapsed in February 2001, the president moved to prohibit the workers temporarily from carrying out their threat to strike, arguing that such an action would unfairly hurt U.S. travelers. In October 2002 he invoked the Taft-Hartley Act to order longshore workers on the West Coast back to work, after a slowdown had prompted dock-owners to shut down ports all along the coast.

Finally, in January 2003, labor leaders were angered by the administration's refusal to allow 60,000 new federal airport safety screeners to unionize. The administration countered that collective bargaining agreements would make the new workforce much less flexible and could hamper the government's ability to change work assignments and implement other moves to respond quickly to terrorist threats.

Current Issues

With its conservative board in place in 2003, the NLRB was poised to review a number of recent controversial rulings that were made under the more liberal, Clinton-appointed board. These included the 1999 Epilepsy Foundation decision, where the board held that nonunion workers could demand that a coworker be present during any questioning that could lead to disciplinary action or firing. In the past, only union employees enjoyed these rights (referred to as "Weingarten rights.")

Likewise, the new board may revisit an issue it dealt with in 2000: whether temporary workers can join a union representing permanent employees and create a single collective bargaining unit. Some felt that the decision had created great difficulties for firms, because temporary and permanent workers often had different needs and hence had difficulty bargaining together.

Other old NLRB rulings that might come up for rehearing include the 1999 decision allowing residents, interns, and other medical personnel to unionize, and a 1998 ruling expanding the number of situations under which employees can use the mail to vote in elections to determine whether workers unionize.

The NLRB also was expected to examine a number of new, important issues, including the legal limitations on employee e-mail use. Previously, the board ruled that employees cannot be fired for writing e-mails on work-related issues—such as pay, vacation, or unionization—regardless of what they wrote. But a ruling was expected on whether unions could use a business's e-mail to contact the firm's workers.

Meanwhile, relations between the president and organized labor remained chilly. Most recently, the administration proposed strict new financial disclosure rules for unions in an effort to crack down on corruption. The move enraged union leaders, many of whom charged that the new regulations were meant to intimidate them. Even unions that have, in the past, supported the president—most notably the Teamsters—have distanced themselves from the White House over the new requirements.

AGENCY ORGANIZATION

Biographies

ROBERT J. BATTISTA, CHAIRMAN

Appointment: Nominated by President George W. Bush and confirmed by the Senate for a term that expires on December 16, 2007.

Education: University of Notre Dame, B.A., 1961; University of Michigan Law, J.D., 1964.

Political Affiliation: Republican.

Previous Career: Battista practiced employment and labor relations law since 1965 with the Detroit firm Butzel Long. He was the former chair of the Labor Employment and Law section of the Michigan Bar Association, a member of the Advisory Committee of the Michigan Employment Relations Commission, and is a fellow with the College of Labor and Employment Lawyers.

WILMA B. LIEBMAN, BOARD MEMBER

Appointment: Reappointed by President George W. Bush and confirmed by the Senate to a second term that will expire on August 27, 2006. She previously served as a member from November 14, 1997 to December 16, 2002.

Born: April 3, 1950, Philadelphia, PA.

Education: Barnard College, B.A., 1971; George Washington University Law Center, J.D., 1974.

Profession: Lawyer.

Political Affiliation: Democrat.

Previous Career: Before her appointment to the NLRB Board, Liebman served as Deputy Director of the Federal Mediation and Conciliation Service.

PETER C. SCHAUMBER, BOARD MEMBER

Appointment: Nominated by President George W. Bush and confirmed by the Senate for a term that will expire on August 27, 2005.

Education: Georgetown University 1964, B.S; Georgetown University Law, J.D., 1968.

Political Affiliation: Republican.

Previous Career: Before joining NLRB, Schaumber practiced as a labor arbitrator serving on a number of industry panels and through national arbitration rosters.

DENNIS P. WALSH, BOARD MEMBER

Appointment: Nominated by President George W. Bush and confirmed by the Senate for a term expiring December 16, 2004. He previously served as a member from December 30, 2000, to December 20, 2001.

Born: Aug. 27, 1954.

Education: Hamilton College, B.A., 1976; Cornell Law School, J.D., 1983.

Profession: Lawyer.

Political Affiliation: Democrat.

Previous Career: Prior to his appointment Walsh was chief counsel to member Wilma B. Liebman, and from 1994–1997, he was chief counsel to member Margaret A. Browning. Formerly he was a associate at the Philadelphia firm Spear, Wilderman, Borish, Endy, Browning and Spear.

R. ALEXANDER ACOSTA, BOARD MEMBER

Appointment: Nominated by President George W. Bush and confirmed by the Senate for a term that expires August 27, 2003.

Education: Harvard College, B.A.; Harvard Law School, J.D.

Political Affiliation: Republican.

Previous Career: Prior to his appointment Acosta served as principal deputy assistant attorney general at the Civil Rights Division of the Department of Justice. He specialized in labor issues and appellate practice at the Washington office of Kirkland and Ellis and served as a fellow in legal studies at the Ethics and Public Policy Center.

Headquarters and Divisions

BOARD

The NLRB has two principal functions under the National Labor Relations Act, as amended: (1) preventing statutorily defined unfair labor practices on the part of employers and labor organizations or their agents; and (2) conducting secret ballot elections among employees in appropriate collective-bargaining units to determine whether they desire to be represented by a labor organization.

The NLRB is further responsible for conducting secret ballot elections among employees who have been covered by a union-shop agreement, when requested by 30 percent of the employees, to determine whether they wish to revoke their union's authority to make such agreements; determining, in cases involving jurisdictional disputes, which of the competing groups of workers is entitled to perform the work involved; and conducting secret ballot elections among employees concerning the final settlement offers of employers in national emergency labor disputes.

The board exercises full and final authority over the Office of the Solicitor, Office of the Inspector General, Office of Representative Appeals, and Division of Information. The board appoints administrative law judges and exercises authority over the Division of Administrative Law Judges subject to the Administrative Procedures Provisions of Title 5, U.S. Code, and the National Labor Relations Act, as amended. Each board member supervises staff counsel, each staff being under the immediate supervision of the chief counsel of the respective board member.

NATIONAL LABOR RELATIONS BOARD

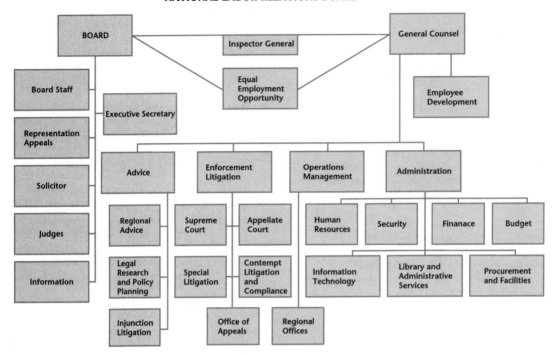

Along with the general counsel, the board approves the budget, opens new offices, and appoints the director of administration, regional directors, and officers-in-charge.

Chair

Robert J. Battista .... (202) 273-1770

Fax .... (202) 273-4270

Board Members

Wilma B. Liebman .... (202) 273-1700

Peter C. Schaumber .... (202) 273-1790

Dennis P. Walsh .... (202) 273-1740

R. Alexander Acosta .... (202) 273-1070

Board Staff

Chief Counsel to the Chair

Harold J. Datz .... (202) 273-1770

Chief Counsel to Member Liebman

John F. Colwell .... (202) 273-1700

Chief Counsel to Member Schaumber

James R. Murphy .... (202) 273-1790

Chief Counsel to Member Walsh

Gary W. Shinners .... (202) 273-1740

Chief Counsel to Member Acosta

Peter Winkler .... (202) 273-1070

Division of Administration

Directs the administrative management functions of the agency. Responsible for financial management functions; personnel management; mail, graphic, printing, editorial and transportation services; information technology services, including computer services and statistical analyses of case activity; library and records management; procurement; facilities and communications management; and an occupational health and safety program.

Director

Gloria J. Joseph .... (202) 273-3890

Library and Administrative Services Branch

Vanita C.S. Reynolds .... (202) 273-3920

Budget Branch

Lisa Bevels .... (202) 273-3970

Finance Branch

Karl Rohrbaugh .... (202) 273-4230

Information Technology Branch

Louis B. Adams .... (202) 273-4030

Human Resources Branch

Catherine McCoy .... (202) 273-3900

Procurement and Facilities Branch

Angela F. Crawford .... (202) 273-4040

Security Branch

Eugene Lott Jr. .... (202) 273-1990

DIVISION OF ADMINISTRATIVE LAW JUDGES

Conducts all hearings in unfair labor practice cases and other hearings as assigned. Also rules on pretrial motions, requests for extension of time to file briefs, proposed findings, and conclusions. The chief, deputy chief, and associate chief administrative law judges designate administrative law judges to conduct hearings, make rulings, assign dates for hearings, and maintain a calendar of cases to be heard.

Chief Administrative Law Judge

Robert A. Giannasi .... (202) 501-8800

Fax .... (202) 501-8686

Atlanta Branch Office

401 W. Peachtree St. N.W., #1708

Atlanta, GA 30308-3510

(404) 331-6652

William N. Cates, associate chief administrative law judge

New York Branch Office

120 W. 45th St., 11th Floor

New York, NY 10036-5503

(212) 944-2941

Joel P. Biblowitz, associate chief administrative law judge

San Francisco Branch Office

901 Market St., #300

San Francisco, CA 94103-1779

(415) 356-5255

William L. Schmidt, associate chief administrative law judge

OFFICE OF THE EXECUTIVE SECRETARY

Serves as administrative manager of the board's judicial affairs. Assigns cases to individual board members to initiate the judicial process; represents the board in dealing with parties to cases; receives, dockets, and acknowledges formal documents filed with the board; issues and serves board decisions and orders on the parties to all cases; and certifies copies of all documents that are part of the board's files or records.

Advises the board on interlocutory appeals and requests for special permission to appeal and advises regional offices about procedural matters in representation cases.

Communicates on behalf of the board with employees, employers, labor organizations, Congress, other agencies, and the public.

Executive Secretary

Vacant .... (202) 273-1940

Docket Order and Issuance Section

Vacant .... (202) 273-1940

OFFICE OF THE GENERAL COUNSEL

Supervises the agency's attorneys, regional offices, and headquarters divisions and offices (except those under the direct supervision of the board: the administrative law judges, staff counsel to board members, executive secretary, and solicitor). Investigates charges, issues complaints, and prosecutes those complaints before the board. On behalf of the board, prosecutes injunction proceedings; handles U.S. Court of Appeals proceedings, miscellaneous litigation, and efforts to obtain compliance with board orders. Together with the members of the board, the general counsel determines budget requests, appoints agency personnel, and administers the equal employment opportunity program. The general counsel is independent from the board.

General Counsel

Arthur F. Rosenfeld .... (202) 273-3700

DIVISION OF ENFORCEMENT LITIGATION

Represents the agency in litigation before the U.S. Supreme Court, U.S. Court of Appeals, and federal district courts, including contempt litigation and enforcement and review of board decisions.

The division's Office of Appeals reviews appeals of refusals by regional directors to issue complaints in unfair labor practice cases and on occasion hears informal supportive or opposing oral presentations by counsel or other representatives of parties involved in such litigation, before recommending the action to be taken by the general counsel. The office also advises the general counsel on further legal action in appeals cases stemming from regional directors' refusals to provide documents under the Freedom of Information Act.

Associate General Counsel

John H. Ferguson .... (202) 273-2950

Fax .... (202) 273-4244

Appeals

Yvonne T. Dixon .... (202) 273-3760

Supreme Court Branch

John Arbab .... (202) 273–2957

DIVISION OF ADVICE

Handles circuit court appeals cases from district courts; advises the general counsel in appeal and contempt matters; assists in injunction litigation under special circumstances; and makes recommendations for the general counsel to the board on handling requests for injunction.

The Regional Advice Branch advises the general counsel and regional directors on special issues of law and policy and performs legal research. This branch prepares the general counsel's quarterly reports and guideline memoranda on important legal issues for regional directors and the public.

The Research and Policy Planning Branch analyzes, digests, and indexes all board and related court decisions for publication and internal agency use. This branch is responsible for legal information retrieval systems. It also coordinates compliance with the Freedom of Information Act.

Associate General Counsel
  Barry J. Kearney .... (202) 273-3800
  Fax .... (202) 273-4275
Injunction Litigation
  Judith L. Katz .... (202) 273-3810
Regional Advice Branch
  David A. Colangelo .... (202) 273-3831
Research and Policy Planning Branch
  Jacqueline A. Young .... (202) 273–3840

OFFICE OF EQUAL EMPLOYMENT OPPORTUNITY

Processes all complaints of alleged discrimination within the NLRB. Carries out its responsibilities under Title VII of the Civil Rights Act of 1964, the Rehabilitation Act of 1973, the Equal Pay Act of 1963, the Age Discrimination in Employment Act of 1967, and the Civil Rights Act of 1991.

Also monitors the agency's affirmative action employment plan and the agency's federal equal opportunity recruitment program plan. Offers advice and assistance to all managers, supervisors, and employees on EEO matters and issues.

Director
  Robert J. Poindexter .... (202) 273-3891
Deputy Director
  Lori Suto-Goldsby .... (202) 273-0761

DIVISION OF INFORMATION

See Information Sources.

OFFICE OF THE INSPECTOR GENERAL

Investigates allegations of waste, fraud, abuse, and mismanagement in federal programs and conducts audits of internal agency matters. Also recommends steps to increase the NLRB's effectiveness and efficiency.

Inspector General
  Jane E. Altenhofen .... (202) 273–1960
Counsel to Inspector General
  David P. berry .... (202) 273–1964
Supervisory Auditor
  Emil T. George.......................... (202) 275–1966

OFFICE OF THE SOLICITOR

Advises the board on questions of law and procedure, on intervention in court proceedings to protect the board's jurisdiction, on the board's exercise of its discretion regarding injunctive relief, and on enforcement of board orders. Makes recommendations to the board on summary judgments, advisory opinions concerning the board's jurisdiction, and formal settlement proposals. Also advises the board on internal labor relations matters. Serves as the board's liaison with Congress, the White House, state officials, other agencies, and members of the bar.

Solicitor
  Jeffrey D. Wedekind .... (202) 273-2910

DIVISION OF OPERATIONS MANAGEMENT

Responsible for the operation and administration of all regional, resident, and subregional offices, including case processing; and coordinates these operations with the case handling and administrative operations of the general counsel. Also provides advice to the general counsel on major policy questions.

Associate General Counsel
  Richard Siegel .... (202) 273-2900

Regional Offices

REGION 1

(Boston)
Boston Federal Office Bldg., 6th Floor
10 Causeway St.
Boston, MA 02222-1072
(617) 565-6700
Fax (617) 565-6725
Rosemary Pye, regional director

REGION 2

(New York)
Jacob K. Javits Federal Bldg., #3614
26 Federal Plaza
New York, NY 10278-0104
(212) 264-0300
Fax (212) 264-8427
Celeste Mattina, regional director

REGION 3

(Buffalo)
Federal Bldg., #901
111 W. Huron St.
Buffalo, NY 14202-2387
(716) 551-4931
Fax (716) 551-4972
Vacant, regional director

REGION 4

(Philadelphia)
One Independence Mall
615 Chestnut St., 7th Floor
Philadelphia, PA 19106-4404
(215) 597-7601
Fax (215) 597-7658
Dorothy L. Moore-Duncan, regional director

REGION 5

(Baltimore)
The Appraisers Store Bldg., 8th Floor
103 S. Gay St.
Baltimore, MD 21202-4026
(410) 962-2822
Fax (410) 962-2198
Wayne Gold, regional director

REGION 6

(Pittsburgh)
William S. Moorehead Federal Bldg., #1501
1000 Liberty Ave.
Pittsburgh, PA 15222-4173
(412) 395-4400
Fax (412) 395-5986
Gerald Kobell, regional director

REGION 7

(Detroit)
Patrick V. McNamara Federal Bldg., #300
477 Michigan Ave.
Detroit, MI 48226-2569
(313) 226-3200
Fax (313) 226-2090
Stephen M. Glasser, regional director

REGION 8

(Cleveland)
Anthony J. Celebrezze Federal Bldg., #1695
1240 E. 9th St.
Cleveland, OH 44199-2086
(216) 522-3716
Fax (216) 522-2418
Frederick Calatrello, regional director

REGION 9

(Cincinnati)
Federal Office Bldg., #3003
550 Main St.
Cincinnati, OH 45202-3271
(513) 684-3686
Fax (513) 684-3946
Richard L. Ahearn, regional director

REGION 10

(Atlanta)
233 Peachtree St. N.E.
Harris Tower, #1000
Atlanta, GA 30303-1531
(404) 331-2896
Fax (404) 331-2858
Martin M. Arlook, regional director

REGION 11

(Winston-Salem)
Republic Square, #200
4035 University Parkway
Winston-Salem, NC 27106-3323
(336) 631-5201
Fax (336) 631-5210
Willie L. Clark Jr., regional director

REGION 12

(Tampa)
South Trust Plaza, #530
201 E. Kennedy Blvd.
Tampa, FL 33602-5824
(813) 228-2641
Fax (813) 228-2874
Rochelle Kentov, regional director

REGION 13
(Chicago)
200 W. Adams St., #800
Chicago, IL 60606-5208
(312) 353-7570
Fax (312) 886-1341
Elizabeth Kinney, regional director

REGION 14
(St. Louis)
1222 Spruce St., #8.302
St. Louis, MO 63103-2829
(314) 539-7770
Fax (314) 539-7794
Ralph R. Tremain, regional director

REGION 15
(New Orleans)
1515 Poydras St., #610
New Orleans, LA 70112-3723
(504) 589-6361
Fax (504) 589-4069
Rodney D. Johnson, regional director

REGION 16
(Fort Worth)
Federal Office Bldg., #8A24
819 Taylor St.
Fort Worth, TX 76102-6178
(817) 978-2921
Fax (817) 978-2928
Curtis Wells, regional director

REGION 17
(Kansas City)
8600 Farley St., #100
Overland Park, KS 66212-4677
(913) 236-3000
Fax (913) 967-3010
F. Rozier Sharp, regional director

REGION 18
(Minneapolis)
Towle Bldg., #790
330 2nd Ave. South
Minneapolis, MN 55401-2221
(612) 348-1757
Fax (612) 348-1785
Ronald M. Sharp, regional director

REGION 19
(Seattle)
Henry M. Jackson Federal Bldg., #2948
915 2nd Ave.
Seattle, WA 98174-1078
(206) 220-6300
Fax (206) 220-6305
Vacant, regional director

REGION 20
(San Francisco)
901 Market St., #400
San Francisco, CA 94103-1735
(415) 356-5130
Fax (415) 356-5156
Robert H. Miller, regional director

REGION 21
(Los Angeles)
888 S. Figueroa St., 9th Floor
Los Angeles, CA 90017-5449
(213) 894-5200
Fax (213) 894-2778
Victoria E. Aguayo, regional director

REGION 22
(Newark)
20 Washington Pl., 5th Floor
Newark, NJ 07102-2570
(973) 645-2100
Fax (973) 645-3852
Gary T. Kendellen, regional director

REGION 24
(San Juan)
La Torre de Plaza, #1002
525 F.D. Roosevelt Ave.
San Juan, PR 00918-1002
(787) 766-5347
Fax (787) 766-5478
Marta Figueroa, regional director

REGION 25
(Indianapolis)
Minton-Capehart Federal Bldg., #238
575 N. Pennsylvania St.
Indianapolis, IN 46204-1577
(317) 226-7430
Fax (317) 226-5103
Roberto G. Chavarry, regional director

REGION 26
(Memphis)
Mid-Memphis Tower Bldg., #800
1407 Union Ave.
Memphis, TN 38104-3627
(901) 544-0018
Fax (901) 544-0008
Ronald K. Hooks, regional director

REGION 27
(Denver)
North Tower, 7th Floor
600 17th St.
Denver, CO 80202-5433
(303) 844-3551
Fax (303) 844-6249
B. Allan Benson, regional director

REGION 28
(Phoenix)
2600 N. Central Ave., #1800
Phoenix, AZ 85004-2212
(602) 640-2160
Fax (602) 640-2178
Cornele A. Overstreet, regional director

REGION 29
(Brooklyn)
One Metro Tech Center, 10th Floor
Jay St. and Myrtle Ave.
Brooklyn, NY 11201-4201
(718) 330-7713
(718) 330-7579
Alvin P. Blyer, regional director

REGION 30
(Milwaukee)
Henry S. Reuss Federal Plaza, #700
310 W. Wisconsin Ave.
Milwaukee, WI 53203-2211
(414) 297-3861
Fax (414) 297-3880
Philip E. Bloedorn, regional director

REGION 31
(Los Angeles)
11150 W. Olympic Blvd., #700
Los Angeles, CA 90064-1824
(310) 235-7351
Fax (310) 235-7420
James J. McDermott, regional director

REGION 32
(Oakland)
1301 Clay St., #300N
Oakland, CA 94612-5211
(510) 637-3300
Fax (510) 637-3315
Alan B. Reichard, regional director

REGION 34
(Hartford)
280 Trumbull St., 21st Floor
Hartford, CT 06103-3503
(860) 240-3522
Fax (860) 240-3564
Peter B. Hoffman, regional director

■ CONGRESSIONAL ACTION

Congressional Liaison
Lester A. Heltzer........................ (202) 273-1940

Committees and Subcommittees

HOUSE APPROPRIATIONS COMMITTEE
Subcommittee on Labor, Health and Human Services, and Education
2358 RHOB, Washington, DC 20515
(202) 225-3508

HOUSE EDUCATION AND THE WORKFORCE COMMITTEE
Subcommittee on Employer-Employee Relations
2181 RHOB, Washington DC 20515
(202) 225-4527

HOUSE GOVERNMENT REFORM AND OVERSIGHT COMMITTEE

Subcommittee on Human Resources
B372 RHOB, Washington DC 20515
(202) 225-2548

SENATE APPROPRIATIONS COMMITTEE

Subcommittee on Labor, Health and Human Services, and Education
SD-184, Washington, DC 20510
(202) 224-7230

SENATE LABOR AND HUMAN RESOURCES COMMITTEE

SD-428 Washington, DC 20510
(202) 224-6770

Legislation

The NLRB administers the following acts in full or in part:

National Labor Relations Act of 1935 (Wagner Act) (49 Stat. 449, 29 U.S.C. 151). Signed by the president July 5, 1935. Defined rights of employees to bargain collectively and strike; determined unfair labor activities that employers are forbidden from practicing.

Labor-Management Relations Act of 1947 (Taft-Hartley Act) (61 Stat. 136, 29 U.S.C. 141). Signed by the president June 23, 1947. Added provisions to the 1935 act protecting employers as well as employees.

Labor-Management Reporting and Disclosure Act of 1959 (Landrum-Griffin Act) (73 Stat. 519, 29 U.S.C. 401). Signed by the president Sept. 14, 1959. Established an employee bill of rights and reporting requirements for union activities.

Postal Reorganization Act of 1970 (84 Stat. 719, 39 U.S.C. 1201-1209). Signed by the president Aug. 12, 1970. Provided NLRB jurisdiction over labor disputes and representation elections in the U.S. Postal Service.

The National Labor Relations Act Amendments of 1974 (88 Stat. 395, 29 U.S.C. 152). Signed by the president July 26, 1974. Repealed the exemption for nonprofit hospital employees under the National Labor Relations Act as amended by the Taft-Hartley Act.

▨ INFORMATION SOURCES

Internet

The NLRB's Internet site is maintained by the Government Printing Office. It can be reached at: http://www.nlrb.gov. The site lists publications that are available to the public; it provides regional contact information; weekly summary and decisions by the board are obtainable; and forms used to file charges are available for download.

Telephone Contacts

Consult the NLRB Division of Information (below).

Information and Publications

KEY OFFICES

NLRB Division of Information
1099 14th St. N.W., Room 9400
Washington, DC 20570-0001
(202) 273-1991
David B. Parker, director
Mary M. Davis, public inquiry assistant

Provides general information to the media and the general public; arranges for agency personnel to speak before groups; issues news releases and a weekly summary of board and administrative law judges' decisions; distributes publications. General information also is available from the regional offices.

Freedom of Information
1099 14th St. N.W., Room 10610
Washington, DC 20570-0001
(202) 273-3840
Jacqueline A. Young, FOI officer

PUBLICATIONS

For a complete listing of publications regarding the NLRB and their prices, please call the Government Printing Office at (202) 512-1800. The Division of Information at the NLRB distributes a full catalog and limited quantities of free pamphlets. These pamphlets include (*available online):

A Career in Labor: Management Relations as an Attorney

A Career in Labor: Management Relations as a Field Examiner

The National Labor Relations Board and You (Representation cases)*

The National Labor Relations Board and You (Unfair labor practices)*

*The National Labor Relations Board: What It Is, What It Does**

*Your Government Conducts An Election**

Other publications, including subscription services, must be purchased from the Superintendent of Documents, U.S. Government Printing Office (GPO): see appendix, Ordering Government Publications. Titles for sale include:

Annual Report of the National Labor Relations Board.

Classified Index of National Labor Relations Board Decisions and Related Court Decisions. Quarterly; covers all board, administrative law judge, and NLRB-related court decisions issued during the period. Available as a subscription service.

Decisions and Orders of the National Labor Relations Board. Contact the NLRB Division of Information for information on latest volumes available.

A Guide to Basic Law and Procedures Under the National Labor Relations Act.*

The Guide For Hearing Officers in NLRB Representation and Section 10(k) Proceedings. Designed to assist agency employees in preparing for and conducting hearings in representation cases pursuant to Section 9(c) and in jurisdictional disputes, pursuant to Section 10(k) of the National Labor Relations Act.

Index of Court Decisions Relating to the National Labor Relations Act.

National Labor Relations Board Casehandling Manual. Provides complete, updated general counsel procedural and operational guidelines to NLRB regional offices in processing cases received under the National Labor Relations Act. The three-part manual is available as a subscription service.

NLRB Election Report. Lists the outcome of secret ballot voting by employees in NLRB-conducted representation elections in cases closed for each month. Compiled from results following resolution of post-election objections and/or challenges. Available as a subscription service; published monthly.

An Outline of Law and Procedure in Representation Cases. Reference guide to the law and administrative policy applicable to representation proceedings at various stages of processing by the NLRB.

Rules and Regulations and Statements of Procedure of the National Labor Relations Board, Series 8, as amended. Sold as a subscription service; includes updates for an indefinite period.

Weekly Summary of NLRB Cases.* Weekly subscription service containing a summary of each published NLRB decision in unfair labor practice and representation election cases; lists decisions of NLRB administrative law judges and directions of elections by NLRB regional directors.

DATA AND STATISTICS

Information Technology Branch
NLRB Division of Administration
1099 14th St. N.W., Room 7202
Washington, DC 20570-0001
(202) 273-4030
Louis B. Adams, chief information officer

Maintains the NLRB's computerized databases; prepares regular and special reports on case activity for the use of agency staff and the public. Much of this information appears in summary form in the *Annual Report.* More specific data is contained in the internal information system, which provides an accounting of all cases processed in the agency including median elapsed days and volume of cases at different stages of case handling. Statistical reports are generated monthly and summaries are published annually.

Research and Policy Planning Branch
NLRB Division of Advice
1099 14th St. N.W., #10612
Washington, DC 20570-0001
(202) 273-3840
Jacqueline A. young, Assistant General Counsel

Maintains a Legal Research System that provides indexes of board decisions, court decisions, and related legal information. Reports are issued quarterly or bimonthly and are available from the GPO.

MEETINGS
In accordance with the Government in the Sunshine Act, NLRB oral arguments and advisory committee meetings are open to the public. Meetings scheduled to consider specific litigation or the drafting of an opinion on a pending case are closed to the public.

For more information on scheduled board meetings, contact the NLRB Division of Information; (202) 273-1991.

Reference Resources

LIBRARIES

NLRB Library
1099 14th St. N.W., Room 8000
Washington, DC 20570-0001
(202) 273-3720
Kenneth Nero, librarian
Hours: 8:30 a.m to 5:00 p.m.

Open to the public. Participates in the interlibrary loan program.

Public Information Room
1099 14th St. N.W., Room 9700
Washington, DC 20570-0001
(202) 273-2840
Bonita G. Newman, chief of records
Appointment recommended

Maintains for public inspection the decision papers of the agency, including regional director's decisions, judge's decisions, appeals and advice papers, and regional director dismissal letters. Photocopying facilities are not available, but arrangements may be made to purchase copies.

RULES AND REGULATIONS
NLRB rules and regulations are published in the *Code of Federal Regulations,* Title 29, parts 100–199. Proposed rules, new final rules, and amendments to the *Code of Federal Regulations* are published in the daily *Federal Register. (See appendix for details on how to obtain and use these publications.)*

Other Information Sources

RELATED AGENCIES

DOL Bureau of Labor Statistics
2 Massachusetts Ave. N.E.
Washington, DC 20212
(202) 691-7800
Fax (202) 691-7797
Internet: http://www.bls.gov
Katharine G. Abraham, assistant commissioner

Gathers and analyzes data relating to labor and industry, including employment, unemployment, industrial relations, industrial safety, and wages and prices.

DOL Office of Labor-Management Standards
See p. 571.

NONGOVERNMENTAL ORGANIZATIONS
The following are some key organizations that monitor the NLRB and labor relations issues.

American Arbitration Association
355 Madison Ave., 10th Fl.
New York, NY 10017-4605
(212) 716-5800
Fax (212) 716-5905
Internet: http://www.adr.org

AFL-CIO
Government Affairs
815 16th St. N.W.
Washington, DC 20006
(202) 637-5000
Fax (202) 637-5058
Internet: http://www.aflcio.org

Center on National Labor Policy
5211 Port Royal Rd.
North Springfield, VA 22151
(703) 321-9180
Fax (703) 321-9325

George Meany Center for Labor Studies
10000 New Hampshire Ave.
Silver Spring, MD 20903
(301) 431-6400
Fax (301) 434-0371
Internet: http://www.georgemeany.org

National Association of Manufacturers
Human Resource Policy
1331 Pennsylvania Ave. N.W., #1500N
Washington, DC 20004-1790
(202) 637-3000
Fax (202) 637-3182
Internet: http://www.nam.org

U.S. Chamber of Commerce
Domestic Policy
1615 H St. N.W.
Washington, DC 20062-2000
(202) 659-6000
Internet: http://www.uschamber.com

PUBLISHERS
The following companies and organizations publish on the NLRB and related issues through books, periodicals, or electronic media.

American Law Institute-American Bar Association
Committee on Continuing Professional Education
4025 Chestnut St.
Philadelphia, PA 19104
(800) CLENEWS
Fax (215) 243-1664
Internet: http://www.ali-aba.org

Bureau of National Affairs (BNA), Inc.
1231 25th St. N.W.
Washington, DC 20037
(800) 372-1033
Internet: http://www.bna.com

West Group
610 Opperman Dr.
Eagan, MN 55123
(800) 344-5008
Fax (800) 741-1414
Internet: http://www.westgroup.com

ILR Press
Cornell University Press
P.O. Box 6525
750 Cascadilla St.
Ithaca, NY 14851-6525
(607) 277-2211
Fax (800) 688-2877
Internet: http://www.ilr.cornell.edu/depts/ILRpress

Industrial and Labor Relations Review
201 ILR Research Bldg.
Cornell University
Ithaca, NY 14853-3901
(607) 255-2733
Fax (607) 255-8016
Internet: http://www.ilr.cornell.edu/depts/ilrrev/

Industrial Relations: A Journal of Economy and Society
Institute of Industrial Relations
University of California
2521 Channing Way, #5555
Berkeley, CA 94720-5555
(510) 642-5452
Fax (510) 642-6432
Internet: http://violet.berkeley.edu/~iir/

Prentice Hall
P.O. Box 11701
Des Moines, IA 50336-1071
(800) 643-5506
Fax (800) 835-5327
Internet: http://www.prenhall.com

Occupational Safety and Health Administration

200 Constitution Ave. N.W., Washington, DC 20210
Internet: http://www.osha.gov

■ INTRODUCTION

The Occupational Safety and Health Administration (OSHA) was established as an agency within the Labor Department by the Occupational Safety and Health Act of 1970. The assistant secretary of labor for occupational safety and health, who is nominated by the president and confirmed by the Senate, directs the agency.

Responsibilities

OSHA performs the following:

▪ Encourages employers and employees to reduce hazards in the workplace by improving existing safety and health programs or by implementing new ones.

▪ Establishes "separate but dependent responsibilities and rights" for employers and employees to improve safety and health conditions.

▪ Maintains reporting and record-keeping procedures to monitor job-related injuries and illnesses.

▪ Develops and enforces mandatory job safety and health standards.

▪ Encourages the states to assume responsibility for establishing and administering their own occupational safety and health programs.

▪ Monitors federal agency safety programs and receives an annual report from each agency about its job safety and health efforts.

▪ Establishes advisory committees when necessary to assist in developing standards.

▪ Imposes emergency temporary standards when workers are in danger due to exposure to new toxic substances or hazards.

▪ Grants variances for special circumstances.

▪ Provides free on-site consultation services to small businesses to assist them in meeting OSHA standards.

Powers and Authority

OSHA regulations and standards extend to all employers and their employees in the fifty states, the District of Columbia, Puerto Rico, and all other territories under federal jurisdiction.

As defined by the Occupational Safety and Health Act, an employer is any "person engaged in a business affecting commerce who has employees, but does not include the United States or any state or political subdivision of a state." Therefore, the act covers employers and employees in varied fields such as construction, longshoring, agriculture, law, medicine, charity and disaster relief, organized labor, and private education. Coverage includes religious groups to the extent that they employ workers for secular purposes. Self-employed persons, family-owned and operated farms, and workplaces already protected by other federal agencies are not subject to OSHA regulations.

Federal agencies also are exempted from OSHA regulations and enforcement provisions, but each agency is required to establish and maintain an effective and comprehensive job safety and health program of its own. Such a program must be based, in part, upon consultations with representatives of its employees and be consistent with OSHA standards for private employers. OSHA monitors federal agency programs, and each agency must submit an annual report to OSHA on the status of job safety and health efforts.

STANDARDS

One of OSHA's major tasks is developing standards to protect workers. The agency's standards fall into four major categories—general industry, maritime, construction, and agriculture. When it first started operating, OSHA adopted many of the consensus standards developed over the years by the American National Standards Institute and the National Fire Protection Association. These standards, however, frequently either were outdated or represented minimum rather than ideal degrees of protection. OSHA has worked to update, revise, and add to these standards to cover as many potential workplace hazards as possible.

OSHA can begin standards-setting procedures on its own initiative or on petitions from other parties, including the secretary of the Health and Human Services Department, the National Institute for Occupational Safety and Health, state and local governments, any nationally recognized standards-producing organization, employer or labor representatives, or any other interested person.

If OSHA determines that a standard is needed, it may call on its two standing advisory committees or appoint ad hoc committees to develop specific recommendations. The ad hoc committees, limited to a life span of 270 days, include representatives of labor, management, and state and federal agencies, as well as occupational safety and health professionals and the general public. Meetings and records of the committees are open to the public.

Notices of committee meetings are published in the *Federal Register* at least seven days in advance and include the location of the meeting and a staff member to contact for additional information.

Anyone wishing to participate in a committee meeting should notify the Division of Consumer Affairs in advance. The division requests that participating persons provide them with at least twenty copies of statements to be presented or an estimate of the time required to speak and an outline of the view to be presented. Participation is limited to a designated time period and is subject to the discretion of the administrative law judge who presides over the meeting. The judge may call for additional opinions to be offered by anyone attending the meeting.

Usually the standards development process follows the rules set out in the Administrative Procedure Act. There must be publication of proposals in the *Federal Register*, followed by an adequate period of time for comments. After all evidence from committee meetings, hearings, and written submissions has been analyzed from a legal, technical, environmental, and economic viewpoint, OSHA must publish in the *Federal Register* either a final rule or a standard based on updated information or technological advances in the field.

The legislation creating OSHA stressed that its standards should be feasible and based on research, experiments, demonstrations, past experience, and the latest available scientific data.

In some critically dangerous situations OSHA is authorized to set emergency temporary standards that take effect immediately. In those cases, OSHA must determine that workers are in grave danger due to exposure to toxic substances or new hazards and that an emergency standard is needed to protect them. After publication of such an emergency standard, regular standard-setting procedures must be initiated and completed within six months.

Any person adversely affected by a final or emergency standard may file a petition within sixty days of the rule's issuance for judicial review of the standard with the U.S. Court of Appeals for the circuit in which the person lives or has his or her principal place of business. Filing an appeals petition, however, does not delay enforcement of a standard unless the court specifically orders an injunction.

Employers may apply to OSHA for a variance from a standard or regulation if they lack the means to comply with it readily, or if they can prove that their facilities or methods of operation provide employee protection that is "at least as effective as" that required by OSHA. Standard or regulation variances may be temporary or permanent, depending on the situation.

To ensure that all workers are protected, the Occupational Safety and Health Act includes a provision making it the duty of all employers to provide a safe and healthful workplace. Thus, even if a specific standard has not been developed, all workers have at least minimum protection.

INSPECTIONS AND INVESTIGATIONS

To enforce its standards and regulations, OSHA is authorized under the Occupational Safety and Health Act to conduct workplace inspections. Every establishment covered by the act is subject to inspection by OSHA safety and health compliance officers. States with their own occupational safety and health programs conduct inspections using qualified compliance officers.

With very few exceptions, inspections are conducted without advance notice. Before 1978 OSHA compliance officers were allowed to enter a workplace without a search warrant. However, in May 1978 the Supreme Court ruled that an employer has the right to refuse admission to an OSHA inspector who does not have a warrant. The ruling has not had a dramatic effect on the agency; most employers are willing to admit the compliance officers without a warrant. Should an employer refuse, a warrant can be obtained from a federal court relatively quickly. OSHA need not indicate a specific unsafe condition it is looking for to obtain a warrant. The agency need only indicate that the premises to be inspected have been chosen on the basis of a neutral plan to enforce OSHA standards.

Because OSHA has limited personnel to conduct workplace inspections, the agency has established a system of inspection priorities. Imminent danger situations are given top priority, followed in descending order by: investigations of fatalities and catastrophes resulting in hospitalization of five or more employees; investigations of employee complaints of alleged violation of standards or unsafe or unhealthful working conditions; inspections aimed at specific high-hazard industries, occupations, or health substances; and follow-up inspections to determine whether previously cited violations have been corrected.

An employer has the right to accompany an OSHA inspector during a tour of the workplace. An employee representative also may accompany the inspector during the tour. In addition, the inspector must be given the opportunity to interview employees privately.

Employees or their representative may give written notification to the inspector of any violation they believe exists, and they must be provided with a written explanation if no citation is issued respecting the alleged violation. Employees or their representative also have the right to request a special inspection if they feel there are unsafe conditions in their workplace.

When a compliance officer arrives to inspect a workplace, he or she explains the purpose of the visit to the employer and provides copies of the safety and health standards that apply to that particular workplace. A copy of any employee complaint that may be involved also is provided. If so requested, the name of the employee making the complaint will not be revealed.

After reviewing records of deaths, injuries, and illnesses that the employer is required to keep, the inspector determines the route and duration of the inspection. The inspector must keep confidential any trade secrets observed during an inspection.

Following the inspection tour, the compliance officer and the employer hold a closing conference. The compliance officer discusses with the employer what has been found on the inspection and advises the employer of all apparent violations for which a citation may be issued or recommended. During the closing conference the employer may provide the compliance officer with information to help OSHA determine how much time may be needed to correct an alleged violation.

CITATIONS

A citation in writing is issued to the employer if violations are discovered during an inspection. The citation describes the violation and allows a reasonable amount of time for its correction. A copy of the citation must be posted at or near the place of each violation. The compliance officer does not propose penalties.

Many relatively minor, or de minimis, violations are not sufficiently serious to warrant a citation. In such cases the compliance officer discusses the violation with the employer and recommends ways to correct the problem.

Employers who have received citations during an inspection by a compliance officer may request an informal settlement or file a "Notice of Contest" with the OSHA area director if they wish to contest the citation. Once a Notice of Contest is filed, the Occupational Safety and Health Review Commission (an independent government agency that adjudicates disputes) takes over the case from OSHA.

Employees may request an inspection if they believe unsafe conditions exist in their workplace. Employers are not allowed to take any action or discriminate against employees who complain to OSHA. If an inspection is conducted and no citations are issued, the employee or employee representative may request an informal review of the decision not to issue a citation. Also, if the time limit allowed for correction of an unsafe condition seems unreasonably long, the employee or employee representative may submit a written objection to OSHA that will be forwarded to the Occupational Safety and Health Review Commission.

When an OSHA compliance officer finds that there exists an imminent danger—defined as "a condition or practice that could reasonably be expected to cause death or serious physical harm before such condition or practice can be abated"—the officer asks the employer to take immediate steps voluntarily to protect workers, including removal of employees from the dangerous area if necessary.

If the employer refuses to take immediate action, a temporary restraining order or injunction requiring that steps be taken to correct, remove, and avoid the danger may be obtained from a U.S. district court.

ENFORCEMENT REVIEW

The Occupational Safety and Health Review Commission has responsibility for reviewing contested inspections. After an inspection or investigation has been completed and any citations issued, OSHA notifies the employer in writing of the period of time allowed to correct the violation (abatement period) and the proposed penalty, if any, for each violation. All of this information is turned over to the review commission. An employer has fifteen days to contest a citation or a proposed penalty, as do employees or their representative. Usually a notice of contest filed by employees challenges the reasonableness of the abatement period.

If no notice of contest is filed, the citation and proposed penalties become the final order of the commission. If a citation is contested, the review commission usually holds a hearing before an administrative law judge. After listening to the evidence and considering all arguments, the judge prepares a decision and mails copies of it to the parties involved. The judge also files all material related to the case with the commission.

The judge's decision becomes final thirty days after the commission receives it, unless a petition for discretionary review is filed. If such a petition is filed, the three-member commission reviews the administrative law judge's decision. In a few cases the commission will initiate a review of a decision even if a petition for discretionary review has not been filed.

Employers also may file a petition requesting modification of the abatement period specified in a citation. Such petitions are handled in much the same manner as a notice of contest.

PENALTIES

OSHA only proposes penalties; the final orders imposing them are issued by the Occupational Safety and Health Review Commission. The law requires the review commission to consider four factors when determining civil penalties: (1) the size of the business involved; (2) the gravity of the violation; (3) the good faith of the employer; and (4) the employer's history of previous violations.

No penalties are imposed for minor violations. For an "other than serious violation," one that has a direct relationship to job safety and health but probably would not cause death or serious injury, a fine of up to $1,000

may be imposed. If reinspection shows failure to correct the violation, penalties of up to $1,000 per day may be added.

For "serious violations," when there is substantial probability of death or serious physical harm and the employer knows about the hazard, or should know about it, a penalty of up to $1,000 is mandatory for each violation. Falsifying records, reports, and applications can bring a fine of $10,000 and six months in jail. Violations of posting requirements can bring a civil penalty of $1,000.

Assaulting a compliance officer or interfering with a compliance officer in the performance of his or her duties is a criminal offense, subject to a fine of not more than $5,000 and imprisonment for not more than three years.

For employers who willfully or repeatedly violate the law, penalties of up to $10,000 for each violation may be assessed. If an employer is convicted of a willful violation that has resulted in the death of an employee, the employer may be fined not more than $10,000 and/or imprisoned for up to six months. A second conviction doubles the maximum penalties.

RECORD KEEPING AND REPORTING

OSHA requires employers of eleven or more employees to maintain records of occupational injuries and illnesses. Employers with ten or fewer employees must keep such records only if selected by the Bureau of Labor Statistics to participate in periodic statistical surveys.

An occupational injury is any injury, such as a cut, fracture, sprain, or amputation, that results from a work-related accident or from exposure involving a single incident in the work environment. An occupational illness is any abnormal condition or disorder, other than one resulting from an occupational injury, caused by exposure to environmental factors associated with employment. Included are acute and chronic illnesses that may be caused by inhalation, absorption, ingestion, or direct contact with toxic substances.

Employers must record all occupational illnesses. Injuries must be recorded if they result in death (regardless of the length of time between the injury and death and regardless of the length of the illness); one or more lost workdays; restriction of work or motion; loss of consciousness; transfer to another job; or medical treatment (other than first aid).

Two record-keeping forms are used for data that must be maintained on a calendar-year basis. They are not sent to OSHA but are retained at the establishment and kept available for OSHA inspections for at least five years following the end of the year recorded.

The records required are a log of occupational illnesses and injury (OSHA No. 200) and a supplementary record of injury and illness (OSHA No. 101). Certain employers are chosen by OSHA to participate in the annual statistical survey (OSHA No. 200S).

In addition, if an on-the-job accident occurs that results in the death of an employee or in the hospitalization of five or more employees, the employer by law must report the accident in detail to the nearest OSHA office within forty-eight hours.

STATE PROGRAMS

OSHA's legislation requires the agency to encourage states to develop and operate their own occupational safety and health programs. These plans must be at least as effective as the federal program. By 2000 twenty-four states had OSHA-certified programs.

OSHA retains the authority to enforce federal regulations in the state until the proposed state program is fully operational. Once the state has demonstrated that within three years its program will be as effective as the federal program, the plan may be approved by OSHA. The state in this interim period must exhibit legislative, administrative, regulatory, and procedural commitment to occupational safety as well as a sufficient number of enforcement personnel to meet OSHA's requirements. When a state plan is approved, OSHA agrees to pay up to 50 percent of the cost of operations.

The agency continues to receive summaries of enforcement and compliance activities from the state and submits an annual evaluation of progress to the state. When the state program has operated at a fully effective level for at least one year, final OSHA approval may be granted. At that time, agency enforcement authority will cease but monitoring activities continue to ensure compliance with federal standards.

If the state program does not continue to provide adequate safety and health protection, OSHA either can reintroduce federal enforcement personnel in the appropriate areas or begin proceedings to withdraw federal approval of the program.

Critics maintain that some state plans provide grossly inadequate enforcement of workplace safety and health standards. State officials reject such criticism, saying that their programs conduct more safety inspections than the federal agency. Some state officials also argue that they get insufficient federal funds. The federal contribution to state programs in 2000 composed about 20 percent of OSHA's total budget.

CONSULTATION AND TRAINING

OSHA has developed a consultation program to help businesses comply with safety standards. Of the states administering OSHA-approved job safety and health programs, only one does not provide on-site consultation. For states without OSHA-approved plans, OSHA has issued rules under which they too may offer such consultation, using state personnel.

On-site consultation is intended primarily to provide aid to small businesses that do not have their own safety and health staffs. A consultative visit consists of an opening conference, an inspection tour of the workplace, a closing conference, and a written summary of findings. During the inspection tour the consultant explains to the employer which OSHA standards apply to the company and the technical language and application of the appropriate standards. The consultant also points out where the employer is not in compliance and may suggest ways to eliminate identified hazards.

No citations are issued and no penalties are proposed for alleged violations discovered during the consultation. An employer, however, must agree to eliminate hazardous conditions identified by the consultant. Failure to abide by this agreement can result in referral of the employer's establishment to the enforcement staff for inspection.

OSHA also offers training to safety and health specialists through its Training Institute in Des Plaines, Ill., and through its field offices. In addition, OSHA has endorsed vocational safety and health training programs at schools of business administration throughout the country.

Background

OSHA was created by Congress in 1970 after years of debate over workplace safety and worker health. During the early 1960s the Labor Department came under increasing criticism for weak enforcement of a 1936 law directing the department to ensure safe work standards for federal contractors. Congress held hearings on the matter in 1964, and the following year the Public Health Service published a study drawing attention to health threats arising from new technologies.

President Lyndon B. Johnson endorsed a legislative package of safety and health measures in 1968, but business opposition defeated it, charging usurpation of states' rights by the federal government. In 1969 President Richard Nixon offered a bill, the Occupational Safety and Health Act, that gave the states the option to administer standards set by the federal government. Passage the following year created the agency, which was given a broad mandate "to assure so far as possible every working man and woman in the nation safe and healthful working conditions and to preserve our human resources."

Twenty-three states immediately chose to conduct their own OSHA programs. By law these programs had to be "at least as effective" as the federal health and safety regulations.

EARLY HISTORY

As required by Congress, OSHA's start-up health and safety standards were adopted from existing federal regulations and national consensus standards set by groups such as the American National Standards Institute and the National Fire Protection Association. The wholesale adoption of some 4,400 job safety and health rules during OSHA's first month of operation later proved to be a major source of irritation, especially for business. Even at the time, it was generally recognized that many of these standards were "outdated, unnecessarily specific and unrelated to occupational health and safety," according to a 1985 Office of Technology Assessment (OTA) report. The OTA was a nonpartisan research arm of Congress.

Business complained that penalties for first violations were unfair and that the cost of compliance was at times so burdensome as to drive small companies into bankruptcy. The paperwork requirements imposed on employers also came under attack as excessive and time-consuming. At the same time, labor groups complained that the agency's enforcement activities were sporadic and weak and that it failed to reduce workplace hazards significantly.

From 1974 to 1976 OSHA stepped up its efforts to develop health standards for substances linked to illnesses such as cancer and lung disease. Although evidence sometimes was inconclusive, OSHA often set stringent standards without waiting for more concrete scientific data. These standards required employers to reduce worker exposure to certain substances to the lowest feasible levels, even if the agency was not sure that those levels were necessary to prevent significant risk. Critics charged that OSHA paid little attention to how much the regulations cost affected industries.

STREAMLINING OSHA

The first wave of limitations on OSHA came in 1976, when Congress decided to exempt most small businesses— those with ten or fewer employees—from record-keeping requirements. In early 1977 President Jimmy Carter, who had made deregulation a theme of his presidential campaign, appointed Eula Bingham to head OSHA. In an effort to reduce complaints about the agency, Bingham pledged to adopt a set of "common sense" priorities and to make fundamental changes in administration and regulation policy. She promised to focus attention on the most dangerous industries and devote less time to inspecting small businesses (except those with a higher than average rate of serious injury).

Under Bingham, who served until 1981, streamlining and consolidation became the operative words in OSHA's efforts to develop safety standards. Nearly 1,000 safety standards were revoked during the first month of fiscal 1977. OSHA staff members also worked to simplify the rules and regulations in the areas of construction, fire protection, and electricity. Inspections became concentrated on the most dangerous industries, with less than 5 percent of inspections being done in small businesses.

During this period the agency further increased its emphasis on the development of health standards designed to protect workers from toxic substances, such as carcinogens and cotton dust. In a setback for the agency, however, the Supreme Court in two July 1980 cases (*Marshall v. American Petroleum Institute, Industrial Union Department* and *AFL-CIO v. American Petroleum Institute*) ruled that OSHA's standard for worker exposure to benzene was invalid because the rule was unsupported by sufficient evidence that it was necessary to protect the health of workers. Broadly applied, these decisions meant that OSHA could no longer require employers to reduce worker exposure to hazards to the lowest feasible levels unless it proved that a significant risk to workers existed above those levels. OSHA had to prove not only that the substance being regulated was hazardous but also that a significant risk existed above the exposure levels it set as permissible in its standards.

OSHA IN THE 1980S

Despite the reforms initiated by Bingham, OSHA remained a favorite target of labor and business. As a candidate for president in 1980, Ronald Reagan promised to abolish the agency. Once in office, however, he failed to muster the political support to fulfill his pledge.

Reagan's choice to head the agency, Thorne G. Auchter, shared his commitment to reduce the federal presence in workplace health and safety matters. As did many other Reagan appointees, he emphasized cost effectiveness and voluntary, rather than mandatory, compliance. Supporting this philosophy, the Reagan administration in January 1981 froze a number of pending OSHA regulations, including a safety standard limiting exposure to lead in the workplace and a requirement that employers pay workers who accompany federal safety officials on inspection tours.

The agency also announced that it would forgo inspections of businesses that reported below-average numbers of injuries. This move would allow the agency to concentrate on high-hazard companies. Critics maintained that this policy provided business with a powerful incentive to underreport. In 1983 an AFL-CIO report called the program of targeting plants with poor records a "paper tiger" and complained that inspectors spent too much time inspecting records rather than touring plants.

OSHA had been directed since its inception to balance worker health and safety against costs incurred by employers. President Reagan elevated cost-benefit analysis to even greater importance in 1981 when he issued Executive Order 12291, which required federal rulemaking agencies to show that "the potential benefits to society for [a proposed] regulation outweigh the potential costs." Unlike the previous orders, which only directed regulatory agencies to evaluate the economic impact of their decisions, Reagan's order made the application of cost-benefit analysis an explicit requirement.

The order's application to OSHA regulations, however, was soon declared invalid by the Supreme Court in *American Textile Manufacturing Institute v. Donovan*, a case involving permissible limits of cotton dust in textile mills. During the Carter administration, OSHA had issued a new standard to protect textile workers from byssinosis, or brown lung, which is caused by breathing cotton particles. Textile industry representatives argued that OSHA had exceeded its authority because it had not conducted an analysis to show that the benefits of the regulation exceeded the costs. Labor union representatives argued that the 1970 act required no such analysis. The Reagan administration asked the Supreme Court to refer the case back to OSHA for modification in accordance with cost-benefit analysis. But the Court denied the request and in June 1981 upheld OSHA's cotton-dust standard, saying that cost-benefit analysis was not required by the Occupational Safety and Health Act.

Although the ruling was hailed at the time as one of the most significant in the history of regulatory law, it did not deter Auchter's commitment to curb federal health and safety regulations. Following the Court decision, he announced that the agency would consider four points in issuing future regulations: whether a significant health risk existed; whether the proposed standard would protect workers from that risk; whether the standard was economically feasible for the industry affected; and whether the standard was cost effective—that is, was the least costly way to achieve the desired goal.

Applying Auchter's four-point guideline, OSHA made a number of controversial recommendations to postpone or revise existing regulations. It reopened the cotton-dust debate in June 1983 by proposing revisions to the regulations upheld by the Supreme Court. OSHA also proposed to revoke 194 safety and health standards that the agency said were unenforceable because they used the word "should" rather than "shall."

Auchter's zeal for curbing OSHA rulemaking appeared to wane by 1983. In the summer of that year, OSHA suddenly decided to set a stricter emergency standard for asbestos, bypassing normal rulemaking procedures. Auchter also promised additional safety standards and health standards by the end of 1984. Critics pointed out that OSHA's increased regulatory activities coincided with a scandal at the Environmental Protection Agency in which its top administrator and her entire management team were forced to resign.

John A. Pendergrass began his tenure as head of OSHA in May 1986 at a time when President Reagan was signaling his interest in improving ties with organized labor. Under Pendergrass, the most visible signs of OSHA's change in direction came in the form of high-profile health and safety regulation enforcement that produced record proposed fines against some of the country's biggest employers. Among them were Chrysler, General Motors, Ford, General Dynamics, Caterpillar, Union Carbide, and IBP, the nation's leading meatpacker. In all, OSHA proposed fines totaling $24.7 million for health and safety violations in fiscal 1987, almost five times the amount proposed in 1982.

Most of the large fines, however, as critics noted, were settled for half of the proposed amount or less. And most of the fines were imposed for record-keeping violations, not hazardous workplaces. Pendergrass maintained that he was more interested in encouraging companies to improve their record keeping and fostering a spirit of cooperation between government and business than collecting big fines. Sensitive to criticism of the agency's enforcement efforts, Pendergrass in March 1988 announced that OSHA's manufacturing safety inspectors would start checking factory floors in high-hazard businesses, rather than simply checking office records of injuries and illnesses, the procedure at the time.

A month later, a number of the agency's scientists and compliance officers, under subpoena to testify, criticized OSHA's performance during hearings before a Senate committee. Among the problems outlined for the committee:

- OSHA had been slow to issue workplace safety standards, often taking years to issue a final rule. Many of the standards had to be completed under court order.

- Top administration officials, including those in the Office of Management and Budget (OMB), had either weakened OSHA safety proposals or had made them unenforceable.

- OSHA compliance officers, responsible for on-site inspections, had been pressured to rush their work to meet inspection quotas.

- The agency lacked the budget and personnel to enforce the regulations already on the books.

Under the glare of congressional scrutiny, OSHA became more activist in the last year of the Reagan administration. In January 1989, in the first overhaul of exposure limits since the passage of the Occupational Safety and Health Act in 1970, OSHA issued new exposure standards for nearly four hundred hazardous materials used in workplaces. Lumping so many substances together in a single package marked a major shift in the agency's approach to rulemaking. In the past, OSHA had developed exposure limits for toxic substances on a case-by-case basis, thus inviting endless debate over technical issues. By bundling four hundred substances into one package, the agency hoped to disarm critics who would think twice about challenging the entire package just to object to a handful of the new standards. However, this approach was overturned by the Eleventh Circuit Court of Appeals in 1992, because OSHA had not made a separate scientific case for gauging the health risks of each individual chemical.

OSHA IN THE 1990S

The administration of President George Bush had what seemed to be a split personality in its policy toward OSHA. The administration worked hard to defeat a congressional effort to beef up OSHA's enforcement powers and called for more cost-benefit analysis in issuing health and safety regulations. At the same time, OSHA, headed by Gerard F. Scannell, issued one of the most controversial rules to date—one dealing with blood-borne pathogens. The public comment period on the rule went on for more than a year, and the agency received more comments on the proposed rule than any other in its history. The rule, which went into effect in March 1992, was largely aimed at preventing people, primarily health care workers, from contracting the HIV or hepatitis B viruses while on the job.

In other signs of activism under Bush, OSHA proposed the largest fine in its history, $7.3 million, against USX Corp., for more than two thousand alleged safety, health, and record-keeping violations; worked out an agreement with the Sara Lee Corp.'s thirty-one meat processing plants to seek ways to reduce repetitive motion injuries; and issued final, controversial rules requiring companies to ensure that machinery shut down for maintenance cannot be turned on while employees work on it. Also OSHA, in an important policy shift, began referring flagrant cases of willful exposure of employees to hazards of all kinds to the Justice Department for criminal prosecution. OSHA has always had this authority but had seldom used it.

However, OSHA under Bush, as it had been under Reagan, was greatly restricted by the enormous oversight power held by OMB. Between 1981 and 1990 OMB changed, disapproved, or forced the withdrawal of more than 40 percent of the Labor Department's proposed regulations—most of which were generated by OSHA. Defenders of OMB's regulatory oversight powers maintained that the review process served as a necessary check and balance over rulemaking by agencies under the president's authority. Critics countered that OMB had become a super-regulatory agency, operating outside the normal rulemaking procedures.

A 1991 fire that killed twenty-five people in a North Carolina chicken-processing plant was the impetus behind the efforts of some Democratic members of Congress to strengthen OSHA's enforcement powers, which began a battle with Republicans over changes to OSHA. In 1992 the House Education and Labor Committee approved tough legislation that would have overhauled OSHA and increased supervisor liability and criminal penalties for violations. Though the measure had enthusiastic support among Democrats, Republicans and Labor Secretary Lynn Martin opposed it, thus derailing further action.

Many supporters of OSHA hailed the start of the Democratic administration of Bill Clinton in 1993, sure that it would mean a more effective federal bureaucracy. In September 1993 Clinton issued Executive Order 12866, which limited OMB's role in regulatory overview. But the presence of a Democrat in the White House was not enough to push through the OSHA overhaul bill. Although the Education and Labor Committee approved the bill in 1994 (as it had in 1992), the measure did not move further in the House, and the Senate never acted on a similar bill.

In testimony before the House Appropriations Subcommittee on Labor, Health, and Human Services in March 1994, Joseph Dear, Clinton's pick to be assistant secretary of Labor for OSHA, pledged to reinvigorate and rededicate OSHA to saving workers' lives and preserving their health. As one indication, the Clinton administration pushed through a substantial increase in OSHA's budget—$311.6 million for fiscal 1995, up from $297.2 in fiscal 1994.

Under Dear, the agency initiated standards for certain workplace hazards that earlier had been overshadowed by OSHA's emphasis on accidents and company noncompliance. When the Centers for Disease Control issued a report in 1993 stating that tuberculosis (TB) transmission was a recognized risk in health care facilities, OSHA began work on a rule designed to protect health care workers from exposure to TB. The final rule was promulgated in September 1996. In 1995 OSHA began to develop specific guidelines to prevent workplace violence, which was on the rise. The guidelines would address both the dangers posed from the outside because of lax security and staffing requirements as well as the problem of increasing violence among coworkers, which was in part attributed to poor management strategies.

As part of the Clinton administration's "Reinventing Government" initiative, OSHA's inspection programs were restructured to focus on the most dangerous workplaces. The agency also streamlined procedures for complaints, eliminated obsolete regulations, and began to rewrite guidelines and requirements in nonbureaucratic language. To improve cooperation between OSHA and state agencies and with inspected businesses and industry, OSHA undertook a redesign of its field offices. A pilot program launched in Maine targeted the state's two hundred most unsafe workplaces, giving companies the option of adopting a voluntary safety partnership with OSHA or else facing stiffer penalties.

OSHA has long been a target of antiregulatory groups, and it faced a particularly forceful challenge from the

Republican 104th Congress. For many in the Republican majority and the business community OSHA remained a symbol of the invasiveness of the federal government. In 1995 and 1996 various legislative proposals advanced in Congress to ease safety regulations on small businesses, apply cost-benefit analysis requirements to worker safety regulations, limit inspections to those workplaces where worker complaints had been filed, and eliminate the National Institute of Occupational Safety and Health (NIOSH), the research arm of OSHA. Both supporters and critics of these proposals claimed that these changes would make OSHA more of a training and advisory body than an enforcement agency.

None of these major initiatives became law, although the Congress was able to pass in 1996 the Small Business Regulatory Enforcement Fairness Act, which simply required OSHA to be more responsive to the needs of small businesses. As part of the rulemaking process, the law required OSHA to collect advice and recommendations from small businesses to improve analyses of the impact of proposed regulations.

In addition to its congressional efforts at restructuring the agency, the new Republican majority also attacked OSHA's budget, cutting it by $6 million to $304.9 million in fiscal 1996. Despite President Clinton's request for $340 million, Congress cut OSHA's budget further to $298 million in fiscal 1997. Efforts to expand voluntary safety partnerships stalled due to reduced funds for employer and worker training, as did plans for further redesign of field offices.

In December 1996 Dear resigned to become the chief of staff for Washington state governor Gary Locke. Almost one year later, in November 1997, Charles N. Jeffress, the former OSHA director for North Carolina, was sworn in as the new head of the agency.

Jeffress almost immediately jumped into the fray when, a month after formally assuming his job, he announced a controversial policy for encouraging voluntary compliance among businesses that have bad health and safety records. Under the plan, the owners of the twelve thousand work sites that had injury rates twice the national average or higher would be asked by the agency to voluntarily institute new, rigorous plans aimed at improving worker safety and health. In exchange for agreeing to comply, companies would significantly reduce the likelihood of a surprise OSHA inspection. Those businesses that did not opt for voluntary compliance would inevitably be inspected. OSHA officials and others argued that the plan would let the agency focus on the very worst employers while allowing others to fix their own problems.

Although 87 percent of the targeted work sites volunteered to establish the new safety plans, many in the business community opposed the policy. The U.S. Chamber of Commerce, the National Association of Manufacturers, and other business groups argued that there was nothing "voluntary" about complying with the plan, because non-compliance guaranteed inspection. The business groups succeeded in 1998 in getting a federal court to stop the new program temporarily and force OSHA to revert to its old, random inspection regime. In April 1999 the U.S. Court of Appeals in Washington ruled that the new safety program was essentially a new federal regulation and should have, under the Administrative Procedures Act, been open to public comment before it was finalized.

OSHA IN THE 2000S

Soon after President George W. Bush took office in 2001, it became clear that the new administration's approach to workplace safety issues would differ considerably from that of the Clinton administration. Almost immediately, Republican leaders in Congress, with support from the White House, moved to overturn high-profile ergonomics regulations, which had been finalized in November 2000 after a decade of study and controversy.

The draft ergonomics regulations—aimed at preventing musculoskeletal disorders caused by repetitive motions such as typing or lifting—had been issued under Dear. But opposition from Congress, with the support of big business, had forced delays in the publication of final rules. At the end of Clinton's term, Jeffress issued the final regulations. The move left the new rules in a precarious place, because lawmakers had been unable to find a compromise.

The final regulations would have applied to about 102 million workers and would have required employers to inform their employees about musculoskeletal disorders such as carpal tunnel syndrome and tendonitis. Businesses would have had to adjust job conditions when an injury occurred and allow workers who were unable to work to continue receiving up to 90 percent of their pay for ninety days.

Capital Hill Republicans overturned the final Clinton ergonomics rule through an unusual legislative procedure known as the Congressional Review Act. That procedure, which allows Congress to overturn any regulation by simple majorities in each chamber within a limited time frame, had never before been used successfully to rescind a rule.

Any Congressional Review Act resolution bans an agency from issuing a similar regulation that is in "substantially the same form." But new Labor secretary Elaine L. Chao said that she would work to create a more flexible program to "address injuries before they occur, through prevention and compliance assistance."

Regardless of Chao's promise, the action produced howls of protest from organized labor and many of their Democratic allies, who charged that the new administration was paying back big business for their support in the

2000 election at the expense of worker safety. But business groups and others countered that the causes of ergonomic injuries were still too vague to impose a broad and expensive mandate on businesses.

Another Clinton-era workplace-safety proposal that was dropped early on by the Bush administration would have banned smoking in virtually all workplaces. The rule, which never went into effect, was vigorously opposed by the tobacco industry, but had the support of the nation's public health community. OSHA announced it was setting aside the proposed rule so that it could "devote its resources to other projects." It also noted that nearly 70 percent of all workplaces were already smoke-free.

The first year of the new administration also saw the appointment of John Henshaw as OSHA's new head. While Henshaw came from the business sector—working on health and safety issues for a number of chemical companies—organized labor praised the nominee's relevant experience. He was confirmed by the Senate in August 2001.

But in the opening months of 2002, labor unions and OSHA were once again at odds. The fight concerned the new ergonomic policy the administration had promised after proposed Clinton-era rules had been repealed by Congress a year earlier. The new policy called for companies to take voluntary steps to reduce repetitive injuries as opposed to the mandatory requirements contained in earlier, rejected rules. OSHA hoped to assist employers by developing ergonomic guidelines for major industries, especially those with high rates of repetitive stress injuries such as meatpacking and nursing home care. Enforcement would be beefed up to encourage companies to take the steps needed to reduce ergonomic injuries and punish those that ignored the issue and allowed workers to be hurt. Finally, OSHA would create a National Advisory Committee on Ergonomics to help it set guidelines and conduct research on how best to reduce repetitive stress injuries.

Henshaw described the voluntary industry guidelines as a win/win for employers and employees. Unlike the "one-size-fits-all" approach of the rescinded rules, he said, the plan would give businesses flexibility to tailor their ergonomic efforts to their specific needs. All in all, he said, the new plan would allow businesses to better protect workers and save money.

But unions and their allies in Congress criticized the plan as a gift to big business and little more than window dressing for workers. "Today's announcement rejects substantive protections for America's workers in favor of small symbolic gestures," said Sen. Edward M. Kennedy, a Massachusetts Democrat and a strong labor supporter.

Current Issues

In spite of the criticism, OSHA has started to move ahead with its ergonomics plan. For instance, in January 2003, the ergonomics advisory committee convened for the first time. It has been charged with using the latest scientific research to come up with practical recommendations for reducing ergonomic injuries.

The agency has also issued its first set of ergonomic guidelines—for the nursing home industry. Included in the guidelines were suggestions on how to minimize the stress from lifting nursing home patients, a prime cause of ergonomic injuries for workers in the industry.

On other fronts, the agency recently announced a new initiative to crack down on repeat and severe workplace safety violators. Under the plan, OSHA inspectors were to coordinate visits if a suspect firm had multiple workplace sites and follow-up inspections were to be mandated for serious violators of OSHA regulations.

Along this line, OSHA also has beefed up its overall inspections process. OSHA inspectors visited 37,493 workplaces in fiscal 2002, up from 35,800 the year before. Fines for serious violations also rose, from $930 in fiscal 2001 to $977 the following year.

The administration has proposed an additional $4.2 million for enforcement as part of its $450 million OSHA budget request for fiscal 2004. The overall request was $13 million or 3 percent higher than the 2003 budget and included more funding for outreach and education, especially to Spanish-speaking workers.

OSHA also has been playing a role in the war on terrorism. The agency sent about one thousand staff members to New York in the months following the Sept. 11, 2001, attacks to ensure the health and safety of the workers charged with cleaning up the World Trade Center site. More recently, OSHA has been working with employers to devise evacuation plans in the event of another terrorist attack. The guidelines were expected in 2003. In addition, assistant secretary Henshaw announced the creation of a new position—Special Assistant for Emergency Preparedness—to coordinate the agency's antiterrorism efforts.

■ AGENCY ORGANIZATION

Headquarters and Divisions

ASSISTANT SECRETARY OF LABOR FOR OCCUPATIONAL SAFETY AND HEALTH

Advises and assists the secretary of labor on all matters related to worker safety and health and provides

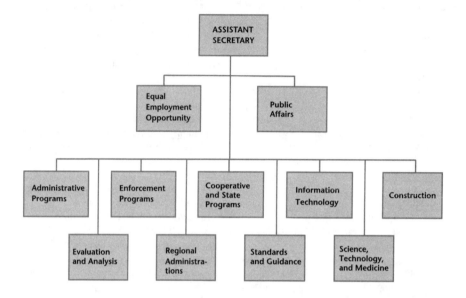

executive direction for developing and enforcing safety and health standards. Holds final authority over all departments within OSHA and provides leadership and direction for public affairs, policy analysis, legislative and interagency affairs, equal employment opportunities, and regional programs.

Assistant Secretary
John Lester Henshaw (designate) ...... (202) 693-2000
Deputy Assistant Secretaries
Gary Visscher .... (202) 693-1900
R. Davis Layne .... (202) 693-1900

OFFICE OF PUBLIC AFFAIRS
See Information Sources.

OFFICE OF EQUAL EMPLOYMENT OPPORTUNITY
Develops, implements, and monitors internal affirmative action plans. Initiates and conducts surveys to determine the effectiveness of existing programs and counsels employees as well as management officials on career development, opportunities available, and the complaint and appeals procedure. Works in cooperation with the Office of Personnel Management and the Labor Department's Equal Employment Opportunity Office.

Director
Betty Gillis-Robinson .... (202) 693-2150
Fax .... (202) 693-1687

DIRECTORATE OF ADMINISTRATIVE PROGRAMS
Responsible for general administrative services: housekeeping, personnel, labor-management relations, budgeting, contract management, and data processing. Compiles data and conducts studies on program policies and coordination with other management groups.

Director
David Zeigler .... (202) 693-1600
Fax .... (202) 693-1660
Administrative Services
Patricia Adamik .... (202) 693-2121
Management Systems and Organization
Zoltan Bagdy .... (202) 693-2002
Personnel Programs
Doug Goodell .... (202) 693-1800
Program Budgeting and Financial Management
James Digan .... (202) 693-1600

DIRECTORATE OF ENFORCEMENT PROGRAMS
Maintains occupational safety and health compliance directives and assistance programs for general industry, maritime, construction, health, and other areas; oversees an occupational safety and health program administered by federal agencies and submits evaluations and a summary report to the president; administers an antidiscrimination program that protects the rights of employees to make safety complaints; and conducts the cargo gear accreditation program.

Director

Richard Fairfax......................... (202) 693-2100

Fax...................................... (202) 693-1681

Federal Agency Programs

Thomas Marple .... (202) 693-2122

General Industry Enforcement

Arthur Buchanan...................... (202) 693-1850

Health Enforcement

Melody Sands........................... (202) 693-2190

Maritime Enforcement

Steve Butler............................ (202) 693-2086

Investigative Assistance

John Spear .... (202) 693-2199

DIRECTORATE OF CONSTRUCTION

Advises OSHA on construction safety and engineering. Acts as technical construction adviser to the assistant secretary and supports all headquarters and regional organizations with regard to construction activities. Also serves as the focal point for requests for information from industry, labor, and other interest groups regarding OSHA's construction program.

Director

Russell B. Swanson..................... (202) 693-2020

Construction Services

Stewart Burkhammer.................. (202) 693-2020

Engineering Services

Mohammad Ayub...................... (202) 693-2346

Construction Standards and Compliance Assistance

Noah Connell........................... (202) 693-2345

DIRECTORATE OF COOPERATIVE AND STATE PROGRAMS

Develops, evaluates, and analyzes the performance of the state occupational safety and health programs. Trains and advises employers, employees, and their representative organizations on how to recognize, avoid, and prevent unsafe and unhealthful working conditions. Administers OSHA partnership programs including the premier recognition Voluntary Protection Programs.

Director

Paula White........................... (202) 693-2200

Fax...................................... (202) 693-1671

Small Business Assistance

Tyna Coles............................. (202) 693-2213

Outreach Services and Alliances

Lee Anne Jillings...................... (202) 693-2340

Partnerships and Recognition

Cathy C. Oliver .... (202) 693-2213

State Programs

Barbara Bryant .... (202) 693-2244

OSHA Training Institute (Des Plaines, IL)

Henry Payne........................... (847) 297-4810

Training and Education (Des Plaines, IL)

Henry Payne........................... (847) 297-4810

DIRECTORATE OF EVALUATIONS AND ANALYSES

Evaluates and advises the assistant secretary on OSHA programs and policies, monitors congressional activities, and analyzes OSHA-related legislation. Also maintains liaison with other regulatory agencies such as the National Institute for Occupational Safety and Health, the Environmental Protection Agency, the Food and Drug Administration, and the Consumer Product Safety Commission.

Director

Frank Frodyma (acting) .... (202) 693-2400

Fax...................................... (202) 693-1641

Evaluations and Analyses

John Lewis (acting) .... (202) 693-1915

Program Review

John Martonik......................... (202) 693-2400

Regulatory Analysis

Robert Burt............................ (202) 693–1952

Statistical Analyses

Joe Dubois............................. (202) 693–1702

DIRECTORATE OF INFORMATION TECHNOLOGY

Director

Cheryle Greenaugh..................... (202) 693–1818

Management Data Systems

Lissa Scott............................. (202) 693–1700

Data Systems

Diane Childress........................ (801) 524–7900

DIRECTORATE OF STANDARDS AND GUIDANCE

Studies and evaluates occupational safety standards. Is aided by the National Institute of Occupational Safety and Health and has responsibilities similar to those of the Directorate of Health Standards Programs.

Director

Steve Witt.............................. (202) 693–1950

Fax...................................... (202) 693-1663

Engineering Safety

Vacant.................................. (202) 693-2277

Safety Systems

Lee Smith.............................. (202) 693-2255

Maritime Safety Standards

Paul Bolan .... (202) 693-2086

Physical Hazards

Michael Seymour....................... (202) 693-2092

Chemical Hazards - Nonmetal

William Perry........................... (202) 693-2090

Biological Hazards

Caroline Freeman .... (202) 693-2091

Chemical Hazards - Metal

Amanda Edens .... (202) 693-2093

DIRECTORATE OF SCIENCE, TECHNOLOGY, AND MEDICINE

Provides technical guidance and support to OSHA compliance staff and oversees development of technical manuals and interactive software advisers for employers and employees. Maintains laboratories to analyze toxic substances and health hazards in the workplace and to test newly developed hazard detection equipment. Makes decisions on granting standards variances based on recommendations of the Directorate of Health Standards Programs and the Directorate of Safety Standards Programs.

Director

Ruth McCully........................... (202) 693-2300

Fax...................................... (202) 693-1644

Ergonomic Support

Vacant.................................. (202) 693-2333

Occupational Health Nursing

Elise Handleman .... (202) 693-2120

Occupational Medicine

Vacant.................................. (202) 693-2323

Science and Technology Assessment

David Ippolito.......................... (202) 693-2095

Technical Data Center

Vacant.................................. (202) 693-2350

Technical Programs and Coordination Activities

Maryann Garahan...................... (202) 693-2110

OSHA Maintenance and Calibration Laboratory

435 Elm St., #500

Cincinnati, OH 45202

(513) 684-3721

Bob Williams, director

Provides for development, evaluation, calibration, and repair of hazard measurement instrumentation and equipment.

Salt Lake Technical Center

P.O. Box 65200

Salt Lake City, UT 84165

(801) 487-0521

Jimmy Roberts, director

Robert Curtis, Health Response Team director

Conducts analyses, tests, and studies of all samples submitted by safety and health compliance officers and others to evaluate toxicity and the existence of health hazards. Health Response Team investigates accidents involving major health issues, fatalities, and catastrophes that receive nationwide attention.

ADVISORY COMMITTEES

Two standing advisory committees and a varying number of special ad hoc committees make specific recommendations on the development of standards. All advisory committees must have members representing employers, employees, and state and federal agencies. The occupational safety and health professions as well as the general public also may be represented. Ad hoc committees are specially appointed to develop standards in specific areas and are limited in duration to 270 days.

Advisory Committee on Construction Safety and Health

Tim Nichols, chair

Contact

Bruce Swanson .... (202) 693-2020

Advises the secretary of labor on the formulation of construction safety and health standards and related regulations.

National Advisory Committee on Occupational Safety and Health (NACOSH)

Kathleen M. Rest, chair

Contact

Catherine Sutter........................ (202) 693-2400

Advises the secretary of labor and the secretary of health and human services on matters regarding the administration of the Occupational Safety and Health Act.

Regional Offices

These offices monitor state safety and health programs and oversee area office compliance personnel. They coordinate regional activities with the Labor Department's Office of the Solicitor, the Field Operations Coordinator, National Institute of Occupational Safety and Health, and the Small Business Administration. There are area offices located within the regions that conduct inspections and provide compliance assistance and training to employers and employees.

REGION 1

(CT, MA, ME, NH, RI, VT)

JFK Federal Bldg., #E340

Boston, MA 02203

(617) 565-9860

Marthe Kent, regional administrator

REGION 2
(NJ, NY, PR, VI)
201 Varick St., #670
New York, NY 10014
(212) 337-2378
Patricia Clark, regional administrator

REGION 3
(DC, DE, MD, PA, VA, WV)
Curtis Center, #740 West
170 S. Independence Mall West
Philadelphia, PA 19106-3309
(215) 861-4900
Richard Soltan, regional administrator

REGION 4
(AL, FL, GA, KY, MS, NC, SC, TN)
61 Forsyth St. S.W.
Atlanta, GA 30303
(404) 562-2300
Cindy A. Coe, regional administrator

REGION 5
(IL, IN, MI, MN, OH, WI)
230 S. Dearborn St., #3244
Chicago, IL 60604
(312) 353-2220
Mike Connor, regional administrator

REGION 6
(AR, LA, NM, OK, TX)
525 Griffin St., #602
Dallas, TX 75202
(214) 767-4731
John Miles, regional administrator

REGION 7
(IA, KS, MO, NE)
City Center Square
1100 Main St., #800
Kansas City, MO 64105
(816) 426-5861
Charles Atkins, regional administrator

REGION 8
(CO, MT, ND, SD, UT, WY)
1999 Broadway, #1690
Denver, CO 80202-5716
(303) 844-1600
Adam Finkel, regional administrator

REGION 9
(AS, AZ, CA, GU, HI, NV)
71 Stevenson St., #420
San Francisco, CA 94105
(415) 975-4310
Frank Strasheim, regional administrator

REGION 10
(AK, ID, OR, WA)
1111 Third Ave., #715
Seattle, WA 98101-3212
(206) 553-5930
Richard Terrill, regional administrator

■ CONGRESSIONAL ACTION

Congressional Liaison
John Lewis .... (202) 693–2400

Committees and Subcommittees

HOUSE APPROPRIATIONS COMMITTEE
Subcommittee on Labor, Health and Human Services, and Education
2358 RHOB, Washington, DC 20515
(202) 225-3508

HOUSE EDUCATION AND THE WORKFORCE COMMITTEE
2181 RHOB, Washington, DC 20515
(202) 225-4527
Subcommittee on Workforce Protections
2181 RHOB, Washington, DC 20515
(202) 225-4527

HOUSE SMALL BUSINESS COMMITTEE
Subcommittee on Regulatory Reform and Paperwork Reduction
B363 RHOB, Washington, DC 20515
(202) 226-2630

SENATE APPROPRIATIONS COMMITTEE
Subcommittee on Labor, Health, Human Services, and Education
SD-184, Washington, DC 20510
(202) 224-7230

SENATE LABOR AND HUMAN RESOURCES COMMITTEE
SD-428, Washington, DC 20510
(202) 224-5375

SENATE SMALL BUSINESS COMMITTEE
SR-428A, Washington, DC 20510
(202) 224-5175

Legislation

OSHA was established by the **Occupational Safety and Health Act of 1970** (84 Stat. 1590, 29 U.S.C. 553, 651-678). In addition to creating OSHA, the act set up the Occupational Safety and Health Review Commission and the National Institute for Occupational Safety and Health.

The legislation gives OSHA the power to promulgate and enforce worker safety and health standards, conduct inspections and investigations, require employers to keep detailed records on worker injuries and illnesses, and provide education and training.

When OSHA became operational in 1971 it adopted the standards issued under several earlier acts. (The legal administration of these acts remains with the Labor Department.) As OSHA develops its own standards, they supersede the standards issued under the following acts:

Longshore and Harbor Workers' Compensation Act (44 Stat. 1444, 33 U.S.C. 941). Signed by the president March 4, 1927. Provided benefits for injured and disabled workers and dependents of deceased workers.

Walsh-Healey Act (49 Stat. 2036, 41 U.S.C. 35). Signed by the president May 13, 1936. Provided benefit and labor standards for persons employed by federal contractors.

The National Foundation on the Arts and the Humanities Act (79 Stat. 845, 20 U.S.C. 951). Signed by the president Sept. 29, 1965. Provided health and safety standards for performers and personnel engaged in any project or production authorized under this act.

Service Contract Act of 1965 (79 Stat. 1034, 41 U.S.C. 351). Signed by the president Oct. 22, 1965. Provided labor standards for persons employed by federal contractors.

Construction Safety Act (83 Stat. 96, 40 U.S.C. 333). Signed by the president Aug. 9, 1969. Promoted health and safety in the building trades and construction industry for all federal and federally financed or assisted construction projects.

Small Business Regulatory Enforcement Fairness Act of 1996 (110 Stat. 857, 5 U.S.C. 601 note). Signed by the president March 29, 1996. Required SBA to assist small businesses with regulatory compliance through community information clearinghouses and resource centers; to establish a Small Business and Agriculture Regulatory Enforcement Ombudsman, and to establish a Small Business Regulatory Fairness Board in each SBA regional office. Required all federal agencies promulgating new regulation to submit cost-benefit reports and small business economic impact reports to Congress for review. The act gave Congress authority, through passage of a joint resolution of disapproval, to deny the enactment of the proposed regulation. The president could override the decision of Congress if the regulation affected national security, national health, or if necessary to implement an international trade agreement.

■ INFORMATION SOURCES

Internet

Agency Web Site: http://www.osha.gov. Provides information on OSHA offices, programs, publications, and statistics. The public can also search through multiple databases at the agency's Web site.

Telephone Contacts

DOL Locator .... (202) 866–4–USA–DOC
Emergency .... (800) 321-6742

Information and Publications

KEY OFFICES

OSHA Public Affairs
200 Constitution Ave. N.W.
Washington, DC 20210
(202) 693-1999
Fax (202) 693-1634
Bonnie Friedman, director

Provides general information about OSHA to the news media and the public; publishes and distributes consumer information leaflets. Handles Freedom of Information requests for documents of a general nature.

To request documents related to a specific incident, contact the FOI officer in the area or regional office serving the location where the incident occurred. If an initial request for information is denied by either an area office or the national office, an appeal may be made to the solicitor of the Labor Department *(see Other Information Sources)*.

Responsible for developing the OSHA consumer affairs program to give employers and employees a greater role in the rulemaking process. Provides information on upcoming meetings and works to increase public comment on new proposals.

OSHA Publications Office

200 Constitution Ave. N.W., Room N3101
Washington, DC 20210
(202) 693-1888
Fax (202) 693-2498

Distributes publications and training materials; provides a catalog.

Freedom of Information

Contact OSHA Public Affairs, above. More information on FOI is available at the agency's Web site.

GRANTS

OSHA makes grants to state agencies to administer and enforce federally approved state programs for occupational safety and health. Arrangements for statistical operating grants are handled for OSHA by the Bureau of Labor Statistics; funds are also available from the National Institute for Occupational Safety and Health (*see Related Agencies, p. 276*).

PUBLICATIONS

Consumer Information

The OSHA Office of Public Affairs develops documents describing hazards, standards, and OSHA programs and policies. Topics include job safety and health, eye protection, indoor air quality, OSHA consultation services, general record-keeping requirements, protection against asbestos, carbon monoxide poisoning, cotton dust, field sanitation standards, grain handling facilities standards, and hazardous waste/emergency response. OSHA also produces a four-color magazine, *Job Safety and Health Quarterly*, available by subscription from GPO.

The public can download many of these publications via the agency's Web site.

Other General Publications

For information and specific titles, contact the OSHA Publications Office at Room N3101, Washington, DC 20210 or the nearest regional office. Many publications are available through the OSHA Web site, which contains the most recent listings.

Titles available include:

All About OSHA. An outline of OSHA's activities and policies.

How to Prepare for Workplace Emergencies. Details basic steps needed to prepare for handling emergencies such as accidental releases of toxic gases, chemical spills, fires, explosions, and personal injuries.

You Have a Right to a Safe and Healthful Workplace. It's the Law! Official poster required by law to be posted prominently in the workplace.

Maritime Standards: Parts 1911–1925. Contains all job safety and health rules and regulations pertaining to maritime terminals and longshoring operations.

OSHA: Employee Workplace Rights. Lists fourteen rights covered in the Occupation Safety and Health Act of 1970. Also includes employee responsibilities.

Worker Exposure to AIDS and Hepatitis B. Gives history of AIDS (acquired immune deficiency syndrome) and HBV (hepatitis B) and the risk the viruses present to workers, especially in health care; recommends practices for protection.

Many OSHA titles are also available from the U.S. Government Printing Office (GPO): see appendix, Ordering Government Publications. Topics include general health and safety guidelines for various industries; electrical hazards; emergency response and preparedness requirements; ergonomics; workplace violence; and materials on handling and storage.

Training Program Materials

OSHA has various training materials to help both employers and employees understand OSHA requirements. These include audio cassette/slide packets and programmed courses of instruction. The following may be purchased from the National Technical Information Service (NTIS) or its National Audiovisual Center division (NAC): see appendix, Ordering Government Publications. See OSHA's Web site at www.osha.gov for up-to-date information and listings.

DATA AND STATISTICS

Office of Management Data Systems

Department of Labor, OSHA
200 Constitution Ave. N.W.
Washington, DC 20210
(202) 693-1700
Lissa Scott, director

Maintains inspection reports, citation and penalty data, notices of contest, complaints, and penalty payment amounts. Also maintains other data, many of which are produced by the Bureau of Labor Statistics (BLS) or the National Institute for Occupational Safety and Health (NIOSH): see Related Agencies. Data collections include:

Annual Survey of Occupational Injuries and Illnesses. Data collected by industry category on deaths, lost workdays, nonfatal cases not resulting in lost workdays, and seven categories of specific illnesses. For details contact the BLS.

Criteria Documents. Prepared by NIOSH and used by OSHA to develop new standards. Available at the OSHA Technical Data Center (see below) and at all area and regional offices; or contact NIOSH.

Supplementary Data System. Data from reports of injuries and illnesses that are submitted to state workers' compensation programs. Major categories of data collected are: characteristics of the injury or illness, the firm, the worker, and the work situation. For details contact the BLS.

Work Injury Reports. Profiles of characteristics associated with selected types of workplace injuries. Compiled from questionnaires completed by injured workers. For more information contact the BLS.

MEETINGS

Schedules of upcoming advisory committee meetings are published in the *Federal Register* at least seven days in advance of the meeting. (See appendix for details on how to use the *Federal Register*.) Records of previous meetings are available for review by the public in the OSHA Technical Data Center.

Reference Resources

LIBRARY

OSHA Technical Data Center

200 Constitution Ave., N.W., Room N2625
Washington, DC 20210
(202) 693-2350
Fax (202) 219-5046
Chris Aaron, director
Hours: 8:15 a.m. to 4:45 p.m.

Open to the public; no appointment needed. Houses transcripts of advisory committee meetings, reports, opinions, periodicals and books on safety and health issues. Interlibrary loan service is available.

DOCKETS

Department of Labor, OSHA

200 Constitution Ave. N.W., Room N2625
Washington, DC 20210
(202) 693-2350
Fax (202) 693-1648
Elaine Bynum, docket officer
Hours: 10:00 a.m. to 4:00 p.m.

All records of hearings dealing with proposed standards or standards development are available for public inspection in this office.

RULES AND REGULATIONS

OSHA rules, regulations, and standards are published in the *Code of Federal Regulations,* Title 29. Proposed regulations and standards, new final rules, and standards and updates to the *Code of Federal Regulations* are published in the daily *Federal Register. (See appendix for information on how to obtain and use these publications.)*

OSHA standards are divided into three major categories—General Industry, Maritime, and Construction. Copies of each category of rules may be obtained from the Government Printing Office as on the OSHA Web site at www.osha.gov.

Other Information Sources

RELATED AGENCIES

DOL Bureau of Labor Statistics

Office of Safety, Health, and Working Conditions
    Statistics
2 Massachusetts Ave. N.E.
Washington, DC 20212
(202) 691-6179
Fax (202) 691-6196
Internet: http://www.bls.gov
William L. Weber, assistant commissioner

Provides many of the statistics used by OSHA.

DOL Office of the Solicitor

200 Constitution Ave. N.W.
Washington, DC 20210
(202) 693-5261
Judith E. Kramer (acting), solicitor

Divisions include the Office of the Solicitor for OSHA. The co-counsel for administrative law provides information on the Freedom of Information appeals process for OSHA.

National Institute for Occupational Safety and Health (NIOSH)
Centers for Disease Control and Prevention
4676 Columbia Pkwy., Mail Stop C13
Cincinnati, OH 45226
(800) 35-NIOSH (toll-free)

Conducts research and evaluation studies of occupational injuries and hazardous substances in the workplace. These criteria are used by OSHA for the basis of its standards development process. Also operates the Clearinghouse for Occupational Safety and Health Information (COSHI) and the Registry of Toxic Effects of Chemical Substances (RTECS). (The Centers for Disease Control and Prevention, which includes NIOSH, is a component of the Health and Human Services Department.)

Most NIOSH documents can be ordered through the above toll-free number. NIOSH criteria documents are available, upon request, for inspection and copying at all OSHA regional and area offices, at the OSHA Technical Data Center, and at NIOSH field offices. They also may be purchased from the U.S. Government Printing Office (GPO): see appendix, Ordering Government Publications.

Funds are available from NIOSH to any public or private institution wishing to conduct research in the field of occupational safety and health or to develop specialized professional personnel with training in occupational medicine, nursing, industrial hygiene, and safety.

Further information on application and award procedures may be obtained from:

National Institute for Occupational Safety and Health
Grants Program Activity
1600 Clifton Rd.
Atlanta, GA 30333
(404) 639-3343
Roy Fleming, research science director

Occupational Safety and Health Review Commission
Office of Information
1120 20th St. N.W., 9th Floor
Washington, DC 20006
(202) 606-5398
Linda Whitsett, information officer

An independent adjudicatory agency (not connected with the Labor Department). All citations issued by OSHA compliance and enforcement officers are subject to appeal to the review commission. For further information on agency administration and proceedings, contact this office.

NONGOVERNMENTAL ORGANIZATIONS
The following are some key organizations that monitor OSHA and issues of occupational health and safety.

American Industrial Health Council
2001 Pennsylvania Ave. N.W., #760
Washington, DC 20006
(202) 833-2131
Fax (202) 833-2201

American Industrial Hygiene Association
2700 Prosperity Ave., #250
Fairfax, VA 22031
(703) 849-8888
Fax (703) 207-3561
Internet: http://www.aiha.org

National Association of Manufacturers
Risk Management
1331 Pennsylvania Ave. N.W., #1500N
Washington, DC 20004-1790
(202) 637-3000
Fax (202) 637-3182
Internet: http://www.nam.org

National Safety Council
112 Spring Lake Dr.
Itasca, IL 60143-3201
(630) 285-1121
Fax (630) 285-1315
Washington office
1019 19th St. N.W., #401
Washington, DC 20036-5105
(202) 293-2270
Fax (202) 293-0032
Internet: http://www.nsc.org

Public Citizen Health Research Group
1600 20th St. N.W.
Washington, DC 20009
(202) 588-1000
Fax (202) 588-7796
Internet: http://www.citizen.org

U.S. Chamber of Commerce
1615 H. St. N.W.
Washington, DC 20062
(202) 659-6000
Fax (202) 463-5836
Internet: http://www.uschamber.org

PUBLISHERS

The following companies and organizations publish on OSHA and related issues through books, periodicals, or electronic media.

Board of Certified Safety Professionals
208 Burwash Ave.
Savoy, IL 61874
(217) 359-9263
Fax (217) 359-0055
Internet: http://www.bcsp.com

Cambridge Scientific Abstracts
7200 Wisconsin Ave.
Bethesda, MD 20814
(800) 843-7751
(301) 961-6700
Fax (301) 961-6720
Internet: http://www.csa.com

Charles C. Thomas Publisher, Ltd.
P.O. Box 19265
2600 S. First St.
Springfield, IL 62794-9265
(800) 258-8980
Fax (217) 789-9130
Internet: http://www.ccthomas.com

Commerce Clearing House (CCH), Inc.
2700 Lake Cook Rd.
Riverwoods, IL 60015
(847) 267-7000
Fax (847) 267-7878
Internet: http://www.cch.com

Merritt Professional Publishing Co.
1661 Ninth St.
Santa Monica, CA 90406
(800) 638-7597
Fax (310) 396-4563
Internet: http://merritpub.com

Pergamon Press
P.O. Box 945
New York, NY 10159-0945
(888) 437-4636
Fax (212) 633-3680
Internet: http://www.elsevier.nl

Securities and Exchange Commission

450 5th St. N.W., Washington, DC 20549
Internet: http://www.sec.gov

■ INTRODUCTION

The Securities and Exchange Commission (SEC) is an independent regulatory agency established by the Securities Exchange Act of 1934. The commission is composed of five members, not more than three of whom may be members of the same political party. The commissioners are nominated by the president and confirmed by the Senate for five-year terms. The president also designates one of the members to serve as chair.

Responsibilities

The SEC functions as both a regulatory and investigatory agency. Its role is to police the securities markets and protect investors, both through public disclosure of information about corporate activities and securities transactions and through enforcement actions.

Because the nation's financial markets are closely interlinked and because the SEC does not have jurisdiction over all aspects of them, the agency works closely with other regulators. Among those are the Treasury Department, which regulates trading in federal government securities; the Commodity Futures Trading Commission (CFTC), which regulates commodity traders and exchanges *(p. 312)*; the Federal Reserve System, which regulates bank holding companies and foreign banks and oversees monetary policy *(p. 166)*; the Office of the Comptroller of the Currency, which regulates federally chartered banks *(p. 692)*; and the Office of Thrift Supervision, which regulates savings and loans *(p. 704)*.

In a world securities market that is becoming increasingly linked, the SEC also works with foreign securities regulators to investigate and prevent fraud, to enhance public disclosure of foreign corporate financial activity, and to harmonize international financial reporting.

GLOSSARY

Broker—A person who acts as an agent for customers in selling or buying securities for their accounts.

Dealer—A person who acts as a principal rather than as an agent in buying or selling securities. Typically, a dealer buys for his own account and sells to a customer from his own inventory.

Holding company—A corporation organized to hold the stock of other corporations; usually a holding company owns or controls a dominant interest in one or more other corporations and is able to influence or dictate the management policies of the other corporations.

Insider trading—Violation of the antifraud provisions of federal securities laws; occurs when an individual profits in the stock market on the basis of confidential corporate secrets. For example, an insider could profit from knowledge of an impending corporate takeover, which would drive up the takeover target's stock price, or of a soon-to-be released disappointing earnings report, which typically would drive a stock price down.

Institutional investor—Commonly used phrase for bank mutual funds, insurance companies, pension funds, and large corporate investment accounts that, because of the size and frequency of their transactions, are eligible for preferential commissions and other services from broker-dealers.

Junk bonds—Colloquial expression for high-yield, high-risk bonds. Because they have received a low, or speculative, rating from the companies that rate bonds, these bonds pay a higher interest rate to attract buyers.

Margin trading—Purchasing securities that are paid for in part with a loan taken out using the same securities as collateral, in the hope that the price of the securities will increase, allowing the purchaser to pay off the loan and make a profit. Also called "buying on margin."

Mutual fund—An investment organization that issues stock to raise capital, which it then invests in other securities to generate funds for its operating costs and profits for its investors.

Program trading—Defined by the New York Stock Exchange as buy or sell orders for a group of fifteen or more stocks. Commonly, program trading employs the use of computers both to determine the optimum time for such trades and to execute them. Strategies include index arbitrage, the simultaneous trading of Big Board stocks and stock-index futures contracts to profit from brief price disparities, and tactical asset allocation, which uses futures contracts to shift money among equities, bonds, and other types of investments.

Selling short—Borrowing securities and selling them in anticipation of a market decline; if the market goes down, the securities may be bought back at a lower price and returned to the party from which they were borrowed, with the short seller keeping the profit.

Tender offer—A public offer to purchase stock (usually the controlling interest) in a corporation within a specified time period and at a stipulated price, usually above the market price.

In its effort to regulate the securities markets, the SEC:

- Requires broad disclosure of facts concerning public offerings of securities listed on national securities exchanges and certain securities traded over-the-counter (a market for buying and selling stock among broker-dealers without going through a stock exchange).

- Requires detailed periodic reports on the financial condition of companies that have made public securities offerings. Monitors and works with the Financial Accounting Standards Board, a private, self-regulatory association of public accountants that develops rules for corporate financial reporting.

- Regulates the trading of securities on the eight national securities exchanges and on over-the-counter markets; oversees the operations and rules of securities exchanges and the National Association of Securities Dealers (NASD), each of which functions as a self-regulatory organization; oversees the operations and rules of various clearing corporations that handle settlement of securities transactions.

- Requires securities brokers, dealers, and investment advisers to register with the SEC and regulates their activities.

- Enforces disclosure requirements in the soliciting of proxies for meetings of security holders by companies whose securities are listed on exchanges, public utility holding companies and their subsidiaries, and investment companies.

- Investigates securities fraud, stock manipulation, and other violations of securities laws; imposes administrative sanctions for such violations and seeks judicial injunctive remedies and criminal prosecution.

- Supervises the activities of mutual funds (including money market funds) and other investment companies.

- Regulates the provisions of trust indentures under which debt securities are sold to the public.

- Regulates the purchase and sale of securities, utility properties, and other assets by registered public utility holding companies and their electric and gas utility subsidiaries; also regulates reorganizations, mergers, and consolidations of public utility holding companies.

- Advises federal courts regarding corporate reorganization proceedings under Chapter 11 of the Federal Bankruptcy Code.
- Regulates cash and exchange tender offers.
- Requires government securities dealers to register with the agency to improve protection for investors in the market for government securities; monitors records of government securities transactions to guard against fraud and other illegal trading activities.
- Enforces record-keeping provisions of the Foreign Corrupt Practices Act, which prohibits public companies from bribing officials of foreign governments.
- Oversees the Securities Investor Protection Corporation.
- Works toward the establishment of a national market system for securities and for the prompt and accurate clearance and settlement of transactions in securities.

Powers and Authority

Legislation enacted since the establishment of the SEC has required various companies, individuals, and institutions to register with the commission. Supervising these registrants is one of the commission's major tasks.

The Securities Act of 1933 requires that before a public offering of securities is made by a company, or any person controlling such a company, a registration statement must be filed with the SEC by the issuer. The statement must contain an adequate and accurate disclosure of the material facts concerning the company and the securities it proposes to sell. Generally, statements include a description of the registrant's properties and business, a description of the significant provisions of the security to be offered for sale and its relationship to the registrant's other capital securities, information about the management of the registrant, and financial statements certified by independent public accountants. The information contained in registration filings becomes public immediately, but sales of securities may not start until the effective date of the filing, which on average occurs about thirty-five days after the filing is made.

Security registration statements are reviewed for compliance with disclosure requirements by the Division of Corporation Finance. If the statement appears to be incomplete or inaccurate, and the issuing company takes no action to correct it, the commission has the authority to advance or suspend the statement's effective date. A hearing may be held if intentionally misleading information is included in the filing. If evidence of a deliberate attempt to conceal and mislead is developed during the hearing, a stop order barring the security from the market may be issued.

However, a stop order is not a permanent bar to the sale of securities. The order must be lifted and the statement

declared effective if amendments are filed correcting the statement in accordance with the stop order decision.

The registration requirement applies to securities of both domestic and foreign private stock issues offered for sale in the United States, as well as to securities of foreign governments or their instrumentalities. Exempted from the registration requirement are (1) private offerings to a limited number of persons or institutions who have access to the kind of information registration would disclose; (2) offerings restricted to the residents of the state in which the issuing company is organized and doing business; (3) securities of municipal, state, federal, and other government instrumentalities, of charitable institutions, of banks and of carriers subject to the Interstate Commerce Act; (4) offerings by smaller businesses of up to $7.5 million made in compliance with regulations of the commission; and (5) offerings of "small business investment companies."

In October 1980 Congress passed the Small Business Investment Incentive Act, which amended securities laws to make it easier for small companies to issue stock. The legislation exempted from registration certain employee benefit and retirement plans.

The Securities Exchange Act of 1934 requires the registration of "national securities exchanges" (those having a substantial trading volume) and of brokers and dealers who conduct an over-the-counter securities business in interstate commerce.

To register, exchanges must show that they are able to comply with the provisions of the statute and the rules and regulations of the commission and that they operate under rules that adequately protect the investing public. While exchanges establish their own self-regulatory rules, the commission may "alter or supplement" them if it finds that the rules fail to protect investors.

Registered brokers and dealers must conform to business practices and standards prescribed by various laws and by the commission. The Office of Filings and Information Services, with assistance from the Division of Market Regulation, examines applications from brokers and dealers.

In 1986 Congress amended the Securities Exchange Act of 1934 to require all government securities dealers to register with the SEC. The Public Utility Holding Company Act of 1935 requires registration of interstate holding companies that are engaged through their subsidiaries in the electric utility business or in the retail distribution of natural or manufactured gas. Registered holding companies are subject to regulation by the commission.

The Investment Company Act of 1940 requires registration of mutual funds: companies that engage in the business of investing, reinvesting, and trading in securities and whose own securities are offered, sold to, and held by the investing public. Mutual funds and other investment companies are required to disclose their financial condition and investment policies. They are prohibited from changing the nature of their business or investment policies without the approval of the stockholders.

REPORTING REQUIREMENTS

Any company whose securities are registered with the SEC must file an annual report and other periodic reports with the commission to keep the information in the original filing up to date. The data in these reports are available to the public at the offices of the SEC, at the exchanges, and online. These reports also are used extensively by publishers of securities manuals, securities advisory services, investment advisers, trust departments, and securities brokers and dealers. There are penalties for filing false reports, as well as a provision for recovery by investors who suffer losses in the purchase or sale of registered securities due to incorrect information in the reports.

Proxies

When management or a group of stockholders is soliciting proxies for any reason, reports must be filed disclosing all the facts concerning the matters on which they are asked to vote. When a contest for control of the management of a corporation is involved, the rules require disclosure of the names and interests of all participants in the proxy contest. Proxy material must be filed in advance with the commission to permit staff review and to ensure that any interested securities holder may have access to it before the vote.

Acquisition

Amendments to the Securities Exchange Act of 1934 require that any effort to acquire control of a company through a tender offer or other planned stock acquisition be reported to the SEC. This applies to anyone attempting to obtain more than 5 percent of a company's equity securities.

Insider Trading

Officers, directors, and holders of more than 10 percent of a company's registered securities must file a report with the commission showing the amount of holdings. A report also must be filed for any month during which there is any change in the holdings.

INVESTIGATION AND ENFORCEMENT

Disclosure requirements of the federal securities laws, including registration and reporting requirements, are intended to safeguard the integrity of U.S. securities markets. It is the duty of the commission under the laws it administers to investigate complaints or other indications of possible law violations in securities transactions, most of which arise under the Securities Act of 1933 and the Securities Exchange Act of 1934 as amended. Investigation and enforcement work is the primary responsibility of the commission's Division of Enforcement.

Most of the commission's investigations are conducted privately; the facts are developed to the fullest extent possible through informal inquiry, interviewing of witnesses, examination of brokerage records, trading data, and other documents, and by similar means. The commission, however, has the authority to issue subpoenas requiring sworn testimony and the production of books, records, and other documents pertinent to the subject under investigation. In the event of refusal to respond to a subpoena, the commission may apply to a federal court for an order compelling compliance.

Inquiries and complaints from investors as well as news stories provide leads for detection of law violations in securities transactions. Violations also may be uncovered by unannounced inspections of the books and records of brokers and dealers by the SEC regional offices to determine whether the business practices of the companies being examined conform to prescribed rules. Inquiries into market fluctuations in particular stocks, when those fluctuations appear to be influenced by factors other than known developments affecting the issuing company or broad market trends, also may reveal securities laws violations.

The more general types of investigations concern the unregistered sales of securities subject to the registration requirement of the Securities Act of 1933, and misrepresentation or omission of material facts concerning securities offered for sale (whether or not registration is required). The antifraud provisions of the law apply equally to the purchase of securities, whether involving outright misrepresentations or the withholding or omission of pertinent facts to which the seller was entitled. For example, it is unlawful in certain situations to purchase securities from another person while withholding material information that would indicate that the securities have a value substantially greater than the purchase price. Such provisions of the law apply not only to transactions between brokers and dealers and their customers, but also to the reacquisition of securities by an issuing company or its "insiders."

Other types of inquiries relate to the manipulation of the market prices of securities; the misappropriation or unlawful pledging of customers' funds or securities; the conduct of a securities business while insolvent; the purchase or sale of securities by a broker-dealer, from or to customers, at prices not reasonably related to the current market prices; and violation by the broker-dealer of a responsibility to treat customers fairly.

The most common of the latter type of violation involves broker-dealers who, on gaining the trust and confidence of customers and thereby establishing a relationship demanding the highest degree of integrity, takes secret profits in their securities transactions with or for the customers over and above the agreed brokerage (agency) commission. For example, the broker-dealers may have purchased securities from customers at prices far below, or sold securities to customers at prices far above, their current market value. Or the firm may engage in large-scale buy and sell transactions for the customer's account (churning) to generate increased commissions.

STATUTORY SANCTIONS

SEC investigations are essentially fact-finding inquiries. The facts developed by the staff are considered by the commission only in determining whether there is prima facie evidence of a law violation and whether an action should be commenced to determine if a violation actually occurred and if some sanction should be imposed. If the facts show possible fraud or other law violation, the laws provide several courses of action or remedies:

Civil Injunction

The commission may apply to an appropriate U.S. district court for an order enjoining those acts or practices alleged to violate the law or commission rules. The SEC also may issue cease and desist orders against persons who it believes are violating securities laws or commission rules when it fears continued activity would be significantly harmful to investors or the public interest, or would result in substantial dissipation or conversion of assets.

Very often the SEC secures consent agreements, in which an accused party voluntarily agrees not to engage in prohibited practices, while not admitting to prior violations. Such consent agreements have the effect of court-ordered injunctions. And the parties who agree to them can be subject to more severe sanctions if they do not adhere to the terms.

Civil Fines

For cases where the SEC believes a fraud or other securities law violation has occurred, it may seek civil fines as punishment. The authority to seek fines is relatively new (except in cases of insider trading, for which civil penalties have existed since 1984). It was granted by Congress in 1990 because the standard of proof for civil actions is less than that for criminal prosecution and thus often easier and quicker to meet.

Criminal Prosecution

If fraud or other willful law violation is indicated, the SEC may refer the facts to the Department of Justice (DOJ) with a recommendation for criminal prosecution of the offending persons. Through local U.S. attorneys, frequently assisted by SEC attorneys, the DOJ may present the evidence to a federal grand jury and seek an indictment.

Administrative Remedy

The commission may, after a hearing, issue orders that suspend or expel members from exchanges or from the over-the-counter dealers association; deny, suspend, or revoke the registrations of broker-dealers; censure firms or individuals for misconduct; or bar individuals (temporarily or permanently) from employment with a registered firm.

All of the sanctions mentioned above may be applied to any person who engages in securities transactions that violate the law, whether or not the person is engaged in the securities business. The administrative remedy is invoked in the case of exchange or association members, as well as registered brokers, dealers, or individuals who may associate with any such firm. In an administrative proceeding, the commission issues an order specifying the acts or practices alleged to have been committed in violation of law and directing that a hearing be held. At the hearing, counsel for the Division of Enforcement (normally a regional office attorney) undertakes to establish for the record those facts that support the charge. The respondents have full opportunity to cross-examine the witnesses and to present evidence in their defense.

The initial decision in such a proceeding is delivered to the respondents by an agency administrative law judge and can be appealed to the full five-member SEC. The commission's final opinion in a proceeding of this type can be appealed directly to a federal court of appeals.

Background

The origins of the SEC may be traced to the stock market crash of Oct. 29, 1929. The crash and the ensuing economic depression focused public attention on the way securities were bought and sold during the feverish trading years of the 1920s. There were widespread reports of stock manipulations designed to make large profits quickly for small groups or "pools" of wealthy investors. Unscrupulous dealers and brokers promoted offers of securities that they knew to be almost worthless.

Public outrage at the practices on Wall Street caused the Senate in 1931 to pass a resolution calling for an extensive investigation of securities trading. The investigation led to passage of the Securities Act of 1933, also known as the "truth-in-securities" bill. The act required anyone offering securities for sale in interstate commerce or through the mails to file information with the Federal Trade Commission (FTC) on the financial condition of the issuing company. A prospectus containing a summary of the filed information had to be given to potential investors.

The Securities Exchange Act of 1934 created the SEC and transferred to it the functions that had been assigned to the FTC under the 1933 law. The 1934 act required companies whose securities were traded on national exchanges to file periodic financial reports. The measure also required that exchanges and over-the-counter dealers and brokers conduct business in line with principles of fair and equitable trade. Those who failed to comply could be forced to do so by the SEC.

Agitation for increased regulation of securities markets, primarily emanating from the administration of President Franklin D. Roosevelt, continued through the 1930s. The first three SEC chairs, Joseph P. Kennedy, James M. Landis, and William O. Douglas, provided strong leadership for the new agency. Douglas, who served as chair from 1937 until his appointment to the Supreme Court in 1939, was especially effective in forcing the reorganization of the New York Stock Exchange (NYSE), altering the character of the nation's largest exchange from a private men's club to a public institution.

Beginning in 1935 Congress passed a number of laws that greatly expanded the powers of the SEC. The first was the Public Utility Holding Company Act, which required utility companies to register with the SEC and submit to its regulation. That act was followed in 1938 by the addition of a new section to federal bankruptcy law, authorizing the commission to assist federal courts in the administration of corporations undergoing reorganization as a result of bankruptcy. In 1939 Congress passed the Trust Indenture Act, which was followed in 1940 by two related bills: the Investment Company Act and the Investment Advisers Act, requiring investment companies and advisers to register with the SEC.

From 1940 until the early 1960s, Congress showed little interest in securities regulation, primarily because the securities markets functioned smoothly. However, as the U.S. economy began to boom and international trade increased, the need for new industrial plants also grew. This development required commensurate growth in capital markets, from traditional banking to stocks, bonds, and other forms of investment. In response, the SEC in 1963 recommended numerous administrative and legislative changes to give added protection to investors. Chief among the recommendations were tightening regulations for over-the-counter trading, raising the quality of securities sales personnel, increasing supervision of brokers, and granting the SEC more flexibility in disciplining violators.

Most of the recommendations were incorporated in the Securities Acts Amendments of 1964. The amendments generally extended the same information disclosure requirements to companies whose stock was traded over-the-counter as already applied to those whose securities were traded on the national exchange. The law also required dealers in over-the-counter markets either to join the NASD or to accept SEC supervision. In addition, the NASD was required to adopt written standards of training,

experience, and competence for its members and to establish minimum capital requirements for member firms.

The SEC then turned its attention to mutual funds. Neither the Investment Company Act nor the Investment Advisers Act had ever been substantially amended, and the acts were no longer adequate to deal with the multibillion-dollar industry. Passage of new legislation, however, was delayed until 1970.

While the SEC was concentrating on over-the-counter markets and mutual funds, other problems were emerging in the securities markets. The troubles stemmed, in part, from general economic conditions: prevailing high interest rates on debt instruments made equity stocks less attractive investments, and recession undercut corporate profits. But the primary difficulty lay in the failure of the industry and federal regulations to keep pace with the vast expansion of trading volume and the changing character of the securities market.

One such change was the growing importance of stock investments by institutions such as pension funds, insurance companies, banks, and other organizations that managed large portfolios. Institutional investors accounted for most of the rising stock market activity during the 1960s, and the existing exchange structure had difficulty adjusting to their rising prominence.

One problem involved the fixed brokerage commission rates that U.S. stock exchanges had been setting since the NYSE was founded in 1792. That system had prevented investors from negotiating the best possible price for stock transaction services offered by exchange members, thus curtailing competition among brokers who held stock exchange seats. During the 1960s institutional investors began to seek alternative ways to cut brokerage costs, including attempts to obtain stock exchange seats for themselves or affiliated firms that could offer preferential treatment. The NYSE, the most significant securities auction market in the nation, refused to admit institutional members and insisted that fixed brokerage rates were necessary as an incentive for holding expensive exchange seats and as protection for smaller firms and investors.

At the same time, the securities markets were becoming increasingly fragmented as more and more shares listed on the NYSE were traded in other regional exchanges or on the so-called "third market" (over-the-counter trading through securities dealers outside the exchanges). The situation complicated investors' efforts to find the best available price for stocks.

Stock markets encountered other problems as well, among them rapidly rising trading volume that occasionally overwhelmed an outmoded system for clearing and settling stock transactions. In fact, a 1968–1970 "paperwork crisis" almost closed down the markets. That development, along with inadequate capitalization for many firms and other difficulties, forced more than 100 brokerage firms into liquidation.

These problems worked to undermine public confidence in stock markets. Relatively low investment returns after 1968 discouraged stock purchases, and the growing dominance of institutional investors suggested to many potential investors that individuals making small investments were at a disadvantage. As a result, the number of persons investing directly in stocks began falling for the first time in many years.

SEC IN THE 1970S

To restore confidence in the securities markets, Congress passed the Securities Investor Protection Act of 1970. The law created the Securities Investor Protection Corporation (SIPC), a nonprofit membership organization that provided coverage for loss of cash and securities left on deposit with brokers who became insolvent. Although the SIPC was an independent, nongovernmental corporation, it was subject to close supervision by the SEC.

The SEC also promulgated a series of rules under its existing powers of supervision over the self-regulatory exchanges and the NASD. In 1973 the SEC adopted rules that ordered: (1) creation of a consolidated tape communications system for reporting the prices and volume of all transactions in listed stocks, whether sold on the NYSE, other exchanges, or the third market; (2) a limit on institutional membership on stock exchanges for firms that conducted at least 80 percent of their business with nonaffiliated persons; and (3) replacement of fixed exchange commission rates with fully competitive fees on most transactions after May 1, 1975.

Congress in 1975 gave final approval to amendments to the Securities Act intended to encourage development of a national system for buying and selling stocks. The amendments banned practices that restricted investors' access to the nation's stock exchanges and the over-the-counter markets. While preserving the self-regulatory framework established under the Securities Exchange Act of 1934, the legislation significantly enlarged SEC oversight of the stock exchanges and the NASD.

Provisions prohibiting exchange members from buying or selling stocks for themselves or for an affiliated company and provisions upholding the SEC's earlier abolition of fixed brokerage commissions significantly changed the operation of the stock exchanges. Other major provisions extended SEC regulation to firms that process securities transaction paperwork and to banks that underwrite and trade state and local government bonds. The bill also required that banks, insurance companies, and other large-scale institutional investors be subject to certain SEC disclosure requirements.

SEC IN THE 1980S

In the 1980s a series of high-profile insider trading cases the SEC brought against well-known traders rocked Wall Street and captured banner headlines in newspapers throughout the country. As part of its crackdown on insider trading, the SEC sought to stiffen penalties for the offense. Existing law in the early 1980s empowered the SEC to order an inside trader to pay back illegal profits. In 1982 the commission sought legislation increasing the fine up to three times the value of an inside trader's illegal profits. The Insider Trading Sanctions Act was signed into law in 1984.

The serious nature of the SEC cases in the late 1980s led Congress to further stiffen the penalties for insider trading violations. In November 1988 Congress passed the Insider Trading and Securities Fraud Enforcement Act raising the penalty for each violation of insider trading to ten years in prison from five years and increasing potential fines to $1 million from $100,000. The legislation also authorized the SEC to pay bounties for information leading to an SEC insider trading case. The bill also included severe fines for Wall Street firms that do not supervise their employees.

Earlier, on Oct. 19, 1987, one of the worst stock market drops in history occurred. (The Dow Jones Industrial Average fell 508 points, losing 22.6 percent of its value.) An SEC staff study echoed the views of many market observers that sophisticated program trading strategies employed by institutional investors and brokerage firms accelerated and worsened the market's fall.

These trading strategies often used stock-index futures, a product developed and traded on the Chicago futures markets and regulated by the CFTC. Index futures were tied to the value of an index of stock prices, such as the S&P 500, and essentially allowed investors to bet on the direction of the stock market. Unlike most commodity futures contracts, stock-index futures were settled for cash, not the underlying commodity when they came due. They were created and often used by institutional investors who wanted to hedge against the possibility that the stock market would move adversely to their stock investments.

The SEC asked Congress for jurisdiction over stock-index futures, but because of political pressure from the futures industry, all that resulted were modified circuit breakers that stopped the use of computer-assisted trades after a 50-point rise or fall in the Dow Jones average. Pressure to reform the financial markets returned following a major drop in the stock market in October 1989. The next year, President George Bush signed into law the Market Reform Act, which gave the SEC authority to order trading halts and take other steps to protect the integrity of the stock markets in times of emergency. It required brokers and dealers to keep records of large securities transactions and gave the SEC authority to require reports of such transactions.

The SEC also stepped up its pursuit of accounting fraud during the 1980s. Despite its enforcement efforts, however, the agency came under heavy criticism from some members of Congress for its policy of encouraging the accounting industry to regulate its affairs through industry groups such as the Financial Accounting Standards Board and the American Institute of Certified Public Accountants.

A bill enacted in 1990 to grant the SEC authority to seek civil monetary penalties in cases of securities law violations also gave federal courts the power to bar anyone convicted of a securities law violation from serving as an officer or a director of a public company. Following disclosures during the savings and loan debacle in the late 1980s that accounting firms had been complicit in allowing weak thrifts to disguise their financial difficulties to regulators, some members of Congress attempted to make outside auditors responsible for reporting evidence of financial fraud to the SEC.

The SEC moved slowly in developing the national market system, as mandated by the 1975 legislation. In January 1983 the commission formally approved the modest beginnings of such a system, which it called the Intermarket Trading System. The system consists of a permanent electronic linkage of the NASD's automated quotation system for trading over-the-counter stocks, the Nasdaq, and the eight U.S. exchanges. During its first year of operation, more than one billion shares of stock were traded through the system. The linkage also meant investors could obtain faster and more complete information about a stock's trading activity.

In late 1984 the commission approved new rules relaxing the standards used by the NASD to determine stocks eligible for use as collateral for margin loans by broker-dealers. Following the October 1987 market crash, additional concerns arose over the clearing and settling of stock transactions, and the time it took (typically five business days) to close trades. The 1990 Market Reform Act gave the SEC authority to develop a national system for clearance and settlement. In a move toward that end, in 1993 the SEC issued a rule requiring settlement of stock trades handled by registered brokers and dealers within three business days. The change went into effect in 1995.

SEC IN THE 1990S

One arena where the SEC had exercised limited regulatory control before the 1990s involved so-called penny stocks—small, low-cost issues not traded on exchanges. Abuses and fraud continued to crop up in this market during the 1980s as individuals sought higher-yielding investments and more money flowed into all securities markets.

In 1990, as part of a bill enacted to grant the SEC authority to seek civil penalties, Congress increased the SEC's authority in the penny stock area. Generally, the law required the SEC to more closely monitor this market and to require brokers and dealers in penny stocks to provide buyers with a risk-disclosure document explaining that these stocks were often difficult to trade because the market for them was small and less liquid.

Congress in 1993 followed the lead of the SEC and imposed new disclosure requirements on brokers who put together deals to convert limited partnerships into public corporations. Often these restructurings involved real estate and oil and gas drilling ventures that had greatly declined in value. More than 2,000 partnerships worth billions of dollars were "rolled up" in the 1980s and 1990s. In many cases there were allegations that the results often enriched the general partners who managed the ventures and left limited partners holding stock whose prices fell precipitously.

The SEC and NASD had issued rules requiring broad disclosure of rollup proposals and to allow limited partners greater opportunity to communicate with each other about rollup deals. The bill enacted in 1993 essentially codified those rules and extended them to brokers not otherwise subject to SEC or NASD jurisdiction. It also allowed dissenters to a rollup to demand cash or other compensation rather than stock. Congress has refused to adopt other legislative proposals, including one that would have required independent "fairness opinions" of a rollup's worth.

President Bill Clinton appointed Arthur Levitt Jr. chair of the SEC in 1993. Levitt, a former American Stock Exchange (Amex) chair, thrived in the deregulatory environment of the 1990s and was confirmed for a second five-year term in April 1998. He oversaw the slashing of dozens of securities rules and regulations considered redundant. At the same time, Levitt furthered the agency's efforts to build confidence in the securities market by allocating more staff to enforcement offices. In 1995 the agency moved most of its employees who formerly studied small business filings to a new centralized office of compliance inspections, and examinations in Washington, D.C.

To protect investors' principal against rapid interest rate changes similar to those seen in 1994, the SEC in 1996 under Levitt's leadership approved a rule to tighten safeguards over money market funds that invest in tax-exempt municipal securities. The new rule placed stricter requirements on these funds to diversify, to improve credit quality, and to limit investments in more volatile securities. For example, a money market fund investing in tax-exempt securities in a single state could invest no more than 5 percent of its portfolio with a single issuer in that state. The rule also prohibited investments in certain interest-sensitive securities, such as inverse floater bonds that pay more interest as rates fall, and less as they rise.

Under pressure from House Republicans to further reduce securities regulations, the SEC spent much of 1996 making changes to simplify corporate offering procedures. Dozens of rules considered duplicative and obsolete were eliminated, while new rules were passed to make it easier for small companies to raise capital. The changes revamped insider trading rules designed to prevent the illegal manipulation of a company's securities when new financial products were being issued. Historically, corporate officers and directors were not allowed to turn profits within six months on transactions involving the companies' securities.

Under the rule changes approved in May 1996, corporate insiders would be exempt from the trading restrictions on many routine transactions involving employee-benefit plans, dividend reinvestment plans, and other investment plans, as long as the transactions were approved by the company's board, a panel of outside directors, or by shareholders. The new rules also narrowed the time frame in which trading restrictions apply during a new offering and exempted more than 2,000 large, actively traded companies from the restrictions altogether.

In June 1997 the Supreme Court issued a 6–3 ruling that made it easier for the SEC and the DOJ to prosecute investors who improperly benefited from confidential information by establishing a broader definition of insider trading. The Court defined insider trading as the illegal buying or selling of securities for personal gain using misappropriated information, regardless of the source of the information. This definition extended to those who profited from confidential information even if they did not work for the company or obtained the information from representatives of the company.

In what many financial experts considered a monumental achievement of Levitt's tenure, the SEC unanimously approved new rules for the Nasdaq. Phased in during 1997, the new rules narrowed the trading spreads (the differences between the prices at which dealers offer to buy and sell stock) by forcing Nasdaq dealers to (1) publicly display all investor limit orders; (2) notify the public of the absolute best prices for stocks, which had been available only to institutions and dealers, through such systems as Instinet and Nasdaq's SelectNet; and (3) expand the size of any offered block of stock at the best market price to include a customer's limit order at the same price.

Dealers complained that such tightening of trading spreads would expose them to massive losses, so the SEC postponed a decision on its most controversial proposal: a "price-improvement" rule that would have obligated dealers to improve prices in investors' favor if the market shifted after the customer orders were placed.

In a related move, the SEC in 1997 took action to revamp the U.S. trading system's long-standing practice of expressing stock prices in fractional terms. For more than two centuries, U.S. exchanges had quoted stock prices in increments of eighths of a dollar, such as 1/8 (12.5 cents). Critics said the fractional pricing system hurt small investors by keeping stock spreads artificially high. Fractional pricing also complicated trading between U.S. and foreign exchanges, because most of the world's industrialized countries expressed stock prices in decimal units.

Congress in March 1997 introduced a bill requiring a switchover to decimal units, but the legislative approach proved to be unnecessary. In June 1997 the governing board of the NYSE voted to phase out fractional pricing and to start expressing stock prices in dollars and cents as soon as it could revamp its computer system. In the interim, the NYSE, Nasdaq, Amex, and some regional exchanges started quoting prices in increments of 1/16 of a dollar, or 6.25 cents.

The SEC endorsed the concept of decimal pricing, but in October 1997 it recommended that the nation's exchanges delay the conversion until after Jan. 1, 2000, because of the potential for computer problems associated with the rollover from 1999 to 2000. However, fears about the so-called "Y2K" bug proved to be unfounded. The NYSE and Amex began trading in decimals in January 2001, and a number of regional exchanges soon followed suit. Nasdaq, the last major U.S. exchange to switch over to decimals, completed its conversion on April 9, 2001.

While the conversion to decimal pricing was hailed by many investors and lawmakers on Capitol Hill, it nevertheless prompted some complaints from stock market participants who struggled to adapt to the new system. Institutional investors, such as mutual funds, said that the decimal pricing units made it easier for floor traders to engage in "front-running," the practice of outbidding the institutions by a penny in an effort to drive up the price of a stock. Some in the industry said that the NYSE's rules, not decimalization, were to blame.

In early 1996 the SEC further refined its controversial stance on campaign contributions by bond dealers. In trying to combat the practice known as "pay to play," in which bond dealers contribute to state and local officials' campaigns in hopes of winning bond business, the SEC had set a $250 limit on contributions to candidates in jurisdictions where the bond dealers are entitled to vote. If their contributions exceeded that limit, their firms were barred from doing business in that jurisdiction for two years.

In February 1996 the SEC approved a Municipal Securities Rulemaking Board proposal to scrap the previous position that municipal dealers could not contribute to a governor running for president until the candidate was on the ballot in jurisdictions where the donors live. This became an issue when the SEC blocked municipal-bond dealers from contributing to California governor Pete Wilson's short-lived presidential campaign the year before.

In the waning months of the Clinton administration, Levitt proposed expanding the "pay to play" rule to bar money managers for public pension funds from making political contributions to government officials who hire financial advisers. But the SEC took no action to expand the rule before Clinton left office in January 2001.

International Agreements

The SEC took its first enforcement action against a Russian investment fund in 1996, charging a Moscow-based fund with making an illegal public offering of securities without registering as an investment company under federal securities laws. Russ-Invest settled with the SEC without admitting wrongdoing and agreed not to raise money from American investors. The case was unusual because the SEC has made a point of trying to accommodate foreign firms that have different standards for accounting and disclosure to encourage participation in the U.S. market and to sustain a sense of cooperation with other countries, especially in enforcement issues. More than 800 foreign filers joined the U.S. public securities market in 1996, up from 650 two years before.

The SEC had been nurturing its foreign relationships for nearly two decades. In 1982 the agency negotiated an agreement with Switzerland aimed at helping U.S. law enforcement authorities get around Swiss bank secrecy laws in investigating suspected illegalities. This agreement was followed by similar arrangements with Japan and Britain. In 1988 the commission signed a memorandum of understanding with three Canadian provinces permitting U.S. and Canadian officials to conduct full-scale investigations upon the request of their foreign counterparts. The SEC also worked with the International Organization of Securities Commissions to develop an international disclosure system. This system is based on the mutual recognition of each participating country's disclosure, accounting, and auditing requirements.

In 1990, to facilitate such international cooperation, Congress passed a law that permitted the SEC to exchange information with foreign enforcement agencies and insulated the SEC from Freedom of Information Act requests for information obtained from foreign sources. The law also gave the SEC and stock exchanges authority to bar persons convicted abroad of securities violations from U.S. exchanges. Acknowledging the reluctance of many foreign countries to submit to stiff U.S. financial reporting requirements, early in 1990 the SEC moved to allow privately placed securities to be traded freely among large investors and to permit foreign companies to issue private placements in the United States.

Investor Awareness

The SEC took several more steps in the latter part of the 1990s to protect the millions of Americans pouring money into the market through mutual funds, their 401(k) and other retirements plans, and other methods that rely on investment advisors. Levitt called "appalling" the financial literacy levels of many of these new entrants to the market and the American public as a whole, and the SEC moved to require both greater disclosure of the risks and that sellers communicate investment information in "plain English."

In January 1997 the SEC adopted new rules to require any company trading or raising money in domestic markets to publicly disclose its potential losses that could be caused by sudden shifts in financial markets, such as volatility in stock prices, exchange rates, or interest rates.

Levitt also pressed for the use of straightforward and easy-to-understand language in introductory and other sections of investment documents. In January 1998 the SEC approved a rule requiring companies and mutual funds to write the cover page, summary, and risk factor sections of their prospectuses in simple, concise language that even the most novice investors would be able to understand. Two months later, the SEC moved to allow mutual fund companies, for the first time, to sell shares to investors using only a short profile of the fund rather than distributing the full prospectus to potential buyers before making a sale. The latter move, combined with the plain English requirement, was intended to make it easier for the average investor to choose among competing mutual funds, the number of which had grown to 8,000 in 1998.

In April 2000 the commission extended its plain English initiative to investment advisers, requiring them to give clients an easily understandable brochure outlining their services. The rule, billed as the most significant commission initiative in regulating advisers since the Investment Advisers Act of 1940, also created an Internet database that allowed consumers to look up information on the services and fees of all registered financial advisers, and on any disciplinary actions taken against them.

The SEC also continued its efforts to give investors more information about the operation of mutual funds. In January 2001 the commission announced it would require mutual funds to disclose standardized after-tax returns so investors could compare tax consequences when choosing an investment. That same month the commission also signaled it expected mutual fund names to reflect the makeup of their portfolios accurately. It released specifications about the percentage of stocks or bonds that funds would have to own to include the term in their name. The most controversial of the recent agency rules designed to maximize investor information was known as "fair disclosure" or "Regulation FD." It barred public companies from releasing important corporate information to a select audience and not also to the general public.

EDGAR System

To help investors obtain accurate, up-to-date information, the commission in 1983 took the first steps toward making the periodic corporate reports filed with it available to the public in electronic form through the Electronic Data Gathering, Analysis, and Retrieval system (EDGAR).

It took more than a decade and cost about $111 million, but EDGAR finally was up and running full speed by 1996, with corporate filings of some 16,000 public companies available online. The SEC estimated that EDGAR eliminated more than 12 million pages of corporate material annually, and savvy investors with a personal computer and a phone line could daily monitor the financial details of any public company.

In July 1998 the SEC launched a three-year modernization of the EDGAR system that aimed to reduce costs and effort associated with the preparation and submission of SEC required documents and improve the presentation of the information. The project was designed to convert the EDGAR system to an Internet-based system using HTML as the official filing format. By November 2000 filers were required to submit information directly to the Internet.

In addition, the SEC updated its own Web site. The agency launched a new version in February 2001. The SEC Web site holds about 1.7 million documents and averages one million "hits" a day.

Managing Competition

In the late 1990s and early 2000s, the SEC spent an increasing amount of its time adjusting to the new financial landscape. With many foreign exchanges consolidating and adapting new technology that attracted new customers, the SEC tried to ensure that U.S. exchanges were not left behind. The commission also attempted to get a handle on new financial products sanctioned by legislation that broke down the barriers between banks, stock brokerages, and insurance companies and that recognized futures-based products.

In December 1999 the commission adopted a rule that gave all regulated stock exchanges, such as the Nasdaq, full access to shares listed at the venerable NYSE. The rule expanded the Intermarket Trading System to give the NASD and other traders access to companies that had been listed on the NYSE before 1979, including mammoth corporations such as General Electric and IBM. The move was seen as a first step to allowing Electronic Communications Networks, such as Island and Archipelago, unimpeded access to traditional exchanges. These networks allow traders to keep buying and selling after the stock markets close, by matching sell and buy orders.

SEC IN THE 2000S

The SEC faced new challenges at the dawn of the new century, such as how to best regulate the burgeoning practice of Internet-based trading. The average number of online trades soared from about 455,000 per day in the first quarter of 1999 to more than 1.24 million per day in the first quarter of 2000, an increase of 173 percent. Likewise, the number of investors opening online trading accounts nearly doubled from 8.6 million in the first quarter of 1999 to more than 17.4 million in the second quarter of 2000.

The popularity of online trading spawned a host of Internet-based stock manipulation schemes. Some hustlers used the Internet to run "pump and dump" operations, driving up their stock prices by posing as interested investors, or "shills," on anonymous Internet message boards. Others conned unwary online traders out of their money using "spam" e-mails, electronic newsletters, and bogus Web sites.

The SEC launched five nationwide "Internet sweeps" beginning in 2000 in an effort to shut down companies and individuals engaged in such activities. By 2001 the agency had brought 200 enforcement actions against Web sites that gave out faulty information. The SEC also launched a campaign to educate investors about the potential risks of online trading. The initiative was effective in reducing the number of consumer complaints lodged with the SEC over Internet trading by 75 percent, according to a July 2001 report by the General Accounting Office.

The SEC also took action to strengthen its conflict-of-interest regulations for independent auditors. The ambitious, but controversial, move was prompted by an internal SEC review, made public in January 2000, that alleged widespread violations of auditor independence rules by employees of accounting giant PricewaterhouseCoopers (PwC). The review found that many PwC employees owned stock in companies they were hired to audit. Likewise, it found that PwC employees hired as auditors routinely negotiated lucrative consulting contracts with their clients for other professional services, such as tax advice and information technology services.

Alarmed by the findings, the SEC in March began talking with PwC and the other "Big Five" accounting firms about revamping the conflict of interest rules governing the accounting profession. The SEC initiated formal rulemaking on the topic in May and held several public hearings on the matter throughout the summer. The hearings were often adversarial in nature. Initially, Levitt sought to prohibit accounting firms from providing information technology and other nonaudit services to their audit clients altogether. Levitt maintained that audit firms might ignore or conceal their clients' financial problems so as not to jeopardize their lucrative nonaudit business ventures. The accounting firms, conversely, argued that performing nonaudit consulting services made them better auditors, because they learned more about their clients' businesses.

In November 2000, after a tumultuous public comment period, the SEC unveiled an updated conflict of interest rule that amounted to a compromise between what it and the accounting industry wanted. The rule, which was formally adopted in February 2001, allowed accounting firms to continue to design information technology systems and to provide other nonaudit consulting services to their audit clients. However, it imposed a host of disclosure requirements on companies that maintain nonaudit business relationships with their auditors. Specifically, the rule required companies to disclose publicly how much they paid their auditors for both audit and nonaudit services. In addition, the rule required companies to disclose publicly any concerns they might have regarding their auditors' independence.

The SEC quickly showed that it intended to rigorously enforce the new regulation. The same month the rule was approved, the commission sanctioned KPMG, one of the "Big Five" accounting firms. The SEC said that KPMG had compromised its independence in a 1996 audit of Porta Systems, a telecommunications equipment manufacturer that was being run by a KPMG BayMark, an affiliate of the accounting firm.

New Leadership

After George W. Bush arrived at the White House, Levitt stepped down from the commission in February 2001. Bush's nominee to succeed Levitt was Harvey L. Pitt, a private-practice securities lawyer who served as the SEC's general counsel in the 1970s. Supporters said Pitt was eminently qualified for the job, but critics argued that he was too beholden to corporate interests to be an effective advocate for small investors. As a securities lawyer, critics noted, Pitt routinely advised Wall Street brokerage houses, accounting firms, corporate executives, and the NYSE on how to avoid getting into trouble with the SEC. But Pitt shrugged off such criticism and told lawmakers at his confirmation hearing that he would push for a review of the nation's securities laws, saying many were obsolete and imposed unfair burdens on market participants. Pitt was confirmed by the Senate in August 2001.

Pitt had been on the job only a few weeks when terrorists attacked the World Trade Center towers in New York City in September 2001. The attacks posed a host of daunting challenges for the SEC. The commission's northeast regional office in Lower Manhattan was destroyed in the attack, but incredibly no SEC employees were killed in the assault. Furthermore, because the office stored backup copies of its records at an off-site location, its investigations of securities firms in the New York area were unaffected by the tragedy.

The nation's securities markets also temporarily shut down, but the SEC played a key role in reestablishing their operations. Immediately following the attacks, Pitt and other SEC officials met in New York City with the leaders of the nation's major markets, securities firms, and banks to devise a strategy and a timetable for reopening the markets. The nation's fixed-income and futures markets resumed trading just two days after the tragedy. The NYSE, Nasdaq, and the other major equities and options markets reopened six days after the attacks.

The SEC also for the first time in its history invoked certain "emergency powers" that it holds under the Securities Exchange Act of 1934. For example, the commission temporarily relaxed a regulation so that public companies could repurchase more of their own stock. The move, which was rescinded in mid-October, was designed to provide companies with greater stability and liquidity in a time of market uncertainty.

The SEC later began working with the Treasury Department on an antimoney laundering initiative designed to identify and choke off funds flowing to terrorist groups such as al Qaeda, which had carried out the attacks. The SEC's participation in the project was mandated by the USA PATRIOT Act, a comprehensive antiterrorism bill passed by Congress in the wake of the attacks.

Corporate Scandals

Another national crisis landed on the SEC's doorstep shortly after the terrorist attacks: a rash of business meltdowns and accounting scandals that wiped out many investors' life savings and raised serious questions about the integrity and soundness of corporate America. The crisis began in October 2001, when Enron Corp., one of the nation's largest public companies, unexpectedly reported a $618 million third-quarter loss and a $1.2 billion writedown in shareholder equity. The SEC launched investigations of the Texas-based energy-trading company and its accounting firm, Arthur Andersen. The SEC soon found that Enron's once-mighty financial empire had been built on dubious accounting schemes and shady business arrangements, such as off-the-books partnerships designed to hide losses from investors and federal securities regulators. Enron filed for bankruptcy protection in December 2001, wiping out many employees' pension funds and socking investors with huge losses.

In the congressional hearings that followed, officials from Enron and Andersen blamed each other for the debacle. In the end, both companies collapsed. In March 2002 the DOJ indicted the Andersen firm for obstruction of justice. Andersen, admitting that its employees had destroyed thousands of Enron records after learning that the SEC had begun investigating its client, contended that it should not be criminally prosecuted as a firm. A jury disagreed, finding Andersen guilty in June 2002. By 2003 the firm was teetering on the brink of extinction.

Enron did not fare much better. In 2003 the company's creditors were seeking more than $200 billion from the bankrupt firm, and some Enron executives had been brought up on federal charges. In August 2002 the SEC and the DOJ filed fraud charges against former Enron executive Michael J. Kopper, alleging that he used complex structures, hidden payments, and secret loans to enrich himself and to make Enron appear more profitable than it was. Kopper pleaded guilty to wire fraud and money laundering and agreed to hand over $12 million in illicit profits. In October Enron's former chief financial officer, Andrew S. Fastow, was brought up on similar charges. He pleaded not guilty. More charges were expected in the Enron case.

But Enron was only the tip of the corporate-scandal iceberg. In July 2002 WorldCom, the nation's second-largest long-distance telephone carrier, filed for bankruptcy protection after admitting that it had overstated its earnings for five quarters by $3.8 billion. The company later reported additional accounting errors and increased the total overstatement to approximately $9 billion. The bankruptcy filing and alleged corporate fraud by WorldCom was, by far, the largest in U.S. history. The SEC moved to charge WorldCom and four of its former employees with numerous violations of U.S. securities laws.

Other corporate scandals soon followed: Adelphia Communications, Dynergy, Global Crossing, Halliburton, Rite Aid, Tyco International, and Xerox, to name a few. The SEC filed fraud charges against each of these companies in 2002. In most cases, the SEC also brought charges against individual executives of these companies. While the details of these cases varied, each revolved around allegations that the defendants purposely and knowingly overstated their earnings to bolster their stock prices and enrich themselves.

Calls for Reform

Congressional leaders and federal regulators in Washington responded to the corporate scandals with a host of divergent proposals for reform. Of the various proposals, bills introduced by Democratic lawmakers called for the strongest crackdown on malfeasance by public companies and the accounting industry. Most Republicans, at least initially, backed weaker measures. SEC chair Pitt sided openly with the Republicans. But after WorldCom's implosion made it clear that the Enron debacle had not been an isolated incident, Republicans rushed to embrace many of the

tougher reform provisions advocated by the Democrats. In July lawmakers passed an anticorporate fraud measure named after the sponsors of two competing bills, Sen. Paul Sarbanes of Maryland and Rep. Michael Oxley of Ohio, President Bush signed the Sarbanes-Oxley Act into law on July 30, 2002, calling the bill "the most far-reaching reforms of American business practices since the time of Franklin Delano Roosevelt."

Among its other provisions, Sarbanes-Oxley made it a criminal offense—punishable by up to twenty years in prison—to knowingly destroy or falsify records pertaining to SEC or other federal investigations. The law also created new criminal penalties for knowingly filing false financial reports. It also prohibited companies from hiring outside accountants to perform certain nonaudit consulting services contemporaneously with their official bookkeeping duties.

The most sweeping provision of the Sarbanes-Oxley Act created a new entity, the Public Company Accounting Oversight Board (PCAOB), to oversee the audits of public companies. The act empowers the PCAOB to inspect the auditing firms performing those audits, to set rules and standards for such audits, and to impose meaningful sanctions if warranted. To safeguard the board's independence, the act mandated that it be funded by fees from public companies. Moreover, no more than two of its five members were to be accountants. The act granted the SEC "general oversight and enforcement authority" over the board, including the approval of its rules and the appointment of its members.

Ironically, Pitt was forced to resign as SEC chair as a result of his efforts to appoint the first chair of the PCAOB. Pitt's controversial choice for the job, former FBI and CIA director William H. Webster, was initially approved by the SEC on Oct. 25, 2002, in a bitterly divided 3–2 vote. A political firestorm, however, soon developed when it became known that Webster had once headed the audit committee of a company accused of fraud by the SEC. Pitt, who had known about but had not shared that information about Webster with his fellow SEC commissioners, tendered his resignation on Nov. 5, having served just fifteen months of his six-year term. Webster stepped down as chair of the PCAOB a week after Pitt resigned.

Current Issues

President Bush's choice to succeed Pitt, William H. Donaldson, said at his Senate confirmation hearing in February 2003 that he would "call on corporate America and Wall Street" to make honesty, integrity, and regard for shareholders' interests the motivating factors for all business decisions. Donaldson cofounded a Wall Street investment bank and ran the NYSE from 1990 to 1995. Despite his ties to Wall Street and corporate America, Donaldson did not elicit the kind of criticism that dogged his predecessor Pitt.

In May 2003, after considering the results of a thorough background check, Donaldson and his fellow SEC commissioners unanimously appointed William J. McDonough, a former president of the Federal Reserve Bank of New York, to be chair of the fledgling PCAOB.

The PCAOB, which began meeting in October 2002, has been in the process of adopting the rules by which it will work. In June 2003 the board approved a set of strict ethics rules in an apparent effort to stave off any conflicts of interest that could tarnish its work. The rules, which must be approved by the SEC before they can take effect, generally prohibit all board and staff members from either owing, or being owed, any money from any "former employer, business partner, publisher or client." Members of the PCAOB and their spouses and dependents were also prohibited from receiving any profit or payments from a public accounting firm, other than proceeds from an already established retirement plan. In addition, the rules prohibited board members and staff from having any financial interests in public accounting firms. Likewise, they instructed PCAOB employees to "avoid investments that affect or reasonably create the appearance of affecting their independence or objectivity." Personal investments were not otherwise restricted by the rules.

The SEC, meanwhile, has nearly completed the lengthy rulemaking process required by the landmark Sarbanes-Oxley Act. Early in 2003, for example, the commission adopted rules for one of the most controversial sections of the act: consulting services prohibited to independent auditors. The rules defined nine nonaudit services that could potentially impair an auditor's independence, such as investment banking services, legal services, and the design and implementation of financial information systems. The SEC also recently adopted Sarbanes-Oxley-mandated rules relating to financial experts on audit committees; trading during pension fund blackout periods; retention of audit records; and standards of conduct for corporate attorneys, among other matters.

The SEC was projected to get a big boost in funding in fiscal year 2004 to carry out its many tasks. The White House's budget request of $841.5 million for the SEC would be the largest amount ever appropriated for the commission. SEC chair Donaldson told lawmakers early in 2003 that the commission needed the large appropriation to pay for the additional enforcement activities mandated by the Sarbanes-Oxley Act.

Indeed, the SEC continued to make headlines in its crackdown on corporate crime. On June 2003 the SEC filed securities fraud charges against lifestyle entrepreneur Martha Stewart and her former stockbroker, Peter Bacanovic. The SEC alleged that Stewart committed illegal insider trading when she sold stock in a biopharmaceutical company, ImClone Systems, Inc., in December 2001, after receiving an unlawful tip from Bacanovic. Stewart and Bacanovic were also indicted on criminal charges in the matter. Both have pleaded not guilty.

■ AGENCY ORGANIZATION

Biographies

WILLIAM H. DONALDSON, CHAIRMAN

Appointment: Appointed by President George W. Bush on Feb. 18, 2003.

Education: Yale University, B.A., 1953; Harvard Graduate School of Business Administration, M.B.A., 1958.

Profession: Business Management.

Political Affiliation: Republican.

Previous Career: Prior to the appointment Mr. Donaldson served as CEO of a private investment firm that he originally founded in 1981. Simultaneously he served as Chairman of the Board of the Carnegie Endowment for International Peace. Prior to that he headed the nation's largest providers of health insurance and related benefits until his retirement in 2001. From 1990–1995, Mr. Donaldson also served as Chairman and CEO of the New York Stock Exchange.

PAUL S. ATKINS, COMMISSIONER

Appointment: Appointed by President George W. Bush on July 29, 2002.

Education: Wofford College, A.B., 1980; Vanderbilt University, J.D., 1983.

Profession: Lawyer.

Political Affiliation: Republican.

Previous Career: Before joining the SEC, Atkins assisted financial services firms in improving their compliance with SEC regulations and worked with law enforcement agencies to investigate and rectify situations where investors had been harmed. Atkins also served on the staff of two former chairmen of the SEC, Richard C. Breeden and Arthur Levitt.

CYNTHIA A. GLASSMAN, COMMISSIONER

Appointment: Appointed by President George W. Bush on January 28, 2002.

Education: Wellesley College, B.A.; University of Pennsylvania, M.A., Ph.D.

Profession: Professor, Economist.

Political Affiliation: Republican.

Previous Career: Before joining the SEC, Glassman spent over thirty years in the public and private sectors

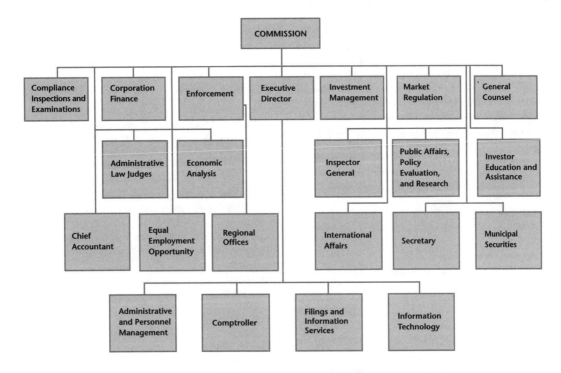

focusing on financial services regulatory and public policy issues. She spent the first twelve years of her career at the Federal Reserve. Glassman, spent one year on assignment to the U.S. Department of the Treasury as Senior Economist in the Office of Capital Markets Legislation during the Carter administration. Glassman also taught economics at the University of Cambridge, England, where she remains as a Senior Member of Lucy Cavendish College.

HARVEY J. GOLDSCHMID, COMMISSIONER
Appointment: Appointed by President George W. Bush to a term expiring June 5, 2004.

Education: Columbia College, B.A., 1962; Columbia University School of Law, J.D., 1965.

Profession: Professor, Lecturer.

Political Affiliation: Democrat.

Previous Career: Before joining the SEC, Goldschmid served as Dwight Professor of Law at Columbia University School of Law. He is the author of numerous publications on corporate, securities, and antitrust law. From 1980–1993 Goldschmid served as reporter for the American Law Institute's Corporate Governance Project. He also served as Chair of the Nominating Committee (2000–2001), and

completed a term as Treasurer and member of the Executive Committee in 1998.

ROEL C. CAMPOS, COMMISSIONER
Appointment: Nominated by President George W. Bush, and confirmed by the Senate on July 25, 2002.

Education: U.S. Air Force Academy, B.S., 1971; UCLA, M.B.A., 1972; Harvard Law, J.D., 1979.

Profession: Military Officer, Lawyer.

Political Affiliation: Democrat.

Previous Career: Before joining the SEC, Campos was an officer in the U.S. Air Force. Campos was also a principal owner of El Dorado Communications and served as an executive with the radio broadcasting company in Houston. He also worked in Los Angeles for major law firms as a corporate transactions/securities lawyer and litigator. In 1985 he served as a federal prosecutor for several years in the U.S. Attorney's Office in Los Angeles.

Headquarters and Divisions

COMMISSION
The commission promulgates rules and regulations related to the statutes it administers and holds hearings on

proposed changes in regulations. It considers results of staff investigations to determine if there is sufficient evidence of violation of the law to warrant prosecution or administrative sanctions. The commission can apply for civil injunctions ordering a halt to alleged violations; it can recommend criminal prosecution; or it can issue orders suspending or expelling members from exchanges and over-the-counter associations. The commission is empowered to deny, suspend, or revoke the registration of broker-dealers and censure individuals for misconduct. It can bar individuals (temporarily or permanently) from employment with firms registered with the SEC. The commission also can order stock exchanges and dealers' associations to comply with its rules and guidelines under penalty of the judicial and administrative sanctions mentioned. The office of the chair also handles SEC congressional liaison work.

Chairman
    William H. Donaldson .... (202) 942–0100
    Fax .... (202) 942–9646
Commissioners
    Paul S. Atkins .... (202) 942–0700
    Cynthia A. Glassman .... (202) 942–0600
    Harvey J. Goldschmid .... (202) 942–0800
    Roel C. Campos .... (202) 942–0500
Legislative Affairs
    Jane O. Cobb .... (202) 942–0010

OFFICE OF ADMINISTRATIVE LAW JUDGES

The administrative law judges conduct hearings on administrative proceedings instituted by the SEC and appeals of proceedings instituted by others.

Chief Judge
    Brenda Murray .... (202) 942–0399

OFFICE OF THE CHIEF ACCOUNTANT

Responsible for all accounting and auditing matters related to the statutes administered by the SEC. Recommends that administrative proceedings be instituted, when necessary, against accountants who should be disqualified from practice before the SEC, and issues periodic releases on changes in SEC-approved accounting practices.

Chief Accountant
    Vacant .... (202) 942–4400
    Fax .... (202) 942–9656

OFFICE OF COMPLIANCE INSPECTIONS AND EXAMINATIONS

Conducts all compliance inspection programs of brokers, dealers, self-regulatory organizations, investment companies, investment advisers, clearing agencies, and transfer agents.

Director
    Lori A. Richards .... (202) 942–7400
    Fax .... (202) 942–9641
Broker-Dealer Examinations and Oversight/
Self-Regulatory Organization Inspections Office
    Mary Ann Gadziala .... (202) 942–0087
Investment Company/Investment Adviser
Examinations and Oversight
    Gene A. Gohlke .... (202) 942–0540

DIVISION OF CORPORATION FINANCE

Responsible for examining all registration statements of securities offered for public sale for compliance with standards of adequate disclosure set forth in the Securities Act of 1933. Also seeks full and fair disclosure in the solicitation of proxies, in tender offer filings, and in any other matters on which shareholders are asked to vote. Processes issuers' periodic reports and applications for the registration of securities on any national securities exchange as well as registrations of certain over-the-counter securities.

Director
    Alan Beller .... (202) 942–2800
    Fax .... (202) 942–9525
Deputy Director
    Martin Dunn .... (202) 942–2890
Deputy Director
    Shelley Parratt .... (202) 942–2830
Associate Director
    Paula Dubberly .... (202) 942–2825
Associate Director, Chief Accountant
    Carol Stacey .... (202) 942–2960
Chief Counsel, Legal
    Vacant .... (202) 942–2900
Operations
    Vacant .... (202) 942–2830
Regulatory Policy
    Mauri Osheroff .... (202) 942–2840
Small Business
    Gerald Laporte .... (202) 942–2990
International Corporate Finance
    Paul Dudek .... (202) 942–2990

OFFICE OF ECONOMIC ANALYSIS

Assists the SEC in establishing regulatory policy by analyzing economic developments that affect the securities markets. Evaluates the impact on financial markets of proposed SEC actions and coordinates recommendations to the commission on policy matters that affect several SEC divisions and offices.

Chief Economist

Lawrence E. Harris..................... (202) 942–8020

Fax..................................... (202) 942–9657

Deputy Chief Economist

Jonathan Sokobin...................... (202) 942–7198

DIVISION OF ENFORCEMENT

Supervises and conducts all of the enforcement activities required by each of the acts administered by the SEC. Reviews cases with the general counsel to determine which ones should be referred to the Justice Department for criminal prosecution. Supervises operations of the regional offices.

Director

Stephen M. Cutler..................... (202) 942–4500

Fax..................................... (202) 942–9636

Chief Counsel

Joan McKown.......................... (202) 942–4530

Internet Enforcement

John Reed Stark....................... (202) 942–4803

Chief Litigation Counsel

David Kornblau........................ (202) 942–4818

Chief Accountant, Corporate Practices

Vacant................................. (202) 942–4510

Regional Operations

James Clarkson........................ (202) 942–4580

OFFICE OF EQUAL EMPLOYMENT OPPORTUNITY

Develops, implements, and monitors internal affirmative action plans. Initiates and conducts surveys to determine the effectiveness of existing programs and counsels employees as well as management officials on career development, and the complaint and appeals procedure.

Director

Debra K. Balducchi .... (202) 942–0040

Fax..................................... (202) 942–9547

OFFICE OF THE EXECUTIVE DIRECTOR

The executive director acts as the chief administrative officer for the commission. For the purposes of budget authority and management, the executive director oversees the entire SEC staff; for policymaking purposes, the executive director is responsible for the administrative offices only.

Executive Director

James McConnell...................... (202) 942–4300

Fax..................................... (202) 942–9588

OFFICE OF ADMINISTRATIVE AND PERSONNEL MANAGEMENT

Prints SEC reports, brochures, and other materials; provides supplies to offices; and prints and maintains the

SEC telephone directory. Also responsible for all areas of personnel management, including recruitment, placing, staffing, position classification, wage administration, employee-management relations, employee development and training, and health and incentive awards.

Associate Executive Director

Jayne L. Seidman....................... (202) 942–4000

Fax..................................... (202) 914–0592

Employee and Labor relations

Mark Raisher.......................... (202) 942–4090

Publishing

Scott Mackert.......................... (202) 942–4055

OFFICE OF FINANCIAL MANAGEMENT

Responsible for the financial management and programming functions of the commission. The comptroller serves as SEC liaison with the Office of Management and Budget, congressional appropriations committees, the Treasury Department, and the General Accounting Office.

Comptroller

Margaret J. Carpenter................. (202) 942–0340

Fax..................................... (703) 914–0172

OFFICE OF INFORMATION TECHNOLOGY

Receives all public documents filed with the SEC. Recommends action against delinquent companies; examines insider reports and registration applications of broker-dealers and investment advisers; and calculates fees. Also keeps all SEC official records and operates and maintains the SEC's electronic data processing facilities.

Associate Executive Director

Vacant................................. (202) 942–8800

Fax..................................... (703) 914–2621

Central Systems

Vacant................................. (202) 942–8621

Network Engineering Group

Vacant................................. (202) 942–8800

Program and Resource Management

Leanne Vaeth.......................... (202) 942–8800

Applications and Software Management

Lewis Walker.......................... (202) 942–8811

Customer Support

Derek Scarbrough..................... (202) 942–8823

Technical Architecture Group

Sanjeev Purohit....................... (202) 942–7715

Security Group

Mark Brickman........................ (202) 942–7761

OFFICE OF THE GENERAL COUNSEL

Represents the commission in legal proceedings and reviews cases with the Division of Enforcement to determine which ones should be referred to the Justice Department for criminal prosecution. Interprets questions of law for the commission, assists in the preparation of SEC comments to Congress on pending legislation, and helps draft proposed legislation. Also reviews all SEC releases and speeches dealing with SEC statutes.

General Counsel
    Giovanni Prezioso .... (202) 942–0900
    Fax .... (202) 942–9625
Adjudication
    Anne Chafer .... (202) 942–0950
Appellate Litigation and Bankruptcy
    Jacob Stillman .... (202) 942–0930
Legal Policy
    Meredith Mitchell .... (202) 942–0834
Counseling and Regulatory Policy
    Diane Sanger .... (202) 942–0960
Litigation and Administrative Practice
    Richard Humes .... (202) 974–0940
Ethics Counsel
    Barbara Hannigan .... (202) 942–0970

OFFICE OF THE INSPECTOR GENERAL

Conducts independent internal audits and investigations of the commission's operations.

Inspector General
    Walter Stachnik .... (202) 942–4461
    Fax .... (202) 942–9653
Deputy Inspector General
    Nelson Egbert .... (202) 942–4462

OFFICE OF INTERNATIONAL AFFAIRS

Negotiates protocols between the SEC and foreign securities regulators and coordinates enforcement programs according to those agreements. Also handles inquiries from SEC offices and the general public regarding international securities regulation.

Director
    Vacant .... (202) 942–2770
    Fax .... (202) 942–9524

DIVISION OF INVESTMENT MANAGEMENT

Administers the Investment Company Act of 1940, the Investment Advisers Act of 1940, and other statutes that apply to investment companies. Registers investment companies. Also examines and processes periodic reports and proxy soliciting material required by the Securities Exchange Act of 1934. Has authority to grant, deny, or revoke prior grants of requests for confidential treatment of information filed by investment companies. Office of Public Utility Regulation analyzes legal, financial, accounting, engineering, and other problems arising under the Public Utility Holding Company Act.

Director
    Paul Roye .... (202) 942–0720
Deputy Director
    Cynthia Fornelli .... (202) 942–0720
Associate Director (Chief Counsel)
    Douglas J. Scheidt .... (202) 942–0666
Chief Counsel (International Issues)
    Alison Fuller .... (202) 942–0660
Chief Counsel (Financial Institutions)
    Elizabeth Osterman .... (202) 942–0660
Chief Accountant
    Brian Bullard .... (202) 942–0590
Associate Director - Disclosure and Insurance Product Regulation
    Susan Nash .... (202) 942–0630
Enforcement Liaison
    Barbara Chretien-Dar .... (202) 942–0535
Legal and Disclosure
    Barry D. Miller .... (202) 942–0663
    Disclosure and Review #1
    Michael A. Lainoff .... (202) 942–0589
    Disclosure and Review #2
    Frank J. Donaty .... (202) 942–0585
    Insurance Products
    William J. Kotapish .... (202) 942–0670
    Disclosure Regulation
    Paul G. Cellupica .... (202) 942–0721
Regulatory Policy and Investment Regulation
    Robert E. Plaze .... (202) 942–0716
    Regulatory Policy
    Hunter C. Jones .... (202) 942–0690
    Investment Adviser Regulation Task Force
    Jennifer Sawin .... (202) 942–0719
Associate Director - Public Utility and Investment Company Regulation
    David B. Smith .... (202) 942–0525
    Financial Analysis
    Paul Goldman .... (202) 942–0510
    Investment Company Regulation
    Nadya B. Boytblat .... (202) 942–0564
    Public Utility Regulation
    Catherine A. Fisher .... (202) 942–0545

DIVISION OF MARKET REGULATION

Responsible for administering the SEC's program to facilitate the establishment of a national market system. Also responsible for the registration and regulation of brokers, dealers, municipal securities dealers, securities information processors, transfer agents, and self-regulatory organizations (any national securities exchange, registered clearing agency, or registered securities association). This function involves, among other things, the oversight of the conduct of registered broker-dealers and the evaluation, oversight, and inspection of self-regulatory organizations. Works to establish a national system for the clearance and settlement of securities transactions.

Director
Annette Nazareth...................... (202) 942–0090
Fax................................... (202) 942–9643
Senior Special Counsel
David Shillman........................ (202) 942–0072
Risk Management and Control
Michael A. Macchiaroli................ (202) 942–0770
Market Supervision
Belinda Blaine........................ (202) 942–0180

OFFICE OF PUBLIC AFFAIRS

The public information and legislative liaison office of the commission. Responds to requests for information and assistance from Congress, the news media, and the public. Produces the annual report to Congress, publishes the daily *SEC News Digest,* and supervises the production and distribution of SEC publications and audiovisual materials. It provides speakers for various forums.

Director
Vacant................................ (202) 942–0020
Fax................................... (202) 942–9654
Deputy Director
Heibert Perone .... (202) 942–0020
Deputy Director
John Heine............................ (202) 942–0022
Senior Public Affairs Specialist
Carol Patterson....................... (202) 942–0020

OFFICE OF THE SECRETARY

Prepares and maintains the record of all official commission actions. The commissioners have delegated to the secretary responsibility for the commission's rules of practice.

Secretary
Jonathan Katz .... (202) 942–7070

OFFICE OF INVESTOR EDUCATION AND ASSISTANCE

Serves and assists individual investors. Investor assistance specialists are available to answer questions and analyze complaints. However, the office cannot coerce a brokerage firm to resolve complaints. Actions taken by the office are not a substitute for private individuals taking action on their own. Individuals who have unresolved complaints are urged to seek counsel under federal and state laws.

Director
Susan Ferris Wyderko.................. (202) 942–7240

OFFICE OF FILINGS AND INFORMATION SERVICES

Responsible for the receipt and initial handling of all public documents filed with the commission. Also responsible for keeping the commission's official records, development and implementation of the commission's records management program, and authentication of all documents produced for administrative or judicial proceedings.

Associate Executive Director
Kenneth Fogash .... (202) 942–8938

Regional Offices

NORTHEAST REGION
(CT, DC, DE, MA, MD, ME, NH, NJ, NY, PA, RI, VA, VT, WV)
The Woolworth Building
233 Broadway
New York, NY 10279
(646) 428–1500
Wayne Carlin, regional director

Boston District
73 Tremont St., #600
Boston, MA 02108–3912
(617) 424–5900
Juan Marcel Marcelino, district administrator

Philadelphia District
The Curtis Center, #1005E
601 Walnut St.
Philadelphia, PA 19106–3322
(215) 597–3100
Arthur S. Gabinet, district administrator

SOUTHEAST REGION
(AL, FL, GA, LA, MS, NC, PR, SC, TN, VI)
801 Brickwell Ave., #1800
Miami, FL 33131
(305) 982–6300
David Nelson, regional director

Atlanta District
3475 Lenox Rd. N.E., #1000
Atlanta, GA 30326–1232
(404) 842–7600
Richard Wessel, district administrator

MIDWEST REGION
(IA, IL, IN, KY, MI, MN, MO, OH, WI)
175 W. Jackson Blvd., #900
Chicago, IL 60604
(312) 353–7390
Mary Keefe, regional director

CENTRAL REGION
(AR, CO, KS, ND, NE, NM, OK, SD, TX, UT, WY)
1801 California St., #1500
Denver, CO 80202–2648
(303) 844–1000
Randall Fons, regional director

Fort Worth District
801 Cherry St., #1900
Fort Worth, TX 76102
(817) 978–3821
Harold F. Degenhardt, district administrator

Salt Lake District
500 Key Bank Tower
50 S. Main St., #500
Salt Lake City, UT 84144–0402
(801) 524–5796
Kenneth D. Israel, district administrator

PACIFIC REGION
(AK, AZ, CA, GU, HI, ID, MT, NV, OR, WA)
5670 Wilshire Blvd., 11th Floor
Los Angeles, CA 90036–3648
(323) 965–3998
Randall R. Lee, regional director

San Francisco District
44 Montgomery St., #1100
San Francisco, CA 94104
(415) 705–2500
Helane Morrison, district administrator

■ CONGRESSIONAL ACTION

Congressional Liaison
Estee Levine............................(202) 942–0014

Committees and Subcommittees

HOUSE APPROPRIATIONS COMMITTEE
Subcommittee on Commerce, Justice, State, and
Judiciary
H309 CAP, Washington, DC 20515
(202) 225–3351

HOUSE BANKING AND FINANCIAL SERVICES COMMITTEE
Subcommittee on Capital Markets, Securities, and
Government-Sponsored Enterprises
2129 RHOB, Washington, DC 20515
(202) 226–0469

HOUSE COMMERCE COMMITTEE
Subcommittee on Oversight and Investigations
2125 RHOB, Washington, DC 20515
(202) 225–2927

Subcommittee on Telecommunications, Trade, and
Consumer Protection
2125 RHOB, Washington, DC 20515
(202) 225–2927

SENATE APPROPRIATIONS COMMITTEE
Subcommittee on Commerce, Justice, State, and
Judiciary
S146A CAP, Washington, DC 20510
(202) 224–7277

SENATE BANKING, HOUSING, AND URBAN AFFAIRS COMMITTEE
Subcommittee on Securities
SD-534, Washington, DC 20510
(202) 224–7391

SENATE GOVERNMENTAL AFFAIRS COMMITTEE
Permanent Subcommittee on Investigations
SR-100, Washington, DC 20510
(202) 224–3721

Legislation
The SEC was created by the **Securities Exchange Act of 1934** (48 Stat. 881, 15 U.S.C. 78a). Signed by the president June 6, 1934. The act required any company whose securities are traded on national exchanges or over-the-counter to file registration applications and annual and periodic reports with the SEC that detail the economic health of the company. The act also set up the following requirements: proxy solicitations must disclose all information concerning the matter to be voted on; individuals or firms making a tender offer to buy up stock in a company, as well as individuals urging stockholders to accept or reject a tender offer, must provide full information to stockholders; corporate officers or insiders and large (10 percent) stockholders must report changes in their holdings; a company may recover profits earned by insiders on the sale or purchase of the company stock; and all national exchanges and all brokers and dealers who conduct business over-the-counter must register with the SEC and comply with principles of trade as enforced by the commission.

The legislation creating the SEC also gave the commission responsibility for administering the **Securities Act of 1933** (48 Stat. 74, 15 U.S.C. 77a). Signed by the president May 27, 1933. This act, originally administered by the Federal Trade Commission, required any firm or individual issuing securities for sale in interstate commerce or through the mails to file financial and other data about the issuer and the securities offered with the SEC before the securities can be placed on the market. Offerings exempt from the registration requirement include: private offerings to a small number of individuals or institutions who are familiar with the securities being offered and who do not plan to redistribute them; offerings restricted to residents of the state in which the issuing company is located and engaged in business; securities of municipal, state, federal, and other governmental bodies (but not foreign governments or their instrumentalities), charitable institutions, banks, and carriers subject to the Interstate Commerce Act; offerings not in excess of certain amounts and made in compliance with SEC regulations (such as small business offerings under $500,000); and offerings of small business investment companies.

Public Utility Holding Company Act of 1935 (49 Stat. 803, 15 U.S.C. 79). Signed by the president Aug. 26, 1935. Required public utility (gas and electric) holding companies to register with the SEC and to file reports containing detailed data about organization, financial structure, and operations. Required the companies to operate as coordinated, integrated systems confined to a single area or region. Regulated the functions, activities, expansion, and operations of utility holding companies generally.

Trust Indenture Act of 1939 (53 Stat. 1149, 15 U.S.C. 77aaa). Signed by the president Aug. 3, 1939. Established conditions for the sale of debt securities issued under trust indentures; required that the indenture trustee be free from all conflicts of interest.

Investment Advisers Act of 1940 (54 Stat. 847, 15 U.S.C. 80b-l). Signed by the president Aug. 22, 1940. Required that all individuals engaged in the business of advising others on security transactions register with the commission and maintain books in accordance with commission rules. Empowered the SEC to enact rules to prevent fraudulent, deceptive, or manipulative acts and practices. Gave the SEC power to suspend or revoke registration of individuals found guilty of dishonest or illegal practices.

Investment Company Act of 1940 (54 Stat. 789, 15 U.S.C. 80a-l). Signed by the president Aug. 22, 1940. Required all investment companies to register with the SEC and regulated their activities to ensure fair treatment of all clients.

Securities Investor Protection Act of 1970 (84 Stat. 1636, 15 U.S.C. 78o) Signed by the president Dec. 30, 1970. Established the Securities Investor Protection Corp. (SIPC) as an independent nongovernmental corporation, subject to close supervision by the SEC.

Securities Acts Amendments of 1975 (89 Stat. 97, 15 U.S.C. 78a note). Signed by the president June 4, 1975. Directed the SEC to encourage development of a national system for buying and selling stocks. Enlarged SEC oversight powers over the stock exchanges and its indirect oversight responsibility for over-the-counter markets.

Foreign Corrupt Practices Act of 1977 (91 Stat. 1494, 15 U.S.C. 78a note). Signed by the president Dec. 19, 1977. An amendment to the Securities Act. Prohibited U.S. companies from making payments to foreign officials for the purpose of winning business contracts or to influence laws or regulations of other governments. The SEC was given responsibility for enforcing the bribery ban and can seek civil injunctions against violators. The legislation also required firms to maintain records that accurately reflect their transactions and dispositions of assets.

Bankruptcy Reform Act of 1978 (92 Stat. 2625, 11 U.S.C. 1101, et seq.). Signed by the president Nov. 6, 1978. Authorized the SEC to aid the federal courts in the administration of corporations reorganizing as a result of bankruptcy.

Small Business Investment Incentive Act of 1980 (94 Stat. 2275, 15 U.S.C. 80a). Signed by the president Oct. 21, 1980. Amended the Securities Acts to exempt certain small- and medium-sized businesses from securities law registration requirements.

Insider Trading Sanctions Act of 1984 (98 Stat. 1264, 15 U.S.C. 78a note). Signed by the president Aug. 10, 1984. Authorized the SEC to seek a civil penalty of up to three times the profit gained or loss avoided as a result of insider trading. Allowed an increase in the maximum fine for a criminal violation.

Shareholder Communications Act of 1985 (99 Stat. 1737, 15 U.S.C. 78n note). Signed by the president Dec. 28, 1985. Required banks, associations, and fiduciaries to disseminate proxy materials.

Government Securities Act of 1986 (100 Stat. 3208, 15 U.S.C. 78a). Signed by the president Oct. 28, 1986. Tightened federal regulation of brokers and dealers who trade in government securities and mortgage pools.

Insider Trading and Securities Fraud Enforcement Act of 1988 (102 Stat. 4677, 15 U.S.C. 78a note). Signed by the president Nov. 19, 1988. Increased civil and criminal penalties for persons who trade stocks using substantive, nonpublic information.

Securities Enforcement Remedies and Penny Stock Reform Act of 1990 (Remedies Act) (104 Stat. 931, 15 U.S.C. 78a note). Signed by the president Oct. 15, 1990. Amended the federal securities laws to provide additional enforcement remedies for violations and to eliminate abuses in transactions in penny stocks.

Market Reform Act of 1990 (104 Stat. 963, 15 U.S.C. 78a note). Signed by the president Oct. 16, 1990. Provided measures to enhance financial market stability, authorized increased monitoring of risks posed to SEC-regulated firms by their holding company, and set provisions for the institution of a large trader reporting system by the SEC to facilitate analysis of market developments.

Futures Trading Practices Act of 1992 (106 Stat. 3590, 7 U.S.C. 1 note). Signed by the president Oct. 28, 1992. Amended the Commodity Exchange Act to improve the regulation of futures and options traded under rules and regulations of the Commodity Futures Trading Commission.

North American Free Trade Agreement Implementation Act (107 Stat. 2057, 19 U.S.C. 3301 note). Signed by the president Dec. 8, 1993. Implemented the North American Free Trade Agreement (NAFTA). Required each party (United States, Canada, and Mexico) to grant most-favored-nation treatment to financial service providers and investors of the other parties.

Government Securities Act Amendments of 1993 (107 Stat. 2344, 15 U.S.C. 78a note). Signed by the president Dec. 17, 1993. Amended the government securities provisions of the Securities Exchange Act of 1934. Regulated sales practices and required disclosure by government securities dealers and brokers that are not financial institutions if their accounts are not insured by the Securities Investor Protection Corp.

Telemarketing and Consumer Fraud and Abuse Prevention Act (108 Stat. 1545, 15 U.S.C. 6101 et seq.). Signed by the president Aug. 16, 1994. Directed the SEC to prescribe rules that would prohibit deceptive telemarketing acts and practices by brokers and dealers.

Unlisted Trading Privileges Act of 1994 (108 Stat. 4081, 15 U.S.C. 78a note). Signed by the president Oct. 22, 1994. Amended the Securities Exchange Act of 1934 to enable a national securities exchange to extend unlisted trading privileges for corporate securities.

Private Securities Litigation Reform Act of 1995 (109 Stat. 737, 15 U.S.C. 78a note). Signed by the president. Amended the Securities Act of 1933 and the Securities Exchange Act of 1934. Prohibited the SEC from using disgorgement funds resulting from actions in the federal court to pay for legal expenses incurred by private parties seeking distribution of such funds. Authorized the SEC to seek injunctive relief or money penalties against aiders and abettors of securities laws violations. Directed the SEC to make recommendations to the Congress to protect senior citizens and qualified retirement plans from securities fraud and abusive or unnecessary securities fraud litigation.

Telecommunications Act of 1996 (110 Stat. 56, 47 U.S.C. 609 note). Signed by the president Feb. 8, 1996. Title I amended the Public Utility Holding Company Act of 1935 to allow the SEC to determine that a registered holding company providing telecommunications, information, and other related services through a single-purpose subsidiary is an "exempt telecommunications company" (ETC). The relationship between an ETC and a registered holding company will remain subject to SEC's jurisdiction. If a registered holding company or its subsidiary acquires or holds the securities or an interest in the business of an ETC, it must file with the SEC the following information: (1) investments and activities by the registered holding company, or any subsidiary thereof, with respect to the ETCs; and (2) any activities of an ETC within the holding company system that are reasonably likely to have a material impact on the financial or operational condition of the holding company system.

Capital Markets Efficiency Act of 1996 (110 Stat. 3417, 15 U.S.C. 78a note). Signed by the president Oct. 11, 1996. Part of a larger bill. Section 102 directs the SEC to study and to report to the Congress on the extent to which uniformity of state regulatory requirements for securities has been achieved for non-covered securities. Section 108 amended the Securities Exchange Act of 1934 to mandate the SEC and certain self-regulatory organizations to coordinate their examination functions according to prescribed guidelines in order to avoid duplication in the process.

Investment Company Act Amendments of 1996 (110 Stat. 3432, 15 U.S.C. 78a note). Signed by the president Oct. 11, 1996. Part of a larger bill. Section 208 repealed the SEC's authority to bring an action in a U.S. district court for injunctive relief against a violator of unlawful adoption of a name that is materially deceptive or misleading. Section 210 authorized the SEC to provide exemptions from certain investment advisory performance fee contract restrictions to the extent that an exemption relates to a contract with any person that the SEC determines does not need the statutory protections.

Investment Advisers Supervision Coordination Act (110 Stat. 3437, 15 U.S.C. 78a note). Signed by the president Oct. 11, 1996. Part of a larger bill. Section 303 amended the Investment Advisers Act of 1940 to exempt from SEC registration requirements investment advisers subject to a state securities regulator, unless they manage at least $25 million in assets and serve as advisers to certain federally registered investment companies.

Securities and Exchange Commission Authorization Act of 1996 (110 Stat. 3441, 15 U.S.C. 78a note). Signed by the president Oct. 11, 1996. Part of a larger bill. Required the SEC to collect transaction fees and securities registration fees to recover costs to the federal government related to securities registration and market regulation and supervision. Also required national securities exchanges to pay the SEC an annual exchange-traded securities fee and an off-exchange-trades of last-sale-reported securities fee. Fee rates and due dates are to be published in the *Federal Register*. (*See appendix for information on ordering and using this publication.*)

Gramm-Leach-Bliley Act (113 Stat. 1338, 12 U.S.C. 1811 note). Signed by the president Nov. 12, 1999. Repealed provisions of the Banking Act of 1933 and the Bank Holding Act of 1956 to allow affiliations between banks and any financial company, including brokerage and insurance firms. Amended the Securities Exchange Act of 1934 to extend SEC regulation of securities to the securities activities of banks.

Investor and Capital Markets Fee Relief Act (115 Stat. 2390, 15 U.S.C. 78a note). Signed by the president Jan. 16, 2002. Reduced fees on the purchase and sale of securities, on trades of single stock futures, on merger and tender offers, and on security registration fees. Eliminated fees on Trust Indenture applications. Required the SEC to adjust its fees annually after fiscal 2002 to account for changing market conditions. Increased SEC staff salaries by authorizing the SEC to establish an employee compensation system outside of the existing federal civil service system.

Uniting and Strengthening America by Providing Appropriate Tools Required to Intercept and Obstruct Terrorism Act of 2002 (USA Patriot Act). (115 Stat. 272, 18 U.S.C. 1 note). Signed by the president on Oct. 26, 2001. Directed certain federal agencies to investigate and curtail money laundering and other activities that might be undertaken to finance terrorist actions. Required securities brokers and dealers to submit reports regarding suspected money-laundering transactions.

Sarbanes-Oxley Act (116 Stat. 745, 15 U.S.C. 7201 note). Signed by the president July 30, 2002. Established the Public Company Accounting Oversight Board (PCAOB) to police accounting firms and granted the SEC enforcement authority over the board. Amended the Securities Exchange Act of 1934 to prohibit accounting companies from conducting many consulting services for public companies they audit. Directed the SEC to establish rules requiring attorneys to report discovery of corporate wrongdoing to the company's chief legal counsel or CEO and, if necessary, its directors. Required the SEC to conduct a study of corporations' use of off-balance-sheet transactions.

▨ INFORMATION SOURCES

Internet
Agency Web Site: http://www.sec.gov.
FTP Server: ftp.sec.gov.

Both Internet addresses provide access to EDGAR (Electronic Data Gathering, Analysis, and Retrieval). For details about this system, see Reference Resources, below.

A wide range of contact information, including regional and district offices and a listing of e-mail addresses, is provided.

Telephone Contacts
Recorded Information .... (202) 942–8088
TDD .... (202) 942–8092
Publications Orders (recording) .... (202) 942–4046
Washington Service Bureau .... (800) 955–5216
Personnel Locator .... (202) 942–4150
Investor Information Service .... (800) 732–0330
Public Reference .... (202) 942–8090

Information and Publications

KEY OFFICES

SEC Public Affairs
450 5th St. N.W.
Washington, DC 20549
(202) 942–0020
Fax (202) 942–9654
Vacant, director

Issues news releases on important commission decisions, suspensions of trading, and other areas related to the SEC. Also issues the daily *SEC News Digest.* To subscribe, see Publications, below.

SEC Office of Filings and Information Services
450 5th St. N.W.
Washington, DC 20549
(202) 942–8938
TDD (202) 942–7065
Kenneth Fogash, associate executive director

Responsible for the receipt and initial handling of all public documents filed with the commission. Also responsible for keeping the commission's official records, development and implementation of the commission's records management program, and authentication of all documents produced for administrative or judicial proceedings.

Freedom of Information and Privacy Act Operations
450 5th St. N.W.
Washington, DC 20549
(202) 942–4320
Vacant, FOI/Privacy Act officer

To expedite, write "FOIA Request" on the envelope, identify the records desired as specifically as possible, and explain briefly why the records are needed. A pamphlet describing the FOI procedure is listed under Publications, below.

SEC Publications Unit

450 5th St. N.W.
Washington, DC 20549
(202) 272–7040
Printing Branch (202) 942–4040
Orders (recording) (202) 942–4046

Provides selected SEC publications to the public.

PUBLICATIONS

The SEC Publications Section provides the following free titles; note that the recorded order line requires a specific title.

Arbitration Procedures. Explains procedures for disputes with brokerage firms involving financial claims.

Beware of Penny Stock Fraud. Describes warning signs of fraud in the sale of penny stocks.

Consumers Financial Guide. Explains how investors can get help from the SEC.

EDGAR. Describes the SEC's electronic filing system and how companies can use it.

How to Make a FOIA Request. Explains how to obtain information not available in the Public Reference Room.

Information on Bounties. Explains SEC bounties for people who provide information leading to the recovery of a civil penalty from an insider trader.

Investigate Before You Invest. Discusses factors to consider before investing in securities.

Penny Stock Telephone Fraud. How to recognize and avoid it.

Q&A: Small Business and the SEC. Discusses capital formation and the federal securities laws.

Regulation S-K. Standard instructions for filing forms under the 1933 and 1934 acts and the Energy Policy and Conservation Act.

Regulation S-X. Form and requirements for financial statements of the 1933, 1934, and 1935 acts, the Investment Company Act, and the Energy Policy and Conservation Act.

Work of the SEC. Describes the history of the SEC, the laws it administers, and its structure.

The following texts of statutes are free, but a 9"x12" self-addressed, stamped envelope must accompany the order.

Investment Advisers Act of 1940
Investment Company Act of 1940
Public Utility Holding Company Act of 1935
Securities Exchange Act of 1934

The following are selected SEC publications that may be purchased from the U.S. Government Printing Office (GPO): see appendix, Ordering Government Publications.

Annual Report to Congress. Contains statistical data on all aspects of SEC operations, transactions, cases filed and handled, and major problem areas in the securities markets. Past editions also are available for purchase.

Official Summary. Monthly; summary of security transactions and holdings reported by "insiders" (officers, directors, and others) pursuant to provisions of federal securities laws.

Official Summary of Security Transactions and Holdings. Monthly; summary of insider trading activities.

What Every Investor Should Know. Informational brochure on investments.

DATA AND STATISTICS

The Office of Economic Analysis conducts research on various aspects of the securities markets and compiles statistics on the industry. The data are published in the SEC annual report.

Financial and other data included in registration statements, reports, applications, and similar documents filed with the commission are available for inspection in the SEC's Public Reference Room. Copies may be obtained for a fee. Estimates of the cost of copies of specific reports or other information may be obtained from Bechtel, 9430 Key West Ave., Rockville MD 20850; (202) 272–8090 (Public Reference Room) or (301) 417–3000 (MD).

The Public Reference Rooms of the New York and Chicago regional offices also have copies of current annual and other periodic reports (including financial statements) filed by companies whose securities are listed on exchanges. They have copies of the registration statements (and subsequent reports) filed by those companies required to register under the Securities Exchange Act and whose securities are traded on over-the-counter markets.

Prospectuses covering recent public offerings of securities registered under the Securities Act of 1933 may be examined in all regional offices.

Copies of broker-dealer and investment adviser registrations and Regulation A notifications and offering circulars may be examined in the regional office in which they were filed.

MEETINGS

Advance notice of open commission meetings is published the preceding week in the *SEC News Digest.* The Office of the Secretary also provides information as well as audiotapes of open meetings; (202) 942–7070. There is no mailing list for minutes, but they can be requested by mail or picked up in person.

Closed meetings also are announced in the *Digest.* Agendas generally are not published, although in some cases the subject of the meeting is revealed. Agendas of open meetings also are available at the meeting itself.

Reference Resources

LIBRARIES

SEC Library
450 5th St. N.W.
Washington, DC 20549
(202) 942–7090
Cynthia Plisch, library director
Hours: 9:00 a.m. to 5:00 p.m.

Open to the public. No appointment required.

SEC Public Reference Room
450 5th St. N.W., Room 1024
Washington, DC 20549
(202) 942–8090
TTD (202) 942–8092
Valerie Lenyear, branch chief
Hours: 9:00 a.m. to 5:00 p.m.

Contains all filed reports required by the statutes administered by the SEC. These include securities registration statements; information on proxy solicitations; reports on insider trading; and registration statements and/or annual and periodic reports of corporations, national exchanges, over-the-counter brokers and dealers, public utility holding companies, investment companies, and investment advisers. Maintains hard copy of reports and statements for the preceding quarter, and microfiche for reports and statements after 1979 (earlier materials must be ordered from storage). Also maintains reference copies of selected SEC publications and distributes a free *User's Guide to the Public Reference Room.*

This material is available for public inspection and copying. The SEC has a contract for all copying in the Public Reference Room with Discloser Inc., a firm that provides and maintains the machines. Copies are 24 cents plus tax at self-serve machines or 34 cents plus tax for microfiche copies made by Discloser. Individuals may arrange with Discloser to have certain specified materials copied and mailed. Contact Discloser Inc., 4561 River Rd., Bethesda, MD 20816; (202) 272–8090 (Public Reference Room); (301) 951–1300 (MD); or (800) 638–8241.

Many companies offer a service to search SEC files for clients. A list of these companies is available; their representatives work daily in the Public Reference Room and can be contacted there in person.

The Public Reference Rooms located in the Chicago and New York regional offices contain complete information only for their region.

ONLINE

EDGAR
The Electronic Data Gathering, Analysis, and Retrieval (EDGAR) Database, which contains publicly available filings submitted to the SEC from 1994 to the present, is accessible via the agency's Internet addresses and via terminals in the Public Reference Room. It also can be accessed directly from LEXIS/NEXIS, the private contractor that operates the EDGAR dissemination system; 9443 Springboro Pike, Miamisburg, OH 45342; (800) 227–9597.

Since 1994, all businesses that file information with the SEC have been required to use EDGAR. Features include:

Workload Teleprocessing Display (WRKD). Provides an up-to-date listing of filings made by registrants.

Securities Reporting System. An index that provides information on securities transactions by company officers, directors, and beneficial owners.

Proposed Sale of Securities Inquiry (PSSI). Contains information filed on Form 144, which is a notice of the proposed sale of certain securities.

Proceedings and Litigation Action Display (PLAD). Contains public litigation data on federal, state, Canadian, National Association of Securities Dealers, and stock exchange actions.

The public portion of these filings is available in hard copy or on microfiche at the Public Reference Room. Manuals on how to use this system and on how to file via EDGAR are available for reference use at the Public Reference Room or can be requested from Customer Support at the Office of Information Technology; (202) 942–4310. Queries about EDGAR can also be directed by e-mail to webtech@sec.gov.

RULES AND REGULATIONS
SEC rules and regulations are published in the *Code of Federal Regulations,* Title 17. Proposed rules, new final rules, and updates to the *Code of Federal Regulations* are published in the daily *Federal Register. (See appendix for information on how to obtain and use these publications.)*

Other Information Sources

RELATED AGENCY

Securities Investor Protection Corp. (SIPC)
805 15th St. N.W., Suite 800
Washington, DC 20005
(202) 371–8300
Fax (202) 371–6728
Clifford Hudson, chair
Michael Don, president
Stephen Harbeck, general counsel

An independent nongovernmental corporation under the supervision of the SEC and Congress, which was set up in 1970 to protect customers against loss in the event of the financial failure of a securities dealer or broker.

The SIPC provides information to the public, including a pamphlet called *How SIPC Protects You.*

NONGOVERNMENTAL ORGANIZATIONS

The following are some key organizations that monitor the SEC and securities issues.

American Institute of Certified Public Accountants

1211 Avenue of the Americas
New York, NY 10036-8775
(212) 596–6200
Fax (212) 596–6213
Internet: http://www.aicpa.org

Council of Institutional Investors

1730 Rhode Island Ave. N.W., #512
Washington, DC 20036
(202) 822–0800
Fax (202) 822–0801
Internet: http://www.cii.org

Financial Accounting Standards Board

Box 5116
401 Merritt #7
Norwalk, CT 06856-5116
(203) 847–0700
Fax (203) 849-9714
Internet: http://rutgers.edu/accounting/raw/fasb

Investment Company Institute

1401 H St. N.W., #1200
Washington, DC 20005–2148
(202) 326–5800
Fax (202) 326–5806
Internet: http://www.ici.org

Investor Responsibility Research Center

1350 Connecticut Ave. N.W., #700
Washington, DC 20036–1701
(202) 833–0700
Fax (202) 833–3555
Internet: http://www.irrc.org

NASD Regulation, Inc.

11 Penn Center
1835 Market St., 19th Floor
Philadelphia, PA 19103
(215) 665–1180
Fax (215) 496–0434
Internet: http://www.nasdr.com

Nasdaq Stock Market, Inc.

1735 K St. N.W.
Washington, DC 20006
(202) 728–8000
(800) 289–9999
Fax (202) 496–2696
Internet: http://www.nasdaq.com

National Association of Securities Dealers (NASD)

1735 K St. N.W.
Washington, DC 20006–1506
(202) 728–8000
Fax (202) 496–2696
Internet: http://www.nasd.com

New York Stock Exchange

11 Wall St.
New York, NY 10005
(212) 656–3000
Internet: http://www.nyse.com
  Washington office
  801 Pennsylvania Ave. N.W., #630
  Washington, DC 20004
  (202) 293–5740
  Fax (202) 331–4158

PUBLISHERS

The following companies and organizations publish on the SEC and related issues through books, periodicals, or electronic media.

American Law Institute–American Bar Association

Committee on Continuing Legal Education
4025 Chestnut St.
Philadelphia, PA 19104
(800) CLENEWS
Fax (215) 243–1664
Internet: http://www.ali-aba.org

Bureau of National Affairs (BNA), Inc.
1231 25th St. N.W.
Washington, DC 20037
(202) 452–4200
Fax (800) 253–0332
Internet: http://www.bna.com

CDA Investment Technologies
(Thomson Publishing)
1455 Research Blvd.
Rockville, MD 20850
(301) 545–4000
Fax (301) 545–4900
Internet: http://www.cda.com

Commerce Clearing House (CCH), Inc.
2700 Lake Cook Road
Riverwoods, IL 60015
(847) 267–7000
Fax (847) 267–7878
Internet: http://www.cch.com

DIAL/DATA Database
Track Data Corp.
56 Pine St., 7th Floor
New York, NY 10005
(800) 275–5544
Fax (212) 612–2241
Internet: http://www.tdc.com

Dow Jones & Co.
Publications Dept.
170 At the Commons
Shrewsbury, NJ 07072
(732) 389–8700
Fax (732) 389–8701
Internet: http://www.dowjones.com

Little, Brown and Co.
3 Center Plaza
Boston, MA 02108–2084
(800) 759–0190
Fax (617) 263–2871
Internet: http://www.pathfinder.com/twep/little`brown/
Publishes *Securities Regulation* (11 vols.).

Matthew Bender & Co., Inc.
1275 Broadway
Albany, NY 12204
(800) 223–1940
Fax (800) 544–6572
Internet: http://www.bender.com

Media General Financial Services
P.O. Box 85333
Richmond, VA 23293
(804) 649–6587
Fax (804) 649–6097
Internet: http://www.mgfs.com

Prentice Hall
P.O. Box 11701
Des Moines, IA 50336–1071
(800) 643–5506
Fax (800) 835–5327
Internet: http://www.prenhall.com

Standard and Poor's Corp.
25 Broadway
New York, NY 10004
(212) 208–8000
Internet: http://www.mcgraw-hill.com/financial-markets
  Blue List Division
  65 Broadway
  New York, NY 10006
  (212) 770–4300
  Fax (212) 425–6864
  Internet: http://www.bluelist.com

Towers Data Systems
Valport System
6707 Democracy Blvd., #310
Bethesda, MD 20817
(800) 464–4976
Fax (301) 530–6011
Internet: http://www.towersdata.com/products/products_
  valport.asp

Value Line
220 E. 42nd St.
New York, NY 10017
(800) 654–0508
Fax (212) 907–1913
Internet: http://www.valueline.com

West Group
115 Pfingsten Rd.
Deerfield, IL 60015
(800) 221–9428
Fax (847) 948–7005
Internet: http://www.westgroup.com

Other Regulatory Agencies

Architectural and Transportation Barriers Compliance Board

1331 F St. N.W., Suite 1000, Washington, DC 20004–1111
Internet: http://www.access-board.gov

The Architectural and Transportation Barriers Compliance Board (ATBCB), referred to as the Access Board, was created under Section 502 of the Rehabilitation Act of 1973 to enforce the provisions of the Architectural Barriers Act (ABA) of 1968. The ABA requires that all facilities owned, rented, or funded in any part by the federal government after September 1969 be accessible to and usable by persons with disabilities.

Since enactment of the Americans with Disabilities Act (ADA) of 1990, the Access Board has been responsible for developing ADA Accessibility Guidelines (minimum accessibility guidelines for places of public accommodation, commercial facilities, state and local government facilities, and transportation vehicles and facilities) and for offering training and technical assistance to individuals and organizations on how to remove architectural, transportation, and communication barriers.

The Access Board is an independent federal agency with twenty-five board members. The president appoints thirteen public members (a majority of whom must be people with disabilities) to four-year terms. The remaining twelve board members represent the departments of Commerce, Defense, Education, Health and Human Services, Housing and Urban Development, Interior, Justice, Labor, Transportation, and Veterans Affairs; the General Services Administration; and the U.S. Postal Service. An executive director heads the Access Board staff.

The Access Board establishes minimum guidelines and requirements for standards under the ADA. It proposes alternative solutions to barriers facing persons with disabilities in housing, transportation, communications, education, recreation, and public attitudes. Along these lines, it also determines what federal, state, and local governments and other public or private agencies and groups are doing to eliminate barriers.

In October 2000 the Access Board published accessibility guidelines for newly built or altered play areas under ADA. The guidelines address play areas provided at schools, parks, child care facilities (except those based in the operator's home, which are exempt), and other facilities subject to the ADA.

Under the ADA, the Access Board is responsible for developing and maintaining accessibility guidelines for transportation vehicles. When it originally issued the ADA Accessibility Guidelines for Transportation Vehicles, the Access Board reserved requirements for passenger vessels pending further study and gathering of information. In August 1998 the Access Board created the Passenger Vessel Access Advisory Committee to provide recommendations for a proposed rule addressing accessibility guidelines for newly constructed and altered passenger vessels covered by the ADA. The committee completed its work in November 2000 and submitted its report to the Access Board. Final action is pending.

The Access Board offers training and technical assistance to individuals and organizations on the removal of architectural, transportation, and communication barriers and ensures that public conveyances can be used by persons with disabilities. It also prepares plans for adequate transportation and housing for persons with disabilities, including proposals to cooperate with other agencies, organizations, and individuals working toward such goals.

In August 1998 President Bill Clinton signed into law the Rehabilitation Act Amendments of 1998 that covered access to federally funded programs and services. In December the Access Board issued accessibility standards for electronic and information technology under Section 508 of the Rehabilitation Act, as amended. Enforcement of Section 508 began in June 2001.

The law strengthened section 508 of the Rehabilitation Act and required access to electronic and information technology provided by the federal government. The law applied to all federal agencies when they develop, procure, maintain, or use electronic and information technology. Federal agencies had to ensure that this technology was accessible to employees and members of the public with disabilities to the extent it did not pose an undue burden. Section 508 listed various means for disseminating information, including federal Web sites. The law empowered the Access Board to develop accessibility standards for such technology for incorporation into regulations that govern federal procurement practices. The law also provided a complaint process under which complaints concerning access to technology will be investigated by the responsible federal agency.

In 2000 the Access Board and the American Institute of Architects (AIA) unveiled a Web-based education course on the Access Board's ADA Accessibility Guidelines (ADAAG). The course focuses on supplements to ADAAG that cover public facilities, including courthouses and prisons, and building elements designed for children's use. The AIA is making this course available on its Web site to train architects.

In 2002 Congress passed an election reform bill that was intended to prevent the type of ballot controversies that arose in the presidential election of 2000, particularly in the state of Florida. The Help America Vote Act of 2002 established requirements for voting systems used in federal elections that would allow voters to verify and correct their selections before casting a ballot, remove language barriers, and permit provisional voting where eligible voters were not listed on official registration lists. The bill also contained key provisions on improving access to polling places and voting systems for persons with disabilities. The law required every precinct in the country to have at least one voting machine or system accessible to persons with disabilities, including those with vision impairments, by Jan. 1, 2006.

The measure created a new independent entity, the Election Assistance Commission, to oversee the development of guidelines for voting systems that were to include provisions for accessibility. The guidelines were to be developed through several advisory bodies, with the Access Board represented on some of these entities.

The Access Board may conduct investigations, hold public hearings, and issue orders to comply with the ABA. An order is final and binding on any federal department, agency, or instrumentality of the United States. The Access Board responds to all complaints it receives about an inaccessible federally funded building or facility. The board first tries to resolve complaints informally. If necessary, legal proceedings before an administrative law judge may be initiated.

It is not necessary to file a complaint to obtain information and assistance from the board. The agency maintains extensive files on bibliographies, products, and other resources on accessibility; it also may direct inquiries to officials in state, local, or other federal agencies or private organizations.

The ATBC reports annually to the president and Congress on investigations, actions, and extent of compliance with the ABA.

■ KEY PERSONNEL

Executive Director
Lawrence Roffee . . . . (202) 272–0080
Compliance and Enforcement
Jeff Hill . . . . (202) 272–0080
General Counsel
James Raggio . . . . (202) 272–0080
Technical and Information Services
David Capozzi . . . . (202) 272–0080

■ INFORMATION SOURCES

Internet

Agency Web Site: http://www.access–board.gov. Includes information on ATBCB guidelines and publications.
E-mail: info@access-board.gov

Telephone Contacts

Personnel Locator . . . . (202) 272–0080
Agency Fax . . . . (202) 272–0081
Technical Assistance (toll-free) . . . . (800) 872–2253
TDD (toll-free) . . . . (800) 993–2822

Information and Publications

KEY OFFICES

ATBCB Public Affairs
1331 F St. N.W., #1000
Washington, DC 20004–1111
(202) 272–0026
David Yanchulis, contact

Issues news releases, prepares and distributes the board's annual report, and answers or refers general questions. Distributes ATBCB publications, which are free and often available in alternative formats such as Braille, large type, cassette, and floppy disk.

Freedom of Information

1331 F St. N.W., #1000
Washington, DC 20004–1111
(202) 272–0042
Elizabeth Stewart, contact

PUBLICATIONS

Various publications, including all ATBCB guidelines and standards, are available free from the ATBCB and its Web site. These publications include:

About the Architectural Barriers Act and Other Disability Rights' Laws.

ADA Accessibility Guidelines and the Uniform Federal Accessibility Standards. Provides design criteria for the construction and alteration of buildings and facilities. Checklists, manuals, and technical bulletins related to these documents are also available.

ADA Accessibility Guidelines for Transportation Vehicles. Provides accessibility requirements for buses, vans, rail vehicles, and other modes of public transportation.

Telecommunications Act Accessibility Guidelines.

Standards for Electronic and Information Technology.

Access Currents. The Boards bimonthly newsletter.

A checklist of publications is available. For further information contact the ATBCB or visit its Web site.

MEETINGS

The board meets six times a year usually in Washington, D.C.; public hearings may be held in different locations around the country to give people with disabilities outside the Washington area the opportunity to express their opinions to the board.

After each meeting, the board publishes *Access Currents* to cover actions taken at the meeting. It can be obtained through the Public Affairs office, or interested individuals can subscribe to it by e-mailing their names and mailing addresses to news access-board.gov.

Reference Resources

LIBRARY

ATBCB Library

1331 F St. N.W., #1000
Washington, DC 20004–1111
(202) 272–0021
Forrest J. Pecht, librarian
Hours: 9:00 a.m. to 5:00 p.m.

RULES AND REGULATIONS

ATBCB rules and regulations are published in the *Code of Federal Regulations,* Title 36, parts 1151 (bylaws), 1191 (buildings), 1192 (vehicles), 1193 (telecommunication products) and 1194 (electronic and information technology). Proposed rules, new final rules, and updates to the *Code of Federal Regulations* are published in the daily *Federal Register.* (See appendix for information on how to obtain and use these publications.)

▉ LEGISLATION

The ATBCB administers the following laws:

Architectural Barriers Act of 1968 (82 Stat. 718, 42 U.S.C. 4151 et seq.). Signed by the president Aug. 12, 1968. Ensured that buildings and facilities designed, constructed, altered, or leased with certain federal funds after September 1969 are accessible to people with disabilities.

Rehabilitation Act of 1973 (87 Stat. 355, 29 U.S.C. 792). Signed by the president Sept. 26, 1973. Established the ATBCB to enforce disability access laws. Barred discrimination by the federal government against persons with disabilities.

Fair Housing Amendments Act of 1988 (102 Stat. 1619, 42 U.S.C. 3601 note). Signed by the president Sept. 13, 1988. Prohibited discrimination in the sale or rental of housing to persons with disabilities.

Americans with Disabilities Act of 1990 (104 Stat. 327, 42 U.S.C. 1201 note). Signed by the president July 26, 1990. Titles II and III provided Americans with disabilities, including those with AIDS, the same rights to jobs, public transportation, and public accommodations that women and racial, religious, and ethnic minorities receive under the Civil Rights Act of 1964.

Telecommunications Act of 1996 (110 Stat. 56, 47 U.S.C. 609 note). Signed by the president Feb. 8, 1996. Gave the ATBCB additional authority to set guidelines for telecommunications equipment and customer premises equipment.

Rehabilitation Act Amendments of 1998 (29 U.S.C. 794 d). Signed by the president Aug. 7, 1998. Section 508, as amended by the Workforce Investment Act of 1998, required federal agencies to make their electronic and information technology accessible to people with disabilities. The law applied to all federal agencies when they develop, procure, maintain, or use electronic and information technology.

Help America Vote Act of 2002 (42 U.S.C. 15301 et seq.). Signed by the president Nov. 7, 2002. Required voting systems to be accessible for individuals with disabilities. Established the Election Assistance Commission to serve as a national clearinghouse and resource for the compilation of information and review of procedures with respect to the administration of federal elections.

Commodity Futures Trading Commission

3 Lafayette Center, 1155 21st St. N.W., Washington, DC 20581
Internet: http://www.cftc.gov

The Commodity Futures Trading Commission (CFTC) was established in 1975 as an independent agency to administer the Commodity Exchange Act of 1936. The 1974 legislation establishing the CFTC authorized its operations for four years. Congress extended authorization for an additional four years in 1978 and 1982, for three years in 1986, for two years in 1992, and for five years in 1995 and 2000. Its mandate is to regulate commodity futures and option markets in the United States.

The purpose of the commission is to further the economic utility of futures markets by encouraging their efficiency, ensuring their integrity, and protecting participants against abusive trade practices, fraud, and deceit. The objective is to enable the markets to serve their designated function: to provide a price discovery mechanism and a means of offsetting price risk to contribute to better planning, more efficient distribution and consumption, and more economical marketing.

The commission is composed of five members appointed by the president and confirmed by the Senate, with one member designated as chair. Members serve five-year terms arranged so that one term expires each year. No more than three members of the commission may belong to the same political party.

The CFTC is funded by an annual appropriation by Congress. The CFTC has authority to charge the industry fees for services such as approval of contracts and the registration of leverage commodities.

The commission oversees futures and options trading on sixteen exchanges and trading in certain off-exchange trade options. A futures contract is a firm commitment to deliver or to receive a specified quantity and grade of a commodity during a designated month, with the price being determined by public auction among exchange members. A futures option is a unilateral contract that enables the holder to buy or sell a futures contract at a set price at a specified time, regardless of the market price of that commodity.

The commission routinely monitors the trading in more than 130 actively traded futures contracts, including physical commodities such as lumber, precious metals, petroleum products, coffee, frozen concentrated orange juice, livestock, grains, and pork bellies; financial instruments, such as currencies, Treasury bonds, and Eurodollars; various indices in stocks, currencies, and other commodities; and options on futures contracts and options on physical commodities. In recent years new futures contracts have been offered in various other nontraditional commodity areas such as seafood, dairy products, crop yields, and energy commodities, such as oil and natural gas.

The 1982 authorizing legislation delineated the jurisdictions of the CFTC and the Securities and Exchange Commission, affirming exclusive CFTC authority over commodity futures contracts and options on futures, including futures and options on so-called exempted securities, such as instruments of the Government National Mortgage Association and Treasury bills, but not on municipal securities.

The 1982 law also required the industry's self-regulatory group, the National Futures Association (NFA), to begin actively sharing regulatory responsibilities with the CFTC. The CFTC has since delegated to the NFA authority to register brokers and certain commodity professionals, to audit records and bank accounts, and to enforce compliance of member firms to rules and regulations of both the NFA and CFTC.

The Commodity Futures Modernization Act of 2000 created a flexible structure for regulation of futures trading, codified an agreement between the CFTC and the Securities and Exchange Commission to repeal the eighteen-year-old ban on trading single stock futures, and provided legal certainty for the over-the-counter derivatives markets. The law, which reauthorized the CFTC for five years, also clarified the Treasury Amendment exclusion and specifically granted the CFTC authority over retail foreign exchange trading.

The Patriot Act of 2001, which amended the Bank Secrecy Act, was adopted in response to 2001 terrorist attacks. The Patriot Act was intended to strengthen U.S. measures to prevent, detect, and prosecute international money laundering and the financing of terrorism. These efforts included new antimoney laundering tools that affected the banking, financial, and investment communities. Under the act, persons who were required to be registered as futures commission merchants, introducing brokers, commodity pool operators, and commodity trading advisors were subject to new requirements for establishing antimoney laundering programs, reporting suspicious activity, verifying the identity of customers, and dealing with certain types of accounts involving foreign persons.

The commission has five major operating units: (1) the Division of Enforcement investigates allegations of fraud or manipulation and conducts all other enforcement proceedings; (2) the Division of Economic Analysis monitors trading, reviews proposed futures contracts, and conducts or sponsors research on futures markets; (3) the Division of Trading and Markets performs market analysis and supervises audit procedures; (4) the Office of the General Counsel acts as the CFTC's legal advisor and represents the Commission in appellate litigation and certain trial-level cases, including bankruptcy proceedings that involve futures industry professionals; and (5) the Office of the Executive Director formulates and implements the management and administrative policies and functions of the agency.

Specific responsibilities of the commission include:

Regulating Exchanges. All exchanges on which commodities are traded for future delivery are regulated by the commission. The commission reviews and approves rules and may require a market to change its rules or practices. In emergencies the CFTC may direct an exchange to take action to maintain or restore orderly markets. Under commission rules, procedures must be developed to settle customer complaints against members and employees of exchanges.

Approving Futures Contracts. The commission must approve all futures and options contracts traded on exchanges. Contracts must reflect normal market flow and commercial trading practices in the actual commodity being traded and provide for a broad deliverable supply. A limit may be imposed on the number of contracts a single speculator may trade or hold.

Regulation of Futures Professionals. Companies and individuals who handle customer funds or give trading advice must apply for registration through the National Futures Association (NFA), a self-regulatory organization approved by the commission. The CFTC also seeks to protect customers by requiring registrants to disclose market risks and past performance information to prospective customers, by requiring that customer funds be kept in accounts separate from those maintained by the firm for its own use, and by requiring customer accounts to be adjusted to reflect the current market value at the close of trading each day. In addition, the CFTC monitors registrant supervision systems, internal controls, and sales practice compliance programs. Further, all registrants are required to complete ethics training.

Protecting Customers. The commission sets minimum financial requirements for futures brokers and option dealers and requires that customer funds be segregated from company funds. The commission operates a reparation process to adjudicate and settle customer complaints.

Monitoring Information. The commission requires that information provided by exchanges, such as volume and open interest, be timely and accurate. It monitors market letters, reports, and statistics provided by traders, brokers, trading advisers, and commodity pool operators. The commission analyzes written complaints of staff-detected problems and enforces the law by filing cases in federal district court or through administrative proceedings before agency administrative law judges. Enforcement actions may lead to the loss of trading rights or a substantial fine.

■ KEY PERSONNEL

Chair and Commissioner
James E. Newsome......................(202) 418-5050
Commissioners
Barbara Pederson Holum..............(202) 418-5070
Walter Lukken..........................(202) 418-5040
Sharon Brown-Hruska.................(202) 418-5060
Office of Chief Economist
James Overdahl.........................(202) 418-5260
Enforcement
Gregory Mocek.........................(202) 418-5320
Counsel
Marcia Blase............................(202) 418-5030
Secretariat
Jean Webb...............................(202) 418-5100
Executive Director
Madge Bollinger.......................(202) 418-5160
General Counsel
Patrick J. McCarty.....................(202) 418-5120

Inspector General

A. Roy Lavik .... (202) 418–5110

Division of Clearing and Intermediary Oversight

Jane Kang Thorpe .... (202) 418–5430

Division of Market Oversight

Michael Gorham........................(202) 418–5260

■ INFORMATION SOURCES

Internet

Agency Web Site: http://www.cftc.gov.

Telephone Contacts

Personnel Locator .... (202) 418-5000

Fax .... (202) 418-5521

Information and Publications

KEY OFFICES

CFTC Office of External Affairs

Three Lafayette Centre
1155 21st St. N.W.
Washington, DC 20581
(202) 418-5080
Alan Sobba, director
Internet: http://www.cftc.gov
Toll-free complaint line (866) 366–2382

Issues press releases and media advisories; publishes newsletters and pamphlets of general information.

Freedom of Information

Three Lafayette Centre
1155 21st St. N.W.
Washington, DC 20581
(202) 418-5105
Eileen Donovan, FOI officer

Complaints Section

Three Lafayette Centre
1155 21st St. N.W.
Washington, DC 20581
(202) 418-5250
R. Britt Lenz, director

Reparation is available for any valid claim filed within two years after the violation occurs. To obtain a pamphlet detailing the reparation procedure or to file a claim, contact this office.

REPORTS AND PUBLICATIONS

Available from CFTC Public Affairs unless otherwise specified. Titles include:

Annual Report. Summation of commission activities during the year.

CFTC Regulations. Title 17 of the *Code of Federal Regulations,* revised annually in April; available from the U.S. Government Printing Office (GPO): see appendix, Ordering Government Publications.

Foreign Instrument Approvals & Exemptions.

Regulatory and Self-Regulatory Authorities That Have Received Exemptions Under CFTC Rule 30.10.

The CFTC: An Active Partner in Global Cooperation Through Information-Sharing with Other Financial Regulators.

Futures and Option Contracts Approved by the Commodity Futures Trading Commission as of September 30, 2000.

The Commitments of Traders Report (COT).

Speculative Limits, Hedging, and Aggregation.

The CFTC Market Surveillance Program.

Commodity Trading Advisors and Commodity Pool Operators.

The CFTC's Large-Trader Reporting System.

Economic Purposes of Commodity Futures Trading.

Futures & Options: What You Should Know Before You Trade.

The Reparations Program.

2002 Annual Report to Congress.

FY 2004 President's Budget.

FY 2004 Annual Performance Plan.

Report on the Study of the Commodity Exchange Act and the Commission's Rules and Orders Governing the Conduct of Registrants Under the Act.

Report on Futures Industry Response to September 11th.

Opportunities for Strategic Change: Commodity Futures Trading.

Commission Strategic Plan 2000–2005.

FY 2001 Inventory of Commercial Activities Performed by CFTC Employees.

Five-Year Plan for Information Resources Management FY 2000–2004.

The Commitments of Traders Report.

Deliveries on CBOT U.S. Treasury Bond/Note Futures.

Bank Participation in Futures and Options Market Reports.

Cotton "on-call" Report.

Historical Cotton "on-call" Reports.

Selected Futures Commission Merchants (FCMs) Financial Reports.

Report on Cattle Futures Trading During March/April 2002; prepared by CFTC Market Surveillance: Staff Report; USDA Timeline of Events; Appendices to Staff Report; Updated Appendices to Staff Report (06/21/02).

The Global Competitiveness of U.S. Futures Markets Revisited.

Policy Alternatives Relating to Agricultural Trade Options and Other Agricultural Risk-Shifting Contracts.

A Study of the Global Competitiveness of U.S. Futures Markets.

OTC Derivative Markets and Their Regulation.

DATA AND STATISTICS

The commission releases a biweekly *Commitments of Traders Compressed Reports* that shows, for each commodity traded, current trading statistics, including a breakdown of speculative and hedge positions among large (reportable) traders and aggregate positions for small (non-reporting) traders. *Data from Commitments of Traders Compressed Reports* are available to the public through a variety of intermediaries. For a list of providers or information on how to obtain historical COT data, contact the Division of Economic Analysis, (202) 418-5260.

MEETINGS

The CFTC meets in executive session in the Hearing Room at its headquarters. Meetings are open to the public unless the subject of the meeting is exempt under the Government in the Sunshine Act.

Notices of scheduled commission meetings are announced in advance, usually in news releases and always in the *Weekly Advisory,* mailed each Friday. They also are posted on CFTC's Internet home page. The office of the secretariat keeps an up-to-date list of meetings; (202) 418-5100.

Reference Resources

LIBRARY

CFTC Library
Three Lafayette Centre
1155 21st St. N.W.
Washington, DC 20581
(202) 418-5255
Daniel May, librarian

Generally closed to the public. Interlibrary loan service is available to authorized libraries.

DOCKETS

CFTC Office of Proceedings
Three Lafayette Centre
1155 21st St. N.W.
Washington, DC 20581
(202) 418-5508
Tempest Thomas, proceedings clerk

Documents Office of the Secretariat
Three Lafayette Centre
1155 21st St. N.W.
Washington, DC 20581
(202) 418-5100
Jean Webb, director

Public records and documents of the CFTC are available for inspection in these offices.

RULES AND REGULATIONS

Rules and regulations of the CFTC are published in the *Code of Federal Regulations,* Title 17, chapter 1. Proposed regulations, new final regulations, and updates to the *Code of Federal Regulations* are published in the daily *Federal Register.* (See appendix for details on how to obtain and use these publications.)

▉ LEGISLATION

The CFTC carries out its responsibilities under:

Grain Futures Act (42 Stat. 998, 7 U.S.C. 1-17). Signed by the president Sept. 21, 1922. Empowered the secretary of agriculture to give markets the federal authority to trade commodities, or to revoke markets' authority.

Commodity Exchange Act (49 Stat. 1491, 7 U.S.C. chap. 1). Signed by the president June 15, 1936. Established the Commodity Exchange Authority in the Agriculture Department to regulate commodity brokerage activities and commodity fraud.

Commodity Futures Trading Commission Act of 1974 (88 Stat. 1389, 7 U.S.C. 4a). Signed by the president Oct. 23, 1974. Amended the Commodity Exchange Act and established the CFTC as an independent agency to replace the Commodity Exchange Authority.

Futures Trading Act of 1978 (92 Stat. 865, 7 U.S.C. chap. 1). Signed by the president Sept. 30, 1978. Reauthorized the CFTC to Sept. 30, 1982.

Futures Trading Act of 1982 (96 Stat. 2294, 7 U.S.C. chap. 1). Signed by the president Jan. 11, 1983. Reauthorized the CFTC to Sept. 30, 1986.

Futures Trading Act of 1986 (100 Stat. 3556, 7 U.S.C. chap. 1). Signed by the president Nov. 10, 1986. Reauthorized the CFTC to Sept. 30, 1989.

Futures Trading Practices Act of 1992 (106 Stat. 3590. 7 U.S.C. 1 note). Signed by the president Oct. 28, 1992. Reauthorized the CFTC to Sept. 30, 1994. Required futures exchanges to put in place electronic or computerized systems to audit and monitor all floor trades. Authorized the CFTC to exempt certain new financial instruments, such as swaps or hybrids, from regulations applied to other futures products.

Commodity Futures Modernization Act (114 Stat. 2763, 7 U.S.C. chap. 1). Signed by the president Dec. 21, 2000. Created a flexible structure for the regulation of futures trading, codified an agreement between the CFTC and the SEC to repeal the ban on trading single stock futures, and provided regulation for the over-the-counter derivatives markets.

Uniting and Strengthening America by Providing Appropriate Tools Required to Intercept and Obstruct Terrorism Act of 2002 (USA Patriot Act) (115 Stat. 272, 18 U.S.C. 1 note). Signed by the president on Oct. 26, 2001. (Sec. 321) Required registered securities brokers and dealers, futures commission merchants, commodity trading advisors, and commodity pool operators to file reports of suspicious financial transactions and share monetary instruments transactions records upon request of a U.S. intelligence agency for use in the conduct of intelligence or counterintelligence activities to protect against international terrorism.

◾ REGIONAL OFFICES

EASTERN REGION
140 Broadway, 19th Floor
New York, NY 10005
(646) 746–9700

CENTRAL REGION
525 W. Monroe St., #1100
Chicago, IL 60661
(312) 596–0700
Fax (312) 353–9126

SOUTHWESTERN REGION
4900 Main St., #721
Kansas City, MO 64112
(816) 931–7600
Fax (816) 931–9643

MINNEAPOLIS OFFICE - SOUTHWESTERN REGION
510 Grain Exchange Building
Minneapolis, MN 55415
(612) 370–3255
Fax (612) 370–3257

Selected Self-Regulatory Organizations
National Futures Association
200 W. Madison St.
Chicago, IL 60606
Toll-free (800) 621–3570
or (800) 676–4NFA
www.nfa.futures.org

Regulated Markets
Brokertec Futures Exchange
1 Evertrust Plaza
Jersey City, NJ 07302
(201) 209–7800
www.btecfutures.com

Chicago Board of Trade
141 W. Jackson Blvd.
Chicago, IL 60604
(312) 435–3500
www.cbot.com

Chicago Board Options Exchange
400 S. LaSalle St.
Chicago, IL 60605
(877) THE–CBOE

Chicago Mercantile Exchange
30 S. Wacker Dr.
Chicago, IL 60606
(312) 930–1000
www.cme.com

The Island ECN
50 Broad St., 6th Floor
New York, NY 10004
(212) 231–5000
www.island.com

Kansas City Board of Trade
4800 Main St., #303
Kansas City, MO 64112
(816) 753–7500
www.kcbt.com

Minneapolis Grain Exchange
400 S. Fourth St.
Minneapolis, MN 55415
(612) 338–6212
www.mgex.com

Nasdaq Liffe Markets, LLC
1 Liberty Plaza
165 Broadway, 50th Floor
New York, NY 10006
(212) 858–4453
www.nqlx.com

New York Board of Trade
1 North End Ave.
New York, NY 10282
www.nybot.com

New York Mercantile Exchange
1 North End Ave.
New York, NY 10282
(212) 299–2000
www.nymex.com

OneChicago
141 W. Jackson Blvd., #2208-A
Chicago, IL 60604
(312) 424–8500
www.onechicago.com

onExchange, Inc.
1 Alewife Center
Cambridge, MA 02140
(617) 665–9100
www.onexchange.com

Farm Credit Administration

1501 Farm Credit Dr., McLean, VA 22102–5090
Internet: http://www.fca.gov

The Farm Credit Administration (FCA) is an independent agency responsible for examining and regulating the activities of the Farm Credit System (FCS), a nationwide system of borrower-owned financial institutions organized as cooperatives. Under the Farm Credit Act of 1971, it is empowered to issue cease-and-desist orders, levy civil money penalties, remove officers and directors of system institutions, and place such institutions into conservatorship or receivership. The FCA, however, does not mediate disputes between borrowers and FCS financial institutions.

The FCA is the safety and soundness regulator of the FCS. FCA charters, regulates, and examines the 147 banks, associations, and service corporations of the FCS. FCS institutions make loans to agricultural producers and their cooperatives nationwide.

FCA policy is set by a three-member board, appointed by the president and confirmed by the Senate. The chair is designated the chief executive officer. Board members serve six-year terms and are not eligible for reappointment. The FCA board members also serve on the board of the Farm Credit System Insurance Corporation.

The Farm Credit System (FCS) is a network of borrower-owned lending institutions and related service organizations serving all fifty states and the Commonwealth of Puerto Rico. These institutions specialize in providing credit and related services to farmers, ranchers, and producers or harvesters of aquatic products. Loans may also be made to finance the processing and marketing activities of these borrowers. In addition, loans may be made to rural homeowners, certain farm-related businesses, and agricultural, aquatic, and public utility cooperatives.

All FCS banks and associations are governed by boards of directors elected by the stockholders who are farmer-borrowers of each institution. Federal law also requires that at least one member of the board be elected from outside the FCS by the other directors. FCS institutions, unlike commercial banks or thrifts, do not take deposits.

As of January 2003, the FCS was composed of the following lending institutions:

- Five Farm Credit Banks (FCBs) that provide loan funds to eighty-one Agricultural Credit Associations (ACAs), and thirteen Federal Land Credit Associations (FLCAs). PCAs make short- and intermediate-term loans, ACAS make short-, intermediate-, and long-term loans, and FLCAs make long-term loans.

- One Agricultural Credit Bank (ACB), which has the authority of an FCB and provides loan funds to five ACAs. In addition, the ACB makes loans of all kinds to agricultural, aquatic, and public utility cooperatives and is authorized to finance U.S. agricultural exports and provide international banking services for farmer-owned cooperatives.

The following FCS entities also are examined and regulated by FCA:

- The Federal Farm Credit Banks Funding Corporation (Funding Corporation) is an entity owned by the FCS banks that markets the securities the banks sell to raise loan funds. FCS institutions obtain the majority of their loan funds through the sale of these securities in the nation's capital markets. These securities, chiefly bonds and discount notes, are offered by the Funding Corporation through a nationwide group of securities dealers and dealer banks.

- The Farm Credit System Financial Assistance Corporation (Assistance Corporation) was created by the Agricultural Credit Act of 1987 and chartered in 1988 to provide needed capital to the FCS through the purchase of preferred stock issued by FCS institutions that received financial assistance authorized by the Farm Credit System

Assistance Board. Approximately $1.26 billion in funds were provided by the Assistance Corporation, and its authority to raise additional funds expired on Dec. 31, 1992. This entity is managed by the same board of directors as the Funding Corporation and will continue to operate until all funds used to provide the assistance are repaid.

- The Federal Agricultural Mortgage Corporation, also known as Farmer Mac, provides a secondary market for agricultural real estate and rural housing mortgages. It guarantees the timely payment of principal and interest on securities representing interests in, or obligations backed by, mortgage loans secured by first liens on agricultural real estate or rural housing. It also guarantees securities backed by the "guaranteed portions" of farm ownership and operating loans, rural business and community development loans, and certain other loans guaranteed by the U.S. Department of Agriculture. Farmer Mac also purchases or commits to purchase qualified loans or securities backed by qualified loans directly from lenders.

Service corporations organized under the Farm Credit Act of 1971 are also examined and regulated by the FCA. These include (1) the Farm Credit Finance Corporation of Puerto Rico, which uses tax incentives offered to investors to provide low-interest funding (other than that from the Funding Corporation) to the Puerto Rico Farm Credit, ACA; (2) the Farm Credit Leasing Services Corporation (Leasing Corporation), which provides equipment leasing services to eligible borrowers, including agricultural producers, cooperatives, and rural utilities. The Leasing Corporation is owned primarily by two FCS banks—CoBank, ACB and AgFirst Farm Credit Bank (the other banks are nonvoting stockholders); (3) Farm Credit Financial Partners, Inc., which provides support services to the associations affiliated with CoBank, ACB, and the Western Farm Credit Bank; and (4) the FCS Building Association (FCSBA), which acquires, manages, and maintains facilities to house FCA's headquarters and field office staff. The FCSBA was formed in 1981 and is owned by the FCS banks. The FCA Board oversees the FCSBA's activities on behalf of its owners; (5) AgVantis Inc. provides technology-related and other support services to the associations affiliated with the Farm Credit Bank of Wichita. AgVantis, which was chartered by FCA in August 2001, is owned by the bank and its affiliated associations.

The Office of Examination monitors the financial activities of the Farm Credit System. Field operations are managed by directors located in Bloomington, Minn.; Dallas, Texas; Denver, Colo.; McLean, Va.; Sacramento, Calif., and the Special Examination and Supervision Division (SESD), located in McLean, Va. In addition, the SESD is responsible for managing the FCA's enforcement activities. The office examines the corporations within the FCS.

The regional offices examine the FCS institutions within their jurisdictions under the supervision of the Office of Examination. The Agricultural Credit Act of 1987 required the FCA to draft new examination regulations, update its examination manual, and analyze the quality of financial disclosure information provided to stockholders.

The Office of General Counsel (OGC) provides legal advice and services to the FCA Board and agency staff. OGC renders legal opinions relating to the powers, duties, and authorities of the agency and FCS institutions. It also provides legal support for the development and promulgation of FCA regulations and legislation affecting the agency. In addition, OGC represents the agency in enforcement proceedings initiated by FCA, in proceedings before other administrative bodies, and, in coordination with the Department of Justice, in other litigation. OGC also processes requests under the Freedom of Information Act and the Privacy Act and reviews agency compliance with other federal laws.

The Office of Inspector General is an independent office within FCA established by law to conduct, supervise, and coordinate audits, investigations, and operations reviews relating to FCA's programs and operations; review existing and proposed legislation and regulations and to make recommendations to the Congress concerning the impact on the economy and efficiency of programs and operations administered by FCA or the prevention and detection of fraud and abuse; and keep the chair of the agency and Congress fully and currently informed.

The Office of the Ombudsman, established in 2003, serves as an effective, neutral, and confidential resource and liaison for the public.

In January 2001 the FCA proposed to amend its regulations to provide procedures for requesting national charters. The proposed rule would also require each association with a national charter to extend sound and constructive credit to eligible and creditworthy customers in its Local Service Area (LSA). In addition, the FCA proposed to establish controls through new business planning requirements for an association with a national charter. FCA formerly withdrew this regulation from the Unified Agenda on Oct. 11, 2001.

▓ KEY PERSONNEL

Board

Michael M. Reyna, chair .... (703) 883–4005

Fax .... (703) 790–5241

Members

Douglas L. Flory .... (703) 883–4011

Nancy O. Pellett .... (703) 883–4008

Secretary to the Board

Jeanette Brinkley .... (703) 883–4009

Chief Administrative Officer
Philip Shebest............................(703) 883–4135
Chief Financial Officer
W. B. Erwin ....(703) 883–4099
Chief Information Officer
Doug Valcour ....(703) 883–4300
Equal Employment Opportunity
Eric Howard ....(703) 883–4481
Examination
Roland E. Smith ....(703) 883–4160
General Counsel
Charles Rawls...........................(703) 883–4020
Inspector General
Stephen Smith ....(703) 883–4030
Policy and Analysis
Michael V. Dunn........................(703) 883–4414

■ INFORMATION SOURCES

Internet

Agency Web Site: http://www.fca.gov. Includes information on the FCA and its board members.

Telephone Contacts

Personnel Locator ....(703) 883–4000
TDD...(703) 883–4444

Information and Publications

KEY OFFICES

FCA Communications and Public Affairs

1501 Farm Credit Dr.
McLean, VA 22102-5090
(703) 883–4056
Hal C. DeCell III, director (Acting)

FCA Congressional and Legislative Affairs

(703) 883–4056
Hal C. DeCell III, director
(Serves as FCA's liaison with Congress)

Answers general questions about the FCA and the Farm Credit System, and provides information and publications.

Freedom of Information

1501 Farm Credit Dr.
McLean, VA 22102–5090
(703) 883–4020
Fax (703) 790–0052
Debra Buccolo, FOI officer

PUBLICATIONS

Communications and Public Affairs distributes a number of FCA publications, including the FCA annual performance and accountability report. Other published works include *Farm Credit Administration Strategic Plan,* and *Office of Inspector General Semiannual Report.* A complete catalogue of publications is available at http://www.fca.gov.

A copy of the Farm Credit Act (P.L. 92–181), as amended, the regulations of the FCA, and one year's updates to this information, are available for $50 from the FCA Mail Center; (703) 883–4291.

REGULATIONS

FCA regulations are published in the *Code of Federal Regulations,* Title 12, parts 600–621. Proposed regulations, new final regulations, and updates to the *Code of Federal Regulations* are published in the daily *Federal Register.* (See appendix for details on how to obtain and use these publications.)

FCA regulations and the Farm Credit Act of 1971, as amended, are available on FCA's Web site: www.fca.gov, in a searchable database posted under Legal Info.

■ LEGISLATION

The FCA carries out its responsibilities under:

Farm Credit Act of 1971 (85 Stat. 583, 12 U.S.C. 2001). Signed by the president Dec. 10, 1971. Recodified all previous laws governing federal land banks, federal land bank associations, federal intermediate credit banks, production credit associations, and banks for cooperatives. Authorized loans to commercial fishermen and rural home owners. Reduced loan-to-value ratios and authorized variable rate loans, lease financing, and loans for farm-related services.

Farm Credit Act Amendments of 1980 (94 Stat. 3437, 12 U.S.C. 2012). Signed by the president Dec. 24, 1980. Amended the Farm Credit Act of 1971 to permit Farm Credit System institutions to improve their services. Authorized banks for cooperatives to engage in international lending transactions and authorized federal land banks and production credit associations to finance basic processing and marketing activities of farmers.

Farm Credit Act Amendments of 1985 (99 Stat. 1678, 12 U.S.C. 2001 note). Signed by the president Dec. 23, 1985. Amended the Farm Credit Act of 1971 to restructure and reform the Farm Credit System. Gave the Farm Credit System broader authority to use its own resources to shore up weak system units. Authorized the FCA to reorganize and regulate the Farm Credit System. Authorized the secretary of the Treasury to guarantee bonds issued by the Farm Credit System Financial Assistance Corporation.

Agricultural Credit Act of 1987 (101 Stat. 1568, 12 U.S.C. 2162). Signed by the president Jan. 6, 1988. Provided credit assistance to farmers, strengthened the Farm Credit System, and facilitated the establishment of secondary markets for agricultural loans. Provided for mandated and voluntary mergers between Farm Credit System institutions. Expanded borrower rights provisions of the 1971 act and established a corporation to insure rates and bonds issued by system institutions after 1993.

Food, Agriculture, Conservation, and Trade Act Amendments of 1991 (105 Stat. 1818, 7 U.S.C. 1421 note). Signed by the president Dec. 13, 1991. Gave the FCA regulatory control over the Federal Agricultural Mortgage Corporation (Farmer Mac), a secondary market for agricultural loans. Authorized Farmer Mac to borrow money with unsecured notes in order to purchase securities.

Farm Credit Banks and Associations Safety and Soundness Act of 1992 (106 Stat. 4102, 12 U.S.C. 2277a). Signed by the president Oct. 28, 1992. Amended Farm Credit System Insurance Corporation authority and provided for a separate board of directors, effective Jan. 1, 1996. Expanded the lending powers of banks for cooperatives.

Farm Credit System Reform Act of 1996 (110 Stat. 162, 12 U.S.C. 2001 note). Signed by the president Feb. 10, 1996. Reduced regulatory burdens on Farm Credit System institutions. Repealed a previous law to create a separate Farm Credit Insurance Corporation Board, and authorized rebates of excess Insurance Fund interest earnings. Provided new operational authorities for the Federal Agricultural Mortgage Corporation.

■ FARM CREDIT BANKS

MID-ATLANTIC AND SOUTHEAST REGION
(AL, DC, DE, FL, GA, KY, LA, MD, MS, NC, OH, PA, PR, SC, TN, VA, WV)
AgFirst Farm Credit Bank
1401 Hampton St.
P.O. Box 1499
Columbia, SC 29202
(803) 799–5000
E.A. "Andy" Lowrey, president and chief executive officer

MIDWEST REGION
(AR, IA, IL, IN, KY, MI, MN, MO, ND, NE, OH, SD, TN, WI, WY)
AgriBank, FCB
375 Jackson St.
P.O. Box 64949
St. Paul, MN 55164
(651) 282–8800
William J. Collins, chief executive officer

CENTRAL PLAINS REGION
(CO, KS, NM, OK)
Farm Credit Bank of Wichita
245 N. Waco St.
P.O. Box 2940
Wichita, KS 67201
(316) 266–5100
Jerold Harris, president and chief executive officer

SOUTH CENTRAL REGION
(Long-term financing for AL, LA, MS, TX; short-term financing for northwest LA, NM, TX)
Farm Credit Bank of Texas
6210 Hwy. 290 E.
P.O. Box 15919
Austin, TX 78761
(512) 465–0400
Larry Doyle, chief executive officer

SOUTHWEST REGION
(AZ, CA, HI, eastern ID, NV, UT)
Western Farm Credit Bank
3636 American River Dr.
P.O. Box 13106
Sacramento, CA 95813–4106
(916) 485–6000
Jerold L. Harris, president and chief executive officer
(Under joint management with the Farm Credit Bank of Wichita; direct correspondence, inquiries to Wichita, KS address)

■ AGRICULTURAL CREDIT BANK

COBANK
(Serves cooperatives nationwide and associations in AK, CT, ID, MA, ME, MT, NH, NJ, NY, OR, RI, VT, WA)
5500 S. Quebec St.
Englewood, CO 80111
  Mailing address:
    P.O. Box 5110
    Denver, CO 80217
(303) 740–4000
Douglas D. Sims, chief executive officer

■ FIELD OFFICES

NATIONAL HEADQUARTERS
1501 Farm Credit Dr.
McLean, VA 22102-5090
(703) 883–4160
Roland E. Smith, director and chief examiner

BLOOMINGTON FIELD OFFICE

2850 Metro Dr., #729
Bloomington, MN 55425–1415
(952) 854–7151
Chester Slipek, director

DALLAS FIELD OFFICE

511 East Carpenter Freeway, #650
Irving, TX 75062–3930
(972) 869–0550
Sharon Wilhite, director

DENVER FIELD OFFICE

3131 S. Vaughn Way, #250
Aurora, CO 80014–3507
(303) 696–9737
Steve Weisz, director

MCLEAN FIELD OFFICE

1501 Farm Credit Dr.
McLean, VA 22102–5090
(703) 883–4497
Ronald Boehr, director

SACRAMENTO FIELD OFFICE

2180 Harvard St., #300
Sacramento, CA 95815
(916) 648–1118
David E. Kuhler, director

◼ CORPORATIONS

FARM CREDIT LEASING SERVICES CORPORATION

1600 Colonnade
5500 Wayzata Blvd.
Minneapolis, MN 55416–1252
(763) 797–7400
Steven J. Montgomery, president and chief executive officer

FEDERAL FARM CREDIT BANKS FUNDING CORPORATION/ FARM CREDIT SYSTEM FINANCIAL ASSISTANCE CORPORATION

10 Exchange Pl., #1401
Jersey City, NJ 07302
(201) 200–8000
James Brickley, president

FARM CREDIT SYSTEM INSURANCE CORPORATION

1501 Farm Credit Dr.
McLean, VA 22102
(703) 883–4380
Mary A. Creedon-Connelly, chief operating officer

FEDERAL AGRICULTURAL MORTGAGE CORPORATION (FARMER MAC)

1133 21st St., NW, #600
Washington, DC 20036-3332
(202) 872–7700
Henry Edelman, president and chief executive officer

Federal Election Commission

999 E St. N.W., Washington, DC 20463
Internet: http://www.fec.gov

The Federal Election Commission (FEC) is an independent regulatory agency. It administers and enforces the provisions of the Federal Election Campaign Act of 1971, as amended. The act requires the disclosure of sources and uses of funds in campaigns for any federal office, limits the size of individual contributions, and provides for partial public financing of presidential elections. Partial funding is available to primary election candidates on a matching basis if they meet certain requirements. Full funding for the general election is available to qualified candidates.

The commission is composed of six members appointed by the president and confirmed by the Senate. The commissioners serve staggered six-year terms and no more than three commissioners may be members of the same political party. The chair and vice chair must be members of different political parties; they are elected annually by their fellow commissioners.

The commission staff is headed by a staff director. Other senior staff members include a general counsel, inspector general, and assistant staff directors for audit, reports analysis, public disclosure, information, and administration.

The Presidential Election Campaign Fund Act of 1971 authorized the commission to certify payments to presidential campaigns from the Presidential Election Campaign Fund. (This money comes from taxpayers who have indicated on their federal tax returns that they wish $3 of their taxes to be contributed to the fund.)

The act, as amended, requires campaign committees, political action committees (PACs), and parties to file periodic financial reports. It also establishes limits on the size and type of contributions a candidate may receive. Contributions from national banks, corporations, labor organizations, government contractors, and nonresident foreign nationals are prohibited. Also prohibited are contributions of cash (currency) in excess of $100, contributions from one person given in the name of another, and contributions exceeding legal limits *(box, p. 324)*.

Any candidate for federal office and any political group or committee formed to support a candidate must register with the FEC; the committee treasurer must periodically file reports on campaign finances with the secretary of the Senate (candidates for Senate seats), the House clerk's office (candidates for House seats), or the FEC. Individuals and committees making independent expenditures on behalf of or against a candidate also must file reports. In addition, campaign reports must be submitted to the secretary of state (or equivalent office) in the state where the nomination or election is sought or where the political committee's headquarters is located. Reports are made available to the public within forty-eight hours of their receipt.

To register with the FEC, candidates and committees must submit a statement of candidacy that designates a principal campaign committee. (This committee must be registered by filing a statement of organization within ten days; PACs and party committees also register by filing a statement of organization.) Other financial disclosure documents submitted include a report of receipts and expenditures, a statement of independent expenditures on behalf of or against a candidate, and a statement of any debt settlements. Disclosure statements also must be filed showing costs incurred on behalf of candidates by corporations, labor organizations, membership organizations, and trade associations for certain partisan communication, conducted within their own particular organization.

Independent expenditures are payments for communications that advocate the election or defeat of a candidate, but made without the cooperation of the particular candidate or campaign committee. Independent expenditures

CONTRIBUTION LIMITS

Recipients

Donors	Candidate Committee	PAC[1]	State, District, and Local Party Committee[2]	National Party Committee[3]	Special Limits
Individual	$2,000* per election[4]	$5,000 per year	$10,000 per year combined limit	$25,000* per year	Biennial limit of $95,000* ($37,500 to all candidates and $57,500[5] to all PACs and parties)
State, District, and Local Party Committee[2]	$5,000 per election combined limit	$5,000 per year combined limit	Unlimited transfers to other party committees		
National Party Committee[3]	$5,000 per election	$5,000 per year	Unlimited transfers to other party committees		$35,000* to Senate candidate per campaign[6]
PAC Multicandidate[7]	$5,000 per election	$5,000 per year	$5,000 per year combined limit	$15,000 per year	
PAC Not Multicandidate[7]	$2,000* per election	$5,000 per year	$10,000 per year combined limit	$25,000* per year	

Source: Federal Election Commission.

*These limits will be indexed for inflation, starting in 2005.

1. These limits apply to both separate segregated funds (SSFs) and political action committees (PACs). Affiliated committees share the same set of limits on contributions made and received.

2. A state party committee shares its limits with local and district party committees in that state unless a local or district committee's independence can be demonstrated. These limits apply to multicandidate committees only.

3. A party's national committee, Senate campaign committee, and House campaign committee are each considered national party committees, and each have separate limits, except with respect to Senate candidates—see Special Limits column.

4. Each of the following is considered a separate election with a separate limit: primary election, caucus or convention with the authority to nominate, general election, runoff election, and special election.

5. No more than $37,500 of this amount may be contributed to state and local parties and PACs.

6. This limit is shared by the national committee and the Senate campaign committee.

7. A multicandidate committee is a political committee that has been registered for at least six months, has received contributions from more than fifty contributors and—with the exception of a state party committee—has made contributions to at least five federal candidates.

---

greater than $250 per calendar year must be reported to the FEC. Independent expenditures may not be regulated except for disclosure.

FEC staff members review the reports for errors or omissions; if any are found, the campaign or committee is requested to provide additional information. If this information is not supplied, the FEC has the authority to begin a formal investigation. If, after the investigation, the commission decides that violations of the law did occur, it has the authority to negotiate a conciliation agreement with the party in question. Failure to negotiate an agreement within legal parameters allows the FEC to seek enforcement of the law and the imposition of civil penalties in U.S. District Court.

These procedures to enforce compliance also apply to cases in which the FEC discovers a violation of campaign finance law. FEC investigations of alleged violations can spring from an audit or routine review of a report or from a complaint sent to the FEC from another group or individual.

If candidates or committees have questions concerning the finance laws as they relate to specific campaigns, they may request an advisory opinion from the commission. Advisory opinion requests and advisory opinions are available for public inspection at the Public Records Office (see p. 327).

The commission also administers provisions of the law covering the public financing of presidential primaries and general elections. Public funds are also made available to national party committees for their nominating conventions. Candidates who accept public campaign funds must adhere to spending limits imposed by the Federal Election

Campaign Act Amendments of 1976 (FECA). The limits are adjusted each campaign season to account for inflation. The commission provides matching grants to presidential primary candidates who have raised more than $5,000 in individual contributions of $250 or less from individuals in twenty different states and who agree to limit expenditures.

The FEC determines a candidate's eligibility for public funds. If eligible, the candidate or committee is certified by the commission to the Treasury Department. After receiving subsequent submissions for matching funds, the commission certifies specific amounts to be paid from the fund. The Treasury is responsible for the actual disbursement of money.

For the 2000 primary campaign season the FECA set the limit at $40 million, up from $37.09 million in 1996. Each major-party presidential nominee was eligible for a $67.56 million grant for the 2000 general election, up from $61.82 million in 1996. The candidate had to agree to limit expenditures to $67.56 million and could not accept any private contributions for the general election campaign. Candidates are allowed to accept private contributions to pay for certain legal and accounting fees. Candidates may reject public funds entirely, freeing them to spend as much as they like. The limits on the size of contributions remain the same, however. George W. Bush did not receive matching funds; his campaign raised and spent in excess of $90 million by July 31, 2000.

As of February 2003, FEC auditors predict a primary matching fund entitlement of $36.6 million on Jan. 2, 2004, and a $66.4 million entitlement for the full election cycle. This estimate is subject to variables, specifically the number of candidates opting to accept public funding, the amounts of matchable money raised, and how early they are able to raise it.

Because of the alleged campaign finance violations arising from the 1996 elections, the FEC had to deal with more cases than ever before. Despite being rejected by Congress for additional funding and failing to receive additional help from the Justice Department, the FEC has made technological improvements to increase the efficiency of the commission.

In January 1997 the commission began distributing FECFile, software that would enable filers to submit their reports electronically via computer disks. In February 1998 filers were able to submit their reports through the postal service, via computer disks, via a modem, or through e-mail. These innovative steps have enabled the FEC to review more cases in less time and consequently have allowed the general public faster access to these reports.

In October 2000 the FEC implemented a new voluntary Alternative Dispute Resolution (ADR) program designed to promote compliance with the campaign finance law (FECA) and FEC regulations by encouraging settlements outside the normal enforcement context. Bilateral negotiations through ADR are oriented toward reaching an expedient resolution with a mutually agreeable settlement that is both satisfying to the respondent(s) and in compliance with the Federal Election Campaign Act (FECA). Resolutions reached through direct and, when necessary, mediated negotiations are submitted to the commissioners for final approval. If a resolution is not reached in bilateral negotiation, the case proceeds to mediation. It should be noted that cases resolved through ADR are not precedent-setting cases.

The FEC also operates the Office of Election Administration. That office, scheduled to become the Election Assistance Commission in 2003, collects information on election procedures and makes it available to federal, state, and local election officials (see p. 326).

On March 27, 2002, President George W. Bush signed into law the Bipartisan Campaign Reform Act of 2002 (BCRA), which made many substantial and technical changes to the federal campaign finance law. The new law banned the national parties and federal candidates from raising and spending soft money. It also broadened the definition of issue ads to include any ad that referred to a specific federal candidate sixty days before a general election and thirty days before a primary. It barred the use of corporate or union money for such ads and required that the names of major backers of the ads be disclosed.

The legislation made a number of other changes. The limit on individual contributions to a federal candidate was raised from $1,000 to $2,000 per election, with an overall two-year-election-cycle limit of $37,500 for contributions to candidates and $57,500 to other committees, up from an aggregate annual limit of $25,000. Political parties were barred from making independent expenditures on behalf of a candidate if they made coordinated expenditures for that candidate. Most of the changes became effective Nov. 6, 2002; however, changes involving contribution limits took effect with regard to contributions made on or after Jan. 1, 2003.

The FEC and its Office of Election Administration serve as the primary federal agency charged with providing assistance in the administration of federal elections by state and local governments. In order to aid election officials with the acquisition of reliable voting equipment, the FEC promulgated the 1990 Voting System Standards (VSS) to ensure that machines used for voting meet certain baseline criteria for accuracy, reliability, and durability. States adopt VSS on a voluntary basis as voting systems are subject to state regulation. In April 2002 the FEC approved the updated 2002 VSS for release and publication.

KEY PERSONNEL

Chair (position rotates annually)
    Ellen Weintraub .... (202) 694–1035
Vice Chairman
    Bradley Smith ....(202) 694–1011
Commissioners
    Scott Thomas .... (202) 694–1055
    David Mason ....(202) 694-1050
    Michael Toner .... (202) 694-1045
    Darryl Wold ....(202) 694-1045
Administration
    Sylvia Butler ....(202) 694–1240
Audit
    Joseph Stoltz .... (202) 694–1200
Congressional Affairs
    Christina VanBrakle ....(202) 694–1006
Data Systems Development
    Vacant .... (202) 694–1250
Equal Employment Opportunity
    Patricia Brown .... (202) 694–1228
General Counsel
    Lawrence Norton .... (202) 694–1650
Enforcement
    Rhonda Vosdingh .... (202) 694–1650
Litigation
    Richard Bader ....(202) 694–1650
Policy
    Rosemary Smith .... (202) 694–1650
Public Financing, Ethics, and Special Projects
    Gregory Baker .... (202) 694–1650

Information Division
    Gregory Scott .... (202) 694–1100
Inspector General
    Lynne McFarland .... (202) 694–1015
Personnel
    Bill Fleming .... (202) 694–1080
Planning and Management
    John O'Brien ....(202) 694–1216
Press
    Ronald M. Harris .... (202) 694–1220
Public Disclosure
    Patricia Young .... (202) 694–1120
Reports Analysis
    John Gibson ....(202) 694–1130
Secretary
    Mary Dove .... (202) 694–1040
Staff Director
    Jim Pehrkon ....(202) 694–1007
    Management
    Allison Doone .... (202) 694–1215
Audit & Review
    Robert Costa ....(202) 694–1181

INFORMATION SOURCES

Internet

Agency Web Site: http://www.fec.gov. Includes information on FEC publications and services, elections, candidates, PACs, and guidelines for political contributions.

The FEC also operates the Direct Access Program, an electronic tracking system of the financial activities of federal candidates, PACs, and political parties. The charge is $20 per hour. For more information contact the FEC Data Systems Division, (202) 694–1250.

Telephone Contacts

Fax ....(202) 219–3880
Fax-on-demand .... (202) 501–3413
Toll-free .... (800) 424–9530

Information and Publications

KEY OFFICES

FEC Information Division

999 E St. N.W.
Washington, DC 20463
(202) 694–1100
Toll-free (800) 424–9530
Fax-on-demand (202) 501–3413
Kevin Salley, deputy assistant staff director

Provides all public information on the FEC, including publications. Handles inquiries from candidates and committees as well as the general public and operates a toll-free number for queries and publication orders from outside the Washington area. Fax-on-demand service provides automatic faxes of selected FEC documents.

FEC Press Office

999 E St. N.W.
Washington, DC 20463
(202) 694–1220
Ron Harris, press officer

Handles all liaison with the media and answers and refers questions from media representatives. Also handles Freedom of Information requests.

Office of Election Administration

999 E St. N.W.
Washington, DC 20463
(202) 694–1095
Penelope Bonsall, director

Compiles and distributes election administration information to help federal, state, and local election officials develop and improve federal election procedures and systems.

FEC General Counsel

999 E St. N.W.
Washington, DC 20463
(202) 694–1650
Lawrence Norton, general counsel

Handles complaints alleging violations of the Federal Election Campaign Act, as amended, or FEC regulations. Complaints must be in writing, sworn to and notarized, and must contain the name, address, and telephone number of the person making the complaint; a statement of the facts; and evidence concerning the complaint. Complaints must be signed by the person making the complaint and must include a statement indicating whether the complaint is made at the suggestion of or on the behalf of any other person. For information on procedure, contact the Information Division, above.

Freedom of Information

Contact the FEC Press Office, above.

PUBLICATIONS

FEC publications available from the Information Division include an annual report and a free monthly newsletter, *The FEC Record*. The commission also makes available numerous campaign guides for political committees and candidates.

The National Clearinghouse for Election Administration publishes several reports and a quarterly *FEC Journal of Election Administration*. Contact the clearinghouse for subscription information *(above)*.

Several Bipartisan Campaign Reform Act resources, including the BCRA Campaign Guide Supplement, are available for download at http://www.fec.gov/pages/bcra/major_resources_bcra.htm.

Federal Elections 2000 is available at http://www.fec.gov/pubrec/fe2000/cover.htm. Hard copies may be ordered from the National Technical Information Service (NTIS), U.S. Department of Commerce, 5285 Port Royal Road, Springfield, VA 22161. Online orders may be placed at http://www.ntis.gov.

The following reports from the National Clearinghouse on Election Administration are available for purchase from the U.S. Government Printing Office (GPO); see appendix, Ordering Government Publications. Titles include:

Ballot Access. Four volumes.
Bilingual Election Services. Two volumes.
Campaign Finance Law 2002. Summary of state laws.

Computerizing Election Administration. Two volumes.
Contested Elections and Recounts. Three volumes.
Election Case Law, 1997.
Election Directory, 2003.
Federal Elections Titles 2002. Also available for '82, '84, '86, '88, '90, '92, '94, and '96.
Voter Information and Education Programs. Two volumes.

DATA AND STATISTICS

The best source for statistical data is the *FEC Reports on Financial Activity*. It can be purchased from the Public Records Office.

MEETINGS

The commission is required by law to meet once each month; however, it generally holds weekly meetings. Dates and agendas are published in the *Federal Register* and posted on a bulletin board in the Public Records Office. Commission meetings are open to the public unless they deal with pending compliance cases and personnel matters. Up-to-date information on changes in agenda or schedule may be obtained from the Information Division, the Public Records Office, or the Press Office.

Reference Resources

LIBRARIES

FEC Library

999 E St. N.W.
Washington, DC 20463
(202) 694–1600
Leta Holley, librarian
Hours: 9:00 a.m. to 5:00 p.m.

FEC Public Records Office

999 E St. N.W.
Washington, DC 20463
(202) 694–1120
Patricia Young, assistant staff director

Maintains and makes available to the public all campaign finance reports filed by federal candidates and committees since 1972. Copies of campaign reports may be requested in person, by mail, or by phone. There is a minimal charge for this service.

Open to the public from 9:00 a.m. to 5:00 p.m. During reporting deadline periods and at certain other times the office is open for extended evening and weekend hours.

The Public Records Office also makes available the following reference materials:

- Statistical summaries of campaign finance reports.
- Computer indexes and cross indexes to help locate documents.
- Advisory opinion requests and texts of advisory opinions.
- Completed compliance cases.
- Audit reports.
- Press releases.
- Copies of court cases filed by the FEC.
- The Multi-Candidate Committee Index (MCC), which lists political action committees (PACs) that may make contributions at the highest level.
- Commission memoranda, agendas of all commission meetings, agenda items, and minutes.

Secretary of the Senate

Office of Public Records
SH-232
Washington, DC 20510
(202) 224–0322

Maintains for public inspection microfilm copies of original campaign finance reports filed by candidates for the U.S. Senate and their committees.

Legislative Resource Center

Office of the Clerk of the House
1036 LHOB
Washington, DC 20515
(202) 226–5200

Maintains copies of campaign finance reports filed by candidates for the U.S. House of Representatives and their committees.

State Records Offices

Campaign finance reports must also be filed with the secretary of state or equivalent official in each state. See list below.

RULES AND REGULATIONS

FEC rules and regulations are contained in the *Code of Federal Regulations,* Title 11, various parts. Proposed rules, updates to the *Code of Federal Regulations,* and new final rules are published in the daily *Federal Register.* (See appendix for information on how to obtain and use these publications.)

A publication issued by the commission, *FEC Regulations,* is available from the Information Division.

■ LEGISLATION

The FEC carries out its responsibilities under:

Federal Election Campaign Act of 1971 (86 Stat. 3, 2 U.S.C. 431 note). Signed by the president Feb. 7, 1972. Established detailed spending limits and disclosure procedures. This act was the first comprehensive revision of federal campaign legislation since the Corrupt Practices Act of 1925.

Federal Election Campaign Act Amendments of 1974 (88 Stat. 1263, 2 U.S.C. 431 note). Signed by the president Oct. 15, 1974. Amended the Federal Election Campaign Act of 1971 by instituting limits on how much an individual can contribute to a candidate, how much candidates can spend in primary and general elections, and how much political parties are allowed to spend on candidates and nominating conventions. The amendments set up the FEC to enforce the provisions of the act. They also established public funding of presidential elections. Partial funding is available during the primaries to candidates who meet certain requirements. Full funding is available to qualified candidates for the general election. In the *Buckley v. Valeo* decision of 1976, the Supreme Court found parts of the 1974 act unconstitutional.

Federal Election Campaign Act Amendments of 1976 (90 Stat. 475, 2 U.S.C. 431 note). Signed by the president May 11, 1976. Reorganized the commission in a form that is constitutional. This law required that the commissioners be appointed by the president and confirmed by the Senate, established new contribution limits for individuals and political committees, and cut off matching funds for presidential candidates who receive less than a specific percentage of the votes cast during the primaries. No limit was imposed on spending for congressional races, and individual candidates were exempted from any limits on contributions they make to themselves.

Federal Election Campaign Act Amendments of 1979 (93 Stat. 1339, 2 U.S.C. 431 note). Signed by the president Jan. 8, 1980. Changed reporting and registration requirements that apply to political committees and candidates. Generally the amendments simplified paperwork requirements and removed some restrictions on party assistance to federal candidates and on volunteer activities.

Bipartisan Campaign Reform Act of 2002 (P.L. 107-155). Signed by the president March 27, 2002. Title I: Reduction of Special Interest Influence amended the Federal Election Campaign Act of 1971 (FECA) with respect to soft money to prohibit: (1) a national committee of a political party from soliciting or receiving contributions or making expenditures not subject to FECA; (2) a national, state, district, or local committee of a political party from soliciting or donating funds to a tax-exempt organization; and (3) a candidate for federal office from soliciting or receiving funds not subject to FECA. Restricted use of broadcast electioneering communication that was coordinated with a candidate (or his or her authorized committee), or a federal, state, or local political party or committee. Increased the limit on individual contributions to a federal candidate from $1,000 to $2,000 per election.

■ STATE RECORDS OFFICES

The FEC has no regional offices. However, campaign finance reports are also available at the office of the secretary of state (or equivalent office) in the state or territory where a candidate is seeking nomination or election, or where the campaign headquarters is located. The following state offices maintain copies of campaign records for public inspection; those marked by an asterisk also offer direct computer access to the FEC disclosure database.

ALABAMA*
Elections Division
Office of the Secretary of State
State Capitol, #E-204
600 Dexter Ave.
Montgomery, AL 36104
(334) 242–7210

ALASKA*
Office of the Lieutenant Governor
State Capitol, #315
120 Fourth St.
Juneau, AK 99801
(907) 465–3520

AMERICAN SAMOA
Election Office
P.O. Box 3970
Pago Pago, AS 96799
(684) 633–2522

ARIZONA*
Office of the Secretary of State
State Capitol, West Wing, 7th Floor
1700 W. Washington
Phoenix, AZ 85007–2808
(602) 542–4285

ARKANSAS*
Elections Division
Office of the Secretary of State
State Capitol Building, #026
Little Rock, AR 72201
(501) 682–5070 or (800) 482–1127

CALIFORNIA*
Political Reform Division
Office of the Secretary of State
1500 11th St., #495
Sacramento, CA 95814
(916) 653–6224

COLORADO*
Elections Division
Office of the Secretary of State
1560 Broadway, #200
Denver, CO 80202
(303) 894–2680

CONNECTICUT*
Elections Division, Campaign Finance Unit
Office of the Secretary of State
30 Trinity St.
Hartford, CT 06106
(860) 509–6100 or (800) 540–3764

DELAWARE*
Office of the Secretary of State
Townsend Bldg.
Dover, DE 19901
(302) 739–4111
  Mailing Address:
    P.O. Box 898
    Dover, DE 19903

DISTRICT OF COLUMBIA*
Office of Campaign Finance
Reeves Municipal Center, #420
2000 14th St. N.W.
Washington, DC 20009
(202) 939–8717

FLORIDA*
Division of Elections
Office of the Secretary of State
The Capitol, #1801
Tallahassee, FL 32399–0250
(850) 488–7690

GEORGIA*
Elections Division
Office of the Secretary of State
2 Martin Luther King Jr. Dr. S.E.
West Tower, #1104
Atlanta, GA 30334–1505
(404) 656–2871

GUAM
Election Commission
P.O. Box BG
Agana, GU 96932
(671) 477–9791

HAWAII*
Campaign Spending Commission
235 S. Beretania St., #300
Honolulu, HI 96813–2437
(808) 586–0285

IDAHO*
Elections Division
Office of the Secretary of State
203 State House
Boise, ID 83720
(208) 334–2852

ILLINOIS*
State Board of Elections
1020 S. Spring St.
Springfield, IL 62704
(217) 782–4141
  Mailing Address:
  P.O. Box 4187
  Springfield, IL 62708

State Board of Elections
100 W. Randolph St., #14–100
Chicago, IL 60601
(312) 814–6440

INDIANA*
Indiana Election Commission
302 W. Washington St., #E032
Indianapolis, IN 46204–2767
(317) 232–3939 or (800) 622–4941

IOWA*
Iowa Ethics and Campaign Disclosure Board
514 E. Locust St., #104
Des Moines, IA 50309
(515) 281–4028

KANSAS*
Elections Division
Office of the Secretary of State
State Capitol, 2nd Floor
300 Southwest 10th Avenue
Topeka, KS 66612–1594
(785) 296–4561

KENTUCKY*
Registry of Election Finance
140 Walnut St.
Frankfort, KY 40601
(502) 573–2226

LOUISIANA*
Elections Division
Office of the Secretary of State
State Capitol, 19th Floor
Baton Rouge, LA 70804
(504) 342–4970
  Mailing Address:
  P.O. Box 94125
  Baton Rouge, LA 70804–9125

MAINE*
Commission on Governmental Ethics and
  Election Practices
State Office Bldg., #114
135 State House Station
Augusta, ME 04333
(207) 287–6219

MARYLAND*

State Administrative Board of Election Laws
11 Bladen St.
Annapolis, MD 21401
(410) 974–3711 or (800) 222–8683
  Mailing Address:
    P.O. Box 231
    Annapolis, MD 21401–0231

MASSACHUSETTS*

Public Records Division
Office of the Secretary of the Commonwealth
1 Ashburton Place, #1719
Boston, MA 02108
(617) 727–2832

MICHIGAN*

Elections Bureau
Office of the Secretary of State
208 N. Capitol Ave., 4th Floor
Lansing, MI 48918–1700
(517) 373–2540
  Mailing Address:
    P.O. Box 20126
    Lansing, MI 48901–0726

MINNESOTA*

Elections Division
Office of the Secretary of State
180 State Office Building
100 Constitution Ave.
St. Paul, MN 55155–1299
(612) 215–1440

MISSISSIPPI*

Office of the Secretary of State
401 Mississippi St.
Jackson, MS 39201
(601) 359–1350 or (800) 829–6786
  Mailing Address:
    P.O. Box 136
    Jackson, MS 39205–0136

MISSOURI*

Missouri Ethics Commission
221 Metro Dr., Suite A
Jefferson City, MO 65109
(573) 751–2020 or (800) 392–8660
  Mailing Address:
    P.O. Box 1370
    Jefferson City, MO 65102

MONTANA*

Commission of Political Practices
1205 Eighth Ave.
P.O. Box 202401
Helena, MT 59620–2401
(406) 444–2942

NEBRASKA*

Accountability and Disclosure Commission
State Capitol, 11th Floor
Lincoln, NE 68509
(402) 471–2522
  Mailing Address:
    P.O. Box 95086
    Lincoln, NE 68509–4608

NEVADA*

Office of the Secretary of State
101 North Carson Street, #3
Carson City, NV 89701–4786
(702) 687–3176

NEW HAMPSHIRE*

Office of the Secretary of State
State House, #204
Concord, NH 03301
(603) 271–3242

NEW JERSEY*

Elections Division
Department of State
20 W. State St., CN 304
Trenton, NJ 08625–0304
(609) 292–3761

NEW MEXICO*
Office of the Secretary of State
State Capitol Building, #420
Santa Fe, NM 87503
(505) 827–3620 or (800) 477–3632

NEW YORK*
State Board of Elections
Swan St. Bldg., Core 1
6 Empire State Plaza, #201
Albany, NY 12223–1650
(518) 474–8200

NORTH CAROLINA*
Campaign Reporting Office
State Board of Elections
133 Fayetteville St. Mall, #100
Raleigh, NC 27601
(919) 733–7173
  Mailing Address:
  P.O. Box 2169
  Raleigh, NC 27602–2169

NORTH DAKOTA*
Office of the Secretary of State
Capitol Bldg., FL 1
600 E. Boulevard Ave.
Bismarck, ND 58505–0500
(701) 328–2900

OHIO
Elections Division
Office of the Secretary of State
30 E. Broad St., 14th Floor
Columbus, OH 43266–0418
(614) 466–2585

OKLAHOMA*
Ethics Commission
2300 N. Lincoln Boulevard, Room B-5
Oklahoma City, OK 73105–4812
(405) 521–3451

OREGON*
Elections Division
Office of the Secretary of State
141 State Capitol
Salem, OR 97310–0722
(503) 986–1518

PENNSYLVANIA*
Bureau of Commissions, Elections, and Legislation
304 North Office Bldg.
Harrisburg, PA 17120–0029
(717) 787–5280

PUERTO RICO
State Elections Commission
P.O. Box 9066525
San Juan, PR 00906–6525
(809) 724–4979

RHODE ISLAND*
Elections Division
Office of the Secretary of State
100 N. Main St.
Providence, RI 02903
(401) 222–2340

SOUTH CAROLINA*
State Election Commission
2221 Devine St., #105
Columbia, SC 29205
(803) 734–9060
  Mailing Address:
  P.O. Box 5987
  Columbia, SC 29250

SOUTH DAKOTA*
Office of the Secretary of State
204 State Capitol Bldg.
Pierre, SD 57501–5070
(605) 773–3537

TENNESSEE*

Registry of Election Finance
404 James Robertson Pkwy., #1614
Nashville, TN 37243–1360
(615) 741–7959

TEXAS*

Texas Ethics Commission
201 E. 14th Street, 10th Floor
Austin, TX 78701
(512) 463–5800 or (800) 325–8506
 Mailing Address:
  P.O. Box 12070, Capitol Station
  Austin, TX 78711–2070

UTAH*

Office of the Lieutenant Governor
State Capitol, #203
Salt Lake City, UT 84114–0601
(801) 538–1040 or (800) 995–8683

VERMONT*

Office of the Secretary of State
109 State St.
Montpelier, VT 05609–1101
(802) 828–2464

VIRGIN ISLANDS

Board of Elections
P.O. Box 6038, Emancipation Garden Station
Charlotte Amalie, VI 00801–6038
(340) 774–3107

VIRGINIA*

State Board of Election
200 N. Ninth St., #101
Richmond, VA 23219–3497
(804) 786–6551

WASHINGTON*

Public Disclosure Commission
711 Capitol Way, #403
P.O. Box 40908
Olympia, WA 98504–0908
(360) 753–1111

WEST VIRGINIA*

Office of the Secretary of State
Bldg. 1, #157-K
1900 Kanawha Blvd. East
Charleston, WV 25305–0770
(304) 558–6000

WISCONSIN*

Wisconsin Elections Board
132 E. Wilson St., #300
Madison, WI 53702–0001
(608) 266–8005
 Mailing Address:
  P.O. Box 2973
  Madison, WI 53701–2973

WYOMING

Elections Division
Office of the Secretary of State
Capitol Bldg.
Cheyenne, WY 82002–0020
(307) 777–7378

Federal Housing Finance Board

1777 F St. N.W., Washington, DC 20006
Internet: http://www.fhfb.gov

The Federal Housing Finance Board (FHFB), also called the Finance Board, is an independent regulatory agency that supervises the Federal Home Loan Bank (FHLB) system and operates an affordable housing program. Four board members are appointed by the president for seven-year terms, and the fifth member is the Secretary of the Department of Housing and Urban Development, or the secretary's designee.

The Finance Board regulates the twelve FHLBs that were created in 1932 to improve the supply of funds to local lenders that, in turn, finance loans for home mortgages. The Finance Board ensures that the FHLBs, which are privately capitalized, government-sponsored enterprises, operate in a safe and sound manner, carry out their housing and community development finance mission, and remain adequately capitalized and able to raise funds in the capital markets.

The FHFB was created in August 1989 by the Financial Institutions Reform, Recovery and Enforcement Act (FIRREA) to assume some of the responsibilities of the abolished Federal Home Loan Bank Board.

The FHLB system, consisting of twelve district banks, became a part of the FHFB and also became a source of funds for the former Resolution Trust Corporation (RTC). FIRREA required these district banks to contribute to a $1.2 billion thrift bailout fund managed by the Resolution Funding Corporation (REFCORP). REFCORP raised $30 billion by issuing thirty-year bonds.

These banks also are required to contribute funds to the Affordable Housing Program (AHP). This program lends money to member banks below market cost to finance purchase and renovation of housing for families with incomes at 80 percent or below the median for their community.

From 1990 to 1993 AHP received $50 million from this levy; during the mid- to late 1990s the total was raised several times until it reached $300 million.

Under the Financial Services Modernization Act of 1999, the annual $300 million funding formula for the REFCORP obligations of the FHLBs was changed to 20 percent of annual net earnings. A district bank may seek a temporary suspension of these payments if the bank is financially unstable. A similar program, the Community Investment Program, lends money to member banks at the cost of funds plus a small overhead, for families with incomes at 115 percent or below the median for their community. The Community Investment Program also supports mixed-use commercial housing projects.

The district banks also pay the administrative expenses of the Finance Board. The Finance Board regulates the activities of the district banks, ensuring that they operate in a safe and sound manner while meeting these new financial obligations.

Today, the FHLBs and their 7,929 member-owners, which constitute the FHLB system, form a cooperative partnership that continues to help finance the country's urban and rural housing and community development needs. The members of the FHLB system include commercial banks, insured savings and loan associations, mutual savings banks, credit unions, and insurance companies. Members must be primarily home financing institutions that reinvest the funds as home mortgages.

The Financial Services Modernization Act of 1999, also known as the Gramm-Leach-Bliley Act, directly affected the operation of the FHFB:

▪ Governance of the FHLBs was decentralized from the Finance Board to the individual FHLBs. The directors of each FHLB, rather than the Finance Board, now elect their own chair and vice chair, and a statutory limit was placed on FHLB directors' compensation.

- A new, permanent capital structure for the FHLBs was established. Two classes of stock were authorized, redeemable on six-month and five-year notices. FHLBs must meet a 5 percent leverage minimum tied to total capital and a risk-based requirement tied to permanent capital.
- Banks with less than $500 million in assets may use long-term advances for loans to small businesses, small farms, and small agribusinesses.
- The stock purchase requirements for banks and thrifts was equalized.
- Voluntary membership for federal savings associations took effect six months after enactment.

■ KEY PERSONNEL

Chair
John T. Korsmo . . . . (202) 408–2622
Board Members
Mel Martinez, secretary of housing
and urban development . . . . (202) 708–2817
J. Timothy O'Neill . . . . (202) 408–2953
Franz Leichter . . . . (202) 408–2986
Allan I. Mendelowitz . . . . (202) 408–2587
General Counsel
Arnold Intrater . . . . (202) 408–2570
Supervision
Stephen M. Cross . . . . (202) 408–2562
Resource Management
Judith Hofmann . . . . (202) 408–2586
Inspector General
Edward Kelley . . . . (202) 408–2544

■ INFORMATION SOURCES

Internet
The Federal Housing Finance Board maintains a Web site at: http://www.fhfb.gov

Telephone Contacts
Personnel Locator . . . . (202) 408–2500
Fax . . . . (202) 408–2950

Information and Publications

KEY OFFICES

FHFB Public Affairs
1777 F St. N.W.
Washington, DC 20006
(202) 408–2817
Carter Wood, special assistant

Answers questions for the press and the public.

Freedom of Information
1777 F St. N.W.
Washington, DC 20006

MEETINGS
The schedule may be obtained by contacting:

Mary Gottlieb
1777 F St. N.W.
Washington, DC 20006
(202) 408–2826

Reference Resources
A searchable data base of Finance Board decision documents of all kinds, plus information on such topics as board meetings, rules and regulations, the monthly interest rate survey, and Federal Home Loan Bank policies and programs is available at the Finance Board Web site, www.fhfb.gov.

DOCKETS

Office of General Counsel
1777 F St. N.W.
Washington, DC 20006
(202) 408–2826

The Finance Board maintains records of rulemakings, administrative proceedings, and docket information. Information must be requested in writing.

RULES AND REGULATIONS
FHFB rules and regulations are published in the *Code of Federal Regulations,* Title 12, parts 910, 912, 931–944, 950, 955. Proposed regulations, new final regulations, and updates to the *Code of Federal Regulations* are published in the daily *Federal Register.* (See appendix for details on how to obtain and use these publications.)

■ LEGISLATION
Federal Home Loan Bank Act of 1932 (FHLBA) (47 Stat. 725, 12 U.S.C. 1421–1449). Signed by the president July 22, 1932. Created the Federal Home Loan Bank Board and the Federal Home Loan Bank System, which included federally chartered institutions insured by the Federal Savings and Loan Insurance Corporation and mutual savings banks.

Financial Institutions Reform, Recovery and Enforcement Act of 1989 (FIRREA) (101 Stat. 183, 12 U.S.C. 1811 note). Signed by the president Aug. 9, 1989. Abolished the Federal Home Loan Bank Board and distributed its responsibilities to other agencies; established the FHFB and the Office of Thrift Supervision. Created the Affordable Housing Program.

Financial Services Modernization Act of 1999 (113 Stat. 1338, 12 U.S.C. 1811 note). Signed by the president on Nov. 12, 1999. Title VI: Federal Home Loan Bank System Modernization Act of 1999 amended the FHLBA to expand FHLB membership parameters to make a federal savings association's membership in the FHLB system voluntary instead of mandatory. Empowered the FHFB to charge an FHLB or any executive officer or director with violation of law or regulation in connection with the granting of any application or other request by the bank, or any written agreement between the bank and the FHFB and other provisions.

▉ REGIONAL BANKS

REGION 1
(CT, MA, ME, NH, RI, VT)
Federal Home Loan Bank of Boston
One Financial Center, 20th Floor
P.O. Box 9106
Boston, MA 02205–9106
(617) 542–0150
Michael Jessee, president

REGION 2
(NJ, NY, PR, VI)
Federal Home Loan Bank of New York
101 Park Ave.
New York, NY 10178
(212) 681–6000
Alfred DelliBovi, president

REGION 3
(DE, PA, WV)
Federal Home Loan Bank of Pittsburgh
601 Grant St.
Pittsburgh, PA 15219
(412) 288–3400
James Roy, president

REGION 4
(AL, DC, FL, GA, MD, NC, SC, VA)
Federal Home Loan Bank of Atlanta
1475 Peachtree St. N.E.
P.O. Box 105565
Atlanta, GA 30348
(404) 888–8000
Raymond R. Christman, president

REGION 5
(KY, OH, TN)
Federal Home Loan Bank of Cincinnati
221 E. 4th St., #1000
P.O. Box 598
Cincinnati, OH 45201–0598
(513) 852–7500
David H. Hehman, president

REGION 6
(IN, MI)
Federal Home Loan Bank of Indianapolis
8250 Woodfield Crossing Blvd.
P.O. Box 60
Indianapolis, IN 46206–0060
(317) 465–0200
Martin Heger, president

REGION 7
(IL, WI)
Federal Home Loan Bank of Chicago
111 E. Wacker Dr., #700
Chicago, IL 60601
(312) 565–5700
Alex Pollock, president

REGION 8
(IA, MN, MO, ND, SD)
Federal Home Loan Bank of Des Moines
907 Walnut St.
Des Moines, IA 50309
(515) 281–1000
Patrick J. Coaway, president

REGION 9

(AR, LA, MS, NM, TX)
Federal Home Loan Bank of Dallas
5605 N. McArthur Blvd.
Irving, TX 75038
  Mailing address:
    P.O. Box 619026
    Dallas, TX 75261–9026
(972) 944–8500
Terry Smith, president

REGION 10

(CO, KS, NE, OK)
Federal Home Loan Bank of Topeka
120 E. 6th St.
2 Townsite Plaza
Topeka, KS 66603
(913) 233–0507
Andrew Setter, president

REGION 11

(AZ, CA, NV)
Federal Home Loan Bank of San Francisco
600 California St., #300
P.O. Box 7948
San Francisco, CA 94120
(415) 616–1000
Dean Schultz, president

REGION 12

(AK, GU, HI, ID, MT, OR, UT, WA, WY)
Federal Home Loan Bank of Seattle
1501 4th Ave., #1900
Seattle, WA 98101–1693
(206) 340–2300
Norman B. Rice, president

Federal Maritime Commission

800 N. Capitol St. N.W., Washington, DC 20573
Internet: http://www.fmc.gov

The Federal Maritime Commission (FMC) is an independent regulatory agency within the executive branch. It began operations Aug. 12, 1961, as the result of Reorganizational Plan No. 7 issued by President John F. Kennedy.

The FMC has five commissioners nominated by the president and confirmed by the Senate. No more than three of the commissioners may be members of the same political party. The president designates one of the commissioners to serve as chair with all commissioners serving five-year terms.

The FMC is responsible for regulating the ocean commerce of the United States, a role formerly held by the Federal Maritime Board. The board was abolished by the reorganization that created the FMC. The other chief function of the former maritime board, promoting the nation's merchant marine, was transferred to the Transportation Department's Maritime Administration (MARAD: see p. 663).

The FMC consists of six offices that are directly responsible to the chair. They are the offices of the secretary, inspector general, general counsel, managing director, administrative law judges, and equal employment opportunity. Three bureaus report to the managing director and are responsible for the direct administration and coordination of FMC regulatory functions and other activities:

▪ Bureau of Trade Analysis, formerly known as Bureau of Economics and Agreement Analysis, reviews agreements and monitors the concerted activities of common carriers by water under the standards of the Shipping Act of 1984.

The bureau also reviews and analyzes service contracts, monitors rates of government controlled carriers, reviews carrier published tariff systems under the accessibility and accuracy standards of the Shipping Act of 1984, and responds to inquiries or issues that arise concerning service contracts or tariffs. The bureau also is responsible for competition oversight and market analysis, focusing on activity that is substantially anticompetitive and market distorting in violation of the Shipping Act of 1984.

An integral part of the bureau's responsibilities is the systematic surveillance of carrier activity and commercial conditions in the U.S. liner trades. Accordingly, the bureau administers a variety of monitoring programs, and other research efforts, designed to apprise the commission of current trade conditions, emerging commercial trends, and carrier pricing and service activities.

The Bureau of Trade Analysis also maintains an agreement library of carrier and terminal agreements on file with the commission and publishes Carrier Agreements in the U.S. Oceanborne Trades.

▪ The Bureau of Enforcement, formed through the merger of the former Hearing Counsel and Bureau of Investigations, participates as trial counsel in formal adjudicatory proceedings, nonadjudicatory investigations, rulemaking proceedings when designated by commission order, and other proceedings initiated by the commission. The bureau also participates in formal complaint proceedings where intervention is permitted and appropriate, and monitors all other formal proceedings in order to identify major regulatory issues and to advise the managing director and the other bureaus.

The bureau also participates in the development of commission rules and regulations. Through investigative personnel, the bureau conducts investigations into and monitors the activities of ocean common carriers, nonvessel operating common carriers (NVOCCs), freight forwarders, shippers, ports and terminals, and other persons to ensure compliance with the statutes and regulations administered by the commission. Investigations are conducted into alleged violations of the full range of statutes and regulations administered by the commission.

The bureau maintains a headquarters office in Washington, D.C., as well as area representatives in Los Angeles, Miami, New Orleans, New York, and Seattle. The area representatives also serve other major port cities and transportation centers within their respective areas on a regular rotating basis.

▪ The Bureau of Consumer Complaints and Licensing provides information and referrals in response to a wide range of informal inquiries, provides guidance with respect to licensing and bonding, and, where appropriate, advises inquiring persons about various means available to resolve complaints, both informally and formally. The bureau attempts to facilitate conflict resolution through informal and nonbinding approaches in an effort to avoid the expense of litigation. The bureau also licenses ocean transportation intermediaries; administers the ocean transportation intermediary bonding program by setting policies and guidelines and reviewing financial instruments that evidence financial responsibility; certifies that owners and operators of passenger vessels in U.S. trades have evidenced financial responsibility to satisfy liability incurred for nonperformance of voyages or death or injury to passengers and other persons; responds to consumer inquiries and complaints; and oversees a program of alternative dispute resolution and provides mediation and other dispute resolution services where appropriate.

The Shipping Act of 1984 expedited FMC procedures so that agreements between U.S. ocean liner companies (also known as conferences) that met the act's requirements were automatically approved by the FMC. The Shipping Act deregulated the shipping industry because such conferences were no longer subject to prior review by the FMC, and the agreements were exempted from U.S. antitrust laws.

The 1984 act protects the rights of shippers and consumers by expanding the powers of shippers to bargain with shipping cartels (conferences) for the best rates.

The FMC can still intervene if it believes the enactment of an agreement would exploit its grant of antitrust immunity and to ensure that agreements do not otherwise violate the 1984 act or result in an unreasonable increase in transportation cost or unreasonable reduction in service. However, the commission no longer has the authority to approve or disapprove general rate increases or individual commodity rate levels in U.S. foreign commerce except with regard to certain foreign government-owned carriers.

Charges of discriminatory treatment (by terminal operators, forwarders, etc.) are initially filed with the Office of the Secretary. The charges are then investigated and may result in formal administrative proceedings adjudicated by an administrative law judge. In addition, formal complaints may be filed seeking reparations or other remedies. Formal complaint proceedings, investigations, and other administrative proceedings can include a prehearing conference, a formal hearing before an administrative law judge, the judge's decision, oral argument before the commissioners, and a final report. The decisions of the commission may be appealed to the U.S. Court of Appeals.

The FMC reported that the act's reform did not bring about the negative consequences that some opponents had predicted. There were no sharp rate increases, no curtailment of shipping services, or loss of independent carrier competition. In fact, ocean freight rates have fallen since 1984. Most carriers advocate a renewal of the act with few amendments because it allows them to discuss rates with their competition without violating U.S. antitrust laws. Shippers approve of their ability to enter into service contracts with the carriers. Service contracts provide valuable leverage to control shipping rates.

In 1993 the FMC implemented the Automated Tariff Filing and Information System (ATFI) to alleviate paperwork burdens on the government and the shipping industry. The system became fully operational in 1994. In 1995 more than 1,100 tariffs were filed electronically. All paper tariffs have been either converted to the new electronic format or canceled.

During 1995, the FMC increased its cooperation with the U.S. Customs Service. The FMC now has online access to Customs' Automated Commercial Environment database, the Automated Broker Interface module of which provides investigators with information on shipping transactions that had been very difficult to obtain.

The Shipping Act of 1984 was amended by the Ocean Shipping Reform Act (OSRA) of 1998. OSRA was the culmination of a nearly four-year effort to update and revise the Shipping Act, with virtually all segments of the industry represented in the legislative reform process. The following are major provisions of OSRA:

▪ Provide shippers and common carriers greater choice and flexibility in entering into contractual relationships with shippers for ocean transportation and intermodal services. The most significant improvement is the right of members of ocean carrier agreements to negotiate and enter into service contracts with one or more shippers independent of the agreement.

▪ Reduce the expense of the tariff filing system and privatize the function of publishing tariff information while maintaining current tariff enforcement and common carriage principles with regard to tariff shipments.

▪ Protect U.S. exporters from disclosure to their foreign competitors of their contractual relationships with common carriers and proprietary business information, including targeted markets.

- Exempt new assembled motor vehicles specifically from tariff and service contract requirements and provide the FMC with greater flexibility to grant general exemptions from provisions of the 1984 Act.
- Reform the licensing and bonding requirements for ocean freight forwarders and NVOCCs and consolidate the definitions of those two entities under the term ocean transportation intermediary.

In September 2001 the commission issued its two-year study on the regulatory and economic impact of OSRA. The study provided a general regulatory and economic overview of ocean shipping and examined several key issues: service contract developments, agreement and voluntary service contract guideline activities, ocean transportation intermediary licensing and bonding, and tariff publication. Other issues covered included controlled carriers, restrictive shipping practices by foreign governments, port trucking, and e-commerce. The study's closing observations identify issues meriting continuing attention and offer several suggestions for possible legislative consideration. The study is available on the FMC Web site.

▨ KEY PERSONNEL

Chair
Steven R. Blust..........................(202) 523–5911
Commissioners
Joseph E. Brennan......................(202) 523–5723
Harold J. Creel Jr........................(202) 523–5712
Rebecca F. Dye..........................(202) 523–5715
Delmond J.H. Won.....................(202) 523–5721
Administrative Law Judge
Norman D. Kline ....(202) 523–5750
Equal Employment Opportunity
Alice M. Blackmon ....(202) 523–5806
General Counsel
David R. Miles (Acting)................(202) 523–5740
Ethics Counsel
Christopher Hughey....................(202) 523–5740
Inspector General
Tony P. Kominoth ....(202) 523–5863
Secretary
Bryant L. VanBrakle....................(202) 523–5725
Executive Director
Bruce A. Dombrowski..................(202) 523–5800
Budget and Financial Management
Karen E. Douglass......................(202) 523–5770
Human Resources
Harriette Charbonneau ....(202) 523–5773
Information Resources Management
George D. Bowers.......................(202) 523–5835

Management Services
Michael H. Kilby........................(202) 523–5900
Bureau of Consumer Complaints and Licensing
Sandra L. Kusomoto....................(202) 523–5787
Consumer Complaints
Joseph T. Farrell ....(202) 523–5807
Passenger Vessels and Information Processing
Anne E. Trotter ....(202) 523–5818
Transportation Intermediaries
Ralph W. Freibert.......................(202) 523–5843
Bureau of Enforcement
Vern W. Hill.............................(202) 523–5783
Bureau of Trade Analysis
Florence A. Carr ....(202) 523–5796
Agreements
Jeremiah D. Hospital ....(202) 523–5793
Economics and Competitive Analysis
Karen V. Gregory ....(202) 523–5845
Service Contracts and Tariffs
Mamie H. Black..........................(202) 523–5856

▨ INFORMATION SOURCES

Internet
Agency Web site: http://www.fmc.gov. Includes information on many offices and programs, FMC regulations, and forms that can be downloaded.

Telephone Contacts
Personnel Locator ....(202) 523–5773
Fax...(202) 523–3782
Inspector General Hotline ....(202) 523–5865

Information and Publications

KEY OFFICES

FMC Public Information
Office of the Secretary
800 N. Capitol St. N.W.
Washington, DC 20573
(202) 523–5707

Issues news releases and answers or refers general questions. Distributes the commission's annual reports.

Freedom of Information
Office of the Secretary
800 N. Capitol St. N.W.
Washington, DC 20573
(202) 523–5725
Bryant L. VanBrakle, secretary

FMC Informal Inquiries, Complaints, and Informal Dockets

Office of Consumer Complaints
800 N. Capitol St. N.W.
Washington, DC 20573
(202) 523–5807
Joseph Farrell, director

Provides general information of interest to consumers and answers consumer complaints or refers them to the appropriate office within the commission.

PUBLICATIONS

The annual report is available from FMC Public Information; other FMC publications are available from the Government Printing Office (GPO): see appendix, Ordering Government Publications. Titles available include:

FMC Reports, Vols. 26, 27, and 28
Section 18 Report on the Shipping Act of 1984

MEETINGS

The commissioners hold periodic meetings at 800 N. Capitol St. N.W., Washington, DC 20573. The agenda for each meeting is posted in the Office of the Secretary (202) 523–5725. Agendas are posted on the agency's Web site at www.fmc.gov and also are published in the *Federal Register* and trade publications.

Reference Resources

LIBRARY

FMC Library

800 N. Capitol St. N.W., #1085
Washington, DC 20573
(202) 523–5762
David Vespa, librarian

Collection specializes in maritime law. Open to the public from 8:30 a.m. to 5:00 p.m., Monday to Friday.

DOCKETS

800 N. Capitol St. N.W.
Washington, DC 20573
(202) 523–5760

Maintains dockets for FMC rulemakings and other regulatory proceedings. Open to the public from 8:30 a.m. to 5:00 p.m.

RULES AND REGULATIONS

FMC rules and regulations are published in the *Code of Federal Regulations*, Title 46, parts 500 to end. Proposed rules, new final rules, and updates to the *Code of Federal Regulations* are published in the daily *Federal Register*. (See appendix for information on how to obtain and use these publications.)

▎ LEGISLATION

Legislation the FMC administers includes:

Merchant Marine Act of 1920 (41 Stat. 988, 46 U.S.C. 13). Signed by the president June 5, 1920. Section 19 empowered the commission to make rules and regulations to reduce the effect on American shippers of unfavorable rules made by foreign countries.

Public Law 89–777 (80 Stat. 1356, 46 U.S.C. 362). Signed by the president Nov. 6, 1966. Authorized the FMC to require evidence of adequate financial resources from owners or operators of vessels with accommodations for fifty or more passengers that take on passengers at U.S. ports to cover judgments for personal injury or death and to repay passengers if the voyage fails to take place.

Shipping Act of 1984 (98 Stat. 67, 46 U.S.C. 1701 note). Signed by the president March 20, 1984. Title I of the Ocean Shipping Reform Act of 1998 (112 Stat. 1902), signed by the president Oct. 14, 1998, made comprehensive amendments to the Shipping Act of 1984. Granted carriers participating in conferences or cooperative agreements automatic immunity from antitrust prosecution. The FMC could seek a federal court injunction against any agreement that it believed unnecessarily raised transportation costs or limited services. The act also provided for licensing and bonding Ocean Transportation Intermediaries, the confidential filing of service contracts, and the publication of ocean freight rates.

Omnibus Trade and Competitiveness Act of 1988 (102 Stat. 1107, 19 U.S.C. 2901 note). Signed by the president Aug. 23, 1988. Included the Foreign Shipping Practices Act of 1988 (102 Stat. 1570, 46 U.S.C. app. 1710a). Authorized the FMC to take action against foreign ocean carriers whose practices or whose government's practices result in adverse conditions affecting the operations of U.S. carriers.

▎ REGIONAL OFFICES

FMC Bureau of Enforcement

In 1996, the former field offices were replaced with five area representatives.

HEADQUARTERS
800 N. Capitol St. N.W., #900
Washington, DC 20573
(202) 523–5783
Fax (202) 523–5785
Michael F. Carley, area representative

LOS ANGELES
P.O. Box 230
839 S. Beacon St., #320
San Pedro, CA 97033-0230
(310) 514–4905
Oliver E. Clark, area representative

MIAMI
909 S.E. First Ave., #705
Miami, FL 33131
(305) 536–4316
Andrew Margolis, area representative
Eric O. Mintz, area representative

NEW ORLEANS
423 Canal St., #309B
New Orleans, LA 70130
(504) 589–6662
Alvin N. Kellogg, area representative

NEW YORK
P.O. Box 3461
Church St. Station
New York, NY 10008
Emanuel J. Mingione, area representative

SEATTLE
FMC c/o U.S. Customs
#7 S. Nevada St., #100
Seattle, WA 98134
(206) 553–0221
Michael A. Moneck, area representative

National Credit Union Administration

1775 Duke St., Alexandria, VA 22314–3428
Internet: http://www.ncua.gov

The National Credit Union Administration (NCUA), an independent agency within the executive branch, was created by a 1970 amendment to the Federal Credit Union Act of 1934. Administration of the original Federal Credit Union Act, which authorized the federal government to charter credit unions, was shifted among several agencies before the creation of the NCUA in 1970.

A three-member board governs the agency. Members of the board are nominated by the president and confirmed by the Senate for six-year terms.

The credit union movement in the United States dates from 1909, when Massachusetts passed the first state credit union law. Since then, all states have passed similar laws.

A credit union is a cooperative association designed to promote thrift among its members. Membership is limited to persons having a common bond of occupation or association and to groups within a well-defined neighborhood, community, or rural district. The credit union accumulates funds from savings to make loans to members for useful purposes at reasonable interest rates.

A credit union is managed by a board of directors and committees made up of members. After expenses and legal reserve requirements are met, most of the earnings of a credit union are returned to the members as dividends on share holdings.

There are two types of credit unions: federal credit unions, chartered by the NCUA; and state credit unions, chartered by state agencies.

The NCUA:

- Approves or disapproves applications for federal credit union charters.
- Issues charters when applications are approved.
- Examines federal credit unions to determine financial condition.
- Supervises and regulates all federally insured credit unions.
- Regulates the operations of the Central Liquidity Facility, the central bank for loans.
- Administers the National Credit Union Share Insurance Fund (NCUSIF), which was authorized in 1970. All federally chartered credit unions are insured by NCUSIF. In addition, the fund insures the member accounts in 97 percent of state-chartered credit unions. This insurance coverage is limited to $100,000 per account. The NCUA board formulates standards and requirements for insured credit unions.

Unprofitable assets and assets of liquidated credit unions are managed and sold by the Asset Liquidation Management Center.

In 1998 the banking industry and the credit unions battled over credit union membership. The banking industry sought to limit credit union membership to groups with a common bond of enterprise. In February 1998 the Supreme Court, in a 5–4 decision, ruled that credit unions had overstepped their bounds by accepting members and groups that did not have a common bond with the credit union's chartering organization. However, the credit unions won a major victory with passage of the Credit Union Membership Access Act in August 1998. This act amended the Federal Credit Union Act to add multiple common bond credit unions to the current permissible categories of single common bond and community credit unions. However, the new act limited membership of multiple bond credit unions to 3,000.

The American Bankers Association filed suit against NCUA shortly after the NCUA adopted changes to the chartering and field of membership policies in compliance with the Credit Union Membership Access Act of 1998. Early legal decisions favored NCUA, but the American Bankers Association filed an appeal in May 2000. In November 2001 the U.S. Court of Appeals dismissed the American Bankers Association suit against NCUA's field of membership regulation issued pursuant to the Credit Union Membership Access Act.

Terrorist attacks in New York and Washington in September 2001 prompted immediate efforts by the federal government to further restrict the methods of moving funds internationally that may assist terrorists accomplish their goals. On October 26, 2001, President George W. Bush signed the Uniting and Strengthening America by Providing Appropriate Tools Required to Intercept and Obstruct Terrorism Act of (USA PATRIOT ACT) 2001. Title III of the PATRIOT ACT, International Money Laundering Abatement and Financial Anti-Terrorism Act of 2001, strengthened money-laundering laws, including funds held in credit unions.

■ KEY PERSONNEL

Chair of the Board
Dennis Dollar .... (703) 518–6300
Board Members
JoAnn Johnson (Vice Chair) .... (703) 518–6300
Deborah Matz .... (703) 518–6300
Secretary to the Board
Rebecca Baker .... (703) 518–6300
Chief Financial Officer
Dennis Winans .... (703) 518–6570
Fax .... (703) 518–6664
Deputy Financial Officer/NCUA
Ronald Aaron .... (703) 518–6570
Deputy Financial Officer/NCUSIF
Karen White .... (703) 518–6570
Community Development Credit Union
Anthony LaCreta .... (703) 518–6610
Fax .... (703) 518–6680
Corporate Credit Unions
Kent Buckham .... (703) 518–6640
Fax .... (703) 518–6665
Equal Employment Opportunity
Marilyn G. Gannon .... (703) 518–6325
Manager
Robert N. French .... (703) 518–6325
Examination and Insurance
David M. Marquis .... (703) 518–6360
Fax .... (703) 518–6666
Deputy Director
Tawanna Y. James .... (703) 518–6360

Executive Director
J. Leonard Skiles .... (703) 518–6320
Fax .... (703) 518–6661
Deputy Executive Director
Vacant .... (703) 518–6320
Director of Strategic Planning
James L. Patrick .... (703) 518–6315
General Counsel
Robert M. Fenner .... (703) 518–6540
Fax .... (703) 518–6667
Deputy General Counsel
James J. Engel .... (703) 518–6540
FOIA Officer
Dianne M. Salva .... (703) 518–6540
Associate General Counsel for Litigation and Liquidations
Allan H. Meltzer .... (703) 518–6540
Associate General Counsel for Operations
Shelia Albin .... (703) 518–6540
Special Counsel
Hattie M. Ulan .... (703) 518–6540
Human Resources
Sherry Turpenoff .... (703) 518–6510
Fax .... (703) 518–6668
Inspector General
Herb Yolles .... (703) 518–6350
Fax .... (703) 518–6670
Counsel
Sharon Separ .... (703) 518–6350
Investment Services
Vacant .... (703) 518–6620
Fax .... (703) 518–6663
Chief Information Officer
Douglas Verner .... (703) 518–6440
Fax .... (703) 518–6689
Systems and Customer Services
Jeryl Fish .... (703) 518–6440
Product Services
Gail Halkias .... (703) 518–6440
Training and Development
Leslie Armstrong (acting) .... (703) 518–6630
Fax .... (703) 518–6672

■ INFORMATION SOURCES

Internet
Agency Web Site: http://www.ncua.gov.

The NCUA also operates an electronic bulletin board system (BBS) that contains press releases, proposed regulations, legal opinions, and manuals from the agency.

For assistance .... (800) 518–6335
For modem access only .... (703) 518–6480

Telephone Contacts

Toll-free .... (800) 827–3255
Fax... (703) 518–6319
Personnel Locator .... (703) 518-6510
Inspector General's Hotline............... (703) 518-6357
Procurement.............................. (703) 518-6410

Information and Publications

KEY OFFICES

NCUA Public and Congressional Affairs
1775 Duke St.
Alexandria, VA 22314–3428
(703) 518–6330
Fax (703) 518–6330
Clifford R. Northup, director

Answers questions for the press and the public. Issues news releases; maintains a mailing list.

Freedom of Information
NCUA Office of General Counsel
1775 Duke St.
Alexandria, VA 22314–3428
(703) 518–6540
Dianne M. Salva, FOI officer

PUBLICATIONS

NCUA Office of Administration
Attn: Publications
1775 Duke St.
Alexandria, VA 22314–3428
(703) 518–6410
Michael Kole, director

Handles publications orders. Charges vary and prepayment is required. A complete list of publications is available. Titles include:
Annual Report of the Central Liquidity Facility
Annual Report of the National Credit Union Administration

Annual Report of the National Credit Union Share Insurance Fund
Federal Credit Union Act
Federal Credit Unions
NCUA-Credit Union Directory
Your Insured Funds

Technical publications include:
The Federal Credit Union Bylaws
NCUA Regulatory Handbook (compliance activities)
NCUA User's Guide (financial performance report)

Reference Resources

LIBRARY

NCUA Library
1775 Duke St.
Alexandria, VA 22314–3428
(703) 518–6540
Jackie Minor, library technician

A legal library located in the Office of the General Counsel. Open to the public from 8:00 a.m. to 4:00 p.m. An appointment is required.

RULES AND REGULATIONS

NCUA rules and regulations are published in the *Code of Federal Regulations*, Title 12, parts 700–760. Proposed regulations, new final regulations, and updates to the *Code of Federal Regulations* are published in the daily *Federal Register*. (See appendix for details on how to obtain and use these publications.)

The *Annual Report* of the NCUA also reports on regulatory actions taken by the agency during the previous year.

■ LEGISLATION

The NCUA carries out its responsibilities under:

Federal Credit Union Act (48 Stat. 1216, 12 U.S.C. 1751). Signed by the president June 26, 1934. Authorized the federal government to charter credit unions.

Federal Credit Union Act Amendments of 1970 (84 Stat. 994, 12 U.S.C. 1781). Signed by the president Oct. 19, 1970. Provided insurance coverage for member accounts in state and federally chartered credit unions.

Financial Institutions Regulatory and Interest Rate Control Act of 1978 (92 Stat. 3641, 12 U.S.C. 226 note). Signed by the president Nov. 10, 1978. Reorganized the NCUA and expanded the authority of bank regulators.

Depository Institutions Deregulation and Monetary Control Act of 1980 (94 Stat. 132, 12 U.S.C. 226 note). Signed by the president March 31, 1980. Extended reserve requirements to all financial institutions, phased out interest rate ceilings over a six-year period, and allowed thrift institutions to offer a wide range of financial services.

Deficit Reduction Act of 1984 (98 Stat. 1203, 12 U.S.C. 1781). Signed by the president July 18, 1984. Clarified the guidelines of the National Credit Union Share Insurance Fund; Central Liquidity Fund given tax-exempt status.

Competitive Equality Banking Act of 1987 (101 Stat. 552, 12 U.S.C. 226 note). Signed by the president Aug. 10, 1987. Streamlined credit union operations; exempted the NCUA from Gramm-Rudman-Hollings budget restrictions.

Financial Institutions Reform, Recovery, and Enforcement Act of 1989 (103 Stat. 183, 12 U.S.C. 1881 note). Signed by the president Aug. 9, 1989. Enhanced the regulatory and enforcement powers of federal financial institutions' regulatory agencies; established internal pay scale system; clarified the NCUA's powers as a liquidating agent and conservator.

Truth in Savings Act (105 Stat. 2334, 12 U.S.C. 4301 note). Signed by the president Dec. 19, 1991. Subtitle F of the FDIC Improvement Act of 1991 provided uniformity in the disclosure of terms and conditions on which interest is paid and fees are assessed in connection with savings accounts.

Small Business Regulatory Enforcement Fairness Act (110 Stat. 857, 5 U.S.C. 601 note). Signed by the president March 29, 1996. Amended the Regulatory Flexibility Act of 1980 and the Equal Access to Justice Act of 1985. Required the NCUA to prepare an economic analysis outlining any major impact a regulation may have on a significant number of small credit unions; required the NCUA to publish a compliance guide regarding the rules covered by the act; and provided for congressional and GAO review of all agency regulations.

Examination Parity and Year 2000 Readiness for Financial Institutions Act (112 Stat. 32, 12 U.S.C. 1461 note, 12 U.S.C. 1811 note). Signed by the president on March 20, 1998. Provided authority to the NCUA to supervise credit union organizations and institutions that provide services affected by the year 2000 computer problem.

Credit Union Membership Access Act (1751 Stat., 12 U.S.C.). Signed by the president Aug. 7, 1998. Amended the Federal Credit Union Act to add multiple common bond credit unions to the current permissible categories of single common bond and community credit unions. Limited a multiple common bond credit union group to fewer than 3,000 members. Directed the NCUA board to prescribe regulations defining "well-defined local community, neighborhood, or rural district" for the purposes of membership criteria.

Uniting and Strengthening America by Providing Appropriate Tools Required to Intercept and Obstruct Terrorism Act of 2001 (USA PATRIOT ACT) (115 Stat. 272, 18 U.S.C. 1 note). Signed by the president on Oct. 26, 2001. Title III amended federal law governing monetary transactions to prescribe procedural guidelines under which the secretary of the Treasury could require domestic financial institutions and agencies to take specified measures to combat money laundering. Required any credit union to record and report requirements for monetary instrument transactions.

◼ REGIONAL OFFICES

REGION 1
(CT, MA, ME, NH, NY, RI, VT)
9 Washington Sq.
Albany, NY 12205
(518) 862–7400
Mark Treichel, director

REGION 2
(DC, DE, MD, NJ, PA, VA)
1775 Duke St., #4206
Alexandria, VA 22314–3437
(703) 519-4600
Ed Dupcak, director

REGION 3
(AL, AR, FL, GA, KY, LA, MS, NC, PR, SC, TN, VI)
7000 Central Pkwy., #1600
Atlanta, GA 30328
(678) 443–3000
Alonzo Swann III, director

REGION 4
(IL, IN, MI, MO, OH, WI, WV)
4225 Naperville Rd., #125
Lisle, IL 60532-3658
(630) 955–4100
Melinda Love, director

REGION 5
(AZ, CO, IA, KS, MN, ND, NE, NM, OK, SD, TX)
4807 Spicewood Springs Rd., #5200
Austin, TX 78759–8490
(512) 349–5600
Jane Walters, director

REGION 6
(AK, AS, CA, GU, HI, ID, MT, NV, OR, WA, UT, WY)
2300 Clayton Rd., #1350
Concord, CA 94520
(925) 363–6200
Robert E. Blatner, director

AMAC (Asset Management Assistance Center)
4807 Spicewood Springs Rd., #5100
Austin, TX 78759-8490
(512) 231-7900
Mike Barton, president

National Mediation Board

1301 K St. N.W., Suite 250 East, Washington, DC 20572
Internet: http://www.nmb.gov

The National Mediation Board (NMB), established by the 1934 amendments to the Railway Labor Act of 1926, is an independent agency that performs a central role in facilitating harmonious labor-management relations within two of the nation's key transportation modes—the railroads and airlines.

The board has three members who are nominated by the president and confirmed by the Senate to three-year terms; the board members select a chair annually among themselves.

The board is responsible for the mediation of disputes over wages, hours, and working conditions that arise between rail and air carriers and organizations representing their employees. If a dispute arises among the employees of a carrier concerning the representation of the employees in negotiations, the board investigates and determines to whom such powers should be granted.

Either the carriers or the employee organizations may request mediation, or the board may intercede on its own initiative. The board mediates until the dispute is settled or until it determines that its efforts are unsuccessful, at which time it tries to persuade both parties to submit to arbitration. If either party refuses to arbitrate, the board states that mediation has failed. After a thirty-day cooling off period, the employer is entitled to change rates of pay, rules, or working conditions, and employees may strike.

If, in the opinion of the board, a labor dispute seriously threatens to interrupt interstate commerce, the board notifies the president. The president may, in turn, appoint an emergency board to investigate the dispute. During an investigation a strike is barred. There have only been five airline presidential emergency boards since 1978. In 2002

one presidential emergency board was created to investigate a strike threatened at United Airlines. United and its union workers eventually reached agreement without a strike or lock-out.

Individual grievances arising under labor-management agreements in the railroad industry are handled by the National Railroad Adjustment Board and public law boards. These are paid for by the NMB. There are no publicly funded boards for the airline industry; the NMB merely appoints a neutral referee on request.

Historically, some 97 percent of all NMB mediation cases have been successfully resolved without interruptions to public service. Since 1980, only slightly more than 1 percent of cases have involved a disruption of service.

The elimination of the Interstate Commerce Commission (ICC) at the end of 1995 raised questions about the status of certain companies that the ICC categorized as "express carriers." In particular, Federal Express, a package delivery company, had been covered by the Railway Labor Act, while its principal competitor, United Parcel Service (UPS), fell under the National Labor Relations Act. Legislation in 1996 preserved this controversial distinction, but in September 2000 the NMB certified that UPS flight dispatchers were covered under the Railway Labor Act. Future action on the subject could shift companies under the NMB's jurisdiction to that of the National Labor Relations Board (NLRB). Most likely, jurisdiction will be determined on a case-by-case basis.

In 2002 the NMB handled fifty-nine mediation cases. Fifty-five (93 percent) reached tentative contract agreements with forty-five days or less of negotiation. Forty-nine cases (80 percent) reached tentative contract agreements in one year or less.

KEY PERSONNEL

Chair
Francis L. Duggan .... (202) 692–5019

Board Members
Edward Fitzmaurice .... (202) 692–5016
Harry Hoglander .... (202) 692–5022

Chief of Staff
Benetta Mansfield .... (202) 692–5030

Deputy Chiefs of Staff
Larry Gibbons .... (202) 692–5060
Daniel Rainey .... (202) 692–5051

Arbitration
Roland Watkins .... (202) 692–5055

Chief Financial Officer
June King .... (202) 692–5010

Hearing Officers
Mary L. Johnson .... (202) 692–5040
Eileen Hennessey .... (202) 692–5040
Susanna Pequinot .... (202) 692–5040

INFORMATION SOURCES

Internet

The NMB maintains its Web site at: http://www.nmb.gov.

Telephone Contacts

Switchboard .... (202) 692–5000
Fax .... (202) 692–5080
TDD .... (202) 692–5001

Information and Publications

KEY OFFICES

NMB Information Contacts
1301 K St. N.W., Suite 250 East
Washington, DC 20572
(202) 692–5050
Don West, public affairs officer
(202) 692–5050
Judy Femi, Freedom of Information officer

PUBLICATIONS

NMB Publications Contact
1301 K St. N.W., Suite 250 East
(202) 692–5000
Florine Kellogg, publications contact

Titles available include:
Annual Report of the National Mediation Board Including the Report of the National Railroad Adjustment Board
Determinations of the National Mediation Board
The Railway Labor Act (U.S. Code Provisions)

Reference Resources

DOCUMENTS

Documents Office
1301 K St. N.W., Suite 250 East
Washington, DC 20572
(202) 692–5030
Susan Brown, director

Copies of collective bargaining agreements between labor and management of various rail and air carriers, and copies of the determinations issued by the board, are available for inspection.

NMB rules and regulations are published in the *Code of Federal Regulations*, Title 29, parts 1200–1209. Proposed regulations, new final rules, and updates to the *Code of Federal Regulations* are published in the daily *Federal Register*. (See appendix for details on how to obtain and use these publications.)

LEGISLATION

The National Mediation Board exercises its authority under amendments to the **Railway Labor Act** (48 Stat. 1185, 45 U.S.C. 151–158, 160–162). The amendments creating the board were signed by the president June 21, 1934.

REGIONAL OFFICE

NATIONAL RAILROAD ADJUSTMENT BOARD
844 N. Rush St.
Chicago, IL 60611
(312) 751–4688

National Transportation Safety Board

490 L'Enfant Plaza East S.W., Washington, DC 20594
Internet: http://www.ntsb.gov

The National Transportation Safety Board (NTSB) was created by the Department of Transportation Act of 1966 and began operations in April 1967. Originally it was an autonomous agency within the Department of Transportation. In 1974 Congress passed the Independent Safety Board Act that granted NTSB independent status. The board began operations under the new act on April 1, 1975.

The board is composed of five members appointed by the president and confirmed by the Senate. Board members serve five-year terms; two members are designated by the president to serve as chair and vice chair for two-year terms. No more than three members of the board may be of the same political party. At least three members must be appointed on the basis of demonstrated knowledge of accident reconstruction, safety engineering, human factors, transportation safety, or transportation regulation.

The NTSB headquarters are in Washington, with regional offices for aviation, highway, and railroad accidents. The NTSB:

- Investigates, determines accident cause, makes safety recommendations, and reports the facts and circumstances of all U.S. civil aviation accidents; all railroad accidents in which there is a fatality or substantial property damage, or in which involve a passenger train; all pipeline accidents in which there is a fatality or substantial property damage; highway accidents involving issues with wide-ranging safety significance; major marine casualties and marine accidents involving a public vessel and a nonpublic vessel; and other catastrophic transportation accidents.
- Investigates and reports on the transportation of hazardous materials.
- Makes recommendations on matters pertaining to transportation safety and works to prevent accidents by conducting special studies.

- Assesses techniques of accident investigation.
- Publishes recommended procedures for accident investigations, establishing regulations governing the reporting of accidents and evaluating the effectiveness of the transportation safety efforts of other government agencies.
- Reviews on appeal the suspension, amendment, modification, revocation, or denial of any certificate or license issued by the secretary or any of the administrators of the Department of Transportation.

Since the board's creation, more than 80 percent of the NTSB's recommendations have been implemented. The NTSB has issued more than 11,600 recommendations in all transportation modes to more than 2,200 recipients.

The NTSB can only make safety recommendations; it has no authority to impose them or to take action. For example, in response to two unsolved crashes involving Boeing 737 aircraft—in 1991 at Colorado Springs, and in 1994 near Pittsburgh—the NTSB recommended that the FAA require airlines to retrofit planes with new flight data recorders, which would allow more extensive data to be recovered in the future. The NTSB recommended retrofitting 737s by the end of 1995 and most other planes by the end of 1997. In April 1995 the FAA adopted the substance of the NTSB's recommendations but not its timetable; in July 1996 NTSB chair James Hall remarked that retrofits were still not slated to conclude before the year 2000.

In the 1990s the NTSB faced intense and ever-increasing pressure from the media to solve high-profile cases quickly; such accidents as the collision of two passenger trains at Silver Spring, Md., in February 1996, and the crash of a TWA 747 off East Moriches, Long Island, in July 1996, have been followed by daily press conferences with the NTSB officials in charge of the investigation. Reaction to the Long Island crash—most notably from victims' families—forced the NTSB to coordinate its accident investigation to an unusual extent with the effort to recover bodies.

Following those highly publicized investigations in 1996, the NTSB was assigned the role of coordinating the resources of the federal government and other organizations to support the efforts of the local and state authorities and the airlines to meet the needs of aviation disaster victims and their families. Family counseling, victim identification and forensic services, communication with foreign governments, and translation services are among the services with which the federal government can help local authorities and the airlines deal with a major aviation disaster.

In cases where criminal action is suspected, the NTSB works closely with the FBI; once sabotage has been proved, as in the October 1995 derailment of Amtrak's Sunset Limited in Hyder, Ariz., the FBI officially takes over the investigation. The NTSB also worked with the FBI in investigating the four flights that were hijacked and crashed by terrorists on Sept. 11, 2001.

Although the NTSB does not have enforcement authority, the NTSB's administrative law judges conduct formal hearings and issue initial decisions on appeals from all FAA certificate actions and civil penalty actions involving pilots, engineers, mechanics, and repair personnel. Also covered are petitions for certification that have been denied by the FAA.

The NTSB Academy, established in 2001, is a new NTSB organization currently under development. The academy's building is under construction in Ashburn, Va., and is expected to be ready in late summer 2003. The academy's main purpose is to train NTSB investigators and employees. Most courses will be geared to the investigation of aviation accidents.

The Rail Passenger Disaster Family Assistance Act of 2003 was introduced in March 2003. The act would authorize the NTSB to establish a director of family support services for families of rail accident victims. Action was pending in the 108th Congress.

◼ KEY PERSONNEL

Chair
Ellen G. Engleman .... (202) 314–6020
Fax .... (202) 314–6018
Vice Chair
Mark Rosenker .... (202) 314–6020
Board Members
Carol Carmody .... (202) 314–6050
Fax .... (202) 314–6035

Richard Healing .... (202) 314–6030
Fax .... (202) 314–6035
John J. Goglia .... (202) 314–6660
Fax .... (202) 314–6035
Administrative Law Judges
William Fowler Jr., chief .... (202) 314–6150
Fax .... (202) 314–6158
Aviation Safety
John Clark .... (202) 314–6300
Fax .... (202) 314–6309
Equal Employment Opportunity
Fara Guest .... (202) 314–6190
Fax .... (202) 314–6260
General Counsel
Ron Battocchi .... (202) 314–6080
Fax .... (202) 314–6090
Government Affairs
Brenda Lee Yager .... (202) 314–6100
Fax .... (202) 314–6110
Managing Director
Daniel Campbell .... (202) 314–6060
Fax .... (202) 314–6070
Research and Engineering
Vernon Ellingstad .... (202) 314–6500
Fax .... (202) 314–6598
Safety Recommendations
Elaine Weinstein .... (202) 314–6170
Fax .... (202) 314–6178

◼ INFORMATION SOURCES

Internet
Agency Web site: http://www.ntsb.gov. Offers press releases, as well as information on recent transportation accidents and a list of the improvements in transportation safety that are highest priorities for the NTSB.

Telephone Contacts
Switchboard .... (202) 314–6000
Main Fax .... (202) 314–6018

Information and Publications

KEY OFFICES

NTSB Public Affairs
490 L'Enfant Plaza East S.W.
Washington, DC 20594
(202) 314–6100
Fax (202) 314–6110
Jamie Finch, director

Provides information about the NTSB, including press releases.

Freedom of Information

NTSB Office of Administration
490 L'Enfant Plaza East S.W.
Washington, DC 20594
(202) 314–6540
(800) 877–6799
Melba Moye, FOI contact

PUBLICATIONS

Titles available include the annual report, accident report series, transportation accident briefs, transportation safety recommendations, transportation special reports, initial decisions, board opinions and orders in safety enforcement and seamen cases, and the transportation abstract newsletter. Some documents are available on the agency's Internet site; others may be ordered from the National Technical Information Service (NTIS) by calling (800) 553-6847. See appendix, Ordering Government Publications. Some later publications, including the *List of Most Wanted Safety Regulations*, are available online through the NTSB Web site.

The Public Inquiries Section maintains a mailing list for those who wish to receive the news digest on a continuing basis; (202) 314-6551 or (800) 877-6799.

DATA AND STATISTICS

The NTSB's annual report contains statistical data on accidents, accident rates, and fatalities.

Reference Resources

DOCKETS

NTSB Public Inquiries Section

490 L'Enfant Plaza East S.W.
Washington, DC 20594
(202) 314–6551
(800) 877–6799
Melba Moye, records management officer

Handles all requests for files on aviation, highway, rail, pipeline, and marine accidents investigated by the NTSB.

NTSB Docket Section

490 L'Enfant Plaza East S.W.
Washington, DC 20594
(202) 314–6551
(800) 877–6799

Handles all requests for information on appeals cases of air and marine personnel.

RULES AND REGULATIONS

NTSB rules and regulations are published in the *Code of Federal Regulations*, Title 49, parts 800–850. Proposed regulations, new final regulations, and updates to the *Code of Federal Regulations* are published in the daily *Federal Register*. (See appendix for details on how to obtain and use these publications.)

The *National Transportation Safety Board Annual Report to Congress* reports on accident investigations and safety study actions taken by the agency during the previous year.

▪ LEGISLATION

Federal Aviation Act of 1958 as amended (72 Stat. 731, 49 U.S.C. 1411). Signed by the president Aug. 23, 1958. Required the Civil Aeronautics Board to investigate and report on accidents involving civil aircraft. (These responsibilities were acquired by the NTSB in 1966.)

Department of Transportation Act of 1966 (80 Stat. 931, 49 U.S.C. 1651). Signed by the president Oct. 15, 1966. Created the Department of Transportation and established the National Transportation Safety Board as an independent agency within the department.

Independent Safety Board Act of 1974 (88 Stat. 2166, 49 U.S.C. 1901). Signed by the president Jan. 3, 1975. Established the NTSB as a totally separate agency.

Independent Safety Board Act Amendments of 1981 (95 Stat. 1065, 49 U.S.C. 1901). Signed by the president Nov. 3, 1981. Gave board investigations priority over other federal agency investigations; allowed NTSB employees to examine or test any item necessary to investigations.

Aviation Insurance Program (96 Stat. 1453, 49 U.S.C. 1902 note). Signed by the president Oct. 14, 1982. Amended the Independent Safety Board Act of 1974 by requiring that at least three members of the board have expertise in the fields of accident reconstruction, safety engineering, human factors, transportation safety, or transportation regulation.

Aviation Drug-Trafficking Control Act (98 Stat. 2315, 49 U.S.C. app. 1301). Signed by the president Oct. 19, 1984. Authorized the board to review on appeal the revocation of certain certificates or licenses issued by the FAA administrator because of aircraft transportation of controlled substances.

Airport and Airway Safety and Capacity Expansion Act of 1987 (101 Stat. 1528, 49 U.S.C. app. 2201). Signed by the president Dec. 30, 1987. Authorized the board to require the reporting of accidents and aviation incidents involving public aircraft other than aircraft of the armed forces and the intelligence agencies.

Independent Safety Board Act Amendments of 1988 (102 Stat. 876, 877; 49 U.S.C. app. 1901). Signed by the president July 19, 1988. Authorized an emergency fund of $1 million for necessary expenses, not otherwise provided, for the purpose of accident investigations.

National Transportation Safety Board Amendments of 1996 (110 Stat. 3452, 49 U.S.C. 1101 note). Signed by the president on Oct. 11, 1996. Prohibited the NTSB from disclosing records or information relating to its participation in foreign aircraft accident investigations. Further prohibited NTSB from providing safety-related information that was unrelated to NTSB's accident or incident investigation authority, if such disclosure would inhibit the voluntary provision of that type of information. Authorized the NTSB to conduct training of its employees in subjects necessary for the proper performance of accident investigations.

Aviation Disaster Family Assistance Act of 1996 (49 U.S.C. 1136), which was signed by the president on Oct. 9, 1996; and **Foreign Air Carrier Support Act of 1997** (49 U.S.C. 41313), which was signed by the president on Dec. 16, 1997. Gave the NTSB the authority to coordinate federal services to victims of major aviation accidents and their families.

■ REGIONAL OFFICES

NTSB/Aviation

NORTHEAST
2001 Route 46, #203
Parsippany, NJ 07054
(973) 334–6420
Robert Pearce, director

SOUTHEAST
8405 N.W. 53rd St., #B-103
Miami, FL 33166
(305) 597–4610
Jorge Prellezo, director

NORTH CENTRAL
31 West 775 North Ave.
West Chicago, IL 60185
(630) 377–8177
Carl Dinwiddie, director

SOUTH CENTRAL
624 Six Flags Dr., #150
Arlington, TX 76011
(817) 652–7800
Tim Borson, director

NORTHWEST
19518 Pacific Hwy. South, #201
Seattle, WA 98188
(206) 870–2200
Keith McGuire, director

SOUTHWEST
1515 W. 190th St., #555
Gardena, CA 90248
(310) 380–5660
Gary Mucho, director

NTSB/Highway

NORTHEAST
2001 Route 46, #203
Parsippany, NJ 07054
(973) 334–6615
Vacant, director

SOUTHEAST
Atlanta Federal Center
60 Forsyth St. S.W., #3M25
Atlanta, GA 30303–3104
(202) 314–6419
Bruce Magladry, director (operating out of Washington, DC headquarters)

CENTRAL
624 Six Flags Dr., #150
Arlington, TX 76011
(817) 652–7840
Kenneth Rogers, director

WESTERN
1515 W. 190th St., #555
Gardena, CA 90248
(310) 380–5461
Ron Robinson, director

NTSB/Railroad

EASTERN

Atlanta Federal Center
60 Forsyth St. S.W., #3M25
Atlanta, GA 30303–3104
(404) 562-1655
Mark Garcia, director

CENTRAL

31 West 775 North Ave.
West Chicago, IL 60185
(630) 377–8177
Russell Seipler, director

WESTERN

1515 W. 190th St., #555
Gardena, CA 90248
(310) 380–5453
Dave Watson, director

Nuclear Regulatory Commission

11555 Rockville Pike, Rockville, MD
Mailing address: Washington, DC 20555
Internet: http://www.nrc.gov

The Nuclear Regulatory Commission (NRC) was created by the Energy Reorganization Act of 1974 and began operation in January 1975. It took over the nuclear regulatory and licensing functions of the Atomic Energy Commission (AEC), which was abolished. The other functions of the AEC, primarily nuclear research and development, were taken over by the Energy Research and Development Administration (later incorporated into the Department of Energy).

The commission is headed by five commissioners appointed by the president and confirmed by the Senate. No more than three commissioners may be members of the same political party. Commissioners serve five-year terms; the president names one commissioner to serve as chair.

Specifically, the NRC:

- Licenses the construction and operation of nuclear reactors and commercial fuel cycle facilities.
- Licenses the possession, use, transportation, handling, packaging, and disposal of nuclear materials.
- Regulates licensed activities including ensuring that measures are taken for the physical protection of nuclear facilities and materials.
- Develops and implements rules and regulations for licensed nuclear activities.
- Conducts public hearings on radiological safety, environmental, common defense, security, and antitrust matters.
- Develops effective working relationships with states and monitors their regulation of nuclear materials.
- Licenses the export and import of nuclear equipment and materials.

The Energy Reorganization Act of 1974 mandated three offices within the commission responsible for the following areas: nuclear reactor regulation, nuclear material safety and safeguards, and nuclear regulatory research.

The Office of Nuclear Reactor Regulation licenses nuclear reactors used for testing, research, and power generation. A construction permit must be granted before construction can begin on a nuclear facility and an operating license must be issued before fuel can be loaded and the reactor started. License applications are reviewed to determine whether the proposed facility can be built and operated without undue risk to public safety and health. Environmental impact is also considered. Applicants are investigated to determine if they are properly insured against accidents. No application to construct a new nuclear plant has been approved since 1979.

An applicant may apply for a Limited Work Authorization (LWA) if a favorable initial decision has been issued on environmental and site suitability issues but not on the possible effects on public health and safety. The LWA enables the applicant to begin work on plant construction, but there is no guarantee that the final construction permit will later be authorized. Complete construction of the site may be carried out only after a licensing board has made favorable findings regarding health and safety matters.

Public hearings on applications for construction permits are mandatory. The proceedings are conducted by an Atomic Safety and Licensing Board in communities near proposed nuclear facilities. Notices of hearings are published in the *Federal Register,* posted in the nearest public document room, and published in local newspapers. Interested parties petition the licensing board for the right to participate in public hearings. The two types of participation are:

Limited appearance—an informal submission of a written statement to be included in the hearing record or oral presentation at the hearing.

Evidentiary appearance—petitioning the commission to become an "intervenor" in the case, with full rights in the hearing including cross-examination of witnesses.

Through more standardized reactor designs, in the future the revised licensing process will allow for early resolution of licensing issues and will result in one license, rather than two, being issued by the NRC for the construction of new nuclear plants.

The Office of Nuclear Material Safety and Safeguards ensures that public health and safety, national security, and environmental factors are considered in the licensing and regulation of nuclear facilities. Safeguards are reviewed and assessed against possible threats, thefts, and sabotage.

The Office of Nuclear Regulatory Research conducts research in nuclear safety, safeguards, and environmental assessment to support agency licensing activities and the commission's decision-making process. Its functions include developing and recommending nuclear safety standards in the licensed uses of nuclear facilities and materials and preparing standards for the preparation of environmental impact statements.

The Office of State and Tribal Programs is responsible for establishing and maintaining effective communications and working relationship between the NRC and states, local government, other federal agencies, and American Indian tribe organizations. It serves as the primary contact for policy matters between NRC and these external groups, and it keeps the agency appraised of these groups' activities as they may affect NRC.

Other offices within the NRC assist the agency in carrying out its mission but are not required under the commission's establishing legislation.

The Office of Enforcement monitors compliance with regulatory requirements. Current enforcement policy forbids operations by any licensees with inadequate levels of protection. The Office of Enforcement may issue written violation notices, assign civil penalties, order a licensee to "cease and desist," and modify, suspend, or revoke licenses.

The Office of Investigations monitors the investigations of licensees, applicants, contractors, or vendors, including the investigation of all allegations of wrongdoing by other than NRC employees and contractors.

Office of Nuclear Security and Incident Response, established in April 2002, develops overall agency policy and provides management direction for evaluation and assessment of technical issues involving security at nuclear facilities. The office operates as the agency interface on security matters with the departments of Energy and Homeland Security, the Federal Emergency Management Agency, the intelligence and law enforcement communities, and other federal agencies.

Elements of the NRC also serve an advisory function. The Advisory Committee on Reactor Safeguards provides advice on the safety of proposed and existing nuclear facilities. Licensing boards for the NRC are formed from members of the Atomic Safety and Licensing Board Panel. The Advisory Committee on Nuclear Waste advises the NRC on nuclear waste management.

The economic, regulatory, and political climate has discouraged construction of new plants since the Three Mile Island accident in 1979. That accident brought orders on new nuclear plants to a halt. Moreover, changes mandated after Three Mile Island greatly increased construction costs for the plants on order, adding to the financial burdens of an industry already plagued by cost overruns and construction mismanagement.

The NRC faces competing, perhaps contradictory, demands to improve its enforcement of safety regulations and to cut costs. When the media criticized the agency in March 1996 for overlooking safety violations for some years at the Millstone reactor in Connecticut, NRC chair Shirley Jackson acknowledged that problems existed, but stressed that they were being addressed. By May the nationwide review she ordered of nuclear plants' refueling procedures had found that fourteen other reactors had safety violations similar to those at the Millstone facility.

In 1995 Jackson also moved to review NRC rules implemented in 1990 and 1992, which sought to increase reactor safety by requiring psychological services for nuclear-plant employees who were thought to be experiencing stress or abusing drugs. These rules appeared to have had an unintended consequence, by giving management leeway to subject workers to psychological examinations whenever they raise safety concerns—and thus allegedly opening a loophole for retaliation against whistleblowers.

In 1996 Jackson announced several major organizational changes within the NRC. The Office of the Chief Financial Officer and the Office of the Chief Information Officer were established. Under Jackson, the NRC also moved to let nuclear plants conduct their own examinations of prospective reactor operators. This shift was projected to save the agency at least $3 million a year. Consumer advocates feared it could lower standards for operators at a time when the challenges to avert accidents are increasing.

In 1998 the NRC and the Department of Energy (DOE) began a pilot program to test the feasibility of NRC external regulation of DOE nuclear facilities. The pilot program tested regulatory concepts at specific DOE nuclear facilities, through simulated regulations, by evaluating a facility and its standards, requirements, procedures, practices, and activities against the standards that NRC determined would ensure safety. The overall conclusion of the NRC task force was that most of the technical, policy, and regulatory issues involved in NRC oversight of the DOE nuclear facilities studied as part of the pilot program could be handled adequately within the existing NRC regulatory structure.

At the turn of the millennium, the NRC was concerned that the race toward electric utility deregulation might compromise safety as well as bring about financial problems for nuclear power plants. Some industry watchers predicted that the deregulation of electricity prices would cause so much financial pressure that a large percentage of operating nuclear plants would be forced to shut down before the end of their forty-year licenses. Despite these dire predictions, nuclear plants have not shut down as some had predicted and have continued to apply for license renewal. In 2002 there were 103 operating commercial nuclear power plants in the United States. U.S. nuclear power plants contributed approximately one-fifth of the total electricity generation in the nation.

As U.S. nuclear power plants age, the future problems of managing nuclear waste from facilities that are decommissioned has remained unsolved for many years. In 2002, after many years of debate, a permanent nuclear waste repository at a site beneath Yucca Mountain in the Nevada desert was approved. However, lawsuits to determine whether the Yucca Mountain site will be built have been ongoing. In the meantime the Energy Department has begun work on a massive license application that will be submitted to the NRC in 2004. The commission's review was expected to be complete by 2008. If approved, the license would authorize DOE to construct the repository, marking the first step in a three-pronged process that would require separate NRC approvals to build, operate, and eventually close the facility.

The Yucca Mountain project, scheduled to begin operations in 2010, has been a multifaceted endeavor. Besides the license application and scientific studies, the DOE must formulate and implement a plan for transporting used nuclear fuel and defense waste to the Nevada site, approximately 90 miles north of Las Vegas. The department will cooperate with local, state, tribal, and federal agencies to develop a transportation plan by mid-2003.

Following the terrorist attacks of September 2001, security at nuclear facilities became the leading issue for the NRC. Sen. Harry Reid introduced legislation in 2002 to amend the Atomic Energy Act of 1954 to establish a task force on nuclear infrastructure security to examine the protection of sensitive nuclear facilities from potential terrorist threats. NRC chair Richard Meserve generally supported the bill but expressed his concern that the proposed bill did not provide the necessary procedural flexibility to issue many new regulatory requirements and continue to protect sensitive information. Meserve did not want to see sensitive information made available to the public, and possibly terrorists. The bill, however, did not pass that year.

The NRC, however, has not waited for legislation to begin to improve security measures. Since the terrorist attacks the NRC has been engaged in a comprehensive review of its programs and security of the nuclear facilities and activities it regulates. The NRC made a number of significant changes to its regulatory programs and issued orders to licensees to improve security in the interim period while the commission completed its comprehensive review. The NRC established a new Office of Nuclear Security and Incident Response to focus and coordinate the agency's efforts in the security and emergency preparedness areas. The NRC established a threat advisory system for NRC licensees, the NRC Threat Advisory and Protective Measures System, based on guidance from the Office of Homeland Security.

In January 2003 Senator Reid reintroduced his bill as the Nuclear Security Act of 2003, which had many of the same provisions of the earlier legislation. The act would direct the president to (1) promulgate regulations establishing the Nuclear Infrastructure Antiterrorism Team to protect sensitive nuclear facility perimeters; and (2) establish a training program for National Guard, state, and local law enforcement agency response to threats against a sensitive nuclear facility. The legislation would authorize trained security guards and employees of NRC certificate holders to carry firearms at NRC facilities. Action on this legislation is pending.

■ KEY PERSONNEL

Chairman
    Nils J. Diaz .... (301) 415–1759
Commissioners
    Vacant .... (301) 415–8420
    Greta J. Dicus .... (301) 415–1820
    Edward McGaffigan .... (301) 415–1800
    Jeffrey S. Merrifield .... (301) 415–1855
Administration
    Michael L. Springer .... (301) 415–6222
Atomic Safety and Licensing Board Panel
    G. Paul Bollwerk III .... (301) 415–7454
Commission Appellate Adjudication
    John F. Cordes Jr. .... (301) 415–1600
Congressional Affairs
    Dennis K. Rathbun .... (301) 415–1776
Chief Financial Officer
    Jesse L. Funchess .... (301) 415–7322
Chief Information Officer
    Ellis W. Merschoff .... (301) 415–8700
Enforcement
    Frank J. Congel .... (301) 415–2741

Executive Director for Operations
William D. Travers......................(301) 415–1700
General Counsel
Karen D. Cyr...........................(301) 415–1743
Inspector General
Hubert T. Bell...........................(301) 415–5930
International Programs
Janice Dunn Lee.......................(301) 415–1780
Investigations
Guy P. Caputo..........................(301) 415–2373
Nuclear Material Safety and Safeguards
Martin J. Virgilio......................(301) 415–7800
Nuclear Reactor Regulation
Samuel J. Collins.......................(301) 415–1270
Nuclear Regulatory Research
Ashok Thadani.........................(301) 415–6641
Secretary of the Commission
Annette L. Vietti-Cook................(301) 415–1969
Small Business and Civil Rights
Corenthis B. Kelley....................(301) 415–7380
State and Tribal Programs
Paul H. Lohaus........................(301) 415–3340
Advisory Committee on Medical Use of Isotopes
Manuel D. Cergueira..................(301) 415–0191
Advisory Committee on Nuclear Waste
George Hornberger.....................(301) 415–6816
Advisory Committee on Reactor Safeguards
George Apostolakis....................(301) 415–6807

▓ INFORMATION SOURCES

Internet

Agency Web site: http://www.nrc.gov. Includes a wide range of information on the NRC and on nuclear reactors and materials.

The NRC Public Document Room also operates the Bibliographic Retrieval System (BRS), an online database with citations of public documents since 1978 and the full text of selected documents from 1995 onward. The Public Document Room also offers an electronic bulletin board (BBS) that is accessible via FedWorld; for access to the BBS, call (703) 487–4086.

Telephone Contacts

Personnel Locator..........................(301) 415–7000
Main Fax...................................(301) 415–7010
or......................................(301) 415–7020
Toll-free Number..........................(800) 368–5642
Public Document Room...................(800) 397–4209
or......................................(202) 415-4737

Information and Publications

KEY OFFICES

NRC Public Affairs
Washington, DC 20555
(301) 415–8200
Fax (301) 415–2234 or (301) 415–3716
E-mail: opa@nrc.gov
William Beecher, director

Answers general questions from the public and the press; issues publications and news releases; coordinates requests for speakers and/or participants for seminars and lectures.

Freedom of Information
NRC Office of Administration
Washington, DC 20555
(301) 415–7169
Carol Ann Reed, FOI officer

PUBLICATIONS

NRC publications are available from the NRC Public Document Room (see Libraries) or by contacting one of the following:

NRC Sales
P.O. Box 37082
Washington, DC 20013
Fax (202) 512–2250

National Technical Information Service (NTIS) or U.S. Government Printing Office (GPO). See appendix, Ordering Government Publications.

A quarterly listing of abstracts for all NRC reports is available through the NTIS and the GPO; fees vary. Also available:

Licensee Event Report Compilation. Monthly; arranged by facility name and by event date for each facility.

Nuclear Regulatory Commission Issuances. Monthly; includes opinions, decisions, denials, memoranda, and orders of the commission, the Atomic Safety and Licensing Board, and the administrative law judge.

Nuclear Regulatory Commission's Regulatory Guides. Description of methods acceptable for implementing specific requirements of NRC regulations; published in ten subject areas.

Nuclear Regulatory Commission's Rules and Regulations. Loose-leaf set of the information contained in Title 10, parts 0–199, *Code of Federal Regulations,* and replacement pages, issued as supplements, reflecting amendments to rules.

Nuclear Regulatory Commission's Telephone Directory. Biannual.

Public Document Room Accession List. Weekly and monthly description of information received and generated by the NRC, including docketed and nondocketed material. Available free from NRC's Public Document Room.

MEETINGS

Advisory Committee Meetings

Schedules of upcoming advisory committee meetings are published in the *Federal Register* at least seven days in advance of the meeting (see appendix for how to use the *Federal Register*). Records of previous meetings are available for review in the NRC Public Document Room. Contact NRC Public Affairs for the meeting schedule.

Commission Meetings

The commissioners usually meet several times a week in the commissioner's conference room at NRC headquarters in Rockville, MD. Meetings are open to the public unless the subject of the meeting is exempt under the Government in the Sunshine Act.

Notices of meetings are posted in the NRC Public Document Room and in the *Federal Register.*

Subjects to be covered are published in the *Federal Register* one week before each meeting. The NRC also maintains a recorded message service with details of upcoming meetings: (301) 415–1292.

Reference Resources

LIBRARIES

NRC Public Document Room

1 White Flint North, 1st Fl.
11555 Rockville Pike
Rockville, MD 20852
(301) 415-4737
Fax (301) 415-3548
Telephone reference: (800) 397–4209
E-mail: pdr@nrc.gov
Hours: 7:45 a.m. to 4:15 p.m., Monday through Friday.

Provides NRC publications. Houses all material on NRC licensing cases and facilities; rulemaking proceedings; research, topical, and periodic reports; regulatory guides;

judicial decisions; and reports to Congress. Maintains the Bibliographic Retrieval System (BRS), an online database; conducts free searches of the BRS and trains clients in how to use it. The training tutorial, as well as the BRS itself, is accessible online from remote locations.

NRC Technical Library

11545 Rockville Pike
Rockville, MD
(Mailing address: Washington, DC 20555)
(301) 415–5610
Hours: 7:30 a.m. to 4:15 p.m., Monday through Friday.
Eileen Chen, section chief

Maintains a collection of technical materials published by the NRC and other sources.

DOCKETS

Contact the NRC Public Document Room: (301) 415–4737.

RULES AND REGULATIONS

NRC rules, regulations, and standards are published in the *Code of Federal Regulations,* Title 10, parts 0–199. Proposed regulations and standards, new final rules and standards, and updates to the *Code of Federal Regulations* are published in the daily *Federal Register.* (See appendix for information on how to obtain and use these publications.)

■ LEGISLATION

The NRC exercises authority under the following legislation, as amended:

Atomic Energy Act of 1954 as amended (68 Stat. 919, 42 U.S.C. 2011). Signed by the president Aug. 30, 1954. Established the Atomic Energy Commission, which was the forerunner of the NRC, and set out the basic authority for the regulation of nuclear energy.

Energy Reorganization Act of 1974 as amended (88 Stat. 1242, 42 U.S.C. 5841). Signed by the president Oct. 11, 1974. Abolished the Atomic Energy Commission, transferring its powers to the NRC and the Energy Research and Development Administration (now Department of Energy).

Clean Air Act Amendments (91 Stat. 685, 42 U.S.C. 7401). Signed by the president Aug. 7, 1977. Gave the Environmental Protection Agency and the NRC authority to set air quality standards for radioactive substances and emissions.

Nuclear Non-Proliferation Act of 1978 (92 Stat. 120, 22 U.S.C. 3201). Signed by the president Mar. 10, 1978. Established a more effective framework to ensure worldwide development of peaceful nuclear activities and prevent the export by any nation of equipment, technology, or nuclear materials that contribute to proliferation.

Uranium Mill Tailings Radiation Control Act of 1978 as amended (92 Stat. 3021, 42 U.S.C. 7901 note). Signed by the president Nov. 8, 1978. Authorized the NRC to regulate the handling and disposal of wastes from the processing of uranium.

Reorganization Plan No. 1 (H. Doc. 96–288, as amended by H. Doc. 96–307). Effective June 16, 1980. Increased the authority of the NRC chair to oversee nuclear power plant emergencies and to control staff operations.

Low-Level Radioactive Waste Policy Act of 1980 (94 Stat. 3347, 42 U.S.C. 2021b). Signed by the president Dec. 23, 1980. Established a federal program for the interim storage of spent nuclear fuel away from the reactor. Title III established NRC's duties and policy regarding storage and licensing of waste storage facilities.

Nuclear Waste Policy Act of 1982 (96 Stat. 2201, 42 U.S.C. 10101 note). Signed by the president Jan. 7, 1983. Established a deadline for establishing a permanent underground repository for high-level nuclear waste.

Low-Level Radioactive Waste Policy Amendments Act of 1985 (99 Stat. 1842, 42 U.S.C. 2021). Signed by the president Jan. 15, 1986. Imposed strict deadlines for states or regions to set up disposal facilities for low-level radioactive wastes; approved compacts among 37 states to join together for the disposal of such wastes.

Solar, Wind, Waste, and Geothermal Power Production Incentives Act of 1990 (104 Stat. 2834, 16 U.S.C. 791a note). Signed by the president Nov. 15, 1990. Amended the Atomic Energy Act of 1954 by providing a single-step process for licensing uranium enrichment. Directed the NRC to prescribe regulations for the control, ownership, or possession of any equipment or device, or important component part, that is capable of separating uranium isotopes or enriching uranium in isotope 235.

Energy Policy Act of 1992 (106 Stat. 2776, 42 U.S.C. 13201). Signed by the president Oct. 24, 1992. Title VIII specifically dealt with the NRC's responsibilities regarding the disposal/storage of high-level radioactive waste. Section 801b established NRC requirements and criteria regarding nuclear waste disposal, particularly at the Yucca Mountain site. Section 803 required that the NRC, along with the DOE and the EPA, submit plans for the management of nuclear waste. Created the United States Enrichment Corporation (USEC), a government-owned corporation, as a first step in transferring the uranium enrichment business to the private sector.

USEC Privatization Act (110 Stat. 1321-335, 42 U.S.C. 2011 note). Signed by the president April 26, 1996. Required the Board of Directors of the United States Enrichment Corporation (USEC) to sell the assets of the corporation to a private-sector entity. The new private owner would be responsible for the operation of two gaseous diffusion plants in Kentucky and Ohio, and the development of the atomic vapor laser isotope separation (AVLIS) technology. Amended the Atomic Energy Act of 1954, as amended, with respect to certification of gaseous diffusion plants and licensing of an AVLIS enrichment facility. Provided that NRC would not issue a license or certificate to the corporation or its successor if the corporation is owned, controlled, or dominated by a foreign corporation or government.

■ REGIONAL OFFICES

REGION 1
(CT, DC, DE, MA, MD, ME, NH, NJ, NY, PA, RI, VT)
475 Allendale Rd.
King of Prussia, PA 19406
(610) 337–5000
Hubert Miller, regional administrator

REGION 2
(AL, FL, GA, KY, MS, NC, PR, SC, TN, VA, VI, WV)
Atlanta Federal Center
61 Forsyth St. N.W., 23T85
Atlanta, GA 30303
(404) 562–4400
Luis Reyes, regional administrator

REGION 3
(IA, IL, IN, MI, MN, MO, OH, WI)
801 Warrenville Rd.
Lisle, IL 60532–4351
(630) 829–9500
James E. Dyer, regional administrator

REGION 4
(AK, AR, AS, AZ, CA, CO, GU, HI, ID, KS, LA, MT, ND, NE, NM, NV, OK, OR, SD, TX, UT, WA, WY)
611 Ryan Plaza Dr., #400
Arlington, TX 76011–8064
(817) 860–8100
Thomas D. (Pat) Gwynn, (acting) regional administrator

Pension Benefit Guaranty Corporation

1200 K St. N.W., Washington, DC 20005
Internet: http://www.pbgc.gov

The Employee Retirement Income Security Act of 1974 (ERISA) extended federal regulatory control of private pension and welfare plans. The Welfare and Pension Plans Disclosure Act of 1958 had required only the filing of annual reports and the disclosure of the operation and administration of pension plans. ERISA is administered by three government agencies: the Pension Benefit Guaranty Corporation (PBGC), the Employee Benefits Security Administration (PWBA) of the Department of Labor (*p. 612*), and the Internal Revenue Service (IRS) of the Treasury Department (p. 697).

The PWBA administers and enforces ERISA's fiduciary standards and its requirements on reporting and disclosure, employee protection, and enforcement. The IRS administers and enforces standards for funding, participation, and vesting of individuals covered by pension plans. The PBGC is responsible for pension plan insurance programs.

ERISA does not require businesses to establish private pension and welfare plans; however, if an employer wishes to continue a plan or intends to establish a new plan, guidelines and standards promulgated under the statute must be followed. The basic provisions of ERISA are the following:

- Employees cannot be forced to work for an unreasonable amount of time before becoming eligible for participation in a pension plan.
- Benefit pension plans must meet minimum funding standards.
- Operators of pension and welfare plans must file a copy of the plan with the PWBA and must file an annual or triennial financial report; both the plan and the report may be inspected by the public (see Information Sources, below).
- Pension plan participants must be provided with summaries of the plan's provisions and be informed of any changes made regarding benefits.
- Individuals with a fiduciary responsibility for handling a pension plan's funds and assets must meet certain standards of conduct and avoid conflict of interest.

Pension plans not covered by the provisions of ERISA include government plans (including Railroad Retirement Act plans and plans of some international organizations); certain church plans; plans maintained solely to comply with workers' compensation laws, unemployment compensation laws, or disability insurance laws; plans operated outside the United States primarily for nonresident aliens; and excess benefit plans (those that provide benefits or contributions above those allowed for tax-qualified plans) that are unfunded. Tax-qualified plans are those in which the assets are not taxable until they are distributed.

A ruling by the Supreme Court broadened the PBGC's powers to protect the pensions of American workers by affirming the government's authority to order corporations to reinstate terminated retirement plans. The ruling involved the LTV Corp., a Dallas-based steel and aerospace manufacturing company that filed for bankruptcy in 1986. Its pension plans were terminated by the PBGC, which assumed LTV's pension payment responsibilities. But when LTV's financial condition improved, the PBGC in 1987 ordered the company to resume responsibility for its pension plans. LTV refused, saying it should be held liable only after it fully recovered financially. LTV's refusal was initially upheld by a federal district judge and a U.S. Court of Appeals.

In 1990 the Supreme Court's reversal of the two lower courts made it harder, if not impossible, for corporations to use bankruptcy laws to "dump" their unfunded pension liability on the PBGC so they can have more cash for their creditors. The ruling also improved the financial outlook for the PBGC; the government had warned that the agency's future was threatened if it could not order firms to restore abandoned pension benefits and that it could suffer a financial crisis similar to that facing the government's insurance program for the savings and loan industry.

The PBGC was created by Title IV of ERISA. The PBGC ensures that participants in the pension plans it insures will receive at least basic retirement benefits in the event that the plan does not have sufficient funds to pay. The PBGC's termination insurance program covers single-employer, private-defined benefit pension plans—plans whose benefits are determined by using a formula including factors such as age, length of service, and salary. The agency, under its insurance program, also protects the pension benefits of the approximately eight million participants in multiemployer pension plans. Multiemployer plans are based on collective bargaining agreements involving a union and two or more employers. These plans usually cover an industry, skilled trade, or craft in a particular geographic area.

Congress enacted legislation in 1980 to define PBGC liability in the event of multiemployer plan failures. If a multiemployer plan becomes insolvent, the PBGC can provide financial assistance for the period of insolvency but does not take over administration of the plan. An employer who contributes to a multiemployer plan and subsequently withdraws from that plan is liable to the plan for a portion of the plan's unfunded vested benefits. This is called the employer's "withdrawal liability." The legislation also increased the PBGC premium paid by a plan for each participant to $2.60 per year. The premium has been increased incrementally from $1.00 in 1980 to the present rate.

The PBGC is a nonprofit corporation wholly owned by the federal government. It is financed by premiums levied against covered pension plans, the assets of plans it places into trusteeship, and investment income. The corporation is administered by a board of directors and an executive director. The board is composed of the secretaries of labor, commerce, and the Treasury; the labor secretary serves as chair.

A seven-member advisory committee, made up of two labor representatives, two business representatives, and three public members, advises the corporation on various matters related to the PBGC's insurance programs. The committee is appointed by the president.

When a covered single-employer pension plan terminates, the PBGC determines whether the plan will be able to pay basic benefits to all entitled participants. If it can, the corporation ensures that the fund's assets are used properly; if it cannot pay the benefits, the PBGC takes over, makes up the difference in assets, administers the fund, and distributes the basic benefits.

In cases involving the termination of an insufficiently funded plan, the employer or plan sponsor is liable to the PBGC for the insufficiency. The PBGC also may force a plan to terminate if the plan is unable to pay benefits or if the long-term losses to the insurance program would be unreasonable. In that case, the corporation takes over the pension plan to assure continued payments of benefits to participants.

To protect the benefits of U.S. workers and retirees, President Bill Clinton signed the Retirement Protection Act of 1994, which accelerated funding for underfunded pension plans, improved disclosure, and strengthened the pension insurance program. The act required certain underfunded plans to notify participants and beneficiaries annually of the plan's funding status and the limits of PBGC's guarantee.

In fiscal year 2002, PBGC became trustee of 144 terminated single-employer plans covering 187,000 people, up from 104 plans and 89,000 participants in fiscal year 2001. This represented the largest one-year increase in the number of people owed guaranteed benefits by PBGC. PBGC paid more than $1.5 billion in benefits during the year, nearly 50 percent more than the record amount it paid during the previous year. By the end of 2002, PBGC was responsible for the pensions of 783,000 participants, including those who have not yet retired.

PBGC launched its Pension Search Directory on the Internet in December 1996. Within five years, the program had located more than 10,000 people owed about $34 million from terminated defined benefit pension plans.

■ KEY PERSONNEL

Chair
Elaine L. Chao . . . . (202) 693–6000
Board Members
Donald Evans . . . . (202) 482–2112
John W. Snow . . . .(202) 622–1100
Office of the Inspector General
Robert Emmons . . . . (202) 326–4030
Executive Director
Steven A. Kandarian . . . .(202) 326–4010
Assistant Executive Director for Legislative Affairs
Vince Snowbarger . . . . (202) 326–4010
Assistant Executive Director and Chief Technology Officer
Rick Hartt . . . .(202) 326–4010
Information Resources Management Department
Cris Birch . . . . (202) 326–4130
Communications and Public Affairs Department
Randy Clerihue . . . . (202) 326–4040
Corporate Finance and Negotiations Department
Andrea Schneider . . . .(202) 326–4070

Deputy Executive Director and Chief Operating Officer
Joseph Grant............................(202) 326–4010
Corporate Policy and Research Department
Stuart Sirkin ....(202) 326–4080
Insurance Operations Department
Bennie Hagans.........................(202) 326–4050
General Counsel
James Keightley........................(202) 326–4020
Deputy Executive Director and Chief Financial Officer
Hazel Broadnax........................(202) 326–4170
Contracts and Control Review Department
Marty Boehm...........................(202) 326–4161
Financial Operations Department
Theodore J. Winter Jr...................(202) 326–4060
Deputy Executive Director and Chief Management Officer
John Seal ....(202) 326–4180
Budget Department
Henry Thompson ....(202) 326–4120
Facilities and Service Department
Janet Smith.............................(202) 326–4150
Human Resources Department
Sharon Barbee-Fletcher ....(202) 326–4110
Participant and Employer Appeals Department
Harriet Verburg........................(202) 326–4090
Procurement Department
Robert Herting..........................(202) 326–4160
Process Change Consulting Group
Kathleen Blunt.........................(202) 326–4180

■ INFORMATION SOURCES

Internet
Agency Web site: http://www.pbgc.gov. Includes information on PBGC offices and programs, including news releases.

Telephone Contacts
Personnel locator ....(202) 326–4110
Fax...(202) 326–4153
TDD.......................................(202) 326–4115

Information and Publications

KEY OFFICES

PBGC Communications and Public Affairs
1200 K St. N.W.
Washington, DC 20005
(202) 326–4040
Fax (202) 326–4042
Randy Clerihue, director

Answers general questions and issues PBGC publications to the general public.

Freedom of Information
1200 K St. N.W.
Washington, DC 20005
(202) 326–4040
E. William FitzGerald, FOIA officer

PBGC Customer Service Center
(202) 326–4100
Toll-free (800) 400–7242

Answers questions about specific pension plans that have been taken over by the PBGC.

PUBLICATIONS
Titles available from PBGC Communications and Public Affairs include:
PBGC Annual Report.
PBGC Fact Sheet.
Your Guaranteed Pension. Answers to commonly asked questions about pension plans.
Divorce Orders & PBGC.
Pension Insurance Data Book.
The PBGC also publishes a series of technical materials, including actuarial tables and mortality rate bulletins.

DATA AND STATISTICS
See the *Annual Report to the President and Congress* for data and statistics on the operations of the PBGC.

Reference Resources

DOCKETS

PBGC Disclosure Room
1200 K St. N.W.
Washington, DC 20005
(202) 326–4040
Hours: 9:00 a.m. to 4:30 p.m.

Dockets for selected PBGC regulations and rulings, cases litigated, news releases, and a list of all terminated pension plans may be inspected and copied at this office.

RULES AND REGULATIONS
PBGC rules and regulations are published in the *Code of Federal Regulations*, Title 29, parts 2601–2671. Proposed rules, new final rules, and updates to the *Code of Federal Regulations* are published in the daily *Federal Register*. (See

appendix for information on how to obtain and use these publications.)

■ LEGISLATION

The legislation that established regulation of employee benefit plans is the **Employee Retirement Income Security Act of 1974** (88 Stat. 829, 29 U.S.C. 1001). Signed by the president Sept. 2, 1974, the statute, known as ERISA, authorized mandatory minimum federal standards for pension and welfare plans and created the PBGC.

ERISA did not require the establishment of pension plans; rather, it specified minimum requirements for existing or proposed plans. The requirements applied to vesting formulas, capitalization of the fund, participation in the fund, and the responsibilities of the fund's operators.

The law required that operators of pensions make reports on the conditions of their funds and inform participants of changes in the fund.

ERISA also provided for the establishment of tax-deferred plans for retirement income by individuals not covered by a pension plan.

Multi-Employer Pension Plan Amendments Act of 1980 (94 Stat. 1208, 29 U.S.C. 1001). Signed by the president Sept. 26, 1980, the amendments to ERISA and to the **Internal Revenue Code of 1954** (68a Stat. 3, 26 U.S.C. 1) strengthened the funding requirements for multi-employer pension plans and replaced the termination insurance program with an insolvency-based benefit protection plan covering multiemployer plans only.

Retirement Equity Act of 1984 (98 Stat. 1426, 29 U.S.C. 1001 note). Signed by the president Aug. 23, 1984. Provided for greater equity in private pension plans for workers and their spouses and dependents.

Single-Employer Pension Plan Amendments Act of 1986 (100 Stat. 82, 29 U.S.C. 1001). Signed by the president April 7, 1986. Strengthened the PBGC single-employer insurance fund that covers individual firms and prevented companies from terminating their pension plans arbitrarily.

Pension Protection Act of 1987 (101 Stat. 1330–1333, 26 U.S.C. note 1). Signed by the president Dec. 22, 1987. Barred employers from deducting contributions to "overfunded" pension funds, defined as funds with assets exceeding 150 percent of current liability.

Retirement Protection Act of 1994 (108 Stat. 4809). Signed by the president on Dec. 8, 1994. Amended the Employee Retirement Income Security Act of 1974 (ERISA) requirements for pension plan funding, including: (1) minimum funding, revising additional funding requirements for single-employer plans; (2) limitation on changes in current liability assumptions; (3) anticipation of bargained benefit increases; (4) modification of the quarterly contribution requirement; and (5) exceptions to the excise tax on nondeductible contributions.

Postal
Rate
Commission

1333 H St. N.W., Suite 300, Washington, DC 20268
Internet: http://www.prc.gov

The Postal Rate Commission (PRC) is an independent agency created by the Postal Reorganization Act of 1970, as amended by the Postal Reorganization Act Amendments of 1976. The major responsibility of the commission is to consider proposed changes in postal rates, fees, and mail classifications and to submit recommended decisions to the governors of the United States Postal Service (USPS). The commission is responsible for scheduling public hearings on rate changes, soliciting comments, and publishing proposals in the *Federal Register.*

The commission also may issue advisory opinions to the USPS on proposed nationwide changes in postal services. The PRC has appellate jurisdiction to review Postal Service decisions to close or consolidate small post offices. Rate and classification decisions made by the commission may be appealed to the U.S. Court of Appeals.

The PRC has five members nominated by the president and confirmed by the Senate. Members serve six-year terms. The president designates the chair and the commission annually elects one of its members to be vice chair. No more than three commissioners can be members of the same political party.

When the USPS asks the PRC for a recommended decision on proposed postal rate and fee increases, the Postal Reorganization Act of 1970 requires the PRC to submit its recommended decision within ten months. Some PRC recommendations proceed more quickly, however. For example, in December 1995 the USPS sent the PRC a proposal to discount the rate for small prebarcoded first-class and priority mail parcels, which can be processed by automated equipment. The PRC transmitted its recommended decision, an approval, within three months, and these changes were in effect by the end of April 1996.

The Postal Reorganization Act's promise of a more businesslike approach to providing the nation's mail service prompted considerable concern over the fate of small post offices, particularly rural ones. Section 101(b) of the Postal Reorganization Act reflects this concern by providing that no small post office shall be closed simply for operating at a deficit, it being the specific intent of the Congress that effective postal services be insured to residents of both urban and rural communities.

The Postal Reorganization Act as originally enacted did not provide any role for the commission in small post office closings. It contemplated only Postal Service involvement. However, the early-to-mid 1970s saw mounting concern and frustration over inflammatory GAO reports and USPS administrative proposals to close up to 6,000 small post offices. In response, Congress amended the Postal Reorganization Act in 1976 to provide for commission review of appeals of post office closings or consolidations brought to it by affected persons.

The perpetual struggle between the PRC and the USPS continued into 2001. The PRC denied a request by USPS to further increase postage rates to raise $1 billion a year above the levels set on Jan. 7, 2001. (The rate for first class mail had increased by one cent to thirty-four cents on Jan. 7, 2001.) The PRC rejected most of the items in the request, recommending only increases in the rates for certified mail and for certain books and catalogs. These increases would provide $83 million of additional revenue.

In March 2002 the PRC approved an unusual settlement that allowed postal rates to increase on June 30, 2002. The settlement was offered in a PRC proceeding considering a USPS request for rate increases. The request had been developed before the terrorist attacks of Sept. 11.

However, the PRC recognized that the events of September and October 2001, in particular the disruption caused by the use of the mail to distribute lethal anthrax spores, had a significant impact on USPS operations and finances.

In the rate increase request, the USPS had joined with mailer groups, postal employee organizations, competitors, and the Office of Consumer Advocate that represents the interests of the general public to offer a proposal that increased rates by 7.7 percent. The settlement raised rates for first-class letters by three cents, to 37 cents. The postcard rate increased by two cents to 23 cents.

This was the first time a postal rate case had been resolved through settlement. Normally, the numerous conflicting interests engage in complex litigation to determine whether rate increases are justified. Federal law requires the USPS to break even from operations. As part of the settlement, the USPS agreed to defer any additional increases until the summer of 2003.

However, in November 2002 the Postal Service announced some good news about future postal hikes. A financial review of USPS contributions since 1971 to the Civil Service Retirement System revealed that the Postal Service had been paying too much into its retirement fund. Legislation passed in April 2003 corrected the imbalance and allowed the Postal Service to reduce its debt. This also allowed USPS to forecast that another postal rate increase would not be needed until 2006.

▓ KEY PERSONNEL

Chair
George Omas .... (202) 789–6801

Vice Chair
Dana B. Covington .... (202) 789–6868

Commissioners
Vacant .... (202) 789-6868
Tony Hammond .... (202) 789–6805
Ruth Y. Goldway .... (202) 789–6810

Chief Administrative Officer and Secretary
Steven W. Williams .... (202) 789–6840
  Fax .... (202) 789–6886

General Counsel
Stephen Sharfman .... (202) 789–6820

Rates, Analysis, and Planning
Robert Cohen .... (202) 789–6850

▓ INFORMATION SOURCES

Internet

Agency Web site: http://www.prc.gov. Includes information on PRC opinions and decisions.

Telephone Contacts

Switchboard .... (202) 789–6800
Fax .... (202) 789–6861

Information and Publications

KEY OFFICES

PRC Information Office

1333 H St. N.W., #300
Washington, DC 20268
(202) 789–6840
Fax (202) 789–6886
Steven W. Williams, public information contact
Gary J. Sikora, assistant administrative officer

Handles all requests for information from the press and the public, including Freedom of Information requests.

Consumer Advocate

1333 H St. N.W., #300
Washington, DC 20268
(202) 789–6830
Shelley Dreifuss, officer

Represents the public interest in rate and classification proceedings before the commission. Letters and comments should be directed to this office.

Freedom of Information

Contact the PRC Information Office, above.

PUBLICATIONS

The PRC Information Office provides information on PRC studies and other publications; selected documents are available from the agency's Internet site.

DATA AND STATISTICS

Many PRC publications include data and statistics on specific aspects of the Postal Service.

Reference Resources

DOCKETS

PRC Dockets Section

1333 H St. N.W., #300
Washington, DC 20268
(202) 789–6846
Joyce Taylor, contact
Hours: 8:00 a.m. to 5:00 p.m.

RULES AND REGULATIONS

PRC rules and regulations are published in the *Code of Federal Regulations*, Title 39, part 3001. Proposed rules, new final rules, and updates to the *Code of Federal Regulations* are published in the daily *Federal Register*. (See appendix for information on how to obtain and use these publications.)

■ LEGISLATION

The PRC carries out its responsibilities under the following legislation:

Postal Reorganization Act of 1970 (84 Stat. 759, 39 U.S.C. 3601). Signed by the president Aug. 12, 1970. Created the USPS as an independent government corporation and abolished the Cabinet-level Post Office Department. Established the PRC to advise the USPS on rates and mail classification.

Postal Reorganization Act Amendments of 1976 (90 Stat. 1303, 39 U.S.C. 101). Signed by the president Sept. 24, 1976. This act made some administrative changes in the PRC but had no effect on the powers of the commission.

Small Business Administration

409 3rd St. S.W., Washington, DC 20416
Internet: http://www.sba.gov

The Small Business Administration (SBA) is an independent federal agency created by the Small Business Act of 1953. The SBA operates under the Small Business Investment Act of 1958. This legislation was enacted to "aid, counsel, assist and protect insofar as is possible the interests of small business concerns in order to preserve free competitive enterprise, to ensure that a fair proportion of the total purchases and contracts for supplies and services for the government be placed with small business enterprises, and to maintain and strengthen the overall economy of the nation."

With a portfolio of business loans, loan guarantees, and disaster loans worth more than $45 billion, in addition to a venture capital portfolio of $13 billion, SBA is the nation's largest single financial backer of small businesses. The SBA offered management and technical assistance to more than one million small business owners.

America's twenty-five million small businesses employ more than 50 percent of the private workforce, generate more than half of the nation's gross domestic product, and are the principal source of new jobs in the U.S. economy.

The SBA makes loan guaranties and offers management counseling and training to all types of small businesses. Eligibility for SBA assistance requires that the business be independently owned and operated, not dominate its field, and meet SBA's size standard. The SBA makes long-term and low-interest loans under the Physical Disaster Loan Program to small or large businesses and to homeowners who suffer uninsured losses in natural disasters declared by the president or SBA administrator. It also provides loan assistance to businesses to control or abate air and water pollution.

The SBA also provides venture capital to small businesses by licensing, regulating, and providing financial assistance to small business investment companies (SBICs) and section 301(d) licensees (formerly minority enterprise small business investment companies). SBICs are privately owned companies that provide management assistance, equity financing, and long-term loans.

The Office of Government Contracting refers small businesses to prime government contractors and uses several options to ensure small business participation in assorted federal projects.

The Office of Advocacy researches the economic role of small business, analyzes proposed laws and rules affecting small business, reports the results of its research to the government and the small business community, and interacts with state and local governments.

The agency also operates the Small Business Answer Desk, a toll-free information center that handles inquiries and addresses the concerns of businesspeople.

The SBA's Office of Business and Community Initiative cosponsors courses and conferences, prepares informational leaflets and booklets, and encourages small business management research. It arranges workshops and courses for established and prospective businesspersons and enlists retired and active businesspersons to assist small businesses. The Office of Small Business Development Centers provides assistance and training to businesspeople through nearly 1,000 small business development center service locations.

The Office of International Trade provides information and assistance to small business owners new to exporting and those already exporting but planning to expand their markets.

The SBA operates several specialized programs to encourage small business development. The Office of Technology manages a program to encourage technological innovation and research by small businesses, including the Small Business Technology Transfer program. The Office of Veterans Business Development monitors and reviews the SBA's programs for special consideration for veterans, supports conferences tailored to the special needs of veterans, and advocates programs to benefit veteran small business. The Office of Women's Business Ownership provides support, training, and advocacy for women entrepreneurs and businesses owned primarily by women. The Office of Women's Business Ownership also runs the women's business centers. Each women's business center provides assistance or training in finance, management, marketing, procurement, and the Internet, as well as addressing specialized topics such as home-based businesses, corporate executive downsizing, and welfare-to-work.

The Small Business Welfare to Work Initiative program helps small businesses by connecting them to local service providers and job-ready workers. Targets efforts toward small businesses in industries that are experiencing labor shortages. Also provides entrepreneurial counseling and training to people currently or formerly on welfare who are interested in starting businesses as a means to their self-sufficiency. The Welfare to Work Initiative is a function of the SBA's Office of Entrepreneurial Development.

The Office of Minority Enterprise Development, under section 8(a) of the Small Business Act, assists in the expansion of minority-owned and -controlled small businesses by providing them with business development and assistance and the opportunity to pursue government contracts with SBA's help. The largest percentage of all contracting moving through the 8(a) program is the result of self-marketing by the participants, who are encouraged to initiate communication with federal buyers to stimulate contracts. The SBA works alongside federal purchasing agents and program participants, functioning as the prime contractor and subcontracting work assignments to 8(a) firms. The agency has channeled more than $55 billion in federal contracting to 8(a) firms and their employees since the program was created in 1969.

Since 1996 Congress has worked to facilitate the relationship between the federal government and small business. The most notable initiative was the passage of the Small Business Regulatory Enforcement Fairness Act of 1996. This legislative mandate required, among other things, that federal agencies promulgating new regulations prepare a cost-benefit analysis of the proposed regulation(s), prepare a report outlining the economic impact of the proposed regulation on a significant number of small businesses, and submit these reports to Congress for review. If Congress did not approve of the proposed regulation, it could pass a joint resolution of disapproval and bar the regulation from enactment. However, the president could enact the regulation if necessary to protect national security, protect the public health, or to implement an international trade agreement.

The act also required SBA to assist small businesses with compliance through community information clearinghouses and resource centers; to establish a Small Business and Agriculture Regulatory Enforcement Ombudsman; and to establish a Small Business Regulatory Fairness Board in each SBA regional office.

All federal agencies are subject to the requirements of the HUBZone (historically underutilized business zone) Empowerment Contracting program, which was enacted into law as part of the Small Business Reauthorization Act of 1997. The program, which falls under the auspices of the SBA, provides federal contracting opportunities for qualified small businesses located in distressed areas and encourages economic development in historically underutilized business zones through the establishment of preferences.

A small business must meet all of the following criteria to qualify for the HUBZone program: it must be located in a "historically underutilized business zone" or HUBZone; it must be owned and controlled by one or more U.S. citizens; and at least 35 percent of its employees must reside in a HUBZone.

◼ KEY PERSONNEL

Administrator
    John D. Whitmore Jr. (acting) . . . . (202) 205–6605
    Fax . . . . (202) 205–6802
Advocacy
    Susan M. Walthall (acting) . . . . (202) 205–6533
    Fax . . . . (202) 205–6928
Business Initiatives
    Monika Harrison . . . . (202) 205–6665
    Fax . . . . (202) 205–7416
Congressional and Legislative Affairs
    Karen Hontz (acting) . . . . (202) 205–6700
    Fax . . . . (202) 205–7374
Capital Access
    Jeanne M. Sclater . . . . (202) 205–6657
    Fax . . . . (202) 205–7230
Financial Assistance
    Jane P. Butler . . . . (202) 205–6490
    Fax . . . . (202) 205–7722
International Trade
    Jean Smith (acting) . . . . (202) 205–6720
    Fax . . . . (202) 205–7272
Investments
    Henry Haskins (acting) . . . . (202) 205–6510
    Fax . . . . (202) 205–6959
Small Business Development Centers
    Johnnie Albertson . . . . (202) 205–6766
    Fax . . . . (202) 205–7727

Veterans Affairs

William Elmore........................(202) 205–6773

Fax....................................(202) 205–7292

TDD...................................(202) 205–5988

Women's Business Ownership

Wilma Goldstein (acting).............(202) 205–6673

Fax....................................(202) 205–7287

Entrepreneur Development

Gail McGrath (acting)................(202) 205-6706

Fax....................................(202) 205–6903

General Counsel

Robert Gangwere (acting) ....(202) 205–7649

Fax....................................(202) 205–6846

**Government Contracting and Minority Enterprise
Development**

William Fisher (acting) ....(202) 205–6459

Fax....................................(202) 205–5206

Government Contracting

Luz Hopewell ....(202) 205–6460

Fax....................................(202) 205–7534

Business Development

Della Ford.............................(202) 205–6410

Fax....................................(202) 205–6028

Hearings and Appeals

David Kohler (acting) ....(202) 401–8203

Fax....................................(202) 205–7059

Inspector General

Phyllis Fong...........................(202) 205–6586

Fax....................................(202) 205–7382

Office of Administration

Thomas Dumaresq....................(202) 205–6630

Fax....................................(202) 205–7125

Office of Technology

Maurice Swinton ....(202) 205–6450

Fax....................................(202) 205–6390

Public Communications

Barbara Manning (acting) ....(202) 205–6740

Fax....................................(202) 205–6913

**Small Business and Agriculture
Regulatory Enforcement Ombudsman**

Jim VanWert (acting) ....(202) 205-7024

▨ INFORMATION SOURCES

Internet

Agency Web site: http://www.sba.gov. Provides information on SBA programs and access to SBA publications.

The SBA's resource library can be accessed at www.sba.gov/library/pubs.html.

Telephone Contacts

Personnel Locator ....(202) 205–6600

Small Business Answer Desk..............(800) 827–5722

Fraud and Abuse Hotline ....(800) 767–0385

Information and Publications

KEY OFFICES

SBA Public Communications Office

Media and Editorial Services

409 3rd St. S.W.

Washington, DC 20416

(202) 205–6740

Fax (202) 205–6901

Janie Dymond, contact

Handles press inquiries and issues news releases; maintains a media mailing list.

Freedom of Information

SBA Hearings and Appeals

409 3rd St. S.W.

Washington, DC 20416

(202) 401–8203

Lisa J. Babcock, chief of FOIA/PA

PUBLICATIONS

The annual report may be obtained by calling the SBA Answer Desk, 1-800-UASKSBA (1-800-827-5722). Most publications are also available from one of the 70 SBA field offices located in nearly every major city in the country.

Reference Resources

LIBRARIES

SBA Law Library

409 3rd St. S.W.

Washington, DC 20416

(202) 205–6849

Imelda Kish, law librarian

Open to the public

Hours: 10:00 a.m. to 4:00 p.m.

SBA Reference Library
409 3rd St. S.W.
Washington, DC 20416
(202) 205–7033
Margaret Hickey, reference librarian
Open to the public

Hours (subject to change): 8:30 a.m. to 11:30 a.m. and 12:30 p.m. to 4:30 p.m.

RULES AND REGULATIONS

SBA rules and regulations are published in the *Code of Federal Regulations*, Title 13, part 101. Proposed regulations, new final regulations, and updates to the *Code of Federal Regulations* are published in the daily *Federal Register*. (See appendix for details on how to obtain and use these publications.)

■ LEGISLATION

The SBA carries out its responsibilities under the following legislation:

Small Business Act (72 Stat. 384, 15 U.S.C. 631). Signed by the president July 30, 1953. Created and organized the SBA, declared the agency's policy, and defined small business concerns.

Small Business Investment Act of 1958 (72 Stat. 689, 15 U.S.C. 661). Signed by the president Aug. 21, 1958. Made equity capital and long-term credit more readily available for small business concerns.

Disaster Relief Act of 1970 (84 Stat. 1744, 42 U.S.C. 4401). Signed by the president Dec. 31, 1970. Revised and expanded federal relief programs that deal with victims of natural disasters.

Consolidated Farm and Rural Development Act (87 Stat. 24, 7 U.S.C. 1969). Signed by the president April 20, 1973. Guaranteed and set interest rates for loans made as a result of natural disasters.

Regulatory Flexibility Act of 1980 (94 Stat. 1164, 5 U.S.C. 601 note). Signed by the president Sept. 19, 1980. Required the federal government to anticipate and reduce the impact of rules and paperwork requirements on small businesses.

Small Business Investment Incentive Act of 1980 (94 Stat. 2275, 15 U.S.C. 80a). Signed by the president Oct. 21, 1980. Amended the Securities Act to exempt certain small and medium-sized businesses from securities laws registration requirements.

Business Opportunity Development Reform Act of 1988 (102 Stat. 3853, 15 U.S.C. 631 note). Signed by the president Nov. 15, 1988. Amended the Small Business Act to reform the Capital Ownership Development Program (8(a)) to abolish the noncompetitive contract award system, stiffened criminal penalties for persons who establish "front companies" posing as minority businesses, and restricted minority businessowners' ability to sell 8(a) contracts to nonminority enterprises.

Omnibus Trade and Competitiveness Act of 1988 (102 Stat. 1107, 19 U.S.C. 2901). Signed by the president Aug. 23, 1988. Enhanced SBA's ability to promote international trade among small businesses and provided new financing authority for export purposes.

Fair Labor Standards Amendments of 1989 (103 Stat. 938, 29 U.S.C. 201 note). Signed by the president Nov. 17, 1989. Amended the Fair Labor Standards Act of 1938 to increase the minimum wage.

Americans with Disabilities Act of 1990 (104 Stat. 327, 42 U.S.C. 12101). Signed by the president July 26, 1990. Declared that it was discriminatory, on the basis of disability, to deny opportunities or to afford them unequally, to provide opportunities less effectively, to assist an organization or individual that discriminates, or to otherwise limit opportunities enjoyed by others.

Civil Rights Act of 1991 (105 Stat. 1071, 42 U.S.C. 1981 note). Signed by the president Nov. 21, 1991. Amended the Civil Rights Act of 1964 to strengthen and improve federal civil rights laws, to provide for damages in cases of intentional employment discrimination, and to clarify provisions regarding disparate impact actions.

Small Business Credit and Business Opportunity Enhancement Act of 1992 (106 Stat. 986, 15 U.S.C. 631 note). Amended Small Business Investment Act of 1958 to improve operations of small business investment companies.

Family and Medical Leave Act of 1993 (107 Stat. 6, 29 U.S.C. 2601 note). Signed by the president Feb. 5, 1993. Established certain requirements for family and medical leave for permanent employees.

Small Business Lending Enhancement Act of 1995 (109 Stat. 295, 15 U.S.C. 631 note). Signed by the president Oct. 12, 1995. Amended the Small Business Act to reduce the level of participation by the SBA in loans guaranteed under the act on a deferred basis. Directed the SBA, with respect to each guaranteed loan made from the proceeds of development company debentures issued by qualified state or local development companies, to assess and collect a fee for such loans.

Small Business Regulatory Enforcement Fairness Act of 1996 (110 Stat. 857, 5 U.S.C. 601 note). Signed by the president March 29, 1996. Required SBA to assist small businesses with regulatory compliance through community information clearinghouses and resource centers; to establish a regulatory enforcement ombudsman; and to establish a regulatory fairness board in each SBA regional office. Required all federal agencies promulgating new regulations to submit cost-benefit reports and small business economic impact reports to Congress for review.

Small Business Programs Reauthorization Act of 2000 (P.L. 106-554). Signed by the president Dec. 21, 2000. Amended the portions of the Small Business Act to qualify as a HUBZone small business concern: (1) an Alaska Native Corporation owned and controlled by Alaska Natives; (2) a small business that is wholly owned by one or more Native American tribal governments; or (3) a small business owned in part by one or more tribal governments if all other owners are either U.S. citizens or small businesses. Reauthorized the National Women's Business Council.

Small Business Technology Transfer Program Reauthorization Act of 2001 (115 Stat. 263, 15 U.S.C. 631 note). Signed by the president on Oct. 15, 2001. Amended the Small Business Act to increase and extend through 2009 the authorization of appropriations for the Small Business Technology Transfer Program.

Small Business Paperwork Relief Act of 2002 (P.L. 107-198). Signed by the president on June 28, 2002. Required the director of the Office of Management and Budget (OMB) to publish annually in the *Federal Register*, and make available on the Internet, a list of regulatory compliance assistance resources available to small businesses.

■ REGIONAL OFFICES

REGION 1

(CT, MA, ME, NH, RI, VT)
10 Causeway St., #812
Boston, MA 02222–1093
(401) 528-4562
Jeffrey Butland, regional administrator

REGION 2

(NJ, NY, PR, VI)
26 Federal Plaza, #3108
New York, NY 10278
(212) 264–1450
Michael J. Pappas, regional administrator

REGION 3

(DC, DE, MD, PA, VA, WV)
Robert M.C. Nix Federal Bldg., 5th Floor
900 Market St.
Philadelphia, PA 19107
(215) 580–2700
Allegra McCullough, regional administrator

REGION 4

(AL, FL, GA, KY, MS, NC, SC, TN)
233 Peachtree St., #1800
Atlanta, GA 30303
(404) 331–4999
Noby Fowler, regional administrator

REGION 5

(IL, IN, MI, MN, OH, WI)
500 W. Madison, #1240
Chicago, IL 60661
(312) 353–4508
Judith Roussel, regional administrator

REGION 6

(AR, LA, NM, OK, TX)
4300 Amon Carter Blvd., #108
Fort Worth, TX 76155
(510) 324-5871, ext. 225
Joseph Montes, regional administrator

REGION 7

(IA, KS, MO, NE)
323 W. 8th St., #307
Kansas City, MO 64105–1500
(816) 374–6380, ext. 225
Samuel Jones, regional administrator

REGION 8

(CO, MT, ND, SD, UT, WY)
721 19th St., #400
Denver, CO 80202–2599
(303) 844–0500
Elten Ringsak, regional administrator

REGION 9

(AZ, CA, GU, HI, NV)
455 Market St., #200
San Francisco, CA 94105–2939
(415) 744–2118
Bruce Thompson, regional administrator

REGION 10

(AK, ID, OR, WA)
1200 Sixth Ave., #1805
Seattle, WA 98101–1128
(206) 553–0291
Conrad Lee, regional administrator

Social Security Administration

6401 Security Blvd., Baltimore, MD 21235
Internet: http://www.ssa.gov

The Social Security Administration (SSA) administers the Social Security system that ensures workers income after they retire or become disabled. Some benefits also are provided to families of workers who die while employed. In addition, the SSA administers the supplemental security income (SSI) program for the aged, blind, and disabled. The SSA operates ten regional offices and over 1,300 local offices. All SSA programs are administered through its local offices.

Legislation signed into law in August 1994 made the SSA independent from the Department of Health and Human Services in March 1995. The administration is headed by a commissioner who is appointed by the president and confirmed by the Senate. The commissioner has a fixed six-year term and is not removable except for wrongdoing. The 1994 law also created a seven-member bipartisan advisory board that makes recommendations to the president and Congress.

The president appoints three members and Congress appoints four.

The SSA is authorized to regulate eligibility requirements for the following programs:

- Social Security retirement benefits.
- Social Security disability payments.
- Social Security survivor benefits.
- Supplemental security income programs for the aged, blind, and disabled.
- Income maintenance payments in Puerto Rico, Guam, the Virgin Islands, and the Northern Marianas.

Individuals dissatisfied with a determination of eligibility may appeal to an SSA administrative law judge. The administrative law judge's opinion may, in turn, be appealed to the SSA Appeals Council.

The basic Social Security program is financed by contributions from employees, employers, and the self-employed to special trust funds. Funds are paid out on a regular basis when a worker retires, is disabled, or dies. Part of the contributions go to a hospital trust fund to help finance the Medicare program administered by the Centers for Medicare and Medicaid Services (see p. 519).

The SSA also conducts research on the social, health, and financial problems of the aged, the blind, the poor, and the disabled.

An important issue facing SSA is the solvency of the Social Security and Medicare trust funds. Each year the Trustees of the Social Security and Medicare trust funds report in detail on their financial condition.

In its 2003 annual report to Congress, the trustees announced the projected point at which tax revenues would fall below program costs was 2018, and the projected point at which the trust funds would be exhausted was 2042. To rectify the future shortage, the trust funds in 2003 required another $3.5 trillion, earning interest at Treasury rates, to pay all scheduled benefits over the next seventy-five years. This obligation grew $200 billion from 2002. However, reform of the Social Security and Medicare programs continued to be a political hot potato in Washington, with no overhaul proposal garnering wide support.

The Supplementary Medical Insurance (SMI) Trust Fund, which pays doctor's bills and other outpatient expenses, is expected to remain adequately funded into the indefinite future, but only because current law sets financing each year to meet the next year's expected costs. Although the rate of growth of SMI costs has moderated in recent years, outlays have still increased 38 percent during the past five years, or about 5 percent faster than the economy as a whole. Despite the significant improvement in the financial outlook for Medicare, the projected increases in medical care costs still make finding solutions to Medicare's financing problems more difficult than for Social Security.

The Balanced Budget Act of 1997 established the Bipartisan Commission on Medicare to address the future of Medicare. In March 1999 the commission recommended (1) designing a premium support system that would allow beneficiaries to choose from among competing comprehensive health plans in a system based on a blend of existing government protections and market-based competition; (2) improving the current Medicare program incrementally, including providing federal funding of pharmaceutical coverage through Medicaid for all seniors living at up to 135 percent of the poverty level; and (3) combining Part A and Part B Trust Funds into a single Medicare Trust Fund while developing a new concept of solvency for Medicare. With the changing of administrations in 2001, the implementation of the commission's recommendations remains uncertain.

Under provisions of the Social Security Amendments of 1983, the normal retirement age for Social Security increased for 150 million working Americans beginning in January 2000. Although sixty-two remains the earliest age at which individuals can retire and collect reduced benefits, the age for collecting full Social Security benefits will gradually increase from age sixty-five to sixty-seven over a twenty-two-year period. The increase in the retirement age was included in the Social Security Amendments of 1983.

The increase in the full retirement age begins with individuals born in 1938 whose normal retirement age will be sixty-five and two months. The age increases in two-month increments for workers born between 1939 and 1943 until the retirement age reaches sixty-six and remains there for all workers born through 1954. For those born after 1954, the retirement age begins to increase again in two-month increments until it reaches age sixty-seven for those born in 1960 or later.

An additional provision of the 1983 law will give workers who continue working, and delay collecting Social Security benefits until after their normal retirement age, higher benefits. The amount of the increase, known as the "delayed retirement credit," is determined by a set percentage and increases the longer retirement is delayed. Currently, workers born in 1938 who delay retirement receive a 6.5 percent credit for each year they do not collect benefits. The yearly credit will increase to 8 percent for those born in 1943 or later. For individuals who work a partial year, the yearly percentage is broken into monthly increments. The increase stops at age seventy, regardless of when a worker starts collecting benefits.

▓ KEY PERSONNEL

Commissioner
Jo Anne B. Barnhart
(Baltimore office)........................(410) 965–3120
Fax......................................(410) 966–1463
(Washington office)....................(202) 358–6000
Fax......................................(202) 358–6077

Finance, Assessment, and Management
Dale Sopper............................(410) 965–2910
Fax......................................(410) 965–0201

Litigation
Caroline Lott...........................(410) 965–1507
Fax......................................(410) 965–4170

Policy
Paul Van de Water (acting)............(410) 966–6756
Fax......................................(410) 966–1909

Operations
Mary Glenn-Croft......................(410) 965–1880
Fax......................................(410) 966–7941

Disabilities and Income Security Programs
Vacant..................................(410) 965–4623
Fax......................................(410) 965–9063

Communications and Public Affairs
Jim Courtney Jr. (acting)..............(410) 965–1720
Fax......................................(410) 965–3903

International Programs
Joseph A. Gribbin......................(410) 965–7389
Fax......................................(410) 966–9797

Legislation and Congressional Affairs
Robert Wilson (acting)................(410) 965–3737
Fax......................................(410) 966–3168

Program Benefits
Fritz Streckewald......................(410) 965–6212
Fax......................................(410) 965–8582

Chief Actuary
Stephen Goss...........................(410) 965–3000
Fax......................................(410) 965–6693

Hearings and Appeals
(5101 Leesburg Pike, Falls Church, VA 22041)
Rita Geier..............................(703) 605–8200
Fax......................................(703) 605–8201

Systems
Bill Gray...............................(410) 965–7747
Fax......................................(410) 966–4383

▓ INFORMATION SOURCES

Internet
Agency Web site: http://www.ssa.gov. Includes information on specific SSA offices and programs, and offers various SSA publications. Much of the information also is available in Spanish.

Telephone Contacts

Personnel Locator .... (410) 965–3368
Toll-free Information.......................(800) 772–1213

Information and Publications

KEY OFFICES

SSA Office of Public Inquiries

6401 Security Blvd.
Baltimore, MD 21235
(410) 965–2738
Fax (410) 966–6166
Toll-free (800) 772–1213
Charles H. Mullen, associate commissioner

The central point for consumer inquiries about the SSA and its various programs. (The administration encourages individuals to seek help from their local SSA office before contacting the headquarters.)

SSA Press Office

6401 Security Blvd.
Baltimore, MD 21235
(410) 965–8904
Fax (410) 966–9973
Washington office (202) 358–6018
Fax (202) 358–6077
Jim Courtney Jr., press officer

Serves as the central point for media inquiries about the SSA and its various programs. Issues news releases; arranges press conferences and interviews for SSA officials.

Freedom of Information

6401 Security Blvd.
Baltimore, MD 21235
(410) 965–3134
Fax (410) 966–0869
Randolph W. Gaines, executive director

PUBLICATIONS

All SSA local offices can provide SSA publications, including brochures on types of coverage available and the SSA annual report. Information regarding all SSA publications also may be obtained by calling (800) 772–1213.

DATA AND STATISTICS

SSA Office of Research, Evaluation, and Statistics

6401 Security Blvd.
Baltimore, MD 21235
(410) 965–2841
Fax (410) 965–3308
Susan Grad (acting), associate commissioner

Washington Office

International Trade Commission Building
500 E St. S.W., 9th Floor
Washington, DC 20254
(202) 358–6220
Fax (202) 358–6181
Susan Grad (acting), associate commissioner

Provides information on selected SSA reports and bulletins. These include the *Social Security Bulletin*, which contains data on employment and earnings, beneficiary and benefit payments, use of health services, and other topics related to SSA programs; the SSA's *Annual Statistical Supplement*; and reports on specific topics.

Reference Resources

LIBRARY

SSA Library

6401 Security Blvd.
Baltimore, MD 21235
(410) 965–6113
Fax (410) 966–2027
Eugene Macowski, chief librarian

Not open to the public on a regular basis. Students and others doing research, however, can make arrangements to use the SSA collection.

RULES AND REGULATIONS

Most SSA rules and regulations are published in the *Code of Federal Regulations*, Title 20, parts 401–450; other rules and regulations are distributed throughout the *Code of Federal Regulations*, primarily in Titles 26, 42, and 45.

Proposed regulations, new regulations, and updates to the *Code of Federal Regulations* are published in the *Federal Register*. (See appendix for information on how to obtain and use these publications.)

■ LEGISLATION

The SSA carries out its responsibilities under:

Social Security Act (49 Stat. 620, 42 U.S.C. 301). Signed by the president Aug. 14, 1935. Authorized the SSA to set, maintain, and enforce eligibility requirements for SSA-administered benefits. Amendments over the years have both expanded and restricted benefits available to various categories of recipients.

Social Security Administrative Reform Act of 1994 (108 Stat. 1464, 42 U.S.C. 1305 note). Signed by the president Aug. 15, 1994. Established the Social Security Administration as an independent agency and made other improvements in the old-age, survivors, and disability insurance program.

The Contract with America Advancement Act of 1996 (110 Stat. 847, 5 U.S.C. 601 note). Signed by the president March 29, 1996. Prohibited the SSA from providing disability insurance and supplemental security income eligibility to individuals whose drug addiction or alcoholism is a contributing factor to the finding of disability. Established the position of chief actuary, to be appointed by, and report directly to, the commissioner, and be subject to removal only for cause.

The Omnibus Consolidated Rescissions and Appropriations Act of 1996 (110 Stat. 1321). Signed by the president April 26, 1996. Provided the SSA with permanent debt collection authorities. Required recurring federal payments to persons who began receiving them after July 1996 to be paid by electronic funds transfer (EFT).

Ticket to Work and Work Incentives Improvement Act of 1999 (113 Stat. 1860, 42 U.S.C. 1305 note). Signed by the president on Dec. 17, 1999. Directed the commissioner to establish a Ticket to Work and Self-Sufficiency Program within one year that would provide Social Security disability beneficiaries with a ticket they may use to obtain vocational rehabilitation (VR) services, employment services, and other support services. Established a Work Incentives Advisory Panel within the SSA.

■ REGIONAL OFFICES

REGION 1

(CT, MA, ME, NH, RI, VT)
John F. Kennedy Federal Bldg., #1900
Boston, MA 02203

(617) 565–2870
Manuel J. Vaz, regional commissioner

REGION 2

(NJ, NY, PR, VI)
26 Federal Plaza, #40–102
New York, NY 10278
(212) 264–3915
Beatrice M. Disman, regional commissioner

REGION 3

(DC, DE, MD, PA, VA, WV)
300 Spring Garden St.
Philadelphia, PA 19123
(215) 597–5157
 Mailing Address:
  P.O. Box 8788
  Philadelphia, PA 19101
Larry G. Massanari, regional commissioner

REGION 4

(AL, FL, GA, KY, MS, NC, SC, TN)
61 Forsyth St. S.W.
Atlanta, GA 30303
(404) 562–5600
Paul Barnes, regional commissioner

REGION 5

(IL, IN, MI, MN, OH, WI)
600 W. Madison St., 10th Floor
Chicago, IL 60661
(312) 353–8277
James Martin, regional commissioner

REGION 6

(AR, LA, NM, OK, TX)
1301 Young St., #500
Dallas, TX 75202
(214) 767–4210
Horace L. Dickerson Jr., regional commissioner

REGION 7

(IA, KS, MO, NE)
601 E. 12th St., #436
Kansas City, MO 64106
(816) 936–5700
Michael Grochowski, regional commissioner

REGION 8

(CO, MT, ND, SD, UT, WY)
1961 Stout St., #1355
Denver, CO 80294
(303) 844–2388
James C. Everett, regional commissioner

REGION 9

(AS, AZ, CA, GU, HI, NV)
1221 Nevin Ave.
Richmond, CA 94804
  Mailing Address:
    P.O. Box 4200
    Richmond, CA 94802
(510) 970–8400
Peter D. Spencer, regional commissioner

REGION 10

(AK, ID, OR, WA)
2201 Sixth Ave., Mail Stop RX-50
Seattle, WA 98121
(206) 615–2103
Carmen Keller, regional commissioner

United States International Trade Commission

500 E St. S.W., Washington, DC 20436
Internet: http://www.usitc.gov or ftp://ftp.usitc.gov

The United States International Trade Commission (USITC) is an independent, nonpartisan, quasi-judicial federal agency created by an act of Congress on Sept. 8, 1916. Initially called the U.S. Tariff Commission, the agency's name was changed to the U.S. International Trade Commission by the Trade Act of 1974.

The USITC is headed by a staff of six commissioners. They are appointed by the president and confirmed by the Senate; the president also designates members to serve as chair and vice chair. The commissioners serve nine-year terms and are not eligible for reappointment, unless they have completed fewer than five years of a term. The chair serves a statutory two-year term. No more than three commissioners may be members of the same political party, and the chair and vice chair must belong to different parties.

The USITC staff includes attorneys, economists, investigators, commodity analysts, computer specialists, and service and production personnel. The staff's primary function is to gather facts and evaluate data to aid the commission in its determinations.

As a fact-finding agency, the commission has broad powers to study and investigate all issues relating to U.S.-foreign trade, its effect on domestic production, employment, and consumption, the competitiveness of U.S. products, and foreign and domestic customs laws. It does not set policy; however, its technical advice forms a basis for economic policy decisions on U.S. international trade. The commission may act on its own initiative or at the request of the president, other government agencies, the Senate Finance Committee, the House Ways and Means Committee, or on behalf of an industry, a company, or a group of workers.

As imports have increased and many domestic producers face what they view as unfair foreign competition, industries continue to file petitions with the commission for relief from foreign competition.

The commission conducts three major types of investigations. First, it examines whether rapidly increasing imports are causing serious injury to U.S. industries. Workers, companies, or other industry representatives may request the investigation. The commission advises the president on what relief, if any, might be needed to help U.S. businesses. The president may decide to do nothing; provide adjustment assistance to workers, companies, or communities hurt by low-cost imports; restrict quantities of imports; negotiate market agreements; impose tariffs; or impose a combination of tariffs, quotas, or other remedies.

Second, the commission investigates whether importers are infringing U.S. patents, copyrights, or trademarks. The commission may begin the investigation on its own or after receiving a complaint under oath from an interested party. If it finds that the unfair practices are harming U.S. businesses, it may issue cease-and-desist orders or ban the article from entering the United States. These orders are effective when issued and become final sixty days after issuance unless disapproved for policy reasons by the president within that sixty-day period.

Third, after receiving a petition from an industry representative or the Commerce Department, the commission investigates whether there are reasonable indications that U.S. industries are threatened or materially injured by imports that are subsidized or sold in the United States at prices lower than foreigners would charge in their home market (a practice known as dumping). At the same time, the International Trade Administration of the Department of Commerce conducts a preliminary investigation to determine whether dumping actually is taking place.

If both preliminary investigations are affirmed, the commission must conduct a final investigation to determine whether a U.S. industry is being materially injured or threatened by unfairly priced imports. If the commission finds that such harm is occurring, the Commerce Department must order that a duty be placed on the imports equal to the amount of the unfair subsidy or price. That duty cannot be lifted by the president.

The USITC is responsible for continually reviewing the Harmonized Tariff Schedule of the United States (HTS), a list of all the specific items that are imported into and exported from the United States, and for recommending modifications to the HTS that it considers necessary or appropriate.

In addition, the USITC:

- Advises the president on the effect of international trade negotiations on U.S. industries and consumers.
- Studies effects of lifting duties on imports from developing nations.
- Investigates the effects of trade with communist countries, including the effect of granting most-favored-nation (MFN) status to those countries.
- Studies the potential effects of imports from nations with state-run economies.
- Advises the president whether agricultural imports interfere with the price support programs of the U.S. Department of Agriculture.
- Monitors import levels.
- Provides the president, Congress, other government agencies, and the general public with technical information on trade and tariff matters.
- Assists in the development of uniform statistical data on imports, exports, and domestic production.
- Conducts studies on trade and tariff issues relating to U.S. foreign trade.

▓ KEY PERSONNEL

Chair
Deanna Tanner Okun .... (202) 708–2880
Vice Chair
Jennifer A. Hillman..................... (202) 708–5482
Commissioners
Marcia E. Miller .... (202) 205–2021
Stephen Koplan........................ (202) 708–2880
Administration and Chief Information Officer
Stephen McLaughlin .... (202) 205–3131
Secretary
Marilyn R. Abbott .... (202) 205–2000
Deputy CIO for Management
Dennis Szymanski .... (202) 205–2513
Finance
Patricia Katsouros .... (202) 205–2682

Facilities Management
Jonathan Brown .... (202) 205–2741
Personnel
Jeri Buchholz........................... (202) 205–2651
Administrative Law Judges
Sidney Harris .... (202) 205–2692
Paul Luckern.......................... (202) 205–2694
Delbert Terrill........................ (202) 708–4051
Charles Bullock .... (202) 205–2681
External Relations
Daniel Leahy.......................... (202) 205–3141
Public Affairs
Margaret O'Laughlin................... (202) 205–1819
Congressional Relations
Nancy Carman......................... (202) 205–3151
Trade Remedy Assistance
John Greer .... (202) 205–2200
Equal Employment Opportunity
Jacqueline Waters...................... (202) 205–2240
General Counsel
Lyn Schlitt............................ (202) 205–3061
Inspector General
Kenneth F. Clarke...................... (202) 205–2210
Operations
Robert Rogowsky .... (202) 205–2230
Economics
Robert Koopman .... (202) 205–3216
Industries
Vern Simpson.......................... (202) 205–3296
Fax .... (202) 205–3161
Information Services
Vacant................................. (202) 205–2513
Investigations
Robert Carpenter .... (202) 205–3160
Tariff Affairs and Trade Agreements
Eugene Rosengarden .... (202) 205–2592
Unfair Import Investigations
Lynn Levine........................... (202) 205–2561

▓ INFORMATION SOURCES

Internet

Agency Web site: http://www.usitc.gov. The ITC's Internet Web site offers 24-hour access to an extensive variety of ITC information resources and workproducts, including: news releases; *Federal Register* notices; most ITC reports and publications, including the Harmonized Tariff Schedule of the United States and congressional bill reports; the ITC DataWeb; the ITC Electronic Document Information System (EDIS—also accessible through www.edis.usitc.gov); information on recent petitions and complaints; the monthly calendar; a section focused on the

ITC's five-year (sunset) reviews; the ITC's rules of practice and procedure, hearing guidelines, an introduction to APO practices at the ITC, and other investigation-related materials; information related to the Freedom of Information Act; and general information about the agency, its work, and its commissioners and staff.

FTP server: ftp://ftp.usitc.gov

Telephone Contacts

Personnel Locator .... (202) 205–2000

Information and Publications

KEY OFFICES

USITC Office of the Secretary
500 E St. S.W.
Washington, DC 20436
(202) 205–2000
Marilyn R. Abbott, secretary

The Office of the Secretary compiles and maintains the ITC's official records, including petitions, briefs, and other legal documents. The office issues ITC notices, reports, and orders, and it schedules and participates in all commission meetings and hearings. The office makes determinations on requests for confidential treatment of information, requests for information to be released under protective order, and requests under the Freedom of Information Act (FOIA). The Office of the Secretary manages distribution of ITC reports and studies.

USITC Office of External Relations
500 E St. S.W.
Washington, DC 20436
(202) 205–3141
Fax (202) 205–2139
Daniel Leahy, director
(202) 205–1819
Fax (202) 205–2186
Margaret O'Laughlin, public affairs officer

The Office of External Relations develops and maintains liaison between the ITC and its varied external customers. The office is the focal point for contacts with the U.S. Trade Representative and other executive branch agencies, Congress, foreign governments, international organizations, the public, and international, national, and local news media.

Freedom of Information
Contact the USITC Office of the Secretary, above.

PUBLICATIONS
Order from the USITC Office of the Secretary by leaving a recorded request: (202) 205–1809.

DATA AND STATISTICS
The ITC DataWeb is an extensive tariff and trade computerized database. The system is relied upon for tariff and trade data by various federal government agencies, congressional offices, various U.S. trade negotiating groups, and U.S. embassies. The ITC DataWeb provides worldwide interactive access to current and historical U.S. trade data. It can be accessed from the ITC's Internet site (www.usitc.gov); DataWeb contact: Peggy MacKnight, (202) 205–3431.

Tariff Schedules of the United States Annotated—Legal document used by the importing business community to ascertain the appropriate commodity classification, dutiable status, statistical treatment, and other fundamental requirements for entry of foreign goods.

MEETINGS
Commission members meet in Room 101, 500 E St. S.W., Washington, DC. Meetings are not held on a regularly scheduled basis, but are open to the public unless the subject of the meeting is considered private or is exempt under the Government in the Sunshine Act.

Notices of commission meetings are listed in the *Federal Register* and are sent to the commission's mailing list. Agendas are published in the *Federal Register*.

The secretary's office keeps the USITC mailing list. Public hearings are also held in Room 101. For details, call (202) 205-2000.

Reference Resources

LIBRARIES

USITC Law Library
500 E St. S.W.
Washington, DC 20436
(202) 205–3287
Hours: 8:30 a.m. to 5:00 p.m.
Stephen Kover, law librarian

Primarily for the use of trade commission attorneys. The collection includes standard reference materials, domestic and international trade laws, and works on the history of trade relations.

USITC Research Library

500 E St. S.W.

Washington, DC 20436

(202) 205–2630

Hours: 8:45 a.m. to 5:00 p.m.

Elizabeth Root, chief

Maintains a general collection of books, theses, working papers, government reports, and periodicals on subjects relating to export-import and trade.

DOCKETS

500 E St. S.W., Room 112

Washington, DC 20436

(202) 205–1802

Ann Jones, deputy secretary

The USITC Docket Office provides nonconfidential files of cases under investigation and recent determinations for public inspection. Also handles requests to inspect the files of older cases.

RULES AND REGULATIONS

USITC rules and regulations are published in the *Code of Federal Regulations*, Title 19, parts 200-212. Proposed regulations, new final regulations, and updates to the *Code of Federal Regulations* are published in the daily *Federal Register*. (See appendix for details on how to obtain and use these publications.)

■ LEGISLATION

The USITC administers the following laws in full or in part:

Revenue Act of 1916 (39 Stat. 795, 19 U.S.C. 1330 and note). Signed by the president Sept. 8, 1916. Established the U.S. Tariff Commission (later renamed the United States International Trade Commission).

Tariff Act of 1930 (46 Stat. 590, 19 U.S.C. 1202). Signed by the president June 17, 1930. Protected U.S. industry from unfair methods of competition and unfair acts in the importation of merchandise into the country.

Agricultural Adjustment Act (48 Stat. 31, 7 U.S.C. 601). Signed by the president May 12, 1933. Established and maintains orderly market conditions for agricultural commodities in interstate commerce.

Trade Expansion Act of 1962 (76 Stat. 872, 19 U.S.C. 1801). Signed by the president Oct. 11, 1962. Authorized adjustment assistance to industries and groups of workers who may be injured by increased imports resulting from foreign trade agreements.

Trade Act of 1974 (88 Stat. 1978, 19 U.S.C. 2101). Signed by the president Jan. 3, 1975. Provided adequate safeguards to American industry and labor against unfair or injurious import competition.

Trade Agreements Act of 1979 (93 Stat. 144, 19 U.S.C. 2501 note). Signed by the president July 26, 1979. Changed U.S. trade laws to carry out the agreements reached during multilateral trade talks in Tokyo. Amended the Tariff Act of 1930 to incorporate protection for U.S. industry against dumped or subsidized merchandise. Repealed the Anti-Dumping Act of 1921, which protected against dumped goods.

Trade and Tariff Act of 1984 (98 Stat. 2498, 19 U.S.C. 54 note). Signed by the president Oct. 30, 1984. Specified several criteria that the commission must use in assessing the threat of injury to U.S. industries from imports. Created a Trade Remedy Assistance Office to inform the public of the remedies and benefits of trade laws. Stipulated that if the president does not follow the commission's advice on how to aid industries hurt by imports, Congress may enact the commission's recommendations by joint resolution. However, the president may veto that joint resolution.

The Omnibus Trade and Competitiveness Act of 1988 (100 Stat. 1107, 19 U.S.C. 2901 note). Signed by the president Aug. 23, 1988. Amended Section 201 of the Trade Act of 1974 to place a greater emphasis on industry adjustment to import competition in granting relief. Changed the antidumping and countervailing duty law with respect to release of business proprietary information under protective orders.

United States Postal Service

475 L'Enfant Plaza West S.W., Washington, DC 20260
Internet: http://www.usps.gov

The United States Postal Service (USPS) is an independent agency in the executive branch. Created by the Postal Reorganization Act of 1970, it replaced the Post Office Department. The USPS regulates all aspects of the mail.

The service is administered by an eleven-member board of governors; nine members are appointed by the president and confirmed by the Senate. The nine members select and appoint the postmaster general, who serves as the tenth member of the board and as chief executive officer of the service. The ten board members then appoint a deputy postmaster who serves as the eleventh board member. The appointed members serve staggered nine-year terms. No more than five of the nine appointees may belong to the same political party.

The authority to regulate the mail was given to the USPS through a group of federal laws known as the private express statutes. These statutes give the USPS the exclusive right to carry letters subject to certain exceptions and also protect USPS revenues, which enables the Postal Service to provide service throughout the country at uniform rates as mandated by law.

Violations of these statutes are punishable by fine, imprisonment, or both. The statutes also may be enforced by means of an injunction.

Although repeal of all, or part of, the private express statutes often has been considered, Congress is concerned that repealing postal monopoly laws could result in a significant decline of mail volume handled by the USPS. Private companies likely would concentrate on service to high-density areas and large-volume business mailers. Individuals, particularly those outside metropolitan areas, would not have alternate services available to them and would have to pay more for service.

The Postal Service provides information to consumers and businesses on mail rates and classification. Recommendations on domestic mail rates and classification matters are handled by the Postal Rate Commission (PRC) *(see p. 365)*, another independent agency created by the Postal Reorganization Act of 1970.

The Postal Service also sets standards for several areas related to mail delivery, including the size of individual pieces of mail, bulk mailings, mail chutes, mail boxes in apartment houses, lockers for parcels, and postage meters.

The appropriations that the USPS receives from Congress are annual "revenue forgone" appropriations as authorized under the Postal Reorganization Act of 1970. Revenue forgone appropriations reimburse the USPS for handling certain public service second-, third-, and fourth-class mails at rates lower than those paid by regular commercial mailers as determined by Congress. These appropriations are not used to subsidize other postal operations.

The USPS enforces the laws and regulations governing the mail system through its Inspection Service. The Inspection Service is authorized by law to protect, audit, and police three areas of the postal service:

- The personnel, property, equipment, revenue, and technology that make up the assets of the USPS.
- The safety and security of the environment in which mail delivery and related postal business is conducted.
- The overall integrity of the postal system.

The Inspection Service conducts internal audits of postal operations and investigates alleged violations of the private express statutes and individuals suspected of mail fraud and mail theft. There are approximately 2,000 postal inspectors stationed throughout the United States who enforce more than 200 federal laws covering investigations of crimes that adversely affect or fraudulently use the U.S. mail and postal system. The service uses forfeiture procedures as a law enforcement tool in child pornography, mail fraud, and drug and money-laundering cases.

During 2002, postal inspectors arrested 10,828 criminal suspects, with 54 percent of the arrests for mail theft. Mail fraud investigations resulted in 1,634 arrests, approximately $2 billion in court-ordered and voluntary restitution, and 780 civil or administrative actions. Inspectors arrested 249 suspects for child sexual exploitation offenses related to the mail.

The service's role in investigations involving the illegal transport of controlled substances through the mail has increased with the passage of the Anti-Drug Abuse Act of 1988. During 2002 the Inspection Service arrested 1,385 suspects for drug trafficking and money laundering via the mail.

The Inspection Service has five operations support groups *(see p. 388)* and maintains crime labs in Washington, D.C., Chicago, Memphis, Tenn., San Bruno, Ca., and New York City.

In 1996 the postmaster general's intention not to raise the price of the first-class stamp until the year 2000 made for some controversial proposals to raise USPS revenue. One was to rent space at post offices for private companies to erect cellular telephone towers, construction that would in some cases take advantage of the exemption of federal property from local zoning laws. Another proposal was to raise the rents on post office boxes, doubling them in small towns and charging additional fees to "nonresidents." The latter proposal was not endorsed by the Postal Rate Commission.

During the late 1990s the USPS began investing more than $5 billion to improve and expand the capability of its operating systems. The total five-year investment plan concentrated resources in two main categories: new technologies that produce labor savings or achieve cost avoidance; and customer service programs that generate revenue or enhance competitiveness in the marketplace. USPS implemented an overnight express mail service and a two-day (not guaranteed) priority mail service to compete with private express carriers. Current technology that has improved postal operations includes barcoding flat mail, remote encoding technology, and handwriting recognition software.

In October 2001 the nation and the Postal Service were shocked by the discovery that deadly anthrax had been sent through the mail, resulting in the deaths of several people, including two Washington, D.C., postal workers. The Postal Service shut down mail facilities and instituted precautionary procedures throughout its entire system, greatly increasing its costs. The administration provided an immediate $175 million in funding, with an additional $500 million coming through the Department of Defense Emergency Supplemental Appropriations Act and $87 million through the Supplemental Act for Further Recovery from and Response to Terrorist Attacks on the United States. Congress also appropriated funds for the purchase of biohazard detection and prevention equipment.

In March 2002 the PRC approved an unusual settlement that allowed postal rates to increase on June 30, 2002. In the rate increase request, the USPS had joined with mailer groups, postal employee organizations, competitors, and the Office of Consumer Advocate that represents the interests of the general public to offer a proposal that increased rates by 7.7 percent. The rates for first-class letters increased by 3 cents, to 37 cents. The postcard rate increased by 2 cents to 23 cents. As part of the settlement, the USPS agreed to not raise rates again until the summer of 2003.

In November 2002, however, the Postal Service was able to change that forecast. After completing a financial review of its contributions since 1971 to the Civil Service Retirement System, the Postal Service discovered that it had been overpaying into its retirement fund. Congress passed legislation in April 2003 to correct the imbalance, change the way the Postal Service calculated its retirement payments, and reduce the Postal Service debt. This allowed the USPS to forecast that future postal hikes would be deferred until 2006.

◼ KEY PERSONNEL

Postmaster General
John E. Potter...........................(202) 268–2550
Fax......................................(202) 268–4860
Deputy Postmaster General
John Nolan..............................(202) 268–2525
Chief Operating Officer
Patrick Donahoe........................(202) 268–4841
Chief Postal Inspector
Lee Heath...............................(202) 268–4267
Government Relations
Ralph Moden............................(202) 268–2505
Diversity Development
Murry Weatherall.......................(202) 268–6566
General Counsel
Mary Anne Gibbons.....................(202) 268–2950
Fax......................................(202) 268–6981
Information Technology
Robert L. Otto..........................(202) 268–6900
Fax......................................(202) 268–4492
Labor Relations
Anthony J. Vegliante....................(202) 268–7853
Fax......................................(202) 268–3074

■ INFORMATION SOURCES

Internet

Agency Web site: http://www.usps.gov. Includes consumer and business information on postal rates and regulations. An interactive feature allows the user to check the correct ZIP+4 for any U.S. address.

Telephone Contacts

Personnel Locator .... (202) 268–2000
Complaints Hotline .... (800) 275–8777
Fraud and Abuse Hotline .... (800) 372–8347

Information and Publications

KEY OFFICES

USPS Consumer Affairs
475 L'Enfant Plaza West S.W.
Washington, DC 20260–2200
(202) 268–2281
Fax (202) 268–2281
Francia G. Smith, consumer advocate

Provides information to consumers on USPS services and products. Receives and attempts to settle consumer grievances. Unresolved complaints are referred to Postal Service officials.

USPS Public Affairs and Communications
475 L'Enfant Plaza West S.W.
Washington, DC 20260
(202) 268–2143
Azeezaly Jaffer, media relations

Provides the media with all public information about the Postal Service.

Forensic and Technical Services Division
USPS Inspection Service
22433 Randolph Dr.
Dulles, VA 20104–1000
(703) 406–7100
Fax (703) 406–7115
Roy Geffen, director

Provides scientific and technical expertise to the criminal and security investigations of the USPS Inspection Service. Processes information requests for all USPS crime labs.

Freedom of Information
Payroll Accounting/Records
475 L'Enfant Plaza West S.W.
Room 8650
Washington, DC 20260–5240
(202) 268–2608
Betty Sheriff, FOIA/PA officer

USPS Corporate Information Services
475 L'Enfant Plaza West S.W.
Room 2800
Washington, DC 20260–1540
(202) 268–2832
Pete Stark, manager

Produces and provides information on many USPS publications (see below for ordering information).

PUBLICATIONS

A list of USPS publications, the *Directives and Forms Catalog (Pub. 223)*, is available from:

NJ Material Distribution Center
U.S. Postal Service
2 Brick Plant Rd.
South River, NJ 08877–9998
(732) 613–2301
Fax (732) 613–2310

A number of USPS general publications and handbooks are available free at main post offices. These include:
A Consumer's Directory of Postal Services and Products (Pub. 201)
A Consumer's Guide to Postal Crime Prevention (Pub. 300)
Express Mail Users Guide (Pub. 161)
Mailing Free Matter for Blind and Visually Handicapped Persons (Pub. 347)

The National ZIP Code and Post Office Directory (Pub. 65) may be purchased from the U.S. Government Printing Office (GPO): see appendix, Ordering Government Publications. The GPO also offers USPS publications on a subscription basis. Titles include:
Domestic Mail Manual. Updates on domestic addressing, packaging, rates, classification regulations, and presort mail.
International Mail Manual. Updates on international regulations and mail services and rates for every country.

Postal Bulletin. Biweekly newspaper that contains current orders, new rates, classifications, and items of interest to USPS personnel and stamp collectors.

The USPS publishes a monthly magazine for customers who generate large quantities of mail. Subscriptions are available from:

Memo to Mailers
475 L'Enfant Plaza West S.W.
Room 10523
Washington, DC 20260
(202) 268–7280
Jon Leonard, editor

The *Comprehensive Statement on Postal Operations,* an annual USPS report to Congress, is available from USPS Government Relations, (202) 268–2505, or by contacting the USPS Library, (202) 268–2905. The annual report also is available on the web site: http://www.usps.gov/ history/anrpt97.

DATA AND STATISTICS

USPS Payroll Accounting/Records
475 L'Enfant Plaza West S.W.
Room 8650
Washington, DC 20260
(202) 268–2608
Betty Sheriff, FOIA/PA officer

Provides information on databases maintained by the Postal Service. These include files on consumer complaints, delivery service analyses, mail fraud and prohibited mailings, lost mail, revenue, the ZIP code system, budget, bulk mailings, second-class, controlled circulation publications, and rural routes.

Reference Resources

LIBRARY

USPS Library
475 L'Enfant Plaza West S.W.
Room 11800
Washington, DC 20260
(202) 268–2900
Bob Gardner, USPS corporate librarian
Hours: 9:00 a.m. to 4:00 p.m.

DOCKETS
Materials related to enforcement actions, rate cases, and other administrative proceedings are maintained at the USPS Library. Information on dockets and regulatory matters may also be obtained from Betty Sheriff, USPS Payroll Accounting/Records, (202) 268–2608.

RULES AND REGULATIONS
USPS rules and regulations are published in the *Code of Federal Regulations,* Title 39, parts 1–3003. Proposed rules, new final rules, and updates to the *Code of Federal Regulations* are published in the daily *Federal Register.* (See appendix for information on how to obtain and use these publications.)

For information on how to obtain postal regulation manuals, contact Dani Oddone, USPS Corporate Information Services, (202) 268–2849.

■ LEGISLATION
The Postal Service carries out its responsibilities under:

Postal Reorganization Act (84 Stat. 719, 39 U.S.C. 101). Signed by the president Aug. 12, 1970. Created the USPS and the PRC. Transferred the powers to regulate the distribution of mail from the Post Office Department to the USPS. (A description of the private express statutes also can be found under these cites: 84 Stat. 727, 39 U.S.C. 601–606; 84 Stat. 727, 18 U.S.C. 1693–1699, 1724–1725.)

The Postal Reorganization Act removed appointment of postmasters from the influence of Congress.

Mail Order Consumer Protection Amendments of 1983 (97 Stat. 1316–1317, 39 U.S.C. 3005, 3013). Signed by the president Nov. 30, 1983. Strengthened the investigatory and enforcement powers of the USPS by authorizing certain inspection authority by providing for civil penalties for misleading advertisements that use the mail. Required semiannual reports summarizing investigative activities.

Inspector General Amendments of 1988 (101 Stat. 2524, 5 U.S.C. appendix). Signed by the president Oct. 18, 1988. Elevated the Postal Inspector Office to an Office of Inspector General within the USPS. The inspector general reports to the postmaster general and Congress regarding problems and deficiencies relating to the USPS and suggests corrections needed.

Anti-Drug Abuse Act of 1988 (101 Stat. 4362, 18 U.S.C. 3061; 102 Stat. 4363, 21 U.S.C. 881). Signed by the president Nov. 18, 1988. Gave the Inspection Service additional civil and criminal forfeiture authority incident to postal-related drug and money-laundering investigations as agreed to by the attorney general. Proceeds from forfeiture activities are deposited in the Postal Service Fund.

Act of Dec. 12, 1989 (103 Stat. 1944, 39 U.S.C. 2005a). Signed by the president Dec. 12, 1989. Raised the USPS's borrowing authority limitations from $10 billion in fiscal year 1990 to $15 billion for fiscal year 1992 and each fiscal year thereafter.

Omnibus Reconciliation Act (103 Stat. 2133, 39 U.S.C. 2009a). Signed by the president Dec. 19, 1989. Excluded the USPS from the federal budget and exempted it from inclusion in calculating the federal deficit under the Balanced Budget and Emergency Deficit Control Act of 1985.

Postal Civil Service Retirement System Funding Reform Act of 2003 (P.L. 108-18). Signed by the president April 11, 2003. Required that the USPS change the way it calculated its contributions to the Civil Service Retirement and Disability Fund.

■ REGIONAL OFFICES

U.S. Postal Service

GREAT LAKES AREA
(IL, IN, MI)
244 Knollwood Dr., 4th Floor
Bloomingdale, IL 60117–1000
(630) 539–5858
Fax: (630) 539–7171
Danny Jackson, vice president, area operations

NEW YORK AREA
(New York City, northern NJ)
142–02 20th Ave., #318
Flushing, NY 11351–0001
(718) 321–5823
Fax: (718) 321–7150
David L. Solomon, vice president, area operations

NORTHEAST AREA
(CT, MA, ME, NH, NY, RI, VT)
6 Griffin Rd. North
Windsor, CT 06006–7010
(860) 285–7040
Fax: (860) 285–1253
Jon Steele, vice president, area operations

PACIFIC AREA
(CA, HI)
1125 Rancho Carmel Dr.
San Diego, CA 92197–0100
(858) 674–3100
Fax: (858) 674–3101
Al Iniguez, vice president, area operations

EASTERN AREA
(DE, southern NJ, OH, PA)
5315 Campbell's Run Rd.
Pittsburgh, PA 15277–7010
(412) 494–2510
Fax: (412) 494–2582
Alexander Lazaroff, vice president, area operations

MID-ATLANTIC AREA
(DC, KY, MD, NC, SC, VA, WV)
2800 Shirlington Rd., 12th Floor
Arlington, VA 22206–7000
(703) 824–7050
Henry Penky, vice president, area operations

CAPITAL METRO AREA
16501 Shady Grove Rd.
Gaithersburg, MD 20898-9998
(301) 548–1403
Fax: (301) 548–1434
Jerry D. Lane, manager

SOUTHEAST AREA
(AL, FL, GA, MS, TN)
225 N. Humphreys Blvd.
Memphis, TN 38166–0100
(901) 747–7333
Fax: (901) 747–7444
William J. Brown, vice president, area operations

SOUTHWEST AREA
(AR, LA, OK, TX)
P.O. Box 224748
Dallas, TX 75222–4748
(214) 819–8650
Fax: (214) 905–9227
George L. Lopez, vice president, area operations

WESTERN AREA
(AK, AZ, CO, ID, MT, NM, NV, OR, UT, WA, WY)
1745 Stout St., #1000
Denver, CO 80299–1000
(303) 391–5101
Fax: (303) 313–5102
Sylvester Black, vice president, area operations

Inspection Service, Operations Support Groups

BALA CYNWYD
(DC, DE, KY, MD, NC, OH, PA, SC, VA, WV)
P.O. Box 3000
Bala Cynwyd, PA 19004–3609
(610) 668–4500

CHICAGO
(CO, IA, IL, IN, KS, MI, MN, MO, ND, NE, SD, UT, WI,
  WY)
222 S. Riverside Plaza, #1250
Chicago, IL 60606–6100
(312) 669–5650

JERSEY CITY
(CT, MA, ME, NH, NJ, NY, PR, RI, VI, VT)
2 Gateway Center, 9th Floor
Newark, NJ 07175–0001
(973) 693–4500

MEMPHIS
(AL, AR, FL, GA, LA, MS, OK, TN, TX)
225 N. Humphreys Blvd.
Memphis, TN 38161–0001
(901) 747–7700

SAN FRANCISCO
(AK, AZ, CA, HI, ID, MT, NM, NV, OR, WA)
P.O. Box 882528
San Francisco, CA 94188–2528
(415) 778–5800

Departmental Agencies

Agriculture Department

14th St. and Independence Ave. S.W., Washington, DC 20250
Internet: http://www.usda.gov

Agricultural Marketing Service

14th St. and Independence Ave. S.W., Washington, DC 20250
Mailing address: P.O. Box 96456, Washington, DC 20090-6456
Internet: http://www.ams.usda.gov

In 1922 the Bureau of Markets was combined with another bureau to form the Bureau of Agricultural Economics. In 1939 this bureau was incorporated into the Agricultural Marketing Service (AMS). The AMS is one of several service and regulatory units within the U.S. Department of Agriculture (USDA). The AMS is under the jurisdiction of the assistant secretary of agriculture for marketing and regulatory programs and is headed by an administrator appointed by the secretary of agriculture. Serving under the administrator is a deputy administrator responsible for management and marketing programs.

Responsibilities at the AMS are shared by eight units; each unit supervises marketing and regulatory activities for a particular segment of the agriculture industry. The specific areas are cotton, dairy products, fruits and vegetables, livestock and seed, poultry, tobacco, science and technology, and transportation and marketing.

The regulatory activities of the AMS are the broadest of any of the agencies within the USDA. The agency administers programs designed to promote order and efficiency in marketing agricultural products and regulates fair trading of fruits and vegetables and truth-in-labeling of seeds. The agency also prohibits discrimination against members of producers' organizations and protects the rights of plant breeders. By agreement with groups of producers, the AMS issues marketing orders to manage the flow of agricultural commodities to the marketplace.

AMS regulatory programs include:

- Administration of the Perishable Agricultural Commodities Act, which prohibits unfair and fraudulent practices in the marketing of fresh and frozen fruits and vegetables. The act requires licensing of interstate dealers and specifies that any labels on containers be accurate.

- Administration of the Federal Seed Act, which requires that all agricultural and vegetable seeds shipped interstate be truthfully labeled. It prohibits false advertising and imports of seed lots containing undesirable components.

- Administration of the Plant Variety Protection Act, which protects the "inventions" of breeders of plants that reproduce sexually. Protection extends for eighteen years and prohibits others from using the new plant without the breeder's permission.

- Administration of the Agricultural Fair Practices Act, which makes it unlawful for handlers of agricultural commodities to discriminate against farmers who belong to a producers association.

- Administration of the Export Fruit Acts, which authorize regulation of the quality of exported apples, pears, grapes, and plums to protect the reputation of U.S. produced fruit in international markets.

- Administration of the Egg Products Inspection Act, which assures that eggs and egg products that reach consumers are unadulterated and provides continuous inspection in all plants that process liquid, dried, or frozen egg products.

The AMS also operates programs to help producers and handlers market their products efficiently and ensure that high quality is maintained. These include a market news service, grading standardization and classification programs, research and promotion programs, administration of a system of marketing orders and agreements, and transportation programs.

The Market News service provides current information to the agricultural commodities industry to encourage an orderly marketing and distribution system. Information in the reports covers prices and demand, current supply, location, quality, and condition. Much of this information covers national trends.

The Transportation and Marketing Programs division assists in the development of an efficient transportation system for rural communities to move commodities through the nation's highways, railroads, airports, and waterways into the domestic and international marketplace. The division also oversees the responsibilities of the National Organic Standards Board. The AMS develops standards to be used in classifying certain farm products. These include fresh and processed fruits and vegetables, livestock, wool, mohair, tobacco, cotton, and naval stores. Grading services are offered to buyers and sellers. The AMS also tests and classifies seeds.

The AMS purchases food for distribution through programs of the Food and Nutrition Service (p. 410) such as the school lunch program, nutrition programs for the elderly, and the supplemental food program for women, infants, and children.

A government-wide food quality assurance program helps make sure the federal government buys its food as efficiently and economically as possible. The program eliminates overlap and duplication among federal agencies in government food purchase specifications. It also encourages bidding by food processors on government contracts. In its procurement programs, the AMS applies federal law giving minority and women-owned businesses certain preferences.

Research and promotion programs, designed to improve the quality of agricultural commodities and develop new markets, are sponsored by the agricultural industries monitored by the USDA and authorized by congressional acts for each commodity. The programs conducted under AMS supervision are funded by the producers, either through direct assessments or by deducting funds from price support payments. Laws have been passed authorizing research and promotion programs for beef, cotton, dairy products, fluid milk, eggs, floral products, honey, lamb, mohair, pork, potatoes, watermelon, and wool.

The AMS is responsible for shell surveillance inspections mandated by the Egg Products Inspection Act. The inspections enhance fair competition and facilitate marketing of consumer-grade eggs by assuring the proper disposition of "restricted eggs," (i.e., checked and dirty eggs, leaking eggs, incubator rejects, loss and inedible eggs). The inspections, performed by the USDA and cooperating state agencies, are conducted at least once each calendar quarter.

Authorized by the Agricultural Marketing Act of 1937, marketing agreements and orders are issued by the AMS to help stabilize markets for a number of farm commodities, chiefly milk, fruits, vegetables, and specialty crops such as peanuts, kiwifruit, and avocados. Through these programs individual farmers can organize to solve common market-

ing problems. AMS specialists make sure the orders operate in the public interest and within legal bounds.

The programs are voluntary and are initiated and designed by farmers. A marketing order may be issued by the secretary of agriculture only after a public hearing at which farmers, marketers, and consumers may testify, and after farmers vote approval through a referendum.

Marketing orders enable the agriculture industry to regulate the handling and marketing of its products to prevent market shortages and gluts without direct control over pricing. In addition, marketing orders can keep high quality produce on the market, standardize packs or containers, regulate the weekly flow to the market, establish reserve pools for storable commodities, and authorize advertising, research, and development.

The Science and Technology Program division provides centralized scientific support to AMS programs including laboratory analyses and quality assurance, coordination of scientific research conducted by other agencies for the AMS, and statistical and mathematical consulting services. The Science and Technology Program division also issues certificates of protection for new varieties of sexually reproduced plants. In addition, it administers USDA's pesticide record-keeping program.

The Farm Security and Rural Investment Act of 2002 adjusted many of the programs regulated under AMS. These included programs dealing with peanuts, dairy, commodity purchases, sheep research and promotion, caneberry marketing orders, farmers markets, organic classification, cotton classing, country of origin labeling, and salmon promotion.

▉ KEY PERSONNEL

Administrator
  A. J. Yates .... (202) 720–5115
Associate Administrator
  Kenneth C. Clayton .... (202) 720–4276
  Fax .... (202) 720–8477
Compliance and Analysis Programs
  David N. Lewis .... (202) 720–4638
Cotton
  Norma McDill .... (202) 720–3193
Dairy
  Richard McKee .... (202) 720–4392
Fruit and Vegetable
  Robert Keeney .... (202) 720–4722
Legislative and Regulatory Review Staff
  Chris Sarcone .... (202) 720–3203
Livestock and Seed
  Barry Carpenter .... (202) 720–5705
Poultry
  Howard Magwire .... (202) 720–4476

Public Affairs
 Billy Cox .... (202) 720–8998
Science and Technology
 Robert Epstein .... (202) 720–5231
Tobacco
 John Duncan III .... (202) 205–0567
Transportation and Marketing
 Barbara Robinson .... (202) 690–1300

■ INFORMATION SOURCES

Internet

Agency Web site: http://www.ams.usda.gov/. Includes information on AMS programs, offices, and publications.

Telephone Contacts

Personnel Locator .... (202) 720–8732

Information and Publications

KEY OFFICES

AMS Public Affairs Staff

1400 Independence Ave. S.W.
South Bldg., Room 3510-S
Washington, DC 20090-0273
(202) 720–8998
Fax (202) 720–7135
Billy Cox, director
Zipora Bullard, FOI officer
(202) 720–3203

Issues publications, news releases, and speeches related to the AMS and provides audio-visual material to news media. Maintains mailing lists; handles Freedom of Information requests.

Market news on specific agricultural products is available from the following contacts. The mailing address for branches based in Washington is P.O. Box 96456, Washington, DC 20250.

AMS Cotton Market News Branch

3275 Appling Rd.
Memphis, TN 38133
(901) 384–3016
Stokes Quisenberry, chief

AMS Dairy Market Information Branch

1400 Independence Ave. S.W.
South Bldg., Room 2764
(202) 720–7461
John P. Rourke, chief

AMS Fruit and Vegetable Market News Branch

1400 Independence Ave. S.W.
South Bldg., Room 2503-S
(202) 720–2745
Terry Long, chief

AMS Livestock and Grain Market News Branch

1400 Independence Ave. S.W.
South Bldg., Room 2623-S
(202) 720–6231
John Van Dyke, chief

AMS Poultry Market News Branch

1400 Independence Ave. S.W.
South Bldg., Room 3960-S
(202) 720–6911
Grover T. Hunter, chief

AMS Tobacco Market Information and Program Analysis Branch

1400 Independence Ave. S.W.
Room 506, Annex
(202) 205–0489
Henry R. Martin, chief

PUBLICATIONS

Contact the AMS Public Affairs Staff at (202) 720–8998. Information is also available on the agency's Internet site.

DATA AND STATISTICS

The AMS Public Affairs Staff provides information on AMS statistical material.

MEETINGS

Notices of administrative proceedings—hearings before the administrative law judges, public hearings on marketing orders, and hearings on proposed rules and regulations—are published in the *Federal Register*. Information about administrative hearings, marketing orders, and other programs also may be obtained from the AMS Information Staff: (202) 720–8998.

Reference Resources

LIBRARY

National Agricultural Library

10301 Baltimore Blvd.
Beltsville, MD 20705–2351
(301) 504–5755
Pamela Andre, director
Hours: 8:00 a.m. to 4:30 p.m.

The USDA also maintains a reference center at the main Agriculture Department building. The collection consists primarily of periodicals, reference volumes, and databases.

D.C. Reference Center

1400 Independence Ave. S.W.
South Bldg., Room 1052-S
Washington, DC 20250
(202) 720–3434
Janet Wright, chief
Hours: 8:00 a.m. to 4:30 p.m.

DOCKETS

AMS Legislative and Regulatory Review Staff

1400 Independence Ave. S.W.
South Bldg., Room 3510-S
P.O. Box 96456
Washington, DC 20090-6456
(202) 720–3203
Hours: 8:00 a.m. to 4:30 p.m.

Information on public dockets related to AMS rule-making and regulations may be obtained at this office.

RULES AND REGULATIONS

AMS rules and regulations are published in the *Code of Federal Regulations,* Title 7, various parts. Proposed rules, new final rules, and updates to the *Code of Federal Regulations* are published in the daily *Federal Register. (See appendix for information on how to obtain and use these publications.)*

■ LEGISLATION

All of the laws administered by the AMS are listed in the publication, *Compilation of Statutes Relating to the Agricultural Marketing Service and Closely Related Activities.* Additional information is available from the AMS legislative liaison, Christine Sarcone, at (202) 720-3203.

Legislation administered by the AMS includes:

U.S. Cotton Standards Act (42 Stat. 1517, 7 U.S.C. 51-65). Signed by the president March 4, 1923. Authorizes the secretary of agriculture to establish and promote the use of official U.S. cotton standards.

Produce Agency Act (44 Stat. 1355, 7 U.S.C. 491-497). Signed by the president March 3, 1927. Prohibits destruction or dumping of farm products by commissions, merchants, and others.

Wool Standards Act (45 Stat. 593, 7 U.S.C. 415b-d). Signed by the president May 17, 1928. Authorizes the use of certain funds for wool standardization and grading work.

Perishable Agricultural Commodities Act (46 Stat. 531, 7 U.S.C. 499a-499t). Signed by the president June 10, 1930. Prohibits unfair or fraudulent practices in the marketing of fresh or frozen fruits and vegetables. Required licenses for dealers, commission merchants, brokers, shippers, and agents who deal with fresh or frozen fruits and vegetables. It also impresses a trust on the commodities and sales proceeds for the benefit of unpaid sellers.

Export Apple Act (48 Stat. 123, 7 U.S.C. 581-590). Signed by the president June 10, 1933. Requires inspection of fresh apples exported from the U.S. to determine they meet minimum quality specifications.

Tobacco Inspection Act (49 Stat. 735, 7 U.S.C. 511-511q). Signed by the president Aug. 23, 1935. Establishes and maintains standards of classification for tobacco and provided for official tobacco inspections.

Act of August 24, 1935 (49 Stat. 750, 7 U.S.C. 612c). Signed by the president Aug. 24, 1935. Authorizes purchase, export, and diversion programs to expand market outlets for surplus farm commodities. Provided for limited price assistance to farmers and for increased use of agricultural products among low-income groups.

Agricultural Marketing Agreement Act of 1937 (50 Stat. 246, 7 U.S.C. 601, 602, 608a-e, 610, 612, 614, 624, 627, 671-674). Signed by the president June 3, 1937. Authorizes establishment of marketing orders and agreements to regulate milk handling and to set minimum prices for farmers; regulated quality and quantity of containers and shipments of certain fruits, vegetables, nuts, and hops. Regulates the import of certain of these commodities whenever domestic shippers are subject to quality regulations under marketing orders.

Federal Seed Act (53 Stat. 1275, 7 U.S.C. 1551-1611). Signed by the president Aug. 9, 1939. Requires truth-in-labeling and advertising of seeds shipped in interstate commerce.

Agricultural Marketing Act of 1946 (60 Stat. 1087, 7 U.S.C. 1621-1627). Signed by the president Aug. 14, 1946. Provides basic authority for many AMS functions. Authorizes federal standards for farm products, grading, and inspection services, market news services, cooperative agreements, transportation services, market expansion activities, and consumer education.

Export Grape and Plum Act (74 Stat. 734, 7 U.S.C. 591-599). Signed by the president Sept. 2, 1960. Requires inspection of export shipments of fresh grapes and plums for which quality specifications have been established.

Agricultural Fair Practices Act (82 Stat. 93, 7 U.S.C. 2301-2306). Signed by the president April 16, 1968. Prohibits unfair trade practices by processors and handlers who deal with farmers, prohibiting discriminating activities against members of a producer association. Protects farmers rights to organize and join cooperatives.

Plant Variety Protection Act (84 Stat. 1542, 7 U.S.C. 2321-2331). Signed by the president Dec. 24, 1970. Encourages the development of novel varieties of sexually (by seed) reproduced or tuber propagated plants by providing protection to developers of such plants.

Egg Products Inspection Act (84 Stat. 1620, 21 U.S.C. 1031-1056). Signed by the president Dec. 29, 1970. Provides for a shell surveillance program to ensure the proper disposition of restricted (dirty, cracked, leaking) eggs.

Dairy and Tobacco Adjustment Act of 1983 (97 Stat. 1149, 7 U.S.C. 511r). Signed by the president Nov. 29, 1983. Requires all imported tobacco, with the exception of cigar and oriental tobacco, be inspected for grade and quality.

Organic Foods Production Act of 1990 (104 Stat. 3935, 7 U.S.C. 6501-6522). Signed by the president Nov. 28, 1990. Authorizes a program of national standards for the production and certification of organically produced foods. Established a National Organic Standards Board to provide recommendations on implementation of the act and to develop a list of allowed and prohibited substances.

Various Commodity Research and Promotion Laws authorizing self-help industry-financed programs to carry out national promotion and research efforts. These laws apply to avocadoes (7 U.S.C. 7801-7813), beef (7 U.S.C. 2901-2911), canola (7 U.S.C. 7441-7452), cotton (7 U.S.C. 2101-2118), dairy (7 U.S.C. 4501-4513), eggs (7 U.S.C. 2701-2718), flowers (7 U.S.C. 4301-4319), fluid milk (7 U.S.C. 6401-6417), fresh cut flowers and greens (7 U.S.C. 6801-6814), honey (7 U.S.C. 4601-4613), kiwifruit (7 U.S.C. 7461-7473), limes (7 U.S.C. 6201-6212), mushrooms (7 U.S.C. 6101-6112), pecans (7 U.S.C. 6001-6013), popcorn (7 U.S.C. 7481-7491), pork (7 U.S.C. 4801-4819), potatoes (7 U.S.C. 2611-2627), sheep (7 U.S.C. 7101-7111), soybeans (7 U.S.C. 6301-6311), watermelons (7 U.S.C. 4901-4916), and wheat (7 U.S.C. 3401-3417).

Farm Security and Rural Investment Act of 2002 (2002 Farm Bill) (116 Stat. 1348, 7 U.S.C. 7901 note). Signed by the president on May 13, 2002. Provided that all peanuts marketed in the United States, including imported ones, be officially inspected and graded. Eliminated the termination date of the Fluid Milk Promotion Act. Required mandatory country of origin labeling for beef, lamb, pork, fish, perishable agricultural commodities, and peanuts after a two-year voluntary program. Required the establishment of a national organic certification cost-share program.

■ FIELD OFFICES

Each of the Marketing Program Divisions has several field offices. For field office phone numbers, contact the program directors at the Washington headquarters office.

Marketing Program Divisions

The physical address in Washington is listed for each division. The mailing address for these offices is 1400 Independence Ave., SW, Washington, DC 20250.

COTTON

1400 Independence Ave. S.W., #2641-S
(202) 720–3193
Norma McDill, director

DAIRY

1400 Independence Ave. S.W., #2968-S
(202) 720–4392
Richard McKee, director

FRUIT AND VEGETABLE

1400 Independence Ave. S.W., #2077-S
(202) 720–4722
Robert C. Keeney, director

LIVESTOCK AND SEED

1400 Independence Ave. S.W., #2092-S
(202) 720–5705
Barry L. Carpenter, director

POULTRY

1400 Independence Ave. S.W., #3932-S
(202) 720–4476
Howard Magwire, director

SCIENCE AND TECHNOLOGY

1400 Independence Ave. S.W., #3507-S
(202) 720–5231
Robert Epstein, director

TOBACCO

300 12th St. S.W., Annex #502
(202) 205–0567
John P. Duncan III, director

TRANSPORTATION AND MARKETING

1400 Independence Ave. S.W., #2510-S
(202) 690–1300
Barbara Robinson, director

Animal and Plant Health Inspection Service

14th St. and Independence Ave. S.W., Washington, DC 20250
Mailing address: Stop 3407, Washington, DC 20250
Internet: http://www.aphis.usda.gov

The Animal and Plant Health Inspection Service (APHIS) was created in 1972 as an agency within the U.S. Department of Agriculture (USDA). APHIS is under the jurisdiction of the assistant secretary of agriculture for marketing and regulatory programs; it is run by an administrator who is appointed by the secretary of agriculture. APHIS is responsible for programs to eradicate diseases and pests that affect animals and plants, for animal and plant health and quarantine programs, and for the control of depredating animals. The agency also regulates the agricultural products of biotechnology and enforces certain humane laws.

APHIS regulates the entry of agricultural products into the United States by inspecting all shipments at major air, sea, border, and offshore points of entry. Cargoes of plants and plant products are examined. Inspectors also examine general cargo for agricultural pests and for prohibited animal products. APHIS inspectors can refuse entry of infested plants or can demand that plants be quarantined or treated prior to entry.

Inspectors also work in several foreign countries where they examine and certify shipments of agricultural products to the United States (primarily plant products, fruits, and vegetables). Domestic plants for export are certified to be pest free before they are shipped abroad.

The Homeland Security Act of 2002 transferred to the new Homeland Security Department the Department of Agriculture functions relating to agricultural import and entry inspection activities under specified animal and plant protection laws. On March 1, 2003, APHIS's Agricultural Quarantine Inspection (AQI) program was transferred to the Department of Homeland Security's Border and Transportation Security Directorate. Only the AQI program moved to Homeland Security; the rest of APHIS remained a part of the Department of Agriculture.

APHIS programs concerning plant pests and diseases concentrate on control and eradication. These programs usually are carried out in cooperation with the affected states.

Surveys are made of various areas throughout the country to determine pest activity, population, and spread. When evidence of a dangerous pest is found, an emergency may be declared; emergency regulations designed to prevent the spread of the pest may go into effect and an areawide quarantine may be invoked.

APHIS control programs are carried out in cooperation with the states to prevent the spread of pests and plant diseases. Control efforts may take the form of chemical sprays, introduction of a pest's natural enemy into an infested area, and release of sterilized insect pests to reduce the population.

APHIS performs similar functions to protect animal health. APHIS personnel maintain quarantine stations for the care of imported animals. The staff issues permits for importation of animals and the interstate transportation of imported animals. The service inspects and certifies livestock and poultry to be exported. APHIS also licenses privately owned bird quarantine stations and approves processing plants in the United States that handle restricted animal materials and byproducts. Processing facilities are inspected frequently to ensure that the materials do not pose a threat to the domestic animal population.

APHIS works to control and eradicate diseases that infect domestic animals. In cooperation with affected states, APHIS officials establish programs to monitor and control diseases.

Maladies that are or have been the object of APHIS disease programs include brucellosis, bovine tuberculosis, trichinosis, exotic Newcastle disease, avian mycoplasm, scrapie, equine infectious anemia, and salmonella enteritis.

APHIS also administers regulation under the Animal Welfare Act. In 1966, responding to complaints about suffering and neglected dogs and cats supplied to research institutions and focusing on the problem of "petnapping," Congress passed the Laboratory Animal Welfare Act. Four years later, a much more comprehensive piece of legislation—the Animal Welfare Act (AWA)—was enacted. This law expanded coverage to most other warm-blooded animals used in research; to animals in zoos and circuses and marine mammals in sea life shows and exhibits; and to animals sold in the wholesale pet trade. The law does not cover retail pet shops, game ranches, livestock shows, rodeos, state or county fairs, or dog and cat shows.

The AWA has been amended four times. A 1976 amendment extended the scope of the act to include care and treatment while animals are being transported via common carriers. It also outlawed animal fighting ventures, such as dog or cock fights, unless specifically allowed by state law. The 2002 Farm Bill amended AWA to exclude rats, mice, and birds bred for research purposes from the definition of animal in the AWA.

Under the Horse Protection Act, APHIS protects horses by enforcing a statute that forbids "soring" of horses in interstate commerce. (Soring is the willful bruising of the front feet of a horse that causes the horse to lift the tender hooves high off the ground, creating a dancing step admired in horse shows.)

APHIS regulates the manufacture of biological products used in the treatment of animals, including genetically engineered biologics, to assure that the products are safe, pure, potent, and effective. APHIS issues licenses to manufacturers of biologics, surveys production techniques, and inspects production facilities. The agency also regulates the interstate movement and import of genetically engineered plants and microorganisms that are or may be plant pests.

The Animal Damage Control Program, now the Wildlife Services Program, was transferred in 1986 from the U.S. Fish and Wildlife Service to APHIS. Under the Animal Damage Control Act of 1931, APHIS is authorized to protect livestock and crops from depredating mammals and birds. This program protects forests, range lands, and many kinds of wildlife, including endangered species, from animal damage. In addition, the program helps protect human health and safety through control of animal-borne diseases and hazards to aircraft caused by birds.

Following the terrorist attacks of September 2001 and the anthrax attacks in the weeks that followed, Congress and the administration of George W. Bush enacted the Agricultural Bioterrorism Protection Act of 2002. The law required the Agriculture Department to establish and maintain a list of biological agents and toxins that could pose a severe threat to animal or plant health. The FBI was responsible for conducting security risk assessments of individuals seeking access to listed agents and toxins and individuals or entities seeking to register under the act.

■ KEY PERSONNEL

Administrator
  Bobby Acord............................ (202) 720–3668
  Fax..................................... (202) 720–3054
Associate Administrator
  Peter Fernandez .... (202) 720–3861
Animal Care (Riverdale)
  Chester Gipson .... (301) 734–4980
Wildlife Services
  William H. Clay .... (202) 720–2054
International Services
  Ralph Iwamota .... (202) 720–7593
  Executive Correspondence (Riverdale)
  Felicia Stepney......................... (301) 734–8898
Organizational and Professional Development (Riverdale)
  Andrea M. Morgan (acting)........... (301) 734–5100
Budget and Accounting
  John Neesen .... (301) 734–8635
Plant Protection and Quarantine
  Richard L. Dunkle...................... (202) 720–5601
  Biological Assessment and Taxonomic Support
  Rebecca Bech .... (301) 734–8896
Policy and Program Development
  Kevin A. Shea.......................... (202) 720–6907
Veterinary Services
  Ron DeHaven........................... (202) 720–5193

■ INFORMATION SOURCES

Internet
Agency Web site: http://www.aphis.usda.gov. Includes many APHIS publications and information on program activities.

Telephone Contacts
Personnel Locator (Riverdale, MD)....... (301) 734–8010

Information and Publications

KEY OFFICES

APHIS Legislative and Public Affairs
South Bldg., Room 1147
14th St. and Independence Ave. S.W.
Stop 3407
Washington, DC 20250
(202) 720–2511
Ralph R. Harding, director

Answers general questions from the public, the media, and Congress. Refers specific questions on APHIS programs to the proper office. Divisions include:

APHIS Legislative Services
(202) 720–3981
Lynn Quarles, deputy director

Provides liaison services between the agency and Congress.

APHIS Public Affairs
4700 River Rd.
Riverdale, MD 20737
(301) 734–7799
Bethany Jones, assistant director

Issues news releases on actions taken by APHIS and recent developments concerning plant and animal diseases. Maintains a mailing list.

Freedom of Information
Executive Correspondence
4700 River Rd.
Riverdale, MD 20737
(301) 734–7776
Christina Myers, assistant director

Handles/processes all APHIS correspondence.

APHIS Management Services Division
4700 River Rd., Unit 1
Riverdale, MD 20737
(301) 734–5524

Provides ordering information on APHIS publications and data.

PUBLICATIONS
The APHIS Management Services Division distributes *Available Information from the Animal and Plant Health In-spection Service*. This list includes pamphlets and brochures on all aspects of APHIS's work: agricultural quarantines, plant pest control, animal welfare, livestock and poultry diseases, foreign animal diseases, identification of cattle and swine, animal import and export, and veterinary biologics.

Some APHIS publications are also available via the agency's Internet site (including some in Spanish).

DATA AND STATISTICS
Statistical information on the work of APHIS is available in the publications listed below. For details on ordering, contact the APHIS Management Services Division.

Foreign Animal Disease Report. Issued quarterly.

Strategic Plan: Meeting Producer and Public Needs. Assesses APHIS's role in the future of U.S. agriculture and plant and animal health.

This is APHIS. A general description of the programs carried out by APHIS.

Travelers' Tips. Lists what food, plant, and animal products can be brought into the United States from foreign countries.

Uniform Methods and Rules for Bovine Tuberculosis Eradication. Describes the cooperative state/federal bovine tuberculosis eradication program.

Uniform Methods and Rules for Brucellosis Eradication. Describes the cooperative state/federal brucellosis eradication program.

Reference Resources

LIBRARIES

APHIS Public Reading Room
14th St. and Independence Ave. S.W.
South Bldg., Room 1141-S
Stop 3499
Washington, DC 20250
(202) 690–2817
Judy Lee, program specialist
Hours: 7:00 a.m. to 4:30 p.m.

Maintains records of APHIS public hearings and administrative proceedings for public inspection. Some materials concerning APHIS are also available from:

National Agricultural Library
10301 Baltimore Blvd.
Beltsville, MD 20705–2351
(301) 504–5755
Pamela Andre, director
Hours: 8:00 a.m. to 4:30 p.m.

The USDA also maintains a reference center at the main Agriculture Department building. The collection consists primarily of periodicals, reference volumes, and databases.

D.C. Reference Center
14th St. and Independence Ave. S.W.
South Bldg., Room 1052-S
Washington, DC 20250
(202) 720–3434
Janet Wright, chief
Hours: 8:00 a.m. to 4:30 p.m.

DOCKETS
Contact the APHIS Public Reading Room. Address comments on proposed regulations to:

APHIS Policy and Program Development Division
Regulatory Analysis and Development Branch
4700 River Rd.
Unit 118, #3-C-71
Riverdale, MD 20737
(301) 734–8682
Cynthia Howard, chief

RULES AND REGULATIONS
APHIS rules and regulations are published in the *Code of Federal Regulations,* Title 7, parts 300–399 and Title 9, parts 1–199. Proposed rules, new final rules, and updates to the *Code of Federal Regulations* are published in the daily *Federal Register. (See appendix for information on how to obtain and use these publications.)*

▨ LEGISLATION
Legislation administered by APHIS includes:

Act of Aug. 30, 1890 (26 Stat. 416, 21 U.S.C. 101). Signed by the president Aug. 30, 1890. Prohibited the importation of certain animals except at quarantine stations and authorized the slaughter of animals that have been diagnosed to be diseased.

Plant Quarantine Act of 1912 (37 Stat. 319, 7 U.S.C. 151). Signed by the president Aug. 20, 1912. Set standards for the importation of nursery stock and established procedures for importing plants; also known as the Nursery Stock Quarantine Act. This act was later amended by the Plant Quarantine Act Amendment (96 Stat. 2276, 7 U.S.C. 159). Signed by the president Jan. 8, 1983. Permitted APHIS to restrict the importation of plants without holding a public hearing.

Mexican Border Act of 1942 (56 Stat. 40, 7 U.S.C. 149). Signed by the president Jan. 31, 1942. Authorized inspection and cleaning of vehicles and materials that enter the country from Mexico.

Federal Plant Pest Act (71 Stat. 31, 7 U.S.C. 150aa). Signed by the president May 23, 1957. Authorized regulation of movement of any plant pest from a foreign country into or through the United States; authorized inspections and seizures.

Act of July 2, 1962 (76 Stat. 129, 21 U.S.C. 134). Signed by the president July 2, 1962. Established procedure standards for the interstate transportation of animals exposed to communicable diseases.

Animal Welfare Act (80 Stat. 350, 7 U.S.C. 2131). Signed by the president Aug. 24, 1966. Amended by the **Animal Welfare Act of 1970** (84 Stat. 1560, 7 U.S.C. 2131), signed by the president Dec. 24, 1970, and the **Animal Welfare Act Amendments of 1976** (90 Stat. 417, 7 U.S.C. 2131 note), signed by the president April 22, 1976. Established minimum standards for transportation, purchase, sale, housing, care, handling, and treatment of certain animals used for research experiments or exhibition.

Act of May 6, 1970 (84 Stat. 202, 21 U.S.C. 135). Signed by the president May 6, 1970. Authorized the establishment of an international quarantine station.

Horse Protection Act of 1970 (84 Stat. 1404, 15 U.S.C. 1821). Signed by the president Dec. 9, 1970. Prohibited the "soring" (the bruising of the front feet) of horses shipped interstate.

Food Security Act of 1985 (99 Stat. 1650, 7 U.S.C. 2131 note). Signed by the president Dec. 23, 1985. Established more stringent standards of care for regulated animals, including a suitable physical environment for primates and exercise for dogs.

Continuing Appropriations Act for Fiscal Year 1987 (100 Stat. 3341–3347, 7 U.S.C. 426). Signed by the president Oct. 30, 1986. Authorized the transfer of funds from the Interior Department to the USDA to carry out the responsibilities authorized in the **Animal Damage Control Act of 1931** (46 Stat. 1468, 7 U.S.C. 426), signed by the president March 2, 1931. Authorized APHIS to conduct investigations and tests as necessary to determine the best methods of eradication or control in national areas of mountain lions, wolves, coyotes, bobcats, prairie dogs, gophers, ground squirrels, jack rabbits, and other animals injurious to agriculture, forestry, wild game animals, livestock, and other domestic animals.

Farm Security and Rural Investment Act of 2002 (2002 Farm Bill) (116 Stat. 1348, 7 U.S.C. 7901 note). Signed by the president on May 13, 2002. Established a grant program for security upgrades at colleges and universities. Established a felony provision under the Plant Protection Act. Amended definition of animal under the Animal Welfare Act (AWA) to exclude rats, mice, and birds bred for research. Authorized APHIS to conduct research on transmissible spongiform encephalopathy in deer, elk, and moose, and chronic wasting disease.

Agricultural Bioterrorism Protection Act of 2002 Signed by the president on June 12, 2002. Directed the establishment of a list of biological agents and toxins that could pose a severe threat to animal or plant health. Set forth provisions for the regulation of (1) transfers of listed agents and toxins; (2) possession and use of listed agents and toxins; (3) registration, identification, and maintenance of database of listed toxins; and (4) security and safeguard of persons possessing, using, or transferring a listed agent. Directed the secretary of agriculture and the secretary of health and human services to coordinate activities regarding overlap agents and toxins.

Homeland Security Act of 2002 (P.L. 107-296). Signed by the president on Nov. 25, 2002. Created the Department of Homeland Security. Section 421 transferred to the Department of Homeland Security the Agriculture Department functions relating to agricultural import and entry inspection activities under specified animal and plant protection laws.

■ REGIONAL OFFICES

Animal Care

EASTERN REGION
(AL, CT, DC, DE, FL, GA, IL, IN, KY, MA, MD, ME, MI, MN, MS, NC, NH, NJ, NY, OH, PA, PR, RI, SC, TN, VA, VI, VT, WI, WV)
920 Main Campus Rd., #200
Raleigh, NC 27606-5210
(919) 716-5532
Elizabeth Goldentyer, regional director

WESTERN REGION
(AK, AR, AZ, CA, CO, GU, HI, IA, ID, KS, MO, MT, NE, ND, NM, OK, OR, SD, TX, UT, WA, WY)
2150 Centre Ave., Bldg. A, #143
Ft. Collins, CO 80526
(970) 498–1100
Robert M. Gibbons, regional director

Wildlife Services

EASTERN REGION
(AL, AR, CT, DC, DE, FL, GA, IA, IL, IN, KY, LA, MA, MD, ME, MI, MO, MN, MS, NC, NH, NJ, NY, OH, PA, PR, RI, SC, TN, VA, VI, VT, WI, WV)
920 Main Campus Rd., #200
Raleigh, NC 27606-5210
(919) 716-5632
Charles Brown, regional director

WESTERN REGION
(AK, AS, AZ, CA, CO, GU, HI, ID, KS, MT, ND, NE, NM, NV, OK, OR, SD, TX, UT, WA, WY)
12345 W. Alameda Pkwy., #204
Lakewood, CO 80228
(303) 236–5828, ext. 222
Michael Worthen, regional director

Plant Protection and Quarantine Program

EASTERN REGION
(AL, CT, DE, FL, GA, IL, IN, KY, MA, MD, ME, MI, MN, MS, NC, NH, NJ, NY, OH, PA, PR, SC, TN, VA, VT, WI, WV)
920 Main Campus Rd., #200
Raleigh, NC 27606-5210
(919) 716–5676
Jerry Fowler, regional director

WESTERN REGION
(AK, AZ, CA, CO, GU, HI, ID, MT, NV, OR, UT, WA, WY)
9580 Micron Ave., #1
Sacramento, CA 95827
(970) 494–7575
James R. Reynolds, regional director

Veterinary Services

EASTERN REGION

(AL, CT, DC, DE, FL, GA, IL, IN, KY, MA, MD, ME, MI,
MN, MS, NC, NH, NJ, NY, OH, PA, PR, RI, SC, TN, VA,
VI, VT, WI, WV)
920 Main Campus Rd., Suite 200
Raleigh, NC 27606
(919) 716–5570
Dr. William Buisch, regional director

WESTERN REGION

(AK, AZ, CA, CO, GU, HI, ID, MT, NM, NV, OR, UT,
WA, WY)
384 Inverness Dr. South, #150
P.O. Box 3857
Englewood, CO 80155
(970) 494–7385
Jose Diez, regional director

Farm Service Agency

14th St. and Independence Ave. S.W., Washington, DC 20250
Mailing address: P.O. Box 2415, Washington, DC 20013
Internet: http://www.fsa.usda.gov

The Farm Service Agency (FSA) was created in 1994 by a reorganization of the U.S. Department of Agriculture (USDA). It combines the farm loan section of the former Farmers Home Administration (FmHA) with the former Agricultural Stabilization and Conservation Service (ASCS). In addition, the FSA administers most functions of the government-owned and operated corporation, the Commodity Credit Corporation (CCC). The FSA formerly administered crop insurance programs through the Federal Crop Insurance Corporation (FCIC). In 1996 the Risk Management Agency (RMA) was created as a separate agency within USDA. RMA now administers the functions of the FCIC.

The FSA is headed by an administrator who reports to the under secretary of agriculture for farm and foreign agricultural services. The administrator is appointed by the president and confirmed by the Senate. After its creation in 1994, the FSA was briefly known as the Consolidated Farm Service Agency. Major program areas of the FSA include commodity programs, farm loans, conservation programs, price support, and disaster assistance.

Commodity programs. The CCC operates commodity programs to stabilize the price and supply of agricultural products, in particular wheat, corn, cotton, peanuts, rice, tobacco, milk, sugar beets and sugar cane, wool, mohair, honey, barley, oats, grain sorghum, rye, soybeans, and other oilseeds.

The CCC is a wholly owned government corporation that is now administered by the FSA. It was created in 1933 and incorporated in 1948 as a federal corporation within the USDA by the Commodity Credit Corporation Charter Act. It is managed by an eight-member board of directors appointed by the president and confirmed by the Senate. The secretary of agriculture serves as chair of the CCC board of directors and as an *ex officio* director. The other seven board members are appointed by the president and designated according to their positions in the USDA. The corporation staff, including president, executive vice president, secretary of the board, and general counsel, are also senior officials of the USDA.

The FSA makes CCC loans to eligible farmers using the stored crop as collateral. Many of these loans are "nonrecourse." When market prices are higher than the loan rate, a farmer may pay off the loan and market the commodity; when prices are below the loan levels, the farmer can forfeit or deliver the commodity to the government to discharge the loan in full. Hence the loans promote orderly marketing by providing farmers with income while they hold their crops for later sale. In most cases, to qualify for payments, commodity loans, and purchases, a farmer must participate in the acreage reduction, allotment, or quota programs in effect for the particular crop. The CCC also has authority to license and inspect warehouses and other facilities that store insured commodities.

The CCC is capitalized at $100 million and has authority to borrow up to $30 billion. Funds are borrowed from the federal Treasury and also may be borrowed from private lending agencies.

Commodities acquired by the CCC under the various commodity stabilization programs are sold in this country and abroad, transferred to other government agencies, and donated to domestic and foreign agencies. The Foreign Agricultural Service *(see p. 421)* administers CCC export activities.

Other commodity programs administered by the FSA include:

- Dairy Refund Payment Program. Provides producers refunds of the reduction in the price received for milk during a calendar year. The Dairy Indemnity Payment Program makes producers eligible for payments if milk has been contaminated by residues of chemical or toxic substances.

- Emergency Programs. Provide feed to farmers in areas struck by natural disasters; provide emergency conservation assistance to restore damaged farm lands; and operate emergency programs to promote food production during national emergencies.
- Grain Reserve Program. Grain owned by farmers is held in reserve through the CCC to stabilize the grain market and to ensure an adequate supply.

Farm loans. Like its predecessor, the Farmers Home Administration (FmHA), the FSA makes direct and guaranteed loans to farmers who are temporarily unable to obtain private, commercial credit. Farmers who qualify receive loan guarantees, whereby a local agricultural lender makes and services the loan and the FSA guarantees the loan up to a maximum of 90 percent. For farmers who cannot qualify for loan guarantees, the FSA makes direct loans, which in most cases are administered by the FSA at the local level.

In support of its farm loan programs, the FSA provides credit counseling and supervision to its direct borrowers. The agency also assesses the feasibility of these borrowers' farming operations and provides further loan services to borrowers whose accounts are delinquent.

Unlike FSA's commodity loans, these loans can only be approved for those who have repayment ability; the farm loans are fully secured and are "nonrecourse." The goal of FSA farm credit operations is to graduate its customers to commercial credit.

Conservation programs. The FSA operates most of the programs of the former Agricultural Stabilization and Conservation Service (ASCS), many of which pertain to commodities and are discussed above. The FSA now administers two major voluntary land-use programs designed to protect, expand, and conserve farm lands, wetlands, and forests:

Conservation Reserve Program (CRP). Targets the most fragile farmland by encouraging farmers to plant a permanent vegetative cover, rather than crops. In return, the farmer receives an annual rental payment for the term of the multiyear contract.

Agricultural Conservation Program (ACP). Provides cost-sharing to farmers and ranchers who carry out conservation and environmental protection practices, particularly to prevent soil erosion and contamination of water resources.

Other ASCS conservation programs, including the Wetlands Reserve, Water Bank, Colorado River Basin Salinity Control, and Forestry Incentives programs, are now part of a different USDA agency, the Natural Resources Conservation Service (NRCS).

The FSA also conducts the Emergency Haying and Grazing Assistance program. Haying and grazing of certain conservation reserve program acreage may be made available in areas suffering from weather-related natural disaster. Requests have to be made by the FSA county committees through the state committees and finally decided by the deputy administrator for farm programs.

Another is the Emergency Conservation Program (ECP). ECP shares with agricultural producers the cost of rehabilitating eligible farmlands damaged by the natural disaster. During severe drought, ECP also provides emergency water assistance for livestock and for existing irrigation systems for orchards and vineyards. ECP may be made available in areas without regard to a presidential or secretarial emergency disaster designation.

Price support. The Farm Service Agency Price Support Division (PSD) offers a variety of programs that assist farmers and ranchers in managing their businesses, from marketing loans to price support programs. The Federal Agriculture Improvement and Reform Act of 1996 (FAIRA) provided transition payments, nonrecourse marketing assistance loans, and loan deficiency payments for the 1996–2002 feed grain crops, wheat, rice, cotton, soybeans, and minor oilseeds. The 2002 Farm Bill amended FAIRA to direct the secretary of agriculture to enter into contracts with eligible owners and producers of eligible cropland for both direct and counter-cyclical payments in crop years 2002 through 2006. USDA, in conjunction with Texas A&M University, developed new computer-based tools to help producers analyze the economic consequences of the bill's updating options. Information about these tools is available on the USDA web site.

Disaster assistance. FSA offers a number of programs that assist farmers and ranchers in recovering from weather-related setbacks. Two of these programs include the Noninsured Crop Disaster Assistance Program and the Emergency Loans Program. The Noninsured Crop Disaster Assistance Program is for crops for which crop insurance is not available. It provides assistance for farmers who grow such crops, limiting their losses from natural disaster and helping to manage their overall business risk. Eligible crops include agricultural commodities that are grown for food; planted and grown for livestock consumption, including but not limited to grain and seeded and native forage crops; grown for fiber, except for trees; and specialty crops, such as aquaculture, floriculture, ornamental nursery, Christmas trees, turf for sod, industrial crops, and seed crops used to produce NAP-eligible crops.

FSA also provides low-interest emergency loan assistance to eligible farmers to help cover production and physical losses in counties declared as disaster areas. The FSA administrator may also authorize emergency loan assistance to cover physical losses only. Borrowers are eligible to borrow up to 80 percent of the actual production loss or 100 percent of actual physical loss. Emergency loans are traditionally made to producers in declared disaster areas where drought, floods, and other natural disasters have had devastating effects. The 2002 Farm Bill allowed farmers and ranchers located in declared quarantine areas to also apply for emergency loans.

KEY PERSONNEL

Administrator
James R. Little . . . . (202) 720–3467
Fax . . . . (202) 720–9105
Associate Administrator
Verle Lanier . . . . (202) 690–0153
Economic and Policy Analysis
Larry Walker . . . . (202) 720–3451
Civil Rights (Agriculture Dept.)
Sharon Lynn Holmes . . . . (202) 401–7220
General Counsel (Agriculture Dept.)
James Michael Kelly . . . . (202) 720–7219
Legislative Liaison
Mary Helen Askins (acting) . . . . (202) 720–3865
Commodity Credit Corporation Chair
Ann Veneman . . . . (202) 720–3631
Fax . . . . (202) 205–2883
President
J.B. Penn . . . . (202) 720–3111
Fax . . . . (202) 720–8254
Controller (Alexandria, VA)
Kristine M. Chadwick . . . . (703) 305–1386
Fax . . . . (703) 305–2842
Secretary
Verle Lanier (acting) . . . . (202) 690–0153
Fax . . . . (202) 418–9125
Commodity Operations
Bert D. Farish . . . . (202) 720–3217
Fax . . . . (202) 720–8055
Procurement and Donations
Steve Mikkelsen . . . . (202) 720–5074
Warehouse and Inventory
Steve Gill . . . . (202) 720–2121
Kansas City Commodity Office
(P.O. Box 419205, Kansas City, MO 64141)
George Aldaya . . . . (816) 926–6301
Farm Loan Programs
Carolyn Cooksie . . . . (202) 720–4671
Fax . . . . (202) 690–3573
Loan Making
James Radintz . . . . (202) 720–1632

Loan Servicing
A. Veldon Hall . . . . (202) 690–0155
Program Development and Economic Enhancement
Bobby Reynolds . . . . (202) 720–7719
Farm Programs
John A. Johnson . . . . (202) 720–7641
Fax . . . . (202) 720–4726
Production, Emergency, and Compliance
Diane Sharp . . . . (202) 720–9882
Conservation and Environmental Protection
Robert Stephenson . . . . (202) 720–6221
Price Support
Grady Bilberry . . . . (202) 720–7901
Tobacco
John Truluck III. . . . . (202) 720–7413
Management
John Williams . . . . (202) 720–3438
Fax . . . . (202) 690–0439
State Operations
Douglas W. Frago . . . . (202) 690–2807
Fax . . . . (202) 690–3309

INFORMATION SOURCES

Internet
Agency Web site: http://www.fsa.usda.gov. Includes news releases and extensive information on FSA programs.

Telephone Contacts
Personnel Locator . . . . (202) 720–8732

Information and Publications

KEY OFFICES

FSA Public Affairs Staff
USDA/FSA
1400 Independence Ave., SW, Stop 0506
Washington, DC 20250
(202) 720–7807
Eric Parsons, director

Provides all public and press information on the FSA. Issues news releases on programs, actions, and decisions on pricing; maintains a mailing list. Produces publications, pamphlets, and fact sheets.

Freedom of Information
USDA Farm Service Agency
1400 Independence Ave., SW, Stop 0506
Washington, DC 20250
(202) 720–5534
Diane Korwin, FOIA officer

PUBLICATIONS

Contact the FSA Public Affairs Staff for leaflets and fact sheets on agricultural policies, problems, and programs; and pamphlets on FSA operations.

DATA AND STATISTICS

FSA statistical publications, including reports on the Commodity Credit Corporation and specific programs, are available from the FSA Public Affairs Staff.

Publications of special interest include:

Annual Report of the Commodity Credit Corporation. Covers operations of the CCC during the preceding year.

Commodity Fact Sheets. Includes provisions and selected basic data for individual agricultural commodity programs, including dairy, feed grains, sugar, tobacco, cotton, peanuts, and rice.

Reference Resources

LIBRARY

National Agricultural Library
10301 Baltimore Blvd.
Beltsville, MD 20705–2351
(301) 504–5755
Pamela Andre, director
Hours: 8:00 a.m. to 4:30 p.m.

The USDA also maintains a reference center at the main Agriculture Department building. The collection consists primarily of periodicals, reference volumes, and databases.

D.C. Reference Center
14th St. and Independence Ave. S.W.
South Bldg., Room 1052
Washington, DC 20250
(202) 720–3434
Janet Wright, chief
Hours: 8:00 a.m. to 4:30 p.m.

RULES AND REGULATIONS

FSA rules and regulations are published in the *Code of Federal Regulations,* Title 7, parts 701–799. Proposed rules, new final rules, and updates to the *Code of Federal Regulations* are published in the daily *Federal Register. (See appendix for information on how to obtain and use these publications.)*

■ LEGISLATION

Following are the act that established the FSA and the laws pertaining to the FSA's program areas.

Department of Agriculture Reorganization Act of 1994 (108 Stat. 3178). Signed by the president Oct. 13, 1994. Consolidated the direct farm programs of the Agricultural Stabilization and Conservation Service and the Commodity Credit Corporation with those of the Federal Crop Insurance Corporation and the Farmers Home Administration into a new Agriculture Service Agency (now the FSA).

Crop Insurance:

Federal Crop Insurance Corporation Act of 1938 (7 U.S.C. 1501). Signed by the president Feb. 16, 1938. Established the FCIC as an agency of the USDA.

Federal Crop Insurance Reform Act of 1994 (7 U.S.C. 1501 note). Signed by the president Oct. 13, 1994. Overhauled the crop insurance program. Established catastrophic level (CAT) coverage as a requirement to participate in certain FSA programs; also established the Noninsured Crop Disaster Assistance Program for crops not yet insurable.

Agricultural Market Transition Act (110 Stat. 896, 7 U.S.C. 7201). Signed by the president April 4, 1996. Part of the Federal Agriculture Improvement and Reform Act of 1996. Under title I (the act itself), subtitle H (miscellaneous commodity provisions), section 193 amended the Federal Crop Insurance Act to direct the secretary of agriculture to offer catastrophic risk protection in a State through the local Department of Agriculture offices if sufficient coverage is unavailable. Provided for the transfer of current policies to private insurers and established a crop insurance pilot project. Section 194 established the Office of Risk Management to oversee the Federal Crop Insurance Corporation and related crop insurance matters. Section 195 established a revenue insurance pilot program. Section 196 directed the secretary to operate a noninsured crop disaster assistance program through the FSA for food or fiber crops not covered by the federal crop insurance catastrophic risk protection program.

Agricultural Research, Extension, and Education Reform Act of 1998 (112 Stat. 523). Signed by the president June 23, 1998. Title V (agricultural program adjustments), subtitle C (crop insurance) amended the Federal Crop Insurance Corporation Act of 1938 to make permanent the Federal Crop Insurance Corporation's authority to pay expenses from the insurance fund. Directed the corporation to establish and implement procedures for responding to regulatory inquiries.

Commodity Programs:

U.S. Warehouse Act (39 Stat. 486, 7 U.S.C. 241). Signed by the president Aug. 11, 1916. Authorized licenses for warehouses that store agricultural products; provides for inspection of warehouses and products. These functions formerly were carried out by the Agricultural Marketing Service; they were transferred to the ASCS in January 1985.

Commodity Credit Corporation Charter Act (62 Stat. 1070, 15 U.S.C. 714 note). Signed by the president June 29, 1948. Established the CCC as an agency of the USDA. The CCC originally was created in 1933 as an agency of the federal government under the corporation laws of Delaware; in 1939 it was transferred to the USDA by a reorganization plan. The 1948 act authorized the agency to support the prices of commodities through loans, purchases, and payments.

Agricultural Act of 1949 (63 Stat. 1051, 7 U.S.C. 1446a, 1427). Signed by the president Oct. 31, 1949. This act, together with the **Agricultural Act of 1956** (70 Stat. 188, 7 U.S.C. 1851a), signed by the president May 28, 1956, authorized the CCC to make domestic donations to the military, the Veterans Administration, schools, and nonprofit institutions.

Agricultural Trade Development and Assistance Act (68 Stat. 454, 7 U.S.C. 1427). Signed by the president July 10, 1954. Authorized the CCC to finance the sale and export of agricultural commodities for relief donations abroad; also authorized the CCC to trade excess commodities for materials required abroad by other federal agencies. This act was amended and later known as the **Food for Peace Act** (80 Stat. 1526, 7 U.S.C. 1691). Signed by the president Nov. 11, 1966. Promoted agricultural trade; donated food, fertilizers, and technology to foreign countries to combat hunger; and encouraged economic development in developing countries.

Agricultural Act of 1954 (68 Stat. 910, 7 U.S.C. 1781). Signed by the president Aug. 28, 1954. Included the **National Wool Act**, which established mohair and wool price stabilization by authorizing payments to producers.

Dairy Farmers Indemnity Payments, as amended (82 Stat. 750, 7 U.S.C. 450j). Signed by the president Aug. 13, 1968. Authorized indemnity payments to dairy farmers who had to remove their milk from commercial markets because it contained residues of chemicals, toxic substances, or nuclear radiation.

Food and Agriculture Act of 1977 (91 Stat. 913, 7 U.S.C. 1308). Signed by the president Sept. 23, 1977. Established revised price supports and loan levels for various agricultural commodities.

Food and Agriculture Act of 1977 (91 Stat. 953, 7 U.S.C. 1427). Signed by the president Sept. 29, 1977. Provided a farmer-owned grain reserve program for wheat and feed grains to isolate grain stocks from the market to counter the price-depressing effects of these surplus stocks.

Agricultural Trade Act of 1978 (92 Stat. 1685, 7 U.S.C. 1707a). Signed by the president Oct. 21, 1978. Authorized the CCC to finance agricultural export sales to expand and maintain foreign markets for certain U.S. agricultural commodities.

Agriculture and Food Act of 1981 (95 Stat. 1213, 7 U.S.C. 1281). Signed by the president Dec. 22, 1981. Basic statute administered by the ASCS. Extended, expanded, and revised the subsidy, allotment, and set-aside programs established by earlier legislation (including the Agricultural Act of 1949 and the farm bills of 1965, 1970, 1973, and 1977).

Extra Long Staple Cotton Act of 1983 (97 Stat. 494, 7 U.S.C. 1421 note). Signed by the president Aug. 26, 1983. Authorized the ASCS to make deficiency payments to producers of extra long staple cotton. Lowered the federal commodity loan rate for extra long staple cotton and authorized paid acreage reduction programs for the cotton crop.

Export Administration Amendments Act of 1985 (99 Stat. 158, 15 U.S.C. 4053). Signed by the president July 12, 1985. Authorized the CCC to exchange commodities for petroleum and petroleum products and other materials vital to the national interest.

Food Security Act of 1985 (99 Stat. 1354, 7 U.S.C. 1281 note). Signed by the president Dec. 23, 1985. Authorized new programs: Targeted Export Assistance, Conservation Reserve, and Export Enhancement. Amended the Food for Peace Act to allow the use of accrued foreign currencies to encourage development of private enterprise in developing countries. Extended, expanded, and revised income and price support programs, set-aside and acreage reduction programs, and voluntary paid land diversion programs.

Continuing Appropriations Act, Fiscal 1988 (101 Stat. 1329–335, 15 U.S.C 714). Signed by the president Dec. 22, 1988. Increased the CCC's borrowing authority from $25 billion to $30 billion.

Food, Agriculture, Conservation, and Trade Act of 1990 (104 Stat. 3359, 7 U.S.C. 1421 note). Signed by the president Nov. 28, 1990. Adjusted the formula for determining price supports on various commodities and the rules for the operation of grain reserves. Limited the total acreage eligible for diversion and deficiency payments on certain crops. Expanded planting flexibility.

Farm Security and Rural Investment Act of 2002 (2002 Farm Bill) (116 Stat. 1348, 7 U.S.C. 7901 note). Signed by the president on May 13, 2002. Amended the Federal Agriculture Improvement and Reform Act of 1996 (FAIRA) to direct the secretary of agriculture to enter into contracts with eligible owners and producers of eligible cropland for both direct and countercyclical payments in crop years 2002 through 2006. Required owner or producer compliance with appropriate conservation, wetlands, planting flexibility, and agricultural use requirements. Authorized the Milk Income Loss Contract (MILC) Program for dairy producers. Authorized the Hard White Wheat Incentive Program through 2005. Required that USDA operate the sugar program at no net cost to taxpayers, thus avoiding forfeitures to the CCC.

Farm Loans:

Bankhead-Jones Farm Tenant Act (50 Stat. 525, 7 U.S.C. 1010). Signed by the president July 22, 1937. Provided loan authorization to cover costs of resource conservation and development projects.

Farmers Home Administration Act (60 Stat. 1062, 7 U.S.C. 451 note). Signed by the president Aug. 14, 1946. Changed the name of the Farm Security Administration to the Farmers Home Administration and continued government loan programs established under that agency and the Resettlement Administration. Gave FmHA authority to insure loans made by banks, other agencies, and private individuals.

Consolidated Farm and Rural Development Act (75 Stat. 307, 7 U.S.C. 1921). Signed by the president Aug. 8, 1961. Authorized the FmHA to prescribe terms and conditions for making loans and grants and to require that the lender and the borrowers comply with applicable federal laws and regulations.

Rural Development Act of 1972 (86 Stat. 657, 7 U.S.C. 1006). Signed by the president Aug. 30, 1972. Empowered the FmHA to guarantee loans made by commercial lenders for farming and other purposes.

Agricultural Credit Act of 1978 (92 Stat. 420, 7 U.S.C. 1921 note). Signed by the president Aug. 4, 1978. Amended the Consolidated Farm and Rural Development Act to allow the FmHA to make or guarantee loans to farmers hurt by shortages of credit from normal sources or by a cost-price squeeze (when costs of producing goods rise faster than prices charged for them). It also expanded eligibility for farm loans to family corporations, cooperatives, and partnerships; and increased loan limits to $200,000 for insured and $300,000 for guaranteed real estate loans.

Emergency Agricultural Credit Act of 1984 (98 Stat. 138, 7 U.S.C. 1921). Signed by the president April 10, 1984. Authorized the FmHA to raise loan limits on new farm operating direct loans from $100,000 to $200,000, and on guaranteed loans from $200,000 to $400,000; and increased the maximum repayment period for rescheduled or consolidated emergency and operating loans from 7 to 15 years from the date of the original note.

Food Security Act of 1985 (99 Stat. 1518, 7 U.S.C. 1281 note). Signed by the president Dec. 23, 1985. Changed farm loan eligibility requirements and provided additional protections for borrowers undergoing serious financial difficulty. Two of three FmHA county committee members were to be elected by farmers in the community instead of being appointed.

Agricultural Credit Act of 1987 (101 Stat. 1568, 12 U.S.C. 2001 note). Signed by the president Jan. 6, 1988.

Permitted FmHA farmer program loans to be reduced to the recovery value of the borrower's collateral if the farmer has a feasible plan to continue the farming operation. Expanded preservation loan servicing programs. Established an independent appeals unit. Authorized the USDA to certify and issue grants to assist agricultural loan mediation programs in states upon a governor's request.

Food, Agriculture, Conservation, and Trade Act of 1990 (104 Stat. 3359, 7 U.S.C. 1421 note). Signed by the president Nov. 28, 1990. Modified delinquent farm-borrower debt relief provisions of the 1987 Agricultural Credit Act and instituted new procedures to strengthen borrowers' prospects for success. Transferred some FmHA programs to the new Rural Development Administration.

Agricultural Credit Improvement Act of 1992 (106 Stat. 4142, 7 U.S.C. 1921 note). Signed by the president Oct. 28, 1992. Established a program of targeted farm ownership and operating assistance for qualified beginning farmers and ranchers. Limited the number of years that borrowers are eligible for FmHA assistance and created a new lender-certified program for guaranteed farm loans. Established safeguards to ensure against discrimination on the basis of gender in FmHA farm lending practices.

Federal Agriculture Improvement and Reform Act of 1996 (110 Stat. 888, 7 U.S.C. 7201 note). Signed by the president April 4, 1996. Amended the Consolidated Farm and Rural Development Act of 1961 (CFRDA). Title VI (credits), subtitle A (farm ownership loans) revised direct farm ownership loan provisions. Subtitle B (operating loans) revised farm operating loan provisions. Authorized line-of-credit loans. Subtitle C (emergency loans) revised emergency loan provisions. Subtitle D (administrative provisions) authorized the secretary to enter into farm loan service contracts with eligible financial institutions through FY 2002; reduced loan service notice requirements; set property sale provisions; revised cash flow margin and loan termination provisions; prohibited direct operating loans to delinquent borrowers and limited borrowing ability of persons who have received debt forgiveness. Title VII (rural development), subtitle B (amendments to CFRDA) authorized loan guarantees to family farmers for cooperative stock purchases.

Farm Security and Rural Investment Act of 2002 (2002 Farm Bill) (116 Stat. 1348, 7 U.S.C. 7901 note). Signed by the president on May 13, 2002. Nonrecourse Marketing Assistance Loans and Loan Deficiency Payments: amended FAIRA to direct the secretary of agriculture to make nonrecourse marketing assistance loans and loan deficiency payments available to producers of specified commodities through crop year 2006 (upland cotton through crop year 2007).

Conservation Programs:

Food Security Act of 1985 (99 Stat. 1354, 7 U.S.C. 1281 note). Signed by the president Dec. 23, 1985. Established the Conservation Reserve program and other conservation provisions.

Food, Agriculture, Conservation, and Trade Act of 1990 (104 Stat. 3359, 7 U.S.C. 1421 note). Signed by the president Nov. 28, 1990. Incorporated previous conservation programs into the Agricultural Resource Conservation Program.

Federal Agriculture Improvement and Reform Act of 1996 (110 Stat. 888, 7 U.S.C. 7201 note). Signed by the president April 4, 1996. Title III amended the Food Security Act of 1985, the Food, Agriculture, Conservation, and Trade Act of 1990, the Cooperative Forestry Assistance Act of 1978, and the Agriculture and Food Act of 1981. Established the National Natural Resource Conservation Foundation, a conservation-related nonprofit corporation.

Farm Security and Rural Investment Act of 2002 (2002 Farm Bill) (116 Stat. 1348, 7 U.S.C. 7901 note). Signed by the president on May 13, 2002. Conservation Security: amended the Food Security Act of 1985 to establish a conservation security program from FY 2003 through 2006 to assist conservation practices on production land.

◼ REGIONAL OFFICES

FSA KANSAS CITY COMMODITY OFFICE

6501 Beacon Dr.
Kansas City, MO 64133-4676
(816) 926–6301
George Aldaya, director

Provides information on commodity sales and purchases. Directs many of the functions of the Commodity Credit Corporation (CCC).

FSA operates state and county offices. FSA county offices are the primary points of contact for participation in programs and are listed in telephone directories under "U.S. Department of Agriculture." FSA state offices supervise the county offices and are usually located in the state capital or near the state land-grant university.

Food and Nutrition Service

3101 Park Center Dr., Alexandria, VA 22302
Internet: http://www.fns.usda.gov

The Food and Nutrition Service (FNS) was established in 1969 to administer the food assistance programs of the U.S. Department of Agriculture (USDA). Formerly known as the Food and Consumer Service (FCS), Secretary of Agriculture Dan Glickman announced the name change on Nov. 25, 1997. The FNS is under the jurisdiction of the assistant secretary of agriculture for food, nutrition, and consumer services. The FNS is headed by an administrator who is appointed by the secretary of agriculture. The administrator is aided by an associate administrator and four deputy administrators responsible for the agency program areas: the food stamp program, special nutrition programs, financial management, and overall department management.

The agency administers fifteen nutrition programs and conducts nutrition education to inform consumers about the link between diet and health. FNS programs include the food stamp program; the special supplemental food program for women, infants, and children (WIC); a nutrition program and a commodity supplemental food program for the elderly; commodity distribution to charitable institutions; the emergency food assistance program (TEFAP), which distributes food to soup kitchens and food banks; and the national school breakfast and lunch programs. In 2003 about 28 million children were participating in the FNS's school meals programs.

The FNS also administers programs that supply milk to school children free or at reduced prices, provide nutritional training for food service personnel and children, supply commodity foods to Native American families who live on or near reservations and to Pacific Islanders, provide cash and coupons to participants in Puerto Rico and the Northern Marianas, supply WIC participants with coupons to purchase fresh fruits and vegetables at autho-

rized farmers markets, supply food for special children's summer programs, and provide food for child and adult day-care centers.

The Good Samaritan Food Donation Act, passed in October 1996, encouraged the donation of food and grocery products to nonprofit organizations such as homeless shelters, soup kitchens, and churches for distribution to needy individuals. Through the Food Recovery and Gleaning program, FNS joined with key nonprofit organizations and community-based groups to recover surplus food for distribution to food banks. The Good Samaritan Food Donation Act limited liability for donors.

The 2002 Farm Bill affected many of the functions of FNS, including the food stamp, child nutrition, special nutrition, food distribution, and supplemental nutrition programs. The bill partially restored food stamp benefits to legal aliens, regardless of date of entry into the United States. Previously, legal aliens were required to have been in the country on Aug. 22, 1996. The bill also simplified food stamp eligibility requirements and established, as an independent entity of the legislative branch, the Congressional Hunger Fellows Program.

The Agricultural Marketing Service (p. 392) acts as the purchasing agent for the FNS to obtain the commodities donated to schools and other institutions.

The FNS also:

- Sets eligibility requirements for recipients in the food stamp program.

- Approves applications from food sellers who wish to participate in the food stamp program.

- Establishes procedures for states to follow in administering food stamp programs.

- Sets standards for certifying households applying for benefits.

- Sets requirements for the composition of school lunches and breakfasts.
- Establishes eligibility requirements for children in programs for free and reduced price meals.
- Establishes requirements for supplemental food programs.
- Provides commodity foods for shelters and other mass feeding sites and issues emergency food stamps during disasters.

FNS programs are administered through the agency's regional offices. These offices coordinate all FNS programs through state agricultural, educational, welfare, and health agencies. The states determine most details regarding distribution of food benefits and eligibility, and FNS funding covers most of the states' administrative costs. Certain special nutrition programs are administered directly by FNS if states choose not to administer them.

KEY PERSONNEL

Administrator
Roberto Salazar.......................... (703) 305–2062
Fax...................................... (703) 305–2908
Associate Administrator
George A. Braley .... (703) 305–2062
Analysis and Evaluation
Alberta C. Frost .... (703) 305–2017
Family Program Staff
Steven Carlson.......................... (703) 305–2133
Special Nutrition Staff
Peter S. Murano .... (703) 305–2052
Civil Rights
Ramona Pegues.......................... (703) 305–2195
Communications and Governmental Affairs
Scott Mexic .... (703) 305–2281
Staff Office Director
Dan Dager (acting).................... (703) 305–2281
Financial Management
Gary Maupin .... (703) 305–2046
Accounting
Rose McClyde .... (703) 305–2447
Budget
Roger Butler........................... (703) 305–2493
Grants Management
Bob Labbe (acting).................... (703) 305–0901
Food Stamp Program
Kate Coler............................. (703) 305–2026
Benefit Redemption
Thomas O'Connor..................... (703) 305–2756
Program Accountability
Lou Pastura........................... (703) 305–2414

Program Development
Art Foley............................... (703) 305–2494
Information Technology Division
Chris Beavers.......................... (703) 305–2759
Management
Don Arnette........................... (703) 305–2026
Special Nutrition Programs
Peter S. Murano .... (703) 305–2052
Child Nutrition
Stan Garnett........................... (703) 305–2590
Food Distribution
Les Johnson........................... (703) 305–2680
Nutrition and Technical Services
Judy Wilson........................... (703) 305–2585
Supplemental Food Programs
Patricia Daniels....................... (703) 305–2746

INFORMATION SOURCES

Internet

Agency Web site: http://www.fns.usda.gov. FNS programs, news releases, and fact sheets are all available on the agency Web site. Links also are provided to reach other agencies within the USDA.

Telephone Contacts

Personnel Locator.......................... (202) 720–8732
TDD...................................... (202) 720–7808
Other Disabilities
(Braille, large print, audiotape) .... (202) 720–5881

Information and Publications

KEY OFFICES

FNS Communications and Governmental Affairs
3101 Park Center Dr., Room 926
Alexandria, VA 22302
(703) 305–2281
Scott Mexic, director

Issues news releases and publications, including a quarterly newsletter, *Commodity Foods,* which is directed toward school system food service directors. Refers questions on specific FNS programs to the appropriate office.

USDA Office of Communications
14th St. and Independence Ave. S.W.
Room 402A
Washington, DC 20250
(202) 720–4623

Maintains a news release mailing list for FNS.

Freedom of Information
Management Branch
FNS Information Resources Management Division
3101 Park Center Dr., Room 322
Alexandria, VA 22302
(703) 305–2244
Sara Bradshaw, FOIA officer

PUBLICATIONS
Publishing and Audiovisual Branch
FNS Governmental Affairs and Public Information
3101 Park Center Dr., #814
Alexandria, VA 22302
(703) 305–2000
Christopher Kocsis, team leader

Provides a list and ordering information for FNS publications, most of which are about the food and nutrition programs the agency administers. There is a fee for some publications.

DATA AND STATISTICS

News Branch
FNS Governmental Affairs and Public Information
3101 Park Center Dr., #819
Alexandria, VA 22302
(703) 305–2286
Vacant, team leader

Provides information on how to obtain copies of reports and databases.

Data and statistics available to the public in FNS's *Food Program Update* include:
- Monthly report of food stamp participation and coupon issuance.
- Participation in school nutrition programs.
- Participation in special nutrition programs.
- Receipt and distribution of donated commodities by state agencies.

Statistics on the programs provided by the FNS also are contained in the following publications *(see Publications, above, for ordering information)*:

Annual Historical Review

Characteristics of Food Stamp Households (current edition)

Reference Resources

LIBRARY

National Agricultural Library
10301 Baltimore Blvd.
Beltsville, MD 20705–2351
(301) 504–5755
Pamela Andre, director
Hours: 8:00 a.m. to 4:30 p.m.

The USDA also maintains a reference center at the main Agriculture Department building. The collection consists primarily of periodicals, reference volumes, and databases.

D.C. Reference Center
14th St. and Independence Ave. S.W.
South Bldg., Room 1052
Washington, DC 20250
(202) 720–3434
Janet Wright, chief
Hours: 8:00 a.m. to 4:30 p.m.

DOCKETS
Management Branch
FNS Information Technology Division
3101 Park Center Dr.
Alexandria, VA 22302
(703) 305–2754
Chris Beavers, director

Maintains dockets, containing all materials pertaining to FNS rulemakings and other regulatory proceedings, for public inspection.

RULES AND REGULATIONS
FNS (formerly FCS) rules and regulations are published in the *Code of Federal Regulations*, Title 7, parts 210–299. Proposed rules, new final rules, and updates to the *Code of Federal Regulations* are published in the daily *Federal Register*. *(See appendix for information on how to obtain and use these publications.)*

■ LEGISLATION
The FNS carries out its responsibilities under:

National School Lunch Act (60 Stat. 230, 42 U.S.C. 1751). Signed by the president June 4, 1946. Set standards for school lunch programs and established eligibility requirements for children and institutions participating in the program.

Food Stamp Act of 1964 (78 Stat. 703, 7 U.S.C. 2011). Signed by the president Aug. 31, 1964. Set eligibility requirements for food stamp program participants, including recipients, vendors, food stores, and states.

Child Nutrition Act of 1966 (80 Stat. 885, 42 U.S.C. 1771). Signed by the president Oct. 11, 1966. Authorized the regulation of school breakfast programs, established requirements for supplemental food programs, and provided for nutrition education and training programs for students and food service personnel.

Food Stamp Act of 1977 (91 Stat. 951, 7 U.S.C. 2011). Signed by the president Sept. 29, 1977. Tightened eligibility requirements for food stamps and allowed their free distribution.

Emergency Jobs Appropriations Act of 1983, Title II (97 Stat. 13, 7 U.S.C. 612c note). Signed by the president March 24, 1983. Authorized the FCS (now the FNS) to distribute the Commodity Credit Corporation's excess food supplies.

National Nutrition Monitoring and Related Research Act of 1990 (104 Stat. 1034, 7 U.S.C. 5301 note). Signed by the president Oct. 22, 1990. Directed the secretaries of agriculture and health and human services to develop a national nutrition-monitoring plan. Established an advisory council to publish dietary guidelines and coordinate nutritional advice issued by federal agencies.

Food, Agriculture, Conservation, and Trade Act of 1990 (104 Stat. 3359, 7 U.S.C. 1421 note). Signed by the president Nov. 28, 1990. Reauthorized the food stamp program for five years. Established new standards for the calculation of income in determining food stamp eligibility. Authorized online electronic benefit transfer systems as a replacement for food stamp coupons. Strengthened reporting requirements and imposed fines for fraud and misuse of food stamps by retail and wholesale food operations.

WIC Farmers' Market Nutrition Act of 1992 (106 Stat. 280, 42 U.S.C. 1771 note). Signed by the president July 2, 1992. Established a program to promote the use of fresh fruits and vegetables in the WIC program.

Child Nutrition Amendments of 1992 (106 Stat. 911, 42 U.S.C. 1751 note). Signed by the president Aug. 5, 1992. Authorized the FCS (now the FNS) to reimburse homeless shelters that provide meals to children under the age of six.

Mickey Leland Childhood Hunger Relief Act (107 Stat. 672, 7 U.S.C. 2011 note). Signed by the president Aug. 10, 1993. Expanded the food stamp program. Restructured benefit eligibility requirements to allow increased deductions for housing costs and removed reporting requirement on income earned by family members in high school.

The Good Samaritan Food Donation Act (P.L. 104-210). Signed by the president on Oct. 1, 1996. Encouraged the donation of food and grocery products to nonprofit organizations such as homeless shelters, soup kitchens, and churches for distribution to needy individuals. Promoted food recovery by limiting the liability of donors to instances of gross negligence or intentional misconduct. Stated that, absent gross negligence or intentional misconduct, persons, gleaners, and nonprofit organizations shall not be subject to civil or criminal liability arising from the nature, age, packaging or condition of apparently wholesome food or apparently fit grocery products received as donations. Also established basic nationwide uniform definitions pertaining to donation and distribution of nutritious foods and helps assure that donated foods meet all quality and labeling standards of federal, state, and local laws and regulations.

Farm Security and Rural Investment Act of 2002 (2002 Farm Bill) (116 Stat. 1348, 7 U.S.C. 7901 note). Signed by the president on May 13, 2002. Title IV simplified various food stamp eligibility requirements, including restoring eligibility to qualified aliens who were receiving disability benefits regardless of date of entry. Titles I, III, IV, and X established, as an independent entity of the legislative branch, the Congressional Hunger Fellows Program. Authorized the president to provide U.S. agricultural commodities and financial and technical assistance for educational school food programs in foreign countries and for nutrition programs for pregnant women, nursing mothers, and infants and children.

■ REGIONAL OFFICES

NORTHEAST REGION

(CT, MA, ME, NH, NY, RI, VT)
10 Causeway St., #501
Boston, MA 02222–1069
(617) 565–6370
Frances Zorn, regional administrator

MID-ATLANTIC REGION

(DC, DE, MD, NJ, PA, PR, VA, VI, WV)
Mercer Corporate Park
300 Corporate Blvd.
Robbinsville, NJ 08691–1598
(609) 259–5025
Christopher Martin, regional administrator

SOUTHEAST REGION

(AL, FL, GA, KY, MS, NC, SC, TN)
61 Forsyth St. S.W., #8T36
Atlanta, GA 30303-3415
(404) 562–1800
Virgil L. Conrad, regional administrator

MIDWEST REGION
(IL, IN, MI, MN, OH, WI)
77 W. Jackson Blvd., 20th Floor
Chicago, IL 60604–3507
(312) 353–6664
Theodore O. Bell, regional administrator

MOUNTAIN PLAINS REGION
(CO, IA, KS, MO, ND, NE, SD, UT, WY)
1244 Speer Blvd., #903
Denver, CO 80204–3581
(303) 844–0300
William Ludwig, regional administrator

SOUTHWEST REGION
(AR, LA, NM, OK, TX)
1100 Commerce St., #5-A-6
Dallas, TX 75242–9980
(214) 290–9800
Ruthie Jackson, regional administrator

WESTERN REGION
(AK, AS, AZ, CA, GU, HI, ID, MP, NV, OR, WA)
550 Kearney St., #400
San Francisco, CA 94108–2518
(415) 705–1310
Allen Ng, regional administrator

Food Safety and Inspection Service

14th St. and Independence Ave. S.W., Washington, DC 20250
Internet: http://www.fsis.usda.gov

The Food Safety and Inspection Service (FSIS) is an agency within the U.S. Department of Agriculture (USDA) under the jurisdiction of the under secretary for food safety. The FSIS is headed by an administrator appointed by the secretary of agriculture.

The FSIS regulates the meat, poultry, and egg products industries by inspecting all meat, poultry, and egg products plants that ship goods in interstate and foreign commerce. The service also administers laws that ensure that these products are accurately labeled.

Slaughtering and processing plants must receive FSIS approval of facilities, equipment, and procedures before they may operate. The FSIS sets food standards for all products containing more than 3 percent fresh meat or at least 2 percent cooked poultry meat. The Food and Drug Administration (FDA) oversees the labeling of most other food products. Food standards set requirements on the kinds and amounts of ingredients used in the manufacture of processed foods and assure the consumer that a product sold under a particular name has certain characteristics.

The service cooperates with other USDA agencies, such as the Agricultural Marketing Service and the Animal and Plant Health Inspection Service, and with other federal agencies with food safety responsibilities, such as the FDA and the Environmental Protection Agency. In July 1996, the FSIS entered into an agreement with the Public Health Service (PHS) in the Department of Health and Human Services, under which PHS commissioned corps officers can be assigned to scientific positions at FSIS. Flexible deployment rules allow the officers to assist FSIS staff in instantly responding to emergencies, such as a foodborne illness outbreak, and shifting priorities within the agency. These additional officers also enhance FSIS capabilities for rapid response during heightened security alerts or an actual threat to food security.

Reorganization. A thorough reorganization of FSIS took place late in 1996. Existing divisions were replaced by four major operating units: the Office of Public Health and Science; the Office of Management; the Office of Field Operations; and the Office of Policy, Program Development, and Evaluation. In addition, three units became responsible directly to the administrator: the Legislative Liaison staff; the Food Safety, Executive Management, and Coordination staff; and the Food Safety Education and Communications staff. This reorganization was designed to allow FSIS to implement the new Pathogen Reduction and Hazard Analysis and Critical Control Points (HACCP) regulations. A brief look at each of the operating units is provided below.

Office of Public Health and Science. Provides expert scientific analysis, advice, data, and recommendations on all matters involving public health and science of concern to FSIS. Maintains liaison with other federal, state, and local public health officials. Leads and coordinates all traceback and investigation recall activities whenever meat, poultry, and egg products are associated with foodborne illness outbreaks. Designs, develops, and oversees passive and active surveillance systems to collect data and information regarding foodborne illness and pathogens and analyzes such information to assess the use and efficacy of prevention measures in the human population. Provides microbiological, chemical, and toxicological expertise, leadership, quality assurance, and control for the agency. Operates field service laboratories.

Office of Management. Provides administrative services in the areas of budget and finance, personnel management, administrative services, employee and organizational development, automated information systems, labor management relations, civil rights, planning, and internal controls to meet the needs of the agency.

Office of Field Operations. Manages a program of regulatory oversight and inspection pursuant to meat, poultry, and egg products laws to ensure that covered products are safe, wholesome, and properly labeled. Participates in the planning and formulation of the agency's policy. Plans and coordinates FSIS cooperative activities to assist states in administering meat, poultry, and egg products inspection programs. Conducts reviews of foreign inspection programs and products to assure that federal requirements are met.

Office of Policy, Program Development, and Evaluation. Develops and recommends all domestic and international policy for the agency. Develops and reviews product, process, and technology compounds used by industry. Provides statistical support for the agency. Develops and evaluates programs, inspection methods, systems, and techniques. Provides leadership in identifying food safety production activities. Develops and drafts proposed and final regulations for publication in the *Federal Register*.

■ KEY PERSONNEL

Administrator
Garry L. McKee.......................... (202) 720–7025
Fax....................................... (202) 720–0158
Food Safety Education Staff
Susan D. Conley........................ (301) 504–9605
Legislative Liaison
Linda Swacina .... (202) 720–3897
USDA Meat and Poultry Hotline
Bessie Berry............................. (301) 504–6258
Public Health and Science
Karen Hulebak .... (202) 720–2644
Fax....................................... (202) 690–2980
Food Hazard Surveillance
Margaret Nunnery...................... (202) 501–7515
Emerging Pathogens and Zoonotic Diseases
William James........................... (202) 501–7321
Emergency Response
Jesse Majkowski........................ (202) 501–7521
Microbiology
Ann Marie McNamara................. (202) 501–7607
Chemistry and Toxicology
Pat Basu.................................. (202) 501–7319
Epidemiology and Risk Assessment
Ruth Etzel............................... (202) 501–7472

Scientific Research Oversight
Richard Ellis............................ (202) 501–7625
Policy, Program Development, and Evaluation
Margaret Glavin........................ (202) 720–2709
Fax....................................... (202) 720–2025
Animal Production Food Safety
Bonnie Buntain......................... (202) 690–2683
International Policy Development
Mark Manis.............................. (202) 720–6400
Domestic Policy Development and Evaluation
Jane Roth .... (202) 720–6735
Labeling, Product, and Technical Standards
Charles Edwards........................ (202) 205–0675
Labeling and Compound Review
Robert Post .... (202) 205–0279
Regulations Development and Analysis
Daniel Engeljohn....................... (202) 720–5627
Inspection Systems
Arshad Hussain......................... (202) 720–3219
Management
Yvonne Davis........................... (202) 720–4425
Fax....................................... (202) 690–1742
Human Resources
Marlin Waller........................... (202) 720–4827
Automated Information Systems
Stephanie Thomas .... (202) 720–2987
Administrative Services
Glen Durst............................... (202) 720–3551
Budget and Finance
Mike Zimmerer......................... (202) 720–3367
Field Operations
William C. Smith....................... (202) 720–8803
Fax....................................... (202) 720–5439
Compliance and Investigation
Don Edwards............................ (202) 418–8874
Evaluation and Enforcement
Scott Safian .... (202) 418–8872
Federal/State Relations
William Leese........................... (202) 418–8900
Resource Management
Ray Bolyard............................. (202) 418–8925
Emergency Programs
George Bickerton....................... (202) 418–8910

■ INFORMATION SOURCES

Internet
Agency Web site: http://www.fsis.usda.gov. Links to various FSIS programs are available. Publications and the latest news are also maintained at the site.

Telephone Contacts

Personnel Locator........................(202) 720–8732
Meat and Poultry Hotline..............(800) 535–4555
Also, toll-free...........................(888) MPHotline

Information and Publications

Key Offices
Congressional and Public Affairs Staff
14th St. and Independence Ave. S.W.
South Bldg., Room 1175
Washington, DC 20250
(202) 720–9113
(202) 720–3897
Fax (202) 720–5704
Rob Larew, director

Answers general questions about inspection, food safety, and labeling, and refers technical queries to the appropriate office within the agency. Issues news releases and consumer publications on FSIS actions. Issues publications and other informational materials for consumers.

Freedom of Information
Food Safety Executive Management Staff
South Bldg., Room 1164
14th St. and Independence Ave. S.W.
Washington, DC 20250
(202) 690–3881
Fax (202) 205–0158
Barbara McNiff, director

PUBLICATIONS
FSIS Food Safety Education Staff
5601 Sunrise Ave.
Mail Drop 5268
Beltsville, MD 20705
(301) 504–9605
Fax (301) 504–0203

Issues publications and other informational materials about FSIS programs and the safe handling of meat, poultry, and egg products. Selected publications are also available for viewing or for download at the FSIS Web site.

Titles published by the FSIS include:

Federal Facilities' Requirements for Small Existing Meat Plants. Aids plant owners and operators of small meat plants applying for federal inspection.

FSIS Facts: How to Get USDA Approval of Equipment, Facilities, Chemicals and Packaging for Meat and Poultry Products. Foreign Plants Certified to Export Meat to the United States—Annual Report

FSIS Facts: Meat and Poultry Inspection. Annual report of the agency.

Meat and Poultry Inspection Directory. Semiannual. Lists plants regulated by federal inspection laws, including establishment numbers, addresses, phone numbers, and type of operation.

Issuances of the Meat and Poultry Inspection (MPI) Program. Monthly; includes bulletins, directives, and updates of the *MPI Inspection Manual* and regulations.

Meat and Poultry Inspection Manual. Lists regulations covering slaughter and processing.

U.S. Inspected Meat and Poultry Packing Plants: A Guide to Construction and Layout. Interprets inspection regulations and guidelines for designing, building, and maintaining slaughter plants operating under federal inspection.

DATA AND STATISTICS
For types of data and statistics available from the FSIS, contact Food Safety Education: (301) 504–9605

Reference Resources

LIBRARY

National Agricultural Library
10301 Baltimore Blvd.
Beltsville, MD 20705–2351
(301) 504–5755
Pamela Andre, director
Hours: 8:00 a.m. to 4:30 p.m.

The USDA also maintains a reference center at the main Agriculture Department building. The collection consists of periodicals, reference volumes, and databases.

D.C. Reference Center
South Bldg., Room 1052
14th St. and Independence Ave. S.W.
Washington, DC 20250
(202) 720–3434
Janet Wright, chief
Hours: 8:00 a.m. to 4:30 p.m.

DOCKETS

Public Reading Room
Cotton Annex Bldg., #103
300 12th St. S.W.
Washington, DC 20250
(202) 720–7377
Fax (202) 205–0381
Diane Moore, hearing clerk
Hours: 8:00 a.m. to 4:30 p.m.

Public dockets containing all public materials related to FSIS rulemakings, standard settings, and other regulatory proceedings may be inspected in this office. An electronic reading room is also available on the FSIS Web site.

RULES AND REGULATIONS

FSIS rules and regulations are published in the *Code of Federal Regulations,* Title 9, parts 301–390. Proposed rules, standards, and guidelines are published in the daily *Federal Register. (See appendix for information on how to obtain and use these publications.)*

For specific handbooks of FSIS regulations, see Publications above.

▨ LEGISLATION

The FSIS administers the following statutes:

Poultry Products Inspection Act (71 Stat. 441, 21 U.S.C. 451). Signed by the president Aug. 28, 1957. Provided for regulation of the processing and distribution of poultry and poultry products. This act was amended by the **Wholesome Poultry Products Act** (82 Stat. 791, 21 U.S.C. 451). Signed by the president Aug. 18, 1968. Authorized the secretary of agriculture to assist state agencies in developing and administering poultry product inspection programs equal to federal inspection programs for poultry products sold as human food only within a particular state.

Talmadge-Aiken Act (76 Stat. 663, 7 U.S.C. 450). Signed by the president Sept. 28, 1962. Provided for coordination between the federal government and the states to regulate agricultural products and to control or eradicate plant and animal diseases and pests.

Wholesome Meat Act (81 Stat. 584, 21 U.S.C. 601). Signed by the president Dec. 15, 1967. Revised the **Federal Meat Inspection Act of 1907.** Provided for the regulation, by inspection and labeling, of meat and meat products in interstate and foreign commerce. Later amended by the **Agriculture and Food Act of 1981, Title XVIII** (95 Stat. 1213, 7 U.S.C. 1281 note). Signed by the president Dec. 22, 1981.

Humane Methods of Slaughter Act of 1978 (92 Stat. 1069, 21 U.S.C. 601). Signed by the president Oct. 10, 1978. Set standards for slaughtering livestock and poultry to ensure humane treatment; prohibited importation of meat or meat products unless such livestock were slaughtered in a humane manner.

Food Security Act of 1985, Title XVII (99 Stat. 1633, 21 U.S.C. 466). Signed by the president Dec. 23, 1985. Required that imported poultry and meat products be subject to the same inspection, sanitary, quality, species verifica-

tion, and residue standards applied to products produced in the United States. Any meat or poultry product not meeting U.S. standards is not permitted entry into the United States.

Omnibus Trade and Competitiveness Act of 1988 (102 Stat. 1408, 21 U.S.C. 620). Signed by the president Aug. 23, 1988. Known as the Reciprocal Meat Inspection Requirement, this section required that the agriculture secretary and the U.S. trade representative recommend that the president restrict the importation of meat products from foreign countries that apply standards for the importation of meat articles from the United States that are not based on public health concerns.

NAFTA Implementation Act (107 Stat. 2057, 19 U.S.C. 3301 note). Signed by the president Dec. 8, 1993. Implemented the North American Free Trade Agreement (NAFTA) between the United States, Mexico, and Canada. Required U.S. inspections to recognize "equivalent" sanitary meat and poultry inspection measures of both Canada and Mexico.

Department of Agriculture Reorganization Act of 1994 (108 Stat. 3178). Signed by the president Oct. 13, 1994. Created the new position of under secretary for food safety.

Federal Agricultural Improvement and Reform Act of 1996 (7 U.S.C. 7201 note). Signed by the president April 4, 1996. Established the Safe Meat and Poultry Inspection Panel. However, funding for the panel was not included in the 1999 appropriations bill.

Farm Security and Rural Investment Act of 2002 (2002 Farm Bill) (116 Stat. 1348, 7 U.S.C. 7901 note). Signed by the president on May 13, 2002. Amended the Agricultural Marketing Act of 1946 to require a retailer of a covered commodity (beef, lamb, pork, wild or farm-raised fish, perishable agricultural commodities, or peanuts—but not processed beef, lamb, and pork items or frozen entrees containing beef, lamb, and pork) to inform consumers at the final point of sale of a commodity's country of origin.

▨ REGIONAL OFFICES

Food Safety and Inspection Service

Technical Service Center
1299 Farman St.
Landmark Center, #300
Omaha, NE 68102
(402) 221–7400
Fax (402) 221–7438
Michaelle Fisher, director

District 5

(CA)
620 Central Ave., Bldg. 2C
Alameda, CA 94501
(510) 337–5074
Fax (510) 337–5081
Murli Prasad, manager

District 10

(AK, AS, GU, HI, ID, MP, OR, WA)
530 Center St. N.E., #405
Salem, OR 97301
(503) 399–5831
Fax (503) 399–5636
Helmut W. Blume, manager

District 15

(AZ, CO, NM, NV, UT)
655 S. Broadway, Suite B
Boulder, CO 80303
(303) 497–5411
Fax (303) 497–7306
Ronald K. Jones, manager

District 20

(MN, MT, ND, SD, WY)
Butler Square West, # 989-C
100 N. 6th St.
Minneapolis, MN 55403
(612) 370–2400
Fax (612) 370–2411
Nathaniel Clark, manager

District 25

(IA, NE)
11338 Aurora Ave.
Des Moines, IA 50322
(515) 727–8960
Fax (515) 727–8991
Jerry J. Booth, manager

District 30

(KS, MO)
4920 W. 15th St.
Lawrence, KS 66049
(785) 841–5600
Fax (785) 841–5623
William M. Walker, manager

District 35

(AR, LA, OK)
Country Club Center, Bldg. B, #201
4700 S. Thompson
Springdale, AR 72764
(501) 751–8412
Fax (501) 751–9049
Cordell H. Schilmoeller, manager

District 40

(TX)
1100 Commerce St., #5F41
Dallas, TX 75242
(214) 767–9116
Fax (214) 767–8230
Alan F. Knox (acting), manager

District 45

(MI, WI)
2810 Crossroads Dr., #3500
Madison, WI 53718
(608) 240–4080
Fax (608) 240–4092
James W. Blank, manager

District 50

(IN, IL)
1919 S. Highland Ave., #115C
Lombard, IL 60148
(630) 620–7474
Fax (630) 620–7599
David E. Green, manager

District 55

(KY, OH, WV)
155 E. Columbus St., #200
Pickerington, OH 43147
(614) 833–1405
Fax (614) 833–1067
Ellis L. Jones, manager

District 60

(PA)
701 Market St., #2-B South
Philadelphia, PA 19106–1516
(215) 597–4219 or
(800) 637–6681
Fax (215) 597–4217
Joseph Priore, manager

District 65

(NJ, NY)
230 Washington Ave. Extension
Albany, NY 12203
(518) 452–6870
(800) 772–7033
Fax (518) 452–3118
Louis Leny, district manager

District 70

(CT, MA, ME, NH, PR, RI, VI, VT)
411 Waverly Oaks Rd.
Bldg. 3, #331
Waltham, MA 02452
(781) 398–2291
Fax (781) 736–1843
Jan T. Behney, manager

District 75

(DC, DE, MD, VA)
5601 Sunnyside Ave., #1–228 B
Greenbelt, MD 20705–5200
(301) 504–2136
Fax (301) 504–2140
Perfecto Santiago, manager

District 80

(NC, SC)
6020 Six Forks Rd.
Raleigh, NC 27609
(919) 844–8400
Fax (919) 844–8411
Karen W. Henderson, manager

District 85

(FL, GA)
100 Alabama St. S.W., #3R90
Atlanta, GA 30303
(404) 562–5900
Fax (404) 562–5877
Lewis Burgman, manager

District 90

(AL, MS, TN)
715 S. Pear Orchard Rd., #101
Ridgeland, MS 39157
(601) 965–4312
Fax (601) 965–4993
Mariano-Loret de Mola, manager

Foreign Agricultural Service

14th St. and Independence Ave. S.W., Washington, DC 20250
Internet: http://www.fas.usda.gov

The Foreign Agricultural Service (FAS) was established in 1953 as an agency within the U.S. Department of Agriculture (USDA). It is under the jurisdiction of the under secretary of agriculture for farm and foreign agricultural services. The FAS is primarily an information and promotion agency. The service represents U.S. agricultural interests overseas by gathering information about crop production and supply and demand abroad. It then distributes this data to U.S. producers and exporters. The FAS also provides information about U.S. products and supplies to foreign importers and cooperates with U.S. exporters on projects to establish and expand export markets.

The administrator of the FAS is appointed by the secretary of agriculture and is assisted by an associate administrator and five deputy administrators. The deputy administrators are responsible for commodity and marketing programs, export credits, foreign agricultural affairs, international trade policy, and international cooperation and development.

The main function of the FAS is to gather information about foreign agriculture to assist U.S. exporters of commodities. The FAS receives reports from agricultural attachés and officers in more than eighty locations around the world. Trade information sent to Washington from FAS personnel overseas is used to map strategies for improving market access, pursuing U.S. rights under trade agreements, and developing programs and policies to make U.S. farm products more competitive. The FAS publishes nearly 200 commodity reports annually that present a world picture of production, consumption, and trade flows for about 100 crop and livestock commodities. These reports analyze changes in international trading conditions and indicate market opportunities for U.S. exporters *(see Publications; Data and Statistics, p. 423)*.

In addition, the agency collects information on export sales from private exporters of agricultural commodities; this material is compiled in the weekly publication, *U.S. Export Sales*.

To aid in the promotion of U.S. agricultural products abroad, the FAS operates several programs designed to stimulate contacts between domestic producers and foreign markets.

The FAS cooperates with states and industry representatives in promoting U.S. agricultural products through exhibits at trade shows, advertisements in the trade press, and diplomatic liaison. The FAS operates AgExport Services to provide U.S. firms with a wide range of export services.

The largest FAS promotional programs are the Foreign Market Development Cooperator (FMD) Program and the Market Access Program (MAP). FAS provides assistance to exporters through practical marketing information and services to help them locate buyers. Additionally, FAS supports U.S. participation in several major trade shows and a number of single-industry exhibitions each year.

FAS cooperates with other USDA agencies, U.S. universities, and other organizations to promote U.S. agriculture's global competitiveness. FAS also coordinates USDA's international training and technical assistance programs and serves as the department's liaison with international food and agriculture organizations.

FAS coordinates and directs USDA's responsibilities in international trade negotiations, working closely with the U.S. Trade Representative's office in this effort. During international negotiations, FAS staff represents U.S. agricultural interests. This representation extends to bilateral and regional trade arrangements, as well as the World Trade Organization (WTO), successor to the General Agreement on Tariffs and Trade (GATT). The FAS also has a permanent representative at the WTO.

USDA shares administration of U.S. food aid programs with the U.S. Agency for International Development to help needy people around the world. USDA channels food aid through three programs. Title I of Public Law 480 (Food for Peace) provides for long-term concessional sales of U.S. agricultural commodities to support economic growth in countries that need food assistance. Food for Progress, authorized by the Food for Progress Act of 1985, provides commodities to countries with commitments to expanding free enterprise in their agricultural communities. Section 416(b) programs, authorized by the Agricultural Act of 1949, as amended, provide for donations of surplus Commodity Credit Corporation commodities abroad.

FAS administers the Commodity Credit Corporation Export Credit Sales Guarantee Program, designed to facilitate the export of U.S. agricultural commodities (other CCC activities are administered by the Farm Service Agency). FAS also is responsible for all USDA export credit and market development programs and acts as principal foreign sales spokesperson for the department.

The 2002 Farm Bill amended provisions of the 1996 Farm Bill and made adjustments to FAS's export credit guarantee programs, market development programs, the Export Enhancement Program, food aid and development programs, technical barriers to trade, and trade-related programs in other titles. A long-range agricultural trade strategy that identifies export growth opportunities was to be prepared.

■ KEY PERSONNEL

Administrator
Ellen Terpstra (acting) .... (202) 720–3935
Fax .... (202) 690–2159
Associate Administrator/General Sales Manager
W. Kirk Miller (acting) .... (202) 720–5691
Civil Rights
Mae Johnson .... (202) 720–7233
Fax .... (202) 720–2658
Legislative Affairs
Sharon McClure (acting) .... (202) 720–6829
Fax .... (202) 720–8097
Commodity and Marketing Programs
Frank Lee .... (202) 720–4761
Fax .... (202) 690–3606
Agricultural Export Services
Dan Berman .... (202) 720–6343
Fax .... (202) 690–9509
Dairy, Livestock, and Poultry
Howard Wetzel .... (202) 720–8031
Fax .... (202) 720–0617

Forest Products
Scott Reynolds .... (202) 720–0638
Fax .... (202) 720–8461
Grain and Feed
Robert Remenschneider .... (202) 720–6219
Fax .... (202) 720–0340
Horticultural and Tropical Products
Frank Tarrant .... (202) 720–6590
Fax .... (202) 720–3799
Marketing Operations
Denise Huttenlocker .... (202) 720–4327
Fax .... (202) 720–9361
Cotton, Oilseeds, Tobacco, and Seeds
Larry Blum .... (202) 720–9516
Fax .... (202) 720–0965
Production Estimates and Crop Assessment
Allen L. Vandergriff .... (202) 720–0888
Trade Assistance and Promotion Office
Leslie Burket .... (202) 720–5138
Export Credits
Mary Chambliss .... (202) 720–6301
Fax .... (202) 690–1595
Lawrence McElvain .... (202) 720–6211
Fax .... (202) 720–0938
Program Development
Robin Tilsworth .... (202) 720–4221
Foreign Agricultural Affairs
Lyle J. Sebranek .... (202) 720–6138
Fax .... (202) 720–6063
International Cooperation and Development
Howard Anderson (acting) .... (202) 690–0776
Fax .... (202) 720–6103
Development Resources
Howard Anderson .... (202) 690–1924
Food Industries
Frank Fender .... (202) 690–3737
International Organizations
Lynn Reich .... (202) 690–1823
Research and Scientific Exchange
Carol Kramer Le Blanc .... (202) 690–4872
International Trade Policy
Patricia Sheikh .... (202) 720–6887
Fax .... (202) 720–0069
Asia and the Americas
Brian Grunenfelder .... (202) 720–1289
Fax .... (202) 690–0069
Europe, Africa, and the Middle East
Bob Macke .... (202) 720–1340
Import Policies and Programs
Richard Blabey .... (202) 720–2916
Multilateral Trade Negotiations
Debra Henke .... (202) 720–1324

Vacant.................................. (202) 720–1301

Fax.................................... (202) 720–0677

INFORMATION SOURCES

Internet

Agency Web site: http://www.fas.usda.gov. Includes information on FAS and on international agricultural trade.

Telephone Contacts

Personnel Locator.......................... (202) 720–8732

Information and Publications

KEY OFFICES

FAS Public Affairs Division

14th St. and Independence Ave. S.W.
Washington, DC 20250
(202) 720–7115
Fax (202) 720–1727
Maureen Quinn, director

Issues news releases and other items of interest to the public and the news media.

Freedom of Information

FAS Information Division
14th St. and Independence Ave. S.W., Room 5711
Washington, DC 20250
(202) 720–3101
Donald Washington, FOI officer

PUBLICATIONS

Most FAS publications are available from the National Technical Information Service (NTIS): see appendix, Ordering Government Publications. Titles include:

AgExporter. Monthly magazine analyzes conditions affecting U.S. agricultural trade and highlights market development and export promotion activities. Condenses data from agricultural attachés around the world.

Foreign Agriculture Circulars. Published periodically on various commodities and trade topics. Each circular has its own mailing list and is subject to a user fee.

U.S. Export Sales. Weekly report; summarizes sales and exports of selected U.S. agricultural commodities by country based on reports from private exporters.

DATA AND STATISTICS

The main job of the FAS is to collect and distribute information about foreign crop production and the demand for U.S. agricultural products abroad. Topics include trade, consumption of commodities, weather, and political and economic developments that affect U.S. agriculture. Publications of special interest include the FAS periodicals *AgExporter, U.S. Export Sales,* the *Foreign Agriculture Circulars (see Publications, above),* and the Attaché reports.

Reference Resources

DOCKETS

FAS has limited regulatory authority; consequently there is no central place where FAS rulemaking dockets are kept. If a regulation applies to a particular commodity or function of the FAS, contact the office responsible for the commodity or function.

RULES AND REGULATIONS

FAS rules and regulations are published in the *Code of Federal Regulations,* Title 7, parts 1520 and 1540. Proposed rules, new final rules, and updates to the *Code of Federal Regulations* are published in the daily *Federal Register. (See appendix for information on how to obtain and use these publications.)*

LEGISLATION

The FAS carries out its responsibilities under the following legislation:

Agricultural Adjustment Act of 1933 (48 Stat. 31, 7 U.S.C. 601). Signed by the president May 12, 1933. Authorized the FAS to administer import quotas for several commodities whenever the president determines that imports pose a threat to the well-being of U.S. farmers.

Agricultural Trade Development and Assistance Act of 1954 (68 Stat. 454, 7 U.S.C. 1427). Signed by the president July 10, 1954. Granted authority to the general sales manager, authorized the sale and export of agricultural commodities for relief abroad, and authorized the trading of excess commodities for long-term credit with foreign governments.

Agriculture and Consumer Protection Act of 1973 (87 Stat. 221, 7 U.S.C. 1281 note). Signed by the president Aug. 10, 1973. Authorized the FAS to monitor the export sales contracts of certain designated commodities.

Meat Import Act of 1979 (93 Stat. 1291, 19 U.S.C. 1202 note). Signed by the president Dec. 31, 1979. Authorized the FAS to administer import quotas on beef. Under a "countercyclical" formula, quotas are to be imposed when domestic supplies are plentiful; when supplies decline, more foreign beef would be allowed to enter the country.

Agriculture Improvement and Reform Act of 1996 (7 U.S.C. 7201 note). Signed by the president April 4, 1996.

Capped funding for several agricultural export and market promotion programs. Gave statutory authority to the Foreign Market Development Program, which helps develop overseas markets.

Farm Security and Rural Investment Act of 2002 (2002 Farm Bill) (116 Stat. 1348, 7 U.S.C. 7901 note). Signed by the president on May 13, 2002. All trade programs were reauthorized through 2007. New programs included the McGovern-Dole International Food for Education and Nutrition Program, the Biotechnology and Agricultural Trade Program that addressed nontariff barriers to U.S. exports, a Technical Assistance for Specialty Crops Program, and an online Exporter Assistance Initiative.

◼ REGIONAL OFFICES

The FAS does not have regional offices in the United States. However, it maintains more than 80 offices overseas. All of the country officers below can be reached via U.S. or APO addresses. For those listed as c/o FAS, the address is USDA Foreign Agricultural Service, Washington, DC 20250–6000.

ALGERIA

American Embassy, Algiers
c/o FAS
Carol M. (Merritt) Chesley, agricultural attaché (resident in Rabat)

ANGOLA

American Ebassy, Luanda
Office of Agricultural Affairs
State Department
Washington, DC 20521–2550
Richard B. Helm, agricultural counselor (resident in Pretoria)

ARGENTINA

American Embassy, Buenos Aires
Unit 4325
APO AA 34034–0001
David J. Menger, agricultural counselor

AUSTRALIA

American Embassy, Canberra
PSC 277
APO AP 96549
Randy Zeitner, agricultural counselor

AUSTRIA

American Embassy, Vienna
State Department AGR
Washington, DC 20521–9900
Robert Curtis, agricultural counselor

BANGLADESH

American Embassy, Dhaka
c/o FAS
Wayland Beeghly, agricultural counselor (resident in New Delhi, India)

BELGIUM

American Embassy, Brussels
PSC 82, Box 002
APO AE 09724
Philip Letarte, agricultural counselor (resident in the Netherlands)

U.S. Mission to the European Union (Brussels)
FAS USEU
(same address as embassy)
Mary Revelt, agricultural minister-counselor

BELIZE

American Embassy, Belize City
Unit 3305
APO AA 34024
Suzanne E. Heinen, agricultural counselor (resident in Guatemala)

BOLIVIA

American Embassy, La Paz
Office of Economic Affairs
Unit 3918
APO AA 34032
Daryl Brehm, agricultural attaché (resident in Peru)

BRAZIL

American Embassy, Brasilia
Unit 3500
APO AA 34030
William W. Westman, agricultural counselor

American Consulate, Sao Paulo
Edificio Suarez Trade
Alameda Santoa 2224
Conjunto 11
Sao Paulo, SP
Brazil
Marc Lower, director

BULGARIA

American Embassy, Sofia
Office of Agricultural Affairs
State Department
Washington, DC 20521–5740
Holly S. Higgins, agricultural attaché

BURMA

American Embassy, Rangoon
Box B
APO AP 96545–0002
Maurice House, agricultural counselor (resident in
    Bangkok, Thailand)

CANADA

American Embassy, Ottawa
P.O. Box 5000
Ogdensburg, NY 13669–0430
Norval E. Francis Jr., agricultural minister-counselor

CARIBBEAN BASIN COUNTRIES

Agricultural Trade Office, Miami
909 S.E. First Ave., #720
Miami, FL 33131
Magaret Bauer, director

CHILE

American Embassy, Santiago
Unit 4118
APO AA 34033
Lewis J. Stockard, agricultural counselor

CHINA

American Embassy, Beijing
PSC 461, Box 50
FPO AP 96521–0002
Larry Senger, agricultural minister-counselor

Agricultural Trade Office
American Consulate, Guangzhou
State Department
Washington, DC 20521–4090
Sam Wong, director

Agricultural Trade Office
American Consulate, Shanghai
PSC 461, Box 200
FPO AP 96521–0002
LaVerne E. Brabant, director

COLOMBIA

American Embassy, Bogota
AGR Section
Unit 5119
APO AA 34038
David G. Salmon, agricultural attaché

COSTA RICA

American Embassy, San Jose
Unit 2507
APO AA 34020
Alan Hrapsky, agricultural attaché

CÔTE D' IVOIRE

American Embassy, Abidjan
c/o FAS
Bruce Zanin, agricultural attaché

CZECH REPUBLIC

American Embassy, Prague
PSC 115, Unit 1330
APO AE 09213–1330
Robert Curtis, agricultural counselor (resident in Vienna,
    Austria)

DENMARK

American Embassy, Copenhagen
PSC 73
APO AE 09716
Philip Letarte, agricultural counselor (resident in
    Netherlands)

DOMINICAN REPUBLIC

American Embassy, Santo Domingo
Unit 5530
APO AA 34041–5530
Kevin Smith, agricultural attaché

ECUADOR

American Embassy, Quito
Unit 5336
APO AA 34039–3420
Larry D. Fuell, agricultural attaché (resident in Lima)

EGYPT

American Embassy, Cairo
Unit 64900, Box 22
APO AE 09839–4900
Thomas Pomeroy, agricultural counselor

EL SALVADOR

American Embassy, San Salvador
Unit 3113
APO AA 34023
Frank A. Coolidge, agricultural counselor (resident in
  Guatemala)

FRANCE

American Embassy, Paris
PSC 116, Box A-218 (Agr.)
APO AE 09777
Frank J. Piason, agricultural minister-counselor

GERMANY

American Embassy, Bonn
PSC 117, Box 385
APO AE 09080
Peter O. Kurn, agricultural minister-counselor

Agricultural Trade Office, Hamburg
State Department
Washington, DC 20521–5180
Jeffrey W. Jones, director

GHANA

American Embassy, Accra
c/o FAS
David I. Rosenbloom, agricultural counselor (resident in
  Lagos, Nigeria)

GREECE

American Embassy, Athens
PSC 108, Box 7 (Agr.)
APO AE 09842
Elizabeth Berry, agricultural counselor (resident in Rome)

GUATEMALA

American Embassy, Guatemala City
Unit 3305
APO AA 34024
Frank A. Coolidge, agricultural counselor

HONDURAS

American Embassy, Tegucigalpa
Unit 2941
APO AA 34022–2941
Frank A. Coolidge, agricultural counselor (resident in
  Guatemala)

HONG KONG

Agricultural Trade Office, Hong Kong
PSC 464, Box 30
FPO AP 96522–0002
Howard Wetzel, director

HUNGARY

American Embassy, Budapest
Office of Agricultural Affairs
State Department
Washington, DC 20521–5270
Robert Curtis, agricultural counselor (resident in Vienna,
  Austria)

INDIA

American Embassy, New Delhi
c/o FAS
Wayland Beeghly, agricultural counselor

INDONESIA

American Embassy, Jakarta
Box 1, Unit 8129
APO AP 96520–0001
Kent D. Sisson, agricultural counselor

IRELAND

American Embassy, Dublin
c/o FAS
Thomas A. Hamby, agricultural minister-counselor
  (resident in United Kingdom)

ISRAEL

American Embassy, Tel Aviv
Unit 7228
APO AE 09830
Thomas Pomeroy, agricultural counselor (resident in
  Cairo, Egypt)

ITALY

American Embassy, Rome
PSC 59, Box 13
APO AE 09624
Elizabeth Berry, agricultural counselor

U.S. Mission to the U.N. Agencies for Food and
Agriculture
(same address as embassy, Rome)
David P. Lambert, agricultural attaché

American Consulate General, Milan
PSC 59, Box 100 M
APO AE 09624
Robert Curtis, director

JAMAICA

American Embassy, Kingston
c/o FAS
Kevin Smith, agricultural attaché (resident in Santo
  Domingo, Dominican Republic)

JAPAN
American Embassy, Tokyo
Unit 45004, Box 226
APO AP 96337–5004
Suzanne K. Hale, agricultural minister-counselor

Agricultural Trade Office, Tokyo
Unit 45004, Box 241
APO AP 96337–5004
Terrence Barber, senior director

Agricultural Trade Office, Osaka
Unit 45004, Box 239
APO AP 96337–5004
Daniel A. Martinez, senior director (resident in Tokyo)

JORDAN
American Embassy, Amman
P.O. Box 354
APO AE 09892–0200
Thomas Pomeroy, agricultural counselor (resident in
   Cairo, Egypt)

KAZAKSTAN
American Embassy, Almaty
U.S. Agriculture Department
Washington, DC 20521–7030
James Dever, agricultural attaché (resident in Pakistan)

KENYA
American Embassy, Nairobi
Unit 64100, Box 351
APO AE 09831–4100
Fred Kessel, agricultural attaché

KOREA
American Embassy, Seoul
Unit 15550
APO AP 96205–0001
Grant A. Pettrie, agricultural minister-counselor

Agricultural Trade Office, Seoul
(same address as embassy)
Daryl A. Brehm, director

LATVIA
American Embassy, Riga
PSC 78, Box R
APO AE 09723
Lana S. Bennett, agricultural attaché (resident in
   Stockholm, Sweden)

MALAYSIA
American Embassy, Kuala Lumpur
APO AP 96534–8152
Bernadette (Bonnie) Borris, agricultural attaché

MEXICO
American Embassy, Mexico City
(same address as Laredo, below)
William L. Brant III, agricultural minister-counselor

Agricultural Trade Office, Nuevo Laredo
Mexico Agricultural Trade Office
P.O. Box 3087
Laredo, TX 78044–3087
Chad Russell, director

MOROCCO
American Embassy, Rabat
PSC 74, Box 002
APO AE 09718
Carol Merritt Chesley, agricultural attaché

NETHERLANDS
American Embassy, The Hague
PSC 71, Box 1000
APO AE 09715
Philip Letarte, agricultural counselor

NEW ZEALAND
American Embassy, Wellington
PSC 467, Box 1
FPO AP 96531–1001
David B. Young, agricultural attaché

NICARAGUA
American Embassy, Managua
Unit 2703, Box 2
APO AA 34021
Alan Hrapsky, agricultural attaché (resident in San Jose,
   Costa Rica)

NIGERIA
American Embassy, Lagos
c/o FAS
David I. Rosenbloom, agricultural counselor

NORWAY
American Embassy, Oslo
APO AE 09707
Lana S. Bennett, agricultural counselor (resident in
   Stockholm, Sweden)

PAKISTAN

American Embassy, Islamabad
Unit 62200, Box 16
APO AE 09812–2200
James Dever, agricultural attaché

PANAMA

American Embassy, Panama City
Unit 0945, Junet Bldg.
APO AA 34002–9945
Alan Hrapsky, agricultural attaché (resident in San Jose, Costa Rica)

PERU

American Embassy, Lima
Unit 3785, FAS
APO AA 34031
Larry D. Fuell, agricultural attaché

PHILIPPINES

American Embassy, Manila
FPO AP 96515
Charles Alexander, agricultural counselor

POLAND

American Embassy, Warsaw
State Department
Washington, DC 20521–5010
James J. Higgiston, agricultural counselor

PORTUGAL

American Embassy, Lisbon
PSC 83, Box FAS
APO AE 09726
Lloyd J. Fleck, agricultural counselor (resident in Spain)

ROMANIA

American Embassy, Bucharest
State Department
Washington, DC 20521–5260
Holly S. Higgins, agricultural attaché (resident in Bulgaria)

RUSSIA

American Embassy, Moscow
PSC 77 Agr.
APO AE 09721
Margaret E. (Peg) Shursland, senior agricultural attaché

American Consulate General, Vladivostok
(same address as Moscow)
Geoffrey W. Wiggins, agricultural minister and counselor (resident in Moscow)

SAUDI ARABIA

American Embassy, Riyadh
Unit 61307
APO AE 09803–1307
Quintin Gray, director

American Consulate General, Jeddah
Unit 62112
APO AE 09811–2112
John H. Wilson, director (resident in Riyadh)

SENEGAL

American Embassy, Dakar
State Department
Washington, DC 20521–2130
Bruce Zanin, agricultural attaché (resident in Abidjan, Côte d'Ivoire)

SERBIA-MONTENEGRO

American Embassy, Belgrade
Office of Agricultural Affairs
State Department
Washington, DC 20521–5070
Jamie Rothschild, agricultural attaché (resident in Sofia, Bulgaria)

SINGAPORE

American Embassy, Singapore
PSC 470
FPO AP 96534–0001
Bernadette (Bonnie) Borris, director

SOUTH AFRICA

American Embassy, Pretoria
c/o FAS
Richard B. Helm, agricultural counselor

American Consulate General, Cape Town
Africa Institute for Policy Analysis, 3rd Floor
Concord House
Buitengracht St.
P.O. Box 5066
Cape Town 8001
South Africa
Michael J. Caughlin Jr., agricultural specialist

SPAIN

American Embassy, Madrid
PSC 61, Box 20
APO AE 09642
Leslie C. O'Connor, agricultural attaché

SWEDEN

American Embassy, Stockholm
c/o FAS
Lana S. Bennett, agricultural counselor

SWITZERLAND

American Embassy, Bern
c/o FAS
Kenneth J. Roberts, agricultural minister-counselor
  (resident in Geneva/USTR)

Office of the U.S. Trade Representative, Geneva
c/o FAS
Kenneth J. Roberts, agricultural minister-counselor

SYRIA

American Embassy, Damascus
c/o FAS
Thomas Pomeroy, agricultural counselor (resident in
  Cairo, Egypt)

TAIWAN

American Institute in Taiwan Taipei
P.O. Box 1612
Washington, DC 20013
Stan Cohen, director

Agricultural Trade Office
American Institute in Taiwan Taipei
P.O. Box 1612
Washington, DC 20013
Daniel A. Martinez, director

THAILAND

American Embassy, Bangkok
Box 41
APO AP 96546–0001
Maurice House, agricultural counselor

TUNISIA

American Embassy, Tunis
c/o FAS
Carol Merritt Chesley, agricultural attaché (resident in
  Rabat)

TURKEY

American Embassy, Ankara
PSC 93, Box 5000
APO AE 09823
Susan Schayes, agricultural counselor

American Consulate General, Istanbul
PSC 97, Box 0002
APO AE 09827–0002
Susan Schayes, agricultural counselor (resident in
  Ankara)

UKRAINE

American Embassy, Kiev
State Department
Washington, DC 20521–5850
James J. Higgiston, agricultural counselor

UNITED ARAB EMIRATES

American Consulate General, Dubai
c/o FAS
Ronald Verdonk, director

UNITED KINGDOM

American Embassy, London
PSC 801, Box 48
FPO AE 09498–4048
Thomas Hamby, agricultural minister-counselor

UZBEKISTAN

American Embassy, Tashkent
State Department
Washington, DC 20520–7110
James Dever, agricultural attaché (resident in Pakistan)

VENEZUELA

American Embassy, Caracas
Unit 4940
APO AA 34037
S. Rod McSherry, agricultural counselor

VIETNAM

American Embassy, Hanoi
PSC 461, Box 400
FPO AP 96521–0002
L. Henry Schmick Jr., agricultural attaché

YEMEN

American Embassy, Sanaa
c/o FAS
Quintin Gray, director (resident in Riyadh, Saudi Arabia)

Forest Service

201 14th St. S.W., Washington, DC 20250
Mailing address: P.O. Box 96090, Washington, DC 20090
Internet: http://www.fs.fed.us

Congress established the Forest Service in 1905 to provide quality water and timber for the nation's benefit. The Forest Service, an agency within the U.S. Department of Agriculture (USDA), is under the jurisdiction of the assistant secretary of agriculture for natural resources and the environment. The Forest Service is administered by a chief who is assisted by six deputy chiefs responsible for business operations, the National Forest System, programs and legislation, research and development, state and private forestry, and international programs.

The Forest Service manages and regulates the use and protection of the nation's 191.6 million-acre National Forest System, with 155 national forests and twenty national grasslands in forty-four states, the Virgin Islands, and Puerto Rico. The agency operates under the concept of multiple use and administers statutes that are aimed at providing sustained yields of renewable resources such as water, livestock forage, wildlife habitat, and timber, as well as preserving wilderness and biodiversity for recreational and scenic purposes. Forest Service programs also oversee protection of national forest lands from wildfires, pest and disease epidemics, floods, erosion, and water and air pollution. The agency administers statutes that regulate:

- Construction of roads and trails through national forests to ensure closely regulated timber harvesting and give the public access to recreation areas.
- Construction and maintenance of facilities on National Forest System lands.
- Removal of oil, gas, uranium, and other minerals of strategic importance, as well as geothermal steam and coal.
- Timber harvesting methods and quantities.
- Use of national forests and range lands as a refuge for threatened and endangered species.
- Use of national forests and grasslands for grazing.

The Forest Service also works with state forestry agencies to develop multiple-use forestry practices on forests and adjacent lands. Through its cooperative state and private forestry programs, the agency provides financial and technical assistance to private landowners to protect and improve the quality of air, water, soil, and open space on nonfederal lands. The research division conducts extensive research on a wide range of forest-related subjects, including long-term natural resources issues of both national and international scope.

A new international forestry division was created under the 1990 Farm Bill to provide assistance to promote sustainable development and global environmental stability, particularly in countries important in global climate change. The service's 1990 Resources Planning Act Program set forth four major long-term objectives: enhancing wildlife, fisheries, and recreation resources, including improved access to public lands by the elderly and people with disabilities; ensuring that commodity production is environmentally acceptable; improving scientific knowledge about natural resources issues, including biological diversity, tropical forestry, sensitive species, and global change; and strengthening ties with other nations to improve resource conservation and better respond to global resources issues.

Since 1908, 25 percent of the USDA's Forest Service revenues from timber receipts have been returned to states in which national forest lands are located to help pay for school services and road maintenance. As revenue from timber sales has steadily declined over the past decade, payments to communities have also declined, thus affecting communities' ability to provide necessary services.

The Secure Rural Schools and Community Self-Determination Act of 2000 stabilized payment levels to their historic high. Instead of the annual flat 25 percent rate, the act directed the secretary of the Treasury to base future payments for FY 2001 through 2006 for eligible states and counties on the average of the three highest annual payment amounts from FY 1986 through 1999. The legislation also created citizen advisory committees and gave local communities the choice to fund restoration projects on federal lands or in counties.

The 2002 Farm Bill amended the Cooperative Forestry Assistance Act of 1978 to direct the secretary to establish in the Forest Service the Office of Tribal Relations. The Tribal Relations Program will ensure indigenous perspectives are an integral part of maintaining and restoring healthy lands for future generations.

▓ KEY PERSONNEL

Chief of the Forest Service
> Dale Bosworth............................ (202) 205–1661
> Fax...................................... (202) 205–1765

Associate Chief
> Sally Collins............................. (202) 205–1491

Chief of Staff
> Chris Pyron............................. (202) 205–1661

Office of Communication
Director
> George D. Lennon....................... (202) 205–8333

Deputy Director
> Walter E. Pierce III .... (202) 205–8333

Business Operations
> Thomas Mills........................... (202) 205–1707

International Programs
> Valdis E. Mezainis...................... (202) 205–1650

National Forest System
> Tom Thompson .... (202) 205–1523
> Fax...................................... (202) 205–1758

Programs, Legislation, and Communication
> Elizabeth Estill.......................... (202) 205–1663

Research and Development
> Robert Lewis............................ (202) 205–1665
> Fax...................................... (202) 205–1530

State and Private Forestry
> Joel Holtrop .... (202) 205–1657
> Fax...................................... (202) 205–1174

▓ INFORMATION SOURCES

Internet

Agency Web site: http://www.fs.fed.us. Provides information on the Forest Service and related topics. Includes a feature for customized information searches.

Telephone Contacts

Personnel Locator......................... (703) 605–5200

Information and Publications

KEY OFFICES

Forest Service Office of Communication

201 14th St. S.W.
P.O. Box 96090
Washington, DC 20090
(202) 205–1760
Fax (202) 205–0885
George Lennon, director

Clearly, simply, and actively communicate with the public about the Forest Service's people and their stewardship of the natural resources entrusted to them.

Executive Services is responsible for the publication and distribution of Forest Service documents that are available to the public, and for organizing and producing audiovisuals and still photography. For more information, call (202) 205–0963.

Media Relations. For information concerning these areas contact Joe Walsh, (202) 205–1294.

Freedom of Information

P.O. Box 96090
Attn: FOI officer
Washington, DC 20090
(703) 605–4910
Rita Morgan, FOI officer

Requests must be submitted in writing.

PUBLICATIONS

The Forest Service produces publications on forestry, natural resources, wood utilization, recreation, and Forest Service programs. Contact Creative Services in Forest Service Office of Communication at (202) 205–1219.

Two particularly useful publications are:
The Principal Laws Relating to Forest Service Activities
Report of the Forest Service

DATA AND STATISTICS

The best source of statistics on the operations of the Forest Service is the agency's annual report, *Report of the Forest Service,* which is available from Creative Services in Forest Service Office of Communication. Please call (202) 205–1219.

Reference Resources

LIBRARY

National Agricultural Library

10301 Baltimore Blvd.
Beltsville, MD 20705–2351
(301) 504–5755
Pamela Andre, director
Hours: 8:00 a.m. to 4:30 p.m.

The USDA also maintains a reference center at the main Agriculture Department building. The collection consists primarily of periodicals, reference volumes, and databases.

D.C. Reference Center

14th St. and Independence Ave. S.W.
South Bldg., Room 1052
Washington, DC 20250
(202) 720–3434
Janet Wright, chief
Hours: 8:00 a.m. to 4:30 p.m.

DOCKETS

Public dockets, containing records of all Forest Service rulemakings and other administrative proceedings, are maintained by the division responsible for the proceeding. Information on where a docket is kept is published in the *Federal Register* in the notice announcing the proceeding. Additional information on a particular docket may be obtained from:

Forest Service Information Resources Management Staff

201 14th St. S.W., Room 800 RPE
P.O. Box 96090
Washington, DC 20090
(703) 235–1488
Marian Connolly, regulatory officer

RULES AND REGULATIONS

Forest Service rules and regulations are published in the *Code of Federal Regulations*, Title 36, parts 200–299. Proposed rules, new final rules, and updates to the *Code of Federal Regulations* are published in the *Federal Register*. (*See appendix for information on how to obtain and use these publications.*)

■ LEGISLATION

Laws administered by the Forest Service are listed in the publication, *The Principal Laws Relating to Forest Service Activities*. Copies may be obtained from Creative Services in the Public Affairs Office.

The statutes authorizing the Forest Service to manage the National Forest System, conduct forestry research, and assist state and private forestries include:

Organic Administration Act (30 Stat. 34, 16 U.S.C. 473–482, 551). Signed by the president June 4, 1897. Provided basic authority for protecting and managing national forest lands.

Act of March 1, 1911 (36 Stat. 961, 16 U.S.C. 480). Signed by the president March 1, 1911. Popularly known as the Weeks Law, this statute authorized the secretary of agriculture to purchase forested, cutover, or denuded lands within watersheds of navigable streams necessary to the regulation and flow of navigable streams or for the production of timber. Lands acquired under this act were permanently reserved as national forest lands.

Clarke-McNary Act (43 Stat. 653, 16 U.S.C. 471b, 499, 505, 564–570). Signed by the president June 7, 1924. Established forest fire prevention programs in cooperation with the states and provided for the production and distribution of forest tree seeds and plants. Authorized the purchase of forests to protect navigable streams and to promote timber production.

Knutson-Vandenberg Act (46 Stat. 527, 16 U.S.C. 576–576b). Signed by the president June 9, 1930. Authorized the establishment of forest tree nurseries and other activities that are necessary to prepare for planting on national forests. The act also required purchasers of national forest timber to make deposits to cover the cost of replanting national forest land that is logged by the purchaser.

Anderson-Mansfield Reforestation and Revegetation Act (63 Stat. 762, 16 U.S.C. 581j). Signed by the president Oct. 11, 1949. Authorized funding for reforestation and revegetation of national forest lands.

Cooperative Forest Management Act (64 Stat. 473, 16 U.S.C. 568c). Signed by the president Aug. 25, 1950. Authorized cooperative efforts in forest management.

Multiple-Use Sustained-Yield Act of 1960 (74 Stat. 215, 16 U.S.C. 528). Signed by the president June 12, 1960. Decreed that national forests are established and administered for recreation, range, timber, watershed, and fish and wildlife purposes.

Wilderness Act (78 Stat. 890, 16 U.S.C. 1121). Signed by the president Sept. 3, 1964. Established a National Wilderness Preservation System composed of federally owned areas designed as "wilderness areas."

National Forest Roads and Trails Systems Act (78 Stat. 1089, 16 U.S.C. 532–538). Signed by the president Oct. 13, 1964. Authorized construction and regulation of roads and trails in national forests.

Wild and Scenic Rivers Act (82 Stat. 906, 16 U.S.C. 127, 1271–1287). Signed by the president Oct. 2, 1968. Protected selected rivers with remarkable scenic, geologic, fish and wildlife, and other values.

Forest and Range Land Renewable Resources Planning Act (88 Stat. 476, 16 U.S.C. 1600–1614). Signed by the president Aug. 17, 1974. A planning and budgetary procedure act that required the Forest Service to prepare long-term programs for the National Forest System. Amended by the **National Forest Management Act of 1976** (90 Stat. 2949, 16 U.S.C. 472a). Signed by the president Oct. 22, 1976. Provided for a coordinated land management planning process that required full public participation in the development and revision of land management plans for each national forest or grassland. Provided comprehensive new authorities for managing, harvesting, and selling national forest timber; and provided direction for bidding on national forest timber, road building associated with timber harvesting, reforestation, salvage sales, and the handling of receipts from timber sales activities.

Federal Land Policy and Management Act of 1976 (90 Stat. 2743, 43 U.S.C. 1752). Signed by the president Oct. 21, 1976. Provided for the use of national forests and grasslands for grazing; authorized the secretary of agriculture to issue grazing permits; and authorized issuances of rights-of-way.

Cooperative Forestry Assistance Act of 1978 (92 Stat. 365, 16 U.S.C. 2101, 1606). Signed by the president July 1, 1978. Authorized the Forest Service to carry out cooperative forestry programs with state and other federal agencies that are directed at the sustained protection and development of all forestry resources.

Alaska National Interest Lands Conservation Act (94 Stat. 2371, 16 U.S.C. 3101 note). Signed by the president Dec. 2, 1980. Provided for the conservation of certain public lands in Alaska, including additional designations of national park, national wildlife refuge, national forest, and national wilderness areas.

Wood Residue Utilization Act of 1980 (94 Stat. 3257, 16 U.S.C. 1600 note). Signed by the president Dec. 19, 1980. Established a program to improve recovery of wood residue in national forests for use as fuel.

National Forest Foundation Act (104 Stat. 2969, 16 U.S.C. 583j note). Signed by the president Nov. 16, 1990. Established a nonprofit foundation to encourage and administer private donations of land to the Forest Service.

Tongass Timber Reform Act (104 Stat. 4426, 16 U.S.C. 539d note). Signed by the president Nov. 28, 1990. Withheld one million acres of the Alaskan Tongass National Forest from timber cutting. Required that long-term contracts between the Forest Service and pulp mills in the region be renegotiated to ensure that timber sales would be profitable for the federal government.

Forest Stewardship Act of 1990 (104 Stat. 3521, 16 U.S.C. 582 note). Signed by the president Nov. 28, 1990. Reauthorized the **Cooperative Forestry Assistance Act of 1978** and established research and conservation programs to support better stewardship of private forests. Created

a private foundation, America the Beautiful, to promote tree planting and conservation activities through grants for planting, protection, and cultivation of trees. Authorized the USDA to provide emergency reforestation assistance to landowners who suffered losses because of damaging weather or wildfire.

Pacific Yew Act (106 Stat. 859, 16 U.S.C. 4801 note). Signed by the president Aug. 7, 1992. Required the harvesting of Pacific yew trees on public lands before those lands are opened to commercial logging. Taxol, a cancer-fighting agent, is derived from the bark of the tree. Directed the Forest Service to inventory yew trees in federal forests and to ensure that yews be harvested in a way to promote new growth.

Secure Rural Schools and Community Self-Determination Act of 2000 (P.L. 106-393). Signed by the president on Oct. 30, 2000. Title I: Secure Payments for States and Counties Containing Federal Lands. Directed the secretary of the Treasury, with respect to timber-related and other revenue sharing payments from Bureau of Land Management and National Forest Service lands, to calculate the full FY 2001 through 2006 payment amounts for eligible states and counties by averaging the safety net payments and the three highest annual 50 percent (BLM) payments or 25 percent (FS) payments, respectively, during the FY 1986 through 1999 eligibility period. Directed the secretary to make payments to eligible states from Forest Service lands for affected counties to use for public education and transportation.

Farm Security and Rural Investment Act of 2002 (2002 Farm Bill) (116 Stat. 1348, 7 U.S.C. 7901 note). Signed by the president on May 13, 2002. Amended the Cooperative Forestry Assistance Act of 1978 to establish the Office of Tribal Relations. Authorized the secretary to provide financial, technical, educational, and related assistance to Native American tribes for: (1) FS coordination respecting resource management, tribal land interests, and traditional and cultural matters; (2) conservation activities; and (3) tribal acquisition of conservation interests from willing sellers. Required the inspector general of the USDA to conduct an investigation independent of the FS whenever a firefighter employed by the FS is killed because of wildfire entrapment or burnover.

▪ REGIONAL OFFICES

NORTHERN REGION

(northern ID, MT, ND, northwestern SD, northern WY)
Federal Building
P.O. Box 7669
Missoula, MT 59807–7669
(406) 329–3316
Vacant, regional forester

ROCKY MOUNTAIN REGION

(CO, KS, NE, southeastern SD, eastern WY)
P.O. Box 25127
Lakewood, CO 80225
(303) 275–5450
Rock D. Cables, regional forester

SOUTHWESTERN REGION

(AZ, NM)
517 Gold Ave. S.W.
Albuquerque, NM 87102
(505) 842–3300
Eleanor S. Towns, regional forester

INTERMOUNTAIN REGION

(southern ID, NV, UT, western WY)
Federal Building #324, 25th St.
Ogden, UT 84401–2310
(801) 625–5605
Jack A. Blackwell, regional forester

PACIFIC SOUTHWEST REGION

(CA, HI)
1323 Club Dr.
Vallejo, CA 94592
(707) 562–9000
Bradley E. Powell, regional forester

PACIFIC NORTHWEST REGION

(OR, WA)
333 S.W. First Ave.
P.O. Box 3623
Portland, OR 97208
(503) 808–2202
Harv Forsgren, regional forester

SOUTHERN REGION

(AL, AR, FL, GA, KY, LA, MS, NC, OK, PR, SC, TN, TX, VA, VI)
1720 Peachtree Rd. N.W.
Atlanta, GA 30309
(404) 347–4177
Elizabeth Estill, regional forester

EASTERN REGION

(CT, DE, IA, IL, IN, MA, MD, ME, MI, MN, MO, NH, NJ, NY, OH, PA, RI, VT, WI, WV)
Henry S. Reuss Federal Plaza, #500
310 W. Wisconsin Ave.
Milwaukee, WI 53203
(414) 297–3765
Robert T. Jacobs, regional forester

ALASKA REGION

Federal Office Building
709 W. 9th St.
P.O. Box 21628
Juneau, AK 99802
(907) 586–8863
James A. Caplan (acting), regional forester

Grain Inspection, Packers, and Stockyards Administration

14th St. and Independence Ave. S.W., Stop 3601
Washington, DC 20250-3601
Internet: http://www.usda.gov/gipsa

The Grain Inspection, Packers, and Stockyards Administration (GIPSA) was created as a unit within the U.S. Department of Agriculture (USDA) in 1994, through the merger of the Federal Grain Inspection Service (FGIS) and the Packers and Stockyards Administration (PSA). GIPSA is headed by an administrator who is appointed by the president and confirmed by the Senate; the administrator reports to the assistant secretary of agriculture for marketing and regulatory programs. The FGIS and the renamed Packers and Stockyards Programs continue to function as distinct divisions of GIPSA.

Federal Grain Inspection Service (FGIS). Created in 1976 to administer the provisions of the Grain Standards Act, the service establishes federal standards for grain and performs inspections to ensure compliance. It also regulates the weighing of all grain that is moved through any export facility in the country.

Standards have been established for corn, wheat, rye, oats, barley, flaxseed, grain sorghum, soybeans, triticale (a hybrid of durum wheat and rye), sunflower seed, and mixed grains.

The FGIS also has authority to establish and enforce standards for rice, dry beans, peas, lentils, and hops under the provisions of the Agricultural Marketing Act of 1946.

The FGIS is divided into four major divisions:

- Compliance ensures through reviews, evaluations, and enforcement actions that regulations are uniformly enacted and followed.
- Field Management directs the operation of FGIS field offices, establishes U.S. standards for grain, rice, and other commodities, and measures the quality of grain as it moves through the market. There currently are twenty-one FGIS field locations (thirteen field offices, two federal/state offices, and six suboffices) in fifteen states and Canada.

- Technical Services develops tests and methods to determine grain quality, recommends specifications and approves grain inspection instrumentation, develops quality control systems, and makes final decisions on inspection appeals.
- International Affairs (OIA) represents GIPSA on committees and task forces concerned with international grain trade policies, and national policy issues relating to the World Trade Organization (WTO), the North American Free Trade Agreement (NAFTA), agricultural biotechnology, and sanitary and phytosanitary (SPS) issues. The staff also serves as GIPSA's liaison with the Foreign Agricultural Service.

Nearly all grain exported from the United States is inspected during loading. The inspections are performed by FGIS personnel or state inspection agencies authorized by the FGIS. Domestic grain is examined by state inspectors or private firms certified by the FGIS administrator.

If a buyer or seller disputes an inspection result, an appeal inspection from the FGIS field office can be requested. This, in turn, may be appealed to the FGIS Board of Appeals and Review.

FGIS personnel, or state inspectors approved by the service, inspect grain and certify weight at export facilities. This process is closely monitored by FGIS field employees. At nonexport facilities, FGIS-approved officials perform weighings upon request under the supervision of the FGIS. Violations of FGIS standards are punishable by fines and imprisonment.

All individuals and companies engaged in large-scale grain export operations must register with the FGIS and supply ownership and management information. Registrants are granted a certificate that must be renewed annually. The certificate may be revoked or suspended by the FGIS administrator if a hearing determines that FGIS standards have been violated.

Packers and Stockyards Programs (PSP). This division of GIPSA carries out its responsibilities under the 1921 Packers and Stockyards Act, which charges the agency with the regulation of livestock and live poultry marketing practices as well as those of meat and poultry packers in interstate or foreign commerce.

The act safeguards farmers, ranchers, and consumers from unfair business practices and protects members of the livestock, poultry, and meat industries from unfair, deceptive, unjustly discriminatory, or monopolistic competition.

The Economic and Statistical Support Staff (ESS) provides economic advice to agency officials on broad policy issues and the economic implications of various programs, policies, and practices of the livestock, meat, poultry, and grain industries. ESS also administers Section 1324 of the Food Security Act of 1985 (Clear Title program) and certifies state central filing systems to notify buyers, commission merchants, and selling agents of lenders' security interests in farm products.

The Office of Field Operations (OFO) is responsible for program and policy implementation, investigations, budget, personnel, supervision, and coordination of regional offices and all activities relating to enforcement of the Packers and Stockyards Act in the regional offices.

The Office of Policy/Litigation Support (OPLS) is responsible for developing regulations, enforcement policies, and procedures and for providing litigation support to the Office of General Counsel. To accomplish these tasks, the office consists of three branches that focus on the core responsibilities of competition, fair trade practices, and financial protection.

The Regional Offices of Packers and Stockyards Programs are located in Atlanta, Ga., Denver, Colo., and Des Moines, Iowa. Each office is responsible for carrying out the activities and functions of the Packers and Stockyards Programs and for investigating potential violations of the Packers and Stockyards Act within its assigned region. The regional offices are located near concentrations of livestock and poultry production and slaughter.

▪ KEY PERSONNEL

Administrator
Donna Reifschneider................... (202) 720–0219
Fax.................................... (202) 205–9237

FEDERAL GRAIN INSPECTION SERVICE
Deputy Administrator
David R. Shipman..................... (202) 720–9170
Fax.................................... (202) 205–9237

Compliance
Neil Porter............................ (202) 720–8262
Fax.................................... (202) 690–2755
Field Management
David Orr............................. (202) 720–0228
Fax.................................... (202) 720–1015
Technical Services
(USDA FGIS Technical Center)
10383 N. Ambassador Dr.
Kansas City, MO 64153-1394
Steven Tanner .... (816) 891–0401
Fax.................................... (816) 891–8070
Commodity Testing Laboratory
Lynn Polston.......................... (816) 891–0444
Board of Appeals and Review
Eurvin Williams....................... (816) 891–0418

PACKERS AND STOCKYARDS PROGRAMS
Deputy Administrator
JoAnn Waterfield...................... (202) 720–7051
Fax.................................... (202) 205–3941
Economic and Statistical Support Staff
Gerald Grinnell....................... (202) 720–7455
Field Operations
Daniel L. VanAckeren................. (202) 720–7063
Policy/Litigation Support
Bruce Boor (acting).................. (202) 720–6951

▪ INFORMATION SOURCES

Internet
Agency Web site: http://www.usda.gov/gipsa. Includes information about GIPSA offices and programs, news releases, and GIPSA publications.

Telephone Contacts
Personnel Locator (DC) .... (202) 720–8732
Personnel Locator (MN)................... (612) 349–5437
(APHIS Field Servicing Office
100 N. 6th St., 5th Floor
Minneapolis, MN 55403)

Information and Publications

KEY OFFICES

GIPSA Public Affairs Office
14th St. and Independence Ave. S.W., Stop 3601
Washington, DC 20090-3601
(202) 720–2533
Gregory J. Hawkins, public affairs specialist

Provides information about GIPSA activities and programs, including the annual report and fact sheets on grain and related commodities.

Freedom of Information
14th St. and Independence Ave. S.W., Room 1647-S
Stop 3604
Washington, DC 20090-3604
(202) 720–8087
Joanne Peterson, FOI officer

14th St. and Independence Ave. S.W., Room 1638-S
Washington, DC 20250
(202) 690–3842
Bruce Boor, FOI officer

PUBLICATIONS
Contact the GIPSA Public Affairs Office. Selected publications also are available for ordering or for downloading on the agency's Internet site.

DATA AND STATISTICS
Contact GIPSA Public Affairs for the FGIS annual report, which includes data on many of the agency's activities.

Reference Resources

LIBRARY

National Agricultural Library
10301 Baltimore Blvd.
Beltsville, MD 20705–2351
(301) 504–5755
Pamela Andre, director
Hours: 8:00 a.m. to 4:30 p.m.

The USDA also maintains a reference center at the main Agriculture Department building. The collection consists of periodicals, reference volumes, and databases.

D.C. Reference Center
South Bldg., Room 1052
14th St. and Independence Ave. S.W.
Washington, DC 20250
(202) 720–3434
Janet Wright, chief
Hours: 8:00 a.m. to 4:30 p.m.

DOCKETS

GIPSA Issuance Management Staff
14th St. and Independence Ave. S.W.
Room 1654-S
Stop 3604
Washington, DC 20090-3604
(202) 720–7486
Tess Butler, manager
Hours: 8:30 a.m. to 4:00 p.m.

Maintains dockets containing the files for GIPSA rule-making proceedings.

RULES AND REGULATIONS
GIPSA rules and regulations are published in the *Code of Federal Regulations,* Title 7, parts 181–229 (PSP) and 800–899 (FGIS). Proposed regulations, new final regulations, and updates to the *Code of Federal Regulations* are published in the daily *Federal Register.* (See appendix for information on how to obtain and use these publications.)

■ LEGISLATION
Department of Agriculture Reorganization Act of 1994 (7 U.S.C. 6901). Signed by the president Oct. 13, 1994. Merged the Federal Grain Inspection Service (FGIS) with the Packers and Stockyards Administration (PSA) to form GIPSA.

The FGIS carries out its responsibilities under:
Agricultural Marketing Act of 1946 (60 Stat. 1087, 7 U.S.C. 1621). Signed by the president Aug. 14, 1946. Authorized the FGIS to provide official inspection and weighing services for rice, dry beans, peas, lentils, hay, straw, hops, and other processed grain products.
U.S. Grain Standards Act of 1976 (90 Stat. 2867, 7 U.S.C. 71 note). Signed by the president Oct. 21, 1976. Amended the **U.S. Grain Standards Act of 1916** (39 Stat. 454, 7 U.S.C. 71), which was signed by the president Aug. 11, 1916. The 1976 act created the FGIS, strengthened the inspection provisions of the original legislation, required supervised weighing of grain and added stiffer penalties for violations. This act was later amended by the **Food and Agriculture Act of 1977** (91 Stat. 913, 7 U.S.C. 1281 note), the **United States Grain Standards Act–Grain Exportation Amendments** (94 Stat. 1870, 7 U.S.C. 75), the **Agriculture and Food Act of 1981** (95 Stat. 1213, 7 U.S.C.

1281 note), the **Omnibus Budget Reconciliation Act of 1981** (95 Stat. 357, 31 U.S.C. 1331), and the **Federal Grain Inspection Program Amendments** (98 Stat. 1831, 7 U.S.C. 79).

Futures Trading Act of 1986 (100 Stat. 3564, 7 U.S.C. 71 note). Signed by the president Nov. 10, 1986. Included the **Grain Quality Improvement Act of 1986.** Established four purposes for grades and standards to guide the work of the FGIS: to facilitate marketing, reflect storability, measure the end-product yield and quality, and provide market incentives.

U.S. Grain Standards Act Amendments of 1993 (107 Stat. 1525, 7 U.S.C. 71 note). Signed by the president Nov. 24, 1993. Authorized inspection and weighing activities in Canadian ports. Authorized a pilot program to permit more than one official agency to carry out inspections within a single geographic area. Extended inspector licensing authority to contract-supervised persons. Enabled the administrator of the FGIS to test weighing equipment and collect related fees. Established Sept. 30, 2000 as the date when the grain standards advisory committee will terminate.

Grain Standards and Warehouse Improvement Act of 2000 (P.L. 106-472). Signed by the president on Nov. 9, 2000. Extended GIPSA authority to implement several provisions of the United States Grain Standards Act (USGSA) from Sept. 30, 2000 to Sept. 30, 2005. Authorized the collection of the tonnage portion of the original inspection and weighing fees, and the fee for supervising official agencies. Also extended authority to maintain an advisory committee.

The PSP carries out its responsibilities under:

Packers and Stockyards Act of 1921, as amended (7 U.S.C. 181-229). Signed by the president Aug. 15, 1921. Gave the secretary authority to regulate competition and trade practices in the livestock, meat packing, and poultry industries. The Packers and Stockyards Administration (PSA), the forerunner of the Packers and Stockyards Programs within GIPSA, was created to administer the act. A 1958 amendment (72 Stat. 1749) substantially expanded the secretary's jurisdiction over auction markets and dealers. A 1976 amendment (90 Stat. 1249) increased financial protection for livestock sellers and made meat wholesalers subject to regulation as packers.

Food Security Act of 1985 (7 U.S.C. 1631). Signed by the president Dec. 23, 1985. Gave the PSA regulatory and certifying power over a new central filing system for notification of liens against farm products.

Poultry Producers Financial Protection Act of 1987 (7 U.S.C. 182 note). Signed by the president Nov. 23, 1987. Expanded the responsibilities of the PSA by adding statutory trust and payment provisions for poultry producers similar to those adopted in 1976 for livestock producers.

Farm Security and Rural Investment Act of 2002 (2002 Farm Bill) (116 Stat. 1348, 7 U.S.C. 7901 note). Signed by the president on May 13, 2002. Section 10502 amended the Packers and Stockyards Act to make any swine contractor subject to the jurisdiction of the act. Persons contracting with others to raise and care for feeder pigs or other swine that were not intended for slaughter were not covered.

◼ REGIONAL OFFICES

Federal Grain Inspection Service

BEAUMONT
1745 Buford St., Suite A
Beaumont, TX 77701–5855
(409) 839-2425
Alfred Broussard, officer in charge

CALIFORNIA
1220 N St., #A–471
Sacramento, CA 95814-5621
(916) 654-0743
Michael Johnson, manager

CEDAR RAPIDS
P.O. Box 74855
Cedar Rapids, IA 52407–4855
(319) 364-0047
Ron Metz, manager

CORPUS CHRISTI
P.O. Box 2942
Corpus Christi, TX 78403–2942
(361) 888-3461
Tom Wane, officer in charge

CROWLEY
P.O. Box 443
Crowley, LA 70527–0443
(337) 262-6694
Wayne M. Melvin, officer in charge

DULUTH/SUPERIOR
P.O. Box 33
Superior, WI 54880
(715) 392-7677
Ted Respet, officer in charge

GRAND FORKS
P.O. Box 13427
Grand Forks, ND 58208-3427
(701) 772-3371
Thomas Wrenn, manager

GREENVILLE
P.O. Box 4824
Greenville, MS 38704–4824
(662) 335-4805
Ken Carter, officer in charge

JONESBORO
1904 Grant Ave., Suite J
Jonesboro, AR 72401–6165
(870) 932-4585
William B. Strickland, officer in charge

KANSAS CITY
6501 Beacon Drive, #180
Stop 1404
Kansas City, MO 64133
(816) 823-4640
Diane Palecek, manager

LEAGUE CITY
1025 E. Main St., #104
League City, TX 77573-2483
(281) 338-2787
Danny Cameron, manager

MINNEAPOLIS
13401 County Rd., #5
Burnsville, MN 55337
(612) 335-4095
Steve Bennett, manager

MONTREAL
715 Peel St., #272
Montreal, Quebec H3C 4L7
Canada
(514) 392-9798
Vacant, manager

MOSCOW
220 E. Fifth St., #212D
Moscow, ID 83843-2964
(208) 882-4833
Robert Peterson, manager

NEW ORLEANS
104 Campus Dr., #200
P.O. Box 640
Destrehan, LA 70047-0640
(985) 764-2324
John Shropshire, manager

PORTLAND
P.O. Box 3837
Portland, OR 97208–3837
(503) 326-7887
Walter Rust, manager

STUTTGART
P.O. Box 137
Stuttgart, AR 72160-0152
(870) 673-2508
Clyde Steves, manager

TOLEDO
1910 Indian Wood Cir., #401
Maumee, OH 43537–4029
(419) 259-6276
David M. Mundwiler, manager

WASHINGTON STATE
3939 Cleveland Ave.
Olympia, WA 98501-4079
(360) 753-9072
John Flemm, manager

WICHITA
7920 W. Kellogg, #200
Wichita, KS 67209-2006
(316) 722-6370
Kenneth Critchfield, manager

Packers and Stockyards Programs

ATLANTA
Richard Russell Bldg.
78 Spring St., #230
Atlanta, GA 30303
(404) 562-5840
Elkin Parker, regional supervisor

DENVER
1 Gateway Center
3950 Lewiston, #200
Aurora, CO 80011
(303) 375-4240
John Barthel, regional supervisor

DES MOINES
Federal Bldg., #317
210 Walnut St.
Des Moines, IA 50309
(515) 323-2579
Jay Johnson, regional supervisor

Natural Resources Conservation Service

14th St. and Independence Ave. S.W., Washington, DC 20250
Internet: http://www.nrcs.usda.gov

The Natural Resources Conservation Service (NRCS) was created in 1994 by a reorganization of the U.S. Department of Agriculture (USDA). It succeeds the former Soil Conservation Service (SCS), a USDA agency established by the Soil Conservation and Domestic Allotment Act of 1935, and combines its functions with various conservation programs previously administered by the Agricultural Stabilization and Conservation Service (ASCS) and the Farmers Home Administration (FmHA).

The NRCS provides technical and financial assistance to conserve natural resources. It works primarily with farmers and ranchers on private lands but also assists the conservation districts of rural and urban governments to reduce erosion, conserve and protect water, and solve other resource problems. Most NRCS employees work in the USDA's local county offices. To accomplish its conservation goals, the NRCS also works with environmental groups, AmeriCorps, and its own Earth Team volunteers. The agency is headed by a chief who reports to the under secretary of agriculture for natural resources and environment.

In addition to technical assistance to landowners and governments, the NRCS conducts various other programs. Many of these involve cooperation with other government agencies and state land-grant universities. In addition to several watershed and flood prevention programs, NRCS programs authorized or reauthorized under the Farm Security and Rural Investment Act of 2002 include:

- Agricultural Management Assistance Program.
- Conservation of Private Grazing Land Program providing technical assistance from the NRCS to owners and managers of private grazing land.
- Conservation Security Program providing financial and technical assistance to conserve soil, water, air, energy, and plant and animal life on tribal and private working lands—cropland, grassland, prairie land, improved pasture and rangeland, as well as certain forested land that is an incidental part of an agriculture operation.
- Environmental Quality Incentive Program helping farmers and ranchers to treat identified soil, water, and related natural resource concerns on eligible land.
- Farmland Protection Program providing matching funds to help purchase development rights to keep productive farm and ranchland in agricultural uses.
- Resource Conservation and Development Program assisting local councils in planning and carrying out programs for conservation.
- Wetlands Reserve Program (formerly ASCS) purchasing easements from agricultural land owners to protect or restore wetlands.
- Wildlife Habitat Incentives Program providing financial incentives to develop habitat for fish and wildlife on private lands.

■ KEY PERSONNEL

Chief
Bryce I. Knight .... (202) 720–7246
Fax .... (202) 720–7690

Management
P. Dwight Holman .... (202) 720–6297
Fax .... (202) 720–2588

Science and Technology
Lawrence E. Clark .... (202) 720–4630
Fax .... (202) 720–7710

Programs
Jose Acevedo .... (202) 720–4527
Fax .... (202) 720–6559

Budget Planning and Analysis
Brenda Thomas .... (202) 720–4533
Conservation Operations
Charles Whitmore (acting)............ (202) 720–1845
Fax...................................... (202) 720–4265
International Programs
Jose Acevedo (acting)................. (202) 720–2218
Fax...................................... (202) 720–0668
Resource Conservation and Community Development
Anne Dubey (acting)................... (202) 720–2847
Fax...................................... (202) 690–0639
Watersheds and Wetlands
Harry Slawter (acting)................. (202) 720–3527
Fax...................................... (202) 720–2143
Soil Survey and Resource Assessment
Maurice Mauschbach................. (202) 690–4616
Fax...................................... (202) 690–4390
Resource Inventory
Wayne M. Maresch..................... (301) 504–2271
Fax...................................... (301) 504–2230
Soils
Wayne M. Maresch (acting) .... (202) 720–1820
Fax...................................... (202) 720–4593
Resource Assessment
Carlos F. Henning..................... (202) 720–8644

■ INFORMATION SOURCES

Internet
Agency Web site: http://www.nrcs.usda.gov. Provides information on NRCS offices and programs, a weekly update on agency activities, and access to the NRCS Data Clearinghouse.

Telephone Contacts
See NRCS Conservation Communication Staff, below.

Information and Publications

KEY OFFICES

NRCS Conservation Communication Staff
14th St. and Independence Ave. S.W.
Washington, DC 20250
(202) 720–3210
Fax (202) 720–1564
Terry Bish, director

NRCS Legislative Affairs Staff
14th St. and Independence Ave. S.W.
Washington, DC 20250
(202) 720–2771
Fax (202) 690–0845
Doug McKalip, director

Freedom of Information
14th St. and Independence Ave. S.W.
Washington, DC 20250
(202) 941–0130
Vacant, FOI officer

PUBLICATIONS
To order publications or request a publications list, contact:

NRCS Publications and Distribution Office
1–888–LANDCARE
945 SW Ankeny Rd.
Ankeny, IA 50021

A selected number of publications can be found on the agency's Web site, www.nrcs.usda.gov.

DATA AND STATISTICS
The NRCS Data Clearinghouse is accessible via the agency's Internet site.

Reference Resources

LIBRARY

National Agricultural Library
10301 Baltimore Blvd.
Beltsville, MD 20705–2351
(301) 504–5755
Peter R. Young, director
Hours: 8:00 a.m. to 4:30 p.m.

The USDA also maintains a reference center at the main Agriculture Department building. The collection consists primarily of periodicals, reference volumes, and databases.

D.C. Reference Center
14th St. and Independence Ave. S.W.
South Bldg., Room 1052
Washington, DC 20250
(202) 720–3434
Hours: 8:00 a.m. to 4:30 p.m.

RULES AND REGULATIONS

NRCS rules and regulations are published in various parts of Titles 7 and 16 of the *Code of Federal Regulations*. Proposed rules, new final rules, and updates to the *Code of Federal Regulations* are published in the *Federal Register*. *(See appendix for information on how to obtain and use these publications.)*

▓ LEGISLATION

Soil Conservation and Domestic Allotment Act (49 Stat. 163, 16 U.S.C. 590a). Signed by the president April 27, 1935. Created the Soil Conservation Service, now NRCS. Authorized the secretary of agriculture to provide loans and payments to farmers and others to improve conservation efforts and prevent erosion.

Watershed Protection and Flood Prevention Act (68 Stat. 666, 16 U.S.C. 1001 note). Signed by the president Aug. 4, 1954. Empowered the FmHA to make loans to state or local organizations to carry out watershed and flood prevention measures.

Water Bank Act (84 Stat. 1468, 16 U.S.C. 1301). Signed by the president Dec. 19, 1970. Provided funds for the improvement and maintenance of wetlands and adjacent natural resource areas; the control of runoff, erosion, and floods; and the promotion of water management techniques.

Soil and Water Conservation Act of 1977 (16 U.S.C. 2001). Signed by the president Nov. 18, 1977. Directed the secretary of agriculture to conduct an appraisal and develop a National Conservation Program every five years.

Cooperative Forestry Assistance Act of 1978 (92 Stat. 367, 16 U.S.C. 2103). Signed by the president July 1, 1978. Authorized the Forestry Incentives Program to provide cost-sharing incentives to encourage development, management, and protection of nonindustrial private forest lands.

Agriculture, Rural Development and Related Agencies Appropriations Act for Fiscal Year 1980 (93 Stat. 835, 16 U.S.C. 590e-1). Signed by the president Nov. 9, 1979. Authorized the experimental Rural Clean Water program to provide cost-sharing and technical assistance for installing measures that control nonpoint source pollution and improve water quality in rural America.

Food Security Act of 1985 (99 Stat. 1518, 7 U.S.C. 1281 note). Signed by the president Dec. 23, 1985. Began a program in which a farmer can sell an easement on highly erodible land for conservation for 50 years in exchange for a reduction of FmHA debt. Required farmers and ranchers who have highly erodible crop land to have a conservation plan to remain eligible for program benefits.

Food, Agriculture, Conservation, and Trade Act of 1990 (104 Stat. 3359, 7 U.S.C. 1421 note). Signed by the president Nov. 28, 1990. Established standards for protection of wetlands in the FmHA inventory.

Department of Agriculture Reorganization Act of 1994 (7 U.S.C. 6901). Signed by the president Oct. 13, 1994. Established the NRCS by combining the Soil Conservation Service with conservation programs from the former ASCS and FmHA.

Federal Agriculture Improvement and Reform Act of 1996 (110 Stat. 888). Signed by the president April 4, 1996. Authorized more than $2.2 billion in additional funding for conservation programs, extended the Conservation Reserve Program and the Wetlands Reserve Program, and created new programs to address high priority environmental protection goals.

Farm Security and Rural Investment Act of 2002 (2002 Farm Bill) (116 Stat. 1348, 7 U.S.C. 7901 note). Signed by the president on May 13, 2002. Authorized several new conservation programs. Amended the Food Security Act of 1985 to establish a conservation security program from FY 2003 through 2006 to assist conservation practices on production land. Amended the Cooperative Forestry Management Act of 1978 to permit local governments or qualified organizations to acquire forest legacy program conservation easements and enhance community fire protection and tree and forest growth and resource conservation.

▓ REGIONAL OFFICES

EAST
(CT, DE, MA, MD, ME, NH, NJ, NY, PA, RI, VT, WV)
11710 Beltsville Dr., Bldg. 2, #100
Beltsville, MD 20705
(301) 504–2300
Richard D. Swenson, regional conservationist

SOUTHEAST
(AL, FL, GA, KY, MS, NC, PR, SC, TN, VA, VI)
1720 Peachtree Rd. N.W., #446–N
Atlanta, GA 30309
(404) 347–6105
Charles Adams (acting), regional conservationist

MIDWEST
(IA, IL, IN, MI, MN, MO, OH, WI)
2820 Walton Commons West, #123
Madison, WI 53718–6797
(608) 224–3001
Charles Whitmore, regional conservationist

SOUTH CENTRAL
(AR, LA, OK, TX)
501 Felix St., Bldg. 23
Felix and Hemphill St.
P.O. Box 6459
Fort Worth, TX 76115
(817) 509–3328
Humberto Hernandez, regional conservationist

NORTHERN PLAINS
(CO, KS, MT, ND, NE, SD, WY)
100 Centennial Mall North, #152
Lincoln, NE 68508
(402) 437–5315
Richard Van Klaveren, regional conservationist

WEST
(AK, AZ, CA, HI, ID, NM, NV, OR, UT, WA)
430 G St., #4165
Davis, CA 95616–4165
(530) 792–5700
Pearlie S. Reed, regional conservationist

Risk Management Agency

14th St. and Independence Ave. S.W., Washington, DC 20250
Internet: http://www.rma.usda.gov

In 1996 the Risk Management Agency (RMA) was created to administer Federal Crop Insurance Corporation programs and other noninsurance-related risk management and education programs that help support U.S. agriculture. Many of these functions were formerly covered under the Farm Services Agency.

Today, the crop insurance program, which is administered by the RMA, helps farmers survive a major crop loss. About two-thirds of the acreage planted to major U.S. crops is insured, covering seventy-six crops and many of their varieties. Crop insurance is sold and serviced by seventeen insurance companies in conjunction with a network of 15,000 agents. The effectiveness of this partnership is evident in that virtually all indemnities are paid within thirty days of a claim.

Federal Crop Insurance Corporation (FCIC). Through the Federal Crop Insurance Corporation (FCIC), the RMA offers all-risk crop insurance to cover unavoidable losses because of insect infestation, adverse weather conditions, plant disease, flood, wildlife, fire, and earthquake.

The management of the corporation is vested in a board of directors subject to the general supervision of the secretary of agriculture. The board consists of the manager of the corporation, the undersecretary of agriculture responsible for the federal crop insurance program, one additional undersecretary of agriculture as designated by the secretary of agriculture, one member who is experienced in crop insurance but not otherwise employed by the federal government, and three active farmers not otherwise employed by the federal government.

Congress first authorized federal crop insurance in the 1930s along with other initiatives to help agriculture recover from the combined effects of the Great Depression and the Dust Bowl. The FCIC was created in 1938 to carry out the program. Initially, the program was started as an experiment, and crop insurance activities were mostly limited to major crops in the main producing areas. Crop insurance remained an experiment until passage of the Federal Crop Insurance Act of 1980.

The 1980 act expanded the crop insurance program to many more crops and regions of the country. It encouraged expansion to replace the free disaster coverage (compensation to farmers for prevented planting losses and yield losses) offered under farm bills created in the 1960s and 1970s, because the free coverage competed with the experimental crop insurance program. To encourage participation in the expanded crop insurance program, the 1980 act authorized a subsidy equal to 30 percent of the crop insurance premium limited to the dollar amount at 65 percent coverage.

The Federal Crop Insurance Reform Act of 1994 significantly changed the way in which government assists producers suffering a major crop loss. Its goal is to replace the uncertainty of ad hoc disaster assistance with the predictability of crop insurance protection. Under the new program, producers must purchase at least the catastrophic level (CAT) of crop insurance of economic significance to participate in other assistance programs through the Farm Service Agency (see p. 403), such as price support and production adjustment programs, certain farm loans, and the Conservation Reserve Program. CAT coverage provides per-acre return similar to the coverage under most previous ad hoc disaster programs. It is fully subsidized by the federal government apart from a nominal processing fee and is available from both commercial insurance agents and local USDA offices.

The FCIC also provides money and policy incentives for producers to purchase additional coverage from commercial insurance agents. For crops that are not yet insurable, the Crop Insurance Reform Act has established a Noninsured Crop Disaster Assistance Program (NAP), which provides benefits similar to CAT coverage. NAP is administered through the Farm Services Agency.

In 1996 Congress repealed the mandatory participation requirement. However, farmers who accepted other benefits were required to purchase crop insurance or otherwise waive their eligibility for any disaster benefits that might be made available for the crop year. These provisions are still in effect.

Participation in the crop insurance program increased significantly following enactment of the 1994 act. In 1998 more than 180 million acres of farmland were insured under the program, more than three times the acreage insured in 1988, and more than twice the acreage insured in 1993. The liability (or value of the insurance in force) in 1998 was $28 billion. The total premium, which includes subsidy, and the premium paid by insured persons (nearly $950 million) were also record figures.

Since 2000 farmer purchases of higher levels of protection and revenue coverage policies have increased. In 2002 more than 50 percent of the insured acreage was insured at 70 percent or higher level of coverage compared to only 9 percent in 1998.

RMA Pilot Programs. New RMA programs are tested on a pilot basis in selected counties to allow the agency to gain insurance experience and test the programs' components. Most pilot programs operate for about two to three years before they are made more broadly available or are converted to permanent program status. However, during a new program's pilot period, expansion into new counties may be approved by the FCIC board of directors. RMA routinely develops, implements, and monitors pilot programs for new crops, new plans of insurance, and new management strategies.

RMA also provides training to farmers to help them acquire the risk management skills needed to compete and win in the global marketplace. The agency is leading a risk management education initiative in cooperation with USDA's Cooperative State Research, Education, and Extension Service; USDA's National Office of Outreach; and the Commodity Futures Trading Commission. With public and private partners, RMA works to find improved risk management strategies, develop educational curricula and materials, and train producers in effective use of risk management tools.

RMA also helps make information on risk management more accessible to farmers and educators by funding the National Ag Risk Education Library, a powerful resource developed by the Center for Farm Financial Management at the University of Minnesota.

■ KEY PERSONNEL

Administrator
Ross J. Davidson .... (202) 690-2533
Fax .... (202) 690-2818

Associate Administrators
Byron E. Anderson .... (202) 690-2533
Fax .... (202) 690-2818
David C. Hatch .... (202) 690-2533
Fax .... (202) 690-2818

Insurance Services
Vacant .... (202) 720-5290

Risk Management Services
Anne Jenkins (acting) .... (814) 624-0737

Regulatory Division
E. Heyward Baker .... (202) 720-4286

Risk Management Education
Craig Witt .... (202) 690-2957

Risk Compliance
Michael Hand .... (202) 720-0642

Risk Operations
Vacant .... (202) 720-8812

Programs Integrity and Internal Controls
Larry Piatz, chief .... (202) 260-4729

Programs Integrity and Internal Controls
Wes Azama, deputy chief

Research and Development (Kansas City, MO)
Timothy B. Witt .... (816) 926-7394

■ INFORMATION SERVICES

INTERNET
Agency Web site: http://www.rma.usda.gov

COMMUNICATIONS
USDA-RMA
1400 Independence Ave. S.W.
Washington, DC 20250
(202) 720–5846
James Callan, director
Terrie Ray, FOIA coordinator
(202) 690-5701

■ DATA ACQUISITION AND ANALYSIS

Director
Garland Westmoreland .... (202) 720–5828

PUBLICATIONS

Many RMA publications, reports, and bulletins are available online in portable document format (pdf) at http://www.rma.usda.gov/pubs.

RMA PUBLICATIONS ORDERS

FSA-KCMO Warehouse
9420 Troost
Kansas City, MO 64131-3055
Fax: (816) 363-1762

DATA AND STATISTICS

National Ag Risk Education Library

The National Ag Risk Education Library is an online, searchable resource developed and maintained by the Center for Farm Financial Management, in the Department of Applied Economics, College of Agriculture, Food and Environmental Sciences at the University of Minnesota. It is accessible at http://www.agrisk.umn.edu.

▩ LEGISLATION

Federal Crop Insurance Corporation Act of 1938 (7 U.S.C. 1501). Signed by the president Feb. 16, 1938. Established the FCIC as an agency of the USDA.

Federal Crop Insurance Reform Act of 1994 (7 U.S.C. 1501 note). Signed by the president Oct. 13, 1994. Overhauled the crop insurance program. Established catastrophic level (CAT) coverage as a requirement to participate in certain FSA programs; also established the Noninsured Crop Disaster Assistance Program (NAP) for crops not yet insurable.

Federal Agriculture Improvement and Reform Act of 1996 (110 Stat. 896, 7 U.S.C. 7201). Signed by the president April 4, 1996. Part of the Federal Agriculture Improvement and Reform Act of 1996. Under title I (the act itself), subtitle H (miscellaneous commodity provisions), section 193 amended the Federal Crop Insurance Act to direct the secretary of agriculture to offer catastrophic risk protection in a state through the local Department of Agriculture offices if sufficient coverage is unavailable. Provided for the transfer of current policies to private insurers and established a crop insurance pilot project. Section 194 established the Office of Risk Management to oversee the Federal Crop Insurance Corporation and related crop insurance matters. Section 195 established a revenue insurance pilot program. Section 196 directed the secretary to operate a noninsured crop disaster assistance program through the FSA for food or fiber crops not covered by the federal crop insurance catastrophic risk protection program.

Agricultural Research, Extension, and Education Reform Act of 1998 (112 Stat. 523, 7 U.S.C. 7926). Signed by the president June 23, 1998. Title V (agricultural program adjustments), subtitle C (crop insurance) amended the Federal Crop Insurance Corporation Act of 1938 to make permanent the Federal Crop Insurance Corporation's authority to pay expenses from the insurance fund. Directed the corporation to establish and implement procedures for responding to regulatory inquiries.

Agricultural Risk Protection Act of 2000 (114 Stat. 358, 7 U.S.C. 1501 note). Signed by the president on June 20, 2000. Amended the Federal Crop Insurance Act to provide greater access to more affordable risk management tools, to improve the efficiency and integrity of the federal crop insurance program, and for other purposes. Amended the Federal Crop Insurance Act to direct the Commodity Credit Corporation to offer optional quality adjustment crop insurance policies (with reduced premiums for nonelecting producers) and to authorize the Commodity Credit Corporation to conduct crop insurance-related research and pilot programs. Amended the Agricultural Research, Extension, and Education Reform Act of 1998 to establish an educational program to improve agricultural producers' risk management skills.

Farm Security and Rural Investment Act of 2002 (2002 Farm Bill) (116 Stat. 1348, 7 U.S.C. 7901 note). Signed by the president on May 13, 2002. Amended the Federal Crop Insurance Act to increase research and development reimbursement funding and education program funding for FY 2002 through 2006. Eliminated funding for the partnerships for risk management education program. Amended the Federal Agricultural Improvement and Reform Act of 1996 to restrict commodity and crop insurance payments, loans, and benefits to qualifying previously cropped land, including conservation reserve land. Amended the Food Security Act of 1985 to include farm storage facility loans, disaster payments, and indemnity payments for producers of commodities on highly erodible land.

▩ REGIONAL OFFICES

BILLINGS, MT, REGIONAL OFFICE

(MT, ND, SD, WY)
2110 Overland Ave., #106
Billings, MT 59102-6440
406-657-6447
Doug Hagel, director

JACKSON, MS, REGIONAL OFFICE

(AR, KY, LA, MS, TN)
8 River Bend Pl.
Jackson, MS 39208
601-965-4771
Rock Davis, director

OKLAHOMA CITY, OK, REGIONAL OFFICE
(NM, OK, TX)
205 NW 63rd St., #170
Oklahoma City, OK 73116
405-879-2700
Ronald L. Berryhill, director

RALEIGH, NC, REGIONAL OFFICE
(CT, DE, MA, MD, ME, NC, NH, NJ, NY, PA, RI, VA, VT, WV)
4407 Bland Rd., #160
Raleigh, NC 27609
919-875-4880
Larry N. Atkinson, director

DAVIS, CA, REGIONAL OFFICE
(AZ, CA, HI, NV, UT)
430 G St., # 4168
Davis, CA 95616-4168
530-792-5870
William Murphy (acting), director

ST. PAUL, MN, REGIONAL OFFICE
(IA, MN, WI)
910 Minnesota World Trade Center
30 East 7th St.
St. Paul, MN 55101-4901
651-290-3304
Craig Rice, director

SPOKANE, WA, REGIONAL OFFICE
(AK, ID, OR, WA)
112 N. University Road, #205
Spokane, WA 99206-5295
509-353-2147
Dave Paul, director

SPRINGFIELD, IL, REGIONAL OFFICE
(IL, IN, MI, OH)
3500 West Wabash, #B
Springfield, IL 62707
217-241-6600
Michael Alston, director

TOPEKA, KS, REGIONAL OFFICE
(CO, KS, MO, NE)
3401 S.W. Van Buren St.
Topeka, KS 66611
785-266-0248
Rebecca Davis, director

VALDOSTA, GA, REGIONAL OFFICE
(AL, FL, GA, PR, SC)
106 South Patterson St., #250
Valdosta, GA 31601-5609
229-219-2200
Mike Moore, director

Regional Compliance Offices

SOUTHERN REGIONAL COMPLIANCE OFFICE
(AR, KY, LA, MS, NM, OK, TN, TX)
1111 West Mockingbird Lane, #280
Dallas, TX 75247-5016
214-767-7700
Billy M. Pryor, director

MIDWEST REGIONAL COMPLIANCE OFFICE
(IL, IN, MI, OH)
Corporate Center North
6905 Corporate Circle
Indianapolis, IN 46278
317-290-3050
Gene Prochaska, director

CENTRAL REGIONAL COMPLIANCE OFFICE
(CO, KS, MO, NE)
6501 Beacon Dr.
Kansas City, MO 64133
816-926-7394
Alvin Gilmore, director

EASTERN REGIONAL COMPLIANCE OFFICE
(AL, CT, DE, FL, GA, MA, MD, ME, NC, NH, NJ, NY, PA, PR, RI, SC, VA, VT, WV)
4407 Bland Rd., #280
Raleigh, NC 27609
919-875-4930
Johnnie F. Perdue, director

WESTERN REGIONAL COMPLIANCE OFFICE
(AK, AZ, CA, HI, ID, NV, OR, UT, WA)
430 G St., # 4167
Davis, CA 95616-4167
530-792-5850
Susan Choy, director

NORTHERN REGIONAL COMPLIANCE OFFICE
(IA, MN, MT, ND, SD, WI, WY)
3440 Federal Dr., #200
Eagan, MN 55122-1301
612-725-3730
Mark Huber, director

Rural Development

**14th St. and Independence Ave. S.W.
Washington, DC 20250–0320
Internet: http://www.rurdev.usda.gov**

The Rural Development mission area was created in 1994 by a reorganization of the U.S. Department of Agriculture (USDA). Rural Development is the successor to two former USDA agencies, the Rural Development Administration (RDA) and the Rural Electrification Administration (REA), and it also handles the rural housing programs of a third former agency, the Farmers Home Administration (FmHA). Following the 1994 reorganization, Rural Development was initially known as Rural Economic and Community Development.

Four agencies make up Rural Development: the Rural Business-Cooperative Service, the Rural Housing Service, the Rural Utilities Service, and the Office of Community Development. Each of these is primarily a lending agency and is headed by an administrator who reports to the under secretary of agriculture for rural development. Administrators are appointed by the president and confirmed by the Senate.

Rural Business-Cooperative Service (RBS). The RBS inherits the business development programs of the RDA and the REA.

Through its business programs, the RBS makes or guarantees a wide range of loans and grants to improve, develop, or finance business, industry, and employment in rural communities. Loans are made primarily through the existing private credit structure, with the RBS guaranteeing lenders against loss up to 90 percent of principal and interest.

Intermediary Relending Program loans are available to nonprofit corporations, public agencies, Native American tribes, and cooperatives: these entities serve in turn as "intermediaries" to provide loans to "ultimate recipients" to finance business and community development projects. Similarly, Rural Technology and Cooperative Development Grants are made to create or finance centers which in turn promote technological and economic development in rural areas. Some other RBS loans and grants, however, are made directly to business owners and entrepreneurs.

Other RBS programs include the Cooperative Services Program, which conducts research and serves as a clearinghouse of information on rural cooperatives; the Land-Grant Institution Initiative, which works with universities on rural economic development projects; the USDA Alternative Agricultural Research and Commercialization Center (AARC), which develops new nonfood uses of agricultural commodities; and the AmeriCorps USDA Rural Development Team, which brings volunteers to specific projects in rural communities. The Community Adjustment and Investment Program (CAIP) under the North American Development Bank (NADBank) lends to businesses in communities with significant levels of workers adversely affected by NAFTA-related trade.

Rural Housing Service (RHS). The RHS inherits the rural housing programs of the FmHA and the rural community loan programs of the RDA and the REA.

The RHS provides direct and guaranteed loans to individuals and local sponsoring organizations for various purposes in rural areas, including community facilities, watershed protection and flood prevention, resource conservation and development, rental and congregate housing, and the construction, purchase, or improvement of housing by rural residents. The RHS also provides grants for many of these projects as well as rental and utility assistance to low-income families in rural areas. Most loans and grants have either an income requirement for individuals or a population requirement for participating communities, two exceptions being the watershed and resource conservation programs.

Rural Utilities Service (RUS). The RUS inherits the electric and telecommunications programs of the REA and the water and waste disposal programs of the RDA.

Under the Rural Electrification Act of 1936, as amended, the RUS Electric Program assures adequate electric service to rural areas by making or guaranteeing loans to nonprofit and cooperative associations and to public bodies for construction and operation of generating plants and transmission and distribution lines.

The RUS Telecommunications Program similarly ensures adequate telephone service in rural areas through loans to commercial companies, public bodies, and cooperative, nonprofit, limited dividend, or mutual associations. The program is now involved in modernizing rural telecommunications, particularly to accommodate use of the Internet. The RUS also operates the Rural Telephone Bank, which makes loans to telephone systems at a rate consistent with the bank's cost in obtaining the money from the U.S. Treasury. The RUS administrator serves as governor of the bank.

Through the Distance Learning and Telemedicine Program, which was established by the Farm Bill of 1990, the RUS provides grants to rural schools and health care providers, for investment in telecommunications facilities and equipment.

The RUS Water and Waste Program makes or guarantees loans to develop water and waste disposal systems in rural areas and towns with a population under 10,000. Funds are available to public entities such as municipalities, counties, special-purpose districts, Native American tribes, and nonprofit corporations. The Waste and Water Program also distributes a variety of related grants, including for repair and replacement of facilities, and provides technical assistance to rural water systems.

The 2002 farm bill authorized creation of the Rural Broadband Loan and Loan Guarantee Program, which is administered by the RUS. For fiscal year 2003 RUS made available $1.4 billion in loans and loan guarantees to provide broadband services in rural communities. These loans were to facilitate deployment of new and innovative technologies to provide two-way data transmission of 200 kbps or more, in communities with populations up to 20,000.

Office of Community Development. As part of the Omnibus Budget Reconciliation Act, the Community Empowerment Program was signed into law in August 1993. The Office of Community Development (OCD) administers the Community Empowerment Program, which offers economic assistance, through grants, to rural communities having high rates of poverty. In the first year, three ru-

ral Empowerment Zones (EZ) and thirty rural Enterprise Communities (EC) were named. Rural EZs received grants of $40 million and rural ECs received special EZ/EC grants of just under $3 million from the Social Services Block Grants (SSBG) program administered by the Department of Health and Human Services.

Round II was enacted into law by the Taxpayer Relief Act of 1997. That act established five new EZs. The eligibility requirements were changed, and a simpler method of determining poverty was adopted. Native American reservation lands were made eligible for Round II. The act did not appropriate grant funds as had been available to Round I EZs and ECs, but did make available a package of tax benefits. Later, however, Congress appropriated first-year grants of $2 million to each of the five EZs and authorized an additional twenty rural ECs and provided them with $250,000 in first-year funding.

Round III was enacted by the Consolidated Appropriations Act of 2001, signed by the president on Dec. 21, 2000, which authorized the secretary of agriculture to designate two more EZs.

OCD also administers the Rural Economic Area Partnership (REAP) program. The REAP Initiative was established as a pilot program to address critical issues related to constraints in economic activity and growth, low-density settlement patterns, stagnant or declining employment, and isolation that has led to disconnection from markets, suppliers, and centers of information and finance.

This pilot project set up a collaborative and citizen-led effort to enhance economic development in areas designated as REAP Zones. In 1995 two zones in North Dakota were initially designated to participate in the REAP initiative. Subsequently, in 1999, two areas in upstate New York were added as the third and fourth REAP Zones. In 2000 an area in Vermont was designated as the fifth zone. Both the North Dakota and the Vermont zones are multicounty in size, while the two in New York are, for the most part, single counties.

◼ KEY PERSONNEL

Under Secretary
Thomas C. Dorr........................ (202) 720–4581
Fax..................................... (202) 720–2080
Deputy Under Secretary Policy and Planning
Gilbert G. Gonzalez.................... (202) 720–4581
Fax..................................... (202) 720–2080
Deputy Under Secretary Operations and Management
(Vacant)............................... (202) 720–4581
Fax..................................... (202) 720–2080

RURAL BUSINESS–COOPERATIVE SERVICE
Administrator
John Rosso .... (202) 690–4730
Fax .... (202) 690–4737
Associate Administrator
(Vacant) .... (202) 690–4730
Fax .... (202) 690–4737

BUSINESS PROGRAMS
Deputy Administrator
William F. Hagy III .... (202) 720–7287
Fax .... (202) 690–0097
Special Projects/Programs Oversight Division
Dwight Carmon .... (202) 690–4100
Business and Industry Division
Carolyn Parker .... (202) 690–4103
Specialty Lenders Division
(Vacant) .... (202) 720–1751

COOPERATIVE SERVICES
Deputy Administrator
James E. Haskell (Acting) .... (202) 720–7558
Fax .... (202) 720–4641
Cooperative Development
John H. Wells .... (202) 720–3350
Cooperative Marketing
Thomas H. Stafford .... (202) 690–0368
Cooperative Resources Management
John R. Dunn .... (202) 690–1374
Statistics and Technical Services
(Vacant) .... (202) 720–3189

RURAL HOUSING SERVICE
Administrator
Arthur Garcia .... (202) 690–1533
Fax .... (202) 690–0500
Associate Administrator
James E. Selmon .... (202) 690–1533
Fax .... (202) 690–0500
Program Support Staff
Richard A. Davis .... (202) 720–9619

SINGLE FAMILY HOUSING
Deputy Administrator
David Villano .... (202) 720–5177
Director, Direct Loan Division
Michael Feinberg (Acting) .... (202) 720–1474
Director, Guaranteed Loan Division
Roger Glendenning .... (202) 720–1452

MULTI–FAMILY HOUSING
Deputy Administrator
James C. Alsop (Acting) .... (202) 720–3773
Processing Division
Carl Wagner .... (202) 720–1604
Portfolio Management Division
Stephanie White .... (202) 720–1615

COMMUNITY PROGRAMS
Deputy Administrator
James C. Alsop .... (202) 720–1500
Direct Loan and Grant Processing
Chadwick Parker .... (202) 720–1502
Guaranteed Loan Processing
C. Barth Miller .... (202) 720–1505

RURAL UTILITIES SERVICE
Administrator
Hilda Gay Legg .... (202) 720–9540
Fax .... (202) 720–1735
Deputy Administrator
Curtis Anderson .... (202) 720–9540
Fax .... (202) 720–1735
Financial Services
Larry Belluzzo .... (202) 720–1265
Program Accounting and Regulatory Analysis
Kenneth Ackerman .... (202) 720–9450
Electric Program
Blaine Stockton Jr. .... (202) 720–9545
Fax .... (202) 690–0717
Northern Regional Division
Sally R. Price .... (202) 720–1420
Southern Regional Division
Robert Ellinger .... (202) 720–0848
Electric Staff
George Bagnall .... (202) 720–1900
Power Supply
Victor Vu .... (202) 720–6436
Telecommunications Program
Roberta Purcell .... (202) 720–9554
Fax .... (202) 720–0810
Advanced Services division
Orren Cameron .... (202) 690–4493
Telecommunications Standards
Gerald Nugent .... (202) 720–8663
Eastern Area Regional Division
Ken Kuchno .... (202) 690–4673
Northwest Area Regional Division
Jerry Brent .... (202) 720–1025
Southwest Area Regional Division
Ken B. Chandler .... (202) 720–0800

Water and Environmental Programs
Gary Morgan .... (202) 690–2670
Fax .... (202) 720–0718
Engineering and Environmental Staff
Glendon D. Deal .... (202) 720–8328
Water Programs Division
(Vacant) .... (202) 720–9583
Portfolio Management Branch
Sewell Feddiman Jr. .... (202) 720–9631

OFFICE COMMUNITY DEVELOPMENT
Deputy Administrator
Luis Luna .... (202) 619–7980
Fax .... (202) 401–7420

OPERATIONS AND MANAGEMENT
Deputy Administrator
Sherie Hinton Henry .... (202) 692–0200
Fax .... (202) 692–0203
Civil Rights Staff
Cheryl Prejean Greaux .... (202) 692–0204
Native American Coordinator
David Saffert .... (202) 720–0400
Budget Division
Deborah Lawrence .... (202) 692–0122
Financial Management Division
John Purcell .... (202) 692–0080
Policy and Analysis Division
William French (Acting Director) ..... (202) 690–9824
Procurement and Administrative Services
Sharon Randolph .... (202) 692–0207
Human Resources
Diana Shermeyer (Acting Director) ... (202) 692–0222
Legislative and Public Affairs
Tim McNeilly (Acting Director) ...... (202) 720–1019
Chief Information Officer
Tom Hannah .... (202) 692–0212
Chief Financial Officer
Christine Burgess (Acting) .... (202) 539–2360
Alternative Dispute Resolution
Bob Lovan .... (202) 690–2583

■ INFORMATION SOURCES

Internet
Agency Web Site: http://www.rurdev.usda.gov. Includes information on Rural Development agencies and programs and links to related economic development Internet sites.

Telephone Contacts
Personnel Locator (USDA) .... (202) 720-8732

Information and Publications

KEY OFFICES

Legislative and Public Affairs
USDA Rural Development
14th St. and Independence Ave. S.W.
Washington, DC 20250
(202) 720–1019
Fax (202) 690–9916
Tim McNeilly (acting), director

Provides public information and responds to general queries.

Freedom of Information
USDA Rural Development
14th St. and Independence Ave. S.W.
Washington, DC 20250
(202) 692-0031
Dorothy Hinden, FOI officer

Records also may be requested at the state offices.

PUBLICATIONS
The Legislative and Public Affairs Staff provides USDA Rural Development fact sheets: (202) 720–1019.

Information and applications for financial assistance are available through state USDA Rural Development offices. This information is available for persons with disabilities (in media including Braille, large print, and audiotape) from the USDA Office of Communications: (202) 720-4623.

Economic Research Service (ERS-NASS)
1800 M St. N.W.
Washington, DC 20036
(202) 694-5050

Reference Resources

LIBRARY

National Agricultural Library
10301 Baltimore Blvd.
Beltsville, MD 20705-2351
(301) 504-5755
Pamela Andre, director
Hours: 8:30 a.m. to 4:30 p.m.

The USDA also maintains a reference center at the main Agriculture Department building. The collection consists primarily of periodicals, reference volumes, and databases.

D.C. Reference Center
14th St. and Independence Ave. S.W.
South Bldg., Room 1052
Washington, DC 20250
(202) 720-3434
Hours: 8:00 a.m. to 4:30 p.m.

DOCKETS

Regulations and Paperwork Management
USDA Rural Development
14th St. and Independence Ave. S.W.
South Bldg., Room 6348S
Washington, DC 20250
(202) 692–0040
Jeanne Jacobs, branch chief
Hours: 8:00 a.m. to 4:30 p.m.

Maintains dockets containing all information and materials pertaining to Rural Development administrative proceedings for public inspection.

RULES AND REGULATIONS

USDA Rural Development rules and regulations are published in the *Code of Federal Regulations,* Title 7, various parts. Proposed rules, new final rules, and updates to the *Code of Federal Regulations* are published in the *Federal Register. (See appendix for information on how to obtain and use these publications.)*

▪ LEGISLATION

Legislation administered by USDA Rural Development includes:

Federal Housing Act of 1949 (63 Stat. 413, 42 U.S.C. 1401). Signed by the president July 15, 1949. Empowered the FmHA to make rural housing loans and to require that buildings constructed comply with federal housing regulations.

Consolidated Farm and Rural Development Act (75 Stat. 307, 7 U.S.C. 1921). Signed by the president Aug. 4, 1961. Authorized the FmHA to prescribe terms and conditions for making loans and grants and to require that lenders and borrowers comply with applicable federal laws and regulations.

Senior Citizens Housing Act (76 Stat. 670, 42 U.S.C. 1471). Signed by the president Sept. 28, 1962. Established a loan program for low-rent apartments for individuals age sixty-two and over and authorized loans for establishment of recreational facilities.

Rural Development Act of 1972 (86 Stat. 657, 7 U.S.C. 1006). Signed by the president Aug. 30, 1972. Authorized the FmHA to guarantee loans made by commercial lenders for farming, housing, and rural business and industry in cities up to 50,000 population. Authorized loans for construction of community facilities, as well as youth loans and industrial site improvement grants.

Rural Housing Amendments of 1983 (97 Stat. 1240, 42 U.S.C. 1441). Signed by the president Nov. 30, 1983. Required the FmHA to revise income definitions to be consistent with the Department of Housing and Urban Development (HUD), and to accept any of the voluntary national model building codes and HUD minimum property standards, in addition to FmHA construction standards. Empowered the FmHA to extend eligible single-family home mortgages from thirty-three years to thirty-eight years, and required the administration to give more priority to persons in the low-income classification.

Housing and Community Development Technical Amendments Act of 1984 (98 Stat. 2218, 42 U.S.C 5301). Signed by the president Oct. 17, 1984. Authorized the FmHA to lend 60 percent of its single-family housing funds to persons in the low-income classification and 40 percent to those in the very low-income classification.

Food, Agriculture, Conservation, and Trade Act of 1990 (104 Stat. 3359, 7 U.S.C. 1421 note). Signed by the president Nov. 28, 1990. Established the RDA as a new agency within the USDA. Consolidated and transferred to the RDA rural development responsibilities previously under the FmHA and other agencies. Authorized the RDA to administer technical assistance and credit programs for rural community facilities, water and waste systems, and business and industry.

Cranston-Gonzalez National Affordable Housing Act (104 Stat. 4079, 42 U.S.C. 12701 note). Signed by the president Nov. 28, 1990. Authorized a guaranteed loan program for rural single-family home ownership. Mandated special targeted housing assistance to underserved areas and modified the rural population standard for housing program eligibility. Created a demonstration program for mortgage payment deferral.

Housing and Community Development Act of 1992 (106 Stat. 3672, 43 U.S.C. 5301 note). Signed by the president Oct. 28, 1992. Increased the income level for applicants eligible to apply for single-family home ownership loans and the percentage of a state's rural multifamily rental housing allocation reserved for nonprofit organizations. Authorized FmHA to require a 5 percent equity contribution by rental housing developers receiving assistance from the agency. Provided housing preservation grant funds for replacement housing. Established a rural housing voucher program and expanded the underserved areas assistance program.

Department of Agriculture Reorganization Act of 1994 (7 U.S.C. 6901). Signed by the president Oct. 13, 1994. Consolidated the missions of the RDA and REA, and the rural housing programs of the FmHA.

Omnibus Budget Reconciliation Act of 1993 (P.L. 103-66). Signed by the president Aug. 10, 1993. Subchapter C: Empowerment Zones, Enterprise Communities, Rural Development Investment Areas provided for the designation of ninety-five tax enterprise communities and nine empowerment zones during calendar years after 1993 and before 1996. Provided for the issuance of enterprise zone facility bonds in enterprise communities and empowerment zones in a manner similar to exempt facility bonds. Allowed a general business tax credit for contributions to selected community development corporations to provide employment of, and business opportunities for, low-income individuals who are residents of the operational area of the community.

Federal Agriculture Improvement and Reform Act of 1996 (110 Stat. 888). Signed by the president April 4, 1996. Title VI (credit), subtitles A, B, and C, revised farm loan provisions with regard to farm ownership loans, operating loans, and emergency loans. Title VII (rural development), subtitle A repealed the rural investment partnerships program, the water and waste facility loan, and the rural wastewater circuit rider programs. Subtitle B established a program under which the secretary may guarantee rural development loans made by a certified lender, and established a rural community advancement program of grants, loans, guarantees, and other assistance to local communities and federally recognized Native American tribes.

Farm Security and Rural Investment Act of 2002 (2002 Farm Bill) (116 Stat. 1348, 7 U.S.C. 7901 note). Signed by the president on May 13, 2002. Amended the Consolidated Farm and Rural Development Act to establish the National Rural Cooperative and Business Equity Fund Act. Authorized qualifying private investors to establish a nonfederal entity, the National Rural Cooperative and Business Equity Fund, to generate and provide equity capital for rural businesses. Amended the Consolidated Farm and Rural Development Act to authorize the establishment of the Rural Endowment Program. Amended the Rural Electrification Act of 1936 to make grants and loans for construction, improvement, or acquisition of facilities and equipment for rural broadband service. Amended the Rural Electrification Act of 1936 to make grants, loans, and loan guarantees to rural electric cooperatives and other rural electric utilities to develop renewable energy, or for rural economic development.

National Rural Development Partnership Act of 2002 (Title VI, Subtitle B of the 2002 Farm Bill). Amended the Consolidated Farm and Rural Development Act to establish the National Rural Development Partnership composed of the National Rural Development Coordinating Committee and state development councils.

■ STATE OFFICES

ALABAMA
Sterling Center
4121 Carmichael Road, Suite 601
Montgomery, AL 36106–3683
(334) 279–3400
Steve Pelham, Director

ALASKA
800 West Evergreen, Suite 201
Palmer, AK 99645
(907)761–7705
Bill Allen, Director

ARIZONA
3003 North Central Avenue, Suite 900
Phoenix, AZ 85012
(602) 280–8700
Eddie Browning, Director

ARKANSAS
Federal Building
700 W. Capitol Avenue, Room 3416
Little Rock, AR 72201–3225
(501) 301–3200
John Allen, Director

CALIFORNIA
430 G Street, Agency 4169
Davis, CA 95616–4169
(530) 792–5800
Paul Venosdel, Director

COLORADO
655 Parfet Room E–100
Lakewood, CO 80215
(303) 236–2801
Ginette Dennis, Director

DELAWARE/MARYLAND
4607 South Dupont Hwy.
P.O. Box 400
Camden, DE 19934–9998
(302) 697–4300
Marlene B. Elliott, Director

FLORIDA/VIRGIN ISLANDS
4440 NW 25th Place
P.O. Box 147010
Gainesville, FL 32614–7010
(352) 338–3402
Charles Clemons, Sr., Director

GEORGIA
Stephens Federal Building
355 E. Hancock Avenue
Athens, GA 30601–2768
(706) 546–2162
F. Stone Workman, Director

HAWAII
Federal Building
154 Waianuenue Avenue, Room 311
Hilo, HI 96720
(808) 933–8302
Larraine Shin, Director

IDAHO
9713 West Barnes Drive
Suite A1
Boise, ID 83709
(208) 378–5600
Michael A. Field, Director

ILLINOIS
Illini Plaza
1817 South Neil Street, Suite 103
Champaign, IL 61820
(217) 398–5235
Douglas A. Wilson, Director

INDIANA
5975 Lakeside Boulevard
Indianapolis, IN 46278
(317) 290–3100
Robert White, Director

IOWA
Federal Building, Room 873
210 Walnut Street
Des Moines, IA 50309
(515) 284–4663
Daniel Brown, Director

KANSAS
1200 SW Executive Drive
P.O. Box 4653
Topeka, KS 66604
(785) 271–2700
Charles R. Banks, Director

KENTUCKY
771 Corporate Drive, Suite 200
Lexington, KY 40503
(859) 224–7300
Kenneth Slone, Director

LOUISIANA
3727 Government Street
Alexandria, LA 71302
(318) 473–7921
Michael B. Taylor, Director

MAINE
967 Illinois Avenue, Suite 4
Bangor, ME 04402–0405
(207) 990–9106
Michael Aube, Director

MASSACHUSETTS/RHODE ISLAND/ CONNECTICUT
451 West Street
Amherst, MA 01002
(413) 253–4300
David H. Tuttle, Director

MICHIGAN
3001 Coolidge Road, Suite 200
East Lansing, MI 48823
(517) 324–5188
Director (Vacant)

MINNESOTA
410 AgriBank Building
375 Jackson Street
St. Paul, MN 55101
(651) 602–7800
Stephen Wenzel, Director

MISSISSIPPI
Federal Building, Suite 831
100 West Capitol Street
Jackson, MS 39269
(601) 965–4316
Nick Walters, Director

MISSOURI
601 Business Loop 70 West
Parkade Center, Suite 235
Columbia, MO 65203
(573) 876–0976
Gregory C. Branum, Director

MONTANA
Unit 1, Suite B
900 Technology Boulevard
Bozeman, MT 59715
(406) 585–2580
W. T. (Tim) Ryan, Director

NEBRASKA

Federal Building, Room 152
100 Centennial Mall N
Lincoln, NE 68508
(402) 437–5551
M. James Barr, Director

NEVADA

1390 South Curry Street
Carson City, NV 89703–5405
(775) 887–1222
Larry J. Smith, Director

NEW JERSEY

Tarnsfield Plaza, Suite 22
790 Woodlane Road
Mt. Holly, NJ 08060
(609) 265–3600
Andrew M.G. Law, Director

NEW MEXICO

6200 Jefferson Street, Room
Albuquerque, NM 87109
(505) 761–4950
Jeff Condrey, Director

NEW YORK

The Galleries of Syracuse
441 South Salina Street
Syracuse, NY 13202
(315) 477–6435
Patrick Brennan, Director

NORTH CAROLINA

4405 Bland Road, Suite 260
Raleigh, NC 27609
(919) 873–2000
John J. Cooper, Director

NORTH DAKOTA

Federal Building, Room 208
220 East Rosser, P.O. Box 1737
Bismarck, ND 58502–1737
(701) 530–2037
Clare Carlson, Director

OHIO

Federal Building, Room 507
200 North High Street
Columbus, OH 43215–2477
(614) 255–2400
Randall Hunt, Director

OKLAHOMA

100 USDA, Suite 108
Stillwater, OK 74074
(405) 742–1000
Brent J. Kisling, Director

OREGON

101 SW Main Street, Suite 1410
Portland, OR 97204–3222
(503) 414–3300
Lynn Schoessler, Director

PENNSYLVANIA

1 Credit Union Place, Suite 330
Harrisburg, PA 17110–2996
(717) 237–2184
Byron E. Ross, Director

PUERTO RICO

IBM Building, Suite 601
654 Munos Rivera Avenue
Hato Rey, PR 00918–6106
(787) 766–5095
Jose A. Otero–Garcia, Director

SOUTH CAROLINA

Strom Thurmond Federal Building
1835 Assembly Street, Room 1007
Columbia, SC 29201
(803) 765–5163
Charles D. Sparks, Director

SOUTH DAKOTA

Federal Building, Room 210
200 4th Street SW
Huron, SD 57350
(605) 352–1100
Lynn Jensen, Director

TENNESSEE

3322 West End Avenue, Suite 300
Nashville, TN 37203–1071
(615) 783–1300
Mary (Ruth) Tackett, Director

TEXAS

Federal Building
101 South Main, Suite 102
Temple, TX 76501
(254) 742–9700
Bryan Daniel, Director

UTAH

Wallace F. Bennett Fed. Bldg.
125 South State Street, Room 4311
Salt Lake City, UT 84138
(801) 524–4320
John R. Cox, Director

VERMONT/NEW HAMPSHIRE

City Center, 3rd Floor
89 Main Street
Montpelier, VT 05602
(802) 828–6002
Jolinda LaClair, Director

VIRGINIA

Culpepper Building, Suite 238
1606 Santa Rosa Road
Richmond, VA 23229
(804) 287–1552
Joseph Newbill, Director

WASHINGTON

1835 Blacklake Boulevard, SW, Suite B
Olympia, WA 98512–5715
(360) 704–7715
Jackie J. Gleason, Director

WEST VIRGINIA

75 High Street
P.O. Box 678
Morgantown, WV 26505
(304) 284–4861
Jenny N. Phillips, Director

WISCONSIN

4949 Kirschling Court
Stevens Point, WI 54481
(715) 345–7600
Frank Frassetto, Director

WYOMING

100 East B, Federal Building, Room 1005
P.O. Box 820
Casper, WY 82602
(307) 261–6300
John E. Cochran, Director

Commerce Department

14th St. and Constitution Ave. N.W., Washington, DC 20230
Internet: http://www.doc.gov

Bureau of Industry and Security

14th St. and Constitution Ave. N.W., Washington, DC 20230
Internet: http://www.bxa.doc.gov

The Commerce Department's Bureau of Export Administration (BXA) was established in 1987 to stem proliferation of weapons of mass destruction without unnecessarily impeding U.S. export growth. In 2002 the BXA changed its name to the Bureau of Industry and Security (BIS) to reflect more accurately the broad scope of the agency's responsibilities. The change in name did not substantively affect its activities, nor those of its sister organization, the International Trade Administration, which remained responsible for the Commerce Department's trade promotion and policy activities.

To accomplish its mission, the BIS controls exports and re-exports of dual-use commodities and technical data from the United States and its territories and possessions. Dual-use commodities are items of a primarily civilian nature that also have potential military applications. Under the authority of the Export Administration Act (EAA), controls on these commodities and technologies are maintained for reasons of national security, foreign policy, and short supply. For example the EAA includes export controls designed to address national security and foreign policy issues, such as protecting human rights and combating terrorism.

The BIS administers the Export Administration Regulations (EAR), which specify rules for the submission of export license applications. The BIS also administers export controls on commercial encryption products under EAR. These regulations were extensively revised in 1995 for the first time in more than forty years.

The BIS maintains controls for purposes of nuclear nonproliferation pursuant to section 309 (C) of the Nuclear Nonproliferation Act of 1978, as well as limiting the proliferation of chemical and biological weapons and missile technology, in cooperation with other governments.

The agency is divided into two principal divisions: Export Administration, which serves as the federal government's licensing agency for dual-use commodities and technical data; and Export Enforcement, which executes administrative, civil, and criminal sanctions against parties who violate U.S. export control laws, including the antiboycott provisions of the EAA.

In 1995 President Bill Clinton announced a new policy for controlling the export of high-performance computers (HPCs). The new policy focused on (1) limiting the acquisition of computational capabilities by potential adversaries and countries of proliferation concern, and (2) ensuring that U.S. domestic industries supporting computing capabilities important for national security could compete in markets of limited security or proliferation risks.

In 1998 the White House swiftly directed the BIS to implement far-reaching sanctions against India and Pakistan following nuclear weapons tests by both countries. Export and re-export licenses for dual-use items relating to nuclear or missile proliferation, such as computers and software, were denied indefinitely to both countries' governments and nongovernment entities. Export and re-export licenses for dual-use items of other purposes were screened by the BIS on a case-by-case basis.

On March 17, 2000, the *Federal Register* published a rule that removed fifty-one Indian entities and modified one entity's listing. In addition, this rule revised the license review policy for items classified as EAR99 (items that are subject to EAR, but are not listed on the Commerce Control List) to Indian and Pakistani government, private, and parastatal entities from a presumption of denial to a presumption of approval. However, a prohibition remained imposed on exports and re-exports to certain government, parastatal, and private entities in India and Pakistan that were determined to continue nuclear or missile activities.

The issue of U.S. exports of HPCs, commercial satellites, and related technology to China also made headlines in 1998. Questions were raised whether such exports assisted China's weapons research. In response to these concerns, the Commerce Department tightened computer export regulations to China and a host of other countries in February 1998. The National Defense Authorization Act of 1998 (passed in November 1997) required that advance notices of all exports and re-exports of HPCs must be given to the BIS. These notices are forwarded to the Defense, Energy, and State departments. If none of the agencies object to the notices within ten days, the export will proceed. If an objection is raised, the notice will be converted to a license application.

Following a review in 1999 by all relevant security and nonproliferation agencies and private-sector experts, it became apparent that the growth in widely available computer hardware capabilities was outpacing the ability of export control policy to keep up. The biggest challenge to the ability to control computer hardware effectively was the capabilities of end-users to network large clusters of computers. This was a challenge for the administration of George W. Bush taking office in 2001.

The United States and India on Feb. 5, 2003, signed a Statement of Principles for U.S.-India High Technology Commerce. The statement, which recognized the untapped potential for U.S.-India high-technology commerce, also acknowledged both governments' commitment to preventing the proliferation of sensitive goods and technologies and noted the need to facilitate high-technology trade consistent with laws and national security and foreign policy objectives.

In January 2003 the Commerce Department announced a new regulation to streamline export controls on general purpose microprocessors that were used worldwide in technology and commercial applications such as personal computers and cell phones. Under the new rule, a license will only be required to export general purpose microprocessors to terrorist countries or for military uses in countries posing national security concerns. The BIS published the regulation after consultation with the Departments of State and Defense.

■ KEY PERSONNEL

Under Secretary for Export Administration
Kenneth I. Juster .... (202) 482–1455
Fax .... (202) 482–2387
Deputy Under Secretary
Karen K. Bhatia .... (202) 482–1427

Administration
Miriam Cohen .... (202) 482–1900
Fax .... (202) 482–1418
Chief Counsel
John A. Dyck .... (202) 482–5301
Fax .... (202) 482–0085
Export Administration
Assistant Secretary
James Jochum .... (202) 482–5491
Fax .... (202) 482–3911
Chemical/Biological Controls and Treaty Compliance
Steven Goldman .... (202) 482–3825
Exporter Services
Eileen Albanese .... (202) 482–0436
Nonproliferation Controls and Treaty Compliance
Steven Goldman .... (202) 482–4188
Strategic Industries and Economic Security
Dan Hill .... (202) 482–4506
Strategic Trade and Foreign Policy Controls
Bernie Kritzer .... (202) 482–4196
Export Enforcement
Assistant Secretary
Vacant .... (202) 482–1561
Fax .... (202) 482–4173
Antiboycott Compliance
Dexter Price .... (202) 482–5914
Enforcement Analysis
Thomas Andrukonis .... (202) 482–4255
Export Enforcement
Mark Menefee .... (202) 482–2252

■ INFORMATION SOURCES

Internet
Agency Web Site: http://www.bis.doc.gov. The agency also operates the Export License Application and Information Network (ELAIN), which accepts export license applications electronically.

The Government Printing Office's Export Administration Regulation Web site: http://w3.access.gpo.gov/bis/index.html contains an up-to-date database of the entire Export Administration Regulations (EAR), including the Commerce Control List, the Commerce Country Chart, and a link to the Denied Persons List. EAR revisions are incorporated into this site. This Web site also includes a table with all the *Federal Register* notices that revise the text of the EAR since its complete revision on March 25, 1996.

The NTIS EAR Marketplace Web site http://bxa.fedworld.gov also offers an up-to-date EAR database that is searchable using a "user-friendly" search engine. In addition, the EAR Marketplace has a combined, downloadable, and searchable version of the Entity List, the Debarred List, and the Specially Designated Nationals List.

Telephone Contacts

Personnel Locator . . . . (202) 482–2000
Antiboycott Advice Line . . . . (202) 482–2381
Enforcement Hotline . . . . (800) 424–2890
Exporter Counseling Center
Electronic License Voice Information
  System (ELVIS) . . . . (202) 482–4811
System for Tracking Export License
  Applications (STELA) . . . . (202) 482–2752

Information and Publications

KEY OFFICES

BIS Congressional and Public Affairs
14th St. and Constitution Ave. N.W., #3897
Washington, DC 20230
(202) 482–2721
Fax (202) 482–2421
Scott Kaminis, director

Provides all basic information about the BIS.

BIS Exporter Services
Export Seminar Staff
14th and Pennsylvania Ave. N.W., #1099-C
Washington, DC 20230
(202) 482–6031
Linda Powers Oldenbuttel, (acting) director

Programs advise the exporting community on export control, export licensing, and defense conversion issues. For Western Region programs, call (714) 660–144.

PUBLICATIONS
Visit the BIS website at www.bis.doc.gov
BIS Annual Report
Export Administration:
Export Administration Annual Report on Foreign Policy Export Controls
  Offsets in Defense Trade
  U.S. Export Administration Regulations

Reference Resources

LIBRARY

Commerce Department
14th St. and Constitution Ave. N.W.
Washington, DC 20230
(202) 482–5511
Vera Whisenton, director
Open to the public
Hours: 1:00 p.m. to 4:00 p.m.

RULES AND REGULATIONS
BIS rules and regulations are published in the *Code of Federal Regulations*, Title 15, parts 768–799. Proposed regulations are published in the daily *Federal Register*. *(See appendix for details on how to obtain and use these publications.)*

■ LEGISLATION
The BIS carries out its trade regulation responsibilities under:

Export Administration Act of 1979 (93 Stat. 503, 50 U.S.C. 4001 note). Signed by the president Sept. 29, 1979. Extended the earlier act of 1969, which prohibited export of goods, including technology, that could threaten U.S. national security.

Export Administration Amendments of 1985 (99 Stat. 120, 50 U.S.C. app. 2401 note). Signed by the president July 12, 1985. Reauthorized and amended the Export Administration Act of 1979 to make American exporters more competitive and to protect U.S. national security. To make U.S. exporters more competitive, the law decontrolled the export of low-tech items and liberalized licensing where similar products are available in the international market. To protect U.S. national security interests, the law expanded export enforcement authority.

The Omnibus Trade and Competitiveness Act of 1988 (100 Stat. 1170, 19 U.S.C. 2901 note). Signed by the president Aug. 23, 1988. Amended section 201 of the Trade Act of 1974 to place a greater emphasis on industry adjustment to import competition in granting relief. Changed the antidumping and countervailing duty law to provide new provisions relating to the release of business proprietary information under protective orders.

1998 National Defense Authorization Act (111 Stat. 1029, 50 U.S.C. app. 2404 note). Signed by the president Nov. 18, 1997. Set export controls on high performance computers (HPCs). Required exporters to give BXA advance notice of all exports and re-exports of certain HPCs from the United States to Tier 3 countries (as listed in the *Code of Federal Regulations*). BXA must refer the notice to the secretary of defense, secretary of energy, secretary of state, and the director of Arms Control and Disarmament Agency. (ACDA was abolished in 1998. Its operations were absorbed by the State Department.)

Export Administration Modification and Clarification Act of 2000 (P.L. 106-508). Signed by the president on Nov. 13, 2000. Reauthorized the Export Administration Act. Amended the Export Administration Act of 1979 to increase the civil penalties for violations of the export control requirements contained in such act.

■ FIELD OFFICES

Office of Export Enforcement

CALIFORNIA
2601 Main St., #310
Irvine, CA 92714–6299
(949) 251–9001
Earl Estram, special agent in charge
96 N. Third St., #250
San Jose, CA 95112-5572
(408) 291–4204
Julie Salcido, special agent in charge

FLORIDA
200 E. Las Olas Blvd., #1260
Fort Lauderdale, FL 33301
(954) 356–7540
Roy Gilfix, special agent in charge

ILLINOIS
2400 E. Devon St., #300
Des Plaines, IL 60018
(312) 353–6640
Wendy Hauser, special agent in charge

MASSACHUSETTS
10 Causeway St., #350
Boston, MA 02222
(617) 565–6030
John McKenna, special agent in charge

NEW YORK
1200 S. Ave., #104
Staten Island, NY 10314
(718) 370–0070
Sidney Simon, special agent in charge

TEXAS
525 S. Griffin St., #622
Dallas, TX 75202
(214) 767–9294
George Richardson, special agent in charge

VIRGINIA
381 Elden St., #1125
Herndon, VA 20170
(703) 487–9300
John Wanat, special agent in charge

Economic Development Administration

14th St. and Constitution Ave. N.W., Washington, DC 20230
Internet: http://www.doc.gov/eda

The Economic Development Administration (EDA) is an agency within the Commerce Department. It was created by the Public Works and Economic Development Act of 1965 to administer programs providing assistance to states, counties, cities, and communities suffering from substantial, persistent, or potential unemployment and underemployment.

The EDA provides assistance to local and state governments as well as to private nonprofit organizations. Its programs include planning grants, technical assistance, public works, research grants, economic adjustment assistance, trade adjustment assistance, postdisaster economic recovery, and sudden and severe economic dislocations, such as military base closings.

The EDA also responds to community needs and priorities that create private-sector jobs and leverage private-sector capital.

The EDA is headed by the assistant secretary of commerce for economic development, who is supported by the deputy assistant secretary for program operations and six regional directors.

The six regional directors are responsible for coordinating with local communities in economic planning and development of Overall Economic Development Programs (OEDPs), which are related to the needs of designated areas and districts served by the regional offices; managing EDA resources available for the economic development of designated areas and districts; and processing and approving applications for assistance. The regional directors monitor approved projects.

The EDA has economic development representatives, primarily located away from the regional offices, who are responsible for providing information about the agency's programs and activities. They also assist prospective ap-plicants in preparing applications for financial assistance. The economic development representatives report to their respective regional directors.

In 1990 the EDA, which had not had a standing authorization since 1982, was reauthorized through fiscal year 1993. Both the Reagan and the Bush administrations proposed abolishing the EDA, arguing that it was limited in scope and should be funded by state or local governments, but Congress has kept the agency alive through appropriations bills. The Clinton administration, in contrast, sought to revitalize the agency, and under the Democrat-controlled 103rd Congress, the administration won spending increases for the EDA. In November 1998 the EDA was reauthorized for five years.

However, conservatives, who have long criticized the EDA's efforts as inappropriate interference in the private sector, again sought to eliminate the agency during the 104th Congress. A major reason for the agency's survival during the Republican-controlled Congress was the personal advocacy of Rep. Harold K. Rogers (R-Ky.), chair of the Appropriations subcommittee that provided funding for the Commerce Department. Rogers, who represented an economically troubled district, was a determined champion of the program's efforts to generate economic development through public works projects and technical assistance grants.

Between 1965 and 1999, EDA distributed more than $16 billion in grants across all programs, including local public works and special initiatives such as responding to natural disasters and defense conversion, and generated more than $36 billion in private investment. EDA estimates that its public works investments currently generate about $10 million in private-sector investment and $10 million in local tax base for every $1 million of EDA funds.

■ KEY PERSONNEL

Assistant Secretary for Economic Development
David A. Sampson .... (202) 482–5081
Fax...................................... (202) 273–4781

Chief Operating Officer
David M. Bearder .... (202) 482–5081
Fax...................................... (202) 273–4781

Senior Advisor
Sandy K. Baruah...................... (202) 482–5081
Fax...................................... (202) 273–4781

Chief Counsel
Claudia Nadig .... (202) 482–4687

Communications and Congressional Liaison
Nat Wienecke.......................... (202) 482–2309
Fax...................................... (202) 501-4828

Program Operations
Sandy K. Baruah...................... (202) 482–3081
Fax...................................... (202) 501–8007

Economic Adjustment
David Witschi .... (202) 482–2659
Fax...................................... (202) 482-3742

Planning and Development Assistance
Anthony J. Mayer...................... (202) 482–2127
Fax...................................... (202) 482-0466

Compliance Review
Frank Monteferrante.................. (202) 482–4208
Fax...................................... (202) 482-0995

Public Works
David McIlwain .... (202) 482–5265
Fax...................................... (202) 219-9007

Program Research and Evaluation
Nat Wienecke.......................... (202) 482–2309
Fax...................................... (202) 501-4828

Research and National Technical Assistance
John McNamec........................ (202) 482–4085
Fax...................................... (202) 501-4828

Budget
Deborah Simmons .... (202) 482–0547

Operations Review and Analysis
Patricia A. Flynn...................... (202) 482–3688

Finance and Administration Office
Mary Pleffner .... (202) 482–5891
Fax...................................... (202) 273–4781

Accounting
Joseph A. Henry....................... (202) 482–5271
Fax...................................... (202) 482–2838

Information Systems
Louise McGlathery..................... (202) 482–0526
Fax...................................... (202) 482–3096

Liquidation
Kenneth Kukovich .... (202) 482–4965
Fax...................................... (202) 482–2217

■ INFORMATION SOURCES

Internet
Agency web site: http://www.doc.gov/eda. Includes a brief overview of EDA activities, contact information, and vital current issues.

Telephone Contacts
Personnel Locator......................... (202) 482–2000

Information and Publications

KEY OFFICES

EDA Communications and Congressional Liaison
14th St. and Constitution Ave. N.W., #7814A
Washington, DC 20230
(202) 482–2309
Nat Wienecke, OAS

Provides public information. Issues news releases and publications.

Freedom of Information
EDA Office of the Chief Counsel
14th St. and Constitution Ave. N.W., #7001
Washington, DC 20230
(202) 482–5442
Claudia Nadig, Chief Counsel

PUBLICATIONS
EDA Communications and Congressional Liaison provides publications, including the *Program Description Book* and the *EDA Annual Report.*

DATA AND STATISTICS
See Publications, above.

Reference Resources

LIBRARY

Commerce Department
14th St. and Constitution Ave. N.W.
Washington, DC 20230
(202) 482–5511
Vera Whisenton, director
Open to the public
Hours: 1:00 p.m. to 4:00 p.m.

RULES AND REGULATIONS
EDA rules and regulations are published in the *Code of Federal Regulations*, Title 13, parts 301–318. Proposed

rules, new final rules, and updates to the Code of Federal Regulations are published in the daily *Federal Register. (See appendix for information on how to obtain and use these publications.)*

▪ LEGISLATION

The EDA carries out its responsibilities under the **Public Works and Economic Development Act of 1965** (79 Stat. 552, 42 U.S.C. 312). Signed by the president Aug. 26, 1965. Established the EDA to provide aid to economically distressed areas of the country.

Economic Development Administration and Appalachian Regional Development Reform Act of 1998 (112 Stat. 3596). Signed by the president on Nov. 13, 1998. Title I: Economic Development Administration Reform Act of 1998 amended the Public Works and Economic Development Act of 1965 to replace titles I through VI with the provisions of this act. Directed the secretary of commerce to cooperate with states and other entities to ensure that federal economic development programs are compatible with and further the objectives of state, regional, and local economic development plans and comprehensive economic development strategies. Directed the secretary to promulgate regulations for intergovernmental review of proposed economic development projects. Authorized the secretary to enter into economic development cooperation agreements with two or more adjoining states. Set forth provisions similar to existing provisions of law authorizing grants to eligible recipients for acquisition or development of public works and development facilities. Retained a limitation that prohibits more than 15 percent of the amounts made available for such assistance from being expended in any one state.

▪ REGIONAL OFFICES

ATLANTA
(AL, FL, GA, KY, MS, NC, SC, TN)
401 W. Peachtree St. N.W., #1820
Atlanta, GA 30308–3002
(404) 730–3002
William J. Day Jr., regional director

AUSTIN
(AR, LA, NM, OK, TX)
903 San Jacinto Blvd., #121
Austin, TX 78701
(512) 916–5595
Pedro R. Garza, regional director

CHICAGO
(IL, IN, MI, MN, OH, WI)
111 N. Canal St., #855
Chicago, IL 60606–7204
(312) 353–7706
Robert Sawyer, regional director

DENVER
(CO, IA, KS, MO, MT, ND, NE, SD, UT, WY)
1244 Speer Blvd., #670
Denver, CO 80204
(303) 844–4715
Anthony Preite, regional director

PHILADELPHIA
(CT, DC, DE, MA, MD, ME, NH, NJ, NY, PA, PR, RI, VA, VI, VT, WV)
Independence Square West, #140 S
Philadelphia, PA 19106
(215) 597–4603
Paul Raetsch, regional director

SEATTLE
(AK, AS, AZ, CA, GU, HI, ID, MP, NV, OR, WA, Marshall Islands, Micronesia, Palau)
915 Second Ave., #1856
Seattle, WA 98174
(206) 220–7660
A. Leonard Smith, regional director

International Trade Administration

14th St. and Constitution Ave. N.W., Washington, DC 20230
Internet: http://www.ita.doc.gov

The International Trade Administration (ITA), formerly the Industry and Trade Administration, was established Jan. 2, 1980. The ITA grew out of a presidential directive aimed at consolidating the federal government's nonagricultural trade functions, particularly export promotion, in a single agency. The functions of the ITA are to expand exports, to improve enforcement of U.S. trade laws, and to upgrade government trade activities in line with the Multilateral Trade Negotiations agreements signed by the United States in 1979.

Supervision of the ITA is vested in the under secretary for international trade and a deputy under secretary. The agency's role in export promotion includes the responsibility for U.S. commercial attachés in most major countries; the secretary of commerce is an *ex officio* nonvoting member of the board of the Export-Import Bank. In addition, the ITA has responsibility for implementing trade agreements, antidumping investigations, imposition of countervailing duties and embargoes, and national security trade investigations.

ITA activities are divided into four principal areas, each directed by an assistant secretary.

The Market Access and Compliance (MAC) Section concentrates on market access. It maintains country specialists, organized by region, whose expertise is available to American business. With expertise on nearly 200 countries, MAC provides critical, in-depth information enabling U.S. firms, particularly small- and medium-sized companies, to benefit fully from market access openings resulting from the more than 200 trade agreements, which the United States concluded between 1995 and 2000. MAC manages bilateral economic commissions, reviews issues relating to international economic sectors, implements and monitors agreements, and coordinates departmental participation in the World Trade Organization (WTO) and other international organizations.

The Import Administration Section investigates dumping complaints to determine whether foreign goods are being sold in the United States at less than fair value and investigates countervailing duty petitions to determine whether foreign governments are subsidizing their exports to the United States. It administers the foreign trade zones program and conducts an industrial mobilization program to ensure availability of materials essential to national defense.

The Trade Development Section provides U.S. firms with analysis of the international market to help expand exports of industrial products and services. To develop and implement strategies for export expansion, the section collects and analyzes information on trade policy and foreign industry. The Trade Development Program includes industry analysis and trade promotion organized by specific industry sectors: basic industries; service industries and finance; technology and aerospace; textiles, apparel, and consumer goods; and tourism.

The ITA manages the U.S. Commercial Service, which assists American traders in countries around the world, and gathers information on foreign commercial and industrial trends for the benefit of American businesses. The service, through its district offices, furnishes information, technical assistance, and counseling to the local business community. The service has 105 U.S. Export Assistance Centers throughout the U.S. It also maintains more than 150 international offices overseas. In 2002 U.S. Commercial Service facilitated more than $23 billion in U.S. exports.

KEY PERSONNEL

Under Secretary for International Trade
Grant Aldonas.......................... (202) 482–2867
Fax...................................... (202) 482–4821

Deputy Under Secretary
Timothy J. Hauser...................... (202) 482–3917
Fax...................................... (202) 482–2925

Administration and Chief Financial Officer
Linda Cheatham....................... (202) 482–5855
Fax...................................... (202) 208–6825

Chief Counsel for Import Administration
John McInerney........................ (202) 482–1434
Fax...................................... (202) 482–4912

Chief Counsel for International Commerce
Eleanor Roberts Lewis .... (202) 482–0937
Fax...................................... (202) 482–4076

Legislative and Intergovernmental Affairs
Vacant.................................. (202) 482–3015
Fax...................................... (202) 482–0900

Import Administration
Assistant Secretary
Vacant.................................. (202) 482–1780
Fax...................................... (202) 482–0947

Anti-Dumping Investigations
Richard Moreland...................... (202) 482–1768

Statutory Import Programs
Frank Creel .... (202) 482–1660

Foreign Trade Zones
Dennis Puccinelli (acting) .... (202) 482–2862

Market Access and Compliance
Assistant Secretary
Peter Hale (acting) .... (202) 482–3022
Fax...................................... (202) 482–5444

Policy Coordination
Peter Hale.............................. (202) 482–5341

Africa and the Near East
Gerald Feldman (acting).............. (202) 482–4925

Asia and the Pacific
Phil Agress............................. (202) 482–5251

Europe
Charles Ludolph....................... (202) 482–5638

Japan
Bob Francis............................ (202) 482–4527

Western Hemisphere
Regina Vargo .... (202) 482–5324

Trade Development
Assistant Secretary
Johnathan Menes (acting) .... (202) 482–1461
Fax...................................... (202) 482–5697

Advocacy Center
Jay Brandes (acting)................... (202) 482–3896

Trade and Economic Analysis
Jonathan C. Menes.................... (202) 482–5145

Export Promotion Coordination
Gary Enright........................... (202) 482–4501

Planning Coordination and Resource Management
Robert W. Pearson .... (202) 482–4921

Basic Industries
Henry Misisco (acting) .... (202) 482–0614

Environmental Technologies Exports
Carlos Montoulieu (acting) .... (202) 482–5225

Service Industries and Finance
A. Everette James..................... (202) 482–5261

Transportation and Technology Industries
Henry Misiseo (acting) .... (202) 482–1872

Textiles, Apparel, and Consumer Goods Industries
Michael Hutchinson (acting)......... (202) 482–3737

Tourism
Heleno Marano........................ (202) 482–0140

U.S. Commercial Service
Assistant Secretary and Director General
Maria Cino .... (202) 482–5777
Fax...................................... (202) 482–5013

Domestic Operations
Thomas Strauss (acting)............... (202) 482–4767

Export Promotion Services
Mary Fran Kirchner................... (202) 482–6220

International Operations
Larry Jensen .... (202) 482–6228

INFORMATION SOURCES

Internet

Agency Web Site: www.export.gov. A comprehensive site providing information on all trade agency programs and services, trade statistics, and links to Internet sites devoted to specific countries and regions.

The Trade Information Center (TIC) is a comprehensive resource for information on all federal government export assistance programs. The center is operated by the ITA for the twenty federal agencies that make up the Trade Promotion Coordinating Committee (TPCC). These agencies are responsible for managing the government's export promotion programs and activities. The TIC can be reached by a toll-free number: (800) 872-8723. The center is open Monday through Friday from 8:30 a.m. to 5:30 p.m. More information is available via its Web site at http://www.trade.gov/td/tic.

Telephone Contacts

Personnel Locator......................... (202) 482–2000
Trade Information Center................ (800) 872–8723

The Trade Information Center number also activates the Global Export Market Information System, an automated fax retrieval system with information on export promotion programs, regional markets, and international trade agreements. The caller presses "1" for the automated fax system or "2" to speak with a Trade Information Center specialist.

Information and Publications

KEY OFFICES

ITA Public Affairs
14th St. and Constitution Ave. N.W.
Washington, DC 20230
(202) 482–3809
Fax (202) 482–5819
Julie Cram (acting), director

ITA Legislative and Intergovernmental Affairs
14th St. and Constitution Ave. N.W.
Washington, DC 20230
(202) 482–3015
Fax (202) 482–0900
Vacant, director

ITA Publications Division
14th St. and Constitution Ave. N.W.
Washington, DC 20230
(202) 482–5487
Fax (202) 482–5819
John Ward, director

Produces and distributes ITA publications.

ITA Trade Information Center
14th St. and Constitution Ave. N.W.
Washington, DC 20230
(202) 482–0543
Toll-free (800) 833–8723
TDD (800) 833–8723
Fax (202) 482–4473

Counsels U.S. businesses on exporting. Similar services are provided by ITA's export assistance centers.

PUBLICATIONS

The ITA Publications Division *(see above)* can provide information on how to order. Titles available include:

Business America. Monthly magazine available by subscription.

U.S. Foreign Trade Highlights. Annual; contains statistics on U.S. foreign trade.

DATA AND STATISTICS

Most information available from the ITA can be obtained from the National Trade Data Bank, which can be accessed via the agency's main Internet site or at http://www.stat-usa.gov. The data also are available on CD-ROM from the National Technical Information Service (NTIS): see appendix, Ordering Government Publications.

Reference Resources

LIBRARY

COMMERCE DEPARTMENT
14th St. and Constitution Ave. N.W.
Washington, DC 20230
(202) 482–5511
Vera Whisenton, director
Open to the public
Hours: 1:00 p.m. to 4:00 p.m.

RULES AND REGULATIONS

ITA rules and regulations are published in the *Code of Federal Regulations,* Title 15, chapter 3 and Title 19, chapter 3. Proposed regulations are published in the daily *Federal Register. (See appendix for details on how to obtain and use these publications.)*

The annual report of the secretary of commerce reports on regulatory actions taken during the previous year.

▪ LEGISLATION

The ITA carries out its trade regulation responsibilities under:

Trade Agreements Act of 1979 (93 Stat. 144, 19 U.S.C. 2051). Signed by the president July 26, 1979. Approved and implemented the agreements reached in the Multilateral Trade Negotiations; its purpose is to expand U.S. foreign trade. The law overhauled the U.S. countervailing duty law, which was designed to protect domestic industry against foreign government subsidies on imported goods; and speeded up investigations and imposition of penalties under both the countervailing duty law and antidumping statutes.

Export Trading Company Act of 1982 (96 Stat. 1233, 15 U.S.C. 4001 note). Signed by the president Oct. 8, 1982. Encouraged exports by facilitating the formation of export trading companies, export trade associations, and the export trade services generally.

Trade and Tariff Act of 1984 (98 Stat. 2948, 19 U.S.C. 1654 note). Signed by the president Oct. 30, 1984. Amended the laws that govern international trade and investment, authorized the negotiation of trade agreements, extended trade preferences, and changed the tariff treatment of certain articles. Three of the act's titles are especially pertinent to the ITA. Title VI changed trade laws concerning antidumping and countervailing duties. Title VIII gave the president enforcement authority for bilateral steel agreements. Title IX gave the president the authority to seek the reduction or elimination of international trade barriers to U.S. wine exports.

The Omnibus Trade and Competitiveness Act of 1988 (100 Stat. 1107, 19 U.S.C. 2901 note.) Signed by the president Aug. 23, 1988. Amended section 201 of the Trade Act of 1974 to place a greater emphasis on industry adjustment to import competition in granting relief. Changed the antidumping and countervailing duty law to provide new provisions relating to release of business proprietary information under protective orders.

Export Enhancement Act of 1992 (106 Stat. 2199, 15 U.S.C. 4727). Signed by the president Oct. 21, 1992. Established the Trade Promotion Coordinating Committee (TPCC) to coordinate and promote the export financing activities of the United States, develop trade promotion policies and programs, and act as a central source of information on federal export promotion and export financing programs.

Freedom Support Act (106 Stat. 3322, 22 U.S.C. 5812). Signed by the president Oct. 24, 1992. Enhanced opportunities for trade and facilitated foreign investment in the independent states of the former Soviet Union.

Trade and Development Act of 2000 (P.L. 106-200). Signed by the president on May 18, 2000. Directed the International Trade Administration to take specified action to encourage the export of U.S. goods and services to sub-Saharan African countries.

▓ EXPORT ASSISTANCE CENTERS

Note: A complete listing of export assistance centers, including district and local offices, can be found at http://www.ita.doc.gov/uscs/domfld.html.

ALABAMA
950 22nd St. North, #707
Birmingham, AL 35203
(205) 731–1331
George Norton, director

ALASKA
3601 C St., #700
Anchorage, AK 99503
(907) 271–6237
Charles Becker, director

ARIZONA
2901 N. Central Ave., #970
Phoenix, AZ 85012
(602) 640–2513
Frank Woods, director

ARKANSAS
425 W. Capitol Ave., #700
Little Rock, AR 72201
(501) 324–5794
Lon Hardin, director

CALIFORNIA
101 Park Center Plaza, #1001
San Jose, CA 95113
(408) 271–7300
James S. Kennedy, director

One World Trade Center, #1670
Long Beach, CA 90831
(310) 980–4550
Joe Sachs, director

COLORADO
1625 Broadway, #680
Denver, CO 80202
(303) 844–6622
Nancy Charles-Parker, director

CONNECTICUT
213 Court St., #903
Middletown, CT 06457–3348
(860) 838–6950
Carl Jacobsen, director

DELAWARE
Served by the Philadelphia Center

FLORIDA
5600 N.W. 36th St., #617
Miami, FL 33166
(305) 526–7425
John McCartney, director

GEORGIA
285 Peachtree Center Ave. N.E., #200
Atlanta, GA 30303–1229
(404) 657–1900
Samuel Troy, director

HAWAII

300 Ala Moana Blvd., #4106
P.O. Box 50026
Honolulu, HI 96850
(808) 541–1782
Amer Kayani, manager

IDAHO

700 W. State St., 2nd Floor
Boise, ID 83720
(208) 334–3857
Steve Thompson, manager

ILLINOIS

55 W. Monroe St., #2440
Chicago, IL 60603
(312) 353–8045
Mary Joyce, director

INDIANA

11405 N. Pennsylvania St., #106
Carmel, IN 46032
(317) 582–2300
Dan Swart, manager

IOWA

210 Walnut St., #817
Des Moines, IA 50309
(515) 284–4222
Allen Patch, director

KANSAS

151 N. Volutsia
Wichita, KS 67214–4695
(316) 269–6160
George D. Lavid, manager

KENTUCKY

601 W. Broadway, #634B
Louisville, KY 40202
(502) 582–5066
John Autin, director

LOUISIANA

365 Canal St., #2150
New Orleans, LA 70130
(504) 589–6546
David Spann, director

MAINE

Maine International Trade Center
511 Congress St.
Portland, ME 04101
(207) 541–7400
Jeffrey Porter, manager

MARYLAND

401 E. Pratt St., #2432
Baltimore, MD 21202
(410) 962–4539
Michael Keaveny, director

MASSACHUSETTS

164 Northern Ave., #307
Boston, MA 02210
(617) 424–5990
Frank J. O'Connor, director

MICHIGAN

211 W. Fort St., #2220
Detroit, MI 48226
(313) 226–3650
Nell Hesse, director

MINNESOTA

45 S. 7th Ct., #2240
Minneapolis, MN 55402
(612) 348–1638
Ronald Kramer, director

MISSISSIPPI

704 E. Main St.
Raymond, MS 39154
(601) 857–0128
Hanson Ford, manager

MISSOURI

8182 Maryland Ave., #303
St. Louis, MO 63105
(314) 425–3302
Randall J. LaBounty, director

MONTANA

Served by the Boise, ID Center

NEBRASKA

11135 O St.
Omaha, NE 68137
(402) 221–3664
Meredith Bond, manager

NEVADA
1755 E. Plumb Ln., #152
Reno, NV 89502
(702) 784–5203
Jere Dabbs, manager

NEW HAMPSHIRE
17 New Hampshire Ave.
Portsmouth, NH 03801
(603) 334–6074
Susan Berry, manager

NEW JERSEY
3131 Princeton Pike
Bldg. 6, #100
Trenton, NJ 08648
(609) 989–2100
Rod Stuart, director

Gateway 1, 9th Floor
Newark, NJ 07102
(201) 645–4789
Tom Rosengren, director

NEW MEXICO
c/o Dept. of Economic Development
P.O. Box 20003
Santa Fe, NM 87504–5003
(505) 827–0350
Susan Necessary, manager

NEW YORK
20 Exchange Place, 40th Floor
New York, NY 10048
(212) 809–2642
John Lavelle, director

NORTH CAROLINA
521 E. Morehead St., #435
Charlotte, NC 28202
(704) 333–4886
Roger Fortner, director

NORTH DAKOTA
Served by the Minneapolis, MN Center

OHIO
36 E. 7th St., #2650
Cincinnati, OH 45202
(513) 684–2944
Michael Miller, director
600 Superior Ave. East, #700
Cleveland, OH 44114
(216) 522–4750
Clem Von Koschembahr (acting), director

OKLAHOMA
301 N.W. 63rd St., #330
Oklahoma City, OK 73116
(405) 231–5302
Ronald Wilson, director

OREGON
121 S.W. Salmon St., #242
Portland, OR 97204
(503) 326–3001
Scott Goddin, director

PENNSYLVANIA
615 Chestnut St., #1501
Philadelphia, PA 19106
(215) 597–6101
Maria Galindo, director

PUERTO RICO
525 F.D. Roosevelt Ave., #905
San Juan, PR 00918
(787) 766–5555
J. Enrique Vilella, director

RHODE ISLAND
1 W. Exchange St.
Providence, RI 02903
(401) 528–5104
Raimond Meerbach, director

SOUTH CAROLINA
1835 Assembly St., #172
Columbia, SC 29201
(803) 765–5345
Ann Watts, director

SOUTH DAKOTA

2001 S. Summit Ave., #SS–29A
Sioux Falls, SD 57197
(605) 330–4264
Cinnamon King, manager

TENNESSEE

404 James Robertson Pkwy., #114
Nashville, TN 37219
(615) 736–5161
Michael Speck, director

TEXAS

2050 N. Stemmons Fwy., #170
P.O. Box 420069
Dallas, TX 75207
(214) 767–0542
Bill Schrage, director

500 Dallas St., #1160
Houston, TX 77002
(713) 718–3062
James Cook, director

UTAH

324 S. State St., #221
Salt Lake City, UT 84111
(801) 524–5116
Stan Rees, director

VERMONT

National Life Bldg., Drawer 20
Montpelier, VT 05609
(802) 828–4508
James Cox, director

VIRGINIA

704 E. Franklin St., #550
Richmond, VA 23219
(804) 771–2246
William Davis Coale Jr., director

WASHINGTON

2001 Sixth Ave., #650
Seattle, WA 98121
(206) 553–5615
Laura McCall (acting), director

WEST VIRGINIA

405 Capitol St., #807
Charleston, WV 25301
(304) 347–5123
Harvey Timberlake, director

WISCONSIN

517 E. Wisconsin Ave., #596
Milwaukee, WI 53202
(414) 297–3473
Paul Churchill, director

WYOMING

Served by the Denver, CO Center

National Institute of Standards and Technology

Administration Bldg., Gaithersburg, MD 20899
Internet: http://www.nist.gov

Created by an act of Congress in 1901, the National Institute of Standards and Technology (NIST), which was called the National Bureau of Standards until 1988, works to promote U.S. economic growth by working with industry to develop and apply technology, measurements, and standards. The institute's programs also are directed toward reducing or removing technical barriers that impede the prompt introduction or exploitation of new technologies. An agency of the Commerce Department's Technology Administration, the NIST does not formally regulate industry.

NIST has an operating budget of about $864 million and operates primarily in two locations: Gaithersburg, Md. (headquarters) and Boulder, Colo. NIST employs more than 3,000 scientists, engineers, technicians, business specialists, and administrative personnel. About 1,600 guest researchers complement the staff. In addition, NIST partners with 2,000 manufacturing specialists and staff at affiliated centers around the country.

The Advanced Technology Program (ATP) provides cost-shared awards to industry to develop high-risk technologies that can enable significant commercial progress. The ATP provides funding to individual companies and to industry-led joint ventures. The program seeks to build bridges between basic research and product development. It accelerates technologies that otherwise are unlikely to be developed in time to compete in rapidly changing markets without such a partnership of industry and government.

The Manufacturing Extension Partnership (MEP) helps small and medium-sized companies to adopt new technologies. The MEP aids these companies through manufacturing extension centers in all fifty states and Puerto Rico and linking technologies and programs that connect participants into a nationwide system. This includes links to outreach and technical assistance programs of other federal, state, and local organizations.

The Malcolm Baldrige National Quality Award is part of a quality outreach program. The award program encourages continuous improvements in quality management by large U.S. manufacturers, service companies, and small businesses.

NIST's laboratory effort is planned and implemented in cooperation with industry and focuses on infrastructural technologies, such as measurements, standards, evaluated data, and text methods. It consists of eight laboratories listed below.

Building and Fire Research Laboratory focuses on improving the life-cycle quality of constructed facilities, reducing economic and human losses due to natural disasters and hazards such as fire, and improving the productivity of the U.S. construction industry. The laboratory was called in to investigate the disastrous terrorist attack at the World Trade Center in New York City on Sept. 11, 2001. The investigation, which began in August 2002, was expected to take two years. In 2002 the National Construction Safety Team Act was signed into law. The act required NIST to establish National Construction Safety Teams for deployment within forty-eight hours after events causing the failure of a building that has resulted in or posed significant potential for substantial loss of life.

Chemical Science and Technology Laboratory develops the calibration and measurement standards for a range of instruments and processes and produces Standard Reference Materials and Standard Reference Data to improve the quality, efficiency, and productivity of chemical measurements. The lab also is working to develop new technologies to monitor the environment and to minimize waste produced by the manufacturing process.

Information Technology Laboratory advises and assists industry in developing computer standards that satisfy users' needs and accommodate innovations. In addition, laboratory personnel help federal agencies in planning computer security programs, increasing awareness of the need for computer security, and carrying out computer security training. The Computer Security Resource Center, a clearinghouse of cyber security research, is available at http://csrc.nist.gov.

Computer System Security and Privacy Advisory Board (CSSPAB) was created by the Computer Security Act of 1987. The board examines issues affecting the security and privacy of sensitive (unclassified) information in federal (executive branch) computer and telecommunications systems. The board's authority does not extend to private sector systems or federal systems that process classified information. The membership of the board consists of twelve members and a chair.

Electronics and Electrical Engineering Laboratory provides the fundamental basis for all U.S. electrical measurements. Institute programs are tailored to meet measurement needs in the manufacture of semiconductor, magnetic, radio-frequency, microwave, optical, optoelectronics, and superconducting products, as well as electrical power systems.

Manufacturing Engineering Laboratory works with the nation's manufacturing sector to develop and apply technology, measurements, and standards in areas ranging from advanced machine tool controllers to enterprise integration and from single-point diamond turning to fabricating the next generation of integrated circuits.

Materials Science and Engineering Laboratory conducts research and provides information to further materials science and related technology development. Separate research initiatives address ceramics, metals, polymers, composites, and superconductors.

Physics Laboratory conducts research in the areas of quantum, electron, optical, atomic, molecular, and radiation physics. This research is complemented by work in quantum metrology and efforts to improve the accuracy and precision of time and frequency standards.

Technology Services was established as a new organization within the NIST to join, under one umbrella, traditional NIST standards and measurement services with the newly assigned extramural technology transfer activities. This office provides technical support and, in some cases, financial assistance to U.S. industry and state governments to help commercialize products that are based on new scientific discoveries.

Some NIST research is conducted at laboratories in Boulder, Colo. These laboratories work in specific areas of electronics and electrical engineering, chemical science and technology, physics, materials science and engineering, and information technology.

▓ KEY PERSONNEL

Office of the Director
Director
  Arden L. Bement Jr. .... (301) 975–2300
  Fax .... (301) 869–8972
Deputy Director
  Karen H. Brown .... (301) 975–2300
Chief Information Officer
  Cita Furlani (acting) .... (301) 975–6500
Civil Rights
  Mirta-Marie M. Keys (acting) .... (301) 975–2037
Congressional and Legislative Affairs
  Verna Hines .... (301) 975–3080
Counsel
  Michael Rubin .... (301) 975–2803
International and Academic Affairs
  B. Stephen Carpenter .... (301) 975–3069
Program
  Michael P. Casassa (acting) .... (301) 975–2667
National Quality Program
  Harry Hertz............................ (301) 975–2360
Administration and Chief Financial Officer
  Jorge Urrutia .... (301) 975–2390
  Fax .... (301) 926–7203
Acquisition and Assistance
  Phyllis A. Bower (acting) .... (301) 975–6348
Human Resources Management
  Ellen Dowd .... (301) 975–3000
Facilities Services
  Susan Carscadden .... (301) 975–3301
Management and Organization
  Sharon Bisco .... (301) 975–4054
Occupational Health and Safety
  Rosamond A. Rutledge-Burns......... (301) 975–5818
Plant
  Robert Moore .... (301) 975–6900
Financial Operations
  John McGuffin .... (301) 975–2291
Financial Policy
  William A. Smoot .... (301) 975–2550
Boulder Laboratory Director
  Vacant................................. (303) 497–3237
Laboratories
Building and Fire Research
  Jack E. Snell........................... (301) 975–5900
  Fax .... (301) 975–4032
Chemical Science and Technology
  Hratch G. Semerjian .... (301) 975–8300
  Fax .... (301) 975–3845

Electronics and Electrical Engineering
William E. Anderson.................. (301) 975–2220
Fax...................................... (301) 975–4091
Information Technology
Susan Zevin (acting).................. (301) 975–2900
Fax...................................... (301) 840–1857
Manufacturing Engineering
Dale E. Hall............................ (301) 975–3400
Fax...................................... (301) 948–5668
Materials Science and Engineering
Leslie E. Smith........................ (301) 975–5658
Fax...................................... (301) 926–8349
Physics
Katharine Gebbie...................... (301) 975–4201
Fax...................................... (301) 975–3048
Manufacturing Extension Partnership
Kevin Carr............................. (301) 975–5454
Fax...................................... (301) 963–6556
Technology Services
Richard F. Kayser..................... (301) 975–4500
Calibration Program
John Rumble Jr. (acting).............. (301) 975–2203
Information Services
Mary-Diedre Corragio................ (301) 975–2786
Measurement Services
John Rumble Jr. .... (301) 975–2203
Metric Program
Kenneth S. Butcher................... (301) 975–4859
Standard Reference Data Program
John Rumble........................... (301) 975–2200
Standards Services
Mary H. Saunders..................... (301) 975–4000
Technology Partnerships
Bruce E. Mattson...................... (301) 975–3850

■ INFORMATION SOURCES

Internet
Agency Web Site: http://www.nist.gov. Provides information on NIST programs, products, and services; an interactive feature that allows customized information searches; and links to related Internet sites maintained by government and professional organizations.

Telephone Contacts
Public Inquiries......................... (301) 975–NIST
Personnel Locator .... (301) 975–2000
Advanced Technology Program .... (800) ATP-FUND
EU Hotline.............................. (301) 921–4164
WTO Hotline........................... (301) 975–4041

Information and Publications

KEY OFFICES

NIST Communications and Inquiries
Administration Bldg., Room A902
100 Bureau Dr., Stop 3460
Gaithersburg, MD 20899-3460
(301) 975–NIST
Fax (301) 926–1630
Sharon Shaffer, chief

Answers general questions and provides information about NIST publications.

NIST Media Liaison Group
Administration Bldg., Room A900
100 Bureau Dr., Stop 3460
Gaithersburg, MD 20899-3460
(301) 975–3025
Fax (301) 926–1630
Michael Newman, chief

Provides general or detailed information about the NIST and its research to the news media.

Freedom of Information
Administration Bldg., Room A1105
100 Bureau Dr., Stop 3220
Gaithersburg, MD 20899-3220
(301) 975–4054
Fax (301) 926–7203
Sharon Bisco, FOIA officer

PUBLICATIONS
The institute issues monographs, handbooks, technical notes, and special series on standard reference data, building science, and Federal Information Processing Standards. The institute also publishes a bimonthly technical journal, *Journal of Research of the National Institute of Standards and Technology;* and a quarterly newsletter, *Technology at a Glance.* For ordering information, call (301) 975-NIST or see the agency Web site: http://www.nist.gov.

DATA AND STATISTICS
See www.nist.gov/data

NIST *Standard Reference Materials Program*
100 Bureau Dr., Stop 2321
Bldg. 202, Room 112
Gaithersburg, MD 20899-2321
(301) 975–6776
Fax (301) 926–4342
John Rumble Jr. (acting), chief

Provides an online catalogue of more than 1,300 different Standard Reference Materials (SRMs) available at the NIST. SRMs are well-characterized, homogeneous, stable materials, or simple artifacts with specific properties measured and certified by the NIST. They are used in a variety of measurement applications, including the evaluation of the accuracy of test methods, improvement of measurement compatibility among different laboratories, and establishment of measurement traceability to the NIST. See www.nist.gov/srm

National Center for Standards and Certification Information

100 Bureau Dr., Stop 2150
Bldg. 820, Room 164
Gaithersburg, MD 20899-2150
(301) 975–4040
Fax (301) 926–1559
Carmina Londono, chief

Provides up-to-date information on standards and certification programs. Maintains an extensive collection of U.S. military and other federal government specifications, U.S. industry and national standards, international standards, and selected foreign national standards. Also maintains information on World Trade Organization (WTO) activities that may affect U.S. trade opportunities with other countries that are signatories to the Agreement on Technical Barriers to Trade (Standards Code). See http://ts.nist.gov/ts/htdocs/210/ncsci/ncsci.htm

NIST Standard Reference Data Program

100 Bureau Dr., Stop 2310
North Bldg. 820, Room 110
Gaithersburg, MD 20899-2310
(301) 975–2208
Fax (301) 926–0416
John Rumble, chief

NIST provides well-documented data to scientists and engineers for use in technical problem solving, research, and development. These recommended values are based on data extracted from the world's literature, assessed for reliability, and then evaluated to select the preferred value. To increase the usefulness and accessibility of these data, NIST has developed a series of personal computer databases with interactive programs, search routines, and other calculational and graphical software features. See www.nist.gov/data

NIST Calibration Program

100 Bureau Dr., Stop 2330
North Bldg. 820, Room 235
Gaithersburg, MD 20899-2330
(301) 975–2002
Fax (301) 869–3548
John Rumble Jr. (acting), chief

NIST provides more than 500 different services to ensure that manufacturers and other users of precision instruments achieve measurements of the highest possible quality. Calibration services, available for a fee, encompass seven major areas: dimensional measurements; mechanical, including flow, acoustic, and ultrasonic; thermodynamics; optical radiation; ionizing radiation; electromagnetics, including direct current, alternating current, radio frequency, and microwave; and time and frequency. See www.ts.nist.gov/calibrations

NIST Metric Program

100 Bureau Dr., Stop 2000
North Bldg. 820, Room 321
Gaithersburg, MD 20899-2000
(301) 975–3690
Fax (301) 948–1416
Kenneth S. Butcher, chief

Seeks to accelerate the nation's transition to the metric system as the preferred system of weights and measures for U.S. trade and commerce. Helps foster the metric transition activities of all federal agencies; provides leadership and assistance on metric conversion to other organizations; and disseminates educational information to increase understanding of the metric system and to identify and remove barriers to metric usage. See http://ts.nist.gov/ts/htdocs/200/202/mpo_home.htm

Reference Resources

LIBRARY

NIST Information Services

Administration Bldg., Room E104
Gaithersburg, MD 20899-0001
(301) 975–2786
Fax (301) 869–8071
Mary-Deidre Corragio, chief
See http://nvl.nist.gov

Provides information on physics, chemistry, mathematics, engineering, and related technologies. Also has a small legal collection on federal practice and a rare books collection on the history of the development of metrology in the Western world. See also Data and Statistics (above). See http://nvl.nist.gov

ONLINE

See also Publications *(p. 442)*.

The NIST Internet site, http://www.nist.gov, provides information on NIST programs, products, and services, with links to related sites.

Computer Security Resource Clearinghouse

Provides information on computer viruses, software reviews, computer security alerts, and publications on the NIST Web site at http://csrc.nist.gov. For assistance, contact the computer security division of the NIST at (301) 975-2934.

Building and Fire Research Laboratory Information

Features computer programs developed by the NIST's Building and Fire Research Laboratories. The programs can be accessed from the Building and Fire Research Laboratory Web site at http://www.bfrl.nist.gov

RULES AND REGULATIONS

NIST rules and regulations are published in the *Code of Federal Regulations,* Title 15, chapter 2. Proposed regulations, new final regulations, and updates to the *Code of Federal Regulations* are published in the daily *Federal Register. (See appendix for details on how to obtain and use these publications.)*

LEGISLATION

The NIST carries out its responsibilities under:

"Organic Act" of the National Bureau of Standards (31 Stat. 1449, 15 U.S.C. 271). Signed by the president March 3, 1901. Established the National Bureau of Standards.

Standard Reference Data Act (82 Stat. 339, 15 U.S.C. 290). Signed by the president July 11, 1968. Gave the secretary of commerce primary responsibility for the collection, compilation, critical evaluation, publication, and dissemination of standard reference data on the properties of materials.

Radiation Control Health and Safety Act of 1968 (82 Stat. 1173, 42 U.S.C. 263). Signed by the president Oct. 18, 1968. Under this act the National Bureau of Standards provided standards and procedures to protect the public from the harmful effects of radiation. One program pro-

vided services for the accurate measurement of radiation dosage in cancer treatment.

Federal Fire Prevention and Control Act (88 Stat. 1535, 15 U.S.C. 201). Signed by the president Oct. 29, 1974. Established the Center for Fire Research to study building design and methods of reducing the effects of fire on victims, including methods of testing and certifying smoke detectors.

Federal Non-nuclear Energy Research and Development Act (88 Stat. 1878, 42 U.S.C. 5901). Signed by the president Dec. 31, 1974. Authorized the National Bureau of Standards to evaluate promising energy-related inventions submitted by individuals and small companies seeking grants from the Energy Department.

Earthquake Hazards Reduction Act of 1977 (91 Stat. 1098, 42 U.S.C. 7701). Signed by the president Oct. 7, 1977. Required the National Bureau of Standards to assist and cooperate with the Housing and Urban Development Department, other federal agencies and state and local building departments in continuing the development, testing, and improvement of model seismic design and construction provisions for local building codes.

Trade Agreements Act of 1979 Title IV (93 Stat. 144, 19. U.S.C. 2501 note). Signed by the president July 26, 1979. Approved and implemented the trade agreements negotiated under the Trade Act of 1974. The objective of this act was to foster and promote an open international trading system. Title IV, Technical Barriers to Trade (standards), deals with federal standards-related activities and established within the Commerce Department a single Standards Information Center.

National Materials and Minerals Policy, Research and Development Act of 1980 (94 Stat. 2305, 30 U.S.C. 1601 note). Signed by the president Oct. 21, 1980. Provided for a national policy on materials and for strengthening the materials research, development and production capability of the United States.

Stevenson-Wydler Technology Innovation Act of 1980 (94 Stat. 2311, 15 U.S.C. 3701–3714). Signed by the president Oct. 21, 1980. Promoted U.S. technological innovation for the achievement of national economic, environmental, and social goals. Required each federal laboratory to establish an Office of Research and Technology Application to facilitate technological transfer to the private sector.

Malcolm Baldrige National Quality Improvement Act of 1987 (101 Stat. 725, 14 U.S.C. 3711a). Signed by the president Aug. 20, 1987. Established the Malcolm Baldrige National Quality Award to be made periodically to companies and other organizations judged to be deserving of special recognition for substantially benefiting the economic or social well-being of the United States through improvements in the quality of their goods and services resulting from the effective practice of quality management.

Computer Security Act of 1987 (P.L. 100-235). Signed by the president on Jan. 8, 1988. Directed the establishment of a computer standards program for federal computer systems, including guidelines for the security of such systems. Established a Computer System Security and Privacy Advisory Board within the Department of Commerce to report on issues relating to computer systems security and privacy. Amended the Federal Property and Administrative Services Act of 1949 to require the secretary to promulgate standards and guidelines pertaining to federal computer systems on the basis of standards developed by the bureau.

The Omnibus Trade and Competitiveness Act of 1988 (100 Stat. 1107, 15 U.S.C. 271 et seq.). Signed by the president Aug. 23, 1988. Reauthorized and expanded the mission of the National Bureau of Standards and renamed it the National Institute for Standards and Technology (NIST). Established a number of regional outreach centers through which the NIST could demonstrate new manufacturing technology to small and medium-sized businesses. Formalized industrial technology services at the NIST to improve the availability of federal technology at the state and local levels. Authorized the establishment of the Advanced Technology Program to promote U.S. economic growth and competitiveness.

National Institute of Standards and Technology Authorizations Act for Fiscal Year 1989 (102 Stat. 2589, 15 U.S.C. 3704 note). Signed by the president Oct. 24, 1988. Amended the Stevenson-Wydler Technology Innovation Act of 1980 to create a Technology Administration within the Commerce Department, to be headed by an under secretary for technology. The Technology Administration included the National Institute of Standards and Technology, the National Technical Information Service, and the Office of Technology Policy (formerly the Office of Productivity, Technology and Innovation). The objective was to keep the United States competitive in world markets by stimulating U.S. industrial productivity, technology, and innovation.

High-Performance Computing Act of 1991 (105 Stat. 1594, 15 U.S.C. 5524). Signed by the president Dec. 9, 1991. Implemented a National High-Performance Computing Program under which the NIST is to conduct basic and applied measurement research to support networks, develop and propose standards and guidelines, measurement techniques, and test methods, and be responsible for developing benchmark tests and standards for high-performance computing systems and software.

American Technology Preeminence Act of 1991 (105 Stat. 7, 15 U.S.C. 271, 271n, 3701, 3717). Signed by the president Feb. 14, 1992. Amended the Omnibus Trade and Competitiveness Act of 1988 relative to the Advanced Technology Program, by modifying the fund allocation guidelines for the program. Also amended various provisions of the Stevenson-Wydler Technology Innovation Act of 1980. Established a National Quality Council to establish national goals and priorities for quality performance in all sectors of the economy nationwide.

National Technology Transfer and Advancement Act of 1995 (110 Stat. 775, 15 U.S.C. 3701 note). Signed by the president March 7, 1996. Amended the Stevenson-Wydler Technology Innovation Act of 1980 with respect to inventions made under Cooperative Research and Development Agreements (CRADAs). Guaranteed collaborating industry partners' right to choose an exclusive license for a field of use for any invention created under a CRADA. Required that federal agencies pay each year to federal employee inventors first $2,000 and thereafter at least 15 percent of the royalties received for inventions.

Next Generation Internet Research Act of 1998 (112 Stat. 2919, 15 U.S.C. 5501 note). Signed by the president on Oct. 28, 1998. Amended the High-Performance Computing Act of 1991 to authorize appropriations for fiscal years 1999 and 2000 for the Next Generation Internet program. Program objectives included increasing Internet capabilities and improving Internet performance; developing an advanced testbed network connecting research sites; and developing advanced Internet applications that meet national goals and agency mission needs.

National Construction Safety Team Act (P.L. 107-231). Signed by the president on Oct. 1, 2002. Authorized the establishment of National Construction Safety Teams for deployment within forty-eight hours after events causing the failure of a building that has resulted in or posed significant potential for substantial loss of life. Granted a team investigation priority over any other investigation of any other federal agency, with the exception of related investigations conducted by the National Transportation Safety Board or building failures that may have been caused by criminal acts. This legislation gave NIST no regulatory authority over the adoption of building standards, codes, and practices but rather charged the agency with reporting its findings to Congress.

Homeland Security Act of 2002 (P.L. 107-296). Signed by the president on Nov. 25, 2002. Amended the National Institute of Standards and Technology Act to revise and expand the mandate of NIST to develop standards, guidelines, and associated methods and techniques for information systems. Renamed the Computer System Security and Privacy Advisory Board as the Information Security and Privacy Board and required it to advise the director of OMB (instead of the secretary of Commerce) on information security and privacy issues pertaining to federal government information systems.

Cyber Security Research and Development Act (P.L. 107-305). Signed by the president on Nov. 27, 2002. Amended the National Institute of Standards and Technology Act (NISTA) to require the NIST director, through the director of the Office for Information Security Programs, to establish a program of assistance to institutions of higher education that enter into partnerships with for-profit entities to support research to improve computer and network security. Amended NISTA to authorize appropriations to enable the Information Security and Privacy Board to (1) identify emerging issues related to computer security, privacy, and cryptography;

(2) convene public meetings, and (3) publish and disseminate information.

REGIONAL OFFICE

NIST BOULDER
325 S. Broadway
Boulder, CO 80303
Internet: http://www.boulder.nist.gov

Public and Business Affairs
(303) 497–3246
Fred P. McGehan, public affairs officer

National Oceanic and Atmospheric Administration

14th St. and Pennsylvania Ave. N.W., Washington, DC 20230
Internet: http://www.noaa.gov

The National Oceanic and Atmospheric Administration (NOAA), within the Commerce Department, was established by Reorganization Plan No. 4 on Oct. 3, 1970.

The agency's principal functions are to explore, map, and chart the global ocean and its living resources and to manage, use, and conserve those resources. The agency describes, monitors, and predicts conditions in the atmosphere, ocean, sun, and space environment; reports the weather of the United States and its possessions; issues warnings against impending destructive natural events; disseminates environmental data through a system of meteorological, oceanographic, geophysical, and solar-terrestrial data centers; manages and conserves living marine resources and their habitats, including certain endangered species and marine mammals; and develops policy on ocean management and use along the coastline of the United States and provides grants for marine research, education, and advisory services. The agency also plays a substantial role in the federal research effort on the potential for global climate change.

The National Ocean Service coordinates coastal zone management and information; conducts marine environmental quality and pollution research, development and monitoring; and directs programs to produce charts and related information for safe navigation of the nation's waterways, territorial seas, and national airspace.

Within NOS, the Office of Ocean and Coastal Resource Management (OCRM) has the primary responsibility of developing resource management plans for the nation's coastal zone. OCRM administers the provisions of the Coastal Zone Management Act of 1972 and is responsible for designating and managing the nation's network of marine sanctuaries. OCRM also administers the National Estuarine Research Reserve System and the National Ocean Minerals and Energy Program.

The National Weather Service program prepares and delivers weather predictions and warnings and exchanges information with international organizations such as the World Meteorological Organization and the International Civil Aviation Organization. The National Weather Service has six regional offices. Presently, the National Weather Service is undergoing a modernization plan that will replace the outdated equipment of the 1960s with the most modern technological advances, which include Next Generation Radar (NEXRAD), Automated Surface Observing Stations (ASOS), more sophisticated weather satellites, and a computerized system for the processing and communication of weather information. These tools will enable the operational forecaster to pinpoint the location and timing of severe storms more accurately.

The National Marine Fisheries Service works to rebuild and maintain sustainable fisheries; promote the recovery of protected species; and protect and maintain the health of coastal marine habitats. To advance these goals, the service measures the social and economic effects of fishing practices and regulations, enforces fishing laws, and manages fish and marine mammals. Fisheries service scientists also research the biology and populations status of marine animals and assess their habitat needs.

The National Environmental Satellite, Data, and Information Service is responsible for the NOAA's environmental satellite and data management programs. The program includes management services to develop and operate civilian satellite systems for observing land, ocean, atmospheric, and solar conditions required by governments, commerce, industry, and the general public. The office operates the Satellite Operational Control Center and Command and Data Acquisition facilities to control and track the satellites and to read their data. NOAA's satellite service also operates the mission control center for an international search and rescue network.

The Office of Oceanic and Atmospheric Research is responsible for coordinating the NOAA's oceanic and atmospheric research and development programs. The office conducts research to further the understanding of phenomena such as the El Niño ocean current, global warming, and ozone depletion. The office also coordinates NOAA programs with the Office of Science and Technology Policy; the Federal Coordinating Council for Science, Engineering and Technology Policy; the National Science Foundation; the National Academy of Sciences; universities; international scientific organizations; and other groups.

NOAA also houses the nation's seventh uniformed service, the NOAA Corps, a force of 299 commissioned officers who operate a sixteen-ship research fleet and pilot NOAA research and hurricane warning aircraft.

▨ KEY PERSONNEL

Under Secretary and Administrator
Conrad C. Lautenbacher, Jr., USN
(Ret.).................................... (202) 482–3436
Assistant Secretary and Deputy Administrator
Dr. James Mahoney.................... (202) 482–3567
Chief Financial and Administrative Officer
Sonya Stewart.......................... (202) 482–2291
Civil Rights
Alfred Corea........................... (301) 713–0500
Chief Scientist
Vacant................................. (202) 482–2977
General Counsel
James Walpole.......................... (202) 482–4080
Legislative Affairs
Mary Beth Nethercutt.................. (202) 482–4981
NOAA Corps
Rear Adm. Evelyn Fields............... (301) 443–1045
Policy and Strategic Planning
James Burgess, Acting Dir............. (202) 482–5916
Public and Constituent Affairs
Jordan P. St.John...................... (202) 482–5647
National Environmental Satellite, Data, and Information Service
  Assistant Administrator
  Greg Withee........................... (301) 457–5115
  Climatic Data
  Thomas Karl........................... (704) 271–4476
  Geophysical Data
  Michael Loughridge.................... (303) 497–6215

Oceanographic Data
  Kurt Schuebele........................ (301) 713–3267
Executive Operation Officer
  Ralph Coulin.......................... (301) 457–5115
Integrated Program Office
  John Cunningham...................... (303) 427–2070
Research and Applications
  James Purdom.......................... (301) 763–8127
Satellite Data Processing and Distribution
  Helen Wood............................ (301) 457–5120
Satellite Operations
  Kathy Kelly............................ (301) 457–5130
Systems Development
  Gary K. Davis.......................... (301) 457–5277
National Marine Fisheries Service
  Assistant Administrator
  Dr. William Hogarth................... (301) 713–2239
  Enforcement
  Dale Jones............................. (301) 427–2300
  Habitat Conservation
  Rollie Schmitten....................... (301) 713–2325
  Industry and Trade
  Linda Chavez.......................... (301) 713–2379
  Intergovernmental and Recreational Activities
  Richard Schaefer...................... (301) 427–2014
  Protected Resources
  Don Knowles.......................... (301) 713–2332
  Science and Technology
  William Fox........................... (301) 713–2367
  Sustainable Fisheries
  Clarence Pautzke...................... (301) 713–2334
National Ocean Service
  Assistant Administrator
  Margaret Davidson (acting).......... (301) 713–3074
  Coast Survey
  Capt. David MacFarland.............. (301) 713–2770
  Ocean and Coastal Resource Management
  Jeffrey Benoit......................... (301) 713–3155
  Ocean Resources, Conservation, and Assessment
  Don Scavia............................ (202) 713–2989
National Weather Service
  Assistant Administrator
  John J. Kelly Jr. .... (301) 713–0689
  Deputy Assistant Administrator (Operations)
  John Jones............................ (301) 713–0711
  Hydrology
  Frank Richards........................ (301) 713–1658
  Meteorology
  Louis Ucellini......................... (301) 713–0700
National Centers for Environmental Prediction
  Louis Ucellini......................... (301) 763–8016

National Hurricane Center (1320 S. Dixie Hwy., #631,
Coral Gables, FL 33146)
Max Mayfield...........................(305) 229–4470
Systems Development
Douglas Sargeant......................(301) 713–0745
Systems Operations
Walter Telesetsky ....(301) 713–0165
Oceanic and Atmospheric Research
Assistant Administrator
Dave Evans.............................(301) 713–2458
Environmental Research Laboratories
James Rasmussen......................(301) 713–2458
Resources Management
Mary Anne Whitcomb.................(301) 713–2454
Program Development and Coordination
William Hooke ....(301) 713–0460

▮ INFORMATION SOURCES

Internet

Agency Web Site: http://www.noaa.gov. Provides information on NOAA programs, with links to data centers and other divisions of NOAA.

Telephone Contacts

Personnel Locator..........................(301) 713–4000

Information and Publications

KEY OFFICES

NOAA Public and Constituent Affairs

14th St. and Pennsylvania Ave. N.W., Room 6013
Washington, DC 20230
(202) 482–5647
Vacant, director

Answers questions, distributes publications, and issues news releases. Maintains a mailing list.

Freedom of Information

AT-IMS 2
6010 Executive Blvd., Room 714
Rockville, MD 20852
(301) 443–8967
Marcia Kregg, FOI officer

PUBLICATIONS

Distribution Division

NOAA National Ocean Service
6501 Lafayette Avenue (N/ACC3)
Riverdale, MD 20737-1199
(800) 638–8975
DC area (301) 436–6990
Fax orders (301) 436–6829

Offers nautical and aeronautical charts and publications. Chart catalogs are free upon request.

DATA AND STATISTICS

National Environmental Satellite, Data, and Information Service (NESDIS)

Satellite Data Processing and Distribution Office
Suitland and Silver Hill Roads
Federal Office Bldg. 4
Suitland, MD 20233
(301) 457–5120
Helen Wood, director

Manages all U.S. civil operational remote-sensing satellite systems and provides a variety of space-derived and environmental data and information products and services. Operates polar-orbiting, geostationary, and land satellites to provide real-time products to users. Also gathers data collected by global and national organizations for processing and dissemination by its three data centers, listed below.

National Climatic Data Center

Federal Bldg.
Asheville, NC 28801
(704) 271–4476
Thomas Karl, director

A central source of historical weather information. Data available include sky cover, visibility, precipitation, pressure, high and low temperature, wind direction, wind speed, degree days, and humidity. NCDC provides worldwide satellite cloud photos and analyses, infrared imagery, and data and computer-derived products from operational and experimental environmental satellites.

National Geophysical Data Center
325 Broadway
Boulder, CO 80303
(303) 497–6215
Michael Loughridge, director

Provides solid earth geophysical data on accelerograms, earthquakes, tsunamis, volcanos, magnetic surveys, and secular change. Provides marine geology and geophysical data on seismic reflection, bathymetry, gravimetrics, geomagnetic total field measurements, cores, samples, sediments, and heat flow. Also provides solar-terrestrial physics data on the ionosphere, solar activity, geomagnetic variation, auroras, cosmic rays, airglow, and ice and snow.

National Oceanographic Data Center
1315 East-West Hwy.
Silver Spring, MD 20910
(301) 713–3267
Henry Frey, director

Provides the world's largest collection of oceanographic data. Data available include temperature, salinity, conductivity, oxygen, inorganic phosphate, total phosphorus, nitrite-nitrogen, nitrate-nitrogen, silicate-silicon, and pH. Also available is information on ocean pollution and on surface currents, plankton standing crop, chlorophyll concentrations, and rates of primary productivity. Special databases are available, such as the one for ocean thermal energy conversion.

Reference Resources

LIBRARY

NOAA Library and Information Services Division
1315 East-West Hwy.
Silver Spring, MD 20910
(301) 713–2600

Headquarters library; maintains a collection of current books, journals, and monographs dealing with oceanic and atmospheric phenomena.

RULES AND REGULATIONS

NOAA rules and regulations are published in the *Code of Federal Regulations*, Title 15 (general regulations), Title 50, parts 201–295 (marine mammals and fisheries), parts 401–453 (joint regulations with the U.S. Fish and Wildlife Service) and parts 601–680 (fisheries conservation and management). Proposed regulations, new final regulations, and updates to the *Code of Federal Regulations* are published in the daily *Federal Register*. *(See appendix for details on how to obtain and use these publications.)*

■ LEGISLATION

The NOAA carries out its responsibilities under:

Whaling Convention Act of 1949 (64 Stat. 421, 16 U.S.C. 916). Signed by the president Aug. 9, 1950. Provided for the licensing, enforcement of regulations, and research to assist the International Whaling Commission established in 1946.

Tuna Convention Acts of 1950 (64 Stat. 777, 16 U.S.C. 951). Signed by the president Sept. 7, 1950. Provided authority to the secretary of commerce to issue regulations to protect the tuna population to ensure the maximum sustained catch.

Fur Seal Act of 1966 (80 Stat. 1149, 16 U.S.C. 1151). Signed by the president Nov. 2, 1966. Amended earlier laws providing for management of the fur seal herd and administration of the Pribilof Islands. Implemented the protocol on fur seals signed by the United States, Canada, Japan, and the Soviet Union.

Public Law 92–205 (85 Stat. 735, 15 U.S.C. 330). Signed by the president Dec. 18, 1971. Required persons engaged in weather modification activities to submit to the secretary of commerce reports describing these activities. A 1976 amendment to the act provided for research into weather modification technology.

Marine Mammal Protection Act of 1972 (86 Stat. 1027, 16 U.S.C. 1361). Signed by the president Oct. 21, 1972. Established a moratorium on the taking of marine mammals and a ban on the importation of marine mammals and marine mammal products with certain exceptions. Amended in 1994 to strengthen the law's provisions protecting marine mammals from incidental harm in commercial fishing.

Marine Protection, Research and Sanctuaries Act of 1972 (86 Stat. 1052, 32 U.S.C. 1401). Signed by the president Oct. 23, 1972. Established a system for regulating the dumping of materials into ocean waters and for the transportation of these materials. Authorized research into ocean dumping, including the long-range effects of pollution, overfishing and man-induced changes of ocean ecosystems.

Coastal Zone Management Act of 1972 (86 Stat. 1280, 16 U.S.C. 1451). Signed by the president Oct. 27, 1972. Authorized the secretary of commerce to make grants and contracts with any coastal state for developing and implementing a management program for the coastal zone and for acquiring and operating estuarine sanctuaries. Later amendments dealt with impacts resulting from coastal energy activities.

Endangered Species Act of 1973 (87 Stat. 884, 16 U.S.C. 1531). Signed by the president Dec. 28, 1973. Provided for the conservation of endangered species of fish, wildlife, and plants by identifying these species and implementing plans for their survival.

Fishery Conservation Management Act of 1976 (90 Stat. 331, 16 U.S.C. 1801). Signed by the president April 13, 1976. Extended the U.S. exclusive fishery zone to 200 from 12 nautical miles and set limits on foreign vessels fishing within these waters. This act has been amended numerous times.

Deep Seabed Hard Minerals Resources Act (94 Stat. 553, 30 U.S.C. 1401). Signed by the president June 28, 1980. Established a framework for the development and deployment of deep seabed mining technologies and authorized the NOAA to issue licenses for exploration and permits for commercial recovery.

Ocean Thermal Energy Conversion Act of 1980 (94 Stat. 974, 42 U.S.C. 9109). Signed by the president Aug. 3, 1980. Authorized the NOAA to issue licenses and regulations for research into the conversion to energy of differences in ocean temperatures. Research and development authority was left to the Energy Department.

Comprehensive Environmental Responses Compensation and Liability Act of 1980 (94 Stat. 2767, 42 U.S.C. 9601 note). Signed by the president Dec. 11, 1980. This act, commonly referred to as "Superfund," designated the president as trustee for natural resources. The president delegated his trusteeship for marine resources to the NOAA.

Oceans Act of 1992 (106 Stat. 5039, 16 U.S.C. 1431). Signed by the president Nov. 4, 1992 Amended the Marine Mammal Protection Act of 1972. Title III established a program to examine trends of marine mammal population and ensure effective responses to strandings and catastrophic events involving marine mammals.

Airport and Airways Improvement Act (108 Stat. 698, 26 U.S.C. 9502). Signed by the president Aug. 23, 1994. Authorized the secretary of transportation to reimburse NOAA from the Airport and Airway Trust Fund for the cost of providing the Federal Aviation Administration with aviation weather reporting services.

Homeland Security Act of 2002 (P.L. 107-296). Signed by the president Nov. 25, 2002. Transferred to Homeland Security the functions, personnel, assets, and liabilities of the Integrated Hazard Information System of the National Oceanic and Atmospheric Administration, which was renamed FIRESAT.

National Oceanic and Atmospheric Administration Commissioned Officers Corps Act of 2002 (P.L. 107-372). Signed by the president Dec. 19, 2002. Applied certain specified provisions of federal law pertaining to the armed forces to the NOAA Commissioned Officer Corps, including ones dealing with leave, retirement, or separation for physical disability, and with computation of retired pay. Allowed the president to transfer NOAA vessels, equipment, stations, and officers to a military department in times of emergency, and prescribed rules for such cooperation.

◼ REGIONAL OFFICES

National Marine Fisheries Service

NORTHEAST REGION
(CT, DC, DE, IL, IN, MA, MD, ME, MI, MN, NH, NJ, NY, OH, PA, RI, VA, WV)
1 Blackburn Dr.
Gloucester, MA 01930
(978) 281–9300
Patricia Kurkul, regional administrator

SOUTHEAST REGION
(AL, FL, GA, LA, MS, NC, PR, SC, TX)
9721 Executive Center Dr. North
St. Petersburg, FL 33702
(813) 570–5301
Joe Powers (acting), regional administrator

NORTHWEST REGION
(CO, ID, MT, ND, OR, SD, UT, WA, WY)
7600 Sand Point Way N.E.
BIN C15700, Bldg. 1
Seattle, WA 98115
(206) 526–6150
Donna Darm (acting), regional administrator

SOUTHWEST REGION
(AZ, CA, GU, HI, NV)
501 W. Ocean Blvd. #4200
Long Beach, CA 90802
(562) 980–4000
Rebecca Lent, regional administrator

ALASKA REGION
(AK)
P.O. Box 21668
Juneau, AK 99802–1668
(907) 586–7221
James Balsiger, regional administrator

National Weather Service

EASTERN REGION
(CT, DC, DE, MA, MD, ME, NC, NH, NJ, NY, OH, PA,
  RI, SC, VA, VT, WV)
630 Johnson Ave., #1836
Bohemia, NY 11716–2626
(516) 244–0100
Dean Gulezian, director

SOUTHERN REGION
(AL, AR, FL, GA, LA, MS, NM, OK, PR, TN, TX, VI)
819 Taylor St., #10A26
Fort Worth, TX 76102–6171
(817) 978–2651
Bill Proeuza, director

CENTRAL REGION
(CO, KS, KY, IA, IL, IN, MI, MN, MO, ND, NE, SD, WI,
  WY)
601 E. 12th St., #1836
Kansas City, MO 64106–2897
(816) 426–5400
Dennis McCarthy, director

WESTERN REGION
(AZ, CA, ID, MT, NV, OR, UT, WA)
125 S. State St., #1210
Salt Lake City, UT 84147–1102
(801) 524–5122
Vicki Nadolski, director

ALASKA REGION
(AK)
222 W. Seventh Ave., #23, Room 517
Anchorage, AK 99513–7575
(907) 271–5136
Rich Przywarty, director

PACIFIC REGION
(GU, HI)
737 Bishop St., #2200
Honolulu, HI 96813
(808) 532–6416
Richard Hagemeyer, director

Patent and Trademark Office

2011 S. Clark Place, Arlington, VA 22202
Mailing address: Washington, DC 20231
Internet: http://www.uspto.gov

On April 10, 1790, President George Washington signed the first patent bill. Three years earlier, the Constitutional Convention had given Congress the power to "promote the process of science and useful arts by securing for limited times to authors and inventors the exclusive right to their respective writings and discoveries."

The U.S. Patent Office became an actual entity in 1802 when an official in the State Department was designated as superintendent of patents. In 1849 the Patent Office was moved to the Interior Department, and in 1925 its authority was transferred to the Commerce Department. The name of the agency was changed on Jan. 2, 1975, to the Patent and Trademark Office (PTO). The functions of the PTO are to examine and issue patents on new and useful inventions and to examine and register trademarks used with goods and services in interstate commerce.

The PTO examines applications for three kinds of patents: design patents (issued for fourteen years from the date of application), plant patents (issued for twenty years from the date of application), and utility patents (issued for twenty years). Patents provide inventors with exclusive rights to the results of their creative efforts. The patent system is intended to give incentive to invent, to invest in research and development, to commercialize new technology, and to make public inventions that otherwise would be kept secret. PTO received 326,081 utility, plant, and reissue (UPR) applications in FY 2001. Increases in the number of applications in communications, information processing, and biotechnology led to the 11.2 percent growth over the previous year. For FY 2002, UPR applications were expected to increase another 12 percent, with the high-technology areas leading this growth.

In FY 2001 PTO received 232,939 trademark applications, including 296,388 classes for registration, marking the second highest level of filings ever recorded. A trademark consists of any distinctive word, name, symbol, or device used by manufacturers, merchants, or businesses to identify goods or services or to distinguish them from those manufactured or sold by others. Trademarks, registered for twenty years with renewal rights, are examined by the PTO to ensure compliance with various statutory requirements to prevent unfair competition and consumer deception.

In addition, the office sells printed copies of issued documents, hears and decides appeals from prospective inventors and trademark applicants, participates in legal proceedings involving the issue of patent or trademark registration, and helps to represent the United States in international patent policy matters. The PTO maintains a list of agents and attorneys who are qualified to practice before it.

▨ KEY PERSONNEL

Undersecretary of Commerce for Intellectual Property and Director
James E. Rogan . . . . (703) 305–8600
Fax . . . . (703) 305–8664

Deputy Undersecretary of Commerce for Intellectual Property and Deputy Director
Jon W. Dudas . . . . (703) 305–8700

Chief Information Officer
Doug Bourgeois . . . . (703) 305–9400

Congressional Liaison
Janie Cooksey . . . . (703) 305–9310

Corporate Planning and Budget
Michelle Picard, (acting) . . . . (703) 305–4217

Enrollment and Discipline
Harry Moatz.......................... (703) 306–4097
External Affairs
Lois E. Boland .... (703) 305-8700
General Counsel
James Toupin .... (703) 305-9035
Chief Financial Officer and Chief Administrative Officer
Jo-Anne Barnard .... (703) 305–9200
Fax................................... (703) 305–8825
Administrative Services
John Hassett .... (703) 305–8183
Civil Rights
Marie Campo.......................... (703) 305–8292
TDD .... (703) 305–8059
Finance
Michelle Picard....................... (703) 305–8360
Human Resources
Diane Atchinson (acting)............. (703) 305–8062
Procurement
Michael Anastasio..................... (703) 305–8219
Patent Appeals and Interferences
Bruce H. Stoner Jr..................... (703) 308–9797
Patents
Commissioner
Nicholas Godici .... (703) 305–8800
Fax................................... (703) 305–8825
Trademarks (2900 Crystal Dr., Arlington, VA 22202-3513)
Commissioner
Anne H. Chasser .... (703) 306-3109
Fax................................... (703) 308–7220

▨ INFORMATION SOURCES

Internet
Agency Web Site: http://www.uspto.gov. Includes agency information, forms that can be downloaded, searchable databases of patents, and links to other intellectual property office web sites.

Telephone Contacts
Automated Help Desk .... (703) 308–9000
Personnel Locator .... (703) 308–4455
TDD...................................... (703) 305–7785
General Inquiries......................... (800) 786–9199
Washington, D.C. area .... (703) 308–4357

Information and Publications

KEY OFFICES
Mailing address for PTO offices is P.O. Box 1450, Alexandria, VA 22313-1450.

PTO Public Affairs
2121 Crystal Dr., #0100
Arlington, VA 22202
(703) 305–8341
Richard Maulsby, director

Answers questions, distributes publications, issues news releases and responds to press inquiries.

Freedom of Information
Crystal Park, PK-2
2121 Crystal Dr.
Arlington, VA 22202
(703) 305–9035
Fax (703) 308–5258

PTO Publications
Crystal Park 3
2231 Crystal Dr.
Arlington, VA 22202
(703) 305–8594
Fax (703) 305–4372
Richard Bawcombe, director

Maintains a list of current information available to the public.

PTO Search and Information Resources
Crystal Park 3, Room 702
Arlington, VA 22202
(703) 308–3105
Fax (703) 308–6879
Frederick Schmidt, administrator

Publishes reports on patent activity; maintains patent files and databases.

PUBLICATIONS
Most U.S. PTO publications are no longer available but may be downloaded from the USPTO Web site: www.uspto.gov

DATA AND STATISTICS

PTO Search and Information Resources maintains a patent file that contains more than 6.5 million distinct U.S. patents. These are classified and cross-referenced into approximately 158,000 categories of technology. The technology assessment and forecast program maintains a master database covering all U.S. patents.

Reference Resources

LIBRARIES

See also Data and Statistics, above.

PTO Library

Crystal Plaza, Bldg. 3, 2nd Floor
2021 S. Clark Pl.
Arlington, VA 22202
(703) 308–0808
Kristin Vajs, manager
Hours: 7:30 a.m. to 6:00 p.m. (5:00 p.m. for public)

Contains material of a scientific or technical nature.

Public Patent Search Room

Crystal Plaza, Bldg. 3
2021 S. Clark Pl.
Arlington, VA 22202
(703) 308–0595
Edith Wilkniss, manager
Hours: 8:00 a.m. to 8:00 p.m.

Trademark Search Library

2900 Crystal Dr.
South Tower Bldg. 2, B30
Arlington, VA 22202
(703) 308–9800
Marilyn Ricks, chief, trademark search branch
Hours: 8:00 a.m. to 5:00 p.m.

Library of Congress Copyright Office

James Madison Bldg., Room 401
1st St. and Independence Ave. S.E.
Washington, DC 20540
(202) 707–3000
Marybeth Peters, register of copyrights

Provides information on copyright registration procedures, requirements, and copyright law. Registers copyright claims; maintains records of copyright registrations and transfers. Copyright files are open to the public for research, or searches may be conducted by the library staff for a fee. The Copyright Office is not permitted to give legal advice. For information on Copyrights see Library of Congress.

RULES AND REGULATIONS

PTO proposed regulations, new final regulations, and updates to the *Code of Federal Regulations* are published in the daily *Federal Register. (See appendix for details on how to obtain and use these publications.)*

■ LEGISLATION

The PTO carries out its responsibilities under authority granted in the following legislation:

Trademark Act of 1946, as amended (60 Stat. 427, 15 U.S.C. 1051). Signed by the president July 5, 1946. Revised and codified earlier statutes pertaining to the protection of trademarks used in interstate commerce.

Title 35 of the U.S. Code. Established the PTO and the U.S. patent system. All amendments related to patent legislation were covered under this title. Authorized the administration of patent laws, derived from the act of July 19, 1952, and subsequent enactment. Made available revenues from fees, to the extent provided for in appropriations acts, to the commissioner to carry out the activities of the office. Authorized the PTO to charge international fees for activities undertaken pursuant to the Patent Cooperation Treaty. Authorized the deployment of automated search systems of the office to the public.

44 U.S.C. 1337-1338 of the U.S. Code. Authorized the PTO to print patents, trademarks, and other matters relating to the business of the office.

Intellectual Property and Communications Omnibus Reform Act of 1999 (15 U.S.C. 11225). Signed by the president on Nov. 29, 1999. (Part of Consolidated Appropriations Act, FY 2000.) Title III: Anticybersquatting Consumer Protection Act amended the Trademark Act of 1946 to make liable in a civil action by the owner of a trademark any person who, with a bad faith intent to profit from that trademark, registers or uses a domain name which is (1) identical or confusingly similar to a distinctive mark; (2) dilutive of a famous mark; or (3) is a protected trademark, word, or name. Title IV: American Inventors Protection Act of 1999 provided protection for inventors against deceptive practices of certain invention promotion companies. Reduced certain patent fees and emphasized that trademark fees could only be used for trademark-related activities. Protected against patent infringement for a party who had, in good faith, commercially used the subject matter before the effective filing date. Established the PTO as an agency within the Department of Commerce, subject to the policy direction of the secretary of commerce. Provided authority for the electronic filing, maintenance, and publication of documents.

Technology, Education, and Copyright Harmonization Act of 2002 (P.L. 107-273). Signed by the president Nov. 2, 2002. Intellectual Property and High Technology Technical Amendments Act of 2002 amended federal patent and trademark law, as amended by the Intellectual Property and Communications Omnibus Reform Act of 1999 (IPCORA) and the American Inventor's Protection Act (AIPA), to specify that third-party requesters were persons who may invoke reexamination of a patent in light of new evidence affecting its patentability. Subtitle D: Madrid Protocol Implementation Act amended the Trademark Act of 1946 to set forth the Madrid Protocol concerning the international registration of trademarks. Authorized the owner of a basic application for trademark registration pending before, or of a basic registration granted by, the PTO who is a U.S. national, is domiciled in the United States, or has a real and effective industrial or commercial establishment in the United States to file an international application with the PTO.

Defense
Department

The Pentagon, Washington, DC 20301
Internet: http://www.defenselink.mil

Army Corps of Engineers

20 Massachusetts Ave. N.W., Washington, DC 20314
Internet: http://www.usace.army.mil

The Army Corps of Engineers regulates all construction projects in the navigable waterways of the United States. It also regulates the use of special areas, designating both danger zones (areas that may be used by the Defense Department for military exercises), and restricted areas (areas that are reserved for special uses).

In addition, the corps promulgates regulations governing the transportation and dumping of dredged materials in navigable waters.

The corps is a division of the Army Department, within the Defense Department. The chief of engineers is the army's chief engineer and the commander of the corps of engineers and is appointed by the president and confirmed by the Senate.

The majority of the corps' responsibilities involve water resource development projects. The corps develops, plans, and builds various structures—dams, reservoirs, levees, harbors, waterways, and locks—to protect areas from floods, reduce transportation costs, supply water for municipal and industrial use, generate hydroelectric power, create recreational areas, improve water and wildlife quality, and protect the shorelines of oceans and lakes.

The Army Corps of Engineers also provides assistance to state, local, and nonfederal water resource management groups, as well as to foreign countries.

Corps regulatory activities are administered by the Directorate of Civil Works. The directorate has primary responsibility for granting permits for structures or work in or affecting the navigable waters of the United States, for the discharge of dredged or fill materials in navigable waters, and for the transportation of dredged material to ocean dumping grounds. This nationwide civil works organization, consisting of 650 officers and more than 35,000 civilians, works to ensure, through administrative proceedings and the solicitation of public comments, that proposed construction projects are not contrary to the public interest. The directorate is located in eleven divisions, forty districts, and hundreds of area, project, and resident engineer offices worldwide.

Public benefit is determined by judging each proposal against several factors, including conservation, economics, aesthetic and cultural value, navigation, recreation, agricultural and mineral value, and private property rights.

The Directorate of Military Programs manages all Army construction, installations, family housing, real estate, facilities requirements, and real property maintenance.

The directorate also is responsible for a major portion of construction programs for the Air Force.

KEY PERSONNEL

Commander
Lt. Gen. Robert B. Flowers............. (202) 761–0000
Fax.................................... (202) 761–1683
Deputy Commander
Col. Michael J. Walsh .... (202) 761–0002
Commander's Staff Group
Lt. Col. Ed Gulley .... (202) 761–1130
Chief of Engineers Office
Col. Douglas Horn .... (703) 693–4400
Civil Works
Maj. Gen. Robert Griffin.............. (202) 761–0099
Corporate Information
Wilbert Barrios........................ (202) 761–0273
Human Resources
Susan Duncan .... (202) 761–0558

Logistics
Gary L. Anderson .... (202) 761–5455
Military Programs
Maj. Gen. James Cheatham (acting) .. (202) 761–0379
Real Estate
Linda D. Garvin .... (202) 761–0483
Research and Development
Michael J. O'Connor .... (202) 761–1839
Resource Management
Stephen Coakley .... (202) 761–0077
Chief Counsel
Robert M. Andersen .... (202) 761–0018
Engineer Inspector General
Lt. Col. Willie A. James .... (703) 428–6572
Safety and Occupational Health
Robert E. Stout .... (202) 761–8566
Audits
John E. Templeton .... (202) 761–0061
Security and Law Enforcement
Lt. Col. Terrence P. Ryan .... (202) 761–8725
History
Paul K. Walker .... (703) 761–0360
Contracting
Bunny Greenhouse .... (202) 761–0566
Small Business
Judith W. Blake .... (202) 761–8789
Equal Employment Opportunity
John S. Sellmansberger .... (202) 761–0095

■ INFORMATION SOURCES

Internet

Agency Web Site: http://www.usace.army.mil. Provides information on Corps of Engineers activities, news releases, and links to related government Internet sites.

Telephone Contacts

Information .... (202) 761–0660
Switchboard/Locator .... (703) 545–6700

Information and Publications

KEY OFFICES

OFFICE OF PUBLIC AFFAIRS
Office of the Chief of Engineers
441 G St. N.W.
Washington, DC 20314–1000
(202) 761–0010
Fax (202) 761–1803

Provides information on operations of the Army Corps of Engineers. Answers or refers all questions about the corps and issues news releases and publications.

FREEDOM OF INFORMATION
Office of the Chief Counsel
441 G St. N.W.
Washington, DC 20314–1000
(202) 761–8557
Richard Frank, FOI contact

PUBLICATIONS

Information about corps publications may be obtained from the Office of Public Affairs or the nearest regional office.

Three Army Corps of Engineers publications that are particularly useful are:

Annual Civil Works Report

Digest of Water Resources Policies. Describes all corps policies, powers, and regulations.

Regulatory Program Applicant Information. Provides information on obtaining corps permits.

DATA AND STATISTICS

The best source of data and statistics related to the corps is the *Annual Civil Works Report*. Detailed information also is contained in the *Digest of Water Resources Policies.* Both publications are available from the Office of Public Affairs.

In addition, units of the corps produce reports on proposed projects; contact the Directorate of Civil Works or the Office of Public Affairs to find out which office within the corps has specific types of information needed.

Reference Resources

LIBRARY
441 G St. N.W.
Washington, DC 20314–1000
(703) 428–7430
Lee Porter, chief
Hours: 8:30 a.m. to 4:00 p.m.

RULES AND REGULATIONS

Army Corps of Engineers rules and regulations are published in the *Code of Federal Regulations,* Title 33, parts 203–399 and Title 36, parts 312–330. Proposed rules, final rules, and updates to the *Code of Federal Regulations* are published in the daily *Federal Register. (See appendix for information on how to obtain and use these publications.)*

Corps of Engineers regulations and policies are outlined in the *Digest of Water Resources Policies,* available from the Office of Public Affairs.

▨ LEGISLATION

Regulatory statutes administered by the Army Corps of Engineers include:

Rivers and Harbors Act of 1899 (30 Stat. 1151, 33 U.S.C. 403). Signed by the president March 3, 1899. Authorized regulation of all construction work in the navigable waters of the United States.

Rivers and Harbors Act of 1917 (40 Stat. 250, 33 U.S.C. 1). Signed by the president Aug. 8, 1917. Authorized the secretary of the army to regulate navigable waters of the United States as public necessity may require for the protection of life, property, and operations of the United States in channel improvement.

Army Act of July 9, 1918, Chapter XIX (40 Stat. 892, 33 U.S.C. 3). Signed by the president July 9, 1918. Authorized issuance of danger zone regulations to protect lives and property on navigable waters.

Federal Water Pollution Control Act Amendments of 1972 (Clean Water Act) (86 Stat. 816, 33 U.S.C. 1251). Vetoed by the president Oct. 17, 1972; veto overridden Oct. 18, 1972. Empowered the Army Corps of Engineers to issue permits for the disposal of dredged or fill material at specified sites. Amended in 1977.

Marine Protection, Research and Sanctuaries Act of 1972 (86 Stat. 1052, 33 U.S.C. 1401). Signed by the president Oct. 23, 1972. Authorized the corps to issue permits for transportation of dredged material to be dumped in ocean waters.

Water Resources Development Act of 1999 (113 Stat. 269, 33 U.S.C. 2201 note). Signed by the president on Aug. 17, 1999. Provided for the conservation and development of water and related resources. Authorized the secretary of the army to construct various projects for improvements to rivers and harbors of the United States, and for other purposes.

▨ REGIONAL DIVISIONS AND HEADQUARTERS

The areas served by most of these offices are determined by watersheds rather than political boundaries.

NORTH ATLANTIC DIVISION

Fort Hamilton
Military Community, Northwest Division
General Lee Ave., Bldg. 405
Brooklyn, NY 11252
(718) 765–7000
Brig. Gen. Merdith W. B. Temple, commander

MISSISSIPPI VALLEY DIVISION

1400 Walnut St.
P.O. Box 80
Vicksburg, MS 39181–0080
(601) 634–5760
Brig. Gen. Don T. Riley, commander

GREAT LAKES AND OHIO RIVER DIVISION

550 Main St.
P.O. Box 1159
Cincinnati, OH 45201–1159
(513) 684–3002
Brig. Gen. Steven R. Hawkins, commander

Ohio River Regional Headquarters
Same as the division.

PACIFIC OCEAN DIVISON

Fort Shafter, Bldg. 230
Honolulu, HI, 96858–5440
(808) 438–1500
Brig. Gen. Ronald L. Johnson, commander

SOUTH ATLANTIC DIVISION

77 Forsyth St. S.W.
Atlanta, GA 30303–6801
(404) 562–5006
Brig. Gen. Peter T. Madsen, commander

SOUTH PACIFIC DIVISION

333 Market St., #923
San Francisco, CA 94105–2195
(415) 977–8322
Brig. Gen. Robert L. Davis, commander

SOUTHWESTERN DIVISON

1114 Commerce St., #407
Dallas, TX 75242–0216
(214) 767–2502
Brig. Gen. Robert Crear, commander

NORTHWESTERN DIVISION
220 N.W. 8th Ave.
P.O. Box 2870
Portland, OR 97208–2870
(503) 808–3700
Brig. Gen. David A. Fastabend, commander

Missouri River Regional Office
12565 W. Center Rd.
P.O. Box 103
Omaha, NE 68144
(402) 697–2675
Lawrence Cieslik, assistant commander

North Pacific Regional Headquarters
Same as the division.

Energy Department

1000 Independence Ave. S.W., Washington, DC 20585
Internet: http://www.energy.gov

Energy Efficiency and Renewable Energy

1000 Independence Ave. S.W., Washington, DC 20585
Internet: http://www.eren.doe.gov

The Office of Energy Efficiency and Renewable Energy (EREN) is responsible for developing and directing Department of Energy (DOE) programs to increase the production and use of renewable energy such as solar, biomass, wind, geothermal, and alcohol fuels. Headed by an assistant secretary, EREN works to improve the energy efficiency of buildings, transportation, and industrial systems through financial and technological support of long-term research and development.

EREN reorganized in July 2002; the new structure includes eleven programs:

Biomass Program. Includes major programs for developing and improving technology for biomass power; for making biofuels such as ethanol (from biomass residues as well as grain) and renewable diesel; and for making plastics and chemicals from renewable, biobased materials.

Building Technologies Program. Conducts research and development on technologies and practices for energy efficiency, working closely with the building industry and manufacturers; promotes energy and money-saving opportunities to builders and consumers; and works with state and local regulatory groups to improve building codes and appliance standards.

Distributed Energy and Electric Reliability Program. Works with industry stakeholders to streamline the integration of distributed energy systems with the electricity grid. Distributes energy resources support and strengthens the central-station model of electricity generation, transmission, and distribution.

Federal Energy Management. Provides information and technical assistance, creates partnerships, and leverages resources for reducing energy use in federal buildings and operations. Provides information on project financing and guidelines for federal procurement of energy efficient products.

FreedomCAR and Vehicle Technologies Program. Provides information about transportation energy efficiency measures in the United States. Includes transportation rules and legislation, information on the latest technological advances, and tips on how to drive greener today. FreedomCAR, a government-industry program for the advancement of high-efficiency vehicles, focuses on fuel cells and hydrogen produced from renewable energy sources.

Geothermal Energy Program. Offers research and development support for U.S. industry to establish geothermal and hydrothermal energy as an economically competitive contributor to the U.S. energy supply. Geothermal resources range from shallow ground to hot water and rock several miles below Earth's surface, and even farther down to the extremely high temperatures of molten rock called magma.

Hydrogen, Fuel Cells & Infrastructure Technologies Program. Integrates activities in hydrogen production, storage, and delivery with transportation and stationary fuel cell activities.

Industrial Technologies Program. Focuses on applying energy efficiency, renewable energy, and other pollution prevention options in the industrial sector. Research and development programs conducted by the office are focused on seven industries: agriculture, aluminum, chemicals, forest products, glass, metalcasting, and steel.

Solar Energy Technology Program. Accelerates the development of solar technologies as energy sources. These technologies include Photovoltaic cells, which convert sunlight directly into electricity; concentrating solar power technologies use reflective materials to concentrate the sun's heat energy; and low-temperature solar collectors used directly for hot water or space heating for residential, commercial, and industrial facilities.

Weatherization and Intergovernmental Program. Provides consumers and decision makers with information on cost, performance, and financing energy efficiency and renewable energy projects. The Weatherization Assistance Program offers financial assistance to improve energy efficiency in low-income housing.

Wind and Hydropower Technologies Program. Conducts and coordinates research and development with industry and other federal agencies for wind energy research program, wind turbine research and development, and hydropower projects.

▪ KEY PERSONNEL

Assistant Secretary
David Garman........................... (202) 586–9220
Fax... (202) 586–9260
Principal Deputy Assistant Secretary
Douglas L. Faulkner.................... (202) 586–9220
Board of Directors
Robert Dixon .... (202) 586–1394
Mark Ginsberg .... (202) 586–1394
Thomas Gross .... (202) 586–1394
Office of Communications Outreach
Nancy Jeffery .... (202) 586–9373
Deputy Assistant Secretary for Technology Development
Richard Moorer .... (202) 586–5523
Office of Solar Energy Technology Program
Raymond Sutula........................ (202) 586–8064
Office of Wind and Hydropower Technologies Program
Peter Goldman .... (202) 586–1995
Office of Geothermal Technologies Program
Leland (Roy) Mink..................... (202) 586–5463
Office of Distributed Energy and Electricity Reliability Program
William Parks............................ (202) 586–2093
Office of Biomass Program
Douglas Kaempf........................ (202) 586–5264
Office of Industrial Technologies Programs
Buddy Garland .... (202) 586–7547
Office of Freedomcar and Vehicle Technologies Program
Ed Wall................................... (202) 586–0410
Office of Hydrogen and Fuel Cells Infrastructure Technology Program
Steve Chalk .... (202) 586–9118
Office of Building Technologies Program
Michael McLebe........................ (202) 586–9155

Office of Weatherization and Intergovernmental Program
John Millhone........................... (202) 586–4564
Office of Federal Energy Management Program
Beth Shearer .... (202) 586–5772
Deputy Assistant Secretary for Business Administration
John Sullivan .... (202) 586–5390
Office of Program Executive Support
Steve Lee .... (202) 586–0836
Office of Planning, Budget Formulation, and Analysis
Sam Baldwin............................ (202) 586–0927
Office of Information and Business Management Systems
Robert Brener .... (202) 586–2201

PUBLICATIONS
Contact the DOE Office of Public Affairs or the National Energy Information Center.

DATA AND STATISTICS

National Energy Information Center
1000 Independence Ave. S.W., #IE-248
Washington, DC 20585
(202) 586–8800
TDD (301) 903-2323
Sandra Wilkins, team leader

The Energy Information Administration (EIA), which was created in 1977 as the DOE's independent statistical and analytical agency, collects and publishes data; prepares analyses on energy production, consumption, and prices; and makes energy supply and demand projections. The *EIA Publications Directory,* containing titles and abstracts, is available to the public and is the best source of published information from the DOE.

Reference Resources

LIBRARY

Energy Department
1000 Independence Ave. S.W., #GA-138
Washington, DC 20585
(202) 586–9534
Joanne Graham, chief
Hours: 8:30 a.m. to 5:00 p.m.

Open to the public, but due to security measures a photo identification card is required.

RULES AND REGULATIONS

Conservation and renewable energy rules and regulations are published in the *Code of Federal Regulations*, Title 10, various parts. Proposed rules, final rules, and updates to the *Code of Federal Regulations* are published in the daily *Federal Register*. *(See appendix for information on how to obtain and use these publications.)*

▐ LEGISLATION

EREN's responsibilities fall under the following legislation:

Federal Energy Administration Act of 1974 (88 Stat. 96, 15 U.S.C. 761). Signed by the president May 7, 1974. Created the Federal Energy Administration.

Federal Non-nuclear Energy Research and Development Act of 1974 (88 Stat. 1878, 42 U.S.C. 5901). Signed by the president Dec. 31, 1974. Provided federal support for programs of research and development of fuels and energy.

Energy Policy and Conservation Act (89 Stat. 871, 42 U.S.C. 6201 note). Signed by the president Dec. 22, 1975. Authorized the DOE to coordinate activities among the federal agencies to reduce energy consumption in federal buildings and operations.

Energy Conservation and Production Act (90 Stat. 1125, 42 U.S.C. 6801 note). Signed by the president Aug. 14, 1976. Encouraged implementation of energy conservation measures and reauthorized the Federal Energy Administration.

Energy Research and Development Administration Appropriations (91 Stat. 191, 42 U.S.C. 7001 note). Signed by the president June 3, 1977. Included the **National Energy Extension Service Act** (Title V), which established a federal/state partnership to provide small-scale energy users with technical assistance to facilitate energy conservation and the use of renewable resources.

Department of Energy Organization Act (91 Stat. 566, 42 U.S.C. 7101 note). Signed by the president Aug. 4, 1977. Established the Department of Energy within the executive branch.

Department of Energy Act of 1978–Civilian Applications (92 Stat. 47, codified in scattered sections of 42 U.S.C.). Signed by the president Feb. 25, 1978. Authorized funds for fiscal year 1978 for energy research and development programs of the DOE.

National Energy Conservation Policy Act (92 Stat. 3206, 42 U.S.C. 8201 note). Signed by the president Nov. 9, 1978. Authorized federal matching grant programs to assist public or nonprofit schools and hospitals to make energy-conserving improvements in their facilities and operating practices.

Public Utility Regulatory Policies Act of 1978 (92 Stat. 3117, 16 U.S.C. 2601). Signed by the president Nov. 9, 1978.

Required utilities to give customers information about energy conservation devices. Provided funds to schools and hospitals to install energy-saving equipment and provided grants and government-backed loans to low-income families for home energy conservation.

Emergency Energy Conservation Act of 1979 (93 Stat. 749, 42 U.S.C. 8501 note). Signed by the president Nov. 5, 1979. Granted authority to the president to create an emergency program to conserve energy.

Department of Interior Appropriations (93 Stat. 970, 42 U.S.C. 5915). Signed by the president Nov. 27, 1979. Established the Energy Security Reserve of $19 billion until expended to stimulate domestic commercial production of alternative fuels such as ethanol and ammonia fertilizer plants.

Energy Security Act of 1980 (94 Stat. 611, 42 U.S.C. 8701). Signed by the president June 30, 1980. Established a five-year multibillion-dollar program for developing synthetic fuels, including the establishment of the U.S. Synthetic Fuels Corporation; expanded the use of biomass, alcohol fuels, and urban waste; ordered the president to set energy targets; instituted renewable energy initiatives; established an energy conservation and solar bank in the Department of Housing and Urban Development; expanded the use of geothermal energy; and established a program to study the problems of acid rain and carbon dioxide associated with coal burning.

Ocean Thermal Energy Conversion Act of 1980 (94 Stat. 974, 42 U.S.C. 9101). Signed by the president Aug. 3, 1980. Established a legal framework to govern operations of ocean thermal energy conversion plants and extended to such facilities the federal financing aid, including loan guarantees, available to shipbuilders.

Ocean Thermal Energy Conversion Research, Development and Demonstration Act (94 Stat. 941, 42 U.S.C. 9001). Signed by the president Aug. 17, 1980. Provided funds for an accelerated research and development program by the DOE on ocean thermal energy conversion.

Wind Energy System Act of 1980 (94 Stat. 1139, 42 U.S.C. 9201). Signed by the president Sept. 8, 1980. Authorized spending to accelerate the development of wind energy systems.

Renewable Energy Industry Development Act (98 Stat. 1211, 42 U.S.C. 6201 note). Signed by the president July 18, 1984. Established the Committee on Renewable Energy Commerce and Trade to promote and assist U.S.-developed renewable energy technology to compete within the international marketplace.

Energy Policy Act of 1992 (106 Stat. 2776, 42 U.S.C. 13201 note). Signed by the president Oct. 24, 1992. Set strategy for economic growth and national security by promoting conservation and efficient use of energy along with increased domestic production.

Biomass Research and Development Act of 2000 (114 Stat. 428, 7 U.S.C. 7624 note). Signed by the president on June 22, 2000. Directed the secretary of agriculture and the secretary of energy to cooperate and coordinate research and development activities with respect to production of biobased industrial products. Established the Biomass Research and Development Board to coordinate federal programs for the promotion and use of biobased industrial products. Also established the Biomass Research and Development Technical Advisory Committee.

■ FIELD OFFICES

Department of Energy

The following offices are the sites of major DOE operations, not part of EREN itself. They do not serve specific regions.

ALBUQUERQUE
P.O. Box 5400
Albuquerque, NM 87185-5400
(505) 845-0011
Richard E. Glass, operations manager

CHICAGO
9800 S. Cass Ave.
Argonne, IL 60439
(630) 252-2110
Marvin E. Gunn Jr., operations manager

GOLDEN
1617 Cole Blvd.
Golden, CO 80401-3393
(303) 275-4788
Frank M. Stewart, operations manager

IDAHO
850 Energy Dr.
Idaho Falls, ID 83401-1563
(208) 526-1322
Beverly Cook, operations manager

MIAMISBURG
P.O. Box 3020
Miamisburg, OH 45343-3020
(937) 865-3977
Susan R. Brechbill, operations manager

NEVADA
P.O. Box 98518
Las Vegas, NV 89193-8518
(702) 295-3211
Kathleen Carlson, operations manager

OAK RIDGE
200 Administration Rd.
Oak Ridge, TN 37830
(865) 576-4444
G. Leah Dever, operations manager

OAKLAND
1301 Clay St., #700N
Oakland, CA 94612-5208
(510) 637-1801
Camille Yuan-Soo Hoo, operations manager

RICHLAND
825 Jadwin Ave.
Richland, WA 99352
(509) 376-7395
Keith A. Klein, operations manager

ROCKY FLATS
10808 Hwy. 93, #1A
Golden, CO 80403
(303) 966-2025
Barbara Mazurowski, operations manager

SAVANNAH RIVER
Road 1A
Aiken, SC 29802
(803) 725-2277
Greg Rudy, operations manager

Environmental Management

1000 Independence Ave. S.W., Washington, DC 20585
Internet: http://www.em.doe.gov

The Office of Environmental Management (EM) was established by the secretary of energy in October 1989 to consolidate responsibility within the Department of Energy (DOE) for environmental management activities. EM was called the Office of Environmental Restoration and Waste Management until 1994. EM is headed by an assistant secretary and is responsible for environmental cleanup, compliance, and waste management activities.

DOE and the Environmental Protection Agency share responsibility for transportation of hazardous wastes or radioactive and hazardous waste mixtures generated at facilities operated by DOE under the authority of the Atomic Energy Act. These responsibilities are delineated in the 1984 DOE/EPA Memorandum of Understanding on Responsibilities for Hazardous and Radioactive Mixed Waste Management. DOE agreed to comply with Resource Conservation and Recovery Act (RCRA) requirements for hazardous waste transporters that require transporters to obtain an EPA identification number for the waste, comply with the manifest system, and deal with hazardous waste discharges. These regulations incorporate and require compliance with Department of Transportation provisions for labeling, marking, placarding, proper container use, and discharge reporting.

The EM program is responsible for cleaning up 114 sites involved with research, development, production, and testing of nuclear weapons. Taken together, these sites encompass an area of more than two million acres—equal to the combined size of Rhode Island and Delaware. At the beginning of FY 2002, the DOE had completed active cleanup at seventy-four of these sites.

In addition, the EM program is responsible for safely disposing of 88 million gallons of radioactive liquid waste, 2,500 metric tons of spent nuclear fuel, 135,000 cubic meters of transuranic waste, and more than 1 million cubic meters of low level waste.

EM is divided into seven main offices, each managed by a deputy assistant secretary. The following is a brief overview of EM's key components:

Office of Site Closure. The Office of Site Closure (OSC) works to achieve closure of sites in a manner that is safe, cost-effective, and coordinated with stakeholders. OSC provides site guidance and direction, resource allocation, site analysis, policy evaluation, program performance measures, and performance monitoring at the Ohio Sites, the Oak Ridge Sites, the Rocky Flats Environmental Technology Site, and cleanup sites under the purview of the Albuquerque, Chicago, Nevada, and Oakland Operations Offices.

Environmental Restoration, formerly a separate office within EM, now functions under OSC. Environmental restoration involves the cleanup of inactive facilities and sites contaminated by waste generated from past operations, directs the assessment and cleanup of inactive sites and surplus facilities contaminated from previous defense and nondefense-related programs. Environmental Restoration activities are categorized as either remedial actions or decommissioning.

Remedial actions include the assessment and cleanup of inactive hazardous substance release sites. Some remedial actions address contaminated surface water, but most activities involve contaminated soil and groundwater.

Decommissioning activities ensure the safe caretaking of surplus nuclear facilities until they are decontaminated for reuse or completely removed. Although some decommissioning activities involve soil and ground contamination, most are concerned with reactors, hot cells, processing plants, and storage tanks.

OSC works closely with the Office of Integration and Disposition to ensure that complex-wide issues, lessons learned, and initiatives are reflected in site strategies and plans.

Office of Integration and Disposition. The Office of Integration and Disposition (OID), formerly Nuclear Material and Facilities Stabilization, manages the transition of contaminated facilities and equipment from other DOE programs or offices to the EM organization. This process includes developing criteria that facilities must meet before the transition, deactivating surplus facilities, and negotiating the future use of facilities. This office also manages worker retraining programs and economic development of former hazardous wastes sites.

OID identifies disposition pathways for excess nuclear materials, spent nuclear fuels, legacy wastes and remediation wastes, analyses options with stakeholder input, and facilitates decision making between offices and programs. OID also implements multisite services such as support for pollution prevention/waste management analyses, deactivation and decommissioning efforts, transportation, transuranic waste disposal at the Waste Isolation Pilot Plant, and the foreign research reactor spent nuclear fuel acceptance program.

Office of Science and Technology. Develops and applies cost-efficient methods of minimizing and/or eliminating chemical and nuclear waste and managing waste more efficiently and safely. Programs involve research, development, demonstration, and testing and evaluation activities designed to produce innovative technologies to meet national needs for regulatory compliance, and reduce risks to the environment and to public health.

Office of Project Completion. The Office of Project Completion (OPJ) provides resource allocation, program analysis, policy evaluation, and performance monitoring of activities at the Idaho and Savannah River Sites, and for the Office of River Protection and Richland Operations Office, both located at the Hanford Site. OPJ functions, many of which were performed under the former Waste Management office, include reduction of high- or moderate-risk conditions associated with nuclear operations; protection of workers, the public, and the environment from radiological and nonradiological hazards; safe management of spent nuclear fuel, and surplus hazardous and nuclear materials; treatment, storage, transportation, and disposal of radioactive, hazardous, and sanitary wastes; deactivation of facilities to attain lowest surveillance and maintenance costs; remediation of contaminated land; disposition of facilities to alternate future use or final decontamination and decommissioning; and operational oversight for the infrastructure facilities and programs as needed to support business line missions.

Office of Management and Information. Responsible for administrative management, such as personnel administration, general administrative support services and training, and career development. Also responsible for acquisition, procurement, automatic data processing, and information resources management.

Office of Safety, Health and Security. The Office of Safety, Health and Security (OSHS) is responsible for program overview and evaluation, policy development, technical support, and assistance in the areas of safety and health, safeguards and security, and quality assurance for EM. OSHS works to educate EM personnel about their responsibilities in the areas of safety, security, and quality. In addition, OSHS administers risk management, quality assurance, package certification, emergency management, and characterization management.

Office of Policy, Planning, and Budget. Provides critical analysis on policy and planning issues associated with environmental compliance and cleanup activities, waste management, nuclear materials and facilities stabilization, overall budget and priority setting, and nuclear nonproliferation policy. This office also is responsible for the review and coordination of intersite, interagency, and international planning related to these issues.

The agency's 1998 *Paths to Closure* report estimated a life-cycle cost of $147 billion for the ending of all EM cleanup programs. That estimate was, however, too optimistic, as estimated costs rose over the subsequent years. A 2002 review of EM programs found that the life-cycle costs had risen to an estimated $220 billion. The review also made recommendations for restructuring the agency.

On May 19, 2003, the DOE announced plans for a reorganization of the EM. Core functions outlined in the 2002 review would serve as the framework for the daily work activities of the EM staff. The organization will consist of three key elements: Line Management (Operations Oversight), Mission Programs (Logistics/Waste Disposal Enhancements and Environmental Cleanup and Acceleration) and Management Support (Performance Intelligence/Improvement and Business Operations). The reorganization was expected to occur sometime after July 2003.

■ KEY PERSONNEL

Assistant Secretary
    Carolyn L. Huntoon (acting) .... (202) 586–7709
      Fax .... (202) 586–7757
Principal Deputy Assistant Secretary
    James M. Owendoff .... (202) 586–7710
Integration and Disposition
    Gene Schmitt (acting) .... (202) 586–5151

Management and Information
Barbara Male .... (202) 586–1665
Nuclear Material and Facility Stabilization
David Huizenga .... (202) 586–5151
Policy, Planning, and Budget
Vacant .... (202) 586–8754
Project Completion
Vacant .... (202) 586–0370
Science and Technology
Gerald Boyd .... (202) 586–6382
Site Closure
James Fiore .... (202) 586–6331
Site Operations
Michael Oldham .... (202) 586–0738
Waste Management
Mark W. Frei........................... (202) 586–0370

▧ INFORMATION SOURCES

Internet
Agency Web Site: http://www.em.doe.gov. Features schedules for conferences and courses, press releases and regulatory news, and information on job opportunities and relocation assistance.

Telephone Contacts
Personnel Locator .... (202) 586–5000
Environmental Hotline .... (800) 541–1625
Washington, DC, area..................... (202) 586–4073

Information and Publications

KEY OFFICES

DOE Office of Public Affairs
1000 Independence Ave. S.W.
Washington, DC 20585
(202) 586–4940
Jeanne Lopatto, director

Answers questions from the public and news organizations.

DOE Press Office
1000 Independence Ave. S.W.
Washington, DC 20585
(202) 586–5806
Lisa Cutler, director

Handles press inquiries and issues press releases.

Environmental Hotline
DOE Office of the Inspector General
1000 Independence Ave. S.W., Room 5D-031
Washington, DC 20585
(800) 541–1625 (toll free)
(202) 586–4073 (Washington, DC, area)
Greg Friedman, inspector general

The hotline is for reporting fraud, waste, abuse, or environmental matters that concern the DOE.

Freedom of Information
DOE Freedom of Information Reading Room
1000 Independence Ave. S.W., Room 1E-190
Washington, DC 20585
(202) 586–6020
Abel Lopez, FOI officer

The FOI Reading Room is open from 9:00 a.m. to 4:00 p.m. Visitors are required to arrange for a DOE escort to use the Reading Room.

PUBLICATIONS
Contact the DOE Office of Public Affairs or the National Energy Information Center.

DATA AND STATISTICS

National Energy Information Center
1000 Independence Ave. S.W.
Washington, DC 20585
(202) 586–8800
TDD (202) 586–1181
John Weiner, director

The Energy Information Administration (EIA), which was created in 1977 as the DOE's independent statistical and analytical agency, collects and publishes data; prepares analyses on energy production, consumption, prices, and resources; and makes energy supply and demand projections. The *EIA Publications Directory*, containing titles and abstracts, is available to the public and is the best source of published information from the DOE.

Reference Resources

LIBRARY

Energy Department
1000 Independence Avenue S.W., Room GA-138
Washington, DC 20585
(202) 586–9534
Joanne Graham, chief
Hours: 8:30 a.m. to 5:00 p.m.

Open to the public, but due to security measures a photo identification card is required.

Center for Environmental Management Information

470 L'Enfant Plaza S.W., #112
Washington, DC 20585
(202) 863–5084
(800) 736–3282
Hours: 9:00 a.m. to 6:00 p.m.

Open to the public and has a library, an interactive database, and an educational outreach program. Houses many EM publications.

RULES AND REGULATIONS

EM rules and regulations are published in the *Code of Federal Regulations,* Title 10, Section 200-end, various parts; and Title 40, Sections 260 and 300, various parts. Proposed rules, final rules, and updates to the *Code of Federal Regulations* are published in the daily *Federal Register. (See appendix for information on how to obtain and use these publications.)*

◼ LEGISLATION

Environmental Management carries out its responsibilities under:

National Environmental Policy Act of 1969 (83 Stat. 852, 42 U.S.C. 4321). Signed by the president Jan. 1, 1969. Established a broad national environmental policy and required that federal agencies provide environmental impact statements regarding any major federal action or legislative proposal.

Toxic Substances Control Act, as amended (90 Stat. 2003, 15 U.S.C. 2601). Signed by the president Oct. 11, 1976. Required the federal government to regulate the manufacture, processing, distribution in commerce, use, or disposal of chemical substances and mixtures that may present an unreasonable risk to the public health or the environment.

Resource Conservation and Recovery Act of 1976 (RCRA) (90 Stat. 2807, 42 U.S.C. 6923). Signed by the president Oct. 21, 1976. Authorized the Environmental Protection Agency to regulate the treatment, storage, transportation, and disposal of hazardous wastes. Set standards for the transportation of certain types of hazardous wastes and the cleanup of hazardous waste sites.

Department of Energy Organization Act (91 Stat. 566, 42 U.S.C. 7101 note). Signed by the president Aug. 4, 1977. Established the DOE within the executive branch.

Executive Order 12038. Issued by the president Feb. 7, 1978. Transferred responsibilities of the Federal Energy Administration, the Energy Research and Development Administration, and the Federal Power Commission to the DOE.

Uranium Mill Tailings Radiation Control Act of 1978, as amended (92 Stat. 3021, 42 U.S.C. 7901). Signed by the president Nov. 8, 1978. Provided a remedial action program to stabilize, dispose of, and control uranium mill tailings to prevent or minimize radon diffusion into the environment and other health hazards.

Comprehensive Environmental Responses, Compensation and Liability Act of 1980 (Superfund) (94 Stat. 2767, 42 U.S.C. 9601). Signed by the president Dec. 11, 1980. Required the identification and cleanup of inactive hazardous waste sites by responsible parties. Allowed state cleanup standards to be substituted for federal standards if the state imposed more stringent requirements. Amended by the **Superfund Amendments and Reauthorization Act of 1986** (100 Stat. 1613, 42 U.S.C. 9601 note). Signed by the president Oct. 17, 1986. These two acts limited or prohibited many formerly acceptable waste management practices.

Nuclear Waste Policy Act of 1982, as amended (96 Stat. 2201, 42 U.S.C. 10101 note). Signed by the president Jan. 7, 1983. Provided for the development of federal repositories for the disposal of high-level radioactive waste and spent fuel, and established a research program regarding the disposal of high-level radioactive waste and spent nuclear fuel.

Low-Level Radioactive Waste Policy Amendments Act of 1985 (99 Stat. 182, 42 U.S.C. 2021). Signed by the president Jan. 15, 1986. Imposed strict deadlines for states or regions to set up disposal facilities for low-level radioactive wastes; approved compacts among thirty-seven states to join together for the disposal of such wastes.

Energy Policy Act of 1992 (106 Stat. 2276, 42 U.S.C. 13201 note). Signed by the president Oct. 24, 1992. Set strategy for economic growth and national security by promoting conservation and efficient use of energy along with increased domestic production.

◼ FIELD OFFICES

Environmental Management has no field or regional offices. However, the DOE maintains field offices, which do not serve specific regions.

Environment, Safety, and Health

1000 Independence Ave. S.W., Washington, DC 20585
Internet: http://www.eh.doe.gov

The Office of Environment, Safety, and Health (ESH) was created by the secretary of energy in September 1985. Headed by an assistant secretary, it is responsible for ensuring the compliance by Department of Energy (DOE) facilities with applicable environmental laws and regulations and protecting the safety and health of DOE employees and the public. The ESH also develops DOE policy regarding the effects of national environmental policy on U.S. energy industries and energy supply and demand. The office is divided into six divisions headed by deputy assistant secretaries:

Planning and Administration. Performs financial and administrative functions, gathers and updates information from field offices, and maintains the ESH computer-assisted information tracking system, which contains environmental and safety information on all DOE facilities. The office monitors compliance and progress in the completion of corrective activities managed by the DOE Office of Environmental Management *(see p. 500)*.

Environment. Provides environmental oversight of DOE's programs, activities, and facilities. It also assists the DOE in negotiating compliance agreements with the Environmental Protection Agency and state governments. Provides assistance to DOE program and field offices in resolving current and oncoming compliance issues through interaction and coordination with internal and external entities. The NEPA Policy and Assistance Oversight Program ensures mandatory DOE compliance with the Resource Conservation and Recovery Act (RCRA), Comprehensive Environmental Responses, Compensation and Liability Act (CERCLA), Emergency Planning and Community Right-to-Know Act (EPCRA), and National Environmental Policy Act (NEPA).

Health Studies. Develops and recommends policies and standards related to radiation protection, industrial hygiene, and occupational medicine. It also manages a health physics and industrial hygiene graduate fellowship program.

The Office of Epidemiological Studies collects and maintains occupational and community health surveillance data and conducts epidemiological studies, including mortality studies of DOE contract workers, the potential health effects of energy production, and ecological studies of offsite populations.

Performance Assessment and Analysis. Provides the assistant secretary for ESH with an evaluation of the department's effectiveness, vulnerabilities, and trends in protecting the public, the worker, and the environment. This division also serves as the focal point for the collection, analysis, and dissemination of environment, safety, and health performance data, including the department-wide process for planning, budget and execution targets inspections of critical areas of performance based on results of analyses.

Planning and Administration. Provides administrative support to ESH policy development, oversight, and corporate programs. Controls budgeting, procurement, and personnel management.

Safety and Health. Develops, manages, and directs comprehensive programs that assist line management in continuous improvements for protecting the health and safety of workers at all DOE facilities. Works with the Office of Planning and Administration to establish training criteria and ensure the adequacy of training to DOE and contractor employees. Serves as DOE's liaison with the Department of Labor's Occupational Safety and Health Administration.

KEY PERSONNEL

Assistant Secretary
Beverly A. Cook .... (202) 586–6151
Fax .... (202) 586–0956
Environment
Raymond Berube .... (202) 586–5680
Environmental Policy and Guidance
Andrew Lawrence .... (202) 586–6740
NEPA Policy and Compliance
Carol Borgstrom .... (202) 586–4600
Health and Safety
(19901 Germantown Rd., Germantown, MD 20874)
Rick Jones (acting) .... (301) 903–5532
Price Anderson Enforcement
Stephen Schinki .... (301) 903–0100
Regulatory Liaison
Harry J. Pettengill .... (301) 903–5639
Worker Protection Policy Programs
C. Rick Jones .... (301) 903–6061
Health Studies
(19901 Germantown Rd., Germantown, MD 20874)
Steven Cary .... (301) 903–5926
Chief Science Officer
Vacant .... (301) 903–5835
Nuclear and Facility Safety Policy
Richard Black .... (301) 903–3465
Oversight
(19901 Germantown Rd., Germantown, MD 20874)
Raymond Hardwick (acting) .... (202) 586–0307
Environment, Safety, and Health Inspections
Ed Blockwood .... (301) 903–0124
Planning and Administration
Geoffrey Judge .... (202) 586–9024
Budget and Administration
Geoffrey Judge (acting) .... (301) 903–5577
Technical/ Professional Development
Veronica Parham .... (202) 586–0509

INFORMATION SOURCES

Internet
Agency Web Site: http://www.eh.doe.gov. This site, called Technical Information Service (TIS), is a collection of information services that includes publications, regulatory information, and databases.

Telephone Contacts
Personnel Locator .... (202) 586–5000
Environmental Hotline .... (800) 541–1625
Washington, DC, area .... (202) 586–4073

Information and Publications

KEY OFFICES

DOE Office of Public Affairs
1000 Independence Ave. S.W.
Washington, DC 20585
(202) 586–4940
Jeanne Lopatto, director

Answers questions from the public and news organizations.

Press Information
DOE Press Office
1000 Independence Ave. S.W.
Washington, DC 20585
(202) 586–5806
Gerry Schiermeyer, director

Environmental Hotline
DOE Office of the Inspector General
1000 Independence Ave. S.W., Room 5D-031
Washington, DC 20585
(800) 541–1625 (toll free)
(202) 586–4073 (Washington, DC, area)
John C. Layton, inspector general

Handles inquiries or concerns regarding specific DOE facilities.

Freedom of Information
DOE Freedom of Information Reading Room
1000 Independence Ave. S.W., Room 1E-190
Washington, DC 20585
(202) 586–3142
Carolyn Lawson, FOI officer

The FOI Reading Room is open from 9:00 a.m. to 4:00 p.m. Visitors are required to arrange for a DOE escort to use the Reading Room.

PUBLICATIONS
Contact the DOE Office of Public Affairs or the National Energy Information Center. In addition, a number of publications are available for viewing and downloading at the EHS Web site.

DATA AND STATISTICS

National Energy Information Center
1000 Independence Ave. S.W.
Washington, DC 20585
(202) 586–8800
TDD (202) 586–1181
John Weiner, director

The Energy Information Administration (EIA), which was created in 1977 as the DOE's independent statistical and analytical agency, collects and publishes data; prepares analyses on energy production, consumption, prices and resources; and makes energy supply and demand projections. The *EIA Publications Directory,* containing titles and abstracts, is available to the public and is DOE's best source of published information.

Reference Resources

LIBRARY

Energy Department
1000 Independence Avenue S.W., Room GA-138
Washington, DC 20585
(202) 586–9534
Joanne Graham, chief
Hours: 8:30 a.m. to 5:00 p.m.

Open to the public; a photo identification card is required.

RULES AND REGULATIONS
ESH rules and regulations are published in the *Code of Federal Regulations,* Title 10, Sections 200–1060, various parts. Proposed rules, final rules, and updates to the *Code of Federal Regulations* are published in the daily *Federal Register. (See appendix for information on how to obtain and use these publications.)*

■ LEGISLATION
The ESH carries out its responsibilities under:
Department of Energy Organization Act (91 Stat. 566, 42 U.S.C. 7101 note). Signed by the president Aug. 4, 1977. Established the DOE within the executive branch.

Executive Order 12038. Issued by the president Feb. 7, 1978. Transferred responsibilities of the Federal Energy Administration, the Energy Research and Development Administration, and the Federal Power Commission to the DOE.

Executive Order 12088. Issued by the president Oct. 13, 1978. Required that all federal facilities and activities comply with applicable pollution control standards and required each agency to submit an annual pollution control plan to the president.

Comprehensive Environmental Responses, Compensation and Liability Act of 1980 (Superfund) (94 Stat. 2767, 42 U.S.C. 9601). Signed by the president Dec. 11, 1980. Required the identification and cleanup of inactive hazardous waste sites by responsible parties. Allowed state cleanup standards to be substituted for federal standards if the state imposed more stringent requirements. Amended by the **Superfund Amendments and Reauthorization Act of 1986** (100 Stat. 1613, 42 U.S.C. 9601 note). Signed by the president Oct. 17, 1986. These two acts limited or prohibited many formerly acceptable waste management practices.

Price Anderson Amendments Act of 1988 (102 Stat. 1066, 43 U.S.C. 2011 note). Signed by the president Aug. 20, 1988. Amended the Atomic Energy Act of 1954 to establish a comprehensive, equitable, and efficient mechanism for full compensation of the public in the event of a DOE accident involving nuclear materials.

Energy Policy Act of 1992 (106 Stat. 2776, 42 U.S.C. 13201 note). Signed by the president Oct. 24, 1992. Set strategy for economic growth and national security by promoting the conservation and efficient use of energy along with increased domestic production.

■ FIELD OFFICES
ESH has no field or regional offices. However, the DOE maintains operations offices, which do not serve specific regions *(for addresses, see p. 464).*

Fossil Energy

1000 Independence Ave. S.W., Washington, DC 20585
Internet: http://fossil.energy.gov

The Department of Energy's (DOE) Fossil Energy Office is responsible for research and development programs involving fossil fuels. The regulatory responsibilities of the Fossil Energy Office are carried out primarily by three divisions: Oil and Natural Gas, Coal and Power, and Petroleum Reserves.

Oil and Natural Gas develops policy and regulations, conducts administrative law proceedings to determine whether to authorize imports and exports of natural gas, and intervenes in Federal Energy Regulatory Commission proceedings involving natural gas issues *(p. 145)*. Oil and Natural Gas carries out its responsibilities under the Natural Gas Act.

Coal and Power authorizes the export of electricity and issues permits for the construction and operation of electric transmission lines that cross international borders. (The federal government does not regulate the import of electric energy or commercial arrangements between the United States and foreign utilities.) Coal and Power also is responsible for certifying that new electric power plants are constructed or operated with the capability to use coal or another alternate fuel as a primary energy source. This provision was required by the Power Plant and Industrial Fuel Use Act. In 1989 the regulatory authority to implement provisions of the act was transferred from the Economic Regulatory Administration to Fossil Energy. This division also administers the Clean Coal Technology Program.

Petroleum Reserves oversees the Strategic Petroleum Reserve and the Naval Petroleum and Oil Shale Reserves. The Office of Strategic Petroleum Reserves (SPR) is authorized by the Energy Policy and Conservation Act of 1975, which was enacted following the energy crisis in the United States that resulted from the OPEC oil embargo of 1973–1974. The SPR was established to give the United States a backup supply if it lost access to foreign oil markets. The Office of Naval Petroleum and Oil Shale Reserves is authorized by the Naval Petroleum Reserves Production Act of 1976.

At the beginning of 2003 the SPR held more than 600 million barrels of crude oil with the capacity to hold 700 million barrels. It was the largest emergency oil stockpile in the world. Together, the facilities and crude oil represented more than a $20 billion national investment.

■ KEY PERSONNEL

Assistant Secretary
Carl Michael Smith .... (202) 586–6660
Fax..................................... (202) 586–7847
Principal Deputy Assistant Secretary
Vacant................................. (202) 586–6660
Strategic Planning
Raymond Braitsch...................... (202) 586–9682
Communications
Robert Porter.......................... (202) 586–6503
Budget and Financial Management
Charles J. Roy.......................... (202) 586–8977
Human Resources and Program Support
Edward Kilroy .... (301) 903–2617
Coal and Power Systems
George Rudins......................... (202) 586–1650
Natural Gas and Petroleum Technology
James Slutz............................ (202) 586–5600
Fax..................................... (202) 586–6221
Naval Petroleum and Oil Shale Reserves
Anton R. Dammer .... (202) 586–4685
Strategic Petroleum Reserve
John Shages............................ (202) 586–4410

INFORMATION SOURCES

Internet

Agency Web Site: http://www.fossil.energy.gov. Includes information on speeches and events, scientific and technical reports, and budgets.

Telephone Contacts

Personnel Locator .... (202) 586–5000

Information and Publications

KEY OFFICES

Fossil Energy Office of Communications
1000 Independence Ave. S.W., Room 4G-085
Washington, DC 20585
(202) 586–6503
Robert C. Porter, director

Handles questions on congressional or industrial relations and questions from the media.

Freedom of Information
Fossil Energy
1000 Independence Ave. S.W., Room 1G-051
Washington, DC 20585
(202) 586–5955
Abeo Lopez, director

PUBLICATIONS

Available from the Fossil Energy Office of Communications unless otherwise specified.

National Energy Information Center
1000 Independence Ave. S.W.
Washington, DC 20585
(202) 586–8800
TDD (202) 586–1181
Sandra Wilkins, team leader

The Energy Information Administration (EIA), which was created in 1977 as the DOE's independent statistical and analytical agency, collects and publishes data; prepares analyses on energy production, consumption, prices, and resources; and makes energy supply and demand projections. The *EIA Publications Directory,* containing titles and abstracts, is available to the public and is the best source of published information from the DOE.

Reference Resources

LIBRARY

Energy Department
1000 Independence Avenue S.W., Room GA-138
Washington, DC 20585
(202) 586–9534
Joanne Graham, chief
Hours: 8:30 a.m. to 5:00 p.m.

Open to the public, but due to security measures a photo identification card is required.

DOCKETS

Natural Gas Docket Room
1000 Independence Ave. S.W., Room 3F0-70
Washington, DC 20585
(202) 586–9478
Larine Moore, manager
Hours: 8:00 a.m. to 4:30 p.m.

RULES AND REGULATIONS

Fossil Energy rules and regulations are published in the *Code of Federal Regulations,* Title 10, parts 205, 500–516, and 590. Proposed regulations, new final regulations, and updates to the *Code of Federal Regulations* are published in the daily *Federal Register.* (*See appendix for details on how to obtain and use these publications.*)

LEGISLATION

Fossil Energy carries out its responsibilities under:

Federal Power Act, as amended (49 Stat. 839, 16 U.S.C. 824a(e)). Signed by the president Aug. 26, 1935. Required any person desiring to transmit any electric energy from the United States to a foreign country to obtain an authorizing order from the Federal Power Commission.

Natural Gas Act (52 Stat. 822, 15 U.S.C. 717b). Signed by the president June 21, 1938. Required any person desiring to export any natural gas from the United States to a foreign country or to import any natural gas from a foreign country to the United States to obtain an authorizing order from the Federal Power Commission.

Executive Order 10485. Issued by the president Sept. 3, 1953. Empowered the Federal Power Commission to receive and approve all applications of permits for facilities to transmit electric energy or natural gas between the United States and a foreign country provided that the construction and operation of such facility is in the public interest.

Energy Supply and Environmental Coordination Act of 1974, as amended (88 Stat. 246, 15 U.S.C. 791). Signed by the president June 22, 1974. To encourage the use of coal and alternative fuels instead of petroleum and natural gas, this act required the Federal Energy Administration to prohibit certain existing power plants from using petroleum and natural gas as primary energy sources.

Energy Policy and Conservation Act (89 Stat. 881, 42 U.S.C. 6231). Signed by the president Dec. 22, 1975. Authorized the creation of the Strategic Petroleum Reserves to reduce the disruptions in petroleum supplies and to carry out the obligations of the United States in the event of a national emergency.

Naval Petroleum Reserves Production Act of 1976 (90 Stat. 303, 42 U.S.C. 6501 note). Signed by the president April 5, 1976. Directed that the reserves be produced at their maximum efficient rates of production for six years with a provision that the president could extend production in three-year increments if continued production was determined to be in the national interest.

Department of Energy Organization Act (91 Stat. 566, 42 U.S.C. 7101 note). Signed by the president Aug. 4, 1977. Established the DOE within the executive branch.

Executive Order 12038. Issued by the president Feb. 7, 1978. Transferred responsibilities of the Federal Energy Administration and the Federal Power Commission to the DOE.

Power Plant and Industrial Fuel Use Act of 1978 (92 Stat. 3289, 42 U.S.C. 8301 et seq.). Signed by the president Nov. 9, 1978. Prohibited the use of petroleum and natural gas by power plants and major fuel-burning installations. Much of the act was repealed by the **1978 Amendments** (101 Stat. 310, 42 U.S.C. 8301 et seq.). Signed by the president May 21, 1987. The amendments limited the act's application to new baseload power plants that generate electricity for resale. Currently, no new electric power plant may be operated as a baseload power plant without the capability to use coal or another alternate fuel as a primary energy source. The act was amended again by the **Omnibus Budget Reconciliation Act of 1981** (95 Stat. 614, 42 U.S.C. 8341). Signed by the president Aug. 13, 1981. Required the DOE to monitor natural gas consumption by every U.S. electric utility and to publish biannual summaries.

Public Utility Regulatory Policies Act of 1978 (PURPA) (92 Stat. 3117, 16 U.S.C. 2601 note). Signed by the president Nov. 9, 1978. Required annual reports to Congress on the rate-reform initiatives of state regulatory commissions and nonregulated utilities.

Energy Policy Act of 1992 (106 Stat. 2775, 42 U.S.C. 13201 note). Signed by the president Oct. 24, 1992. Set strategy for economic growth and national security by promoting the conservation and efficient use of energy along with increased domestic production.

▓ FIELD OFFICES

ALBANY RESEARCH CENTER
1450 Queen Ave. S.W.
Albany, OR 97312
(541) 967–5893
George Dooley III, director

NATIONAL ENERGY TECHNOLOGY LABORATORY
Morgantown Center
3610 Collins Ferry Rd.
P.O. Box 880
Morgantown, WV 26507–0880
(304) 285–4764
Rita A. Bajura, director

PITTSBURGH CENTER
626 Cochrans Mill Rd.
P.O. Box 10940
Pittsburgh, PA 15236–0940
(412) 892–6122
Rita A. Bajura, director

NATIONAL PETROLEUM TECHNOLOGY OFFICE
Williams Center Tower 1
One W. 3rd St., #1400
Tulsa, OK 74103
(918) 699–2001
William F. Lawson, director

NAVAL PETROLEUM AND OIL SHALE RESERVES
907 N. Poplar St.
Casper, WY 82601
(307) 261–5161
Clarke D. Turner, director

STRATEGIC PETROLEUM RESERVE PROJECT MANAGEMENT OFFICE
900 Commerce Rd. E.
New Orleans, LA 70123
(504) 734–4201
William C. Gibson Jr., project manager

Health and Human Services Department

200 Independence Ave. S.W., Washington, DC 20201
Internet: http://www.os.dhhs.gov

Administration for Children and Families

901 D St. S.W., Washington, DC
370 L'Enfant Promenade S.W., Washington, DC 20447
Internet: http://www.acf.dhhs.gov

The Administration for Children and Families (ACF), within the Department of Health and Human Services, is responsible for federal programs that promote the economic and social well-being of families, children, individuals, and communities. Originally created by the secretary of Health and Human Services (HHS) in 1986 as the Family Support Administration (FSA), the ACF was created when the FSA merged with the Office of Human Development Services in 1991.

▉ WELFARE REFORM

The most prominent division of the ACF, the Office of Family Assistance, is the principal agency designated to carry out welfare—the federal programs that provide temporary financial assistance to needy families with dependent children. This office saw its mission transformed by the Personal Responsibility and Work Opportunity Reconciliation Act of 1996, a law designed to "end welfare as we know it," in the words of both President Bill Clinton and the Republicans in Congress. The law replaced the Aid to Families with Dependent Children (AFDC) program with a new plan called Temporary Assistance for Needy Families (TANF). Whereas AFDC provided direct cash assistance to families, TANF consists of block grants to the states, which were required to have their own welfare reform plans in place by July 1, 1997. New features of TANF include a requirement that most adult recipients must be working within two years of beginning welfare assistance, and a lifetime limit of five cumulative years of cash assistance for each family. States can exempt up to 20 percent of their caseload from this five-year limit, but alternatively they can impose a shorter time limit on welfare recipients. States have the option of further re-strictions: they can deny benefits to children born to welfare recipients, can deny benefits to unwed parents under age eighteen (unless they live with an adult and stay in school), and can maintain recipients who move in from another state at the benefit level that applied in their former state for one year. However, states must still follow the former AFDC rules with regard to eligibility for Medicaid.

The welfare reform law has many other provisions, some of which do not apply as specifically to the ACF, though they affect the agency's caseload significantly. The law denies most federal benefits to legal immigrants who are not citizens as well as to both legal and illegal aliens. It also tightens eligibility for food stamps, Supplemental Security Income (SSI) for disabled children, and the Earned Income Tax Credit. These restrictions account for most of the $54.1 billion savings that the new law was expected to provide through fiscal year 2002. The new law consolidates most federal child care funding into a block grant. It also provides for stronger child support enforcement, through a computer registry of child support cases against which employers must check new hires.

Welfare reform also places increased responsibilities on the ACF's Office of State Systems, which coordinates development of the automated systems that states will need to implement the new law and that are federally funded. In addition to integration of state welfare programs, State Systems is helping develop electronic benefits transfer for the payment of federal benefits.

The Food Stamp Reauthorization Act of 2002 amended the Personal Responsibility and Work Opportunity Reconciliation Act of 1996 to make all legal immigrant children, regardless of U.S. entry date, eligible for the SSI and food stamp programs, beginning in FY 2004.

OTHER ACF PROGRAMS

The ACF also performs its regulatory responsibilities through the following offices:

Community Services. This office is responsible for the distribution of Community Services Block Grants, which are used to provide services to local communities to assist low-income persons, including the elderly. It also administers the Social Service Block Grant program and carries out the Low Income Home Energy Assistance Program (LIHEAP) to assist low-income households in meeting the costs of home energy.

Child Support Enforcement. This office administers the program to ensure that children are supported by their parents. It locates absent parents, establishes paternity when necessary, establishes child support obligations, and enforces child support orders. The 1996 law requires states to establish a computerized registry of child support orders and a registry of new hires by employers (to verify compliance with child support responsibilities). The law gave states authority to suspend driver's licenses and professional licenses of "deadbeat" parents. The law also provides for centralized collection and disbursement of payments within states.

Refugee Resettlement. This office helps refugees achieve economic self-sufficiency within the shortest time possible. It provides a comprehensive program of cash, medical assistance, and social services. Unlike other noncitizens, refugees and those granted asylum are exempted from the new 1996 restrictions on welfare benefits.

Administration on Children, Youth, and Families (ACYF). ACYF is responsible for several programs that affect the well-being of low-income children and their families. Head Start provides education, social, medical, dental, nutrition, and mental health services to preschool children from low-income families. The Child Care and Development Block Grant funds state efforts to provide quality child care services for vulnerable family members who work, train for work, or attend school. Under the 1996 law, most of the federal child care and family preservation programs that were formally administered separately have been consolidated into the block grants.

Administration on Developmental Disabilities. This office manages grant programs that help people with developmental disabilities to reach maximum potential through increased independence, productivity, and community integration.

Administration for Native Americans. This office promotes the goal of social and economic self-sufficiency of American Indians, Alaskan Natives, Native Hawaiians, and other Native American Pacific Islanders, including Native Samoans.

President's Committee on Mental Retardation. This committee acts in an advisory capacity to the president and secretary on matters relating to programs and services for people with mental retardation.

Head Start Bureau. The bureau administers the Head Start program for preschool children from low-income families. Head Start provides children with activities that help them grow mentally, emotionally, socially, and physically. It provides comprehensive development services for America's low-income, preschool children ages three to five and social services for their families.

KEY PERSONNEL

Assistant Secretary
Wade F. Horn . . . . (202) 401–9200
Fax . . . . (202) 401–5770
Deputy Assistant Secretary, Operations
Laurence J. Love . . . . (202) 401–9200
Deputy Assistant Secretary, Policy and External Affairs
Martin Dannenfelser . . . . (202) 401–9200
Deputy Assistant Secretary, Administration
Curtis L. Coy . . . . (202) 401–9238
Child Support Enforcement
Sherri Z. Heller . . . . (202) 401–9370
Community Services
Clarence H. Carter . . . . (202) 401–9333
Family Assistance
Andrew Bush . . . . (202) 401–9275
Planning, Research, and Evaluation
Howard L. Rolston . . . . (202) 401–9220
Refugee Resettlement
Nguyen Van Hanh . . . . (202) 401–9246
State Systems
Vacant . . . . (202) 401–6960
Administration on Children, Youth, and Families
(330 C St. S.W., Washington, DC. Mailing address:
P.O.Box 1182, Washington, DC 20013)
Commissioner
Joan E. Ohl . . . . (202) 205–8347
Fax . . . . (202) 205–9721
Child Care Bureau
Shannon Christian . . . . (202) 690–6782
Children's Bureau
Susan Orr . . . . (202) 205–8618
Family and Youth Services Bureau
Vacant . . . . (202) 205–8086
Head Start Bureau
Wendy M. Hill . . . . (202) 205–8572

Administration on Developmental Disabilities
(200 Independence Ave. S.W., Washington, DC 20201)
Commissioner
Patricia A. Morrissey.................. (202) 690–6590
Fax..................................... (202) 690–6904
TDD .... (202) 690–6415
Administration for Native Americans
(200 Independence Ave. S.W., Washington, DC 20201)
Commissioner
Quanah Crossland Stamps .... (202) 690–7776
Fax..................................... (202) 690–7441
President's Committee on Mental Retardation
(330 Independence Ave. S.W., Washington, DC 20201)
Executive Director
Sally Atwater........................... (202) 619–0634
Fax..................................... (202) 205–9519
Child Abuse and Neglect
(200 Independence Ave. S.W., Washington, DC 20201)
Director
Catherine Nolan....................... (202) 260–5140

INFORMATION SOURCES

Internet
Agency Web Site: http://www.acf.dhhs.gov. Includes general information about ACF programs and administrative services, as well as information on welfare reform and links to child support information from various states.

Telephone Contacts
Domestic Violence Hotline .... (800) 799–SAFE
National Adoption Center .... (800) 862–3678
National Runaway Hotline................ (800) 621–4000

Information and Publications

KEY OFFICES

ACF Public Affairs
370 L'Enfant Promenade S.W.
Washington, DC 20447
(202) 401–9215
Fax (202) 205–9688
Vacant, director

Handles or refers general inquiries about ACF programs.

PUBLICATIONS
Selected fact sheets, including welfare reform information, are available on the agency's Web site.

DATA AND STATISTICS
Requests can be referred by ACF Public Affairs. Selected statistics are available via the agency's Web site.

RULES AND REGULATIONS
ACF rules and regulations are published in the *Code of Federal Regulations,* Title 42, parts 601–799. Proposed regulations, new final regulations, and updates to the *Code of Federal Regulations* are published in the daily *Federal Register.* (*See appendix for details on how to obtain and use these publications.*)

LEGISLATION
The ACF carries out its responsibilities under the following major laws:

Social Security Act, Title IV (49 Stat. 627, 42 U.S.C. 601). Signed by the president Aug. 14, 1935. Established the Aid to Families with Dependent Children (AFDC) program. Amendments over the years have both expanded and restricted benefits available to various categories of recipients. This legislation and its amendments also provide for most other programs administered by the ACF.

Personal Responsibility and Work Opportunity Reconciliation Act of 1996 (42 U.S.C. 1305 note). Signed by the president Aug. 22, 1996. Overhauled the AFDC program, replacing it with Temporary Assistance for Needy Families (TANF). Established time limits and work requirements for receipt of welfare assistance, shifted funding of welfare to block grants to states, required states to establish their own welfare plans by July 1, 1997, and provided for strengthened enforcement of child support payments.

Child Abuse Prevention and Enforcement Act (114 Stat. 35, 42 U.S.C. 3711 note). Signed by the president on March 10, 2000. Amended the Crime Identification Technology Act of 1998 to authorize the use of funds to upgrade the capability of the criminal justice system to deliver timely and accurate criminal record information to child welfare agencies and programs related to the protection of children, including protection against child sexual abuse and placement of children in foster care.

Strengthening Abuse and Neglect Courts Act of 2000 (P.L. 106-314). Signed by the president on Oct. 17, 2000. Directed the attorney general to award grants to help improve the data collection and case-tracking systems of state and local abuse and neglect courts.

Food Stamp Reauthorization Act of 2002 (Title IV of the 2002 Farm Bill) (116 Stat. 1348, 7 U.S.C. 7901 note). Signed by the president on May 13, 2002. Amended the Personal Responsibility and Work Opportunity Reconciliation Act of 1996 to make all legal immigrant children, regardless of U.S. entry date, eligible for the SSI and food stamp programs, beginning in FY 2004. Allowed legal immigrants who could demonstrate sixteen quarters of work history to become eligible for such programs. Eliminated the seven-year eligibility limit for food stamp benefits for refugees and SSI benefits for blind or disabled aliens who were lawfully residing in the United States on Aug. 22, 1996.

▪ REGIONAL OFFICES

REGION 1

(CT, MA, ME, NH, RI, VT)
John F. Kennedy Federal Bldg., #2000
Boston, MA 02203
(617) 565–1020
Hugh Galligan, administrator

REGION 2

(NJ, NY, PR, VI)
26 Federal Plaza, #4048
New York, NY 10278
(212) 264–2890
Mary Ann Higgins, administrator

REGION 3

(DC, DE, MD, PA, VA, WV)
150 S. Independence, Public Ledger Bldg.
Mall West, # 864
Philadelphia, PA 19101
(215) 861–4000
David Lett, administrator

REGION 4

(AL, FL, GA, KY, MS, NC, SC, TN)
Atlanta Federal Center
61 Forsyth St. SW, # 4M60
Atlanta, GA 30303
(404) 562–2900
Carlis Williams, administrator

REGION 5

(IL, IN, MI, MN, OH, WI)
233 N. Michigan Ave., #400
Chicago, IL 60601
(312) 353–2510
Joyce Thomas, administrator

REGION 6

(AR, LA, NM, OK, TX)
1301 Young St., #914
Dallas, TX 75202
(214) 767–9648
Leon McCowan, administrator

REGION 7

(IA, MO, NE)
Federal Office Bldg. #384
601 E. 12th St., #384
Kansas City, MO 64106
(816) 426–3981
Linda Lewis, administrator

REGION 8

(CO, MT, ND, SD, UT, WY)
1961 Stout St., #924
Denver, CO 80294–3538
(303) 844–3100
Beverly Turnbo, administrator

REGION 9

(AS, AZ, CA, GU, HI, MP, NV)
50 United Nations Plaza, #450
San Francisco, CA 94102
(415) 437–8400
Sharon Fujii, administrator

REGION 10

(AK, ID, OR, WA)
2201 Sixth Ave., #600, MS #RX-70
Seattle, WA 98121
(206) 615–2547
Stephen Henigson, administrator

Office for Civil Rights

330 Independence Ave. S.W., Washington, DC 20201
Internet: //www.os.dhhs.gov/ocr/

The Office for Civil Rights (OCR) in the Department of Health and Human Services (HHS) is responsible for ensuring (through the enforcement of various civil rights laws and regulations) that the beneficiaries of federal financial assistance provided by HHS receive services and benefits without discrimination. Services and benefits are provided through state agencies, nursing homes, skilled nursing facilities, medical laboratories, hospitals, day care centers, social service agencies, and other providers.

Any person who believes that he or she has been discriminated against in the provision of services because of age, race, color, disability, national origin, religion, or sex may file a complaint with the OCR. Discrimination in the provision of services includes the denial of services, the provision of services in a different manner, segregation in the provision of services, and otherwise providing services and benefits in a manner that treats groups of individuals receiving assistance under the same program differently.

The OCR is under the supervision of a director, who reports to the secretary of HHS. The director is responsible for the overall coordination of the agency's civil rights activities. The director is also the HHS secretary's special assistant for civil rights and serves as the secretary's chief advisor on all departmental civil rights matters. The office comprises policy and procedural staff headquartered in Washington and local staff in ten regional offices (*addresses below*).

COMPLAINTS

Any person with a complaint that discrimination exists in any program funded by HHS should notify the OCR. Complaints involving schools, colleges, and universities should be filed with the Department of Education. A writ-ten complaint usually should be filed with the regional office that serves the state in which the alleged discrimination occurred. Complaints may also be filed at OCR headquarters office.

Letters of complaint should contain the following information: who was discriminated against and in what way (grounds); which individual or institution was allegedly responsible for the discrimination; date of the alleged discriminatory action; person to contact for further information; the name, address, and telephone number of the person making the complaint; and as much background information as possible. Citizens may ask the nearest regional office for help in writing a complaint.

COMPLIANCE

The OCR conducts compliance reviews of institutions that receive HHS funds. These reviews determine whether policies or practices exist that are discriminatory in nature.

If the review indicates that probable discrimination exists, the OCR staff notifies the institution in writing, indicating the particular areas of noncompliance and advising the institution of its responsibility to prepare and submit a plan for correcting the situation. If an institution submits a plan that is unsatisfactory in any respect, the OCR will inform the institution of its deficiency.

ENFORCEMENT

If an institution refuses to correct discriminatory practices, the HHS will either initiate proceedings for the termination of the institution's federal financial assistance or refer the matter to the Department of Justice with a recommendation for appropriate legal action.

Termination proceedings begin with an administrative hearing before a federal administrative law judge. The judge's initial decision is subject to review by a departmental reviewing authority. A final appeal may be made to the secretary of HHS. Before becoming effective, termination orders are reported to the congressional committees with authority over the affected funds. Termination orders may be appealed to the U.S. District Court.

HEALTH INSURANCE PROTECTION

Recognizing the rapid evolution of health information systems, Congress moved to protect the privacy of health information by passing the Health Insurance Portability and Accountability Act of 1996 (HIPAA). HIPAA's administrative simplification provisions were designed to improve the health care system by facilitating the electronic exchange of information with respect to certain financial and administrative transactions carried out by health plans, health care clearinghouses, and health care providers. To implement these provisions, the statute directed HHS to adopt a suite of uniform, national standards for transactions, unique health identifiers, code sets for the data elements of the transactions, security of health information, and electronic signature.

HHS published a proposed rule concerning privacy standards for individually identifiable health information in November 1999. After reviewing and considering more than 52,000 public comments in response to the proposal, HHS issued a final rule on Dec. 28, 2000, establishing "Standards for Privacy of Individually Identifiable Health Information." The OCR is the HHS office responsible for implementing and enforcing the privacy regulation.

The new protections give patients greater access to their medical records and more control over how their personal information is used by their health plans and health care providers. Consumers will get a notice explaining how their health plans, doctors, pharmacies, and other health care providers use, disclose, and protect their personal information. In addition, consumers will have the ability to see and copy their health records and to request corrections of any errors included in their records. Consumers may file complaints about privacy issues with their health plans or providers or with the OCR.

KEY PERSONNEL

Director
  Richard M. Campanelli .... (202) 619–0403
  Principal Deputy Director
  Robinsue Frohboese .... (202) 619–0403

Deputy Director
  Robinsue Frohboese (acting) .... (202) 619–0403
Executive Staff Assistant to the Director
  Veronica Williams .... (202) 619–0403
Associate General Counsel for Civil Rights
  George Lyon .... (202) 619–0900
Program Policy and Training Division
  Claudia Schlosberg (acting) .... (202) 619–0553
Resource Management Division
  Steve Melov .... (202) 619–0503
Voluntary Compliance and Outreach Division
  Johnny Nelson .... (202) 619–2742
Senior Health Information Privacy Policy Specialist
  Susan McAndrew .... (202) 260–3314

INFORMATION SOURCES

Internet

Agency Web Site: http://www.os.hhs.gov/ocr. Features information on regulations and how to file a complaint, fact sheets on the legal rights of various groups, and frequently asked questions.

Telephone Contacts

Personnel Locator .... (202) 619–0257
Hotline .... (800) 368–1019
  Privacy Hotline .... (866) 627–7748
  TDD .... (800) 527–7697
Fax .... (202) 619–3818

Information and Publications

KEY OFFICES

Program Policy and Training Division
200 Independence Ave. S.W., #509-F
Washington, DC 20201
(202) 619–0553
Claudia Schlosberg (acting), director
(202) 619–3197
Larry Velez, OCR FOIA coordinator

Answers questions about the office and its activities. Handles Freedom of Information requests; requests for agency personnel to speak before group meetings; and prepares news releases, publications, and other informational materials concerning the civil rights compliance programs. Maintains a mailing list.

PUBLICATIONS

Contact the OCR Program, Policy and Training Division for specific publications or to receive information on a regular basis. Materials available include factsheets and posters on civil rights laws enforced by OCR. Titles include:

Know Your Civil Rights
Your Rights Under Title VI
Your Rights Under Section 504S
Your Rights Under the Americans With Disabilities Act
Your Rights Under the Age Discrimination Act

DATA AND STATISTICS

Contact the OCR Policy and Special Projects Staff.

Reference Resources

LIBRARY

The OCR Program, Policy and Training Division handles reference requests.

RULES AND REGULATIONS

OCR rules and regulations are published in the *Code of Federal Regulations*, Title 45, parts 80–86. Proposed regulations, new final regulations, and updates to the *Code of Federal Regulations* are published in the daily *Federal Register*. (*See appendix for details on how to obtain and use these publications.*)

▨ LEGISLATION

The OCR administers the following laws in full or in part:

Hospital Survey and Construction Act (78 Stat. 447, 42 U.S.C. 291c(e)). Signed by the president July 1, 1944. Also known as the Hill-Burton Act. Ensured that federally assisted hospital or health care facilities provide services to all persons residing in the community without discrimination based on race, color, national origin, or method of payment.

Civil Rights Act of 1964, Title VI (78 Stat. 241, 42 U.S.C. 2000d). Signed by the president July 2, 1964. Prohibited discrimination based on race, color, or national origin in programs receiving federal financial assistance.

Comprehensive Alcohol Abuse and Alcoholism Prevention Treatment and Rehabilitation Act of 1970, Section 321 (84 Stat. 1848, 42 U.S.C. 4581). Signed by the president Dec. 30, 1970. Prohibited hospital discrimination against alcoholics in admissions or treatment solely because of alcohol abuse.

Health Manpower Training Act of 1971, Title VII (84 Stat. 1355, 42 U.S.C. 292d). Signed by the president Nov. 18, 1971. Amended the Public Health Service Act to bar sex discrimination in admissions to health training programs.

Drug Abuse Offense and Treatment Act of 1972 (86 Stat. 65, 21 U.S.C. 1171–1180). Signed by the president March 21, 1972. Prohibited hospitals receiving federal assistance from refusing admission or treatment to anyone needing emergency care solely because that person is dependent on or addicted to drugs.

Education Amendments of 1972, Title IX (86 Stat. 235, 20 U.S.C. 1681–1686). Signed by the president June 23, 1972. Prohibited sex discrimination in federally assisted education programs.

Rehabilitation Act of 1973, Title V, Section 504 (87 Stat. 355, 29 U.S.C. 701). Signed by the president Sept. 26, 1973. Prohibited discrimination against the handicapped in programs receiving federal financial assistance.

Age Discrimination Act of 1975 (89 Stat. 713, 42 U.S.C. 3001). Signed by the president Nov. 28, 1975. Prohibited discrimination because of age in programs receiving federal financial assistance.

Omnibus Budget Reconciliation Act of 1981 (95 Stat. 357, 31 U.S.C. 1331). Signed by the president Aug. 31, 1981. Established block grant programs to be administered by the HHS secretary. Authorizations for six of the seven grant programs included sex and religion provisions along with the existing nondiscrimination requirements.

Child Abuse Amendments of 1984 (98 Stat. 1761, 42 U.S.C. 10406). Signed by the president Oct. 9, 1984. Extended and improved provisions of laws relating to child abuse, neglect, and adoption. Section 307(a) prohibited discrimination on the basis of age, handicap, sex, race, color, or national origin in participating in programs or receiving funds made available under this act.

Civil Rights Act of 1991 (105 Stat. 1071, 42 U.S.C. 1981 note). Signed by the president Nov. 21, 1991. Promoted the goals of ridding the workplace of discrimination on the basis of race, color, sex, religion, national origin, and disability.

Health Insurance Portability and Accountability Act of 1996 (110 Stat. 1936, 42 U.S.C. 201 note). Signed by the president on Aug. 21, 1996. Directed the secretary of health and human services to submit to specified congressional committees detailed recommendations on standards with respect to the privacy of individually identifiable health information.

▨ REGIONAL OFFICES

REGION 1

(CT, MA, ME, NH, RI, VT)
John F. Kennedy Federal Bldg., #1875
Boston, MA 02203
(617) 565–1340
TDD (617) 565–1343
Peter Chan (acting), regional manager

REGION 2
(NJ, NY, PR, VI)
26 Federal Plaza, #3312
New York, NY 10278
(212) 264–3313
TDD (212) 264–2355
Michael Carter, regional manager

REGION 3
(DC, DE, MD, PA, VA, WV)
150 S. Independence Mall West, #372
Philadelphia, PA 19106
(215) 861–4441
TDD (215) 861–4440
Paul Cushing, regional manager

REGION 4
(AL, FL, GA, KY, MS, NC, SC, TN)
Atlanta Federal Center, #3B70
Atlanta, GA 30303
(404) 562–7886
TDD (404) 331–2867
Roosevelt Freeman, regional manager

REGION 5
(IL, IN, MI, MN, OH, WI)
233 North Michigan, #240
Chicago, IL 60601
(312) 886–2359
TDD (312) 353–5693
Lisa Simeone, regional manager

REGION 6
(AR, LA, NM, OK, TX)
1301 Young St., #1169
Dallas, TX 75202
(214) 767–4056
TDD (214) 767–8940
Ralph Rouse, regional manager

REGION 7
(IA, KS, MO, NE)
601 E. 12th St., #248
Kansas City, MO 64106
(816) 426–7278
TDD (816) 426–7065
Fred Lang (acting), regional manager

REGION 8
(CO, MT, ND, SD, UT, WY)
1961 Stout St., #1185 FOB
Denver, CO 80294
(303) 844–2024
TDD (303) 844–3439
Velveta Howell, regional manager

REGION 9
(AS, AZ, CA, GU, HI, MP, NV)
50 United Nations Plaza, #322
San Francisco, CA 94102
(415) 437–8310
TDD (415) 437–8311
Ira Pollack, regional manager

REGION 10
(AK, ID, OR, WA)
2201 Sixth Ave., #900
Seattle, WA 98121
(206) 615–2287
TDD (206) 615–2296
Linda Yuu Connor (acting), regional manager

Other Health and Human Services Department Offices

ADMINISTRATION ON AGING

1 Massachusetts Ave., N.W., 5th Floor
Washington, DC 20201
Internet: http://www.aoa.gov

Assistant Secretary
Josefina Carbonell..................... (202) 401–4634
Fax................................... (202) 357–3556
Deputy Assistant Secretary for Policy and Programs
Edwin Walker.......................... (202) 619–3032
Management
Mike Mangano .... (202) 357–3430
Director of Center for Communications and Consumer Services
Carol Crecy........................... (202) 401–4541
Director of Center for Planning and Policy Development
John Wren .... (202) 357–3460
American Indian, Alaskan, and Native Hawaiian Programs
M. Yvonne Jackson.................... (202) 357–3501
Budget and Finance
Steve Hagy............................ (202) 357–3420
Grants Management
Margaret Tolson....................... (202) 357–3440

The Administration on Aging is the principal agency designated to carry out the provisions of the Older Americans Act of 1965, as amended. The agency directly assists the secretary in all matters pertaining to problems of the aging. Specifically, the agency advocates for the needs of older persons in program planning and policy development within the Department of Health and Human Services and in other federal agencies; gives priority to older persons in greatest economic or social need; develops standards and issues best practice guidelines; disseminates information; provides technical assistance; and initiates policy related to services funded by the department and provided to older persons. The agency also administers a program of formula grants to states to establish state and community programs for older persons; administers a program of grants to American Indians, Alaskan Natives, and Native Hawaiians to establish programs for older Native Americans; provides policy and procedural direction, advice, and assistance to states and Native American grantees to promote the development of state and Native American-administered, community-based systems of comprehensive social services for older persons; and administers other programs that provide legal services, training, long-term care, and nutrition services for older Native Americans.

The agency's Internet site has general information about the administration, as well as links to more specific information on how to get help in caring for older people, including federal programs and Internet resources for the aging.

CENTERS FOR MEDICARE AND MEDICAID SERVICES

7500 Security Blvd.
Baltimore, MD 21244
Internet: http://cms.hhs.gov/

Administrator
Thomas A. Scully...................... (202) 690–6726
Fax................................... (202) 690–6262

Deputy Administrator
Leslie Norwalk (acting) .... (202) 690–5727
Press
Rob Sweezy .... (410) 786–5110
Equal Opportunity and Civil Rights
Ramon Suris-Fernandez .... (410) 786-5109
Office of Strategic and Regulatory Affairs
Jacquelyn Y. White .... (202) 690–8390
Freedom of Information
(7500 Security Blvd., Baltimore, MD 21244)
Director, Office of Information Services
Tim Love
Legislation
Robert Foreman .... (202) 690–5960
Fax .... (202) 690–8168
Health Plans and Providers
(7500 Security Blvd., Baltimore, MD 21244)
Director, Center for Medicare Management
Tom Grissom .... (410) 786–4164
Fax .... (202) 690–2505
Mark Miller .... (410) 786–4164
Fax .... (410) 786–5010
Medicaid and State Operations
(7500 Security Blvd., Baltimore, MD 21244)
Dennis Smith (acting) .... (202) 690–7428
Fax .... (202) 358–3403
Internal Customer Support
(7500 Security Blvd., Baltimore, MD 21244)
Ellen Gochnauer .... (410) 786–1051
Fax .... (410) 786–7585
Information Services
Tim Love .... (410) 786–1800
Financial Management
Michelle Snyder .... (410) 786–5448
Clinical Standards and Quality
Sean Tunis .... (410) 786–6841
Office of Research, Development, and Information
(7500 Security Blvd., Baltimore, MD 21244)
Stuart Guterman .... (410) 786–0948
Fax .... (410) 786–6511
Center for Beneficiary Choices
(7500 Security Blvd., Baltimore, MD 21244)
Gail McGrath .... (410) 786–2140
Fax .... (410) 786–5487
Office of Operations Management
Brenda Sykes .... (410) 786–4160
Fax .... (410) 786–1347
Office of HIPAA Standards
Jared Adair .... (410) 786–4160
Fax .... (410) 786–1347
Office of the Actuary
Rick Foster .... (410) 786–6347
Fax .... (410) 786–1295

The Centers for Medicare and Medicaid Services (CMS) are responsible for oversight of the Medicare program, the federal portion of the Medicaid program, and related federal medical care quality control activities. Originally created as the Health Care Financing Administration (HCFA) in 1977, the administration of George W. Bush renamed the agency the CMS on July 1, 2001.

The name change reflected the reform efforts undertaken to make the CMS more responsive and effective for its Medicare and Medicaid beneficiaries. In October 2001 the CMS launched a Medicare 800 number (800-633-4227) that provided service to beneficiaries twenty-four hours a day, seven days a week. The CMS also launched a national media campaign to give seniors and other Medicare beneficiaries more information about their Medicare and Medicaid benefits to help them make informed health care choices.

The CMS was restructured around three centers to focus on its distinct lines of business. The Center for Medicare Management focuses on the management of the traditional fee-for-service Medicare program, including development and implementation of payment policy and management of the Medicare carriers and fiscal intermediaries. The Center for Beneficiary Choices focuses on providing beneficiaries with the information they need to make their health care decisions. This center also includes management of the Medicare+Choice program, consumer research and demonstrations, and grievance and appeals. The Center for Medicaid and State Operations focuses on programs administered by the states, including Medicaid, the State Children's Health Insurance Program, private insurance, survey and certification and the Clinical Laboratory Improvement Amendments.

Medicare helps pay hospital and supplementary medical bills for people aged sixty-five or older. Medicare also pays for medical services for persons with permanent kidney failure or persons who have been Social Security or Railroad Retirement Board disability beneficiaries for more than two years. Medicaid is jointly funded by the federal government and the states. It finances health care for the financially disadvantaged.

▓ OFFICE OF THE INSPECTOR GENERAL

330 Independence Ave. S.W.
Washington, DC 20201
Internet: oig.hhs.gov

Inspector General
Vacant .... (202) 619–3148
Fax .... (202) 619–0521

Principal Deputy Inspector General
Dennis Duquette (acting) .... (202) 619–3148
Deputy Inspector General for Airport Services
George Grob .... (202) 619–3155
Deputy Inspector General, Evaluation and Inspectors
Joseph E. Vegrin .... (202) 619–0480
Deputy Inspector General for Investigations
Vicki L. Shepard .... (202) 619–3208
Deputy Inspector General, Office of Counsel to the Inspector General
Lewis Morris .... (202) 205–0602
External Affairs
Kimberly Bryant .... (202) 205–9523

The OIG was established to carry out the mission of promoting economy, efficiency, and effectiveness through the elimination of waste, abuse, and fraud. The organization:

- Conducts and supervises audits, investigations, inspections, and evaluations relating to HHS programs and operations.
- Indentifies systemic weaknesses giving rise to opportunities for fraud and abuse in HHS programs and operations and making recommendations to prevent their recurrence.
- Leads and coordinates activities to prevent and detect fraud and abuse in HHS programs.
- Detects wrongdoers and abusers of HHS programs and beneficiaries so appropriate remedies may be brought to bear.
- Keeps the Secretary and Congress fully and currently informed about problems and deficiencies in the administration of such programs and operations and about the need for and progress of corrective action, including imposing sanctions against providers of health care under Medicare and Medicaid who commit certain prohibited acts.

In support of its mission, the OIG carries out and maintains an internal quality assurance system and a peer review system with other OIGs that include periodic quality assessment studies and quality control reviews, to provide reasonable assurance that applicable laws, regulations, policies, procedures, standards, and other requirements are followed; are effective; and are functioning as intended in OIG operations.

▓ PUBLIC HEALTH AND SCIENCE

200 Independence Ave. S.W.
Washington, DC 20201
Internet: http://www.osophs.dhhs.gov/ophs

Assistant Secretary for Health
Richard H. Carmona (acting) .... (202) 690–7694
Fax .... (202) 690–6960
Principal Deputy Assistant Secretary for Health
Cristina Beato .... (202) 690–7694
Fax .... (202) 690–6960
Disease Prevention and Health Promotion
Elizabeth Majestic (acting) .... (202) 401–6295
Fax .... (202) 205–9478
HIV/AIDS Policy
Christopher Bates (acting) .... (202) 690–5560
Fax .... (202) 690–7560
International and Refugee Health
(5600 Fishers Lane, Rockville, MD 20857)
Thomas Novotny .... (301) 443–1774
Minority Health
(1101 Wootton Parkway, The Tower Building, Rockville, MD 20852)
Nathaniel Stinson .... (301) 443–5084
Fax .... (301) 594–0767
Human Research Protections
(1101 Wootton Parkway, The Tower Building, Rockville, MD 20852)
Bernard Schwetz (acting) .... (301) 436–7005
Fax .... (301) 402–0527
Population Affairs
(5600 Fishers Lane, Rockville, MD 20857)
Denise Shervingon .... (301) 594–4000
President's Council on Physical Fitness and Sports
Penelope Royall (acting) .... (202) 690–5187
Fax .... (202) 690–5211
Research Integrity
(1101 Wootton Parkway, The Tower Building, Rockville, MD 20852)
Chris Pascal .... (301) 443–3400
Fax .... (301) 443–5341
Surgeon General
(5600 Fishers Lane, Parklawn Building, Rockville, MD 20857)
Richard H. Carmona .... (301) 443–4000
Fax .... (301) 443–8590
Women's Health
Wanda K. Jones .... (202) 690–7650
Fax .... (202) 690–7172
National Vaccine Program
Bruce Gellin .... (202) 205–1832
Fax .... (202) 690–4631

The Office of Public Health and Science (OPHS) was created in 1995 through a reorganization within the Department of Health and Human Services (HHS) which affected the Office of the Secretary and the Public Health Service (PHS). The reorganization designated the eight PHS agencies as Operating Divisions reporting directly to the secretary, established the OPHS within the Office of the Secretary, and abolished the Office of the Assistant Secretary for Health. The position of assistant secretary for health has been retained; the assistant secretary directs the OPHS and serves as the secretary's senior advisor for public health and science.

The OPHS serves as the focal point for leadership and coordination across HHS for public health and science; provides direction to program offices within OPHS and other HHS components; and provides advice and counsel on public health and science issues to the secretary.

The OPHS also provides advice on broad-based health assessments to better define public health problems; assists in the design and implementation of strategies to sustain and improve national health conditions; recommends policy and analyzes legislation; and maintains specialized staffs that examine major public health and science issues.

The name "Public Health Service," as newly defined, applies to the OPHS, the ten regional offices of HHS, and the following eight Operating Divisions: Agency for Health Care Policy and Research, Agency for Toxic Substances and Disease, Centers for Disease Control and Prevention, Food and Drug Administration (p. 205), Health Resources and Services Administration, Indian Health Service, National Institutes of Health, and Substance Abuse and Mental Health Administration.

The OPHS Internet site includes information on the various component offices and programs of the OPHS.

▓ REGIONAL OFFICES

The following regional offices serve all HHS agencies.

REGION 1
(CT, MA, ME, NH, RI, VT)
John F. Kennedy Federal Bldg., #2100
Boston, MA 02203–0001
(617) 565–1500
Betsy F. Rosenfeld (acting), regional director

REGION 2
(NJ, NY, PR, VI)
26 Federal Plaza
New York, NY 10278–0022
(212) 264–4600
Gilberto Cardona, regional director

REGION 3
(DC, DE, MD, PA, VA, WV)
150 S. Independence Mall West, #436
Philadelphia, PA 19106
(215) 861-4633
Dalton G. Paxman, regional director

REGION 4
(AL, FL, GA, KY, MS, NC, SC, TN)
61 Forsyth St. S.W., #5B95
Atlanta, GA 30303
(404) 562-6888
J. Jarrett Clinton (acting), regional director

REGION 5
(IL, IN, MI, MN, OH, WI)
233 N. Michigan Ave., #1300
Chicago, IL 60601
(312) 353–5160
Steven R. Postic, regional director

REGION 6
(AR, LA, NM, OK, TX)
1301 Young St., #1124
Dallas, TX 75202
(214) 767–3301
James A. Doss (acting), regional director

REGION 7
(IA, KS, MO, NE)
601 E. 12th St., #210
Kansas City, MO 64106–2898
(816) 426–2821
Linda Vogel, regional director

REGION 8
(CO, MT, ND, SD, UT, WY)
1961 Stout St., #1076
Denver, CO 80294–1185
(303) 844–3372
Jane Wilson, regional director

REGION 9
(AS, AZ, CA, GU, HI, NV)
50 United Nations Plaza, #431
San Francisco, CA 94102–4988
(415) 437-8500
Ronald Banks, regional director

REGION 10
(AK, ID, OR, WA)
2201 Sixth Ave., #1208
Seattle, WA 98121–1832
(206) 615–2010
Patrick O'Carroll, regional director

Homeland Security Department

3801 Nebraska Ave. N.W., 20395
Internet: http://www.dhs.gov

Bureau of Citizenship and Immigration Service

425 Eye St. N.W., Washington, DC 20536
Internet: http://www.bcis.gov/

The Homeland Security Act of 2002 established the Bureau of Citizenship and Immigration Services (BCIS) within the Department of Homeland Security (DHS) on March 1, 2003. The BCIS assumed the service and benefit functions of the old Immigration and Naturalization Service (INS). The investigation and enforcement activities of INS transferred to the Bureau of Immigration and Customs Enforcement (ICE) *(see p. 536)*; the Border Patrol transferred to the Bureau of Customs and Border Protection (CBP) *(see p. 529)*.

The BCIS is headed by the director of BCIS, who reports directly to the deputy secretary for homeland security.

The bureau allows the DHS to improve the administration of benefits and immigration services for applicants by exclusively focusing on immigration and citizenship services. This new bureau includes approximately 15,000 employees and contractors working in approximately 250 headquarters and field offices around the world. BCIS local offices are still located in the old INS locations, including Application Support Centers and Service Centers. In 2003 there was no immediate plans for changes in office locations.

The BCIS is responsible for the administration of immigration and naturalization adjudication functions and establishing immigration services policies and priorities. These functions include

- Adjudication of immigrant visa petitions.
- Adjudication of naturalization petitions.
- Adjudication of asylum and refugee applications.
- Adjudication performed at the service centers.
- All other adjudication performed by the old INS.

In the 1990s the issue of immigration became highly politicized, with regard to both legal and illegal immigrants, and at both the national and state levels. In such a climate, the increasing efficiency of the INS—in fiscal 1996 it processed a record 1.3 million citizenship applications, 240,000 of which were rejected—has been seen by some as a political gesture, rather than an example of the "reinvention" sought by President Bill Clinton. Republicans in Congress charged that the INS was rushing to swear in new citizens to bolster the ranks of the Democratic Party.

In October 1996 a subcommittee of the House Government Oversight and Reform began examining FBI files for 50,000 new citizens, on the assumption that these files would reveal criminal records that should have disqualified these people from naturalization. In response, INS Commissioner Doris Meissner pointed to another record the agency had set during her tenure: the INS had removed 100,000 criminals from the United States in three years, as well as some 60,000 other illegal aliens. In December 1997 Congress passed a law "to establish a program in local prisons to identify, prior to arraignment, criminal aliens and aliens who are unlawfully present in the United States."

In the mid-1990s the Republican-controlled Congress also passed sweeping reforms that affected immigrants. The Personal Responsibility and Work Opportunity Reconciliation Act of 1996 (the Welfare Act) denied many public benefits to legal and illegal immigrants. The Illegal Immigration Reform and Immigration Responsibility Act of 1996 tightened requirements for family-based immigration. The act also charged the INS to establish a verification system for most federal public benefits.

The Food Stamp Reauthorization Act of 2002 amended the Welfare Act to make all legal immigrant children, regardless of U.S. entry date, eligible for the supplemental security income (SSI) and food stamp programs, beginning in FY 2004. The SSI program is administered by the Social Security Administration *(see p. 374)*. The food stamp program is administered by the Department of Health and Human Services' Administration for Children and Families *(see p. 510).*

Between 1993 and 2000, nearly 6.9 million immigrants applied for citizenship, more than the total in the previous forty years combined. The INS's pending caseload of naturalization applications grew to more than 2 million in 1998. Faced with this unprecedented workload, INS undertook a two-year initiative to clear the naturalization backlog and restore timely processing of citizenship applications. By the end of 2002 (before its transition to the BCIS), the pending caseload had dropped to nearly 600,000—the lowest it has been since November 1996.

■ KEY PERSONNEL

Director
Eduardo Aguirre (acting) .... (202) 514–4600
  Fax .... (202) 305–0134
Assistant Secretary
Michael Petrucelli .... (202) 514–3200
Director of Operations
Bill Yates .... (202) 514–6442
Principal Legal Advisor
Mark D. Wallace .... (202) 514–2895
Assistant Commissioner for Budget
Suzanne H. Wilson (acting) .... (202) 514–3206
Assistant Commissioner for Human Resource Management
Rick Hastings .... (202) 514–3636
Benefits
Michael L. Aytes .... (202) 514–3156
International Affairs
Renee Harris (acting) .... (202) 305–2798

■ INFORMATION SOURCES

Internet

Agency Web Site: http://www.bcis.gov. Includes an overview of the agency, frequently asked questions, press releases, BCIS regulations, employer information, and links to other federal Internet sites. Data and statistics on immigration and foreign-born population are also accessible through the agency's Web site. BCIS forms are also accessible and may be downloaded from the BCIS Web site.

Telephone Contacts

Personnel Locator .... (202) 514–2525
BCIS Forms Request Line .... (800) 870–3676
Unfair Employment Hotline .... (800) 255–7688

Information and Publications

KEY OFFICES

BCIS General Information Office
425 Eye St. N.W.
Washington, DC 20536
(202) 514–2607

Answers general questions; provides information to the public on how to obtain benefits under immigration law. The Headquarters' Ask Immigration Information Line is an automated telephone service with information on visas, immigration, green cards, citizenship, and other matters; dial (202) 514–4316. Outside the Washington area, dial (800) 375-5283.

BCIS Public Affairs
425 Eye St. N.W., Room 7021
Washington, DC 20536
(202) 514–2648
Fax (202) 514–1776
Russ Bergeron, director

Answers questions from the press. Issues news releases and media information materials.

Freedom of Information
425 Eye St. N.W.
Washington, DC 20536
(202) 514–1722
Magda Ortiz, FOI officer

DOJ Public Affairs
10th St. and Pennsylvania Ave. N.W., Room 1228
Washington, DC 20530
(202) 514–2007

Distributes publications describing the department's organization, functions, and legal procedures, including the BCIS. The attorney general's annual report also covers the policies and programs of the BCIS.

PUBLICATIONS

For most publications, contact DOJ Public Affairs.

Teachers' manuals and textbooks on citizenship, written at various reading levels, are available to candidates for naturalization. They are distributed free to public schools and are available for purchase from the Government Printing Office (GPO): see appendix, Ordering Government Publications.

Reference Resources

LIBRARIES

BCIS Public Reading Room
425 Eye St. N.W., 2nd Floor Ullico Bldg.
Washington, DC 20536
(202) 514–1722
Pamela Ball, contact
Hours: 8:00 a.m. to 4:30 p.m.

Maintains BCIS annual reports, statistical reports on aliens and immigrants, interim decisions of the Board of Immigration Appeals, booklets describing immigration forms, and information on immigration regulations. Call ahead for appointment.

BCIS History Office
425 Eye St. N.W., Room 1100
Washington, DC 20536
(202) 514–2837
Marian Smith, contact

Maintains a collection on the history of the BCIS and immigration in general. Open to the public by appointment only.

▮ LEGISLATION

The BCIS carries out its responsibilities under:

Immigration and Nationality Act, as amended (66 Stat. 163, 8 U.S.C. 1101). Signed by the president June 27, 1952. Contained virtually all of the law relating to the entry of aliens and to the acquisition and loss of U.S. citizenship.

Immigration Act of 1990 (104 Stat. 4978, 8 U.S.C. 1101 note). Signed by the president Nov. 29, 1990. Implemented major changes affecting immigrants and nonimmigrants, Filipino World War II veterans desiring U.S. citizenship, and El Salvadoran nationals, and others with immigration concerns. Revised the numerical limits and preference system regulating immigration, empowered the attorney general to issue final determinations on applications for U.S. citizenship, and charged INS with issuing certificates of naturalization.

Immigration and Nationality Technical Corrections Act of 1994 (108 Stat. 4305, 8 U.S.C. 1101). Signed by the president Oct. 25, 1994. Made numerous specific changes to the Immigration and Nationality Act. Allowed U.S. visas for visits from officials of Taiwan; gave equal treatment to women in conferring U.S. citizenship to children born abroad.

Personal Responsibility and Work Opportunity Reconciliation Act of 1996 (The Welfare Act) (110 Stat. 2260, 8 U.S.C. 1601). Signed by the president Aug. 22, 1996. Restricted the access of legal and illegal immigrants to many public benefits.

Illegal Immigration Reform and Immigration Responsibility Act of 1996 (110 Stat. 3009-5468, U.S.C. 1101 note). Signed by the president Sept. 30, 1996. Changed the public charge of inadmissibility standard for prospective immigrants and greatly strengthened the financial responsibility of petitioners for family-based immigrants as well as for some employment-based immigrants. Required the INS to establish a verification system for most federal public benefits. Required INS to verify status of aliens and naturalized citizens for federal, state, or local government agencies.

Torture Victims Relief Act of 1998 (13 Stat. 1301, 22 U.S.C. 2151 note). Signed by the president on Oct. 30, 1998. Recognized that a significant number of refugees and asylees entering the United States have been victims of torture and required INS to give those claiming asylum prompt consideration of their applications for political asylum.

Intercountry Adoption Act of 2000 (114 Stat. 825, 42 U.S.C. 14901 note). Signed by the president on Oct. 6, 2000. Amended the Immigration and Nationality Act to include under its definition of "child" an adopted child.

The Child Citizenship Act (CCA) (114 Stat. 1631, 8 U.S.C. 1101 note). Signed by the president on Oct. 30, 2000. Amended the Immigration and Nationality Act to provide automatic U.S. citizenship for a child born outside the United States when the following conditions are met: (1) at least one parent is a U.S. citizen; (2) the child is under eighteen years old; and (3) the child is residing in the United States in the legal and physical custody of the citizen parent pursuant to a lawful admission for permanent residence.

Legal Immigration Family Equity Act (LIFE Act) (7 U.S.C. 1101 note). Signed by the president on Dec. 21, 2000. Amended the Immigration and Nationality Act to accord nonimmigrant status to certain aliens: (1) with pending or approved but unavailable visa petitions who are the spouses or unmarried sons and daughters of permanent resident aliens; and (2) with approved but unavailable visa petitions who are the spouses of U.S. citizens or minor children of such spouses.

Food Stamp Reauthorization Act of 2002 (Title IV of the 2002 Farm Bill) (116 Stat. 1348, 7 U.S.C. 7901 note). Signed by the president on May 13, 2002. Amended the Personal Responsibility and Work Opportunity Reconciliation Act of 1996 to make all legal immigrant children, regardless of U.S. entry date, eligible for the SSI and food stamp programs, beginning in FY 2004.

Homeland Security Act of 2002 (P.L. 107-296). Signed by the president Nov. 25, 2002. Created the Department of Homeland Security (DHS). Gave DHS exclusive authority to issue, administer, and enforce regulations with respect to the Immigration and Nationality Act (INA). Authorized the BCIS to (1) establish the policies for performing and administering transferred INS functions; (2) establish national immigration services policies and priorities; and (3) implement a managerial rotation program.

Bureau of Customs and Border Protection

1300 Pennsylvania Ave. N.W., Washington, DC 20229
Internet: http://www.customs.gov

The Bureau of Customs and Border Protection (CBP) became an official agency of the Department of Homeland Security (DHS) on March 1, 2003, combining employees from the Department of Agriculture (Agriculture and Quarantine Inspections), the Immigration and Naturalization Service (INS) inspection services, the Border Patrol, and the U.S. Customs Service (USCS). CBP, which is organized within the DHS Border and Transportation Directorate. The investigative and enforcement functions of the Customs Service were transferred to the Bureau of Immigration and Customs Enforcement (ICE) (see p. 536).

CBP is headed by a commissioner who is appointed by the president and confirmed by the Senate. The Customs Service commissioner originally transferred as the commissioner for CBP.

To accomplish its mission of inspecting goods and people crossing the U.S. borders, CBP has a workforce of more than 42,000 employees, including inspectors, canine enforcement officers, border patrol agents, trade specialists, and mission support staff.

The CBP Transition Management Office, a temporary office, is responsible for ensuring a smooth integration of the four component agencies of CBP. This integration involves merging enforcement, trade, culture, operations, budget, human resources, training, and public affairs elements. The budgets of all components total more than $6.7 billion.

CBP works with the trade community to develop, enhance, and maintain security processes throughout the global supply chain and to stem the illegal export of equipment, technology, and munitions to unauthorized destinations. Cooperation between the United States and other nations is needed to allow placement of U.S. inspectors in foreign ports to screen containers before it enters the United States.

As the single unified U.S. border agency, CBP's mission is to improve security and facilitate the flow of legitimate trade and travel. The strategy to accomplish this mission includes

- Improving targeting systems and expanding advance information regarding people and goods arriving in the United States.
- Partnering with foreign governments as well as with the private sector.
- Deploying advanced inspection technology and equipment.
- Increasing staffing for border security.
- Working in concert with other agencies to coordinate activities with respect to trade fraud, intellectual property rights violations, controlled deliveries of illegal drugs, and money laundering.

The key CBP offices are the following:

Office of Field Operations. Manages more than 25,000 employees with more than 19,000 dedicated and vigilant inspectors that protect U.S. borders. Operates twenty field operations offices; 317 ports of entry; fourteen preclearance stations in Canada and the Caribbean; and agricultural quarantine inspection at all ports of entry in order to protect the health of U.S. plant and animal resources. Manages core CBP programs such as border security and facilitation, which handle interdiction and security, passenger operations, targeting and analysis, and canine enforcement.

Office of Trade Relations. Serves as the liaison between industry and CBP officials. Fosters positive relationships with the trade community.

Office of International Affairs. Operates international activities and programs and for conducting customs bilateral and multilateral relations with other countries. Manages the operations of the Customs foreign attachés and advisory teams.

Office of Intelligence. Produces all-source intelligence products for CBP and serves as the CBP liaison to the intelligence community and other federal law enforcement agencies. Detects and identifies criminal, drug, and alien smuggling; detects terrorist groups attempting to cross U.S. borders; and disseminates strategic, operational, and tactical intelligence on criminal and terrorist groups to CBP border security units for use in targeting and interdiction.

Office of Regulations and Rulings. Develops, implements, and evaluates bureau-wide programs, policies, and procedures pertaining to regulations and rulings issued by and affecting customs. Provides informed compliance information to members of the trade community.

▒ KEY PERSONNEL

Commissioner of Customs
Robert C. Bonner .... (202) 927–1000
Deputy Commissioner of Customs
Douglas M. Browning .... (202) 927–1010
Border Interdiction Committee (BIC)
William S. Heffelfinger III .... (202) 927–0230
Chief Counsel
Alfonso Robles .... (202) 927–6900
Fax .... (202) 927–6940
Congressional Affairs
Richard Quinn (acting) .... (202) 927–1760
Fax .... (202) 927–2152
Finance
John Eichelberger .... (202) 927–0600
Fax .... (202) 927–9286
National Finance Center
(6026 Lakeside Blvd., Indianapolis, IN 42678–1988)
Thomas Smith .... (317) 298–1200
Budget
Carol Johnson .... (202) 927–0310
Financial Management
Mari Boyd .... (202) 927–0620
Financial Systems Division
(6026 Lakeside Blvd., Indianapolis, IN 42678–1988)
Tom Garrison .... (317) 298–1520
Logistics
Martha Heggestad (acting) .... (202) 927–0120
Procurement
Gregory Doyle .... (202) 927–0990
Planning
Vacant .... (202) 927–7700
Fax .... (202) 927–0172

Public Affairs
Dennis Murphy .... (202) 927–1770
Fax .... (202) 927–1393
Trade Ombudsman
Eula D. Walden .... (202) 927–1440
Fax .... (202) 927–1969
Special Assistant to the Commissioner, Equal Opportunity
Linda Batts .... (202) 927–0210
Fax .... (202) 927–1476
Strategic Trade
Deborah J. Spero .... (202) 927–0570
Fax .... (202) 927–2110
Laboratories and Scientific Services
Ira Reese (acting) .... (202) 927–1060
Field Operations
Jayson P. Ahern .... (202) 927–0100
Fax .... (202) 927–0837
Anti-Smuggling
James Engleman .... (202) 927–0520
Mission Support Services
Anne Scott .... (202) 927–0958
Outbound Process
Allen Gina .... (202) 927–6060
Passenger Programs
Robert Jacksta .... (202) 927–0530
Process Analysis and Requirements
John Considine .... (202) 927–0415
Trade Compliance
Elizabeth Durant .... (202) 927–0300
Human Resources Management
Robert M. Smith .... (202) 927–1250
Fax .... (202) 927–1712
Investigations
Richard J. Hoglund (acting) .... (202) 927–1600
Labor and Employee Relations
Mari Yonkers .... (202) 927–2688
Staffing and Compensation
Sue Zaner .... (202) 927–3550
Information and Technology
S.W. Hall Jr. .... (202) 927–0680
Fax .... (202) 927–0172
Software Development Division
Jerry Russomano .... (703) 921–7700
Applied Technology
John Pennella .... (202) 927–1420
Automated Commercial Environment
Mike George .... (703) 921–7190
Program Management Staff
Mary Eichelberger .... (703) 921–7197
Systems Operations
Luke McCormack .... (703) 921–6086

Intelligence Division
James Corcoran .... (202) 927–0330
Fax .... (202) 927–1738
Intelligence Support Branch
Janet Gunther .... (202) 927–1772
National Security Branch
Ralph Joseph .... (202) 927–1773
Internal Affairs
William A. Keefer .... (202) 927–1800
Fax .... (202) 927–1434
International Affairs
Donald K. Shruhan Jr. .... (202) 927–0400
Fax .... (202) 927–2064
International Policy and Program Division
Bylle Patterson .... (202) 927–1480
International Training and Assistance
Patricia McCauley .... (202) 927–0430
Program Management Staff
David Roseman .... (202) 927–5840
Investigations
Richard J. Hoglund (acting) .... (202) 927–1600
Fax .... (202) 927–1948
Administration, Planning, and Policy
John E. Eichelberger .... (202) 927–1410
Air Interdiction
Charles Stallworth II .... (202) 927–0024
Foreign Operations
Mark Robinson .... (202) 927–0640
Investigative Operations
Richard Mercier .... (202) 927–1500
Planning and Policy
Lucrezia Rotolo .... (202) 927–1193
Regulations and Rulings
Michael Schmitz .... (202) 572–8700
Fax .... (202) 927–1873
Commercial Rulings
John A. Durant .... (202) 927–0760
Disclosure Law
Lee Kramer .... (202) 927–2333
Duty and Refund Determination
William Rosoff .... (202) 927–2077
Entry Procedures and Carriers
Larry Barton .... (202) 927–2320
General Classification
Marrin Amernick .... (202) 927–2388
Intellectual Property Rights
Joanne Stump .... (202) 927–2330
International Agreements Staff
Myles B. Harmon .... (202) 927–2256
International Trade Compliance
Sandra L. Bell .... (202) 927–0760
Legal Reference Staff
Karen Taylor .... (202) 927–2258

National Commodities Specialist
(New York)
Robert Swierupski .... (212) 637–7000
Operational Oversight
Linda E. Kane .... (202) 927–0760
Penalties
Charles D. Ressin .... (202) 927–2344
Regulations
Harold Singer .... (202) 927–2340
Special Classification and Marketing
Myles Harmon .... (202) 927–2310
Textile
John Elkins .... (202) 927–2380
Training and Development
Marjorie Budd .... (202) 927–0730
Fax .... (202) 927–0886
Value
Virginia Brown .... (202) 927–2399

▮ INFORMATION SOURCES

Internet

Agency Web Site: http://www.customs.gov. Offers information on importing and exporting in the United States, traveling internationally, the USCS's enforcement activities, auctions held by the Customs Service, and access to quota reports and press releases.

The USCS also operates an electronic bulletin board system (CEBB) that contains information for importers and others interested in global trade issues. It also has currency conversion rates for fifty countries that are updated daily. The bulletin board can be accessed via the USCS Web site or directly using a modem.
For assistance .... (703) 921–6236

Telephone Contacts

Personnel Locator .... (202) 354–1000
Hotline (to report smuggling) .... (800) BE–ALERT

Information and Publications

KEY OFFICES

Freedom of Information
USCS Investigations Office
1300 Pennsylvania Ave. N.W.
Washington, DC 20229
(202) 927–0970
Fax (202) 927–0327
Gloria Marshall, FOI director

USCS Legal Reference Staff
1300 Pennsylvania Ave. N.W.
Washington, DC 20229
(202) 927–2271
Thomas Budnik, branch chief

Maintains a legal precedent retrieval system.

PUBLICATIONS

Contact the USCS Public Information Staff or any regional office for free pamphlets and brochures on import regulations. Topics include importing procedures, foreign trade zones, importing cars, and customs recommendations for visitors. Titles include:

Know Before You Go (No. 512)
Importing into the United States (No. 504)
Importing and Exporting a Car (No. 520)
Visiting the U.S. (No. 511)
GSP and the Traveler (No. 515)
International Mail Imports (No. 514)
Moving Household Goods to the U.S. (No. 518)
U.S. Customs in Brief (No. 506)
Protectors of Independence
U.S. Import Requirements

The agency's annual report and its monthly magazine, *Customs Today,* are also available. Many USCS publications also may be obtained from the U.S. Government Printing Office (GPO): see appendix, Ordering Government Publications.

Reference Resources

LIBRARY

USCS Library
1300 Pennsylvania Ave. N.W., Room 7.5B
Washington, DC 20229
(202) 927–1350
Fax (202) 482–1460
Patricia Dobrosky, director
Hours: 9:00 a.m. to 5 p.m.
Open to the public by appointment only.

RULES AND REGULATIONS

USCS rules and regulations are published in the *Code of Federal Regulations,* Title 19, parts 4–199. Proposed regulations, new final regulations, and updates to the *Code of Federal Regulations* are published in the daily *Federal Register. (See appendix for details on how to obtain and use these publications.)*

▌ LEGISLATION

The CBP carries out its responsibilities through authority granted in:

Unfair Competition Act (39 Stat. 798, 15 U.S.C. 71). Signed by the president Sept. 8, 1916. Restricted the importation of articles at less than market value and established import restrictions against countries that prohibit the importation of U.S. goods.

Customs Bureau Act (44 Stat. 1381, 19 U.S.C. 2071). Signed by the president March 3, 1927. Established the Customs Bureau as an agency within the Treasury Department to assess and collect duties on imports.

Tariff Act of 1930 (46 Stat. 763, 19 U.S.C. 1202). Signed by the president June 17, 1930. Established rules and regulations relating to assessment and collection of duty, protection of revenue, entry of vessels, clearance of passengers, exclusion of prohibited merchandise, and regulation of customhouse brokers.

Anti-Smuggling Act (49 Stat. 517, 19 U.S.C. 1701). Signed by the president Aug. 5, 1935. Gave the USCS special enforcement authority to cope with smuggling.

Customs Courts Act of 1970 (84 Stat. 274, 28 U.S.C. 1541). Signed by the president June 2, 1970. Streamlined the judicial machinery of the customs courts by allowing formerly separate appeals of customs court decisions concerning classification of merchandise and collection of customs revenues to be handled by one court.

Trade Act of 1974 (88 Stat. 1978, 19 U.S.C. 2101). Signed by the president Jan. 3, 1975. Gave the USCS additional enforcement responsibilities with respect to antidumping, countervailing duties, and unfair import practices.

Customs Procedural Reform and Simplification Act (92 Stat. 888, 19 U.S.C. 1654 note). Signed by the president Oct. 3, 1978. Streamlined the Custom Service's procedures to expedite international travel and trade. Allowed the USCS to release goods to importers immediately upon presentation of appropriate entry documents, raised the personal duty exemption for returning U.S. residents and amended the Tariff Act of 1930 to remove unduly harsh penalty assessments.

Trade Agreements Act of 1979 (93 Stat. 144, 19 U.S.C. 2501 note). Signed by the president July 26, 1979. Transferred dumping and countervailing duties authority from the USCS to the Commerce Department.

Money Laundering Control Act of 1986 (100 Stat. 3207, 18 U.S.C. 981). Signed by the president Oct. 27, 1986. Prohibited the transport or attempted transport of funds obtained through the commission of a crime or intended for use in a crime. Prohibited the structuring of financial transactions in order to evade federal reporting requirements. Authorized the seizure and forfeiture of cash or other property derived from criminal activity.

United States-Canada Free-Trade Agreement Implementation Act of 1988 (102 Stat. 1851, 19 U.S.C. 2112 note). Signed by the president Sept. 28, 1988. Set a ten-year schedule to phase out tariffs between the United States and Canada. Provided new mechanisms for solving trade disputes.

North American Free Trade Agreement Implementation Act (107 Stat. 2057, 19 U.S.C. 3301 note). Signed by the president Dec. 8, 1993. Implemented the North American Free Trade Agreement (NAFTA), which opened trade borders with Canada, the United States, and Mexico. Title VI, the Customs Modernization Act, amended the Tariff Act of 1930 to revise customs procedures with respect to electronic transmission of forged, altered, or false data to the Customs Service with regard to the entry of imported merchandise; to set penalties for failure to declare imported controlled substances and for fraud, gross negligence, and negligence; to restrict unlawful unloading or transshipment; and to handle the seizure of imported merchandise.

Anticounterfeiting Consumer Protection Act of 1996 (110 Stat. 1836, 18 U.S.C. 2311 note). Signed by the president July 2, 1996. Made trafficking in goods or services bearing counterfeit marks a predicate offense under the Racketeer Influenced and Corrupt Organizations Act (RICO). Gave the USCS authority to establish civil penalties and fines for importing, selling, or distributing merchandise bearing a counterfeit American trademark.

Trade Act of 2002 (116 Stat. 933, 19 U.S.C. 3801 note). Signed by the president Aug. 6, 2002. Title III, the Customs Border Security Act of 2002, provided Customs officers with immunity from lawsuits stemming from personal searches of people entering the country, as long as the officers conduct the searches in good faith and follow federal inspection procedures. Allowed officers to search unsealed, outbound U.S. mail and packages weighing sixteen ounces or more for unreported monetary instruments, weapons of mass destruction, firearms, and other contraband. Required USCS and the Agriculture Department to establish a procedure to identify and prohibit violators of tariffs on sugar, syrups, or related products.

Maritime Transportation Security Act of 2002 (116 Stat. 2064, 46 U.S.C. 2101 note). Signed by the president Nov. 25, 2002. Required the Department of Transportation (DOT) to develop antiterrorism plans at U.S. ports and foreign ports where U.S.-bound shipments originate. Authorized funds through 2008 for research and development to improve the ability of the USCS to inspect cargo, including improving its ability to inspect merchandise on vessels arriving in U.S. ports; purchasing equipment to detect explosives, chemical and biological agents, and nu-

clear materials; and improving tags and seals on shipping containers. Authorized the USCS to issue rules requiring shippers to electronically provide information on cargo shipped to or from the United States before it arrives.

Homeland Security Act of 2002 (P.L. 107-296). Signed by the president Nov. 25, 2002. Established the Department of Homeland Security (DHS). Transferred the INS inspection services, the Border Patrol, the Agriculture and Quarantine Inspections program, and inspection elements of the USCS into the CBP within the DHS.

▮ REGIONAL OFFICES

Customs Management Centers

NORTH ATLANTIC
(CT, MA, ME, NH, RI, VT)
10 Causeway St., #801
Boston, MA 02222
(617) 565–6200
Philip Spayd, director

NEW YORK
(downstate NY)
1 Penn Plaza, 11th Floor
New York, NY 10119
(646) 733–3100
Susan Mitchell, director

BUFFALO FIELD OFFICE
(upstate NY)
4455 Genesee St.
Buffalo, NY 14225
(716) 626–0400
Michael D'Ambrosio, director

MID-ATLANTIC
(DC, DE, MD, NJ, PA except Erie, northern VA)
102 S. Gay St., #715
Baltimore, MD 21202
(410) 962–6200
Steven Knox, director

SOUTH ATLANTIC
(GA, NC, SC, all but northern VA)
1691 Phoenix Blvd., #270
College Park, GA 30349
(770) 994–4100
Robert Gomez, director

NORTH FLORIDA

(northern FL)
1624 E. Seventh Ave., #300
Tampa, FL 33605
(813) 228–2381
Denise Crawford, director

SOUTH FLORIDA

(southern FL)
909 S.E. First Ave., #980
Miami, FL 33131
(305) 810–5120
Thomas Winkowski, director

CARIBBEAN

(PR, VI)
1 La Puntilla St., #203
San Juan, PR 00901
(787) 729–6950
Marcelino Borges, director

GULF

(AL, AR, LA, MS, TN)
423 Canal St., #337
New Orleans, LA 70130
(504) 670–2404
James A. Hynes, director

MID-AMERICA

(IA, IL, IN, KS, KY, southern MN, MO, NE, OH, Erie
region of PA, southern SD, all but northwestern WI)
610 S. Canal St., #900
Chicago, IL 60607
(312) 983–9100
Anne Lombardi, director

WEST GREAT LAKES

(MI)
613 Abbott St., #300
Detroit, MI 48226
(313) 226–2955
Kevin Weeks, director

EAST TEXAS

(OK, northern and eastern TX)
2323 S. Shepard St., #1200
Houston, TX 77019
(713) 387–7200
Robert Trotter, director

SOUTH TEXAS

(central and southern TX)
109 Shiloh Dr., #300
Laredo, TX 78045
(956) 753–1700
Gurdit Dhillon, director

WEST TEXAS/NEW MEXICO

(NM, western TX)
9400 Viscount Blvd., #104
El Paso, TX 79925
(915) 633–7300
Luis Garcia, director

NORTHWEST GREAT PLAINS

(northern ID, northern MN, MT, ND, northern SD, WA,
northwestern WI)
1000 Second Ave., #2200
Seattle, WA 98104–1049
(206) 553–6944
Thomas Hardy, director

NORTH PACIFIC

(AK, CO, all but northern ID, OR, WY)
8337 N.E. Alderwood Rd., #200
Portland, OR 97220
(503) 326–7625
James Tong, director

MID-PACIFIC

(northern and central CA, HI, northern NV, UT)
33 New Montgomery St., 16th Floor
San Francisco, CA 94105
(415) 744–1530
Thomas O'Brien, director

LOS ANGELES FIELD OPERATIONS
(southern CA except San Diego region, southern NV)
1 World Trade Center, #705
Long Beach, CA 90831
(562) 980–3100
John Heinrich, director

ARIZONA
(AZ)
4740 N. Oracle Ave., #310
Tucson, AZ 85705
(520) 407–2300
Donna De La Torre, director

SOUTHERN CALIFORNIA
(San Diego region and Mexican border of CA)
610 W. Ash St., #1200
San Diego, CA 92101
(619) 557–5360, ext. 100
Adele Fasano, director

Bureau of Immigration and Customs Enforcement

425 Eye St., N.W., Washington, DC 20536
Internet: http://www.bice.immigration.gov

On March 1, 2003, the Homeland Security Act of 2002 created the Department of Homeland Security (DHS) and transferred the enforcement and investigation arms of the U.S. Customs Service, the investigative and enforcement functions of Immigration and Naturalization Service (INS), and the entire operation of Federal Protective Services (FPS) into the Bureau of Immigration and Customs Enforcement (ICE). ICE is a component of the Directorate of Border and Transportation Security established within the DHS.

The service and benefit functions of the Immigration and Naturalization Service (INS) transferred into the Bureau of Citizenship and Immigration Services (BCIS) *(see p. 525)*; the inspection functions of the U.S. Customs Service were organized as the Bureau of Customs and Border Protection (CBP) *(see p. 529)*.

Backed by a workforce of nearly 14,000, ICE is the investigative arm of DHS. The agency combines the investigative, detention and removal, and intelligence functions of the former INS with the investigative, intelligence, and air and marine functions of the former Customs Service.

The bureau is led by an assistant secretary who reports directly to the DHS under secretary for border and transportation security.

On May 16, 2003, the ICE announced a reorganization plan scheduled to go into effect by July 2003. The reorganization plan establishes a structure that supports five distinct operational divisions of ICE: Investigations; Detention and Removal; Intelligence, Air and Marine Interdiction; and Federal Protective Service. All these components will report directly to the assistant secretary of ICE.

At the field level, the plan creates a special agent in charge (SAIC) structure for ICE investigations, following the model of other federal law enforcement agencies. Under the plan, twenty-five veteran law enforcement officers will be designated as interim SAICs. Each will be responsible for directing ICE investigative operations and resources in a specific geographic area of the United States.

The field reorganization plan also aligns the reporting structures of detention and removal field units with the interim SAIC offices. In addition, the plan aligns ICE field intelligence units with the interim SAIC offices. The old field regions and offices of the FPS and Air and Marine Interdiction Divisions will remain essentially intact under the plan.

ICE's immigration enforcement component deters illegal migration, prevents immigration-related crimes, and removes individuals, especially criminals, who are unlawfully present in the United States. This mandate is carried out by the Immigration Investigations, Detention and Removal, and Intelligence programs.

Immigration Investigations is charged with investigating violations of the criminal and administrative provisions of the Immigration and Nationality Act, as well as other related immigration law provisions. The staff of special agents, immigration agents, and support personnel perform their duties at field offices, in task force offices, and at domestic and foreign duty posts.

The Detention and Removal program is charged with the supervision, detention, and removal of aliens who are in the United States unlawfully or who are found to be deportable or inadmissible. These activities pertain to enforcing the departure of these individuals when available relief has been exhausted.

ICE's Intelligence Division is responsible for coordinating intelligence activities, including managing the collection, analysis, and dissemination of intelligence;

conducting intelligence-related liaison activities with the intelligence and law enforcement community; and providing contributions to DHS intelligence assessments and reports.

Operational and tactical control of investigative and intelligence operations is divided geographically by areas of responsibility. The SAICs are responsible for the administration and management of all investigative-related customs enforcement activities within the geographic boundaries of the office.

Traditionally, the primary mission of customs enforcement has been to combat various forms of smuggling. Over time however, this mission has been expanded to other violations of law involving terrorist financing, money laundering, arms trafficking (including weapons of mass destruction), technology exports, commercial fraud, and child pornography, to name a few. Customs enforces more than 400 different laws and regulations including those of forty other agencies.

ICE's customs enforcement mission is not limited to conducting investigations. The mission of the Air and Marine Interdiction Division (AMID) is to detect and intercept suspect air and marine targets and to provide surveillance support to investigative entities.

KEY PERSONNEL

Undersecretary
Asa Hutchinson .... (202) 282–8000
Fax .... (202) 282–8407
Assistant Secretary
Michael Garcia (acting) .... (202) 514–1900
Director of Operations
Michael Dougherty .... (202) 514–1900
General Counsel
Victor Cerda (acting) .... (202) 514–2895
Executive Associate Commissioner–Management
George H. Bohlinger .... (202) 514–3182
Assistant Commissioner for Budget
Suzanne H. Wilson (acting) .... (202) 514–3206
Equal Employment Opportunity
Diane Weaver .... (202) 514–2824
Assistant Commissioner for Human Resource Management
Rick Hastings .... (202) 514–3636
Assistant Commissioner for Training and Career Development
Jill Arndt (acting) .... (202)616-2674
Chief Information Officer
Scott Hastings .... (202) 514–2547
Acquisition Management
Priscilla Hunt .... (202) 514–2082

Data Systems
Raj Vellore (acting) .... (202) 514–4517
Assistant Commissioner for Office of Records Services
Dominick Gentile .... (202) 514–2989
Assistant Commissioner for Systems Integration
Alan Shelton .... (202) 514–4477
Director of Intelligence
Jeff Casey .... (202) 514–2960
Investigations
John Clark (acting) .... (202) 514–0078
Benefits
Eunice Chicks .... (202) 514–3245

INFORMATION SOURCES

Internet
Agency Web Site: http://www.bice.immigration.gov. Includes an overview of the agency, frequently asked questions, press releases, BICE regulations, employer information, and links to other federal Internet sites.

Telephone Contacts
Personnel Locator .... (202) 514–2525

Information and Publications

KEY OFFICES

BICE General Information Office
425 Eye St. N.W.
Washington, DC 20536
(202) 514–2607

Answers general questions; provides information to the public.

BICE Public Affairs
425 Eye St. N.W., Room 7021
Washington, DC 20536
(202) 514–2648
Fax (202) 514–1776
Russ Bergeron, director

Answers questions from the press. Issues news releases and media information materials.

Freedom of Information
425 Eye St. N.W.
Washington, DC 20536
(202) 514–1722
Magda Ortiz, FOI officer

DOJ Public Affairs
10th St. and Pennsylvania Ave. N.W., Room 1228
Washington, DC 20530
(202) 514–2007

Distributes publications describing the department's organization, functions, and legal procedures. The attorney general's annual report also covers the policies and programs of the BICE.

PUBLICATIONS

For most publications, contact DOJ Public Affairs.

Teachers' manuals and textbooks on citizenship, written at various reading levels, are available to candidates for naturalization. They are distributed free to public schools and are available for purchase from the Government Printing Office (GPO): see appendix, Ordering Government Publications.

Reference Resources

LIBRARIES

BICE Public Reading Room
425 Eye St. N.W., 2nd Floor Ullico Bldg.
Washington, DC 20536
(202) 514–1722
Pamela Ball, contact
Hours: 8:00 a.m. to 4:30 p.m.

Maintains BICE annual reports, statistical reports on aliens and immigrants, interim decisions of the Board of Immigration Appeals, booklets describing immigration forms, and information on immigration regulations. Call ahead for appointment.

BICE History Office
425 Eye St. N.W., Room 1100
Washington, DC 20536
(202) 514–2837
Marian Smith, contact

Maintains a collection on the history of the BICE and immigration in general. Open to the public by appointment only.

■ LEGISLATION

The ICE carries out its immigration investigation and enforcement responsibilities under:

Immigration and Nationality Act, as amended (66 Stat. 163, 8 U.S.C. 1101). Signed by the president June 27, 1952. Contained virtually all of the law relating to the entry of aliens and to the acquisition and loss of U.S. citizenship.

Immigration and Nationality Technical Corrections Act of 1994 (108 Stat. 4305, 8 U.S.C. 1101). Signed by the president Oct. 25, 1994. Made numerous specific changes to the Immigration and Nationality Act. Allowed U.S. visas for visits from officials of Taiwan; gave equal treatment to women in conferring U.S. citizenship to children born abroad.

Amendments to the Violent Crime Control and Law Enforcement Act of 1994 (110 State 1214, 18 U.S.C. 1). Signed by the president April 24, 1996. Directed the criminal alien identification system to be used to identify and locate deportable aliens who have committed aggravated felonies; the system was to be transferred from the attorney general to the commissioner of the INS.

Homeland Security Act of 2002 (P.L. 107-296). Signed by the president Nov. 25, 2002. Created the Department of Homeland Security (DHS) and transferred to ICE all old INS functions performed under the following programs: (1) the Border Patrol program; (2) the detention and removal program; (3) the intelligence program; (4) the investigations program; and (5) the inspections program. Granted the secretary of homeland security exclusive authority to issue regulations with respect to the Immigration and Nationality Act (INA) and its administration and enforcement.

The ICE carries out its customs investigation and enforcement responsibilities through authority granted in:

Tariff Act of 1930 (46 Stat. 763, 19 U.S.C. 1202). Signed by the president June 17, 1930. Established rules and regulations relating to assessment and collection of duty, protection of revenue, entry of vessels, clearance of passengers, exclusion of prohibited merchandise, and regulation of customhouse brokers.

Anti-Smuggling Act (49 Stat. 517, 19 U.S.C. 1701). Signed by the president Aug. 5, 1935. Gave the USCS special enforcement authority to cope with smuggling.

Money Laundering Control Act of 1986 (100 Stat. 3207, 18 U.S.C. 981). Signed by the president Oct. 27, 1986. Prohibited the transport or attempted transport of funds obtained through the commission of a crime or intended for use in a crime. Prohibited the structuring of financial transactions in order to evade federal reporting requirements. Authorized the seizure and forfeiture of cash or other property derived from criminal activity.

United States-Canada Free-Trade Agreement Implementation Act of 1988 (102 Stat. 1851, 19 U.S.C. 2112 note). Signed by the president Sept. 28, 1988. Set a ten-year schedule to phase out tariffs between the United States and Canada. Provided new mechanisms for solving trade disputes.

North American Free Trade Agreement Implementation Act (107 Stat. 2057, 19 U.S.C. 3301 note). Signed by the president Dec. 8, 1993. Implemented the North American Free Trade Agreement (NAFTA), which opened trade borders with Canada, the United States, and Mexico. Title VI, the Customs Modernization Act, amended the Tariff Act of 1930 to revise customs procedures with respect to electronic transmission of forged, altered, or false data to the Customs Service with regard to the entry of imported merchandise; to set penalties for failure to declare imported controlled substances and for fraud, gross negligence, and negligence; to restrict unlawful unloading or transshipment; and to handle the seizure of imported merchandise.

Anticounterfeiting Consumer Protection Act of 1996 (110 Stat. 1836, 18 U.S.C. 2311 note). Signed by the president July 2, 1996. Made trafficking in goods or services bearing counterfeit marks a predicate offense under the Racketeer Influenced and Corrupt Organizations Act (RICO). Gave the USCS authority to establish civil penalties and fines for importing, selling, or distributing merchandise bearing a counterfeit American trademark.

Trade Act of 2002 (116 Stat. 933, 19 U.S.C. 3801 note). Signed by the president Aug. 6, 2002. Title III, the Customs Border Security Act of 2002, provided Customs officers with immunity from lawsuits stemming from personal searches of people entering the country, as long as the officers conduct the searches in good faith and follow federal inspection procedures. Allowed officers to search unsealed, outbound U.S. mail and packages weighing sixteen ounces or more for unreported monetary instruments, weapons of mass destruction, firearms, and other contraband.

Homeland Security Act of 2002 (P.L. 107-296). Signed by the president Nov. 25, 2002. Established in the Department of Homeland Security. Transferred to ICE the U.S. Customs Service from the Department of the Treasury, but with certain customs revenue functions remaining with the secretary of the treasury. Authorized the secretary of the treasury to appoint up to twenty new personnel to work with DHS personnel in performing customs revenue functions.

Federal Emergency Management Agency

500 C St. S.W., Washington, DC 20472
Internet: http://www.fema.gov

The Federal Emergency Management Agency (FEMA) was established in 1979 as an independent agency of the federal government. The Homeland Security Act of 2002 transferred FEMA into the Department of Homeland Security (DHS) in 2003, where it remains as an independent agency.

FEMA programs include response to and recovery from major natural disasters and man-made emergencies, emergency management planning, flood-plain management, hazardous materials planning, and dam safety. Other activities include off-site planning for emergencies at commercial nuclear power plants and the Army's chemical stockpile sites, emergency food and shelter funding for the homeless, plans to ensure the continuity of the federal government during national security emergencies, and coordination of the federal response to major terrorist incidents.

FEMA's 2,600 full-time employees work at agency headquarters in Washington, D.C., at regional and area offices across the country, at the Mount Weather Emergency Operations Center, and at the FEMA training center in Emmitsburg, Md. FEMA also has nearly 4,000 standby disaster assistance employees who are available to help out after disasters. Often FEMA works in partnership with other organizations that are part of the nation's emergency management system. These partners include state and local emergency management agencies, twenty-seven federal agencies, and the American Red Cross.

KEY PERSONNEL

Undersecretary
Michael D. Brown .... (202) 646–3900
Fax .... (202) 646–3930
Information Technology Services
Rose Parkes .... (202) 646–3006
Mitigation
Anthony S. Lowe .... (202) 646–3003
Response and Recovery
Trey Reid .... (202) 646–3162
Eric Tolbert .... (202) 646–3692
U.S. Fire Administration
R. David Paulison .... (301) 447-1080

Transportation Security Administration

400 7th St., S.W., Washington, DC 20590
Internet: http://www.tsa.gov

The Aviation and Transportation Security Act (ATSA) established the Transportation Security Administration (TSA) within the Department of Transportation (DOT) on Nov. 19, 2001. Although TSA's initial focus was on aviation security, the agency was also given the responsibility of providing security for the entire national transportation system, including rail, land, maritime, transit, and pipeline elements. The Homeland Security Act of 2002 transferred the TSA into the newly created Department of Homeland Security (DHS).

TSA, as part of the Border and Transportation Security Directorate, works with other DHS organizations, such as the Coast Guard, the Bureau of Customs and Border Protection, the Information Analysis and Infrastructure Protection Directorate, and the Science and Technology Directorate to address surface and maritime transportation security issues. TSA also maintains a close alliance with the Department of Transportation.

The TSA, created out of the aftermath of 2001 terrorist attacks on New York and Washington, D.C., was first tasked by the Congress to establish and deploy a qualified and fully trained federal security workforce in all of the nation's 429 commercial airports by Nov. 19, 2002, TSA's one-year anniversary. Over the following year TSA trained a workforce of 45,000 federal screeners, placed them at U.S. airports and met its deadline. TSA also met congressional mandates for passenger and baggage screening operations, which were federalized. By 2003 the TSA was screening 100 percent of checked and unchecked baggage at U.S. airports.

In the first year of service, TSA screeners intercepted more than 4.8 million prohibited items at passenger security checkpoints. Intercepted items included 1,101 firearms, nearly 1.4 million knives, and nearly 2.4 million other sharp objects including scissors, box cutters, incendiary or flammable objects, and clubs.

TSA recruits, trains, and deploys a professional cadre of federal air marshals. The agency, through its Federal Flight Deck Officer training, also provides intensive forty-eight-hour training to volunteer commercial pilots who function as federal law enforcement officers, with jurisdiction limited to the flight deck, or cockpit. These pilots complement the federal air marshals deployed within the aircraft and are authorized to act only if the cockpit is threatened.

On May 5, 2003, the TSA and the DOT issued an interim final rule on the transport of hazardous materials. The rule requires background checks on commercial drivers before certification to transport hazardous materials. Under the rule, approximately 3.5 million commercial drivers with hazardous material endorsements will be required to undergo a routine background check that includes a review of criminal, mental health, and FBI records. The checks also verify that the driver is a U.S. citizen or a lawful permanent resident.

The TSA issues and administers Transportation Security Regulations (TSRs). Many TSRs are former rules of the Federal Aviation Administration (FAA) that were transferred to TSA when TSA assumed FAA's civil aviation security function on Feb. 17, 2002.

TSA's Office of Maritime and Land Security divisions include:

Transportation Passenger Security Division. Protects passengers within the national transportation system and ensures the freedom of movement of people through the system. The division consists of four branches: Maritime Passenger Security; Rail Passenger Security; Highway Passenger Security; and Mass Transit Passenger Security.

Transportation Infrastructure Security Division. Protects the infrastructure of the national transportation system and ensures the freedom of movement of people and commerce through the system. The division consists of six branches: Maritime Infrastructure Security; Rail Infrastructure Security; Highway Infrastructure Security; Mass Transit Infrastructure Security; Pipeline Infrastructure Security; and the Credentialing Program Office.

Cargo Security Division. Ensures the security of cargo throughout the national transportation system. Currently, security improvements for cargo operations are limited by the lack of regulatory authority and resources available for the surface modes. The division consists of five branches: Maritime Cargo Security; Rail Cargo Security; Highway Cargo Security; Air Cargo Security; and the Fusion Center.

Response Planning and Preparedness Division. Oversees program implementation; recommends improvements to regulatory, statutory, and policy documents; and performs internal process troubleshooting and interagency liaison. The division consists of four branches: Readiness Standards and Evaluation; ISAC/Intelligence Coordination; Intermodal Exercises; and Plans.

Stakeholder Relations Division. Maintains effective two-way communications with both internal and external partners and stakeholders, including federal, state, and local governments and agencies; Congress; trade and industry associations and organizations; public organizations and private businesses; the general public; foreign governments; and international businesses and organizations. The Stakeholder Relations Division consists of three branches: Domestic; International; and Governmental.

Performance Standards and Resource Management Division. Serves as division support for all resource issues, including preparing budget requests, responding to congressional reviews, answering industry inquiries, and performing indepth evaluations of programs. Also administers the TSA grants program.

▪ KEY PERSONNEL

Administrator
    Adm. James Loy......................... (571) 227–2800
Deputy Administrator
    Steve McHale........................... (571) 227–2800
Acting Director for Legislative Affairs
    Leslie Adam............................ (571) 227–2829

▪ INFORMATION SOURCES

Internet

Agency Web Site: http://www.tsa.gov. Includes an overview of the agency, frequently asked questions, press releases, regulations, employer information, traveler and consumer information, and links to other federal Internet sites.

Telephone Contacts

Employment................................ (800) 887–1895
Security Violations and Concerns......... (866) 289–9673
General Aviation Operators/
    Maintainers.............................. (866) 427–3287

TSA Public Affairs

425 Eye St. N.W., Room 7021
Washington, DC 20536
(571) 227–2829
Robert Johnson, director

Answers questions from the press. Issues news releases and media information materials.

▪ LEGISLATION

Uniting and Strengthening America by Providing Appropriate Tools Required to Intercept and Obstruct Terrorism Act of 2002 (USA Patriot Act). (115 Stat. 272, 18 U.S.C. 1 note). Signed by the president on Oct. 26, 2001. Amended the federal transportation code to require background checks on individuals before certification to transport hazardous materials.

Aviation and Transportation Security Act (P.L. 107-71). Signed by the president Nov. 19, 2001. Amended federal transportation law to establish the TSA within the DOT. Authorized the TSA to provide for civil aviation security; day-to-day federal security screening operations for passenger air transportation; maritime, rail, and other surface transportation security, especially during a national emergency; and the management of security information, including notifying airports of possible terrorists.

Maritime Transportation Security Act of 2002 (116 Stat. 2064, 46 U.S.C. 2101 note). Signed by the president Nov. 25, 2002. Required the creation of a National Maritime Transportation Security Plan for deterring and responding to a transportation security incident.

Homeland Security Act of 2002 (P.L. 107-296). Signed by the president Nov. 25, 2002. Transferred the TSA to the DHS. Title XIV amended federal law to establish a two-year pilot program to deputize volunteer pilots of air carriers as federal law enforcement officers and provide training, supervision, and equipment for such officers.

United States Coast Guard

2100 2nd St. S.W., Washington, DC 20593
Internet: http://www.uscg.mil

The U.S. Coast Guard is the federal government's primary maritime law enforcement agency. The Coast Guard is a branch of the armed forces formerly under the jurisdiction of the Department of Transportation (DOT), but it was transferred to the jurisdiction of the Department of Homeland Security (DHS) with enactment of the Homeland Security Act of 2002. During time of war, or by presidential order, the Coast Guard operates as a part of the U.S. Navy.

The Coast Guard regulates vessels, sets and enforces safety standards, and prescribes license requirements for merchant marine personnel. Standards apply to vessels built in or under the jurisdiction of the United States.

The commandant of the Coast Guard is appointed by the president; the Senate confirms the nomination.

The Marine Safety Council, chaired by the Coast Guard's chief counsel, provides oversight and guidance for the Coast Guard's regulatory activity. Units within the Coast Guard bring proposals for regulations to the council, whose members also include the assistant commandants of three other Coast Guard offices: Marine Safety and Environmental Protection; Operations; and Systems. The council determines whether or not the proposed regulation will be approved.

Areas for which the Coast Guard is responsible include:

Boating safety. Regulations are issued by the Coast Guard to establish minimum boating safety standards, to require use of safety equipment, and to prevent damage to vessels and structures in navigable waters.

Bridges. The Coast Guard regulates the construction, maintenance, and operation of bridges across U.S. navigable waters.

Deep-water ports. The construction, ownership, and operation of deep-water ports (offshore installations used to transfer oil from supertankers to shore facilities) are regulated by the Coast Guard.

Great Lakes. Registration is required of pilots of domestic and foreign vessels on the Great Lakes. There also are regulations that prescribe permissible rates and charges for pilot services.

Merchant marine personnel. The Coast Guard develops and regulates licensing procedures for masters, mates, chief engineers, and assistant engineers of merchant ships. It also certifies merchant mariners.

Navigation. Navigation aids, including lighthouses, fog signals, lightships, buoys, and beacons, are installed and maintained by the Coast Guard.

The Coast Guard also operates a fleet of ice-breaking vessels to assist marine transportation, prevent flooding, and aid U.S. polar installations and research teams.

Outer continental shelf (OCS). The Coast Guard regulates the design, construction, and maintenance of structures built on the OCS.

Passenger vessels. Vessels that carry passengers must pass Coast Guard inspections. In addition, the design, construction, and alteration of passenger ships is regulated, and limits are established on the number of passengers cargo vessels may carry. Operators are licensed by the Coast Guard.

Search and rescue. The Coast Guard operates a search and rescue network that is responsible for saving lives and protecting property on the high seas. It enforces federal laws and treaties related to the high seas and conducts investigations.

Vessel documentation. The Coast Guard administers vessel documentation statutes and operates a system to register U.S. vessels sold or transferred to U.S. citizens abroad.

Water pollution. The Coast Guard boards and examines vessels carrying oil and other hazardous materials. It requires proof and issues certificates of responsibility to owners and operators of vessels that may be liable to the United States for the costs of removing oil and other hazardous materials from the navigable waters of the United States, adjoining shorelines, and waters of the contiguous zone.

The Coast Guard's new homeland security role includes

- Protecting ports, the flow of commerce, and the marine transportation system from terrorism.
- Maintaining maritime border security against illegal drugs, illegal aliens, and weapons of mass destruction.
- Keeping Coast Guard units at a high state of readiness and keeping marine transportation open for the transit of assets and personnel from other branches of the armed forces.
- Protecting against illegal fishing and indiscriminate destruction of living marine resources.
- Preventing and responding to oil and hazardous material spills—both accidental and intentional.
- Coordinating efforts and intelligence with federal, state, and local agencies.

■ KEY PERSONNEL

Commandant
Adm. Thomas H. Collins .... (202) 267–2390
Fax .... (202) 267–4158
Vice Commandant
Vice Adm. Thomas Barrett .... (202) 267–2385
Chief Administrative Law Judge
Joseph Ingolia .... (202) 267–2940
Congressional Affairs
Capt. Joel Whitehead .... (202) 366–4280
Civil Rights
Walter Somerville .... (202) 267–1562
Chief of Staff
Vice Adm. Thad Allen .... (202) 267–1642
Acquisition
Rear Adm. Ralph Utley .... (202) 267–2007
Chief Counsel
Rear Adm. John Crowley .... (202) 267–1617
Finance and Procurement
Robert Horowitz .... (202) 267–6681
Resources
Rear Adm. Richard Houch .... (202) 267–1088
Human Resources
Rear Adm. Ken Venuto .... (202) 366–0905
Marine Safety and Environmental Protection
Rear Adm. Tom Gilmour .... (202) 267–2220

Operations
Rear Adm. Dave Belz .... (202) 267–0977
Operations Policy
Rear Adm. Jeff Hathaway .... (202) 366–2267
Systems
Rear Adm. Erroll Brown .... (202) 267–1844
Information and Technology
Rear Adm. Cliff Pearson .... (202) 267–2767

■ INFORMATION SOURCES

Internet
Agency Web site: http://www.uscg.mil. Features news releases and information on recruiting, programs and services, and the history of the Coast Guard.

Telephone Contacts
General Information .... (202) 267–2229
Personnel Locator .... (202) 267–1340
Boating Safety Hotline .... (800) 368–5647

Information and Publications

KEY OFFICES

USCG Public Affairs Staff
2100 2nd St. S.W.
Washington, DC 20593
(202) 267–1587
Fax (202) 267–4307
Capt. Jeff Karonis, chief
Robert Browning, historian

Provides general information on operations, answers or refers questions, and issues news releases. The Office of the Coast Guard Historian can also answer general questions.

USCG Office of Boating Safety
2100 2nd St. S.W.
Washington, DC 20593
(202) 267–1077
Fax (202) 267–4285
Capt. Scott Evans, chief

Maintains a mailing list for U.S. Coast Guard consumer advisory newsletters. Contact this office to be placed on the mailing list.

Freedom of Information

Program Support Division
2100 2nd St. S.W., GSII-2
Washington, DC 20593-0001
(202) 267–2324
Donald Taylor, FOI officer

PUBLICATIONS

USCG Public Affairs provides publications on boating safety, the merchant marine, environmental topics, and related subjects (does not issue a general list). Consumer publications also are available through the Coast Guard's district offices.

The Coast Guard publishes a monthly magazine, *Proceedings of the Marine Safety Council*, intended for the maritime industry, which reports on new and proposed Coast Guard regulations and provides other articles on the promotion of maritime safety. For subscription information, contact: Editor, Proceedings of the Marine Safety Council, U.S. Coast Guard (G-CMC), Washington, DC 20593. For the Transportation Department's annual report, which includes regulatory activities of the U.S. Coast Guard, contact DOT Public Affairs; (202) 366–4570.

Reference Resources

LIBRARY

USCG Law Library

Transportation Administrative Services Center (TASC)
2100 2nd St. S.W., Room B726
Washington, DC 20593
(202) 267–2536
Fax (202) 267–4204
Rowena Robinson, technical information specialist
Hours: 9:00 a.m. to 4:00 a.m.

DOT Library

Transportation Administrative Services Center (TASC)
400 7th St. S.W., Room 2200
Washington, DC 20590
(202) 366–0746
Clara Smith, chief of information services
Hours: 8:00 a.m. to 4:00 p.m.

DOCKETS

Regulations and Administrative Law Division

2100 2nd St. S.W., Room 3406
Washington, DC 20593
(202) 267–1477
Hours: 9:30 a.m. to 2:00 p.m.

Maintains documents and comments relating to Coast Guard rulemaking and other administrative procedures for public inspection.

RULES AND REGULATIONS

Major Coast Guard rules and regulations are published in the *Code of Federal Regulations*, Title 33, parts 1–199, Title 46, parts 1–199 and parts 401–403, Title 49, parts 420–453, and certain parts of Title 16 and Title 21. Proposed rules, final rules, notices, and updates to the *Code of Federal Regulations* are published in the daily *Federal Register*. *(See appendix for information on how to obtain and use these publications.)*

See also Publications, above.

◼ LEGISLATION

The Coast Guard was established under Title 14 of the United States Code. It administers the following statutes:

Dangerous Cargo Act (R.S. 4472, 46 U.S.C. 170). Signed by the president Feb. 28, 1871. Provided authority to regulate the carriage of explosives and hazardous substances on vessels.

Bridge Laws (34 Stat. 84, 28 Stat. 362, 54 Stat. 467, 60 Stat. 847; 33 U.S.C. 491, 499, 511, 525). Signed by the president March 3, 1899. As amended, authorized the Coast Guard to approve the location and navigational clearance of bridges built across navigable waters. Also authorized the regulation of drawbridges and provided partial funding for the costs of altering obstructive bridges.

Merchant Marine Act of 1920 (41 Stat. 998, 46 U.S.C. 882). Signed by the president June 5, 1920. Set the number of passengers cargo vessels may carry and established rules of behavior for corporate-owned U.S. vessels.

Act of June 25, 1936 (49 Stat. 1922, 46 U.S.C. 738). Signed by the president June 25, 1936. Established the ice patrol service under the administration of the Coast Guard; required that vessel operators crossing the north Atlantic Ocean give public notice of regular routes and any changes in routes.

Motorboat Act of 1940 (54 Stat. 163, 46 U.S.C. 526). Signed by the president April 25, 1940. Established safety regulations for motorboats and required licensing of motorboat operators.

Outer Continental Shelf Lands Act (67 Stat. 462, 43 U.S.C. 1333). Signed by the president Aug. 7, 1953. Authorized the Coast Guard to establish and enforce safety standards on the outer continental shelf lands.

Act of May 10, 1956 (70 Stat. 151, 46 U.S.C. 390). Signed by the president May 10, 1956. Authorized the Coast Guard periodically to inspect passenger vessels and to establish guidelines for design, construction, alteration, and repair of vessels.

Great Lakes Pilotage Act of 1960 (74 Stat. 259, 46 U.S.C. 216). Signed by the president June 30, 1960. Required registration of pilots of foreign and domestic vessels on the Great Lakes; set rates and charges for pilot services.

Oil Pollution Act of 1961 (75 Stat. 402, 33 U.S.C. 1001). Signed by the president Aug. 30, 1961. Prohibited discharge of oil or oily mixtures into navigable waters.

Department of Transportation Act (80 Stat. 931, 49 U.S.C. 1655). Signed by the president Oct. 15, 1966. Transferred the Coast Guard to the DOT. Established lighting requirements, provided procedures for ships passing one another, established anchorage grounds for safe navigation, required alteration of bridges obstructing navigation, established regulations governing the operation of drawbridges, set reasonable rates for tolls, and required approval of plans and locations for the construction of bridges.

Federal Boat Safety Act of 1971 (85 Stat. 213, 46 U.S.C. 1451 et seq.). Signed by the president Aug. 10, 1971. Empowered the Coast Guard to issue regulations to establish minimum boating safety standards and to require the installation of safety equipment.

Ports and Waterways Safety Act of 1972 (86 Stat. 424, 33 U.S.C. 1221). Signed by the president July 10, 1972. Established safety measures to prevent damage to vessels and structures on navigable waters.

Port and Tanker Safety Act (92 Stat. 1471, 33 U.S.C. 1221, 46 U.S.C. 391a). Signed by the president July 10, 1972. Provided for the port safety program, which includes the establishment of vessel traffic services, issuance of regulations to protect the environment, and authority to regulate various activities in the nation's ports. Also authorized inspection and regulation of tank vessels.

Federal Water Pollution Control Act Amendments of 1972 (86 Stat. 816, 33 U.S.C. 1251 et seq.). Signed by the president Oct. 18, 1972. Authorized inspections of vessels carrying oil or other hazardous materials; required clean up of spills in navigable waters of oil or other hazardous materials; and established standards of performance for marine sanitation devices.

Federal-Aid Highway Act of 1973 (87 Stat. 267, 33 U.S.C. 526a). Signed by the president Aug. 13, 1973. Established guidelines for toll increases used for bridge construction.

Deepwater Port Act of 1974 (88 Stat. 2126, 33 U.S.C. 1501). Signed by the president Jan. 3, 1975. Required licensing and regulation of deep-water port facilities.

Fishery Conservation Management Act (90 Stat. 331, 16 U.S.C. 1801). Signed by the president April 13, 1976. Authorized enforcement and regulation of fishery conservation management zones.

Clean Water Act of 1977 (91 Stat. 1566, 33 U.S.C. 1251). Signed by the president Dec. 27, 1977. Raised liability limit on oil spill cleanup costs. Amended the Federal Water Pollution Control Act Amendments of 1972.

Outer Continental Shelf Lands Act Amendments of 1978 (92 Stat. 629, 43 U.S.C. 1811). Signed by the president Sept. 18, 1978. Imposed liabilities for oil spills associated with the ocean's outer continental shelf.

Deep Seabed Hard Mineral Resources Act of 1980 (94 Stat. 553, 30 U.S.C. 1401). Signed by the president June 28, 1980. Established an interim program to encourage and regulate the development of hard mineral resources of the deep seabed by the United States.

Drug Interdiction Act of 1980 (94 Stat. 1159, 21 U.S.C. 955). Signed by the president Sept. 15, 1980. Facilitated enforcement by the Coast Guard of laws relating to the importation of illegal drugs.

Recreational Boating and Safety and Facilities Act of 1980 (94 Stat. 1983, 46 U.S.C. 1451). Signed by the president Oct. 14, 1980. Amended the Federal Boat Safety Act of 1971 to improve recreational boating safety and facilities through the development, administration, and financing of a national recreational safety and facilities improvement program.

Oil Pollution Act of 1990 (104 Stat. 484, 33 U.S.C. 2701 note). Signed by the president Aug. 18, 1990. Provided for environmental safeguards in oil transportation and addressed wide-ranging problems associated with preventing, responding to, and paying for oil spills.

Maritime Transportation Security Act of 2002 (116 Stat. 2064, 46 U.S.C. 2101 note). Signed by the president Nov. 25, 2002. Required the DOT to develop antiterrorism plans at U.S. ports and foreign ports where U.S.-bound shipments originate. Required the DOT to establish a maritime intelligence program to work in conjunction with the Coast Guard to help identify suspicious vessels before they enter U.S. ports. Authorized the Coast Guard to block ships from entering U.S. ports if they failed to meet security standards. Amended the Ports and Waterways Safety Act to authorize the use of Coast Guard personnel as sea marshals on facilities or vessels to deter or respond to acts of terrorism.

Title III, the Coast Guard Personnel and Maritime Safety Act of 2002, authorized the Coast Guard to borrow up to $100 million from the Oil Spill Liability Trust Fund for emergency oil cleanups; increased penalties for negligent operation of recreational and commercial vehicles; and modified several personnel rules to improve officer retention and enhance morale.

Homeland Security Act of 2002 (P.L. 107-296). Signed by the president Nov. 25, 2002. Transferred to the DHS the authorities, functions, personnel, and assets of the Coast

Guard, which was to be maintained as a distinct entity within DHS. Required the commandant of the Coast Guard to report directly to the secretary of homeland security. Prohibited any of the above conditions and restrictions from applying to the Coast Guard when it was operating as a service in the Navy.

▨ REGIONAL OFFICES

ATLANTIC AREA
431 Crawford St.
Portsmouth, VA 23704–5004
(757) 398–6287
Vice Adm. J. Hull, commander

PACIFIC AREA
Coast Guard Island
Alameda, CA 94501–5100
(510) 437–3324
Vice Adm. T. Cross, commander

DISTRICT 1
(CT, MA, ME, NH, NJ, downstate NY, RI, VT)
408 Atlantic Ave.
Boston, MA 02110
(617) 223–8480
Rear Adm. V. Crea, commander

DISTRICT 5
(DC, DE, MD, NC, most of PA, VA)
431 Crawford St.
Portsmouth, VA 23704–5004
(757) 398–6287
Vice Adm. S. Brice-O'Hara, commander

DISTRICT 7
(most of FL, GA, SC)
909 S.E. First Ave.
Miami, FL 33131–3050
(305) 536–5654
Rear Adm. H. Johnson, commander

DISTRICT 8
(AL, AR, CO, FL panhandle, IA, KS, KY, LA, MO, MS, ND, NE, NM, OK, SD, TN, TX, WV, WY; areas of IL, IN, MN, OH, and WI not adjacent to Great Lakes)
501 Magazine St.
New Orleans, LA 70130
(504) 589–6298
Rear Adm. R. Duncan, commander

DISTRICT 9
(MI; Great Lakes area of IL, IN, MN, NY, OH, PA, and WI)
1240 E. Ninth St.
Cleveland, OH 44199–2060
(216) 902–6001
Rear Adm. R. Silva, commander

DISTRICT 11
(AZ, CA, NV, UT)
Coast Guard Island
Alameda, CA 94501–5100
(510) 437–3324
Rear Adm. K. Eldridge, commander

DISTRICT 13
(ID, MT, OR, WA)
915 Second Ave.
Seattle, WA 98174–1067
(206) 220–7237
Rear Adm. J. Garrett, commander

DISTRICT 14
(HI)
300 Ala Moana Blvd.
Honolulu, HI 96850–4982
(808) 541–2121
Rear Adm. C. Wurster, commander

DISTRICT 17
(AK)
P.O. Box 25517
Juneau, AK 99802–1217
(907) 463–2065
Rear Adm. J. Underwood, commander

Housing and Urban Development Department

451 7th St. S.W., Washington, DC 20410
Internet: http://www.hud.gov

Office of Fair Housing and Equal Opportunity

451 7th St. S.W., Washington, DC 20410
Internet: http://www.hud.gov/offices/fheo

The Department of Housing and Urban Development (HUD) is the primary federal agency responsible for programs concerned with housing needs and improving and developing the nation's communities.

The assistant secretary for fair housing and equal opportunity is the principal adviser to the HUD secretary on matters concerning civil rights and equal opportunity in housing, employment, lending, and business.

The office administers the fair housing program authorized by Title VI and Title VII of the Civil Rights Act of 1964; Title VIII of the Civil Rights Act of 1968; Sections 501, 504, and 505 of the Rehabilitation Act of 1973; the Age Discrimination Act of 1975, as amended; Executive Orders 11063, 11246, 11478, 12259, 12432, and 12892; the Age Discrimination Act of 1967; Section 3 of the Housing and Urban Development Act of 1968, as amended; Section 109 of the Housing and Community Development Act of 1974; the Fair Housing Amendments Act of 1988; and the Americans with Disabilities Act of 1990.

These ensure that HUD programs operate to further the goals of equal opportunity by providing for the coordination, planning, monitoring, and review of programs to increase training, employment, and business opportunities for lower income and minority group residents of HUD-assisted housing programs.

Persons who believe they have been victims of discrimination prohibited by the Fair Housing Act may file a complaint with Office of Fair Housing and Equal Opportunity (FHEO). FHEO will investigate to determine if there has been a violation of the Fair Housing Act. If FHEO finds that the act has been violated, several actions may be taken.

First, HUD will try to reach an agreement with the person or parties named in the complaint (the respondent).

A conciliation agreement must protect both the victim and the public interest. If an agreement is signed, HUD will take no further action. However, if HUD has reasonable cause to believe that a conciliation agreement is breached, HUD will recommend that the attorney general file suit.

If, after investigating a complaint, HUD finds reasonable cause to believe that discrimination occurred, the case will be heard in an administrative hearing within 120 days, unless the complainant or the respondent wants the case to be heard in federal district court. Either way, there is no cost to the complainant. Both the administrative law judge and the federal district court may award actual and punitive damages.

In addition, the attorney general may file a suit in a federal district court if there is reasonable cause to believe a pattern or practice of housing discrimination is occurring.

■ KEY PERSONNEL

Assistant Secretary
Carolyn Y. Peoples...................... (202) 708–4252
Fax...................................... (202) 708–4483
General Deputy Assistant Secretary
Floyd O. May .... (202) 708–4211
Fax...................................... (202) 708–4483
Enforcement and Programs
Deputy Assistant Secretary
David H. Eazel.......................... (202) 619–8046
Fax...................................... (202) 708–2703
Economic Opportunity
Linda Thompson (Acting)............. (202) 708–6385
Policy and Program Evaluation
Bryan Greene.......................... (202) 708–1145

**Operations and Management
Deputy Assistant Secretary**
Karen A. Newton...................... (202) 708–0768

■ INFORMATION SOURCES

Internet
Agency Web site: www.hud.gov/offices/fheo. Includes information about the Fair Housing Act and on what to do if your rights have been violated. HUD also maintains the following online service:

HUD User
P.O. Box 23268
Washington, DC 20026
(800) 245–2691
(301) 495–5863

Provides some HUD publications pertaining to fair housing for a fee. Custom searches of an online database of housing and urban development information are available for a fee. HUD USER hosts its own homepage at http://www.huduser.org.

Telephone Contacts
Personnel Locator.......................... (202) 708–1112
Housing Discrimination Hotline .... (800) 669–9777

Information and Publications

KEY OFFICES

HUD Program Information Center
451 7th St. S.W., Room 8141
Washington, DC 20410
(202) 708–1420
Julie Lovitt, project manager

Handles inquiries from the public and refers all local callers with fair housing and equal opportunity complaints to the proper Washington area authorities. Distributes publications, including brochures and various research studies. Also operates the Housing Discrimination Hotline to hear complaints and respond to fair housing questions.

HUD Public Affairs
451 7th St. S.W., Room 10136
Washington, DC 20410
(202) 708–0980
Diane Leneghan Tomb, assistant secretary of public affairs

Issues news releases and answers questions from the public and the press. To be added to the mailing list, contact the Field Operations and Special Resources Division; (202) 708–3990.

Freedom of Information
HUD Office of the Executive Secretary
451 7th St. S.W., Room 10139
Washington, DC 20410
(202) 708–3054
Dorothy Fason, assistant director

PUBLICATIONS

HUD Customer Service
451 7th St. S.W., Room B-100
Washington, DC 20410
(800) 767–7468
Fax orders (202) 708–2313

Distributes HUD publications, including brochures and various research studies. Titles available include:
Fair Housing—Equal Opportunity for All
Fair Housing—The Law in Perspective
Fair Housing, U.S.A.
You Have a Right to Live Where You Want to Live
Are You a Victim of Fair Housing?

Reference Resources

LIBRARY

Housing and Urban Development Department
451 7th St. S.W., Room 8141
Washington, DC 20410
(202) 708–3728
Julie Lovitt, director

Related materials are also available at regional offices. The headquarters library is open to the public from 8:45 a.m. to 5:15 p.m.

RULES AND REGULATIONS
FHEO rules and regulations are published in the *Code of Federal Regulations,* Title 24, parts 100–199. Proposed regulations, new final regulations, and updates to the *Code of Federal Regulations* are published in the daily *Federal Register.* (*See appendix for details on how to obtain and use these publications.*)

LEGISLATION

FHEO exercises its authority under:

Executive Order 11063. Issued by the president Nov. 20, 1962. Directed HUD to institute policies and actions to prevent discrimination because of race, color, creed, national origin, or sex in the sale, leasing, rental, or other disposition of residential property and related facilities owned, operated, or assisted financially by the federal government and in housing loans insured or guaranteed by the federal government.

Title VI of The Civil Rights Act of 1964 (78 Stat. 241, 42 U.S.C. 2000d). Signed by the president July 2, 1964. Prohibited discrimination in programs or activities receiving federal financial assistance on the basis of race, color, religion, national origin, or sex.

Civil Rights Act of 1968, Title VIII (82 Stat. 81, 42 U.S.C. 3601). Signed by the president April 11, 1968. Also known as the Fair Housing Act. Prohibited discrimination in the sale or rental of most housing.

Section 3 of the Housing and Urban Development Act of 1968, as amended (82 Stat. 476, 12 U.S.C. 1701u). Signed by the president Aug. 1, 1968. Provided for maximum employment and training opportunities on HUD-assisted housing projects for lower-income residents of the metropolitan areas where these projects are located. The act also gave maximum work contract opportunities on these projects to individuals and firms located in or owned by persons residing in the housing project areas.

Section 504 of the Rehabilitation Act of 1973 (87 Stat. 355, 29 U.S.C. 794). Signed by the president Sept. 16, 1973. Prohibited discrimination based on handicap in federally assisted and conducted programs and activities.

Section 109 of the Housing and Community Development Act of 1974 (88 Stat. 633, 42 U.S.C. 5309). Signed by the president Aug. 22, 1974. Prohibited discrimination in any federally funded activity, including employment, benefits, and services, and any program or activity that receives a loan guarantee under the title.

Executive Order 12259. Issued by the president Dec. 31, 1980. Provided the secretary of HUD with a leadership role in the administration of any federal programs and activities relating to housing and urban development to further new housing throughout the United States.

Fair Housing Amendments Act of 1988 (102 Stat. 1619, 42 U.S.C. 3601 note). Amended Title 8 of the Civil Rights Act of 1968 to prohibit housing discrimination against disabled people and families with young children.

Americans with Disabilities Act of 1990 (104 Stat. 327, 42 U.S.C. 12101 et seq.). Signed by the president July 25, 1990. Ensured that all programs, services, and regulatory activities relating to state and local public housing and housing assistance are available to people with disabilities.

Executive Order 12892. Issued by the president Jan. 17, 1994. Requires all federal executive agencies to administer housing and urban development programs in a manner that affirmatively furthers fair housing.

Multifamily Property Disposition Reform Act of 1994 (108 Stat. 342, 12 U.S.C. 1701). Signed by the president Apr. 11, 1994. Amended section 203 of the Housing and Community Development Amendments of 1978 to provide for the disposition of multifamily properties owned by HUD.

Home Ownership and Equity Protection Act of 1994 (P.L. 103-325). Signed by the president Sept. 23, 1994. Amended the Truth in Lending Act to require a creditor to disclose specified lending data to a consumer in connection with reverse mortgage transactions. Directed the Federal Reserve to conduct periodic public hearings on the home equity loan market and the adequacy of existing consumer protection laws.

Executive Order 13217. Issued by the president June 18, 2001. Required federal agencies to evaluate and revise their policies and programs to improve the availability of community-based living arrangements for persons with disabilities.

REGIONAL OFFICES

Housing and Urban Development Department

NEW ENGLAND
(CT, MA, ME, NH, RI, VT)
10 Causeway St., #308
Boston, MA 02222–1092
(617) 994–8300
Toll-free (800) 827–5005
Marcella O. Brown, director

NEW YORK/NEW JERSEY
(NJ, NY)
26 Federal Plaza
New York, NY 10278–0068
(212) 264–1290
Toll-free (800) 496–4294
Stanley Seidenfeld, director

MID-ATLANTIC
(DC, DE, MD, PA, VA, WV)
100 Penn Square East
Philadelphia, PA 19107–3380
(215) 656–0647
Toll-free (888) 799–2085
Wanda S. Nieves, director

SOUTHEAST/CARIBBEAN

(AL, FL, GA, KY, MS, NC, PR, SC, TN, VI)
75 Spring St. S.W.
Atlanta, GA 30303–3388
(404) 331–5140
Toll-free (800) 440–8091
Gregory B. King, director

MIDWEST

(IL, IN, MI, MN, OH, WI)
77 W. Jackson Blvd.
Chicago, IL 60604–3507
(312) 353–7776
Toll-free (800) 765–9372
Barbara Knox, director

SOUTHWEST

(AR, LA, NM, OK, TX)
801 Cherry St.
P.O. Box 2905
Fort Worth, TX 76113–2905
(817) 978–5900
Toll-free (800) 560–8913
Garry Sweeney, director

GREAT PLAINS

(IA, KS, MO, NE)
400 State Ave.
Kansas City, MO 66101–2406
(913) 551–6958
Toll-free (800) 743–5323
Robbie Herndon, director

ROCKY MOUNTAINS

(CO, MT, ND, SD, UT, WY)
633 17th St.
Denver, CO 80202–3607
(303) 672–5437
Toll-free (800) 877–7353
Evelyn Meininger, director

PACIFIC/HAWAII

(AS, AZ, CA, GU, HI, NV)
450 Golden Gate Ave.
P.O. Box 36003
San Francisco, CA 94102–3448
(415) 436–6568
Toll-free (800) 347–3739
Charles E. Hauptman, director

NORTHWEST/ALASKA

(AK, ID, OR, WA)
909 First Ave., #200
Seattle, WA 98104–1000
(206) 220–5170
Toll-free (800) 877–0246
Judith Keeler, director

Office of Housing

451 7th St. S.W., Washington, DC 20410
Internet: http://www.hud.gov/offices/hsg

The assistant secretary for housing, who is also the federal housing commissioner, directs the Department of Housing and Urban Development (HUD) housing and mortgage insurance programs. These include the federally insured Federal Housing Administration (FHA) loans. These programs include the production, financing, and management of new and substantially rehabilitated housing and the conservation and rehabilitation of existing housing. The Office of Housing insures mortgages on single-family homes; multifamily rental, condominium, and cooperative projects; land purchased for residential development; nursing homes; group practice facilities and hospitals; and loans for property improvements and the purchase of manufactured (mobile) homes. The office directs special programs for the housing needs of low-income families; the elderly; disabled and mentally ill individuals; veterans; disaster victims; and prospective home buyers who are marginal credit risks.

The Office of Housing's basic missions are to create homeownership opportunities and to provide affordable rental housing for low- and moderate-income families. The National Homeownership Strategy, created in 1994, promotes homeownership through the cooperative effort of HUD, state and local governments, and private nonprofit and profit-making entities. The 2002 homeownership rate reached just under 70 percent—the highest annual rate in U.S. history. Housing works to ensure the availability of affordable rental housing through the administration of the multifamily insurance programs and Section 8 rental assistance programs.

As previously underserved borrowers were able to buy homes for the first time, many were falling victim to predatory lending practices in a segment of the mortgage lending market. Predatory mortgage lending practices strip borrowers of home equity and threaten families with foreclosure. The Home Ownership and Protection Act of 1994 was enacted to prevent low-income consumers from losing their homes as a result of predatory lending practices.

The Office of Housing is responsible for funding and for regulatory activities in connection with housing counseling, real estate settlement procedures, interstate land sales registration, and manufactured home construction and safety standards.

Interstate Land Sales. Authorized by Title XIV of the Housing and Urban Development Act of 1968, as amended, the Interstate Land Sales Registration Program protects consumers against land fraud and questionable sales practices of land developers and promoters. The Housing Office is responsible for administering the Interstate Land Sales Full Disclosure Act. The act prohibits developers and their agents from selling or leasing any lot in a subdivision of 100 or more nonexempt lots without submitting complete information about the land to the purchaser and to HUD.

Subdivisions of twenty-five or more lots are subject to antifraud provisions of the Interstate Land Sales Full Disclosure Act. Willful violation may result in criminal penalties of imprisonment for not more than five years or a fine of not more than $10,000 or both. The Housing Office can take legal action through any federal court serving the district where the defendant resides, does business or has other ties, or where the transaction occurred. HUD may seek an injunction against any developer who is demonstrably violating or about to violate the law. HUD also may suspend a developer's registration if he or she omits or misrepresents facts in a statement of record or property report.

Manufactured (Mobile) Home Construction and Safety Standards. The Housing Office is authorized to issue federal construction and safety standards to protect manufactured homeowners by Title VI of the Housing and Community Development Act of 1974 and the Housing and Community Development Act of 1977. HUD issues these standards to improve the quality of manufactured homes and to decrease property damage, insurance costs, and the number of personal injuries resulting from manufactured home accidents. The standards, which apply to mobile homes built after June 1976, preempt existing state and local codes and standards that do not meet federal standards.

HUD-authorized inspection agencies must approve every manufactured home design and inspect construction operations in approximately 400 manufactured housing plants. Standards may be enforced either by HUD or by various state agencies set up for the program. The manufacturer is required to notify the consumer if a manufactured home does not conform to federal standards. The manufacturer must correct any defects that might present an unreasonable risk of injury or death. Use of the mails or interstate commerce to sell or lease substandard manufactured homes is prohibited and may result in civil and criminal penalties.

Manufacturers construct an estimated 250,000 manufactured homes yearly in accordance with federal standards. Each year, HUD handles approximately 400 consumer complaints while state agencies process 5,000 to 6,000 additional grievances.

Real Estate Settlement Procedures Act. Under the Real Estate Settlement Procedures Act of 1974 (RESPA), HUD defends the interests of home buyers by regulating real estate transactions to reduce the settlement costs of mortgage loans. This is achieved through the prohibition of abusive practices such as referral fees and kickbacks, the limitation of escrow accounts, and the requirement of full disclosure to home buyers and sellers.

The law requires that lenders provide prospective borrowers of federally related loans (such as those offered by federally insured institutions) with a booklet—prepared by HUD—containing information about real estate transactions, settlement services, cost comparisons, and relevant consumer protection laws. Borrowers must receive good-faith estimates of settlement costs at the outset of a transaction and, at settlement, all parties are entitled to an itemized statement of costs incurred in the transaction.

In July 2002 HUD issued a proposed rule under the RESPA to simplify and improve the process of obtaining home mortgages and reduce settlement costs for consumers. The rule would require mortgage brokers to provide disclosures concerning their functions and fees, while protecting consumers from illegal fees. According to HUD's economic analysis, the rule would ultimately save consumers an estimated $8 billion a year or approximately

$700 per loan transaction. HUD's final RESPA rule was expected to be completed by summer 2003.

In January 2003 HUD issued a proposed rule to strengthen HUD's regulations concerning the responsibilities of FHA-approved lenders in the selection of appraisers for properties that would be the security for FHA-insured mortgages. The proposed rule would hold lenders strictly accountable for the quality of their appraisals. The rule also would require appraisals that do not meet FHA requirements to be subject to the imposition of sanctions by the HUD Mortgagee Review Board. HUD's final ruling was expected after all public comments was received and reviewed.

In May 2003 HUD issued a final rule addressing property flipping, the practice whereby a property recently acquired is resold for a considerable profit with an artificially inflated value, often abetted by a lender's collusion with the appraiser. The final rule established requirements regarding the eligibility of properties to be financed with FHA mortgage insurance. The new requirements made flipped properties ineligible for FHA-insured mortgage financing, thus precluding FHA home purchasers from becoming victims of predatory flipping activity.

■ KEY PERSONNEL

Assistant Secretary for Housing–Federal Housing Commissioner
    John C. Weicher .... (202) 708–3600
    Fax .... (202) 708–2580
General Deputy Assistant Secretary
    Sean G. Cassidy .... (202) 708–3600
Counsel
    Eliot Horowitz .... (202) 708–0579
Government Sponsored Enterprise
    Sandra Fostek .... (202) 708–2224
    Fax .... (202) 708–6259
    Fax .... (202) 401–8860
Deputy Assistant Secretary for Multifamily Housing Programs
    John Coonts .... (202) 708–2495
    Fax .... (202) 708–2583
Associate Deputy Assistant Secretary for Multifamily Housing Programs
    Janet Golrick .... (202) 708–2495
Housing Assistance and Grant Administration
    Willie Spearmon .... (202) 708–3700
Housing Assistance and Contract Administrative Oversight
    Gerri Burson .... (202) 708–2866
Multifamily Development
    Michael McCullough .... (202) 708–3000

Asset Management
Beverly Miller............................. (202) 708–3730
Program Systems Management
Stephen A. Martin...................... (202) 708–4135
Deputy Assistant Secretary for Operations
Michael Hill .... (202) 708–1104
Business Development
Dawn Kuhn............................. (202) 708–1104
Management
Maureen Hilleary........................ (202) 708–1014
Deputy Assistant Secretary for Single Family Housing
Frederick Douglas...................... (202) 708–3175
Fax...................................... (202) 708–2582
Associate Deputy Assistant Secretary for Single Family Housing
Vernice Buell............................ (202) 708–3175
Consumer and Regulatory Affairs
Vacant.................................. (202) 708–4560
Lender Activities and Program Compliance
Phillip Murray.......................... (202) 708–1515
Single Family Asset Management
Joe McCloskey.......................... (202) 708–1672
Single Family Program Management
Vance Morris .... (202) 708–2121
FHA Comptroller
Keith Cole............................... (202) 401–8800
Fax...................................... (202) 401–2664
Deputy Comptroller
George Rabil (acting) .... (202) 401–8800
Financial Services
Samuel Connor......................... (202) 708–1046
Budget and Field Resources
Vacant.................................. (202) 401–8975
Financial Analysis and Reporting
George Rabil............................ (202) 755–7500
Evaluation
Judy May............................... (202) 755-7500
Systems and Technology
Ronald E. Carupi....................... (202) 401–0450

▓ INFORMATION SOURCES

Internet
Agency Web site: http://www.hud.gov/offices/hsg. Features general information on renting and buying single-family and multi-family homes; also includes information on neighborhood networks and the Real Estate Settlement Procedures Act. HUD also maintains the following online service:

HUD User
P.O. Box 6091
Rockville, MD 20849
(800) 245–2691
(301) 251–5154

Some reports, resource guides, kits, executive summaries, case studies, and guidebooks published by HUD are available from HUD USER for a fee. Custom searches of an online database containing information about all aspects of housing and urban development are available for a fee. HUD USER hosts its own homepage at http://www.huduser.org.

Telephone Contacts
Personnel Locator......................... (202) 708–1112

Information and Publications

KEY OFFICES

HUD Program Information Center
451 7th St. S.W., Room 8141
Washington, DC 20410
(202) 708–1420
Julie Lovitt, project manager

Handles inquiries from the public and refers local callers with housing complaints to the proper Washington area authorities. Distributes publications including brochures and various research reports.

HUD Public Affairs
451 7th St. S.W., Room 10136
Washington, DC 20410
(202) 708–0685
Jerry Brown, assistant secretary of public affairs

Answers questions from the public and the press about the Housing Office and its activities, distributes several publications and policy amendments, and issues news releases. To be added to the mailing list, contact Field Operations and Special Resources; (202) 708–3990.

Freedom of Information
HUD Office of the Executive Secretariat
451 7th St. S.W., Room 10139
Washington, DC 20410
(202) 708–3054
Dorothy Fason, assistant director

HUD Customer Service/Distribution Center

451 7th St. S.W., #B-100
Washington, DC 20410
(800) 767–7468
Fax orders (202) 708–2313

Distributes publications including brochures, research studies, and publications on manufactured housing standards, real estate settlement procedures, and interstate land sales.

Publications available include:

Annual Report. Lists major activities of the programs administered by HUD, including statistical information on the Government National Mortgage Association.

Digest: Office of the Inspector General: Report to the Congress. Lists audits and actions taken by the inspector general. Published semiannually.

Programs of HUD. Describes HUD programs including the nature of the programs, eligibility requirements, distribution of aid, information sources, current status, and the funding of the program. Lists regional and field offices.

Reference Resources

LIBRARY

Housing and Urban Development Department

451 7th St. S.W., Room 8141
Washington, DC 20410
(202) 708–3728
Julie Lovitt, project manager
Hours: 8:45 a.m. to 5:15 p.m.

Materials related to the Office of Housing are available here and at regional offices.

REGULATORY BARRIERS CLEARINGHOUSE

HUD's Regulatory Barriers Clearinghouse (RBC) was created to support state and local governments and other organizations seeking information about laws, regulations, and policies affecting all aspects of affordable housing. RBC supports the collection and dissemination of resources that can help identify and address regulatory barriers in each individual state and community. RBC is available at http://www.huduser.org/rbc.

RULES AND REGULATIONS

Office of Housing rules and regulations are published in the *Code of Federal Regulations,* Title 24, parts 100–199. Proposed regulations, new final regulations, and updates to the *Code of Federal Regulations* are published in the daily *Federal Register.* (*See appendix for details on how to obtain and use these publications.*)

▨ LEGISLATION

The Office of Housing carries out its responsibilities under numerous pieces of legislation; among the most important are the following:

National Housing Act of 1934 (48 Stat. 1246, 12 U.S.C. 1702). Signed by the president June 27, 1934. Authorized mortgage insurance, rehabilitation, health facilities, and other financial and related assistance programs.

U.S. Housing Act of 1937 (50 Stat. 888, 42 U.S.C. 1401). Signed by the president Sept. 1, 1937. Authorized the low-income housing programs.

Housing Act of 1959 (73 Stat. 654, 12 U.S.C. 1701q). Signed by the president Sept. 23, 1959. Strengthened laws governing programs to improve housing and renew urban communities such as the FHA Insurance Program, urban renewal, and low-rent public housing. Section 202 provided for a direct-loan program for the construction of housing for the elderly.

Housing and Urban Development Act of 1965 (79 Stat. 451, 42 U.S.C. 3535). Signed by the president Aug. 10, 1965. Strengthened financial assistance provisions for low- and moderate-income families in existing housing laws to promote orderly urban development and to improve living conditions in urban areas. Title I authorized the rent supplement programs.

Housing and Urban Development Act of 1968 (82 Stat. 476, 12 U.S.C. 1701 note). Signed by the president Aug. 1, 1968. Amended the National Housing Act of 1934. Section 106(a) authorized HUD to provide advice and technical assistance with regard to construction, renovation, and operation of low- and moderate-income housing.

Interstate Land Sales Full Disclosure Act (82 Stat. 590, 15 U.S.C. 1701). Signed by the president Aug. 1, 1968. Title XIV of the Housing and Urban Development Act of 1968. Established regulations for the sale or lease of subdivision lots. Required sellers to make available certain information about the land involved and to furnish purchasers with a property report approved by HUD.

Lead-Based Paint Poisoning Prevention Act (84 Stat. 2078, 42 U.S.C. 4801). Signed by the president Jan. 13, 1971. Provided for federal assistance to communities to develop local programs to eliminate causes of lead-based paint poisoning. Prohibited the use of lead-based paint in federal or federally assisted construction or renovation.

Housing and Community Development Act of 1974 (88 Stat. 633, 42 U.S.C. 5301). Signed by the president

Aug. 22, 1974. Section 8 created the Housing Assistance Payments Program, which provided housing assistance payments to participating private owners and public housing agencies to provide decent housing for low-income families at affordable costs.

National Mobile Home Construction and Safety Standards Act of 1974 (88 Stat. 700, 42 U.S.C. 5401). Signed by the president Aug. 22, 1974. Title VI of the Housing and Community Development Act of 1974 established federal standards for the construction, design, performance, and safety of mobile homes.

Real Estate Settlement Procedures Act of 1974 (88 Stat. 1724, 12 U.S.C. 2601). Signed by the president Dec. 22, 1974. Provided for disclosure of the nature and costs of real estate settlement services.

Housing and Community Development Act of 1987 (101 Stat. 1815, 42 U.S.C. 5301 note). Signed by the president Feb. 5, 1988. Authorized funding for housing and community development for fiscal years 1988 and 1989. Permanently extended Federal Housing Administration authority to insure home mortgage loans. Provided incentives and rules to improve maintenance and safety of public housing.

Cranston-Gonzalez National Affordable Housing Act of 1990 (104 Stat. 4079, 42 U.S.C. 12701). Signed by the president Nov. 28, 1990. Reformed low-income housing programs to expand home ownership. Brought state and local government into a new housing investment partnership with the federal government and the private sector to provide for affordable housing.

Omnibus Budget Reconciliation Act of 1990 (42 U.S.C. 1437f). Authorized a series of reforms to FHA single family programs to insure the actuarial soundness of the Mutual Mortgage Insurance Fund.

Housing and Community Development Act of 1992 (106 Stat. 3672, 42 U.S.C. 5301 note). Signed by the president Oct. 28, 1992. Increased the maximum mortgage amount in FHA single family insurance programs; provided for a regulatory structure for government-sponsored enterprises; and implemented programs to reduce the risk of lead-based paint poisoning in public housing.

Multifamily Property Disposition Reform Act of 1994 (108 Stat. 342, 12 U.S.C. 1701). Signed by the president Apr. 11, 1994. Amended section 203 of the Housing and Community Development Amendments of 1978 to provide for the disposition of multifamily properties owned by HUD.

Home Ownership and Equity Protection Act of 1994 (P.L. 103-325). Signed by the president Sept. 23, 1994. This legislation sought to prohibit predatory lending practices against low-income and minority consumers by amending the Truth in Lending Act to require a creditor to disclose specified lending data to a consumer in connection with reverse mortgage transactions. Also directed the board of governors of the Federal Reserve to conduct periodic public hearings on the home equity loan market and the adequacy of existing consumer protection laws.

FHA Downpayment Simplification Act of 2002 (P.L. 107-326). Signed by the president Dec. 4, 2002. Amended the National Housing Act to make the existing FHA single-family down payment provisions permanent. Required that original lenders, in conjunction with an FHA-insured loan, provide prospective borrowers with a one-page analysis of other mortgage products for which they would qualify, including information about rates, insurance premiums, other costs and fees, and mortgage insurance premium termination.

▓ REGIONAL OFFICES

HUD maintains 10 regional offices *(for addresses, see pp. 551–552)*.

Office of Public and Indian Housing

451 7th St. S.W., Washington, DC 20410
Internet: http://www.hud.gov/offices/pih

The Office of Public and Indian Housing (PIH) is responsible for directing HUD's low-income public housing program and coordinating all departmental housing and community development programs for Indians and Alaskan Natives. The low-income housing program provides financial and technical assistance for the development, operation, and management of public housing, including assistance to Indian Housing Authorities (IHAs) for low-income Native American families residing in Native American areas and reservations. PIH also provides operating subsidies for Public Housing Authorities (PHAs) and IHAs.

The provision of assistance for Indian Housing Authorities is authorized by the U.S. Housing Act of 1937, as amended. IHAs must be established before they can receive any HUD assistance. IHAs are corporate, public bodies established by tribal ordinance or state law. They plan, construct, purchase, lease, and manage properties. HUD's role is to administer the federal government's participation in the Indian Housing Program.

PIH is also responsible for administering the following programs:

- The Capital Fund to provide funds to PHAs for the development, financing, and modernization of public housing projects.
- The Resident Opportunities and Self Sufficiency Program and drug-free neighborhood programs.
- The HOPE VI Program.
- Housing Choice Voucher Programs (Section 8) and the Moderate Rehabilitation Program.
- The Indian Community Development Block Grant Program to develop Indian and Alaskan Native Communities and to aid families with low and moderate income.

Under the assistant secretary for PIH, grants are awarded to PHAs and IHAs for the construction, acquisition, and operation of Public and Indian Housing Programs. The HOME Investment Partnership, created by the National Affordable Housing Act of 1990, is a federally funded project that awards funds to federally recognized Indian Tribes and Alaskan Native villages to expand the supply of affordable housing.

PIH also oversees PHAs and IHAs to ensure they comply with HUD lead-based paint testing and removal regulations.

The Quality Housing and Work Responsibility Act of 1998 (QHWRA) authorized a new public housing home-ownership program. PIH issued a final rule outlining the program's regulations, which went into effect in April 2003. The program makes public housing dwelling units available for purchase by low-income Native American families as their principal residence.

KEY PERSONNEL

Assistant Secretary for Public and Indian Housing
Michael Liu . . . . (202) 708–0950
Fax . . . . (202) 619–8478
General Deputy Assistant Secretary
Paula Blunt (acting) . . . . (202) 708–0950
Administration and Budget/Chief Financial Officer
Robert Dalzell . . . . (202) 708–0440
Field Operations
David Ziaya . . . . (202) 708–4016
Grants Management Center
Michael Diggs . . . . (202) 358–0221

Native American Programs
Rodger Boyd............................ (202) 401–7914
Policy, Program, and Legislative Initiatives
Rod Solomon........................... (202) 708–0713
Public Housing and Voucher Programs
William O. Russell..................... (202) 708–1380
Public Housing Investments
Milan Ozdinec......................... (202) 401–8812
Section 8 Financial Management Center
Kevin Jones, (acting) director......... (816) 426–6197
Special Applications Center
Ainars Rodins .... (312) 886–9754
Troubled Agency Recovery
David Ziaya............................ (202) 708–1141

■ INFORMATION SOURCES

Internet
Agency Web site: http://www.hud.gov/offices/pih. Includes general information on public housing, application kits, and frequently asked questions. HUD also maintains the following online service:

HUD User
P.O. Box 6091
Rockville, MD 20849
(800) 245–2691
(301) 251–5154

Provides some HUD publications pertaining to public and Indian housing for a fee. Custom searches of an online database of housing and urban development information are available for a fee. HUD USER hosts its own homepage at http://www. huduser.org.

Telephone Contacts
Personnel Locator......................... (202) 708–1112
Housing Discrimination Hotline .... (800) 669–9777

Information and Publications

KEY OFFICES

HUD Program Information Center
451 7th St. S.W., Room 8141
Washington, DC 20410
(202) 708–1420
Julie Lovitt, project manager

Handles inquiries from the public and refers all local callers with fair housing and equal opportunity com-

plaints to the proper Washington area authorities. Distributes publications, including brochures and various research studies. Also operates the Housing Discrimination Hotline to hear complaints and respond to fair housing questions.

HUD Public Affairs
451 7th St. S.W., Room 10136
Washington, DC 20410
(202) 708–0980
Diane Leneghan Tomb, assistant secretary of public affairs

Issues news releases and answers questions from the public and the press. To be added to the mailing list, contact Field Operations and Special Resources: (202) 708–3990.

Freedom of Information
HUD Office of the Executive Secretariat
451 7th St. S.W., Room 10139
Washington, DC 20410
(202) 708–3054
Dorothy Fason, assistant director

PUBLICATIONS

HUD Customer Service/Distribution Center
451 7th St. S.W., Room B-100
Washington, DC 20410
(800) 767–7468
Fax orders (202) 708–2313

Distributes HUD publications, including brochures and various research studies. Titles available include:
The Community Development Block Grant Program for Native Americans
Housing Programs for Native Americans
The Home Program for Native Americans

Reference Resources

LIBRARY

Housing and Urban Development Department
451 7th St. S.W., Room 8141
Washington, DC 20410
(202) 708–3728
Julie Lovitt, project manager

Related materials are also available at regional offices. The headquarters library is open to the public from 8:45 a.m. to 5:15 p.m.

RULES AND REGULATIONS

PIH rules and regulations are published in the *Code of Federal Regulations*, Title 24, parts 85 and 100–199. Proposed regulations, new final regulations, and updates to the *Code of Federal Regulations* are published in the daily *Federal Register*. *(See appendix for details on how to obtain and use these publications.)*

■ LEGISLATION

U.S. Housing Act of 1937 (50 Stat. 888, 42 U.S.C. 1401). Signed by the president Sept. 1, 1937. Authorized HUD to provide financial and technical assistance to Indian Housing Authorities for the operation, development, and management of housing for lower income Native American families living in Indian areas or reservations.

Housing and Community Development Act of 1974 (88 Stat. 633, 42 U.S.C. 5301). Signed by the president Aug. 22, 1974. Established the Section 8 Rental Certificate Program, which provided housing assistance payments to participating private owners and public housing agencies to provide decent housing for low income families at affordable costs. Also authorized the Indian Community Development Block Grant Programs.

Cranston-Gonzalez National Affordable Housing Act (104 Stat. 4079, 42 U.S.C. 12701). Signed by the president Nov. 28, 1990. Created the Home Investment Partnership to expand the supply of decent and safe affordable housing. Funds are awarded competitively to federally recognized Indian tribes and Alaskan Native villages.

The Public and Assisted Housing Drug Elimination Act of 1990 (101 Stat. 4245, 42 U.S.C. 11901 note). Signed by the president Nov. 28, 1990. Authorized HUD to make grants to PHAs and IHAs for use in eliminating drug-related crime in public housing projects.

Native American Housing Assistance and Self-Determination Act of 1996 (110 Stat. 4016, 25 U.S.C. 4101 note). Signed by the president on Oct. 26, 1996. Title I provided grants to carry out affordable housing programs for Native Americans.

The Quality Housing and Work Responsibility Act of 1998 (112 Stat. 2487). Signed by the president on Oct. 21, 1998. Amended the Public and Assisted Housing Drug Elimination Act of 1990 to make Native American tribes eligible to receive grants for elimination of drug-related crime in public housing. Also contained Native American housing grants and loan guarantees.

■ REGIONAL OFFICES

Office of Public and Indian Housing

EASTERN/WOODLANDS
(All states east of the Mississippi River and IA)
Chicago Office of Native American Programs
77 W. Jackson Blvd.
Chicago, IL 60604–3507
(312) 353–6236
Kevin Fitzgibbons, administrator

SOUTHERN PLAINS
(AR, KS, LA, MO, OK, TX except Isleta del Sur)
Oklahoma City Office of Native American Programs
500 W. Main St., #400
Oklahoma City, OK 73102
(405) 553–7520
Wayne Simms, administrator

NORTHERN PLAINS
(CO, MT, ND, NE, SD, UT, WY)
Denver Office of Native American Programs
633 17th St.
Denver, CO 80202–3607
(303) 672–5465
Randy Akens, administrator

SOUTHWEST
(AZ, CA, NM, NV; Isleta del Sur, TX)
Phoenix Office of Native American Programs
400 N. Fifth St., #1600
Phoenix, AZ 85004–2361
(602) 379–4156
Raphael Mecham, administrator

NORTHWEST
(ID, OR, WA)
Seattle Office of Native American Programs
909 First Ave., #300
Seattle, WA 98104–1000
(206) 220–5270
Ken Bowring, administrator

ALASKA
Alaska Office of Native American Programs
949 E. 36th Ave., #401
Anchorage, AK 99508–4135
(907) 271–4633
Marlin Knight, administrator

Other Housing and Urban Development Department Offices

▨ OFFICE OF COMMUNITY PLANNING AND DEVELOPMENT

451 7th St. S.W.
Washington, DC 20410
Internet: http://www.hud.gov/offices/cpd

Information
(HUD Public Affairs)...................... (202) 708–0980
Assistant Secretary for Community Planning and
Development
    Roy A. Bernardi .... (202) 708–0270
    Fax.................................... (202) 708–3336
Deputy Assistant Secretary
  Economic Development
    Don Mains............................. (202) 708–1506
  Grant Programs
    Nelson Bregon......................... (202) 401–6367
  Operations
    Bill Eargle............................ (202) 708–2690

The Office of Community Planning and Development (CPD) administers economic and community development grant programs, housing rehabilitation programs, special purpose grants, and homeless assistance programs. Community Development Block Grants are used to develop urban areas. Grants are given to state or local governments primarily to benefit people of low and moderate income. The CPD provides a number of financial and technical assistance programs to state and local governments to stimulate effective planning and management of community development programs. It also administers the Uniform Relocation Assistance and Real Property Acquisitions Policy Act of 1970.

In another capacity, the CPD is coordinator of environmental duties that the Department of Housing and Urban Development (HUD) shares with other federal agencies and with the Council on Environmental Quality. In particular, the CPD stresses the prudent use of energy by HUD clients, especially those with low and moderate incomes. The CPD assistant secretary assures departmental compliance with the National Environmental Policy Act of 1969, the National Historic Preservation Act of 1966, and other laws and executive orders.

The agency's Internet site contains general information about community plans, Empowerment Zones and Enterprise Communities, and community connections; also featured are CPD funding applications, consolidated planning software, and a *Guidebook on Military Base Reuse and Homeless Assistance.*

▨ GOVERNMENT NATIONAL MORTGAGE ASSOCIATION

451 7th St. S.W.
Washington, DC 20410
Internet: http://www.ginniemae.gov

President
    Ronald Rosenfeld...................... (202) 708–0926
    Fax.................................... (202) 708–0490
Executive Vice President
    George S. Anderson.................... (202) 708–0926

The Government National Mortgage Association (GNMA), also known as Ginnie Mae, is a U.S. government corporation created in 1968 through an amendment to Title III of the National Housing Act. GNMA was established to support the government's housing objectives by providing liquidity in the secondary mortgage market for federally insured mortgages originating from the Federal Housing Administration (FHA) and Department of Veterans Affairs (VA).

GNMA's principal activity in supporting those objectives is with its Mortgage-Backed Securities Program (MBS), which provides the necessary liquidity and attempts to attract new sources of financing for residential loans. Through this program, GNMA facilitates the use of mortgage collateral for securities by guaranteeing the payment of principal and interest in a timely manner.

In 1993 Congress authorized GNMA to undertake a Real Estate Mortgage Investment Conduit (REMIC), a trust consisting of mortgage-backed securities.

The agency's Internet site provides links to GNMA I Mortgage-Backed Securities, GNMA II Mortgage-Backed Securities, and a housing resources clearinghouse.

■ OFFICE OF HEALTHY HOMES AND LEAD HAZARD CONTROL

451 7th St. S.W., Room P-3202
Washington, DC 20410
Internet: http://www.hud.gov/offices/lead

Director
David E. Jacobs......................... (202) 755–1785
ext. 102
Fax..................................... (202) 755–1000

Planning and Standards
Warren Friedman .... (202) 755–1785
ext. 159

Program Management
Matt Ammon.......................... (202) 755–1785
ext. 158

The Office of Healthy Homes and Lead Hazard Control, established by the Residential Lead-Based Paint Hazard Reduction Act, provides overall direction to HUD's lead-based paint activities and works closely with other HUD offices to develop regulations, guidelines, and policies applicable to departmental programs.

The office also undertakes programs to increase public awareness of the dangers of lead-based paint poisoning. It conducts demonstrations, studies, and standards development; promotes technology improvements in lead-hazard reduction; and encourages, through a grant program, local and state officials to develop cost-effective methods for the reduction of lead-based paint hazards in private housing for both low- and moderate-income families.

Congress established HUD's Healthy Homes Initiative (HHI) in 1999 to develop and implement a program of research and demonstration projects that would address multiple housing-related problems affecting the health of children.

The agency's Internet site features a reference library and a guide for parents, as well as general information about the office and the Lead-Based Paint Hazard Control Grant Program.

Interior Department

1849 C St. N.W., Washington, DC 20240
Internet: http://www.doi.gov

Bureau of Indian Affairs

1849 C St. N.W., Washington, DC 20240
Internet: http://www.doi.gov/bureau-indian-affairs.html

The Bureau of Indian Affairs (BIA), an agency within the Interior Department, was established as part of the War Department in 1824 and transferred to the Interior Department in 1849.

In 1977 the office of the assistant secretary for Indian affairs was created in the Interior Department to centralize the federal government's policy making and advocacy functions with respect to Native Americans. The bureau is directed by the assistant secretary of the interior for Indian affairs, who is appointed by the president and confirmed by the Senate.

The BIA is organized into area offices and field offices under the control of headquarters in Washington, D.C. The central office is responsible for policy and program administration. Twelve area offices assist the central office with budget allocation and service delivery.

The BIA is the principal link between the federal government and the Native American tribes. The BIA has administrative responsibility for 56 million acres of land held in trust for tribes and individuals by the government.

Working with tribal governments, the BIA also provides a range of services and programs for approximately one million American Indians and Alaska natives from 321 federally recognized tribes and 223 native villages in Alaska.

To be eligible for participation in programs administered by the BIA, a Native American tribe must have a statutory relationship with the U.S. government. The tribe is required to have an elected governing body and a constitution subject to approval by the secretary of the interior.

Each tribe sets its own rules to determine who is eligible to vote and to be an enrolled member of the tribe. Only those enrolled members living on or near trust lands, currently half of the nation's total Indian population, are considered part of the service population of the bureau.

The BIA encourages each tribe to assume administration of reservation programs. Under the Indian Self-Determination and Education Assistance Act of 1975, the individual tribes may assume control of reservation programs.

The BIA also seeks to offer Native American people educational opportunities responsive to their individual needs and cultural backgrounds. The BIA funds a federal Indian school system and gives financial assistance to public school systems that have substantial Indian enrollment.

The BIA works to promote Native American economic development and assists tribes in preserving their natural resources. The bureau oversees the development of mineral resources on Indian lands; the Department of the Interior's Minerals Management Service collects royalties from mineral leasing on Native American lands *(see p. 573)*.

During the past decade Native Americans have questioned the Interior's accounting of its land royalties. Since the passage of the Dawes Act in 1887, which allowed the government to take over the management of 90 million acres of land belonging to individual Native Americans and set up individual trust accounts for them, some records have been lost, destroyed, or not kept in the first place.

Congress passed the American Indian Trust Fund Management Reform Act of 1994 to require the proper management of Native American trust funds. The Office of the Special Trustee for American Indians (OST) also was created to improve the accountability and management of Native Americans funds held in trust by the federal government. As trustee, the Department of the Interior has the primary fiduciary responsibility to manage both tribal trust funds and Individual Indian Monies (IIM) accounts, as well as the resources that generate the income for those accounts.

However, in 1996 a group of Native Americans filed a lawsuit against Interior, to recover money from the government for trust fund beneficiaries. U.S. District Judge Royce C. Lamberth ruled that the United States had grossly mismanaged the trust funds. In February 1999 Lamberth held Secretary of Interior Bruce Babbitt and other Clinton administration officials in contempt of court for failing to produce records involved in the case. In 2002 Judge Lamberth held George W. Bush's secretary of interior, Gale Norton, in contempt of court, citing four instances in which the Interior Department committed fraud on the court. In 2003 the case was still unresolved in the federal courts.

■ KEY PERSONNEL

Assistant Secretary
  Aurene Martin (acting) .... (202) 208–7163
  Fax .... (202) 208–6334
Deputy Assistant Secretary
  Aurene Martin .... (202) 208–7163
Alcohol and Substance Abuse Prevention
  Velma Mason .... (202) 219–9737
American Indian Trust
  Jim Pace (acting) .... (202) 208–3338
Audit and Evaluation
  Jerome Fiely (acting) .... (202) 208–1916
Solicitor (Interior Dept.)
  Timothy Elliott (acting) .... (202) 208–4423
Associate Solicitor for Indian Affairs
  Vacant .... (202) 208–3401
Deputy Commissioner
  Terry Virden .... (202) 208–5116
Economic Development
  Ray Brown (acting) .... (202) 208–5324
Equal Employment Opportunity
  John C. Nicholas .... (703) 235–0655
Indian Gaming Management
  George Skibine .... (202) 219–4066
Congressional and Legislative Affairs
  Jackie Cheek .... (202) 208–5706
Law Enforcement
  Bob Ecoffey .... (202) 208–5786
Indian Education Programs
  William Mehojah Jr. .... (202) 208–6123
Tribal Services
  Mike Smith (acting) .... (202) 208–3463
Management and Administration
  Debbie Clark (acting) .... (202) 208–4174
Trust Responsibilities
  Larry Scrivner (acting) .... (202) 208–5831

■ INFORMATION SOURCES

Internet

Agency Web site: http://www.doi.gov/bureau-indian-affairs.html. Includes general information about the bureau and the Indian Health Service, a list of tribal leaders, and a section devoted to Indian ancestry.

Telephone Contacts

Personnel Locator .... (202) 208–3100

Information and Publications

KEY OFFICES

BIA Public Affairs
1849 C St. N.W., Room 4542-MIB
MS 4542-MIB
Washington, DC 20240
(202) 208–3710
(202) 219–4152, media
Nedra Darling, director

Provides information and publications to the media, the Indian community, and the general public.

Freedom of Information
1849 C St. N.W., MS 4040
Washington, DC 20240
(202) 208–2977
Willie Chisolm, FOI coordinator

PUBLICATIONS

Contact BIA Public Affairs for fact sheets, brochures, pamphlets, and a newsletter for Indian tribes and organizations.

Reference Resources

LIBRARY

Interior Department
1849 C St. N.W.
Washington, DC 20240
(202) 208–5815
Frank Herch, director
Hours: 7:45 a.m. to 5:00 p.m.

The BIA does not have its own library, but material on Indian affairs is housed in the Interior Department Library.

RULES AND REGULATIONS

BIA rules and regulations are published in the *Code of Federal Regulations*, Title 25 and Title 41, parts 14H-1 through 14H-90. Proposed regulations, new final regulations, and updates to the *Code of Federal Regulations* are published in the daily *Federal Register*. (*See appendix for details on how to obtain and use these publications.*)

▓ LEGISLATION

The BIA carries out its responsibilities under:

Snyder Act of 1921 (42 Stat. 208, 25 U.S.C. 13). Signed by the president Nov. 2, 1921. Authorized general, nonspecific funding for the benefit, care, and assistance of Native Americans.

Indian Reorganization Act of 1934 (48 Stat. 984, 25 U.S.C. 461). Signed by the president June 18, 1934. Allowed Native Americans to reorganize as constitutional governments with elected governing bodies.

Indian Self-Determination and Education Assistance Act of 1975 (88 Stat. 2203, 25 U.S.C. 450). Signed by the president Jan. 4, 1975. Gave Native American parents and communities greater control over education and training designed to promote further self-determination. Allowed Native American tribes to run programs previously run for them by the federal government.

Tribally Controlled Community College Assistance Act of 1978 (92 Stat. 1325, 25 U.S.C. 1801). Signed by the president Oct. 17, 1978. Provided financial assistance to American Indian-controlled institutions of higher education.

Education Amendments of 1978 (92 Stat. 2143, 20 U.S.C. 2701). Signed by the president Nov. 1, 1978. Amended the **Elementary and Secondary Education Act of 1965** (91 Stat. 911, 20 U.S.C. 241). Title IX increased control of Native American tribes in determining educational needs of children.

Indian Child Welfare Act of 1978 (92 Stat. 3069, 25 U.S.C. 1901). Signed by the president Nov. 8, 1979. Strengthened tribal and parental rights in the custody of children. Promoted the continuation of Native American culture by discouraging the forced placement of tribal children in nontribal foster homes.

Indian Gaming Regulatory Act of 1988 (102 Stat. 2467, 25 U.S.C. 2701 note). Signed by the president Oct. 17, 1988. Prohibited casino gambling and parimutuel betting on reservations unless the tribe enters into a compact with the state for the operation of such activities.

Indian Employment, Training, and Related Services Demonstration Act of 1992 (106 Stat. 2302, 25 U.S.C.

3401). Signed by the president Oct. 23, 1992. Authorized tribal governments to integrate all federally funded employment, training, and related services programs into a single, comprehensive program.

Indian Tribal Justice Act (107 Stat. 2004, 25 U.S.C. 3601). Signed by the president Dec. 3, 1993. Created an office of Tribal Justice Support within the BIA to assist tribes in developing and maintaining tribal justice systems.

American Indian Trust Fund Management Reform Act of 1994 (108 Stat. 4239, 25 U.S.C. 42). Signed by the president Oct. 25, 1994. Amended federal law to provide for the proper management of Native American trust funds. Required the Interior Department to account for daily and annual balances of trust funds and provide periodic performance statements. Established the Office of the Special Trustee for American Indians to develop a comprehensive reform plan of the secretary's trust responsibilities to Native American tribes.

▓ REGIONAL OFFICES

GREAT PLAINS
(ND, NE, SD)
115 Fourth Ave. S.E.
Aberdeen, SD 57401–4384
(605) 226–7343
Alice Harwood, regional director

SOUTHWEST
(CO, NM)
P.O. Box 26567
Albuquerque, NM 87125–6567
(505) 346–7590
Robert Baracker, regional director

SOUTHERN PLAINS
(KS, western OK, TX)
WCD Office Complex
P.O. Box 368
Anadarko, OK 73005–0368
(405) 247–6673, ext. 314
Dan Deerinwater, regional director

ROCKY MOUNTAIN
(MT, WY)
316 N. 26th St.
Billings, MT 59101
(406) 247–7943
Keith Beartusk, regional director

EASTERN REGIONAL OFFICE

(AL, CT, FL, LA, ME, MS, NC, NY)
3701 N. Fairfax Dr.
MS 260-VASQ
Arlington, VA 22203
(703) 235–3006
Franklin Keel, regional director

ALASKA

(AK except Metlakatla)
P.O. Box 25520
709 W. 9th St.
Juneau, AK 99802
(800) 645–8397
Niles Cesar, regional director

MIDWEST

(IA, MI, MN, WI)
One Federal Dr., #550
Minneapolis, MN 55111–4007
(612) 713–4400
Larry Morrin, regional director

EASTERN OKLAHOMA

(eastern OK)
101 N. Fifth St.
Muskogee, OK 74401–6206
(918) 687–2296
Vacant, regional director

NAVAJO

(Navajo reservations in AZ, NM)
Navajo Area Office
P.O. Box 1060
Gallup, NM 87305
(505) 863–8314
Elouise Chicharello, regional director

WESTERN

(AZ, NV, UT: except Navajo reservations)
P.O. Box 10
Phoenix, AZ 85001
(602) 379–6600
Wayne Nordwall, regional director

NORTHWEST

(Metlakatla, AK; ID, MT, OR, WA)
911 11th Ave. N.E.
Portland, OR 97232
(503) 231–6702
Stanley Speaks, regional director

PACIFIC

(CA)
2800 Cottage Way
Sacramento, CA 95814
(916) 978–6000
Ronald Jaeger, regional director

Bureau of Land Management

1849 C St. N.W., Washington, DC 20240
Internet: http://www.blm.gov

The Bureau of Land Management (BLM), an agency within the Department of the Interior, was created in 1946 when Congress combined the functions of the General Land Office (created in 1812) and the U.S. Grazing Service (created in 1934) into a single bureau.

The BLM consists of a headquarters staff in Washington and twelve state offices. It is headed by a director appointed by the president who works under the supervision of the assistant secretary of the interior for land and minerals management.

Resources managed by the BLM include timber, minerals, oil and gas, geothermal energy, wildlife habitats, endangered plant and animal species, range land vegetation, recreation areas, lands with cultural importance, wild and scenic rivers, designated conservation and wilderness areas, and open-space lands. Under authority of the Wild Horse and Burro Act of 1971, BLM manages programs protecting and allowing for the adoption of wild horses and burros.

The BLM is responsible for administering more than 261 million acres of public lands, located mainly in the western United States and Alaska. Most of these lands are original public domain lands, which became federal property in territorial expansions, such as the Louisiana Purchase in 1803 or the Mexican Cession in 1848, and have never been privately owned.

The bureau is responsible for the development of mineral resources found on an additional 300 million acres of land, including lands administered by other federal agencies and certain private lands where mineral rights are reserved to the United States.

In addition, the BLM regulates federal grazing lands, protects and preserves timberland for permanent forest production, manages and protects wild horses and burros living on public lands, controls erosion on public lands, and issues permits for mineral exploration purposes.

The BLM also leases lands for development of designated mineral deposits, grants rights of way through federal lands for pipelines and other uses, and issues permits for excavation of archeological sites.

BLM is one of five federal agencies that fight wildfires in cooperation with state agencies and local fire departments. The other federal agencies are the Agriculture Department's Forest Service and the Interior Department's Fish and Wildlife Service, National Park Service, and Bureau of Indian Affairs. The agencies' wildland fire-fighting activities are coordinated through the National Interagency Fire Center in Boise, Idaho.

■ KEY PERSONNEL

Assistant Secretary
    Rebecca Watson .... (202) 208–5676
    Fax .... (202) 208–3144
Director
    Kathleen Clarke .... (202) 208–3801
    Fax .... (202) 208–5242
    Deputy Director
    Fran Cherry .... (202) 208–6731
    Jim Hughes .... (202) 208–6731
Communications
    Vacant .... (202) 208–6913
    Fax .... (202) 208–6769
Legislative Affairs
    Nancy Smith .... (202) 452–5010
Business and Fiscal Resources
    Vacant .... (202) 208–4864
    Fax .... (202) 208–5964

Human Resources
Vacant.................................. (202) 501–6723
Fax...................................... (202) 501–6718

Equal Employment Opportunity
Michelle Stroman .... (202) 452–5090

Renewable Resources and Planning
Vacant................................. (202) 208–4896
Fax..................................... (202) 208–5010

Planning Assessment and Community Support
Anne Aldrich .... (202) 452–7793

Rangelands, Soils, Water, Wild Horse and Burro Group
Tim Reuwsaat .... (202) 452–7749

Fish, Wildlife, Forest and Woodlands Group
Vacant.................................. (202) 452–7761

Cultural Heritage, Wilderness, Special Areas and Paleontology
Marilyn Nickels........................ (202) 452–0330

Recreation
Vacant.................................. (202) 452–7738

Minerals, Realty and Resource Protection
Vacant................................. (202) 208–4201
Fax..................................... (202) 208–4800

Law Enforcement
Vacant .... (202) 452–5118

Protection and Response
Bernie Hyde .... (202) 452–5057

Fluid Minerals
Del Fortner .... (202) 452–0340

Solid Minerals
Brenda Aird........................... (202) 452–0350

Lands and Realty
Vacant................................. (202) 452–7775

◼ INFORMATION SOURCES

Internet
Agency Web site: http://www.blm.gov. Features state-by-state information, a national map, a calendar of events, and a directory of public contacts.

Telephone Contacts
Personnel Locator......................... (202) 208–3100

Information and Publications

KEY OFFICES

BLM Public Affairs
1849 C St. N.W., Room 406–LS
Washington, DC 20240
(202) 452–5125
Celia Boddington, manager

Answers questions for the press and the public. Distributes publications and issues news releases; maintains a mailing list.

Freedom of Information
1849 C St. N.W.
Washington, DC 20240
(202) 452–5013
John Livornese, FOI specialist

Write and underline "Freedom of Information Request" on the envelope address.

PUBLICATIONS
BLM Public Affairs distributes single copies of bureau publications to individuals free of charge. No catalogue or list of publications is available.

Publications cover the following subject areas: cadastral (land) surveying; forest resource management; lands studies; public lands law and statistics; range management; wildlife habitat management; watershed management; minerals management; mineral, oil, gas, and geothermal leasing; minerals operations; and the history, development, administration, conservation, and use of public lands.

DATA AND STATISTICS
See Publications, above.

Reference Resources

LIBRARIES

BLM Library
Bldg. 50, Denver Federal Center
Denver, CO 80225
(303) 236–6650
Barbara Campbell, chief librarian
Hours: 6:30 a.m. to 4:00 p.m.

Collection includes monographs, serials, periodicals, technical reports, government documents, directives, and an extensive collection of pamphlets and reprints. Makes interlibrary loans and provides both in-person and telephone reference service.

Interior Department Library
1849 C St. N.W.
Washington, DC 20240
(202) 208–5815
John Sherrod, manager
Hours: 7:45 a.m. to 5:00 p.m.

Also houses material on land management.

RULES AND REGULATIONS

BLM rules and regulations are published in the *Code of Federal Regulations,* Title 43, parts 1000 to end. Proposed regulations, new final regulations, and updates to the *Code of Federal Regulations* are published in the daily *Federal Register. (See appendix for details on how to obtain and use these publications.)*

■ LEGISLATION

The BLM administers public lands through a framework of public laws, the most comprehensive being:

Federal Land Policy and Management Act of 1976 (90 Stat. 2744, 43 U.S.C. 1701). Signed by the president Oct. 21, 1976. Restated the policy of the United States to retain and manage federal land for its protection, preservation, and use by the public. Directed land use planning, governed grants and use of right of way over public land, directed review of lands for possible wilderness designation, and amended the Taylor Grazing Act with respect to livestock management, *inter alia.*

The BLM also administers the following laws in full or in part:

Act of May 18, 1796, as amended (1 Stat. 465, 43 U.S.C. 751 et seq.). Signed by the president May 18, 1796. Established the public land survey system of square mile sections and 36-section townships for use in the settlement, disposal, and use of public lands.

Act of May 10, 1872 (R.S. 2319, 30 U.S.C. 22 et seq.). Signed by the president May 10, 1872. Permitted entry on public lands for location of hard rock minerals.

Allotted Indian Land Leasing Act of 1909 (35 Stat. 783, 25 U.S.C. 396). Signed by the president March 3, 1909. Provided for leasing and management of allotted Native American mineral lands through Interior Department regulations.

Mineral Leasing Act (41 Stat. 437, 30 U.S.C. 181). Signed by the president Feb. 25, 1920. Permitted the leasing of public lands for the exploration and development of specified minerals, chiefly oil, gas, and coal.

Recreation and Public Purposes Act (44 Stat. 741, 43 U.S.C. 869). Signed by the president June 14, 1926. Allowed the sale or lease of public lands to federal instrumentalities, territories, states, counties, municipalities, and political subdivisions and to nonprofit organizations and associations for recreational and other uses. Reserved mineral rights on leased lands for the U.S. government.

Right-of-Way Leasing Act of 1930 (46 Stat. 373, 30 U.S.C. 301). Signed by the president May 21, 1930. Provided for the leasing of oil and gas deposits in or under railroads and other rights of way.

Taylor Grazing Act (48 Stat. 1269, 43 U.S.C. 315). Signed by the president June 28, 1934. Provided the ba-

sic legislative authority governing the management and protection of the vacant public land of the United States.

Omnibus Tribal Leasing Act of 1938 (52 Stat. 347, 25 U.S.C. 396a). Signed by the president May 11, 1938. Provided for leasing of unallotted (tribal) lands through Interior Department regulations.

Materials Act (61 Stat. 681, 30 U.S.C. 601). Signed by the president July 31, 1947. Authorized the secretary of the interior to dispose of certain surface mineral materials and timber found on public land.

Mineral Leasing Act for Acquired Lands (61 Stat. 13, 30 U.S.C. 351–359). Signed by the president Aug. 7, 1947. Permitted the leasing of acquired lands for exploration and development of specified minerals.

Submerged Lands Act of 1953 (67 Stat. 29, 43 U.S.C. 1301). Signed by the president May 22, 1953. Extended the boundaries of coastal states seaward for three miles.

Outer Continental Shelf Lands Act (67 Stat. 462, 43 U.S.C. 1331). Signed by the president Aug. 7, 1953. Established Interior Department authority for leasing and managing minerals in the Outer Continental Shelf.

Wilderness Act of 1964 (78 Stat. 890, 16 U.S.C. 1131). Signed by the president Sept. 3, 1964. Directed the secretary of the interior to review areas within the National Wildlife Refuge and National Park Systems in order to recommend to the president new additions for the National Wilderness Preservation System.

Wild and Scenic Rivers Act (82 Stat. 906, 16 U.S.C. 1271). Signed by the president Oct. 2, 1968. Described procedures and limitations for control of lands in federally administered components of the National Wild and Scenic Rivers System and for dealing with disposition of lands and minerals under federal ownership.

National Trails System Act (82 Stat. 919, 16 U.S.C. 1241). Signed by the president Oct. 2, 1968. Established the National Recreational and National Scenic Trails systems.

Geothermal Steam Act of 1970 (84 Stat. 1566, 30 U.S.C. 1001). Signed by the president Dec. 24, 1970. Regulated the leasing of lands for the development and utilization of geothermal steam and associated geothermal resources.

Alaska Native Claims Settlement Act (85 Stat. 688, 43 U.S.C. 1601 et seq.). Signed by the president Dec. 18, 1971. Established right and method for Alaska natives to form local and regional corporations to receive title to 40 million acres of public land.

Federal Coal Leasing Act of 1976 (90 Stat. 1083, 30 U.S.C. 201). Signed by the president Aug. 4, 1976. Amended the coal leasing provision of the 1920 Mineral Leasing Act. Provided for a coal exploration program by the Interior Department and for issuance of coal exploration licenses.

Payments in Lieu of Taxes Act (90 Stat. 1032, 31 U.S.C. 6901). Signed by the president Oct. 20, 1976. Directed the interior secretary to make payments to local jurisdictions where entitled land is located.

Federal Land Policy and Management Act of 1976 (P.L. 94-579). Signed by the president Oct. 21, 1976. Required that public lands be retained in federal ownership unless it is determined that disposal of a particular parcel will serve the national interest.

Public Range Lands Improvement Act of 1978 (92 Stat. 1803, 43 U.S.C. 1901). Signed by the president Oct. 25, 1978. Provided for the protection and improvement of public range lands.

Archaeological Resources Protection Act of 1979 (93 Stat. 721, 92 U.S.C. 4151). Signed by the president Oct. 31, 1979. Established civil and criminal penalties for damaging or removing archaeological resources found on public and Indian lands.

Alaska National Interest Lands Conservation Act of 1980 (94 Stat. 2430, 43 U.S.C. 1631 et seq.). Signed by the president Dec. 2, 1980. Divided public lands in Alaska into national parks and wildlife refuges, and areas subject to special management and study. Established provisions for disposing of Alaska lands to Native Corporations and the state of Alaska.

Mineral Lands–Production of Oil from Tar Sand Act of 1981 (95 Stat. 1070, codified in scattered sections of 30 U.S.C.). Signed by the president Nov. 16, 1981. Provided for the leasing of tar sand deposits and oil and gas leasing.

Federal Oil and Gas Royalty Management Act of 1982 (96 Stat. 2447, 30 U.S.C. 1701). Signed by the president Jan. 12, 1983. Ensured that all energy and mineral resources originating on public lands and on the Outer Continental Shelf are accounted for under the secretary of the interior.

Omnibus Budget Reconciliation Act/Federal Reform Oil and Gas Leasing Act of 1987 (101 Stat. 1330–256, 30 U.S.C. 226b). Signed by the president Dec. 22, 1987. Overhauled the system of leasing federal lands, other than those offshore, for oil and gas drilling and production.

Federal Land Exchange Facilitation Act of 1988 (102 Stat. 1086, 43 U.S.C. 1716). Signed by the president Aug. 20, 1988. Streamlined land-exchange procedures between the BLM and the U.S. Forest Service.

Uranium Mill Tailings Remedial Action Amendments Act of 1988 (102 Stat. 3192, 42 U.S.C. 7916). Signed by the president Nov. 5, 1988. Allowed the Interior Department to transfer BLM lands to the DOE for surveillance and maintenance of slightly radioactive mill tailings.

■ STATE OFFICES

ALASKA

222 W. Seventh Ave., #13
Anchorage, AK 99513–7599
(907) 271–5080
Henri Bisson, director

ARIZONA

222 N. Central Ave.
Phoenix, AZ 85004-2203
(602) 417–9528
Elaine Zielinski, director

CALIFORNIA

2800 Cottage Way, #W-1834
Sacramento, CA 95825
(916) 978–4610
Mike Pool, director

COLORADO

2850 Youngfield St.
Lakewood, CO 80215–7093
(303) 239–3700
Ron Wenker, director

EASTERN UNITED STATES

(All states east of the Mississippi River)
7450 Boston Blvd.
Springfield, VA 22153
(703) 440–1700
Mike Nedd, director

IDAHO

1387 S. Vinnell Way
Boise, ID 83709–1657
(208) 373–4001
K. Lynn Bennett, director

MONTANA

(MT, ND, SD)
5001 Southgate St.
Billings, MT 59101
(406) 896–5069
Marty Ott, director

NEVADA
1340 Financial Way
Reno, NV 89502
(702) 861–6590
Bob Abbey, director

NEW MEXICO
(KS, NM, OK, TX)
1474 Rodeo Rd.
P.O. Box 27115
Santa Fe, NM 87502–0115
(505) 438–7514
Linda Rundell, director

OREGON
(OR, WA)
1515 S.W. Fifth Ave.
P.O. Box 2965
Portland, OR 97208–2965
(503) 952–6024
Elaine Brong, director

UTAH
324 S. State St.
P.O. Box 45155
Salt Lake City, UT 84145–0155
(801) 539–4010
Sally Wisely, director

WYOMING
(NE, WY)
5353 Yellowstone Rd.
P.O. Box 1828
Cheyenne, WY 82003
(307) 775–6001
Bob Bennett, director

Minerals Management Service

1849 C St. N.W., Washington, DC 20240
Internet: http://www.mms.gov

The Minerals Management Service (MMS) was established as an agency within the Department of the Interior on Jan. 19, 1982. The office is headed by a director who is appointed by the secretary of the interior and who reports to the assistant secretary for land and minerals management.

The service was created for two purposes. First, it is responsible for collecting revenues generated from mineral leases offshore and on federal and Native American lands throughout the country through the Royalty Management Program. Second, through the Offshore Minerals Management Program, the service is charged with the orderly development of America's offshore energy and mineral resources while properly safeguarding the environment. These energy and mineral resources include, among others, oil, gas, coal, and sulphur.

Bonuses, rents, and royalties (onshore and offshore) from nearly 70,000 leases can amount to several billion dollars each year—an amount that peaked to more than $10 billion in 1983. These revenues totaled over $6 billion in 2002 and nearly $127 billion since the agency was created in 1982. Totals fluctuate with market prices, amount of production, and number of lease sales.

These funds, one of the largest federal revenue sources outside the Treasury Department, in turn are distributed to Native American tribes and to allotted states in which the minerals were found. In 2002 MMS distributed more than $753 million to thirty-three states for mineral production on federal lands located within their borders and from federal offshore lands adjacent to their shores. Other recipients of funds include the Land and Water Conservation Fund, the Historic Preservation Fund, and the Reclamation Fund of the Treasury.

The Bureau of Land Management *(see p. 568)* within the Interior Department oversees the leasing of minerals management on federal lands; the Interior Department's Bureau of Indian Affairs *(see p. 564)* works with the MMS on royalty management functions on Native American lands.

◼ KEY PERSONNEL

Assistant Secretary
Vacant.................................... (202) 208–5676
Fax...................................... (202) 208–3144
Director
Johnnie Burton......................... (202) 208–3500
Fax...................................... (202) 208–7242
Deputy Director
Walter Cruikshank..................... (202) 208–3500
Administration and Budget
Robert Brown.......................... (202) 208–3220
Equal Employment and Development Opportunity
Pat Callas.............................. (703) 787–1313
Minerals Revenue Management
Lucy Querques Denett................. (202) 208–3415
Offshore Compliance and Asset Management
John Russo............................. (303) 275–7400
Onshore Compliance and Asset Management
Deborah Gibbs Tschudy.............. (303) 275–7200
Royalty in Kind
Milt Dial............................... (303) 275–7400
Offshore Minerals Management
Thomas Readinger..................... (202) 208–3530
Deputy Associate Director
Robert Labelle......................... (703) 787–1700
Policy Management and Improvement
George Triebsch....................... (202) 208–3398

▓ INFORMATION SOURCES

Internet

Agency Web site: http://www.mms.gov. Includes general information about the MMS and the collection and distribution of revenues. Also includes a reading room and a section on science and the environment.

Telephone Contacts

Personnel Locator .... (202) 208–3100

Information and Publications

KEY OFFICES

MMS Office of Public Affairs
1849 C St. N.W., #4230
Washington, DC 20240
(202) 208–3985
Nicolette Humphries, (acting) chief

Responsible for dissemination of news and publications regarding the MMS.

MMS Office of Congressional Affairs
1849 C St. N.W.
Washington, DC 20240
(202) 208–3985
Lyn Herdt, chief

Freedom of Information
MMS Office of Administration
381 Elden St., MS 2053
Herndon, VA 20170–4817
(703) 787–1242
Ginny Morgan, FOIA officer

Requests must be in writing; write "Freedom of Information Request" on the envelope.

PUBLICATIONS

The MMS does not have a central office for publications; however, the Technical Publications Unit (TPU) within Offshore Information Services operates a scientific and technical publications program. The TPU publishes informal documents that by law must be released quickly; these are short-term documents with a narrow focus. Formal documents—more in-depth materials of a wider rang-

ing and longer term interest—also are published. To obtain such documents contact:

MMS Technical Publications Unit
381 Elden St.
Herndon, VA 22070
(703) 787–1030
Douglas Slitor, unit chief

Three times a year, the MMS publishes *MMS Today*, which provides general information for the service's constituency, including news on proposed regulations, MMS policy, and major personnel changes. Copies can be obtained from:

MMS Today
Office of Public Affairs
1849 C St. N.W., MS 4213
Washington, DC 20240
(202) 208–3985
Walter Bonora, editor

DATA AND STATISTICS

Statistical and technical publications are available from the Technical Publications Unit. Some data are also available on the MMS Web site.

Reference Resources

LIBRARY

Interior Department
1849 C St. N.W.
Washington, DC 20240
(202) 208–5815
John Sherrod, manager
Hours: 7:45 a.m. to 5:00 p.m.

The MMS does not have its own library, but materials on mineral leasing and royalty management are kept in the Interior Department Library.

RULES AND REGULATIONS

MMS rules and regulations are published in the *Code of Federal Regulations*, Title 30, parts 201–260. Proposed regulations, new final regulations, and updates to the *Code of Federal Regulations* are published in the daily *Federal Register*. (*See appendix for details on how to obtain and use these publications.*)

■ LEGISLATION

The MMS administers the following laws in full or in part:

Outer Continental Shelf Lands Act Amendments of 1978 (92 Stat. 629, 43 U.S.C. 1801). Signed by the president Sept. 18, 1978. Gave the secretary of the interior authority to expedite exploration and development of Outer Continental Shelf minerals.

Federal Oil and Gas Royalty Management Act of 1982 (96 Stat. 2447, 30 U.S.C. 1701 note). Signed by the president Jan. 12, 1983. Sought to ensure that all oil and gas originating on public lands and on the Outer Continental Shelf are properly accounted for under the direction of the secretary of the interior.

Outer Continental Shelf Lands Act Amendments of 1985 (100 Stat. 147, 43 U.S.C. 1301 note). Signed by the president April 7, 1986. Divided $6.4 billion in revenues from offshore oil and gas formations that straddle federal-state boundaries.

Oil Pollution Prevention, Response, Liability, and Compensation Act (104 Stat. 484, 33 U.S.C. 2701). Signed by the president Aug. 18, 1990. Established limitations on liability for damages from oil spillage. Created a fund to pay for cleanup and compensation costs not covered otherwise.

Federal Oil and Gas Royalty Simplification and Fairness Act of 1996 (110 Stat. 1700, 30 U.S.C. 1701 et seq.).Signed by the president on Aug. 13, 1996. Amended the Federal Oil and Gas Royalty Management Act of 1982 to revise and expand the guidelines for delegating the collection of oil and gas receipts and related activities to a state upon its request. Excluded Native American lands and privately owned minerals from the purview of this act.

Mineral Revenue Payments Clarification Act of 2000 (P.L. 106-393). Signed by the president on Oct. 30, 2000. Amended the Mineral Leasing Act respecting federal oil and gas revenue distributions to prohibit state amounts from being reduced by federal administrative or other costs.

■ REGIONAL OFFICES

ALASKA REGION
949 E. 36th Ave.
Anchorage, AK 99508–4302
(907) 271–6010
John Goll, regional director

GULF OF MEXICO REGION
1201 Elmwood Park Blvd.
Jefferson, LA 70123–2394
(504) 736–2589
Chris Oynes, regional director

PACIFIC REGION
770 Paseo Camarillo
Los Angeles, CA 93010
(805) 389–7520
Lisle Reed, regional director

ROYALTY MANAGEMENT PROGRAM
Sixth Ave. and Kipling St.
Bldg. 85, Denver Federal Center
Denver, CO 80225
(303) 231–3162
Lucy Querques Denett, associate director

LEASING DIVISION
381 Elden St.
Herndon, VA 22070
(703) 787–1300
Rene Orr, director

United States Fish and Wildlife Service

1849 C St. N.W., Washington, DC 20240
Internet: http://www.fws.gov

The U.S. Fish and Wildlife Service (FWS) was created within the Interior Department by Reorganization Plan No. 3 in 1940. Its predecessor agency, the Bureau of Fisheries, was created in 1871, initially as an independent agency and later within the Department of Commerce. A second agency, the Bureau of Biological Survey, was established in 1885 in the Department of Agriculture. The two bureaus and their functions were transferred to the Department of the Interior in 1939 and were consolidated into one agency in 1940. The FWS is under the jurisdiction of the assistant secretary of the interior for fish, wildlife, and parks.

The service is the lead federal agency for fish and wildlife and is composed of a headquarters staff in Washington, D.C., seven regional offices, and field units. FWS manages the 95 million-acre National Wildlife Refuge System of nearly 540 National Wildlife Refuges and thousands of small wetlands and other special management areas. Under the fisheries program it also operates sixty-nine National Fish Hatcheries, sixty-four fishery resource offices, and seventy-eight ecological services field stations. FWS enforces wildlife laws through a nationwide network of wildlife law enforcement agents.

The service is responsible for conservation and management of fish and wildlife resources and their habitats, including migratory birds, endangered species, certain marine mammals, and fresh water and anadromous fisheries. It regulates hunting of migratory birds and preserves wetlands for waterfowl and other species within the National Wildlife Refuge System.

In 1993 some of the research, monitoring, and information transfer programs of the service were consolidated in a new nonregulatory Department of Interior bureau, the National Biological Survey (NBS). Subsequently renamed the National Biological Service, the NBS was transferred to the U.S. Geological Survey in 1996.

The United States is a signatory of the Convention of International Trade in Endangered Species of Wild Fauna and Flora (CITES), a treaty among party nations dedicated to protecting endangered fish, wildlife, and plants from commercial exploitation and illegal global trade. The Office of Law Enforcement of the FWS administers CITES through the Endangered Species Act. The office also enforces the Lacey Act, which makes it unlawful to sell any wildlife taken, possessed, transported, or sold in violation of any law, treaty or regulation of the United States.

■ KEY PERSONNEL

Assistant Secretary
Judge Craig Manson .... (202) 208–5347
Deputy Assistant Secretary
Paul Hoffman and David P. Smith .... (202) 208–4416
Director
Steven A. Williams .... (202) 208–4717
Fax .... (202) 208–6965
Deputy Director
Marshall Jones .... (202) 208–4545
Solicitor (Interior Dept.)
Vacant .... (202) 208–4813
Assistant Solicitor for Fish and Wildlife
Charles Raynor .... (202) 208–6172
External Affairs
Tom O. Melius .... (202) 208–6541
Duck Stamp Office
Vaugn Collins .... (703) 358–2000
Federal Aid
Kris LaMontagne .... (703) 358–2156

Congressional and Legislative Affairs
Alexandra Pitts.......................... (202) 208–5403
Ecological Services
Gary D. Frazer.......................... (202) 208–4646
Fisheries
Dr. Mamie Parker .... (202) 208–6394
International Affairs
Kenneth Stansell........................ (703) 358–6393
Law Enforcement
Kevin Adams .... (202) 208–3809
Migratory Birds and State Programs
Paul Schmidt .... (202) 208–3195
Planning and Budget
Denise Sheehan......................... (202) 208–3736
Refuges
William Hartwig .... (202) 208–5333

▦ INFORMATION SOURCES

Internet

Agency Web site: http://www.fws.gov. Features the mission of the service, locations of offices, and information on activities nationwide.

Telephone Contacts

Personnel Locator.......................... (202) 208–7220

Information and Publications

KEY OFFICES

FWS Public Affairs

1849 C St. N.W., Room 3240
Washington, DC 20240
(202) 208–5634
Megan Durham, chief

Answers questions for the press and the public, distributes publications and photographs, and issues news releases. Provides information on public use of wildlife refuges and fish hatcheries; also issues information on the annual "Duck Stamp" art competition and annual migratory bird hunting regulations.

FWS Extension and Publications

Publications Unit
National Conservation Training Center
Route 1, Box 166
Shepherdstown, WV 25443
(304) 876–7203
John Fisher, chief

Distributes scientific and technical reports, refuge leaflets, and general interest materials.

PUBLICATIONS

Titles available from FWS Extension and Publications:
Careers
Conserving the Nature of America
The Duck Stamp Story
Endangered and Threatened Wildlife and Plants
Facts About Federal Wildlife Laws
50 Years Restoring America's Wildlife
Restoring America's Sport Fisheries
Visitor's Guide to the National Wildlife Refuge System

DATA AND STATISTICS

FWS Public Affairs maintains data and statistics on topics including endangered and threatened wildlife and plants; hunting and fishing license sales by the states; federal aid for fish and wildlife restoration; and results of National Survey of Fishing, Hunting, and Wildlife Associated Recreation.

Reference Resources

LIBRARY

Interior Department

1849 C St. N.W.
Washington, DC 20240
(202) 208–5815
George Franchois, manager/librarian
Hours: 7:45 a.m. to 5:00 p.m.

RULES AND REGULATIONS

FWS rules and regulations are published in the *Code of Federal Regulations,* Title 50, parts 1–96, 401–453. Proposed regulations, new final regulations, and updates to the *Code of Federal Regulations* are published in the daily *Federal Register.* (*See appendix for details on how to obtain and use these publications.*)

▦ LEGISLATION

The FWS exercises its authority under:

Lacey Act of 1900 (31 Stat. 187, 16 U.S.C. 667). Signed by the president May 25, 1900. Stated that the duties of the Department of the Interior include conservation, preservation, and restoration of birds and other wildlife.

Migratory Bird Treaty Act (40 Stat. 755, 16 U.S.C. 703). Signed by the president July 3, 1918. Implemented the 1916 Convention between the U.S. and Great Britain (for Canada) for the protection of migratory birds, thereby establishing a federal responsibility for protection of this natural resource.

Migratory Bird Conservation Act (45 Stat. 1222, 16 U.S.C. 715). Signed by the president Feb. 28, 1929. Implemented treaties between the U.S. and other countries for the protection of migratory birds.

Fish and Wildlife Coordination Act (48 Stat. 401, 16 U.S.C. 661). Signed by the president March 10, 1934. Authorized the secretary of the interior to assist federal, state, and other agencies in development, protection, rearing, and stocking fish and wildlife on federal lands, and to study effects of pollution on fish and wildlife.

Migratory Bird Hunting and Conservation Stamp Act (48 Stat. 452, 16 U.S.C. 718). Signed by the president March 16, 1934. Also known as the Duck Stamp Act. Required waterfowl hunters to have a valid federal hunting stamp.

Refuge Revenue Sharing Act (49 Stat. 383, 16 U.S.C. 715). Signed by the president June 15, 1935. Established the procedure for sharing with counties the revenue derived from sales of products from refuges located within the counties.

Federal Aid in Wildlife Restoration Act (50 Stat. 917, 16 U.S.C. 699). Signed by the president Sept. 2, 1937. Provided federal aid to states for game restoration work.

Bald Eagle Protection Act (54 Stat. 250, 16 U.S.C. 668). Signed by the president June 8, 1940. Provided for the protection of bald eagles and golden eagles by prohibiting, except under specified conditions, the taking, possession of, and commerce in such birds.

Federal Aid in Sport Fish Restoration Act (64 Stat. 430, 16 U.S.C. 777). Signed by the president Aug. 9, 1950. Provided federal aid to the states for management and restoration of sport fish.

Fish and Wildlife Act of 1956 (70 Stat. 1119, 16 U.S.C. 742). Signed by the president Aug. 8, 1956. Established a comprehensive national fish and wildlife policy; directed a program of continuing research, extension, and information services on fish and wildlife.

Sikes Act (74 Stat. 1052, 16 U.S.C. 670a-o). Signed by the president Sept. 15, 1960. Provided for cooperation by the Interior and Defense Departments with state agencies in planning, development, and maintenance of fish and wildlife resources on military reservations throughout the United States.

Refuge Recreation Act (76 Stat. 653, 16 U.S.C. 460). Signed by the president Sept. 28, 1962. Permitted recreational use of refuges, hatcheries, and other conservation areas when such use does not interfere with the area's primary purpose.

Anadromous Fish Conservation Act (79 Stat. 1125, 16 U.S.C. 757). Signed by the president Oct. 30, 1965. Authorized the secretaries of commerce and the interior to enter into agreements with the states and other interests for conservation, development, and enhancement of anadromous fish.

National Wildlife Refuge System Administration Act of 1966 (80 Stat. 927, 16 U.S.C. 668). Signed by the president Oct. 15, 1966. Provided guidelines and directives for administration and management of all areas in the National Wildlife Refuge System.

Marine Mammal Protection Act of 1972 (86 Stat. 1027, 16 U.S.C. 1361). Signed by the president Oct. 21, 1972. Established a federal responsibility for conservation of marine mammals and vested in the Department of the Interior responsibility for management of certain animals.

Endangered Species Act of 1973 (87 Stat. 884, 16 U.S.C. 1531). Signed by the president Dec. 28, 1973. Provided for the conservation of threatened and endangered species of fish, wildlife, and plants by federal action and establishment of state programs.

Fish and Wildlife Improvement Act of 1978 (92 Stat. 3110, 16 U.S.C. 7421). Signed by the president Nov. 8, 1978. Authorized establishment of a law enforcement training program for state fish and wildlife law enforcement personnel and research to improve enforcement.

Fish and Wildlife Conservation Act of 1980 (94 Stat. 1322, 16 U.S.C. 2901). Signed by the president Sept. 29, 1980. Provided federal aid to the states for the management and restoration of nongame species.

Alaska National Interest Lands Conservation Act of 1980 (94 Stat. 2377, 16 U.S.C. 410hh). Signed by the president Dec. 2, 1980. Designated certain public lands in Alaska as units of the national park, national wildlife refuges, wild and scenic rivers, national wilderness preservation, and national forest systems. Provided management guidance for land use issues.

National Fish and Wildlife Foundation Establishment Act (98 Stat. 107, 16 U.S.C. 3701). Signed by the president March 26, 1984. Established the National Fish and Wildlife Foundation to encourage and administer donations of real or personal property in connection with fish and wildlife programs and activities in the United States.

Coastal Barrier Improvement Act of 1990 (104 Stat. 2931, 16 U.S.C. 3501 note). Signed by the president Nov. 16, 1990. Added 700,000 acres along the Atlantic and Gulf coasts, Great Lakes shores, Florida Keys, Puerto Rico, and Virgin Islands to the national barrier island system. Established mechanisms to allow states and localities to bring coastal areas into the system for protection.

Nonindigenous Aquatic Nuisance Prevention and Control Act of 1990 (104 Stat. 4761, 16 U.S.C. 4701 note). Signed by the president Nov. 29, 1990. Established a program to monitor and control the spread of introduced aquatic nuisance species such as the zebra mussel in the Great Lakes.

Coastal Wetlands Planning, Protection, and Restoration Act (104 Stat. 4761, 16 U.S.C. 3953). Signed by the president Nov. 29, 1990. Established a conservation and restoration program for Louisiana coastal wetlands. Authorized a national program matching grants for state wetlands conservation projects.

Wild Bird Conservation Act of 1992 (106 Stat. 2224, 16 U.S.C. 4901 note). Signed by the president Oct. 23, 1992. Established a federal system to limit or prohibit the importation of endangered exotic wild birds.

National Wildlife Refuge System Improvement Act of 1997 (111 Stat. 1252, 16 U.S.C. 668dd). Signed by the president Oct. 9, 1997. Amended the National Wildlife Refuge System Administration Act of 1966 by reinforcing the National Wildlife Refuge System's authority to administer the national networks of lands and waters under its protection. Recognized and supported wildlife-dependent recreation.

Migratory Bird Treaty Reform Act of 1998 (112 Stat. 2956, 16 U.S.C. 710 note). Signed by the president Oct. 30, 1998. Amended the Migratory Bird Treaty Act to make it unlawful for persons to take migratory birds by the aid of baiting.

▨ REGIONAL OFFICES

REGION 1
(CA, HI, ID, NV, OR, WA)
911 N.E. 11th Ave.
Portland, OR 97232–4181
(503) 231–6118
David B. Allen, regional director

REGION 2
(AZ, NM, OK, TX)
500 Gold Ave. S.W.
Albuquerque, NM 87102
(505) 248–6282
Dale Hall, regional director

REGION 3
(IA, IL, IN, MI, MN, MO, OH, WI)
One Federal Dr.
BHW Federal Bldg.
Fort Snelling, MN 55111–4056
(612) 713–5301
Robyn Thorson, regional director

REGION 4
(AL, AR, FL, GA, KY, LA, MS, NC, PR, SC, TN, VI)
1875 Century Blvd., NE, #400
Atlanta, GA 30345
(404) 679–4000
Samuel Hamilton, regional director

REGION 5
(CT, DC, DE, MA, MD, ME, NH, NJ, NY, PA, RI, VA, VT, WV)
300 Westgate Center Dr.
Hadley, MA 01035–9589
(413) 253–8300
Vacant, regional director

REGION 6
(CO, KS, MT, ND, NE, SD, UT, WY)
P.O. Box 25486
Denver, CO 80225
(303) 236–7920
Ralph Morgenweck, regional director

REGION 7
(AK)
1011 E. Tudor Rd.
Anchorage, AK 99503
(907) 786–3542
Rowan Gould, regional director

United States Geological Survey

National Center, 12201 Sunrise Valley Dr., Reston, VA 22092
Internet: http://www.usgs.gov

The U.S. Geological Survey (USGS) was established in the Department of the Interior by the act of March 3, 1879, which provided for "the classification of the public lands and the examination of the geological structure, mineral resources, and products of the national domain." Authorization was expanded in 1962 to include activities outside the limits of the United States.

The headquarters staff is located in Reston, Va. Other offices include major regional centers in Denver, Colo., and Menlo Park, Calif.; five mapping centers; water resources offices in fifty states, Puerto Rico, the Virgin Islands, and Guam; and five Earth Science Information Centers. The USGS operates under the jurisdiction of the assistant secretary of the interior for water and science.

The objectives of the USGS are to perform surveys, investigations, and research covering topography, geology, the identification of potential natural hazards (such as earthquakes and landslides), the mineral, water, and energy resources of the United States, water quality assessment, and water use.

The USGS prepares and publishes reports and maps including topographic, orthophoto, geologic, and mineral resource maps and various databases related to cartography and the earth sciences. The survey cooperates with other agencies in researching mineral and water resources and other earth science activities.

In October 1996 the USGS absorbed the National Biological Service (NBS), a nonregulatory Department of Interior bureau that was created in 1993 as the National Biological Survey. Renamed the Biological Resources division of the USGS, this agency continues to perform the same research, monitoring, and information transfer programs that it was charged with as a separate agency.

▓ KEY PERSONNEL

Assistant Secretary for Water and Science
  Bennett W. Raley .... (202) 208–3186
Deputy Assistant Secretary
  Tom Weimer .... (202) 208–4812
Solicitor (Interior Dept.)
  William G. Myers III. .... (202) 208–4423
Deputy Solicitor (Interior Dept.)
  Timothy Elliott .... (202) 208–4423
Director
  Charles G. Groat .... (703) 648–7411
    Fax .... (703) 648–4454
Deputy Director
  Robert E. Doyle .... (703) 648–7412
Equal Opportunity
  Fred Gonzalez .... (703) 648–7770
Biology
  Sue Haseltine .... (703) 648–4050
Geography
  Barbara Ryan .... (703) 648–7419
Geology
  P. Patrick Leahy .... (703) 648–6600
Water
  Robert Hirsch .... (703) 648–5215

▓ INFORMATION SOURCES

Internet

Agency Web site: http://www.usgs.gov. Includes fact sheets, selected data and publications, and information on ordering products.

Telephone Contacts

Personnel Locator	(202) 208–3100
Map Orders	(888) ASK–USGS
Fax-on-Demand	(703) 648–4888

Information and Publications

KEY OFFICES

USGS Office of Communications
119 National Center
12201 Sunrise Valley Dr.
Reston, VA 22092
(703) 648–4599
Barbara Wainman, chief

Public Affairs Office
119 National Center
12201 Sunrise Valley Dr.
Reston, VA 22092
(703) 648–4460
Scott Harris, chief

Congressional Liaison Officer
Tim West .... (703) 648–4455

Prepares news releases, feature articles, and related visual material describing the survey's activities. Maintains a mailing list.

USGS Earth Science Information Center
507 National Center
12201 Sunrise Valley Dr.
Reston, VA 22092
(703) 648–5422
Steve Shivers (acting), chief

Answers questions about the survey's activities and programs. Distributes USGS publications; provides information on bureau mapping activities and on the availability of maps produced by other federal and state agencies. For more information, visit the homepage at http://mapping.usgs.gov/esic/esic.html.

Freedom of Information
807 National Center
12201 Sunrise Valley Dr.
Reston, VA 22092
(703) 648–7313
John Cordyack, FOI officer

PUBLICATIONS
Technical and scientific reports and maps are listed in the permanent catalogues, *Publications of the Geological Survey.* Volumes cover 1879–1961, 1962–1970, 1971–1981, and 1981–2000 annually. More recent publications from the USGA can be found in New Publications of the United States Geological Survey at http:/pubs.usgs.gov/publications/index.shtml

These reports and maps are available by calling 1-888-ASK-USGS.

USGS Mailing List Unit
582 National Center
12201 Sunrise Valley Dr.
Reston, VA 22092

Distributes the free monthly catalog, *New Publications of the U.S. Geological Survey.*

DATA AND STATISTICS

Earth Resources Observation System (EROS) Data Center
Sioux Falls, SD 57198
(605) 594–6123
Donald Lauer, chief

Receives, processes, and distributes remote sensing data acquired by satellite and aircraft. Conducts and sponsors research to apply data findings in areas including mapping, geography, mineral and land resources, water resources, and environmental monitoring. For more information, visit the homepage at http://edcwww. cr.usgs.gov.

National Earthquake Information Service
MS-967, Box 25046
Denver Federal Center
Denver, CO 80225
(303) 273–8500
Waverly Person, chief

Provides information on earthquakes and earthquake-locating technology to the media, disaster agencies, research scientists, and the public. For more information, visit the homepage at http://gldss7.cr.usgs.gov.

Reference Resources

USGS Library
950 National Center
12201 Sunrise Valley Dr.
Reston, VA 22092
(703) 648–4305
Nancy Blair, chief librarian
Hours: 8:00 a.m. to 4:00 p.m.

Facilities for examining reports, maps, and publications of the USGS are located here and at the following locations:

Central Region
Box 25046, MS 914
Federal Center
Denver, CO 80225
(303) 236–1000

Western Region
345 Middlefield Rd., MS 955
Menlo Park, CA 94025
(650) 329–5027

Astrogeology Collection
2255 N. Gemini Dr.
Flagstaff, AZ 86001
(520) 556–7272

RULES AND REGULATIONS

USGS rules and regulations are published in the *Code of Federal Regulations,* Title 30, Part 400. Proposed regulations, new final regulations, and updates to the *Code of Federal Regulations* are published in the daily *Federal Register.* (*See appendix for details on how to obtain and use these publications.*)

Legislation

The USGS carries out its responsibilities under:

Act of March 3, 1879, as amended (20 Stat. 394, 43 U.S.C. 31A). Signed by the president March 3, 1879. Established the USGS.

Earthquake Hazards Reduction Act of 1977 (91 Stat. 1098, 42 U.S.C. 7701). Signed by the president Oct. 7, 1977. Designed to reduce the risks of life and property from future earthquakes in the United States through the establishment and maintenance of an effective earthquake hazards reduction program.

Water Resources Research Act of 1984 (98 Stat. 97, 42 U.S.C. 10301). Vetoed by the president Feb. 21, 1984; veto overridden March 22, 1984. Authorized Interior Department grants for water research projects and programs at land grant colleges.

Continental Scientific Drilling and Exploration Act of 1988 (102 Stat. 1760, 43 U.S.C. 31 note). Signed by the president Sept. 22, 1988. Established an interagency program to research the composition, structure, dynamics, and evolution of the continental crust, and how such processes affect natural phenomena such as earthquakes and volcanic eruptions.

National Geologic Mapping Act of 1992 (106 Stat. 166, 43 U.S.C. 31a). Signed by the president May 18, 1992. Established the National Cooperative Geologic Mapping Program. Also established a national geologic map database to be a national archive.

National Geologic Mapping Reauthorization Act of 1997 (111 Stat. 1107, 43 U.S.C. 31a note). Signed by the president Aug. 5, 1997. Amended the National Geologic Mapping Act of 1992 to establish a national cooperative geologic mapping program between the USGS and state geological surveys. Established a geologic mapping advisory committee to advise the director of the USGS on the planning and the implementation of the program.

◾ REGIONAL OFFICES

U.S. Geological Survey

EASTERN REGION
(AL, CT, DC, DE, FL, GA, IL, IN, KY, MA, MD, ME, MI, MS, NC, NH, NJ, NY, OH, PA, PR, RI, SC, TN, VA, VI, VT, WI, WV)
1700 Leetown Rd.
Kearneysville, WV 25430
(304) 724–4521
Bonnie A. McGregor, regional director

CENTRAL REGION
(AR, CO, IA, KS, LA, MN, MO, MT, ND, NE, NM, OK, SD, TX, WY)
Denver Federal Center, Bldg. 810
P.O. Box 25046
Denver, CO 80225–0046
(303) 202–4740
Thomas J. Casadevall, regional director

WESTERN REGION
(AK, AZ, CA, HI, ID, NV, OR, UT, WA)
909 1st Ave., 8th Fl., MS150
Seattle, WA 98104
(206) 220–4600
John Buffington, regional director

Other Interior Department Offices

▉ NATIONAL PARK SERVICE

1849 C St. N.W.
Washington, DC 20240
Internet: http://www.nps.gov

Director
    Frances P. Mainella (designate) .... (202) 208–4621
    Fax .... (202) 208–7889
    TDD .... (202) 208–4817
Public Affairs
    David Barna .... (202) 208–6843
    Fax .... (202) 219–0910

The National Park Service was established in the Interior Department in 1916. Its fundamental objective is to conserve the scenery, natural and historic objects, and wildlife in the nation's parks and to provide for the enjoyment of these resources without impairing them for future generations. The service administers an extensive system of national parks, monuments, historic sites, and recreation areas. It develops and implements park management plans and staffs the areas under its administration.

The service seeks to convey the natural values and the historical significance of these areas to the public through talks, tours, films, exhibits, and publications. It operates campgrounds and other visitor facilities and provides lodging, food, and transportation services in many areas. The service also manages historic preservation and recreation programs.

The Service Center in Denver provides planning, architectural, engineering, and other professional services. A center for production of museum exhibits, audiovisual materials, and publications is located in Harpers Ferry, W.V. In 2003 the National Park Service administered 388 sites.

The NPS Web site provides general information on the Park Service and maps and descriptions of specific park properties.

▉ BUREAU OF RECLAMATION

1849 C St. N.W.
Washington, DC 20240
Internet: http://www.usbr.gov

Information .... (202) 208–4215
Commissioner
    John W. Keys III .... (202) 513-0501
    Fax .... (202) 513-0314
Chief of Staff
    Robert Quint .... (202) 513-0501

In 1902, when Congress authorized "the reclamation of arid and semi-arid lands in the West," the secretary of the interior gave this task to the U.S. Geological Survey (USGS). In 1907 the Reclamation Service (now the Bureau of Reclamation) was separated from the USGS.

The bureau is responsible for water and power resource development protection and management in the seventeen western states. Projects include municipal and industrial water services, irrigation water service, hydropower generation, flood control, river regulation, outdoor recreational opportunities, fish and wildlife enhancement, and water quality improvement. Programs are financed both through taxes levied upon direct beneficiaries of these projects and from the Treasury Department's Reclamation Fund.

In cooperation with other agencies, the Bureau of Reclamation prepares and reviews environmental impact statements for proposed federal water resource projects and provides technical assistance to foreign countries in water resource development and utilization.

The bureau has five regional offices in the western United States. The agency's Internet site includes organizational information, searchable databases, lists of upcoming events, and a searchable index.

▓ OFFICE OF SURFACE MINING

1951 Constitution Ave. N.W.
Washington, DC 20240
Internet: http://www.osmre.gov/osm.htm

Fax-on-demand............................ (202) 219–1703
Director
   Jeffrey D. Jarrett .... (202) 208–4006
   Fax.................................... (202) 219–3106
Communications
   Michael Gauldin .... (202) 208–2565

The Office of Surface Mining (formerly Surface Mining Reclamation and Enforcement) was established in the Interior Department by the Surface Mining Control and Reclamation Act of 1977.

Its primary mission is to administer a nationwide program that protects society and the environment from the adverse effects of coal mining operations, set national standards for regulating surface effects of coal mining, and assist states in implementing regulatory programs.

In addition, the Office of Surface Mining supports reclamation of coal mines abandoned prior to the passage of the 1977 act.

The responsibilities of the office are carried out through monitoring the activities of coal-producing states and providing technical support and research capabilities.

The headquarters are in Washington, D.C., with regional offices in Pittsburgh and Denver and field offices in coal-producing states.

The agency's Web site includes news releases, information on the environment and citizen involvement, and lists of state and federal regulations.

Justice
Department

10th St. and Constitution Ave. N.W., Washington, DC 20530
Internet: http://www.usdoj.gov

Antitrust Division

950 Pennsylvania Ave. N.W., Washington, DC 20530
Internet: http://www.usdoj.gov/atr/index.html

The Antitrust Division, a unit within the Justice Department, is headed by the assistant attorney general for antitrust, who is responsible for investigating and prosecuting cases under federal antitrust laws.

Many actions that restrain and monopolize trade or reduce competition are violations of antitrust laws. Enforcement activities of the division include investigating possible antitrust violations by the civil investigative process and by conducting grand jury proceedings, preparing and prosecuting antitrust cases, prosecuting appeals, and negotiating and enforcing final judgments. Two major areas of enforcement activity are (1) investigation, detection, and criminal prosecution of price fixing and (2) investigation and civil litigation to prevent anticompetitive mergers and bid rigging.

The division represents the United States in judicial proceedings to review certain orders of the Federal Communications Commission (p. 100), the Federal Maritime Commission (p. 338), and the Nuclear Regulatory Commission (p. 355).

The Antitrust Division serves as the administration's principal authority for competition policy in regulated industries and advises government departments and agencies on the competitive implications of their policies. From time to time the division participates in regulatory proceedings involving competition in transportation, energy, agriculture, communication, banking, health care, and professional and occupational licensing.

In certain circumstances, and at the written request of interested parties, the division reviews proposed private business plans and offers a statement of its enforcement intentions under the antitrust law with regard to the proposed conduct.

The Antitrust Division provides guidance to the business community, much of it jointly with the Federal Trade Commission (p. 194). This guidance includes new and subsequently revised and expanded joint statements of policy regarding the health care industry, the licensing of intellectual property, international operations, and an accelerated individual business review process.

Staff members of the Antitrust Division participate in interagency committees on government trade policy. The division represents the United States on the Restrictive Business Practices Committee of the Organization for Economic Cooperation and Development (OECD). It also maintains, through the State Department, a liaison with foreign governments on antitrust enforcement matters that have an impact on trade with other nations. The Web site features links to foreign antitrust enforcement agencies.

In 1993 the Antitrust Division implemented a new Corporate Leniency Policy under which a corporation can avoid criminal prosecution for antitrust violations by confessing its role in the illegal activities, fully cooperating with the division, and meeting other specified conditions. In 1994 the division also implemented a Leniency Policy for Individuals under which persons who approach the division on their own behalf, not as part of a corporate proffer or confession, may seek leniency for reporting illegal antitrust activity of which the division has not previously been made aware.

In May 1998, in one of the most noted antitrust cases in years, the United States filed a suit against Microsoft, alleging the software giant had violated the Sherman AntiTrust Act. After lengthy legal proceedings and unsuccessful mediation efforts, a federal district court judge in April 2000 held that Microsoft had engaged in a series of anticompetitive acts to protect and maintain its Windows operating system monopoly and to monopolize the market for Web browsers. The court ordered Microsoft to submit a plan to reorganize itself into two separate firms: an operating system business and an applications business.

In 2001 a federal appeals court overturned the breakup order but still ruled that Microsoft was an illegal monopoly. The software maker giant then cut a deal with the administration of George W. Bush the following year. Under the agreement, Microsoft remained whole in exchange for lifting license restrictions on its operating system, which would allow Microsoft competitors to gain more equal footing within the software market. The court also ordered that Microsoft not retaliate against original equipment manufacturers and other vendors, including Internet access providers.

▓ KEY PERSONNEL

Assistant Attorney General
R. Hewitt Pate (acting)................. (202) 514–2401
Fax..................................... (202) 514-6543
Operations/Merger Enforcement
Constance Robinson .... (202) 514–3544
Executive Office
Thomas King .... (202) 514–2421
Legal Policy
Robert A. Potter....................... (202) 514–2512
Principal Deputy Assistant Attorney General
Vacant................................. (202) 514–2410
Fax.................................... (202) 616–7320
Appellate
Catherine O'Sullivan.................. (202) 514–2413
Foreign Commerce
Edward Hand.......................... (202) 514–2464
Telecommunications Task Force
Laury Bobbish........................ (202) 514–5621
Deputy Assistant Attorney General
Deborah Majoras..................... (202) 514–1157
Fax.................................... (202) 514–6543
Civil Task Force
James R. Wade........................ (202) 616–5935
Computers and Finance
Nancy M. Goodman .... (202) 307–6200
Transportation, Energy, and Agriculture
Roger Fones........................... (202) 307–6351
Deputy Assistant Attorney General
James Griffin .... (202) 514–3543
Fax.................................... (202) 307–9978
Litigation 1
Anthony Nanni........................ (202) 307–6694

Deputy Assistant Attorney General
Vacant................................ (202) 307–2032
Fax................................... (202) 514–0306
Litigation 2
J. Robert Kramer II.................... (202) 307–0924
Merger Task Force
Craig W. Conrath .... (202) 307–0001
Health Care Task Force
Gail Kursh .... (202) 307–5799
Economics Deputy Assistant Attorney General
Joseph Farrell......................... (202) 514–2408
Fax................................... (202) 514–0306
Competition Policy
Kenneth Heyer .... (202) 307–6341
Economic Litigation
Norman Familant..................... (202) 307–6323
Economic Regulatory
George Rozanski .... (202) 307–6603

▓ INFORMATION SOURCES

Internet
Agency Web site: http://www.usdoj.gov/atr/index.html. The site contains updated information on the most recent antitrust news or issues.

Telephone Contacts
Personnel Locator.......................... (202) 514–2000

Information and Publications

KEY OFFICES

Antitrust Division Public Affairs
10th St. and Constitution Ave. N.W.
Washington, DC 20530
(202) 616–2007
Fax (202) 616–0904
Gina Talamona, director

Answers general public and press questions. To be placed on a mailing list to receive news releases and reports on antitrust issues, contact DOJ Public Affairs, below.

Freedom of Information
Antitrust Division
Liberty Place, #200
Washington, DC 20530
(202) 514–2692
Fax (202) 616–4529
Ann Lea Harding, FOI officer

Antitrust Documents Group

Antitrust Division
325 7th St. N.W., #215
Washington, DC 20530
(202) 514–2481
Fax (202) 514–3763
Janie Ingalls, contact

Provides Antitrust Division publications.

DOJ Public Affairs

10th St. and Pennsylvania Ave. N.W., #228
Washington, DC 20530
(202) 514–2007

Distributes general information brochures about the department's organization, functions, and legal procedures. Maintains a mailing list for antitrust issues.

PUBLICATIONS

Contact the Antitrust Division's Antitrust Documents Group or DOJ Public Affairs. Current titles include:

Annual Report of the Attorney General of the United States

Antitrust Enforcement Guidelines for International Operations

Antitrust Guidelines for the Licensing of Intellectual Property

Customer Service in the Antitrust Division

Digest of Business Reviews

Health Care Enforcement Policy Statements

Legal Activities

Opening Markets and Protecting Competition for America's Businesses and Consumers

Reference Resources

LIBRARY

Antitrust Division Library

555 4th St. N.W., Room 1B615
Washington, DC 20001
(202) 514–5870
Fax (202) 514–9099
Blane Dessy, librarian
Hours: 8:30 a.m. to 5:00 p.m.

Houses legal, business, and reference materials. May be used by the public only with prior permission.

RULES AND REGULATIONS

Antitrust Division rules and regulations are published in the *Code of Federal Regulations,* Title 28, parts 0.40–0.49.

Proposed regulations, new final regulations, and updates to the *Code of Federal Regulations* are published in the daily *Federal Register. (See appendix for details on how to obtain and use these publications.)*

The annual report of the attorney general details the regulatory actions taken by the division during the previous year. Single copies of the report are available from DOJ Public Affairs: (202) 514–2007.

■ LEGISLATION

The Antitrust Division exercises its responsibilities under:

Sherman Antitrust Act (26 Stat. 209, 15 U.S.C. 1). Signed by the president July 2, 1890. Prohibited restraint of trade and the monopolization of interstate trade or commerce.

Wilson Tariff Act of 1894 (15 U.S.C. §§8-11). Declared illegal the importation of any article into the United States that was in restraint of lawful trade or free competition in lawful trade or commerce.

Clayton Act (38 Stat. 730, 15 U.S.C. 12). Signed by the president Oct. 15, 1914. Outlawed mergers or acquisitions that could substantially lessen competition or help to create monopolies.

Hart-Scott-Rodino Antitrust Improvement Act of 1976 (90 Stat. 1383, 15 U.S.C. 1311 note). Signed by the president Sept. 30, 1976. Required enterprises to notify the Antitrust Division and the Federal Trade Commission before engaging in mergers or acquisitions exceeding certain minimum sizes.

Export Trading Company Act of 1982 (96 Stat. 1233, 15 U.S.C. 40001). Signed by the president Oct. 8, 1982. Encouraged exports by facilitating the formation and operation of export trade companies, associations, and services. The Antitrust Division and the secretary of commerce determine if appropriate standards are met for the issuance of a certificate conferring a limited antitrust exemption.

Antitrust Amendments Act of 1990 (104 Stat. 2879, 15 U.S.C. 1 note). Signed by the president Nov. 16, 1990. Amended the Sherman Antitrust Act to increase the maximum criminal fines for corporations from $1 million to $10 million.

National Cooperative Research and Production Act of 1993 (NCRPA) (107 Stat. 117, 15 U.S.C. 4301 note). Signed by the president June 10, 1993. Permitted parties participating in joint research and development ventures to limit their possible antitrust damage exposure to actual damages if they filed notification with the attorney general and the Federal Trade Commission.

International Antitrust Enforcement Assistance Act of 1994 (108 Stat. 4597, 15 U.S.C. 6201 note). Signed by the president Nov. 2, 1994. Authorized the Justice Department and the FTC to negotiate reciprocal assistance agreements with foreign antitrust enforcement authorities.

Charitable Gift Annuity Antitrust Relief Act of 1995 (109 Stat. 687, 15 U.S.C. 1 note). Signed by the president Dec. 5, 1995. Provided antitrust protection to qualified charities that issue charitable gift annuities by creating a specific statutory exemption.

Telecommunications Act of 1996 (47 U.S.C. 609 note). Signed by the president Feb. 8, 1996. Gave the Antitrust Division a role in FCC proceedings on "Baby Bell" applications to provide in-region long-distance telephone services.

Antitrust Technical Corrections Act of 2002 (P.L. 107-273). Signed by the president Nov. 2, 2002. Repealed provisions requiring depositions for use in lawsuits filed under the Sherman Act to be open to the public. Repealed provisions of the Wilson Tariff Act that authorized any person injured by reason of anything prohibited by such act to sue to recover damages. Amended the Sherman Act to apply the prohibitions against monopolizing trade or commerce among the states or with foreign nations to monopolizing trade or foreign commerce in or among any U.S. territories and the District of Columbia.

Antitrust Modernization Commission Act of 2002 (P.L. 107-273). Signed by the president on Nov. 2, 2002. Established the Antitrust Modernization Commission to study and report to Congress and the president on issues and problems relating to the modernization of the antitrust laws.

▇ FIELD OFFICES

ATLANTA
(AL, FL, GA, MS, NC, SC, TN, PR, VI)
75 Spring St. S.W., #1176
Atlanta, GA 30303–3308
(404) 331–7100
John T. Orr Jr., chief

CHICAGO
(CO, IA, IL, IN, KS, western MI, MO, MN, ND, NE, SD, WI)
209 S. LaSalle St., #600
Chicago, IL 60604–1204
(312) 353–7530
Marvin N. Price Jr., chief

CLEVELAND
(KY, eastern MI, OH, WV)
55 Erieview Plaza, #700
Cleveland, OH 44114–1816
(216) 522–4070
Scott M. Watson, chief

DALLAS
(AR, LA, NM, OK, TX)
1601 Elm St., #4950
Dallas, TX 75201–4717
(214) 880–9401
Alan A. Pason, chief

NEW YORK
(CT, MA, ME, NH, northern NJ, NY, RI, VT)
26 Federal Plaza, #3630
New York, NY 10278–0140
(212) 264–0390
Ralph T. Giordano, chief

PHILADELPHIA
(DE, MD, southern NJ, PA, VA)
Curtis Center, One Independence Sq. West
7th and Walnut Sts., #650
Philadelphia, PA 19106–2424
(215) 597–7405
Robert E. Connolly, chief

SAN FRANCISCO
(AK, AZ, CA, HI, ID, MT, NV, OR, UT, WA, WY)
450 Golden Gate Ave., #10-0101
Box 36046
San Francisco, CA 94102–3478
(415) 436–6660
Christopher S. Crook, chief

Bureau of Alcohol, Tobacco, Firearms, and Explosives

650 Massachusetts Ave. N.W., Washington, DC 20226
Internet: http://www.atf.gov

The Bureau of Alcohol, Tobacco, and Firearms (ATF), a law enforcement and regulatory bureau within the Treasury Department since 1972, became the Bureau of Alcohol, Tobacco, Firearms, and Explosives (also ATF), within the Justice Department on Jan. 24, 2003. The Homeland Security Act of 2002, which created the Department of Homeland Security, also called for the reorganization of the ATF. The old ATF's law enforcement functions relating to firearms, explosives, and arson were transferred to the Justice Department, while the functions relating to the regulation and collection of revenue from the alcohol and tobacco industries remained at Treasury in the form of a new agency, the Alcohol and Tobacco Tax and Trade Bureau (*p. 689*).

The move of the ATF's law enforcement functions to the Justice Department accomplished a goal that many reformers had sought for years: the consolidation of all major federal law enforcement agencies within the Justice Department. In January 2003 Bradley A. Buckles, the director of the ATF, said that the ATF "is now a pure law enforcement agency, and now part of a department that is dedicated to effective law enforcement."

Under the Justice Department, the ATF continues to perform the law enforcement and regulatory functions relating to firearms, explosives, and arson, which were originally transferred to the bureau from the Internal Revenue Service in 1972 legislation. The ATF continues to work closely with other Justice Department law enforcement agencies, especially the Federal Bureau of Investigation (FBI). It also administers the U.S. Criminal Code provisions concerning alcohol and tobacco smuggling and diversion.

The ATF director is appointed by the attorney general. Although the headquarters of the ATF are in Washington, D.C., most of its personnel are stationed in area and district offices nationwide. The ATF field operations offices across the country are responsible for investigating the illegal use of firearms, ammunition, and explosives; operations carried on without a license or permit; and crimes of arson with an interstate nexus.

In addition, the ATF enforces federal explosives laws and develops methods to locate bombs before an explosion and to trace the source of explosives after detonation. The Church Arson Prevention Act of 1996 authorized funds for additional ATF agents for the investigation of church fires.

The bureau provides technical and scientific services to state and local law enforcement officials. It is the central agency for all gun tracing; approximately half of all ATF gun traces are for state and local law enforcement officials.

ATF lab technicians also are available to perform ink analysis and other technical operations to aid local law enforcement agencies in gathering evidence for criminal prosecutions.

■ KEY PERSONNEL

Director
  Bradley A. Buckles .... (202) 927–8700
  Fax .... (202) 927–8876
Deputy Director
  Richard J. Hankinson .... (202) 927–8710
Congressional Liaison
  Charles Higman .... (202) 927–8490
Chief Counsel
  Stephen Rubenstein .... (202) 927–8209
  Fax .... (202) 927–8673

Administration and Ethics
Eleanor R. Loos.........................(202) 927–8237
Disclosure and Forfeiture
Richard S. Isen.........................(202) 927–8213
Litigation
Imelda Koett...........................(202) 927–8229
Field Operations
Paul M. Snabal.........................(202) 927–7970
Fax....................................(202) 927–7756
Field Management Staff
Karl Anglin............................(202) 927–8090
Intelligence
Theodore Baltas........................(202) 927–8010
Special Operations
Phillip Durham.........................(202) 927–8020
Inspection
Malcolm W. Brady......................(202) 927–7800
Fax....................................(202) 927–8685
Management
William T. Earle.......................(202) 927–8400
Fax....................................(202) 927–8786
Acquisition and Property Management
Etrain Fernandez.......................(202) 927–8820
Administrative Programs
Harry Pass.............................(202) 927–8830
Financial Officer
Vivian Baran...........................(202) 927–8400
Personnel
John Duelos............................(202) 927–8556
Management Analysis Staff
Everett Tabourn.......................(202) 927–7834
Firearms, Explosives, and Arson
John P. Malone.........................(202) 927–7940
Arson and Explosives Programs
Carson Carroll.........................(202) 927–7930
Firearms Programs
Gary Thomas...........................(202) 927–7770
Science and Technology
Marquerita R. Moccia..................(202) 927–8390
Fax....................................(202) 927–8863
Audit Services
Francis Frande.........................(202) 927–7832
Information Services
Vacant.................................(202) 927–7231
Science and Technology Staff
Gail Davis.............................(202) 927–1610
Laboratory Services
(Rockville, MD)
Michael Ethridge.......................(301) 762–9800
Training and Professional Development
Mark Logan............................(202) 927–9380
Fax....................................(202) 927–0752

Career Development
Ray Rowley ....(202) 565–4570

■ INFORMATION SOURCES

Internet
Agency Web site: http://www.atf.gov. Offers access to many ATF publications, including the agency newsletter; information on ATF program areas, including firearms, explosives, tobacco, and alcohol; and the ATF most wanted persons list.

Telephone Contacts
Personnel Locator ....(202) 927–7777
Arson Hotline ....(888) 283–3473
Bomb Hotline ....(888) 283–2662
Report Illegal Firearms Activity...........(800) 283–4867
Firearms Theft Hotline ....(800) 800–3855
Report Stolen, Hijacked, or
Seized Cigarettes ....(800) 659–6242
Other Criminal Activity ....(888) ATF-TIPS

Information and Publications

KEY OFFICES

Public and Governmental Affairs
650 Massachusetts Ave. N.W.
Washington, DC 20226
(202) 927–8500
Fax (202) 927–8868
Kathran Kiernan, assistant director

Answers questions for the press and the public. Distributes publications and issues news releases.

Freedom of Information
ATF Disclosure Branch
650 Massachusetts Ave. N.W.
Washington, DC 20226
(202) 927–8480
Fax (202) 927–8866
Dorothy Chambers, chief

Firearms Tracing Center
Serves all local, state, and federal agencies upon request. A gun trace by the bureau provides law enforcement officials with the history of the firearm, from the manufacturer or importer through wholesale and retail dealers to the first retail purchase. Firearms retailers are required by the bureau to maintain files on purchasers including name,

address, physical characteristics, and form of identification used to verify identity.

To request a firearms trace, call (304) 274–4100 or (800) 788–7133. (Only law enforcement agents may request a firearms trace.)

For information pertaining to Title II weapons that fall under the National Firearms Act, call (202) 927–8330.

For information on firearms applications and licensing, call the National Licensing Center at (404) 679–5040.

PUBLICATIONS

ATF Distribution Center

P.O. Box 5950
Springfield, VA 22150
(703) 455–7801

Handles requests for publications, pamphlets, posters, and audio-visual materials. Subjects covered include explosives, firearms, distilled spirits, and alcohol fuels. Titles include:

ATF Bulletin (quarterly magazine)
ATF: Explosives, Laws, and Regulations
ATF Summary Statistics
Bomb Threats and Bomb Techniques
Church Threat Assessment Guide
Explosives Federal Agency Directory
Federal Firearms Licensee Information
Federal Firearms Regulations
Firearms and Ammunitions Curios and Relics List
Gauging Manual (distilled spirits)
Gun Dealer Licensing and Illegal Gun Trafficking
Regulations Under the Federal Alcohol Administration Act
State Laws and Published Ordinances: Firearms
Youth Crime Gun Interdiction Initiative

Reference Resources

LIBRARY

See Dockets (below).

DOCKETS

ATF Reading Room

650 Massachusetts Ave. N.W., Room 4412
Washington, DC 20226
(202) 927–7890
Fax (202) 927–3253
Delona Foster, librarian
Hours: Open to the public between 10:00 a.m. and 12:00 p.m. However, appointments can be made with the librarian between 7:30 a.m. and 4:00 p.m.

Public dockets, containing records of all ATF rulemakings and other administrative proceedings, are available for public inspection by appointment only.

RULES AND REGULATIONS

ATF rules and regulations are published in the *Code of Federal Regulations,* Title 27, parts 1–299. Proposed regulations, new final regulations, and updates to the *Code of Federal Regulations* are published in the daily *Federal Register.* *(See appendix for details on how to obtain and use these publications.)*

▮ LEGISLATION

The ATF exercises its authority under:

Title VII of Omnibus Crime Control and Safe Streets Act of 1968 (82 Stat. 197, 18 U.S.C. app., sec. 1201). Signed by the president June 19, 1968. Prohibited the shipment of firearms in interstate or foreign commerce by convicted felons.

Gun Control Act of 1968 (82 Stat. 1213, 18 U.S.C. 921). Signed by the president Oct. 22, 1968. Amended the National Firearms Act of 1934 that regulated machine guns and shotguns used by gangsters. Repealed the Federal Firearms Act of 1938 and set record-keeping and eligibility requirements for the purchase and sale of firearms.

Title XI of Organized Crime Control Act of 1970 (84 Stat. 922, 18 U.S.C. 841). Signed by the president Oct. 15, 1970. Established a system of federal controls over the interstate and foreign commerce of explosive materials through licenses and permits to curb the misuse of explosives.

Arms Export Control Act of 1976 (90 Stat. 744, 22 U.S.C. 2778, sec. 38). Signed by the president June 30, 1976. Gave the president discretionary authority to control the import and export of defense articles and services. Empowered him to designate which items were to be considered as defense related, and authorized him to promulgate regulations for the import and export of such items.

Anti-Arson Act of 1982 (96 Stat. 1319, 18 U.S.C. 1124). Signed by the president Oct. 12, 1982. Amended Title 18 of the U.S. Code and Title XI of the Organized Crime Control Act of 1970 (84 Stat. 922, 18 U.S.C. 841) to clarify crimes and penalties involving explosives and fire.

Comprehensive Crime Control Act of 1984 (98 Stat. 1837, 18 U.S.C. 921). Signed by the president Oct. 12, 1984. Required federal judges to follow new sentencing guidelines and restricted use of the insanity defense. Increased penalties for drug trafficking and reestablished anticrime grants for states.

Brady Handgun Violence Prevention Act (107 Stat. 1536, 18 U.S.C. 921). Signed by the president Nov. 30, 1993. Provided a waiting period before purchasing a handgun and established a background check system for the transfer of any firearm.

Violent Crime Control and Law Enforcement Act of 1994 (108 Stat. 1796, 42 U.S.C. 13701 note). Signed by the president Sept. 13, 1994. Increased funding for police hiring, prison construction, and prevention programs. Banned the possession and manufacture of nineteen types of assault weapons. Adopted the "three strikes and you're out" provision.

Church Arson Prevention Act (109 Stat. 1492, 18 U.S.C. 242). Signed by the president Aug. 6, 1996. Expanded the circumstances under which the federal government can become involved in prosecuting those who damage religious property. Authorized funds for additional ATF agents for investigation of church fires.

Homeland Security Act of 2002 (116 Stat. 2135, 6 U.S.C. 101 note). Signed by the president Nov. 25, 2002. Created the Bureau of Alcohol, Tobacco, Firearms, and Explosives by transferring the Bureau of Alcohol, Tobacco, and Firearms' law enforcement functions relating to firearms, explosives, and arson from the Treasury Department to the Justice Department.

▣ REGIONAL OFFICES

Law Enforcement District Offices

ATLANTA
(GA)
2600 Century Pkwy.
Atlanta, GA 30345–3104
(404) 679–5170

BALTIMORE
(DE, MD)
31 Hopkins Plaza
Federal Bldg., 5th Floor
Baltimore, MD 21201
(410) 962–0897

BOSTON
(CT, MA, ME, NH, RI, VT)
10 Causeway St., #253
Boston, MA 02222–1047
(617) 565–7042

CHARLOTTE
(NC, SC)
6701 Carmel Rd., #200
Charlotte, NC 28226
(704) 716–1800

CHICAGO
(IL, northern IN)
300 S. Riverside Plaza, #350 S
Chicago, IL 60606
(312) 353–6935

COLUMBUS
(OH)
37 W. Broad St., #200
Columbus, OH 43215
(614) 469–5303

DALLAS
(OK, northern TX)
1114 Commerce St., #308
Dallas, TX 75242
(469) 277–4318

DETROIT
(MI)
1155 Brewery Park Blvd., #300
Detroit, MI 48207–2602
(313) 393–6000

HOUSTON
(southern TX)
15355 Vantage Pkwy. West, #210
Houston, TX 77032
(281) 421–3440

KANSAS CITY
(IA, KS, MO, NE)
2600 Grand Ave., #200
Kansas City, MO 64108
(816) 421–3440

LOS ANGELES
(southwestern AZ, southern CA)
350 S. Figueroa St., #800
Los Angeles, CA 90071
(213) 894–4812

LOUISVILLE
(southern IN, KY, western WV)
600 Dr. Martin Luther King Pl., #311
Louisville, KY 40202
(502) 582–5211

MIAMI
(FL)
5225 N.W. 87th Ave., #300
Miami, FL 33178
(305) 597–4800

NASHVILLE

(AL, TN)
5300 Maryland Way, #200
Brentwood, TN 37027
(615) 565–1400

NEW ORLEANS

(AR, LA)
Heritage Plaza, #1008
111 Veterans Blvd.
Metairie, LA 70005
(504) 841–7000

NEW YORK

(northern NJ, NY, PR)
241 37th St., 3rd Floor
Brooklyn, NY 11232
(212) 466–5145

PHILADELPHIA

(southern NJ, PA, eastern WV)
U.S. Custom House, #607
Second and Chestnut Sts., #504
Philadelphia, PA 19106
(215) 597–7266

PHOENIX

(all but southwestern AZ, NM)
3003 N. Central Ave., #1010
Phoenix, AZ 85012
(602) 776–5400

ST. PAUL

(MN, MT, ND, SD, WI)
1870 Minnesota World Trade Center
30 E. 7th St.
St. Paul, MN 55101
(651) 290–3092

SAN FRANCISCO

(northern CA, CO, NV, UT)
221 Main St., 11th Floor
San Francisco, CA 94105
(415) 744–7001

SEATTLE

(AK, HI, ID, OR, WA, WY)
915 Second Ave., #806
Seattle, WA 98174
(206) 220–6440

WASHINGTON, DC

(DC, VA)
607 14th St. N.W., #620
Washington, DC 20005
(202) 927–8810

Civil Rights Division

950 Pennsylvania Ave. N.W., Washington, DC 20530
Internet: http://www.usdoj.gov/crt

The Civil Rights Division is a unit within the Justice Department that was established in 1957 in response to the need to ensure effective enforcement of federal civil rights laws. The division is headed by an assistant attorney general appointed by the president and confirmed by the Senate.

The division enforces the federal civil rights laws that prohibit discrimination on the basis of race, color, religion, sex, or national origin in the areas of voting, education, employment, credit, and housing; in the use of public facilities and accommodations; and in the administration of all federally assisted programs. Laws prohibiting discrimination on the basis of disability in the areas of employment and education are enforced by this division. It is responsible for protecting the constitutional rights of the mentally disabled, state prisoners, and psychiatric hospital patients.

The division also enforces federal criminal statutes that prohibit violations of individual civil rights and interference with federally secured rights. It is responsible for coordinating the civil rights enforcement programs of federal agencies and offers assistance to agencies to help them identify and eliminate policies and programs that discriminate on the basis of sex. (See also HUD Office of Fair Housing and Equal Opportunity, *p. 549;* HHS Office for Civil Rights, *p. 515;* and Equal Employment Opportunity Commission, *p. 79.*)

In May 1994, after the levels of violence against reproductive health care clinics began escalating across the country, Congress enacted the Freedom of Access to Clinic Entrances Act. This act established federal criminal penalties and civil remedies for "certain violent, threatening, obstructive, and destructive conduct that is intended to injure, intimidate, or interfere with persons seeking to obtain or provide reproductive health care services." The division is responsible for enforcing the provisions of the act.

■ KEY PERSONNEL

Assistant Attorney General
Ralph F. Boyd Jr......................... (202) 514–2151
    Fax.................................... (202) 307–1379
    TDD .... (202) 514–0716
Chief of Staff
    Vacant.................................. (202) 514–4127
Deputy Assistant Attorneys General
    Robert Neil Driscoll................... (202) 353–0742
    Loretta King .... (202) 616–1278
    Brad Schlozman........................ (202) 305–8060
    J. Michael Wiggins .... (202) 514–8696
Special Assistants to the Assistant Attorney General
    Vacant
Counsels to the Assistant Attorney General
    Vacant
Administrative Management Section
    DeDe Greene .... (202) 514–4224
    Fax.................................... (202) 514–1783
Appellate
    David K. Flynn .... (202) 514–2195
    Fax.................................... (202) 514–8490
Coordination and Review
    Merrily A. Friedlander .... (202) 307–2222
    Fax.................................... (202) 307–0595
Criminal
    Al Moskowitz.......................... (202) 514–3204
    Fax.................................... (202) 514–8336

Disability Rights

John Wodatch .... (202) 307–2227
Fax .... (202) 307–1189
TDD .... (202) 514–0383

Educational Opportunities

Jeremiah Glassman .... (202) 514–4092
Fax .... (202) 514–8337

Employment Litigation

Katherine A. Baldwin .... (202) 514–3831
Fax .... (202) 514–1105

Housing and Civil Enforcement

Joan A. Magagna .... (202) 514–4713
Fax .... (202) 514–5116

Special Litigation

Steven H. Rosenbaum .... (202) 514–6255
Fax .... (202) 514–6273

Voting

Joseph Rich .... (202) 514–6018
Fax .... (202) 307–3961

Special Counsel for Immigration-Related Unfair Employment Practices

John Trasvina .... (202) 616–5594
Fax .... (202) 616–5509

▪ INFORMATION SOURCES

Internet

Agency Web site: http://www.usdoj.gov/crt. Includes general agency information, selected speeches and legal cases.

The Civil Rights Division also operates an electronic bulletin board system (BBS) that contains information about the rights of disabled people. It also covers discrimination based on sex, race, or disability.

For modem access only .... (202) 514–6193

Telephone Contacts

ADA Information .... (800) 514–0301
TDD .... (800) 514–0383
Personnel Locator .... (202) 514–3934
TDD Locator .... (202) 472–1953
Special Counsel Information .... (800) 255–7688
TDD .... (800) 237–2515

Information and Publications

KEY OFFICES

DOJ Public Affairs

950 Pennsylvania Ave. N.W., Room 1228
Washington, DC 20530
(202) 514–2007
Fax (202) 514–5331

Answers questions about the Civil Rights Division for the press. Distributes publications and issues news releases. Maintains a mailing list for news releases and other reports on civil rights.

Freedom of Information

FOIA/PA Branch
DOJ Civil Rights Division
950 Pennsylvania Ave. N.W.
(NALC 311)
Washington, DC 20530
(202) 514–4210
Fax (202) 514–6195
Nelson D. Hermilla, chief

PUBLICATIONS

Contact DOJ Public Affairs. Titles include:
Annual Report of the Attorney General of the United States
Legal Activities

Reference Resources

LIBRARY

The Department of Justice maintains an internal library that is not open to the public. Telephone: (202) 616-5564.

RULES AND REGULATIONS

Civil Rights Division rules and regulations are published in the *Code of Federal Regulations*, Title 28, parts 0.50–0.52. Proposed regulations, new final regulations, and updates to the *Code of Federal Regulations* are published in the daily *Federal Register*. *(See appendix for details on how to obtain and use these publications.)*

▪ LEGISLATION

The Civil Rights Division carries out its responsibilities under:

Civil Rights Act of 1960 (74 Stat. 88, 42 U.S.C. 1971). Signed by the president May 6, 1960. Strengthened provisions of the Civil Rights Act of 1957 for court enforcement of voting rights and required preservation of voting records. Contained limited criminal penalty provisions relating to bombing and to obstruction of federal court orders (aimed primarily at school desegregation orders).

Civil Rights Act of 1964 (78 Stat. 243, 42 U.S.C. 2000a). Signed by the president July 2, 1964. Prohibited discrimination in public accommodations and in programs receiving federal assistance. Prohibited discrimination by employers and unions. Established the Equal Employment Opportunity Commission and strengthened enforcement of voting laws and desegregation of schools and public facilities.

Voting Rights Act of 1965 (79 Stat. 445, 42 U.S.C. 1971). Signed by the president Aug. 6, 1965. Authorized the attorney general to appoint federal examiners to register voters in areas of marked discrimination. Strengthened penalties for interference with voter rights.

Civil Rights Act of 1968 (82 Stat. 81, 42 U.S.C. 3601). Signed by the president April 11, 1968. Prohibited discrimination in the sale or rental of approximately 80 percent of all housing. Protected persons exercising specified rights, such as attending school or working, and civil rights workers urging others to exercise their rights. Included antiriot provisions.

Equal Credit Opportunity Act (88 Stat. 1521, 15 U.S.C. 1691). Signed by the president Oct. 28, 1974. Prohibited credit discrimination against women. Amended in 1975 to include discrimination based on age, race, color, religion, or national origin.

Institutionalized Persons Act of 1980 (94 Stat. 349, 42 U.S.C. 1997). Signed by the president May 23, 1980. Authorized the federal government to file suit against states to protect the rights of persons confined in state institutions.

Americans with Disabilities Act (104 Stat. 327, 42 U.S.C. 1201 note). Signed by the president July 26, 1990. Provided disabled Americans, including those with AIDS, the same rights to jobs, public transportation, and public accommodations that women and racial, religious, and ethnic minorities receive under the Civil Rights Act of 1964.

Civil Rights Act of 1991 (105 Stat. 1071, 42 U.S.C. 1981 note). Signed by the president Nov. 21, 1991. Strengthened protection in the workplace against bias and harassment on the basis of race, color, sex, religion, national origin, or disability. Allowed for greater damage awards in successful lawsuits.

EEOC Education, Technical Assistance, and Training Revolving Fund Act of 1992 (106 Stat. 2102, 42 U.S.C. 200a). Signed by the president Oct. 14, 1992. Amended the Civil Rights Act of 1964 to establish the EEOC Education, Technical Assistance, and Training Revolving Fund.

Violent Crime Control and Law Enforcement Act of 1994 (108 Stat. 1796). Signed by the president Sept. 13, 1994. Prohibited any federal law enforcement officers from depriving persons of their constitutional or federal rights. Authorized the attorney general to bring a civil action against such officers to eliminate such practices.

Congressional Accountability Act of 1995 (109 Stat. 3, 2 U.S.C. 1301 note). Signed by the president Jan. 23, 1995. Applied provisions of several laws to the legislative branch, including the Fair Labor Standards Act of 1938, Title VII of the Civil Rights Act of 1964, and the Age Discrimination in Employment Act of 1967. Required all personnel actions affecting covered employees to be made free from any discrimination based on race, color, religion, sex, national origin, age, or disability.

Presidential and Executive Office Accountability Act (110 Stat. 4053, 3 U.S.C. 401 note). Signed by the president Oct. 26, 1996. Provided for the application of several laws to the Executive Office of the President, the Executive Residence, and the Official Residence of the Vice President. These laws included the Fair Labor Standards Act of 1938, Title VII of the Civil Rights Act of 1964, Title I of the Americans with Disabilities Act of 1990, and the Age Discrimination in Employment Act of 1967. Amended the Government Employee Rights Act of 1991 to repeal its rights, protections, and remedies with respect to employment of presidential appointees.

Executive Order 13160. Issued by the president June 23, 2000. Prohibited discrimination on the basis of race, sex, color, national origin, disability, religion, age, sexual orientation, and status as a parent in federally conducted education and training programs.

Executive Order 13166. Issued by the president Aug. 11, 2000. Required federal agencies to assess and address the needs of otherwise eligible persons seeking access to federally conducted programs and activities who, because of limited English proficiency, cannot fully and equally participate in or benefit from those programs and activities.

Victims of Trafficking and Violence Protection Act of 2000 (114 Stat. 1464, 22 U.S.C. 7101 note). Signed by the president Oct. 28, 2000. Enacted to combat trafficking of persons, especially into the sex trade, slavery, and slavery-like conditions in the United States and countries around the world through prevention, through prosecution and enforcement against traffickers, and through protection and assistance to victims of trafficking.

Help America Vote Act of 2002 (116 Stat. 1666, 42 U.S.C. 15301 note). Signed by the president Oct. 29, 2002. Required voting systems to be accessible for individuals with disabilities.

Drug Enforcement Administration

700 Army-Navy Dr., Arlington, VA 22202
Mailing Address: Washington, DC 20537
Internet: http://www.usdoj.gov/dea

The Drug Enforcement Administration (DEA) was established as an agency within the Justice Department by Reorganization Plan No. 2 of 1973. The reorganization merged into one agency the Bureau of Narcotics and Dangerous Drugs, the Office for Drug Abuse Law Enforcement, the Office of National Narcotic Intelligence, divisions of the Bureau of Customs that had drug investigative responsibilities, and divisions of the Office of Science and Technology related to drug enforcement. The DEA administrator reports to the U.S. attorney general.

The DEA coordinates the drug enforcement activities of other federal agencies and works with them to control the supply of illicit drugs. These agencies include the Federal Bureau of Investigation, Bureau of Customs and Border Protection *(p. 529)*, Bureau of Immigration and Customs Enforcement *(p. 536)*, Internal Revenue Service *(p. 697)*, Bureau of Alcohol, Tobacco, Firearms, and Explosives *(p. 590)*, U.S. Coast Guard *(p. 542)*, Federal Aviation Administration *(p. 641)*, and the U.S. Army Criminal Investigation Command.

In carrying out its responsibilities the DEA:

- Acts as the lead agency responsible for the development of overall federal drug enforcement strategy, programs, planning, and evaluation.
- Investigates and prepares for the prosecution of major violators of controlled substances laws operating at the interstate and international levels in keeping with established drug priority goals.
- Manages a national narcotics intelligence system in cooperation with federal, state, and foreign officials to collect, analyze, and disseminate strategic and operational intelligence information.
- Seizes and forfeits assets derived from, traceable to, or intended to be used for illicit drug trafficking.

- Enforces the provisions of the Controlled Substances Act that pertain to the manufacture, distribution, and dispensing of legally produced controlled substances.
- Maintains liaison with the United Nations, INTERPOL, and other organizations on matters relating to international narcotics control programs.
- Is responsible for programs associated with drug law enforcement counterparts in foreign countries under the policy guidance of the secretary of state and U.S. ambassadors abroad.
- Coordinates and cooperates with federal, state, and local law enforcement officials on mutual drug enforcement efforts including interstate and international investigations.
- Coordinates and cooperates with other federal, state, and local agencies, and with foreign governments, in programs designed to reduce the availability of illicit drugs on the U.S. market through nonenforcement methods such as crop eradication, crop substitution, and training of foreign officials.

The DEA has twenty-one domestic field divisions, each managed by a special agent in charge (SAC). Subordinate to these divisions are more than 200 resident offices and six district offices, with at least one office located in every state. The El Paso Intelligence Center and the Office of Training at Quantico, Va., are managed by a SAC.

The DEA operates several regional forensic laboratories, a special testing and research laboratory, and an aviation unit that provides air support throughout the United States and in foreign countries. Overseas, the DEA maintains seventy-nine offices in fifty-eight countries.

In 2002 the DEA State and Local Task Force Program consisted of 207 state and local task forces. These task forces were staffed by more than 1,172 DEA special agents and

1,916 state and local police officers. Participating state and local officers were deputized to perform the same functions as DEA special agents.

KEY PERSONNEL

Administrator
Karen P. Tandy........................... (202) 307–8000
Deputy Administrator
Vacant.................................. (202) 307–7345
Administrative Law Judge
Mary Ellen Bittner .... (202) 307–8188
Chief Counsel
Cynthia R. Ryan .... (202) 307–7322
Congressional and Public Affairs
Christopher Battle..................... (202) 307–7363
  Congressional Affairs
  Emmitt Highland (acting)............. (202) 307–7423
  Demand Reduction
  John J. Lunt........................... (202) 307–7936
Intelligence Division
Steven W. Casteel Jr..................... (202) 307–3607
  Intelligence Policy and Management
  Judith Bertini......................... (202) 307–8748
Operational Support Division
William B. Simpkins .... (202) 307–4730
  Administration
  James M. Whetstone................... (202) 307–7708
  Forensic Sciences
  Thomas J. Janovsky .... (202) 307–8866
  Information Systems
  Dennis R. McCrary.................... (202) 307–3653
Human Resources
Catherine J. Kasch..................... (202) 307–4000
  Board of Professional Conduct
  Eli Madrid .... (202) 307–8980
  Equal Employment Opportunity
  Barbara Lewis .... (202) 307–8888
Operations Division
Rogelio Guevara....................... (202) 307–7340
  Diversion Control
  Laura M. Nagel .... (202) 307–7165
  Special Operations
  Joseph D. Keefe........................ (703) 488–4205
  International Operations
  Martin W. Pracht...................... (202) 307–4266
Financial Management
Frank M. Kalder .... (202) 307–7330
Chief Inspector for Inspections
John Driscoll (acting)................. (202) 307–7358
  Deputy Chief Inspector, Professional Responsibility
  John Driscoll .... (202) 307–8232

INFORMATION SOURCES

Internet
Agency Web site: http://www.dea.gov. Features general information about the administration, trends and statistics, a list of DEA fugitives, and employment opportunities.

Telephone Contacts
Personnel Locator .... (202) 307–4133
Automated Information .... (202) 307–1000

Information and Publications

KEY OFFICES

DEA Public Affairs Section
Washington, DC 20537
(202) 307–7977
Will Glasby, chief

Answers general questions and press queries.

FREEDOM OF INFORMATION
DEA Freedom of Information Division
Washington, DC 20537
(202) 307–7600
Kathy Myrick, chief

PUBLICATIONS
For information, contact the DEA Demand Reduction Section: (202) 307–7938.

DATA AND STATISTICS
The DEA Public Affairs Section provides information on the availability of the following computer data bank systems:

Asset Seizures and Forfeitures. Information includes statistics on seizures and forfeitures of assets seized by the DEA or referred to the DEA by another agency. System is being expanded to provide data by judicial districts.

Defendant Data. Data includes statistics on arrests, dispositions, and sentencing of defendants arrested by the DEA. Reports can be generated in a variety of formats.

Drug Removals. Drug removal statistics reflect the total of all drugs purchased, seized, or otherwise obtained through DEA investigations. Data are reported by net weight and displayed in four major categories: heroin, cocaine, cannabis, and dangerous drugs.

Reference Resources

LIBRARY

DEA Library
700 Army-Navy Dr.
Arlington, VA 22202
(202) 307–8932
Rosemary Russo, chief librarian
Hours: 8:00 a.m. to 5:00 p.m.

Maintains an extensive collection of research materials related to the history, study, and control of narcotic and dangerous drugs. Materials for research purposes are only available for DEA employees.

RULES AND REGULATIONS

DEA rules and regulations are published in the *Code of Federal Regulations,* Title 21, parts 1300 to end. Proposed regulations, new final regulations, and updates to the *Code of Federal Regulations* are published in the daily *Federal Register. (See appendix for details on how to obtain and use these publications.)*

■ LEGISLATION

The DEA carries out its responsibilities under:

Controlled Substances Act of 1970 (84 Stat. 1236, 21 U.S.C. 801). Signed by the president Oct. 27, 1970. Required registration of persons engaged in the manufacture and distribution of controlled substances; established criteria for determining abuse potential of drugs; provided for increased research into drug abuse and development of drug abuse prevention programs; strengthened existing drug laws.

Reorganization Plan No. 2 of 1973 (Executive Order No. 11727, 38 F.R. 18357). Signed by the president July 6, 1973. Established the DEA within the Department of Justice.

Narcotic Addict Treatment Act of 1974 (88 Stat. 124, 125, 42 U.S.C. 801). Signed by the president May 14, 1974. Required registration of narcotic treatment and drug rehabilitation programs with the DEA; established record-keeping and security requirements for these programs.

Comprehensive Crime Control Act of 1984, Title II (98 Stat. 2044, 21 U.S.C. 853). Signed by the president Oct. 12, 1984. Gave the attorney general emergency authority to require tight control of new chemical substances when such action was determined "necessary to avoid an imminent hazard to public safety." Authorized the attorney general to establish programs to help states reduce the amount of drugs diverted from medical channels to the black market.

Gave federal prosecutors new authority to seize the assets and profits of drug traffickers. Increased maximum fines and prison sentences for certain drug offenses.

Anti-Drug Abuse Act of 1988 (102 Stat. 4181, 21 U.S.C. 1501 note). Signed by the president Nov. 18, 1988. Created the Office of National Drug Control Policy and allowed for the death penalty for major drug traffickers who intentionally killed someone as part of their drug-related transactions. Authorized $2.7 billion to be split evenly between drug enforcement and treatment.

Domestic Chemical Diversion Control Act of 1993 (107 Stat. 2333, 21 U.S.C. 801). Signed by the president Dec. 17, 1993. Modified the so-called "legal" exemption of the Chemical Diversion and Trafficking Act of 1988. Established a registration system for distributors, importers, and exporters of listed chemicals.

■ FIELD DIVISIONS

ATLANTA
(GA, NC, SC, TN)
75 Spring St. S.W., #800
Atlanta, GA 30303
(404) 893–7000
Michael W. Ferguson, special agent in charge

CARIBBEAN
(PR, VI, Caribbean except Bahamas)
P.O. Box 2167
San Juan, PR 00922–2167
(787) 775–1700
Jerome Harris, special agent in charge

CHICAGO
(most of IL, IN, MN, ND, WI)
230 S. Dearborn St., #1200
Chicago, IL 60604
(312) 353–7875
Richard Sanders, special agent in charge

DALLAS
(OK, northern TX)
10160 Technology Blvd. E.
Dallas, TX 75220
(214) 366–6900
Sherri Strange, special agent in charge

DETROIT
(KY, MI, OH)
431 Howard St.
Detroit, MI 48226
(313) 234–4000
Michael A. Braun, special agent in charge

HOUSTON

(southern TX)
1433 W. Loop South, #600
Houston, TX 77027
(713) 693–3000
Kevin Whaley, special agent in charge

LOS ANGELES

(southern CA, GU, HI, NV)
255 E. Temple St., 20th Floor
Los Angeles, CA 90012
(213) 621–6700
Michele M. Leonhart, special agent in charge

MIAMI

(FL, Bahamas)
8400 N.W. 53rd St.
Miami, FL 33166
(305) 590–4870
Thomas W. Raffanello, special agent in charge

ST. LOUIS

(IA, southern IL, KS, MO, NE, SD)
317 S. 16th St.
St. Louis, MO 63103
(314) 538–4600
William J. Renton Jr., special agent in charge

BOSTON

(CT, MA, ME, NH, RI, VT)
15 New Sudbury St., Suite E400
Boston, MA 02203–0402
(617) 557–2100
Mark R. Trouville, special agent in charge

NEW ORLEANS

(AL, AR, LA, MS)
3838 N. Causeway Blvd., #1800
Metairie, LA 70002
(504) 840–1100
James Craig, special agent in charge

NEW YORK

(NY)
99 10th Ave.
New York, NY 10011
(212) 337–3900
Anthony P. Placido, special agent in charge

NEWARK

(NJ)
80 Mulberry, 2nd Fl.
Newark, NJ 07102
(973) 273–5000
Alexander J. Gourley Jr., special agent in charge

PHILADELPHIA

(DE, PA)
600 Arch St., #10224
Philadelphia, PA 19106
(215) 861–3474
James M. Kasson, special agent in charge

PHOENIX

(AZ)
3010 N. Second Ave., #301
Phoenix, AZ 85012
(602) 664–5600
Errol J. Chavez, special agent in charge

DENVER

(CO, NM, UT, WY)
115 Inverness Dr. East
Engelwood, CO 80112–5116
(303) 705–7300
Jeffrey D. Sweetin, special agent in charge

SAN DIEGO

(CA, Mexican border)
4560 Viewridge Ave.
San Diego, CA 92123
(858) 616–4001
Michael Vigil, special agent in charge

SAN FRANCISCO

(northern CA)
450 Golden Gate Ave.
P.O. Box 36035
San Francisco, CA 94102
(415) 436–7900
Stephen Delgado, special agent in charge

SEATTLE

(AK, ID, MT, OR, WA)
400 2nd Ave. West
Seattle, WA 98119
(206) 553–5443
John M. Bott, special agent in charge

WASHINGTON, DC

(DC, MD, VA, WV)
800 K St. N.W., 5th Floor
Washington, DC 20001
(202) 305–8500
R.C. Gamble, special agent in charge

EL PASO

(Western TX, NM)
660 Mesa Hills Dr., #2000
El Paso, TX 79912
(915) 832–6000
Sandallo Gonzalez, special agent in charge

EL PASO INTELLIGENCE CENTER

11339 SSG Sims St.
El Paso, TX 79908–8098
(915) 760–2000
James Mauromatis, special agent in charge

OFFICE OF TRAINING

DEA/FBI Academy
P.O. Box 1475
Quantico, VA 22134–1475
(703) 640–1631
Gary E. Wade, special agent in charge

Office of Justice Programs

810 7th St. N.W., Washington, DC 20531
Internet: http://www.ojp.usdoj.gov

Formerly the Office of Justice Assistance, Research and Statistics, and the Law Enforcement Assistance Administration before that, the Office of Justice Programs (OJP) was established by the Justice Assistance Act of the Comprehensive Crime Control Act of 1984. It is headed by an assistant attorney general nominated by the president and confirmed by the Senate. The OJP is responsible for the coordination of the Bureau of Justice Assistance, the Bureau of Justice Statistics, the National Institute of Justice, the Office of Juvenile Justice and Delinquency Prevention, and the Office for Victims of Crime.

Through the programs developed and financed by its bureaus and offices, OJP works to form partnerships among federal, state, and local government officials. Program bureaus and offices award formula grants to state agencies, which, in turn, subgrant funds to units of state and local government. Formula grant programs—drug control and system improvement, juvenile justice, victims compensation, and victims assistance—are administered by state agencies. Discretionary grant funds are announced in the *Federal Register*, and applications are made directly to the sponsoring OJP bureau or office.

The Violent Crime and Law Enforcement Act of 1994 significantly expanded the responsibilities of the Office of Justice Programs. The bureaus and program offices of the OJP implemented the majority of the act's provisions, which included the Violent Crime Reduction Trust Fund to provide for 100,000 new police officers and strengthen community policing; a ban on the manufacture of various military-type assault weapons; the expansion of the federal death penalty to cover more than sixty offenses; and enactment of mandatory life sentences for federal offenders with three or more convictions for serious violent felonies or drug trafficking crimes.

The Bureau of Justice Assistance (BJA) is authorized to provide federal financial and technical assistance to states, local governments, and private nonprofit organizations for criminal justice programs. The BJA administers the Justice Department's programs for the donation of surplus federal property for correctional purposes and the payment of benefits to the survivors of public safety officers killed in the line of duty. A clearinghouse of information is maintained by the BJA.

The Bureau of Justice Statistics (BJS) compiles, analyzes, and distributes a number of criminal justice statistical reports, including the Report to the Nation on Crime and Justice and the *National Crime Survey*.

The National Institute of Justice (NIJ) is the principal research and development agency in the Department of Justice. NIJ responsibilities include evaluating the effectiveness of justice programs and supporting basic research and development on criminal justice issues. The institute administers the National Criminal Justice Reference Service, which distributes information about the OJP and the Office of National Drug Control Policy and maintains a computerized database on law enforcement and criminal justice information.

The Office of Juvenile Justice and Delinquency Prevention (OJJDP) administers federal programs relating to missing and exploited children and to juvenile delinquency. The OJJDP's missing children's assistance program maintains a national resource center and clearinghouse to provide technical assistance to public and private agencies in locating and recovering missing children. It awards federal grants and contracts for research and service projects and operates a national toll-free hotline to assist in locating missing children. The Federal Coordinating Council on Juvenile Justice and Delinquency Prevention reviews federal policies on juvenile justice and advises the OJJDP administrator. As designated by the Juvenile Justice and Delinquency Prevention Act of 1974, the council is composed of nine statutory members representing the following federal agencies: Departments of Justice, Education, Health and Human Services, Housing and Urban Development, and Labor; the Office of National Drug Control Policy; Bureau of Citizenship and Immigration Services; the Corporation for National Service; and the Office of Juvenile Justice and Delinquency Prevention. The council also includes nine practitioner members, representing disciplines that focus on youth.

The Victims of Crime Act of the Comprehensive Crime Control Act of 1984 established a crime victims fund in the Department of Treasury to be administered by the attorney general through OJP's Office for Victims of Crime (OVC). Sources for the fund include federal criminal fines, penalty assessment fees, and forfeited bonds and collateral. Grants from the fund are given to the states both to finance their crime victim compensation programs and to allow them to award funds to local crime victim assistance programs. In addition, OVC sponsors training to sensitize criminal justice practitioners to victims' needs.

Crime victim compensation is a direct reimbursement to, or on behalf of, a crime victim for the following crime-related expenses: medical costs, mental health counseling, funeral and burial costs, lost wages, or loss of support. Other expenses that may be compensated include eyeglasses or other corrective lenses, dental services and devices, prosthetic devices, and crime scene cleanup.

OJP also includes the Office on Violence Against Women, the Executive Office for Weed and Seed, the Office of the Police Corps, and Law Enforcement Education. OJP's American Indian and Alaska Native Affairs Desk coordinates programmatic activity across the bureaus and program offices and serves as an information resource center for American Indian and Alaskan Native criminal justice interests.

▓ KEY PERSONNEL

Assistant Attorney General
Deborah J. Daniels .... (202) 307–5933
Fax .... (202) 514–7805
Deputy Assistant Attorney General
Cheri Nolan .... (202) 307–5933
Budget and Management Services
Kimberly Orben (acting) .... (202) 514–9337
Civil Rights
Michael Alston (acting) .... (202) 307–0692
Comptroller
Cynthia Schwimer .... (202) 307–3186

Corrections Program
Larry Meachum .... (202) 307–3914
Drug Courts Program
Marilyn Roberts .... (202) 616–5001
Executive Office for Weed and Seed
Robert Samuels (acting) .... (202) 307–1357
General Counsel
Rafael A. Madan .... (202) 307–0790
Personnel
Leah Hollander .... (202) 616–3272
Violence Against Women Grants Office
Diane Stuart (acting) .... (202) 307–0728
Bureau of Justice Assistance
Director
Richard R. Nedelkoff .... (202) 514–6278
Fax .... (202) 305–1367
Program Development
Timothy J. Murray .... (202) 514–5943
Deputy Director for Planning
Harri Kramer .... (202) 514–6094
State and Local Assistance
Vacant .... (202) 305–2088
Bureau of Justice Statistics
Director
Lawrence A. Greenfield .... (202) 616–3281
Fax .... (202) 307–5846
Intergovernmental Assistance Programs
Vacant .... (202) 307–0765
National Statistical Programs
Lawrence A. Greenfeld .... (202) 616–3281
Planning, Management, and Budget
Maureen A. Henneberg .... (202) 616–3282
Publication Development and Verification
Tom Hester .... (202) 616–3283
Publications and Electronic Dissemination
Marilyn Marbrook .... (202) 616–3283
Research and Public Policy Issues
Patrick A. Langan .... (202) 616–3490
National Institute of Justice
Director
Sarah V. Hart .... (202) 307–2942
Fax .... (202) 307–6394
Research and Evaluation
Thomas Feucht .... (202) 307–2949
Development and Communication
John Schwarz .... (202) 305–4893
Planning and Management Staff
Douglas Homer .... (202) 514–3928
Science and Technology
John Morgan .... (202) 305–0995

Office for Victims of Crime

Director
John Gillis .... (202) 307–5983
Fax .... (202) 514–6383

Federal Crime Victims
Thomas Kilmartin .... (202) 616–3568

Legal Counsel
Vacant .... (202) 616–3585

Special Projects
Joye Whatley .... (202) 305–1715

Office of Juvenile Justice and Delinquency Prevention

Administrator
J. Robert Flores .... (202) 307–5911
Fax .... (202) 307–2093

Research and Program Development
Kathi Grasso .... (202) 619–7567

Special Emphasis
Jim Burch .... (202) 307–5914

State and Tribal Assistance Division
Roberta E. Dorn .... (202) 616–3660

Training and Technical Assistance
Donna Ray .... (202) 616–3572

Information Dissemination and Planning Unit
Catherine M. Doyle .... (202) 514–9208

Concentration of Federal Efforts
Kim Budnick .... (202) 307–5911

▮ INFORMATION SOURCES

Internet

Agency Web site: http://www.ojp.usdoj.gov. Features information on OJP divisions and programs, including the Bureau of Justice Assistance, the Bureau of Justice Statistics, and the Office of Juvenile Justice and Delinquency Prevention.

Telephone Contacts

Personnel Locator .... (202) 514–2000
Drug and Crime Data .... (800) 666–3332
National Victims Resource Center .... (800) 627–6873
OJP Information Fax .... (202) 307–0091

See Publications (below) for toll-free order numbers.

Information and Publications

KEY OFFICES

OJP Congressional and Public Affairs

810 7th St. N.W., #6338
Washington, DC 20531
(202) 307–0703
Fax (202) 514–5958
Harri J. Kramer, director

Answers questions about the OJP and its activities. Distributes publications and issues news releases. Maintains a mailing list.

Freedom of Information

810 7th St. N.W., #5400
Washington, DC 20531
(202) 307–0790
Dorothy A. Lee, FOI officer

PUBLICATIONS

Data and publications are available from the following toll-free numbers. See also the National Criminal Justice Reference Service (below).

National Institute of Justice .... (800) 851–3420
Office of Juvenile Justice and
   Delinquency Prevention .... (800) 638–8736
Office for Victims of Crime .... (800) 627–6872
Office of National Drug Control
   Policy .... (800) 666–3332
Bureau of Justice Assistance .... (800) 688–4252
Bureau of Justice Statistics .... (800) 732–3277

DATA AND STATISTICS

National Criminal Justice Reference Service (NCJRS)

2277 Research Blvd.
P.O. Box 6000
Rockville, MD 20849
(301) 519–5063
Fax (301) 251–5212
Electronic bulletin board (301) 738–8895 (modem)
Internet: http://www.ncjrs.org/ncjhome.htm
E-mail: askncjrs@ncjrs.org

A clearinghouse for information on criminal justice issues; serves all offices of the OJP as well as the Office of National Drug Control Policy and the Executive Office for Weed and Seed. Conducts searches of its database to provide information requested by organizations or individuals. Information is available in the following forms: automated matching of a user's interest area with literature in the NCJRS system; hard-copy documents; search and retrieval on specific and general questions; referral to other information and reference services; indexes; and Internet services. There is a charge for some services.

The NCJRS also distributes research titles, including final reports; manuals; law enforcement equipment studies; statistics on custody, prisoners, and other corrections issues; community crime prevention programs; juvenile justice; crime victim services; illicit drugs; and audiovisual materials listings.

The NCJRS abstracts database can be accessed through the NCJRS homepage at http://www.ncjrs.org/database.htm. This service is free of charge and provides summaries of criminal justice literature including government reports, journal articles, and books. The database can be purchased on CD-ROM by calling (800) 851–3420.

National Law Enforcement and Corrections Technology Center (NLECTC)

P.O. Box 6000
Rockville, MD 20849–1160
(301) 251–5060
Toll-free (800) 248–2742
Fax (301) 251–5149
Internet: http://www.nlectc.org
E-mail: nlectc@aspensys.com

Administered by the National Institute for Justice. Provides information about law enforcement and corrections equipment and technology. Helps identify needs; initiates partnerships among private and public organizations to develop technologies; tests and evaluates products.

Reference Resources

LIBRARIES

OJP Online Research and Information Center (ORIC)

810 7th St. N.W., #3700
Washington, DC 20531
(202) 307–6742
Scott Hertzberg, librarian
Appointment should be made with librarian prior to visit.

NCJRS Research and Information Center

2277 Research Blvd.
Rockville, MD 20850
(301) 519–5063
Hours: Open Wednesday through Friday by appointment only.

Houses the main library collection of the National Criminal Justice Reference Service. Open to criminal justice professionals and graduate students.

DOJ Response Center

1100 Vermont Ave., 6th Floor
Washington, DC 20530
(202) 307–1480
(800) 421–6770 (outside Washington area)

Provides technical information to applicants for grants administered by the OJP.

RULES AND REGULATIONS

OJP rules and regulations are published in the *Code of Federal Regulations,* Title 28, parts 18–20, 30, and 32. Proposed regulations, new final regulations, and updates to the *Code of Federal Regulations* are published in the daily *Federal Register. (See appendix for details on how to obtain and use these publications.)*

■ LEGISLATION

The OJP carries out its responsibilities under:

Civil Rights Act of 1964 (78 Stat. 252, 42 U.S.C. 2000d). Signed by the president July 2, 1964. Title IV barred discrimination based on race, color, or national origin in any program or activity receiving federal assistance.

Omnibus Crime Control and Safe Streets Act of 1968 (82 Stat. 197, 42 U.S.C. 3701). Signed by the president June 19, 1968. Provided grants to law enforcement agencies [through the now-defunct Law Enforcement Assistance Administration.]

Rehabilitation Act of 1973 (87 Stat. 357, 29 U.S.C. 701). Signed by the president Sept. 26, 1973. Extended basic federal aid programs to the disabled.

Juvenile Justice and Delinquency Prevention Act of 1974 (88 Stat. 1109, 42 U.S.C. 5601). Signed by the president Sept. 7, 1974. Established the Office of Juvenile Justice and Delinquency Prevention. Amended in 1984 to establish a program for missing and exploited children.

Public Safety Officers' Benefits Act of 1976 (90 Stat. 1346, 42 U.S.C. 3701 note). Signed by the president Sept. 29, 1976. Authorized the provision of a $100,000 benefit to the survivors of public safety officers killed as a result of a personal injury sustained in the line of duty. Currently administered by the Bureau of Justice Assistance.

Justice System Improvement Act of 1979 (93 Stat. 1167, 42 U.S.C. 3711). Signed by the president Dec. 27, 1979. Created the Office of Justice Assistance, Research, and Statistics and brought under its jurisdiction the Law Enforcement Assistance Administration (now defunct), the National Institute of Justice, and the Bureau of Justice Statistics. Also provided for grants to states, local governments, and nonprofit organizations for criminal justice purposes.

Comprehensive Crime Control Act of 1984 (98 Stat. 1837, 18 U.S.C. 1 note). Signed by the president Oct. 12, 1984. Provisions of the act included those under the **Justice Assistance Act** (98 Stat. 2077, 42 U.S.C. 3711 note), which established the OJP to coordinate the activities of several units within the Department of Justice. Also created the Bureau of Justice Assistance to administer a new program of block grants for anticrime projects. The **Victims of Crime Act** (98 Stat. 2170, 42 U.S.C. 10601 note) established a crime victims fund in the Treasury to provide financing for victim compensation and victim assistance programs.

Anti-Drug Abuse Act of 1988 (102 Stat. 4181, 21 U.S.C. 1501 note). Signed by the president Nov. 18, 1988. Authorized over $2 billion to prevent the manufacturing, distribution, and use of illegal drugs; to increase drug treatment and education programs; and to strengthen local law enforcement efforts. Created a cabinet-level "drug czar" position.

Crime Control Act of 1990 (104 Stat. 4789, 18 U.S.C. 1 note). Signed by the president Nov. 29, 1990. Provided for federal debt collection and prosecution of fraud at financial institutions. Also provided further protection for children from child abuse and child pornography.

Violent Crime Control and Law Enforcement Act of 1994 (108 Stat. 1796, 42 U.S.C. 13701 note). Signed by the president Sept. 13, 1994. Provided funding to hire 100,000 new police officers and build new boot camps and prisons. Expanded the federal death penalty and enacted mandatory life imprisonment for federal offenders with three or more serious violent felonies or drug trafficking crimes.

Juvenile Justice and Delinquency Prevention Act of 2002 (P.L. 107-273). Signed by the president Nov. 2, 2002. Amended the Juvenile Justice and Delinquency Prevention Act to repeal certain provisions and to establish the Juvenile Delinquency Prevention Block Grant Program.

Other Justice Department Offices

CRIMINAL DIVISION

950 Pennsylvania Ave. N.W.
Washington, DC 20530
Internet: http://www.usdoj.gov/criminal/

Assistant Attorney General
    Michael Chertoff .... (202) 514–7200
DOJ Public Affairs
    Barbara Comstock .... (202) 514–2007

The Criminal Division of the Justice Department is the unit responsible for coordinating the development and enforcement of the majority (more than 900) of federal criminal statutes (except those specifically assigned to the Antitrust, Civil Rights, Environment and Natural Resources, or Tax Divisions). It is headed by an assistant attorney general who is appointed by the president with the advice and consent of the Senate.

The division handles certain civil matters related to its criminal jurisdiction under federal liquor, narcotics, counterfeiting, gambling, firearms, customs, and immigration laws. It investigates and prosecutes criminal offenses involving subversive activities including treason, espionage, sedition, and Nazi war crimes. The division approves or monitors sensitive areas of law enforcement such as participation in the Witness Security Program and the use of electronic surveillance. The Criminal Division also is responsible for civil litigation resulting from petitions for writs of habeas corpus by members of the Armed Forces, actions brought on behalf of federal prisoners, and legal issues concerning national security, such as counter espionage.

Prosecution of cases usually is handled in the field by one or more of the division's ninety-three U.S. attorneys.

The division focuses most of its prosecution efforts on organized crime, white-collar crime and fraud, official corruption and public integrity, and major narcotics trafficking.

The agency's Web site provides an overview of the Criminal Division.

FEDERAL BUREAU OF PRISONS

320 1st St. N.W.
Washington, DC 20534
Internet: http://www.bop.gov

Director
    Harley G. Lappin .... (202) 307–3250
    Fax .... (202) 514–6878
BOP Public Affairs
    Linda Wines Smith .... (202) 307–3198
    Inmate Locator Service .... (202) 307–3126
    NIC Information Center .... (800) 877–1461

The Federal Bureau of Prisons was established in 1930 to provide more progressive and humane care for federal inmates, to professionalize the prison service, and to ensure consistent and centralized administration of the federal prison system. The mission of the Bureau of Prisons is to protect society by confining offenders in the controlled environments of prisons and community-based facilities that are safe, humane, cost-efficient, and appropriately secure, and that provide work and other self-improvement opportunities to assist offenders in becoming law-abiding citizens.

The bureau is responsible for the custody and care of federal offenders. The agency confines these offenders in Bureau-operated correctional institutions or detention centers, as well as through agreements with State and local governments and through contracts with privately operated community correction centers, detention centers, prisons, and juvenile facilities. At the end of 2000 the Bureau operated 102 institutions and was responsible for the confinement of approximately 168,000 federal offenders in bureau-operated and privately operated facilities.

The Bureau of Prisons' headquarters, or Central Office, is located in Washington, D.C. The Central Office is composed of nine divisions that are responsible for establishing national policy; developing and reviewing programs; providing training and technical assistance to the field; and coordinating agency operations in the various disciplines (administration, correctional programs, community corrections and detention, health services, industries and education, human resources, legal issues, information resource management and public affairs, and program review). The Bureau has created six regions and has given direct responsibility for overseeing day-to-day operations of the prisons to a regional office, headed by a regional director. In conjunction with the Central Office, the regional offices also provide administrative oversight and support to the institutions and community corrections offices. Institution wardens have responsibility for managing the prisons and report to their prospective regional director. Community corrections offices oversee community corrections centers and home confinement programs.

Staff training is an integral part of Bureau of Prisons employee development. Introductory training is conducted at the Bureau's Staff Training Academy in Glynco, Ga.; specialized professional training is conducted at the Management and Specialty Training Center in Aurora, Colo., and at the Staff Training Academy's Specialty Training Center in Artesia, N.M.

The National Institute of Corrections (NIC) provides technical assistance, training, and information to State and local correctional agencies throughout the country. NIC has four divisions (Jails, Prisons, Community Corrections, and Academy), and it operates a clearinghouse known as the NIC Information Center. NIC provides training to State and local correctional personnel and to Bureau employees at its Academy in Longmont, Colo.

■ UNITED STATES PAROLE COMMISSION

5550 Friendship Blvd., #420
Chevy Chase, MD 20815
Internet: http://www.usdoj.gov/uspc

Chair

Edward F. Reilly .... (301) 492–5990

Fax .... (301) 492–5543

DOJ Public Affairs

Thomas W. Hutchison, (acting) .... (202) 492–5953

Fax .... (301) 492–5543

The U.S. Parole Commission is an independent unit within the Justice Department. The agency was created by Congress in 1930 as the U.S. Board of Parole. The commission administers the parole system for federal prisoners and is responsible for developing a federal parole policy. The Parole Phaseout Act of 1996, effective Oct. 2, 1996, extended the life of the agency until Nov. 1, 2002. However, the Department of Justice Appropriations Authorization Act of 2002 extended the United States Parole Commission for an additional three years.

The commission:

• Determines parole eligibility for federal prisoners.

• Imposes conditions on the release of any prisoner from custody.

• Revokes parole or mandatory release judgments.

• Discharges offenders from supervision and terminates prison sentences prior to expiration of the supervision period.

Hearing examiners at headquarters conduct hearings with eligible prisoners and make parole recommendations to the commission. The Bureau of Prisons makes arrangements for hearings and implements release orders *(see p. 608).*

Under commission regulations, all federal prisoners serving a maximum term of more than one year are afforded parole hearings within 120 days of confinement; hearings for prisoners with minimum terms of parole eligibility of ten years or more are conducted during the month prior to completion of the minimum term.

Appeals for parole revocation decisions may be taken up with the regional commissioner and then with the National Appeals Board. The commission also is required to review periodically cases of all released prisoners to determine the appropriateness of terminating future sentences earlier than the term imposed by the court.

The agency's Web site provides a brief overview of the Parole Commission.

Status of the Parole Commission. The commission has been steadily phased down since passage of the Sentencing Reform Act of 1984 and implementation of the U.S. Sentencing Guidelines on Nov. 1, 1987. The agency has closed its former regional offices; beginning in February 1996 all functions were consolidated at the Chevy Chase headquarters. The number of commissioners has also been reduced, from the original nine to three in October 1996, with corresponding reductions in staff. The Parole Phase-out Act of 1996 provided for further reductions. The law also required the attorney general to report to Congress yearly, beginning in 1998, whether it is more cost-effective for the commission to remain a separate agency or whether its functions and personnel should be assigned elsewhere.

The Department of Justice Appropriations Authorization Act of 2002 extended the commission for an additional three years. The legislation directed the attorney general to establish a committee within DOJ to evaluate the merits and feasibility of transferring the commission's functions regarding the supervised release of District of Columbia offenders to other entities outside DOJ.

Labor Department

200 Constitution Ave. N.W., Washington, DC 20210
Internet: http://www.dol.gov

Employee Benefits Security Administration

200 Constitution Ave. N.W., Washington, DC 20210
Internet: http://www.dol.gov/ebsa

The Employee Benefits Security Administration (EBSA) is responsible for administering the Title I provisions of the Employee Retirement Income Security Act of 1974 (ERISA). Before January 1986, EBSA was known as the Pension and Welfare Benefits Administration (PWBA). At the time of its name change, EBSA was upgraded to a subcabinet position with the establishment of assistant secretary and deputy assistant secretary positions.

The EBSA has primary responsibility for ERISA's requirements on fiduciary standards, reporting and disclosure, employee protection, and enforcement. The agency develops rules and regulations on the standards of conduct of individuals who operate employee benefit plans or manage pension plan funds. It also oversees requirements designed to protect the benefits of workers, including health plan benefits, and employees' rights to information about their plans. These requirements include continuation of health care benefits as established by the Consolidated Omnibus Budget Reconciliation Act of 1985 (COBRA) and extended by the Health Insurance Portability and Accountability Act of 1996 (HIPAA).

The Child Support Performance and Incentive Act of 1998 is intended to help children gain access to coverage under their noncustodial parents' employer-based group health plans. The act provides a uniform National Medical Support Notice to be used by the states in carrying out their responsibilities in child support enforcement. The National Medical Support Notice also allows administrators of group health plans to determine readily that medical child support orders are qualified under section 609(a) of ERISA.

Under its enforcement authority, the EBSA monitors and investigates the administration of these plans to ensure compliance with the requirements of ERISA. The agency has authority to enforce ERISA through voluntary compliance to resolve any violations of law or by bringing civil actions in federal courts.

Criminal prosecutions based on violations of ERISA are directed by the Government Regulations and Labor Section of the Justice Department's Criminal Division. (For further information on regulation of pension plans, see Pension Benefit Guaranty Corporation, *p. 361.*)

■ KEY PERSONNEL

Assistant Secretary
Ann L. Combs .... (202) 693-8300
Fax .... (202) 219–5526

Deputy Assistant Secretary for Policy
Paul Zurawski .... (202) 693–8300

Deputy Assistant Secretary for Program Operations
Alan Lebowitz .... (202) 693–8315

Senior Policy Adviser
Morton Klevan .... (202) 693–8315

Chief Accountant
Ian Dingwall .... (202) 693–8361

Congressional Liaison (Labor Dept.)
Kristine Iverson .... (202) 693-4600

Enforcement
Virginia Smith .... (202) 693–8440

Exemption Determinations
Ivan Strasfeld .... (202) 693–8542

Information Management
John P. Helms .... (202) 693–8602

Participant Assistance
Sharon S. Watson .... (202) 693–8631

Policy and Research Analysis
Joseph Piacentini...................... (202) 693–8427
Regulations and Interpretations
Robert J. Doyle........................ (202) 693–8502
Health Plan Standards and Compliance Assistance
Daniel Maguire........................ (202) 693–8318

▓ INFORMATION SOURCES

Internet

Agency Web site: http://www.dol.gov/ebsa. Information about EBSA includes publications, media releases, and regulations the agency enforces.

Telephone Contacts

Personnel Locator........................ (202) 693–5000

Information and Publications

KEY OFFICES

EBSA Program Information

200 Constitution Ave. N.W., Room N5656
Washington, DC 20210
(202) 693–8664

Provides general information about the agency.

Freedom of Information

200 Constitution Ave. N.W., Room N5625
Washington, DC 20210
(202) 693–8630
Sharon Watson, FOI officer

PUBLICATIONS

EBSA Public Affairs distributes a list of available publications and studies of the agency. EBSA publications are available through the brochure request line at (800) 444–EBSA or on the agency Web site at www.dol.gov/ebsa.

EBSA titles include:
How to File a Claim for Your Benefits
Protect Your Pension—A Quick Reference Guide
Top 10 Ways to Beat the Clock and Save for Retirement
What You Should Know About Your Pension Rights
Simple Retirement Solutions for Small Business
How to Obtain Employee Benefit Documents from the Labor Department
Health Benefits Under COBRA
Q&A for Dislocated Workers

DATA AND STATISTICS

Contact Policy and Research.
200 Constitution Ave. N.W., #N5718
Washington, DC 20210
(202) 693–8410

Reference Resources

LIBRARIES

Wirtz Labor Library

200 Constitution Ave. N.W., Room N2445
Washington, DC 20210
(202) 693–6600
Open to the public.
Hours: 8:15 a.m. to 4:45 p.m., M–F

EBSA Public Disclosure Room

200 Constitution Ave. N.W., Room N1513
Washington, DC 20210
(202) 693–8673
Hours: 8:15 a.m. to 4:45 p.m., M–F

Maintains annual financial reports and descriptions of plan requirements for pension and welfare plans required by ERISA for public inspection. The agency sends copies of specific reports to individuals upon phone request. A nominal fee is charged for copying.

RULES AND REGULATIONS

EBSA rules and regulations are published in the *Code of Federal Regulations,* Title 29, various parts. Proposed rules, new rules, and updates to the *Code of Federal Regulations* are published in the daily *Federal Register. (See appendix for information on how to obtain and use these publications.)*

▓ LEGISLATION

The EBSA is responsible for the following statutes:

Employee Retirement Income Security Act of 1974 (88 Stat. 829, 29 U.S.C. 1001). Signed by the president Sept. 2, 1974. Empowered the agency to enforce provisions regulating individuals who operate pension funds.

Multi-Employer Pension Plan Amendments of 1980 (94 Stat. 1208, 29 U.S.C. 1001). Signed by the president Sept. 26, 1980. Amended ERISA to strengthen the funding requirements for multi-employer pension plans.

Retirement Equity Act of 1984 (98 Stat. 1426, 29 U.S.C. 1001). Signed by the president Aug. 23, 1984. Provided for greater equity in private pension plans for workers and their spouses and dependents.

Consolidated Omnibus Budget Reconciliation Act of 1985 (COBRA) (29 U.S.C. 1162). Signed by the president April 1986. Guaranteed continuation of health care coverage for eighteen months for workers who lose their jobs (twenty-nine months for disabled workers), and for the worker's spouse and dependent children if they are covered when employment is terminated.

Single-Employer Pension Plan Amendments of 1986 (100 Stat. 82, 29 U.S.C. 1001). Signed by the president April 7, 1986. Prevented companies from terminating their pension plans arbitrarily.

Pension Protection Act of 1987 (101 Stat. 1330–1333, 26 U.S.C. note 1). Signed by the president Dec. 22, 1987. Barred employers from the act of deducting contributions to "overfunded" pension funds, which are defined as funds with assets exceeding 150 percent of current liability.

Health Insurance Portability and Accountability Act of 1996 (HIPAA) (110 Stat. 1936, 42 U.S.C. 201 note). Signed by the president Aug. 21, 1996. Limited the circumstances in which employers can use preexisting conditions to deny new workers health care benefits. Extended COBRA coverage to workers who become disabled within the first sixty days of coverage and to children born to or adopted by workers during the period of coverage.

Child Support Performance and Incentive Act of 1998 (112 Stat. 645, 42 U.S.C. 1305 note). Signed by the president July 16, 1998. Directed the enforcement of a child support order for health care coverage. Prescribed enforcement guidelines for enrollment of the child in the health care coverage of the noncustodial parent's employer.

◼ REGIONAL OFFICES

ATLANTA
(AL, FL, GA, MS, NC, PR, SC, TN)
61 Forsyth St. S.W., #7B54
Atlanta, GA 30303
(404) 562–2156
Howard Marsh, regional director

BOSTON
(northern CT, MA, ME, NH, central and western NY, RI, VT)
JFK Bldg., #575
Boston, MA 02203
(617) 565–9600
James Benages, regional director

CHICAGO
(northern IL, northern IN, WI)
200 W. Adams St., #1600
Chicago, IL 60606
(312) 353–0900
Kenneth Bazar, regional director

CINCINNATI
(southern IN, KY, MI, OH)
1885 Dixie Hwy., #210
Fort Wright, KY 41011–2664
(859) 578–4680
Joseph Menez, regional director

DALLAS
(AR, LA, NM, OK, TX)
525 Griffin St., #900
Dallas, TX 75202–5025
(214) 767–6831
Steve Eichen, regional director

KANSAS CITY
(CO, IA, southern IL, KS, MN, MO, MT, ND, NE, SD, WY)
1100 Main St., #1200
Kansas City, MO 64105–2112
(816) 426–5131
Gregory Egan, regional director

LOS ANGELES
(AS, AZ, southern CA, GU, HI)
1055 E. Colorado Blvd., #200
Pasadena, CA 91101–2341
(626) 229–1000
Billy Beaver, regional director

NEW YORK

(southern CT, northern NJ, eastern NY)
33 Whitehead St., 12th Floor, #1200
New York, NY 10004
(212) 607–8600
Frank Clisham, regional director

PHILADELPHIA

(DC, DE, MD, southern NJ, PA, VA, WV)
Curtis Center, #870W
170 S. Independence Mall West
Philadelphia, PA 19106–3317
(215) 861–5300
Mabel Capolongo, regional director

SAN FRANCISCO

(AK, northern CA, ID, NV, OR, UT, WA)
71 Stevenson St., #915
P.O. Box 190250
San Francisco, CA 94119–0250
(415) 975–4600
Bette Briggs, regional director

Employment Standards Administration

200 Constitution Ave. N.W., Washington, DC 20210
Internet: http://www.dol.gov/esa

The Employment Standards Administration (ESA) is an agency within the Labor Department with regulatory authority over employment standards programs. The assistant secretary of labor for employment standards is the administrator of the ESA. Responsibilities are carried out by its main offices: the Office of Federal Contract Compliance Programs; the Office of Workers' Compensation Programs; the Wage and Hour Division; and the Office of Labor-Management Standards, which before 1996 was the Office of the American Workplace. ESA also includes support offices that handle administrative management, program development, and accountability functions.

The ESA has the regulatory authority to correct a wide range of unfair employment practices. It enforces laws and regulations that require fair wages and working conditions for all workers, compensation to certain workers who are injured on their jobs, equal employment opportunity on the part of all federal contractors and subcontractors, and extensive reporting on the activities of labor unions.

Office of Federal Contract Compliance Programs (OFCCP). The OFCCP administers Executive Order 11246, section 503 of the Rehabilitation Act of 1973, and section 402 of the Vietnam-Era Veterans Readjustment Assistance Act of 1974.

Executive Order 11246 prohibits discrimination by federal contractors and subcontractors against employees on the basis of race, color, religion, national origin, and sex. It also directs federal contractors and subcontractors to take affirmative action to hire and promote groups that have been targets of previous discrimination.

Executive Order 11246, as amended, applies to employers in any of the following groups: contractors or subcontractors that provide the federal government with more than $10,000 worth of supplies, services, or labor; contrac-

tors or subcontractors that have had more than $10,000 worth of government contracts in any twelve-month period; any firm that serves as an issuing or paying agent of U.S. savings bonds and notes; and any firm that serves as a depository of federal funds in any amount.

In addition, the order applies to all contractors and subcontractors that hold federally assisted contracts in excess of $10,000 and to a construction contractor's or subcontractor's construction employees who are engaged in on-site construction, including those construction employees who work on a nonfederal or nonfederally assisted construction site.

Contractors with fifty or more employees who also have a contract of $50,000 or more must develop a written affirmative action program. Contractors with contracts or subcontracts of $2,500 or more are covered by rules for persons with disabilities, and those with contracts of $10,000 or more are covered by rules for veterans.

The office also administers programs under section 503 of the Rehabilitation Act of 1973, as amended, that requires federal contractors and subcontractors to take affirmative action to hire and promote qualified persons with disabilities, Vietnam-era veterans, and disabled veterans.

The Americans with Disabilities Act (ADA) prohibits discrimination against persons with disabilities. The office enforces provisions under ADA with regard to government contractors.

Enforcement actions can result from either compliance reviews or complaints. Violations of federal compliance standards can result in partial or total cancellation or suspension of contracts, and violators may be declared ineligible for further government contract work. The agency may order remedies such as reimbursement of back pay or imposition of retroactive seniority.

Complaints against employers should be filed with the OFCCP regional offices. The regional offices also offer technical assistance to government contractors and subcontractors to help them comply with employment laws.

Office of Labor-Management Standards (OLMS). The OLMS safeguards the financial integrity and internal democracy of labor unions by working cooperatively with unions in the areas of administration and regulation.

The OLMS administers the Labor-Management Reporting and Disclosure Act (LMRDA) of 1959, which requires labor organizations to file copies of their constitutions, bylaws, and annual financial reports. All of these materials are available for public inspection.

Unions are required to follow certain rules in election of union officers, administration of labor union trusteeships, protection of the rights of union members, and handling of union funds. In addition, employers must report any expenditures intended to interfere with or restrain the right of employees to form a union or bargain collectively.

Employers must file reports if they arrange with labor relations consultants to obtain certain information about employees' union activities. Labor relations consultants must file reports if they agree to perform these services for employers.

The OLMS attempts, through technical assistance, to encourage compliance with the act. The office can, however, bring suit in U.S. District Court to force compliance.

The OLMS also enforces portions of the Civil Service Reform Act of 1978 and the Foreign Service Act of 1980, which established standards of conduct for federal employee unions similar to those established for public unions by the Labor-Management Reporting and Disclosure Act. Unions representing U.S. Postal Service employees became subject to the LMRDA with the passage of the Postal Reorganization Act of 1970. Mass transit employees are protected as well under the Urban Mass Transportation Act of 1964 and under section 5333(b) of Title 49 U.S. Code.

Formerly part of the Office of the American Workplace, the OLMS retains its network of regional offices.

Office of Workers' Compensation Programs (OWCP). The OWCP administers claims under three major disability programs, each aimed at mitigating—through income replacement and medical benefit payments—the financial burden on certain workers, their dependents, or survivors resulting from work-related injuries, diseases, or deaths.

These three programs are: the Federal Employees' Compensation Act, which provides benefits to civilian employees of the federal government and to other designated groups; the Longshore and Harbor Workers' Compensation Act of 1927, which provides similar protection to private sector workers engaged in certain maritime industries; and the Black Lung Benefits Reform Act of 1977, which provides benefits to the nation's coal miners.

Wage and Hour Division (WHD). The WHD administers the Fair Labor Standards Act (FLSA) and a number of other labor standards statutes. The FLSA is the federal law of most general application concerning wages and hours of work. It requires that all covered and nonexempt employees be paid not less than $5.15 an hour (as of Sept. 1, 1997) and not less than one-and-a-half times their regular rates of pay for all hours worked in excess of forty in a work week.

The child labor provisions of the FLSA set a basic sixteen-year minimum age for employment; however, persons fourteen and fifteen years of age may be employed outside school hours in a variety of nonmanufacturing and nonhazardous occupations. Minors under age fourteen may engage only in employment that is exempt from the FLSA or that is not covered by its child labor provisions.

The FLSA requires that employers keep records on all employees and make the records available upon request. Although the FLSA does not specify the form of these records, it does require that the records contain certain types of information identifying the employee and listing hours worked and wages paid. Records must be kept for three years.

The division receives complaints from workers across the country; compliance officers in regional and local offices investigate and, if necessary, correct the situation.

The division also prohibits the following practices: the withholding of more than a limited amount of money from a worker's wages to settle a debt (garnishment) and the firing of an employee because earnings have been garnished for only one debt; the payment by federal contractors of less than the prevailing wage rates and fringe benefits for workers on government construction projects or contracts for goods and services; and the exploitation of migrant workers. Farm labor contractors are required to register with the ESA; contractors, their employees, and other employers of migrant workers must observe certain rules in the employment of migrant workers.

■ KEY PERSONNEL

Assistant Secretary
Victoria A. Lipnic .... (202) 693-0200
Fax .... (202) 693-0218

Deputy Assistant Secretary
Dixon M. Wilson .... (202) 693-0200

Equal Employment Opportunity
Kate Dorrell .... (202) 693-0024

Management, Administration, and Planning
Anne Baird-Bridges .... (202) 693-0423

Federal Contract Compliance Programs
Charles E. James Sr. .... (202) 693-0101
Fax .... (202) 693-1304
Policy, Planning, and Program Development
James I. Melvin .... (202) 693-1135
Program Operations
Harold Busch .... (202) 693-1072
Management and Administrative Programs
Michelle P. Ouellet .... (202) 693-0101
Labor-Management Standards
Don Todd .... (202) 693-0123
Administrative Management and Technology
Ed Hilz .... (202) 693-0125
Enforcement
Lary Yud .... (202) 693-1239
Interpretations and Standards
Kay H. Oshel .... (202) 693-0123
Liaison, Compliance Assistance, and Training
Joseph O. Fuchs (acting) .... (202) 693–0123
Statutory Programs
Kelley Andrews .... (202) 693-1182
Wage and Hour Division
Tammy McCutchen .... (202) 693-0051
Enforcement Policy
Michael Ginley .... (202) 693-0745
Planning and Analysis
Nancy Flynn .... (202) 693-0551
Wage Determination
William Gross .... (202) 693-0062
Workers' Compensation Programs
Shelby Hallmark .... (202) 693-0031
Fax .... (202) 693-1378
Coal Mine Workers' Compensation
James DeMarce .... (202) 693-0046
Federal Employees' Compensation
Deborah Sanford .... (202) 693-0040
Longshore and Harbor Workers' Compensation
Michael Niss .... (202) 693-0038
Planning, Policy, and Standards
Cecily Rayburn .... (202) 693-0032
Energy Employees' Occupational Illness Compensation
Peter Turcic .... (202) 693-0081

▪ INFORMATION SOURCES

Internet
Agency Web site: http://www.dol.gov/esa. Features information about ESA's offices and programs, press releases, and regulatory documents.

Telephone Contacts
Personnel Locator .... (202) 693-3444

Information and Publications

KEY OFFICES

ESA Public Affairs
200 Constitution Ave. N.W., Room S3325
Washington, DC 20210
(202) 693–0023
Vacant, director

Responds to general consumer questions and refers technical questions to the appropriate office within the administration. Also issues news releases on actions taken by ESA offices. Publishes and distributes most ESA publications and answers queries from the news media. Maintains a mailing list for news releases.

Freedom of Information
ESA Management, Administration, and Planning
200 Constitution Ave. N.W., Room S30-13C
Washington, DC 20210
(202) 693–0006
Dorothy Chester, FOI/Privacy Act Coordinator

Forwards FOI requests to the staff contact for each unit of the ESA.

Complaints
Allegations of discrimination by federal contractors and questions concerning employment standards laws, minimum wages, and legal limits on hours worked should be directed to the nearest ESA regional office (*addresses, p. 617*).

PUBLICATIONS
ESA publications are listed in *Publications of the U.S. Department of Labor,* available free from DOL Information and Public Affairs: (202) 693-4650. Requests for copies of ESA publications should be directed to ESA Public Affairs. Current ESA titles include:
Black Lung Benefits
Compliance Guide to the Family and Medical Leave Act
EEO and Affirmative Action Guidelines for Federal Contractors
Employee Polygraph Protection Act of 1988
Employment of Workers with Disabilities in Supported Work Programs
Employment Relationship Under the Fair Labor Standards Act

FarmWorkers and the Federal Wage and Hour Law
Federal Minimum Wage and Overtime Pay Standards
Major Programs of the Employment Standards Administration
Wage Garnishment Law
When Injured at Work
Workers' Compensation for Federal Employees

DATA AND STATISTICS

The best sources of data and statistics on the ESA are the agency's reports to Congress on the laws it administers. Copies may be requested through ESA Public Affairs.

The Office of Federal Contract Compliance Programs maintains data that measure compliance of federal contractors with the Labor Department's guidelines on equal employment opportunity. Summaries of findings are available through a freedom of information request.

Federal Procurement Data Center

7th and D Sts. S.W., #5652
Washington, DC 20407
(202) 401–1529

Within the General Services Administration. Compiles information on all companies doing business with the government. Collects procurement data from all federal executive agencies that use appropriated money. Data include type of business, material purchased, name of contractor, purchase cost, and method of contracting. The center also compiles detailed data on all government procurement transactions over $25,000 and aggregate data for all government procurement transactions under $25,000.

Quarterly standard reports containing aggregate figures are available to the public at no cost. These reports include the number of transactions involving union contracts, types of contracts, and whether or not transactions included contract bidding. Special reports may be requested from the center for a fee.

Reference Resources

LIBRARIES

Labor Department

200 Constitution Ave. N.W., Room N2445
Washington, DC 20210
(202) 219–6992
Dorothy Weed, director
Open to the public
Hours: 8:15 a.m. to 4:45 p.m.

Labor Financial Reports Disclosure Room

200 Constitution Ave. N.W., Room N5610
Washington, DC 20210
(202) 693-0125
Emma Weaver, disclosure officer
Hours: 8:30 a.m. to 4:00 p.m.

Labor organizations' reports, constitutions, and bylaws required by the LMRDA may be inspected and copied. OLMS also will send copies of specific reports to individuals upon phone request; a nominal fee is charged for this service.

DOCKETS

ESA maintains dockets for all rulemakings and other administrative proceedings. However, there is no central ESA office where docket materials may be examined and copied. During an administrative proceeding, notices in the *Federal Register* will inform interested parties where the docket is maintained and which unit within the agency is responsible for the administrative proceeding.

RULES AND REGULATIONS

ESA rules and regulations, including those for OLMS, are published in the *Code of Federal Regulations* under various parts of Titles 20, 29, and 41. Proposed rules, new final rules, and updates to the *Code of Federal Regulations* are published in the daily *Federal Register*. *(See appendix for information on how to obtain and use these publications.)*

The ESA has a compliance manual for use by staff members in the local offices located across the country. Copies of the manual are available to contractors and other interested parties. Contact ESA Public Affairs for details.

■ LEGISLATION

The ESA has administrative responsibilities over the following legislation:

FEDERAL CONTRACT COMPLIANCE

Statutes administered by the OFCCP include:

Executive Order 11246, issued by the president Sept. 28, 1965. The order instructed government agencies to guarantee that contractors and subcontractors doing government work did not discriminate against employees because of race, color, religion, or national origin; it was amended in 1967 to prohibit sex discrimination by Executive Order 11375.

Rehabilitation Act of 1973, Section 503 (87 Stat. 393, 29 U.S.C. 793). Signed by the president Sept. 26, 1973.

Required that federal contractors take affirmative action to hire and promote persons with disabilities.

Vietnam-Era Veterans Readjustment Assistance Act of 1974, Section 402 (88 Stat. 1593, 38 U.S.C. 2012). Signed by the president Dec. 3, 1974. Assured quality treatment for Vietnam veterans and disabled veterans of all wars.

Immigration Reform and Control Act of 1986 (100 Stat. 3359, 8 U.S.C. 1101 note). Signed by the president Nov. 6, 1986. Title I amended the Immigration and Nationality Act and the Migrant and Seasonal Agricultural Worker Protection Act to make it unlawful for a person or other entity to knowingly hire, recruit, or refer for a fee any alien workers who are unauthorized to work in the United States and those who do not possess proper working permits.

Americans with Disabilities Act of 1990 (104 Stat. 327, 42 U.S.C. 12101 note). Signed by the president July 26, 1990. Title I prohibited discrimination by an employer against any qualified individual with a disability in the job application procedures, hiring or discharge, compensation, advancement, training, and other terms, conditions, and privileges of employment.

Family and Medical Leave Act of 1993 (107 Stat. 6, 29 U.S.C. 2601 note). Signed by the president Feb. 5, 1993. Established certain requirements for unpaid family and medical leave for permanent employees.

LABOR-MANAGEMENT STANDARDS

Statutes administered by the OLMS include:

Labor-Management Reporting and Disclosure Act of 1959 (73 Stat. 524, 29 U.S.C. 431). Signed by the president Sept. 14, 1959. Required labor organizations to file annual reports and copies of their constitutions and bylaws with the Labor-Management Services Administration.

Civil Service Reform Act of 1978 (92 Stat. 1111, 5 U.S.C. 1101 note). Signed by the president Oct. 31, 1978. Provided for the reorganization of the Civil Service Commission. Title VII governs labor-management relations in the federal government. This title established the Federal Labor Management Relations Authority to take over the responsibilities given to the Federal Labor Relations Council and the assistant secretary of labor for labor-management relations under Executive Order 11491, issued in October 1969.

Foreign Service Act of 1980 (94 Stat. 2071, 22 U.S.C. 3901 note). Signed by the president Oct. 17, 1980. Created a Foreign Service Labor Relations Board to hear employee disputes and grievances. Established a Senior Foreign Service and provided for pensions and survivors benefits for spouses of former foreign service employees.

Transportation Equity Act for the 21st Century (TEA-21) (112 Stat. 107, 23 U.S.C. 101 note). Signed by the president June 9, 1998. Provided for three new transportation programs that require employee protections under section 5333(b) of Title 49 U.S. Code. These are the Job Access and Reverse Commute Program (section 3037), the Over-the-Road Bus Accessibility Program (section 3038), and the State Infrastructure Bank Program (section 1511).

WAGE AND HOUR

Statutes administered by the WHD include:

Davis-Bacon Act (46 Stat. 1949, 40 U.S.C. 276a). Signed by the president March 3, 1931. Required payment of prevailing wages to employees of contractors or subcontractors working on government construction projects.

Fair Labor Standards Act (52 Stat. 1060, 29 U.S.C. 201). Signed by the president June 25, 1938. Established standards for a minimum wage, overtime pay, and child labor.

Service Contract Act (79 Stat. 1034, 41 U.S.C. 351). Signed by the president Oct. 22, 1965. Required that contractors and subcontractors working for the government under a service contract (services include jobs like security services, maintenance, laundry) pay prevailing minimum wages to their employees.

Consumer Credit Protection Act of 1968 (82 Stat. 146, 15 U.S.C. 1601). Signed by the president May 29, 1968. Set a limit on the amount a creditor may have taken out of a worker's wages to pay off a debt (garnishment); prohibited the firing of a worker because earnings have been garnished for a single debt.

Migrant and Seasonal Agricultural Worker Protection Act (96 Stat. 2583, 29 U.S.C. 1801 note). Signed by the president Jan. 14, 1983. Repealed the **Farm Labor Contractor Registration Act of 1963** (78 Stat. 920, 7 U.S.C. 2401) to distinguish between migrant crew leaders and agricultural employers. The act continued basic federal workers' protections regardless of the employer's status. The law distinguished between migrant and seasonal agricultural workers and provided exemptions for labor unions and small and family businesses.

Immigration Reform and Control Act of 1986 (100 Stat. 3359, 8 U.S.C. 1101 note). Signed by the president Nov. 6, 1986. Allowed the imposition of employer sanctions. Provided for the legalization of some aliens residing illegally in the United States.

Employee Polygraph Protection Act of 1988 (102 Stat. 646, 29 U.S.C. 2001 note). Signed by the president June 27, 1988. Prevented most employers engaged in interstate commerce from using lie detector tests either for pre-employment screening or during the course of employment. Federal, state, and local governments as well as employers in certain sensitive industries, such as the manufacture of controlled substances, were excluded from the requirements.

Fair Labor Standards Amendments of 1989 (103 Stat. 938, 29 U.S.C. 201 note). Signed by the president Nov. 17, 1989. Increased the minimum wage and raised the annual volume test for enterprises covered under the Fair Labor Standards Act to $500,000.

Family and Medical Leave Act of 1993 (107 Stat. 6, 29 U.S.C. 2601 note). Signed by the president Feb. 5, 1993. Established 12 weeks of unpaid, job-protected leave for all eligible employees for specified family and medical reasons.

Minimum Wage Increase Act of 1996 (110 Stat. 1928, 29 U.S.C. 201 note). Increased the minimum wage from $4.25 an hour to $5.15 an hour.

WORKERS' COMPENSATION

Statutes administered by the OWCP include:

Federal Employees' Compensation Act (39 Stat. 742, 5 U.S.C. 8101). Signed by the president Sept. 7, 1916. Original workers' compensation bill required that federal employees receive a certain level of medical benefits and other compensation.

Longshore and Harbor Workers' Compensation Act of 1927 (44 Stat. 1424, 33 U.S.C. 901). Signed by the president March 4, 1927. Provided benefits for workers disabled by injuries suffered on the navigable waters of the United States or adjacent areas used for loading, unloading, repairing, or building vessels. Amended in 1972 and 1984.

Black Lung Benefits Reform Act of 1977 (92 Stat. 95, 30 U.S.C. 801 note). Signed by the president March 1, 1978. Amended by the **Black Lung Benefits Revenue Act of 1981** (95 Stat. 1635, 26 U.S.C. 1 note) and the **Black Lung Benefits Amendments of 1981** (95 Stat. 1643, 30 U.S.C. 801 note). Both signed by the president Dec. 29, 1981. The original act expanded and made permanent the government's temporary program to compensate coal miners disabled by pneumoconiosis (black lung disease). The 1981 amendments increased the taxes paid by coal mine operators to the Black Lung Disability Trust Fund to bring it to solvency; they established more stringent eligibility requirements to ensure that future benefits are awarded only to miners who suffer from black lung disease.

■ REGIONAL OFFICES

REGION 1
(CT, MA, ME, NH, RI, VT)
1 Congress St., 11th Floor
Boston, MA 02114–2023
Federal Contract Compliance Programs
(Serviced by Northeast Region)
Wage and Hour Division
(617) 565–2091
Corllis L. Sellers (acting), regional administrator

Workers' Compensation Programs
(617) 624–6677
Vacant, regional director
Dorothy L. Reed, director

REGION 2
(NJ, NY, PR, VI)
201 Varick St., #750
New York, NY 10014–4811
Federal Contract Compliance Programs
(Northeast Region)
(646) 264–3170
James R. Turner Jr., regional director
Wage and Hour Division
(212) 337–2006
Corllis L. Sellers, regional administrator
Workers' Compensation Programs
(646) 264–3100
Vacant, regional director

REGION 3
(DC, DE, MD, PA, VA, WV)
3535 Market St., #15210
Philadelphia, PA 19104–3309
Federal Contract Compliance Programs
(Mid-Atlantic Region)
(215) 861-5765
Joseph J. DuBray Jr., regional director
Wage and Hour Division
(215) 596–1185
Corllis L. Sellers, regional administrator
Workers' Compensation Programs
(215) 861–5402
R. David Lotz, regional director

REGION 4
(AL, FL, GA, KY, MS, NC, SC, TN)
1375 Peachtree St. N.E., #662
Atlanta, GA 30367–2302
Federal Contract Compliance Programs
(Southeast Region)
(404) 893–4545
Vacant, regional director
Wage and Hour Division
(404) 562–2202
Alfred Perry, regional administrator
Workers' Compensation Programs
214 N. Hogan St., #1026
Jacksonville, FL 32202
(904) 357–4750
Nancy Ricker, regional director

REGION 5

(IL, IN, MI, MN, OH, WI)
230 S. Dearborn St., 8th Floor
Chicago, IL 60604
Federal Contract Compliance Programs
(Midwest Region)
(312) 596–7010
Sandra S. Zeigler, regional director
Wage and Hour Division
(312) 596-7180
Timothy J. Reardon, regional administrator
Workers' Compensation Programs
(312) 596-7129
Nancy Jensen, regional director

REGION 6

(AR, CO, LA, NM, OK, TX, WY)
525 S. Griffin St., #800
Dallas, TX 75202–5007
Federal Contract Compliance Programs
(Southwest & Rocky Mountain Region)
(972) 850–2550
Fred Azua Jr., regional director
Wage and Hour Division
(214) 767–6895
M. Jose Villarreal Jr., regional administrator
Workers' Compensation Programs
(972) 850–2330
E. Martin Walker, regional director

REGION 7

(IA, KS, MO, NE)
1100 Main St.
Kansas City, MO 64105
Federal Contract Compliance Programs
(Serviced by Midwest Region)
Wage and Hour Division
(816) 426–5386
Timothy J. Reardon, regional administrator
Workers' Compensation Programs
(216) 357–5100
Nancy Jensen, regional director

REGION 8

(MT, ND, SD, UT)
1801 California St., #920
Denver, CO 80202–2614
Federal Contract Compliance Programs
(Serviced by Southwest & Rocky Mountain Region)
Wage and Hour Division
(Serviced by Region 6)
Workers' Compensation Programs
(972) 850–2411
E. Martin Walker, regional director

REGION 9

(AK, AZ, CA, GU, HI, ID, NV, OR, WA)
71 Stevenson St., #930
San Francisco, CA 94105
Federal Contract Compliance Programs
(Pacific Region)
(415) 848–6969
Woody Gilliland, regional director
Wage and Hour Division
(415) 975–4510
George Friday Jr., regional administrator
Workers' Compensation Programs
(415) 848–6859
Edward Bounds, regional director

Office of Labor-Management Standards

ATLANTIC REGION

(CT, DE, MA, ME, NH, NJ, NY, PA, RI, VT)
801 Arch St., #415
Philadelphia, PA 19107
(215) 597–4960
Eric Feldman, regional director

GREAT LAKES REGION

(IA, IL, KS, MI, MN, MO, ND, NE, SD, WI)
1100 Main St., #950
Kansas City, MO 64105
(816) 426–2547
Kamil Bishara, regional director

GULF COAST REGION

(AL, AR, FL, GA, LA, MS, OK, SC, TN, TX)
61 Forsyth St. S.W., #8B95
Atlanta, GA 30367
(404) 562–2083
Ronald Lehman, regional director

OHIO-POTOMAC REGION

(DC, IN, KY, MD, NC, OH, VA, WV)
1730 K St. N.W., #558
Washington, DC 20006
(202) 254–6510
Robert Merriner, regional director

PACIFIC REGION

(AK, AZ, CA, CO, HI, ID, MT, NM, NV, OR, UT, WA, WY)
71 Stevenson St., #725
San Francisco, CA 94105
(415) 975–4020
C. Russell Rock, regional director

Employment and Training Administration

200 Constitution Ave. N.W., Washington, DC 20210
Internet: http://www.doleta.gov

The Employment and Training Administration (ETA) is an agency within the Department of Labor under the jurisdiction of the assistant secretary of labor for employment and training. The ETA funds and regulates training and employment programs administered by state and local agencies and is responsible for the employment service and the unemployment insurance systems.

Following passage of the Personal Responsibility and Work Opportunity Reconciliation Act of 1996 (The Welfare Reform Act), greater emphasis was placed on welfare-to-work and job training. As a result of the act, welfare recipients have been required to move into the work force. The training programs administered by the Employment and Training Administration have seen increased enrollment and increased funding.

Apprenticeship. The administration establishes standards for apprenticeship programs and promotes the development of such programs in industry and among individuals. It provides technical assistance and advisory services to private industry in establishing and registering high-skill quality training programs, protects the welfare of apprentices, insures equal employment opportunity, and provides for credentialing of training programs and participants.

Employment and Training Programs. The ETA administers employment and training programs under the Job Training Partnership Act of 1982 (JTPA). The JTPA replaced the Comprehensive Employment and Training Act (CETA), which expired Sept. 30, 1982. Operating through block grant funding to the states, the JTPA entails the following:

- Private industry and state and local governments work together to plan, monitor, and assess programs.
- The majority of federal funds are allocated to job training programs, where the ETA concentrates its efforts.
- A dislocated worker program offers retraining and other services to displaced workers who are unlikely to return to their former jobs.
- More job training and placement responsibility is given to the U.S. Employment Service and affiliated offices.

Under the act, the ETA also administers national employment and training programs including Job Corps; programs for special targeted groups such as persons with disabilities and the economically disadvantaged; and programs for Native Americans and migrant workers. The ETA administers the Senior Community Service Employment Program for older workers, which is authorized by Title V of the Older Americans Act of 1965 (amended in 1967 and 1969).

Unemployment Insurance. The ETA monitors state unemployment insurance programs to ensure compliance with federal laws and regulations; assists states with administration of unemployment programs; and establishes formulas to determine the amount of money needed to administer state unemployment services.

United States Employment Service. Through its network of employment service officers, the U.S. Employment Service (USES) helps the jobless find employment, and employers find workers. State and local labor market information is provided to facilitate the working of the labor market. Veterans of the armed forces receive priority in job training and placement services.

The USES aids workers displaced by foreign trade competition and ensures that the admission of aliens into the nation's workplace does not hurt U.S. workers.

Since 1979, employers under the Targeted Jobs Tax Credit have received an income tax break by hiring workers the USES has certified as hard to employ, such as individuals with disabilities or economically disadvantaged individuals.

In most major metropolitan areas, a daily updated computerized job bank lists local job openings.

In local areas the USES encourages local job service employer committees to suggest ways local offices can serve local industry and the community more effectively.

Trade Act Programs. Trade Act programs are available to assist individuals who have become unemployed as a result of increased imports (Trade Adjustment Assistance). These programs include assistance to workers who are laid off or forced into part-time work as a result of a shift of U.S. production to Mexico or Canada or as a result of increased imports from these countries arising from the North American Free Trade Agreement (NAFTA). These workers include family farmers and farm workers who do not qualify for unemployment compensation. State governors and the Department of Labor are responsible for investigating worker layoffs to determine if trade adjustment assistance is applicable. The trade act program offers on-site services to workers threatened by layoffs, such as employment counseling, job placement, job training, income support, and relocation allowances.

▓ KEY PERSONNEL

Assistant Secretary
Emily S. DeRocco .... (202) 693-2700
Fax .... (202) 693-2725
Deputy Assistant Secretaries
Mason M. Bishop .... (202) 693–2700
David G. Dye .... (202) 693–2700
Thomas M. Dowd .... (202) 693–2700
Congressional Liaison (Labor Dept.)
Kristine Iverson .... (202) 693-4600
EEO Coordinator
Jan T. Austin .... (202) 693-3370
Financial and Administrative Management
Anna Goddard .... (202) 693-2800
Comptroller
Jack Rapport .... (202) 693-2742
Grants and Contract Management
Anna Goddard .... (202) 693-3300
Human Resources
Anna Goddard .... (202) 693-3922

Management and Information Services
Joseph Paslawski .... (202) 693–5741
Adult Services
Grace A. Kilbane .... (202) 693-3500
Fax .... (202) 693-5428
Apprenticeship and Training
Anthony Swoope .... (202) 693-3500
Trade Adjustment Assistance
Shirley M. Smith .... (202) 693-3560
Field Operations
David Lah .... (202) 693-3604
Policy and Research
Maria Flynn .... (202) 693-3700
Performance Management and Evaluation
Eric R. Johnson .... (202) 693-3650
Planning, Policy, and Legislation
Maria Flynn .... (202) 693-3640
Research and Demonstration
Maria Flynn .... (202) 693-3630
U.S. Employment Service
Anthony Dias .... (202) 693-3046
Workforce Investment
Grace A. Kilbane .... (202) 693-3031
Job Corps
Richard Trigg .... (202) 693-3000
National Programs
John R. Beverly III. .... (202) 693-3840
Workforce Securities
Cheryl Atkinson .... (202) 693-3029
Fax .... (202) 693-3229
Fiscal and Actuarial Services
Ronald Wilus .... (202) 693–2930
Legislation
Jerry Hildebrand .... (202) 693–3028
Program Development and Implementation and Unemployment Insurance
Betty Castillo .... (202) 693-3032
Performance and Management
Darlyne W. Bryant .... (202) 693–2995

▓ INFORMATION SOURCES

Internet
Agency Web site: http://www.doleta.gov. Features general information about the ETA and specific information about ETA programs.

Telephone Contacts
DOL Employee Locator (Toll-free) .... (866) 487–2365

Information and Publications

KEY OFFICES

ETA Office of Public Affairs

200 Constitution Ave. N.W., #N4665
Washington, DC 20210
(202) 693–3984
Lorette Post, director

Provides general information, answers or refers questions, and issues news releases.

ETA Office of Trade Adjustment Assistance

200 Constitution Ave. N.W., Room C-5311
Washington, DC 20210
(202) 693–3577
Ed Tomchick, director

Provides information on the NAFTA Transitional Adjustment Assistance Program.

Freedom of Information

200 Constitution Ave., N.W., #N4471
Washington, DC 20210
(202) 693-2770
Patsy Files, FOI coordinator

DATA AND STATISTICS

The ETA publishes several reports that contain data and statistical materials; all are available from the GPO *(see Publications)*. Reports include:

Area Trends in Employment and Unemployment
Training and Employment Report of the Secretary of Labor

Each state and local employment agency gathers and distributes information on employment and unemployment within its area.

Reference Resources

LIBRARY

Labor Department

200 Constitution Ave. N.W., Room N2445
Washington, DC 20210
(202) 693–6600
Linda K. Parker, labor librarian and C.O.T.R.
Open to the public.
Hours: 8:15 a.m. to 4:45 p.m.

DOCKETS

Each main office within the ETA keeps copies of dockets containing materials and information related to rulemakings and other administrative proceedings for which it is responsible.

RULES AND REGULATIONS

ETA rules and regulations are published in the *Code of Federal Regulations,* Title 20, parts 601–699, and Title 29, various parts. Proposed rules, new final rules, and updates to the *Code of Federal Regulations* are published in the daily *Federal Register. (See appendix for information on how to obtain and use these publications.)*

■ LEGISLATION

Statutes administered by the ETA include:

Wagner-Peyser Act (48 Stat. 113, 29 U.S.C. 49). Signed by the president June 3, 1933. Established a national system of ETA employment offices and authorized the secretary of labor to establish the system's operating standards.

Social Security Act (49 Stat. 620, 42 U.S.C. 301). Signed by the president Aug. 14, 1935. Certified states that had unemployment compensation laws approved under the Federal Unemployment Tax Act to receive payments from the Treasury Department.

Federal Unemployment Tax Act (68A Stat. 439, 26 U.S.C. 23). Signed by the president Aug. 16, 1954. Established a state system providing unemployment compensation to eligible individuals. The ETA would ensure state compliance with national program standards.

Trade Act of 1974 (88 Stat. 1978, 19 U.S.C. 2101). Signed by the president Jan. 3, 1975. Authorized the ETA to certify for benefit payments workers unemployed because of U.S. trade agreements.

Job Training Partnership Act (JTPA) (96 Stat. 1322, 29 U.S.C. 1501). Signed by the president Oct. 13, 1982. Authorized the ETA to provide job training and other employment services to economically disadvantaged and unskilled youths and adults and to dislocated workers. The JTPA replaced the Comprehensive Employment and Training Act, which expired Sept. 30, 1982.

Economic Dislocation and Worker Adjustment Assistance Act (102 Stat. 1524, 29 U.S.C. 1501 note). Signed by the president Aug. 23, 1988. Replaced Title III of the **Job Training Partnership Act** and created a new training program for workers who lost their jobs because of economic factors, including plant closings and mass layoffs, and for divorced or widowed displaced homemakers with no salable job skills.

Indian Employment, Training, and Related Services Demonstration Act of 1992 (25 U.S.C. 3401). Signed by the president Oct. 23, 1992. Authorized tribal governments to integrate all federally funded employment, training, and related services programs into a single, comprehensive program.

North American Free Trade Agreement Implementation Act (107 Stat. 2057, 19 U.S.C. 3301 note). Signed by the president Dec. 8, 1993. Title V of this act established a Transitional Adjustment Assistance program for workers in companies affected by imports from Canada or Mexico or by shifts of U.S. production to those countries because of NAFTA.

Workforce Investment Act of 1998 (112 Stat. 936, 20 U.S.C. 9201 note). Signed by the president Aug. 7, 1998. Established federal aid programs for vocational education, adult education, and job training at state and local levels. Also established the Twenty-First Century Workforce Commission to study information technology in the U.S. workforce.

▨ REGIONAL OFFICES

REGION 1 - BOSTON
JFK Federal Bldg., #E-350
Boston, MA 02203
(617) 788–0170
Joseph Stoltz, regional administrator

REGION 1 - NEW YORK
201 Varick St., #755
New York, NY 10014
(212) 337–2139
Patrick Rowe (acting), regional administrator

REGION 2 - PHILADELPHIA
The Curtis Center
170 South Independence Mall West, #825-East
Philadelphia, PA 19106-3315
(215) 861–5205
Lenita Jacobs-Simmons, regional administrator

REGION 3 - ATLANTA
Atlanta Federal Center
61 Forsyth St. S.W., #6M12
Atlanta, GA 30303
(404) 562–2092
Helen Parker, regional administrator

REGION 4 - DALLAS/DENVER
Federal Building, #317
525 Griffin St.
Dallas, TX 75202
(214) 767–8263
Joseph C. Juarez, regional administrator

REGION 5 - CHICAGO/KANSAS CITY
230 South Dearborn St., #628
Chicago, IL 60604
(312) 596–5400
Byron Zuidema, regional administrator

REGION 6 - SAN FRANCISCO/SEATTLE
71 Stevenson St., #830
San Francisco, CA 94119–3767
(415) 975–4610
Armando Quiroz, regional administrator

Mine Safety and Health Administration

4015 Wilson Blvd., Arlington, VA 22203
Internet: http://www.msha.gov

In 1910, following a decade in which the number of coal mine fatalities exceeded 2,000 annually, Congress established the Bureau of Mines as a new agency in the Interior Department. The bureau was charged with the responsibility to conduct research and to reduce accidents in the coal mining industry, but was given no inspection authority until 1941, when Congress empowered federal inspectors to enter mines. In 1947 Congress authorized the formulation of the first code of federal regulations for mine safety. The Federal Coal Mine Safety Act of 1952 provided for annual inspections in certain underground coal mines, and gave the bureau limited enforcement authority, including power to issue violation notices and imminent danger withdrawal orders. The last incarnation under the Interior Department was the Mining Enforcement and Safety Administration.

The Federal Mine Safety and Health Amendments Act of 1977 (the Mine Act) established the Mine Safety and Health Administration (MSHA) as an agency within the Department of Labor under the jurisdiction of the assistant secretary of labor for mine safety and health.

The MSHA develops and promulgates mandatory safety and health standards, ensures compliance with such standards, proposes penalties for violating standards, investigates accidents, and cooperates with the states in developing mine safety and health programs.

MSHA technical support engineers, based at three U.S. sites, investigate and survey conditions that affect mine workers' health and safety, such as ventilation, radiation, dust, noise, industrial hygiene, ground support, and mine wastes. The agency also operates the National Mine Health and Safety Academy in Beckley, W.Va., to train its inspectors and technical support personnel as well as profession-als from the mining industry. MSHA also works with the National Institute of Occupational Safety and Health on various safety and health research projects.

The Mine Act provides that MSHA inspectors shall inspect each surface mine at least twice a year and each underground mine at least four times a year (seasonal or intermittent operations are inspected less frequently) to determine whether an imminent danger exists and whether there is compliance with health and safety standards or with any citation, order, or decision issued under the Mine Act. The Mine Act provides for criminal sanctions against mine operators who willfully violate safety and health standards. MSHA initially investigates possible willful violations; if evidence of such a violation is found, the agency turns its findings over to the Justice Department for prosecution.

Before any citation or order is assessed, the operator or miners' representative can confer with an MSHA supervisor about any disagreement with the inspector's findings. If the disagreement cannot be resolved on this level, the operator is entitled to a hearing before an administrative law judge with the Federal Mine Safety and Health Review Commission. An operator or miners' representative who disagrees with any other enforcement action by MSHA also is entitled to a hearing. The administrative law judge's decision can be appealed to the commissioners and thereafter to the U.S. Court of Appeals.

All MSHA activities are aimed at preventing and reducing mine accidents and occupational diseases. While health and safety standards apply to all types of mining, coal mining and metal and nonmetal mining are administered separately. Several specific MSHA programs are described under Data and Statistics, below.

■ KEY PERSONNEL

Assistant Secretary
David D. Lauriski...................... (202) 693–9414
Fax..................................... (202) 693–9401

Deputy Assistant Secretary for Operations
John R. Correll .... (202) 693–9414

Deputy Assistant Secretary for Policy
John R. Caylor.......................... (202) 693–9414

Congressional and Legislative Affairs
Regina Flahie .... (202) 693–9434

Diversity Outreach and Employee Safety
Michael Thompson .... (202) 693–9880

Administration and Management
David Meyer........................... (202) 693–9800

Budget and Finance
Thomas Charboneau .... (202) 693–9810

Human Resources
Joe Stormer............................ (202) 693–9855

Management Services
Melissa Stoehr .... (202) 693–9825

Coal Mine Safety and Health
Ray McKinney.......................... (202) 693–9501

Health
Melinda Pon .... (202) 693–9510

Safety
Erik Sherer............................. (202) 693–9528

Educational Policy and Development
Jeffrey Duncan......................... (202) 693–9570

Policy and Program Coordination
Douglas Altizer Jr...................... (202) 693–9570

Metal and Nonmetal Mine Safety and Health
Robert Friend.......................... (202) 693–9600

Health
Carol Jones .... (202) 693–9630

Safety
Thomas Loyd........................... (202) 693–9640

Technical Support
Mark E. Skiles .... (202) 693–9470

Standards, Regulations, and Variances
Marvin Nichols........................ (202) 693–9440

Assessments
Stephen Webber........................ (202) 693–9700

Policy and Systems
A. Keith Watson .... (202) 693–9700

Technical Compliance and Investigations
Carolyn James.......................... (202) 693–9700

■ INFORMATION SOURCES

Internet

Agency Web site: http://www.msha.gov. Includes news releases, speeches, special reports, and congressional testi-mony; information on safety and health, including mining accidents and injuries; and employment opportunities with MSHA.

Telephone Contacts

Personnel Locator .... (202) 219–5000
TDD....................................... (202) 693–9899

Information and Publications

KEY OFFICES

MSHA Information and Public Affairs

1100 Wilson Blvd., #2354
Arlington, VA 22209
(202) 693–9400
Katharine Snyder, director

Provides general information. Issues press releases, de-cisions, reports, and statements for use by the media. Main-tains a mailing list for news releases. Also handles Freedom of Information requests.

RELATED MINING AGENCIES

Federal Mine Safety and Health Review Commission

601 New Jersey Ave., N.W.
Washington, DC 20001
(202) 434–9900

Handles disputes arising under the Federal Mine Safety and Health Act.

DOL Workers' Compensation Programs

Division of Coal Mine Workers' Compensation (see p. 618)

Administers the black lung benefits program, certifies benefit payments, and maintains beneficiary rolls.

PUBLICATIONS

MSHA Information and Public Affairs provides vari-ous fact sheets on mining health and safety; many publi-cations are obtainable via the MSHA Web Site. Technical reports, instruction guides, safety manuals, and the *Cat-alog of Training Products for the Mining Industry* are also available from:

National Mine Health and Safety Academy

Office of Academy Services
1301 Airport Rd.
Beaver, WV 25813-9426
(304) 256–3252
Fax (304) 256–3299

DATA AND STATISTICS

Statistics are posted on MSHA's Web site at www.msha.gov. MSHA Offices that gather data and statistics include:

Civil Penalty Program. Determines assessments and keeps track of the status of cases and the collection of fines. Contact Stephen Webber, MSHA Office of Assessments, 1100 Wilson Blvd., Arlington, VA 22209: (202) 693–9700.

Program Evaluation and Informational Resources (PEIR). Conducts internal reviews and evaluates the effectiveness of agency programs and conducts follow-up reviews to ensure that appropriate corrective actions have been taken. Another function of PEIR is to collect, analyze, and publish data obtained from mine operators on the prevalence of work-related injuries and illnesses in the mining industry. PEIR is also responsible for support and training for all MSHA automated information systems, data communications networks, and ADP equipment.

Reference Resources

LIBRARIES

All reference and the resource material pertaining to the MSHA is housed in the libraries of the Labor Department:

MSHA ACADEMY LEARNING RESOURCE CENTER

The technical information center and library maintains books, journals, newspapers, technical reports, audiovisual materials, and other information related to mine health and safety. The library gives academy students and clients immediate and easy access to information sources.

Labor Department
200 Constitution Ave. N.W., Room N2445
Washington, DC 20210
(202) 219–6992
Cindy Wolff, director
Open to the public
Hours: 8:15 a.m. to 4:45 p.m.

RULES AND REGULATIONS

A full listing of all current regulations is published in the *Code of Federal Regulations,* Title 30, parts 1–199. Proposed rules, new final rules, and updates to the *Code of Federal Regulations* are published in the daily *Federal Register. (See appendix for information on how to obtain and use these publications.)*

▌ LEGISLATION

The MSHA exercises authority under the following legislation:

Federal Mine Safety and Health Act of 1977, as amended (91 Stat. 1290, 30 U.S.C. 801). Signed by the president Nov. 9, 1977. Combined metal and nonmetal mines under the same authority as coal mines, transferred the Mining Enforcement and Safety Administration from the Interior Department to the Labor Department and reorganized it as the MSHA. Established the Mine Safety and Health Review Commission to adjudicate disputes.

Waste Isolation Pilot Plant Land Withdrawal Act (106 Stat. 4777). Signed by the president Oct. 30, 1992. Required periodic inspections of the Waste Isolation Pilot Plant project by the MSHA. Required the results to be submitted for review to the secretary of energy.

▌ REGIONAL OFFICES

MSHA/Metal and Nonmetal Mine Safety and Health

NORTHEASTERN DISTRICT
(CT, DE, MA, MD, ME, NH, NJ, NY, PA, RI, VA, VT, WV)
Thorn Hill Industrial Park, #40
547 Keystone Dr.
Warrendale, PA 15086-7573
(724) 772-2333
James Petrie, district manager

SOUTHEASTERN DISTRICT
(AL, FL, GA, KY, MS, NC, PR, SC, TN, VI)
135 Gemini Circle, #212
Birmingham, AL 35209
(205) 290–7294
Mike Davis, district manager

NORTH CENTRAL DISTRICT
(IA, IL, IN, MI, MN, OH, WI)
515 W. First St., #333
Duluth, MN 55802–1302
(218) 720–5448
Felix Quintana, district manager

SOUTH CENTRAL DISTRICT
(AR, LA, MO, NE, NM, OK, TX)
1100 Commerce St., #462
Dallas, TX 75242–0499
(214) 767–8401
Edward Lopez, district manager

ROCKY MOUNTAIN DISTRICT

(AZ, CO, KS, MT, ND, NE, SD, UT, WY)
P.O. Box 25367, DFC
Denver, CO 80225
(303) 231–5465
Irvin T. Hooker, district manager

WESTERN DISTRICT

(AK, CA, HI, ID, NV, OR, WA)
2060 Peabody Road
Vacaville, CA 95687
(707) 447–9844
Lee Ratliff, district manager

MSHA/Coal Mine Safety and Health

DISTRICT 1

(anthracite coal regions of PA)
The Stegmaier Building, #034
7 N. Wilkes-Barre Blvd.
Wilkes-Barre, PA 18702
(570) 826–6321
John Kuzar, district manager

DISTRICT 2

(bituminous coal regions of PA)
319 Paintersville Rd.
Hunker, PA 15639
(724) 925–5150
Cheryl McGill, district manager

DISTRICT 3

(MD, OH, northern WV)
5012 Mountaineer Mall
Morgantown, WV 26505
(304) 291–4277
Timothy J. Thompson, district manager

DISTRICT 4

(southern WV)
100 Bluestone Rd.
Mt. Hope, WV 25880
(304) 877–3900
Edwin P. Brady, district manager

DISTRICT 5

(VA)
P.O. Box 560
Norton, VA 24273
(540) 679–0230
Ray McKinney, district manager

DISTRICT 6

(eastern KY)
100 Fae Ramsey Ln.
Pikeville, KY 41501
(606) 432–0944
Bill G. Foulck, district manager

DISTRICT 7

(central KY, NC, SC, TN)
3837 S. U.S. Hwy. 25E
Barbourville, KY 40906
(606) 546–5123
Joseph W. Pavlovich, district manager

DISTRICT 8

(IA, IL, IN, MI, MN, northern MO, WI)
2300 Willow St., #200
Vincennes, IN 47591
(812) 882–7617
James Oakes, district manager

DISTRICT 9

(all states west of the Mississippi River except IA, MN, northern MO)
P.O. Box 25367, DFC
Denver, CO 80225–0367
(303) 231–5458
John A. Kuzar, district manager

DISTRICT 10

(western KY)
100 YMCA Dr.
Madisonville, KY 42431
(502) 821–4180
Carl Boone, district manager

DISTRICT 11

(GA, AL, MS, FL)
135 Gemini Circle, #213
Birmingham, AL 35209
(205) 290–7300
Frank Young, district manager

BEAVER

1301 Airport Rd.
Beaver, WV 25813
(304) 256–3223
Jesse Cole, mine emergency unit coordinator

Veterans' Employment and Training Service

200 Constitution Ave. N.W., Washington, DC 20210
Internet: http://www.dol.gov/vets

The Veterans' Employment and Training Service (VETS), a component of the Department of Labor, is administered by the assistant secretary for veterans' employment and training. The assistant secretary is responsible for seeing that the policies of the secretary of labor regarding national employment and training programs for veterans are carried out by the local public employment services and private-sector contractors. The assistant secretary also is responsible for promulgating policies, procedures, and training opportunities mandated by legislation for veterans and other eligible persons, with priority services given to disabled and Vietnam-era veterans.

Through a nationwide field staff, supervision and technical assistance is provided to state job services and private contractors to ensure that counseling, referral, and placement services are provided to all veterans and to other eligible persons. Service to disabled and Vietnam-era veterans is provided by Disabled Veterans' Outreach Program specialists and Local Veterans' Employment representatives who are stationed in many local offices throughout the state job service system.

VETS and the Office of Veterans' Reemployment Rights within the Department of Veterans Affairs assist veterans, reservists, members of the National Guard, and rejectees in exercising reinstatement rights to the job they left to enter military service and to the right to any increased wages or benefits added during their absence in the military service.

Cooperative agreements with the Department of Veterans Affairs provide other services and benefits to veterans.

■ KEY PERSONNEL

Assistant Secretary
Frederico Juarbe Jr. .... (202) 693–4700
Fax .... (202) 693–4754
Deputy Assistant Secretary
Charles S. Ciccolella .... (202) 693–4700
Operations and Programs
Stanley A. Seidel .... (202) 693–4707
Agency Management and Budget
Hary Puente-Duany .... (202) 693–4750

■ INFORMATION SOURCES

Internet
Agency Web site: http://www.dol.gov/vets. Features media releases, statutory and regulatory information, and information about grants and VETS activities.

Telephone Contacts
Personnel Locator .... (202) 219–5000

Information and Publications

KEY OFFICES

VETS Information Office
200 Constitution Ave. N.W., Room S1316
Washington, DC 20210
(202) 693–4745
Gordon Berg, public affairs specialist

Freedom of Information

Contact Gordon Berg, (202) 693-4745.

PUBLICATIONS

Contact the VETS Information Office. Some publications are available via the agency's Internet site.

DATA AND STATISTICS

Contact the VETS Information Office for the Labor Department's annual report, the best source of data and statistics on VETS.

Reference Resources

LIBRARY

Labor Department

200 Constitution Ave. N.W., Room N2445
Washington, DC 20210
(202) 219–4482
Dorothy Weed, director
Open to the public.
Hours: 8:15 a.m. to 4:45 p.m.

RULES AND REGULATIONS

VETS rules and regulations are published in the *Code of Federal Regulations* under various parts of Titles 29 and 38. Proposed rules, new rules, and updates to the *Code of Federal Regulations* are published in the daily *Federal Register. (See appendix for information on how to obtain and use these publications.)*

◼ LEGISLATION

VETS is responsible for:

Uniformed Services Employment and Reemployment Rights Act. Guaranteed the rights of veterans to return to their former jobs with no loss of status, pay, or seniority.

Workforce Investment Act (Section 168). Veterans Workforce Investment Program set up grant program designed to meet the employment and training needs of service-connected disabled veterans, Vietnam veterans, and veterans recently separated from military service and veterans awarded a campaign or expedition medal or badge.

Veterans Compensation, Education, and Employment Amendments of 1982 (96 Stat. 1429, 38 U.S.C. 101 note). Signed by the president Oct. 14, 1982. Transferred responsibility for enforcement of the Vietnam Era Veterans Readjustment Assistance Act of 1974 to the office of the assistant secretary of labor for veterans' employment and training.

Veterans' Employment, Training, and Counseling Amendments of 1988 (102 Stat. 556, 38 U.S.C. 101 note). Signed by the president May 20, 1988. Extended a veteran's job-training program for two years and provided additional funding for 1,600 local veterans' employment representatives nationwide.

Veterans' Education and Employment Programs (105 Stat. 48, 38 U.S.C. 2010). Signed by the president Mar. 22, 1991. Amended section 2010 of 38 U.S.C. to establish within the Department of Labor an Advisory Committee on Veterans Employment and Training.

◼ REGIONAL OFFICES

REGION 1

(CT, ME, MA, NH, RI, VT)
JFK Federal Bldg., #E-315
Government Center
Boston, MA 02114–2023
(617) 565–2080
David Houle, regional administrator

REGION 2

(NJ, NY, PR, VI)
201 Varick St., #766
New York, NY 10014–4811
(212) 337–2211
Vacant, regional administrator

REGION 3

(DC, DE, MD, PA, VA, WV)
The Curtis Center, #770W
170 S. Independence Mall West
Philadelphia, PA 19106
(215) 861-5390
Joseph Minor, regional administrator

REGION 4

(AL, FL, GA, KY, MS, NC, SC, TN)
Sam Nunn Federal Center
61 Forsyth St. S.W., #6-T85
Atlanta, GA 30303
(404) 562-2305
William J. Bolls Jr., regional administrator

REGION 5

(IL, IN, MI, MN, OH, WI)
230 S. Dearborn St., #1064
Chicago, IL 60604
(312) 353–0970
Ronald G. Bachman, regional administrator

REGION 6

(AR, LA, NM, OK, TX)
525 Griffin St., #858
Dallas, TX 75202–5028
(214) 767–4987
Lester L. Williams Jr., regional administrator

REGION 7

(IA, KS, MO, NE)
City Center Sq. Bldg., #860
1100 Main St.
Kansas City, MO 64106–2009
(816) 426–7151
Lester L. Williams Jr., regional administrator

REGION 8

(CO, MT, ND, SD, UT, WY)
1999 Broadway, #1730
Denver, CO 80202–2614
(303) 844-1178
Ronald G. Bachman, regional administrator

REGION 9

(AZ, CA, GU, HI, NV)
71 Stevenson St., #705
San Francisco, CA 94105
(415) 975–4700
Rex Newell, regional administrator

REGION 10

(AK, ID, OR, WA)
1111 Third Ave., #900
Seattle, WA 98101–3212
(206) 553–4831
Rex Newell, regional administrator

State
Department

2201 C St. N.W., Washington, DC 20520
Internet: http://www.state.gov

Bureau of Consular Affairs

2201 C St. N.W., Washington, DC 20520
Internet: http://travel.state.gov

The purpose of the Bureau of Consular Affairs is to administer laws, formulate regulations, and implement policies relating to the broad range of consular services provided to U.S. citizens abroad. Four main offices implement these responsibilities: the Office of Overseas Citizens Services, the Passport Services Office, the Visa Services Office, and the Office of Children's Issues.

The Office of Overseas Citizens Services advises and supports U.S. embassies and consulates around the world in such matters as deaths, arrests, robberies, citizenship and nationality, federal benefits, notarization of documents, international parental child abduction, and international adoptions. To assist the traveling public, the Office of Overseas Citizens Services issues consular information sheets, travel warnings, and public announcements concerning conditions in countries where Americans may be planning to visit or reside.

The Passport Services Office issues passports to U.S. citizens and is responsible for administering laws, formulating regulations, and recommending and implementing policies relating to the determination of U.S. citizenship and nationality. In 2002 the Bureau of Consular Affairs, through fourteen U.S. passport agencies and one processing center, issued more than 7.4 million U.S. passports to American citizens planning to travel overseas.

The Office of Visa Services oversees the issuance of immigrant (IV) and nonimmigrant (NIV) visas to the United States by consular officers as governed by the Immigration and Nationality Act, as amended. Visa Services provides liaison between the State Department and Foreign Service posts on visa matters, interprets visa laws and regulations, and acts as a point of contact for the public. Visa Services publishes an annual report which provides statistics on recent immigration into the United States.

The Office of Children's Issues formulates, develops, and coordinates policies and programs and provides direction to foreign service posts on international parental child abduction and international adoption. It also fulfills U.S. treaty obligations relating to the abduction of children.

The office offers general information and assistance regarding the adoption process in more than sixty countries. Because adoption is a private legal matter within the judicial sovereignty of the nation where the child resides, the State Department cannot intervene on behalf of an individual U.S. citizen in foreign courts.

Since the late 1970s, the Bureau of Consular Affairs has taken action in more than 8,000 cases of international parental child abduction. The Office of Children's Issues works closely with parents, attorneys, other government agencies, and private organizations in the United States to prevent international abductions. Forty-four countries (including the United States) have joined the Hague Convention on the Civil Aspects of International Child Abduction. The convention discourages abduction as a means of resolving a custody matter, by requiring (with few exceptions) that the abducted child be returned to the country where he/she resided before the abduction.

The Bureau of Consular Affairs informs the public of its activities through publications on international travel, through its hotline numbers, and through its Web site.

KEY PERSONNEL

Assistant Secretary
Maura Harty............................ (202) 647–9576
Fax..................................... (202) 647–0341
Principal Deputy Assistant Secretary
Daniel B. Smith........................ (202) 647–9577
Fax..................................... (202) 647–0341
Executive Director
Joanne Arzt............................ (202) 663-2500
Overseas Citizens Services
Diane Andruch........................ (202) 647–6541
Fax..................................... (202) 647–3732
   Managing Director
   Michele T. Bond..................... (202) 647–9018
   American Citizens Services and Crisis Management
   Elizabeth Kirincich.................... (202) 647–9019
   Children's Issues
   Michelle Bernier-Toth .... (202) 312–9749
   Policy Review and Interagency Liaison
   Edward Betancourt.................... (202) 312–9723
Passport Services
   Deputy Assistant Secretary
   Frank Moss .... (202) 647–5366
   Fax................................... (202) 647–0341
   Managing Director
   Ann M. Barrett....................... (202) 663–2423
   Passport Policy and Advisory Services
   John Hotchner......................... (202) 663-2427
   Special Issuance Agency
   Barbara Chesman .... (202) 955–0202
   Information Management and Liaison
   Richard McLevey...................... (202) 663-2409
Visa Services
   Janice Jacobs.......................... (202) 647–9584
   Fax................................... (202) 647-0341
   Managing Director
   Catherine Barry....................... (202) 663–1153
   Field Support and Liaison
   Michael Regan......................... (202) 663–1160
   Legislation, Regulation, and Advisory Assistance
   Stephen Fischel....................... (202) 663–1184
   Public and Diplomatic Liaison
   Lisa Piascik .... (202) 663–3579

INFORMATION SOURCES

Internet

Agency Web site: http://travel.state.gov. Includes passport and visa information, travel warnings, the text of selected publications, and links to many U.S. embassies and consulates abroad. For assistance, call Public Affairs at (202) 647-1488.

Telephone Contacts

Personnel Locator .... (202) 647–4000
Fax-on-demand .... (202) 647–3000
Overseas Citizens Services
   American Citizens Services............ (202) 647–5225
   Children's Issues...................... (202) 312–9749
Passport Services
   General Information................... (900) 225-5674
                                          (888) 362-8668
   Diplomatic/Congressional/Official
     Travel .... (202) 955–0198
Visa Services
   General Information................... (202) 663–1225
   Immigration Visas .... (202) 334–0700
   Priority Dates Hotline .... (202) 663–1541

Information and Publications

KEY OFFICES

Policy Coordination and Public Affairs
Bureau of Consular Affairs
2201 C St. N.W.
Washington, DC 20520–4818
(202) 647–1488
Fax (202) 647–6074
Edward Vazquez, director

Handles press inquiries, legislative affairs, and public outreach. Publishes the *Tips for Travelers* series and other travel documents.

Visa Services
Bureau of Consular Affairs
2201 C St. N.W., Room 6811
Washington, DC 20520–4818
(202) 663–1153
Fax (202) 663–1247
Catherine Barry, managing director

Publishes an annual report that is a record of recent immigration into the United States. It details all aspects of immigration, including methods of staying in the United States permanently or temporarily, recent immigration legislation, the different classes of immigrants, and statistical tables on immigration and visa issuances.

Freedom of Information

State Department
A/RPS, SA-2
515 22nd St., N.W.
Washington, DC 20522
(202) 261-8314
Margaret Grafeld, director

PUBLICATIONS

For the annual report on immigration, contact Visa Services. Other publications are available free via the agency's Internet sites and fax-on-demand service; they can also be purchased from the U.S. Government Printing Office (GPO). For the GPO and the Consumer Information Center (CIC), which distributes some of the titles below, see appendix, Ordering Government Publications. Consular Affairs publications include:

A Safe Trip Abroad
Overseas Citizens Services
HIV Testing Requirements for Entry into Foreign Countries
Medical Information for Americans Traveling Abroad
Foreign Entry Requirements
Tips for Women Traveling Alone
Tips for Travelers With Disabilities
Advance Fee Business Scams
Sending Money Overseas to a U.S. Citizen in an Emergency
Tips for Americans Residing Abroad
Tips for Older Americans
Tips for Travelers (pamphlets on Canada, the Caribbean, Central and South America, China, Mexico, the Middle East and North Africa, Russia and the Newly Independent States, South Asia, and Sub-Saharan Africa)
Travel Warning on Drugs Abroad
Your Trip Abroad

DATA AND STATISTICS

Contact Visa Services, above, for the annual report on immigration.

Reference Resources

LIBRARY

State Department
2201 C St. N.W.
Washington, DC 20520
(202) 647–1099
Fax (202) 647–2971
Daniel Clemmer, librarian
Hours: 8:15 a.m. to 5:00 p.m.

Open to State Department employees only. Some exceptions for unusual circumstances may be made.

RULES AND REGULATIONS

Bureau of Consular Affairs rules and regulations are published in the *Code of Federal Regulations,* Title 8, part 1101 et seq. Proposed rules, new final rules, and updates to the *Code of Federal Regulations* are published in the daily *Federal Register. (See appendix for information on how to obtain and use these publications.)*

◼ LEGISLATION

The Bureau of Consular Affairs carries out its responsibilities under:

Immigration and Nationality Act, as amended (66 Stat. 163, 8 U.S.C. 1101). Signed by the president June 27, 1952. Contained virtually all of the law relating to the entry of aliens and to the acquisition and loss of U.S. citizenship.

Immigration Act of 1990 (104 Stat. 4978, 8 U.S.C. 1101 note). Signed by the president Nov. 29, 1990. Implemented major changes affecting immigrants and nonimmigrants, Filipino World War II veterans desiring U.S. citizenship, El Salvadoran nationals, and others with immigration concerns.

Immigration and Nationality Technical Corrections Act of 1994 (108 Stat. 4305, 8 U.S.C. 1101). Signed by the president Oct. 25, 1994. Made numerous specific changes to the Immigration and Nationality Act. Allowed U.S. visas for visits from officials of Taiwan. Gave equal treatment to women in conferring U.S. citizenship to children born abroad.

◼ REGIONAL OFFICES

Passport Services

BOSTON
(MA, ME, NH, upstate NY, RI, VT)
10 Causeway St., #247
Boston, MA 02222-1094
(617) 878-0900

CHARLESTON
1269 Holland St.
Charleston, SC 29405
(Not open to the general public.)

CHICAGO
(IL, IN, MI, WI)
230 S. Dearborn St., #380
Chicago, IL 60604-1564
(312) 341-6020

HONOLULU

(AS, GU, HI, MP, Micronesia)
300 Ala Moana Blvd., #I-330
Box 50185
Honolulu, HI 96850-1330
(808) 522-8283

HOUSTON

(KS, OK, NM, TX)
1919 Smith St., #1100
Houston, TX 77002-8049
(713) 751-0294

LOS ANGELES

(Southern CA, southern NV)
11000 Wilshire Blvd., #1000
Los Angeles, CA 90024-3615
(310) 575-5700

MIAMI

(FL, GA, PR, SC, VI)
51 S.W. First Ave., 3rd Floor
Miami, FL 33120-1680
(305) 539-3600
(Accepts applications from those traveling in two weeks, or who need foreign visas to travel.)

NEW ORLEANS

(AL, AR, IA, KY, LA, MO, MS, NC, OH, TN, all but northern VA)
365 Canal St., #1300
New Orleans, LA 70130-6508
(504) 412-2600

NEW YORK

(New York City, Long Island)
376 Hudson St.
10th Floor
New York, NY 10014-4896
(212) 206-3500
(Accepts only emergency applications from those leaving within two weeks.)

PHILADELPHIA

(DE, NJ, PA, WV)
200 Chestnut St., #103
Philadelphia, PA 19106-2970
(215) 418-5937

SAN FRANCISCO

(AZ, central and northern CA, northern NV, UT)
95 Hawthorne St., 5th Floor
San Francisco, CA 94105
(415) 538-2700

SEATTLE

(AK, CO, ID, MN, MO, ND, NE, OR, SD, WA, WY)
915 Second Ave., #992
Seattle, WA 98174-1091
(206) 808–5700
(Only accepts applications for passports for those traveling within 14 days.)

CONNECTICUT

(CT; Westchester County, NY)
50 Washington St.
Norwalk, CT 06856
(203) 299-5443

WASHINGTON

(DC, MD, northern VA)
1111 19th St. N.W.
Washington, DC 20522-1705
(202) 647–0518

NATIONAL PASSPORT CENTER

31 Rochester Ave.
Portsmouth, NH 03801-2900
(603) 334-0500
(Handles all applications for passports by mail and some of the workload from the regional agencies. Not open to the general public.)

Transportation Department

400 7th St. S.W., Washington, DC 20590
Internet: http://www.dot.gov

Federal Aviation Administration

800 Independence Ave. S.W., Washington, DC 20591
Internet: http://www.faa.gov

The Federal Aviation Administration (FAA), an agency within the Department of Transportation (DOT), establishes and enforces rules and regulations for safety standards covering all aspects of civil aviation. Major areas under FAA regulatory control are the manufacture, maintenance, and operation of aircraft; the training and certification of air personnel (pilots, flight engineers, navigators, aviation mechanics, air traffic controllers, parachute riggers, and aircraft dispatchers); security measures at airports; domestic and international air traffic; and noise and exhaust emissions from aircraft (in cooperation with the Environmental Protection Agency). The FAA also develops air traffic rules and regulations and allocates the use of U.S. airspace.

The Office of Airport Safety and Standards serves as the principal organization of FAA responsible for all airport program matters pertaining to standards for airport design, construction, maintenance, operations, safety, and data, including ensuring adequacy of the substantive aspects of FAA rulemaking actions relating to the certification of airports.

An important function of the FAA is the operation and maintenance of an air traffic control network. The network consists of air route traffic control centers and airport control towers, staffed by air traffic controllers and flight service stations, which provide weather briefings and other aeronautical information.

The FAA promotes civil aviation abroad by the assignment of technical groups, the training of foreign nationals, and the exchange of information with foreign governments. It provides technical representation at conferences, including participation in the International Civil Aviation Organization and other international organizations.

The FAA's Office of Security and Investigations is responsible for preventing criminal acts such as air piracy, hijacking, sabotage, and extortion. The administration requires all airports to maintain security systems to screen airline passengers. It also investigates selected aviation accidents in cooperation with the National Transportation Safety Board (p. 350) to determine their causes.

The FAA inspects commercial aircraft for safety violations. In response to accidents involving aging aircraft and to public concern, the FAA developed corrosion inspection standards for particular aircraft. Industry observers and the general public continue to voice concerns about the present air traffic control system. Suggestions for improvement include establishing the FAA as an independent agency, adding runways to existing airports, and building more airports in less-congested airspace.

Drug testing of pilots, flight attendants, and other personnel became mandatory in December 1989. Legislation passed that same year prohibited smoking on almost all flights in the United States.

The 1993 Capital Investment Plan (CIP) addressed problems and improvements for the National Airspace System (NAS). Because the NAS is a complex conglomeration of integrated systems, the CIP is based on incremental improvements designed to respond to changing requirements. A major focus of the plan is commitment to a satellite-based navigation system that uses a global positioning system (GPS) as its foundation. This system of twenty-four satellites provides positioning information to airplanes, and allows aircraft to make curved approaches to airports, fly more efficient routes, and obtain positional information anywhere in the world.

In 1994 the FAA opened the national Air Traffic Control System Command Center near Dulles International Airport in northern Virginia. The Air Traffic Management Center tracks and manages the flow of more than 50,000 daily flights within the United States.

Passenger safety on domestic and international flights is a major focus of the FAA. The deaths of 259 people in the 1988 explosion of a Pan Am 747 over Lockerbie, Scotland, caused by a bomb hidden in a portable tape player, initiated a reassessment of airport security. The Aviation Security Improvement Act of 1990 mandated the implementation of several recommendations from the President's Commission on Aviation Security and Terrorism, set up to investigate the Lockerbie disaster. Provisions included the establishment of federal security managers as the FAA liaison with airport managers and law enforcement officials, and provisions for notifying passengers of terrorist threats to flights.

In July 1996 security measures were heightened once again following the explosion of a TWA 747 bound for Paris from New York. In the wake of the mysterious crash, the FAA called for more intensive screening of passengers on international flights, more thorough screening of carry-on baggage for domestic and international flights, and implementation of a series of classified security measures. However, the cause of the crash was later determined to be mechanical.

As a result of the 1996 crash of a ValuJet DC-9, caused by improperly capped oxygen generators, the FAA asked the Research and Special Programs Administration (RSPA), which designates federal policies in transporting hazardous materials, to ban the transportation of all "oxidizers" and "oxidizing materials" in specific compartments on passenger and cargo aircraft.

In the wake of the terrorist attacks on the World Trade Center Towers and the Pentagon in September 2001, the airline industry experienced significant changes in security measures. President George W. Bush signed sweeping aviation security legislation that removed airport security from the jurisdiction of the airlines and made it a federal responsibility. The Aviation and Transportation Security Act, signed into law two months after the attacks, created the Transportation Security Administration (TSA), which hires and manages the thousands of workers who screen passengers and baggage. The law also mandated random deployment of armed federal "sky marshals" on commercial flights, permitted pilots to carry guns after specialized training, and required physical security improvements in planes and airports. In November 2002 the TSA was integrated into the Department of Homeland Security.

In 2003, after a highly publicized 2002 incident of two pilots who were prevented from flying a commercial plane because they were drunk, the FAA established new procedures for dealing with drunk pilots. The FAA was also troubled to see that in 2002 the rate of commercial pilots failing sobriety tests doubled (twenty-two commercial pilots failed alcohol tests) from the previous year. New regulations require that pilots who fail sobriety tests to have their medical and airman's certificates revoked immediately, effectively grounding them. Grounded pilots must then wait a year and go through rehabilitation to restore their medical certificates, and they must retake all the required written and flight tests to restore their airman's certificate.

■ KEY PERSONNEL

Administrator
Marion C. Blakey .... (202) 267–3111
Fax .... (202) 267–5047

Deputy Administrator
Bobby Sturgell .... (202) 267–8111

Financial Services
John F. Hennigan .... (202) 267–9105
Fax .... (202) 267–5801

Performance Management
Tim Lawler .... (202) 267–7140

Human Resources
Glenda Tate .... (202) 267–3456

Civil Rights
Fanny Rivera .... (202) 267–3254
Fax .... (202) 267–5565

Chief Counsel
Andrew B. Steinberg .... (202) 267–3222
Fax .... (202) 267–3227

Government and Industry Affairs
David Balloff .... (202) 267–3277
Fax .... (202) 267–8210

System Safety
Christopher A. Hart .... (202) 267–3611
Fax .... (202) 267–5496

Air Traffic Services
Steven J. Brown .... (202) 267–7111
Fax .... (202) 267–5716

Air Traffic
Steve Zaidman .... (202) 267–8181
Fax .... (202) 267–5015

Air Traffic Systems Requirements
James H. Washington .... (202) 385–7500

Systems Capacity
Paula R. Lewis .... (202) 267–7370
Fax .... (202) 267–5767

Independent Test and Evaluation
A. Martin Phillips . . . . (202) 267–3341
Fax . . . . (202) 267–5669
Runway Safety
William S. Davis . . . . (202) 385–4778
Fax . . . . (202) 385–4772
Terminal Business Service
William R. Voss . . . . (202) 264–4000
Fax . . . . (202) 554–9837
Airway Facilities
Alan Moore . . . . (202) 267–8181
Airports
Woodie Woodward . . . . (202) 267–9471
Fax . . . . (202) 267–5301
Airport Planning and Programming
Catherine Lang . . . . (202) 267–8775
Fax . . . . (202) 267–5302
Airport Safety and Standards
David Bennett . . . . (202) 267–3053
Security and Investigation
Lynn Osmus . . . . (202) 267–7211
Fax . . . . (202) 267–5738
Free Flight
John Thorton . . . . (202) 220–3300
Fax . . . . (202) 220–3312
Commercial Space Transportation
Patti Smith . . . . (202) 267–7793
Fax . . . . (202) 267–5450
Space Systems Development Division
Herbert Bachner . . . . (202) 267–7859
Licensing and Safety Division
Jay Garvin . . . . (202) 385–4700
Systems Engineering and Training Division
Hugh Q. Cook . . . . (202) 493–5244
Counsel to the Administrator
Louise E. Maillett . . . . (202) 267–7417
Fax . . . . (202) 267–5047
Aviation Policy and Plans
John M. Rodgers . . . . (202) 267–3274
Environment and Energy
Carl Burlesen . . . . (202) 267–3576
International Aviation
Ava L. Wilkerson . . . . (202) 267–3213
Regulation and Certification
Nicholas A. Sabatini . . . . (202) 267–3131
Fax . . . . (202) 267–9675
Accident Investigation
Steven B. Wallace . . . . (202) 267–9612
Aircraft Certification
John Hickey . . . . (202) 267–8235
Aerospace Medicine
Jon L. Jordan . . . . (202) 267–3535

Flight Standards Service
James L. Bailough . . . . (202) 267–8237
Rulemaking
Anthony Fazio . . . . (202) 267–9677
Information Services
Daniel J. Mehan . . . . (202) 493–4570
Region and Center Operations
Ruth Leverenz . . . . (817) 222–5001
Fax . . . . (202) 267–5015
Research and Acquisitions
Charles Keegan . . . . (202) 267–7222
Fax . . . . (202) 267–5085
Acquisitions
Gilbert B. Devey . . . . (202) 267–8513
Air Traffic Systems Development
Gregory D. Burke . . . . (202) 493–0237
Aviation Research
Herman Rediess . . . . (202) 267–9251
Business Management
Lauraline Gregory . . . . (202) 267–3716
Communications, Navigation, and Surveillance Systems
Daniel P. Salvano . . . . (202) 267–3555
System Architect and Investment Analysis
John A. Scardina . . . . (202) 385–7101
Technical Center
Anne Harlan . . . . (609) 485-6641

■ INFORMATION SOURCES

Internet
Agency Web site: http://www.faa.gov. Includes information on FAA divisions, centers, and regions; news releases; and links to other FAA Internet sites.

The FAA also operates the Federal Information Exchange (FEDIX), an electronic bulletin board system (BBS) that contains news releases, the administrator's speeches, procurement notices, legal information, FAA publications, and educational materials for elementary school programs.

For assistance . . . . (301) 975–0103
For modem access only . . . . (301) 258–0953

Telephone Contacts
Personnel Locator . . . . (202) 366–4000
Consumer Hotline
Toll free . . . . (800) 322–7873
DC area . . . . (202) 267–8592
Safety Hotline
Toll free . . . . (800) 255–1111
DC area . . . . (202) 267–8590

Information and Publications

FAA Public Affairs
800 Independence Ave. S.W., Room 911A
Washington, DC 20591
(202) 267–3883
Greg Martin, assistant administrator

Provides general information. DOT Public Affairs maintains mailing lists for DOT advisories: 400 7th St. S.W., Washington, DC 20590; (202) 366–4570.

FAA Public Inquiry Center
800 Independence Ave. S.W.
Washington, DC 20591
(202) 267–3484
Distributes FAA publications and provides assistance and answers to complaints and inquiries.

HOTLINES
The FAA operates two hotlines, listed above under Telephone Contacts.

FAA Consumer Hotline
Handles complaints about carry-on baggage restrictions, airport security procedures, and child safety seats. Also handles complaints about user services of the FAA, including examinations, aircraft certification, and facility operations. All calls are picked up by an answering machine; calls are returned by an FAA official if the caller leaves a name and telephone number. Questions regarding airline service, such as flight delays, lost luggage, and ticketing, are handled by DOT Aviation Consumer Protection Division; (202) 366–2220.

FAA Safety Hotline
For aviation industry employees with specific knowledge of possible violations of FAA regulations. Callers' identities are confidential. Operates weekdays 8:00 a.m. to 4:00 p.m. Callers may leave a message after business hours; calls are returned by an FAA official if the caller leaves a name and telephone number.

PUBLICATIONS
Contact the FAA Public Inquiry Center for the annual *Guide to Federal Aviation Administration Publications*, which also includes information on materials published by other agencies related to the work of the FAA. Some FAA publications must be ordered from the U.S. Government Printing Office (GPO): see appendix, Ordering Government Publications. Titles available from the FAA Public Inquiry Center include:

Aircraft Information. Statistical and operational information about the characteristics, ownership, and operation of the civil air fleet in the United States.

Aviation Forecast Information. Twelve-year national forecast of aviation activity, published annually. Included are forecasts for enplaned passengers, revenue, passenger miles, cargo, air carrier and general aviation fleet and activity levels, and engine and aircraft production. Also included is a forecast of total air carrier, general aviation, and military activity at FAA-operated air traffic control facilities.

Aviation System Plans. Annual statement of the funding and scheduling of programs needed to meet realistic requirements of aviation for the next decade.

FAA General Aviation News. Bimonthly periodical devoted to aviation safety, written by the staff of the Flight Standards Service, available on a subscription basis.

The Department of Transportation's annual report summarizes all regulatory actions taken by the agency during the previous year. It is available from the GPO or from DOT Public Affairs, 400 7th St. S.W., Washington, DC 20590; (202) 366–4570.

DATA AND STATISTICS

FAA Policy and Plans
Statistic and Forecast Branch
800 Independence Ave. S.W., Room 938
Washington, DC 20591
(202) 267–3355

The FAA publishes statistical and financial reports as well as economic studies on domestic and international air traffic activity, the aviation industry, aviation safety, and air personnel. Publications are described, with ordering information, in the *Guide to Federal Aviation Administration Publications,* available from the Public Inquiry Center.

Reference Resources

LIBRARY

DOT Library
400 7th St. S.W., Room 2200
Washington, DC 20590
(202) 366–0746
Linda Cullen (acting), chief of information services
Hours: 8:00 a.m. to 4:00 p.m.

Section contains copies of FAA rules, regulations, and guidelines; FAA reports; materials on aviation and aviation safety; the *Congressional Record;* law reports and compilations; and technical and scientific aviation periodicals.

DOCKETS

Rules Docket

FAA Office of the Chief Counsel
800 Independence Ave. S.W., #900 East
Washington, DC 20591
(202) 267–3222
Andrew B. Steinberg, chief counsel

Maintains dockets containing official FAA records, correspondence, and materials related to rulemaking and regulations. Most material in the dockets is available for public inspection and copying. Copies of requested material can be mailed; there is a charge for copying. Two other DOT offices also have FAA-related dockets:

U.S. Department of Transportation - Docket Management Facility

400 7th St. S.W., PL-401
Washington, DC 20590
(202) 366–9329
Hours: 9:00 a.m.–5:00 p.m. (M–F)
Docket Management System Web site: www.dms.dot.gov

Maintains docket information concerning air routes. Releases official opinions and orders. Files are open to the public for inspection and copying; an index to the dockets is on file.

The Docket Section prepares two weekly summaries, the *Summary of Application* and the *Summary of Orders and Regulations.* Both are available at the docket room or by subscription from private companies. A list of these companies may be obtained from the Docket Section.

Regulatory Affairs

DOT Office of International Aviation
400 7th St. S.W., Room 6402
Washington, DC 20590
(202) 366–2423
Paul L. Gretch, director

Holds complete listings of all the tariffs (fares) currently in effect for all air carriers operating international passenger service.

Included in the filings are all the regular and promotion (such as super saver and APEX) fares that are charged by airlines for international service. The material is arranged by air carrier.

RULES AND REGULATIONS

FAA rules and regulations are published in the *Code of Federal Regulations,* Title 14, parts 1–199. Proposed rules, final rules, and updated rules and revisions are published in the daily *Federal Register. (See appendix for information on how to obtain and use these publications.)*

The FAA also issues copies of regulations that have been revised. Those most frequently revised are sold to the public on a subscription basis; others are sold separately. This service is available through the GPO: see appendix, Ordering Government Publications.

■ LEGISLATION

The FAA is responsible for the administration of parts of several statutes, most of which are related to aviation safety. The FAA carries out its responsibilities under:

Federal Aviation Act of 1958 (72 Stat. 737, 49 U.S.C. 1301). Signed by the president Aug. 23, 1958. Created the Federal Aviation Agency and gave the agency authority to regulate aviation safety standards, control the nation's navigable airspace, operate air navigation facilities, formulate air traffic rules and regulations, issue certificates of standards for air personnel and aircraft, establish grant programs for the construction and improvement of airports, require registration of aircraft, and establish security provisions for aircraft and airports.

Department of Transportation Act (80 Stat. 931, 49 U.S.C. 1651). Signed by the president Oct. 15, 1966. Created the cabinet-level Department of Transportation (DOT); placed the functions, powers, and authorities of the Federal Aviation Agency in one of the three separate administrations within the DOT; changed the name of the Federal Aviation Agency to the Federal Aviation Administration.

Airport and Airway Improvement Act of 1982 (96 Stat. 671, 49 U.S.C. 2201). Signed by the president Sept. 3, 1982. Authorized the FAA to issue operating certificates to airports to assure safe operation. Authorized a long-range program of planning and construction grants for expansion and improvement of the nation's airports and navigation facilities.

Tax Equity and Fiscal Responsibility Act of 1982 (96 Stat. 324, 26 U.S.C. 1 note). Signed by the president Sept. 3, 1982. Established certain taxes imposed on users of the aviation system to fund construction and improvement projects.

Airport and Airway Safety and Capacity Expansion Act of 1987 (101 Stat. 1486, 49 U.S.C. app. 2201 note). Signed by the president Dec. 30, 1987. Amended the Airport and Airway Improvement Act of 1982 to reauthorize funding for airport programs, including expansion grants, through fiscal year 1992, and airway programs, including funding for air traffic control equipment, through 1990.

Department of Transportation and Related Agencies Appropriations Act (103 Stat. 1098, 49 U.S.C. app. 1374d). Signed by the president Nov. 21, 1989. Banned smoking on virtually all domestic air flights.

Miscellaneous Aviation Amendments (103 Stat. 2060, 49 U.S.C. app. 1475d). Signed by the president Dec. 15, 1989. Extended the authorization for the penalty assessment program.

Aviation Security Improvement Act of 1990 (104 Stat. 3066, 49 U.S.C. app. 2152 note). Signed by the president Nov. 16, 1990. Amended Title III of the Federal Aviation Act of 1958 to add sections 318 and 319, which included measures to strengthen air transport security and ensure the safety of passengers of U.S. air carriers against terrorist threat. Established the position of Civil Aviation Security associate administrator within the FAA.

FAA Civil Penalty Administrative Assessment Act of 1992 (106 Stat. 923, 49 U.S.C. app. 1301 note). Signed by the president Aug. 26, 1992. Amended the Federal Aviation Act of 1958 to authorize the FAA administrator to assess a civil penalty for violations pertaining to civil air flights over security zones, aviation safety regulations, and regulations requiring public notice of existing or proposed construction or repairs which will promote safety in air commerce.

Department of Transportation and Related Agencies Appropriations Act of 1992 (105 Stat. 917, 49 U.S.C. app. 1301 note). Signed by the president Oct. 28, 1991. Required air carriers and foreign air carriers to conduct preemployment, reasonable suspicion, random, and postaccident testing of pilots, crew members, airport security, and air carrier employees to test for alcohol and controlled substances. This law also required testing of FAA employees whose duties include responsibility for safety-sensitive functions.

Antiterrorism and Effective Death Penalty Act of 1996 (110 Stat. 1214, 18 U.S.C. 1 note). Signed by the president April 24, 1996. Title III, International Terrorism Prohibitions, required the FAA administrator to approve security programs used by foreign air carriers operating in the U.S. Required foreign carriers to meet standards used by U.S. carriers and airports.

Air Traffic Management System Performance Improvement Act of 1996 (110 Stat. 3227, 49 U.S.C. 40101 note, 49 U.S.C. 106 note). Signed by the president Oct. 9, 1996. Authorized the administrator to use personnel of other federal agencies. Established the Federal Aviation Management Advisory Council to provide advice and counsel on operational issues and act as an oversight re-

source for management, policy, spending, and regulatory matters. Established the National Civil Aviation Review Commission to analyze alternative financing means for meeting the needs of the aviation system and aviation safety in the United States.

Aviation Medical Assistance Act of 1998 (112 Stat. 47, 49 U.S.C. 44701 note). Signed by the president April 24, 1998. Directed the administrator to reevaluate the medical equipment and supplies carried by air carriers and the training of flight attendants in the use of such equipment.

Aviation and Transportation Security Act (115 Stat. 597, 49 U.S.C. 40101 note). Signed by the president Nov. 19, 2001. Created a Transportation Security Administration (TSA) within the DOT. Gave the TSA jurisdiction over airport security, federalized airport security workers, and mandated random deployment of armed federal "sky marshals" on commercial flights. Also permitted pilots to carry guns after specialized training. Required physical security improvements in planes and airports, including strengthened cockpit doors, mandatory training for flight crews on how to deal with hijacking attempts, and screening of all checked and carry-on baggage. Created a Transportation Security Oversight Board to review emergency security regulations and other actions of the TSA.

Homeland Security Act of 2002 (116 Stat. 2135, 6 U.S.C. 101 note). Signed by the president Nov. 25, 2002. Established the Department of Homeland Security (DHS) and transferred all or significant portions of twenty-two existing agencies to the new department, which is responsible for protecting the United States from terrorist attacks. Integrated the Transportation Security Administration into the border and transportation security division of DHS.

■ REGIONAL OFFICES

NEW ENGLAND
(CT, MA, ME, NH, RI, VT)
12 New England Executive Park
Burlington, MA 01803
(781) 238–7020
Amy Corbett, regional administrator

EASTERN
(DC, DE, MD, NJ, NY, PA, VA, WV)
Fitzgerald Federal Bldg., #207
John F. Kennedy International Airport
Jamaica, NY 11430
(718) 553–3000
Arlene Feldman, regional administrator

SOUTHERN

(AL, FL, GA, KY, MS, NC, PR, SC, TN, VI)
1707 Columbia Ave.
College Park, GA 30337
(404) 305–5000
Carolyn Blum, regional administrator

GREAT LAKES

(IL, IN, MI, MN, ND, OH, SD, WI)
2300 E. Devon Ave., #366
Des Plaines, IL 60018–4686
(847) 294–7294
Cecelia Hunziker, regional administrator

CENTRAL

(IA, KS, MO, NE)
601 E. 12th St., #1501
Kansas City, MO 64106
(816) 426–5626
Chris Blum, regional administrator

SOUTHWEST

(AR, LA, NM, OK, TX)
2601 Meacham Blvd.
Fort Worth, TX 76193–0005
(817) 222–5001
Ruth Leverenz, regional administrator

WESTERN-PACIFIC

(AZ, CA, HI, NV)
15000 Aviation Blvd.
Hawthorne, CA 90044
(310) 725–3550
William Withycombe, regional administrator

NORTHWEST MOUNTAIN

(CO, ID, MT, OR, UT, WA, WY)
1601 Lind Ave. S.W.
Renton, WA 98055–4056
(425) 227–2001
Thomas Busker (acting), regional administrator

ALASKAN

222 W. Seventh Ave., #14
Anchorage, AK 99513
(907) 271–5645
Patrick Poe, regional administrator

Other Field Offices

MIKE MONRONEY AERONAUTICAL CENTER

P.O. Box 25082
Oklahoma City, OK 73125
(405) 954–4521
Lindy Ritz, director

WILLIAM J. HUGHES TECHNICAL CENTER

Atlantic City International Airport
Atlantic City, NJ 08405
(609) 485–6641
Anne Harlan, director

Federal Highway Administration

400 7th St. S.W., Washington, DC 20590
Internet: http://www.fhwa.dot.gov

The Federal Highway Administration (FHWA), an agency within the Department of Transportation (DOT), sets functional safety standards for the design, construction, and maintenance of the nation's highways. It also establishes safety standards for motor carriers engaged in interstate or foreign commerce and provides highway program support to other federal agencies.

The FHWA is headed by an administrator who is appointed by the president and confirmed by the Senate. Serving under the administrator are the deputy administrator, the executive director, and seven associate administrators with functional responsibilities for administration; program development; policy; research and development; and safety and system applications. Also reporting to the administrator are the chief counsel, the director of civil rights, the director of communications, and nine regional administrators.

The FHWA administers the federal highway program, which distributes federal funds to the states to construct and improve the federal-aid highway systems. The National Highway System Designation Act of 1995 designated roughly 160,000 miles of interstate highways and other heavily traveled roads as the National Highway System (NHS). Routes on the NHS receive slightly more than 30 percent of all federal highway aid.

The FHWA regulates highway design and construction to reduce traffic deaths, injuries, and damage to property and to increase the efficiency of traffic movement. FHWA rules and regulations must be followed by the states and communities that receive FHWA matching funds to construct or improve highways.

The FHWA operates the National Highway Institute, which administers a training program for state and local highway employees. In addition, it offers fellowships in highway safety and transportation research and education, and a highway technician scholarship.

The FHWA is responsible for highway beautification programs, the Darien Gap and Alaska Highway programs, the highway construction portions of the Appalachian regional development project, and the territorial highway program. It designs and builds forest highways, national defense access roads, and roads in national parks and Native American reservations, and administers training programs in highway construction for unskilled workers. The FHWA also provides highway engineering services and assistance to other federal agencies and foreign governments.

In 1999 Congress passed the Motor Carrier Safety Improvement Act, which abolished the FHWA Office of Motor Carrier Safety and established the Federal Motor Carrier Safety Administration within the Transportation Department.

■ KEY PERSONNEL

Administrator
Mary E. Peters........................... (202) 366–2146
Fax.................................... (202) 366–3244
Deputy Administrator
J. Richard Capka........................ (202) 366–2241
Executive Director
Frederick (Bud) Wright................ (202) 366–2243
Deputy Executive Director
Vincent F. Schimmoller................ (202) 366–2242
Chief Counsel
Edward V. A. Kussy (acting)........... (202) 366–0740
Fax.................................... (202) 366–7499

Civil Rights
Edward W. Morris Jr. .... (202) 366–0693
Fax .... (202) 366–7239

Public Affairs
Bill Outlaw .... (202) 366–0660
Fax .... (202) 366–7239

Program Quality Coordination
Fred Hempel .... (202) 366–9393
Fax .... (202) 366–7495

Administration
Michael J. Vecchietti .... (202) 366–0604
Fax .... (202) 366–7943

Corporate Management
Ronald C. Marshall .... (202) 366–9393
Fax .... (202) 366–3253

Federal Lands Highway
Arthur E. Hamilton .... (202) 366–7495
Fax .... (202) 366–7495

Infrastructure
King W. Gee .... (202) 366–0371
Fax .... (202) 366–3043

Operations
Jeffrey Paniati .... (202) 366–0408
Fax .... (202) 366–3302

Planning and Environment
Cynthia Burbank .... (202) 366–0116
Fax .... (202) 366–3043

Policy
Charles D. (Chip) Nottingham .... (202) 366–0585
Fax .... (202) 366–9626

Professional Development
Joseph S. Toole .... (202) 366–0500
Fax .... (202) 366–0593

National Highway Institute
Moges Ayele .... (202) 366–0500

Program Development
Butch J. Wlaschin .... (202) 366–9486
Fax .... (202) 366–0371

Research, Development and Technology
Dennis C. Judycki .... (202) 493–3165
Fax .... (202) 493–3170

Safety
George Ostensen .... (202) 366–2288
Fax .... (202) 366–3222

▓ INFORMATION SOURCES

Internet
Agency Web site: http://www.fhwa.dot.gov. Includes information on publications and statistics, procurements, legislation and regulations, and conferences and training.

Telephone Contacts
Personnel Locator .... (202) 366–4000

Information and Publications

KEY OFFICES

FHWA Public Affairs
400 7th St. S.W., #4211-A
Washington, DC 20590
(202) 366–0660
Bill Outlaw, director

Provides public information, answers or refers general questions, and maintains a mailing list for news releases. Acts as media liaison.

FHWA Office of Highway Policy Information
400 7th St. S.W., #3306
Washington, DC 20590
(202) 366–0180
Barna Juhasz, director

Handles statistical reports on highway systems.

Freedom of Information
400 7th St. S.W.
Washington, DC 20590
(202) 366–0534
Kathy Ray, FOIA and audit liaison

FHWA Office of Chief Counsel
400 7th St. S.W.
Washington, DC 20590
(202) 366–0761
Edward V. A. Kussy (acting), chief counsel

Serves as principal FHWA legal officer and advisor, rendering legal services and providing legal advice to headquarters and field offices concerning all aspects of FHWA programs, functions and activities.

PUBLICATIONS
Each office within the FHWA handles publications requests for information pertaining to its functions. Address inquiries to the individual office at the FHWA.

The Research, Development and Technology office handles requests for research publications.

DATA AND STATISTICS
Contact FHWA Public Affairs or the FHWA Office of Highway Policy Information.

Reference Resources

FHWA Law Library
Docket Room
400 7th St. S.W., PL 402
Washington, DC 20590
(202) 366–9392
Hours: 8:00 a.m. to 5:30 p.m.

Maintains dockets and all other materials related to rulemakings and administrative proceedings for inspection and copying.

DOT Library
Transportation Administrative Services Center (TASC)
400 7th St. S.W., Room 2200
Washington, DC 20590
(202) 366–0746
Clara Smith, chief of information services
Hours: 8:00 a.m. to 4:00 p.m.

DOCKETS
Contact the FHWA Law Library, Docket Room (above).

RULES AND REGULATIONS
FHWA rules and regulations are published in the *Code of Federal Regulations,* Title 23, parts 1–999 and 1204–1252, and Title 49, parts 301–399. Proposed rules, new final rules, and updates to the *Code of Federal Regulations* are published in the daily *Federal Register. (See appendix for details on how to obtain and use these publications.)*

A summary of DOT regulatory actions is published semiannually in the *Federal Register.*

■ LEGISLATION

The FHWA carries out its responsibilities under:

Interstate Commerce Act (24 Stat. 379, 49 U.S.C. 1). Signed by the president Feb. 4, 1887. Empowers the FHWA to establish safety standards for all commercial motor carriers engaged in interstate or foreign commerce.

Crimes and Criminal Procedures Act (62 Stat. 738, 18 U.S.C. 831). Signed by the president June 25, 1948. Authorized the FHWA to regulate transportation of dangerous cargoes on U.S. highways.

Highway Safety Act of 1966 (80 Stat. 731, 23 U.S.C. 401). Signed by the president Sept. 9, 1966. Required each state to have a highway safety program that meets federal standards for driver and pedestrian performance and bicycle safety. Authorized the FHWA to provide incentive grants to states that reduce traffic fatalities and to enact legislation requiring the use of seat belts.

Department of Transportation Act (80 Stat. 931, 49 U.S.C. 1651). Signed by the president Oct. 15, 1966. Created the cabinet-level Department of Transportation; transferred authority for safety standards for motor carriers from the Interstate Commerce Commission to the FHWA.

Highway Safety Act of 1970 (84 Stat. 1739, 23 U.S.C. 144). Signed by the president Dec. 31, 1970. Divided responsibility for the Highway Safety Act of 1966 between the National Highway Traffic Safety Administration (NHTSA) and the FHWA. The FHWA was given responsibility for highway safety and design programs and the NHTSA was given authority over vehicle and pedestrian safety.

Intermodal Surface Transportation Efficiency Act of 1991 (ISTEA) (105 Stat. 1914, 49 U.S.C. 101 note). Signed by the president Dec. 18, 1991. Increased funding to enhance transportation efficiency. Authorized funding for incentive programs to improve passenger safety and to prevent drunk driving.

National Highway System Designation Act of 1995 (109 Stat. 568, 23 U.S.C. 101 note). Signed by the president Nov. 28, 1995. Designated roughly 160,000 miles of interstate highways and other heavily traveled roads as the National Highway System (NHS). Repealed the federal cap on highway speed limits, allowing states to set their own speed limits for all roadways.

Transportation Equity Act for the 21st Century (TEA-21) (112 Stat. 154, 23 U.S.C. 143). Signed by the president June 9, 1998. Reauthorized the federal highway, transit, safety, research, and motor carrier programs under the ISTEA from 1998 through 2003. Provided incentives for states to adopt tough .08 blood alcohol concentration standards for drunk driving.

Motor Carrier Safety Improvement Act of 1999 (113 Stat. 1748). Signed by the president Dec. 9, 1999. Title I established the Federal Motor Carrier Safety Administration within the DOT, to be headed by an administrator appointed by the president and confirmed by the Senate.

■ REGIONAL OFFICES

EASTERN RESOURCE CENTER
10 S. Howard St., #4000
Baltimore, MD 21201-1819
(410) 962-0093
Gene K. Fong, director of field services

MIDWESTERN RESOURCE CENTER

19900 Governors Dr., #301
Olympia Fields, IL 60461-1021
(708) 283-3510
Christine Johnson, director of field services

SOUTHERN RESOURCE CENTER

61 Forsyth St. S.W., #17T26
Atlanta, GA 30303-3104
(404) 562-3570
Eugene W. Cleckley, director of field services

WESTERN RESOURCE CENTER

201 Mission St., #2100
San Francisco, CA 94105
(415) 744-3102
Christine Johnson, director of field services

Federal Motor Carrier Safety Administration

400 7th Street S.W., Washington, DC 20590
Internet: http://www.fmcsa.dot.gov

The Federal Motor Carrier Safety Administration (FMCSA) was established within the Department of Transportation on Jan. 1, 2000, pursuant to the Motor Carrier Safety Improvement Act of 1999. Formerly a part of the Federal Highway Administration, the Federal Motor Carrier Safety Administration's primary mission is to prevent commercial motor vehicle-related fatalities and injuries.

FMCSA promotes safety in motor carrier operations through strong enforcement of safety regulations, targeting high-risk carriers and commercial motor vehicle drivers; improving safety information systems and commercial motor vehicle technologies; strengthening commercial motor vehicle equipment and operating standards; and increasing safety awareness. To accomplish these activities, FMCSA works with federal, state, and local enforcement agencies, the motor carrier industry, labor safety interest groups, and others.

The following are programs administered by FMCSA.

Motor Carrier Safety Assistance Program. This is a federal grant program that provides states with financial assistance for roadside inspections and other commercial motor vehicle safety programs. It promotes detection and correction of commercial motor vehicle safety defects, commercial motor vehicle driver deficiencies, and unsafe motor carrier practices before they become contributing factors to crashes and hazardous materials incidents. The program also promotes the adoption and uniform enforcement by the states of safety rules, regulations, and standards compatible with the federal motor carrier safety regulations and federal hazardous materials regulations.

Regulatory Compliance and Enforcement. The FMCSA's compliance reviews and enforcement activities and the states' roadside inspection activities are the principal means of ensuring that the federal motor carrier safety regulations and the federal hazardous materials regulations are enforced. Compliance and enforcement efforts are enhanced through the Performance and Registration Information Systems Management (PRISM) program, a federal and state partnership to improve safety performance or remove high-risk carriers from the nation's highways. Through PRISM, compliance reviews are conducted on unsafe motor carriers and their safety performance is monitored and tracked. Continued poor safety performance may result in a federal operations out-of-service order/unfit determination in conjunction with the suspension and/or revocation of vehicle registration privileges.

Commercial Driver's License Program (CDL). FMCSA develops, issues, and evaluates standards for testing and licensing commercial motor vehicle drivers. These standards require states to issue a commercial driver's license only after drivers pass knowledge and skill tests that pertain to the type of vehicle operated. States are audited every three years to monitor compliance with federal standards; noncompliance could result in loss of federal funding.

Data and Analysis. FMCSA collects and disseminates safety data concerning motor carriers. Data collected by federal safety investigators and state partners from roadside inspections, crashes, compliance reviews, and enforcement activities are indexed by carrier. This information provides a national perspective on carrier performance and assists in determining FMCSA and state enforcement activities and priorities. Combined with data from other sources (including the National Highway Traffic Safety Administration), extensive analysis is performed to determine trends in performance by carrier and other factors such as cargo, driver demographics, location, time, and type of incident. Based on identified trends, FMCSA directs resources in the most efficient and effective manner to improve motor carrier safety.

Research and Technology Program. FMCSA identifies, coordinates, and administers research and development to enhance the safety of motor carrier operations, commercial motor vehicles, and commercial motor vehicle drivers. FMCSA promotes the use of information systems and advanced technologies to improve commercial vehicle safety, simplify government administrative systems, and provide savings to states and the motor carrier industry.

Border and International. FMCSA supports the development of compatible motor carrier safety requirements and procedures throughout North America in the context of the North American Free Trade Agreement (NAFTA). The agency supports programs to improve the safety performance of motor carriers operating in border areas through special grants to states for enforcement activities and, in cooperation with other federal agencies, it supports the development of state safety inspection facilities. FMCSA participates in international technical organizations and committees to share best practices in motor carrier safety.

Hazardous Materials. FMCSA enforces regulations for the safe transportation of hazardous materials by highway and rules governing the manufacture and maintenance of cargo tank motor vehicles, as set forth in Chapter 51 of Title 49 of the U.S. Code.

Licensing and Insurance. With the closing of the Interstate Commerce Commission (ICC), the licensing and insurance responsibility of the ICC were transferred to the Office of Motor Carrier and later to FMCSA.

■ KEY PERSONNEL

Administrator
Annette M. Sandberg (acting)......... (202) 366–2519
Deputy Administrator
Annette M. Sandberg .... (202) 366–2519
Chief Safety Officer
Brian McLaughlin (acting) .... (202) 366–2519
Strategic Planning and Program Evaluation
Sue Halladay........................... (202) 366–0596
Administration
Allen Fisher............................ (202) 366–8773
Chief Counsel
Warren E. Hoemann................... (202) 366–0834
Enforcement and Regulatory Affairs
Suzanne O'Malley..................... (202) 366–1367
Research, Technology and Information Management
Terry Shelton (acting)................. (202) 366–2525
Policy and Program Development
Brian McLaughlin..................... (202) 366–8173
Enforcement and Program Delivery
Steve Barber .... (202) 366–2525

■ INFORMATION SOURCES

Internet
Agency Web site: http://www.fmcsa.dot.gov.

Telephone Contacts
Personnel Locator (DOT) .... (202) 366–4000
Motor Carrier Safety Hotline.......... 1–888–DOT–SAFT (368–7238)

Information and Publications

KEY OFFICES

FMCSA Public and Consumer Affairs
400 7th Street S.W.
Washington, DC 20590
(202) 366-0456
Fax (202) 366-7298
David Longo, director

Freedom of Information
Federal Motor Carrier Safety Administration
FOIA Team
400 7th Street S.W.
Washington, DC 20590
(202) 366-2960
Fax (202) 366-3518
Joy Dunlap, team leader

Rules and Regulations
FMCSA rules and regulations are published in the *Code of Federal Regulations,* Title 49, parts 301-399. Proposed rules, new final rules, and updates to the *Code of Federal Regulations* are published in the daily *Federal Register. (See appendix for details on how to obtain and use these publications.)*

■ LEGISLATION
Tandem Truck Safety Act of 1984/Motor Carrier Safety Act of 1984 (98 Stat. 2829, 49 U.S.C. app. 2311). Signed by the president Oct. 30, 1984. Allowed states to ban large tandem trucks from unsafe sections of interstate highways. Improved uniformity of truck safety laws and broadened DOT enforcement powers to regulate truck safety.

Commercial Motor Vehicle Safety Act of 1986 (100 Stat. 3207-170, 49 U.S.C. app. 2701). Signed by the president Oct. 27, 1986. Required the DOT to issue and enforce state testing and licensing of commercial vehicle operators.

Truck and Bus Safety and Regulatory Reform Act of 1988 (102 Stat. 4527, 49 U.S.C. 2501 note). Signed by the president Nov. 18, 1988. Eliminated exemptions from safety rules for trucks and buses operating in metropolitan commercial zones and required rulemaking from the DOT secretary on the need and methods available to improve operator compliance.

Transportation Equity Act for the 21st Century (TEA-21) (112 Stat. 154, 23 U.S.C. 143). Signed by the president June 9, 1998. Reauthorized the federal highway, transit, safety, research, and motor carrier programs under the Intermodal Surface Transportation Efficiency Act of 1991 (ISTEA) from 1998 through 2003. Provided incentives for states to adopt tough .08 blood alcohol concentration standards for drunk driving.

Motor Carrier Safety Improvement Act of 1999 (113 Stat. 1748). Signed by the president Dec. 9, 1999. Title I established the Federal Motor Carrier Safety Administration within the DOT, to be headed by an administrator appointed by the president and confirmed by the Senate.

▓ REGIONAL OFFICES

EASTERN

10 S. Howard Street, Suite 4000
Baltimore, MD 21201-1819
(410) 962-0097
Joseph Muscara, field administrator

SOUTHERN

61 Forsyth Street SW, Suite 17T75
Atlanta, GA 30303-3104
(404) 562-3600
Jerry Cooper, field administrator

MIDWESTERN

19900 Governors Drive, Suite 210
Olympia Fields, IL 60461-1021
(708) 283-3577
JoAnne R. Haller, field administrator

WESTERN

201 Mission Street, Suite 2100
San Francisco, CA 94105
(415) 744-3088
Nicholas Walsh, field administrator

The administration also maintains division offices in each state.

Federal Railroad Administration

1120 Vermont Ave. N.W., Washington, DC 20590
Internet: http://www.fra.dot.gov

The Federal Railroad Administration (FRA) is an agency within the Department of Transportation (DOT). It has the authority to regulate the safety aspects of U.S. rail transportation.

The FRA is headed by an administrator appointed by the president and confirmed by the Senate. Serving under the administrator are four associate administrators responsible for administration and finance, railroad development, policy and program development, and safety. Other divisions include the offices of budget, chief counsel, and research and development.

The Office of the Associate Administrator for Safety is the principal regulatory unit in the FRA. The regulatory responsibility of the FRA extends to the safety of locomotives, signals, train safety appliances, power brakes, hours of service, and transportation of dangerous articles by railway.

The FRA employs close to 400 inspectors in eight regional offices to monitor safety equipment and procedures. Regulations require that all rail accidents be reported to and investigated by the Office of Safety.

Other FRA programs include rail transportation research and development, financial assistance in the form of grants to the National Railroad Passenger Corporation (Amtrak), and financial assistance (loans and loan guarantees) to railroads and others to promote safe operation and preserve the public interest in the nation's rail system.

Financial assistance takes the form of grant and loan programs for Amtrak and railroads in reorganization in the Midwest and Northeast, grants for state rail safety programs, and subsidies to small freight lines so that they will be able to continue service.

The Transportation Equity Act for the 21st Century (TEA-21), passed in 1998, authorized appropriations for FY 1998 through 2001 for high-speed rail technology activities (including corridor planning). High-speed rail refers to a series of technologies involving trains traveling at top speeds of 90 to 300 mph. A 1997 report to Congress concluded that each of these technologies has potential to solve passenger transportation problems in some of the nation's most well-traveled intercity corridors. FRA administers programs to help develop high-speed rail systems in such corridors.

In December 2000 Amtrak unveiled its new high-speed train service, known as Acela Express, in the Boston-New York-Washington Northeast Corridor. During the four weeks between Dec. 11 and Jan. 5, Acela Express attracted more than 11,000 customers and earned more than $1.25 million in ticket sales, beating projections by 12 percent.

FRA programs related to high-speed rail include research and development on high-speed rail safety and several activities authorized under TEA-21: the Next Generation High-Speed Rail Technology program, which develops and demonstrates technology elements that are important for reducing the cost or improving the effectiveness of high-speed rail through partnerships with states and industry; the Grade Crossing Hazard Elimination Program, which provides grants to states with designated high-speed rail corridors; and the Maglev Deployment Program, which aims to select one rail project for possible construction subsequent to preconstruction planning efforts by several competing states.

▌ KEY PERSONNEL

Administrator
Jon Allan Rutter .... (202) 493–6014
    Fax .... (202) 493–6009

Deputy Administrator
Elizabeth Monro .... (202) 493–6015
Civil Rights
Carl Ruiz................................ (202) 493-6010
Public Affairs
Robert L. Gould .... (202) 493–6024
Fax .... (202) 493–6013
Administration and Finance
Margaret Reid .... (202) 493–6100
Fax .... (202) 493–6169
Budget
D.J. Stadtler .... (202) 493–6150
Financial Services
Gerald K. Schoenauer.................. (202) 493–6141
Human Resources
William Tito .... (202) 493–6110
Chief Counsel
S. Mark Lindsey .... (202) 493–6052
Fax .... (202) 493–6068
Policy and Program Development
Vacant.................................. (202) 493–6400
Fax .... (202) 493–6401
Industry and Intermodal Policy
Jane H. Bachner .... (202) 493–6400
Policy Systems
Raphael Kedar .... (202) 493–6410
Railroad Development
Mark Yachmetz......................... (202) 493–6381
Jo Strang, deputy administrator....... (202) 493–6386
Fax .... (202) 493–6330
Freight Programs
JoAnne McGowan...................... (202) 493–6390
Research and Development
Steven Ditmeyer........................ (202) 493–6347
Safety
George Gavalla (acting)................ (202) 493–6304
Fax .... (202) 493–6309
Safety Analysis
John Leeds .... (202) 493–6327
Safety Assurance and Compliance
Edward Pritchard....................... (202) 493–6321

▨ INFORMATION SOURCES

Internet
Agency Web site: http://www.fra.dot.gov. Includes general agency information and links to specific FRA offices.

Telephone Contacts
Personnel Locator (FRA) .... (202) 493-6000

Information and Publications

KEY OFFICES

FRA Public Affairs
1120 Vermont Ave. N.W.
Washington, DC 20590
(202) 493–6024
Robert L. Gould, Associate Administrator for Public Affairs

Provides public information on the FRA and distributes all FRA publications and news releases.

Freedom of Information
FRA Office of the Chief Counsel
1120 Vermont Ave. N.W. -RCC-20
Washington, DC 20590
(202) 493–6039
Lauren Price, FOIA Officer

PUBLICATIONS
FRA Public Affairs can provide information on publications. *(See above.)*

DATA AND STATISTICS
The FRA annually produces reports and studies that are available to the public. In particular, the Office of Safety releases accident reports and data, including an annual analysis of railroad accidents and incidents. Contact the Office of Safety or the Office of Public Affairs. Some of this information is also available on FRA's Web site.

Reference Resources

LIBRARY

DOT Library
Transportation Administrative Services Center (TASC)
400 7th St. S.W., Room 2200
Washington, DC 20590
(202) 366–0746
Clara Smith, chief of information services
Hours: 8:00 a.m. to 4:00 p.m.

DOCKETS

FRA Office of the Chief Counsel
1120 Vermont Ave. N.W., Mail Stop 10
Washington, DC 20590
(202) 493–6030
Ivornette Lynch, docket clerk
Hours: 9:00 a.m. to 6:00 p.m.

Maintains dockets, containing all material related to FRA rulemakings and other administrative proceedings, for inspection.

RULES AND REGULATIONS

FRA rules and regulations are published in the *Code of Federal Regulations,* Title 49, parts 200–299. Proposed rules, new final rules, and updates to the *Code of Federal Regulations* are published in the daily *Federal Register. (See appendix for information on how to obtain and use these publications.)*

▨ LEGISLATION

Statutes administered by the FRA include:

Department of Transportation Act (80 Stat. 931, 49 U.S.C. 1652). Signed by the president Oct. 15, 1966. Created the FRA and set rail safety standards; provided for inspection of locomotives, signal systems, and mail cars; and set standards for reporting railroad accidents.

Federal Railroad Safety and Hazardous Materials Transportation Control Act of 1970 (84 Stat. 971, 45 U.S.C. 431). Signed by the president Oct. 16, 1970. Required establishment of safety standards for railroads and provided grants to states for safety programs.

Regional Rail Reorganization Act of 1973 (87 Stat. 986, 45 U.S.C. 701). Signed by the president Jan. 2, 1974. Provided funds for rail service continuation, property acquisition, and construction or improvement of facilities.

Railroad Revitalization and Regulatory Reform Act of 1976 (90 Stat. 31, 45 U.S.C. 801). Signed by the president Feb. 5, 1976. Provided financial assistance to rehabilitate and improve railroads.

Staggers Rail Act of 1980 (94 Stat. 1895, 49 U.S.C. 10101 note). Signed by the president Oct. 14, 1980. Provided railroads with more pricing rate flexibility and contract provisions.

Rail Safety Improvement Act of 1988 (102 Stat. 624, 45 U.S.C. 421 note). Signed by the president June 22, 1988. Amended the Federal Railroad Safety Act of 1970 by increasing penalties and liabilities of individuals. Established a program requiring licensing or certification of engineers. Gave the FRA jurisdiction over high-speed rail systems.

Transportation Equity Act for the 21st Century (TEA-21) (112 Stat. 154, 23 U.S.C. 143). Signed by the president June 9, 1998. Amended federal railroad law to authorize appropriations for high-speed rail technology activities. Amended the Railroad Revitalization and Regulatory Reform Act of 1976 to authorize the secretary to provide direct loans and loan guarantees to state and local governments, government-sponsored authorities and corporations, railroads, and joint ventures that include at least one railroad.

▨ REGIONAL OFFICES

REGION 1

(CT, MA, ME, NH, NJ, NY, RI, VT)
55 Broadway, #1077
Cambridge, MA 02142
(617) 494–2302
Mark McKeon, regional director

REGION 2

(DC, DE, MD, OH, PA, VA, WV)
2 International Plaza, #550
Philadelphia, PA 19113
(610) 521–8200
Dave Myers, regional director

REGION 3

(AL, FL, GA, KY, MS, NC, SC, TN)
61 Forsyth St. S.W., #16T20
Atlanta, GA 30303
(404) 562–3800
Fred Dennin, regional director

REGION 4

(IL, IN, MI, MN, WI)
200 W. Adams St.
Chicago, IL 60606
(312) 353–6203
Laurence Hasvold, regional director

REGION 5

(AR, LA, NM, OK, TX)
4100 International Plaza, #450
Hurst, TX 76053
(817) 862–2200
John F. Megary, regional director

REGION 6

(CO, IA, KS, MO, NE)
911 Locust St., #464
Kansas City, MO 64106
(816) 329-3840
Darrell Tisor, regional director

REGION 7

(AZ, CA, HI, NV, UT)
801 I St., #466
Sacramento, CA 95814
(916) 498–6540
Alvin L. Settje, regional director

REGION 8

(AK, ID, MT, ND, OR, SD, WA, WY)
703 Broadway, #650
Vancouver, WA 98660
(206) 696–7536
Dick L. Clairmont, regional director

Federal Transit Administration

400 7th St. S.W., Washington, DC 20590
Internet: http://www.fta.dot.gov

The federal government became actively involved in mass transportation with the enactment of the Housing Act of 1961, which provided limited loans and grants to state and local governments for transit development. The first comprehensive transit legislation, the Federal Transit Act, was signed by President Lyndon B. Johnson in 1964, but the actual forerunner to the Federal Transit Administration (FTA), the Urban Mass Transit Administration (UMTA), was not established until 1968. The UMTA became one of the five modal administrations in the newly created Department of Transportation.

The Federal Transit Act of 1964 established the first comprehensive program of federal assistance for mass transportation, including provisions for matching grants, technical assistance, and research and development. The Federal Transit Assistance Act of 1970 included substantially increased funding and officially designated the FTA to provide consolidated management of all federal mass transit programs.

The Surface Transportation Assistance Act (STAA) of 1982 included a penny a gallon gas tax dedicated to transit. Other major provisions established a separate Mass Transit Account (under the Highway Trust Fund), authorized discretionary contract authority for the trust fund, and created a block grant program funded from the general fund apportionments for fiscal years 1984–1986. Most grant recipients are states and public transit agencies. Major research and demonstration projects are carried out by the FTA under contract to private organizations, including state and local governments.

FTA projects include new techniques of traffic management, crime reduction and safety studies, new computerized techniques for planning needs, and special features to facilitate the use of mass transportation systems by the elderly and handicapped.

In 1991 President George Bush signed the Intermodal Surface Transportation Efficiency Act (ISTEA), which authorized funding for highways, highway safety, and mass transportation through fiscal year 1997. In 1998 ISTEA was reauthorized through 2003 with a budget authority totaling $215 billion.

Following the passage of welfare reform legislation in 1996, the Department of Transportation (DOT) recognized that most welfare recipients (94 percent) do not own automobiles. The 1998 ISTEA reauthorization established the Job Access and Reverse Commute Grant program designed to assist states and localities in developing new or expanded transportation services that connect welfare recipients and other low-income persons to jobs and other employment related services.

▮ KEY PERSONNEL

Administrator
Jennifer L. Dorn........................ (202) 366–4040
Fax..................................... (202) 366–9854
Deputy Administrator
Robert Jamison......................... (202) 366–4325
Administration
Tim Wolgast (acting) .... (202) 366–4007
Fax..................................... (202) 366–7164
Budget and Policy
Bob Tuccillo .... (202) 366–4050
Fax..................................... (202) 366–7116
Budget and Financial Management
Gwen Daniels........................... (202) 366–2918

Policy Development
Bill Menczer .... (202) 366–1698
Chief Counsel
Will Sears .... (202) 366–4063
Fax .... (202) 366–3809
Environment and Regional Operations
Scott Biehl .... (202) 366–4063
General Law
Donald R. Durkee .... (202) 366–4063
Legislation and Regulations
Scott Biehl .... (202) 366–0748
Civil Rights
Michael Winter .... (202) 366–4018
Fax .... (202) 366–3475
Program Management
Hiram J. Walker .... (202) 366–4020
Fax .... (202) 366–7951
Lynn Sahaj .... (202) 366–4020
Research, Demonstration, and Innovation
Barbara Sisson .... (202) 366–4052

■ INFORMATION SOURCES

Internet

Agency Web site: http://www.fta.dot.gov. Includes a search feature, news releases, and information organized by subject and by office.

Telephone Contacts

Personnel Locator .... (202) 366–4000

Information and Publications

KEY OFFICES

Office of Communications & Congressional Affairs
400 7th St. S.W.
Washington, DC 20590
(202) 366–4043
Kristi Clemens, associate administrator

FTA Office of Research, Demonstration and Innovation
400 7th St. S.W., Room 9401
Washington, DC 20590
(202) 366–0201
Marina Dranzak, contact

Distributes FTA publications and technical information; maintains a reference collection.

PUBLICATIONS

Contact the FTA Office of Research, Demonstration and Innovation for pamphlets and brochures including bibliographies, abstracts of project reports, conference proceedings, and the annual directory of research, development, and demonstration projects.

Technical reports and publications on particular mass transit projects are available through the National Technical Information Service (NTIS): see appendix, Ordering Government Publications.

For the Transportation Department's annual report, which lists regulatory actions taken by the FTA, contact DOT Public Affairs, 400 7th St. S.W., Washington, DC 20590; (202) 366–4570.

DATA AND STATISTICS

Technical information is available from FTA Office of Research, Demonstrations and Innovation; (202) 366–4052.

Reference Resources

LIBRARIES

DOT Library
Transportation Administrative Services Center (TASC)
400 7th St. S.W., Room 2200
Washington, DC 20590
(202) 366–0746
Clara Smith, chief of information services
Hours: 8:00 a.m. to 4:00 p.m.

DOCKETS

DOT Office of the General Counsel
Documentary Services Division C-55
400 7th St. S.W., Room PL-401
Washington, DC 20590
(800) 647–5527
Hours: 10:00 a.m. to 5:00 p.m.

RULES AND REGULATIONS

FTA rules and regulations are published in the *Code of Federal Regulations,* Title 49, parts 601–670. Proposed regulations, new final regulations, and updates to the *Code of Federal Regulations* are published in the daily *Federal Register. (See appendix for details on how to obtain and use these publications.)*

■ LEGISLATION

The FTA carries out its responsibilities under:
Federal Transit Act of 1964 (78 Stat. 302, 49 U.S.C. 1601). Signed by the president July 9, 1964. Authorized the

Housing and Home Finance Administration to provide additional assistance for the development of comprehensive and coordinated mass transportation systems.

Reorganization Plan No. 2 of 1968 (82 Stat. 1369, 49 U.S.C. 1608 note). Signed by the president June 30, 1968. Established the FTA as an agency within the DOT.

Federal Transit Assistance Act of 1970 (84 Stat. 962, 49 U.S.C. 1601 note). Signed by the president Oct. 15, 1970. Provided long-term financing for expanded urban mass transportation programs.

Federal Transit Assistance Act of 1974 (88 Stat. 1567, 49 U.S.C. 1604a). Signed by the president Nov. 26, 1974. Authorized grants to state and local agencies to ensure adequate commuter transportation service in urban areas.

Federal Public Transportation Act of 1978 (92 Stat. 2735, 49 U.S.C. 1601 note). Signed by the president Nov. 6, 1978. Authorized mass transit funding for five years. Reorganized the mass transit discretionary grant program.

Surface Transportation Assistance Act of 1982 (96 Stat. 2097, 23 U.S.C. 104 note). Signed by the president Jan. 6, 1983. Amended the Federal Transit Act of 1964. Established mass transit accounts in the Highway Trust Fund for discretionary capital grants and a new Section 9 formula program to replace the Section 5 formula program.

Surface Transportation and Uniform Relocation Assistance Act of 1987 (101 Stat. 133, 49 U.S.C. 1601). Vetoed by the president March 27, 1987; veto overridden April 2, 1987. Authorized mass transit funding through Sept. 30, 1991. Reauthorized existing highway and mass transit policies and programs.

Intermodal Surface Transportation Efficiency Act of 1991 (ISTEA) (105 Stat. 1914, 49 U.S.C. 104 note). Signed by the president Dec. 18, 1991. Authorized funding for highways, highway safety, and mass transportation through fiscal year 1997. Set policy to develop a national intermodal transportation system that is economically efficient and environmentally sound. Title III changed the agency name from the Urban Mass Transit Administration to the Federal Transit Administration.

Transportation Equity Act for the 21st Century (TEA-21) (112 Stat. 154, 23 U.S.C. 143). Signed by the president June 9, 1998. Reauthorized the federal highway, transit, safety, research, and motor carrier programs under the ISTEA from 1998 through 2003. Provided incentives for states to adopt tough .08 blood alcohol concentration standards for drunk driving.

▪ REGIONAL OFFICES

REGION 1
(CT, MA, ME, NH, RI, VT)
55 Broadway, Kendall Square
Cambridge, MA 02142–0193
(617) 494–2055
Richard Doyle, regional administrator

REGION 2
(NJ, NY, VI)
1 Bowling Green, #429
New York, NY 10004-1415
(212) 668-2170
Letitia Thompson, regional administrator

REGION 3
(DC, DE, MD, PA, VA, WV)
1760 Market St., #500
Philadelphia, PA 19103–4124
(215) 656–7100
Herman Shipman, (acting) director

REGION 4
(AL, FL, GA, KY, MS, NC, PR, SC, TN)
61 Forsyth St. S.W., #17T50
Atlanta, GA 30303
(404) 562–3500
Jerry Franklin, regional administrator

REGION 5
(IL, IN, MI, MN, OH, WI)
200 W. Adams St., #2410
Chicago, IL 60606–5232
(312) 353–2789
Joel Ettinger, regional administrator

REGION 6
(AR, LA, NM, OK, TX)
Fritz Lanham Federal Bldg.
819 Taylor St., #8A36
Fort Worth, TX 76102
(817) 978-0550
Robert C. Patrick, regional administrator

REGION 7

(IA, KS, MO, NE)
901 Locust St., #404
Kansas City, MO 64106
(816) 523–0204
Molchtee Ahmad, regional administrator

REGION 8

(AZ, CO, MT, ND, NV, SD, UT, WY)
216 16th St., #650
Denver, CO 80202–5120
(303) 844–3242
Lee O. Waddleton, regional administrator

REGION 9

(AS, CA, GU, HI)
201 Mission St., #2210
San Francisco, CA 94105
(415) 744–3133
Leslie T. Rogers, regional administrator

REGION 10

(AK, ID, OR, WA)
915 Second Ave., #3142
Seattle, WA 98174–1002
(206) 220–7954
Rick Krochalis, regional administrator

Maritime Administration

400 7th St. S.W., Washington, DC 20590
Internet: http://www.marad.dot.gov

The Maritime Administration (MARAD) was transferred to the Department of Transportation (DOT) in 1981. It had been a Commerce Department agency since its establishment under Reorganization Plan No. 21 of 1950. MARAD is responsible for programs that aid the development, promotion, and operation of the U.S. merchant marine. The fleet serves the nation's foreign and domestic shipping needs and provides support as a naval auxiliary to the armed forces in times of national emergency.

MARAD is headed by a maritime administrator assisted by two deputy maritime administrators, a chief counsel, a secretary, and six associate administrators. The associate administrators are responsible for administration; ship financial approvals and cargo preference; port, intermodal, and environmental activities; policy and international trade; shipbuilding and technology development; and national security.

Financial Assistance. MARAD provides financial assistance programs to the U.S. shipping industry.

As originally enacted in 1936, the Federal Ship Financing Guarantees (Title XI) program authorized the federal government to insure private-sector loans or mortgages made to finance or refinance the construction or reconstruction of American-flag vessels in U.S. shipyards. Title XI was amended in 1972 to provide direct government guarantees of the underlying debt obligations for future transactions, with the government holding a mortgage on the equipment financed. The government insures or guarantees full payment of the unpaid principal, interest, mortgage, or obligation in the event of default by the vessel owner.

Capital Construction Fund (CCF). Administered by MARAD it was authorized by the Merchant Marine Act of 1970. This program enables operators to deposit tax-deferred earnings and other monies in CCF accounts to accumulate the large amounts of capital necessary to build, reconstruct, or acquire large ships.

U.S.-flag vessels that are involved in essential foreign trade are eligible for an operating-differential subsidy from MARAD. This subsidy is designed to off-set the higher cost of operating U.S.-flag vessels in foreign trade compared to operating costs of vessels under foreign flags.

Maritime Operations. The Maritime Subsidy Board, whose membership includes the administrator, the administrator's deputy, and the chief counsel, has authority to award, amend, and terminate subsidy contracts for the construction and operation of vessels in the foreign commerce of the United States. It also performs investigations, gathers data from the industry, and holds public hearings. All of the board's decisions are subject to review by the secretary of transportation.

- Reserve Fleet. MARAD maintains a National Defense Reserve Fleet of approximately 300 merchant ships at Ft. Eustis, Va.; Beaumont, Texas; and Suisun Bay, Calif. The ships are preserved for reactivation if needed during a national emergency. In 1975 MARAD established the Ready Reserve Fleet (RRF) with the U.S. Navy. The RRF provides merchant vessels that can be activated for military sealift duties within five to twenty days.

- Emergency Operations. During a national emergency MARAD directs the operation of merchant ships through the National Shipping Authority. The American merchant marine has transported approximately 90 percent of sealift cargoes in U.S. war efforts of the past.

Shipbuilding and Technology Development. Responsibilities of this division include formulating, directing, and coordinating national policies and programs for developing and reviewing the designs of proposed ships;

assisting in the administration of MARAD's shipbuilding contracts; and administering programs that collect, analyze, and maintain data on the relative costs of shipbuilding in the United States and foreign countries.

Maritime Labor, Training and Safety. This division is responsible for MARAD policy regarding labor management relations, training, and safety as it applies to seafaring, longshore, and shipyard workers. To execute these policies, the division directs studies and supervises development and implementation of reports on organized maritime labor; processes nominations for appointments to the U.S. Merchant Marine Academy; administers an assistance program for state maritime academies; and promotes the use of safe practices in the maritime industry and provision of high-quality safety training at the academy.

Maritime Security Program (MSP). On a contingency basis, an active, privately owned, U.S.-flagged, and U.S.-crewed liner fleet is available to assist the Department of Defense (DOD). The MSP was established by the Maritime Security Act of 1996 and provides approximately $100 million in annual funding for up to forty-seven vessels to help offset the higher operating costs of keeping these vessels under U.S. flag registry. MSP payments represent approximately 13 percent of the cost of operating U.S.-flag vessels.

Other Responsibilities. MARAD also is responsible for promoting the U.S. merchant marine and for a variety of other programs. These include the training of officers at the U.S. Merchant Marine Academy at Kings Point, N.Y., and administering the Cargo Preference Act, which requires at least 50 percent of all federal government-generated cargoes to be shipped in U.S.-flag vessels. The agency also operates a National Maritime Research Center at Kings Point.

The Maritime Administration is charged under the American Fisheries Act (AFA) of 1998 with the responsibility of determining whether vessels of 100 feet or greater comply with the new ownership, control, and financing requirements. The AFA raised the U.S. citizen ownership and control threshold that U.S.-flag vessels must meet to be eligible to operate in U.S. waters from 50 percent to 75 percent.

In November 2002 President George W. Bush signed the Maritime Transportation Act, one of the largest maritime bills in decades. The law required the DOT to improve security at U.S. ports and foreign ports where U.S.-bound shipments originate. The legislation was originally introduced in July 2001 to protect ports from illegal activity, including drug trafficking, cargo theft, and smuggling of contraband and aliens. Following the September 2001 terrorist attacks on the United States, concerns about the vulnerability of ports to terrorism accelerated passage of the bill.

■ KEY PERSONNEL

Maritime Administrator
Captain William G. Schabert .... (202) 366–5823
Fax .... (202) 366–3890
Deputy Maritime Administrator
Bruce J. Carlton (acting) .... (202) 366–1719
Administration
Ralph Ferguson (acting) .... (202) 366–5802
Fax .... (202) 366–3889
Accounting
John Hoban .... (202) 366–5852
Acquisition
Timothy P. Roark .... (202) 366–5757
Budget
Lynn Ashe .... (202) 366–5778
Civil Rights
Vontell Tucker .... (202) 366–5111
Information Resources Management
Ronnie Levine .... (202) 366–4181
Management Services
Richard Weaver, Director .... (202) 366–5816
Personnel
Raymond Pagliarini .... (202) 366–4141
Security
C.R. Gibbs .... (202) 366–5816
Chief Counsel
Robert B. Ostrom .... (202) 366–5711
Fax .... (202) 366–7485
Maritime Education Programs
Kris Krusa .... (202) 366–2648
Fax .... (202) 366–9206
National Security
James Caponiti .... (202) 366–5400
Fax .... (202) 366–3954
National Security Plans
Thomas M.P. Christensen .... (202) 366–5900
Sealift Support
Taylor E. Jones II .... (202) 366–2323
Ship Operations
William Trost .... (202) 366–1875
Policy and International Trade
Bruce J. Carlton .... (202) 366–5772
Fax .... (202) 366–3746
International Activities
Vacant .... (202) 366–5773
Policy and Plans
Janice G. Weaver .... (202) 366–4468
Statistical and Economic Analysis
William B. Ebersold .... (202) 366–2267
Port, Intermodal, and Environmental Activities
Margaret D. Blum .... (202) 366–4721
Fax .... (202) 366–6988

Environmental Activities
Michael Carter.......................... (202) 366–8887
Intermodal Development
Richard Walker........................ (202) 366–8888
Ports and Domestic Shipping
Raymond Barberesi................... (202) 366–4357
Cargo Preference
James J. Zok .... (202) 366–0364
Fax...................................... (202) 366–7901
Cargo Preferences
Thomas Harrelson .... (202) 366-4610
Costs and Rates
Michael P. Ferris....................... (202) 366–2324
Ship Financing
Mitchell D. Lax .... (202) 366–5744
Subsidy and Insurance
Edmond Fitzgerald.................... (202) 366–2400
Shipbuilding
Jean E. McKeever...................... (202) 366–5737
Fax...................................... (202) 366–5522
Ship Financial Approvals
Mitchell D. Lax .... (202) 366–5744
Shipbuilding and Marine Technology
Joseph A. Byrne .... (202) 366–1931

▪ INFORMATION SOURCES

Internet
Agency Web site: http://www.marad.dot.gov. Includes news and features, programs and initiatives, education, customer service, and doing business with MARAD.

Telephone Contacts
Personnel Locator.......................... (202) 366–5812
Toll Free................................1(800) 99MARAD

Information and Publications

KEY OFFICES

MARAD Congressional and Public Affairs
400 7th St. S.W.
Washington, DC 20590
(202) 366–5807
Robyn Boerstling, director
Vacant, media relations and public affairs officer

Issues news releases, publications, and texts of speeches given by administration officials. Maintains a mailing list and presents for public inspection the daily "press book,"

which covers all other agency actions that do not warrant a press release.

Freedom of Information
400 7th St. S.W.
Washington, DC 20590
(202) 366–2666
Jeanette Flood, FOI contact

PUBLICATIONS
MARAD Congressional and Public Affairs announces, lists and makes available publications via its Web site.

DATA AND STATISTICS

MARAD Statistical and Economic Analysis Office
400 7th St. S.W.
Washington, DC 20590
(202) 366–2267
William B. Ebersold, director

Collects information on most aspects of the U.S. merchant fleet. Issues reports that are available from MARAD Congressional and Public Affairs.

Reference Resources

LIBRARY

DOT Library
Transportation Administrative Services Center (TASC)
400 7th St. S.W., Room 2200
Washington, DC 20590
(202) 366–0746
Clara Smith, chief of information services
Hours: 8:00 a.m. to 4:00 p.m.

DOCKETS
DOT Office of General Counsel
Documentary Services
400 7th St. S.W.
Washington, DC 20590
(202) 366–9322
(800) 647–5527
Hours: 10:00 a.m. to 5:00 p.m.

Maintains dockets for MARAD rules, orders, and regulations.

RULES AND REGULATIONS
MARAD rules and regulations are published in the *Code of Federal Regulations,* Title 32a, Chapter 18 and

Title 46, parts 201–391. Proposed rules, new final rules, and updates to the *Code of Federal Regulations* are published in the daily *Federal Register. (See appendix for information on how to obtain and use these publications.)*

■ LEGISLATION

MARAD carries out its responsibilities under:

Merchant Marine Act, 1920 (41 Stat. 988, 46 U.S.C. 861). Signed by the president June 5, 1920. Section 867 of this act authorized support for the development of ports and other facilities connected with transport by water.

Merchant Marine Act of 1936 (49 Stat. 1985, 46 U.S.C. 1101). Signed by the president June 29, 1936. Established the subsidy program for the construction and operations of U.S. vessels.

Merchant Ship Sales Act (60 Stat. 41, 50 U.S.C. 1735). Signed by the president March 8, 1946. Gave MARAD authority to approve all sales or transfers of U.S.-flag vessels to a foreign country.

Cargo Preference Act (68 Stat. 832, 46 U.S.C. 1241). Signed by the president Aug. 26, 1954. Required that at least 50 percent of certain government cargoes be shipped on U.S. vessels.

Merchant Marine Act of 1970 (84 Stat. 1018, 46 U.S.C. 1101). Signed by the president Oct. 21, 1970. Overhauled the 1936 act to revitalize the merchant marine.

Shipping Act of 1984 (98 Stat. 67, 46 U.S.C. app. 1701 note). Signed by the president March 20, 1984. Reformed the regulation of liner shipping in U.S. foreign trade.

Food Security Act of 1985 (99 Stat. 1491, 46 U.S.C. 1241f). Signed by the president Dec. 23, 1985. Required that at least 75 percent of certain agricultural cargoes be shipped on U.S. vessels and that the DOT finance any resulting increase in ocean freight charges.

Intermodal Surface Transportation Efficiency Act of 1991 (ISTEA) (105 Stat. 1914, 49 U.S.C. 104 note). Signed by the president Dec. 18, 1991. Set the national policy plan for an economically and environmentally efficient intermodal transport system.

Maritime Security Act of 1996 (110 Stat. 3118, 46 U.S.C. app. 1245 note). Signed by the president Oct. 8, 1996. Amended the Merchant Marine Act of 1936 to mandate establishment of a fleet of active, militarily useful, privately owned vessels to meet national defense and other security requirements and maintain a U.S. presence in international commercial shipping.

American Fisheries Act (P.L. 105-277). Signed by the president Oct. 21, 1998. Amended federal law with regard to eligibility requirements for vessels to operate in certain fisheries.

Maritime Transportation Security Act of 2002 (116 Stat. 2064, 46 U.S.C. 2101). Signed by the president Nov. 25, 2002. Amended the Merchant Marine Act of 1936 to require the DOT to develop antiterrorism plans at U.S. ports and foreign ports where U.S.-bound shipments originate. Required the DOT to develop and maintain an antiterrorism cargo identification, tracking, and screening system. Required the DOT to establish a maritime intelligence program to help identify suspicious vessels before they entered U.S. ports. Authorized the DOT to establish a long-range vessel tracking system using satellite technology. Established a DOT National Maritime Security Advisory Committee to make recommendations for port security improvements.

■ REGIONAL OFFICES

NORTH ATLANTIC

(CT, DE, MA, MD, ME, NH, NJ, downstate NY, eastern PA, PR, RI, VT)
1 Bowling Green #418
New York, NY 10004-1415
(212) 668–3330
Robert McKeon, director

SOUTH ATLANTIC

(eastern FL, GA, NC, SC, VA, WV)
7737 Hampton Blvd., #4D–211
Norfolk, VA 23505
(757) 441–6393
Mayank Jain, director

CENTRAL

(AL, AR, western FL, IA, KS, KY, LA, MO, MS, NE, OK, TN, TX)
501 Magazine St., #1223
New Orleans, LA 70130–3394
(504) 589–2000
John W. Carnes, director

GREAT LAKES

(IL, IN, MI, MN, upstate NY, OH, western PA, WI)
2860 South River Rd., #185
Des Plaines, IL 60018–2413
(847) 298–4535
Doris Bautch, director

WESTERN
(AK, AZ, CA, CO, HI, ID, MT, ND, NM, NV, OR, SD, UT, WA, WY)
201 Mission St., #2200
San Francisco, CA 94105–1905
(415) 744–3125
Francis Johnston, director

U.S. MERCHANT MARINE ACADEMY
Kings Point, NY 11024–1699
(516) 773–5000
Rear Adm. Joseph D. Stewart (U.S.M.S.), superintendent

National Highway Traffic Safety Administration

400 7th St. S.W., Washington, DC 20590
Internet: http://www.nhtsa.dot.gov

The National Highway Traffic Safety Administration (NHTSA) is an agency within the Department of Transportation (DOT). It administers federal programs designed to increase motor vehicle safety and combat the deaths, injuries, and economic losses caused by highway crashes. The administration has authority to issue standards for vehicle safety, fuel economy, damage liability, and theft protection.

The NHTSA is headed by an administrator appointed by the president and confirmed by the Senate. Seven associate administrators serve under the administrator. The associate administrators are responsible for administration, safety assurance, plans and policy, research and development, safety performance standards, traffic safety programs, and regional operations.

The NHTSA:

- Develops mandatory minimum safety standards for domestic and foreign vehicles and vehicle equipment (tires, lights, child restraints) sold in the United States.
- Establishes corporate average fuel economy standards for passenger cars and light-duty vehicles (vans and pickup trucks).
- Administers state and community highway safety grant programs with the Federal Highway Administration (*p. 648*).
- Undertakes research, development, and demonstration of new state and community highway safety grant programs, particularly against drunk driving.
- Enforces compliance with safety and fuel economy standards; identifies safety defects in vehicles and administers manufacturer-recall campaigns for corrective action; enforces federal odometer tampering laws; and operates a toll-free auto safety hotline.

- Issues bumper standards designed to minimize consumer losses associated with low-speed crashes.
- Issues standards requiring certain parts on high-theft vehicle lines to be marked to reduce vehicle thefts.

Vehicles. NHTSA safety standards for vehicles are based on research performed by the agency. The research determines which parts of the vehicle can be improved to provide greater protection in the event of a crash or to reduce the incidence of crashes. The administration also investigates vehicle defects and can order manufacturers to repair flaws that affect the safe performance of the vehicle.

The agency can order manufacturers to include certain safety features in the design of a motor vehicle. In the past, safety features ordered by the NHTSA have included seat belts, safety windshields, dual brake systems, air bags, steering columns able to absorb impact, and high-mounted stop lamps.

The NHTSA operates a toll-free auto safety hotline through which it receives most of its information and complaints on vehicle defects from consumers.

Copies of all complaints not covered by an agency standard are forwarded to vehicle manufacturers and to the NHTSA's Office of Defects Investigation. This office enters complaints into a computer database. If a pattern of complaints develops that points to a possible safety defect, an investigation is conducted to confirm the defect and to determine its cause and severity. The manufacturer may voluntarily recall and repair the product at any time during this agency process. If the process reaches the formal investigation stage without a recall, the NHTSA will issue a public announcement and request comments from the public and the manufacturer. After analysis of this information, the agency will (if it appears necessary) issue an initial determination that a safety defect exists and schedule a public meeting. The public meeting is announced in the *Federal Register* and in the news media, allowing comments from the manufacturer, consumer groups, and other interested parties.

Based on findings from the public meeting, the agency may issue a final determination of a defect and then may order the manufacturer to recall the product. The manufacturer is required to supply the NHTSA with information on how the recall will be carried out and what corrective action will be taken. Consumers must be notified by mail and the defect must be corrected at no charge to the consumer. NHTSA recall orders may be contested by the manufacturer in U.S. District Court. Most investigations leading to a recall are resolved in the early stages with a voluntary recall, but NHTSA has been to court on several occasions to try to force involuntary recalls.

Compliance with NHTSA standards is achieved through the annual outlay of funds for the selected purchase of motor vehicles of all classes as well as the procurement of automotive parts and components, including tires, for testing. Using a precise procedure prepared by agency engineers, compliance testing is accomplished under agency supervision, principally through the use of private (nonfederal) testing facilities. Motor vehicle equipment and motor vehicles that do not comply with the standards are subject to manufacturer recall and substantial civil penalties.

The NHTSA manages programs to ensure that nonconforming foreign vehicles (gray market) are properly modified and certified in conformity with the Federal Motor Vehicle Safety Standards. This is principally accomplished through the engineering review of certification data submitted by registered importers as evidence of compliance and by physical inspections of selected vehicles. The NHTSA can recommend the forfeiture of customs bonds, impose civil penalties, or enter into litigation in its efforts to support certification.

In 1998 NHTSA officials signed an international agreement in Geneva that made possible the development of global regulations concerning the safety performance of motor vehicles and motor vehicle equipment.

Enforcement of the Federal Odometer Tampering Law and Regulations also is an NHTSA responsibility. Investigators at agency headquarters and in regional offices refer cases of odometer fraud to the Department of Justice for criminal prosecution. In addition, each investigator works closely with state agencies in each enforcement region in odometer fraud investigations.

Traffic Safety. The NHTSA supervises a program of grants to states to set up motor vehicle, driver, and pedestrian safety programs. Areas covered by safety programs include effects of alcohol and other drugs on driving ability,

occupant protection, emergency medical services, police traffic services, motorcycle safety, and traffic records.

The NHTSA, through its National Driver Register, maintains a nationwide file on drivers with license sanctions for drunk driving and other serious violations.

In 1995 Congress repealed the federal cap on highway speed limits, allowing states to set their speed limits for all roadways.

Fuel Economy Standards. The NHTSA has authority to prescribe fuel use economy standards—the average number of miles per gallon a manufacturer's fleet has to achieve. The agency has established average fuel economy standards for passenger cars beginning with the 1978 model year and nonpassenger motor vehicles beginning with the 1979 model year. The NHTSA has developed an economic, marketing, and technological database to support and provide information on the fuel economy program.

Fuel economy standards are enforced through tests, inspections, and investigations. The Environmental Protection Agency *(p. 52)* is responsible for the actual testing of automobiles for gas mileage performance. The NHTSA recommends enforcement and compliance actions in conjunction with the Department of Justice and the Federal Trade Commission *(p. 194)*, the agencies that enforce the law requiring that fuel economy rating labels be affixed to new vehicles.

The NHTSA has the authority to fine manufacturers who fail to comply with standards; it offers credits to offset fines to manufacturers who exceed average fuel economy standards.

▉ KEY PERSONNEL

Administrator
    Jeffrey W. Runge........................ (202) 366–2105
    Fax..................................... (202) 366–2106
Deputy Administrator
    Vacant.................................. (202) 366–2775
Chief Counsel
    Jacqueline Glassman.................... (202) 366–9511
Civil Rights
    George Quick........................... (202) 366–0972
Executive Correspondence
    Linda Divelbiss........................ (202) 366–2870
External Affairs
    Scott Brenner.......................... (202) 366–2111
Policy and Operations
    William Walsh.......................... (202) 366–2017
    Fax.................................... (202) 366–2559
Advanced Research and Analysis
    Raymond Owings....................... (202) 366–1537
Advanced Safety Research
    Keith Brewer........................... (202) 366–5662

National Center for Statistics and Analysis
Joseph Carra............................(202) 366–1503
Administration
Delmas Johnson........................(202) 366–1788
Human Resources
Essex Brown............................(202) 366–1784
Contracts and Procurement
Gail Felder.............................(202) 366–0607
Technology and Information Management
Joseph Cassell..........................(202) 366–0136
Planning, Evaluation and Budget
Rose McMurray........................(202) 366–2550
Strategic and Program Planning
Jane Dion..............................(202) 366–1574
Regulatory Analysis and Evaluation
James F. Simmons......................(202) 366–2555
Fiscal Services
Katherine Montgomery................(202) 366–2577
International Policy and Harmonization
Julie Abraham..........................(202) 366–2114
Chief Information Officer
Susan White............................(202) 366–0136
Communications and Consumer Information
Susan Gorcowski.......................(202) 366–9550
Traffic Injury Control
Brian McLaughlin......................(202) 366–1755
Program Development and Delivery
Marilena Amoni........................(202) 366–1755
Impaired Driving and Occupant Protection
Jeffrey Michael.........................(202) 366–4913
Safety Programs
Susan Ryan............................(202) 366–9588
Research and Technology
Richard Compton......................(202) 366–9591
Injury Control Operations and Resources
Marlene Markison......................(202) 366–2121
Vehicle Safety
Ronald Medford........................(202) 366–1810
Rulemaking
Stephen Kratzke.......................(202) 366–1810
Crashworthiness Standards
Roger Saul.............................(202) 366–1740
Crash Avoidance Standards
Claude Harris..........................(202) 366–4931
Planning and Consumer Standards
Noble Bowie...........................(202) 366–0846
Enforcement
Kenneth Weinstein.....................(202) 366–9700
Defects Investigation
Kathleen Demeter......................(202) 366–2850

Vehicle Safety Compliance
Vacant.................................(202) 366–2832
Odometer Fraud Investigation
Richard Morse.........................(202) 366–4761
Applied Research
Joseph Kanianthra.....................(202) 366–4862
Vehicle Research and Test Center
Michael Monk..........................(937) 666–4511
Applied Vehicle and Test Center
William T. Hollowell...................(202) 366–5663

■ INFORMATION SOURCES

Internet

Agency Web site: http://www.nhtsa.dot.gov. Includes general information about NHTSA and sections on "Cars" and "People." Topics covered include vehicle testing, regulations and standards, and research, as well as injury prevention, driver performance, and crash information.

Telephone Contacts

DOT Auto Safety Hotline.................(888) 327–4236
DC area..................................(202) 366–0123
Personnel Locator.........................(202) 366–4000

Information and Publications

KEY OFFICES

Communications and Consumer Information
400 7th St. S.W.
Washington, DC 20590
(202) 366–9550
Susan Gorcowski, director

Provides public information, issues news releases and other materials, and answers general questions on vehicle safety.

Consumer information division responds to written consumer complaints and questions, acts as a clearinghouse for consumer publications on vehicle and pedestrian safety, issues *NHTSA Consumer Advisories* (press releases that contain information on investigations and recalls), and solicits reports from consumers on problems under investigation. DOT Public Affairs handles the distribution of consumer advisories: 400 7th St. S.W., Washington, DC 20590; (202) 366–5576.

Specific questions and complaints concerning vehicle safety should be directed to the DOT toll-free Auto Safety Hotline.

Freedom of Information

NHTSA Office of the Chief Counsel
400 7th St. S.W.
Washington, DC 20590
(202) 366–1834

PUBLICATIONS

Most NHTSA consumer and technical publications can be ordered from:

NHTSA Publications

Resource Center
3341 E. 75th Ave., #F
Landover, MD 20785
Online ordering : www.nhtsa.dot.gov

Materials are available on multiple highway safety topics including:

Occupant Protection
Impaired Driving
Pedestrian, Bicycle, and Motorcycle Safety
Emergency Medical Services
Traffic Law Enforcement

DATA AND STATISTICS

NHTSA National Center for Statistics and Analysis

400 7th St. S.W.
Washington, DC 20590
(202) 366–1503
Joseph Carra, director

The best source of data and statistics on highway traffic safety. See Publications (above) for some specific titles that include NHTSA data and statistics.

Reference Resources

LIBRARIES

NHTSA Technical Information Services

400 7th St. S.W., Room 5110
Washington, DC 20590
e-mail: tis@nhtsa.dot.gov
Fax (202) 493–2833
Hours: 9:30 a.m. to 4:00 p.m.

Contains a small collection of technical literature on highway and vehicle safety. Also performs database searches for a fee.

DOT Library

400 7th St. S.W., Room 2200
Washington, DC 20590
(202) 366–0746
Linda Cullen (acting), director
Hours: 8:00 a.m. to 4:00 p.m.

DOCKETS

The NHTSA Technical Reference Division maintains dockets for NHTSA rulemakings and other administrative proceedings for copying and inspection.

RULES AND REGULATIONS

NHTSA rules and regulations are published in the *Code of Federal Regulations,* Title 49, parts 400–999. Proposed rules, new final rules, and updates to the *Code of Federal Regulations* are published in the daily *Federal Register. (See appendix for information on how to obtain and use these publications.)*

■ LEGISLATION

The NHTSA carries out its responsibilities under:

National Traffic and Motor Vehicle Safety Act of 1966 (80 Stat. 718, 15 U.S.C. 1381). Signed by the president Sept. 9, 1966. Required the establishment of safety standards for all tires and vehicles, domestic and imported, sold in the United States. Authorized research and development programs on auto safety and expanded the national driver registration service to record the names of drivers whose licenses have been suspended or revoked.

Highway Safety Act of 1966 (80 Stat. 731, 23 U.S.C. 401). Signed by the president Sept. 9, 1966. Required states to establish highway safety programs that meet federal standards. Established a grant program to assist states and communities in creating highway safety programs.

Highway Safety Act of 1970 (84 Stat. 1739, 23 U.S.C. 144). Signed by the president Dec. 31, 1970. Divided responsibility for the Highway Safety Act of 1966 between the NHTSA and the Federal Highway Administration (FHWA). The FHWA was given responsibility for highway safety and design programs and the NHTSA was given authority over vehicle and pedestrian safety.

Motor Vehicle Information and Cost Savings Act of 1972 (86 Stat. 947, 15 U.S.C. 1901). Signed by the president Oct. 20, 1972. Authorized the NHTSA to enforce the national speed limit of 55 miles per hour and to set mandatory fuel use standards for motor vehicles. Authorized the agency to impose fines on manufacturers who fail to meet standards. Authorized the agency to perform research on reducing economic losses in car crashes by using diagnostic inspection techniques and prohibited any form of tampering with motor vehicle odometers.

Imported Vehicle Safety Compliance Act of 1988 (102 Stat. 2818, 15 U.S.C. 1381 note). Signed by the president Oct. 31, 1988. Required importers to prove that they are capable of modifying foreign-manufactured vehicles to meet U.S. safety standards.

Intermodal Surface Transportation Efficiency Act of 1991 (ISTEA) (105 Stat. 1914, 49 U.S.C. 101 note). Signed by the president Dec. 18, 1991. Authorized funding for incentive programs to improve occupant safety and to prevent drunk driving. Increased funding to enhance transportation efficiency.

National Highway System Designation Act of 1995 (23 U.S.C. 101 note). Signed by the president Nov. 28, 1995. Designated roughly 160,000 miles of interstate highways and other heavily traveled roads as the National Highway System (NHS). Routes on the NHS receive 30 percent of all federal highway aid initially, with increases to follow. Repealed the federal cap on highway speed limits, allowing states to set their own speed limits for all roadways.

Transportation Equity Act for the 21st Century (TEA-21) (112 Stat. 154, 23 U.S.C. 143). Signed by the president June 9, 1998. Reauthorized the federal highway, transit, safety, research, and motor carrier programs under the ISTEA from 1998 through 2003. Provided incentives for states to adopt tough .08 blood alcohol concentration standards for drunk driving.

Transportation Recall Enhancement, Accountability, and Documentation (TREAD) Act (114 Stat. 1806, 49 U.S.C. 3016 note). Signed by the president Nov. 1, 2000. Directed the DOT to undertake certain activities to improve highway safety.

▪ REGIONAL OFFICES

REGION I
(CT, MA, ME, NH, RI, VT)
Transportation System Center
Kendall Square, Code 903
Cambridge, MA 02142
(617) 494–3427
Heidi Coleman (acting), regional administrator

REGION II
(NJ, NY, PR, VI)
222 Mamaroneck Ave., #204
White Plains, NY 10605
(914) 682–6162
Fax (914) 682–6239
Thomas Louizou, regional administrator

REGION III
(DC, DE, MD, PA, VA, WV)
10 S. Howard St., #4000
Baltimore, MD 21201
(410) 962–0053
Fax (410) 962–2770
Elizabeth Baker, regional administrator

REGION IV
(AL, FL, GA, KY, MS, NC, SC, TN)
61 Forsyth St. S.W., #17T30
Atlanta, GA 30303
(404) 562–3739
Fax (404) 562–3763
Troy Ayers, regional administrator

REGION V
(IL, IN, MI, MN, OH, WI)
19900 Governors Dr., #201
Olympia Fields, IL 60461
(708) 503–8892 ext. 13
Fax (708) 503–8991
Donald J. McNamara, regional administrator

REGION VI
(AR, LA, NM, OK, TX)
819 Taylor St., #8A38
Fort Worth, TX 76102–6177
(817) 978–3653
Fax (817) 978–8339
Georgia S. Chakiris, regional administrator

REGION VII
(IA, KS, MO, NE)
P.O. Box 412515
Kansas City, MO 64141
(816) 329–3900
Fax (816) 329–3910
Romell Cooks, regional administrator

REGION VIII

(CO, MT, ND, SD, UT, WY)
555 Zang St., #430
Lakewood, CO 80228
(303) 969–6917
Fax (303) 969–6294
Louis De Carolis, regional administrator

REGION IX

(AS, AZ, CA, GU, HI, MP, NV)
201 Mission St., #2230
San Francisco, CA 94105
(415) 744–3089
Fax (415) 744–2532
David Manning, regional administrator

REGION X

(AK, ID, OR, WA)
3140 Jackson Federal Building
915 Second Ave.
Seattle, WA 98174
(206) 220–7640
Fax (206) 220–7651
Curtis A. Winston, regional administrator

Research and Special Programs Administration

400 7th St. S.W., Washington, DC 20590
Internet: http://www.rspa.dot.gov

The Research and Special Programs Administration (RSPA) is an agency in the Department of Transportation (DOT). Its main duties are carried out by the following offices: Hazardous Materials Safety; Management and Administration; Pipeline Safety; Research, Technology and Analysis; and the Volpe National Transportation Systems Center. Legal support is provided by the DOT Office of the General Counsel.

Office of Management and Administration. This office plans, develops, coordinates, and implements a comprehensive program of administration and financial management of all elements of RSPA.

Office of Hazardous Materials Safety (OHMS). The OHMS regulates the transportation of hazardous materials by all modes of transportation except bulk transport by water. Designates substances as hazardous materials and monitors shipping and carrier operations and packaging and container specifications in cooperation with the modal offices of the DOT. Operates a centralized system for reporting accidents involving hazardous materials. Written reports must be filed with the Information Systems Branch of the Policy Development and Information Systems Division of the OHMS within fifteen days of an accident. The OHMS has the authority to impose civil penalties of up to $10,000 per violation per day with no maximum fine.

The OHMS also sponsors two outreach programs: the Cooperative Hazardous Materials Enforcement Development Program (through the Initiatives and Training Division) and the Hazardous Materials Emergency Preparedness (HMEP) Grants Program. These programs are designed to foster cooperation among federal, state, and local agencies and the private sector with responsibilities for maintaining hazardous materials transportation safety.

Office of Pipeline Safety (OPS). The OPS develops and enforces design, construction, operations, and maintenance safety regulations for the transportation of gas and hazardous materials by pipeline. Also formulates and issues special exemptions to regulations.

Under the Natural Gas Pipeline Safety Act of 1968, states may acquire regulatory jurisdiction over some or all of their intrastate gas facilities. To enable a state to carry out an effective safety program, the OPS administers a program to pay states up to 50 percent of the actual costs incurred in regulating natural gas pipelines. The Pipeline Safety Act of 1979 authorized the establishment of a similar grant program for liquid gas facilities.

The OPS also reviews state regulation certificates for intrastate pipeline transportation; requires annual examination of pipelines and associated facilities on federal lands; and establishes and enforces standards and regulations to ensure safe construction and operation of pipelines on the Outer Continental Shelf.

The OPS has authority to impose civil penalties of up to $10,000 per day per violation for noncompliance with regulations; the maximum fine is not to exceed a total of $500,000.

Office of Innovation, Research and Education. This office shapes and advances the transportation research, engineering, and education agenda for the secretary of transportation and the president by conducting system-level assessments and policy research; facilitating government, university, and industry partnerships; fostering innovative inter/multimodal research, education and safety training; and managing department-wide strategic transportation research, technology, education, and training programs.

The Innovation, Research and Education University Transportation Centers (UTC) program, initiated in 1987 under the Surface Transportation and Uniform Relocation Assistance Act, authorized the establishment and operation of transportation centers in each of the ten standard federal regions. The Intermodal Surface Transportation Efficiency Act of 1991 (ISTEA) added four additional national centers and six University Research Institutes (URI). The mission of the fourteen UTCs is to advance U.S. expertise and technology transfer. The six URIs each have a specific transportation research and development mandate.

The DOT has implemented a research program in partnership with leading academic institutions, service providers, and industry for remote sensing, such as global positioning systems (GPS), in transportation. The program is designed to serve long-term research for education and workforce development and near-term technology applications to transportation practice. The program combines NASA research expertise in remote sensing with DOT expertise in technology assessment and application to transportation practice.

The Office of Emergency Transportation develops, coordinates, and reviews plans, policies, and programs for achieving and maintaining a high state of preparedness for transportation emergencies, including those caused by national defense needs, natural disasters, and other crisis situations.

Volpe National Transportation Systems Center (TSC). Headquartered in Cambridge, Mass., the TSC is the DOT's research, analysis, and systems engineering facility. Funding is generated through project agreements with various clients within the DOT and other federal agencies, such as the Federal Aviation Administration, the Federal Highway Administration, the Office of the Secretary of Transportation, the Environmental Protection Agency, and the Departments of Defense, Energy, and State. State and local agencies also use the center's resources. The center's four major programs are enhanced safety and security, infrastructure modernization, upgrading of management support systems, and departmental support.

The Volpe Center develops the U.S. Federal Radionavigation Plan (FRP) under the sponsorship of the Transportation Department's Office of the Assistant Secretary for Transportation Policy. The FRP is jointly published every two years by the Transportation Department and the Defense Department. Publication of the FRP is required by law. The FRP sets forth the official U.S. government policy on management, operating plans, and transition schedules for all U.S. government-operated, common-use (civil and military) radionavigation systems.

◼ KEY PERSONNEL

Administrator
vacant .... (202) 366–4433
Fax .... (202) 366–7431
Deputy Administrator
Samuel G. Bonasso .... (202) 366–4461
Chief Counsel
Elaine Joost (acting) .... (202) 366–4400
Civil Rights
Helen Hagin .... (202) 366–9638
Congressional Liaison (RSDA)
Patricia Klinger .... (202) 366–4831
Emergency Transportation
vacant .... (202) 366–5270
Hazardous Materials Safety
Robert McGuire .... (202) 366–0656
Fax .... (202) 366–5713
Enforcement
John O'Connell Jr. .... (202) 366–4700
Exemptions and Approvals
vacant .... (202) 366–4511
HMEP Grants Program
Charles Rogoff .... (202) 366–0001
Initiatives and Training
David Sargent .... (202) 366–4900
International Standards
Bob Richard .... (202) 366–0656
Planning and Analysis
Richard C. Hannon .... (202) 366–4484
Standards
Edward Mazzullo .... (202) 366–8553
Technology
Charles Hochman .... (202) 366–4545
Management and Administration
Edward A. Boigham .... (202) 366–4347
Fax .... (202) 366–7432
Administration
Marie Savoy .... (202) 366–4347
Budget and Programs
James Taylor .... (202) 366–5180
Contracts and Procurement
Lola Ward .... (202) 366–5180
Pipeline Safety
Stacey Gerard .... (202) 366–4595
Fax .... (202) 366–4566
Alaska Natural Gas Pipeline Project
vacant .... (202) 366–4556
Enforcement Compliance and State Operations
G. Tom Fortner .... (202) 366–4595
Program Support
Jeffrey Wiese .... (202) 366–4595

Regulatory Programs
Richard Huriaux .... (202) 366–4046
Research, Technology, and Analysis
Timothy Klein .... (202) 366–4434
Transportation Safety Institute (Oklahoma City)
Frank B. Tupper .... (405) 954–3153
Volpe National Transportation Systems Center (Cambridge, MA)
Richard R. John .... (617) 494–2222
Administratve Services
Philip S. Coonley .... (617) 494–2331
Information and Logistics Management
Karen M. Cronin .... (617) 494–2467
System and Economic Assessment
M.L. Tischer .... (617) 494–2374
Plans and Programs
Frank L. Hassler .... (617) 494–2563
Safety and Security
Robert Ricci .... (617) 494–2343
Environmental Preservation and Systems Modernization
David Lev .... (617) 494–2445
Traffic and Operations Management
Vivian J. Hobbs .... (617) 494–2354

■ INFORMATION SOURCES

Internet
Agency Web site: http://www.rspa.dot.gov. Includes general information about the RSPA and links to related Internet sites.

Telephone Contacts
Personnel Locator .... (202) 366–4000

Information and Publications

KEY OFFICES

RSPA Office of the Administrator
Program and Policy Support Staff
400 7th St. S.W.
Washington, DC 20590
(202) 366–4831
Patricia Klinger, external communications

Answers general inquiries from the public and the press about offices within the RSPA.

Freedom of Information
RSPA, DCR-1
400 7th St. S.W., Room 8419
Washington, DC 20590
(202) 366–9638
Helen Hagin, FOI contact

PUBLICATIONS

RSPA Hazardous Materials Initiatives and Training
400 7th St. S.W.
Washington, DC 20590
(202) 366–4900

Issues fact sheets, brochures, and pamphlets on hazardous materials transportation safety and education, regulations, and incident reporting procedures.

The Hazardous Materials Transportation Safety Newsletter, issued quarterly, summarizes notices of and amendments to recent rules and regulations, as well as DOT penalty actions against violators. Another RSPA publication, the *Emergency Response Guidebook,* is available from any U.S. Government Printing Office bookstore.

All publications are available through this division, which also provides a complete list of current publications and available audio-visual materials.

For the Transportation Department's annual report, which includes regulatory actions of the RSPA, contact DOT Public Affairs, 400 7th St. S.W., Washington, DC 20590; (202) 366–4570.

DATA AND STATISTICS

Bureau of Transportation Statistics
Office of Airline Statistics
Data Administration Division, DAI-20
400 7th St. S.W.
Washington, DC 20590
(202) 366–4373
Donald Bright, chief

Collects and maintains data on the financial and statistical results of air carrier operations in providing scheduled, nonscheduled, and charter air transportation. (Data may be viewed in the office's Reports Reference Room or accessed through a variety of government and private sector services.) Provides a list of private and government sources of aviation data and publishes guidelines for FOIA requests and for obtaining aviation economic data that are already in the public domain.

Technical Reference Center

Volpe National Transportation Systems Center
Kendall Square
Cambridge, MA 02142
(617) 494–2306

Provides data and statistics on transportation research.

Reference Resources

LIBRARY

DOT Library

Transportation Administrative Services Center (TASC)
400 7th St. S.W., Room 2200
Washington, DC 20590
(202) 366–0746
Clara Smith, chief of information services
Hours: 8:00 a.m. to 4:00 p.m.

DOCKETS

RSPA Public Docket Room

400 7th St. S.W., Room 8419
Washington, DC 20590
(202) 366–5046
Hours: 8:30 a.m. to 5:00 p.m.

Maintains dockets containing all materials related to rulemaking activities of the Office of Hazardous Materials Safety and the Office of Pipeline Safety for public inspection. Other offices in the RSPA do not maintain dockets.

RULES AND REGULATIONS

RSPA rules and regulations are published in the *Code of Federal Regulations,* Title 49, parts 100–199. Proposed regulations, new final regulations, and updates to the *Code of Federal Regulations* are published on Monday and Thursday in the *Federal Register. (See appendix for details on how to obtain and use these publications.)*

■ LEGISLATION

The Office of Hazardous Materials Transportation and the Office of Pipeline Safety carry out their responsibilities under authority granted in the following laws:

Mineral Leasing Act of 1920 (41 Stat. 437, 30 U.S.C. 185). Signed by the president Feb. 25, 1920. Authorized inspections of pipelines that have rights-of-way through federal lands.

Department of Transportation Act (80 Stat. 937, 49 U.S.C. 1655). Signed by the president Oct. 15, 1966. Created the cabinet-level Department of Transportation.

Natural Gas Pipeline Safety Act of 1968 (82 Stat. 720, 49 U.S.C. 1671). Signed by the president Aug. 12, 1968. Authorized the secretary of transportation to prescribe safety standards for the transportation of natural and other gas by pipeline.

Deepwater Port Act of 1974 (88 Stat. 2126, 33 U.S.C. 1501). Signed by the president Jan. 3, 1975. Established a licensing and regulatory program governing offshore deepwater ports development.

Hazardous Materials Transportation Act (88 Stat. 2156, 49 U.S.C. 1801). Signed by the president Jan. 3, 1975. Strengthened the laws governing the transportation of hazardous materials.

Hazardous Liquid Pipeline Safety Act of 1979 (93 Stat. 989, 49 U.S.C. 2001). Signed by the president Nov. 30, 1979. Clarified and expanded the authority of the DOT over liquefied natural gas and transportation safety. Established a statutory framework to regulate the transport of hazardous liquids.

Nuclear Waste Policy Act of 1982 (96 Stat. 2241, 42 U.S.C. 10157). Signed by the president Jan. 7, 1982. Assigned responsibility for licensing and regulating the transport of spent nuclear fuel to the DOT.

Comprehensive Omnibus Budget Reconciliation Act of 1986 (100 Stat. 140, 49 U.S.C. app. 1682a). Signed by the president April 7, 1986. Placed responsibility on the DOT for the establishment and collection of fees for natural gas and hazardous materials pipelines.

Comprehensive Environmental Response, Compensation and Liability Act of 1986 (Superfund) (100 Stat. 1695, 42 U.S.C. 9656). Signed by the president Oct. 17, 1986. Made common or contract carriers liable for damages or remedial actions resulting from the release of hazardous materials in transport, unless the carrier can demonstrate a lack of knowledge of the identity or nature of the substance.

Sanitary Food Transportation Act of 1990 (104 Stat. 1213, 49 U.S.C. app. 2801 note). Signed by the president Nov. 3, 1990. Prohibited transportation of most solid waste in refrigerated vehicles used to transport food, and transportation of some nonfood products in cargo tanks used to transport food.

Hazardous Materials Transportation Uniform Safety Act of 1990 (104 Stat. 3244, 49 U.S.C. app. 1801 note). Signed by the president Nov. 16, 1990. Strengthened the Hazardous Materials Transportation Act (HMTA) to include creation of a grant program to provide assistance to state and local governments. Authorized establishing regulations for the safe transportation of hazardous materials in intrastate, interstate, and foreign commerce.

Pipeline Safety Act of 1992 (106 Stat. 3289, 49 U.S.C. app. 1671 note). Signed by the president Oct. 24, 1992. Authorized the DOT to take several near-term actions to protect the environment, increased pipeline inspection requirements, and instituted a national program to inspect underwater pipelines.

Transportation Equity Act for the 21st Century (TEA-21) (112 Stat. 154, 23 U.S.C. 143). Signed by the president June 9, 1998. Reauthorized the federal research and safety programs under the Intermodal Surface Transportation Efficiency Act of 1991 (ISTEA) from 1998 through 2003.

Pipeline Safety Improvement Act of 2002 (116 Stat. 2985, 49 U.S.C. 60101). Signed by the president Dec. 17, 2002. Required the inspection of all major natural gas pipelines in densely populated areas within ten years, followed by reinspections every seven years. Authorized funds for research and development to improve all aspects of pipeline quality. Increased the DOT's authority to require operators to fix pipelines that have a potentially unsafe condition. Gave DOT the authority to increase states' involvement in the oversight of interstate pipeline transportation.

■ REGIONAL OFFICES

The Office of Research, Technology, and Analysis does not maintain independent regional offices. Direct questions concerning this office's regional activities to its main office.

Office of Hazardous Materials Enforcement

EASTERN
(CT, DC, DE, FL, GA, MA, MD, ME, NC, NH, NJ, NY, PA, PR, RI, SC, VA, VT, WV)
820 Bear Tavern Rd., #306
West Trenton, NJ 08628
(609) 989–2256
Colleen Abbenhaus, regional chief

CENTRAL
(IA, IL, IN, KS, KY, MI, MN, MO, ND, NE, OH, SD, WI)
2350 E. Devon Ave., #136
Des Plaines, IL 60018
(847) 294–8580
Kevin Boehne, regional chief

SOUTHWEST
(AL, AR, LA, MS, NM, OK, TN, TX)
2320 LaBranch St., #2118
Houston, TX 77004
(713) 718–3950
Billy Hines, regional chief

WESTERN
(AK, AZ, CA, CO, HI, ID, MT, NV, OR, UT, WA, WY)
3200 Inland Empire Blvd., #230
Ontario, CA 91764
(909) 483–5624
Dan Derwey, regional chief

Office of Pipeline Safety

EASTERN
(CT, DC, DE, MA, MD, ME, NH, NJ, NY, PA, PR, RI, VA, VT, WV)
400 7th St. S.W., #2108
Washington, DC 20590
(202) 366–4580
William H. Gute, regional chief

SOUTHERN
(AL, FL, GA, KY, MS, NC, SC, TN)
61 Forsyth St. S.W., #6T15
Atlanta, GA 30303
(404) 562–3530
Fred A. Joyner, regional chief

CENTRAL
(IA, IL, IN, KS, MI, MN, MO, ND, NE, OH, SD, WI)
1100 Main St., #1120
Kansas City, MO 64105
(816) 426–2654
Ivan A. Huntoon, regional chief

SOUTHWEST
(AR, LA, NM, OK, TX)
2320 La Branch St., #2116
Houston, TX 77004
(713) 718–3746
Rodrick M. Seeley, regional chief

WESTERN
(AK, AZ, CA, CO, HI, ID, MT, NV, OR, UT, WA, WY)
12600 W. Colfax Ave., #A250
Lakewood, CO 80215–3736
(303) 231–5701
Christopher Hoidal, regional chief

Other RSPA Field Offices

TRANSPORTATION SAFETY INSTITUTE
6500 S. MacArthur Blvd.
P.O. Box 25082
Oklahoma City, OK 73125–5050
(405) 954–3153
Frank B. Tupper, director

VOLPE NATIONAL TRANSPORTATION SYSTEMS CENTER
55 Broadway, Kendall Square
Cambridge, MA 02142
(617) 494–3153
Richard John, director

Saint Lawrence Seaway Development Corporation

Massena Office: 180 Andrews St., Massena, NY 13662
Washington Office: 400 7th St. S.W., Washington, DC 20590
Internet: http://www.seaway.dot.gov

The Saint Lawrence Seaway Development Corporation (SLSDC) is a government-owned corporation. Created by an act of Congress in 1954 to oversee the construction of U.S. facilities for the Saint Lawrence Seaway project, it joined the Department of Transportation (DOT) under the Department of Transportation Act of 1966.

The corporation is headed by an administrator who is appointed by the president. The agency's offices are divided between Washington, D.C., and Massena, N.Y. Funding for the corporation is appropriated by Congress.

The corporation is responsible for the operation and maintenance of the section of the Saint Lawrence Seaway within U.S. territorial limits, between the port of Montreal and Lake Erie. It conducts trade development programs and coordinates all activities with its Canadian counterpart, the Saint Lawrence Seaway Management Corporation (successor to the Saint Lawrence Seaway Authority of Canada). Together they develop safety standards and set toll rates for vessels and cargoes passing through the seaway, manage vessel traffic, publish transit regulations, and maintain navigational aids.

In 1997 the SLSDC, along with the U.S. Coast Guard and the SLSA, began to inspect all vessels making their first inbound transit of the seaway in compliance with new environmental laws including the Oil Pollution Act and the Non-Indigenous Aquatic Nuisance Prevention and Control Act of 1990. As a result, in July 1998 the SLSDC was awarded the ISO 9002 certificate by the International Organization for Standardization for its high-quality management standards and vessel inspection services program on the Saint Lawrence Seaway.

■ KEY PERSONNEL

Administrator
Albert Jacquez........................ (202) 366–0091
Fax..................................... (202) 366–7147
Associate Administrator
Salvatore Pisani....................... (315) 764–3211
Fax..................................... (315) 764–3235
Chief Counsel
Marc C. Owen.......................... (202) 366–6823
Chief of Staff
Anita K. Blackman..................... (202) 366–0091
Congressional Liaison (DOT)
Vacant................................. (202) 366–9714
Logistics
Kevin O'Malley........................ (202) 366–0091
Finance
Edward Margosian..................... (315) 764–3275
Trade Development and Public Affairs
Rebecca McGill........................ (202) 366–0091
Administration
Mary Ann Hazel....................... (315) 764–3230

■ INFORMATION SOURCES

Internet
Agency Web site: http://www.seaway.dot.gov. Includes agency news, the current toll schedule, a link to the Saint Lawrence Seaway Management Corporation and general information about the seaway.

Telephone Contacts

Personnel Locator . . . . (202) 366–4000

Information and Publications

KEY OFFICES

SLSDC Office of Trade Development and Public Affairs

400 7th Street S.W., Room 5424
Washington, DC 20590
(202) 366–0091
Rebecca McGill, director

Handles policy matters and general inquiries with a national scope. Most questions concerning the immediate region will be referred to the Massena Public Information Office.

Freedom of Information

180 Andrews St.
P.O. Box 520
Massena, NY 13662–0520
(315) 764–3210
Mary Fregoe, FOI officer

PUBLICATIONS

The SLSDC Office of Trade Development and Public Affairs provides an information package containing general background information on the seaway, maps, fact sheets, and the annual report of the agency.

For the Transportation Department's annual report, which includes regulatory actions taken by the SLSDC, contact DOT Public Affairs, 400 7th St. S.W., Washington, DC 20590; (202) 366–4570.

Reference Resources

LIBRARY

DOT Library

Transportation Administrative Services Center (TASC)
400 7th St. S.W., Room 2200
Washington, DC 20590
(202) 366–0746
Clara Smith, director
Hours: 8:00 a.m. to 4:00 p.m.

DOCKETS

The SLSDC does not have a central office where dockets containing materials related to agency rulemakings and other administrative proceedings may be examined. The best source of information is the director of the office that has jurisdiction over a particular rule. Notices of rulemakings listed in the *Federal Register* include the name of a staff member to contact for additional information and the location where the docket may be inspected.

RULES AND REGULATIONS

SLSDC rules and regulations are published in the *Code of Federal Regulations,* Title 33, parts 400–499. Proposed regulations, new final regulations, and updates to the *Code of Federal Regulations* are published in the daily *Federal Register.* (*See appendix on how to obtain and use these publications.*)

■ LEGISLATION

The SLSDC carries out its responsibilities under authority granted by:

Saint Lawrence Seaway Act, as amended (68 Stat. 92, 33 U.S.C. 981 et seq.). Signed by the president May 13, 1954. Created the Saint Lawrence Seaway Development Corporation.

Ports and Waterways Safety Act of 1972 (86 Stat. 424, 33 U.S.C. 1221). Signed by the president July 10, 1972. Authorized establishment of standards and regulations to promote safety of ports, harbors, and navigable waters of the United States.

Port and Tanker Safety Act of 1978 (92 Stat. 1471, 33 U.S.C. 1221). Signed by the president Oct. 17, 1978. Expanded and strengthened regulations concerning vessel safety standards.

Water Resources Development Act of 1986 (100 Stat. 4102, 33 U.S.C. 2234a). Signed by the president Nov. 17, 1986. Instituted a tax on cargo loaded or unloaded in U.S. ports; revenue from this tax is held by the Harbor Maintenance Trust Fund and appropriated by Congress for the costs of maintaining and operating the Saint Lawrence Seaway.

Maritime Transportation Security Act of 2002 (116 Stat. 2064, 46 U.S.C. 2101). Signed by the president Nov. 25, 2002. Amended the Merchant Marine Act of 1936 to require DOT to develop antiterrorism plans at U.S. ports and foreign ports where U.S.-bound shipments originate. Amended the Ports and Waterways Safety Act of 1972 to authorize the use of qualified armed Coast Guard personnel as sea marshals on facilities or vessels to deter or respond to acts of terrorism. Amended the Ports and Waterways Safety Act to require all commercial vessels entering U.S. waters to provide specified information, including name, route, and a description of any hazardous conditions or cargo.

Surface Transportation Board

1925 K St. N.W., Washington, DC 20423
Internet: http://www.stb.dot.gov

The Surface Transportation Board (STB), an agency within the Department of Transportation (DOT), was created on Jan. 1, 1996, by the ICC Termination Act of 1995. It is the successor to the Interstate Commerce Commission (ICC), an independent agency that had been established in 1887. The STB consists of a chair, a vice chair, and an additional board member, who are appointed by the president and confirmed by the Senate. Commissioners of the ICC whose terms had not expired by the end of 1995 are now board members of the STB.

The STB adjudicates disputes and regulates interstate surface transportation through various laws pertaining to different modes of surface transportation. The STB's general responsibilities include the oversight of firms engaged in transportation in interstate and in foreign commerce to the extent that it takes place within the United States, or between or among points in the contiguous United States and points in Alaska, Hawaii, or U.S. territories or possessions. The principal mission of the board, however, is to facilitate commerce by providing an effective forum for efficient dispute resolution and facilitation of appropriate market-based business transactions through rulemakings and case disposition.

Although some of the former responsibilities of the ICC have been abolished, the STB retains jurisdiction in the following areas:

Railroads. The STB remains responsible for several aspects of the railroad industry: review of railroad mergers, settlement of railroad rate disputes, regulation of some new rail line constructions, transfer of rail lines or trackage rights, and approval of rail line abandonment proposals. Regulation of abandonments has been reduced, although the STB remains involved in the transition of railroad routes to trails or other public rights-of-way.

Water and intermodal carriers. The STB regulates rates for water transportation in the noncontiguous domestic trade, specifically between Alaska and Hawaii and the mainland. The STB also regulates intermodal connections (between rail and water and between motor and water transportation) in the noncontiguous domestic trade.

Motor carriers. The STB has transferred motor licensing and certain other motor functions to the Federal Highway Administration (p. 648); tariff filing has been retained only for the noncontiguous domestic trade. Included in the transfer are most responsibilities for moving van lines. The STB continues to regulate mergers and through-route requirements for the intercity bus industry, although rulings on bus route discontinuances have been eliminated.

Pipelines. The STB continues to regulate rates and practices for surface pipeline carriers.

The STB's first year was dominated by mergers among the nation's leading rail lines. The Santa Fe and Burlington Northern railroads had merged under the ICC in September 1995 to form the country's largest rail carrier, with 31,000 route miles in twenty-seven western and midwestern states. In July 1998 the STB approved the merger of Conrail and CSX, which similarly created a rail system of nearly 30,000 miles in twenty-two eastern states. The mergers also provoked calls for the STB to increase access for competitors on the merged companies' routes, and for the STB to consider "open access" to rail routes, an idea modeled on deregulation developments in the telecommunications and energy utility industries.

KEY PERSONNEL

Chair
Roger Nober............................ (202) 565–1510
Fax...................................... (202) 565–9013

Vice Chair
Vacant.................................. (202) 565–1525
Fax...................................... (202) 565–9018

Board Member
Linda J. Morgan........................ (202) 565–1500
Fax...................................... (202) 565–9015

Compliance and Enforcement
Melvin F. Clemens Jr. .... (202) 565–1573
Fax...................................... (202) 565–9011

Rates and Informal Cases
Lawrence C. Herzig .... (202) 565–1573

Tariffs
Lawrence C. Herzig .... (202) 565–1573

Congressional and Public Services
Dan G. King............................ (202) 565–1592
Fax...................................... (202) 565–9016

Economic, Environmental Analysis and Administration
Leland L. Gardner...................... (202) 565–1526
Fax...................................... (202) 565–9000

Costing and Financial Information
H. Jeff Warren .... (202) 565–1533

Environmental Analysis
Elaine K. Kaiser........................ (202) 565–1538

Research and Analysis
Michael Mosko .... (202) 565–1540

General Counsel
Ellen D. Hanson........................ (202) 565–1558
Fax...................................... (202) 565–9001

Proceedings
David M. Konschnik.................... (202) 565–1600
Fax...................................... (202) 565–9002

Administration
Julia M. Farr........................... (202) 565–1600

Management Information and Legal Support Services
Barbara G. Saddler..................... (202) 565–1656

Legal Counsel I
Beryl Gordon.......................... (202) 565–1600

Legal Counsel II
Joseph H. Dettmar..................... (202) 565–1600

Secretary
Vernon A. Williams.................... (202) 565–1718
Fax...................................... (202) 565–9019

INFORMATION SOURCES

Internet
Agency Web site: http://www.stb.dot.gov. Maintains information on the function of the STB. Publications and selected data are available for viewing or for downloading.

Telephone Contacts
General Information...................... (202) 565–1674
TDD....................................... (800) 877–8339

Information and Publications

KEY OFFICES

STB Congressional and Public Services
1925 K St. N.W., Suite 840
Washington, DC 20423
(202) 565–1592
Fax (202) 565–9016
Dan G. King, director

Provides information for Congress, the press, and the public. Issues press releases; maintains a mailing list. Handles requests related to the Freedom of Information Act.

Helps businesses resolve surface transportation regulation problems. Informs the STB of the nature and status of these problems and advises it of the public interest aspects of rail regulatory actions. Assists individuals, consumer groups, small communities, small shippers, and public utility commissioners participating in STB proceedings.

STB Office of Compliance and Enforcement
1925 K St. N.W., Suite 780
Washington, DC 20423
(202) 565–1573
Melvin F. Clemens Jr., director

Assists shippers, carriers, and the general public with problems involving the availability and provision of essential surface transportation services. Administers regulations related to compliance and conducts compliance surveys. Advises the board on tariff policies and rate adjustments.

STB Office of Proceedings
1925 K St. N.W., Room 626
Washington, DC 20423
(202) 565–1600
David M. Konschnik, director

Provides legal and policy advice to the board. Responsible for accepting, docketing, and processing applications to construct or abandon railroad lines; applications to consolidate or merge; complaints about carrier practices and rates; and rulemaking proceedings approved by the board.

Freedom of Information

Contact STB Congressional and Public Services.

PUBLICATIONS

For information, contact STB Congressional and Public Services. Publications available include:

STB Annual Report to Congress
Abandonments and Alternatives to Abandonments
So You Want to Start a Small Railroad
The STB: Who's Who and What We Do

DATA AND STATISTICS

STB Economics, Environmental Analysis, and Administration

1925 K St. N.W., #500
Washington, DC 20423
(202) 565–1532
Leland Gardner, director

Contact this office for information about available statistical reports and publications. Selected reports, statistics, and data also are available at the agency's Web site.

MEETINGS

Under the Government in the Sunshine Act, board meetings are open to the public unless the subject of the meeting is specific litigation or discussion of an opinion on a pending court case. Notices of scheduled board meetings are listed in the *Federal Register. (See appendix for information on how to obtain and use this publications.)*

Reference Resources

LIBRARY

STB Library

1925 K St. N.W.
Washington, DC 20423
(202) 565–1668
Fax (202) 565–9004
Kelley A. Weber, librarian
Hours: 8:30 a.m. to 5:00 p.m.

Assists the STB and the general public in researching court cases involving surface transportation problems, and cross-referencing significant information such as date, decision, and precedent. Library open to the public.

DOCKETS

STB Docket Room

1925 K St. N.W.
Washington, DC 20423
(202) 565–1684

Records of board proceedings may be examined during business hours.

RULES AND REGULATIONS

STB rules and regulations are published in the *Code of Federal Regulations,* Title 49, parts 1000–end. Proposed rules, new final rules, and updates to the *Code of Federal Regulations* are published in the daily *Federal Register. (See appendix for information on how to obtain and use these publications.)*

■ LEGISLATION

The STB exercises its authority under the **Interstate Commerce Act of 1887** (24 Stat. 379, 49 U.S.C. 1). Signed by the president Feb. 4, 1887. In 1978 Congress passed the **Revised Interstate Commerce Act** (92 Stat. 1337, Subtitle IV, 49 U.S.C. 10101). Signed by the president Oct. 13, 1978. The revision was a recodification of existing laws and did not make any substantive changes in the powers and authority of the ICC. Obsolete language was changed and superseded statutes removed. The following references to the U.S. Code reflect the 1978 revision.

Hepburn Act of 1906 (34 Stat. 584, 49 U.S.C. 10501). Signed by the president June 29, 1906. Extended ICC jurisdiction over express companies, pipelines (except water and gas), and sleeping car companies. It also gave the commission the power to prescribe and enforce reasonable rates, charges, and regulations for the industries it regulated at that time.

Mann-Elkins Act of 1910 (36 Stat. 539, 49 U.S.C. 10501). Signed by the president June 18, 1910. Authorized the commission to suspend and investigate new rate proposals.

Panama Canal Act of 1912 (37 Stat. 566, 15 U.S.C. 31, 46 U.S.C. 11, 49 U.S.C. 10503, 11321, 11914). Signed by the president Aug. 24, 1912. Prohibited railroads from continuing ownership or operation of water lines when competition would be reduced.

Esch Car Service Act of 1917 (40 Stat. 101, 49 U.S.C. 10102). Signed by the president May 29, 1917. Authorized the commission to determine the reasonableness of freight car service rules; prescribe rules in place of those found unreasonable; and in time of emergency, suspend car service rules and direct the car supply to fit the circumstances.

Transportation Act of 1920 (41 Stat. 474, 49 U.S.C. 10501). Signed by the president Feb. 28, 1920. Granted the commission authority to fix minimum as well as maximum rates, to prescribe intrastate rates if necessary to remove discrimination against interstate commerce, and to require that railroads obtain ICC approval for construction and operation of new lines as well as abandonment of existing lines.

Transportation Act of 1940 (54 Stat. 898, 49 U.S.C. 10501). Signed by the president Sept. 18, 1940. Brought coastal, intercoastal, and inland water carriers and freight forwarders under ICC jurisdiction.

Reed-Bullwinkle Act of 1948 (62 Stat. 472, 49 U.S.C. 10706). Signed by the president June 17, 1948. Allowed common carriers by rail, motor, and water, and freight forwarders to join in collective ratemaking activities.

Transportation Act of 1958 (72 Stat. 568, 49 U.S.C. 10501). Signed by the president Aug. 12, 1958. Gave the ICC authority to determine reasonable minimum railroad rates, enlarged ICC jurisdiction over curtailment of railroad services, and exempted truckers of certain agricultural products from ICC rules.

Department of Transportation Act of 1967 (81 Stat. 224, 49 U.S.C. 1652). Signed by the president Sept. 11, 1967. Created the cabinet-level Department of Transportation and transferred to it jurisdiction over carrier safety practices.

Rail Passenger Service Act of 1970 (84 Stat. 1327, 26 U.S.C. 250, 45 U.S.C. 501). Signed by the president Oct. 30, 1970. Gave the ICC authority to establish standards of adequate rail passenger service.

Regional Rail Reorganization Act of 1973 (87 Stat. 985, 31 U.S.C. 856, 45 U.S.C. 11124). Signed by the president Jan. 2, 1974. Reorganized bankrupt railroads in the northeast United States and created the Rail Services Planning Office within the ICC. The new office was responsible for ensuring public participation in the Northeast redevelopment project.

Railroad Revitalization and Regulatory Reform Act of 1976 (90 Stat. 31, 15 U.S.C. 77c, 31 U.S.C. 11, 45 U.S.C.

543, 49 U.S.C. 10501). Signed by the president Feb. 5, 1976. Reduced degree of regulation imposed on rail industry by the ICC. Allowed railroad management more flexibility to raise and lower individual freight rates; imposed strict time limits on the ICC for the processing and disposition of rail-related proceedings; established an Office of Rail Public Counsel in the ICC to ensure that public interest considerations would be fully explored during the decision-making process; and gave permanent status to the Rail Services Planning Office.

Staggers Rail Act of 1980 (94 Stat. 1895, 49 U.S.C. 10101 note). Signed by the president Oct. 14, 1980. Gave railroads increased price-setting flexibility with less regulation by the ICC, limited railroad carriers' immunity from antitrust laws to set rates collectively, and expedited procedures for railroad abandonment of service.

Surface Freight Forwarder Deregulation Act of 1986 (100 Stat. 2993, 49 U.S.C. 10101 note). Signed by the president Oct. 22, 1986. Rescinded licensing requirement for general commodities freight forwarders but maintained requirement for filing cargo liability insurance information. Excluded household goods freight forwarders from this deregulation.

Negotiated Rates Act of 1993 (107 Stat. 2044, 49 U.S.C. 10101 note). Signed by the president Dec. 3, 1993. Set up mechanisms for settlements between bankrupt carriers and former shippers based on the weight of the shipment. Reduced the statute of limitations for filing undercharge claims and exempted from claims those shippers who transported charitable or recyclable goods.

Interstate Commerce Commission Termination Act of 1995 (49 U.S.C. 101 note). Signed by the president Dec. 29, 1995. Abolished the ICC, establishing the Surface Transportation Board within the DOT to handle most of the ICC's surviving regulatory functions.

Transportation Equity Act for the 21st Century (TEA-21) (112 Stat. 154, 23 U.S.C. 143). Signed by the president June 9, 1998. Reauthorized the federal highway, transit, safety, research, and motor carrier programs under the Intermodal Surface Transportation Efficiency Act of 1991 (ISTEA) from 1998 through 2003. Provided incentives for states to adopt tough .08 blood alcohol concentration standards for drunk driving.

Other Transportation Department Offices

■ AVIATION ENFORCEMENT AND PROCEEDINGS

Office of the General Counsel
400 7th St. S.W.
Washington, DC 20590
http://www.dot.gov/ost/ogc/org/aviation

Assistant General Counsel
  Samuel Podberesky.....................(202) 366–9342
  Fax.....................................(202) 366–7152
Deputy Assistant General Counsel
  Dayton Lehman........................(202) 366–9342
Consumer Protection Division
  Assistant Director
  Norman Strickman.....................(202) 366–5957
  Fax.....................................(202) 366–5944

The Office of the Assistant General Counsel for Aviation Enforcement and Proceedings provides legal support to offices that handle airline functions. This includes enforcing Department of Transportation (DOT) rules and regulations governing the obligations of air carriers under the Federal Aviation Act, except those dealing with safety, which are enforced by the Federal Aviation Administration.

The office also conducts administrative proceedings in cases where airlines have failed to follow DOT rules and regulations concerning consumer affairs. The Consumer Protection Division takes action when it believes an airline or charter operator has engaged in unfair or deceptive practices, such as when there is evidence of "bait and switch" sales tactics, or when violations of advertising and overbooking regulations occur and when other consumer-related matters are concerned.

■ AVIATION AND INTERNATIONAL AFFAIRS

400 7th St. S.W.
Washington, DC 20590
Internet:
http://ostpxweb.dot.gov/aviation/intro.htm

Assistant Secretary
  Vacant..................................(202) 366–4551
  Fax.....................................(202) 493–2005
Aviation Analysis
  Randall D. Bennett.....................(202) 366–5903
  Fax.....................................(202) 366–7638
International Aviation
  Paul Gretch...........................(202) 366–2423
  Fax.....................................(202) 366–3694

The Office of the Assistant Secretary for Aviation and International Affairs develops and coordinates policy related to economic regulation of the airline industry, and the office administers the laws and regulations governing U.S. and foreign carrier economic authority to engage in air transportation.

The following divisions are key regulatory offices within Aviation and International Affairs:

• The Office of Aviation Analysis sets and renews subsidy and service levels for essential air service and monitors air carriers' reliability and performance. It represents the public interest in formal hearings concerning carrier fitness, mergers and acquisitions, and employee protection cases. It evaluates applications from companies for new air carrier authority; researches and monitors aviation industry performance; and develops and administers operating authority policies for services by scheduled, charter, cargo, air taxi, commuter, and indirect air carriers. It also aids in rulemakings and legislative proposals concerning essential air service.

- The Office of International Aviation formulates, coordinates, and executes the international aviation policy of the United States and administers economic regulatory functions related to foreign air travel. The office originates international aviation negotiating positions, coordinates negotiating policy and strategy with government agencies and air carriers, and conducts or participates in those negotiations. It also receives complaints from U.S. carriers experiencing difficulties in foreign markets and intervenes to resolve those problems.

In its regulatory function, International Aviation receives, processes, and makes or recommends disposition of all U.S. and foreign carrier requests for economic operating authority between the U.S. and foreign points, and of all tariff filings and fare and rate agreements from these carriers.

■ OFFICE OF HEARINGS

400 7th St. S.W.
Washington, DC 20590
http://www.dot.gov/ost/hearings

Chief Administrative Law Judge
Ronnie A. Yoder . . . . (202) 366–2142
Fax . . . . (202) 366–7536

The Office of Hearings conducts formal proceedings requiring oral evidence concerning the regulatory powers of the Department of Transportation (DOT). The DOT office prosecuting the case normally prepares the exhibits, analyses, and written testimony. At the end of the hearing, the presiding administrative law judge issues an initial recommended decision on the case at hand.

Treasury Department

15th St. and Pennsylvania Ave. N.W., Washington, DC 20220
Internet: http://www.ustreas.gov

Alcohol and Tobacco Tax and Trade Bureau

650 Massachusetts Ave. N.W., Room 8290
Washington, DC 20226
Internet: http://www.ttb.gov

The Homeland Security Act of 2002, which created the Department of Homeland Security, also created the Alcohol and Tobacco Tax and Trade Bureau (TTB) within the Treasury Department on Jan. 24, 2003. The TTB's authority to regulate and collect revenue from the alcohol and tobacco industries previously had been within the Treasury Department's Bureau of Alcohol, Tobacco, and Firearms (ATF) since 1972. The Homeland Security Act also transferred the ATF's law enforcement functions relating to firearms, explosives, and arson to the Justice Department, becoming the Bureau of Alcohol, Tobacco, Firearms, and Explosives (also ATF), within the Justice Department (p. 590).

The TTB continues to regulate and collect revenue from the alcohol and tobacco industries. The agency also provides assistance to states for certain programs and develops consumer protection programs. Offices within the agency are responsible for investigating trade practice violations, issuing licenses and permits, and overseeing tax collection on alcohol and tobacco products. The bureau makes periodic inspections of tobacco manufacturing plants, breweries, and wineries. TTB personnel also monitor the advertising, packaging, and formulation of alcoholic beverages to ensure that the products are safe and that they are accurately labeled.

The regulatory inspectors monitor the annual collection of more than $15 billion in excise taxes on distilled spirits, beer, wine, tobacco products, and firearms. They investigate trade practices that could result in alcohol law violations and administer certain environmental protection programs, such as efforts by regulated industries to curb water pollution.

The TTB also is responsible for regulating the manufacture of alcohol fuels. It issues permits for small-scale and commercial production of alcohol fuels—including gasohol production—for heating and for operating machinery.

The TTB has five major divisions:

Advertising, Labeling and Formulation Division (ALFD). Implements and enforces a broad range of statutory and compliance provisions of the Internal Revenue Code and the Federal Alcohol Administration (FAA) Act, with regard to the formulation and labeling of alcoholic beverages. The FAA Act requires importers and bottlers of beverage alcohol to obtain certificates of label approval or certificates of exemption from label approval (COLAs) for most alcoholic beverages before their introduction into interstate commerce. ALFD ensures that products are labeled in accordance with federal laws and regulations. In addition, ALFD examines alcohol products to ensure that they are manufactured in accordance with federal laws and regulations.

International Trade Division (ITD). Ensures industry compliance with international trade regulations—inclusive of the FAA Act and the Internal Revenue Code. Assists other TTB divisions by providing technical support in matters relating to international trade investigations. Represents the TTB at international trade meetings with foreign country representatives and domestic and foreign alcohol beverage industry members. Functions as an advisor to industry members, and the various federal government branches, and the embassies of international governments.

Alcohol and Tobacco Laboratory (ATL). Provides scientific and technical services to the TTB as well as other federal, state, and local agencies and the regulated industries. The laboratory has two locations: Walnut Creek, Calif., and Beltsville, Md. There are three laboratory sections: the Alcohol Section; the Beverage Alcohol Section; and the Nonbeverage Products Section. The office traces its history back to the first Treasury laboratory established in 1886 for the enforcement of the Oleomargarine Act.

National Revenue Center. Reconciles returns, reports, and claims; screens applications and promptly issues permits; and provides expert technical assistance for industry, the public and government agencies to ensure fair and proper revenue collection and public safety.

Regulations and Procedures Division. Drafts new and revised regulations under the Internal Revenue Code and the FAA Act. Considers requests for alternate methods of complying with the law and regulations and acts on petitions to change the regulations. Issues rulings, procedures, and informational documents to clarify the law and regulations. In conjunction with the TTB Laboratory, resolves technical questions affecting tax classification of regulated products and advises field offices and industry members of findings. Responds to FOIA requests.

▨ KEY PERSONNEL

Administrator
Arthur Libertucci....................... (202) 927–5000
Deputy Administrator
John Manfreda .... (202) 927–5000
Chief Counsel
Robert Tobiassen .... (202) 927–8219
Chief of Staff
Theresa Glasscock..................... (202) 927–5000
Assistant Administrator Headquarters Operations
Susan Stewart.......................... (202) 927–8140
Assistant Administrator Field Operations
John Daffron .... (202) 927–5000
Deputy Assistant Administrator
Vicky McDowell........................ (202) 927–5000
Advertising, Labeling and Formulation Division
Karen Freelove......................... (202) 927–8140
International Trade Division
Sanford Lett (acting).................. (202) 927–8110
Alcohol and Tobacco Laboratory
Sumer Dugar .... (240) 264–3900
National Revenue Center
Roger Bowling.......................... (513) 684–3334
Regulations and Procedures Division
William Foster......................... (202) 927–8210

▨ INFORMATION SOURCES

Internet
Agency Web site: http://www.ttb.gov. Includes an overview of the agency, press releases, regulations, employer information, and links to other federal Internet sites.

KEY OFFICES
Alcohol and Tobacco Tax and Trade Bureau
Office of Public and Governmental Affairs
650 Massachusetts Ave. N.W., Room 5000
Washington, DC 20226
Phone: (202) 927–5000
Laboratory
Walnut Creek, California
Chief, Alcohol Section - SF
Phone: (925) 280–3642
Fax: (925) 280–3651

PUBLICATIONS
Alcohol Fuel Plants
Distilled Spirits for Fuel Use
Importation of Distilled Spirits, Wine, and Beer
Legislative History of the Federal Alcohol Administration Act
Liquor Laws and Regulations for Retail Dealers
Payment of Tax by Electronic Fund Transfer
Regulations Under the Federal Alcohol Administration Act
Viticultural Areas
What You Should Know About Grape Wine Labels

▨ LEGISLATION
The TTB exercises its authority under:

Federal Alcohol Administration Act (49 Stat. 977, 27 U.S.C. 201). Signed by the president Aug. 29, 1935. Defined unlawful trade practices in the alcoholic beverage industry.

Internal Revenue Code of 1954 (68A Stat. 595, 26 U.S.C. 5001). Signed by the president Aug. 16, 1954. Set limits on the tax collected on the manufacture of alcoholic beverages, tobacco products, and firearms.

Distilled Spirits Tax Revision Act of 1979 (93 Stat. 273, 26 U.S.C. 1 et seq.). Signed by the president July 26,

1979. Provided that liquor be taxed solely on the basis of alcohol content and allowed an additional deferral period for payment on spirits bottled in the United States.

Trafficking in Contraband Cigarettes Act (92 Stat. 2463, 18 U.S.C. 2341). Signed by the president Nov. 2, 1978. Prohibited the possession or transportation of contraband cigarettes.

Crude Oil Windfall Profits Tax of 1980 (94 Stat. 278, 26 U.S.C. 5181). Signed by the president April 2, 1980. Amended the Internal Revenue Code and established a new category of distilled spirits plant, the alcohol fuel plant. The TTB is responsible for the licensing of these plants.

Homeland Security Act of 2002 (116 Stat. 2135, 6 U.S.C. 101 note). Signed by the president Nov. 25, 2002. Created the Alcohol and Tobacco Tax and Trade Bureau (TTB) within the Treasury Department. Transferred the ATF's authority to regulate and collect revenue from the alcohol and tobacco industries to the TTB. Transferred the ATF's law enforcement functions to the Justice Department.

Comptroller of the Currency

250 E St. S.W., Washington, DC 20219
Internet: http://www.occ.treas.gov

The Office of the Comptroller of the Currency (OCC) is a bureau of the Treasury Department. Established by the National Bank Act of 1863, it was the first federal agency created to regulate financial institutions *(see also Federal Reserve System, p. 162, and Federal Deposit Insurance Corporation (FDIC), p. 125)*.

The comptroller of the currency is nominated by the president and confirmed by the Senate for a five-year term.

In carrying out its regulatory functions the OCC:

- Grants charters to national banks.
- Supervises and examines nationally chartered banks.
- Takes supervisory actions against national banks that do not conform to laws and regulations or otherwise engage in unsound banking practices.
- Regulates the foreign activities of national banks.
- Issues charters to foreign banks that wish to operate branches in the United States if those branches operate like national banks.
- Approves mergers and consolidations if the resulting financial institution is a nationally chartered bank.
- Approves the conversion of state-chartered banks to national banking institutions.
- Reports on national bank operations and financial conditions.
- Approves plans of national banks to open branches, relocate headquarters, and expand services and facilities.

The comptroller of the currency is required by law to be an *ex officio* member of the FDIC board of directors and the Neighborhood Reinvestment Corporation.

The OCC schedules examinations and visitations according to a bank's condition. National bank examinations are designed to determine the condition and performance of a bank, the quality of operations, and compliance with federal laws. The examination policy of the comptroller places greater emphasis on analysis and interpretation of financial data and banks' internal control systems than on detailed verification procedures.

The comptroller rates banks on a uniform numerical scale of 1 to 5, representing healthy to increasingly troubled banks. Banks with ratings of 3, 4, or 5 are subject to special supervisory action by the OCC, including removal of officers, negotiation of agreements to change existing bank practices, and issuance of cease-and-desist orders to prevent further deterioration.

More than 2,500 national and District of Columbia banks are subject to regulation by the comptroller's office. In addition, nationally chartered financial institutions are required to be members of the Federal Reserve System and must be insured by the FDIC.

National banks may hold investments in foreign financial institutions either directly or through subsidiaries known as Edge Corporations (named after Sen. Walter Edge, R-N.J., 1919–1929, the sponsor of the legislation that allowed their creation).

The OCC is responsible for supervising this international activity. Examiners evaluate the quality of international loan and investment portfolios and analyze foreign exchange activities, reporting procedures, accounting and bookkeeping systems, and the adequacy of internal controls and audit programs.

■ KEY PERSONNEL

Comptroller of the Currency

John D. Hawke Jr. .... (202) 874-4900

    Fax .... (202) 874-4950

Equal Employment Programs

    Vacant .... (202) 874-5360

Minority and Urban Affairs
Glenda B. Cross .... (202) 874-9000
Management and Chief Financial Officer
Edward J. Hanley....................... (202) 874-5080
Fax.................................... (202) 874-5352
Continuing Education and Resource Alternatives
Jennifer C. Kelly....................... (202) 874-4570
Fax.................................... (202) 874-5352
Management Services
William Finister....................... (202) 874-5400
Fax.................................... (202) 874-5436
Workforce Effectiveness
Cynthia T. Pettit....................... (202) 874-4530
Bank Supervision Operations
Leann G. Britton .... (202) 874-5020
Fax.................................... (202) 874-5352
Large Bank Supervision
Delora Ng Jee (San Francisco) .... (415) 545-5981
Douglas Roeder .... (202) 874-4610
Timothy W. Long...................... (202) 874-4610
Bank Supervision Policy
Emory Wayne Rushton .... (202) 874-2870
Fax.................................... (202) 874-5352
Community and Consumer Policy
Ralph E. Sharpe .... (202) 874-5216
Credit Risk
David G. Gibbons...................... (202) 874-5170
Core Policy
Mark L. O'Dell .... (202) 874-5490
International and Economic Affairs
Jonathan L. Fiechter................... (202) 874-5010
Fax.................................... (202) 874-5352
International Banking and Finance
Joseph A. Tuya......................... (202) 874-4741
**Information Technology Services and Chief
Information Officer**
Steven M. Yohai....................... (202) 874-4480
Fax.................................... (202) 874-5252
Information Services
Charles A. Wright .... (202) 874-5443
Customer Services
Vacant................................. (202) 874-4600
Network Services
Harriet A. Antiporowich.............. (301) 324-3180
Chief Counsel
Julie L. Williams....................... (202) 874-5200
Fax.................................... (202) 874-5374
Administrative and Internal Law
David C. Kane.......................... (202) 874-4460
Bank Activities and Structure
Eric Thompson........................ (202) 874-5300
Community and Consumer Law
Michael Bylsma........................ (202) 874-5750

Community Affairs
Anna Alvarez Boyd..................... (202) 874-5556
Congressional Liaison
Carolyn Z. McFarlane................. (202) 874-4840
Enforcement and Compliance
Brian C. McCormally .... (202) 874-4800
Licensing
Steven J. Weiss......................... (202) 874-5060
Litigation
L. Robert Griffin .... (202) 874-5280
Securities and Corporate Practices
Ellen Broadman........................ (202) 874-5210
Public Affairs
Mark A. Nishan (acting)............... (202) 874-4910
Fax.................................... (202) 874-5678
Banking Relations
Gregory C. Golembe................... (202) 874-4671
Communications
Oliver A. Robinson..................... (202) 874-4700
Press Relations
Robert M. Garsson..................... (202) 874-5770

■ INFORMATION SOURCES

Internet
Agency Web site: http://www.occ.treas.gov. Offers press releases, an organizational directory, access to many OCC publications, a complete publications list, and links to related Internet sites.

Telephone Contacts
Personnel Locator.......................... (202) 874-5000
Customer Assistance Hotline............. (800) 613-6743
Public Information Room................. (202) 874–5043

Information and Publications

KEY OFFICES

OCC Public Affairs
250 E St. S.W.
Washington, DC 20219
(202) 874-4910
Mark A. Nishan, acting senior deputy comptroller
Oliver A. Robinson, communications
Robert M. Garsson, press relations
Gregory C. Golembe, banking relations

Serves as the general information and freedom of information office for the OCC. Distributes material on administrative, legal, regulatory, and economic aspects of banking.

OCC Community and Consumer Policy

250 E St. S.W.
Washington, DC 20219
(202) 874-5216
Fax (202) 874-5221
Ralph E. Sharpe, deputy comptroller

Responsible for enforcing consumer laws with respect to national banks. Also advises the OCC on consumer-related policy matters.

OCC Bank Activities and Structure

250 E St. S.W.
Washington, DC 20219
(202) 874-5300
Fax (202) 874-5322
Eric Thompson, director

Provides legal advice on banking law questions to the comptroller, national banks, and the public.

OCC Legislative and Regulatory Activities

250 E St. S.W.
Washington, DC 20219
(202) 874-5090
Fax (202) 874-4889
Karen Solomon, director

Handles legal aspects of banking legislation; maintains information on the status of bills, reports on bills, primary legislative documents, and files on public laws passed in the current and immediately preceding Congresses. Division attorneys are available to speak on banking legislative matters to various groups such as bar associations and foreign bankers.

PUBLICATIONS

Contact OCC Communications for specific publications or a list. (Complete list of publications is available via the agency's Web site.) There is a fee for most publications. Titles available include:

A Citizen's Guide to CRA
Comptroller's Handbook for Asset Management
Comptroller's Handbook for Compliance
An Examiner's Guide to Investment Practices and Products
Quarterly Journal ($120 per annual subscription; single copies also available)
E-Files - The OCC Electronic Library (CD)

DATA AND STATISTICS

Contact the Communications Division at (202) 874–4960 for the OCC *Quarterly Journal*. It is also available online at www.occ.treas.gov. Other sources of data and statistics include *Reports of Condition and Income* and the *Uniform Bank Performance Report (UBPR)*, both of which are available from the FDIC (p. 125).

Reference Resources

LIBRARY

OCC Library

250 E St. S.W.
Washington, DC 20219
(202) 874-4720
Fax (202) 874-5641
Robert Updegrove, administrative librarian

Contains reference volumes dealing with banking legislation and regulation. Public is encouraged to make appointments prior to visits. Government-related materials are available Monday through Friday. Materials not related to the government are available only on Tuesday and Thursday. The library is open from 8:30 a.m. to 4:30 p.m.

DOCKETS

Consult the OCC Library, above.

RULES AND REGULATIONS

OCC rules and regulations are published in the *Code of Federal Regulations,* Title 12, parts 1-199. They are also available on CD, "E-File". Proposed regulations, new final regulations, and updates to the *Code of Federal Regulations* are published in the daily *Federal Register. (See appendix for details on how to obtain and use these publications.)*

▨ LEGISLATION

The OCC administers the following legislation in full or in part:

Fair Housing Act of 1968 (82 Stat. 81, 42 U.S.C. 3601). Signed by the president April 11, 1968. Prohibited discrimination in the sale or rental of housing.

Truth in Lending Act (82 Stat. 146, 15 U.S.C. 1601). Signed by the president May 29, 1968. Required lenders and merchants to inform consumers of total cost of loans and installment purchase plans and to clearly state annual percentage rate. Also prohibited unsolicited distribution of credit cards.

Bank Protection Act of 1968 (82 Stat. 294, 12 U.S.C. 1881). Signed by the president July 7, 1968. Required establishment of minimum security system standards for banking institutions.

Fair Credit Reporting Act (84 Stat. 1128, 15 U.S.C. 1681). Signed by the president Oct. 26, 1970. Regulated credit information and use.

NOW Accounts Act (87 Stat. 342, 12 U.S.C. 1832). Signed by the president Aug. 16, 1973. Regulated interest-bearing checking accounts.

Equal Credit Opportunity Act (88 Stat. 1521, 15 U.S.C. 1691). Signed by the president Oct. 28, 1974. Prohibited credit discrimination against women; amended in 1976 to include discrimination based on age, race, religion, or national origin (90 Stat. 251).

Real Estate Settlement Procedures Act (88 Stat. 1724, 12 U.S.C. 2601). Signed by the president Dec. 22, 1974. Minimized settlement charges for home buyers; confirmed the authority of the Department of Housing and Urban Development to set standards for settlement charges on homes financed through federally guaranteed mortgages.

Home Mortgage Disclosure Act (89 Stat. 1125, 12 U.S.C. 2801). Signed by the president Dec. 31, 1975. Required lending institutions within standard metropolitan statistical areas (SMSAs) to disclose the number and amount of mortgage loans made yearly to determine if banks were discriminating against certain city neighborhoods by refusing to make loans regardless of the creditworthiness of the potential borrower (a practice known as "redlining").

Fair Debt Collection Practices Act (91 Stat. 874, 15 U.S.C. 1692). Signed by the president Sept. 20, 1977. Regulated methods used by debt collection agencies.

Community Reinvestment Act of 1977 (91 Stat. 1147, 12 U.S.C. 2901). Signed by the president Oct. 12, 1977. Required financial institution regulators to encourage the banks under their supervision to meet the credit needs of their communities, including low- and moderate-income neighborhoods.

International Banking Act of 1978 (92 Stat. 607, 12 U.S.C. 3101). Signed by the president Sept. 17, 1978. Provided for the federal regulation of foreign banks in domestic financial markets.

Financial Institutions Regulatory and Interest Rate Control Act of 1978 (92 Stat. 3641, 12 U.S.C. 226 note). Signed by the president Nov. 10, 1978. Prohibited interlocking management and director relationships among financial institutions.

Depository Institutions Deregulation and Monetary Control Act of 1980 (94 Stat. 132, 12 U.S.C. 226 note). Signed by the president March 31, 1980. Extended reserve requirements to all financial institutions; provided for phase-out of interest ceilings by 1986 and allowed thrift institutions to offer an expanded range of financial services; increased federal deposit insurance to $100,000 per depositor.

Garn-St. Germain Depository Institutions Act of 1982 (96 Stat. 1469, 12 U.S.C. 226 note). Signed by the president Oct. 15, 1982. Increased or repealed certain statutory ceilings affecting lending and borrowing by national banks. Simplified statutory restrictions on transactions by bank officials. Permitted the comptroller to dispose of certain unclaimed property recovered from closed national banks and banks in the District of Columbia. Permitted the chartering of certain limited-purpose banks and expanded the powers of bank service corporations (subsidiaries of banks) to deal with the public.

Competitive Equality Banking Act of 1987 (101 Stat. 552, 12 U.S.C. 226 note). Signed by the president Aug. 10, 1987. Granted the Federal Savings and Loan Insurance Corporation (FSLIC) new borrowing authority to reimburse depositors as it shut down bankrupt thrifts. Suspended the expansion of banks into insurance, securities underwriting, and real estate. Eased regulatory requirements for savings and loans in economically depressed areas and required faster clearing of depositors' checks.

Financial Institutions Reform, Recovery and Enforcement Act of 1989 (FIRREA) (103 Stat. 183, 12 U.S.C. 1811 note). Signed by the president Aug. 9, 1989. Approved the use of $50 billion to finance the closing of insolvent savings and loans. Created the Resolution Trust Corporation to manage the disposal of the assets of bankrupt thrifts. FIRREA also dissolved the Federal Home Loan Bank Board, assigning its regulatory responsibilities to the Department of the Treasury and assigning its role in insuring depositors through the Federal Savings and Loan Insurance Corporation to the Federal Deposit Insurance Corporation. Savings and loans were required to maintain a minimum amount of tangible capital equal to 1.5 percent of total assets.

Resolution Trust Corporation Refinancing, Restructuring, and Improvement Act of 1991 (105 Stat. 1761, 12 U.S.C. 1421). Signed by the president Dec. 12, 1991. Provided funding to resolve failed savings associations and working capital for restructuring the Oversight Board and the Resolution Trust Corporation.

Federal Deposit Insurance Corporation Improvement Act of 1991 (FDICA) (105 Stat. 2236, 12 U.S.C. 1811). Signed by the president Dec. 19, 1991. Required the most cost-effective resolution of insured depository institutions and to improve supervision and examinations. It also made available additional resources to the Bank Insurance Fund.

Removal of Regulatory Barriers to Affordable Housing Act of 1992 (106 Stat. 3938, 42 U.S.C. 12705a). Signed by the president Oct. 28, 1992. Encouraged state and local governments to identify and remove regulatory barriers to affordable housing.

Government Securities Act Amendments of 1993 (107 Stat. 2344, U.S.C. Title 15 various parts). Signed by the president Dec. 17, 1993. Extended and revised the government's rulemaking authority under the federal securities laws.

Riegle-Neal Interstate Banking and Branching Efficiency Act of 1994 (108 Stat. 2338, 12 U.S.C. 1811 note). Signed by the president Sept. 29, 1994. Permitted banks to operate networks of branch offices across state lines without having to set up separately capitalized subsidiary banks.

Riegle-Neal Amendments Act of 1997 (111 Stat. 238, 12 U.S.C. 36). Signed by the president July 3, 1997. Required the comptroller of the currency to review actions taken during the preceding year regarding the applicability of state law to national banks and to include review results in its annual report.

Gramm-Leach-Bliley Act (113 Stat. 1338, 12 U.S.C. 1811 note). Signed by the president Nov. 12, 1999. Permitted affiliations between banks and any financial company, including brokerage and insurance firms. Amended the Community Reinvestment Act of 1977 (CRA) to allow regulators to block banks' applications for mergers or acquisitions if they do not have satisfactory CRA ratings.

American Homeownership and Economic Opportunity Act of 2000 (114 Stat. 2944, 12 U.S.C. 1701). Signed by the president Dec. 27, 2000. Established programs to make home ownership more affordable for low- and moderate-income families, the elderly, and the disabled. Title XII, the Financial Regulatory Relief and Economic Efficiency Act of 2000, amended the Federal Deposit Insurance Corporation Improvement Act of 1991 to increase to 100 percent of fair market value the permissible valuation of readily marketable purchased mortgage servicing rights that may be included in calculating a bank's tangible capital, risk-based capital, or leverage limit.

▓ REGIONAL OFFICES

CENTRAL DISTRICT
(IL, IN, KY, MI, OH, WI)
One Financial Place
440 S. LaSalle St., #2700
Chicago, IL 60605
(312) 360-8800
Fax (312) 435-0951
Bert A. Otto, deputy comptroller

MIDWESTERN DISTRICT
(IA, KS, MN, MO, ND, NE, SD)
2345 Grand Blvd., #700
Kansas City, MO 64108-2637
(816) 556-1800
Fax (816) 556-1892
Kay E. Kowitt, deputy comptroller

NORTHEAST DISTRICT
(CT, DC, DE, MA, MD, ME, NH, NJ, NY, PA, PR, RI, VI, VT)
1114 Ave. of the Americas, #3900
New York, NY 10036
(212) 819–9860
Fax (212) 790–4098
Fred D. Finke, deputy comptroller

SOUTHEAST DISTRICT
(AL, FL, GA, MS, NC, SC, TN, VA, WV)
Marquis One Tower, #600
245 Peachtree Center Ave. N.E.
Atlanta, GA 30303
(404) 659–8855
Fax (404) 588-4532
Archie L. Bransford Jr., deputy comptroller

SOUTHWESTERN DISTRICT
(AR, LA, NM, OK, TX)
500 N. Akard St., #1600
Dallas, TX 75201
(214) 720–0656
Fax (214) 720–7000
Archie L. Branford Jr., deputy comptroller

WESTERN DISTRICT
(AK, AZ, CA, CO, GU, HI, ID, MT, NV, OR, UT, WA, WY)
50 Fremont St., #3900
San Francisco, CA 94105-2292
(415) 545-5900
Fax (415) 545-5925
Kay E. Kowitt, deputy comptroller

Internal Revenue Service

1111 Constitution Ave. N.W., Washington, DC 20224
Internet: http://www.irs.gov

The Internal Revenue Service (IRS) is the largest bureau within the Treasury Department. It is responsible for enforcing internal revenue laws, except those falling under the jurisdiction of the Alcohol and Tobacco Tax and Trade Bureau *(p. 689)*.

The office of the commissioner of the Internal Revenue was established in 1862, and Congress first received authority to levy taxes on the income of individuals and corporations in 1913 under the 16th Amendment to the Constitution.

The IRS is headed by a commissioner nominated by the president and confirmed by the Senate. The commissioner is assisted by a deputy commissioner and four chief officers. Each chief officer is responsible for a specific area. The national office develops policies and programs for the administration of internal revenue laws; most of the day-to-day operations are carried out by regional offices, district offices, and service centers across the United States.

The primary responsibility of the IRS is to determine, assess, and collect taxes. The IRS provides services to taxpayers, including help with income tax questions or problems. It also determines pension plan qualifications and rules on the tax status of exempt organizations. To supplement the provisions of the Internal Revenue Code, the service prepares and issues additional rules and regulations. The IRS also conducts research on taxpayer opinions, the simplification of federal tax reporting, and tax compliance.

The IRS encourages the resolution of tax disputes through an independent administrative appeals system rather than through litigation. The appeals system is administered by the office of the regional director of appeals in each region.

The major sources of revenues collected are the individual income, social insurance, and retirement taxes. Other sources of revenue are the corporation income, excise, estate, and gift taxes. The IRS collects more than $2 trillion in taxes each year.

In an effort to increase the effectiveness of the services provided by the IRS, the Citizen Advocacy Panel program was established in 1998. Selected districts in New York City, the Midwest, and the Pacific Northwest established local panels of ordinary citizen volunteers who help identify problems relating to IRS operations and to make recommendations for the improvement of the overall system.

The Internal Revenue Service Restructuring and Reform Act of 1998 brought about a major restructuring of the IRS—the agency's most sweeping overhaul since 1952. At the management level, then Commissioner Charles O. Rossotti added two new deputy commissioner posts for operations and modernization. Also, the Joint Committee on Taxation was given oversight authority of the IRS with regard to reviewing all requests for investigations of the IRS by the General Accounting Office and to approve such requests when appropriate. The act also placed the burden of proof regarding income tax liability upon the IRS rather than the taxpayer.

In October 2000 the IRS officially unveiled its reorganizational structure. The agency's old standard of dividing the nation's taxpayers by geographic boundaries was replaced with a new system centered around four customer-focused divisions, a major reduction from the IRS's thirty-three districts and ten service centers in past years. This new centralized focus helps ensure uniform and consistent practices regardless of where taxpayers live. The new organizational structure also permits the agency to work quickly to solve problems and to meet the needs of specific taxpayer groups. More IRS resources are now devoted to prefiling activities, such as education and outreach to help taxpayers comply with tax law. Postfiling activities focus on problem prevention with targeted enforcement activities for noncompliance.

A key component of the reorganization hinges on computer modernization. The IRS continues to overhaul its 1960s-era, tape-based computer system with a state-of-the-art system. When completed, the project will allow the IRS to deliver tax refunds in days and provide taxpayers up-to-date information on their accounts and improve service in numerous ways. In the meantime the IRS continues its push for more and more taxpayers to file their returns electronically, a process that saves the IRS time and speeds refund checks to recipients. For the 2002 tax year, the IRS estimated that taxpayers would file 43 million individual income tax returns electronically.

Other service improvements will come from the four new divisions, which form the backbone of the new IRS:

- **Wage and Investment** serves individual taxpayers with wage and investment incomes. The division, headquartered in Atlanta, served about 122 million taxpayers in 2003, accounting for 94 million returns. Members of the division focus on educating and assisting taxpayers during all interactions with the IRS.
- **Small Business/Self-Employed** is headquartered in New Carrollton, Md. This diverse group covers taxpayers who are fully or partially self-employed or who own small businesses with assets of less than $10 million. Taxpayers in this group (approximately 45 million in 2003) face some of the most complex tax law requirements and file twice as many forms and schedules as individual taxpayers. This division also focuses on increased education and communication efforts with taxpayers and external stakeholder organizations, such as tax practitioners.
- **Large and Mid-Size Business** serves corporations and partnerships that have assets greater than $10 million. This division, headquartered in Washington, D.C., places an emphasis on helping businesses avoid problems before they occur and streamlining the tax dispute process to ease burdens on businesses.
- **Tax-Exempt/Government Entities** is headquartered in Washington, D.C. The division serves three distinct customer segments—employee plans, tax-exempt organizations, and government entities—representing 3 million customers in 2003. These groups controlled $6.7 trillion in assets.

◾ KEY PERSONNEL

Commissioner
Mark W. Everson...................... (202) 622-9511
Fax...................................... (202) 622-5756
National Public Liaison
Sharon Lane.......................... (202) 622-3359

Equal Opportunity and Diversity
John M. Robinson...................... (202) 622-5400
Legislative Affairs
Floyd Williams .... (202) 622-3720
Taxpayer Advocate
Nina E. Olson........................... (202) 622-6100
Chief Counsel
B. John Williams Jr. .... (202) 622-3300
Fax...................................... (202) 622-4277
Criminal Tax
Barry Finkelstein (acting) .... (202) 622-4460
Income Tax and Accounting
Robert M. Brown....................... (202) 622-4800
Finance and Management
Richard Mihelcic .... (202) 622-3330
Financial Institutes and Products
Lon Smith.............................. (202) 622-3900
General Legal Services
Mark Kaizen .... (202) 283-7900
Large and Mid-Size Business
Linda Burke............................ (202) 283-8604
National Taxpayer Advocate
Carol Campbell......................... (202) 622-4947
Pass-through and Special Industries
Heather C. Maloy .... (202) 622-3000
Procedure and Administration
Deborah A. Butler...................... (202) 622-3400
Small Business and Self-Employed
Tom Thomas (acting).................. (202) 283-2450
Tax-Exempt/Government Entities
Sarah Hall Ingram...................... (202) 622-6000
Wage and Investment
Kirsten Wielebob...................... (202) 622-6958
Deputy Commissioner for Modernization and Chief Information Officer
Vacant.................................. (202) 622-6800
Fax...................................... (202) 622-7153
Information Technology Services
Toni Zimmerman .... (202) 622-0260
Business Systems Modernization
Robert F. Albicker .... (202) 622-7100
Chief Financial Officer
Eileen Powell (acting).................. (202) 622-6400
Fax...................................... (202) 622-2261
Commissioner for Wage and Investment
John Dalrymple .... (202) 622-6860
Fax...................................... (202) 622-8393
Business Systems Planning
Gina Garza............................. (202) 283-0668
Communications
Maureen Allen......................... (404) 338-7102
Customer Assistance, Relationship, and Education
Tyrone Ayres........................... (404) 338-7100

Compliance
Jane Warriner............................ (404) 338-9904
Customer Account Services
Ron Watson.............................. (404) 338-8910
Earned Income Tax Credit Project
Candice Cromling...................... (202) 622-5994
Equal Employment Opportunity and Diversity
Dee Dee Cobb-Byrd.................... (404) 338-7999
Electronic Tax Administration
Terry Lutes.............................. (202) 622-7990
Human Resources
Carol Barnett........................... (404) 338-8751
Strategy and Finance
Mary Davis.............................. (404) 338-8865
Commissioner for Tax-Exempt/Government Entities
Evelyn A. Petschek..................... (202) 283-2500
Fax...................................... (202) 283-9973
Customer Account Services
John Ricketts........................... (513) 263-3733
Deputy Commissioner
Rich Morgante.......................... (202) 283-2700
Exempt Organizations
Steven T. Miller........................ (202) 283-2300
Employee Plans
Carol Gold.............................. (202) 283-2100
Government Entities
Edward Weiler.......................... (202) 283-2900
Business Systems Planning
Bob Wilkerson.......................... (202) 622-2627
Communications
Heather Rosenker...................... (202) 283-7392
Deputy Information Officer
Charles Valentino...................... (202) 283-6557
Compliance
Glen Henderson........................ (202) 622-5100
Equal Employment Opportunity and Diversity
Joanne Finnes.......................... (202) 283-1712
Human Resources
David Krieg............................. (202) 283-0053
Management and Finance
Rich Morgante.......................... (504) 558-3322
Deputy Commissioner of Large and Mid-Size Businesses
Larry R. Langdon....................... (202) 283-8500
Fax...................................... (202) 283-8508
Deputy Commissioner
Deborah M. Nolan...................... (202) 283-8713
Business Systems Planning
Julie Rushin............................ (703) 283-8610
Communications and Liaison
Susan Lindan........................... (202) 283-8589

Equal Opportunity Employment and Diversity
Joanne Johnson-Shaw.................. (202) 283-8628
Field Specialist
Keith Jones............................. (202) 283-8465
Management and Finance
Jim O'Malley........................... (202) 283-8506
Prefiling and Technical Guidance
Gerry Reese............................ (202) 283-8463
Quality Assurance and Performance Management
Arlene Kay.............................. (202) 283-8334
Strategic Research and Program Planning
Dick Teed.............................. (202) 283-8335

■ INFORMATION SOURCES

Internet
Agency Web site: http://www.irs.gov. Offers access to many IRS publications and forms, including all tax forms and instruction manuals; tax tips and tax information for both businesses and individuals; and a register of tax regulations.

Telephone Contacts
Personnel Locator........................ (202) 622-3028
Publications Orders...................... (800) 829-3676
General Information...................... (800) 829-1040
Tax Forms Fax-on-Demand.............. (703) 368-9694
Taxpayer Assistance TDD................ (800) 829-4059

■ INFORMATION AND PUBLICATIONS

KEY OFFICES

IRS Communications Division
1111 Constitution Ave. N.W.
Washington, DC 20224
(202) 622-4010
Frank Keith, director

Answers questions for the press, issues news releases, and maintains a mailing list for media representatives.

Freedom of Information
IRS Freedom of Information Branch
P.O. Box 705, Ben Franklin Station
Washington, DC 20044
(202) 622-6250

PUBLICATIONS

To order, call (800) 829-3676 or (800) 829-1040. The Taxpayer's Guide to IRS Information and Assistance (Publication No. 910) gives information on IRS programs, including Tele-Tax, telephone service for the deaf, information services for the blind, walk-in services, the Outreach and VITA programs, and tax seminars. The guide lists all IRS publications and tax forms available free of charge. Also included are descriptions of films available from the IRS and an order blank for publications and forms. Order blanks also are mailed to taxpayers in their tax form packages.

Titles available include:
Business Use of Your Home (No. 587)
How to Begin Depreciating Your Property (No. 946)
Individual Retirement Arrangements (IRAs) (No. 590)
Introduction to Estate and Gift Taxes (No. 950)
Tax Guide for Small Business (No. 334)
Understanding the Collection Process (No. 594)
Your Federal Income Tax (No. 17)

The weekly *Internal Revenue Bulletin* contains official IRS rulings and procedures as well as Treasury decisions, executive orders, tax conventions, legislation, and court decisions. To subscribe, contact the U.S. Government Printing Office (GPO): see appendix, Ordering Government Publications.

Weekly bulletins are indexed twice a year and published as the *Cumulative Bulletin*, available from the GPO. The four-volume *Bulletin Index-Digest System* is a reference tool for researching matters published in both the weekly Internal Revenue Bulletin and the Cumulative Bulletin since 1953. It is available by subscription from the GPO.

FILMS

Films explaining tax laws and IRS operations may be obtained from any district office. Consult the white pages of the local telephone directory to locate the office in your area.

IRS films cover such topics as tax withholding, information for small businesses, and tax return processing.

DATA AND STATISTICS

Reference Resources
Library
IRS Freedom of Information Reading Room
1111 Constitution Ave. N.W., Room 1569
Washington, DC 20224
(202) 622-6250
Hours: 9:00 a.m. to 4:00 p.m.

Contains IRS public records and documents. Each regional office also maintains a public reading room.

Taxpayer Assistance Numbers

The IRS maintains local toll-free assistance numbers to answer tax law questions and to aid in the preparation of returns. The regional toll-free numbers can be found in local telephone directories under "U.S. Government-Internal Revenue Service."

The IRS also offers TDD assistance: (800) 829-4059. This service operates 9:00 a.m. to 4:30 p.m. year-round, with longer hours depending on the tax season.

During the filing season, IRS local offices extend their hours of telephone assistance for taxpayers who are completing their federal tax forms. The IRS also has a toll-free telephone service called Tele-Tax, which provides recorded tax information tapes on about 150 topics. This service also answers current year refund inquiries beginning March 1 of each year.

A complete listing of the topics available, automated refund information, and the local numbers for Tele-Tax and toll-free telephone assistance are included in the 1040, 1040A, and 1040EZ tax packages.

Taxpayer Counseling

The IRS conducts various programs to help taxpayers fill out their income tax returns:

Outreach Program. Sends IRS speakers to community groups around the country to explain various tax laws and to answer income tax questions during the income tax filing season. The assistance is directed at low- and middle-income individuals.

Volunteer Income Tax Assistance (VITA). Trains volunteers throughout the country to prepare tax returns for the poor, elderly, non-English-speaking, and disabled, as well as members of the Armed Forces. The IRS provides training and materials to private service groups who dispense free tax assistance at local libraries, community centers, and churches.

Tax Counseling for the Elderly (TCE). IRS-trained volunteers from public and nonprofit groups provide tax counseling and tax preparation services for individuals 60 years of age or older, with special attention to the disabled.

Small Business Tax Education (SBTE). Small business owners and self-employed persons attend special tax programs to learn about their federal tax rights and responsibilities.

Understanding Taxes. An introductory tax education course for junior high and high school students.

Taxpayer Information. An information program involving the use of the media to assist and educate taxpayers and increase voluntary compliance.

Consult the IRS Freedom of Information Reading Room, above.

RULES AND REGULATIONS

IRS rules and regulations are published in the *Code of Federal Regulations,* Title 26, parts 1-699. Proposed regulations, new final regulations, and updates to the *Code of Federal Regulations* are published in the daily *Federal Register. (See appendix for details on how to obtain and use these publications.)*

■ LEGISLATION

The IRS carries out its responsibilities under:

Tax Reform Act of 1986 (100 Stat. 2085, 26 U.S.C. 1 et seq.). Signed by the president Oct. 22, 1986. Reduced income tax rates for corporations and individuals, lowering the top rate to 34 percent and 28 percent respectively. Curtailed or eliminated dozens of tax breaks including the elimination of the traditional lower tax rate on capital gains.

Revenue Reconciliation Act of 1993 (107 Stat. 416, 26 U.S.C. 1 et seq.). Signed by the president Aug. 10, 1993. Amended the Tax Reform Act of 1986. Increased income tax top rates to 36 percent for individuals and to 35 percent for corporations.

Taxpayer Bill of Rights 2 (26 U.S.C. 1 note). Signed by the president July 30, 1996. Increased from $100,000 to $1 million the maximum amount of damages taxpayers can recover if wrongly accused in IRS collections actions. Increased the amount taxpayers can recover in attorney's fees if they win a dispute with the IRS. Extended the interest-free period for delinquent payments under $100,000 from ten days to twenty-one days.

Small Business Job Protection Act of 1996 (26 U.S.C. 1 note). Signed by the president Aug. 20, 1996. Increased the tax deduction limit on equipment purchasing by small businesses. Expanded the tip credit for owners of bars and restaurants. Provided a $5,000 tax credit for adoptive parents. Allowed nonworking spouses to save up to $2,000 a year in tax-deferred IRAs.

Health Insurance Portability and Accountability Act of 1996 (42 U.S.C. 201 note). Signed by the president Aug. 21, 1996. Established rules for a pilot program for medical savings accounts. Increased the deduction for health insurance costs for self-employed individuals.

Personal Responsibility and Work Opportunity Reconciliation Act (42 U.S.C. 1305 note). Signed by the president Aug. 22, 1996. Amended the Internal Revenue Code to deny the Earned Income Credit (EIC) to individuals who are not authorized to work in the United States and to those who do not have social security numbers. Authorized the IRS to deny the EIC without appeal.

Internal Revenue Service Restructuring and Reform Act of 1998 (112 Stat. 689, 26 U.S.C. 7801 note). Signed by the president July 22, 1998. Directed the development of a plan to reorganize the IRS by eliminating or modifying the existing national, regional, and district structures. Directed the establishment of organizational units serving particular groups of taxpayers with similar needs. Established the Internal Revenue Service Oversight Board within the Department of the Treasury.

Taxpayer Bill of Rights 3 (112 Stat. 726, 26 U.S.C. 1 note). Signed by the president July 22, 1998. Placed any burden of proof in any court proceeding, regarding the income tax liability of a taxpayer, on the government if the taxpayer has met substantiation requirements. Increased the award cap on the hourly rate of attorney's fees from $110 to $125. Permitted civil damages of up to $100,000 for negligent actions by IRS employees. Suspended the statute of limitations for claiming a refund or credit during periods of a medically determined physical or mental impairment. Required the establishment of procedures to alert married taxpayers of their joint and several liabilities on all appropriate publications and instructions. Authorized the secretary to make grants to provide matching funds for the development, expansion, or continuation of qualified low-income taxpayer clinics.

Ticket to Work and Work Incentives Improvement Act of 1999 (113 Stat. 1860, 42 U.S.C. 1305). Signed by the president Dec. 17, 1999. Expanded health care benefits for the working disabled, extended a variety of business tax breaks, and postponed the implementation of new regulations for organ transplant recipients. Amended the Internal Revenue Code to provide a package of business tax-break extensions, including credits for employers who provide workers with educational assistance or who hire disadvantaged workers or former welfare beneficiaries. Narrowed the "safe harbor" for taxpayers with adjusted gross incomes greater than $150,000 who underpay their estimated taxes.

Economic Growth and Tax Relief Reconciliation Act of 2001 (115 Stat. 38, 26 U.S.C. 1 note). Signed by the president June 7, 2001. Reduced marginal tax rates, repealed the estate tax, reduced taxes for married couples, and increased contribution limits on retirement savings plans. Amended the Internal Revenue Code to create a 10 percent tax bracket, modified the 15 percent bracket and gradually reduced rates for the 28, 31, 36 and 39.6 percent brackets. Included tax breaks for families, including the gradual repeal of a law that phases out the personal exemption for taxpayers with incomes of more than $132,950 ($199,450 for married couples), and a law that phases out the personal exemption beginning in 2006. Increased the child tax credit over ten years, increased the maximum credit given to families that adopt children, and repealed an existing provision that restricted the credit to children with special needs. Reduced the taxes paid by married couples by increasing over five years the size of the standard deduction for couples filing jointly, phasing in an increase in the maximum income that would qualify for the lowest tax bracket, and increasing the income threshold at which the earned income credit is phased out for married couples. Allowed taxpayers to deduct higher education expenses from their taxable incomes, increased the contribution limit on Education Savings Accounts, and increased the student loan interest deduction income limitation. Phased out estate, gift, and generation-skipping taxes over ten years by gradually lowering marginal estate tax rates and increasing the federal estate tax exclusion. Changed the way capital gains are taxed. Increased the limit on annual contributions to traditional and Roth IRAs by 2008, and increased the amounts employers and employees can put into defined-contribution plans.

Victims of Terrorism Tax Relief Act of 2001 (115 Stat. 2427, 26 U.S.C. 1 note). Signed by the president Jan. 23, 2002. Amended the Internal Revenue Code of 1986 to provide tax relief to families of terrorist victims. Applied to victims of the Sept. 11, 2001, terrorist attacks on the United States; the 1995 Oklahoma City bombing; and anthrax-related deaths between September 2001 and January 2002.

Job Creation and Worker Assistance Act of 2002 (116 Stat. 21, 26 U.S.C. 1 note). Signed by the president March 9, 2002. Amended the Internal Revenue Code to authorize funds in fiscal 2002 for a thirteen-week extension of unemployment benefits for workers who exhausted their normal twenty-six weeks of benefits. Title II, the Temporary Extended Unemployment Compensation Act of 2002, allowed businesses to deduct 30 percent of the cost of equipment purchases made from Sept. 11, 2001, through Sept. 10, 2004, and to deduct losses in 2001 and 2002 to offset profits in the previous five years. Established tax breaks and tax-exempt bonds for businesses in New York's "Liberty Zone," the area around the World Trade Center site. Extended fourteen expiring tax credits.

Uniting and Strengthening America by Providing Appropriate Tools Required to Intercept and Obstruct Terrorism Act of 2002 (USA Patriot Act) (115 Stat. 272, 18 U.S.C. 1 note). Signed by the president Oct. 26, 2001. Title III, the International Money Laundering Abatement and Financial Anti-Terrorism Act of 2001, provided enhanced authority to identify, deter, and punish international money laundering. Required additional recordkeeping for particular transactions and the identification of foreign owners of certain accounts at U.S. financial institutions. Required banks to have minimum antimoney laundering due diligence standards for private bank accounts. Barred U.S. depository institutions from establishing, maintaining, administering, or managing correspondent accounts for certain foreign shell banks.

Office of Thrift Supervision

1700 G St. N.W., Washington, DC 20552
Internet: http://www.ots.treas.gov

The Office of Thrift Supervision (OTS) was established as a bureau of the Treasury Department in 1989 as part of a major reorganization of the thrift regulatory structure mandated by the Financial Institutions Reform, Recovery, and Enforcement Act (FIRREA). Today, it has evolved into an entity with about 1,300 staff members who regulate and supervise 1,082 thrifts, with $908 billion in assets, and thrift-holding companies.

Under the Home Owners' Loan Act, the OTS has the authority to charter, examine, supervise, and regulate federal savings associations and federal savings banks. OTS is also authorized to examine, supervise, and regulate state-chartered savings associations belonging to the Savings Association Insurance Fund (SAIF). The OTS carries out that responsibility by adopting regulations governing the savings and loan industry, by examining and supervising thrift institutions and their affiliates, and by taking whatever action is necessary to enforce their compliance with federal laws and regulations.

In addition to overseeing thrift institutions, the OTS regulates, examines, and supervises companies that own thrifts and controls the acquisition of thrifts by such holding companies.

The OTS director is appointed by the president and confirmed by the Senate to a five-year term. The director also serves on the boards of the Federal Deposit Insurance Corporation (FDIC) and the Neighborhood Reinvestment Corporation, an independent corporation chartered by the federal government. The director's office determines policy for OTS and the thrift industry. It also oversees the setting of new regulations governing the industry and individual institutions.

To carry out its mission, the OTS is organized into five major units that report to the director:

- Supervision oversees the examination and supervision of savings institutions by regulatory staff in the agency's five regional offices. The unit develops regulations, directives, and other policies to ensure proper operation of savings institutions and their compliance with federal law and regulations.
- Research and Analysis analyzes and publishes thrift industry data, assesses the risk exposure of financial products sold in capital markets, while determining policy for thrift institutions that buy such securities, and develops regulations dealing with interest rate capital requirements.
- Chief Counsel provides a full range of legal services to the agency, including writing regulations, representing the agency in court, and taking enforcement actions against savings institutions that violate laws or regulations.
- External Affairs includes Public Relations and the Congressional Division. Public Relations is responsible for communicating information about OTS actions and policies to the thrift industry, the public, and the news media. The Congressional Affairs division informs members of Congress on OTS activities and responds to congressional inquiries.
- Administration is responsible for all administrative functions including human resources, the agency's nationwide computer system, agency contracting, and the agency's central records facility and public reading room. This office also responds to Freedom of Information requests.

The OTS is not funded by tax money. Its expenses are met by fees and assessments on the thrift institutions it regulates.

KEY PERSONNEL

Director
James E. Gilleran .... (202) 906–6590
Fax .... (202) 898–6230

Deputy Director
Richard Riccobono .... (202) 906–6583

Ombudsman
Randy Thomas .... (202) 906–7945

Supervision
Scott Albinson .... (202) 906–7849

Accounting Policy
Timothy Stier .... (202) 906–5699

Compliance Policy
Richard Riese .... (202) 906–6134

Economic Analysis
David Malmquist .... (202) 906–5639

Examination Policy
Sonja White .... (202) 906–7857

Supervision Policy
John C. Price .... (202) 906–5745

Supervisory Standards & Review
Michael Finn .... (202) 906–6579

Technology Risk Management
Robert Engebreth .... (202) 906–5631

Chief Counsel
Carolyn Buck .... (202) 906–6251

Business Transactions
John Bowman .... (202) 906–6372

Enforcement
Richard Stearns .... (202) 906–7966

Litigation
Thomas Segal .... (202) 906–7230

Regulations & Legislation
Deborah Dakin .... (202) 906–6445

External Affairs
Kevin Petrasic .... (202) 906–6288

Press Relations
Sam Eskenazi .... (202) 906–6913

FDIC Liaison
Walter B. Mason .... (202) 906–7236

Human Resources & Professional Development
Sue Rendleman .... (202) 906–6050

Diversity Programs
Lynwood Campbell .... (202) 906–5713

Information Systems, Administration & Finance
Timothy Ward .... (202) 906–5666

National Systems
Patrick Berbakos .... (202) 906–6720

Quality Assurance
Barbara Taylor .... (202) 906–7510

Planning, Budget & Finance
Robert W. Beel .... (202) 906–6168

Procurement & Administrative Services
John Connors .... (202) 906–6666

Systems Operations/Telecommunications
Carl Spellacy .... (202) 906–5228

INFORMATION SOURCES

Internet

Agency Web site: http://www.ots.treas.gov. Offers basic information about the mission of OTS. Selected number of publications, press releases, and data are available.

Telephone Contacts

Personnel Locator .... (202) 906–6000
Consumer Hotline .... (202) 842–6929

Information and Publications

KEY OFFICES

OTS External Affairs

Press Relations Branch
1700 G St. N.W.
Washington, DC 20552
(202) 906–6913
Fax (202) 906–7849
Sam Eskenazi, director

Answers questions about the OTS and its activities for the press. Issues news releases and holds quarterly press conferences. Offers subscriptions to the *Cost of Funds Report* ($30.00), which details OTS-regulated and SAIF-insured institutions.

Freedom of Information

FOIA requests are handled by the Dissemination Branch of the Records Management and Information Policy Division. See Publications, below.

PUBLICATIONS

OTS Publications Department

Distribution Center
P.O. Box 753
Waldorf, MD 20604
(301) 645–6264

Titles available include:
Adjustable-Rate Mortgages
Bank Secrecy Act
Compliance: A Self-Assessment Guide
Compliance Activities Handbook
Federal Financial Institutions Examination Council (FFIEC) EDP Manual

Holding Company Handbook
Quarterly Financial Results and Conditions of the Thrift Industry ($40 per year)
Selected Asset and Liability Pricing Tables ($18 per year)
Thrift Activities Handbook
Trust Activities Handbook
Truth in Lending: Discounted Variable Rate Mortgages

OTS Records Management and Information Policy Division

Dissemination Branch
1700 G St. N.W.
Washington, DC 20552
(202) 906–5909
Fax-on-demand (202) 906–6866
Tom Segal, manager

Distributes OTS bulletins, regulations, price tables, testimony and speeches, press releases, OTS public-use forms, and legal opinions. A public reading room is open by appointment only.

DATA AND STATISTICS

See the Dissemination Branch, above.

Reference Resources

LIBRARY

OTS Library

1700 G St. N.W., Basement
Washington, DC 20552
(202) 906–6470
Cheryl Wright, head librarian
Hours: open to public Thursday, 10:00 a.m. to 4:00 p.m.; other days by appointment

Maintains books, working papers, government reports, and periodicals on specific subjects such as savings and loan associations, economics, housing, money, banking, finance, real estate, accounting, and management.

In addition to standard legal references, includes banking and savings and loan laws for the 50 states, history of banking and savings and loan associations, and publications of the U.S. League of Savings Institutions.

DOCKETS

See the Dissemination Branch under Publications, this page.

RULES AND REGULATIONS

OTS rules and regulations are published in the *Code of Federal Regulations*, Title 12, parts 500–599. Proposed regulations, new final regulations, and updates to the *Code of Federal Regulations* are published in the daily *Federal Register*. (*See appendix for details on how to obtain and use these publications.*)

LEGISLATION

The OTS administers the following legislation in full or in part:

Federal Home Loan Bank Act (47 Stat. 725, 12 U.S.C. 1421–1449). Signed by the president July 22, 1932. Created the Federal Home Loan Bank System.

Home Owners' Loan Act of 1933 (48 Stat. 128, 12 U.S.C. 1461). Signed by the president June 13, 1933. Authorized the Federal Home Loan Bank Board to charter, supervise, and examine federal savings and loan associations.

National Housing Act (48 Stat. 1246, 12 U.S.C. 1701). Signed by the president June 27, 1934. Created the Federal Savings and Loan Insurance Corporation to insure accounts; establish reserves and regulate activities of insured institutions; prevent defaults by making loans, purchasing assets, or making contributions; and act as conservator in cases of default.

Truth in Lending Act (82 Stat. 146, 15 U.S.C. 1601). Signed by the president May 29, 1968. Required lenders and merchants to inform consumers of total cost of loans and installment purchase plans and to state annual percentage rate clearly. Also prohibited unsolicited distribution of credit cards.

Bank Protection Act of 1968 (82 Stat. 294, 12 U.S.C. 1881). Signed by the president July 7, 1968. Required the establishment of minimum security system standards for banking institutions.

Fair Credit Reporting Act (84 Stat. 1128, 15 U.S.C. 1681). Signed by the president Oct. 26, 1970. Regulated credit information and use.

NOW Accounts Act (87 Stat. 342, 12 U.S.C. 1832). Signed by the president Aug. 16, 1973. Regulated interest-bearing checking accounts.

Equal Credit Opportunity Act (88 Stat. 1521, 15 U.S.C. 1691). Signed by the president Oct. 28, 1974. Prohibited credit discrimination against women; amended in 1976 to include discrimination based on age, race, religion, or national origin (90 Stat. 251).

Real Estate Settlement Procedures Act (88 Stat. 1724, 12 U.S.C. 2601). Signed by the president Dec. 22, 1974. Minimized settlement charges for home buyers; confirmed the authority of the Department of Housing and Urban Development to set standards for settlement charges on homes financed through federally guaranteed mortgages.

Home Mortgage Disclosure Act (89 Stat. 1125, 12 U.S.C. 2801). Signed by the president Dec. 31, 1975. Required lending institutions within standard metropolitan statistical areas (SMSAs) to disclose the number and amount of mortgage loans made yearly to determine if banks are discriminating against certain city neighborhoods by refusing to make loans regardless of the creditworthiness of the potential borrower (the practice known as "redlining").

Fair Debt Collection Practices Act (91 Stat. 874, 15 U.S.C. 1692). Signed by the president Sept. 20, 1977. Regulated methods used by debt collection agencies.

Housing and Community Development Act of 1977 (91 Stat. 1111, 42 U.S.C. 5301). Signed by the president Oct. 12, 1977. Amended the lending authority of federally chartered savings and loan associations, increasing the amount of money available for conventional home mortgages and home improvement loans.

Community Reinvestment Act of 1977 (91 Stat. 1147, 12 U.S.C. 2901). Signed by the president Oct. 12, 1977. Required financial institution regulators to encourage banks under their supervision to meet the credit needs of their communities, including low- and middle-income neighborhoods.

Housing and Community Development Amendments of 1978, Title VI (92 Stat. 2080, 42 U.S.C. 8101). Signed by the president Oct. 31, 1978. Created the Neighborhood Reinvestment Corporation; its directors include the director of OTS.

Financial Institutions Regulatory and Interest Rate Control Act of 1978 (92 Stat. 3641, 12 U.S.C. 226 note). Signed by the president Nov. 10, 1978. Prohibited interlocking management and director relationships among financial institutions.

Electronic Fund Transfer Act of 1978 (92 Stat. 3728, 15 U.S.C. 1601 note). Signed by the president Nov. 10, 1978. Established rules relating to consumer liability for unauthorized use of an electronic fund transfer card and unsolicited issuance of cards by financial institutions. Prohibited creditors from making automatic repayment of loans a condition of extending credit; overdraft plans were exempted.

Depository Institutions Deregulation and Monetary Control Act of 1980 (94 Stat. 132, 12 U.S.C. 226 note). Signed by the president March 31, 1980. Extended reserve requirements to all financial institutions, provided for phase-out of interest ceilings by 1986 and allowed thrift institutions to offer an expanded range of financial services. Increased insurance coverage for member institutions to $100,000.

Garn-St. Germain Depository Institutions Act of 1982 (96 Stat. 1469, 12 U.S.C. 226 note). Signed by the president Oct. 15, 1982. Expanded the power of federal regulatory agencies to assist troubled banks. Allowed either direct or merger-related assistance to prevent the closing of or to reopen any insured bank; also permitted assistance when severe financial conditions threaten the stability of a significant number of banks or banks with substantial financial resources. Increased the powers of federally chartered savings and loan associations and savings banks (thrift institutions) to conduct a wider range of commercial operations.

Supplemental Appropriations Act of 1983 (97 Stat. 301, 12 U.S.C. 1701 note). Signed by the president July 30, 1983. Created Federal Housing Administration (FHA) programs for alternative mortgages; eliminated rate ceilings in FHA loans; and clarified 1982 federal preemption of state restrictions on due-on-sale clauses and alternative mortgage instruments.

Second Mortgage Market Enhancement Act of 1984 (98 Stat. 1689, 12 U.S.C. 1451). Signed by the president Oct. 3, 1984. Authorized the Federal Home Loan Mortgage Corporation (FHLMC) to purchase manufactured home loans; authorized the FHLMC and the Federal National Mortgage Association to purchase second mortgages; and exempted mortgage-backed securities from state securities laws.

Competitive Equality Banking Act of 1987 (101 Stat. 552, 12 U.S.C. 226 note). Signed by the president Aug. 10, 1987. Granted the Federal Savings and Loan Insurance Corporation new borrowing authority to reimburse depositors as it shut down bankrupt thrifts. Suspended the expansion of banks into insurance, securities underwriting, and real estate. Eased regulatory requirements for savings and loans in economically depressed areas and required faster clearing of depositors' checks.

Financial Institutions Reform, Recovery, and Enforcement Act of 1989 (FIRREA) (103 Stat. 183, 12 U.S.C. 1811 note). Signed by the president Aug. 9, 1989. Approved the use of $50 billion to finance the closing of insolvent savings and loans. Created the Resolution Trust Corporation (RTC) to manage the disposal of the assets of bankrupt thrifts. Dissolved the Federal Home Loan Bank Board, passing its regulatory responsibilities on to the OTS within the Department of the Treasury. Replaced the Federal Savings and Loan Insurance Corporation with the Savings Association Insurance Fund. Required savings and loans to maintain a minimum amount of tangible capital equal to 1.5 percent of total assets.

Federal Deposit Insurance Corporation Improvement Act of 1991 (FDICA) (105 Stat. 2236, 12 U.S.C. 1811). Signed by the president Dec. 19, 1991. Required the most cost-effective resolution of those banks that are insolvent or in danger of failing and improved supervisory and examination procedures. Provided additional resources to Bank Insurance Fund.

Small Business Job Protection Act of 1996 (110 Stat. 1755, 26 U.S.C. 1 note). Signed by the president Aug. 20, 1996. Eliminated use of the section 593 reserve method of accounting for bad debts by savings institutions. Forgave recapture of pre-1988 base year reserves. Required the recapture of post-1987 reserves ratably over a six-year period.

Examination Parity and Year 2000 Readiness for Financial Institutions Act (112 Stat., 12 U.S.C. 1811 note; 12 U.S.C. 1461 note). Signed by the president March 20, 1998. Amended the Home Owners' Loan Act to place under the regulatory authority of the director of the OTS a service corporation or subsidiary owned by a savings association.

Gramm-Leach-Bliley Act (113 Stat. 1338, 12 U.S.C. 1811 note). Signed by the president Nov. 12, 1999. Permitted affiliations between banks and any financial company, including brokerage and insurance firms. Amended the Home Owners' Loan Act of 1933 to prohibit new affiliations between savings and loan holding companies and certain commercial firms. Amended the Electronic Fund Transfer Act of 1978 to mandate fee disclosures to a consumer using an ATM machine. Title VI, the Federal Home Loan Bank System Modernization Act of 1999, amended the 1932 Federal Home Loan Bank Act to make a federal savings association's membership in the Federal Home Loan Bank system voluntary instead of mandatory.

American Homeownership and Economic Opportunity Act of 2000 (114 Stat. 2944, 12 U.S.C. 1701). Signed by the president Dec. 27, 2000. Established programs to make home ownership more affordable for low- and moderate-income families, the elderly, and the disabled. Title XII, the Financial Regulatory Relief and Economic Efficiency Act of 2000, amended the Home Owners' Loan Act of 1933 to repeal savings association liquid asset requirements and to permit a savings and loan holding company to acquire more than 5 percent of the voting shares of a nonsubsidiary savings association or nonsubsidiary savings and loan holding company.

Uniting and Strengthening America by Providing Appropriate Tools Required to Intercept and Obstruct Terrorism Act of 2001 (USA Patriot Act) (115 Stat. 272, 18 U.S.C. 1 note). Signed by the president Oct. 26, 2001. Title III, the International Money Laundering Abatement and Financial Anti-Terrorism Act of 2001, provided enhanced authority to identify, deter, and punish international money laundering. Required additional recordkeeping for particular transactions and the identification of foreign owners of certain accounts at U.S. financial institutions. Required banks to have minimum antimoney laundering due diligence standards for private bank accounts. Barred U.S. depository institutions from establishing, maintaining, administering, or managing correspondent accounts for certain foreign shell banks.

REGIONAL OFFICES

NORTHEAST REGION

(CT, DE, MA, ME, NH, OH, NJ, NY, PA, RI, VT, WV)
10 Exchange Place Center, 18th Floor
Jersey City, NJ 07302
(201) 413–1000
Robert C. Albanese, regional director

SOUTHEAST REGION

(AL, FL, GA, IL, IN, KY, MD, MI, NC, SC, VA, DC, PR, VI)
1475 Peachtree St. N.E.
P.O. Box 105217
Atlanta, GA 30309
(404) 888–0771
John E. Ryan, regional director

MIDWEST REGION

(AR, IA, KS, LA, MN, MO, MS, NE, OK, TN, TX, WI)
225 E. John Carpenter Fwy., #500
Irving, TX 75062
(972) 277–9500
Frederick R. Casteel, regional director

WEST REGION

(AK, AZ, CA, CO, HI, ID, MT, ND, NM, NV, OR, SD, UT, WA, WY, Guam, Northern Mariana Islands)
2001 Junipero Serra Blvd., #650
Daly City, CA 94014
(650) 746–7000
Charles A. Deardorff, regional director

Veterans Affairs Department

810 Vermont Ave. N.W., Washington, DC 20420
Internet: http://www.va.gov

Veterans Affairs Department

810 Vermont Ave. N.W., Washington, DC 20420
Internet: http://www.va.gov

The Department of Veterans Affairs (VA) was elevated to cabinet status on March 15, 1989. The VA was created from the Veterans Administration, which was established as an independent agency in July 1930. The secretary of veterans affairs is appointed by the president and confirmed by the Senate.

The VA administers programs to assist the nation's veterans, their families, and dependents. Most of the programs provide health care to veterans and pensions or other compensation to veterans, their dependents, and survivors. Other programs assist veterans who continue their education. The department also guarantees loans made by commercial lenders to veterans for new homes, condominiums, and mobile or manufactured homes.

The VA guarantees or insures part of each home loan and requires the lending institution to make the loan at a specific rate of interest (usually below the market rate). The department also has authority to provide grants to veterans with permanent disabilities to purchase houses adapted to their needs.

VA officials appraise properties, supervise construction of new homes, and ensure that lenders comply with federal laws and regulations governing access to credit.

The education program provides funds to veterans to pay for education at any high school, vocational, correspondence or business school; junior or teachers college; college or university; professional, scientific or technical institution; or any other institution that furnishes education at the secondary school level or above. These schools must be approved by a state approval agent. The VA reviews the state approval procedure to ensure that the state standards measure up to VA criteria. The VA has no authority to force a state to use its approval standards; it can only refuse to provide the funds to a veteran who wishes to attend a nonapproved school.

The majority of the department's work involves VA hospitals, domiciliaries, clinics, and nursing homes. The VA arranges for the care of some veterans in nonveteran hospitals and homes when space in VA facilities is not available. The VA also performs a wide variety of research and assists in the training of physicians and dentists.

VA benefits include:

- Disability compensation and pensions, including special automobiles, specially adapted housing, and special clothing allowances.
- Vocational rehabilitation programs for disabled veterans.
- Life insurance.

The Veterans Educational Assistance Service ensures that schools and training institutions comply with VA rules and regulations; with the Civil Rights Act of 1964, which prohibits discrimination because of race, color, or national origin in any program that receives federal financial assistance; and with Title IX of the Education Amendments of 1972, which prohibits sex discrimination by an education program that receives federal funds.

Most VA programs are administered through the department's regional offices where assistance and advice to veterans and their dependents can be obtained from the Veterans Assistance Service. (VA regional offices are listed in the booklet, *Federal Benefits for Veterans and Dependents;* see Publications, below.)

The VA also operates the National Cemetery System. Qualified veterans are eligible for a headstone and burial in any national cemetery where space is available. The eligible veteran's next of kin also can receive allowances for private burial, plot, and headstone.

KEY PERSONNEL

Secretary
Anthony J. Principi.................... (202) 273–4800
Fax.................................... (202) 273–4877
Deputy Secretary
Leo S. Mackey Jr. .... (202) 273–4817
Veterans Service Organizations Liaison
Allen "Gunner" Kent................... (202) 273–4835
Board of Contract Appeals
Guy McMichael III.................... (202) 273–6743
Fax.................................... (202) 275–5381
Board of Veterans Appeals
Elijah Dane Clark .... (202) 565–5001
Fax.................................... (202) 565–5787
Congressional Affairs
Gordon H. Mansfield .... (202) 273–5611
Fax.................................... (202) 273–6791
Congressional Liaison
Nurit Erger .... (202) 273–5628
Information and Technology
Vacant................................. (202) 273–4800
General Counsel
Tim McClain .... (202) 273–6660
Fax.................................... (202) 273–6671
Human Resources and Administration
Jacob Lozada.......................... (202) 273–4901
Fax.................................... (202) 273–4914
Administration
Deno Verenes.......................... (202) 273–5356
Equal Opportunity
Gerald Hinch.......................... (202) 273–5888
Human Resources Management
Ventris Gibson........................ (202) 273–9433
Security and Law Enforcement
John Baffa............................. (202) 273–5500
Inspector General
Richard Griffin .... (202) 535–8620
Fax.................................... (202) 565–7936
Management
Vacant................................. (202) 273–5589
Fax.................................... (202) 273–6796
Acquisition and Material Management
Gary Krump .... (202) 273–6029
Budget
D. Mark Catlett........................ (202) 273–5289
Information Resource Management
Vacant................................. (202) 273–8855

National Cemetery Administration
Robin Higgins.......................... (202) 273–5146
Fax.................................... (202) 273–6696
Public Affairs
Richard Arndt......................... (202) 273–5221
Policy and Planning
Dennis M. Duffy .... (202) 273–5033
Fax.................................... (202) 273–5991
Planning
Gary Steinberg........................ (202) 273–5068
Policy
Edward Chow Jr. .... (202) 273–5045
Public and Intergovernmental Affairs
Vacant................................. (202) 273–5750
Fax.................................... (202) 273–5717
Intergovernmental Affairs
Bill McLemore .... (202) 273–5121
Small and Disadvantaged Business Utilization
Scott Denniston .... (202) 565–8124
Fax.................................... (202) 565–8156
Veterans Benefits Administration
Joseph Thompson...................... (202) 273–6763
Fax.................................... (202) 275–3591
Compensation and Pension Service
Robert Epley.......................... (202) 273–7203
Education Service
William D. Fillman.................... (202) 273–7132
Information Management
Adair Martinez........................ (202) 273–7004
Loan Guaranty Service
R. Keith Pedigo .... (202) 273–7331
Directives, Forms, and Publications
Robert Knode.......................... (202) 273–7589
Vocational Rehabilitation and Counseling Service
Julius Williams .... (202) 273–7419
Veterans Health Administration
Thomas Garthwaite.................... (202) 273–5781
Fax.................................... (202) 273–7090
Communications Officer
James Holley.......................... (202) 273–6273

INFORMATION SOURCES

Internet
Agency Web Site: http://www.va.gov. Includes information on benefits, facilities, and special programs, with links to related Internet sites.

Telephone Contacts
Personnel Locator......................... (202) 273–5400

Inspector General
Fraud, Waste, Abuse, and Mismanagement
  Hotline .... (800) 488–8244
Veterans Benefits Administration
Benefits Hotline .... (800) 827–1000
Debt Management Hotline .... (800) 827–0648
Insurance Hotline .... (800) 669–8477

Information and Publications

KEY OFFICES

VA Public Affairs
810 Vermont Ave. N.W.
Washington, DC 20420
(202) 273–5710
Fax (202) 273–5719
Jeffrey Phillips, deputy assistant secretary

Provides general information, issues news releases, and answers queries from the media.

Veterans Benefits Administration
Directives, Forms, and Publications Staff
1800 G St. N.W., #506C
Washington, DC 20006
(202) 273–7586
Fax (202) 275–5947

Operated by the Veterans Benefits Administration. Provides assistance and information to veterans on all programs administered by the VA. Also operates an office in the VA headquarters to answer and refer questions.

Freedom of Information
VA Information Management Service
810 Vermont Ave. N.W.
Washington, DC 20420
(202) 273–8135
Fax (202) 565–8267
Donald Neilson, contact

PUBLICATIONS
Each unit within the VA (e.g., Veterans Benefits) publishes and distributes publications and has a publications control officer. For availability of material on specific topics, contact the appropriate division or unit, or the nearest regional office.

Three basic VA publications are available from the U.S. Government Printing Office (GPO): see appendix, Ordering Government Publications.

Federal Benefits for Veterans and Dependents

Secretary of Veterans Affairs Annual Report
VA History in Brief

Any VA regional office also can provide copies of *A Summary of Department of Veterans Affairs Benefits*

DATA AND STATISTICS
A good source of data and statistics on the VA is the *Secretary of Veterans Affairs Annual Report,* available from the GPO. Most VA statistical information is available on the VA Web site (www.va.gov).

Reference Resources

LIBRARIES

VA Headquarters Library
810 Vermont Ave. N.W.
Washington, DC 20420
(202) 273–8522
Ginny DuPont, director

Holdings include materials on VA history, biomedicine, business, and women veterans. Visitors may obtain more information about the collection by arranging an appointment with the director's office.

VA Law Library
Office of the General Counsel
810 Vermont Ave. N.W., Room 1127
Washington, DC 20420
(202) 273–6558
Fax (202) 273–6645

Collection consists of legal materials related to veterans programs. The library is connected to the WESTLAW computerized database system. Public use is restricted and must be arranged through the office of the chief librarian.

RULES AND REGULATIONS
VA rules and regulations are published in the *Code of Federal Regulations,* Title 38. Updates, revisions, proposed rules, and new final rules are published in the daily *Federal Register. (See appendix for information on how to obtain and use these publications.)*

▪ LEGISLATION
Legislation for which the VA has regulatory responsibility includes:

Veterans Benefits Act (72 Stat. 1105, 38 U.S.C. 101). Signed by the president Sept. 2, 1958. Detailed the full range of veterans benefits. Authorized the VA to establish standards for loans it guarantees or insures.

Veterans Readjustment Benefits Act of 1966 (80 Stat. 12, 38 U.S.C. 101). Signed by the president March 3, 1966. Authorized a system of educational assistance to veterans.

Veterans Health Care Amendments of 1979 (93 Stat. 47, 38 U.S.C. 612A). Signed by the president June 13, 1979. Established a readjustment counseling program for veterans of the Vietnam era.

Veterans Administration Health Care Amendments of 1980 (94 Stat. 1048, 38 U.S.C. Title III). Vetoed by the president Aug. 22, 1980; veto overridden Aug. 26, 1980. Improved and expanded the capability of VA health care facilities to respond to the needs of older veterans.

Veterans Rehabilitation and Education Amendments of 1980 (94 Stat. 2171, 38 U.S.C. 101 note). Signed by the president Oct. 17, 1980. Revised and expanded veterans employment and training programs.

Veterans Health Care, Training, and Small Business Loan Act of 1981 (95 Stat. 1047, 38 U.S.C. 101 note). Signed by the president Nov. 3, 1981. Provided health care for veterans exposed to Agent Orange, a toxic defoliant used in Vietnam.

Veterans Education and Employment Assistance Act of 1984 (98 Stat. 2553, 38 U.S.C. 101 note). Signed by the president Oct. 19, 1984. Established a new educational assistance program for veterans as part of the Department of Defense Authorization Act of 1985.

Veterans Dioxin and Radiation Exposure Compensation Standards Act (98 Stat. 2725, 38 U.S.C. 354 note). Signed by the president Oct. 24, 1984. Required the VA to pay compensation to some veterans exposed to Agent Orange, or to ionizing radiation from atmospheric nuclear tests or from the American occupation of Hiroshima or Nagasaki, Japan.

Veterans Health Care Amendments of 1986 (100 Stat. 372, 38 U.S.C. 101 note). Signed by the president April 7, 1986. Ensured that VA hospital care is provided to service-connected veterans and to lower-income veterans. Veterans with higher incomes may be provided VA health care if space and resources are available, and may be charged for their care.

Department of Veterans Affairs Act (100 Stat. 2635, 38 U.S.C. 201 note). Signed by the president Oct. 25, 1988. Renamed the VA the Department of Veterans Affairs and elevated the agency to an executive department.

Veterans Home Loan Program Amendments of 1992 (106 Stat. 3633, 38 U.S.C. 101 note). Signed by the president Oct. 28, 1992. Authorized the VA to provide home loan benefits for veterans, including guaranteeing adjustable rate mortgages.

Veterans Benefits Act of 1992 (106 Stat. 4320, 38 U.S.C. 101 note). Signed by the president Oct. 29, 1992. Reformed the Dependency and Indemnity Compensation program and made significant improvements in a variety of other veterans' benefits.

Veterans Health Care Act of 1992 (106 Stat. 4943, 38 U.S.C. 101 note). Signed by the president Nov. 4, 1992. Established the Persian Gulf War Veterans Health Registry within the VA. Authorized the VA to provide counseling services to women who suffer the trauma of sexual assault or harassment during their military service.

Persian Gulf War Veterans Benefits Act (108 Stat. 4647, 38 U.S.C. 101 note and 1117 note). Signed by the president Nov. 2, 1994. Authorized the VA to provide disability benefits to veterans suffering from Persian Gulf Syndrome. Established a Center for Women Veterans within the VA to coordinate women's programs. Expanded eligibility for VA-guaranteed home loans.

Amendments to the Persian Gulf War Veterans Benefits Act (110 Stat. 768, 38 U.S.C. 1710e3). Signed by the president Feb. 13, 1996. Extended through Dec. 31, 1996, VA's authority to provide priority hospital care and medical services to Persian Gulf veterans. Extended through Dec. 31, 1997, VA's authority to contract community-based treatment facilities for the care of eligible veterans suffering from alcohol, drug dependence, and abuse disabilities; set forth alternative programs to deal with veterans who are unemployed and/or homeless.

Veterans' Health Care Eligibility Reform Act of 1996 (110 Stat. 3177, 38 U.S.C. 101 note). Signed by the president Oct. 9, 1996. Established the Advisory Committee on the Readjustment of Veterans. Required the Veterans Health Administration to establish a peer review panel to assess the scientific and clinical merit of proposals dealing with mental health and behavioral sciences of veterans.

Veterans' Benefits Improvements Act of 1996 (110 Stat. 3322, 32 U.S.C. 101 note). Signed by the president Oct. 9, 1996. Relaxed some of the requirements needed for veterans to obtain benefits relating to education, housing, memorial affairs, employment, and training.

Veterans' Millennium Health Care and Benefits Act (113 Stat. 1545, 38 U.S.C. 101 note). Signed by the president Nov. 30, 1999. Established a four-year plan requiring the VA to provide institutional care and extended care services to veterans with 70 percent or more service-connected disabilities. Authorized the VA to pay for emergency treatment for uninsured veterans. Required the VA to operate a sexual trauma program through 2004 and to establish specialized mental health treatments for posttraumatic stress and drug abuse. Authorized benefits to spouses of former prisoners of war who were rated completely disabled because of service-connected disabilities. Directed the VA to establish six additional national veterans' cemeteries and to commission a study on improvements to veterans' cemeteries and benefits.

Veterans Claims Assistance Act of 2000 (114 Stat. 2096, 38 U.S.C. 101 note). Signed by the president Nov. 9, 2000. Authorized the VA to help veterans find evidence to use in establishing benefits claims. Required the VA to assist veterans in obtaining medical records and other relevant data at other federal agencies.

Homeless Veterans Comprehensive Assistance Act of 2001 (115 Stat. 903, 38 U.S.C. 101 note). Signed by the president Dec. 21, 2001. Authorized and expanded assistance programs for homeless veterans.

Veterans Education and Benefits Expansion Act of 2001 (115 Stat. 976, 38 U.S.C. 101 note). Signed by the president Dec. 27, 2001. Increased the amounts of veterans' education benefits covered by the Montgomery GI Bill. Repealed the thirty-year presumptive period for respiratory cancers associated with exposure to herbicide agents in Vietnam. Expanded the definition of "undiagnosed illnesses" for Persian Gulf War veterans. Provided a service pension to low-income veterans. Required the VA to give benefit applicants, within three months of their application, information on all benefits available to veterans, dependents, and survivors. Increased the maximum VA home loan guarantee amount. Increased the VA burial and funeral expense benefit for a service-connected death.

Department of Veterans Affairs Emergency Preparedness Act of 2002 (116 Stat. 2024, 38 U.S.C. 101 note). Signed by the president Nov. 7, 2002. Created four national medical-preparedness centers within the VA to conduct research on the detection, diagnosis, prevention, and treatment of illnesses that could result from a biological, chemical, or radiological attack. Authorized the centers to provide laboratory and other medical support services to federal, state, and local authorities during a national emergency. Authorized the VA to provide medical care for people affected by presidentially declared emergencies or disasters.

Veterans Benefits Improvement Act of 2002 (116 Stat. 2820, 38 U.S.C. 101 note). Signed by the president Dec. 6, 2002. Expanded veterans' benefits, including a retroactive increase in the Medal of Honor pension. Authorized increasing the budgets of state agencies that monitor educational institutions and job training facilities for veterans. Extended special monthly compensation to women who needed at least 25 percent of their breast tissue excised as a result of military service. Expanded benefits within other programs.

▨ REGIONAL OFFICES

VA Public Affairs

The Department of Veterans Affairs also maintains benefits offices in each state. For information on these offices, call (800) 827–1000.

REGION 1
(CT, MA, ME, NH, NJ, NY, RI, VT)
245 W. Houston St., #315B
New York, NY 10014
(212) 807–3429
Lawrence M. Devine, regional director

REGION 2
(DC, DE, MD, PA, NC, VA, WV except Huntington)
810 Vermont Ave. N.W.
Washington, DC 20420
(202) 273–5740
Oziel Garza, regional director

REGION 3
(AL, FL except Pensacola, GA, KY, PR, SC, TN)
730 Peachtree St. N.E., #710
Atlanta, GA 30365
(404) 347–3236
Gary Hickman, regional director

REGION 4
(most of IL, IN except Evansville, MI, OH, WI except Superior)
536 S. Clark St., #512
Chicago, IL 60605
(312) 353–4076
Carl H. Henderson, regional director

REGION 5
(CO, IA, KS, MN, MO, MT, NE, ND, SD, UT; parts of ID, IL, IN, WI)
155 Van Gordon St.
Lakewood, CO 80225
(303) 914–5855
Paul Sherbo (acting), regional director

REGION 6
(AK, CA, HI, NV, OR, WA; Pocatello, ID; Philippines)
11301 Wilshire Blvd.
Bldg. 506
Los Angeles, CA 90073
(310) 268–4207
David S. Bayard, regional director

REGION 7
(AR, AZ, LA, MS, NM, OK, TX; Pensacola, FL)
4500 S. Lancaster Rd.
Bldg. 43, #124
Dallas, TX 75216
(214) 767–9270
Rick P. DuCharme, regional director

Regulatory Oversight and Coordination

CONGRESSIONAL BUDGET OFFICE

402 Ford Bldg.
2nd and D Sts. S.W.
Washington, DC 20515
Internet://www.cbo.gov

Director
Dan Crippin .... (202) 226–2700
Fax .... (202) 225–7509
Deputy Director
Barry B. Anderson .... (202) 226–2702
Executive Associate Director
Steven M. Lieberman .... (202) 226–4737
Communications
Melissa Merson .... (202) 226–2602
Administration and Information
William Gainer .... (202) 226–2600
Budget Analysis
Robert Sunshine .... (202) 226–2800
General Counsel
Gail Del Balzo .... (202) 226–2700
Health and Human Resources
Joseph R. Antos .... (202) 226–2671
Macroeconomic Analysis
Robert Dennis .... (202) 226–2750
Macroeconomic and Financial Services
Robert Hirchner .... (202) 226–2940
National Security
Chris Jehn .... (202) 226–2900
Research and Reports
Robert Murphy .... (202) 226–2616
Tax Analysis
Tom Woodward .... (202) 226–2680

The Congressional Budget Office (CBO), a nonpartisan agency in the legislative branch, was established by the Congressional Budget and Impoundment Control Act of 1974. It provides Congress with objective, timely, nonpartisan analyses needed for economic and budget decisions and with the information and estimates required for the congressional budget process. CBO supports the work of the House and Senate Budget Committees, which also were created by the 1974 Congressional Budget Act. CBO's services can be grouped in four categories: helping Congress formulate a budget plan, helping it stay within that plan, assessing the impact of federal mandates, and studying issues related to the budget and to economic policy. It also is responsible for producing the *Annual Report and Economic Outlook* and midsession update each year. CBO is the only part of the legislative branch whose mandate includes making economic forecasts and projections.

CORPORATION FOR NATIONAL AND COMMUNITY SERVICE

1201 New York Ave. N.W.
Washington, DC 20525
Internet: http://www.cns.gov
http://www.nationalservice.org

Chief Executive Officer
Wendy Zenker (acting) .... (202) 606–5000
Fax .... (202) 565–2784
AmeriCorps
Bob Torvestad (acting) .... (202) 606–5000
AmeriCorps Recruiting Information
Vacant .... (800) 942–2677
Learn and Serve America
Amy Cohen (acting) .... (202) 606–5000
Senior Corps
Tess Scannell .... (202) 606–5000
Senior Corps Recruiting
Information .... (800) 424–8867

The Corporation for National and Community Service provides opportunities for Americans of all ages and backgrounds to serve their communities and country through nonprofit organizations, faith-based groups, schools, and local agencies. Volunteers help meet needs in education, the environment, public safety, homeland security, and other critical areas. The Corporation is part of USA Freedom Corps, a White House initiative to foster a culture of citizenship, service, and responsibility.

The Corporation operates the following programs:

- **AmeriCorps.** AmeriCorps provides volunteers with opportunities to serve their communities on a full- or part-time basis, while earning educational awards for college or vocational training. Participants are sponsored and trained by national, state, or local nonprofit organizations to meet the specific needs of the communities they serve. In addition to these local programs, AmeriCorps also offers two national programs, the AmeriCorps National Civilian Community Corps (NCCC) program and the AmeriCorps Volunteers in Service to America (VISTA) program. NCCC is a full-time program in which members work in teams and live together in housing complexes on NCCC campuses. Members help meet the nation's critical needs in education, public safety, the environment, and other human needs. In Americorps*VISTA, individuals work in nonprofit organizations. Rather than providing direct service, such as tutoring or housing renovation, VISTA members work to expand the organization's services by training and recruiting volunteers and helping to establish new community activities.

- **Learn and Serve America.** Learn and Serve America is a grants program that supports teachers and community members who involve young people in service that relates to school studies. Learn and Serve America funds two service-learning programs: one for school-age children and one for undergraduate and graduate students. Learn and Serve America supports service-learning activities for more than 1 million students nationwide. The services ranged from tutoring disadvantaged youth to rehabilitating public housing and helping single mothers strengthen job skills.

- **Senior Corps.** Senior Corps is a network of three programs designed to help older Americans find service opportunities in their communities. The Retired and Senior Volunteers Program (RSVP) encourages older citizens to use their talents and experience in community service. The Foster Grandparent Program offers older citizens opportunities to work with exceptional children and children with special needs. The Senior Companion Program recruits older citizens to help homebound adults, especially seniors with special needs.

COUNCIL OF ECONOMIC ADVISERS

Old Executive Office Bldg., Room 314
Washington, DC 20500
Internet:
http://www.whitehouse.gov/cea/index.html

Chair
Glen Hubbard .... (202) 395–5042
Fax .... (202) 395–6958
Member
Vacant .... (202) 395–5046
Member
Mark B. McClellan (designate) .... (202) 395–5036

The Council of Economic Advisers (CEA) was created by the Employment Act of 1946. It is within the Executive Office of the President. It consists of three members, one designated as chair, who are appointed by the president and confirmed by the Senate. The council and its staff of economists analyze the national economy and its various segments, including economic programs and policies of the federal government; advise the president on economic matters; and prepare the annual *Economic Report of the President* for Congress.

COUNCIL ON ENVIRONMENTAL QUALITY

Old Executive Bldg., Room 360
Washington, DC 20502
Internet: http://www.whitehouse.gov/CEQ/

Chair
James L. Connaughton .... (202) 456–6224
Fax .... (202) 456–6546
Global Environment
Vacant .... (202) 456–6543
Natural Resources
Vacant .... (202) 395–7415
NEPA Oversight
Vacant .... (202) 456–5750
Sustainable Development
Vacant .... (202) 456–6550
Toxics and Environmental Protection
Vacant .... (202) 456–6549

The Council on Environmental Quality (CEQ) was established within the Executive Office of the President by the National Environmental Policy Act (NEPA) of 1969. Additional responsibilities were assigned under the Environment Quality Improvement Act of 1970. The council is headed by a chair who is appointed by the president and confirmed by the Senate. Specific functions of the CEQ include formulating and recommending policies to the president that further environmental quality; analyzing changes and trends in the national environment; reviewing environmental programs of the federal government to determine their soundness; overseeing implementation of NEPA; approving agency environmental regulations; and preparing the president's annual environmental quality report to Congress.

DOMESTIC POLICY COUNCIL

1600 Pennsylvania Ave. N.W.
Washington, DC 20500
Internet: http://www.whitehouse.gov/dpc/

Assistant to the President for Domestic Policy
Margaret LaMontagne .... (202) 456–5594
Fax .... (202) 456–5557
Executive Assistant
Sarah Pfeifer .... (202) 456–5594

The Domestic Policy Council (DPC) was established by an executive order on Aug. 16, 1993. The council is within the Executive Office of the President and composed of cabinet officials and administrators of federal agencies that affect the issues addressed by the DPC. The principal functions of the council include coordinating the domestic policymaking process; ensuring domestic policy decisions and programs are consistent with the president's stated goals; and monitoring the implementation of the domestic policy agenda. The Office of National AIDS Policy (ONAP), the Office of National Drug Control Policy (ONDCP), and the Office of Faith-Based and Community Initiatives (OFBCI) are also affiliated with the Domestic Policy Council. All executive departments and agencies, whether or not represented on the council, coordinate their domestic policy through the council.

▓ FEDERAL TECHNOLOGY SERVICE

General Services Administration
18th and F Sts. N.W.
Washington, DC 20405
Internet: http://www.fts.gsa.gov

Commissioner
(10304 Eaton Pl., Fairfax, VA 22030)
    Sandra N. Bates .... (703) 306–6020
    Fax .... (703) 306–6175
Information Assurance and Critical Infrastructure
Protection
(7th and D Sts. S.W., Washington, DC 20407)
    Sallie McDonald .... (202) 708–7000
    Fax .... (202) 708–5267
Information Technology Integration
(451 7th St. S.W., #4160, Washington, DC 20410)
    Carolyn Cockrell (acting) .... (202) 708–0306
    Fax .... (202) 708–3577

The Federal Technology Service (FTS), formerly the Information Technology Service, is a General Services Administration organization responsible for supporting the National Information Infrastructure, Government Services Information Infrastructure, and National Performance Review. In addition, FTS is responsible for developing a future infrastructure that supports access and interconnectivity among federal agencies and between federal agencies and the public. FTS coordinates and directs a comprehensive, government-wide program for the management, procurement, and use of automated data processing and local telecommunications equipment and services. FTS also plans and directs programs for improving federal records and information management practices. Within

FTS are the Office of Information Security, which provides secure information services for federal government organizations conducting classified, sensitive, diplomatic, or military missions worldwide, and the Office of Information Technology Integration, which plans, manages, and operates government-wide information technology programs.

▓ GENERAL ACCOUNTING OFFICE

441 G St. N.W.
Washington, DC 20548
Internet: http://www.gao.gov

Comptroller General
    David M. Walker .... (202) 512–5500
    Fax .... (202) 512–5507
Chief Operating Officer
    Gene Dodaro .... (202) 512–5600
General Counsel
    Tony Gamboa .... (202) 512–5400
    Fax .... (202) 512–7703
Special Investigations
    Bob Hast .... (202) 512–7455
Chief Mission Support Officer/Chief Financial Officer
    Sallyanne Harper .... (202) 512–5800
Chief Information Officer
    Anthony Cicco .... (202) 512–6623
Controller/Chief Administrative Officer
    Richard Brown .... (202) 512–5535
Customer Relations
    Greg McDonald .... (202) 512–7228
Human Capital Officer
    Jesse Hoskins .... (202) 512–5533
Knowledge Services Officer
    Catherine Teti .... (202) 512–9255
Professional Development Program
    Mark Gebicke .... (202) 512–4126
Congressional Relations
    Helen Hsing .... (202) 512–2639
External Liaison
    Gloria Jarmon .... (202) 512–4707
Field Offices
    Thomas Brew .... (202) 512–7200
Inspector General
    Francis Garcia .... (202) 512–5748
Opportunity & Inclusiveness
    Ron Stroman .... (202) 512–6388
Personnel Appeals Board
    Michael Wolf .... (202) 512–6137
Product & Process Improvement
    Keith Fultz .... (202) 512–3200
Public Affairs
    Jeff Nelligan .... (202) 512–4800

Quality & Risk Management

Mike Gryszkowiec..................... (202) 512–6100

The General Accounting Office (GAO) was established by the Budget and Accounting Act of 1921. The GAO is the investigative arm of Congress and is charged with examining all matters relating to the receipt and disbursement of public funds. The GAO is under the control and direction of the Comptroller General of the United States, who is nominated by the president and confirmed by the Senate for a fifteen-year term.

GAO's mission is to support the Congress in meeting its constitutional responsibilities and to help improve the performance and accountability of the federal government for the benefit of the American people. Nearly all its work is mandated in legislation requested by committee or subcommittee chairs, ranking minority members, or individual members of appropriations, authorizing, budget, or oversight committees.

Most of GAO's work is based on original data collected and analyzed. All of the office's work is conducted in accordance with applicable professional audit and investigation standards.

GAO supports congressional oversight in several ways. It evaluates federal policies and the performance of agencies and programs to determine how well they are working. It oversees government operations through financial and other management audits to determine whether public funds are being spent efficiently, effectively, and in accordance with applicable laws. It conducts investigations to assess whether illegal or improper activities are occurring. It analyzes financing for government activities. It provides legal opinions to determine whether agencies are in compliance with laws and regulations. It conducts analyses to assess needed actions and the implications of proposed actions.

GAO's role is both to meet short-term needs for information and to help the Congress better understand issues that are newly emerging, longer-term in nature, broad in scope, and cutting across government. The Congress looks to GAO to turn assertions and information into facts and knowledge.

Copies of unclassified GAO reports are available from:

U.S. General Accounting Office
P.O. Box 37050
Washington, DC 20013
(202) 512–6000

The first copy of each report and testimony is free; additional copies are $2.00 each. There is a 25 percent discount on orders of 100 or more copies mailed to a single address.

◼ NATIONAL ECONOMIC COUNCIL

1600 Pennsylvania Ave. N.W.
Washington, DC 20500
Internet: http://www.whitehouse.gov/nec/

Assistant to the President and Director, National Economic Council

Lawrence Lindsay .... (202) 456–2800
Fax.................................... (202) 456–0127

The National Economic Council (NEC) was created by an executive order on Jan. 25, 1993. NEC is within the Executive Office of the President and is composed of cabinet members and other high-ranking executive branch officials. The principal functions of the council include coordinating the economic policymaking process; coordinating economic policy advice to the president; ensuring economic policy decisions and programs are consistent with the president's stated goals; and monitoring the implementation of the president's economic policy agenda.

◼ NATIONAL SECURITY COUNCIL

1600 Pennsylvania Ave. N.W.
Washington, DC 20500
Internet: http://www.whitehouse.gov/nsc/

Assistant to the President for National Security Affairs

Condoleezza Rice..................... (202) 456–9491
Fax.................................... (202) 456–9490

Deputy Assistants to the President

Steve Hadley........................... (202) 456–9481
Gary Edson .... (202) 456–9471

Established by the National Security Act of 1947, the National Security Council (NSC) was placed within the Executive Office of the President by Reorganization Plan No. 4 of 1949. The NSC is composed of the president, who chairs the council, the vice president, and the secretaries of state and defense. The chair of the Joint Chiefs of Staff and director of Central Intelligence Agency serve as statutory advisers to the NSC, with other high-ranking executive branch officials, including the assistant to the president for national security affairs, attending council meetings and providing advice.

The NSC advises and assists the president in integrating all aspects of national security policy as it affects the United States—domestic, foreign, military, intelligence, and economic—in conjunction with the National Economic Council.

NATIONAL TELECOMMUNICATIONS AND INFORMATION ADMINISTRATION

Department of Commerce
14th St. and Constitution Ave.
Washington, DC 20230
Internet: http://www.ntia.doc.gov

Assistant Secretary
    John Sopko (acting) .... (202) 482–1840
    Fax .... (202) 482–1635
Institute for Telecommunication Sciences
(325 Broadway, Boulder, CO 80303-3328)
    Val M. O'Day (acting) .... (303) 497–3500
International Affairs
    Robin Layton .... (202) 482–1304
Policy Analysis and Development
    Kelly Levy .... (202) 482–1880
Spectrum Management
    William Hatch .... (202) 482–1850
Telecommunications and Information Applications
    William Cooperman .... (202) 482–5802

The National Telecommunications and Information Administration (NTIA), created in 1978, is an agency within the Department of Commerce that serves as the president's principal adviser on telecommunications and information policy. NTIA manages and coordinates the use of the federal radio frequency spectrum; advances the interests and international competitiveness of the United States through policy analysis, technical guidance, and international representation; provides grants to further the national information infrastructure; maintains the Institute for Telecommunication Sciences, which offers scientific, engineering, and technical expertise to NTIA; and works to bring the benefits of advanced telecommunications technologies to millions of Americans in rural and underserved urban areas.

OFFICE OF COMPLIANCE

110 2nd St. S.E., Room LA 200
Washington, DC 20540-1999
Internet: http://www.compliance.gov

Executive Director
    William W. Thompson II .... (202) 724–9250
    Fax .... (202) 426–1913

General Counsel
    Gary Green .... (202) 724–9250
    Fax .... (202) 426–1663

The Office of Compliance is an independent and neutral agency established in the legislative branch by the Congressional Accountability Act of 1995 to extend federal workplace laws to the employees of Congress and the agencies under its jurisdiction. The office enforces laws pertaining to worker safety, public access, civil rights, overtime pay, fair labor standards, family medical leave, polygraph protection, and plant closing notification.

OFFICE OF GOVERNMENTWIDE POLICY

General Services Administration
18th and F Sts. N.W.
Washington, DC 20405
Internet: http://www.policyworks.gov

Associate Administrator
    G. Martin Wagner .... (202) 501–8880
    Fax .... (202) 501–8898

The Office of Governmentwide Policy (OGP) was established within the General Services Administration (GSA) in December 1995 to consolidate several of the GSA's policymaking activities within one central office. The OGP promotes collaboration between government and the private sector in developing policy; better integration of acquisition, management, and disposal of government property; and the adaptation of private-sector management techniques to government agencies.

OFFICE OF INTERGOVERNMENTAL AFFAIRS

1600 Pennsylvania Ave. N.W., #106 EEOB
Washington, DC 20500

Director
    Ruben Barrales .... (202) 456–2896
    Fax .... (202) 456–7015

The Office of Intergovernmental Affairs serves as a liaison between the Executive Office of the President and state and local governments. The office answers questions and provides information to state and local governments on administration programs and policies.

OFFICE OF MANAGEMENT AND BUDGET

725 17th St. N.W.
Washington, DC 20503
Internet: http://www.whitehouse.gov/omb

Director
Mitchell E. Daniels Jr. .... (202) 395–4742
   Fax .... (202) 395–3888
Deputy Director
Sean O'Keefe........................... (202) 395–4742
Budget Review
Dick Emery .... (202) 395–4630
Economic Policy
Amy Smith .... (202) 395–6190
General Counsel
Jay Lefkowitz .... (202) 395–5044
Information Policy and Technology
Daniel Chenok .... (202) 395–3785
Information and Regulatory Affairs
John D. Graham........................ (202) 395–4852
Management
Vacant.................................. (202) 395–6190

The Office of Management and Budget (OMB) was created in 1970 and was formerly known as the Bureau of the Budget, which was established within the Executive Office of the President in 1939. The OMB's predominant mission is to assist the president in overseeing the preparation of the federal budget and to supervise its administration in executive branch agencies.

In helping to formulate the president's budget plan, the OMB evaluates the effectiveness of agency programs, policies, and procedures; assesses competing funding demands among agencies; and sets funding priorities. In addition, the OMB oversees and coordinates development of regulatory reform proposals, programs for paperwork reduction, and measures for improved agency performance.

The Office of Information and Regulatory Affairs (OIRA) within the OMB was created in 1981 and is primarily responsible for the management of federal information resources, including the collection of information from the public, and for carrying out presidential oversight responsibilities in federal rulemaking activities. It also works to expand interagency coordination and in particular works to reduce unnecessary paperwork and excessive reporting requirements of federal agencies.

The Paperwork Reduction Act of 1980 consolidated within jurisdiction of the OMB director and the OIRA the following information management functions: general information, paperwork clearance, statistical activities, records management, privacy, and automatic data processing and telecommunications related to the collection of information.

The Paperwork Reduction Act also transferred the functions of the former Regulatory Reports Review Group from the General Accounting Office to the OIRA. Those functions include reviewing information requests issued by federal departments and agencies (including independent federal regulatory agencies) to ensure that the proposed data collection is necessary, does not duplicate existing federal collections of information, and does not impose undue or excessive burdens on the public. Any information request sent to nine or more respondents by a federal department must be reviewed by this office. The OIRA also oversees federal information policy, information technology management, and statistical policy activities.

The purpose of joining these functions within one single office was to establish a government-wide policy framework for "information resources management."

President Ronald Reagan's Executive Orders 12291 and 12498, which gave the OMB broad oversight responsibilities over most federal regulatory agencies, were revoked by President Bill Clinton's Executive Order 12866, issued Sept. 30, 1993. Executive Order 12866 provided a comprehensive guide for the writing and issuance of regulations. It listed the responsibilities of the regulating agencies, the vice president, and other policy advisers in the regulatory process *(for text of order, see p. 784)*.

Like Reagan's Executive Order 12291, Clinton's executive order gave the OMB authority to identify duplication, overlap, and conflict in rules, which agencies then were required to rectify; to develop procedures for cost-benefit analysis; to recommend changes in laws authorizing regulatory activity; to monitor compliance with the executive order; and to schedule existing rules for agency review.

As part of its regulatory oversight responsibilities, OMB prepares reports on government agencies for the president. These reports often are available to the public and can be ordered through:

EOP Publications Services
Office of Management and Budget
New Executive Office Bldg., Room 2200
725 17th St. N.W.
Washington, DC 20503
(202) 395–7332
Fax-on-Demand: (202) 395–9068

OFFICE OF NATIONAL AIDS POLICY

736 Jackson Pl.
Washington, DC 20503
Internet:
http://www.whitehouse.gov/onap/aids.html

Director
    Scott Everetz............................ (202) 456–2437
Deputy Director
    Todd Summers .... (202) 456–2437

The Office of National AIDS Policy, headed by the so-called "AIDS Czar," was established within the Executive Office of the President in 1993. The office advises the president and formulates policy on matters related to HIV and AIDS. It coordinates the continuing domestic effort to reduce the number of new infections in the United States, in particular in segments of the population that are experiencing new or renewed increases in the rate of infection. The office also emphasizes the integration of domestic and international efforts to combat HIV/AIDS, and its Interdepartmental Task Force on HIV/AIDS helps to facilitate better communication among the various federal departments and agencies involved in HIV/AIDS policy.

OFFICE OF NATIONAL DRUG CONTROL POLICY

750 17th St. N.W.
Washington, DC 20500
Internet:
http://www.whitehousedrugpolicy.gov/

Director
    John Walters (designate).............. (202) 395–6700
    Fax..................................... (202) 395–6708
Counter-Drug Technology Assessment Center
    Albert Brandenstein.................... (202) 395–6781
Demand Reduction
    Daniel Schecter (acting) .... (202) 395–6751
Supply Reduction
    Robert E. Brown Jr. (acting)........... (202) 395–6741
State and Local Affairs
    Joseph Peters........................... (202) 395–6752

The Office of National Drug Control Policy (ONDCP) was established within the Executive Office of the President by the Anti-Drug Abuse Act of 1988. The office is headed by a director, often called the "Drug Czar," who is appointed by the president and confirmed by the Senate.

Responsibilities of this office include establishing policies and overseeing implementation of a national drug control strategy; recommending changes in the organization, management, budgeting, and personnel allocation of federal agencies involved in drug enforcement activities; and advising the president and National Security Council on drug control policy.

OFFICE OF SCIENCE AND TECHNOLOGY POLICY

1650 Pennsylvania Ave. N.W.
Washington, DC 20502
Internet: http://www.ostp.gov

Director
    Rosina Bierbaum (acting) .... (202) 456–7116
    Fax..................................... (202) 456–6021
National Science and Technology Council
    Gary Ellis .... (202) 456–6100
National Security and International Affairs
    Vacant.................................. (202) 456–2894
Science
    Vacant.................................. (202) 456–6130
Environment
    Vacant.................................. (202) 456–6202
Technology
    Vacant.................................. (202) 456–6046

The Office of Science and Technology Policy (OSTP) was established within the Executive Office of the President by the National Science and Technology Policy, Organization, and Priorities Act of 1976. This office provides expert advice to the president in all areas of science and technology. Through the National Science and Technology Council, the OSTP coordinates science, space, and technology policy and programs across the federal government. OSTP's duties include advising the president and other executive agencies in policy and budget development on questions related to science and technology; coordinates the government's research and development efforts to maximize the return on the public's investment; and advances international cooperation in science and technology.

OFFICE OF THE U.S. TRADE REPRESENTATIVE

600 17th St. N.W., Room 209
Washington, DC 20508
Internet: http://www.ustr.gov

U.S. Trade Representative
Robert B. Zoellick...................... (202) 395–3230
Fax...................................... (202) 395–3911
Deputy U.S. Trade Representatives
Peter Allgeir............................ (202) 395–3230
Limmet F. Deily .... (202) 395–3230
General Counsel
Peter Davison.......................... (202) 395-3150

The Office of the U.S. Trade Representative (USTR) was created by Congress in the Trade Expansion Act of 1962. Originally named the Office of the Special Trade Representative, the office was established as a cabinet-level agency within the Executive Office of the President by the Trade Act of 1974. The USTR sets and administers overall trade policy, serves as the nation's chief trade negotiator, and represents the United States in all major international trade organizations. The USTR has offices in Washington, D.C., and in Geneva, Switzerland. The office in Geneva is organized to cover general World Trade Organization (WTO) affairs, nontariff agreements, agricultural policy, commodity policy, and the harmonized code system. The Geneva deputy USTR is the U.S. ambassador to the WTO and to the United Nations Conference on Trade and Development.

■ REGULATORY INFORMATION SERVICE CENTER

18th F St. N.W., Suite 3033
Washington, DC 20405
http://www.reginfo.gov

Executive Director
Ronald C. Kelly......................... (202) 482–7340
Fax..................................... (202) 482–7360
Project Director
Anne Marie Schramm .... (202) 482–7340
Information........................... (202) 482–7340

Established in June 1981 as part of the General Services Administration, the center works closely with the Office of Management and Budget to provide the president, Congress, and the public with information on federal regulatory policies. Its major project has been to coordinate the development and publication of agency agendas in the "The Unified Agenda of Federal Regulatory and Deregulatory Actions" published twice yearly (in April and October) in the *Federal Register*. The purpose of the agenda is to list government-wide regulatory agendas in a consistent format and to include a comprehensive listing of proposed regulations, not simply those considered "ma-

jor." The agenda includes all executive branch regulatory agencies as well as most independent commissions.

Since December 1995 the center has officially been a division of the GSA's Office of Governmentwide Policy; however, its mission in support of the OMB remains unchanged.

Nongovernmental Organizations

The following are some important organizations that monitor issues of federal regulation, including reform initiatives and proposals to regulate emerging technologies.

ALEXIS DE TOCQUEVILLE INSTITUTION
1611 N. Kent St., #901
Arlington, VA 22209
(703) 351–4969
Fax (703) 351–0090
Internet: http://www.adti.net

ALLIANCE FOR REDESIGNING GOVERNMENT
1120 G St. N.W., #850
Washington, DC 20005-3801
(202) 347–3190
Fax (202) 393–0993
Internet: http://www.napawash.org

THE BROOKINGS INSTITUTION
Center for Public Policy Education
1775 Massachusetts Ave. N.W.
Washington, DC 20036
(202) 797–6000
Fax (202) 797–6004
Internet: http://www.brookings.edu

CATO INSTITUTE
1000 Massachusetts Ave. N.W.
Washington, DC 20001
(202) 842–0200
Fax (202) 842–3490
Internet: http://www.cato.org

COUNCIL FOR CITIZENS AGAINST GOVERNMENT WASTE
1301 Connecticut Ave. N.W., #400
Washington, DC 20036
(202) 467–5300
Toll-free (800) 232–6479
Fax (202) 467–4253
Internet: http://www.govt-waste.org

COUNCIL FOR EXCELLENCE IN GOVERNMENT

1301 K St. N.W., #450W
Washington, DC 20005
(202) 728–0418
Fax (202) 728–0422
Internet: http://www.excelgov.org

FUND FOR CONSTITUTIONAL GOVERNMENT

122 Maryland Ave. N.E.
Washington, DC 20002
(202) 546–3799
Fax (202) 543–3156
Internet: http://epic.org/fcg

GOVERNMENT ACCOUNTABILITY PROJECT

1612 K. St. N.W., #400
Washington, DC 20006
(202) 408–0034
Fax (202) 408–9855
Internet: http://www.whistleblower.org

HERITAGE FOUNDATION

214 Massachusetts Ave. N.E.
Washington, DC 20002
(202) 546–4400
Fax (202) 546–8328
Internet: http://www.heritage.org

INDEPENDENT INSTITUTE

100 Swan Way
Oakland, CA 94621–1428
(510) 632–1366
Toll-free (800) 927–8733
Fax (510) 568–6040
Internet: http://www.independent.org

OMB WATCH

1742 Connecticut Ave. N.W.
Washington, DC 20009
(202) 234–8494
Fax (202) 234–8584
Internet: http://www.ombwatch.org

PRIVATE SECTOR COUNCIL

1101 16th St. N.W., #300
Washington, DC 20036
(202) 822–3910
Fax (202) 822–0638
Internet: http://www.privsect.org

PROJECT ON GOVERNMENT OVERSIGHT

666 11th St. N.W., #500
Washington, DC 20001
(202) 347-1122
Fax (202) 347-1116
Internet: http://www.pogo.org

PUBLIC CITIZEN

1600 20th St. N.W.
Washington, DC 20009
(202) 588–1000
Fax (202) 588–7798
Internet: http://www.citizen.org

REASON FOUNDATION

3415 S. Sepulveda Blvd., #400
Los Angeles, CA 90034
(310) 391–2245
Fax (310) 391–4395
Internet: http://www.reason.org

Appendix

Federal World Wide Web Sites

■ MAJOR REGULATORY AGENCIES

Consumer Product Safety Commission,
http://www.cpsc.gov
Environmental Protection Agency,
http://www.epa.gov
Equal Employment Opportunity Commission,
http://www.eeoc.gov
Federal Communications Commission,
http://www.fcc.gov
Federal Deposit Insurance Corporation,
http://www.fdic.gov
Federal Energy Regulatory Commission,
http://www.ferc.gov
Federal Reserve System,
http://www.federalreserve.gov
Federal Trade Commission, http://www.ftc.gov
Food and Drug Administration, http://www.fda.gov
National Labor Relations Board,
http://www.nlrb.gov
Occupational Safety and Health Administration, http://www.osha.gov
Securities and Exchange Commission,
http://www.sec.gov

■ OTHER REGULATORY AGENCIES

**Architectural and Transportation Barriers
Compliance Board,** http://www.access-board.gov
Commodity Futures Trading Commission,
http://www.cftc.gov
Farm Credit Administration, http://www.fca.gov

Federal Election Commission, http://www.fec.gov
Federal Housing Finance Board,
http://www.fhfb.gov
Federal Maritime Commission, http://www.fmc.gov
National Credit Union Administration,
http://www.ncua.gov
National Mediation Board, http://www.nmb.gov
National Transportation Safety Board,
http://www.ntsb.gov
Nuclear Regulatory Commission,
http://www.nrc.gov
Pension Benefit Guaranty Corporation,
http://www.pbgc.gov
Postal Rate Commission, http://www.prc.gov
Small Business Administration, http://www.sba.gov
Social Security Administration, http://www.ssa.gov
United States International Trade Commission,
http://www.usitc.gov
United States Postal Service, http://www.usps.gov

■ DEPARTMENTAL AGENCIES

Agriculture Department
http://www.usda.gov

Agricultural Marketing Service,
http://www.ams.usda.gov
Animal and Plant Health Inspection Service,
http://www.aphis.usda.gov
Farm Service Agency, http://www.fsa.usda.gov
Food and Nutrition Service,
http://www.fns.usda.gov

Food Safety and Inspection Service,
http://www.fsis.usda.gov
Foreign Agricultural Service,
http://www.fas.usda.gov
Forest Service, http://www.fs.fed.us
**Grain Inspection, Packers, and Stockyards
Administration,** http://www.usda.gov/gipsa
Natural Resources Conservation Service,
http://www.nrcs.usda.gov
Rural Development, http://www.rurdev.usda.gov

Commerce Department

http://www.commerce.gov

Bureau of Industry and Security
http://www.bxa.doc.gov
Economic Development Administration,
http://www.osec.doc.gov/eda
International Trade Administration,
http://www.ita.doc.gov
**National Institute of Standards and Techno-
logy,** http://www.nist.gov
**National Oceanic and Atmospheric Administra-
tion,** http://www.noaa.gov
Patent and Trademark Office,
http://www.uspto.gov

Defense Department

http://www.defenselink.mil/

Army Corps of Engineers, http//www.usace.army.mil

Energy Department

http://www.energy.gov

Energy Efficiency and Renewable Energy,
http://www.eere.energy.gov
Environmental Management,
http://www.em.doe.gov
Environment, Safety, and Health,
http://www.eh.doe.gov
Federal Energy Regulatory Commission,
http://www.ferc.gov
Fossil Energy, http://www.fe.doe.gov

Health and Human Services Department

http://www.os.dhhs.gov

Administration for Children and Families,
http://www.acf.dhhs.gov
Administration on Aging, http://www.aoa.gov
Food and Drug Administration, http://www.fda.gov
Centers for Medicare and Medicaid Services,
http://cms.hhs.gov

Office for Civil Rights, http://www.hhs.gov/ocr
Office of the Inspector General,
http://www.oig.hhs.gov
Public Health and Science,
http://www.osophs.dhhs.gov/ophs

Housing and Urban Development Department

http://www.hud.gov

Community Planning and Development,
http://www.hud.gov/offices/cpd
Government National Mortgage Association,
http://www.ginniemae.gov
Office of Fair Housing and Equal Opportunity,
http://www.hud.gov/offices/fheo
Office of Housing, http://www.hud.gov/offices/hsg
**Office of Healthy Homes and Lead Hazard Con-
trol,** http://www.hud.gov/offices/lead
Office of Public and Indian Housing,
http://www.hud.gov/offices/pih

Interior Department

http://www.doi.gov

Bureau of Indian Affairs,
http://www.doi.gov/bureau-indian-affairs.html
Bureau of Land Management,
http://www.blm.gov
Bureau of Reclamation, http://www.usbr.gov
Minerals Management Service,
http://www.mms.gov
National Park Service, http://www.nps.gov
Office of Surface Mining, http://www.osmre.gov
United States Fish and Wildlife Service,
http://www.fws.gov
United States Geological Survey,
http://www.usgs.gov

Justice Department

http://www.usdoj.gov

Antitrust Division,
http://www.usdoj.gov/atr/index.html
Civil Rights Division, http://www.usdoj.gov/crt/
Criminal Division, http://www.usdoj.gov/criminal/
Drug Enforcement Administration,
http://www.usdoj.gov/dea
Federal Bureau of Prisons, http://www.bop.gov
Immigration and Naturalization Service,
http://www.immigration.gov
Office of Justice Programs,
http://www.ojp.usdoj.gov

United States Parole Commission,
http://www.usdoj.gov/uspc

Labor Department
http://www.dol.gov

Employment and Training Administration,
http://www.doleta.gov
Employment Standards Administration,
http://www.dol.gov/esa
Mine Safety and Health Administration,
http://www.msha.gov
Occupational Safety and Health Administration, http://www.osha.gov
Employee Benefits Security Administration,
http://www.dol.gov/ebsa
Veterans' Employment and Training Service,
http://www.dol.gov/vets

State Department
http://www.state.gov

Bureau of Consular Affairs, http://travel.state.gov

Transportation Department
http://www.dot.gov

Aviation and International Affairs,
http://ostpxweb.dot.gov/aviation
Federal Aviation Administration,
http://www1.faa.gov
Federal Highway Administration,
http://www.fhwa.dot.gov
Federal Railroad Administration,
http://www.fra.dot.gov
Federal Transit Administration,
http://www.fta.dot.gov
Maritime Administration,
http://www.marad.dot.gov
National Highway Traffic Safety Administration, http://www.nhtsa.dot.gov
Research and Special Programs Administration, http://www.rspa.dot.gov
St. Lawrence Seaway Development Corporation, http://www.seaway.dot.gov
Surface Transportation Board,
http://www.stb.dot.gov
United States Coast Guard, http://www.uscg.mil

Treasury Department
http://www.ustreas.gov

Bureau of Alcohol, Tobacco, and Firearms,
http://www.atf.treas.gov

Comptroller of the Currency,
http://www.occ.treas.gov
Internal Revenue Service, http://www.irs.gov
Office of Thrift Supervision,
http://www.ots.treas.gov
United States Customs Service,
http://www.customs.gov

Veterans Affairs Department
http://www.va.gov

■ REGULATORY OVERSIGHT AND COORDINATION

Congressional Budget Office,
http://www.cbo.gov
Corporation for National and Community Service, http://www.cns.gov
Council of Economic Advisors,
http://www.whitehouse.gov/cea/index.html
Council on Environmental Quality,
http://www.whitehouse.gov/CEQ/
Domestic Policy Council,
http://www.whitehouse.gov/dpc/
Federal Emergency Management Agency,
http://www.fema.gov
Federal Technology Service, http://www.fts.gsa.gov
General Accounting Office, http://www.gao.gov
General Services Administration,
http://www.gsa.gov
National Economic Council,
http://www.whitehouse.gov/nec/
National Security Council,
http://www.whitehouse.gov/nsc/
National Telecommunications and Information Administration, http://www.ntia.doc.gov
Office of Compliance, http://www.compliance.gov
Office of Governmentwide Policy,
http://www. policyworks.gov
Office of Management and Budget,
http://www.whitehouse.gov/omb/
Office of National AIDS Policy,
http://www.whitehouse.gov/onap/aids.html
Office of National Drug Control Policy,
http://www.whitehousedrugpolicy.gov
Office of Science and Technology Policy,
http://www.ostp.gov
Office of the U.S. Trade Representative,
http://www.ustr.gov
Regulatory Information Service Center,
http://policyworks.gov/mi/

■ GOVERNMENT PUBLICATIONS OFFICES

Federal Citizen Information Center,
http://www.pueblo.gsa.gov

National Technical Information Service,
http://www.ntis.gov

U.S. Government Printing Office,
http://www.gpo.gov

Ordering Government Publications

In addition to the publications contacts listed in each agency profile, the federal government maintains the following general offices for the distribution of publications.

FEDERAL CITIZEN INFORMATION CENTER (FCIC)

(Pueblo office)
Pueblo, CO 81009
E-mail: catalog.pueblo@gsa.gov
Internet: http://www.pueblo.gsa.gov

(Washington office)
1800 F St. N.W., Room G–142, (XCC)
Washington, DC 20405

Orders:
(202) 501–1794
Fax (202) 501–4281

Part of the General Services Administration. Distributes free publications, including the *Consumer Information Catalog* and consumer booklets from many federal agencies. Also distributes new releases on consumer issues to the media, consumer organizations, and state and local consumer agencies. Orders for publications and catalogs are filled by the Pueblo office; call (888) 878–3256. Orders also can be placed online via the CIC's Web site. The Washington office provides services to the press and other federal agencies.

NATIONAL TECHNICAL INFORMATION SERVICE (NTIS)

Technology Administration
U.S. Department of Commerce
5285 Port Royal Rd.
Springfield, VA 22161
(703) 605–6000
E-mail: orders@ntis.fedworld.gov
Internet: http://www.ntis.gov

Orders:
(800) 553–6847
Fax (703) 605-6900

Part of the Commerce Department's Technology Administration. Distributes or sells publications, subscriptions, and other information from most federal departments, many independent agencies, and a number of foreign governments. Formats include print, CD-ROM, computer tapes and diskettes, online services, and audio- and videocassettes. Distributes numerous print catalogs and the *NTIS OrderNow Catalog on CD-ROM*.

In addition to the main order lines above, key telephone contacts include:

Rush service .... (800) 553–NTIS
TTY .... (703) 487–4639
Subscription section .... (800) 363–2068
Military orders .... (800) 553–NTIS
Tracing an order .... (888) 584–8332

FEDWORLD

Internet: http://www.fedworld.gov

A division of the NTIS and a central access point for federal online information. Provides access to more than 100 federal bulletin board systems (BBS), many of which are not accessible directly via the Internet. Fedworld can be accessed via Telnet, anonymous FTP server, and the World Wide Web.

NATIONAL AUDIOVISUAL CENTER (NAC)

Internet: http://www.ntis.gov/products/types/audiovisual

A division of the NTIS that distributes over 9,000 federal media-based products, including videotapes, audiocassettes, and CD-ROMs. Training materials cover occupational safety and health, foreign languages, law enforcement, and fire services. Educational materials cover topics in history, health, agriculture, and natural resources.

▓ U.S. GOVERNMENT PRINTING OFFICE (GPO)

**732 N. Capitol St. N.W.
Washington, DC 20401**

**Orders:
(202) 512–1800
Fax (202) 512–2250
Internet: http://www.gpo.gov**

Produces publications for Congress and the federal departments and agencies. The Superintendent of Documents distributes or sells products, including catalogs, books, and subscriptions; booklets and other frequently requested publications are generally available from the agencies themselves. An increasing number of GPO products are available in electronic formats. The agency's Web Site provides indexes of GPO products and access to a variety of government databases. The GPO also maintains a network of government bookstores, which stock selected government publications, and a network of Regional Depository Libraries, which receive a copy of all federal government documents that must be made available for public inspection.

In addition to the main order lines above, some key GPO contacts include:

MAIL ORDERS:

Superintendent of Documents
P.O. Box 371954
Pittsburgh, PA 15250–7954

GPO BOOKSTORES

Atlanta
999 Peachtree St. N.E., #120
Atlanta, GA 30309–3964
(404) 347–1900

Denver
1660 Wynkoop St., #130
Denver, CO 80202
(303) 844–3964

Detroit
477 Michigan Ave., #160
Detroit, MI 48226
(313) 226–7816

Houston
801 Travis St., #120
Houston, TX 77002
(713) 228–1187

Jacksonville
100 W. Bay St., #100
Jacksonville, FL 32202
(904) 353–0569

Laurel
8660 Cherry Lane
Laurel, MD 20707
(301) 953–7974

Los Angeles
505 S. Flower St.
Los Angeles, CA 90071–2181
(213) 239–9844

Milwaukee
310 W. Wisconsin Ave., #150W
Milwaukee, WI 53203–2228
(414) 297–1304

Pittsburgh
1000 Liberty Ave., #118
Pittsburgh, PA 15222
(412) 395–5021

Pueblo
201 W. 8th St.
Pueblo, CO 81003
(719) 544–3142

Washington, DC
710 N. Capitol St. N.W.
Washington, DC 20401–0001
(202) 512–0132

How to Use the *Federal Register* and the CFR

The basic tool for finding out about agency rulings, proposed rules, meetings, and adjudicatory proceedings is the *Federal Register,* which is published daily. The *Federal Register* system of publication was established by the Federal Register Act of 1935 (44 U.S.C. Ch. 15) and was further enlarged and amended by the Administrative Procedure Act of 1946 (5 U.S.C. 551).

Contained in the *Federal Register* are federal agency regulations and other legal documents of the executive branch, including presidential documents (among them the texts of proclamations and executive orders).

The system of codifying federal regulations parallels that of legislation. Laws enacted by Congress are compiled annually in the *U.S. Statutes at Large* and are then codified in the U.S. Code by subject titles. Rules and regulations to implement the legislation are published daily in the *Federal Register* and are then codified by subject title in the *Code of Federal Regulations* (CFR), which is updated annually. Working with the *Federal Register* and the CFR, a person may find an up-to-date account of all regulations pertaining to a particular agency or subject.

Organization of the CFR

The CFR, a compilation of the current general and permanent regulations of federal agencies, is divided into fifty titles, according to broad subject areas affected by regulatory action. For example, Title 1 concerns "General Provisions"; Title 3, "The President"; Title 12, "Banks and Banking"; Title 15, "Commerce and Foreign Trade"; Title 21, "Food and Drugs"; and so forth. (The subject of a title may change as regulations are rescinded and different regulations are issued. Not all titles are in use at one time.)

Within each title (consisting of one or more volumes), subjects are further broken down into chapters (numbered in roman capitals as I, II, III, etc.). Chapters are further subdivided into parts, numbered in arabic (1, 2, 3, etc.). Parts are normally assigned to chapters as follows: Chapter I, Parts 1 to 199; Chapter II, Parts 200 to 299; and so forth. Each part contains a number of sections, set off by a decimal point preceded by the symbol §. The notation "§ 32.5" would refer to section 5 of part 32. The "section" is the basic unit of the CFR and ideally consists of a short, simple presentation of one proposition.

As an example: Title 36 of the CFR, composed of one volume, concerns all regulations pertaining to "Parks, Forests, and Public Property." The table of contents of the volume divides the title into eleven chapters. Chapter I contains regulations affecting the "National Park Service, Department of the Interior." There is a table of contents for each chapter, giving the subject matter of each part and the page number on which it may be found. Chapter I of Title 36 contains thirty-seven parts. Part 4 of Chapter I concerns "Vehicles and traffic safety." Within Part 4, there are twenty-one sections. Section 4.3, for example, concerns "Bicycles."

Each CFR volume contains front matter on how to use the code, effective dates and who to contact for further information. The "CFR Index and Finding Aids" is revised annually and is contained in a separate volume. The index section contains a list of CFR titles, chapters, and parts; an alphabetical listing of agencies appearing in the CFR; and lists of current and superseded CFR volumes. The finding aids section consists of additional information and guides to material in the CFR. Included is a parallel table of statutory authorities and rules that lists all sections of the U.S. Code and the *United States Statutes at Large* cited as the rulemaking authority for CFR regulations.

The CFR also publishes monthly a cumulative list of changes in regulations since they were published in the latest annual code. The listing contains the title, chapter, part, and section of the amended regulation and the page number in the *Federal Register* where the change was published. There is no single annual issue of the cumulative list; rather, four of the monthly issues include cumulative lists for certain titles. The December issue contains changes for Titles 1–16; the March issue is the annual revision for Titles 17–27; the June issue contains changes in Titles 28–41; and the September issue notes changes in Titles 42–50.

The entire CFR is revised annually according to the following schedule: Titles 1–16, as of January 1; Titles 17–27, as of April 1; Titles 28–41, as of July 1; Titles 42–50, as of October 1.

The *Federal Register*

Published daily, the *Federal Register* serves to update the *Code of Federal Regulations.* In order to determine the most recent version of a rule, the latest edition of the CFR, the CFR cumulative list of revisions, and the *Federal Register* must be used together.

Each issue of the *Federal Register* includes preliminary pages of finding aids. Documents are arranged under one of five headings: "Presidential Documents," "Rules and Regulations," "Proposed Rules," "Notices," and "Sunshine Act Meetings."

Final Rules. This section on final rules usually contains for each entry the following information: the part (title, chapter, etc.) of the CFR affected; a brief descriptive heading for the change; the agency proposing the action; the type of action involved (for example, a final rule, a termination of rulemaking or proceeding, or a request for further public comment); a brief summary of the nature of the action; the effective date; and the person to contact for further information. This is followed by more or less detailed supplementary information, including the text of the change in the regulation.

Agencies are required to publish rules in the *Federal Register* thirty days before they are to take effect. Exceptions to this requirement, found in section 553 of the Administrative Procedure Act, include: "(1) a substantive rule which grants or recognizes an exemption or relieves a restriction; (2) interpretative rules and statements of policy; or (3) as otherwise provided by the agency for good cause found and published with the rule."

In publishing the supplementary information on the final rule, agencies must summarize comments received about the rule, what action was taken on them, and why. On occasion, agencies may allow further comment on a final rule and will give notice of such in the *Federal Register.*

Proposed Rules. The format for publishing a proposed rule is similar to that for final rules. The entry is headed by the name of the agency initiating the action; the CFR sections affected; a brief descriptive title of the action; the nature of the action (proposed rulemaking, extension of public comment period, etc.); a summary of the proposed rule; the deadlines for receiving public comments and/or dates of public hearings; the person to contact for further information; and a more detailed supplementary section. Also included is the agency's "docket" number under which its files on the proposed action may be identified and examined.

Occasionally, agencies will publish an "advance notice of proposed rulemaking" in cases where a rule is being considered but where the agency has not developed a concrete proposal.

Requests may be made for an extension of the deadline for public comment, but agencies are not required to grant them.

Notices. Contained in this section of the *Federal Register* are documents other than rules or proposed rules that are applicable to the public. Notices of hearings and investigations, committee meetings, agency decisions and rulings, delegations of authority, filing of petitions and applications, issuance or revocation of licenses, and grant application deadlines are examples. Announcements of advisory committee meetings are also required to be published in the "Notice" section. An example of an application notice is a request by an airline company to establish a new route or service. Notice of filings of environmental impact statements are also included in this section.

Sunshine Act Meetings. Notice of open agency meetings are printed in the *Federal Register* in accordance with the provisions of the Government in the Sunshine Act *(see p. 755).* Each entry contains the name of the agency; time, date, and place of the meeting; a brief description of the subject; status (open or closed); the person to contact; and supplementary information. Agencies that have closed a meeting are required to list those that are closed, citing the relevant exemption under the Sunshine Act.

Finding Aids. There are several kinds of finding aids that are published each day in the *Federal Register.* These include:

- Selected Subjects: a list of the subjects affected by rules and proposed rules included in each issue.
- Contents: a comprehensive list of documents in the issue and their page numbers arranged by agency and type of document (rule, proposal, or notice).
- List of CFR parts affected: a numerical guide listing each title of the CFR affected by documents published in the day's issue, giving the citation to the CFR and the page number in that day's *Federal Register* where the action may be found.
- Cumulative list of CFR parts affected—Monthly: rules and proposals that have appeared so far in that

month's *Federal Register,* arranged in similar fashion to the above.

- *Federal Register* Pages and Dates: a parallel table of the inclusive pages and corresponding dates for the *Federal Registers* of the month.

In addition to information provided in each daily *Federal Register,* there are other monthly, quarterly, and annual publications. The first *Federal Register* of each month contains a table of effective dates and time periods for the month. The first issue of each week includes the CFR checklist, which shows the revision date and price of CFR volumes issued to date. The *Federal Register* also publishes a monthly index of all the documents appearing in a given month arranged alphabetically by agency name and thereunder by rules, proposed rules, and notices; broad subject headings are inserted alphabetically among agency headings. The index also includes a list of Freedom of Information Act indexes and a table showing the relationship between *Federal Register* dates and pages. The index is cumulated quarterly and annually.

The *List of CFR Sections Affected* (LSA) directs users to changes to the CFR that were published in the *Federal Register.* Entries for rules are arranged numerically by CFR title, chapter, part, section, and paragraph. A descriptive word or phrase indicates the nature of the amendatory action such as additions, revisions, or removals. The number at the end of each entry gives the page in the *Federal Register* where the amendatory action appears. Proposed rules are listed at the end of the appropriate titles. The proposed rule entries are to the part number. They do not contain a descriptive word or phrase.

The LSA is published monthly in cumulative form and keyed to the annual revision schedule of the CFR volumes. The issues of December, March, June, and September are annual cumulations for certain CFR titles. If a particular LSA is an annual cumulation, a notation appears on the cover.

Each LSA also contains a detailed introductory explanation on how to use the publication. In addition, the LSA contains a parallel table of authorities and rules, which shows additions and removals of authorities, and a table of *Federal Register* issue pages and dates.

The Office of the Federal Register has published a booklet on "The *Federal Register*: What It Is and How to Use It," which may be obtained from the Government Printing Office, and also offers seminars on how to use the *Federal Register.* These are announced in the *Federal Register.*

GPO Access

GPO Access is an online information-dissemination service that provides access to the *Federal Register* (http://www.gpoaccess.gov/fr/index.html) and to the CFR (http://www.gpoaccess.gov/cfr/index.html) using multiple browse and search features. The electronic version of the *Federal Register* is updated daily and includes volumes from fifty-nine (1994) to the present. CFR volumes are added to the online service concurrent with the release of the print editions. Issues are available from 1996 (partial) to the current year. Both publications' documents are available in PDF and ASCII text files. Also available is the *Electronic Code of Federal Regulations* (e-CFR) (http://www.gpo.gov/ecfr/), a daily updated prototype of the CFR that incorporates information from the CFR, *Federal Register,* and *List of CFR Sections Affected.* The e-CFR prototype is a demonstration project and is not an official legal edition of the CFR. e-CFR material is available in HTML and SGML.

Administrative Procedure Act

The Administrative Procedure Act (APA) had its genesis in the proliferation of regulatory agencies during the New Deal. Passed in 1946, the act was the product of a nine-year study of administrative justice by congressional committees, the Justice Department, and lawyers' organizations. On enactment, Pat McCarran, D-Nev., chair of the Senate Judiciary Committee described it as a "bill of rights for the hundreds of thousands of Americans whose affairs are controlled or regulated in one way or another by agencies of the federal government" and said it was designed "to provide guaranties of due process in administrative procedure."

Major provisions of the act:

- Required agencies to publish in the *Federal Register* a description of their organization and rulemaking procedures and to hold hearings or provide other means of public comment on proposed rules.
- Prescribed standards and procedures for agency adjudications, including licensing and injunctive orders. (Among the requirements: adequate notice to parties concerned; separation of prosecution and decision functions through a ban on investigatory or prosecuting officials deciding cases; discretionary authority for agencies to issue declaratory orders.)
- Spelled-out hearing procedures, including a requirement that the proponent of a rule or order should have the burden of proof and that no decision could be made except as supported by "relevant, reliable and probative evidence."
- Provided that any person suffering legal wrong because of any agency action would be entitled to judicial review, except where statutes precluded judicial review or where agency action was by law committed to agency discretion, but required the aggrieved party to exhaust administrative remedies first. The court was to set aside agency actions "unsupported by substantial evidence," and was to review the whole record and take "due account" of the rule of prejudicial error.
- Directed each agency to appoint competent examiners to act as hearing officers and to make, or recommend, decisions.

The act established minimum requirements that all agencies would have to meet. Based on these requirements, agencies have developed their own procedures, which are spelled out in statutes contained in the *Code of Federal Regulations*. Amendments to the APA include the Sunshine Act, the Freedom of Information Act, and the Privacy Act.

The APA divides administrative proceedings into two categories: rulemaking and adjudication. A "rule" is defined by Section 551 as "the whole or a part of an agency statement of general or particular applicability and future effect designed to implement, interpret, or prescribe law or policy or describing the organization, procedure, or practice requirements of an agency...." "Adjudication" is the process of formulating an order, which is defined as a "final disposition ... of an agency in any matter other than rulemaking but including licensing."

Rulemaking

Section 553 sets forward the basic requirements for rulemaking. General notice of a proposed rulemaking is to be published in the *Federal Register,* unless persons subject to the rule "are named and either personally served or otherwise have actual notice thereof in accordance with law. The notice shall include (1) a statement of the time, place, and nature of public rulemaking proceedings; (2) reference to the authority under which the rule is proposed; and (3) either the terms or substance of the proposed rule or description of the subjects and issues involved ...." The APA provides an opportunity for public participation through written or oral comment (the act does not require agencies to hold hearings).

There are two kinds of rulemaking, formal and informal. If a particular statute calls for "on the record" or formal rulemaking, the agency must go through a trial-type procedure. Decisions must be based on the record of transcripts of oral testimony or written submissions. Unlike adjudicatory proceedings, however, the initial and recommended decision of the hearing examiner may be omitted. Under the informal rulemaking process, the decision need not be based on the record and, unless the agency decides otherwise, only the minimum requirements of the APA must be met.

Under Section 553 of the Administrative Procedure Act, a "substantive rule which grants or recognizes an exemption or relieves a restriction" must be published at least thirty days before it becomes effective. However, there are many exceptions to this, among them interpretative rules or general statements of policy. Such notice is not required if it would defeat the purpose of the rule or if immediate action is required to protect property.

Formal Hearings

Where the APA requires a formal hearing—as in a formal rulemaking or adjudicatory proceeding—usually an administrative law judge (hearing examiner) presides and receives evidence. (However, the act also provides that the agency or one or more members of the body that constitutes the agency may do so.) The act requires that each agency "shall appoint as many hearing examiners as are necessary for proceedings required to be conducted" under adjudicatory or formal rulemaking procedures. Hearing examiners, or presiding officers, have the power to administer oaths and affirmations; issue subpoenas authorized by law; rule on offers of proof and receive relevant evidence; regulate the hearings; hold conferences to settle or simplify issues; handle procedural requests; make or recommend decisions; and take other action authorized by agency rules.

Following the hearing, the examiner makes an initial or recommended decision, but it is up to the agency to make the final determination.

Adjudication

In contrast to the more generalized character of rulemaking, adjudication usually involves a more limited number of parties (between the agency and a private party, or between two or more private parties) and is more judicial in nature. Section 554 of the APA requires that the agency notify the affected parties of the hearing's time and place, the statute involved, and the factual dispute that will be decided. The parties involved may submit oral or written evidence, present a defense and rebuttal, and cross-examine witnesses. The hearing examiner is prohibited from consulting any party on an issue of fact unless all parties have a chance to participate.

Judicial Review

Section 702 of the APA provides that: "A person suffering legal wrong because of agency action, or adversely affected or aggrieved by agency action within the meaning of a relevant statute is entitled to judicial review thereof." The reviewing court may "compel agency action unlawfully withheld or unreasonably delayed," and rule unlawful any agency action found to be "arbitrary, capricious, an abuse of discretion, or otherwise not in accordance with law"; unconstitutional; "in excess of statutory jurisdiction, authority or limitations, or short of statutory right"; taken "without observance of procedure required by law"; and unsupported by substantial evidence.

The provisions of the Administrative Procedure Act are contained in the U.S. Code, Title 5, Chapter 5, Subchapter II, and Title 5, Chapter 7.

The following text includes Subchapter II, section 551 and sections 553–559 as well as Chapter 7.

Sections 552, known as the Freedom of Information Act, may be found on p. 747; section 552a, known as the Privacy Act, may be found on p. 769; and section 552b, known as the Government in the Sunshine Act, may be found on p. 755.

SUBCHAPTER II ADMINISTRATIVE PROCEDURE

§ 551. Definitions

For the purpose of this subchapter—

(1) "agency" means each authority of the Government of the United States, whether or not it is within or subject to review by another agency, but does not include—

(A) the Congress;

(B) the courts of the United States;

(C) the governments of the territories or possessions of the United States;

(D) the government of the District of Columbia; or except as to the requirements of section 552 of this title—

(E) agencies composed of representatives of the parties or of representatives of organizations of the parties to the disputes determined by them;

(F) courts martial and military commissions;

(G) military authority exercised in the field in time of war or in occupied territory; or

(H) functions conferred by sections 1738, 1739, 1743, and 1744 of title 12; chapter 2 of title 41; or sections

1622, 1884, 1891–1902, and former section 1641(b)(2), of title 50, appendix;

(2) "person" includes an individual, partnership, corporation, association, or public or private organization other than an agency;

(3) "party" includes a person or agency named or admitted as a party, or properly seeking and entitled as of right to be admitted as a party, in an agency proceeding, and a person or agency admitted by an agency as a party for limited purposes;

(4) "rule" means the whole or a part of an agency statement of general or particular applicability and future effect designed to implement, interpret, or prescribe law or policy or describing the organization, procedure, or practice requirements of an agency and includes the approval or prescription for the future of rates, wages, corporate or financial structures or reorganizations thereof, prices, facilities, appliances, services or allowances therefor or of valuations, costs, or accounting, or practices bearing on any of the foregoing;

(5) "rule making" means agency process for formulating, amending, or repealing a rule;

(6) "order" means the whole or a part of a final disposition, whether affirmative, negative, injunctive, or declaratory in form, of an agency in a matter other than rule making but including licensing;

(7) "adjudication" means agency process for the formulation of an order.

(8) "license" includes the whole or a part of an agency permit, certificate, approval, registration, charter, membership, statutory exemption or other form of permission;

(9) "licensing" includes agency process respecting the grant, renewal, denial, revocation, suspension, annulment, withdrawal, limitation, amendment, modification, or conditioning of a license;

(10) "sanction" includes the whole or a part of an agency—

(A) prohibition, requirement, limitation, or other condition affecting the freedom of a person;

(B) withholding of relief;

(C) imposition of penalty or fine;

(D) destruction, taking, seizure, or withholding of property;

(E) assessment of damages, reimbursement, restitution, compensation, costs, charges, or fees;

(F) requirement, revocation, or suspension of a license; or

(G) taking other compulsory or restrictive action;

(11) "relief" includes the whole or a part of an agency—

(A) grant of money, assistance, license, authority, exemption, exception, privilege, or remedy;

(B) recognition of a claim, right, immunity, privilege, exemption, or exception; or

(C) taking of other action on the application or petition of, and beneficial to, a person;

(12) "agency proceeding" means an agency process as defined by paragraphs (5), (7), and (9) of this section;

(13) "agency action" includes the whole or a part of an agency rule, order, license, sanction, relief, or the equivalent or denial thereof, or failure to act; and

(14) "ex parte communication" means an oral or written communication not on the public record with respect to which reasonable prior notice to all parties is not given, but it shall not include requests for status reports on any matter or proceeding covered by this subchapter.

§ 553. Rule making

(a) This section applies, according to the provisions thereof, except to the extent that there is involved—

(1) a military or foreign affairs function of the United States; or

(2) a matter relating to agency management or personnel or to public property, loans, grants, benefits, or contracts.

(b) General notice of proposed rule making shall be published in the *Federal Register,* unless persons subject thereto are named and either personally served or otherwise have actual notice thereof in accordance with law. The notice shall include—

(1) a statement of the time, place, and nature of public rule making proceedings;

(2) reference to the legal authority under which the rule is proposed; and

(3) either the terms or substance of the proposed rule or a description of the subjects and issues involved. Except when notice or hearing is required by statute, this subsection does not apply—

(A) to interpretative rules, general statements of policy, or rules of agency organization, procedure, or practice; or

(B) when the agency for good cause finds (and incorporates the finding and a brief statement of reasons therefor in the rules issued) that notice and public procedure thereon are impracticable, unnecessary, or contrary to the public interest.

(c) After notice required by this section, the agency shall give interested persons an opportunity to participate in the rule making through submission of written data, views, or arguments with or without opportunity for oral presentation. After consideration of the relevant matter presented, the agency shall incorporate in the rules adopted a concise general statement of their basis and purpose. When rules are required by statute to be made on the record after opportunity for an agency hearing, sections 556 and 557 of this title apply instead of this subsection.

(d) The required publication or service of a substantive rule shall be made not less than 30 days before its effective date, except—

(1) a substantive rule which grants or recognizes an exemption or relieves a restriction;

(2) interpretative rules and statements of policy; or

(3) as otherwise provided by the agency for good cause found and published with the rule.

(e) Each agency shall give an interested person the right to petition for the issuance, amendment, or repeal of a rule.

§ 554. Adjudications

(a) This section applies, according to the provisions thereof, in every case of adjudication required by statute to be determined on the record after opportunity for an agency hearing, except to the extent that there is involved—

(1) a matter subject to a consequent trial of the law and the facts de novo in a court;

(2) the selection or tenure of an employee, except a hearing examiner appointed under section 3105 of this title;

(3) proceedings in which decisions rest solely on inspections, tests, or elections;

(4) the conduct of military or foreign affairs functions;

(5) cases in which an agency is acting as an agent for a court; or

(6) the certification of worker representatives.

(b) Persons entitled to notice of an agency hearing shall be timely informed of—

(1) the time, place, and nature of the hearings;

(2) the legal authority and jurisdiction under which the hearing is to be held; and

(3) the matters of fact and law asserted.

When private persons are the moving parties, other parties to the proceeding shall give prompt notice of issues controverted in fact or law; and in other instances agencies may by rule require responsive pleading. In fixing the time and place for hearings, due regard shall be had for the convenience and necessity of the parties or their representatives.

(c) The agency shall give all interested parties opportunity for—

(1) the submission and consideration of facts, arguments, offers of settlement, or proposals of adjustment when time, the nature of the proceeding, and the public interest permit; and

(2) to the extent that the parties are unable so to determine a controversy by consent, hearing and decision on notice and in accordance with sections 556 and 557 of this title.

(d) The employee who presides at the reception of evidence pursuant to section 556 of this title shall make the recommended decision or initial decision required by section 557 of this title, unless he becomes unavailable to the agency. Except to the extent required for the disposition of ex parte matters as authorized by law, such an employee may not—

(1) consult a person or party on a fact in issue, unless on notice and opportunity for all parties to participate; or

(2) be responsible to or subject to the supervision or direction of an employee or agent engaged in the performance of investigative or prosecuting functions for an agency.

An employee or agent engaged in the performance of investigative or prosecuting functions for an agency in a case may not, in that or a factually related case, participate or advise in the decision, recommended decision, or agency review pursuant to section 557 of this title, except as witness or counsel in public proceedings. This subsection does not apply—

(A) in determining applications for initial licenses;

(B) to proceedings involving the validity or application of rates, facilities, or practices of public utilities or carriers; or

(C) to the agency or a member or members of the body comprising the agency.

(e) The agency, with like effect as in the case of other orders, and in its sound discretion, may issue a declaratory order to terminate a controversy or remove uncertainty.

§ 555. Ancillary matters

(a) This section applies, according to the provisions thereof, except as otherwise provided by this subchapter.

(b) A person compelled to appear in person before an agency or representative thereof is entitled to be accompanied, represented, and advised by counsel or, if permitted by the agency, by other qualified representative. A party is entitled to appear in person or by or with counsel or other duly qualified representative in an agency proceeding. So far as the orderly conduct of public business permits, an interested person may appear before an agency or its responsible employees for the presentation, adjustment, or determination of an issue, request, or controversy in a proceeding, whether interlocutory, summary, or otherwise, or in connection with an agency function. With due regard for the convenience and necessity of the parties or their representatives and within a reasonable time, each agency shall proceed to conclude a matter presented to it. This subsection does not grant or deny a person who is not a lawyer the right to appear for or represent others before an agency or in an agency proceeding.

(c) Process, requirement of a report, inspection, or other investigative act or demand may not be issued, made, or enforced except as authorized by law. A person compelled to submit data or evidence is entitled to retain or, on payment of lawfully prescribed costs, procure a copy or transcript thereof, except that in a nonpublic investigatory proceeding the witness may for good cause be limited to inspection of the official transcript of his testimony.

(d) Agency subpoenas authorized by law shall be issued to a party on request and, when required by rules of procedure, on a statement or showing of general relevance and reasonable scope of the evidence sought. On contest, the court shall sustain the subpoena or similar process or demand to the extent that it is found to be in accordance with law. In a proceeding for enforcement, the court shall issue an order requiring the appearance of the witness or the production of the evidence or data within a reasonable time under penalty of punishment for contempt in case of contumacious failure to comply.

(e) Prompt notice shall be given of the denial in whole or in part of a written application, petition, or other request of an interested person made in connection with any agency proceedings. Except in affirming a prior denial or when the denial is self explanatory, the notice shall be accompanied by a brief statement of the grounds for denial.

§ 556. Hearings; presiding employees; powers and duties; burden of proof; evidence; record as basis of decision

(a) This section applies, according to the provisions thereof, to hearings required by section 553 or 554 of this title to be conducted in accordance with this section.

(b) There shall preside at the taking of evidence—

(1) the agency;

(2) one or more members of the body which comprises the agency; or

(3) one or more hearing examiners appointed under section 3105 of this title.

This subchapter does not supersede the conduct of specified classes of proceedings, in whole or in part, by or before boards or other employees specially provided for by or designated under statute. The functions of presiding employees and of employees participating in decisions in accordance with section 557 of this title shall be conducted in an impartial manner. A presiding or participating employee may at any time disqualify himself. On the filing in good faith of a timely and sufficient affidavit of personal bias or other disqualification of a presiding or participating employee, the agency shall determine the matter as a part of the record and decision in the case.

(c) Subject to published rules of the agency and within its powers, employees presiding at hearings may—

(1) administer oaths and affirmations;

(2) issue subpoenas authorized by law;

(3) rule on offers of proof and receive relevant evidence;

(4) take depositions or have depositions taken when the ends of justice would be served;

(5) regulate the course of the hearing;

(6) hold conferences for the settlement or simplification of the issues by consent of the parties;

(7) dispose of procedural requests or similar matters;

(8) make or recommend decisions in accordance with section 557 of this title; and

(9) take other action authorized by agency rule consistent with this subchapter.

(d) Except as otherwise provided by statute, the proponent of a rule or order has the burden of proof. Any oral or documentary evidence may be received, but the agency as a matter of policy shall provide for the exclusion of irrelevant, immaterial, or unduly repetitious evidence. A sanction may not be imposed or rule or order issued except on consideration of the whole record of those parts thereof cited by a party and supported by and in accordance with the reliable, probative, and substantial evidence. The agency may, to the extent consistent with the interests of justice and the policy of the underlying statutes administered by the agency, consider a violation of section 557(d) of this title sufficient grounds for a decision adverse to a party who has knowingly committed such violation or knowingly caused such violation to occur. A party is entitled to present his case or defense by oral or documentary evidence, to submit rebuttal evidence, and to conduct such cross-examination as may be required for a full and true disclosure of the facts. In rule making or determining claims for money or benefits or applications for initial licenses an agency may, when a party will not be prejudiced thereby, adopt procedures for the submission of all or part of the evidence in written form.

(e) The transcript of testimony and exhibits, together with all papers and requests filed in the proceeding, constitutes the exclusive record for decision in accordance with section 557 of this title and, on payment of lawfully prescribed costs, shall be made available to the parties. When an agency decision rests on official notice of a material fact not appearing in the evidence in the record, a party is entitled, on timely request, to an opportunity to show the contrary.

§ 557. Initial decisions; conclusiveness; review by agency; submissions by parties; contents of decisions; record

(a) This section applies, according to the provisions thereof, when a hearing is required to be conducted in accordance with section 556 of this title.

(b) When the agency did not preside at the reception of the evidence, the presiding employee or, in cases not subject to section 554(d) of this title, an employee qualified to preside at hearings pursuant to section 556 of this title, shall initially decide the case unless the agency requires, either in specific cases or by general rule, the entire record to be certified to it for decision. When the presiding employee makes an initial decision, that decision then becomes the decision of the agency without further proceedings unless there is an appeal to, or review on motion of, the agency within time provided by rule. On appeal from or review of the initial decision, the agency has all the powers which it would have in making the initial decision except as it may limit the issues on notice or by rule. When the agency makes the decision without having presided at the reception of the evidence, the presiding employee or an employee qualified to preside at hearings pursuant to section 556 of this title shall first recommend a decision, except that in rule making or determining applications for initial licenses—

(1) instead thereof the agency may issue a tentative decision or one of its responsible employees may recommend a decision; or

(2) this procedure may be omitted in a case in which the agency finds on the record that due and timely execution of its functions imperatively and unavoidably so requires.

(c) Before a recommended, initial, or tentative decision, or a decision on agency review of the decision of subordinate employees, the parties are entitled to a reasonable opportunity to submit for the consideration of the employees participating in the decisions—

(1) proposed findings and conclusions; or

(2) exceptions to the decisions or recommended decisions of subordinate employees or to tentative agency decisions; and

(3) supporting reasons for the exceptions or proposed findings or conclusions.

The record shall show the ruling on each finding, conclusion, or exception presented. All decisions, including initial, recommended, and tentative decisions, are a part of the record and shall include a statement of—

(A) findings and conclusions, and the reasons or basis therefor, on all the material issues of fact, law, or discretion presented on the record; and

(B) the appropriate rule, order, sanction, relief, or denial thereof.

(d)(1) In any agency proceeding which is subject to subsection (a) of this section, except to the extent required for the disposition of ex parte matters as authorized by law—

(A) no interested person outside the agency shall make or knowingly cause to be made to any member of the body comprising the agency, administrative law judge, or other employee who is or may reasonably be expected to be involved in the decisional process of the proceeding, an ex parte communication relevant to the merits of the proceeding;

(B) no member of the body comprising the agency, administrative law judge, or other employee who is or may reasonably be expected to be involved in the decisional process of the proceeding, shall make or knowingly cause to be made to any interested person outside the agency an ex parte communication relevant to the merits of the proceeding;

(C) a member of the body comprising the agency, administrative law judge, or other employee who is or may reasonably be expected to be involved in the decisional process of such proceeding who receives, or who makes or knowingly causes to be made, a communication prohibited by this subsection shall place on the public record of the proceeding:

(i) all such written communications;

(ii) memoranda stating the substance of all such oral communications; and

(iii) all written responses, and memoranda stating the substance of all oral responses, to the materials described in clauses (i) and (ii) of this subparagraph;

(D) upon receipt of a communication knowingly made or knowingly caused to be made by a party in violation of this subsection, the agency, administrative law judge, or other employee presiding at the hearing may, to the extent consistent with the interests of justice and the policy of the underlying statutes, require the party to show cause why his claim or interest in the proceeding should not be dismissed, denied, disregarded, or otherwise adversely affected on account of such violation; and

(E) the prohibitions of this subsection shall apply beginning at such time as the agency may designate, but in no case shall they begin to apply later than the time at which a proceeding is noticed for hearing unless the person responsible for the communication has knowledge that it will be noticed, in which case the prohibitions shall apply beginning at the time of his acquisition of such knowledge.

(2) This subsection does not constitute authority to withhold information from Congress.

§ 558. Imposition of sanctions; determination of applications for licenses; suspension, revocation, and expiration of licenses

(a) This section applies, according to the provisions thereof, to the exercise of a power or authority.

(b) A sanction may not be imposed or a substantive rule or order issued except within jurisdiction delegated to the agency and as authorized by law.

(c) When application is made for a license required by law, the agency, with due regard for the rights and privileges of all the interested parties or adversely affected persons and within a reasonable time, shall set and complete proceedings required to be conducted in accordance with sections 556 and 557 of this title or other proceedings required by law and shall make its decision. Except in cases of willfulness or those in which public health, interest, or safety requires otherwise, the withdrawal, suspension, revocation, or annulment of a license is lawful only if, before the institution of agency proceedings therefor, the licensee has been given—

(1) notice by the agency in writing of the facts or conduct which may warrant the action; and

(2) opportunity to demonstrate or achieve compliance with all lawful requirements.

When the licensee has made timely and sufficient application for a renewal or a new license in accordance with agency rules, a license with reference to an activity of a continuing nature does not expire until the application has been finally determined by the agency.

§ 559. Effect on other laws; effect of subsequent statute

This subchapter, chapter 7, and sections 1305, 3105, 3344, 4301(2)(E), 5362, and 7521 of this title, and the provisions of section 5335(a)(B) of this title that relate to hearing examiners, do not limit or repeal additional requirements imposed by statute or otherwise recognized by law. Except as otherwise required by law, requirements or privileges relating to evidence or procedure apply equally to agencies and persons. Each agency is granted the authority necessary to comply with the requirements of this subchapter through the issuance of rules or otherwise. Subsequent statute may not be held to supersede or modify this subchapter, chapter 7, sections 1305, 3105, 3344, 4301(2)(E), or 7521 of this title, or the provisions of section 5335(a)(B) of this title that relate to hearing examiners, except to the extent that it does so expressly.

CHAPTER 7—JUDICIAL REVIEW

§ 701. Applications; definitions

(a) This chapter applies, according to the provisions thereof, except to the extent that—

(1) statutes preclude judicial review; or

(2) agency action is committed to agency discretion by law.

(b) For the purpose of this chapter—

(1) "agency" means each authority of the Government of the United States, whether or not it is within or subject to review by another agency, but does not include—

(A) the Congress;

(B) the courts of the United States;

(C) the governments of the territories or possessions of the United States;

(D) the government of the District of Columbia;

(E) agencies composed of representatives of the parties or of representatives of organizations of the parties to the disputes determined by them;

(F) courts martial and military commissions;

(G) military authority exercised in the field in time of war or in occupied territory; or

(H) functions conferred by sections 1738, 1739, 1743, and 1744 of title 12; chapter 2 of title 41; or sections 1622, 1884, 1891–1902, and former section 1641(b)(2), of title 50, appendix; and

(2) "person", "rule", "order", "license", "sanction", "relief", and "agency action" have the meanings given them by section 551 of this title.

§ 702. Right of review

A person suffering legal wrong because of agency action, or adversely affected or aggrieved by agency action within the meaning of a relevant statute, is entitled to judicial review thereof. An action in a court of the United States seeking relief other than money damages and stating a claim that an agency or an officer or employee thereof acted or failed to act in an official capacity or under color of legal authority shall not be dismissed nor relief therein be denied on the ground that it is against the United States or that the United States is an indispensable party. The United States may be named as a defendant in any such action, and a judgment or decree may be entered against the United States: *Provided,* That any mandatory or injunctive decree shall specify the Federal officer or officers (by name or by title), and their successors in office, personally responsible for compliance. Nothing herein (1) affects other limitations on judicial review or the power or duty of the court to dismiss any action or deny relief on any other appropriate legal or equitable ground; of (2) confers authority to grant relief if any other statute that grants consent to suit expressly or impliedly forbids the relief which is sought.

§ 703. Form and venue of proceeding

The form of proceeding for judicial review is the special statutory review proceeding relevant to the subject matter in a court specified by statute or, in the absence or inadequacy thereof, any applicable form of legal action, including actions for declaratory judgments or writs of prohibitory or mandatory injunction or habeas corpus, in a court of competent jurisdiction. If no special statutory review proceeding is applicable, the action for judicial review may be brought against the United States, the agency by its official title, or the appropriate officer. Except to the extent that prior, adequate, and exclusive opportunity for judicial review is provided by law, agency action is subject to judicial review in civil or criminal proceedings for judicial enforcement.

§ 704. Actions reviewable

Agency action made reviewable by statute and final agency action for which there is no other adequate remedy in a court are subject to judicial review. A preliminary, procedural, or intermediate agency action or ruling not directly reviewable is subject to review on the review of the final agency action. Except as otherwise expressly required by statute, agency action otherwise final is final for the purposes of this section whether or not there has been presented or determined an application for a declaratory order, for any form of reconsiderations, or, unless the agency otherwise requires by rule and provides that the action meanwhile is inoperative, for an appeal to superior agency authority.

§ 705. Relief pending review

When an agency finds that justice so requires, it may postpone the effective date of action taken by it, pending judicial review. On such conditions as may be required and to the extent necessary to prevent irreparable injury, the reviewing court, including the court to which a case may be taken on appeal from or on application for certiorari or other writ to a reviewing court, may issue all necessary and appropriate process to postpone the effective date of an agency action or to preserve status or rights pending conclusion of the review proceedings.

§ 706. Scope of review

To the extent necessary to decision and when presented, the reviewing court shall decide all relevant questions of law, interpret constitutional and statutory provisions, and determine the meaning or applicability of the terms of an agency action. The reviewing court shall—

(1) compel agency action unlawfully withheld or unreasonably delayed; and

(2) hold unlawful and set aside agency action, findings, and conclusions found to be—

(A) arbitrary, capricious, an abuse of discretion, or otherwise not in accordance with law;

(B) contrary to constitutional right, power, privilege, or immunity;

(C) in excess of statutory jurisdiction, authority, or limitations, or short of statutory right;

(D) without observance of procedure required by law;

(E) unsupported by substantial evidence in a case subject to sections 556 and 557 of this title or otherwise reviewed on the record of an agency hearing provided by statute; or

(F) unwarranted by the facts to the extent that the facts are subject to trial de novo by the reviewing court. In making the foregoing determinations, the court shall review the whole record or those parts of it cited by a party, and due account shall be taken of the rule of prejudicial error.

Freedom of Information Act

The 1966 Freedom of Information Act (P.L. 89–487) requires executive branch agencies and independent commissions to make available to citizens, upon request, all documents and records—except those that fall into the following exempt categories:

- Secret national security or foreign policy information;
- Internal personnel practices;
- Information exempted by law;
- Trade secrets or other confidential commercial or financial information;
- Interagency or intra-agency memos;
- Personal information, personnel, or medical files;
- Law enforcement investigatory information;
- Information related to reports on financial institutions; and
- Geological and geophysical information.

Following passage of the FOIA, studies of its operation noted that major problems in obtaining information were bureaucratic delay, the cost of bringing suit to force disclosure, and excessive charges levied by the agencies for finding and providing the requested information. Congress in 1974 amended the act to remove some of the obstacles to public access.

Chief among the provisions of the amendments were those allowing a federal judge to review a decision of the government to classify certain material. Another provision set deadlines for the agency to respond to a request for information under the law. Another amendment permitted judges to order payment of attorneys' fees and court costs for plaintiffs who won suits brought for information under the act.

As amended in 1974, the act:

- Required federal agencies to publish their indexes of final opinions on settlements of internal cases, policy statements, and administrative staff manuals—or, if the indexes were not published, to furnish them on request to any person for the cost of duplication. The 1966 law simply required agencies to make such indexes available for public inspection and copying.

- Reworded a provision of the 1966 law to require agencies to release unlisted documents to someone requesting them with a reasonable description. This change was to ensure that an agency could not refuse to provide material simply because the applicant could not give its precise title.

- Directed each agency to publish a uniform set of fees for providing documents at the cost of finding and copying them; the amendment allowed waiver or reduction of those fees when in the public interest.

- Empowered federal district courts to order agencies to produce improperly withheld documents—and to examine the contested materials privately *(in camera)* to determine if they were properly exempted under one of the nine categories. This amendment removed the barrier to court review, which the Supreme Court had pointed out, giving courts the power to hold that a document had been improperly classified and therefore should be released. The government was required to prove that contested material was properly classified.

- Set time limits for agency responses to requests: ten working days for an initial request; twenty working days for an appeal from an initial refusal to produce documents; a possible ten working-day extension that could be granted only once in a single case.

- Set a thirty-day time limit for an agency response to a complaint filed in court under the act, provided that such cases should be given priority attention by the courts at the appeal, as well as at the trial, level.

- Allowed courts to order the government to pay attorneys' fees and court costs for persons winning suits against them under the act.
- Authorized a court to find an agency employee acted capriciously or arbitrarily in withholding information. Such a finding would set into action Civil Service Commission proceedings to determine the need for disciplinary action. If the commission found such a need, the relevant agency would take the disciplinary action which the commission recommended.
- Amended the wording of the national defense and national security exemption to make clear that it applied only to properly classified information, clarifying congressional intent to allow review of the decision to stamp something "classified."
- Amended the wording of the law enforcement exemption to allow withholding only of information which, if disclosed, would interfere with enforcement proceedings, deprive someone of a fair trial or hearing, invade personal privacy in an unwarranted way, disclose the identity of a confidential source, disclose investigative techniques, or endanger law enforcement personnel. Also protected from disclosure all information from a confidential source obtained by a criminal law enforcement agency or by an agency conducting a lawful national security investigation.
- Provided that segregable nonexempt portions of requested material be released after deletion of the exempt portions.
- Required an annual agency report to Congress including a list of all agency decisions to withhold information requested under the act, the reasons, the appeals, the results, all relevant rules, the fee schedule, and the names of officials responsible for each denial of information.
- Required an annual report from the attorney general to Congress listing the number of cases arising under the act, the exemption involved in each case, and the disposition, costs, fees, and penalties of each case.

All agencies of the executive branch have issued regulations to implement the Freedom of Information Act, which may be found in the *Code of Federal Regulations* (consult the general index of the code under "Freedom of Information").

New electronic FOIA provisions. The passage of the Electronic Freedom of Information Act of 1996 amended the FOIA further by expanding coverage to government information stored electronically. In addition, the act specified that federal data should be placed in electronic form when possible. The 1996 act also set about to improve the public's access to government data by speeding up the time government agencies are allowed to take in responding to a request, and by requiring that indexes of government records be made available to the public.

FOIA and the Department of Homeland Security. The Homeland Security Act of 2002, which established the Department of Homeland Security (DHS), granted broad exemption to the FOIA in exchange for the cooperation of private companies in sharing information with the government regarding vulnerabilities in the nation's critical infrastructure. Subtitle B of the act (the Critical Infrastructure Information Act) exempted from the FOIA and other federal and state disclosure requirements any critical infrastructure information that is voluntarily submitted to a covered federal agency for use in the security of critical infrastructure and protected systems, analysis, warning, interdependency study, recovery, reconstitution, or other informational purpose when accompanied by an express statement that such information is being submitted voluntarily in expectation of such nondisclosure protection. The Homeland Security Act required the secretary of DHS to establish specified procedures for the receipt, care, and storage by federal agencies of such critical infrastructure information and to provide criminal penalties for the unauthorized disclosure of such information.

During the 2002 debate over the Homeland Security Act, many lawmakers voiced concern over the fact that the new law shielded companies from lawsuits to compel disclosure; criminalized otherwise legitimate whistleblower activity by DHS employees; and preempted any state or local disclosure laws. On March 12, 2003, Sen. Patrick Leahy introduced the Restoration of Freedom of Information Act of 2003 (Restore FOIA). As proposed, Restore FOIA would

- Limit the FOIA exemption to relevant "records" submitted by the private sector, such that only those that actually pertain to critical infrastructure safety are protected.
- Allow for government oversight, including the ability to use and share the records within and between agencies.
- Allow local authorities to apply their own sunshine laws.
- Not provide civil immunity to companies that voluntarily submit information.
- Not restrict congressional use or disclosure of voluntarily submitted critical infrastructure information.

Legislative action was pending on the Restore FOIA proposal in the 108th Congress (2003–2005).

The following is the text of the Freedom of Information Act, as amended, as it appears in the U.S. Code, Title 5, Chapter 5, Subchapter II, section 552.

§552. Public information; agency rules, opinions, orders, records, and proceedings

(a) Each agency shall make available to the public information as follows:

(1) Each agency shall separately state and currently publish in the *Federal Register* for the guidance of the public—

(A) descriptions of its central and field organization and the established places at which, the employees (and in the case of a uniformed service, the members) from whom, and the methods whereby, the public may obtain information, make submittals or requests, or obtain decisions;

(B) statements of the general course and method by which its functions are channeled and determined, including the nature and requirements of all formal and informal procedures available;

(C) rules of procedure, descriptions of forms available or the places at which forms may be obtained, and instructions as to the scope and contents of all papers, reports, or examinations;

(D) substantive rules of general applicability adopted as authorized by law, and statements of general policy or interpretations of general applicability formulated and adopted by the agency; and

(E) each amendment, revision, or repeal of the foregoing.

Except to the extent that a person has actual and timely notice of the terms thereof, a person may not in any manner be required to resort to, or be adversely affected by, a matter required to be published in the *Federal Register* and not so published. For the purpose of this paragraph, matter reasonably available to the class of persons affected thereby is deemed published in the *Federal Register* when incorporated by reference therein with the approval of the director of the *Federal Register*.

(2) Each agency, in accordance with published rules, shall make available for public inspection and copying—

(A) final opinions, including concurring and dissenting opinions, as well as orders, made in the adjudication of cases;

(B) those statements of policy and interpretations which have been adopted by the agency and are not published in the *Federal Register*;

(C) administrative staff manuals and instructions to staff that affect a member of the public;

(D) copies of all records, regardless of form or format, which have been released to any person under paragraph (3) and which, because of the nature of their subject matter, the agency determines have become or are likely to become the subject of subsequent requests for substantially the same records; and

(E) a general index of the records referred to under subparagraph (D); unless the materials are promptly published and copies offered for sale. For records created on or after November 1, 1996, within one year after such date, each agency shall make such records avail-

able, including by computer telecommunications or, if computer telecommunications means have not been established by the agency, by other electronic means. To the extent required to prevent a clearly unwarranted invasion of personal privacy, an agency may delete identifying details when it makes available or publishes an opinion, statement of policy, interpretation, staff manual, instruction, or copies of records referred to in subparagraph (D). However, in each case the justification for the deletion shall be explained fully in writing, and the extent of such deletion shall be indicated on the portion of the record which is made available or published, unless including that indication would harm an interest protected by the exemption in subsection (b) under which the deletion is made. If technically feasible, the extent of the deletion shall be indicated at the place in the record where the deletion was made. Each agency shall also maintain and make available for public inspection and copying current indexes providing identifying information for the public as to any matter issued, adopted, or promulgated after July 4, 1967, and required by this paragraph to be made available or published. Each agency shall promptly publish, quarterly or more frequently, and distribute (by sale or otherwise) copies of each index or supplements thereto unless it determines by order published in the *Federal Register* that the publication would be unnecessary and impracticable, in which case the agency shall nonetheless provide copies of such index on request at a cost not to exceed the direct cost of duplication. Each agency shall make the index referred to in subparagraph (E) available by computer telecommunications by December 31, 1999. A final order, opinion, statement of policy, interpretation, or staff manual or instruction that affects a member of the public may be relied on, used, or cited as precedent by an agency against a party other than an agency only if—

(i) it has been indexed and either made available or published as provided by this paragraph; or

(ii) the party has actual and timely notice of the terms thereof.

(3) (A) Except with respect to the records made available under paragraphs (1) and (2) of this subsection, each agency, upon any request for records which (i) reasonably describes such records and (ii) is made in accordance with published rules stating the time, place, fees (if any), and procedures to be followed, shall make the records promptly available to any person.

(B) In making any record available to a person under this paragraph, an agency shall provide the record in any form or format requested by the person if the record is readily reproducible by the agency in that form or format. Each agency shall make reasonable efforts to maintain its records in forms or formats that are reproducible for purposes of this section.

(C) In responding under this paragraph to a request for records, an agency shall make reasonable efforts to search for the records in electronic form or format, except when such efforts would significantly interfere with the operation of the agency's automated information system.

(D) For purposes of this paragraph, the term "search" means to review, manually or by automated means, agency records for the purpose of locating those records which are responsive to a request.

(4)(A)(i) In order to carry out the provisions of this section, each agency shall promulgate regulations, pursuant to notice and receipt of public comment, specifying the schedule of fees applicable to the processing of requests under this section and establishing procedures and guidelines for determining when such fees should be waived or reduced. Such schedule shall conform to the guidelines which shall be promulgated, pursuant to notice and receipt of public comment, by the director of the Office of Management and Budget and which shall provide for a uniform schedule of fees for all agencies.

(ii) Such agency regulations shall provide that—

(I) fees shall be limited to reasonable standard charges for document search, duplication, and review, when records are requested for commercial use;

(II) fees shall be limited to reasonable standard charges for document duplication when records are not sought for commercial use and the request is made by an educational or noncommercial scientific institution, whose purpose is scholarly or scientific research; or a representative of the news media; and

(III) for any request not described in (I) or (II), fees shall be limited to reasonable standard charges for document search and duplication.

(iii) Documents shall be furnished without any charge or at a charge reduced below the fees established under clause (ii) if disclosure of the information is in the public interest because it is likely to contribute significantly to public understanding of the operations or activities of the government and is not primarily in the commercial interest of the requester.

(iv) Fee schedules shall provide for the recovery of only the direct costs of search, duplication, or review. Review costs shall include only the direct costs incurred during the initial examination of a document for the purposes of determining whether the documents must be disclosed under this section and for the purposes of withholding any portions exempt

from disclosure under this section. Review costs may not include any costs incurred in resolving issues of law or policy that may be raised in the course of processing a request under this section. No fee may be charged by any agency under this section—

(I) if the costs of routine collection and processing of the fee are likely to equal or exceed the amount of the fee; or

(II) for any request described in clause (ii) (II) or (III) of this subparagraph for the first two hours of search time or for the first one hundred pages of duplication.

(v) No agency may require advance payment of any fee unless the requester has previously failed to pay fees in a timely fashion, or the agency has determined that the fee will exceed $250.

(vi) Nothing in this subparagraph shall supersede fees chargeable under a statute specifically providing for setting the level of fees for particular types of records.

(vii) In any action by a requester regarding the waiver of fees under this section, the court shall determine the matter de novo: *Provided,* That the court's review of the matter shall be limited to the record before the agency.

(B) On complaint, the district court of the United States in the district in which the complainant resides, or has his principal place of business, or in which the agency records are situated, or in the District of Columbia, has jurisdiction to enjoin the agency from withholding agency records and to order the production of any agency records improperly withheld from the complainant. In such a case the court shall determine the matter de novo, and may examine the contents of such agency records in camera to determine whether such records or any part thereof shall be withheld under any of the exemptions set forth in subsection (b) of this section, and the burden is on the agency to sustain its action. In addition to any other matters to which a court accords substantial weight, a court shall accord substantial weight to an affidavit of an agency concerning the agency's determination as to technical feasibility under paragraph (2)(C) and subsection (b) and reproducibility under paragraph (3)(B).

(C) Notwithstanding any other provision of law, the defendant shall serve an answer or otherwise plead to any complaint made under this subsection within thirty days after service upon the defendant of the pleading in which such complaint is made, unless the court otherwise directs for good cause shown.

[(D) Repealed. Pub. L. 98-620, title IV, Sec. 402(2), Nov. 8, 1984, 98 Stat. 3357.]

(E) The court may assess against the United States reasonable attorney fees and other litigation costs reasonably incurred in any case under this section in which the complainant has substantially prevailed.

(F) Whenever the court orders the production of any agency records improperly withheld from the complainant and assesses against the United States reasonable attorney fees and other litigation costs, and the court additionally issues a written finding that the circumstances surrounding the withholding raise questions whether agency personnel acted arbitrarily or capriciously with respect to the withholding, the Special Counsel shall promptly initiate a proceeding to determine whether disciplinary action is warranted against the officer or employee who was primarily responsible for the withholding. The Special Counsel, after investigation and consideration of the evidence submitted, shall submit his findings and recommendations to the administrative authority of the agency concerned and shall send copies of the findings and recommendations to the officer or employee or his representative. The administrative authority shall take the corrective action that the Special Counsel recommends.

(G) In the event of noncompliance with the order of the court, the district court may punish for contempt the responsible employee, and in the case of a uniformed service, the responsible member.

(5) Each agency having more than one member shall maintain and make available for public inspection a record of the final votes of each member in every agency proceeding.

(6) (A) Each agency, upon any request for records made under paragraph (1), (2), or (3) of this subsection, shall—

(i) determine within twenty days (excepting Saturdays, Sundays, and legal public holidays) after the receipt of any such request whether to comply with such request and shall immediately notify the person making such request of such determination and the reasons therefor, and of the right of such person to appeal to the head of the agency any adverse determination; and

(ii) make a determination with respect to any appeal within twenty days (excepting Saturdays, Sundays, and legal public holidays) after the receipt of such appeal. If on appeal the denial of the request for records is in whole or in part upheld, the agency shall notify the person making such request of the provisions for judicial review of that determination under paragraph (4) of this subsection.

(B)(i) In unusual circumstances as specified in this subparagraph, the time limits prescribed in either clause (i) or clause (ii) of subparagraph (A) may be extended by written notice to the person making such request setting forth the unusual circumstances for such extension and the date on which a determination is expected to be dispatched. No such notice shall specify a date that would result in an extension for more than ten working days, except as provided in clause (ii) of this subparagraph.

(ii) With respect to a request for which a written notice under clause (i) extends the time limits prescribed under clause (i) of subparagraph (A), the agency shall notify the person making the request if the request cannot be processed within the time limit specified in that clause and shall provide the person an opportunity to limit the scope of the request so that it may be processed within that time limit or an opportunity to arrange with the agency an alternative time frame for processing the request or a modified request. Refusal by the person to reasonably modify the request or arrange such an alternative time frame shall be considered as a factor in determining whether exceptional circumstances exist for purposes of subparagraph (C).

(iii) As used in this subparagraph, "unusual circumstances" means, but only to the extent reasonably necessary to the proper processing of the particular requests—

(I) the need to search for and collect the requested records from field facilities or other establishments that are separate from the office processing the request;

(II) the need to search for, collect, and appropriately examine a voluminous amount of separate and distinct records which are demanded in a single request; or

(III) the need for consultation, which shall be conducted with all practicable speed, with another agency having a substantial interest in the determination of the request or among two or more components of the agency having substantial subject-matter interest therein.

(iv) Each agency may promulgate regulations, pursuant to notice and receipt of public comment, providing for the aggregation of certain requests by the same requestor, or by a group of requestors acting in concert, if the agency reasonably believes that such requests actually constitute a single request, which would otherwise satisfy the unusual circumstances specified in this subparagraph, and the requests involve clearly related matters. Multiple requests involving unrelated matters shall not be aggregated.

(C)(i) Any person making a request to any agency for records under paragraph (1), (2), or (3) of this subsection shall be deemed to have exhausted his administrative remedies with respect to such request if the agency fails to comply with the applicable time limit provisions of this paragraph. If the government can show exceptional circumstances exist and that the agency is exercising due diligence in responding to the request, the court may retain jurisdiction and allow the agency additional time to complete its review of the records. Upon any determination by an agency to comply with a request for records, the records shall be made promptly available to such person making such request. Any notification of denial of any request for records under this subsection shall set forth the names and titles or positions of each person responsible for the denial of such request.

(ii) For purposes of this subparagraph, the term "exceptional circumstances" does not include a delay that results from a predictable agency workload of requests under this section, unless the agency demonstrates reasonable progress in reducing its backlog of pending requests.

(iii) Refusal by a person to reasonably modify the scope of a request or arrange an alternative time frame for processing a request (or a modified request) under clause (ii) after being given an opportunity to do so by the agency to whom the person made the request shall be considered as a factor in determining whether exceptional circumstances exist for purposes of this subparagraph.

(D)(i) Each agency may promulgate regulations, pursuant to notice and receipt of public comment, providing for multitrack processing of requests for records based on the amount of work or time (or both) involved in processing requests.

(ii) Regulations under this subparagraph may provide a person making a request that does not qualify for the fastest multitrack processing an opportunity to limit the scope of the request in order to qualify for faster processing.

(iii) This subparagraph shall not be considered to affect the requirement under subparagraph (C) to exercise due diligence.

(E)(i) Each agency shall promulgate regulations, pursuant to notice and receipt of public comment, providing for expedited processing of requests for records—

(I) in cases in which the person requesting the records demonstrates a compelling need; and

(II) in other cases determined by the agency.

(ii) Notwithstanding clause (i), regulations under this subparagraph must ensure—

(I) that a determination of whether to provide expedited processing shall be made, and notice of the determination shall be provided to the person making the request, within ten days after the date of the request; and

(II) expeditious consideration of administrative appeals of such determinations of whether to provide expedited processing.

(iii) An agency shall process as soon as practicable any request for records to which the agency has granted expedited processing under this subparagraph. Agency action to deny or affirm denial of a request for expedited processing pursuant to this subparagraph, and failure by an agency to respond in a timely manner to such a request shall be subject to judicial review under paragraph (4), except that the judicial review shall be based on the record before the agency at the time of the determination.

(iv) A district court of the United States shall not have jurisdiction to review an agency denial of expedited processing of a request for records after the agency has provided a complete response to the request.

(v) For purposes of this subparagraph, the term "compelling need" means—

(I) that a failure to obtain requested records on an expedited basis under this paragraph could reasonably be expected to pose an imminent threat to the life or physical safety of an individual; or

(II) with respect to a request made by a person primarily engaged in disseminating information, urgency to inform the public concerning actual or alleged federal government activity.

(vi) A demonstration of a compelling need by a person making a request for expedited processing shall be made by a statement certified by such person to be true and correct to the best of such person's knowledge and belief.

(F) In denying a request for records, in whole or in part, an agency shall make a reasonable effort to estimate the volume of any requested matter the provision of which is denied, and shall provide any such estimate to the person making the request, unless providing such estimate would harm an interest protected by the exemption in subsection (b) pursuant to which the denial is made.

(b) This section does not apply to matters that are—

(1)(A) specifically authorized under criteria established by an Executive order to be kept secret in the interest of national defense or foreign policy and (B) are in fact properly classified pursuant to such Executive order;

(2) related solely to the internal personnel rules and practices of an agency;

(3) specifically exempted from disclosure by statute (other than section 552b of this title), provided that such statute (A) requires that the matters be withheld from the public in such a manner as to leave no discretion on the issue, or (B) establishes particular criteria for withholding or refers to particular types of matters to be withheld;

(4) trade secrets and commercial or financial information obtained from a person and privileged or confidential;

(5) inter-agency or intra-agency memorandums or letters which would not be available by law to a party other than an agency in litigation with the agency;

(6) personnel and medical files and similar files the disclosure of which would constitute a clearly unwarranted invasion of personal privacy;

(7) records or information compiled for law enforcement purposes, but only to the extent that the production of such law enforcement records or information (A) could reasonably be expected to interfere with enforcement proceedings, (B) would deprive a person of a right to a fair trial or an impartial adjudication, (C) could reasonably be expected to constitute an unwarranted invasion of personal privacy, (D) could reasonably be expected to disclose the identity of a confidential source, including a State, local, or foreign agency or authority or any private institution which furnished information on a confidential basis, and, in the case of a record or information compiled by criminal law enforcement authority in the course of a criminal investigation or by an agency conducting a lawful national security intelligence investigation, information furnished by a confidential source, (E) would disclose techniques and procedures for law enforcement investigations or prosecutions, or would disclose guidelines for law enforcement investigations or prosecutions if such disclosure could reasonably be expected to risk circumvention of the law, or (F) could reasonably be expected to endanger the life or physical safety of any individual;

(8) contained in or related to examination, operating, or condition reports prepared by, on behalf of, or for the use of an agency responsible for the regulation or supervision of financial institutions; or

(9) geological and geophysical information and data, including maps, concerning wells.

Any reasonably segregable portion of a record shall be provided to any person requesting such record after deletion of the portions which are exempt under this subsection. The amount of information deleted shall be indicated on the released portion of the record, unless including that indication would harm an interest protected by the exemption in this subsection under which the deletion is made. If technically feasible, the amount of the information deleted shall be indicated at the place in the record where such deletion is made.

(c)(1) Whenever a request is made which involves access to records described in subsection (b)(7)(A) and—

(A) the investigation or proceeding involves a possible violation of criminal law; and

(B) there is reason to believe that (i) the subject of the investigation or proceeding is not aware of its pendency, and (ii) disclosure of the existence of the records could reasonably be expected to interfere with enforcement proceedings, the agency may, during only such time as that circumstance continues, treat the records as not subject to the requirements of this section.

(2) Whenever informant records maintained by a criminal law enforcement agency under an informant's name or personal identifier are requested by a third party according to the informant's name or personal identifier, the agency may treat the records as not subject to the requirements of this section unless the informant's status as an informant has been officially confirmed.

(3) Whenever a request is made which involves access to records maintained by the Federal Bureau of Investigation pertaining to foreign intelligence or counterintelligence, or international terrorism, and the existence of the records is classified information as provided in subsection (b)(1), the Bureau may, as long as the existence of the records remains classified information, treat the records as not subject to the requirements of this section.

(d) This section does not authorize withholding of information or limit the availability of records to the public, except as specifically stated in this section. This section is not authority to withhold information from Congress.

(e)(1) On or before February 1 of each year, each agency shall submit to the Attorney General of the United States a report which shall cover the preceding fiscal year and which shall include—

(A) the number of determinations made by the agency not to comply with requests for records made to such agency under subsection (a) and the reasons for each such determination;

(B)(i) the number of appeals made by persons under subsection (a)(6), the result of such appeals, and the reason for the action upon each appeal that results in a denial of information; and

(ii) a complete list of all statutes that the agency relies upon to authorize the agency to withhold information under subsection (b)(3), a description of whether a court has upheld the decision of the agency to withhold information under each such statute, and a concise description of the scope of any information withheld;

(C) the number of requests for records pending before the agency as of September 30 of the preceding year, and the median number of days that such requests had been pending before the agency as of that date;

(D) the number of requests for records received by the agency and the number of requests which the agency processed;

(E) the median number of days taken by the agency to process different types of requests;

(F) the total amount of fees collected by the agency for processing requests; and

(G) the number of full-time staff of the agency devoted to processing requests for records under this section, and the total amount expended by the agency for processing such requests.

(2) Each agency shall make each such report available to the public including by computer telecommunications, or if computer telecommunications means have not been established by the agency, by other electronic means.

(3) The Attorney General of the United States shall make each report which has been made available by electronic means available at a single electronic access point. The Attorney General of the United States shall notify the Chairman and ranking minority member of the Committee on Government Reform and Oversight of the House of Representatives and the Chairman and ranking minority member of the Committees on Governmental Affairs and the Judiciary of the Senate, no later than April 1 of the year in which each such report is issued, that such reports are available by electronic means.

(4) The Attorney General of the United States, in consultation with the director of the Office of Management and Budget, shall develop reporting and performance guidelines in connection with reports required by this subsection by October 1, 1997, and may establish additional requirements for such reports as the Attorney General determines may be useful.

(5) The Attorney General of the United States shall submit an annual report on or before April 1 of each calendar year which shall include for the prior calendar year a listing of the number of cases arising under this section, the exemption involved in each case, the disposition of such case, and the cost, fees, and penalties assessed under subparagraphs (E), (F), and (G) of subsection (a)(4). Such report shall also include a description of the efforts undertaken by the Department of Justice to encourage agency compliance with this section.

(f) For purposes of this section, the term—

(1) "agency" as defined in section 551(1) of this title includes any executive department, military department, government corporation, government controlled corporation, or other establishment in the executive branch of the government (including the Executive Office of the President), or any independent regulatory agency; and

(2) "record" and any other term used in this section in reference to information includes any information that would be an agency record subject to the requirements of this section when maintained by an agency in any format, including an electronic format.

(g) The head of each agency shall prepare and make publicly available upon request, reference material or a guide for requesting records or information from the agency, subject to the exemptions in subsection (b), including—

(1) an index of all major information systems of the agency;

(2) a description of major information and record locator systems maintained by the agency; and

(3) a handbook for obtaining various types and categories of public information from the agency pursuant to chapter 35 of title 44, and under this section.

Government in the Sunshine Act

A four-year campaign to open the government to more public scrutiny achieved its goal in 1976, with enactment of legislation requiring most federal agencies to open their meetings to the public.

Called "Government in the Sunshine Act," the bill (P.L. 94–409) required for the first time that all multi-headed federal agencies—about fifty of them—conduct their business regularly in public session. The unprecedented open-door requirements embraced regulatory agencies, advisory committees, independent offices, the Postal Service—almost all executive branch agencies except the Cabinet departments.

The only exception to the rule of openness was for discussion of ten kinds of matters, such as court proceedings or personnel problems, specifically listed in the bill.

A separate section of the legislation also placed a ban on informal—*ex parte*—contacts between agency officials and interested outsiders to discuss pending agency business. Calling that provision a sleeper, some Washington lawyers suggested that it could have a broad impact on what had come to be an accepted practice in regulatory proceedings.

The final version of the bill represented a victory for advocates of tough open-meeting requirements. The definition of meetings included almost any gathering, formal or informal, of agency members, including conference telephone calls. Agencies also were required to keep transcripts of closed meetings. However, the bill did allow agencies discussing very sensitive matters, such as monetary policy, to keep either minutes or transcripts.

Among its key features, the bill:
- Required all agencies headed by two or more persons, a majority of whom were appointed by the president and confirmed by the Senate, to open all meetings to the public unless a majority voted to close a meeting. (The Envi-

ronmental Protection Agency is among the single-headed agencies not covered by the act.)
- Defined a meeting as the deliberations of at least the number of members required to take action for an agency where such deliberations determined or resulted in the joint conduct or disposition of agency business.
- Specified that a meeting could be closed only for discussion of the following ten matters: (1) national defense, foreign policy or matters classified by executive order; (2) agency personnel rules and practices; (3) information required by other laws to be kept confidential; (4) trade secrets or financial or commercial information obtained under a pledge of confidentiality; (5) accusation of a crime or formal censure; (6) information whose disclosure would constitute an unwarranted invasion of personal privacy; (7) certain law enforcement investigatory records; (8) bank examination records and similar financial audits; (9) information whose premature disclosure could lead to significant financial speculation, endanger the stability of a financial institution or frustrate a proposed agency action; or (10) the agency's involvement in federal or state civil actions or similar legal proceedings where there was a public record.
- Allowed a meeting to be closed by a majority record vote of all members, barring use of proxies; permitted a single vote to be taken to close a series of meetings on the same subject to be held within a thirty-day period.
- Permitted an agency to close a meeting at the request of a person affected by the agency's deliberations if the discussion could be exempted under exemptions 5, 6, or 7.
- Required an agency to disclose its vote to close a meeting within one day of the vote and to make public in advance of a closed meeting a written explanation of the closing, with a list of all persons expected to attend the closed meeting.

- Permitted agencies that regularly must meet in closed session to devise general regulations to expedite closed meetings and exempted such agencies from many procedural requirements for closed meetings.

- Required advance public notice (seven days) of the date, place, subject matter, and open-closed nature of all meetings, as well as the person to contact for information.

- For closings of meetings, required the general counsel or chief legal officer of an agency to certify it was properly closed according to a specific exemption under the bill.

- Required all agencies to keep and make public complete verbatim transcripts of closed meetings, with deletions of material exempted under the act; agencies closing meetings under exemptions 8, 9, or 10 could elect to keep minutes instead of a transcript.

- Provided for district court enforcement and review of the open-meeting requirements and placed the burden of proof in disputes upon the agency; permitted the court to assess an agency found in violation of the act for the plaintiff's attorneys' fees and court costs and permitted the court to charge a plaintiff for such costs if his suit was found to be "frivolous or dilatory."

- Allowed federal courts reviewing a non-Sunshine agency action, upon request of a party in the proceeding, to inquire into a Sunshine law violation and afford appropriate relief.

- Specified that the provision of this act would take precedence over the Freedom of Information Act (P.L. 93–502) in cases of information requests.

- Required each agency to report annually to Congress the numbers of open and closed meetings, reasons for closings and descriptions of any litigation against an agency under the bill.

- Prohibited *ex parte* communications between agency officials and outsiders affected by pending agency business, required an official to make public any such contact, and made *ex parte* communications grounds for ruling against a party in an agency proceeding.

Agencies covered by the act have established their own regulations to implement it. They are required by the act to publish notice of all meetings—open and closed—in the *Federal Register*.

The following is the text of the Government in the Sunshine Act as it appears in the U.S. Code, Title 5, Chapter 5, Subchapter II, section 552b.

§ 552b. Open meetings

(a) For purposes of this section—

(1) the term "agency" means any agency, as defined in section 552(e) of this title, headed by a collegial body composed of two or more individual members, a majority of whom are appointed to such position by the President with the advice and consent of the Senate, and any subdivision thereof authorized to act on behalf of the agency;

(2) the term "meeting" means the deliberations of at least the number of individual agency members required to take action on behalf of the agency where such deliberations determine or result in the joint conduct or disposition of official agency business, but does not include deliberations required or permitted by subsection (d) or (e); and

(3) the term "member" means an individual who belongs to a collegial body heading an agency.

(b) Members shall not jointly conduct or dispose of agency business other than in accordance with this section. Except as provided in subsection (c), every portion of every meeting of an agency shall be open to public observation.

(c) Except in a case where the agency finds that the public interest requires otherwise, the second sentence of subsection (b) shall not apply to any portion of an agency meeting, and the requirements of subsections (d) and (e) shall not apply to any information pertaining to such meeting otherwise required by this section to be disclosed to the public, where the agency properly determines that such portion or portions of its meeting or the disclosure of such information is likely to—

(1) disclose matters that are (A) specifically authorized under criteria established by an Executive order to be kept secret in the interests of national defense or foreign policy and (B) in fact properly classified pursuant to such Executive order;

(2) relate solely to the internal personnel rules and practices of an agency;

(3) disclose matters specifically exempted from disclosure by statute (other than section 552 of this title), provided that such statute (A) requires that the matters be withheld from the public in such a manner as to leave no discretion on the issue, or (B) establishes particular criteria for withholding or refers to particular types of matters to be withheld;

(4) disclose trade secrets and commercial or financial information obtained from a person and privileged or confidential;

(5) involve accusing any person of a crime, or formally censuring any person;

(6) disclose information of a personal nature where disclosure would constitute a clearly unwarranted invasion of personal privacy;

(7) disclose investigatory records compiled for law enforcement purposes, or information which if written would be contained in such records, but only to the extent that the production of such records or information would (A) interfere with enforcement proceedings, (B)

deprive a person of a right to a fair trial or an impartial adjudication, (C) constitute an unwarranted invasion of personal privacy, (D) disclose the identity of a confidential source and, in the case of a record compiled by a criminal law enforcement authority in the course of a criminal investigation, or by an agency conducting a lawful national security intelligence investigation, confidential information furnished only by the confidential source, (E) disclose investigative techniques and procedures, or (F) endanger the life or physical safety of law enforcement personnel;

(8) disclose information contained in or related to examination, operating, or condition reports prepared by, on behalf of, or for the use of an agency responsible for the regulation or supervision of financial institutions;

(9) disclose information the premature disclosure of which would—

(A) in the case of an agency which regulates currencies, securities, commodities, or financial institutions, be likely to (i) lead to significant financial speculation in currencies, securities, or commodities, or (ii) significantly endanger the stability of any financial institution; or

(B) in the case of any agency, be likely to significantly frustrate implementation of a proposed agency action.

except that subparagraph (B) shall not apply in any instance where the agency has already disclosed to the public the content or nature of its proposed action, or where the agency is required by law to make such disclosure on its own initiative prior to taking final agency action on such proposal; or

(10) specifically concern the agency's issuance of a subpoena, or the agency's participation in a civil action or proceeding, an action in a foreign court or international tribunal, or an arbitration, or the initiation, conduct, or disposition by the agency of a particular case of formal agency adjudication pursuant to the procedures in section 554 of this title or otherwise involving a determination on the record after opportunity for a hearing.

(d)(1) Action under subsection (c) shall be taken only when a majority of the entire membership of the agency (as defined in subsection (a)(1)) votes to take such action. A separate vote of the agency members shall be taken with respect to each agency meeting a portion or portions of which are proposed to be closed to the public pursuant to subsection (c), or with respect to any information which is proposed to be withheld under subsection (c). A single vote may be taken with respect to a series of meetings, a portion or portions of which are proposed to be closed to the public, or with respect to any information concerning such series of meetings,

so long as each meeting in such series involves the same particular matters and is scheduled to be held no more than thirty days after the initial meeting in such series. The vote of each agency member participating in such vote shall be recorded and no proxies shall be allowed.

(2) Whenever any person whose interests may be directly affected by a portion of a meeting requests that the agency close such portion to the public for any of the reasons referred to in paragraph (5), (6), or (7) of subsection (c), the agency, upon request of any one of its members, shall vote by recorded vote whether to close such meeting.

(3) Within one day of any vote taken pursuant to paragraph (1) or (2), the agency shall make publicly available a written copy of such vote reflecting the vote of each member on the question. If a portion of a meeting is to be closed to the public, the agency shall, within one day of the vote taken pursuant to paragraph (1) or (2) of this subsection, make publicly available a full written explanation of its action closing the portion together with a list of all persons expected to attend the meeting and their affiliation.

(4) Any agency, a majority of whose meetings may properly be closed to the public pursuant to paragraph (4), (8), (9)(A), or (10) of subsection (c), or any combination thereof, may provide by regulation for the closing of such meetings or portions thereof in the event that a majority of the members of the agency votes by recorded vote at the beginning of such meeting, or portion thereof, to close the exempt portion or portions of the meeting, and a copy of such vote, reflecting the vote of each member on the question, is made available to the public. The provisions of paragraphs (1), (2), and (3) of this subsection and subsection (e) shall not apply to any portion of a meeting to which such regulations apply: *Provided,* That the agency shall, except to the extent that such information is exempt from disclosure under the provisions of subsection (c), provide the public with public announcement of the time, place, and subject matter of the meeting and of each portion thereof at the earliest practicable time.

(e)(1) In the case of each meeting, the agency shall make public announcement, at least one week before the meeting, of the time, place, and subject matter of the meeting, whether it is to be open or closed to the public, and the name and phone number of the official designated by the agency to respond to requests for information about the meeting. Such announcement shall be made unless a majority of the members of the agency determines by a recorded vote that agency business requires that such meeting be called at an earlier date, in which case the agency shall make public announcement of the time, place, and subject matter of such meeting, and whether open or closed to the public, at the earliest practicable time.

(2) The time or place of a meeting may be changed following the public announcement required by paragraph (1) only if the agency publicly announces such change at the earliest practicable time. The subject matter of a meeting, or the determination of the agency to open or close a meeting, or portion of a meeting, to the public, may be changed following the public announcement required by this subsection only if (A) a majority of the entire membership of the agency determines by a recorded vote that agency business so requires and that no earlier announcement of the change was possible, and (B) the agency publicly announces such change and the vote of each member upon such change at the earliest practicable time.

(3) Immediately following each public announcement required by this subsection, notice of the time, place, and subject matter of a meeting, whether the meeting is open or closed, any change in one of the preceding, and the name and phone number of the official designated by the agency to respond to requests for information about the meeting, shall also be submitted for publication in the *Federal Register*.

(f) (1) For every meeting closed pursuant to paragraphs (1) through (10) of subsection (c), the General Counsel or chief legal officer of the agency shall publicly certify that, in his or her opinion, the meeting may be closed to the public and shall state each relevant exemptive provision. A copy of such certification, together with a statement from the presiding officer of the meeting setting forth the time and place of the meeting, and the persons present, shall be retained by the agency. The agency shall maintain a complete transcript or electronic recording adequate to record fully the proceedings of each meeting, or portion of a meeting, closed to the public, except that in the case of a meeting, or portion of a meeting, closed to the public pursuant to paragraph (8), (9)(A), or (10) of subsection (c), the agency shall maintain either such a transcript or recording, or a set of minutes. Such minutes shall fully and clearly describe all matters discussed and shall provide a full and accurate summary of any actions taken, and the reasons therefor, including a description of each of the views expressed on any item and the record of any rollcall vote (reflecting the vote of each member on the question). All documents considered in connection with any action shall be identified in such minutes.

(2) The agency shall make promptly available to the public, in a place easily accessible to the public, the transcript, electronic recording, or minutes (as required by paragraph (1) of the discussion of any item on the agenda, or of any item of the testimony of any witness received at the meeting, except for such item or items of such discussion or testimony as the agency determines to contain information which may be withheld under subsection (c). Copies of such transcript, or minutes, or a transcription of such recording disclosing the identity of each speaker, shall be furnished to any person at the actual cost of duplication or transcription. The agency shall maintain a complete verbatim copy of the transcript, a complete copy of the minutes, or a complete electronic recording of each meeting, or portion of a meeting, closed to the public, for a period of at least two years after such meeting, or until one year after the conclusion of any agency proceeding with respect to which the meeting or portion was held, whichever occurs later.

(g) Each agency subject to the requirements of this section shall, within 180 days after the date of enactment of this section, following consultation with the Office of the Chairman of the Administrative Conference of the United States[1] and published notice in the *Federal Register* of at least thirty days and opportunity for written comment by any person, promulgate regulations to implement the requirements of subsections (b) through (f) of this section. Any person may bring a proceeding in the United States District Court for the District of Columbia to require an agency to promulgate such regulations if such agency has not promulgated such regulations within the time period specified herein. Subject to any limitations of time provided by law, any person may bring a proceeding in the United States Court of Appeals for the District of Columbia to set aside agency regulations issued pursuant to this subsection that are not in accord with the requirements of subsections (b) through (f) of this section and to require the promulgation of regulations that are in accord with such subsections.

(h)(1) The district courts of the United States shall have jurisdiction to enforce the requirements of subsections (b) through (f) of this section by declaratory judgment, injunctive relief, or other relief as may be appropriate. Such actions may be brought by any person against an agency prior to, or within sixty days after, the meeting out of which the violation of this section arises, except that if public announcement of such meeting is not initially provided by the agency in accordance with the requirements of this section, such action may be instituted pursuant to this section at any time prior to sixty days after any public announcement of such meeting. Such actions may be brought in the district court of the United States for the district in which the agency meeting is held or in which the agency in question has its headquarters, or in the District Court for the District of Columbia. In such actions a defendant shall serve his answer within thirty days after the service of the complaint. The burden is on the defendant to sustain his action. In deciding such cases the court may examine in camera any portion of the transcript, electronic recording, or minutes of a meeting closed to the public, and may take such additional evidence as it deems necessary. The court, having due regard for orderly administration and the public interest, as well as the interests of the parties, may grant such equitable relief as it deems appropriate, including granting an injunction against future violations of this section or ordering the agency to make available to the public such portion of the transcript, recording, or minutes of a meeting as is not authorized to be withheld under subsection (c) of this section.

(2) Any Federal court otherwise authorized by law to review agency action may, at the application of any person properly participating in the proceeding pursuant to other applicable law, inquire into violations by the agency of the requirements of this section and afford such relief as it deems appropriate. Nothing in this section authorizes any Federal court having jurisdiction solely on the basis of paragraph (1) to set aside, enjoin, or invalidate any agency action (other than an action to close a meeting or to withhold information under this section) taken or discussed at any agency meeting out of which the violation of this section arose.

(i) The court may assess against any party reasonable attorney fees and other litigation costs reasonably incurred by any other party who substantially prevails in any action brought in accordance with the provisions of subsection (g) or (h) of this section, except that costs may be assessed against the plaintiff only where the court finds that the suit was initiated by the plaintiff primarily for frivolous or dilatory purposes. In the case of assessment of costs against an agency, the costs may be assessed by the court against the United States.

(j) Each agency subject to the requirements of this section shall annually report to Congress regarding its compliance with such requirements, including a tabulation of the total number of agency meetings open to the public, the total number of meetings closed to the public, the reasons for closing such meetings, and a description of any litigation brought against the agency under this section, including any costs assessed against the agency in such litigation (whether or not paid by the agency).

(k) Nothing herein expands or limits the present rights of any person under section 552 of this title, except that the exemptions set forth in subsection (c) of this section shall govern in the case of any request made pursuant to section 552 to copy or inspect the transcripts, recordings, or minutes described in subsection (f) of this section. The requirements of chapter 33 of title 44, United States Code, shall not apply to the transcripts, recordings, and minutes described in subsection (f) of this section.

(l) This section does not constitute authority to withhold any information from Congress, and does not authorize the closing of any agency meeting or portion thereof required by any other provision of law to be open.

(m) Nothing in this section authorizes any agency to withhold from any individual any record, including transcripts, recordings, or minutes required by this section, which is otherwise accessible to such individual under section 552a of this title.

[1] The Administrative Conference of the United States was abolished by Congress in 1995; the consultation requirement of this provision was not transferred to any other agency.

Paperwork Reduction Act

The Paperwork Reduction Act of 1980 (P.L. 96–511) was enacted during the Carter administration upon the recommendation of the Commission on Federal Paperwork, which issued a report in 1977 calling for major reforms of federal information collection practices. The act was intended to reduce the burden of federal government paperwork, to ensure that information collected by the federal government was necessary, and to establish uniform federal policies and efficient procedures for the collection, storage, and dissemination of information. It established the Office of Information and Regulatory Affairs within the Office of Management and Budget (OMB) to carry out the provisions of the act.

Major provisions of the Paperwork Reduction Act:

- Authorized OMB to develop and implement federal information policies, principles, standards, and guidelines.
- Required agencies to submit to OMB for review and approval any requests for information that will be solicited from ten or more individuals or businesses.
- Provided that agencies must submit to OMB copies of any proposed rule that contains a request for information for review no later than when the rule is published in the *Federal Register.*
- Established a requirement that requests for information must include a control number issued by OMB and must state why the information is being collected.
- Exempted members of the public from penalties for failing to comply with an information request issued after Dec. 31, 1981, that does not display a current OMB control number.
- Required agencies to designate a senior official to carry out their responsibilities under the act.
- Prohibited agencies from requesting information unless they had determined that: the information is necessary for their mission; it is unavailable elsewhere in the federal government; and they have reduced the burden of the request as much as possible.
- Set a goal for reduction of the paperwork burden by 15 percent by Oct. 1, 1982, and by an additional 10 percent by Oct. 1, 1983.
- Established a Federal Information Locator System at OMB to serve as a directory of information resources and an information referral service.
- Required OMB to complete actions on recommendations of the Commission on Federal Paperwork.
- Authorized OMB to oversee compliance with records management provisions of the act and to coordinate records management policies and programs with information collection policies and programs.
- Permitted OMB to monitor compliance with the Privacy Act and to develop and implement policies concerning information disclosure, confidentiality, and security.
- Authorized OMB to develop policies for automatic data processing and telecommunications within the federal government.
- Required OMB to report to Congress annually on implementation of the act.

The following is the text of the Paperwork Reduction Act as it appears in the U.S. Code, Title 44, Chapter 35, Section 3501.

§ 3501. Purpose

The purpose of this chapter is—

(1) to minimize the Federal paperwork burden for individuals, small businesses, State and local governments, and other persons;

(2) to minimize the cost to the Federal Government of

collecting, maintaining, using, and disseminating information;

(3) to maximize the usefulness of information collected by the Federal Government;

(4) to coordinate, integrate and, to the extent practicable and appropriate, make uniform Federal information policies and practices;

(5) to ensure that automatic data processing and telecommunications technologies are acquired and used by the Federal Government in a manner which improves service delivery and program management, increases productivity, reduces waste and fraud, and, wherever practicable and appropriate, reduces the information processing burden for the Federal Government and for persons who provide information to the Federal Government; and

(6) to ensure that the collection, maintenance, use and dissemination of information by the Federal Government is consistent with applicable laws relating to confidentiality, including section 552a of title 5, United States Code, known as the Privacy Act. . . .

§ 3503. Office of Information and Regulatory Affairs

(a) There is established in the Office of Management and Budget an office to be known as the Office of Information and Regulatory Affairs.

(b) There shall be at the head of the Office an Administrator who shall be appointed by, and who shall report directly to, the Director. The Director shall delegate to the Administrator the authority to administer all functions under this chapter, except that any such delegation shall not relieve the Director of responsibility for the administration of such functions. The Administrator shall serve as principal adviser to the Director on Federal information policy.

§ 3504. Authority and functions of Director

(a) The Director shall develop and implement Federal information policies, principles, standards, and guidelines and shall provide direction and oversee the review and approval of information collection requests, the reduction of the paperwork burden, Federal statistical activities, records management activities, privacy of records, interagency sharing of information, and acquisition and use of automatic data processing telecommunications, and other technology for managing information resources. The authority under this section shall be exercised consistent with applicable law.

(b) The general information policy functions of the Director shall include—

(1) developing and implementing uniform and consistent information resources management policies and

overseeing the development of information management principles, standards, and guidelines and promoting their use;

(2) initiating and reviewing proposals for changes in legislation, regulations, and agency procedures to improve information practices, and informing the President and the Congress on the progress made therein;

(3) coordinating, through the review of budget proposals and as otherwise provided in this section, agency information practices;

(4) promoting, through the use of the Federal Information Locator System, the review of budget proposals and other methods, greater sharing of information by agencies;

(5) evaluating agency information management practices to determine their adequacy and efficiency, and to determine compliance of such practices with the policies, principles, standards, and guidelines promulgated by the Director; and

(6) overseeing planning for, and conduct of research with respect to, Federal collection, processing, storage, transmission, and use of information.

(c) The information collection request clearance and other paperwork control functions of the Director shall include—

(1) reviewing and approving information collection requests proposed by agencies;

(2) determining whether the collection of information by an agency is necessary for the proper performance of the functions of the agency, including whether the information will have practical utility for the agency;

(3) ensuring that all information collection requests—

(A) are inventoried, display a control number and, when appropriate, an expiration date;

(B) indicate the request is in accordance with the clearance requirements of section 3507; and

(C) contain a statement to inform the person receiving the request why the information is being collected, how it is to be used, and whether responses to the request are voluntary, required to obtain a benefit, or mandatory;

(4) designating as appropriate, in accordance with section 3509, a collection agency to obtain information for two or more agencies;

(5) setting goals for reduction of the burdens of Federal information collection requests;

(6) overseeing action on the recommendations of the Commission on Federal Paperwork; and

(7) designing and operating, in accordance with section 3511, the Federal Information Locator System.

(d) The statistical policy and coordination functions of the Director shall include—

(1) developing long range plans for the improved performance of Federal statistical activities and programs;

(2) coordinating, through the review of budget proposals and as otherwise provided in this section, the functions of the Federal Government with respect to gathering, interpreting, and disseminating statistics and statistical information;

(3) developing and implementing Government-wide policies, principles, standards, and guidelines concerning statistical collection procedures and methods, statistical data classifications, and statistical information presentation and dissemination; and

(4) evaluating statistical program performance and agency compliance with Government-wide policies, principles, standards, and guidelines.

(e) The records management functions of the Director shall include—

(1) providing advice and assistance to the Administrator of General Services in order to promote coordination in the administration of chapters 29, 31, and 33 of this title with the information policies, principles, standards, and guidelines established under this chapter;

(2) reviewing compliance by agencies with the requirements of chapters 29, 31, and 33 of this title and with regulations promulgated by the Administrator of General Services thereunder; and

(3) coordinating records management policies and programs with related information programs such as information collection, statistics, automatic data processing and telecommunications, and similar activities.

(f) The privacy functions of the Director shall include—

(1) developing and implementing policies, principles, standards, and guidelines on information disclosure and confidentiality, and on safeguarding the security of information collected or maintained by or on behalf of agencies;

(2) providing agencies with advice and guidance about information security, restriction, exchange, and disclosure; and

(3) monitoring compliance with section 552a of title 5, United States Code, and related information management laws.

(g) The Federal automatic data processing and telecommunications functions of the Director shall include—

(1) developing and implementing policies, principles, standards, and guidelines for automatic data processing and telecommunications functions and activities of the Federal Government, and overseeing the establishment of standards under section 111(f) of the Federal Property and Administrative Services Act of 1949;

(2) monitoring the effectiveness of, and compliance with, directives issued pursuant to sections 110 and 111 of such Act of 1949 and reviewing proposed determinations under section 111(g) of such Act;

(3) providing advice and guidance on the acquisition and use of automatic data processing and telecommunications equipment, and coordinating, through the review of budget proposals and other methods, agency proposals for acquisition and use of such equipment;

(4) promoting the use of automatic data processing and telecommunications equipment by the Federal Government to improve the effectiveness of the use and dissemination of data in the operation of Federal programs; and

(5) initiating and reviewing proposals for changes in legislation, regulations, and agency procedures to improve automatic data processing and telecommunications practices, and informing the President and the Congress of the progress made therein.

(h)(1) As soon as practicable, but no later than publication of a notice of proposed rulemaking in the *Federal Register*, each agency shall forward to the Director a copy of any proposed rule which contains a collection of information requirement and upon request, information necessary to make the determination required pursuant to this section.

(2) Within sixty days after the notice of proposed rulemaking is published in the *Federal Register,* the Director may file public comments pursuant to the standards set forth in section 3508 on the collection of information requirement contained in the proposed rule.

(3) When a final rule is published in the *Federal Register,* the agency shall explain how any collection of information requirement contained in the final rule responds to the comments, if any, filed by the Director or the public, or explain why it rejected those comments.

(4) The Director has no authority to disapprove any collection of information requirement specifically contained in an agency rule, if he has received notice and failed to comment on the rule within sixty days of the notice of proposed rulemaking.

(5) Nothing in this section prevents the Director, in his discretion—

(A) from disapproving any information collection request which was not specifically required by an agency rule;

(B) from disapproving any collection of information requirement contained in an agency rule, if the agency failed to comply with the requirements of paragraph (1) of this subsection; or

(C) from disapproving any collection of information requirement contained in a final agency rule, if the Director finds within sixty days of the publication of the final rule that the agency's response to his comments filed pursuant to paragraph (2) of this subsection was unreasonable.

(D) from disapproving any collection of information requirement where the Director determines that the agency has substantially modified in the final rule the collection of information requirement contained in the proposed rule where the agency has not given the Director the information required in paragraph (1), with respect to the modified collection of information requirement, at least sixty days before the issuance of the final rule.

(6) The Director shall make publicly available any decision to disapprove a collection of information requirement contained in an agency rule, together with the reasons for such decision.

(7) The authority of the Director under this subsection is subject to the provisions of section 3507(c).

(8) This subsection shall apply only when an agency publishes a notice of proposed rulemaking and requests public comments.

(9) There shall be no judicial review of any kind of the Director's decision to approve or not to act upon a collection of information requirement contained in an agency rule.

§ 3505. Assignment of tasks and deadlines

In carrying out the functions under this chapter, the director shall—

(1) upon enactment of this Act—

(A) set a goal to reduce the then existing burden of Federal collections of information by 15 per centum by October 1, 1982; and

(B) for the year following, set a goal to reduce the burden which existed upon enactment by an additional 10 per centum;

(2) within one year after the effective date of this Act—

(A) establish standards and requirements for agency audits of all major information systems and assign responsibility for conducting Government-wide or multiagency audits, except the Director shall not assign such responsibility for the audit of major information systems used for the conduct of criminal investigations or intelligence activities as defined in section 4–206 of Executive Order 12036, issued January 24, 1978, or successor orders, or for cryptologic activities that are communications security activities;

(B) establish the Federal Information Locator System;

(C) identify areas of duplication in information collection requests and develop a schedule and methods for eliminating duplication;

(D) develop a proposal to augment the Federal Information Locator System to include data profiles of major information holdings of agencies (used in the conduct of their operations) which are not otherwise required by this chapter to be included in the System; and

(E) identify initiatives which may achieve a 10 per centum reduction in the burden of Federal collections of information associated with the administration of Federal grant programs; and

(3) within two years after the effective date of this Act—

(A) establish a schedule and a management control system to ensure that practices and programs of information handling disciplines, including records management, are appropriately integrated with the information policies mandated by this chapter;

(B) identify initiatives to improve productivity in Federal operations using information processing technology;

(C) develop a program to (i) enforce Federal information processing standards, particularly software language standards, at all Federal installations; and (ii) revitalize the standards development program established pursuant to section 759(f)(2) of title 40, United States Code, separating it from peripheral technical assistance functions and directing it to the most productive areas;

(D) complete action on recommendations of the Commission on Federal Paperwork by implementing, implementing with modification or rejecting such recommendations including, where necessary, development of legislation to implement such recommendations;

(E) develop, in consultation with the Administrator of General Services, a five-year plan for meeting the automatic data processing and telecommunications needs of the Federal Government in accordance with the requirements of section 111 of the Federal Property and Administrative Services Act of 1949 (40 U.S.C. 759) and the purposes of this chapter; and

(F) submit to the President and the Congress legislative proposals to remove inconsistencies in laws and practices involving privacy, confidentiality, and disclosure of information.

§ 3506. Federal agency responsibilities

(a) Each agency shall be responsible for carrying out its information management activities in an efficient, effective, and economical manner, and for complying with the information policies, principles, standards, and guidelines prescribed by the Director.

(b) The head of each agency shall designate, within

three months after the effective date of this Act, a senior official or, in the case of military departments, and the Office of the Secretary of Defense, officials who report directly to such agency head to carry out the responsibilities of the agency under this chapter. If more than one official is appointed for the military departments the respective duties of the officials shall be clearly delineated.

(c) Each agency shall—

(1) systematically inventory its major information systems and periodically review its information management activities, including planning, budgeting, organizing, directing, training, promoting, controlling, and other managerial activities involving the collection, use, and dissemination of information;

(2) ensure its information systems do not overlap each other or duplicate the systems of other agencies;

(3) develop procedures for assessing the paperwork and reporting burden of proposed legislation affecting such agency;

(4) assign to the official designated under subsection (b) the responsibility for the conduct of and accountability for any acquisitions made pursuant to a delegation of authority under section 111 of the Federal Property and Administrative Services Act of 1949 (40 U.S.C. 759); and

(5) ensure that information collection requests required by law or to obtain a benefit, and submitted to nine or fewer persons, contain a statement to inform the person receiving the request that the request is not subject to the requirements of section 3507 of this chapter.

(d) The head of each agency shall establish such procedures as necessary to ensure the compliance of the agency with the requirements of the Federal Information Locator System, including necessary screening and compliance activities.

§ 3507. Public information collection activities — submission to Director; approval and delegation

(a) An agency shall not conduct or sponsor the collection of information unless, in advance of the adoption or revision of the request for collection of such information—

(1) the agency has taken actions, including consultation with the Director, to—

(A) eliminate, through the use of the Federal Information Locator System and other means, information collections which seek to obtain information available from another source within the Federal Government;

(B) reduce to the extent practicable and appropriate the burden on persons who will provide information to the agency; and

(C) formulate plans for tabulating the information in a manner which will enhance its usefulness to other agencies and to the public;

(2) the agency (A) has submitted to the Director the proposed information collection request, copies of pertinent regulations and other related materials as the Director may specify, and an explanation of actions taken to carry out paragraph (1) of this subsection, and (B) has prepared a notice to be published in the *Federal Register* stating that the agency has made such submission; and

(3) the Director has approved the proposed information collection request, or the period for review of information collection requests by the Director provided under subsection (b) has elapsed.

(b) The Director shall, within sixty days of receipt of a proposed information collection request, notify the agency involved of the decision to approve or disapprove the request and shall make such decisions publicly available. If the Director determines that a request submitted for review cannot be reviewed within sixty days, the Director may, after notice to the agency involved, extend the review period for an additional thirty days. If the Director does not notify the agency of an extension, denial, or approval within sixty days (or, if the Director has extended the review period for an additional thirty days and does not notify the agency of a denial or approval within the time of the extension), a control number shall be assigned without further delay, the approval may be inferred, and the agency may collect the information for not more than one year.

(c) Any disapproval by the Director, in whole or in part, of a proposed information collection request of an independent regulatory agency, or an exercise of authority under section 3504(h) or 3509 concerning such an agency, may be voided, if the agency by a majority vote of its members overrides the Director's disapproval or exercise of authority. The agency shall certify each override to the Director, shall explain the reasons for exercising the override authority. Where the override concerns an information collection request, the Director shall without further delay assign a control number to such request, and such override shall be valid for a period of three years.

(d) The Director may not approve an information collection request for a period in excess of three years.

(e) If the Director finds that a senior official of an agency designated pursuant to section 3506(b) is sufficiently independent of program responsibility to evaluate fairly whether proposed information collection requests should be approved and has sufficient resources to carry out this responsibility effectively, the Director may, by rule in accordance with the notice and comment provisions of chapter 5 of title 5, United States Code, delegate to such official the authority to approve proposed requests in specific program areas, for specific purposes, or for all agency purposes. A delegation by the Director under this section shall not preclude the Director from reviewing individual information collection requests if the Director determines that circumstances warrant such a review. The Director shall retain authority to revoke such delegations, both in general and with regard to any specific matter. In acting for the Director, any official to whom approval authority has been delegated under this section shall comply fully with the rules and regulations promulgated by the Director.

(f) An agency shall not engage in a collection of information without obtaining from the Director a control number to be displayed upon the information collection request.

(g) If an agency head determines a collection of information (1) is needed prior to the expiration of the sixty-day period for the review of information collection requests established pursuant to subsection (b), (2) is essential to the mission of the agency, and (3) the agency cannot reasonably comply with the provisions of this chapter within such sixty-day period because (A) public harm will result if normal clearance procedures are followed, or (B) an unanticipated event has occurred and the use of normal clearance procedures will prevent or disrupt the collection of information related to the event or will cause a statutory deadline to be missed, the agency head may request the Director to authorize such collection of information prior to expiration of such sixty-day period. The Director shall approve or disapprove any such authorization request within the time requested by the agency head and, if approved, shall assign the information collection request a control number. Any collection of information conducted pursuant to this subsection may be conducted without compliance with the provisions of this chapter for a maximum of ninety days after the date on which the Director received the request to authorize such collection.

§ 3508. Determination of necessity for information; hearing

Before approving a proposed information collection request, the Director shall determine whether the collection of information by an agency is necessary for the proper performance of the functions of the agency, including whether the information will have practical utility. Before making a determination the Director may give the agency and other interested persons an opportunity to be heard or to submit statements in writing. To the extent, if any, that the Director determines that the collection of information by an agency is unnecessary, for any reason, the agency may not engage in the collection of the information.

§ 3509. Designation of central collection agency

The Director may designate a central collection agency to obtain information for two or more agencies if the Director determines that the needs of such agencies for information will be adequately served by a single collection agency, and such sharing of data is not inconsistent with any applicable law. In such cases the Director shall prescribe (with reference to the collection of information) the duties and functions of the collection agency so designated and of the agencies for which it is to act as agent (including reimbursement for costs). While the designation is in effect, an agency covered by it may not obtain for itself information which it is the duty of the collection agency to obtain. The Director may modify the designation from time to time as circumstances require. The authority herein is subject to the provisions of section 3507(c) of this chapter.

§ 3510. Cooperation of agencies in making information available

(a) The Director may direct an agency to make available to another agency, or an agency may make available to another agency, information obtained pursuant to an information collection request if the disclosure is not inconsistent with any applicable law.

(b) If information obtained by an agency is released by that agency to another agency, all the provisions of law (including penalties which relate to the unlawful disclosure of information) apply to the officers and employees of the agency to which information is released to the same extent and in the same manner as the provisions apply to the officers and employees of the agency which originally obtained the information. The officers and employees of the agency to which the information is released, in addition, shall be subject to the same provisions of law, including penalties, relating to the unlawful disclosure of information as if the information had been collected directly by that agency.

§ 3511. Establishment and operation of Federal Information Locator System

(a) There is established in the Office of Information and Regulatory Affairs a Federal Information Locator System (hereafter in this section referred to as the System) which shall be composed of a directory of information resources, a data element dictionary, and an information referral service. The System shall serve as the authoritative register of all information collection requests.

(b) In designing and operating the System, the Director shall—

(1) design and operate an indexing system for the System;

(2) require the head of each agency to prepare in

a form specified by the Director, and to submit to the Director for inclusion in the System, a data profile for each information collection request of such agency;

(3) compare data profiles for proposed information collection requests against existing profiles in the System, and make available the results of such comparison to—

(A) agency officials who are planning new information collection activities; and

(B) on request, members of the general public; and

(4) ensure that no actual data, except descriptive data profiles necessary to identify duplicative data or to locate information, are contained within the System.

§ 3512. Public protection

Notwithstanding any other provision of law, no person shall be subject to any penalty for failing to maintain or provide information to any agency if the information collection request involved was made after December 31, 1981, and does not display a current control number assigned by the Director, or fails to state that such request is not subject to this chapter.

§ 3513. Director review of agency activities; reporting; agency response

(a) The Director shall, with the advice and assistance of the Administrator of General Services, selectively review, at least once every three years, the information management activities of each agency to ascertain their adequacy and efficiency. In evaluating the adequacy and efficiency of such activities, the Director shall pay particular attention to whether the agency has complied with section 3506.

(b) The Director shall report the results of the reviews to the appropriate agency head, the House Committee on Government Operations, the Senate Committee on Governmental Affairs, the House and Senate Committees on Appropriations, and the committees of the Congress having jurisdiction over legislation relating to the operations of the agency involved.

(c) Each agency which receives a report pursuant to subsection (b) shall, within sixty days after receipt of such report, prepare and transmit to the Director, the House Committee on Government Operations, the Senate Committee on Governmental Affairs, the House and Senate Committees on Appropriations, and the committees of the Congress having jurisdiction over legislation relating to the operations of the agency, a written statement responding to the Director's report, including a description of any measures taken to alleviate or remove any problems or deficiencies identified in such report.

§ 3514. Responsiveness to Congress

(a) The Director shall keep the Congress and its committees fully and currently informed of the major activities under this chapter, and shall submit a report thereon to the President of the Senate and the Speaker of the House of Representatives annually and at such other times as the Director determines necessary. The Director shall include in any such report—

(1) proposals for legislative action needed to improve Federal information management, including, with respect to information collection, recommendations to reduce the burden on individuals, small businesses, State and local governments, and other persons;

(2) a compilation of legislative impediments to the collection of information which the Director concludes that an agency needs but does not have authority to collect;

(3) an analysis by agency, and by categories the Director finds useful and practicable, describing the estimated reporting hours required of persons by information collection requests, including to the extent practicable the direct budgetary costs of the agencies and identification of statutes and regulations which impose the greatest number of reporting hours;

(4) a summary of accomplishments and planned initiatives to reduce burdens of Federal information collection requests;

(5) a tabulation of areas of duplication in agency information collection requests identified during the preceding year and efforts made to preclude the collection of duplicate information, including designations of central collection agencies;

(6) a list of each instance in which an agency engaged in the collection of information under the authority of section 3507(g) and an identification of each agency involved;

(7) a list of all violations of provisions of this chapter and rules, regulations, guidelines, policies, and procedures issued pursuant to this chapter; and

(8) with respect to recommendations of the Commission on Federal Paperwork—

(A) a description of the specific actions taken on or planned for each recommendation;

(B) a target date for implementing each recommendation accepted but not implemented; and

(C) an explanation of the reasons for any delay in completing action on such recommendations.

(b) The preparation of any report required by this section shall not increase the collection of information burden on persons outside the Federal Government.

§ 3515. Administrative powers

Upon the request of the Director, each agency (other than an independent regulatory agency) shall, to the extent practicable, make its services, personnel, and facilities available to the Director for the performance of functions under this chapter.

§ 3516. Rules and regulations

The Director shall promulgate rules, regulations, or procedures necessary to exercise the authority provided by this chapter.

§ 3517. Consultation with other agencies and the public

In development of information policies, plans, rules, regulations, procedures, and guidelines and in reviewing information collection requests, the Director shall provide interested agencies and persons early and meaningful opportunity to comment.

§ 3518. Effect on existing laws and regulations

(a) Except as otherwise provided in this chapter, the authority of an agency under any other law to prescribe policies, rules, regulations, and procedures for Federal information activities is subject to the authority conferred on the Director by this chapter.

(b) Nothing in this chapter shall be deemed to affect or reduce the authority of the Secretary of Commerce or the Director of the Office of Management and Budget pursuant to Reorganization Plan No. 1 of 1977 (as amended) and Executive order, relating to telecommunications and information policy, procurement and management of telecommunications and information systems, spectrum use, and related matters.

(c)(1) Except as provided in paragraph (2), this chapter does not apply to the collection of information—

(A) during the conduct of a Federal criminal investigation or prosecution, or during the disposition of a particular criminal matter;

(B) during the conduct of (i) a civil action to which the United States or any official or agency thereof is a party or (ii) an administrative action or investigation involving an agency against specific individuals or entities;

(C) by compulsory process pursuant to the Antitrust Civil Process Act and section 13 of the Federal Trade Commission Improvements Act of 1980; or

(D) during the conduct of intelligence activities as defined in section 4–206 of Executive Order 12036, issued January 24, 1978, or successor orders, or during the conduct of cryptologic activities that are communications security activities.

(2) This chapter applies to the collection of information during the conduct of general investigations (other than information collected in an antitrust investigation to the extent provided in subparagraph (C) of paragraph (1)) undertaken with reference to a category of individuals or entities such as a class of licensees or an entire industry.

(d) Nothing in this chapter shall be interpreted as increasing or decreasing the authority conferred by Public Law 89–306 on the Administrator of the General Services Administration, the Secretary of Commerce, or the Director of the Office of Management and Budget.

(e) Nothing in this chapter shall be interpreted as increasing or decreasing the authority of the President, the Office of Management and Budget or the Director thereof, under the laws of the United States, with respect to the substantive policies and programs of departments, agencies and offices, including the substantive authority of any Federal agency to enforce the civil rights laws.

§ 3519. Access to information

Under the conditions and procedures prescribed in section 313 of the Budget and Accounting Act of 1921, as amended, the Director and personnel in the Office of Information and Regulatory Affairs shall furnish such information as the Comptroller General may require for the discharge of his responsibilities. For this purpose, the Comptroller General or representatives thereof shall have access to all books, documents, papers and records of the Office.

§ 3520. Authorization of appropriations

There are hereby authorized to be appropriated to carry out the provisions of this chapter, and for no other purpose, sums—

(1) not to exceed $8,000,000 for the fiscal year ending September 30, 1981;

(2) not to exceed $8,500,000 for the fiscal year ending September 30, 1982; and

(3) not to exceed $9,000,000 for the fiscal year ending September 30, 1983.

(b) The item relating to chapter 35 in the table of chapters for such title is amended to read as follows:
"35. Coordination of Federal Information Policy."

(c)(1) Section 2904(10) of such title is amended to read as follows:

"(10) report to the appropriate oversight and appropriations committees of the Congress and to the Director of the Office of Management and Budget annually and at such other times as the Administrator deems desirable (A) on the results of activities conducted pursuant to paragraphs (1) through (9) of this section, (B) on evaluations of responses by Federal agencies to any recommendations resulting from inspections or studies conducted under paragraphs (8) and (9) of this section, and (C) to the extent practicable, estimates of costs to the Federal Government resulting from the failure of agencies to implement such recommendations."

(2) Section 2905 of such title is amended by redesignating the text thereof as subsection (a) and by adding at the end of such section the following new subsection: "(b) The Administrator of General Services shall assist the Administrator for the Office of Information and Regulatory Affairs in conducting studies and developing standards relating to record retention requirements imposed on the public and on State and local governments by Federal agencies."

SEC. 3. (a) The President and the Director of the Office of Management and Budget shall delegate to the Administrator for the Office of Information and Regulatory Affairs all functions, authority, and responsibility under section 103 of the Budget and Accounting Procedures Act of 1950 (31 U.S.C. 18b).

(b) The Director of the Office of Management and Budget shall delegate to the Administrator for the Office of Information and Regulatory Affairs all functions, authority, and responsibility of the Director under section 552a of title 5, United States Code, under Executive Order 12046 and Reorganization Plan No. 1 for telecommunications, and under section 111 of the Federal Property and Administrative Services Act of 1949 (40 U.S.C. 759).

SEC. 4. (a) Section 400A of the General Education Provisions Act is amended by (1) striking out "and" after "institutions" in subsection (a)(1)(A) and inserting in lieu thereof "or," and (2) by amending subsection (a)(3)(B) to read as follows:

"(B) No collection of information or data acquisition activity subject to such procedures shall be subject to any other review, coordination, or approval procedure outside of the relevant Federal agency, except as required by this subsection and by the Director of the Office of Management and Budget under the rules and regulations established pursuant to chapter 35 of title 44, United States Code. If a requirement for information is submitted pursuant to this Act for review, the timetable for the Director's approval established in section 3507 of the Paperwork Reduction Act of 1980 shall commence on the date the request is submitted, and no independent submission to the Director shall be required under such Act."

(b) Section 201(e) of the Surface Mining Control and Reclamation Act of 1977 (30 U.S.C. 1211) is repealed.

(c) Section 708(f) of the Public Health Service Act (42 U.S.C. 292h(f)) is repealed.

(d) Section 5315 of title 5, United States Code, is amended by adding at the end thereof the following:

"Administrator, Office of Information and Regulatory Affairs, Office of Management and Budget."

SEC. 5. This Act shall take effect on April 1, 1981.

Approved December 11, 1980.

Privacy Act

While the Freedom of Information Act was designed to provide the public access to agency documents and proceedings, the 1974 Privacy Act (P.L. 93–579) was designed to give individuals an opportunity to find out what files the government has about them and to challenge, correct, or amend the material. In addition, provisions of the act were designed to protect individual privacy by preventing a person from looking at records involving another individual.

Major provisions of the Privacy Act:

- Permitted an individual access to personal information contained in federal agency files and to correct or amend the information.
- Prevented an agency maintaining a file on an individual from using it or making it available to another agency for a second purpose without the individual's consent.
- Required agencies to maintain records that were necessary and lawful as well as current and accurate and to disclose the existence of all data banks and files they maintain containing information on individuals.
- Prohibited agencies from keeping records that described an individual's exercise of First Amendment rights unless the records were authorized by statute or approved by the individual or were within the scope of an official law enforcement activity.
- Permitted an individual to seek injunctive relief to correct or amend a record maintained by an agency and permitted the individual to recover actual damages when an agency acted in a negligent manner that was "willful or intentional."
- Provided that an officer or employee of an agency who willfully violated provisions of the act should be subject to a fine of not more than $5,000.

- Exempted from disclosure provisions: records maintained by the Central Intelligence Agency; records maintained by law enforcement agencies; Secret Service records; statistical information; names of persons providing material used for determining the qualification of an individual for federal government service; federal testing material; and National Archives historical records.
- Prohibited an agency from selling or renting an individual's name or address for mailing list use.
- Required agencies to submit to Congress and to the Office of Management and Budget any plan to establish or alter any system of records.
- Required the president to submit to Congress by June 30 each year a report on the number of records exempted by each federal agency and the reasons for the exemptions.
- Established a privacy protection study commission composed of seven members to provide Congress and the president information about problems related to privacy in the public and private sectors.
- Made it illegal for any federal, state or local agency to deny an individual any benefit provided by law because he refused to disclose his Social Security account number to the agency. (The provision did not apply to disclosure required by federal statute or to government agencies requiring disclosure of the number before Jan. 1, 1975.)

Following the terrorist attacks of September 11, 2001, Congress enacted two laws that affected privacy issues: the USA Patriot Act (and the Homeland Security Act of 2002. The USA Patriot Act amended the federal criminal code to authorize the interception of wire, oral, and electronic communications for the production of evidence of specified chemical weapons or terrorism offenses and computer fraud and abuse. The act also amended the Foreign

Intelligence Surveillance Act of 1978 (FISA) to require an application for an electronic surveillance order or search warrant to certify that a significant purpose (formerly, the sole or main purpose) of the surveillance was to obtain foreign intelligence information.

The Homeland Security Act of 2002, which established the Homeland Security Department (HSD), exempted from criminal penalties any disclosure made by an electronic communication service to a federal, state, or local governmental entity if made in the good faith belief that an emergency involving danger of death or serious physical injury to any person required disclosure without delay. It also required any government entity receiving such a disclosure to report it to the U.S. attorney general. The act directed the secretary to appoint a senior department official to assume primary responsibility for information privacy policy.

All executive branch agencies have developed their own regulations and procedures for handling the act (consult the *Code of Federal Regulations* under "Privacy Act"), and each agency publishes its procedures for appeal following the denial of a request.

The following is the text of the Privacy Act as it appears in the U.S. Code, Title 5, Chapter 5, Subchapter II, section 552a.

§ 552a. Records maintained on individuals

(a) Definitions

For purposes of this section—

(1) the term "agency" means agency as defined in section 552(e) of this title;

(2) the term "individual" means a citizen of the United States or an alien lawfully admitted for permanent residence;

(3) the term "maintain" includes maintain, collect, use, or disseminate;

(4) the term "record" means any item, collection, or grouping of information about an individual that is maintained by an agency, including, but not limited to, his education, financial transactions, medical history, and criminal or employment history and that contains his name, or the identifying number, symbol, or other identifying particular assigned to the individual, such as a finger or voice print or photograph;

(5) the term "system of records" means a group of any records under the control of any agency from which information is retrieved by the name of the individual or by some identifying number, symbol, or other identifying particular assigned to the individual;

(6) the term "statistical record" means a record in a system of records maintained for statistical research or reporting purposes only and not used in whole or in part in making any determination about an identifiable individual, except as provided by section 8 of title 13; and

(7) the term "routine use" means, with respect to the disclosure of a record, the use of such record for a purpose which is compatible with the purpose for which it was collected.

(b) Conditions of disclosure

No agency shall disclose any record which is contained in a system of records by any means of communication to any person, or to another agency, except pursuant to a written request by, or with the prior written consent of, the individual to whom the record pertains, unless disclosure of the record would be—

(1) to those officers and employees of the agency which maintains the record who have a need for the record in the performance of their duties;

(2) required under section 552 of this title;

(3) for a routine use as defined in subsection (a)(7) of this section and described under subsection (e)(4)(D) of this section;

(4) to the Bureau of the Census for purposes of planning or carrying out a census or survey or related activity pursuant to the provisions of title 13;

(5) to a recipient who has provided the agency with advance adequate written assurance that the record will be used solely as a statistical research or reporting record, and the record is to be transferred in a form that is not individually identifiable;

(6) to the National Archives of the United States as a record which has sufficient historical or other value to warrant its continued preservation by the United States Government, or for evaluation by the Administrator of General Services or his designee to determine whether the record has such value;

(7) to another agency or to an instrumentality of any governmental jurisdiction within or under the control of the United States for a civil or criminal law enforcement activity if the activity is authorized by law, and if the head of the agency or instrumentality has made a written request to the agency which maintains the record specifying the particular portion desired and the law enforcement activity for which the record is sought;

(8) to a person pursuant to a showing of compelling circumstances affecting the health or safety of an individual if upon such disclosure notification is transmitted to the last known address of such individual;

(9) to either House of Congress, or, to the extent of matter within its jurisdiction, any committee or subcommittee thereof, any joint committee of Congress or subcommittee of any such joint committee;

(10) to the Comptroller General, or any of his authorized representatives, in the course of the performance of the duties of the General Accounting Office; or

(11) pursuant to the order of a court of competent jurisdiction.

(c) Accounting of certain disclosures

Each agency, with respect to each system of records under its control shall—

(1) except for disclosures made under subsections (b)(1) or (b)(2) of this section, keep an accurate accounting of—

(A) the date, nature, and purpose of each disclosure of a record to any person or to another agency made under subsection (b) of this section; and

(B) the name and address of the person or agency to whom the disclosure is made;

(2) retain the accounting made under paragraph (1) of this subsection for at least five years or the life of the record, whichever is longer, after the disclosure for which the accounting is made;

(3) except for disclosures made under subsection (b)(7) of this section, make the accounting made under paragraph (1) of this subsection available to the individual named in the record at his request; and

(4) inform any person or other agency about any correction or notation of dispute made by the agency in accordance with subsection (d) of this section of any record that has been disclosed to the person or agency if an accounting of the disclosure was made.

(d) Access to records

Each agency that maintains a system of records shall—

(1) upon request by any individual to gain access to his record or to any information pertaining to him which is contained in the system, permit him and upon his request, a person of his own choosing to accompany him, to review the record and have a copy made of all or any portion thereof in a form comprehensible to him, except that the agency may require the individual to furnish a written statement authorizing discussion of that individual's record in the accompanying person's presence;

(2) permit the individual to request amendment of a record pertaining to him and—

(A) not later than ten days (excluding Saturdays, Sundays, and legal public holidays) after the date of receipt of such request, acknowledge in writing such receipt; and

(B) promptly, either—

(i) make any correction of any portion thereof which the individual believes is not accurate, relevant, timely, or complete; or

(ii) inform the individual of its refusal to amend the record in accordance with his request, the reason for the refusal, the procedures established by the agency for the individual to request a review of that refusal by the head of the agency or an officer designated by the head of the agency, and the name and business address of that official;

(3) permit the individual who disagrees with the refusal of the agency to amend his record to request a review of such refusal, and not later than thirty days (excluding Saturdays, Sundays, and legal public holidays) from the date on which the individual requests such review, complete such review and make a final determination unless, for good cause shown, the head of the agency extends such thirty-day period; and if, after his review, the reviewing official also refuses to amend the record in accordance with the request, permit the individual to file with the agency a concise statement setting forth the reasons for his disagreement with the refusal of the agency, and notify the individual of the provisions for judicial review of the reviewing official's determination under subsection (g)(1)(A) of this section:

(4) in any disclosure, containing information about which the individual has filed a statement of disagreement, occurring after the filing of the statement under paragraph (3) of this subsection, clearly note any portion of the record which is disputed and provide copies of the statement and, if the agency deems it appropriate, copies of a concise statement of the reasons of the agency for not making the amendments requested, to persons or other agencies to whom the disputed record has been disclosed; and

(5) nothing in this section shall allow an individual access to any information compiled in reasonable anticipation of a civil action or proceeding.

(e) Agency requirements

Each agency that maintains a system of records shall—

(1) maintain in its records only such information about an individual as is relevant and necessary to accomplish a purpose of the agency required to be accomplished by statute or by executive order of the President;

(2) collect information to the greatest extent practicable directly from the subject individual when the information may result in adverse determinations about an individual's rights, benefits, and privileges under Federal programs;

(3) inform each individual whom it asks to supply information, on the form which it uses to collect the information or on a separate form that can be retained by the individual—

(A) the authority (whether granted by statute, or by executive order of the President) which authorizes the solicitation of the information and whether disclosure of such information is mandatory or voluntary;

(B) the principal purpose or purposes for which the information is intended to be used;

(C) the routine uses which may be made of the information, as published pursuant to paragraph (4)(D) of this subsection; and

(D) the effects on him, if any, of not providing all or any part of the requested information;

(4) subject to the provisions of paragraph (11) of this subsection, publish in the *Federal Register* at least annually a notice of the existence and character of the system of records, which notice shall include—

(A) the name and location of the system;

(B) the categories of individuals on whom records are maintained in the system;

(C) the categories of records maintained in the system;

(D) each routine use of the records contained in the system, including the categories of users and the purpose of such use;

(E) the policies and practices of the agency regarding storage, retrievability, access controls, retention, and disposal of the records;

(F) the title and business address of the agency official who is responsible for the system of records;

(G) the agency procedures whereby an individual can be notified at his request if the system of records contains a record pertaining to him;

(H) the agency procedures whereby an individual can be notified at his request how he can gain access to any record pertaining to him contained in the system of records, and how he can contest its content; and

(I) the categories of sources of records in the system;

(5) maintain all records which are used by the agency in making any determination about any individual with such accuracy, relevance, timeliness, and completeness as is reasonably necessary to assure fairness to the individual in the determination;

(6) prior to disseminating any record about an individual to any person other than an agency, unless the dissemination is made pursuant to subsection (b)(2) of this section, make reasonable efforts to assure that such records are accurate, complete, timely, and relevant for agency purposes;

(7) maintain no record describing how any individual exercises rights guaranteed by the First Amendment unless expressly authorized by statute or by the individual about whom the record is maintained or unless pertinent to and within the scope of an authorized law enforcement activity;

(8) make reasonable efforts to serve notice on an individual when any record on such individual is made available to any person under compulsory legal process when such process becomes a matter of public record;

(9) establish rules of conduct for persons involved in the design, development, operation, or maintenance of any system of records, or in maintaining any record, and instruct each such person with respect to such rules and the requirements of this section, including any other rules and procedures adopted pursuant to this section and the penalties for noncompliance;

(10) establish appropriate administrative, technical, and physical safeguards to insure the security and confidentiality of records and to protect against any anticipated threats or hazards to their security or integrity which could result in substantial harm, embarrassment, inconvenience, or unfairness to any individual on whom information is maintained; and

(11) at least thirty days prior to publication of information under paragraph (4)(D) of this subsection, publish in the *Federal Register* notice of any new use or intended use of the information in the system, and provide an opportunity for interested persons to submit written data, views, or arguments to the agency.

(f) Agency rules

In order to carry out the provisions of this section, each agency that maintains a system of records shall promulgate rules, in accordance with the requirements (including general notice) of section 553 of this title, which shall—

(1) establish procedures whereby an individual can be notified in response to his request if any system of records named by the individual contains a record pertaining to him;

(2) define reasonable times, places, and requirements for identifying an individual who requests his record or information pertaining to him before the agency shall make the record or information available to the individual;

(3) establish procedures for the disclosure to an individual upon his request of his record or information pertaining to him, including special procedure, if deemed necessary, for the disclosure to an individual of medical records, including psychological records pertaining to him;

(4) establish procedures for reviewing a request from an individual concerning the amendment of any record or information pertaining to the individual, for making a determination on the request, for an appeal within the agency of an initial adverse agency determination, and for whatever additional means may be necessary for each

individual to be able to exercise fully his rights under this section; and

(5) establish fees to be charged, if any, to any individual for making copies of his record, excluding the cost of any search for and review of the record.

The Office of the *Federal Register* shall annually compile and publish the rules promulgated under this subsection and agency notices published under subsection (e)(4) of this section in a form available to the public at low cost.

(g)(1) Civil remedies

Whenever any agency

(A) makes a determination under subsection (d)(3) of this section not to amend an individual's record in accordance with his request, or fails to make such review in conformity with that subsection;

(B) refuses to comply with an individual request under subsection (d)(1) of this section;

(C) fails to maintain any record concerning any individual with such accuracy, relevance, timeliness, and completeness as is necessary to assure fairness in any determination relating to the qualifications, character, rights, or opportunities of, or benefits to the individual that may be made on the basis of such record, and consequently a determination is made which is adverse to the individual; or

(D) fails to comply with any other provision of this section, or any rule promulgated thereunder, in such a way as to have an adverse effect on an individual, the individual may bring a civil action against the agency, and the district courts of the United States shall have jurisdiction in the matters under the provisions of this subsection.

(2)(A) In any suit brought under the provisions of subsection (g)(1)(A) of this section, the court may order the agency to amend the individual's record in accordance with his request or in such other way as the court may direct. In such a case the court shall determine the matter de novo.

(B) The court may assess against the United States reasonable attorney fees and other litigation costs reasonably incurred in any case under this paragraph in which the complainant has substantially prevailed.

(3)(A) In any suit brought under the provisions of subsection (g)(1)(B) of this section, the court may enjoin the agency from withholding the records and order the production to the complainant of any agency records improperly withheld from him. In such a case the court shall determine the matter de novo, and may examine the contents of any agency records in camera to determine whether the records or any portion thereof may be withheld under any of the exemptions set forth in subsection (k) of this section, and the burden is on the agency to sustain its action.

(B) The court may assess against the United States reasonable attorney fees and other litigation costs reasonably incurred in any case under this paragraph in which the complainant has substantially prevailed.

(4) In any suit brought under the provisions of subsection (g)(1)(C) or (D) of this section in which the court determines that the agency acted in a manner which was intentional or willful, the United States shall be liable to the individual in an amount equal to the sum of—

(A) actual damages sustained by the individual as a result of the refusal or failure, but in no case shall a person entitled to recovery receive less than the sum of $1,000; and

(B) the costs of the action together with reasonable attorney fees as determined by the court.

(5) An action to enforce any liability created under this section may be brought in the district court of the United States in the district in which the complainant resides, or has his principal place of business, or in which the agency records are situated, or in the District of Columbia, without regard to the amount in controversy, within two years from the date on which the cause of action arises, except that where an agency has materially and willfully misrepresented any information required under this section to be disclosed to an individual and the information so misrepresented is material to establishment of the liability of the agency to the individual under this section, the action may be brought at any time within two years after discovery by the individual of the misrepresentation. Nothing in this section shall be construed to authorize any civil action by reason of any injury sustained as the result of a disclosure of a record prior to September 27, 1975.

(h) Rights of legal guardians

For the purposes of this section, the parent of any minor, or the legal guardian of any individual who has been declared to be incompetent due to physical or mental incapacity or age by a court of competent jurisdiction, may act on behalf of the individual.

(i)(1) Criminal penalties

Any officer or employee of an agency, who by virtue of his employment or official position, has possession of, or access to, agency records which contain individually identifiable information the disclosure of which is prohibited by this section or by rules or regulations established thereunder, and who knowing that disclosure of the specific material is so prohibited, willfully discloses the material in any manner to any person or agency not entitled to receive it, shall be guilty of a misdemeanor and fined not more than $5,000.

(2) Any officer or employee of any agency who willfully maintains a system of records without meeting the

notice requirements of subsection (e)(4) of this section shall be guilty of a misdemeanor and fined not more than $5,000.

(3) Any person who knowingly and willfully requests or obtains any record concerning an individual from an agency under false pretenses shall be guilty of a misdemeanor and fined not more than $5,000.

(j) General exemptions

The head of any agency may promulgate rules, in accordance with the requirements (including general notice) of sections 553(b)(1), (2), and (3), (c), and (e) of this title, to exempt any system of records within the agency from any part of this section except subsections (b), (c)(1) and (2), (e)(4)(A) through (F), (e)(6), (7), (9), (10), and (11), and (i) if the system of records is—

(1) maintained by the Central Intelligence Agency; or

(2) maintained by an agency or component thereof which performs as its principal function any activity pertaining to the enforcement of criminal laws, including police efforts to prevent, control, or reduce crime or to apprehend criminals, and the activities of prosecutors, courts, correctional, probation, pardon, or parole authorities, and which consists of (A) information compiled for the purpose of identifying individual criminal offenders and alleged offenders and consisting only of identifying data and notations of arrests, the nature and disposition of criminal charges, sentencing, confinement, release, and parole and probation status; (B) information compiled for the purpose of a criminal investigation, including reports of informants and investigators, and associated with an identifiable individual; or (C) reports identifiable to an individual compiled at any stage of the process of enforcement of the criminal laws from arrest or indictment through release from supervision.

At the time rules are adopted under this subsection, the agency shall include in the statement required under section 553(c) of this title, the reasons why the system of records is to be exempted from a provision of this section.

(k) Specific exemptions

The head of any agency may promulgate rules, in accordance with the requirement (including general notice) of sections 553(b)(1), (2), and (3), (c), and (e) of this title, to exempt any system of records within the agency from subsections (c)(3), (d), (e)(1), (e)(4)(G), (H), and (I) and (f) of this section if the system of records is—

(1) subject to the provisions of section 552(b)(1) of this title;

(2) investigatory material compiled for law enforcement purposes, other than material within the scope of subsection (j)(2) of this section: *Provided, however,* That

if any individual is denied any right, privilege, or benefit that he would otherwise be entitled by Federal law, or for which he would otherwise be eligible, as a result of the maintenance of such material, such material shall be provided to such individual, except to the extent that the disclosure of such material would reveal the identity of a source who furnished information to the Government under an express promise that the identity of the source would be held in confidence, or, prior to the effective date of this section, under an implied promise that the identity of the source would be held in confidence;

(3) maintained in connection with providing protective services to the President of the United States or other individuals pursuant to section 3056 of title 18;

(4) required by statute to be maintained and used solely as statistical records;

(5) investigatory material compiled solely for the purpose of determining suitability, eligibility, or qualifications for Federal civilian employment, military service, Federal contracts, or access to classified information, but only to the extent that the disclosure of such material would reveal the identity of a source who furnished information to the Government under an express promise that the identity of the source would be held in confidence, or, prior to the effective date of this section, under an implied promise that the identity of the source would be held in confidence;

(6) testing or examination material used solely to determine individual qualifications for appointment or promotion in the Federal service the disclosure of which would compromise the objectivity or fairness of the testing or examination process; or

(7) evaluation material used to determine potential for promotion in the armed services, but only to the extent that the disclosure of such material would reveal the identity of a source who furnished information to the Government under an express promise that the identity of the source would be held in confidence, or, prior to the effective date of this section, under an implied promise that the identity of the source would be held in confidence.

At the time rules are adopted under this subsection, the agency shall include in the statement required under section 553(c) of this title, the reasons why the system of records is to be exempted from a provision of this section.

(l)(1) Archival records

Each agency record which is accepted by the Administrator of General Services for storage, processing, and servicing in accordance with section 3103 of title 44 shall, for the purposes of this section, be considered to be maintained by the agency which deposited the record and shall be subject to the provisions of this section. The

Administrator of General Services shall not disclose the record except to the agency which maintains the record, or under rules established by that agency which are not inconsistent with the provisions of this section.

(2) Each agency record pertaining to an identifiable individual which was transferred to the National Archives of the United States as a record which has sufficient historical or other value to warrant its continued preservation by the United States Government, prior to the effective date of this section, shall, for the purposes of this section, be considered to be maintained by the National Archives and shall not be subject to the provisions of this section, except that a statement generally describing such records (modeled after the requirements relating to records subject to subsections (e)(4)(A) through (G) of this section) shall be published in the *Federal Register.*

(3) Each agency record pertaining to an identifiable individual which is transferred to the National Archives of the United States as a record which has sufficient historical or other value to warrant its continued preservation by the United States Government, on or after the effective date of this section, be considered to be maintained by the National Archives and shall be exempt from the requirements of this section except subsections (e)(4)(A) through (G) and (e)(9) of this section.

(m) Government contractors

When an agency provides by a contract for the operation by or on behalf of the agency of a system of records to accomplish an agency function, the agency shall, consistent with its authority, cause the requirements of this section to be applied to such system. For purposes of subsection (i) of this section any such contractor and any employee of such contractor, if such contract is agreed to on or after the effective date of this section, shall be considered to be an employee of an agency.

(n) Mailing lists

An individual's name and address may not be sold or rented by an agency unless such action is specifically authorized by law. This provision shall not be construed to require the withholding of names and addresses otherwise permitted to be made public.

(o) Report on new systems

Each agency shall provide adequate advance notice to Congress and the Office of Management and Budget of any proposal to establish or alter any system of records in order to permit an evaluation of the probable or potential effect of such proposal on the privacy and other personal or property rights of individuals or the disclosure of information relating to such individuals, and its effect on the preservation of the constitutional principles of federalism and separation of powers.

(p) Annual report

The President shall submit to the Speaker of the House and the President of the Senate, by June 30 of each calendar year, a consolidated report, separately listing for each Federal agency the number of records contained in any system of records which were exempted from the application of this section under the provisions of subsections (j) and (k) of this section during the preceding calendar year, and the reasons for the exemptions, and such other information as indicates efforts to administer fully this section.

(q) Effect of other laws

No agency shall rely on any exemption contained in section 552 of this title to withhold from an individual any record which is otherwise accessible to such individual under the provisions of this section.

Executive Orders

▪ EXECUTIVE ORDER 12044

(Revoked February 17, 1981)

Improving Government Regulations

As President of the United States of America, I direct each Executive Agency to adopt procedures to improve existing and future regulations.

Section 1. *Policy.* Regulations shall be as simple and clear as possible. They shall achieve legislative goals effectively and efficiently. They shall not impose unnecessary burdens on the economy, on individuals, on public or private organizations, or on State and local governments.

To achieve these objectives, regulations shall be developed through a process which ensures that:

(a) the need for and purposes of the regulation are clearly established;

(b) heads of agencies and policy officials exercise effective oversight;

(c) opportunity exists for early participation and comment by other Federal agencies, State and local governments, businesses, organizations and individual members of the public;

(d) meaningful alternatives are considered and analyzed before the regulation is issued; and

(e) compliance costs, paperwork and other burdens on the public are minimized.

Sec. 2. *Reform of the Process for Developing Significant Regulations.* Agencies shall review and revise their procedures for developing regulations to be consistent with the policies of this Order and in a manner that minimizes paperwork.

Agencies' procedures should fit their own needs but, at a minimum, these procedures shall include the following:

(a) *Semiannual Agenda of Regulations.* To give the public adequate notice, agencies shall publish at least semiannually an agenda of significant regulations under development or review. On the first Monday in October, each agency shall publish in the *Federal Register* a schedule showing the times during the coming fiscal year when the agency's semiannual agenda will be published. Supplements to the agenda may be published at other times during the year if necessary, but the semiannual agendas shall be as complete as possible. The head of each agency shall approve the agenda before it is published.

At a minimum, each published agenda shall describe the regulations being considered by the agency, the need for and the legal basis for the action being taken, and the status of regulations previously listed on the agenda.

Each item on the agenda shall also include the name and telephone number of a knowledgeable agency official and, if possible, state whether or not a regulatory analysis will be required. The agenda shall also include existing regulations scheduled to be reviewed in accordance with Section 4 of this Order.

(b) *Agency Head Oversight.* Before an agency proceeds to develop significant new regulations, the agency head shall have reviewed the issues to be considered, the alternative approaches to be explored, a tentative plan for obtaining public comment, and target dates for completion of steps in the development of the regulation.

(c) *Opportunity for Public Participation.* Agencies shall give the public an early and meaningful opportunity to participate in the development of agency regulations. They shall consider a variety of ways to provide this opportunity, including (1) publishing an advance notice of proposed rulemaking; (2) holding open conferences or public hearings; (3) sending notices of proposed regulations to publications likely to be read by those affected; and (4) notifying interested parties directly.

Agencies shall give the public at least 60 days to comment on proposed significant regulations. In the few instances where agencies determine this is not possible, the regulation shall be accompanied by a brief statement of the reasons for a shorter time period.

(d) *Approval of Significant Regulations.* The head of each agency, or the designated official with statutory responsibility, shall approve significant regulations before they are published for public comment in the *Federal Register.* At a minimum, this official should determine that:

(1) the proposed regulation is needed;

(2) the direct and indirect effects of the regulation have been adequately considered;

(3) alternative approaches have been considered and the least burdensome of the acceptable alternatives has been chosen;

(4) public comments have been considered and an adequate response has been prepared;

(5) the regulation is written in plain English and is understandable to those who must comply with it;

(6) an estimate has been made of the new reporting burdens or recordkeeping requirements necessary for compliance with the regulation;

(7) the name, address and telephone number of a knowledgeable agency official is included in the publication; and

(8) a plan for evaluating the regulation after its issuance has been developed.

(e) *Criteria for Determining Significant Regulations.* Agencies shall establish criteria for identifying which regulations are significant. Agencies shall consider among other things: (1) the type and number of individuals, businesses, organizations, State and local governments affected; (2) the compliance and reporting requirements likely to be involved; (3) direct and indirect effects of the regulation including the effect on competition; and (4) the relationship of the regulations to those of other programs and agencies. Regulations that do not meet an agency's criteria for determining significance shall be accompanied by a statement to that effect at the time the regulation is proposed.

Sec. 3. *Regulatory Analysis.* Some of the regulations identified as significant may have major economic consequences for the general economy, for individual industries, geographical regions or levels of government. For these regulations, agencies shall prepare a regulatory analysis. Such an analysis shall involve a careful examination of alternative approaches early in the decision-making process.

The following requirements shall govern the preparation of regulatory analyses:

(a) *Criteria.* Agency heads shall establish criteria for determining which regulations require regulatory analyses. The criteria established shall:

(1) ensure that regulatory analyses are performed for all regulations which will result in (a) an annual effect on the economy of $100 million or more; or (b) a major increase in costs or prices for individual industries, levels of government or geographic regions; and

(2) provide that in the agency head's discretion, regulatory analysis may be completed on any proposed regulation.

(b) *Procedures.* Agency heads shall establish procedures for developing the regulatory analysis and obtaining public comment.

(1) Each regulatory analysis shall contain a succinct statement of the problem; a description of the major alternative ways of dealing with the problems that were considered by the agency; an analysis of the economic consequences of each of these alternatives and a detailed explanation of the reasons for choosing one alternative over the others.

(2) Agencies shall include in their public notice of proposed rules an explanation of the regulatory approach that has been selected or is favored and a short description of the other alternatives considered. A statement of how the public may obtain a copy of the draft regulatory analysis shall also be included.

(3) Agencies shall prepare a final regulatory analysis to be made available when the final regulations are published.

Regulatory analyses shall not be required in rulemaking proceedings pending at the time this Order is issued if an Economic Impact Statement has already been prepared in accordance with Executive Orders 11821 and 11949.

Sec. 4. *Review of Existing Regulations.* Agencies shall periodically review their existing regulations to determine whether they are achieving the policy goals of this Order. This review will follow the same procedural steps outlined for the development of new regulations.

In selecting regulations to be reviewed, agencies shall consider such criteria as:

(a) the continued need for the regulation;

(b) the type and number of complaints or suggestions received;

(c) the burdens imposed on those directly or indirectly affected by the regulations;

(d) the need to simplify or clarify language;

(e) the need to eliminate overlapping and duplicative regulations; and

(f) the length of time since the regulation has been

evaluated or the degree to which technology, economic conditions or other factors have changed in the area affected by the regulation.

Agencies shall develop their selection criteria and a listing of possible regulations for initial review. The criteria and listing shall be published for comment as required in Section 5. Subsequently, regulations selected for review shall be included in the semiannual agency agendas.

Sec. 5. *Implementation.*

(a) Each agency shall review its existing process for developing regulations and revise it as needed to comply with this Order. Within 60 days after the issuance of the Order, each agency shall prepare a draft report outlining (1) a brief description of its process for developing regulations and the changes that have been made to comply with this Order; (2) its proposed criteria for defining significant agency regulations; (3) its proposed criteria for identifying which regulations require regulatory analysis; and (4) its proposed criteria for selecting existing regulations to be reviewed and a list of regulations that the agency will consider for its initial review. This report shall be published in the *Federal Register* for public comment. A copy of this report shall be sent to the Office of Management and Budget.

(b) After receiving public comment, agencies shall submit their revised report to the Office of Management and Budget for approval before final publication in the *Federal Register.*

(c) The Office of Management and Budget shall assure the effective implementation of this Order. OMB shall report at least semiannually to the President on the effectiveness of the Order and agency compliance with its provisions. By May 1, 1980, OMB shall recommend to the President whether or not there is a continued need for the Order and any further steps or actions necessary to achieve its purpose.

Sec. 6. *Coverage.*

(a) As used in this Order, the term regulation means both rules and regulations issued by agencies including those which establish conditions for financial assistance. Closely related sets of regulations shall be considered together.

(b) This Order does not apply to:

(1) regulations issued in accordance with the formal rulemaking provisions of the Administrative Procedure Act (5 U.S.C. 556, 557);

(2) regulations issued with respect to a military or foreign affairs function of the United States;

(3) matters related to agency management or personnel;

(4) regulations related to Federal Government procurement;

(5) regulations issued by the independent regulatory agencies; or

(6) regulations that are issued in response to an emergency or which are governed by short-term statutory or judicial deadlines. In these cases, the agency shall publish in the *Federal Register* a statement of the reasons why it is impracticable or contrary to the public interest for the agency to follow the procedures of this Order. Such a statement shall include the name of the policy official responsible for this determination.

Sec. 7. This Order is intended to improve the quality of Executive Agency regulatory practices. It is not intended to create delay in the process or provide new grounds for judicial review. Nothing in this order shall be considered to supersede existing statutory obligations governing rulemaking.

Sec. 8. Unless extended, this Executive Order expires on June 30, 1980.

JIMMY CARTER

The White House,
March 23, 1978.

■ EXECUTIVE ORDER 12291
(Revoked September 30, 1993)

Federal Regulation

By the authority vested in me as President by the Constitution and laws of the United States of America, and in order to reduce the burdens of existing and future regulations, increase agency accountability for regulatory actions, provide for presidential over-sight of the regulatory process, minimize duplication and conflict of regulations, and insure well-reasoned regulations, it is hereby ordered as follows:

Section 1. *Definitions.* For the purposes of this Order:

(a) "Regulation" or "rule" means an agency statement of general applicability and future effect designed to implement, interpret, or prescribe law or policy or describing the procedure or practice requirements of an agency, but does not include:

(1) Administrative actions governed by the provisions of Sections 556 and 557 of Title 5 of the United States Code;

(2) Regulations issued with respect to a military or foreign affairs function of the United States; or

(3) Regulations related to agency organization, management, or personnel.

(b) "Major rule" means any regulation that is likely to result in:

(1) An annual effect on the economy of $100 million or more;

(2) A major increase in costs or prices for consumers, individual industries, Federal, State, or local government agencies, or geographic regions; or

(3) Significant adverse effects on competition, employment, investment, productivity, innovation, or on the ability of United States-based enterprises to compete with foreign-based enterprises in domestic or export markets.

(c) "Director" means the Director of the Office of Management and Budget.

(d) "Agency" means any authority of the United States that is an "agency" under 44 U.S.C. 3502(1), excluding those agencies specified in 44 U.S.C. 3502 (10).

(e) "Task Force" means the Presidential Task Force on Regulatory Relief.

Sec. 2. *General Requirements.* In promulgating new regulations, reviewing existing regulations, and developing legislative proposals concerning regulation, all agencies, to the extent permitted by law, shall adhere to the following requirements:

(a) Administrative decisions shall be based on adequate information concerning the need for and consequences of proposed government action;

(b) Regulatory action shall not be undertaken unless the potential benefits to society from the regulation outweigh the potential costs to society;

(c) Regulatory objectives shall be chosen to maximize the net benefits to society;

(d) Among alternative approaches to any given regulatory objective, the alternative involving the least net cost to society shall be chosen; and

(e) Agencies shall set regulatory priorities with the aim of maximizing the aggregate net benefits to society, taking into account the condition of the particular industries affected by regulations, the condition of the national economy, and other regulatory actions contemplated for the future.

Sec. 3. *Regulatory Impact Analysis and Review.*

(a) In order to implement Section 2 of this Order, each agency shall, in connection with every major rule, prepare, and to the extent permitted by law consider, a Regulatory Impact Analysis. Such Analyses may be combined with any Regulatory Flexibility Analyses performed under 5 U.S.C. 603 and 604.

(b) Each agency shall initially determine whether a rule it intends to propose or to issue is a major rule, *provided that,* the Director, subject to the direction of the Task Force, shall have authority, in accordance with Sections 1(b) and 2 of this Order, to prescribe criteria for making such determinations, to order a rule to be treated as a major rule, and to require any set of related rules to be considered together as a major rule.

(c) Except as provided in Section 8 of this Order, agencies shall prepare Regulatory Impact Analyses of major rules and transmit them, along with all notices of proposed rulemaking and all final rules, to the Director as follows:

(1) If no notice of proposed rulemaking is to be published for a proposed major rule that is not an emergency rule, the agency shall prepare only a final Regulatory Impact Analysis, which shall be transmitted, along with the proposed rule, to the Director at least 60 days prior to the publication of the major rule as a final rule;

(2) With respect to all other major rules, the agency shall prepare a preliminary Regulatory Impact Analysis, which shall be transmitted, along with a notice of proposed rulemaking, to the Director at least 60 days prior to the publication of a notice of proposed rulemaking, and a final Regulatory Impact Analysis, which shall be transmitted along with the final rule at least 30 days prior to the publication of the major rule as a final rule;

(3) For all rules other than major rules, agencies shall submit to the Director, at least 10 days prior to publication, every notice of proposed rulemaking and final rule.

(d) To permit each proposed major rule to be analyzed in light of the requirements stated in Section 2 of this Order, each preliminary and final Regulatory Impact Analysis shall contain the following information:

(1) A description of the potential benefits of the rule, including any beneficial effects that cannot be quantified in monetary terms, and the identification of those likely to receive the benefits;

(2) A description of the potential costs of the rule, including any adverse effects that cannot be quantified in monetary terms, and the identification of those likely to bear the costs;

(3) A determination of the potential net benefits of the rule, including an evaluation of effects that cannot be quantified in monetary terms;

(4) A description of alternative approaches that could substantially achieve the same regulatory goal at lower cost, together with an analysis of this potential benefit and costs and a brief explanation of the legal

reasons why such alternatives, if proposed, could not be adopted; and

(5) Unless covered by the description required under paragraph (4) of this subsection, an explanation of any legal reasons why the rule cannot be based on the requirements set forth in Section 2 of this Order.

(e)(1) The Director, subject to the direction of the Task Force, which shall resolve any issues raised under this Order or ensure that they are presented to the President, is authorized to review any preliminary or final Regulatory Impact Analysis, notice of proposed rulemaking, or final rule based on the requirements of this Order.

(2) The Director shall be deemed to have concluded review unless the Director advises an agency to the contrary under subsection (f) of this Section:

(A) Within 60 days of a submission under subsection (c)(1) or a submission of a preliminary Regulatory Impact Analysis or notice of proposed rulemaking under subsection (c)(2);

(B) Within 30 days of the submission of a final Regulatory Impact Analysis and a final rule under subsection (c)(2); and

(C) Within 10 days of the submission of a notice of proposed rulemaking or final rule under subsection (c)(3).

(f)(1) Upon the request of the Director, an agency shall consult with the Director concerning the review of a preliminary Regulatory Impact Analysis or notice of proposed rulemaking under this Order, and shall, subject to Section 8(a)(2) of this Order, refrain from publishing its preliminary Regulatory Impact Analysis or notice of proposed rulemaking until such review is concluded.

(2) Upon receiving notice that the Director intends to submit views with respect to any final Regulatory Impact Analysis or final rule, the agency shall, subject to Section 8(a)(2) of this Order, refrain from publishing its final Regulatory Impact Analysis or final rule until the agency has responded to the Director's views, and incorporated those views and the agency's response in the rulemaking file.

(3) Nothing in this subsection shall be construed as displacing the agencies' responsibilities delegated by law.

(g) For every rule for which an agency publishes a notice of proposed rulemaking, the agency shall include in its notice:

(1) A brief statement setting forth the agency's initial determination whether the proposed rule is a major rule, together with the reasons underlying that determination; and

(2) For each proposed major rule, a brief summary of the agency's preliminary Regulatory Impact Analysis.

(h) Agencies shall make their preliminary and final Regulatory Impact Analyses available to the public.

(i) Agencies shall initiate reviews of currently effective rules in accordance with the purposes of this Order, and perform Regulatory Impact Analyses of currently effective major rules. The Director, subject to the direction of the Task Force, may designate currently effective rules for review in accordance with this Order, and establish schedules for reviews and Analyses under this Order.

Sec. 4. *Regulatory Review.* Before approving any final major rule, each agency shall:

(a) Make a determination that the regulation is clearly within the authority delegated by law and consistent with congressional intent, and include in the *Federal Register* at the time of promulgation a memorandum of law supporting that determination.

(b) Make a determination that the factual conclusions upon which the rule is based have substantial support in the agency record, viewed as a whole, with full attention to public comments in general and the comments of persons directly affected by the rule in particular.

Sec. 5. *Regulatory Agendas.*

(a) Each agency shall publish, in October and April of each year, an agenda of proposed regulations that the agency has issued or expects to issue, and currently effective rules that are under agency review pursuant to this Order. These agendas may be incorporated with the agendas published under 5 U.S.C. 602, and must contain at the minimum:

(1) A summary of the nature of each major rule being considered, the objectives and legal basis for the issuance of the rule, and an approximate schedule for completing action on any major rule for which the agency has issued a notice of proposed rulemaking;

(2) The name and telephone number of a knowledgeable agency official for each item on the agenda; and

(3) A list of existing regulations to be reviewed under the terms of this Order, and a brief discussion of each such regulation.

(b) The Director, subject to the direction of the Task Force, may, to the extent permitted by law:

(1) Require agencies to provide additional information in an agenda; and

(2) Require publication of the agenda in any form.

Sec. 6. *The Task Force and Office of Management and Budget.*

(a) To the extent permitted by law, the Director shall have authority, subject to the direction of the Task Force, to:

(1) Designate any proposed or existing rule as a major rule in accordance with Section 1(b) of this Order;

(2) Prepare and promulgate uniform standards for the identification of major rules and the development of Regulatory Impact Analyses;

(3) Require an agency to obtain and evaluate, in connection with a regulation, any additional relevant data from any appropriate source;

(4) Waive the requirements of Sections 3, 4, or 7 of this Order with respect to any proposed or existing major rule;

(5) Identify duplicative, overlapping and conflicting rules, existing or proposed, and existing or proposed rules that are inconsistent with the policies underlying statutes governing agencies other than the issuing agency or with the purposes of this Order, and, in each such case, require appropriate interagency consultation to minimize or eliminate such duplication, overlap, or conflict;

(6) Develop procedures for estimating the annual benefits and costs of agency regulations, on both an aggregate and economic or industrial sector basis, for purposes of compiling a regulatory budget;

(7) In consultation with interested agencies, prepare for consideration by the President recommendations for changes in the agencies' statutes; and

(8) Monitor agency compliance with the requirements of this Order and advise the President with respect to such compliance.

(b) The Director, subject to the direction of the Task Force, is authorized to establish procedures for the performance of all functions vested in the Director by this Order. The Director shall take appropriate steps to coordinate the implementation of the analysis, transmittal, review, and clearance provisions of this Order with the authorities and requirements provided for or imposed upon the Director and agencies under the Regulatory Flexibility Act, 5 U.S.C. 601 *et seq.*, and the Paperwork Reduction Plan Act of 1980, 44 U.S.C. 3501 *et seq.*

Sec. 7. *Pending Regulations.*

(a) To the extent necessary to permit reconsideration in accordance with this Order, agencies shall, except as provided in Section 8 of this Order, suspend or postpone the effective dates of all major rules that they have promulgated in final form as of the date of this Order, but that have not yet become effective, excluding:

(1) Major rules that cannot legally be postponed or suspended;

(2) Major rules that, for good cause, ought to become effective as final rules without reconsideration. Agencies shall prepare, in accordance with Section 3 of this Order, a final Regulatory Impact Analysis for each major rule that they suspend or postpone.

(b) Agencies shall report to the Director no later than 15 days prior to the effective date of any rule that the agency has promulgated in final form as of the date of this Order, and that has not yet become effective, and that will not be reconsidered under subsection (a) of this Section:

(1) That the rule is excepted from reconsideration under subsection (a), including a brief statement of the legal or other reasons for that determination; or

(2) That the rule is not a major rule.

(c) The Director, subject to the direction of the Task Force, is authorized, to the extent permitted by law, to:

(1) Require reconsideration, in accordance with this Order, of any major rule that an agency has issued in final form as of the date of this Order and that has not become effective; and

(2) Designate a rule that an agency has issued in final form as of the date of this Order and that has not yet become effective as a major rule in accordance with Section 1(b) of this Order.

(d) Agencies may, in accordance with the Administrative Procedure Act and other applicable statutes, permit major rules that they have issued in final form as of the date of this Order, and that have not yet become effective, to take effect as interim rules while they are being reconsidered in accordance with this Order, *provided that,* agencies shall report to the Director, no later than 15 days before any such rule is proposed to take effect as an interim rule, that the rule should appropriately take effect as an interim rule while the rule is under reconsideration.

(e) Except as provided in Section 8 of this Order, agencies shall, to the extent permitted by law, refrain from promulgating as a final rule any proposed major rule that has been published or issued as of the date of this Order until a final Regulatory Impact Analysis, in accordance with Section 3 of this Order, has been prepared for the proposed major rule.

(f) Agencies shall report to the Director, no later than 30 days prior to promulgating as a final rule any proposed rule that the agency has published or issued as of the date of this Order and that has not been considered under the terms of this Order:

(1) That the rule cannot legally be considered in accordance with this Order, together with a brief explanation of the legal reasons barring such consideration; or

(2) That the rule is not a major rule, in which case the agency shall submit to the Director a copy of the proposed rule.

(g) The Director, subject to the direction of the Task Force, is authorized, to the extent permitted by law, to:

(1) Require consideration, in accordance with this Order, of any proposed major rule that the agency has published or issued as of the date of this Order; and

(2) Designate a proposed rule that an agency has published or issued as of the date of this Order, as a major rule in accordance with Section 1(b) of this Order.

(h) The Director shall be deemed to have determined that an agency's report to the Director under subsections (b), (d), or (f) of this Section is consistent with the purposes of this Order, unless the Director advises the agency to the contrary:

(1) Within 15 days of its report, in the case of any report under subsections (b) or (d); or

(2) Within 30 days of its report, in the case of any report under subsection (f).

(i) This Section does not supersede the President's Memorandum of January 29, 1981, entitled "Postponement of Pending Regulations," which shall remain in effect until March 30, 1981.

(j) In complying with this Section, agencies shall comply with all applicable provisions of the Administrative Procedure Act, and with any other procedural requirements made applicable to the agencies by other statutes.

Sec. 8. *Exemptions.*

(a) The procedures prescribed by this Order shall not apply to:

(1) Any regulation that responds to an emergency situation, *provided that,* any such regulation shall be reported to the Director as soon as is practicable, the agency shall publish in the *Federal Register* a statement of the reasons why it is impracticable for the agency to follow the procedures of this Order with respect to such a rule, and the agency shall prepare and transmit as soon as is practicable a Regulatory Impact Analysis of any such major rule; and

(2) Any regulation for which consideration or reconsideration under the terms of this Order would conflict with deadlines imposed by statute or by judicial order, *provided that,* any such regulation shall be reported to the Director together with a brief explanation of the conflict, the agency shall publish in the *Federal Register* a statement of the reasons why it is impracticable for the agency to follow the procedures of this Order with respect to such a rule, and the agency, in consultation with the Director, shall adhere to the requirements of this Order to the extent permitted by statutory or judicial deadlines.

(b) The Director, subject to the direction of the Task Force, may, in accordance with the purposes of this Order, exempt any class or category of regulations from any or all requirements of this Order.

Sec. 9. *Judicial Review.* This Order is intended only to improve the internal management of the Federal govern-

ment, and is not intended to create any right or benefit, substantive or procedural, enforceable at law by a party against the United States, its agencies, its officers or any person. The determinations made by agencies under Section 4 of this Order, and any Regulatory Impact Analyses for any rule, shall be made part of the whole record of agency action in connection with the rule.

Sec. 10. *Revocations.* Executive Orders No. 12044, as amended, and No. 12174 are revoked.

RONALD REAGAN

The White House,
February 17, 1981.

■ **EXECUTIVE ORDER 12498**
(Revoked September 30, 1993)

Regulatory Planning Process

By the authority vested in me as President by the Constitution and laws of the United States of America, and in order to create a coordinated process for developing on an annual basis the Administration's Regulatory Program, establish Administration regulatory priorities, increase the accountability of agency heads for the regulatory actions of their agencies, provide for Presidential oversight of the regulatory process, reduce the burdens of existing and future regulations, minimize duplication and conflict of regulations, and enhance public and Congressional understanding of the Administration's regulatory objectives, it is hereby ordered as follows:

Section 1. *General Requirements.*

(a) There is hereby established a regulatory planning process by which the Administration will develop and publish a Regulatory Program for each year. To implement this process, each Executive agency subject to Executive Order No. 12291 shall submit to the Director of the Office of Management and Budget (OMB) each year, starting in 1985, a statement of its regulatory policies, goals, and objectives for the coming year and information concerning all significant regulatory actions underway or planned; however, the Director may exempt from this Order such agencies or activities as the Director may deem appropriate in order to achieve the effective implementation of this Order.

(b) The head of each Executive agency subject to this Order shall ensure that all regulatory actions are consistent with the goals of the agency and of the Administration, and will be appropriately implemented.

(c) This program is intended to complement the existing regulatory planning and review procedures of agencies and the Executive branch, including the procedures established by Executive Order No. 12291.

(d) To assure consistency with the goals of the Administration, the head of each agency subject to this Order shall adhere to the regulatory principles stated in Section 2 of Executive Order No. 12291, including those elaborated by the regulatory policy guidelines set forth in the August 11, 1983, Report of the Presidential Task Force on Regulatory Relief, "Reagan Administration Regulatory Achievements."

Sec. 2. *Agency Submission of Draft Regulatory Program.*

(a) The head of each agency shall submit to the Director an overview of the agency's regulatory policies, goals, and objectives for the program year and such information concerning all significant regulatory actions of the agency, planned or underway, including actions taken to consider whether to initiate rulemaking; requests for public comment; and the development of documents that may influence, anticipate, or could lead to the commencement of rulemaking proceedings at a later date, as the Director deems necessary to develop the Administration's Regulatory Program. This submission shall constitute the agency's draft regulatory program. The draft regulatory program shall be submitted to the Director each year, on a date to be specified by the Director, and shall cover the period from April 1 through March 31 of the following year.

(b) The overview portion of the agency's submission should discuss the agency's broad regulatory purposes, explain how they are consistent with the Administration's regulatory principles, and include a discussion of the significant regulatory actions, as defined by the Director, that it will take. The overview should specifically discuss the significant regulatory actions of the agency to revise or rescind existing rules.

(c) Each agency head shall categorize and describe the regulatory actions described in subsection (a) in such format as the Director shall specify and provide such additional information as the Director may request; however, the Director shall, by Bulletin or Circular, exempt from the requirements of this Order any class or category of regulatory action that the Director determines is not necessary to review in order to achieve the effective implementation of the program.

Sec. 3. *Review, Compilation, and Publication of the Administration's Regulatory Program.*

(a) In reviewing each agency's draft regulatory program, the Director shall (i) consider the consistency of the draft regulatory program with the Administration's policies and priorities and the draft regulatory programs submitted by other agencies; and (ii) identify such further regulatory or deregulatory actions as may, in his view,

be necessary in order to achieve such consistency. In the event of disagreement over the content of the agency's draft regulatory program, the agency head or the Director may raise issues for further review by the President or by such appropriate Cabinet Council or other forum as the President may designate.

(b) Following the conclusion of the review process established by subsection (a), each agency head shall submit to the Director, by a date to be specified by the Director, the agency's final regulatory plan for compilation and publication as the Administration's Regulatory Program for that year. The Director shall circulate a draft of the Administration's Regulatory Program for agency comment, review, and interagency consideration, if necessary, before publication.

(c) After development of the Administration's Regulatory Program for the year, if the agency head proposes to take a regulatory action subject to the provisions of Section 2 and not previously submitted for review under this process, or if the agency head proposes to take a regulatory action that is materially different from the action described in the agency's final Regulatory Program, the agency head shall immediately advise the Director and submit the action to the Director for review in such format as the Director may specify. Except in the case of emergency situations, as defined by the Director, or statutory or judicial deadlines, the agency head shall refrain from taking the proposed regulatory action until the review of this submission by the Director is completed. As to those regulatory actions not also subject to Executive Order No. 12291, the Director shall be deemed to have concluded that the proposal is consistent with the purposes of this Order, unless he notifies the agency head to the contrary within 10 days of its submission. As to those regulatory actions subject to Executive Order No. 12291, the Director's review shall be governed by the provisions of Section 3(e) of that Order.

(d) Absent unusual circumstances, such as new statutory or judicial requirements or unanticipated emergency situations, the Director may, to the extent permitted by law, return for reconsideration any rule submitted for review under Executive Order No. 12291 that would be subject to Section 2 but was not included in the agency's final Regulatory Program for that year; or any other significant regulatory action that is materially different from those described in the Administration's Regulatory Program for that year.

Sec. 4. *Office of Management and Budget.*

The Director of the Office of Management and Budget is authorized, to the extent permitted by law, to take such actions as may be necessary to carry out the provisions of this order.

Sec. 5. *Judicial Review.*

This Order is intended only to improve the internal management of the Federal government, and is not intended to create any right or benefit, substantive or procedural, enforceable at law by a party against the United States, its agencies, its officers or any person.

RONALD REAGAN

The White House,
January 4, 1985.

EXECUTIVE ORDER 12866

Regulatory Planning and Review

The American people deserve a regulatory system that works for them, not against them: a regulatory system that protects and improves their health, safety, environment, and well-being and improves the performance of the economy without imposing unacceptable or unreasonable costs on society; regulatory policies that recognize that the private sector and private markets are the best engine for economic growth; regulatory approaches that respect the role of State, local, and tribal governments; and regulations that are effective, consistent, sensible, and understandable. We do not have such a regulatory system today.

With this Executive order, the Federal Government begins a program to reform and make more efficient the regulatory process. The objectives of this Executive order are to enhance planning and coordination with respect to both new and existing regulations; to reaffirm the primacy of Federal agencies in the regulatory decision-making process; to restore the integrity and legitimacy of regulatory review and oversight; and to make the process more accessible and open to the public. In pursuing these objectives, the regulatory process shall be conducted so as to meet applicable statutory requirements and with due regard to the discretion that has been entrusted to the Federal agencies.

Accordingly, by the authority vested in me as President by the Constitution and the laws of the United States of America, it is hereby ordered as follows:

Section 1. *Statement of Regulatory Philosophy and Principles. (a) The Regulatory Philosophy.* Federal agencies should promulgate only such regulations as are required by law, are necessary to interpret the law, or are made necessary by compelling public need, such as material failures of private markets to protect or improve the health and safety of the public, the environment, or the well-being of the American people. In deciding whether and how to regulate, agencies should assess all costs and benefits of available regulatory alternatives, including the alternative of not regulating. Costs and benefits shall be understood to include both quantifiable measures (to the fullest extent that these can be usefully estimated) and qualitative measures of costs and benefits that are difficult to quantify, but nevertheless essential to consider. Further, in choosing among alternative regulatory approaches, agencies should select those approaches that maximize net benefits (including potential economic, environmental, public health and safety, and other advantages; distributive impacts; and equity), unless a statute requires another regulatory approach.

(b) *The Principles of Regulation.* To ensure that the agencies' regulatory programs are consistent with the philosophy set forth above, agencies should adhere to the following principles, to the extent permitted by law and where applicable:

(1) Each agency shall identify the problem that it intends to address (including, where applicable, the failures of private markets or public institutions that warrant new agency action) as well as assess the significance of that problem.

(2) Each agency shall examine whether existing regulations (or other law) have created, or contributed to, the problem that a new regulation is intended to correct and whether those regulations (or other law) should be modified to achieve the intended goal of regulation more effectively.

(3) Each agency shall identify and assess available alternatives to direct regulation, including providing economic incentives to encourage the desired behavior, such as user fees or marketable permits, or providing information upon which choices can be made by the public.

(4) In setting regulatory priorities, each agency shall consider, to the extent reasonable, the degree and nature of the risks posed by various substances or activities within its jurisdiction.

(5) When an agency determines that a regulation is the best available method of achieving the regulatory objective, it shall design its regulations in the most cost-effective manner to achieve the regulatory objective. In doing so, each agency shall consider incentives for innovation, consistency, predictability, the costs of enforcement and compliance (to the government, regulated entities, and the public), flexibility, distributive impacts, and equity.

(6) Each agency shall assess both the costs and the benefits of the intended regulation and, recognizing that some costs and benefits are difficult to quantify, propose or adopt a regulation only upon a reasoned determination that the benefits of the intended regulation justify its costs.

(7) Each agency shall base its decisions on the best reasonably obtainable scientific, technical, economic,

and other information concerning the need for, and consequences of, the intended regulation.

(8) Each agency shall identify and assess alternative forms of regulation and shall, to the extent feasible, specify performance objectives, rather than specifying the behavior or manner of compliance that regulated entities must adopt.

(9) Wherever feasible, agencies shall seek views of appropriate State, local, and tribal officials before imposing regulatory requirements that might significantly or uniquely affect those governmental entities. Each agency shall assess the effects of Federal regulations on State, local, and tribal governments, including specifically the availability of resources to carry out those mandates, and seek to minimize those burdens that uniquely or significantly affect such governmental entities, consistent with achieving regulatory objectives. In addition, as appropriate, agencies shall seek to harmonize Federal regulatory actions with related State, local, and tribal regulatory and other governmental functions.

(10) Each agency shall avoid regulations that are inconsistent, incompatible, or duplicative with its other regulations or those of other Federal agencies.

(11) Each agency shall tailor its regulations to impose the least burden on society, including individuals, businesses of differing sizes, and other entities (including small communities and governmental entities), consistent with obtaining the regulatory objectives, taking into account, among other things, and to the extent practicable, the costs of cumulative regulations.

(12) Each agency shall draft its regulations to be simple and easy to understand, with the goal of minimizing the potential for uncertainty and litigation arising from such uncertainty.

Sec. 2. *Organization.* An efficient regulatory planning and review process is vital to ensure that the Federal Government's regulatory system best serves the American people.

(a) *The Agencies.* Because Federal agencies are the repositories of significant substantive expertise and experience, they are responsible for developing regulations and assuring that the regulations are consistent with applicable law, the President's priorities, and the principles set forth in this Executive order.

(b) *The Office of Management and Budget.* Coordinated review of agency rulemaking is necessary to ensure that regulations are consistent with applicable law, the President's priorities, and the principles set forth in this Executive order, and that decisions made by one agency do not conflict with the policies or actions taken or planned by another agency. The Office of Management and Budget (OMB) shall carry out that review function. Within

OMB, the Office of Information and Regulatory Affairs (OIRA) is the repository of expertise concerning regulatory issues, including methodologies and procedures that affect more than one agency, this Executive order, and the President's regulatory policies. To the extent permitted by law, OMB shall provide guidance to agencies and assist the President, the Vice President, and other regulatory policy advisors to the President in regulatory planning and shall be the entity that reviews individual regulations, as provided by this Executive order.

(c) *The Vice President.* The Vice President is the principal advisor to the President on, and shall coordinate the development and presentation of recommendations concerning regulatory policy, planning, and review, as set forth in this Executive order. In fulfilling their responsibilities under this Executive order, the President and the Vice President shall be assisted by the regulatory policy advisors within the Executive Office of the President and by such agency officials and personnel as the President and the Vice President may, from time to time, consult.

Sec. 3. *Definitions.* For purposes of this Executive order:

(a) "Advisors" refers to such regulatory policy advisors to the President as the President and Vice President may from time to time consult, including, among others: (1) the Director of OMB; (2) the Chair (or another member) of the Council of Economic Advisers; (3) the Assistant to the President for Economic Policy; (4) the Assistant to the President for Domestic Policy; (5) the Assistant to the President for National Security Affairs; (6) the Assistant to the President for Science and Technology; (7) the Assistant to the President for Intergovernmental Affairs; (8) the Assistant to the President and Staff Secretary; (9) the Assistant to the President and Chief of Staff to the Vice President; (10) the Assistant to the President and Counsel to the President; (11) the Deputy Assistant to the President and Director of the White House Office on Environmental Policy; and (12) the Administrator of OIRA, who also shall coordinate communications relating to this Executive order among the agencies, OMB, the other Advisors, and the Office of the Vice President.

(b) "Agency," unless otherwise indicated, means any authority of the United States that is an "agency" under 44 U.S.C. 3502(1), other than those considered to be independent regulatory agencies, as defined in 44 U.S.C. 3502(10).

(c) "Director" means the Director of OMB.

(d) "Regulation" or "rule" means an agency statement of general applicability and future effect, which the agency intends to have the force and effect of law, that is designed to implement, interpret, or prescribe law or policy or to describe the procedure or practice requirements of an agency. It does not, however, include:

(1) Regulations or rules issued in accordance with the formal rulemaking provisions of 5 U.S.C. 556, 557;

(2) Regulations or rules that pertain to a military or foreign affairs function of the United States, other than procurement regulations and regulations involving the import or export of non-defense articles and services;

(3) Regulations or rules that are limited to agency organization, management, or personnel matters; or

(4) Any other category of regulations exempted by the Administrator of OIRA.

(e) "Regulatory action" means any substantive action by an agency (normally published in the *Federal Register*) that promulgates or is expected to lead to the promulgation of a final rule or regulation, including notices of inquiry, advance notices of proposed rulemaking, and notices of proposed rulemaking.

(f) "Significant regulatory action" means any regulatory action that is likely to result in a rule that may:

(1) Have an annual effect on the economy of $100 million or more or adversely affect in a material way the economy, a sector of the economy, productivity, competition, jobs, the environment, public health or safety, or State, local, or tribal governments or communities;

(2) Create a serious inconsistency or otherwise interfere with an action taken or planned by another agency;

(3) Materially alter the budgetary impact of entitlements, grants, user fees, or loan programs or the rights and obligations of recipients thereof; or

(4) Raise novel legal or policy issues arising out of legal mandates, the President's priorities, or the principles set forth in this Executive order.

Sec. 4. *Planning Mechanism.* In order to have an effective regulatory program, to provide for coordination of regulations, to maximize consultation and the resolution of potential conflicts at an early stage, to involve the public and its State, local, and tribal officials in regulatory planning, and to ensure that new or revised regulations promote the President's priorities and the principles set forth in this Executive order, these procedures shall be followed, to the extent permitted by law:

(a) *Agencies' Policy Meeting.* Early in each year's planning cycle, the Vice President shall convene a meeting of the Advisors and the heads of agencies to seek a common understanding of priorities and to coordinate regulatory efforts to be accomplished in the upcoming year.

(b) *Unified Regulatory Agenda.* For purposes of this subsection, the term "agency" or "agencies" shall also include those considered to be independent regulatory agencies, as defined in 44 U.S.C. 3502(10). Each agency shall prepare an agenda of all regulations under development or review, at a time and in a manner specified by the Administrator of OIRA. The description of each regulatory action shall contain, at a minimum, a regulation identifier number, a brief summary of the action, the legal authority for the action, any legal deadline for the action, and the name and telephone number of a knowledgeable agency official. Agencies may incorporate the information required under 5 U.S.C. 602 and 41 U.S.C. 402 into these agendas.

(c) *The Regulatory Plan.* For purposes of this subsection, the term "agency" or "agencies" shall also include those considered to be independent regulatory agencies, as defined in 44 U.S.C. 3502(10). (1) As part of the Unified Regulatory Agenda, beginning in 1994, each agency shall prepare a Regulatory Plan (Plan) of the most important significant regulatory actions that the agency reasonably expects to issue in proposed or final form in that fiscal year or thereafter. The Plan shall be approved personally by the agency head and shall contain at a minimum:

(A) A statement of the agency's regulatory objectives and priorities and how they relate to the President's priorities;

(B) A summary of each planned significant regulatory action including, to the extent possible, alternatives to be considered and preliminary estimates of the anticipated costs and benefits;

(C) A summary of the legal basis for each such action, including whether any aspect of the action is required by statute or court order;

(D) A statement of the need for each such action and, if applicable, how the action will reduce risks to public health, safety, or the environment, as well as how the magnitude of the risk addressed by the action relates to other risks within the jurisdiction of the agency;

(E) The agency's schedule for action, including a statement of any applicable statutory or judicial deadlines; and

(F) The name, address, and telephone number of a person the public may contact for additional information about the planned regulatory action.

(2) Each agency shall forward its Plan to OIRA by June 1st of each year.

(3) Within 10 calendar days after OIRA has received an agency's Plan, OIRA shall circulate it to other affected agencies, the Advisors, and the Vice President.

(4) An agency head who believes that a planned regulatory action of another agency may conflict with its own policy or action taken or planned shall promptly notify, in writing, the Administrator of OIRA, who shall forward that communication to the issuing agency, the Advisors, and the Vice President.

(5) If the Administrator of OIRA believes that a planned regulatory action of an agency may be inconsistent with the President's priorities or the principles

set forth in this Executive order or may be in conflict with any policy or action taken or planned by another agency, the Administrator of OIRA shall promptly notify, in writing, the affected agencies, the Advisors, and the Vice President.

(6) The Vice President, with the Advisors' assistance, may consult with the heads of agencies with respect to their Plans and, in appropriate instances, request further consideration or inter-agency coordination.

(7) The Plans developed by the issuing agency shall be published annually in the October publication of the Unified Regulatory Agenda. This publication shall be made available to the Congress; State, local, and tribal governments; and the public. Any views on any aspect of any agency Plan, including whether any planned regulatory action might conflict with any other planned or existing regulation, impose any unintended consequences on the public, or confer any unclaimed benefits on the public, should be directed to the issuing agency, with a copy to OIRA.

(d) *Regulatory Working Group.* Within 30 days of the date of this Executive order, the Administrator of OIRA shall convene a Regulatory Working Group ("Working Group"), which shall consist of representatives of the heads of each agency that the Administrator determines to have significant domestic regulatory responsibility, the Advisors, and the Vice President. The Administrator of OIRA shall chair the Working Group and shall periodically advise the Vice President on the activities of the Working Group. The Working Group shall serve as a forum to assist agencies in identifying and analyzing important regulatory issues (including, among others (1) the development of innovative regulatory techniques, (2) the methods, efficacy, and utility of comparative risk assessment in regulatory decision-making, and (3) the development of short forms and other streamlined regulatory approaches for small businesses and other entities). The Working Group shall meet at least quarterly and may meet as a whole or in subgroups of agencies with an interest in particular issues or subject areas. To inform its discussions, the Working Group may commission analytical studies and reports by OIRA, the Administrative Conference of the United States, or any other agency.

(e) *Conferences.* The Administrator of OIRA shall meet quarterly with representatives of State, local, and tribal governments to identify both existing and proposed regulations that may uniquely or significantly affect those governmental entities. The Administrator of OIRA shall also convene, from time to time, conferences with representatives of businesses, nongovernmental organizations, and the public to discuss regulatory issues of common concern.

Sec. 5. *Existing Regulations.* In order to reduce the regulatory burden on the American people, their families, their communities, their State, local, and tribal governments, and their industries; to determine whether regulations promulgated by the executive branch of the Federal Government have become unjustified or unnecessary as a result of changed circumstances; to confirm that regulations are both compatible with each other and not duplicative or inappropriately burdensome in the aggregate; to ensure that all regulations are consistent with the President's priorities and the principles set forth in this Executive order, within applicable law; and to otherwise improve the effectiveness of existing regulations: (a) Within 90 days of the date of this Executive order, each agency shall submit to OIRA a program, consistent with its resources and regulatory priorities, under which the agency will periodically review its existing significant regulations to determine whether any such regulations should be modified or eliminated so as to make the agency's regulatory program more effective in achieving the regulatory objectives, less burdensome, or in greater alignment with the President's priorities and the principles set forth in this Executive order. Any significant regulations selected for review shall be included in the agency's annual Plan. The agency shall also identify any legislative mandates that require the agency to promulgate or continue to impose regulations that the agency believes are unnecessary or outdated by reason of changed circumstances.

(b) The Administrator of OIRA shall work with the Regulatory Working Group and other interested entities to pursue the objectives of this section. State, local, and tribal governments are specifically encouraged to assist in the identification of regulations that impose significant or unique burdens on those governmental entities and that appear to have outlived their justification or be otherwise inconsistent with the public interest.

(c) The Vice President, in consultation with the Advisors, may identify for review by the appropriate agency or agencies other existing regulations of an agency or groups of regulations of more than one agency that affect a particular group, industry, or sector of the economy, or may identify legislative mandates that may be appropriate for reconsideration by the Congress.

Sec. 6. *Centralized Review of Regulations.* The guidelines set forth below shall apply to all regulatory actions, for both new and existing regulations, by agencies other than those agencies specifically exempted by the Administrator of OIRA:

(a) *Agency Responsibilities.* (1) Each agency shall (consistent with its own rules, regulations, or procedures) provide the public with meaningful participation in the regulatory process. In particular, before issuing a notice of proposed rulemaking, each agency should, where appropriate, seek the involvement of those who are intended to benefit from and those expected to be burdened by any regulation (including, specifically, State, local, and tribal officials). In addition, each agency should afford the public a meaningful opportunity to comment on any proposed regulation, which in most cases should include a comment period of not less than 60 days. Each agency also is directed to explore and, where appropriate, use consensual mechanisms for developing regulations, including negotiated rulemaking.

(2) Within 60 days of the date of this Executive order, each agency head shall designate a Regulatory Policy Officer who shall report to the agency head. The Regulatory Policy Officer shall be involved at each stage of the regulatory process to foster the development of effective, innovative, and least burdensome regulations and to further the principles set forth in this Executive order.

(3) In addition to adhering to its own rules and procedures and to the requirements of the Administrative Procedure Act, the Regulatory Flexibility Act, the Paperwork Reduction Act, and other applicable law, each agency shall develop its regulatory actions in a timely fashion and adhere to the following procedures with respect to a regulatory action:

(A) Each agency shall provide OIRA, at such times and in the manner specified by the Administrator of OIRA, with a list of its planned regulatory actions, indicating those which the agency believes are significant regulatory actions within the meaning of this Executive order. Absent a material change in the development of the planned regulatory action, those not designated as significant will not be subject to review under this section unless, within 10 working days of receipt of the list, the Administrator of OIRA notifies the agency that OIRA has determined that a planned regulation is a significant regulatory action within the meaning of this Executive order. The Administrator of OIRA may waive review of any planned regulatory action designated by the agency as significant, in which case the agency need not further comply with subsection (a)(3)(B) or subsection (a)(3)(C) of this section.

(B) For each matter identified as, or determined by the Administrator of OIRA to be, a significant regulatory action, the issuing agency shall provide to OIRA:

(i) The text of the draft regulatory action, together with a reasonably detailed description of the need for the regulatory action and an explanation of how the regulatory action will meet that need; and

(ii) An assessment of the potential costs and benefits of the regulatory action, including an explanation of the manner in which the regulatory action is consistent with a statutory mandate and, to the extent permitted by law, promotes the President's priorities and avoids undue interference with State, local, and tribal governments in the exercise of their governmental functions.

(C) For those matters identified as, or determined by the Administrator of OIRA to be, a significant regulatory action within the scope of section 3(f)(1), the agency shall also provide to OIRA the following additional information developed as part of the agency's decision-making process (unless prohibited by law):

(i) An assessment, including the underlying analysis, of benefits anticipated from the regulatory action (such as, but not limited to, the promotion of the efficient functioning of the economy and private markets, the enhancement of health and safety, the protection of the natural environment, and the elimination or reduction of discrimination or bias) together with, to the extent feasible, a quantification of those benefits;

(ii) An assessment, including the underlying analysis, of costs anticipated from the regulatory action (such as, but not limited to, the direct cost both to the government in administering the regulation and to businesses and others in complying with the regulation, and any adverse effects on the efficient functioning of the economy, private markets (including productivity, employment, and competitiveness), health, safety, and the natural environment), together with, to the extent feasible, a quantification of those costs; and

(iii) An assessment, including the underlying analysis, of costs and benefits of potentially effective and reasonably feasible alternatives to the planned regulation, identified by the agencies or the public (including improving the current regulation and reasonably viable nonregulatory actions), and an explanation why the planned regulatory action is preferable to the identified potential alternatives.

(D) In emergency situations or when an agency is obligated by law to act more quickly than normal review procedures allow, the agency shall notify OIRA as soon as possible and, to the extent practicable, comply with subsections (a)(3)(B) and (C) of this section. For those regulatory actions that are governed by a statutory or court-imposed deadline, the agency shall, to the extent practicable, schedule rulemaking proceedings so as to permit sufficient time for OIRA to conduct its review, as set forth below in subsection (b)(2) through (4) of this section.

(E) After the regulatory action has been published in the *Federal Register* or otherwise issued to the public, the agency shall:

(i) Make available to the public the information set forth in subsections (a)(3)(B) and (C);

(ii) Identify for the public, in a complete, clear, and simple manner, the substantive changes between the draft submitted to OIRA for review and the action subsequently announced; and

(iii) Identify for the public those changes in the regulatory action that were made at the suggestion or recommendation of OIRA.

(F) All information provided to the public by the agency shall be in plain, understandable language.

(b) *OIRA Responsibilities.* The Administrator of OIRA shall provide meaningful guidance and oversight so that each agency's regulatory actions are consistent with applicable law, the President's priorities, and the principles set forth in this Executive order and do not conflict with the policies or actions of another agency. OIRA shall, to the extent permitted by law, adhere to the following guidelines:

(1) OIRA may review only actions identified by the agency or by OIRA as significant regulatory actions under subsection (a)(3)(A) of this section.

(2) OIRA shall waive review or notify the agency in writing of the results of its review within the following time periods:

(A) For any notices of inquiry, advance notices of proposed rulemaking, or other preliminary regulatory actions prior to a Notice of Proposed Rulemaking, within 10 working days after the date of submission of the draft action to OIRA;

(B) For all other regulatory actions, within 90 calendar days after the date of submission of the information set forth in subsections (a)(3)(B) and (C) of this section, unless OIRA has previously reviewed this information and, since that review, there has been no material change in the facts and circumstances upon which the regulatory action is based, in which case, OIRA shall complete its review within 45 days; and

(C) The review process may be extended (1) once by no more than 30 calendar days upon the written approval of the Director and (2) at the request of the agency head.

(3) For each regulatory action that the Administrator of OIRA returns to an agency for further consideration of some or all of its provisions, the Administrator of OIRA shall provide the issuing agency a written explanation for such return, setting forth the pertinent provision of this Executive order on which OIRA is relying. If the agency head disagrees with some or all of the bases for the return, the agency head shall so inform the Administrator of OIRA in writing.

(4) Except as otherwise provided by law or required by a Court, in order to ensure greater openness, accessibility, and accountability in the regulatory review process, OIRA shall be governed by the following disclosure requirements:

(A) Only the Administrator of OIRA (or a particular designee) shall receive oral communications initiated by persons not employed by the executive branch of the Federal Government regarding the substance of a regulatory action under OIRA review;

(B) All substantive communications between OIRA personnel and persons not employed by the executive branch of the Federal Government regarding a regulatory action under review shall be governed by the following guidelines: (i) A representative from the issuing agency shall be invited to any meeting between OIRA personnel and such person(s);

(ii) OIRA shall forward to the issuing agency, within 10 working days of receipt of the communication(s), all written communications, regardless of format, between OIRA personnel and any person who is not employed by the executive branch of the Federal Government, and the dates and names of individuals involved in all substantive oral communications (including meetings to which an agency representative was invited, but did not attend, and telephone conversations between OIRA personnel and any such persons); and

(iii) OIRA shall publicly disclose relevant information about such communication(s), as set forth below in subsection (b)(4)(C) of this section.

(C) OIRA shall maintain a publicly available log that shall contain, at a minimum, the following information pertinent to regulatory actions under review:

(i) The status of all regulatory actions, including if (and if so, when and by whom) Vice Presidential and Presidential consideration was requested;

(ii) A notation of all written communications forwarded to an issuing agency under subsection (b)(4)(B)(ii) of this section; and

(iii) The dates and names of individuals involved in all substantive oral communications, including meetings and telephone conversations, between OIRA personnel and any person not employed by the executive branch of the Federal Government, and the subject matter discussed during such communications.

(D) After the regulatory action has been published in the *Federal Register* or otherwise issued to the public, or after the agency has announced its decision not to publish or issue the regulatory action, OIRA shall make available to the public all documents exchanged between OIRA and the agency during the review by OIRA under this section.

(5) All information provided to the public by OIRA shall be in plain, understandable language.

Sec. 7. *Resolution of Conflicts.* To the extent permitted by law, disagreements or conflicts between or among agency heads or between OMB and any agency that cannot be resolved by the Administrator of OIRA shall be resolved by the President, or by the Vice President acting at the request of the President, with the relevant agency head (and, as appropriate, other interested government officials). Vice Presidential and Presidential consideration of such disagreements may be initiated only by the Director, by the head of the issuing agency, or by the head of an agency that has a significant interest in the regulatory action at issue. Such review will not be undertaken at the request of other persons, entities, or their agents.

Resolution of such conflicts shall be informed by recommendations developed by the Vice President, after consultation with the Advisors (and other executive branch officials or personnel whose responsibilities to the President include the subject matter at issue). The development of these recommendations shall be concluded within 60 days after review has been requested.

During the Vice Presidential and Presidential review period, communications with any person not employed by the Federal Government relating to the substance of the regulatory action under review and directed to the Advisors or their staffs or to the staff of the Vice President shall be in writing and shall be forwarded by the recipient to the affected agency(ies) for inclusion in the public docket(s). When the communication is not in writing, such Advisors or staff members shall inform the outside party that the matter is under review and that any comments should be submitted in writing.

At the end of this review process, the President, or the Vice President acting at the request of the President, shall notify the affected agency and the Administrator of OIRA of the President's decision with respect to the matter.

Sec. 8. *Publication.* Except to the extent required by law, an agency shall not publish in the *Federal Register* or otherwise issue to the public any regulatory action that is subject to review under section 6 of this Executive order until (1) the Administrator of OIRA notifies the agency that OIRA has waived its review of the action or has completed its review without any requests for further consideration, or (2) the applicable time period in section 6(b)(2) expires without OIRA having notified the agency that it is returning the regulatory action for further consideration under section 6(b)(3), whichever occurs first. If the terms of the preceding sentence have not been satisfied and an agency wants to publish or otherwise issue a regulatory action, the head of that agency may request Presidential consideration through the Vice President, as provided under section 7 of this order. Upon receipt of this request, the Vice President shall notify OIRA and the Advisors. The guidelines and time period set forth in section 7 shall apply to the publication of regulatory actions for which Presidential consideration has been sought.

Sec. 9. *Agency Authority.* Nothing in this order shall be construed as displacing the agencies' authority or responsibilities, as authorized by law.

Sec. 10. *Judicial Review.* Nothing in this Executive order shall affect any otherwise available judicial review of agency action. This Executive order is intended only to improve the internal management of the Federal Government and does not create any right or benefit, substantive or procedural, enforceable at law or equity by a party against the United States, its agencies or instrumentalities, its officers or employees, or any other person.

Sec. 11. *Revocations.* Executive Orders Nos. 12291 and 12498; all amendments to those Executive orders; all guidelines issued under those orders; and any exemptions from those orders heretofore granted for any category of rule are revoked.

WILLIAM J. CLINTON

The White House,
September 30, 1993.

List of Abbreviations

AARC	Alternative Agricultural Research and Commercialization Center	ATF	Bureau of Alcohol, Tobacco, Firearms, and Explosives
ABA	American Bar Association	ATFI	Automated Tariff Filing and Information System
ABA	Architectural Barriers Act of 1968		
ACAs	Agricultural Credit Associations	ATL	Alcohol and Tobacco Laboratory
ACF	Administration for Children and Families	ATP	Advanced Technology Program
ACYF	Administration for Children, Youth, and Families	ATSA	Aviation and Transportation Security Act
		ATV	All-Terrain Vehicle
ADA	Americans with Disabilities Act	AWA	Animal Welfare Act
ADAAG	ADA Accessibility Guidelines		
ADEA	Age Discrimination in Employment Act	BBS	electronic bulletin board system
ADR	Alternative Dispute Resolution	BCIS	Bureau of Citizenship and Immigration Services
AEC	Atomic Energy Commission		
AFDC	Aid to Families with Dependent Children program	BCRA	Bipartisan Campaign Reform Act of 2002
		BIA	Bureau of Indian Affairs
AHP	Affordable Housing Program	BJA	Bureau of Justice Assistance
AIA	American Institute of Architects	BJS	Bureau of Justice Statistics
ALFD	Advertising, Labeling and Formulation Division	BLM	Bureau of Land Management
		BLS	Bureau of Labor Statistics
ALJ	Administrative Law Judge	BOP	Federal Bureau of Prisons
AMA	American Medical Association	BRS	Bibliographic Retrieval System
AMID	Air and Marine Interdiction Division (ICE)	BXA	Bureau of Export Administration
AMS	Agricultural Marketing Service		
ANDA	Abbreviated New Drug Application	CAA	Civil Aeronautics Authority
APA	Administrative Procedure Act of 1946	CAB	Civil Aeronautics Board
APHIS	Animal and Plant Health Inspection Service	CAFE	Corporate Average Fuel Efficiency
		CBO	Congressional Budget Office
AQI	Agricultural Quarantine Inspection	CBP	Customs and Border Protection
ARCP	Agricultural Resource Conservation Program	CCC	Commodity Credit Corporation
ASCS	Agricultural Stabilization and Conservation Service	CCF	Capital Construction Fund
		CCP	Cooperative Compliance Program
ASOS	Automated Surface Observing Stations	CEA	Council of Economic Advisers
ATBCB	Architectural and Transportation Barriers Compliance Board	CEBA	Competitive Equality Banking Act of 1987
		CEQ	Council on Environmental Quality
ATF	Bureau of Alcohol, Tobacco, and Firearms		

CERCLA	Comprehensive Environmental Response, Compensation and Liability Act (Superfund)		ERDA	Energy Research and Development Administration
CETA	Comprehensive Employment and Training Act		EREN	Energy Efficiency and Renewable Energy
			ERISA	Employee Retirement Income Security Act of 1974
CFCs	Chlorofluorocarbons		ERS	Economic Research Service
CFR	Code of Federal Regulations		ESA	Employment Standards Administration
CFTC	Commodity Futures Trading Commission		ESH	Office of Environment, Safety, and Health
CIC	Consumer Information Center		ETA	Employment and Training Administration
CMS	Centers for Medicare and Medicaid Services			
CNS	Corporation for National Service		FAA	Federal Aviation Administration
COBRA	Consolidated Omnibus Budget Reconciliation Act of 1985		Fannie Mae	Federal National Mortgage Association
			Farmer Mac	Federal Agricultural Mortgage Corporation
COSHI	Clearinghouse for Occupational Safety and Health Information		FAS	Foreign Agricultural Service
			FBI	Federal Bureau of Investigation
CPD	Community Planning and Development		FCA	Farm Credit Administration
CPSC	Consumer Product Safety Commission		FCC	Federal Communications Commission
CSAB	Center for the Study of American Business		FCIC	Federal Crop Insurance Corporation
			FCS	Food and Consumer Service
CSRA	Civil Service Reform Act		FCSBA	FCS Building Association
			FDA	Food and Drug Administration
DEA	Drug Enforcement Administration		FDC	Food, Drug, and Cosmetic Act
DHS	Department of Homeland Security		FDIC	Federal Deposit Insurance Corporation
DOE	Department of Energy		FEA	Federal Energy Administration
DOJ	Department of Justice		FEC	Federal Election Commission
DOL	Department of Labor		FECA	Federal Election Campaign Act Amendments of 1976
DOT	Department of Transportation			
DPC	Domestic Policy Council		Fed	Federal Reserve Board
			FEMA	Federal Emergency Management Agency
EAA	Export Administration Act		FEPC	Fair Employment Practices Committee
EDA	Economic Development Administration		FERC	Federal Energy Regulatory Commission
EDGAR	Electronic Data Gathering Analysis and Retrieval system		FFIEC	Federal Financial Institutions Examination Council
EEOC	Equal Employment Opportunity Commission		FGIS	Federal Grain Inspection Service
			FHA	Federal Housing Administration
EFIN	Environmental Financing Information Network		FHEO	Office of Fair Housing and Equal Opportunity
EIA	Energy Information Administration		FHFB	Federal Housing Finance Board
EIS	Environmental Impact Statement		FHLB	Federal Home Loan Bank
ELAIN	Export License Application and Information Network		FHLMC	Federal Home Loan Mortgage Corporation (Freddie Mac)
ELVIS	Electronic License Voice Information System		FHWA	Federal Highway Administration
			FIFRA	Federal Insecticide, Fungicide, and Rodenticide Act
EM	Office of Environmental Management (Energy Dept.)		FIN	Federal Information Network
			FIRREA	Financial Institutions Reform, Recovery, and Enforcement Act of 1989
E-mail PMO	Electronic Messaging Program Management Office			
			FISA	Foreign Intelligence Surveillance Act
EPA	Environmental Protection Agency		FLBA	Federal Land Bank Association
EPA	Equal Pay Act		FLSA	Fair Labor Standards Act
EPUB	Electronic Publishing System		FMC	Federal Maritime Commission
EQC	Environmental Quality Council		FmHA	Farmers Home Administration
ERA	Economic Regulatory Administration		FNS	Food and Nutrition Service

FOI	freedom of information
FOIA	Freedom of Information Act
FOMC	Federal Open Market Committee
FPC	Federal Power Commission
FRA	Federal Railroad Administration
FRCS	Federal Reserve Communications System
Freddie Mac	Federal Home Loan Mortgage Corporation
FRP	Federal Radionavigation Plan
FSA	Family Support Administration
FSA	Farm Service Agency
FSIS	Food Safety and Inspection Service
FSLIC	Federal Savings and Loan Insurance Corporation
FTA	Federal Transit Administration
FTC	Federal Trade Commission
FTS	Federal Technology Service
FWS	United States Fish and Wildlife Service
GAO	General Accounting Office
GATT	General Agreement on Tariffs and Trade
GFN	Good Faith Negotiations
GIPSA	Grain Inspection, Packers, and Stockyards Administration
GNMA	Government National Mortgage Association (Ginnie Mae)
GPO	U.S. Government Printing Office
GPS	Global Positioning System
GSA	General Services Administration
HCFA	Health Care Financing Administration
HEW	Department of Health, Education, and Welfare
HHI	Healthy Homes Initiative
HHS	Department of Health and Human Services
HIPAA	Health Insurance Portability and Accountability Act of 1996
HMEP	Hazardous Materials Emergency Preparedness
HPCs	High Performance Computers
HUBZone	Historically Underutilized Business Zone
HUD	Department of Housing and Urban Development
ICC	Interstate Commerce Commission
ICE	Immigration and Custom Enforcement
IHAs	Indian Housing Authorities
INA	Immigration and Nationality Act
INS	Immigration and Naturalization Service
IRS	Internal Revenue Service
ISDN	Integrated Services Digital Network
ISP	Internet Service Provider
ISTEA	Intermodal Surface Transportation Efficiency Act of 1991

ITA	International Trade Administration
ITD	International Trade Division
ITS	Information Technology Service
ITU	International Telecommunication Union
JOBS	Job Opportunities and Basic Skills program
JTPA	Job Training Partnership Act of 1982
LIHEAP	Low Income Home Energy Assistance Program
LMRDA	Labor-Management Reporting and Disclosure Act
LNG	Liquefied Natural Gas
LPTV	Low-Power Television
LSA	Local Service Area
LWA	Limited Work Authorization
MARAD	Maritime Administration
MBS	Mortgage-Backed Securities
MEDLARS	Medical Literature Analysis and Retrieval System
MFN	Most-favored-nation
MMDS	Multipoint Microwave Distribution Services
MMS	Minerals Management Service
MSHA	Mine Safety and Health Administration
MSPB	Merit Systems Protection Board
NACOSH	National Advisory Committee on Occupational Safety and Health
NAFTA	North American Free Trade Agreement
NASD	National Association of Securities Dealers
NCCC	National Civilian Community Corps
NCE	New Chemical Entity
NCJRS	National Criminal Justice Reference Service
NCUA	National Credit Union Administration
NCUSIF	National Credit Union Share Insurance Fund
NDA	New Drug Application
NEA	National Endowment for the Arts
NEC	National Economic Council
NEDRES	National Environmental Data Referral Service
NEPA	National Environmental Policy Act
NESDIS	National Environmental Satellite, Data, and Information Service
NEXRAD	Next generation radar
NFA	National Futures Association
NGDC	National Geophysical Data Center
NGPA	Natural Gas Policy Act of 1978
NHTSA	National Highway Traffic Safety Administration
NIC	National Institute of Corrections
NIJ	National Institute of Justice

NIOSH	National Institute of Occupational Safety and Health	OLMS	Office of Labor Management Standards
NIRA	National Industrial Recovery Act	OLS	Online Library System
NIST	National Institute of Standards and Technology	OMB	Office of Management and Budget
NLB	National Labor Board	ONAP	Office of National AIDS Policy
NLM	National Library of Medicine	ONDCP	Office of National Drug Control Policy
NLRB	National Labor Relations Board	OPA	Office of Public Affairs
NMB	National Mediation Board	OPHS	Office of Public Health and Science
NOAA	National Oceanic and Atmospheric Administration	OPJ	Office of Project Completion
		OPPT	Office of Pollution Prevention and Toxics
NODC	National Oceanographic Data Center	OPS	Office of Pipeline Safety
NOPR	Notice of Proposed Rulemaking	ORA	Office of Regulatory Activities
NPDES	National Pollution Discharge Elimination System	OSC	Office of Site Closure
		OSHA	Occupational Safety and Health Administration
NPR	National Performance Review	OSHS	Office of Safety, Health and Security
NPS	National Park Service	OSRA	Ocean Shipping Reform Act
NRA	Negotiated Rates Act of 1993	OSTP	Office of Science and Technology Policy
NRC	Nuclear Regulatory Commission	OTA	Office of Technology Assessment
NRCS	Natural Resources Conservation Service	OTC	Over-the-counter
NSC	National Security Council	OTS	Office of Thrift Supervision
NTIA	National Telecommunications and Information Administration	OVC	Office for Victims of Crime
		OWCP	Office of Workers' Compensation Programs
NTIS	National Technical Information Service (Commerce)		
NTSB	National Transportation Safety Board	PAC	Political Action Committee
NVOCC	Nonvessel Operating Common Carrier	PBGC	Pension Benefit Guaranty Corporation
		PCAOB	Public Company Accounting Oversight Board
OAR	Office of Air and Radiation (EPA)	PHAs	Public Housing Authorities
OASHI	Office of AIDS and Special Health Issues	PHS	Public Health Service
OAW	Office of the American Workplace	PIH	Public and Indian Housing
OCA	Office of Consumer Affairs	PRA	Paperwork Reduction Act
OCC	Office of the Comptroller of the Currency	PRC	Postal Rate Commission
OCR	Office for Civil Rights (HHS)	PRISM	Performance and Registration Information Systems Management
OCRM	Ocean and Coastal Resource Management		
OCS	Outer Continental Shelf	PSA	Packers and Stockyards Administration
OCST	Office of Commercial Space Transportation	PSP	Packers and Stockyards Programs
OECD	Organization for Economic Cooperation and Development	PTO	Patent and Trademark Office
		PUHCA	Public Utility Holding Company Act
OFBCI	Office of Faith-Based and Community Initiatives	PURPA	Public Utilities Regulation Policy Act
		PWBA	Pension and Welfare Benefits Administration
OFCCP	Office of Federal Contract Compliance Programs	QHWRA	Quality Housing and Work Responsibility Act of 1998
OGC	Office of General Counsel		
OGP	Office of Governmentwide Policy	RARG	Regulatory Analysis Review Group
OGSM	Office of the General Sales Manager	RBC	Regulatory Barriers Clearinghouse
OHA	Office of Health Affairs	RBS	Rural Business-Cooperative Service
OHMS	Office of Hazardous Materials Safety	RCRA	Resource Conservation and Recovery Act of 1976
OID	Office of Integration and Disposition		
OIG	Office of the Inspector General (HHS)	RDA	Rural Development Administration
OIRA	Office of Information and Regulatory Affairs	REA	Rural Electrification Administration
OJJDP	Office of Juvenile Justice and Delinquency Prevention	REFCORP	Resolution Funding Corporation
		REMIC	Real Estate Mortgage Investment Conduit
OJP	Office of Justice Programs		

RESPA	Real Estate Settlement Procedures Act of 1974		TA	Teaching assistant
RFA	Regulatory Flexibility Act		TANF	Temporary Assistance for Needy Families program
RHS	Rural Housing Service			
RIMS	Records and Information Management System		TASC	Transportation Administrative Services Center
			TCE	Tax Counseling for the Elderly program
RRF	Ready Reserve Fleet		TDD	Telecommunications Device for the Deaf
RSPA	Research and Special Programs Administration (Transportation)		TEA-21	Transportation Equity Act for the 21st Century
			TIRC	Toxicology Information Response Center
RTC	Resolution Trust Corporation		TRR	Trade Regulation Rules
RTECS	Registry of Toxic Effects of Chemical Substances		TSA	Transportation Security Agency
			TSC	Transportation Systems Center
RUS	Rural Utilities Service		TSR	Transportation Security Regulation
			TTB	Alcohol and Tobacco Tax and Trade Bureau
SAC	Special Agent in Charge		TTRC	Training Technology Resource Center
SAIC	Special Agent In Charge			
SAIF	Savings Association Insurance Fund		UMTA	Urban Mass Transportation Administration
SBA	Small Business Administration		URI	University Research Institute
SBIC	Small Business Investment Company		U.S.C.	United States Code
SBREFA	Small Business Regulatory Enforcement Fairness Act		USCS	United States Customs Service
			USDA	United States Department of Agriculture
SBTE	Small Business Tax Education program		USEC	United States Enrichment Corporation
SCS	Soil Conservation Service		USES	United States Employment Service
SEC	Securities and Exchange Commission		USGS	United States Geological Survey
SESD	Special Examination and Supervision Division		USITC	United States International Trade Commission
SIPC	Securities Investor Protection Corporation		USN	United States Navy
SLSDC	Saint Lawrence Seaway Development Corporation		USPS	United States Postal Service
			USTR	Office of the U.S. Trade Representative
SMI	Supplementary Medical Insurance		UTC	University Transportation Center
SMSA	Standard Metropolitan Statistical Area			
SSA	Social Security Administration		VA	Department of Veterans Affairs
SSI	Supplemental Security Income program		VETS	Veterans' Employment and Training Service
STAA	Surface Transportation Assistance Act		VITA	Volunteer Income Tax Assistance program
STB	Surface Transportation Board		VSS	Voting System Standards
STELA	System for Tracking Export License Applications			
			WHD	Wage and Hour Division
Superfund	Comprehensive Environmental Response, Compensation, and Liability Act		WIC	Women, Infants, and Children food program
			WTO	World Trade Organization

Name Index

Coe, Cindy A., 273
Cohen, Amy, 717
Cohen, Miriam, 460
Cohen, Robert, 366
Cohen, Stan, 429
Colangelo, David A., 252
Cole, Jesse, 631
Cole, Keith, 555
Coleman, Heidi, 672
Coleman, Mary, 207
Coler, Kate, 411
Coles, Tyna, 271
Collins, D. Michael, 134
Collins, Sally, 432
Collins, Samuel J., 358
Collins, Thomas H., 544
Collins, Vaugn, 576
Collins, William J., 321
Colwell, John F., 250
Combs, Ann L., 612
Combs, Linda, 68
Compton, Richard, 670
Comstock, Barbara, 608
Condrey, Jeff, 456
Congel, Frank J., 357
Conley, Susan D., 416
Connaughton, James L., 718
Connell, Noah, 271
Connolly, Marian, 433
Connolly, Robert E., 589
Connor, Mike, 273
Connor, Samuel, 555
Connor, Sandra, 183
Connors, Carol, 162
Connors, John, 705
Connors, Thomas A., 181
Conrad, Virgil L., 413
Conrath, Craig W., 587
Considine, John, 530
Cook, Barbara A., 204
Cook, Beverly, 499
Cook, Beverly A., 505
Cook, Hugh Q., 643
Cook, James, 472
Cook, Mike, 70
Cooke, Gregg A., 71
Cooks, Romell, 672
Cooksey, Janie, 486
Cooksie, Carolyn, 405
Coolidge, Frank A., 426
Coonley, Philip S., 676
Coonts, John, 554
Cooper, Erica, 137
Cooper, Jerry, 654
Cooper, John J., 456
Cooperman, William, 721
Copps, Michael J., 112, 113
Corbett, Amy, 646
Corcoran, Howard, 65
Corcoran, James, 531
Cordes, John F., Jr., 357

Cordyack, John, 581
Corea, Alfred, 481
Corey, Beverly, 227
Corrado, Carol, 183
Corragio, Mary-Deidre, 475, 476
Correll, John R., 629
Cosgrove, Kellie, 205
Costa, Robert, 326
Costales, Federico, 93
Cough, Paul F., 66
Coulin, Ralph, 481
Court, Susan, 159
Courtney, Jim, Jr., 375, 376
Covington, Dana B., 366
Cox, Billy, 394
Cox, James, 472
Cox, John R., 457
Coy, Curtis L., 512
Craig, Charles (Wayne), 117
Craig, James, 601
Cram, Julie, 468
Crawford, Angela F., 251
Crawford, Denise, 534
Crawford, Lester, 225
Crea, V., 547
Crear, Robert, 493
Crecy, Carol, 519
Creedon-Connelly, Mary A., 322
Creel, Frank, 467
Creel, Harold J., Jr., 340
Crim, Carol, 225
Cringoli, Michael, 183
Crippin, Dan, 717
Cristofaro, Alexander, 65
Critchfield, Kenneth, 440
Cromling, Candice, 699
Cronin, Karen M., 676
Crook, Christopher S., 589
Cross, Glenda B., 693
Cross, John F., 69
Cross, Stephen M., 335
Cross, T., 547
Crowley, John, 544
Cruikshank, Walter, 573
Cullen, Linda, 644, 671
Cunningham, Barbara A., 69
Cunningham, Geary, 182
Cunningham, John, 481
Cupitt, Larry T., 67
Curry, James, III, 185
Curtis, Robert, 272, 424, 425, 426
Cushing, Paul, 518
Cutler, Lisa, 502
Cutler, Stephen M., 295
Cyr, Karen D., 358

D

D'Ambrosio, Michael, 533
D'Amico, Letterio (Leo), 65
Dabbs, Jere, 471

Daffron, John, 690
Dagen, Gabriel, 206
Dagen, Richard G., 206
Dager, Dan, 411
Dakin, Deborah, 705
Dalrymple, John, 698
Daly, John F., 205
Dalzell, Robert, 558
Dammer, Anton R., 507
Danello, Mary Ann, 46
Daniel, Bryan, 456
Daniels, Deborah J., 604
Daniels, Gwen, 659
Daniels, Mitchell E., Jr., 722
Daniels, Patricia, 411
Daniels, Reuben, 92
Dannenfelser, Martin, 512
Darling, Nedra, 565
Darm, Donna, 484
Dashiell, Emmett D., 67
Datz, Harold J., 250
Davidson, Margaret, 481
Davidson, Ross J., 446
Davis, Anna, 205, 208
Davis, Gail, 591
Davis, Gary K., 481
Davis, Herbert, 136
Davis, Mary, 699
Davis, Mary M., 256
Davis, Mike, 630
Davis, Rebecca, 448
Davis, Richard A., 451
Davis, Robert L., 493
Davis, Rock, 447
Davis, Stacie, 158
Davis, William S., 643
Davis, Yvonne, 416
Davison, Peter, 724
Day, Mark E., 66
Day, William J., Jr., 465
De Carolis, Louis, 673
De La Torre, Donna, 535
de Mola, Mariano-Loret, 420
de Water, Paul Van, 375
Deal, Glendon D., 452
Deardorff, Charles A., 708
DeCell, Hal C., III, 320
Deerinwater, Dan, 566
Degenhardt, Harold F., 298
DeHaven, Ron, 398
Deily, Limmit F., 724
Del Duca, Maureen, 116
Delaware, John, 158
Delgado, Stephen, 601
DelliBovi, Alfred, 336
DeMarce, James, 618
DeMartino, Laura, 204
Demeter, Kathleen, 670
Denett, Lucy Querques, 573, 575
Dennin, Fred, 657
Dennis, Adele, 232

Pleffner, Mary, 464
Plisch, Cynthia, 303
Plummer, C. Landis, 206
Plunkett, Sylvia, 138
Podberesky, Samuel, 686
Poe, Patrick, 647
Poindexter, Robert J., 252
Polakoff, Scott M., 137
Pollack, Ira, 518
Pollock, Alex, 336
Polston, Lynn, 437
Pomeroy, Thomas, 425, 426, 427, 429
Pon, Melinda, 629
Pool, Mike, 571
Poole, William, 179, 186
Porter, Jeffrey, 470
Porter, Lee, 492
Porter, Neil, 437
Porter, Richard, 183
Porter, Robert C., 508
Porter, Robert, 507
Porter, Warren K., Jr., 46
Posey, Philis, 159
Post, Lorette, 626
Post, Robert, 416
Postic, Steven R., 522
Potter, John E., 384
Potter, Robert A., 587
Powell, Bradley E., 435
Powell, Donald, 133, 134
Powell, Eileen, 698
Powell, Michael K., 112, 113
Powers, Joe, 484
Pracht, Martin W., 599
Prasad, Murli, 419
Preiss, Tamara, 115
Preite, Anthony, 465
Prellezo, Jorge, 353
Preuss, Peter W., 67
Prezioso, Giovanni, 296
Price, Dexter, 460
Price, John C., 705
Price, Lauren, 656
Price, Marvin N., Jr., 589
Price, Sally R., 451
Principi, Anthony J., 711
Priore, Joseph, 419
Pritchard, Edward, 656
Prochaska, Gene, 448
Proeuza, Bill, 485
Proger, Robin, 183
Prunella, Warren, 46
Pryor, Billy M., 448
Przywarty, Rich, 485
Puccinelli, Dennis, 467
Puente-Duany, Hary, 632
Purcell, John, 452
Purcell, Mel, 185
Purcell, Roberta, 451
Purdom, James, 481
Purohit, Sanjeev, 295

Putman-Hunter, Sandra, 180
Pye, Rosemary, 252
Pyron, Chris, 432

Q

Quarles, Lynn, 399
Quick, George, 669
Quinn, Maureen, 423
Quinn, Richard, 530
Quint, Robert, 583
Quintana, Felix, 630
Quiroz, Armando, 627
Quisenberry, Stokes, 394
Quist, Edward E., 45

R

Rabil, George, 555
Radebaugh, Day, Jr., 182
Radintz, James, 405
Rados, William, 227
Raetsch, Paul, 465
Raffanello, Thomas W., 601
Raggio, James, 310
Rahtes, John, 117
Rainey, Daniel, 349
Raisher, Mark, 295
Raley, Bennett W., 580
Ralston, Deborah D., 230
Ramm, Wolfhard, 183
Randolph, Sharon, 452
Rapport, Jack, 625
Rarick, Lisa, 231
Rasmussen, James, 482
Rathbun, Dennis K., 357
Ratliff, Lee, 631
Rau, Russel A., 136
Rawls, Charles, 320
Ray, Dale, 46
Ray, Donna, 605
Ray, Kathy, 649
Ray, Terrie, 446
Rayburn, Cecily, 618
Raynor, Charles, 576
Readinger, Thomas, 573
Reams, Gwendolyn Young, 90
Reardon, Timothy J., 622
Rediess, Herman, 643
Redmond, Randall, 47
Reed, Carol Ann, 358
Reed, Dorothy L., 621
Reed, Lisle, 575
Reed, Pearlie S., 444
Reeder, John E., 64
Rees, Stan, 472
Reese, Gerry, 699
Reese, Ira, 530
Regan, Michael, 637
Regas, Diane, 70
Reger, Mark A., 115

Reich, Edward E., 64
Reich, John, 133, 134
Reich, Lynn, 422
Reichard, Alan B., 255
Reid, Margaret, 656
Reid, Trey, 540
Reidhill, Marsha, 181
Reifschneider, Donna, 437
Reilly, Edward F., 609
Reinhart, Vincent R., 181
Reisheimer, David, 183
Reiter, Lawrence W., 67
Remenschneider, Robert, 422
Rendleman, Sue, 705
Renner, Lori, 92
Renton, William J., Jr., 601
Respet, Ted, 439
Ressin, Charles D., 531
Retzer, Joseph D., 66
Reuwsaat, Tim, 569
Revelle, Monica, 226
Revelt, Mary, 424
Reyes, Luis, 360
Reyna, Michael M., 319
Reynolds, Bobby, 405
Reynolds, James R., 401
Reynolds, Scott, 422
Reynolds, Vanita C. S., 250
Ricci, Robert, 676
Riccobono, Richard, 705
Rice, Condoleezza, 720
Rice, Craig, 448
Rice, Norman B., 337
Rice, William W., 71
Rich, Joseph, 596
Richard, Bob, 675
Richards, Frank, 481
Richards, Lori A., 294
Richardson, Bruce, 49
Richardson, George, 462
Ricker, Nancy, 621
Ricketts, John, 699
Ricks, Marilyn, 488
Riese, Richard, 705
Riley, Don T., 493
Rinehart, Charles R., 180
Ringsak, Elten, 373
Ritz, Lindy, 647
Rivera, Fanny, 642
Roark, Timothy P., 664
Robbins, John, 228
Roberts, Jimmy, 272
Roberts, Kenneth J., 429
Roberts, Marilyn, 604
Roberts, Patricia A., 66
Robinson, Barbara, 394, 396
Robinson, Constance, 587
Robinson, Donald, 181
Robinson, John M., 698
Robinson, Mark, 159
Robinson, Oliver A., 693

Subject Index

Note: **Bold** headings indicate the main entries for agencies and executive departments.

consumer protection, 686
drug trafficking, 352
pilots, 642
regulation and deregulation, 19, 29, 686–687
satellites, 641
security, 13, 541–542
smoking, 646
strikes, 348
weather reporting, 484
Airline and aviation industry—related agencies
Federal Aviation Administration, 641–647
International Civil Aviation Organization, 480
National Transportation Safety Board, 350–354
Transportation Security Administration, 541–542
Airport and Airway Improvement Act of 1982, 645
Airport and Airway Safety and Capacity Expansion Act of 1987, 352–353, 645–646
Airport and Airways Improvement Act (1994), 484
Airport and Airway Trust Fund, 484
Air Traffic Control System Command Center, 642
Air Traffic Management Center, 642
Air Traffic Management System Performance Improvement Act of 1996, 646
Alaska, 60, 434, 648
Alaska National Interest Lands Conservation Act (1980), 434, 571, 578
Alaska Native Claims Settlement Act (1971), 570
Alaskan National Wildlife Reserve, 153
Alaskan Tongass National Forest, 434
Alcohol and Tobacco Laboratory (ATL), 689–690
Alcohol and Tobacco Tax and Trade Bureau (TTB), 590, 689–692
Alcoholic beverages, 689
Aldonas, Grant, 467
Alexis de Tocqueville Institution, 724
ALFD. *See* Advertising, Labeling and Formulation Division
ALJs. *See* Administrative law judges
Alleluia Cushion Co., 245
Alliance for Redesigning Government, 724
Allotted Indian Land Leasing Act of 1909, 570
Alternative Agricultural Research and Commercialization Center (AARC), 449
Alternative Dispute Resolution program (ADR), 325
AMA. *See* American Medical Association
Amendment to Consumer Product Safety Act (2002), 48
Amendments to the Persian Gulf War Veterans Benefits Act (1996), 713
American Bankers Association, 343–344
American Bar Association (ABA), 198
American Federation of Labor-Congress of Industrial Organizations (AFL-CIO), 245, 265
American Fisheries Act (AFA; 1998), 664, 666
American Homeownership and Economic Opportunity Act of 2000, 141, 696, 708
American Indian Trust Fund Management Reform Act of 1994, 564–565, 566
American Institute of Architects (AIA), 310
American Institute of Certified Public Accountants, 286
American Inventors Protection Act of 1999, 488
American Medical Association (AMA), 199
American National Standards Institute, 261, 265

American Stock Exchange (Amex), 286
Americans with Disabilities Act of 1990 (ADA), 28, 80, 82, 84, 86, 95, 309, 311, 371, 549, 551, 597, 616, 620
American Technology Preeminence Act of 1991, 478
American Textile Manufacturing Institute v. Donovan (1981), 266
American Trucking Associations, 10
America Online (AOL), 109, 110, 202. *See also* AOL-Time Warner
America the Beautiful Foundation, 434
AmeriCorps, 441, 449, 717
AmeriSource Health Corp., 201
Amex. *See* American Stock Exchange
AMS. *See* Agricultural Marketing Service
Amtrak. *See* National Railroad Passenger Corporation
Anadromous Fish Conservation Act (1965), 578
Analyses. *See also* General Accounting Office
cost-benefit analysis, 3, 8, 9, 10, 11, 12, 14, 20–22, 26, 38, 39, 265–266, 267, 369
costs of, 21
in the regulatory process, 19–22
risk analysis or assessment, 20, 21
Anderson-Mansfield Reforestation and Revegetation Act (1949), 433
Animal and Plant Health Inspection Service (APHIS), 13, 397–402, 415
Animal Damage Control Act of 1931, 398, 400
Animal Damage Control Program, 398
Animal Welfare Act (AWA; 1966), 398, 400–401
Animal Welfare Act Amendments of 1976, 400
Animal Welfare Act of 1970, 400
Annual Report and Economic Outlook (CBO), 717
Anthony, Sheila F., 203, 204
Anti-Arson Act of 1982, 592
Anticounterfeiting Consumer Protection Act of 1996, 533, 539
Anticybersquatting Consumer Protection Act (2000), 488
Anti-Drug Abuse Act of 1988, 384, 386, 600, 607
Anti-Dumping Act of 1921, 382
Anti-Smuggling Act (1935), 532, 538
Antiterrorism and Effective Death Penalty Act of 1996, 646
Antitrust Amendments Act of 1990, 588
Antitrust issues. *See* Business issues; Justice Department
Antitrust Modernization Commission, 589
Antitrust Modernization Commission Act of 2002, 589
Antitrust Technical Corrections Act of 2002, 589
AOL. *See* America Online
AOL-Time Warner, 112
APA. *See* Administrative Procedure Act of 1946
APHIS. *See* Animal and Plant Health Inspection Service
AQI. *See* Agricultural Quarantine Inspection Program
Archaeological Resources Protection Act of 1979, 571
Architectural and Transportation Barriers Compliance Board (ATBCB; Access Board), 309–311
Architectural Barriers Act of 1968 (ABA), 309, 311
ARCO. *See* Atlantic Richfield Company
Arctic National Wildlife Refuge, 60
Arms Control and Disarmament Agency (ACDA), 462
Arms Export Control Act of 1976, 592
Army Act of July 9, 1918, Chapter XIX, 493

Army Corps of Engineers, 5, 491–494
Army Department, 491
Art and entertainment, 5, 36
Arthur Andersen, 290–291. *See also* Enron Corp.
ASCS. *See* Agricultural Stabilization and Conservation
  Service
Ash Council (1971), 23, 24
Ashcroft, John, 13
Asian fiscal crisis, 175
Asset Liquidation Management Center, 343
Assistance Corporation. *See* Farm Credit System Financial
  Assistance Corporation
Associated Gas Distributors v. FERC (1987), 150
ARCO. *See* Atlantic Richfield Company, 202
AT&T, 105, 106, 111. *See also* Bell telephone companies
AT&T wireless, 111
ATBCB. *See* Architectural and Transportation Barriers
  Compliance Board
ATF. *See* Bureau of Alcohol, Tobacco, and Firearms; Bureau
  of Alcohol, Tobacco, Firearms, and Explosives
ATFI. *See* Automated Tariff Filing and Information System
Atkins, Paul S., 292, 294
ATL. *See* Alcohol and Tobacco Laboratory
Atlantic Richfield Company (ARCO), 202
Atomic Energy Act of 1954, 357, 359, 360, 506
Atomic Energy Commission (AEC), 6, 7, 355, 359
Atomic Safety and Licensing Board Panel, 356
ATP. *See* Advanced Technology Program
ATSA. *See* Aviation and Transportation Security Act
Auchter, Thorne G., 265, 266
Auction Reform Act of 2002, 119
Automated Commercial Environment database, 339
Automated Tariff Filing and Information System (ATFI), 339
Automated Telephone Consumer Protection Act of 1991, 118
Automobile issues. *See also* Transportation Department;
  Transportation issues
  air bags, 12
  all-terrain vehicles (ATVs), 40
  auto loans, 132
  auto safety legislation, 6–7
  drinking and driving, 654, 661, 669
  emissions, 11, 52, 53–54, 58, 60, 61, 62, 73, 74
  foreign vehicles, 669, 672
  fuel efficiency, 26, 30, 62, 668, 669
  gasoline, 57, 60
  infant car seats, 41
  safety, 350, 652, 668–669
  sport-utility vehicles (SUVs), 11, 26, 62
  tariffs, 340
  used cars, 199
Aviation and International Affairs, 686–687
Aviation and Transportation Security Act (ATSA; 2001), 541,
  542, 642, 646
Aviation Disaster Family Assistance Act of 1996, 353
Aviation Drug-Trafficking Control Act (1984), 352
Aviation Enforcement and Proceedings, 686
Aviation Insurance Program, 352
Aviation Medical Assistance Act of 1998, 646
Aviation Security Improvement Act of 1990, 642, 646
AWA. *See* Animal Welfare Act

B

Babbitt, Bruce, 565
Bacanovic, Peter, 292
Balanced Budget Act of 1997, 109, 375
Balanced Budget and Emergency Deficit Control Act of 1985,
  387
Bald Eagle Protection Act (1940), 578
Bankhead-Jones Farm Tenant Act (1937), 408
Bank Holding Act of 1956, 141, 301
Bank holding companies (BHCs). *See* Banking issues
Bank Holding Company Act of 1956, 139, 141, 171, 188, 190
Banking Acts of 1933, 1935, 127, 128, 139, 141, 171, 175, 187,
  301
Banking issues
  bank holding companies, 167, 168, 171, 175
  bridge banks, 130
  chartered banks, 692
  checks and payment clearing, 172–173, 174
  commercial banks, 130, 168, 173
  credit unions, 343
  electronic funds transfer, 209
  examinations and reporting, 126–127, 128, 131, 133, 168,
    172, 692, 704
  failures or illegal activity, 127, 127–128, 129–130, 131, 132,
    140, 168, 189
  Farm Credit System, 318
  Federal Home Loan Banks, 336–337
  Federal Reserve banks, 167, 168, 169, 172–173, 178,
    183–187
  foreign and international banking, 129, 140, 167, 168,
    171–172, 174
  fraud, 607
  glossary of banks, 126
  insurance, 125, 127, 128, 129, 130, 131, 133, 189
  interest rates, 130, 167, 170–171, 173, 174, 175, 176
  legislation, 139–141, 334–336, 694–696
  loans and lending, 132, 663
  mergers, 125, 128, 132–133, 139, 168, 171, 188, 189
  monetary policies, 170–171, 178
  national banks, 173
  privacy, 132
  regional banking pacts and interstate banking, 130, 131,
    141, 190
  regulation and deregulation, 128, 129–130, 131, 132,
    167–168, 171–172, 279
  reserves, 174, 178
  Rural Telephone Bank, 450
  savings and loans, 4, 130, 140, 286, 695
  state-chartered banks, 128, 131, 166, 167, 168, 173
Banking issues—related agencies
  Federal Deposit Insurance Corporation, 125–144
  Federal Housing Finance Board, 334–337
  Federal Reserve System, 166–193
  National Credit Union Administration, 343–347
  Office of the Comptroller of the Currency, 692–696
  Office of Thrift Supervision, 704
Bank Insurance Fund (BIF), 125, 131, 132, 133, 140, 189, 707
Bank Mergers Act of 1966, 171, 188
Bank Mergers and Consolidation Act of 1960, 128, 139, 188

appointments and nominations, 23, 40, 42, 43, 60, 62, 87, 88, 110, 112, 132, 133, 134, 175, 176, 177–178, 203, 224, 248, 249, 269, 290, 292
California energy crisis, 154–155
cloning, 223
conservatism, 11
elections of 2000, 325
environmental issues, 60, 61
Executive Orders, 26, 248, 597
freeze and review of regulations, 2–3, 11, 12, 30
Greenspan, Alan and, 176
NLRB and, 248
September 11, 2001, 12–13
Bush (George W.) administration. *See also* individual agencies and departments
antitrust activity, 3
banking issues, 133
budget issues, 25
campaign promises, 12
control of computer hardware, 460
environmental issues, 4, 10–11, 12, 61
FCC and, 110
government personnel issues, 13
Microsoft and, 587
OSHA and, 268, 269
regulatory activity, 11–13, 30
terrorism and counterterrorism, 13, 30
Business and corporate issues. *See also* Employment issues; individual businesses
accounting and auditing, 286, 289–291, 292
advertising, 198, 199, 200, 208, 220, 224
antitrust, 3, 194, 195, 197, 199, 200, 208, 339, 586–587
bankruptcy, 281, 284, 299, 685
Common Sense Initiative, 10
consumer product safety, 35–38, 39, 40, 41, 42–43, 197
contractors, 616–617
corporate average fuel efficiency (CAFE) standards, 26
cost-benefit analyses, 21
costs of regulation, 22
development of technology, 473
EEO reports, 82, 96
employee e-mail use, 248
enterprise zones, 450, 454
environmental quality, 52, 55, 59, 60, 61, 62
FLSA reports, 617
food processing and inspection, 10
Forest Service and, 431–432, 434
Homeland Security Department database, 30–31
lawsuits and sanctions, 17, 37
Malcolm Baldrige National Quality Award, 473, 477–478
medical device manufacturers, 10, 222, 223, 236
mergers and consolidation, 108, 109–110, 111, 125, 128, 147, 197, 199–202, 209, 588, 682
National Labor Board, 243
OSHA and, 263–264, 265, 266, 267, 268–269
overseas agricultural interests, 421–430
participation and representation, 17–18
pensions, 361–362, 612
pharmaceuticals and drugs, 214–216, 218, 222, 223, 235, 236
polygraphs, 620

Project XL, 10
reporting and registration, 82, 96, 217, 235, 268
rules and regulations, 15, 22, 196, 216–217, 268, 274
rural business, 449
scandals, 17, 176, 290–291
securities markets, 284
small businesses, 368–369
temporary workers, 247, 248
toxic release and waste, 57, 74
training and employment programs, 624
workplace inspections, 262
workplace smoking, 269
workplace violence, 267
Business and corporate issues—related agencies
Advanced Technology Program, 473
Employee Benefits Security Administration, 612–615
Equal Employment Opportunity Commission, 79–99
Federal Trade Commission, 194–213
Food and Drug Administration, 214–240
Foreign Agricultural Service, 421–430
Forest Service, 431–435
Internal Revenue Service, 697–703
Justice Department Antitrust Division, 586–589
National Institute of Standards and Technology, 473–479
National Labor Relations Board, 241–259
Occupational Safety and Health Administration, 260–278
Office of Communications Business Opportunities, 113
Pension Benefit Guaranty Corporation, 361–364
Rural Business-Cooperative Service, 449
Small Business Administration, 274, 368–373
Business Opportunity Development Reform Act of 1988, 371
BXA. *See* Bureau of Export Administration
Byington, S. John, 38

C

CAA. *See* Civil Aeronautics Authority
CAB. *See* Civil Aeronautics Board
Cable Communications Policy Act of 1984, 105, 107, 118
Cable Services Bureau, 103
Cable Television Consumer Protection and Competition Act of 1992, 105, 106, 107, 118
CAFE. *See* Corporate average fuel efficiency standards
CAIP. *See* Community Adjustment and Investment Program
California
electricity industry, 3, 19, 154–155, 156
natural gas industry, 152
California Saw and Knife Works (1995), 246
Campaign finance, 287, 288, 323–325. *See also* Federal Election Commission
Campaigns. *See* Elections
Campanelli, Richard M., 516
Campos, Roel C., 293, 294
Canada, 151, 288, 533, 538, 539
Capital Bank & Trust Co., 130
Capital Cities/ABC, 108
Capital Construction Fund (CCF), 663
Capital Investment Plan (CIP), 641
Capital Markets Efficiency Act of 1996, 300
Capital Ownership Development Program, 371
Cardinal Health Inc., 201

Cargo Preference Act (1954), 666
Carter, Jimmy
    appointments and nominations, 38, 39, 83, 105, 265, 55
    budget issues, 39
    Department of Energy, 7
    deregulation under, 265
    Executive Orders, 21, 503, 506, 509, 776–778
    FTC and, 198, 199
Carter (Jimmy) administration, 11, 21, 56, 244
Casellas, Gilbert, 85–86
Castro, Ida L., 86, 87
Caterpillar, Inc., 247, 266
Cato Institute, 724
CBER. *See* Center for Biologics Evaluation and Research
CBO. *See* Congressional Budget Office
CBP. *See* Bureau of Customs and Border Protection
CBS, 108
CCA. *See* Child Citizenship Act, The
CCC. *See* Commodity Credit Corporation
CCF. *See* Capital Construction Fund
CDC. *See* Centers for Disease Control and Prevention
CDL. *See* Commercial Driver's License Program
CDS. *See* Charge Data System
CEA. *See* Council of Economic Advisers
Center for Biologics Evaluation and Research (CBER), 215, 230
Center for Devices and Radiological Health, 230–231, 238
Center for Drug Evaluation and Research, 215, 231
Center for Environmental Management Information, 503
Center for Fire Research, 477
Center for Food Safety and Applied Nutrition, 215, 231–232, 238
Center for Public Policy Education, 724
Center for the Study of American Business (CSAB), 11, 21, 29
Center for Veterinary Medicine, 215, 232
Center for Women Veterans, 713
Centers for Disease Control and Prevention (CDC), 267, 277
Central Intelligence Agency (CIA), 13
Central Sprinkler Corp., 41
CEQ. *See* Council on Environmental Quality
CERCLA. *See* Comprehensive Environmental Response Compensation and Liability Acts of 1980
CETA. *See* Comprehensive Employment and Training Act
CFR. *See* Code of Federal Regulations
CFRDA. *See* Consolidated Farm and Rural Development Act
CFTC. *See* Commodity Futures Trading Commission
Chamber of Commerce, U.S., 10, 199, 268
Chao, Elaine L., 268, 362
CHAP. *See* Chronic hazard advisory panel
Charge Data System (CDS), 96–97
Charitable Gift Annuity Antitrust Relief Act of 1995, 589
Chemical Diversion and Trafficking Act of 1988, 600
Chemical Safety Information, Site Security and Fuels Regulatory Relief Act (1999), 74
Chemical Science and Technology Laboratory, 473
Cheney, Richard B. (Dick), 156, 176
Chevron USA v. NRDC (1984), 28
Chicago Board of Trade, 316
Chicago Mercantile Exchange, 316
Child Abuse Amendments of 1984, 517

Child Abuse Prevention and Enforcement Act (2000), 513
Child Citizenship Act, The (CCA; 2000), 527
Child Nutrition Act of 1966, 413
Child Nutrition Amendments of 1992, 413
Child Protection Amendments of 1966, 36
Children and family issues. *See also* Educational issues
    abducted children, 636
    adopted children, 527, 636
    advertising, 199, 200, 201, 220
    child abuse, 513, 517
    child labor, 617
    child support, 512, 612, 614
    food and nutrition, 393, 410–411
    foreign-born children, 527, 538
    Head Start, 512
    infant formulas, 235
    juvenile justice, 603–604
    medical leave, 371
    missing children, 603, 606
    Native Americans, 566
    pesticides and insecticides, 59, 60, 220
    pharmaceuticals, 236
    product safety, 36, 37, 41, 42
    sexual exploitation, 384
    smoking and tobacco, 220, 221
    television programming, 101, 103, 106, 108–109
    welfare reforms, 511
Children and family issues—related agencies
    Administration for Children and Families, 511–514
    Consumer Product Safety Commission, 35–51
    Employee Benefits Security Administration, 612–615
    Federal Communications Commission, 100–124
    Federal Trade Commission, 194–213
    Food and Nutrition Service, 393, 410–414
    Office of Children's Issues, 636
Children's Bicycle Helmet Safety Act of 1994, 48
Children's Television Act of 1990, 108, 118
Children's Television Report and Policy Statement, 108
Child Safety Protection Act (1994), 41, 48
Child Support Performance and Incentive Act of 1998, 612, 614
China, 460
Chronic hazard advisory panel (CHAP), 36
Chrysler, 266
Church Arson Prevention Act of 1996, 590, 593
CIA. *See* Central Intelligence Agency
Cingular, 111
CIP. *See* Capital Investment Plan
CITES. *See* Convention of International Trade in Endangered Species of Wild Fauna and Flora
Citizen Advocacy Panel Program, 697
Civil Aeronautics Authority (CAA), 6
Civil Aeronautics Board (CAB), 6
Civil Rights Acts of 1957, 1960, 1964, 1968, 1991, 6, 80, 82, 83, 84, 94–95, 371, 517, 549, 551, 596, 597, 606
Civil rights issues. *See also* Justice Department
    discrimination, 80, 81–82, 84, 85, 86, 94, 95, 311, 517, 597
    employment, 79, 80–83, 84, 86–87, 243, 244, 597, 616, 620
    enforcement of laws and regulations, 515–516, 595
    history of, 83

Civil rights issues—related agencies
  Equal Employment Opportunity Commission, 79–99
  Justice Department Civil Rights Division, 595–597
  Office for Civil Rights, 515–518
Civil Service Commission, 5, 620
Civil Service Reform Act of 1978, 617, 620
Civil Service Retirement and Disability Fund, 387
Civil Service Retirement System, 384
Civil War, 173
Clarke-McNary Act (1924), 433
Clayton Act (1914), 195, 197, 208, 588
Clean Air Act (1970), 7, 10, 14, 28, 54, 56, 57, 58, 59, 61, 74
Clean Air Act Amendments (1970, 1977, 1990), 55, 60, 73, 74, 359
Clean Coal Technology Program, 507
Clean Water Acts (1972, 1977), 5, 56, 59, 73, 74, 493, 546
Clearing-house for Occupational Safety and Health Information (COSHI), 277
Clear Skies Initiative (2002), 4, 61, 62
Clinton, Bill
  appointments and nominations, 23, 41, 43, 58, 85, 88, 106, 112, 131, 132, 133, 156–157, 175, 177, 200, 203, 219, 246, 247, 248, 267, 268, 286
  California energy crisis, 154
  environmental issues, 60, 61
  Executive Orders, 25–26, 82, 87, 267, 722, 784–790
  legislation, 171
  NAFTA and, 58
  as a regulatory activist, 8–9, 10, 30
  vetoes, 246
  welfare reform, 511
Clinton (Bill) administration. *See also* individual departments
  AIDS, 220
  approach to regulation, 8–11, 21
  banking issues, 131, 132, 175
  budget issues, 25, 267, 268
  cost and number of regulations, 11, 12
  EDA and, 463
  EEOC and, 87
  environmental issues, 58, 59, 61
  FDA and, 219–220
  federal outreach to stakeholder groups, 18
  labor issues, 246
  Native Americans, 565
  regulation of tobacco, 28
  review of regulations, 2–3, 12
  standards, rules, and goals, 4, 11
  tobacco issues, 220
  trade issues, 459
  use of Internet, 16
Cloning, 223
CNS. *See* Corporation for National Service
Coal. *See* Energy issues
Coastal Barrier Improvement Act of 1990, 578
Coastal Wetlands Planning, Protection, and Restoration Act (1990), 579
Coastal Zone Management Act of 1972, 480, 483
Coast Guard Personnel and Maritime Safety Act of 2002, 546
CoBank, ACB, 319, 321
COBRA. *See* Consolidated Omnibus Budget Reconciliation Act of 1985

Coburn, Tom (R-Okla.), 223
Coca-Cola Co., 86
Code of Federal Regulations (CFR), 217, 736–738
Collins, Sally, 432
Collins, Thomas H., 544
Color Additive Amendments of 1960, 234
Colorado River Basin Salinity Control Program, 404
Columbia University, 247
Combs, Ann L., 612
Commerce and Labor Department, 197
Commerce Committee, Senate, 42
Commerce Control List, 459–460
Commerce Department (DOC), 458–489
  government publications, 733
  grants, 463, 483
  trade promotion and policies, 459
Commerce Department—related agencies
  Bureau of Industry and Security, 459–462
  Economic Development Administration, 463–465
  International Trade Administration, 379, 466–472
  National Institute of Standards and Technology, 473–479
  National Oceanic and Atmospheric Administration, 480–485
  Patent and Trademark Office, 486–489
Commercial Driver's License Program (CDL), 652
Commercial Motor Vehicle Safety Act of 1986, 653
Commercial Space Launch Act of 1984, 8
Commission for Environmental Cooperation, 58–59
Committee on Renewable Energy Commerce and Trade, 498
Committees, House and Senate. *See* individual agencies, departments, and organizations
Commodities Exchange Authority, 6, 315
Commodity Credit Corporation (CCC), 403, 406, 407, 413, 422, 447
Commodity Credit Corporation Charter Act (1948), 403, 407
Commodity Exchange Act (1936), 300, 312, 315
Commodity Futures Modernization Act of 2000, 312–313, 316
Commodity Futures Trading Commission (CFTC), 279, 285, 300, 312–317, 446
Commodity Futures Trading Commission Act of 1974, 312, 315
Common Carrier Bureau, 102, 105
Communications Act of 1934, 100, 102, 104, 105, 106, 118, 119, 209
Communications Satellite Act of 1962, 104, 118, 119
Communications Satellite Corporation (Comsat), 104–105, 118
Community Adjustment and Investment Program (CAIP), 449
Community Empowerment Program, 450
Community Investment Program, 334
Community Reinvestment Act of 1977 (CRA), 129, 132, 140, 172, 188, 695, 696, 707
Community Services, 512
Competitive Equality Banking Act of 1987, 130, 140, 189, 346, 695, 707
Compliance and Information Bureau, 103
Comprehensive Alcohol Abuse and Alcoholism Prevention Treatment and Rehabilitation Act of 1970, 517

Davis-Bacon Act (1931), 620
Davis, Gray, 155
Dawes Act (1887), 564
DCRT. *See* Death Certificate System
DEA. *See* Drug Enforcement Administration, Justice
Department
Dear, Joseph, 267, 268
Death Certificate System (DCRT), 50
Deep Seabed Hard Minerals Resources Act of 1980, 484,
546
Deepwater Port Act of 1974, 546, 677
Defenders of Property Rights, 42
Defense Department (DOD), 490–494
Army Corps of Engineers, 53, 491–494
Army Department, 491
Federal Radionavigation Plan, 675
high-performance computers, 460
Maritime Security Program, 664
radio spectrum, 109
Defense Production Act of 1950, 188
Deficit Reduction Act of 1984, 346
Delaney Amendment (1958), 14, 215, 218, 234, 236
Delaney, James J. (D-N.Y.), 215, 218
Democratic Party. *See also* Carter, Jimmy; Clinton, Bill
EPA and, 59–60
OSHA and, 267, 268–269
regulatory budgets, 25
union political activities, 11
Department of Agriculture Reorganization Act of 1994, 406,
418, 438, 443, 453
Department of Defense Authorization Act of 1985, 713
Department of Defense Emergency Supplementation
Appropriations Act, 384
Department of Energy Act of 1978 - Civilian Applications,
498
Department of Energy Organization Act (1977), 148,
160–161, 498, 503, 506, 509
Department of Interior Appropriations (1979), 498
Department of Justice Appropriations Authorization Act of
2002, 609, 610
Department of Transportation Acts (1966, 1967), 350, 352,
546, 645, 650, 657, 677, 680, 685
Department of Transportation and Related Agencies
Appropriations Acts (1989, 1992), 646
Department of Veterans Affairs Act (1988), 713
Department of Veterans Affairs Emergency Preparedness Act
of 2002, 714
Dependency and Indemnity Compensation Program,
713
Depository Institutions Act (1982), 129
Depository Institutions Deregulation and Monetary Control
Act of 1980, 129, 140, 189, 346, 695, 707
Depository Institutions Deregulation Committee, 140
Depository Institutions Disaster Relief Acts of 1992, 1993,
141, 189
DeRocco, Emily S., 625
Detroit Free Press, 247
Detroit News, 247
DHHS. *See* Health and Human Services Department
DHS. *See* Homeland Security Department
Diaz, Nils J., 357

Dietary Supplement Act of 1992, 236
Dietary Supplement Health and Education Act of 1994, 30,
236
Dill-White Radio Act of 1927, 104
Directorate of Civil Works, 491
Directorate of Military Programs, 491
Disabled Veterans' Outreach Program, 632
Disaster Relief Act of 1970, 371
Disaster relief. *See also* Earthquakes; Emergency entries
FEMA, 13, 356, 540
FSA Emergency Programs, 404–405, 406
Distance Learning and Telemedicine Program, 450
Distilled Spirits Tax Revision Act of 1979, 690–691
Distributed Energy and Electric Reliability Program,
496
DOC. *See* Commerce Department
DOD. *See* Defense Department
DOE. *See* Energy Department
DOI. *See* Interior Department
DOJ. *See* Justice Department
DOL. *See* Labor Department
Dollar, Dennis, 344
Domestic Chemical Diversion Control Act of 1993, 600
Domestic Housing and International Recovery and Financial
Stability Act (1983), 140
Domestic Policy Council (DPC), 718–719
Dominguez, Cari M., 87–88, 89
Donaldson, William H., 291–292, 294
Do-Not-Call Implementation Act (2003), 210
Dorn, Jennifer L., 659
Dorr, Thomas C., 450
DOT. *See* Transportation Department
Douglas, William O., 284
DPC. *See* Domestic Policy Council
Drug Abuse Control Amendments (1965), 234
Drug Abuse Offense and Treatment Act of 1972, 517
Drug Amendments of 1962, 234
**Drug Enforcement Administration, Justice Department
(DEA)**, 598–602
Drug Interdiction Act of 1980, 546
Drug Listing Act of 1972, 235
Drug Price Competition and Patent Term Restoration Act
(1984), 214, 218, 235
Drugs. *See* Crime and criminal issues; Employment issues;
Medical and healthcare issues
Duck Stamp Act (1934), 578
Duggan, Francis L., 349
Duke Energy, 155
Dynegy, 152, 155, 156, 291

E

EAA. *See* Export Administration Act of 1979
Eads, George C., 21
EAR. *See* Export Administration Regulations
EAR Marketplace, 460–461
Earp, Naomi Churchill, 87
Earthquake Hazards Reduction Act of 1977, 477, 582
Earthquakes, 477, 581, 582
Earth Resources Observation System (EROS), 581
Earth Team, 441

FCSBA. *See* FCS Building Association
FCUA. *See* Federal Credit Union Act
FDA. *See* Food and Drug Administration
FDIC. *See* Federal Deposit Insurance Corporation
FDICA. *See* Federal Deposit Insurance Corporation
  Improvement Act of 1991
FEA. *See* Federal Energy Administration
FEC. *See* Federal Election Commission
FECA. *See* Federal Election Campaign Act and Amendments
FECFile, 325, 329
Fed. *See* Federal Reserve System
Federal Agricultural Mortgage Corporation (Farmer Mac),
  319, 321, 322
Federal Agriculture Improvement and Reform Act of 1996
  (FAIRA), 404, 406, 407–408, 409, 418, 443, 447, 454
Federal-Aid Highway Act of 1973, 546
Federal Aid in Sport Fish Restoration Act (1950), 578
Federal Aid in Wildlife Restoration Act (1937), 578
Federal Alcohol Administration (FAA), 689
Federal Alcohol Administration Act (1935), 689, 690
Federal Anti-Tampering Act (1983), 235
Federal Aviation Act of 1958, 352, 645, 646, 686
Federal Aviation Administration (FAA), 641–647
  administrator, 22
  airline disasters, 19, 350
  certification by, 17
  DEA and, 598
  noise regulations, 73
  regulatory negotiation, 29
  transportation regulations, 541, 686
  weather reporting, 484
Federal Aviation Agency, 645
Federal Aviation Management Advisory Council,
  646
Federal Bankruptcy Code, 281
Federal Boat Safety Act of 1971, 546
Federal Bureau of Investigation (FBI), 13, 351, 590, 598
Federal Bureau of Prisons (BOP), 608–609
Federal Cigarette Labeling and Advertising Act (1965), 198,
  208
Federal Citizen Information Center (FCIC), 733
Federal Coal Leasing Act of 1976, 570
Federal Coal Mine Safety Act of 1952, 628
Federal Communications Commission (FCC), 5, 6, 30.
  See also Telecommunications Act of 1996
  agency organization, 101–102, 112–116
  background and history, 100, 104–111
  budgets and personnel, 24, 27, 109, 110, 113–118
  chairmen and commissioners, 100, 105, 109, 110, 111,
    112–113
  Congress and, 102, 103, 106, 110
  congressional action, 118
  cross-ownership rules, 112
  current issues, 111–112
  DOJ and, 586
  FCC University, 110
  glossary, 101
  information sources, 103, 119–124
  legislation, 104, 105, 107, 108, 109, 111, 118–119
  licenses and auctions, 109, 111–112
  responsibilities and authority, 100–104, 110

Federal Coordinating Council on Juvenile Justice and
  Delinquency Prevention, 603–604
Federal Credit Union Act (FCUA; 1934), 343, 345, 346
Federal Credit Union Act Amendments of 1970, 345
Federal Crop Insurance Act of 1980, 406, 445, 447
Federal Crop Insurance Corporation (FCIC), 403, 406,
  445–446, 447
Federal Crop Insurance Corporation Act of 1938, 406,
  447
Federal Crop Insurance Reform Act of 1994, 406, 445, 446,
  447
Federal Deposit Insurance Act (1951), 128, 139, 141, 190
Federal Deposit Insurance Act, Amendment (1983), 140
Federal Deposit Insurance Corporation (FDIC), 6, 168
  agency organization, 133–138
  background and history, 125, 126, 127–133
  board members, 692, 704
  budgets and personnel, 132, 134–138
  chairmen and directors, 125, 131–132, 133–134
  congressional action, 138–139
  current issues, 133
  glossary, 126
  information sources, 141–144
  legislation, 126, 127, 128–129, 130, 131, 132, 139–141
  reforms, 132
  responsibilities and authority, 125–127, 189
Federal Deposit Insurance Corporation Improvement Act of
  1991 (FDICA), 126, 131, 140, 189, 346, 695, 696, 707
Federal Election Campaign Act of 1971 (FECA), 323, 328
Federal Election Campaign Act Amendments of 1974, 1976,
  1979, 325, 328
Federal Election Commission (FEC), 323–333
Federal Emergency Management Agency (FEMA), 13, 356,
  540
Federal Employee's Compensation Acts of 1916, 1927, 617,
  621
Federal Energy Administration (FEA), 7, 498, 509
Federal Energy Administration Act of 1974, 498
Federal Energy Management, 496
Federal Energy Regulatory Commission (FERC), 7, 14, 15,
  16, 19, 507
  agency organization, 156–160
  background and history, 148–156
  budgets and personnel, 157–160
  chairmen and commissioners, 145, 156–157
  congressional action, 160
  current issues, 156
  FERC Orders, 149–151, 152, 154
  glossary, 146
  information sources, 161–165
  legislation, 160–161
  responsibilities and authority, 145–148
Federal Energy Regulatory Commission Member Term Act of
  1990, 161
Federal Environmental Pesticide Control Act of 1972, 55, 73
Federal Express, 348
Federal Farm Credit Banks Funding Corporation (Funding
  Corporation), 318, 322
Federal Financial Institutions Examination Council (FFIEC),
  129, 168
Federal Firearms Act of 1938, 592

responsibilities and authority, 101, 194–198, 200, 203–204, 208, 209–210, 283

Federal Trade Commission Act Amendments of 1994, 197, 209

Federal Trade Commission Acts of 1914, 172, 197, 198, 208

Federal Trade Commission Improvements Acts of 1980, 1994, 197, 208

Federal Transit Act of 1964, 659, 660–661

Federal Transit Administration (FTA), 659–662

Federal Transit Assistance Acts of 1970, 1974, 659, 661

Federal Unemployment Tax Act (1954), 626

Federal Water Pollution Control Act. *See* Clean Water Acts

Federal Water Pollution Control Act Amendments of 1972. *See* Clean Water Acts

Federal Water Power Act of 1920, 148, 161

Fedworld, 734

FEMA. *See* Federal Emergency Management Agency

FEPC. *See* Fair Employment Practices Committee

FERC. *See* Federal Energy Regulatory Commission

Ferguson, Roger W., Jr., 177

Ferris, Charles, 105

FFDCA. *See* Federal Food, Drug and Cosmetic Act of 1938

FFIEC. *See* Federal Financial Institutions Examination Council

FGIS. *See* Federal Grain Inspection Service

FHA Downpayment Simplification Act of 2002, 557

FHEO. *See* Office of Fair Housing and Equal Opportunity

FHFB. *See* Federal Housing Finance Board

FHLBA. *See* Federal Home Loan Bank Act of 1932

FHLBB. *See* Federal Home Loan Bank Board

FHLMC. *See* Federal Home Loan Mortgage Corporation

FHWA. *See* Federal Highway Administration

FIFRA. *See* Federal Insecticide, Fungicide and Rodenticide Act Amendments of 1988

Finance Board. *See* Federal Housing Finance Board

Financial Accounting Standards Board, 286

Financial institutions. *See* Banking issues

Financial Institutions Reform, Recovery, and Enforcement Act (FIRREA; 1989), 130, 140, 334, 336, 346, 695, 704, 707

Financial Institutions Regulatory and Interest Rate Control Act of 1978, 129, 140, 189, 346, 695, 707

Financial Regulatory Relief and Economic Efficiency Act of 2000, 141, 696, 708

Financial services, 17, 130, 175, 284. *See also* Banking issues; Securities and Exchange Commission; Stocks and stock market

Financial Services Modernization Act of 1999 (Gramm-Leach-Bliley Act), 132, 141, 171, 190, 301, 334–335, 336, 696, 708

Firearms, 590–594

Firearms Tracing Center, 591–592

FIRESAT, 484

FIRREA. *See* Financial Institutions Reform, Recovery, and Enforcement Act

Fish and Wildlife Act of 1956, 578

Fish and Wildlife Conservation Act of 1980, 578

Fish and Wildlife Coordination Act (1934), 578

Fish and Wildlife Improvement Act of 1978, 578

Fishery Conservation Management Act (1976), 484, 546

Flammable Fabrics Act (1953), 36, 37, 48, 198

FLCAs. *See* Federal Land Credit Associations

Flory, Douglas L., 319

Flowers, Robert B., 491

FLSA. *See* Fair Labor Standards Act

Fluid Milk Promotion Act, 396

FMC. *See* Federal Maritime Commission

FMCSA. *See* Federal Motor Carrier Safety Administration

FMD. *See* Foreign Market Development Cooperator Program

FmHA. *See* Farmers Home Administration

FNS. *See* Food and Nutrition Service

FOMC. *See* Federal Open Market Committee

Food. *See* Agricultural issues

Food Additives Amendment (Delany Amendment; 1958), 14, 215, 218, 234, 236

Food, Agriculture, Conservation, and Trade Act Amendments of 1991, 321

Food, Agriculture, Conservation, and Trade Act of 1990, 407, 408, 409, 413, 443, 453

Food and Agriculture Act of 1977, 407, 438

Food and Consumer Service (FCS), 410

Food and Drug Act Amendments of 1962, 218

Food and Drug Act of 1906, 31, 214, 217, 234

Food and Drug Administration (FDA). *See also* Medical and healthcare issues

administrative proceedings, 217

agency organization, 225–233

background and history, 214, 217–224

budgets and personnel, 223, 225–234

commissioners, 215, 218, 223, 224

congressional action, 233–234

current issues, 224–225

glossary, 215

grants, 235, 236, 237–238

information sources, 223, 237–240

legislation, 214, 217, 218, 220, 223, 234–236

reforms, 10, 221–223, 235

responsibilities and authority, 214–218, 224, 225, 234, 235, 415

scandals, 218

Food and Drug Administration Act of 1988, 235

Food and Drug Administration Export Reform and Enhancement Act of 1996, 236

Food and Drug Administration Modernization Act of 1997, 214, 221–222, 236

Food and Drug Administration Revitalization Act (1990), 235

Food and Nutrition Service (FNS), 393, 410–414

Food, Drug and Cosmetic Act of 1938. *See* Federal Food, Drug and Cosmetic Act of 1938

Food, Drug and Insecticide Administration, 217

Food for Peace, 422

Food for Peace Act (1966), 407

Food for Progress Act of 1985, 422

Food Marketing Institute, 10

Food Quality Protection Act of 1996, 59, 60, 74, 236

Food Recovery and Gleaning Program, 410

Food Safety and Inspection Service (FSIS), 10, 415–420

Food Security Act of 1985, 400, 407, 408, 409, 418, 437, 439, 443, 447, 666

Food Stamp Acts of 1964, 1977, 413

Food Stamp Reauthorization Act of 2002, 511, 513–514, 525, 527–528

environmental implementation plans, 52
highways, 650
motor vehicle safety programs, 652
occupational safety and health programs, 260, 264
suits in federal court, 28
telephone issues, 106, 111
transportation services, 659
welfare issues, 511
GPO. *See* U.S. Government Printing Office
GPO Access, 738
Grace Culinary Systems, 87
Grade Crossing Hazard Elimination Program, 655
Graham, John, 11–12
Grain Futures Act (1922), 315
Grain Inspection, Packers, and Stockyards Administration (GIPSA), 436–440
Grain Quality Improvement Act of 1986, 439
Grain Reserve Program, 404
Grain Standards Act, 436
Grain Standards and Warehouse Improvement Act of 2000, 439
Gramlich, Edward M., 177
Gramm-Leach-Bliley Act (1999). *See* Financial Services Modernization Act of 1999
Gramm-Rudman-Hollings budget restrictions, 346
Grand Alliance, 108
Great Depression, 128, 129, 173, 445
Great Lakes, 543, 546, 578
Great Lakes Pilotage Act of 1960, 546
Green Party, 6
Greenspan, Alan, 153, 174, 175–177
GSA. *See* General Services Administration
GSEs. *See* Government-sponsored enterprises
GTE Corp., 109
Guidebook on Military Base Reuse and Homeless Assistance (CPD), 561
Gun Control Act of 1968, 592
Guns, 590–594

H

HACCP. *See* Pathogen Reduction and Hazard Analysis and Critical Control Points
Hague Convention on the Civil Aspects of International Child Abduction, 636
Halliburton, 291
Harbor Maintenance Trust Fund, 681
Hart-Scott-Rodino Antitrust Improvement Act of 1976, 209, 588
Harty, Maura, 637
Harvard Center for Risk Analysis, 11
Hasbro, 201
Hatch-Waxman Amendments, 202
Hawke, John D., Jr., 133–134, 692
Hawkins, Augustus F. (D-Calif.), 84
Hazardous and Solid Waste Amendments of 1984, 8, 73
Hazardous Liquid Pipeline Safety Act of 1979, 677
Hazardous Materials Emergency Preparedness Grants Program (HMEP), 674
Hazardous Materials Transportation Act (HMTA; 1975), 677

Hazardous Materials Transportation Uniform Safety Act of 1990, 677
Hazardous Substance Response Trust Fund, 56, 73. *See also* Superfund
H. B. Zachry Co. v. NLRB (1989), 245
HCFA. *See* Health Care Financing Administration
Health. *See* Medical and healthcare issues
Health and Human Services Department (DHHS), 510–522. *See also* Medical and healthcare issues
   background and history, 218
   civil rights issues, 515–516
   current issues, 220
   food stamps, 525–526
   grants, 450, 511, 512, 517, 519
   responsibilities and authority, 30, 261
   secretaries, 221, 223
   Social Security Administration and, 374
Health and Human Services Department—related agencies
   Administration for Children and Families (ACF), 511–514, 526
   Administration on Aging, 519
   Health Care Financing Administration, 519–520
   Office for Civil Rights, 515–518, 595
   Office of Public Health and Science, 521
   Office of the Inspector General, 520
Health Care Financing Administration (HCFA), 374, 519–520
Health Care Safety Net Amendments of 2002, 236
Health, Education and Welfare Department (HEW), 217
Health Insurance Portability and Accountability Act of 1996 (HIPAA), 516, 517, 612, 614, 701
Health issues. *See* Medical and healthcare issues
Health Manpower Training Act of 1971, 517
Health Omnibus Programs Extension of 1988, 235
Healthy Communities Access Program, 236
Healthy Homes Initiative (HHI), 562
Hebert, Curt, Jr., 19, 155
Helfer, Ricki, 131–132
Help America Vote Act of 2002, 310, 311, 597
Henney, Jane E., 224
Henshaw, John, 269
Hepburn Act of 1906, 684
Heritage Foundation, 725
HEW. *See* Health, Education and Welfare Department
HHI. *See* Healthy Homes Initiative
High-Performance Computing Act of 1991, 478
Highway Safety Acts of 1966, 1970, 650, 671
Highway Trust Fund, 659
Hill, Anita, 85
Hill-Burton Act (1944), 517
HIPAA. *See* Health Insurance Portability and Accountability Act of 1996
HMEP. *See* Hazardous Materials Emergency Preparedness Grants Program
HMTA. *See* Hazardous Materials Transportation Act
Holum, Barbara Pederson, 313
HOME Investment Partnership, 558, 560
Homeland Security Act of 2002, 397, 401, 478–479, 484, 525, 528, 533, 536, 538, 539, 540, 541, 542, 546–547, 590, 593, 646, 689, 691

Investments. *See also* Banking issues; Financial services; Stocks and stock market
    complaints, 313, 314
    futures and futures options, 312–313, 316
    insured and uninsured, 132
    USA Patriot Act, 316
Investments—related agencies
    Commodity Futures Trading Commission, 312–317
    Securities and Exchange Commission, 279–305, 312
Investor and Capital Markets Fee Relief Act (2002), 141, 301
IPCORA. *See* Intellectual Property and Communications Omnibus Reform Act of 1999
Iraq, 176
IRS. *See* Internal Revenue Service
ISTEA. *See* Intermodal Surface Transportation Efficiency Act of 1991
ITA. *See* International Trade Administration
ITD. *See* International Trade Division
ITU. *See* International Telecommunication Union

J

Jackson, Shirley, 356
Jackson, Thomas Penfield, 3
Jacobs, David E., 562–
Jacquez, Albert, 680
Japan, 58, 288. *See also* Kyoto accords protocol
Jeffords, James (Ind-Vt.), 12
Jeffress, Charles N., 268
Job Access and Reverse Commute Grant Program, 620, 659
Job Creation and Worker Assistance Act of 2002, 702
Job Training Partnership Act of 1982 (JTPA), 624, 626
Johnson, Lyndon B., 37, 83, 264, 659
Joint Horizontal Merger Guidelines (FTC), 200
Jones-Smith, Jacqueline, 40
JTPA. *See* Job Training Partnership Act of 1982
Juarbe, Frederico, Jr., 632
Judiciary and judicial system. *See also* Supreme Court (U.S.)
    adjudication of agency disputes, 17
    adjudication of rulemaking, 740, 742–744
    class action lawsuits, 81
    customs courts, 532
    judicial review of regulations, 27–28, 740, 744–746
    legal analysis, 19
    National Labor Relations Board, 243
Juster, Kenneth I., 460
Justice Assistance Act (1984), 603, 606
Justice Department (DOJ), 585–610. *See also* Crime and criminal issues
    AT&T lawsuits, 105
    ATV manufacturers lawsuit, 40
    civil rights issues, 515
    Enron Corp., 290–291
    grants, 603, 604, 606–607
    law enforcement, 590
    Microsoft and Intel, 3, 17
    prosecutions, sanctions and penalties, 17, 54, 56, 267, 283, 628, 669
    regulations, 31

state government employment discrimination, 83
tobacco industry lawsuit, 17, 221
Justice Department—divisions
    Antitrust Division, 200, 586–589
    Bureau of Alcohol, Tobacco, Firearms, and Explosives, 590–594
    Civil Rights Division, 595–597
    Criminal Division, 608
    Drug Enforcement Administration, 598–602
    Federal Bureau of Prisons, 608–609
    Office of Justice Programs, 603–607
    U.S. Parole Commission, 609–610
Justice System Improvement Act of 1979, 606
Juvenile Justice and Delinquency Prevention Act of 1974, 604, 606

K

Keller and Heckman, 89
Kennard, William, 109, 110
Kennedy, Edward M. (D-Mass.), 84, 221–222, 269
Kennedy, John F., 23, 83, 338
Kennedy, Joseph P., 284
Kessler, David A., 19, 218, 219, 220
King, Susan, 38
Kirkpatrick, Miles, 198
Knight, Bryce I., 441
Knutson-Vandenberg Act (1930), 433
Kohn, Donald L., 177
Kopper, Michael J., 291
Korean War, 170
Korsmo, John T., 335
KPMG, 290
Kroger Company, 130
Kyoto protocol (1997), 10–11, 12, 59, 60

L

Labeling of Hazardous Art Materials Act (1988), 36, 48
Laboratory Animal Welfare Act, 398
Labor Department (DOL), 611–634
    budget issues, 25
    ergonomics rule, 12
    regulatory review, 30, 267
    secretaries, 267, 268
Labor Department—related agencies
    Employee Benefits Security Administration, 612–615
    Employment and Training Administration, 624–627
    Employment Standards Administration, 616–623
    Mine Safety and Health Administration, 7, 628–631
    Veterans' Employment and Training Service, 632–634
Labor issues. *See* Business and corporate issues; Employment issues
Labor-Management Relations Act of 1947, 256
Labor-Management Reporting and Disclosure Act of 1959 (Landrum-Griffin Act; LMRDA), 244, 256, 617, 620
Labor-Management Services Administration, 620
Labor Policy Association, 246
Lacey Act of 1900, 576, 577
Lamberth, Royce C., 565
LaMontagne, Margaret, 718

Land-Grant Institution Initiative, 449
Landis, James M., 23, 284
Landrum-Griffin Act (1959), 244
Lane company, 42
Lanham Trademark Act of 1946, 208
Lauriski, David D., 629
Lautenbacher, Conrad C., Jr., 481
Lavelle, Rita M., 56
Law enforcement. *See* Crime and criminal issues; Justice
  Department
Law Enforcement Assistance Administration, 603, 606
Law Enforcement Education, 604
Lead-Based Paint Poisoning Prevention Act (1971), 556
Lead Contamination Control Act of 1988, 48
Learn and Serve America, 718
Leary, Thomas B., 203, 204
Leasing Corporation. *See* Farm Credit Leasing Services
  Corporation
Lechmere Inc. v. National Labor Relations Board (1992), 245
Legal Immigration Family Equity Act (LIFE Act), 527
Legislation. *See* individual agencies and departments
Levitt, Arthur, Jr., 286, 288, 289–290
Libraries. *See* individual agencies, departments, and
  organizations
Library of Congress, 5, 489
Libertucci, Arthur, 690
Liebman, Wilma, 248, 249
LIFE Act. *See* Legal Immigration Family Equity Act
LIHEAP. *See* Low Income Home Energy Assistance Program
Lindsay, Lawrence, 720
Lipnic, Victoria A., 617
Little Cigar Act of 1973, 208
Little, James R., 405
Liu, Michael, 558
LMRDA. *See* Labor-Management Reporting and Disclosure
  Act
Lockheed Martin Corp., 201
Longshore and Harbor Workers' Compensation Act (1927),
  274, 617
Loral Corp., 201
Louisiana Purchase (1803), 568
Lowey, Nita M. (D-N.Y.), 223
Low Income Home Energy Assistance Program (LIHEAP),
  512
Low-Level Radioactive Waste Policy Act of 1980, 360
Low-Level Radioactive Waste Policy Amendments Act of
  1985, 360, 503
Loy, James, 542
LTV Corp., 361
Lukken, Walter, 313

M

MAC. *See* Market Access and Compliance Section
Madrid Protocol, 488
Madrid Protocol Implementation Act (2002), 488
Maglev Deployment Program, 655
Magnuson-Moss Warranty-Federal Trade Commission
  Improvement Act (1975), 196, 197, 198
Mail Order Consumer Protection Amendments of 1983, 386
Maine, 267

Malcolm Baldrige National Quality Award, 473, 477–478
Malcolm Baldrige National Quality Improvement Act of
  1987, 477–478
Mammography Quality Standards Act of 1992, 235–236
Mann-Elkins Act of 1910, 104, 684
Manson, Craig, 576
Manufacturing Engineering Laboratory, 474
Manufacturing Extension Partnership (MEP), 473, 475
MAP. *See* Market Access Program
MARAD. *See* Maritime Administration
Marine Mammal Protection Act of 1972, 483, 484
Marine Protection, Research and Sanctuaries Act of 1972, 55,
  73, 74, 483, 493
Marine Safety Council, 543
Maritime Administration (MARAD), 6, 338, 663–667
Maritime Security Act of 1996, 664, 666
Maritime Security Program (MSP), 664
Maritime Subsidy Board, 663
Maritime Transportation Act (2002), 664
Maritime Transportation Security Act of 2002, 533, 542, 546,
  666, 681
Market Access and Compliance Section (MAC), 466, 467
Market Access Program (MAP), 421
Market Reform Act of 1990, 285–286, 299–300
*Marshall v. American Petroleum Institute, Industrial Union
  Department* (1980), 265
Martin, Kevin J., 111, 112–113
Martin, Lynn, 267
Massey, William L., 156–157
Mass Media Bureau, 102, 103, 116
Mass Transit Account, 659
Material Act (1947), 570
Materials Science and Engineering Laboratory, 474
Mattel, 201
MBS. *See* Mortgage-Backed Securities Program
McCain, John (R-AZ), 110, 221
McClellan, Mark B., 224, 225
McDonald's Happy Meals, 42
McDonnell Douglas Corp., 201
McDonough, William J., 292
McGarrity, Thomas, 14–15
McGovern-Dole International Food for Education and
  Nutrition Program, 424
MCI, 105, 111. *See also* WorldCom
McKee, Garry L., 416
McKesson Corp., 201
MDUFMA. *See* Medical Device User Fee and Modernization
  Act
Meat Import Act of 1979, 423
Media issues. *See also* Federal Communications Commission;
  Telecommunications Act of 1996; Telephone and
  telecommunications issues; individual outlets
    advertising, 198, 208, 224, 325
    cable services, 103, 107
    common carrier issues, 102
    cross-ownership rules, 112
    employment and labor issues, 247
    Fairness Doctrine, 103, 105
    licensing, 102, 109, 110
    lotteries and auctions, 105–106, 119
    mass media, 102–103, 107–108

mergers and consolidations, 109–110, 112
pricing, 107
radio, 100, 102–103, 104, 108, 110, 119
regulation and deregulation, 101, 102–103, 104, 105–106,
107–108
television, 101, 103, 106, 108–109, 110, 112, 202
transportation accidents, 350–351
MediaOne, 109
Medical and healthcare issues. *See also* Abortion and family
planning; Tobacco issues
acquired immune deficiency syndrome (AIDS), 84,
235
addictions, 377
advertising, 224
Agent Orange, 713
AIDS and HIV, 220, 223, 267, 723
bar code requirement on medications, 225
brown/black lung, 266, 617, 621
carcinogens and mutagens, 14, 36, 37, 59, 215, 218, 265
drug abuse and treatment, 234, 246, 600
employment and labor issues, 85, 86–87, 245, 246, 247,
248, 617, 621
Ephedra, 30
FTC and, 199, 200, 201, 202
gene therapy, 223
genetic defects and predisposition to disease, 86, 87
genetic engineering, 219
healthcare benefits, 701
hepatitis, 267
hormone replacement therapy, 224–225
imported drugs, 223–224, 235
insurance issues, 516, 517
investigation of Halcion, 17
lead-based paint poisoning, 556, 562
mammography, 235–236
medical devices, 10, 215, 217, 222, 223, 234, 235, 236
medical records, 516
mental health, 85
nuclear power, 355
occupational illnesses and injuries, 10, 263–264, 265, 266,
267
Persian Gulf Syndrome, 713
pesticides, 60, 74
pharmaceuticals and drugs, 30, 214–215, 216–217, 218,
219, 220, 222–225, 234, 235, 236
product-related disorders, 35–36, 219
radiation, 53, 215, 216, 217, 235, 477, 503, 504
regulatory analyses, 20
repetitive motion disorders, 12, 20, 26, 267, 268–269
RU-486, 223
Taxol, 434
thalidomide, 218, 222
tuberculosis, 267
veterans, 713, 714
Viagra, 222
workplace violence, 267
Medical and healthcare issues—related agencies
Food and Drug Administration, 214–240
Mine Safety and Health Administration, 628–631
Occupational Safety and Health Administration, 260–278
Office for Civil Rights, 515–518

Office of Environment, Safety, and Health, 504–506
Office of Workers' Compensation Programs, 617
Medical Device Amendments of 1976, 234
Medical Device User Fee and Modernization Act
(MDUFMA; 2002), 236
Medicare and Medicaid, 31, 221, 374, 375, 511, 520
Meetings and dockets. *See* individual agencies, departments,
and organizations
Meier, Kenneth, 2
Meissner, Doris, 525
Memorandum of Understanding on Responsibilities for
Hazardous and Radioactive Mixed Waste Management
(DOE/EPA), 500
MEP. *See* Manufacturing Extension Partnership
Merchant Marine Act of 1920, 1936, 1970, 341, 545, 663, 666,
681
Merchant Ship Sales Act (1946), 666
Merrill Lynch, 17
Meserve, Richard, 357
Mexican Border Act of 1942, 400
Mexican Cession (1848), 568
Mexico, 58, 539
Meyer Industries, 245
Mickey Leland Childhood Hunger Relief Act (1993), 413
Microsoft, 3, 17, 586–587
Migrant and Seasonal Agricultural Worker Protection Act
(1983), 620
Migratory Bird Conservation Act (1929), 578
Migratory Bird Hunting and Conservation Stamp Act
(1934), 578
Migratory Bird Treaty Act (1918), 577–578, 579
Migratory Bird Treaty Reform Act of 1998, 579
Miller, James, III, 199
Miller, Paul Steven, 87, 88, 89
Miller, W. Kirk, 422
Millstone reactor, 356
Mineral Lands-Production of Oil from Tar Sand Act of 1981,
571
Mineral Leasing Act (1920), 570, 575, 677
Mineral Leasing Act for Acquired Lands (1947), 570
Mineral Revenue Payments Clarification Act of 2000, 575
Minerals Management Service (MMS), 564, 573–575
Mine Safety and Health Administration (MSHA), 7,
628–631
Mine Safety and Health Review Commission, 630
Minimum Wage Increase Act of 1996, 621
Mining and minerals, 7, 484. *See also* Mineral entries
Mining and minerals—related agencies
Bureau of Land Management, 568–572
Bureau of Mines, 628
Minerals Management Service, 573–575
Mine Safety and Health Administration, 628–631
Office of Surface Mining, 584
U.S. Geological Survey, 576, 580–582
Mining Enforcement and Safety Administration, 7, 628, 630
Miscellaneous Aviation Amendments (1989), 646
Mitsubishi Motors, 17, 86
MMS. *See* Minerals Management Service
Monetary Control Act of 1980, 171, 172, 173–174
Money Laundering Control Act of 1986, 532–533, 538
Montgomery GI Bill, 714

Moody's, 153
Moore, Thomas H., 43, 44
Mortgage-Backed Securities Program (MBS), 562
Motorboat Act of 1940, 545
Motor Carrier Act of 1935, 6
Motor Carrier Safety Act of 1984, 653
Motor Carrier Safety Assistance Program, 652
Motor Carrier Safety Improvement Act of 1999, 648, 650, 652, 654
Motor Vehicle Information and Cost Savings Act of 1972, 671
Motor Vehicle Manufacturers v. State Farm (1983), 28
MSHA. *See* Mine Safety and Health Administration
MSP. *See* Maritime Security Program
Multi-Employer Pension Plan Amendments Act of 1980, 364, 613
Multifamily Property Disposition Reform Act of 1994, 551, 557
Multilateral Trade Negotiations, 466
Multiple-Use Sustained-Yield Act of 1960, 433
Municipal Securities Rulemaking Board, 287–288
Muris, Timothy J., 203, 204
Mylan Laboratories, 202

N

NAAG. *See* National Association of Attorneys General
NAC. *See* National Audiovisual Center
NACOSH. *See* National Advisory Committee on Occupational Safety and Health
NAD-Bank. *See* North American Development Bank
Nader, Ralph, 6, 198
NAFTA. *See* North American Free Trade Agreement
NAPA. *See* National Academy of Public Administration
Narcotic Addict Treatment Act of 1974, 600
NAS. *See* National Airspace System
NASA. *See* National Aeronautics and Safety Administration
Nasdaq, 175, 287
National Academy of Public Administration (NAPA), 88
National Advisory Committee for the Flammable Fabrics Act, 39
National Advisory Committee on Ergonomics, 269
National Advisory Committee on Occupational Safety and Health (NACOSH), 272
National Aeronautics and Safety Administration (NASA), 675
National Affordable Housing Act of 1990, 558
National Agricultural Library, 433
National Ag Risk Education Library, 446, 447
National Airspace System (NAS), 641
National Association of Attorneys General (NAAG), 200
National Association of Broadcasters, 110
National Association of Manufacturers, 10, 199, 268
National Association of Securities Dealers, 280, 284, 285, 286
National Audiovisual Center (NAC), 734
National Bank Act (1863), 173, 692
National Biological Survey/Service (NBS), 576, 580
National Bureau of Standards, 473, 477, 478
National Cemetery System, 710–711
National Center for Devices and Radiological Health, 215
National Center for Standards and Certification Information, 476
National Center for Toxicological Research (NCTR), 232, 239

National Civilian Community Corps (NCCC), 717
National Clearinghouse for Election Administration, 325
National Climatic Data Center, 482
National Commission on Orphan Diseases, 235
National Commission on Product Safety, 37
National Commission on the Public Service, Leadership for America: Rebuilding the Public Service, 24
National Conservation Program, 443
National Construction Safety Team Act (2002), 473, 478
National Consumers League, 201
National Cooperative Geologic Mapping Program, 582
National Cooperative Research and Production Act of 1993 (NCRPA), 588
National Credit Union Administration (NCUA), 7, 168, 343–347
National Credit Union share Insurance Fund (NCUSIF), 343, 346
National Crime Survey, 603
National Criminal Justice Reference Service (NCJRS), 603, 605–606
National Currency Act of 1863, 128
National Defense Authorization Act of 1998, 460, 462
National Defense Reserve Fleet, 663
National Do-Not-Call Registry, 202, 210
National Driver Register, 669
National Earthquake Information Service, 581
National Economic Council (NEC), 720
National Electrical Code, 40
National Electronic Injury Surveillance System, 42, 50
National Energy Act (1978), 161
National Energy Conservation Policy Act (1978), 498
National Energy Extension Service Act (1977), 498
National Energy Information Center, 163, 497
National Environmental Data Referral Service (NEDRES), 77
National Environmental Policy Act of 1969 (NEPA), 6, 14, 22, 55, 72, 503, 504, 561, 718
National Environmental Satellite, Data, and Information Service (NESDIS), 480, 481, 482
National Estuarine Research Reserve System, 480
National Firearms Act (1934), 592
National Fire Protection Association, 261, 265
National Fish and Wildlife Foundation, 578
National Fish and Wildlife Foundation Establishment Act (1984), 578
National Fish Hatcheries, 576
National Forest Foundation Act (1990), 434
National Forest Management Act of 1976, 434
National Forest Roads and Trails Systems Act (1964), 433
National Forest System, 431, 434
National Foundation on the Arts and the Humanities Act (1965), 274
National Fraud Information Center, 201
National Futures Association (NFA), 312, 313
National Geologic Mapping Act of 1992, 582
National Geologic Mapping Reauthorization Act of 1997, 582
National Geophysical Data Center, 483
National Health Service Corps (NHSC), 236
National High-Performance Computing Program, 478
National High-Performance Computer Technology Act (1991), 118
National Highway Institute, 648

NPR. *See* National Performance Review; National Public Radio

NRC. *See* Nuclear Regulatory Commission

NRCS. *See* Natural Resources Conservation Service

NRC Threat Advisory and Protective Measures System, 357

NSC. *See* National Security Council

NTIA. *See* National Telecommunications and Information Administration

NTIS. *See* National Technical Information Service

NTSB. *See* National Transportation Safety Board

NTSB Academy, 351

Nuclear energy and weapons. *See also* Energy issues
   controls on, 459
   decommissioning activities, 500, 501
   nuclear testing, 459
   nuclear waste, 74, 501, 503
   thermal pollution, 72–73

Nuclear energy and weapons—related agencies
   Bureau of Industry and Security, 459–461
   Nuclear Regulatory Commission, 7, 16, 19, 355–360, 586
   Office of Environmental Management, 500–503

Nuclear Energy Search Team, 13

Nuclear Infrastructure Antiterrorism Team, 357

Nuclear Nonproliferation Act of 1978, 359–360, 459

Nuclear Regulatory Commission (NRC), 7, 16, 19, 355–360, 586

Nuclear Security Act of 2003, 357

Nuclear Waste Policy Act of 1982, 360, 503, 677

Nursery Stock Quarantine Act, 400

Nutrition Labeling and Education Act (1990), 235

NYSE. *See* New York Stock Exchange

NYU. *See* New York University

O

OASIS. *See* Open Access Same-time Information system

Occupational Safety and Health Act of 1970, 5, 260, 261, 262, 264, 266, 274

Occupational Safety and Health Administration (OSHA). *See also* Labor Department; Medical and healthcare issues; National Institute of Occupational Safety and Health
   agency organization, 269–273
   background and history, 7, 14, 260, 261, 264–269
   budgets and personnel, 11, 21, 25, 26–27, 262, 266, 267, 268, 269, 270–273
   congressional action, 273–274
   cost-benefit analysis, 265–266, 267, 268
   current issues, 269
   directors, 260, 265, 266, 267, 269–270
   grants, 275
   information sources, 274–278
   legislation, 5, 260, 261, 262, 264, 266, 268, 274
   meetings, 261
   reforms, 10, 265, 266–268, 269
   responsibilities and authority, 10, 16–17, 18–19, 29, 260–264, 265–266, 268–269, 274
   standards and goals, 4, 7, 19, 26, 261–262, 265, 266–267, 274

Occupational Safety and Health Review Commission, 262, 263, 274

OCD. *See* Office of Community Development

Ocean Dumping Act (1972), 56

Ocean Pollution Dumping Act of 1988, 74

Oceans Act of 1992, 484

Ocean Shipping Reform Act (OSRA; 1998), 339–340, 341

Ocean Thermal Energy Conversion Act of 1980, 484, 498

Ocean Thermal Energy Conversion Research, Development and Demonstration Act (1980), 498

OCR. *See* Office for Civil Rights

OCRM. *See* Office of Ocean and Coastal Resource Management

OECD. *See* Organization for Economic Cooperation and Development

OEDPs. *See* Overall Economic Development Programs

OFBCI. *See* Office of Faith-Based and Community Initiatives

OFCCP. *See* Office of Federal Contract Compliance Programs

Office Depot, 201

Office for Civil Rights (OCR), 515–518, 595

Office for Drug Abuse Law Enforcement, 598

Office for Information Security Programs, 479

Office for Victims of Crime (OVC), 603, 604–605

Office-Max, 201

Office of Advocacy, 368

Office of Airport Safety and Standards, 641

Office of Aviation Analysis, 686–687

Office of Business and Community Initiative, 368

Office of Children's Health Protection, 64

Office of Children's Issues, 636

Office of Communications Business Opportunities, 113

Office of Community Development (OCD), 449, 450

Office of Community Planning and Development (CPD), 561

Office of Compliance, 36, 721

Office of Consumer Advocate, 366, 384

Office of Economic Analysis, 302

Office of Election Administration, 325, 326–327

Office of Emergency Transportation, 675

Office of Energy Efficiency and Renewable Energy (EREN), 496–499

Office of Energy Projects, 159

Office of Enforcement, 356

Office of Enforcement and Compliance Assurance, 54

Office of Engineering and Technology, 104, 113

Office of Entrepreneurial Development, 369

Office of Environmental Management (EM), 500–503

Office of Environmental Restoration and Waste Management, 500

Office of Environment, Safety, and Health (ESH), 504–506

Office of Equal Employment and Minority Enterprise, 45

Office of Export Enforcement, 462

Office of Fair Housing and Equal Opportunity (FHEO), 549–552, 595

Office of Faith-Based and Community Initiatives (OFBCI), 719

Office of Family Assistance, 511

Office of Federal Contract Compliance Programs (OFCCP), 616–617, 618, 619–620

Office of Federal Operations, 82

Office of Field Operations, 415, 416

Office of Fossil Energy, 507–509

Office of Government Contracting, 368

Office of Governmentwide Policy (OGP), 721, 724

Pipeline Safety Acts of 1979, 1992, 674, 678
Pipeline Safety Improvement Act of 2002, 678
Pitofsky, Robert, 200–201
Pitt, Harvey L., 290, 291
PLAD. *See* Proceedings and Litigation Action Display
Plant Quarantine Act Amendment (1983), 400
Plant Quarantine Act of 1912, 400
Plant Variety Protection Act (1970), 392, 396
Poison Prevention Packaging Act of 1970, 36, 37, 48
"Poison Squad," 217
Political action committees (PACs), 323
Political issues. *See also* Federal Election Commission
    campaigns and elections, 324–325
    immigration, 525
    leadership in regulatory institutions, 23–24
    Medicare and Social Security, 374–375
    political broadcasting, 103
    regulation and rule-making, 2, 4–5, 19, 26
    selection of regulatory personnel, 23
    union activities, 11
Pollution Prevention Act of 1990, 74
Port and Tanker Safety Acts (1972; 1978), 546, 681
Porta Systems, 290
Ports and Waterways Safety Act of 1972, 546, 681
Postal Civil Service Retirement System Funding Reform Act
    of 2003, 387
Postal Rate Commission (PRC), 365–367, 383, 384
Postal Reorganization Act (1970), 244, 256, 365, 367, 383,
    386, 617
Postal Reorganization Act Amendments of 1976, 365,
    367
Post Office Department, 104, 367, 383, 386
Post Roads Act (1866), 104
Potter, John E., 384
Poultry Producers Financial Protection Act of 1987, 439
Poultry Products Inspection Act (1957), 418
Powell, Colin, 110
Powell, Donald E., 132, 133
Powell, Michael K., 110, 111, 112, 113
Power Plant and Industrial Fuel Use Act of 1978, 150, 507,
    509
PRC. *See* Postal Rate Commission
Pregnancy Discrimination Act of 1978, 80, 94
Prescription Drug Marketing Act of 1987, 235
Prescription Drug User Fee Act of 1992 (PDUFA), 236
Presidential and Executive Office Accountability Act (1996),
    597
Presidential Election Campaign Fund, 323
Presidential Election Campaign Fund Act of 1971, 323
Presidents and presidency. *See also* individual presidents and
    administrations
    budget estimates and requests, 24–25
    emergency boards, 348
    executive privilege, 56
    influence on regulation, 24–26, 29
    selection of agency heads and commissioners, 22–23
President's Commission on Aviation Security and Terrorism,
    642
Price Anderson Amendments Act of 1988, 506
PricewaterhouseCooper (PwC), 289
Principi, Anthony J., 711

Privacy Act (1974), 319, 769–775
Privacy issues, 516
Private Radio Services Bureau, 102
Private Sector Council, 725
Private Securities Litigation Reform Act of 1995, 300
Proceedings and Litigation Action Display (PLAD), 303
Procter & Gamble, 219
Produce Agency Act (1927), 395
Product Safety Advisory Council, 39
Product Safety Amendments of 1981, 39
Project on Government Oversight, 725
Proposed Sale of Securities Inquiry (PSSI), 303
PSA. *See* Packers and Stockyards Administration
PSINet, 110
PSSI. *See* Proposed Sale of Securities Inquiry
PTO. *See* Patent and Trademark Office
Public and Assisted Housing Drug Elimination Act of 1990,
    560
Publications and publishers. *See* individual agencies,
    departments, and organizations
Public Citizen, 725
Public Company Accounting Oversight Board (PCAOB),
    291, 292, 301
Public Health Cigarette Smoking Act of 1969, 198, 208
Public Health Security and Bioterrorism Preparedness and
    Response Act of 2002, 74, 236
Public Health Service, 264, 415, 521
Public Health Service Act (1944), 214, 223, 234, 236, 517
Public Law 89-777 (FMC), 341
Public Law 92-205 (weather modification), 483
Public Range Lands Improvement Act of 1978, 571
Public Safety Officers' Benefits Act of 1976, 606
Public Utility Holding Company Act of 1935 (PUHCA), 153,
    281, 284, 299, 300
Public Utility Regulatory Policies Act of 1978 (PURPA), 147,
    161, 498, 509
Public Works and Economic Development Act of 1965, 463,
    465
Puerto Rico, 319, 431
Puerto Rico Farm Credit, ACA, 319
PUHCA. *See* Public Utility Holding Company Act
PURPA. *See* Public Utility Regulatory Policies Act of 1978
PWBA. *See* Pension and Welfare Benefits Administration
PwC. *See* PricewaterhouseCooper

Q

Quality Housing and Work Responsibility Act of 1998
    (QHWRA), 558, 560
Quayle, Dan, 8

R

Racial and minority issues. *See also* Native Americans
    credit opportunities, 188
    employment discrimination, 84, 85, 86
    home mortgages, 188
    housing discrimination, 311
    small businesses, 369
Racketeer Influenced and Corrupt Organizations Act (RICO;
    1970), 533, 539

Radiation Control for Health and Safety Act of 1968, 214, 235, 477

Radio. *See* Federal Communications Commission; Media issues

Radio Act (1912), 104

Rail Passenger Disaster Family Assistance Act, 351

Rail Passenger Service Act of 1970, 685

Railroad Retirement Act, 361

Railroad Revitalization and Regulatory Reform Act of 1976, 657, 685

Railroads. *See also* Transportation issues
    accidents, 350
    high-speed rail, 655, 657
    as a natural monopoly, 3
    price wars, 4
    regulation and deregulation, 5, 29, 684, 685

Railroads—agencies and boards
    Federal Railroad Administration, 655–658
    Surface Transportation Board, 682–685

Rail Safety Improvement Act of 1988, 657

Rail Services Planning Office, 685

Railway Labor Act of 1926, 242, 243, 348

Railway Labor Act amendments (1934), 349

Raley, Bennett W., 580

RARG. *See* Regulatory Analysis Review Group

RBC. *See* Regulatory Barriers Clearinghouse

RBS. *See* Rural Business-Cooperative Service

RCRA. *See* Resource Conservation and Recovery Act

RDA. *See* Rural Development Administration

REA. *See* Rural Electrification Administration

Ready Reserve Fleet (RRF), 663

Reagan, Ronald
    appointments and nominations, 39, 56, 83, 105, 176, 199, 245, 265, 266
    budget issues, 25, 39, 199
    EPA and, 56, 57
    Executive Orders, 25, 26, 265, 722, 778–784
    OSHA and, 265, 266
    reform of rule-making process, 11, 29
    regulation and deregulation, 19, 39

Reagan (Ronald) administration, 8, 11, 20, 39, 218, 245, 463

Real Estate Mortgage Investment Conduit (REMIC), 562

Real Estate Settlement Procedures Act of 1974 (RESPA), 128, 139, 172, 554, 557, 695, 706

REAP Initiative. *See* Rural Economic Area Partnership Initiative

Reason Foundation, 725

Recall Handbook (1989), 37

Reciprocal Meat Inspection Requirement, 418

Reclamation Projects Authorization and Adjustment Act of 1992, 74

Recreational Boating and Safety and Facilities Act of 1980, 546

Recreation and Public Purposes Act (1926), 570

Reed-Bullwinkle Act of 1948, 685

REFCORP. *See* Resolution Funding Corporation

Reference resources. *See* individual agencies, departments, and organizations

Refrigerator Safety Act (1956), 36, 48

Refuge Recreation Act (1962), 578

Refuge Revenue Sharing Act (1935), 578

Regional offices. *See* individual agencies, departments, and organizations

Regional Rail Reorganization Act of 1973, 657, 685

Registry of Toxic Effects of Chemical Substances (RTECS), 277

Regulations and Procedures Division, 690

Regulations and rules. *See also* Executive orders; Standards; individual agencies, departments, and organizations
    accountability, oversight, planning and review, 8, 9, 11–12, 14, 24–28, 30
    administrative personnel, 22–24, 25
    analysis and process, 2, 9, 19–22, 369
    budget issues 24–25, 30
    definition of, 2
    command and control regulation, 4
    costs of, 11
    criticisms of, 15, 23, 24, 37
    deregulation movement, 8
    dispute resolution, 17–20
    economic regulation, 3–5
    enforcement, intervention, and sanctions, 16–17, 30
    history and growth, 5–6, 11, 12
    information, implementation, and monitoring, 16–17
    lawsuits against, 10
    legislation, 13–14
    licenses and permits, 15–16
    net-benefit criteria, 8
    political aspects of, 2, 4–5, 10
    reasons for, 2–5, 18, 19
    reforms and the future, 29–31
    regulatory negotiation, 29–30, 80
    rulemaking and hearings, 14–15, 80, 739–740, 741–742
    social aspects of, 4–5, 6–13
    special goods and services, 4

Regulations Regarding Lawn Darts, 48

Regulatory Analysis Review Group (RARG), 21

Regulatory Barriers Clearinghouse (RBC), 556

Regulatory Compliance and Enforcement Program, 652

Regulatory Flexibility Act of 1980 (RFA), 14, 22, 346, 371

Regulatory Information Service Center, 724

Regulatory Oversight and Coordination, 715–725

Regulatory Reports Review Group, 722

Regulatory Working Group, 9, 26

Rehabilitation Act Amendments of 1998, 309–310, 311

Rehabilitation Act of 1973, 80, 84, 95, 309, 310, 311, 517, 549, 551, 606, 616, 619–620

Reich, John, 133

Reid, Harry (D-Nev.), 357

Reifschneider, Donna, 437

Reilly, William, 57

Reinventing Government, 267, 525

Reliant Energy, 155

REMIC. *See* Real Estate Mortgage Investment Conduit

Removal of Regulatory Barriers to Affordable Housing Act of 1992, 695

Renewable Energy Industry Development Act (1984), 498

Reorganization Plan No. 1 (1980), 360

Reorganization Plan No. 2 (1968, 1973), 598, 600, 661

Reorganization Plan No. 3 (1940, 1970), 72, 576

Reorganization Plan No. 4 (1949), 480, 720

Reorganization Plan No. 7, 338

Sarbanes-Oxley Act (2002), 291, 292, 301

Satellite communications. *See* Federal Communications Commission; Media issues; National Environmental Satellite, Data, and Information Service

Satellite Home Viewer Improvement Act of 1999 (SHVIA), 119

Satellite Operational Control Center and Command and Data Acquisition facilities, 481

Savings Association Insurance Fund (SAIF), 125, 130, 131, 132, 133, 704, 707

SBA. *See* Small Business Administration

SBC. *See* Southwestern Bell Communications

SBTE. *See* Small Business Tax Education

Scandals
  business, 17, 176
  CPSC, 38
  EPA, 25, 56, 266
  FDA, 218

Scanlon, Terrence, 40

Scannell, Gerard F., 267

Schabert, William G., 664

Schaumber, Peter C., 249

Schools. *See* Educational issues

Science and Technology Program, 393

SCS. *See* Soil Conservation Service

Sears, Roebuck and Company, 130

SEC. *See* Securities and Exchange Commission

Second Mortgage Market Enhancement Act of 1984, 707

Secret Service, 13

Section 8. *See* Housing Choice Voucher Programs

Section 8(a). *See* Small Business Act of 1953, 369

Section 8 Rental Certificate Program, 560

Secure Rural Schools and Community Self-Determination Act of 2000, 431–432, 434

Securities Act of 1933, 188, 281, 282, 283, 285, 298–299, 300, 371

Securities Acts Amendments of 1964, 1975, 284, 299

Securities and Exchange Commission (SEC), 6, 17, 312, 313, 316
  agency organization, 292–298
  background and history, 279, 283–291
  budgets and personnel, 292, 294–298
  chairmen and commissioners, 291–294
  congressional action, 298
  current issues, 291–292
  glossary, 280
  information sources, 301–305
  legislation, 298–301
  responsibilities and authority, 279–283, 291
  September 11, 2001, and 290

Securities and Exchange Commission Authorization Act of 1996, 300

Securities Enforcement Remedies and Penny Stock Reform Act of 1990, 299

Securities Exchange Act of 1934, 126, 139, 141, 188, 279, 281, 282, 283–284, 285, 290, 298, 300, 301

Securities Investor Protection Act of 1970, 285, 299

Securities Investor Protection Corporation (SIPC), 281, 285, 299, 300, 303–304

Securities Reporting System, 303

Seminole Tribe v. Florida (1996), 28

Senate (U.S.), 22, 23. *See also* Congress (U.S.)

Senior Citizens Housing Act (1962), 453

Senior Companion Program, 718

Senior Corps, 718

Senior Foreign Service, 620

Sentencing Reform Act of 1984, 609

September 11, 2001, 12, 87, 176, 269, 290, 365–366, 473, 642. *See also* Terrorism and counterterrorism

Service Contract Act (1965), 274, 620

Shalala, Donna, 221

Shareholder Communications Act of 1985, 299

Shelby, Richard C. (R-Al.), 133

Shell Oil Co., 57

Sherman Antitrust Act (1890), 3, 208, 586, 588, 589

Shipping Act of 1984, 338, 339–340, 341, 666

SHVIA. *See* Satellite Home Viewer Improvement Act of 1999

Sierra Club, 55

Sikes Act (1960), 578

Sikes, Alfred, 106

Silverman, Leslie E., 87, 88–89

Simpson, Richard, 38

Single-Employer Pension Plan Amendments Act of 1986, 364, 614

SIPC. *See* Securities Investor Protection Corporation

SLSDC. *See* Saint Lawrence Seaway Development Corporation

Small Business Act of 1953, 368, 369, 371, 372

Small Business Administration (SBA), 74, 274, 368–373

Small Business and Agriculture Regulatory Enforcement Ombudsman, 74, 274

Small Business Answer Desk, 368

Small Business Credit and Business Opportunity Enhancement Act of 1992, 371

Small Business Investment Act of 1958, 368, 371

Small Business Investment Incentive Act of 1980, 281, 299, 371

Small Business Job Protection Act of 1996, 701, 708

Small Business Lending Enhancement Act of 1995, 371

Small Business Liability Protection Act (2002), 74

Small Business Liability Relief and Brownsfields Revitalization Act (2002), 74

Small Business Paperwork Relief Act of 2002, 372

Small Business Programs Reauthorization Act of 2000, 372

Small Business Reauthorization Act of 1977, 369

Small Business Regulatory Enforcement Fairness Act of 1996, 74, 268, 274, 346, 371–372

Small Business Regulatory Fairness Act of 1996, 369

Small Business Regulatory Fairness Board, 74, 274

Small business Tax Education (SBTE), 700

Small Business Technology Transfer Program, 369, 372

Small Business Technology Transfer Program Reauthorization Act of 2001, 372

Small Business Welfare to Work Initiative program, 369

Smith, Carl Michael, 507

Smokeless Tobacco Act (1986), 198

Smokeless Tobacco Health Education Act of 1986, 197

Smoking. *See* Tobacco issues

Snyder Act of 1921, 565

Social issues. *See* Children and family issues; Medical and healthcare issues; Welfare issues

Social Security Act (1935), 377, 513, 626

passenger vessels, 543–544, 545–546
pipelines, 145, 146, 147, 148, 149, 150–152, 682, 684
rural commodities, 392
safety, 350–351, 652–653, 654, 655
shipping, 338–340, 663–664, 666, 681, 682
trucking regulation and deregulation, 29, 541
Transportation issues—related agencies
  Agricultural Marketing Service, 392–397
  Aviation and International Affairs, 686–687
  Aviation Enforcement and Proceedings, 686
  Federal Aviation Administration, 641–647
  Federal Energy Regulatory Commission, 145–165
  Federal Highway Administration, 648–651
  Federal Motor Carrier Safety Administration, 648, 652–654
  Federal Railroad Administration, 655–658
  Federal Transit Administration, 659–662
  Maritime Administration, 6, 338, 663–667
  National Highway Traffic Safety Administration, 7, 668–673
  National Transportation Safety Board, 350–354
  Office of Energy Efficiency and Renewable Energy, 496–499
  Office of Environmental Management, 500–503
  Office of Hearings, 687
  Research and Special Programs Administration, 674–679
  Saint Lawrence Seaway Development Corporation, 680–681
  Surface Transportation Board, 682–685
  Transportation Security Administration, 13, 30, 541–542, 646
Transportation Recall Enhancement, Accountability, and Documentation Act (TREAD; 2000), 672
Transportation Security Administration (TSA), 13, 30, 541–542, 642, 646
TREAD. *See* Transportation Recall Enhancement, Accountability, and Documentation Act
Treasury Department, 131, 590, 688–708
  crime victims fund, 604
  public matching election funds, 325
  responsibilities and authority, 140, 141, 167, 169
Treasury Department—related agencies
  Alcohol and Tobacco Tax and Trade Bureau, 590, 689–692
  Internal Revenue Service, 5, 598, 697–703
  Office of the Comptroller of the Currency, 128, 129, 166, 168, 173, 692–696
  Office of Thrift Supervision, 125, 134, 168, 336, 704–708
Tribally Controlled Community College Assistance Act of 1978, 566
Tribal Relations Program, 432
TRRs (trade regulation rules). *See* Trade issues
Truck and Bus Safety and Regulatory Reform Act of 1988, 654
Truesdale, John C., 247, 248
Truman, Harry S., 82, 244
Trust Indenture Act of 1939, 284, 299
Truth in Lending Act (TILA; 1968), 7, 128, 139, 172, 178, 188, 209, 551, 557, 694, 706
Truth in Savings Act (1991), 172, 346
"Truth-in-securities" bill. *See* Securities Act of 1933
TSA. *See* Transportation Security Administration

TSC. *See* Volpe National Transportation Systems Center
TTB. *See* Alcohol and Tobacco Tax and Trade Bureau
Tuna Convention Act of 1950, 483
Turner Broadcasting Company, 108, 201
Twenty-First Century Workforce Commission, 627
Tyco International, 176, 291

U

UL. *See* Underwriters Laboratories
UMTA. *See* Urban Mass Transportation Administration
Underwriters Laboratories (UL), 41
Unfair Competition Act (1916), 532
Unfunded Mandates Act of 1995, 14, 21
"Unified Agenda of Federal Regulatory and Deregulatory Actions, The," 724
Uniformed Services Employment and Reemployment Rights Act of 1994, 633
Uniform Relocation Assistance and Real Property Acquisitions Policy Act of 1970, 561
Union Carbide, 266
Unions. *See* Business and corporate issues; Employment issues; National Labor Relations Board; individual unions
United Airlines, 348
United Auto Workers, 247
United Nations, 60, 598
United Nations Conference on Trade and Development, 724
United Parcel Service, 348
United States, 58
United States-Canada Free-Trade Agreement Implementation Act of 1988, 533, 538
United States Enrichment Corporation (USEC), 360
United States Statutes at Large, 736
Uniting and Strengthening America by Providing Appropriate Tools Required to Intercept and Obstruct Terrorism Act of 2002. *See* USA Patriot Act
Universal Service Fund, 107
Universal Studios, 112
University of Illinois, 247
University of Michigan, 247
University Research Institutes (URIs), 675
Unlisted Trading Privileges Act of 1994, 300
Upjohn Co., 17
Uranium Mill Tailings Radiation Control Act of 1978, 360, 503
Uranium Mill Tailings Remedial Action Amendments Act of 1988, 571
Urban Mass Transportation Act of 1964, 617
Urban Mass Transportation Administration (UMTA), 659
URIs. *See* University Research Institutes
USA Freedom Corps, 717
U.S. Agency for International Development (USAID), 422
USA Patriot Act (2002), 13, 30, 31, 141, 190, 290, 301, 313, 316, 344, 346, 542, 702, 708
U.S. Army, 57, 598. *See also* Defense Department
U.S. Board of Parole, 609
U.S. Coast Guard (USCG), 6, 13, 52, 543–547, 598, 681
U.S. Cotton Standards Act (1923), 395
U.S. Commercial Service, 466, 467
USCS. *See* U.S. Customs Service
U.S. Customs Service (USCS), 6, 13, 30, 36, 339, 529

USDA. *See* Agriculture Department
USEC. *See* United States Enrichment Corporation
USEC Privatization Act (1996), 360
U.S. Employment Service (USES), 624–625
U.S. Export Assistance Centers, 466
U.S. Fish and Wildlife Service (FWS), 568, 576–579
U.S. Geological Survey (USGS), 576, 580–582
U.S. Government Printing Office (GPO), 734–735
U.S. Grain Standards Act Amendments of 1993, 439
U.S. Grain Standards Act-Grain Exportation Amendments, 438
U.S. Grain Standards Acts of 1916, 1976, 438, 439
U.S. Grazing Service, 568
USGS. *See* U.S. Geological Survey
U.S. Housing Act of 1937, 556, 558, 560
U.S. International Trade Commission (USITC), 379–382
USITC. *See* U.S. International Trade Commission
U.S. Merchant Marine Academy, 664
U.S. Mint, 172
U.S. Navy, 663
U.S. Oceanborne Trades, 338
U.S. Parole Commission, 609–610
U.S. Patent Office, 486. *See also* Patent and Trademark Office
U.S. Postal Service (USPS), 244, 365, 383–388, 617
U.S. Synthetic Fuels Corporation, 498
U.S. Tariff Commission, 379
USTR. *See* Office of the U.S. Trade Representative
U.S. Warehouse Act (1916), 406–407
USX Corp., 267
UTC. *See* Innovation, Research and Education University Transportation Centers Program
Utilization and Quality Control Peer Review Organization Program, 520

V

VA. *See* **Veterans Affairs Department**
Valdez (AK), 57–58
ValuJet, 17
Various Commodity Research and Promotion Laws, 396
Verizon Communications, 109, 111
Verizon Wireless, 111
Vermont, 450
Veterans Administration, 710
Veterans Administration Health Care Amendments of 1980, 713
Veterans Affairs Department (VA), 26, 562, 709–714
Veterans Benefits Acts (1958, 1992), 712, 713
Veterans Benefits Administration, 712
Veterans Benefits Improvement Act of 2002, 714
Veterans Benefits Improvements Act of 1996, 713
Veterans Claims Assistance Act of 2000, 714
Veterans Compensation, Education, and Employment Amendments of 1982, 633
Veterans Dioxin and Radiation Exposure Compensation Standards Act (1984), 713
Veterans Educational Assistance Service, 710
Veterans Education and Benefits Expansion Act of 2001, 714
Veterans Education and Employment Assistance Act of 1984, 713

Veterans Education and Employment Programs, 633
Veterans' Employment and Training Service (VETS), 632–634
Veterans' Employment, Training, and Counseling Amendments of 1988, 633
Veterans Health Administration, 713
Veterans Health Care Act of 1992, 713
Veterans Health Care Amendments of 1979, 1986, 713
Veterans' Health Care Eligibility Reform Act of 1996, 713
Veterans Health Care, Training, and Small Business Loan Act of 1981, 713
Veterans Home Loan Program Amendments of 1992, 713
Veterans issues. *See also* Veterans entries
    cemeteries, 710–711, 713
    disability, 632
    education, 710, 713, 714
    employment, 616, 632, 633
    health care, 713, 714
    home loans, 710, 713
    readjustment assistance, 620
    small business programs, 369
Veterans' Millennium Health Care and Benefits Act (1999), 713
Veterans Readjustment Benefits Act of 1966, 713
Veterans Rehabilitation and Education Amendments, 713
Veterans Workforce Investment Program, 633
VETS. *See* Veterans' Employment and Training Service
Viacom, 112
Victims of Crime Act (1984), 604, 607
Victims of Terrorism Tax Relief Act of 2001, 702
Victims of Trafficking and Violence Protection Act of 2000, 597
Vietnam Era Veterans Readjustment Assistance Act of 1974, 620, 633
Violent Crime Control and Law Enforcement Act of 1994 and Amendments, 538, 593, 597, 603, 607
Violent Crime Reduction Trust Fund, 603
Virgin Islands, 431
Visa Services Office, 636
VISTA. *See* Volunteers in Service to America
VITA. *See* Volunteer Income Tax Assistance
Vitamins and Minerals Amendments (1976), 234
Vivendi Universal, 112
Volcker, Paul A., 174
Volpe National Transportation Systems Center (TSC), 675, 679
Voluntary Assistance Program, 84
Volunteer Income Tax Assistance (VITA), 700
Volunteers in Service to America (VISTA), 717
Voting. *See* Elections
Voting Rights Act of 1965, 597
Voting System Standards (VSS), 325
VSS. *See* Voting System Standards

W

Wage and Hour Division (WHD), 616, 617, 618, 620–621
Wagner Act of 1935, 6, 241, 243–244
Wagner, Curtis, Jr., 155
Wagner-Peyser Act (1933), 626
Wagner, Robert (D-N.Y.), 243

Walker, David M., 719

Walsh, Dennis P., 248, 249

Walsh-Healey Act (1936), 264, 274

Walt Disney, 108

Walters, John, 723

War Department, 564

Wards Cove Packing Co. v. Antonio (1989), 84

Washington, George, 486

Washington University, 11, 22, 29

Waste Isolation Pilot Plant Act (1992), 74

Waste Isolation Pilot Plant Land Withdrawal Act (1992), 630

Water Bank Act (1970), 443

Water Bank Program, 404

Water Pollution Control Act Amendments (1972), 55

Water Power Commission, 6

Water Quality Act of 1987, 73

Water Quality Improvement Act of 1970, 55, 72

Water Resources Development Acts of 1986, 1999, 493, 681

Water Resources Research Act of 1984, 582

Watershed Information Resource System (WIRS), 77

Watershed Protection and Flood Prevention Act (1954), 443

Watson, Rebecca, 568

Weatherization and Intergovernmental Program, 497

Weatherization Assistance Program, 497

Webster, William H., 291

Weeks Law (1911), 433

Weicher, John C., 554

Weidenbaum Center, 22

Weinberger, Caspar, 198

Weintraub, Ellen, 326

Welfare and Pension Plans Disclosure Act of 1958, 361

Welfare issues
    food and nutrition, 410, 411, 412–413
    programs, 511–512
    reform, 511, 513

Welfare issues—related agencies
    Administration for Children and Families, 511–514
    Food and Nutrition Service, 410–414
    Social Security Administration (SSA), 6, 374–378, 511, 525

Welfare Reform Act. *See* Personal Responsibility and Work Opportunity Reconciliation Act of 1996

Western Electric, 105

Western Farm Credit Bank, 319

Westinghouse Corp., 57, 108

Wetlands Reserve Program, 404, 441, 443

Weyerhaeuser (1995), 246

Whaling Convention Act of 1949, 483

WHD. *See* Wage and Hour Division

Wheeler-Lea Act (1938), 197, 208

Wheeler-Lea Amendment (1938), 198

Whitman, Christine Todd, 60–61, 62

Whitman v. American Trucking Associations (2001), 10, 28

Whitmore, John D., Jr., 369

Wholesome Meat Act (1967), 418

Wholesome Poultry Products Act (1968), 418

WIC Farmers' Market Nutrition Act of 1992, 413

Wild and Scenic Rivers Act (1968), 433, 570

Wild Bird Conservation Act of 1992, 579

Wilderness Act of 1964, 433, 570

Wild Horse and Burro Act of 1971, 568

Wildlife Habitat Incentives Program, 441

Wildlife Services Program, 398

Wiley, Harvey W., 217

Wiley, Richard, 105

Williams Transcontinental Gas Pipe Corp., 152

Wilson, Pete, 288

Wilson Tariff Act of 1894, 588, 589

Wind and Hydropower Technologies Program, 497

Wind Energy System Act of 1980, 498

Windows operating system. *See* Microsoft

Wireless Telecommunications Bureau, 102, 116

Wireline Competition Bureau, 115

WIRS. *See* Watershed Information Resource System

Witness Security Program, 608

Women's Health Initiative Study, 225

Women's issues
    abortion and family planning, 223
    credit, 597
    employment discrimination, 84, 85, 86, 88
    hormone replacement therapy, 224–225
    Office of Women's Health, 228
    sexual harassment, 85, 86, 87
    small businesses, 369

Wood, Patrick Henry, III, 155–156

Wood Residue Utilization Act of 1980, 434

Wool Products Labeling Act of 1939, 197, 198, 208

Wool Standards Act (1928), 395

Workforce Investment Act of 1998, 311, 633, 627

Work Incentives Advisory Panel, 377

Workload Teleprocessing Display (WRKD), 303

WorldCom, 17, 109, 110, 176, 291. *See also* MCI

World Meteorological Organization, 480

World Trade Center. *See* September 11, 2001, 422

World Trade Organization (WTO), 421, 436, 466, 724

World War II, 6, 170, 527

World Wide Web (WWW), 729–732. *See also* Internet; individual agencies, departments and organizations

World Wildlife Fund, 57

WRKD. *See* Workload Teleprocessing Display

WTO. *See* World Trade Organization

WWW. *See* World Wide Web

X

Xerox, 176, 291

Y

Yager, Daniel, 246

Yates, A.J., 393

Yucca Mountain (NV), 15, 357

Z

Zenker, Wendy, 717

Zoellick, Robert B., 724